THE HONGKONG BA[NK]
IN THE PERIOD OF DEVELOP[MENT AND]
NATIONALISM, 1941–[   ]
FROM REGIONAL BANK TO MULTINATIONAL GROUP

VOLUME IV OF
THE HISTORY OF THE HONGKONG
AND SHANGHAI BANKING
CORPORATION

THE HISTORY OF THE HONGKONG AND SHANGHAI
BANKING CORPORATION

FRANK H. H. KING

VOLUME I
The Hongkong Bank in Late Imperial China, 1864–1902: On an even keel

VOLUME II
The Hongkong Bank in the Period of Imperialism and War, 1895–1918: Wayfoong, the Focus of Wealth

VOLUME III
The Hongkong Bank between the Wars and the Bank Interned, 1919–1945: return from grandeur

VOLUME IV
The Hongkong Bank in the Period of Development and Nationalism, 1941–1984: from regional bank to multinational group

For a list of contents for each volume, please see pages v–vii.

WILLIAM PURVES, CBE, DSO.
Chairman and chief executive
The Hongkong and Shanghai Banking Corporation Limited, 1986–.

THE HONGKONG BANK IN THE PERIOD OF DEVELOPMENT AND NATIONALISM, 1941–1984

FROM REGIONAL BANK TO MULTINATIONAL GROUP

VOLUME IV OF
THE HISTORY OF THE HONGKONG
AND SHANGHAI BANKING
CORPORATION

FRANK H. H. KING
Professor of Economic History, University of Hong Kong

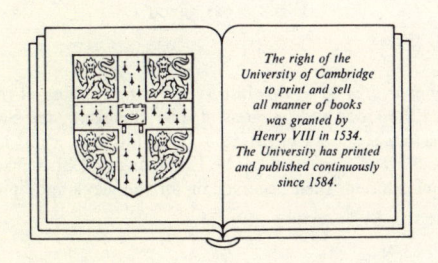

CAMBRIDGE UNIVERSITY PRESS
Cambridge
New York   Port Chester   Melbourne   Sydney

Published by the Press Syndicate of the University of Cambridge
The Pitt Building, Trumpington Street, Cambridge CB2 1RP
40 West 20th Street, New York, NY 10011-4211, USA
10 Stamford Road, Oakleigh, Melbourne 3166, Australia

© The Hongkong and Shanghai Banking Corporation Limited 1991

First published 1991

Printed in Great Britain at the University Press, Cambridge

British Library cataloguing in publication data

King, Frank H. H., 1926–
The History of The Hongkong and Shanghai
Banking Corporation.
Vol. 4: The Hongkong Bank in the period of
development and nationalism, 1941–1984: from regional bank
to multinational group.
1. Hongkong and Shanghai Banking Corporation
– History
I. Title
332.1′2′095125

Library of Congress cataloguing in publication data

King, Frank H. H., 1926–
The Hongkong Bank in the period of development and nationalism, 1941–1984:
from regional bank to multinational group.
(The History of The Hongkong and Shanghai Banking Corporation; v. 4)
Bibliography.
Includes index.
1. Hongkong and Shanghai Banking Corporation – History – 1941–1984.
2. Banks and banking – China – History – Sino–Japanese War, Republic, People's Republic.
3. Banks and banking – Hong Kong – History. 3. Asia – economic conditions.
I. Title. II. King, Frank H. H.
The History of The Hongkong and Shanghai Banking
Corporation; v. 4
HG1571.K56 vol. 4 [HG3354.H65]   332.1′5′095125   S – dc19
[332.1′5′095125]

ISBN 0 521 32709 1

The views and opinions expressed in this history are entirely those of the author and do not
necessarily reflect the views and opinions of The Hongkong and Shanghai Banking
Corporation. This history is a work of private scholarship and, whilst every effort has been
made to ensure the accuracy of facts stated, The Hongkong and Shanghai Banking Corporation
is in no way responsible for their accuracy or for the views and opinions expressed.

CONTENTS OF VOLUMES I, II, III, AND IV

VOLUME I. THE HONGKONG BANK IN LATE IMPERIAL CHINA, 1864–1902: ON AN EVEN KEEL

1 'On an even keel': The Hongkong Bank in history

PART I. THE FOUNDING AND FIRST YEARS OF THE HONGKONG BANK, 1864–1876

2 The Provisional Committee and the founding of the Hongkong Bank, 1864–1865
3 The history of the Hongkong and Shanghae Banking Company, Ltd
4 The Hongkong Bank's special ordinances – to 1873
5 The Court and its policies, 1867–1875
6 Success, crisis, and reorganization, 1867–1876
7 The early Hongkong Bankers

PART II. THE AGE OF JACKSON, 1876–1902, AND THE FALL OF SILVER

8 Jackson's first term, I: recovery and growth, 1876–1882
9 Jackson's first term, II: new capital and growth, 1882–1888
10 The Board, policy, and government, 1876–1888
11 The Bank and its ordinances – revision and renewal, 1882–1890
12 Interregnum, 1889–1893
13 The Bank comes of age: Jackson's second administration, 1893–1902
14 The Hongkong Bank in China, 1874–1895
15 Hongkong Bankers in the age of Jackson

VOLUME II. THE HONGKONG BANK IN THE PERIOD OF IMPERIALISM AND WAR, 1895–1918: WAYFOONG, THE FOCUS OF WEALTH

PART I. THE HONGKONG BANK AS EASTERN EXCHANGE BANK, 1902–1914

1 The Corporation, 1902–1914
2 Branches and agencies – an illustrative survey

v

Contents of Volumes I, II, III, and IV

  3 Hongkong Bankers, 1900–1914
  4 The Hongkong Bank's role in currency and banking reforms

PART II. THE HONGKONG BANK AS MERCHANT BANK, CHINA, 1895–1914

  5 Defeat, indemnity, and railways, 1895–1899
  6 Boxers, indemnity, and railways, 1900–1908
  7 Railways – Rights Recovery, finance, and the Consortium, 1905–1911
  8 Shanghai, revolution, and the Reorganization Loan, 1910–1914

PART III. EPILOGUE: THE BANK, GERMANY, AND THE GREAT WAR

  9 The Bank and Germany prior to 1914
10 The Hongkong Bank in the Great War, 1914–1918, I: the Corporation and staff
11 The Hongkong Bank in the Great War, 1914–1918, II: the Hongkong Bank's relations with Germany

VOLUME III. THE HONGKONG BANK BETWEEN THE WARS AND THE BANK INTERNED, 1919–1945: RETURN FROM GRANDEUR

PART I. ADJUSTING TO THE POST-WAR WORLD, 1919–1927

  1 The Corporation under Sir Newton Stabb, A.G. Stephen, and A.H. Barlow
  2 Grandeur and reality – policy and performance
  3 The years 1923 and 1924: the last hurrah

PART II. SURVIVAL: THE BANK IN THE GREAT DEPRESSION AND AFTER

  4 The Corporation, 1927–1941: the fall of silver and the sterling bank
  5 Hongkong Bankers inter-war, I: policy and managers
  6 Hongkong Bankers inter-war, II: juniors and compradores
  7 The Hongkong Bank and China, 1927–1937
  8 The Hongkong Bank and China's monetary system, 1935–1941
  9 The Corporation and its branches, 1919–1941, I: policy and the European branches
10 The Corporation and its branches, 1919–1941, II: branches in the East – case studies

PART III. THE BANK IN ENEMY HANDS, 1939–1945

11 War in Europe, tension in the East
12 Shutdown – the Bank in the Far East, 1941–1942
13 Clandestine finance, escape, and death

VOLUME IV. THE HONGKONG BANK IN THE PERIOD OF DEVELOPMENT AND NATIONALISM, 1941–1984: FROM REGIONAL BANK TO MULTINATIONAL GROUP

Introduction: from regional bank to multinational group

PART I. THE BABYLONIAN CAPTIVITY OF THE HONGKONG BANK, 1941–1946

1. Head Office, London: Bank operations during the Pacific War
2. The Bank reestablished, 1945–1946
3. Post-war policies and problems: Head Office, Hong Kong
4. The Hongkong Bank and the Republic of China, 1945–1949

PART II. THE CRITICAL YEARS, 1946–1961

5. The Hongkong Bank, policy and performance, 1947–1961
6. The Corporation, 1946–1962
7. Hongkong Bankers and the emergence of Head Office
8. The Hongkong Bank in Hong Kong, 1947–1962
9. The Hongkong Bank in China, 1949–1962
10. The commercial banking branches, 1947–1962
11. Pioneering in Borneo – British North Borneo and Sarawak
12. The Hongkong Bank's new subsidiaries, 1955–1961, and the origins of the Hongkong Bank Group

PART III. CHANGE, GROWTH, AND THE AMERICAN STRATEGY, 1962–1984

13. The Hongkong Bank Group, 1962–1980, I: structure and growth
14. The Hongkong Bank Group, 1962–1980, II: case studies – Hong Kong, London, Iloilo, and Colombo
15. The Hongkong Bank Group, 1962–1980, III: policy, development, and performance
16. The acquisition of Marine Midland Banks, Inc., 1978–1980, I: strategy and initial success, the signing of the Definitive Agreement
17. The acquisition of Marine Midland Banks, Inc., 1978–1980, II: the regulators, Congress, and the final approval
18. 'HongkongBank', the Hongkong Bank Group, 1980–1984

TABLE OF CONTENTS
VOLUME IV

List of illustrations	*page* xxv
List of tables	xxviii
Preface	xxxv
Romanization and terminology; Notes and corrections	
Acknowledgements	xlii
Statement on dollars and exchange	xlvi
Abbreviations	xlvii

INTRODUCTION: FROM REGIONAL BANK TO MULTINATIONAL
    GROUP   1
  Themes for Volume IV   1
    The Bank in its history   2
    Post-war success: explanations   2
        The Hong Kong base; Corporate structure; Personnel; The Bank in a banking system
    Shedding the past   9
        The China Consortium and loans; The legal framework
  The Bank's history, a survey   10

PART I. THE BABYLONIAN CAPTIVITY OF THE
HONGKONG BANK, 1941–1946   17
  1 HEAD OFFICE, LONDON: BANK OPERATIONS DURING THE
      PACIFIC WAR   23
    *The Corporation – the London Committee, the Board, and
    management*   24
        The transfer of Head Office to London   24
            The initial Hong Kong solution; Emergency *ad hoc* measures in London; The Order in Council, 1943; The appointment of Morse as Chief Manager

The Board of Directors and the London Advisory Committee	30
The directors in Hong Kong – their fate; The London Advisory Committee; The Board of Directors, London	
Arthur Morse, Chairman and Chief Manager	33
The significance of a Hongkong Banker as Chairman; Arthur Morse, background and experience; London Office management	
Performance	38
Major indicators; The share market and a bank's losses in war; Exchange banking during the war; Profit and Loss, January 1, 1942 – June 30, 1943	
Hongkong Bank policy and decisions in wartime London	46
Wartime policies and decisions	46
Staff policies	46
The 'working Bank'; The 'Bank interned' and the repatriates; Australian representation and the Bank of New South Wales	
Charity	49
Preparations for post-war developments	51
Staff	51
Development and financial planning	52
The return to the East – timing; Morse's plans for returning Head Office to Hong Kong; Government planning; The Bank's priorities and Hong Kong	
The Hongkong Bank in Free China, 1942–1945	57
The opening of the Chungking agency	57
Foreign banks in China after the end of extrality	59
The Hongkong Bank's wartime presence in China	60
The Hongkong Bank and currency stabilization	62
The Consortium, the British and Chinese Corporation, and merchant banking	64
Branches in South Asia	65
Colombo branch	66
War-related business	66
Colombo, the staff problem in a changing community	67
Labour relations, the beginnings of the post-war East; Local staff and comparative efficiency; The first strike	
India and the Calcutta branch	70
2 THE BANK REESTABLISHED, 1945–1946	74
Prelude to the post-war years	74
The first stage	74

The homecoming	75
The return to the East	78

The reopening of the Bank's offices — 78
Before V-J Day: Europe and the Philippines — 78
    Lyons and Hamburg — 78
    The Philippines — 80
        Manila; The rescue at Los Baños; O.J. Shannon; Iloilo
After V-J Day: the China Coast and Southeast Asia — 84
    Hong Kong — 86
    Shanghai — 89
    China – outports — 90
        Peiping; Canton; Hankow; Swatow
    French Indo-China — 94
        Saigon; Haiphong
    Southeast Asia — 96
        Rangoon and Bangkok; Singapore – then north to Sungei Patani; Batavia
The Bank in Allied occupied countries: Japan and Germany — 102
    Japan: HSBC, SCAP, BCOF, and other acronyms — 102
    Hamburg Branch — 105

3 POST-WAR POLICIES AND PROBLEMS: HEAD OFFICE, HONG KONG — 107

Hongkong Bankers — 107
    General comments — 107
    Post-war realities — 108
    The seniors and their retirement — 109
    Financial problems of local staff — 111
    Salary and related adjustments — 112
    Recruitment — 114

Two key problems — 115
The duress note issue — 117
    The nature of the duress issue — 117
    The decision to recognize the duress issue — 118
    The substance of the negotiations — 119
    The course of the negotiations — 122
        Initial positions and concerns; Official procrastination; An unacceptable offer; The Government's final offer; The actual figures
    The decisions enacted — 128
        The proclamations; The Hongkong Bank Ordinance, No. 8 of

	1946: currency provisions; The Bank Notes and Certificates of Indebtedness Ordinance	
	Consequences	129
Debtor/creditor relations		131
	The problem stated	132
	The Hongkong Bank's position	132
	The Bank versus the Government	134
	The Debtor and Creditor (Occupation Period) Ordinance, No. 24 of 1948	135
	Conclusion	136
Head Office: Hong Kong		137
	The transfer of Head Office	138
	The Order in Council; Ordinance No. 8 of 1946; 'Reconstruction of Records' Ordinance, No. 1 of 1948	
	First meetings	141
	The Board of Directors; The London Advisory Committee	
Postscript: performance, 1945–1946		145

4 THE HONGKONG BANK AND THE REPUBLIC OF CHINA, 1945–1949   149

The Bank as commercial bank in China		151
	The economic setting	151
	The role of the Hongkong Bank	155
	The Bank's business in China	157
	Hankow; Nanking; Mukden; Shanghai	
The Bank as merchant bank in China		165
	The end of the Consortium	165
	The final intervention of Sir Charles Addis; The final decisions; Should China be informed?	
	The British and Chinese Corporation/Chinese Central Railways	167
	The Chinese Central Railways; The British and Chinese Corporation	
	Debt recovery negotiations	172
	The general position; Loans under the Boxer Indemnity Board of Trustees; Loans to the Shanghai Municipal Council; Railway loans, negotiations relative to public issues; Postscript	
	The impact on the Hongkong Bank	180

PART II. THE CRITICAL YEARS, 1946–1961   185

5 THE HONGKONG BANK, POLICY AND PERFORMANCE, 1947–1961   193

A general survey	193
From the Hongkong Bank's accounts	194
The Bank in its region	202
The pressures for change	206
The accounts and the Chairman's statements	207
Explanation and interpretation	207
The annual presentation	207
The balance sheet – adjustments and comparability	209
Reserves	212
Inner reserves – their size, purpose, and uses; A historical note; Reserves policy, 1946–1961	
Other interpretational problems	216
Changes required by the United Kingdom Companies Act; Later changes	
The impact of subsidiary companies on capital structure	218
The incorporation of 'Inc.'	219
Mercantile Bank Limited	219
The British Bank of the Middle East	222
A final adjustment	223
The Group accounts	224
The path to consolidation	224
The impact of later additions	225
The companies; The pooling of Group funds	

6 THE CORPORATION, 1946–1962 — 228

Stability and change – What's in a name?; Examples of change – the capital structure

Legislated change	233
The Hong Kong note issue	233
The Hong Kong Exchange Fund	233
A fixed par of exchange; Exchange operations – a digression; Transferability of certificates of indebtedness	
A government note issue revisited	238
The responsibility for unissued notes	239
Currency legislation in Hong Kong	241
Cancellation of the right to the increased fiduciary issue, 1953; The note issue after the ordinance of 1957	
Capital structure and related changes, 1951–1961	243
The emergency transfer of Head Office	243
The 'bonus' share issue of 1955	244
Ordinance No. 36 of 1957	245
Elimination of double liability and related changes; 'Reserved liability'; The question of management	

Contents

The Board of Directors and the London Advisory Committee	247
The problems of a non-executive board	247
The Board of Directors	250
The Board minutes – a comparison	250
Composition	252
The Board, the Chief Manager, and the Chairman	257
Their respective roles – changes over time; The 1962 succession problem; The remuneration of the Chief Manager – from profit sharing to salary	
The role of the Board of Directors	264
London and the London Advisory Committee	266
The role of the Committee	266
The composition of the Committee	268
Appendix to Chapter 6	
Companies with connections to the Hongkong Bank's Board of Directors, a sample list	272

7 HONGKONG BANKERS AND THE EMERGENCE OF HEAD OFFICE — 275

Chief Managers: the succession	276
General considerations	277
From Sir Arthur Morse to Michael Turner	278
Sir Michael Turner to J.A.H. Saunders	282
Head Office: the Chief Manager and management	284
Foreign staff assignments and accomplishments	285
Head Office	286
Size and impact; Composition and functions; The Inspectorate; Personnel	
Head Office – a second perspective	292
The spirit of Sir Arthur; The working of Head Office – a personal viewpoint; The role of Lady Turner; Signs of change	
Hongkong Bankers – the three tiers	300
The system reviewed	300
Change: factors for and against	302
The second tier – the Portuguese	305
The Chinese staff	309
And the 'Foreign staff'	311
The specifics: 1951, 1954, and 1961 compared	321

8 THE HONGKONG BANK IN HONG KONG, 1947–1962 — 324

A survey of Hong Kong's growth	325
The role of the Bank	329
The Bank, the Government, and responsibility	329

A view to the sea – a cautionary tale	329
The central bank issue	334
Responsibility and loyalty – the broader context	340
The Bank and Hong Kong's industrial development	344
General background	344
Factors favourable to Hong Kong's industrial growth; The Hong Kong open market; Other factors	
The Bank's historical policies and their modification	349
The overall situation, 1948–1953	351
The limitation of risk – and market share	353
Early experiences of Oliphant in Mongkok	354
Banking problems	356
Borrowing short, lending long; Security; Balance sheets; Packing credits; Other adaptations; 'Opinions'	
Inspection	360
The Mongkok office buildings to 1961	362
Branching in Hong Kong – to 1961	364
Factors for and against Hong Kong branching	364
Early developments	369
Developments, 1958–1962 and afterwards	370

9 THE HONGKONG BANK IN CHINA, 1949–1962 — 373

Transition	373
Strike; Business resumed	
Initial adjustment problems and policy	376
Foreign staff discontent	376
The statistics; Personal stories	
'After the break of morn' – the Bank's initial policy in the People's Republic	381
To an 'all-for-all' settlement	383
Developments in the Shanghai branch	384
Revaluation of pre-Liberation accounts; Seconds of exchange; Labour relations	
The Board of Directors' policy for settlement and withdrawal	388
The policy stated; The changing atmosphere	
The Hongkong Bank leaves the Bund	391
China policy restated	391
The 1954 trade mission	392
The agreement and its impact	394
The agreement signed; The terms; Yoxall leaves the Bund; To remain or not?; First post-agreement, post-mission consequences; Uncertainty remains	

	The post-agreement Bank and China	399
	New problems	399
	Moving to new premises; Local staff; Lions and Russians; Corners of foreign fields	
	The Shanghai branch and its Managers, 1958–1966	404
	The Managers	404
	The Shanghai branch at work	405
	On business; On labour relations	
	On life in Shanghai	407
	Miscellaneous comments	408
	The problem of reference matter; Surveillance	
	Hospitality in Peking	410
	Exit from China – the Bank remains	411
10	THE COMMERCIAL BANKING BRANCHES, 1947–1962	412
	The branch networks: the Hongkong Bank, 1947–1961	415
	The initial development	415
	Policy and finance	424
	Foreign staff policy and the branches; Finance and the branches	
	Case studies	432
	Japan	432
	Early staff problems; Japanese bonds and 'face'; The changing pattern of business; The 1955 strike	
	The European offices	438
	London	438
	Hamburg	439
	Lyons/Paris	440
	The Philippines and Iloilo	441
	The Bank in the Philippines	441
	Iloilo, 1946–1965	443
	The post-war business of the Iloilo agency; The expense account comes to Iloilo; Hongkong Bankers, the Bank, and the community	
	The Colombo branch, 1945–1965	453
	The Bank's labour relations; Adjustments in banking; Restrictions and new opportunities, 1956–1965	
11	PIONEERING IN BORNEO – BRITISH NORTH BORNEO AND SARAWAK	463
	The immediate post-war situation	463
	A note on Brunei	
	British North Borneo	466
	Jesselton, 1947	466

Tawau	467
Opening and early business; The coming of competition	
Chief office, Borneo territories	473
Max Haymes in Jesselton; Expansion; Maurice W. Turner, Manager, 1961–1963	
Sarawak, the opening and first operations	478

12 THE HONGKONG BANK'S NEW SUBSIDIARIES, 1955–1961, AND THE ORIGINS OF THE HONGKONG BANK GROUP — 482

General considerations	482
The impact of the Bank's first subsidiaries	482
Policy or chance?	486
The founding and early history of the California subsidiary	489
The founding	489
Agency or branch?	489
The establishment of HBC	490
Directors and management	492
Initial operations, expansion plans, and setback	493
Performance, 1955–1961; Initial 'success' and plans for expansion; Consequences; The limitations of the system	
The acquisition of Mercantile Bank Limited	498
The first approach, April–July 1957	499
Interim: August 1957–September 1958	503
The September meeting; The restructuring of the Mercantile Bank's capital	
The successful negotiations	507
An approach by Chase and the immediate consequences; The Hongkong Bank's second offer; The course of the negotiations; The immediate consequences	
The Hongkong Bank's policy of expansion	517
A background survey	517
Developments to 1959	520
Policy discussions in 1959	522
Frustrated expansion – the Bank's planning efforts	524
Europe; Africa; Elsewhere	
The acquisition of the British Bank of the Middle East	529
Background	529
The rationalization of British Eastern banking; The Hongkong Bank and the Imperial Bank of Persia/BBME in history	
The events to June 1959	531
The negotiations, July–December 1959	535
Tax relief and the preliminary negotiations; The terms of the final agreement	

Identity and the imperial view	540
Group finances	540
The conflict stated	540
The first calculations	542
The Mercantile Bank; The British Bank of the Middle East	
The imperial view vs the status of the BBME in the Gulf	544
The specific BBME proposals	547
The question of branches	549
Postscript: the Hongkong Bank Group	552

PART III. CHANGE, GROWTH, AND THE AMERICAN STRATEGY, 1962–1984 — 555

13 THE HONGKONG BANK GROUP, 1962–1980, I. STRUCTURE AND GROWTH

	565
Shedding a structural heritage	565
The heritage of the Colonial Banking Regulations	566
The trend to conformity	568
Changes in the regulations – general; The current position; Shares and dividends	
Exceptions to conformity	570
General intent and an exception; Maximum share holdings; Disclosure	
The note issue	573
A historical survey of banknotes in Hong Kong; The position of the Hongkong Bank; Changes in the standard	
Changes in corporate organization	578
The historical tradition	578
Changes within the Hongkong Bank	580
Background; Change – and what to preserve	
The structuring of Head Office	583
Developments in the 1960s; Head Office and the subsidiaries; Developments in the 1970s; Technological change	
Head Office and branch management	589
The impact – is this the Hongkong Bank?	590
Branches and geographical expansion	593
The Hongkong Bank and Mercantile Bank, 1962–1971	597
Small branch policies	
Changes in regional coverage	599
Rationalization of branches and intra-Group transfers	
The commercial banking branches of the Hongkong Bank and Mercantile Bank, 1972–1979	604
The changing position of the Mercantile Bank	607

Geographic coverage 608
Macau; New banking, new departures; The British Isles and Chinatowns; Developments in the United States; Korea and Brazil; China

14 THE HONGKONG BANK GROUP, 1962–1980, II. CASE STUDIES: HONG KONG, LONDON, ILOILO, AND COLOMBO 614
Hong Kong 614
Development and policy 614
    'Central banking' 614
    The centenary 615
    Two new branches 616
        Kwun Tong branch; North Point branch in 1965; City offices in other territories – a digression
Financing Hong Kong's industrial development 620
    The statistics and the Bank's share of the market 621
    Lending practices 625
    Internal organizational changes 629
        Mongkok and other branches; The compradore, the new Business Representatives, and the first Chinese Manager; Industrial inspection
London and the integration of two banks 632
    'Londonitis' revisited 632
        The continuing problem; Changes in the 1960s
    London Office – senior management and their role 635
        London's several roles; The problems of the Managers
    London Office – the new building 638
    The representational role – the initial resolution 639
    The London Office – efficiency 641
    The role of the London Advisory Committee 642
    The question of control and the transfer of head offices 645
The Philippines and Sri Lanka 647
The Philippines: Manila and Iloilo 647
    General developments 647
    Iloilo office, the story concluded 648
        The Iloilo fire of 1966; The last years: Iloilo to 1981
Sri Lanka and Colombo 652
    The Hongkong Bank Group and Colombo office 652
        1965–1977; 1977–1980

15 THE HONGKONG BANK GROUP, 1962–1980, III. POLICY, DEVELOPMENT, AND PERFORMANCE 663
Bankers and directors 663

Contents

Personnel: statistics and policy	663
Statistical profile	664
Policy: Foreign staff	667
Recruitment; London and New Beckenham; Terms of service	
Training	671
Regional officers, initial training; Other training	
The Board of Directors and senior management – the Hongkong Bank	674
The Board of Directors	674
Chief executives: the succession	686
Historical background; – Saunders to Sayer; – Sayer to Sandberg; Chief Accountants and the succession – careers compared	
The Hongkong Bank Group – the companies	691
The growing complexity, 1962–1979	691
A survey and explanation, 1962–1979	692
The position in 1979	694
Developments, 1962–1971	697
Expansion and frustration	697
The acquisition of Hang Seng Bank	701
Background; The banking crisis of February 1965; The April crisis; Hang Seng's decision; Saunders' objections and the outcome	
Developments, 1972–1979	706
A survey	706
Hutchison International	708
Merchant banking	714
Wardley Limited; Wardley Canada and Antony Gibbs; The Antony Gibbs Group	
Insurance	717
Finance companies – the Wayfoong Finance Group	719
Other companies	720
Leasing; Wayhong Investment; Guardforce	
Bank and Group: Performance and chronology, 1962–1979	723
General comments	723
Performance defined; The accounts	
A survey of the tables	724
Published shareholders' funds; Profits and dividends; Uses of funds	
Rates of growth	731
The chronology	731
Chief executive – J.A.H. Saunders; – G.M. Sayer; – M.G.R. Sandberg	

16	THE ACQUISITION OF MARINE MIDLAND BANKS, INC., 1978–1980, I. STRATEGY AND INITIAL SUCCESS, THE SIGNING OF THE DEFINITIVE AGREEMENT	762

Introduction to a partnership — 762
The setting — 762
    The transaction described — 762
    The human element — 764
    The timetable — 765
The regulatory and banking environment — 768
    'National treatment' — 768
    Acquisitions by foreign banks — 769
        The nature of the problem; The example of the Standard Chartered Group; Factors behind the acquisitions; Supervisory concerns
    Non-financial activities and national treatment — 773
Three strategies converge — 775
The development of the Hongkong Bank's American strategy — 775
    The first phase — 776
        Focus on California; The Bank's 'philosophy' considered; An America-wide strategy; Hong Kong, November 1976
    The second phase — 781
        The Vancouver Meeting, October 1977; October 1977–January 1978
Marine Midland's search for capital – and a partner — 783
    Background — 783
        1929–1975; The years 1969–1975
    The search for capital — 787
        The capital alternatives; The partnership alternative; the coming of the Hongkong Bank
New York State: the economic policy of the Carey Administration — 790
A deal made: from the first contact to the Definitive Agreement — 791
First contacts — 792
    The immediate prelude — 792
        The schedule to February 1978; The 'dream', partnership, and merger
    First calls and meetings — 794
        Identification by telephone; Washington's birthday weekend, February 17–21, 1978
    The Hawaii meeting, March 17–19, 1978 — 795
        'The spirit of Hawaii'; The course of the meeting
Early reactions — 798
    Back from Hawaii — 798

	First reactions and public relations	799
	Back in New York State; The boards of directors	
	Negotiations and the Definitive Agreement	801
	Early developments	802
	The consequences	803
	The Definitive Agreement – general terms; The role of the subordinated note	
17	THE ACQUISITION OF MARINE MIDLAND BANKS, INC., 1978–1980, II. THE REGULATORS, CONGRESS, AND THE FINAL APPROVAL	807
	The Federal and State regulators – through June 1978	808
	The issues	808
	The negative impact of U.S. legislation on U.S. banking; The non-financial activities of the Hongkong Bank; The Bank's accounts; The Bank's intentions	
	The regulators	812
	The authorities involved	812
	The principals; The 'other' authorities	
	The course of events, May 1978 – June 1979	813
	SEC and full disclosure; The shareholder reaction; The Federal Reserve Bank of New York and the Federal Reserve Board; The New York State Banking Department – (i) developing opposition; – (ii) explanations and reactions	
	The 'Take-over' Bill and its veto	822
	A comparison; The 'Take-over' Bill: background and passage; The Governor's veto	
	The Federal road – the agreement implemented	825
	Preliminaries	826
	Renegotiating the Definitive Agreement	826
	The decision to go National	828
	The withdrawal of HSBC's application	830
	The events; Reactions	
	First steps after the June 1979 decisions	831
	The Federal Reserve Board	831
	The SEC	832
	Before the Comptroller of the Currency	833
	On Capitol Hill	835
	Foreign acquisitions as a political issue	835
	Recent history; The attitude of the regulators	
	The course of events	838
	The Proxmire and Heinz bills; Legislative oversight – the Rosenthal hearings; Laughter on Capitol Hill	
	The charter granted	842

	Contents	xxiii

The hearings	843
The Community Reinvestment Act; Book vs market value of shares	
The 'charade'	845
From delay to approval	847
Appendix to Chapter 17. The timetable	850

18 'HONGKONGBANK', THE HONGKONG BANK GROUP, 1980–1984

	860
The year is 1980	861
The immediate impact of Marine Midland	862
The celebration; The capital/assets problem; The geographical impact; The Hongkong Bank Group	
Other developments in 1980	869
The People's Republic of China; Antony Gibbs; British Bank of the Middle East; Corporate identity	
The Bank's accounts, 1980–1984	874
Background comments; Accounting changes; Capital accounts; Other accounts	
Following the threads to 1984 – (i) corporate development	885
Geographical distribution	887
General developments; The sale of Mercantile Bank Limited; The Americas and Australia	
The Royal Bank of Scotland Group	891
Offers to purchase; Subsequent developments; The Hongkong Bank's position	
The development of the Hongkong Bank Group	896
A survey; Marine Midland and the United States; Developments in Britain	
The 1986 Head Office building	904
Following the threads to 1984 – (ii) shareholders, directors, and the Advisory Committee	908
Shareholders	908
The Board of Directors and the London Committee	909
The Board of Directors; The London Advisory Committee	
Following the threads to 1984 – (iii) Hongkong Bankers	911
The succession	911
Sir Michael Sandberg; William Purves	
Hongkong Bankers – other careers	914
On career specialization; The seniors – contrasting career patterns	
Post-1977 personnel policies	916
New Beckenham; The new policies – 'man management'; Career planning; Regional officers and local staff	

Appendix tables 924
Appendix: The Hongkong and Shanghai Banking Corporation Ordinance 930
Notes 936
Bibliography 954
Index 962

LIST OF ILLUSTRATIONS

FIGURES

I.1	Paid-up capital, 1865–1979	13
I.2	Exchange rate (Hong Kong on London) and the price of silver (London), 1866–1940	15
I.3	Shareholders' funds in dollars and sterling (1865 = 100) 1865–1940	16
II.1	Shareholders' funds and paid-up capital in dollars, 1946–1961	188
II.2	Indices of assets and shareholders' funds, 1946–1962	189
III.1	Indices of assets and shareholders' funds, 1961–1979	563
III.2	Indices of assets and capital resources, 1975–1984	564
13.1	Speedlink for remittances and communication	588
14.1	ETC comes to Sri Lanka	660
15.1	Family tree of insurance interests	718
15.2	Earnings per share: Group	728
15.3	Dividend per share	728
15.4	Profit growth: Group	729
15.5	Shareholders' funds: Group	729
15.6	Total assets: Group	730
15.7	Advance/deposit growth: Group	730
16.1	Marine Midland Banks, Inc.: progress of the transaction	766
18.1	Geographical distribution of assets, 1984	865
18.2	Hexagon and HongkongBank designs	873
18.3	Private banking chart	897

MAPS

1	HongkongBank in 1984, the offices worldwide	xxxii
2	The Hongkong Bank's Asian offices, 1944	22
3	Hong Kong: Statue Square area, 1866–1965	330
4	Hong Kong: the 1980 branch network of the Hongkong Bank: (A) Urban area	598

xxvi   List of illustrations

    (B) New Territories   599
5 Malaysia: the Hongkong Bank's branches, 1980   601

PLATES

Colour

William Purves, CBE, DSO, Chairman and chief executive,
The Hongkong and Shanghai Banking Corporation, 1986–   frontispiece

(*between p. 240 and p. 241*)

1 A general view of Macau, May 29, 1839, by Auguste Borget
2 Sir Arthur Morse, KBE, Chairman and chief executive,
    The Hongkong and Shanghai Banking Corporation, 1941–1953
3 Chinese Imperial Railway 5% Gold Loan of 1899, a £100 bond
4 Hongkong Bank lions – types and uses
5 The Hongkong Bank/Marine Midland Banks definitive
    agreement, at the signing in Buffalo, New York, 1979
6 The Hongkong Bank's 1982 Board of Directors
7 'At Home', Carlingford, the Bangkok Manager's residence
8 Hong Kong, Central, from the southeast, a 1986 view

Black and white (*between p. 80 and p. 81*)

1 Hongkong Bank, Chungking branch: licence to operate, 1943
2 Balance sheet at December 31, 1947; profit and loss account for
    the year 1947
3 Hong Kong officers, post-war: they reopened the Bank
4 A farewell party for Sir Arthur Morse, 1953

(*between p. 496 and p. 497*)

5 Chief executives: Sir Michael Turner, CBE, 1953–1962
6 Group Consolidated Balance Sheet at December 31, 1961
7 Bank buildings – a study in contrasts
8 Inducements: pictures from the 1961 recruiting booklet
9 Chief executives: Sir John Saunders, CBE, DSO, MC, 1962–1972;
    G. R. Sayer, CBE, 1972–1977
10 Tawau, British North Borneo (Sabah), 1953
11 Sports and teamwork – a Hongkong Bank tradition
12 Statue Square: (i) a 1972 view to the sea;
    (ii) a 1972 view from the sea with the 1935 head office building

(*between p. 880 and p. 881*)

13 The Hongkong and Shanghai Banking Corporation, 1984 as seen
    through the published accounts
    (i) Consolidated profit and loss account

(ii) The Hongkong Bank, balance sheet, December 31, 1984
(iii) The Hongkong and Shanghai Banking Corporation, consolidated balance sheet, December 31, 1984
14 The 1986 head office building under construction
15 Chief executives: Sir Michael Sandberg, CBE, 1977–1986

Other illustrations
Sir Thomas Jackson, Bart, KCMG (1841–1915) xxxiv

LIST OF TABLES

		page
I.1	Changes in shares, paid-up capital, and shareholders' funds, 1865–1985	12
1.1	The directors, 1941, and their fate	30
1.2	London Advisory Committee, 1941–1946	32
1.3	Key indicators, 1941–1945	40
1.4	Balance sheet, selected items, 1940, 1942–1946	41
1.5	Certain wartime donations, 1942–1945	50
2.1	Reestablishment of pre-war branches, 1945–1948	79
3.1	Seniority of members of the Eastern staff	110
3.2	Shanghai local staff position, November 1946	112
3.3	The Board and Committee, December 1941 and June 1946	142
3.4	Charity and reconstruction, 1946–1947	144
3.5	Balance sheets: end-1945 and 1946 compared	146
4.1	China: currency conversion rates, 1942–1955	154
II.1	The Hongkong Bank Group: List of principal companies, 1961	186
5.1	HSBC: Capital and dividends, 1946–1961	196
5.2	HSBC: Key indicators, 1947–1961	197
5.3	The Hongkong Bank: Selected balance sheet items and ratios, 1947–1961	198
5.4	The Hongkong Bank: Investments (at under market values)	199
5.5	The Hongkong Bank: 'True' profit estimates, 1947–1961	200
5.6	The Hongkong Bank: Annual accounts, 1951	210
5.7	The Hongkong Bank: 1953 accounts and ratios adjusted	212
5.8	The Hongkong Bank Group: Consolidated accounts: assets and reserves, 1946–1962	220
5.9	The Hongkong Bank Group: Consolidated accounts: capital of subsidiaries, 1955–1961	227
6.1	HSBC: The Board of Directors, 1946–1962	253

6.2	HSBC: Companies represented on the Board of Directors, 1946–1962	257
6.3	HSBC: Charitable donations as listed in minutes, 1949	258
6.4	HSBC: The London Advisory Committee, 1946–1961	269
7.1	The Hongkong Bank: Managers, posts, and Foreign staff, 1950–1962	287
7.2	The Hongkong Bank: Eastern or 'Foreign' staff, 1946–1962	314
7.3	The Hongkong Bank: Seniority distribution of the Foreign staff, 1946–1961	315
7.4	The Hongkong Bank: Offices and their Managers, 1946 and 1961	316
8.1	The Hongkong Bank: Branch profits as reported, 1947–1961	327
8.2	Hong Kong: Banks and banking characteristics, 1954–1980	365
8.3	Hong Kong: The branching networks of the major local bank groups, 1954–1981	366
8.4	HSBC: Spatial pattern of branching in Hong Kong, 1961–1981	367
9.1	HSBC: Closure and reopening of China offices, 1949–1985	382
9.2	China: 1951 conversion rates for pre-Liberation deposits	386
9.3	HSBC: Shanghai branch: business, 1957, 1958	398
10.1	HSBC: Branches, 1947	416
10.2	The Hongkong Bank: Branches, 1946–1961	417
10.3	The Hongkong Bank: Branches, 1946–1962	418
10.4	Hongkong Bank Group: Branches, 1961, the Hongkong Bank and Mercantile Bank	422
10.5	HSBC: Managers who served five years or more at one post, 1946–1961	425
10.6	The Hongkong Bank: Branches, agencies, and their Managers, 1946–1961	426
10.7	The Hongkong Bank: Iloilo branch: Profit and Loss Accounts, 1962–1964	445
10.8	The Hongkong Bank: Iloilo branch: Calculation of theoretical profit	446
12.1	The Hongkong and Shanghai Banking Corporation of California, Inc.: Balance sheets, 1955–1961 – selected items	493
12.2	The Mercantile Bank of India Ltd: Capital structure, 1957	505
12.3	HSBC: Impact of tax concessions relative to the Mercantile Bank	543
12.4	HSBC: Impact of tax concessions relative to the BBME	543
12.5	The British Bank of the Middle East: Shareholders' funds, 1960–1962	549

13.1	The Hongkong Bank Group: Commercial bank branches, 1962–1984: Hongkong Bank, Mercantile Bank, Hongkong Bank of California	594
13.2	Hongkong Bank Group: Branches 1971: Hongkong Bank, Mercantile Bank, Hongkong Bank of California, Hang Seng	605
13.3	Hongkong Bank Group: branches, 1977: Hongkong Bank, Mercantile Bank, Hongkong Bank of California, Hang Seng	606
14.1	Hong Kong: The Hongkong Bank's loans and advances by category	622
14.2	Hong Kong: The Hongkong Bank's shares in loans and advances of all banks	623
14.3	London Advisory Committee, 1962–1985	643
14.4	The Hongkong Bank: Colombo branch: Examination results	657
15.1	The Hongkong Bank: HSBC Foreign staff, 1962 and 1977, HSBC Regional staff, 1977	665
15.2	The Board of Directors, 1962–1985	675
15.3	Principal companies represented on the Board of Directors, 1962–1985	685
15.4	HSBC: Chief Executives from 1876	687
15.5	The Hongkong Bank Group: List of principal companies, 1962	698
15.6	The Hongkong Bank Group: List of principal companies, 1971	699
15.7	The Hongkong Bank Group: List of principal companies, 1976	709
15.8	HSBC: Capital and dividends, 1962–1979	732
15.8A	Hongkong Bank: Sterling dividends, 1962–1971	733
15.9	HSBC: Group consolidated and Hongkong Bank assets compared, 1962–1979	734
15.10	The Hongkong Bank: Selected balance sheet items and ratios, 1962–1979	735
15.11	The Hongkong Bank: Profits and dividends, 1962–1979	736
15.11A	The Hongkong Bank Group: Profits compared, 1962–1979	737
15.12	Companies owned 25% or more (31 December 1979)	747
16.1	Hongkong Bank Group, Hongkong Bank, MMBI: Comparative figures, 1978–1980	763
18.1	Distribution of assets and profits, December 31, 1980	868
18.2	Capital and dividends, 1980–1984	876
18.2A	Capital and dividends, 1980–1984: Capital reconciliation	877
18.2B	Capital and dividends, 1980–1984: Reserve Fund and Share Premium Account reconciliation	878
18.2C	Capital and dividends, 1980–1984: Paid-up capital and number of shares	879

18.3	Group consolidated and Hongkong Bank assets compared, 1980–1984	880
18.4A	The Hongkong Bank: Selected balance sheet items and ratios, 1980–1984	881
18.4B	Selected Group consolidated balance sheet items and ratios, 1980–1984	882
18.5	Profits, ratios, and dividends, 1980–1984	883
18.6	International network, 1984	887
18.7	Principal operating subsidiary and associated companies, 1984	898

APPENDIX TABLES

A.	Chief executives, 1865–1986	924
B.	Directors, Managers, and subsidiary companies, June 1986	926

1 HongkongBank in 1984, the offices worldwide.

For Catherine

Sir Thomas Jackson, Bart, KCMG (1841–1915).

PREFACE

> Which shows what hearts of gold bank authorities had in those days. It was a pleasure to be associated with them.
>
> P.G. Wodehouse, on his career with the Hongkong Bank[a]

'I often wish', the Bank's London Manager, Sir Newton Stabb, wrote in the early 1920s, 'the [China] Consortium were dead and buried.' On December 8, 1941, with the Japanese attack on Hong Kong, the Consortium was at last dead. It was 'buried' in 1946, the year after Sir Charles Addis himself had died. During the Pacific War hopes were not set, as in the Great War, on a return to 'normalcy'; the years from 1895 to 1914 had seen the Hongkong Bank rise to a position of prominence as leader of the China Consortium, but in contrast the inter-war years had forced a 'return from grandeur' to the task of survival. Sir Arthur Morse, as the wartime Chief Manager of the Bank in London exile, would focus on preparing first for reconstruction and then for something new; he planned to take advantage of banking opportunities in a world that was changing, a world that would be described as one of development planning and the new nationalism of colonial and protected territories soon to be independent nations.

Morse and his successors achieved their goals, not through consortiums with political support but through the task they understood clearly, the only task indeed which Stabb himself would recognize and enjoy – banking. The Hong Kong base would prove one key to success; the relatively exemplary economic performance of the region another. In this context the vision of Morse, the tenacity of Sir Michael Turner, the restructuring under Sir John Saunders, the regrouping of forces under G.M. Sayer, and the dramatic American policy and expansion under Sir Michael Sandberg would change the colonially chartered, regional Hongkong Bank into a multinational financial group as shareholders' funds grew from $135.1 million in December 1945 to $20,863 million at the end of 1984.

The business historian might well have echoed Stabb; the history of the Hongkong Bank seemed intertwined with the esoteric politics of the imperial

---

[a] P.G. Wodehouse, 'My Banking Career', *The Hongkong Bank Group Magazine*, No. 6 (Summer 1975), p. 16, reprinted in Volume II, pp. 180–81, of this history.

Ch'ing dynasty, with the personalities and policies of the British Treasury and Colonial Office in London and of the various colonial Governments in the region itself. The labyrinthine negotiations among Powers intent on forcing the pace of world development and the scaremongering of a press promoting an unnecessary war which caught the Bank wholly unprepared in 1914 – as war caught the Bank, for other reasons, in 1941 – were matters which were not so much a complex backdrop as they were an integral part of the corporation's history. Post-1945, however, the history of the Bank, the story of its success, is primarily the story of a corporation, its management, its policies, and its people. Certainly they interact with Governments, but in Hong Kong, for example, the Bank has moved from its virtually solo status as an Eastern exchange bank to become a part, albeit a most influential part, of a banking system servicing a Hong Kong which too has changed in status. It is now the world's third great financial centre, after London and New York.

The shift in emphasis in this the fourth of a four-volume history of The Hongkong and Shanghai Banking Corporation should suggest to the reader certain questions relative to scope and sources. The Bank would find it difficult to cover up, even if it wished to do so, its role in the finance of the then legal opium trade, in which its founders were so interested, or in the China loans from the first in 1874/75 to the Pukow-Sinyang Railway Loan of 1937; the historian's main problem is the plethora of publicly available material on these subjects. Indeed, there are already areas in which information about the post-war Bank is available – for example, capital injections into a less than successful Hongkong Bank of California are recorded in the files of the State Banking Department, and these may be freely consulted by the curious citizen. However, it is certain that the key to the Bank's policies in the more recent past must be found in the archives of the Bank and behind these lie the unwritten thoughts of the men who made policy.

Those familiar with banking in Hong Kong already understand that Hong Kong Government policy does not encourage full disclosure, and the Hongkong Bank does not state 'true' profits; furthermore, the Bank understates shareholders' funds. This has induced financial analysts to try their skills, to calculate what the 'true' position of the Bank must be. I cannot compete with them, although I shall refer to their results. The present history will not solve this particular problem; shareholders will not be surprised to learn that should full disclosure ever be agreed on, the revised figures will come, if permitted, from their Chairman, not from a historian writing a commissioned history. This fact is restated from time to time as a reminder in the text. Yet it obviously leaves the positive questions unanswered: what in fact are the sources for Volume IV and what level of access has been permitted?

To some extent the answers to these questions are found in the Bibliography and, by implication, in the Acknowledgements. Some further comment is, however, necessary.

When the history was commissioned by Sir Michael Sandberg, the tentative cut-off date was set at 1962. In that year Sir Michael Turner resigned as Chief Manager and Chairman; in the rationalization of British post-war overseas banking, it had become clear that Turner's policy had successfully strengthened the Bank through the acquisition of two smaller but important banks, the Mercantile Bank (formerly 'of India') and the British Bank of the Middle East. The Bank was on course; the commissioned history would first tell this story in detail and then summarize later events up to press-time – itself a very movable feast, as it turned out. There were several objections to this decision. The first was that the Bank's most dramatic moments came in 1979 and 1980, when it sought, with eventual success, to acquire, through a concept of partnership, control of a major American bank, Marine Midland Bank, N.A. The facts surrounding this acquisition were in no way confidential; furthermore, those involved were very pleased to fill in the few gaps in the mass of public documentation on a transaction that met with considerable approval and acclaim. Nevertheless Sandberg's American strategy was inconceivable had the Bank remained as it was in 1962. The events of the intervening years had to be explained, if not in full financial detail, then certainly in the context of corporate structure and development. This, moreover, is at least part of what business history should be about.

There had however to be a compromise with a bank's obligation to confidentiality. The end-notes therefore die out before the text, but the consultation of the relevant sources does not. I do not therefore urge a policy of 'Trust me.' Rather I urge that the importance of the story is sufficient to offset the legitimacy of the demand for academic apparatus (but not, I hope, for academic integrity) so that an account of the events by which the Hongkong Bank became one of the world's leading financial institutions can be placed before a legitimately interested audience.

At this point there was an argument. I requested that the book be entitled '*A* history of...'; the publishers and the Bank insisted, successfully it is hardly necessary to add, on '*The* history of...'. The Bank may have feared that, having sponsored so expensive and time-consuming a project, they would be asked to sponsor another. However that may be, both Bank and publisher were mistaken for two reasons. First, and related to the present discussion, a history which cannot always state sources and which cannot, because of the recent nature of the events and their complexity, either explain them in full context or provide the data for further analysis is not a final history – there will be another; perhaps it will be properly entitled to use the definite article. Secondly, the very mass of detail suggests that this must be a very personal history of the Bank.

Sir Michael Sandberg asked me to write the history 'warts and all'; he asked me especially to deal with people, with those who made the Bank successful. Otherwise he set no limits beyond those which are consequent to a publicly recognized policy. In consequence, the commission was open-ended; the choice of material may fairly be termed 'idiosyncratic'. Others may someday write within more strictly defined parameters; perhaps that will be '*The* history...'

There has always been a dual character to this history, thus providing the advantages of a hands-off approach by the Bank supplemented by provision of access and facilities normally associated with a controlled 'in-house' project. On the one hand the research and writing has been a project approved by the several university committees and undertaken within the Centre of Asian Studies, on the other I have been free to move about the Bank, to be a member of the Bank's executive 'mess', and to talk on a confidential basis with present and retired staff. These facilities have been particularly important in the preparation of the present volume. I do not believe that any information has been purposely withheld. If it had been in the interviews and discussions, the fact would have been revealed in the documents, including the Chairman's papers and the Minutes of the Board of Directors, which I have consulted.

My agreement with the Bank stated that in return for full access I would permit the typescript to be read before submission to the publisher; confidential material could then be removed. The typescript was read by the Chairman, Sir Michael Sandberg. Nothing of historical substance has been removed, with the exception of statements which came too close to 'disclosure' or to violation of that confidentiality necessary to protect the interests of customers (or 'constituents', the term traditionally used by the Bank). However, I had my own inhibitions. First, I was unwilling to 'judge' the actions of professionals in an institution which has been successful both for its constituents and for its shareholders unless I felt fully competent to do so, having researched and digested all the relevant information. In more recent years there are few situations in which I considered these requirements to have been fulfilled. Secondly, the arrangements described above, originally designed for a history to end in 1962, were extended to 1980, but not, on my own decision, thereafter. Nevertheless, 'threads' have been followed in Chapter 18 through 1984 – and, where I yielded to temptation, to 1987.

This is the Bank which, in 1956 when I was thirty years of age and a Lecturer in the University of Hong Kong, agreed, after my brief interview with the formidable G.O.W. Stewart, to finance my mortage valued at $10,000. I confess that, as a shareholder and as one who has studied Chinese economic history, I have always considered the Bank an institution key to an understanding of economic events in Treaty Port China, and I have been anxious to write its history. For that reason the preparation of these four volumes has been a work of great professional satisfaction and personal pleasure. Never, I suggest, has a corporation been more open or hospitable to their historian. I hope that my respect for their history and my enjoyment of the assignment have not tempered my critical senses, for that would be a disservice. My own assessment is that these four volumes constitute a fair account as understood by one particular historian who has called Hong Kong his home for some 25 years.

Romanization and terminology

Chinese names and terms (other than Cantonese or other dialect) have been romanized according to the modified Wade-Giles system or as preferred by the person or the times. In this volume the official *pinyin* is used where appropriate. Chinese characters are provided on occasion for the names of bankers who might otherwise be unidentifiable. Readers are referred to the Chinese Glossary in Volume III for other names and terms.

Current banking and other professional terms are to be found in standard technical dictionaries. For traditional China-coast and other unusual terms not defined in the text, readers are referred to the lists in Volumes I through III.

In the oral histories 'pseudo-quotations', that is, quotations used as a narrative device, are not placed within quotation marks.

Notes and corrections

Since the publication of Volumes I through III, the following comments have become necessary.

Volume I. Plate 2C was ascribed to George Chinnery; G.H.R. Tillotson (see Plate 97, p. 87, of his *Fan Kwae Pictures*) states authoritatively that the artist is an unknown European.

David McLean's early life as recounted in Volume I, p. 239, has to be revised in the light of a letter found recently among papers at the home of his grandson, D.C.H. McLean.

McLean served his apprenticeship with the Western Bank of Scotland under William Beveridge, to whom he ascribes his success in banking. Eventually assigned to head office, McLean nevertheless applied to the Oriental Bank for an Eastern 'berth'; the Western Bank failed in 1857 and McLean resolved to go to New Zealand. A last minute check with the Oriental Bank in London, however, revealed that the manager had that day written to offer him a post in either India or China; he abandoned his former plans (and his passage money) and chose China.

The traditional story of the shipwreck, the decision in Ceylon, and the consequential problems of his being unknown to the Oriental's London management is, therefore, incorrect. Certain related comments in Volume I also require amendment.

Table 15.3 (I, 579) is an admittedly incomplete list of family relationships within the Hongkong Bank. However, George H. Townsend (London Office 1874, East in 1878) should be noted as the younger brother of A.M. Townsend. In 1888 George was under house arrest in Manila in connection with the Jurado affair; at the time his brother was Agent New York. George died in Bombay in 1900. A death notice in the *North-China Herald* drew attention to the relationship.

There is a tradition in the A.G. Stephen (Shanghai Manager, 1912–1920; Chief Manager, 1920–d.1924) family that, about 1919/20 during the silver speculations, he was offered a fee of $1 million by J.P. Morgan interests to transfer from the Hongkong Bank; his wife reportedly urged acceptance, but Stephen felt the offer an 'insult' and so confided (as he confided most matters – including the opening exchange rate) to his twin daughters. Instead he attacked (see III, 82–83). 'Tita' (de Gherardi) sensed the extraordinary tension in the months her father out-manoeuvred the American banks in Shanghai.

Although there is no hint in the minutes of the Board of Directors, Stephen's official Bank residence in Shanghai while he was Chief Manager in Hong Kong was undoubtedly required primarily for his wife (see III, 148). Mrs Stephen was a talented violinist; she was also temperamental – she is the 'hysterical prima donna of Shanghai' in Noel Coward's autobiography. And thus Stephen made his last trip to Europe alone; he took the cure at Tarasp where the twins were enschooled and he travelled with them, a dying man, to London (III, 160). They stayed by his bedside until he, feeling the end approaching, ordered them away. They returned, but he sensed their presence and once again sent them out. 'He wished', Tita recalls sadly, 'to spare us.'

Stephen told the twins that he had earlier considered a career in the theatre; while a lad in Scotland he had stepped in to act Hamlet when the lead travelling player had become ill. Family economic considerations prevailed, but Shakespeare remained a vital part of his life. Indeed, his interests were wider; he is the founder of the Bank's art collection (see Tillotson's *Fan Kwae Pictures*).

The illustrations of low denomination tael and tical banknotes in Joe Cribb's *Money in the Bank* are a reminder that the Treasury's long obsession with the question of banknotes of less than $5.00 equivalency in value focused on the

Hong Kong issue; there is apparently no mention in the copious archival material of an offending Shanghai or Bangkok issue. Location would not have affected their impact on the Bank, however, and the Treasury's lack of concern must be ascribed to lack of knowledge. They never asked – and the Bank, true to form, never thought to tell.

Centre of Asian Studies,
University of Hong Kong

March 1, 1987

In consequence of the Hongkong Bank's 1989 registration under the Hong Kong companies act (while remaining subject to the provisions of the Bank's own ordinance/charter), the usual designation 'Limited' is added to the full corporate name. In this volume, the change has been made only in the copyright line (page iv).

Recent research is conclusive that Angelo Luzzatti (II, 302) was born 'Luzzati' and was not, therefore, the nephew or, indeed, any close relation of Luigi Luzzatti.

There has been no reassessment consequent to recent events.

FRANK H. H. KING

New Mexico Military Institute,
Roswell, New Mexico,
U.S.A.

May 1, 1990

ACKNOWLEDGEMENTS

This history was commissioned by The Hongkong and Shanghai Banking Corporation. I am grateful to the Bank's former Chairman, Sir Michael Sandberg, for his willingness not only to commission a history early in his tenure as chief executive officer, but also for his continued support as the project was extended from time to time. This support has been continued by the present Chairman, William Purves.

The history project was jointly sponsored by the Bank and by the University of Hong Kong and undertaken within the Centre of Asian Studies. Rayson L. Huang, Vice-Chancellor, gave full cooperation and encouragement; his successor, Wang Gungwu, continued support for this small part of his inheritance.

Administrative assistance in the University was provided through the Centre of Asian Studies and from the Secretary's Office and Finance Office in the University. I should mention Norman J. Gillanders, Ian A. McKenzie, and all those responsible for handling the accounts. So extensive were my requests for copying that So Wing Cheong and his staff in the University printing office may be excused for supposing that they actually produced these volumes!

The Hongkong Bank supported the project through Group Archives; a succession of Controllers, most recently A.I. Donaldson, the Assistant to the Controller, Margaret Lee, and all members of the Archives staff provided essential support and contacts. From time to time members of the Hongkong Bank staff would provide professional advice and/or hospitality. Catherine King and I recall particularly a dinner at the Junior Mess, Cloudlands, after attending a meeting of members (see Chapter 18).

The final stages of the project were undertaken while I was associated with Merton College which has, as on so many previous occasions, provided a temporary base for study.

Fortunately, Leslie Pressnell, who had accepted the appointment as consultant in 1980, agreed to continue his role through the often extended period of research and writing. His comments and corrections were invaluable.

S.W. Muirhead of the Hongkong Bank and formerly Controller of Archives reread the entire typescript; his familiarity with the archives, with banking in general, and especially with the history of the Mercantile Bank has prevented many serious errors from reaching the published text. Dr Geoffrey Jones continued his constructive interest and his own history of the British Bank of the Middle East provided background and insights.

The contents of the present volume depend less on historical archives than on the more current operational files of the Bank and on interviews with those who made the Bank's history. Nevertheless the researches of D.J.S. King in Germany and of Elizabeth Ng Wai Yee in London were of continued importance. I made further use of the (Sir Charles) Addis papers, now in the Library, School of Oriental and African Studies, and under the care of Rosemary Seton. Once again we acknowledge the kind hospitality and reminiscenses of the late Robina Addis and the additional material provided by Charles P. Addis. Use was also made of the British and Chinese Corporation archives. David King was granted access to certain of the Standard Chartered Bank archives through the courtesy of Sir Peter Graham.

Other important primary sources utilized in this volume include the archives of Siemsen and Co. and the papers of F.T. Koelle. The work of J.R. Jones in preparation for the centenary history covered the years almost to 1960, and much use was made of the contributions which he successfully solicited from retired members of staff and others.

Essential assistance came from those who had made the history of the Bank. Sir Michael Sandberg read chapters in this volume with particular care and both in this and in a series of interviews provided insights which have been incorporated in the history. Without the benefit of these inputs, the volume could not have ventured much beyond a simple chronicling of events in the 1970s and after.

The materials from the London and Shanghai archives selected by F.H. King (no relation) and E.C. Hutchison respectively continued to be useful despite the availability of the records themselves. However, the oral history interviews, the great majority of them undertaken by the experienced Christopher Cook, became increasingly important, and those who assisted are listed in the Bibliography. Claude Fivel-Démoret interviewed retired members of the Lyons staff. Former chief executives Sir Michael Turner, G.M. Sayer, and Sir Michael Sandberg gave permission for their interviews to be quoted. There was also the special contribution of Lady Turner. Certain retired senior officers of the Bank undertook thorough critiques of material in draft chapters concerning which they had personal knowledge. On this account I should give special mention to N.H.T. Bennett, F.C.B. Black, R.G.L. Oliphant, S.W.P. Perry-Aldworth, G.O.W. Stewart, and W.A. Stewart.

Acknowledgements

The story of the Hongkong Bank's acquisition of Marine Midland Banks, Inc. depends on the cooperation not only of the Hongkong Bankers involved but also of virtually all those who participated in the negotiations. These are listed in the Bibliography, and it would be invidious to single out a particular contributor, except perhaps to note the authoritative accounts provided by Edward W. Duffy and John R. Petty, the historical insights into Marine Midland of Karl Hinke, Baldwin Maull, and Arthur Ziegler. Henry C. Wallich, formerly a member of the Board of Governors, Federal Reserve System, also provided access to his grandfather's papers dealing with early banking on the China coast. Well-known and consequently busy investment bankers, legal advisers, and public relations experts were generous with their time, in some cases at least because they were genuinely proud to have been involved in a transaction so satisfactory to all parties (with the one interesting exception) involved. My difficult schedule was coordinated by Carol Donoghue, now an Assistant Vice President in the Bank's New York office.

A similar comprehensive study was made of the Bank's unsuccessful attempt to purchase the Royal Bank of Scotland Group. This story is not fully covered in this history, not so much for reasons of confidentiality, although Britain lacks a Freedom of Information Act, but because the events occurred beyond the year (1980) fixed for the conclusion of the present study. Chapter 18 was originally designed to provide only a brief factual summary of events after the Marine Midland acquisition. The full list of interviewees appears in the Bibliography. I should, nevertheless, refer to my interviews with Sir Michael Herries, William Dacombe, and Sidney Proctor from the Royal Bank of Scotland Group and with Sir Peter Graham from the Standard Chartered Bank, and to the more general guidance of Christopher Baur.

As in previous volumes quotation *in extenso* has been made from papers submitted to the 1981 Hongkong Bank History Conference and published in *Eastern Banking* (London, 1983). This volume is indebted to the writings by Carl T. Smith, Christopher L. Yip, Chee Peng Lim, Phang Siew Nooi and Margaret Boh, Roy C. Ybañez, D.J.S. King, Y.C. Jao, Victor F.S. Sit, S.G. Redding, Y.P. Ngan, and Arthur B. Ziegler – as listed in the Bibliography. Commissioned research reports by Ybañez and H.L.D. Selvaratnam were consulted.

Towards the end of the project research gaps appeared, and Margaret Harcourt Williams was willing to move quickly to meet urgent requirements. Material for the corrections, see pp. xxxix–xl, was provided by D.C.H. McLean and by Tita [Stephen] de Gherardi of Madrid. I am also indebted to Mary [Stephen] Schultz of Roswell, New Mexico, for further insights.

Certain maps and figures were drawn by the Cartographic Unit of the

Acknowledgements

Department of Geography; Mrs D. Lui and her associates in the Centre for Media Resources designed several of the figures; the more recent materials were provided by Group Archives and the Public Affairs Department of the Hongkong Bank. Colleagues in the University of Hong Kong also provided assistance, in addition to contributions to the Hongkong Bank History Conference, especially Y.C. Jao, C.K. Leung, A.Y.C. Lui, K.L. Macpherson, N.J. Miners, Victor F.S. Sit, G.M.G. Stirling, and M. Turnbull.

University of Hong Kong undergraduate research assistants included Lee Chun Wah, Cheng Yim-mei, Kitty Yu Wai Hing, and Pauline Chow Lo Sai. Several assistants came through the American Chamber of Commerce YES Program; Kathryn T. Boland undertook to translate the French oral histories.

I am particularly appreciative of the last-minute comments of Sir Quo Wei Lee relative to the Hongkong Bank's acquisition of Hang Seng Bank (pp. 702–06).

This volume, as with the others, is in part a family project, including the assistance of Roger, David, and Peter King. I could not have completed the history without the editorial assistance of Catherine E. King, who set aside her own interests in the social history of the Treaty Ports and the Bank to help me push these volumes through the several stages of publication. And in this connection we have all to express our appreciation to Anne Rix, who copy edited the first two volumes and then, although fully aware of the difficulties, agreed to continue with the final two volumes on behalf of Cambridge University Press. She did much more than what is usually understood by the term 'copy edit'.

Throughout the project lasting some seven years I have received complete cooperation from both the Group Archives of the Hongkong Bank and the Centre of Asian Studies. In the Archives there has been assistance from Lily Lau Sung and Elaine Wu in Hong Kong and from G. Plastow in London. Margaret Woollam of the Archives staff also read the proofs and detected last minute problems; Anne Cordiero assisted in Singapore. The plates were prepared by Raymond Chan Wing On (Vols. I–III) and Julius Wong Kong Piu (Vol. IV). As for the Centre, the Director, E.K.Y. Chen, and Administrative Officer, Coonoor Kripalani-Thadani, have been responsible for the project. This supervision has been supplemented in a most practical way by Carol Chan Yuen Yee, Sherman Lam Tung Chun, Anita Lau Po Ling, and Cathy Wong Lin Yau, although it is only fair to add that several others were from time to time involved.

FRANK H.H. KING

STATEMENT ON DOLLARS AND EXCHANGE

All dollars in this history
unless specifically stated otherwise
are
HONG KONG DOLLARS.
One billion = 1,000 million
One lac = 1,00,000

The Hong Kong/London exchange rate was quoted as so many shillings and pence per dollar, e.g. $1.00 = 4s 6d. From this it follows that:

A **fall** in exchange will result in a dollar exchanging for fewer shillings and pence and is evidence of a depreciation of the Hong Kong dollar *vis à vis* sterling.

A **rise** (improvement, increase) in exchange will result in a dollar exchanging for more shillings and pence and is evidence of an appreciation of the Hong Kong dollar *vis à vis* sterling.

The Shanghai exchanges were similarly quoted in terms of the Chinese dollar.

'Silver' referred in the popular business jargon of the day to units of account payable in silver bullion or coin. Thus a 'silver' loan is a loan denominated in e.g. Hong Kong dollars or Shanghai taels or dollars.

'Gold' referred to sterling and/or to other currencies on a gold standard.

'The exchanges' or other similar term refers, unless modified, to the foreign exchange rates and the markets which determine the rate at which one currency can be bought in terms of another.

All dollars in this history
unless specifically stated otherwise
are
HONG KONG DOLLARS.

ABBREVIATIONS

Bank	The Hongkong and Shanghai Banking Corporation
BAAG	British Army Advisory Group
B&CC	British and Chinese Corporation
BBME	British Bank of the Middle East
BETRO	British Export Trade Research Organization
BPO	Business Promotion Official
BR	Business Representative
CCR	Chinese Central Railways
CNC	Chinese National Currency
CRA	Community Reinvestment Act
d	penny
EDP	Electronic Data Processing
ETC	Electronic Teller Card
FCBU	Foreign Currency Banking Unit
FDIC	Federal Deposit Insurance Corporation
FECB	Foreign Exchange Control Board (Japan)
FRB	Federal Reserve Board
FRS	Federal Reserve System
FTZ	Free Trade Zone
GAAP	Generally Accepted Accounting Principles
HBC	Hongkong and Shanghai Banking Corporation of California, Incorporated
HSBC	The Hongkong and Shanghai Banking Corporation
IBA	International Banking Act
IBD	Industrial Banking Department
IBRD	International Bank for Reconstruction and Development (World Bank)
ICAC	Independent Commission against Corruption
ICB	International Commercial Bank
ILO	International Labour Organization

IMF	International Monetary Fund
LAC	London Advisory Committee
MBLD	Mercantile Bank Limited
MMB	Marine Midland Bank
MMBI	Marine Midland Banks, Inc.
MMC	Marine Midland Corporation
NYBD	New York State Banking Department
OBU	Offshore Banking Unit
OCBC	Oversea-Chinese Banking Corporation
OCC	Office of the Comptroller of the Currency
P&L	Profit and Loss
P&O	Peninsular and Oriental Steam Navigation Company
P&O Bank	Peninsular and Oriental Bank
PAP	People's Action Party
PLA	People's Liberation Army
PNB	Philippine National Bank
RBSG	Royal Bank of Scotland Group
REIT	Real Estate Investment Trust
s	shilling
SCAP	Supreme Commander Allied Powers
SEC	Securities and Exchange Commission
SMC	Shanghai Municipal Council
UNRRA	United Nations Relief and Rehabilitation Agency

INTRODUCTION: FROM REGIONAL BANK TO MULTINATIONAL GROUP

> Truly Joss take care this bank.
> Shanghai compradore, 1892

At the end of 1984 The Hongkong and Shanghai Banking Corporation was reportedly the world's fourteenth largest banking group as calculated on the basis of shareholders' funds valued at $20.9 billion.[a] With 1,200 offices in 55 countries and a staff of some 45,000, the Hongkong Bank managed assets totalling $481.6 billion (= £53.0 billion or US$61.6 billion). In 1941 all the Bank's Eastern branches this side of India were overrun, and the question of the Bank's survival, never actually in doubt, was nevertheless discussed by the Colonial Office with Arthur Morse, the Acting Chief Manager in London. At the end of the war the Bank moved back to the East; at the time (December 31, 1945) total assets were £94.5 million (= $1,520.0 million) and shareholders' funds £8.4 million (= $135.1 million).[b]

THEMES FOR VOLUME IV

An obvious theme for this, the fourth of a four-volume history of the Hongkong Bank, is the process whereby the corporation not only survived in an increasingly nationalistic East and in the context of intense international banking competition but became a multinational financial organization ranking among the world's twenty largest banks. A related question must be rather bluntly stated: in considering the factors involved in the Bank's post-war development, do the previous three volumes, that is, do the previous 80 years of history, make any difference?

---

[a] Ranking banks by the value of shareholders' funds results in placing Citicorp of New York first, followed by BankAmerica Corp. National Westminister Bank is tenth, Chemical New York Corp. thirteenth, and Manufacturers Hanover Corp. fifteenth. A listing of the top 500 banks can be found in *Euromoney* for June 1985. In this history, one billion = 1,000 million.
[b] The official accounts were then in sterling; the Bank's Head Office had not yet returned to Hong Kong. All dollars in this history are Hong Kong dollars unless specifically stated otherwise.

I

The Bank in its history

The second question will be addressed first. The story of the Bank has been published in a form which permits students of the late Ch'ing period, for example, to focus on Volumes I and II and yet be provided with some information relative to the corporation in later years. Similarly, those specializing in modern banking problems, in the post-war East, or in recent business history will be primarily concerned with Volume IV, and previous events will be summarized in this introduction. But these arrangements are designed for convenience and say more about the cost of each volume than about the continuity of the Bank's history.

When China went off silver in 1935 and Hong Kong followed, the exchange risk which had forced the Bank to maintain 'an even keel', that is, to maintain reserves in both gold (sterling) and silver (dollars), was minimized; the Chief Manager, Sir Vandeleur Grayburn, moved funds to London. Thus the very preservation of the shareholders' funds on the outbreak of the Pacific War was an accident or consequence of the Bank's history, and the consequent assets were the base from which the post-1945 growth began. The use of funds had, however, to be managed by the executives of the Bank and the most senior of these officers had been recruited before the Great War of 1914–1918; Morse himself had come East in 1915. The recruiting process and the training in London had not changed since the 1870s; the socialization process through which management operated and the 'cream' finally rose to the top (to use A.G. Stephen's metaphor) was a unique product of the Hongkong Bank. The parts were not interchangeable; the way Morse operated can only be explained in a historical context. Finally, there is 'good-will', an asset which is capable of quantification and which is admittedly a product of a company's history. The Hongkong Bank had a reputation in the East; it could in consequence command a loyalty – the Bank had itself been loyal to constituents in difficulties – it could 'do things' which newly established banks could not as yet attempt. Certainly this would change; being the doyen in Bangkok, for example, and holding the accounts of the nobility would not seem so important to the treasurers of multinational corporations or even to the new generation of Thai entrepreneurs. Nevertheless, some aura remained; the Bank did not deny its past or the attitudes which had made it respected. Past reputation and present abilities both were responsible for the Bank's recent growth.

Post-war success: explanations
If the Bank cannot be fully understood except in terms of its history, it is then equally true that history alone would not have ensured its post-war success. The Mercantile Bank of India, Ltd., was older; the British Bank of the

Middle East (BBME, formerly the Imperial Bank of Persia) would move into the developing Gulf and yet require a partner. The survival and growth of the Hongkong Bank is a consequence of fortuitous circumstances – the old Shanghai compradore had called it 'joss' – and innovative management which was capable of effecting change without denying the past.

The Hong Kong base

> The Bank would succeed because of its local support.
>
> A.F. Heard, member, Provisional Committee, 1864

First of all, there was the Hong Kong base. When the founding 'Provisional Committee' met in 1864, the Colony's leading merchants were inspired as much or more by the potential of Shanghai and the newly opened Yangtze Valley region and elsewhere in the East as by prospects in Hong Kong itself, but only in Hong Kong (and then with difficulty) could they incorporate with limited liability – hence 'Hongkong and Shanghai'. Then, resisting temptation, both directors and Managers, including London Managers, recognized the importance of Head Office remaining in the East. From this there were two main and one subsidiary consequences: first, the Bank was on hand to finance the unexpected development of Hong Kong, and, second, the British Crown Colony of Hong Kong remained British and its principal bank was enabled to grow undisturbed until it was ready to accept the challenges of international banking. And ancillary to these was the fact that its own home territory proved a low tax area, with provisions which assumed a claim only to income deriving from the territory itself.

The BBME and the Mercantile Bank of India were British overseas banks registered in London and, even before the former's withdrawal from Tehran, each was effectively directed from its principal office in the City. But neither India nor Iran were places friendly to the growth of an alien bank, and, when prosperity came to the Gulf, the BBME was insufficiently financed to take full advantage of it alone. On the contrary, the very prosperity of Hong Kong enriched the Hongkong Bank to the point that diversity in the geographical use of funds became imperative, but its capabilities were still structurally limited. The solution was diversity through acquisition, and the timing was right. The Bank of England, the Treasury, and the Foreign Office would deplore the trade and other economic implications implicit in the disappearance of British overseas banks; there were sad cases, for example, the Ionian Bank. Size was important, yet growth was difficult and consequently rationalization became essential. The British authorities would consequently encourage and facilitate the Hongkong Bank's acquisitions. The Bank, with some show of reluctance, came to accept that the regional limitations imposed by the Treasury in the mid-nineteenth century, limitations virtually unchallenged until the mid 1950s, were no longer tenable. By the end of 1960 the Hongkong Bank was both a major regional bank and a bank holding company whose interests extended beyond the Far East into India, where its presence had previously been marginal, the Middle East, and, less successfully, California. And, having seen what could be done, the Board of Directors sought, unsuccessfully as far as commercial banking was concerned, to move by acquisition into Europe, Canada, and/or Australasia. Although partially frustrated, the efforts, though perhaps inadequately or unsystematically pursued, indicated the essential recognition of what must be done to survive and survive profitably.

The Hongkong Bank's major branches in Ceylon, China, Japan, the Straits Settlements, the Philippines, Siam, and, post-war, India operated virtually as autonomous 'banks', linked by a common capital and staff, under a single Board responsible *de jure* to a single group of shareholders, *de facto* to shareholder interests divided by the fact of registration in London or, alternatively, in the East. To a great extent, therefore, the concept of a 'local bank', considered by A.F. Heard in 1864/65 in relation to the Bank in Hong Kong, has also been relevant to the Bank's activities in each of the territories, and each has a separate history. This remains particularly true today where the Bank is subject to the interplay of political and regulatory factors and is managed largely by local officers with loyalties naturally peculiar to each territory. Although Hong Kong is the logical focus in this volume, the Hong Kong story is paralleled elsewhere. The history of other branches, however, can be only briefly surveyed – as it has been in previous volumes – although supplemented by selected case studies.

Corporate structure

And yet there remained a weak link. The Hongkong Bank's first foreign subsidiary, The Hongkong and Shanghai Banking Corporation of California, Incorporated, ran into immediate management problems from which it never really recovered. A Hongkong Banker with experience on the China coast proved, not surprisingly, to be unqualified to direct a California bank. Even if he had proved qualified, he would have found essential head office support lacking. The regional bank was still 'on-line', without a head office hierarchy, without support services or specialists; it was trying to be an inter-regional bank without the necessary experience or corporate structure.

This deficiency was circumvented at first by retaining the individual identity, staff, and even directors of the two acquired banks. This brought about problems of its own, but it bought time. One major contribution of Sir John Saunders, significantly the first Chief Manager not to have served in the East before the Pacific War, was his ability to direct, or perhaps tolerate, the end of the 'one man' tradition in its extreme form, to give up the reading of all outgoing semi-official correspondence, to move at a relatively early stage into advanced bank technology with all the related organizational implications. Furthermore, he succeeded in re-creating the Board of Directors in a form essential for a modern corporation and in ensuring that an executive director of the Bank would be its Chairman.

Despite these reforms, problems remained. The structural changes had created a potential for success which was not yet fully realized. First, there was as yet no formal planning; the search for subsidiaries seemed *ad hoc*; it became almost opportunistic, which is not to suggest it was not, on the whole, successful or that the new companies thus acquired by the Bank as holding company proved unsound – some did, most did not. In fact, the Bank's particularistic approach to management made the useful accession of a planning officer virtually impractical until 1981, although this would not prevent a small group within Head Office from developing investment banking facilities which became Wardley Limited or in the mid-1970s from planning the American strategy. Nevertheless, the desire to sit back and 'digest' the changes was never more dangerous than in the early 1970s, and hesitations relative to pushing through potential reform to its limits could have had an ultimately serious impact.

The growth of assets placed a focus on the capital/assets ratio, and management struggled throughout, but especially during periods of inflation, to maintain an adequate base of (published) 'primary capital'. The growth of the Reserve Fund in itself was important, but the interrelated problems of capital, reserves, and dividends had to be considered as a whole. One persistent theme in this volume is therefore capital policy and the self-imposed constraints – including a refusal to attempt long-term borrowing or the reluctance to recommend a rights issue.[c] The only alternative remaining was capitalization of published reserves, the latter then being replaced from inner reserves – and variants of this theme. The first capitalization issue, referred to by the Bank as a 'bonus' issue, was in 1955; the second came with the doubling of paid-up capital in 1957 when the double liability of shareholders was eliminated; there was then a centenary bonus issue, and a bonus issue became virtually an annual event. The fast moving events at the end of the 1970s forced a reconsideration, and a rights issue was voted in 1981. Only after 1984 did the Bank raise capital through floating rate, no date bond issues.

[c] A rights issue was actually considered by the Board, but the most telling argument against the proposal was that the Bank had never raised funds in this way and that the Chinese, considering the Bank held unlimited wealth, would misunderstand. The chief executives of the time were sadly unaware of the Bank's history. With only one exception (1865, at a time when capital could in any case only be obtained at par), new capital had always been raised by a rights issue, usually with a joss-assisted timing which can only be described as incredibly fortunate.

This begs the question as to why the Bank was in fact growing. The Bank's policies relative to management of funds has been, one could argue, conservative. Successive chief executives have been reluctant to buy-in funds; the Bank's balance sheet in 1979 reminded U.S. regulators of a 'country bank'. Indeed, the reluctance to engage in liability management, the stress on securing a reliable deposit base remained as important in the 1970s as in 1874/5 when local depositors stayed loyal, held their deposits, and saw the Bank through crisis.

In the East this 'conservatism' was well conceived. The Bank had a certain source of funds. Thus the focus is on use. The immediate response to the question of growth is, therefore, to refer back to the Hong Kong base, to the success (some of the time) of certain economies which the Bank served, and, by the same argument, to the inflow of funds from Chinese in countries with policies unfriendly to capital investment. The Bank grew with its customers. Secondly, under J.A.H. Saunders the Bank for the first time invested deliberately (as opposed to a salvage operation) in equity; while never taking direct control of management, the Bank became directly involved in the affairs of certain of its major constituents. Thirdly, the Bank was on occasion engaged in operations designed to maintain 'confidence' in Hong Kong, buying shares and property when no other buyer could be found; an operation bound to be rewarding should the economy recover – as indeed it has on several occasions. The idea of buying cheap and selling at the peak has occurred to others, but never with greater or more consistent success. Fourthly, high interest rates resulted in a high money income, usually in inflationary periods, suggesting the need to translate to real terms for proper analysis. From these sources the Bank generated sufficient income to require diversification through further investment; the acquisition of 50% or more of the equity of a company required consolidation of the accounts with a consequent increase in leverage, or, expressed another way, a decrease in the vital capital/assets ratio. The argument has turned full cycle.

Personnel

The Bank's traditional personnel policy could not survive the dramatic social, political, and professional changes post-war. The three-tier system – an 'Eastern staff' of British officers recruited only through London, a 'Portuguese' staff of second-line clerks recruited locally, and a 'native' staff recruited by and responsible to a compradore or guarantee shroff – would no longer be tolerated either by a cost-conscious management, a visa-granting sovereign Government, or ambitious young Chinese, Malays, Filipinos, and others throughout Asia.

The traditions of the Eastern (then Foreign then International) staff remained strong; they resisted change. It is difficult to argue with success, and

British anti-intellectualism, against which Sir Charles Addis had argued in the first decade of the century, prevailed in the early post-war years. Even the young man who had passed his second Institute of Bankers examination was regarded with a curious mixture of praise and scorn – 'vellum men', Morse called them. Then came the day when Tokyo office was asked to quote for Eurodollars – and had never heard of them.

Aside from the problem of success there was the problem of numbers. The first attempt at change, designed to overcome this problem, was apparently the easiest, but in fact it may have been psychologically the most difficult – the integration of the three foreign staffs of the Hongkong Bank, the Mercantile Bank, and the BBME. This took nearly twenty years to accomplish. But the need to change was a recurrent theme until in 1977 the whole position was thoroughly reviewed. At this time a key question was considered – aside from the debate relative to pre-professional education ('A' levels or B.A./B.Sc.), what should be the extent of the operational knowledge of an officer intended eventually for senior banking responsibilities? That a senior Accountant can keep a journal is fortunate during a strike of clerks in the early 1950s, but is the skill still relevant? And, if so, at what price?

The decisions stemming from the 1977 review were significant and the new policies decisively implemented, even as the Bank was moving to acquire Marine Midland and consequently come under the scrutiny of the U.S. Comptroller of the Currency. American regulators asked the key question: has this bank the staff and organization adequate for undertaking the responsibilities inherent in being a successful U.S. bank holding company? The response in 1979 was positive.

The second tier virtually took care of itself. The Portuguese of the China coast and Hong Kong, the burghers of Ceylon emigrated. There were too few left to form an employment 'caste' and with the other local employees they stood to benefit from a separate reform – the appointment of local officers.

The compradoric system, so much criticized since the early days of foreign trade with the East, ended not when foreigners were able to handle the compradore's tasks as some nineteenth-century merchants had expected, but when Chinese were admitted to undertake those jobs previously reserved to foreigners. Local officers from the previous second and third tiers were appointed, cautiously, before the end of the 1950s. Their path to full recognition and the acceptance of non-British into the 'International staff', as the equivalent of the old 'Eastern staff' came to be called, is another major theme to be developed below.

The move from a socialized officer-caste required new forms of corporate control. Specialists had to be employed and 'accepted' – or specialist companies acquired to serve the requirements of the Group. London 'training' in the sense described by P.G. Wodehouse (see Volume II) had long ago been faulted, but the inter-war period had not been one sympathetic to personnel innovations. With the growing complexity of the banking profession, not only regional officers would require training; indeed, formal training had to become an integral function of Head Office.

The adjustment of personnel policy, although at first reluctant and deliberately paced, was an essential element in the post-war success of the Hongkong Bank.

The Bank in a banking system

At the same time the Hongkong Bank had to mature in other ways. The founding charter, the 1866 ordinance of incorporation, had placed the Bank within the tradition of colonial banks subject to the Colonial Banking Regulations and, therefore, to the distant supervision of the Treasury through the Colonial Office. There were, however, provisions which required such banks to conform to local banking and, where applicable, company ordinances. Through a chance series of events, Hong Kong did not have an ordinance which attempted real supervision of the banking sector until 1964, and the Hongkong Bank under Morse objected to the very thought of being subjected to any 'general' legislation; the Bank was *sui generis*. This latter position was more a reflection of Morse's strong personality than the legal realities, and when the dangers of an unsupervised banking system became apparent in the early 1960s, Hongkong Bank senior Managers were among the first to recommend specific provisions for effective legislation.

Thus as the Bank was growing, moving out from regional to multinational visibility, so its status was changing from a unique but equivocal position granted by special legislation to membership in and, to some degree at least, leadership in a banking community, subject to its regulatory authorities and its prohibitions. This, however, introduces a further theme: was (or is) the Hongkong Bank a *de facto* central bank in Hong Kong? The answer is a decisive negative, but the argument continues. The Hongkong Bank has admitted responsibilities as the largest commercial bank; full submergence as just one in a system has never occurred – of all its historical heritage, of its uniqueness, for example, the most obvious present manifestation is the Hong Kong note issue, over 80% of which is the responsibility of the Hongkong Bank. How this right survived is certainly a matter which can only be appreciated in the light of developments described in previous volumes. But one point is certain: the right to issue banknotes is irrelevant to the question as to whether the Bank is a central bank. The previous conclusion will survive analysis.

Shedding the past

The China Consortium and loans

The Bank's history also had a negative impact; to this extent the Bank had to shed its past. Before Morse and his colleagues could give their sole attention to post-war development, they were forced to divert part of their energies to matters which in retrospect appear futile, but which at the time seemed only an obvious duty. Furthermore, before the Bank could move freely in an increasingly international business, certain legal peculiarities had to be terminated. That management understood this and undertook the tasks is yet another theme in the Bank's post-war history.

There were naturally the immediate problems created by the war – the duress note issue, debtor/creditor relations – and these are immediately considered in Part I below. But the past was more intrusive than this, and the story must move back to the nineteenth century.

In the heady years from 1895 to 1914 the Hongkong Bank was at the forefront of those who sought to assist China in a reluctant modernization. In the process the Bank was joint-promoter of the British and Chinese Corporation (B&CC) and through this controlled shares in the Chinese Central Railways (CCR) and the relatively short-lived British and Korean Corporation. The Bank financed railway development in China, Siam, and the Philippines; it co-managed public loans to Japan; it financed the Shanghai Municipal Council. The loans to Siam and the Philippines no longer presented problems. Japan was in no condition to meet her obligations; when she was, she did so with a quiet but dramatic gesture to the Hongkong Bank. When the Pacific War was concluded, therefore, Morse looked first to China.

There followed nearly four years of frustration as the National Government recognized many of the obligations but found it impossible to actually make payment. The arguments continued after 'Liberation' through the 1955 'all-for-all' settlement the Bank made with the People's Republic; excluded from this was the matter of frozen U.S. dollar balances, a matter which continued to confuse relations with the new Government into the 1970s. Meanwhile a new relationship was being forged, one which would develop after 1979.

As for the CCR, its problems were merged into those of the B&CC. Again the Bank was frustrated; the small details of company management, the pension of the last widow, had still to be dealt with. And the company as trustee for China bondholders could not be wound up; it appears in the long list of subsidiaries (see Appendix Table B), but it is dormant.

The legal framework

The Hongkong Bank was apparently the last colonially chartered bank under the terms of the Colonial Banking Regulations. The need for such special handling would be obviated by general banking legislation, but, when in 1865 the Hong Kong Legislative Council attempted to include banks within the terms of a general companies ordinance, the ordinance was disallowed.

The Bank's special ordinance of incorporation, as revised, provided, *inter alia*, for the double liability of shareholders. This provision had had no practical significance at least since the crisis of 1874, but, when Sir Michael Turner first faced the question of acquiring the Mercantile Bank in the mid-1950s, he found the matter one of considerable importance. One theme, and one particularly suitable for a history, is the shedding of the colonial legislative heritage, the elimination of features peculiar to the special legislation, and, as already noted, the increasing integration of the Bank within the banking systems of the economies it came to serve.

THE BANK'S HISTORY, A SURVEY[d]

The Hongkong and Shanghai Banking Corporation was founded in 1865. The timing reflected the events since the ending of the Second Sino-British War, the opening of the Yangtze Valley to trade, the growth of Shanghai, and the failure of India or London based exchange banks to serve the intra-regional requirements of the flourishing Treaty Ports of China and Japan and of Hong Kong itself. The specific impetus was the threat of a 'Bank of China', a potentially serious offshoot of the Bombay share speculations, which threatened to preempt the field; accordingly a Provisional Committee of Hong Kong merchants – American, British, German, Norwegian, and Parsee, but excluding at that time Jardine, Matheson and Co. – was quickly assembled by (Sir) Thomas Sutherland, the P&O agent, in August 1864; in March 1865 their new bank was operating with a subscribed capital of $2.5 million.

Although operative, the Bank was not properly incorporated with limited liability by local ordinance until December 1866, by which time the subscribed capital had been increased to $5 million, a sum not fully paid up until 1872. From the first the Bank undertook foreign exchange operations and, in addition to its local interests, quickly became recognized as an Eastern exchange bank with offices in India and London and agents in the United States. There was initial success, but the Bank's previous financing of Hong Kong industrial

---

[d] The purpose of this survey is limited. The assumption is that readers who are interested in the recent history of the Bank may require some bare outline of previous events. For a more thorough survey, readers are referred to Chapter 1, Volume I. For an even more complete account, there are Volumes I–III themselves.

investments and coincident factors in 1874, a year which nearly proved fatal, caused the loss of reserves and the passing of the dividend.

The recovery of the Bank from 1876 was partly the consequence of its previous, conservative write-off policy, and partly the brilliance of the new Chief Manager, (Sir) Thomas Jackson. In 1883 the Bank began a rights issue which would bring paid-up capital to $7.5 million and shareholders' funds to $12.6 million. However a series of setbacks occurred during what proved to be the temporary absence of Jackson, and the Bank's fortunes were restored through an 1890 rights issue. The Bank began the decade with a paid-up capital of $10 million and shareholders' funds of $16.6 million (see Table I.1).

The Hongkong Bank was based in the East where silver was the standard. With the decline in the sterling value of the dollar from 4s:6d in 1872 to 3s:0d in 1888 and 1s:7d in 1902, the year Jackson retired from the East, careful management of the Bank's funds, the need to equate sources and uses by currency area, became an essential policy, referred to as keeping 'on an even keel'. The most important lesson from the failure of major Eastern exchange banks was that funds obtained in sterling should not be 'sent East', where they would be subject to depreciation. The Bank's Hong Kong Head Office and its broad coverage of major ports meant that this problem need not, with care, arise; the Bank had adequate Eastern silver deposits. The Bank did not fear depreciation of silver *per se*; its accounts were in silver, and thus it was able to accept silver deposits without cover and find uses for them. Accordingly it could outbid other Eastern exchange banks for Treasury Chest and Government business; the Bank was building up its reputation as banker to Governments; it was developing an expertise and counselling others on such matters as the currency standard.

The Bank did nevertheless suffer from fluctuations in exchange, and it is certain that its early loan business with Imperial China was one significant factor in its continued growth. The China loans, both Government and railway, became especially important in the 1890s. The Bank suffered through another crisis in 1892/93, Jackson was recalled, and silver had first increased in value and then suddenly continued its decline. The Bank was recovering when China again entered the market. However China's demand for funds during the First Sino-Japanese War in 1894–1895 and the added burden of the post-war indemnity were sufficiently large to attract political attention, and the Bank had to seek partners. Thus began the relationship with the Deutsch-Asiatische Bank, later expanded into the Five Power Groups, the 'China Consortium', which in 1913 would raise £25 million for China's 'reorganization'.

The Bank enjoyed a new-found reputation of international leadership; true to the literary meaning of 'Wayfoong', its Chinese name, the Bank had become a 'focus of wealth'.

Table I.1 *The Hongkong and Shanghai Banking Corporation
Changes in shares, paid-up capital, and shareholders' funds, 1865–1985*

End year[a]	Shares issued	Paid-up capital millions of $	Paid-up capital millions of £	Shareholders' funds millions of $	Shareholders' funds millions of £
1865	20,000	2.5	0.56	2.5	0.56
1866	40,000	2.9	0.65	3.1	0.70
1867	40,000	3.0	0.68	3.4	0.77
1869	40,000	3.5	0.79	4.3	0.97
1870	40,000	4.0	0.90	4.8	1.08
1871	40,000	4.0	0.90	4.8	1.08
1871	40,000	4.5	1.01	5.5	1.24
1872	40,000	5.0	1.13	6.0	1.35
1883	60,000	7.1	1.30	11.7	2.14
1884	60,000	7.5	1.39	12.6	2.23
1890	80,000	9.3	1.59	16.5	2.82
1907	120,000	15.0	1.36	45.8	4.15
1921	160,000	20.0	2.58	81.9	10.58
1955	200,000	25.0	1.56	163.6	10.23
1957	400,000	50.0	3.13	180.1	11.25
1959	498,491	62.3	3.89	240.3	15.02
1960	632,369	79.0	4.94	321.3	20.08
1961	3,161,845	79.0	4.94	321.4	20.09
1965	6,323,690	158.1	9.88	409.2	25.57
1966	6,956,059	173.9	10.87	478.2	29.89
1969	7,651,665	191.3	13.15	591.3	40.65
1970	15,303,330	382.6	26.30	884.4	58.05
1971	16,833,633	420.8	28.93	968.9	66.61
1972	18,517,029	462.9	34.87	1,311.9	98.83
1973	224,272,510	560.7	47.74	1,508.4	128.43
1974	277,651,978	694.1	60.25	1,841.3	159.83
1975	347,064,972	867.7	85.23	1,971.4	193.66
1976	381,771,469	954.4	120.05	2,272.8	285.89
1977	419,948,616	1,049.9	119.44	2,486.4	282.86
1978	461,943,478	1,154.9	117.90	2,877.3	293.75
1979	692,915,217	1,732.3	158.06	3,709.4	338.45
1980	1,114,233,983	2,785.6	227.12	10,326.0	841.91
1981	1,559,927,575	3,899.0	360.00	14,060.0	1,296.00
1982	2,079,903,433	5,199.8	493.00	15,606.0	1,479.00
1983	2,287,893,776	5,719.7	506.00	19,586.0	1,733.00
1984	2,859,867,220	7,149.7	787.00	20,863.0	2,296.00
1985	3,145,853,942	7,864.6	700.00	21,882.0	1,948.00

[a] Years selected are those in which there are changes in paid-up capital.

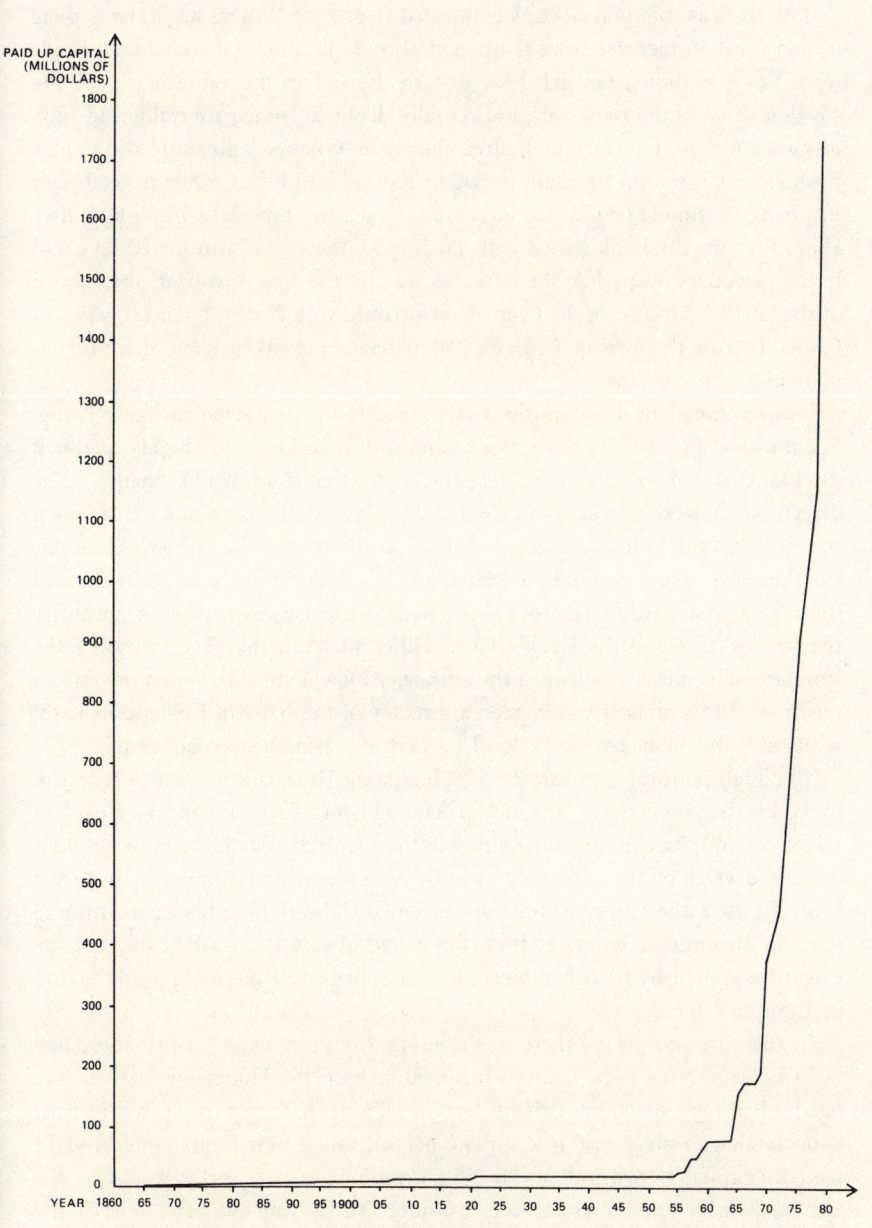

Figure 1.1 The Hongkong and Shanghai Banking Corporation
Paid-up capital, 1865–1979.

The Bank as commercial bank continued to prosper – there was a rights issue in 1907 and an increase in paid-up capital to $15 million (shareholders' funds were $45.8 million); nevertheless, due to the fall in the value of silver, the sterling value of the Bank's capital actually declined from £1.6 million in 1891 to £1.4 million. The various figures shown in Volume I illustrate the Bank's problems as it sought to retain its Hong Kong Head Office while nevertheless inspiring continued confidence in London. This was especially important after 1898, the year the Bank joined with Jardine Matheson to form the B&CC, and in the period to 1914 when the Bank became increasingly involved, as the head of the 'British Group' of the China Consortium, with British financial policy in China. During these years the Bank also managed railway loans to Siam and co-managed loans to Japan.

Despite the Bank's role in the City, Head Office remained in Hong Kong. Sceptics had predicted a move to London if only to find more highly qualified directors, if only to be more responsive to trends in world finance. The directors, however, were sufficiently well-qualified to handle their own businesses, and they delegated actual banking to the Chief Manager. Furthermore, the key London Managers, Sir Ewen Cameron (to 1904) and then Sir Charles Addis (to 1921), established themselves with such authority that many supposed the Bank's Head Office to be in the City; certainly the Foreign Office never challenged the authority by which Addis stated the Bank's position. Addis himself was elected a director of the Bank of England in 1918, while still the Manager of the local branch of a British overseas bank.

The high political exposure of the Hongkong Bank laid it open to criticism by would-be competitors, and the presence of four Germans on the Board of Directors and the close relationship with the Deutsch-Asiatische Bank brought down the wrath of the scaremongers in the years immediately prior to the Great War. In 1914 the German directors resigned. The Bank attempted to purge itself of an undeserved reputation, for it had always been a British bank, its executive staffed by British subjects who had passed through a training period in London Office.

In the post-war period there was a return from grandeur. At first there had been hopes for the New China Consortium, with the Hongkong Bank at the head of a representative British Group. There had also been commercial expectations as silver rose to dramatic heights and a new rights issue brought paid-up capital to $20 million (= £2.58 million) in 1921 – this would be the last such issue for 60 years, the last increase in paid-up capital until the capitalization issue of 1955. The political conditions in China were, however, unstable, and the main tasks of the B&CC and the CCR were debt restructuring and approval of temporary advances to patch up railways already constructed. On the commercial side, silver again declined, and the Bank began once again

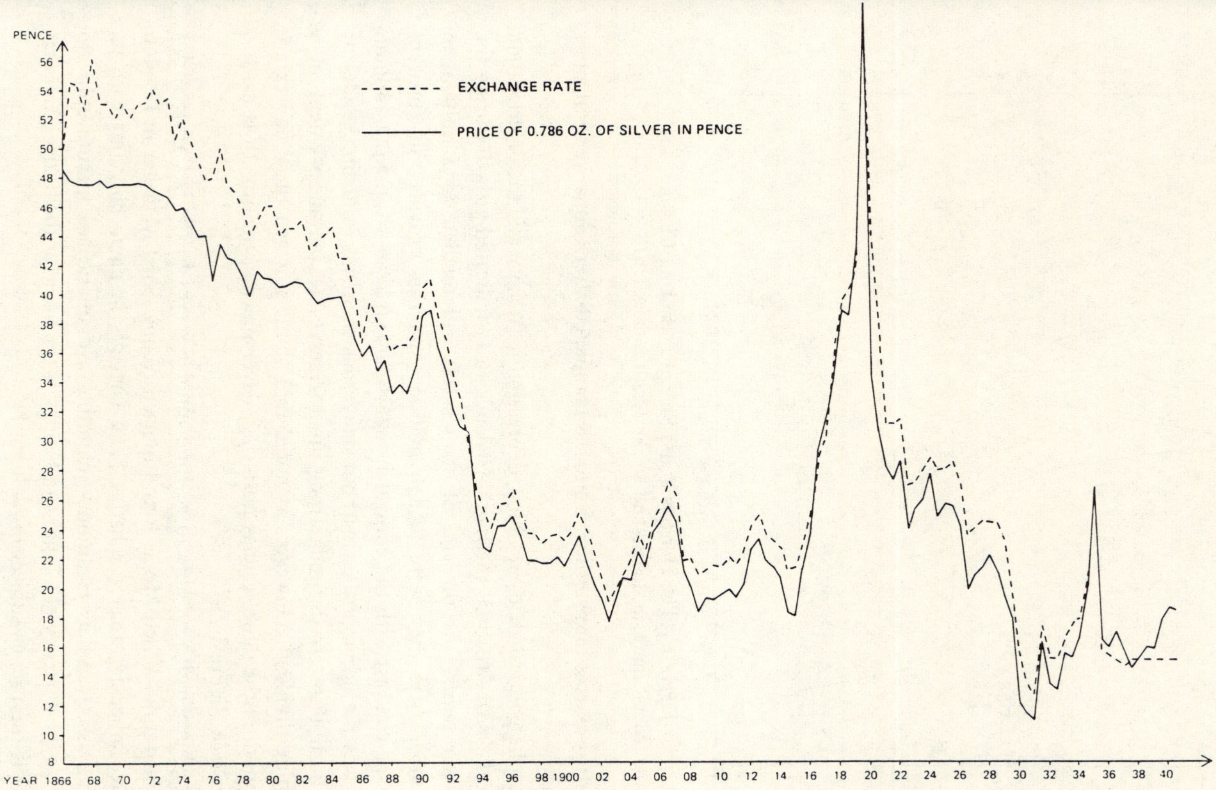

Figure 1.2 The Hongkong and Shanghai Banking Corporation
Exchang rate (Hong Kong on London) and the price of silver (London), 1866–1940.

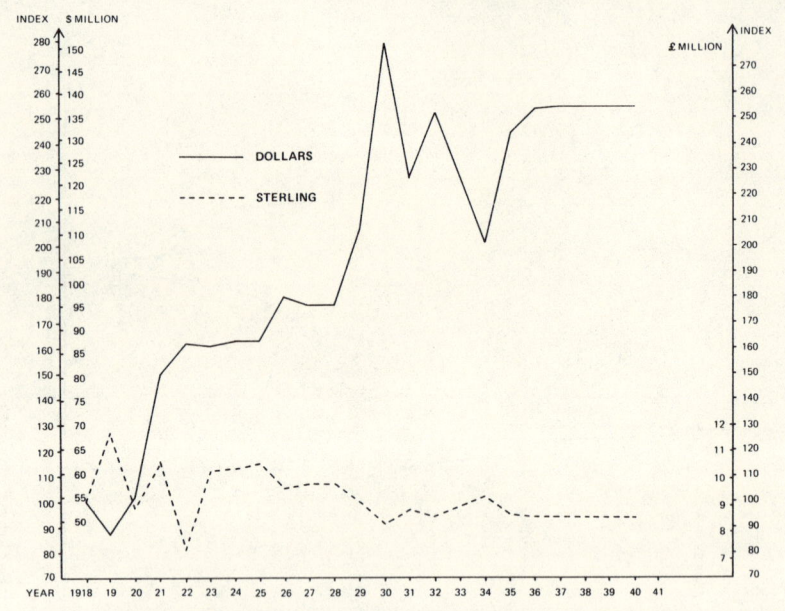

Figure I.3 The Hongkong and Shanghai Banking Corporation
Shareholders' funds in dollars and sterling with indices (1918 = 100), 1918–1941.

to shift resources into sterling, a process completed after China went off silver in 1935.

Despite political chaos in China, depression in Malaya, and the deterioration of the Eastern situation, the Bank's balance sheet indicated growth during the inter-war period. At the end of 1918 assets had totalled $432 million, in December 1940 they were $1,246 million. And this provides an apparent dramatic contrast with the equivalent figure for, say, end-1874, $42.9 million. This was not accomplished without dangerous moments, and Sir Vandeleur Grayburn transferred funds from inner reserves to permit payment of a declining dividend. However, as noted in Volume I, when these figures are measured on the same scale as post-1945 developments, the growth is hard to detect (see Figure I.1).

Grayburn had been able to re-fund inner reserves in the last years of his administration. When Morse found himself Acting Chief Manager in London on December 17, 1941, he had a bank virtually in name only but with its sterling assets and its traditions (including a dramatic last minute effort to stabilize the currency of China) and history as the basis for the future. And that future is the proper subject of Volume IV.

Part I

THE BABYLONIAN CAPTIVITY OF THE HONGKONG BANK, 1941–1946

I trust that never again in the lifetime of any of us here will it be necessary to move our Head Office from this site.
(Sir) Arthur Morse, July 1946,
at the first post-war Annual Meeting of Shareholders in Hong Kong

There was shutdown in the East. In the first few months of the Pacific War all offices of the Bank east of India (except Foochow) had been seized, the Foreign staff interned, and the local staff eventually let loose to make their own way. Those Portuguese who reached Macau were subsidized by remittances from London, but most moved back to the countryside and waited. The story of these initial dramatic events, of the subsequent suffering and death, of the clandestine financial operations in the several camps, the story, that is, of the Bank in captivity has been told in Volume III.

When Sir Vandeleur Grayburn transferred his Assistant Manager, Arthur Morse, to London in 1939, there was no thought of war in the Pacific; Morse was simply one of a series of trusted executives sent in frustrated efforts to 'beef up' London Office. At first he was a 'tertium quid'. Then, through retirement and death and less than six weeks before Pearl Harbor, Morse became the senior London Manager; on December 17, 1941, he was authorized by H. M. Government to assume the title of Acting Chief Manager of the Hongkong and Shanghai Bank. The situation successive chief executives and boards of directors had determined to avoid had become a reality – Head Office was now in London; the Babylonian captivity had begun.

The initial Government decisions called for the Chairman of the London Advisory Committee to become Chairman of the Hongkong Bank; Morse was thus Chairman, *ex officio*. In 1943 the position was regularized by an Order in Council, the members of the London Committee became *de facto* directors and Morse's dual status as Chairman and acting chief executive was regularized; with the death of Sir Vandeleur Grayburn in a Japanese prison hospital, the appointments were substantiated.

As the war progressed several key officers of the Bank reached London Office, among them A.S. Henchman, repatriated from Shanghai, and T.J.J. Fenwick and J.A.D. Morrison, escaped from Hong Kong; they brought the latest information from the East, and a rump Bank continued to operate in China, India, and Ceylon. Morse and his wartime staff worked at several levels. First, as noted, they still had operating branches; the Bank remained, though marginally, in business. London management had also to deal with the Eastern staff and their wives and dependants. They attempted, with little success, to obtain the release, through exchange agreements, of those interned; they then set out to deal with those who had escaped before the Japanese assumed total control or who were simply stranded somewhere in the world. At the same time Morse, a mixture of generosity and sudden moments of economy, sought ways to keep unneeded staff close at hand while yet preserving funds necessary for post-war staff rehabilitation. Nor did he forget local staff in the few cases where they could be reached. As victory approached, Morse made preparations to return to the East as soon as practical.

There were difficult moments. While the patriot anticipated victory in the normal sense, Morse could not be certain that the post-war settlements would provide a clear and immediate role for the Hongkong Bank. Hong Kong itself, some thought, would be Chinese. Occupation plans called for various banking controls which seemed to limit commercial banking prospects. The Japanese had forced the illegal issue of Hongkong Bank notes; their fate and thus the fate of the Bank's reputation were undecided. Although Morse carefully retained a position in Free China's Chungking capital, the 1943 Sino-British Treaty ending extraterritoriality created a mood of uncertainty. And more immediate, no one could forecast the actual physical condition of the great Eastern cities after they had been liberated, possibly on a street-by-street basis, certainly after heavy bombing.

In Morse Grayburn had seen himself reflected; both were tough and determined executives. In the alien world of London Morse proved a fighter. The fate of Hong Kong was not his to decide, but he could ensure the financing of new electricity generating equipment, he could discuss with the representatives of the major hongs their immediate post-war requirements. Meanwhile he and his senior colleagues maintained a running battle with officialdom – the 'duress' note issue and debtor/creditor relations were two major controversies, the terms of the return to the East was yet another. Morse did not win all his battles, but the Hongkong Bank was given an aggressive image which would well suit the needs of economies which, while not as badly damaged as originally expected, were nevertheless in desperate straits.

After the war Morse assumed community leadership; he became, as Sir Michael Sandberg recalls from his junior years, a 'legend in his time'. Only Morse could have determined to use scarce exchange to finance the import of race horses, thereby enhancing the morale of so many people in Hong Kong. At the same time he was arguing, successfully, for the proper conditions for a free economy. In Sir Alexander Grantham, the Governor of Hong Kong, he found an ally.

But along with the dramatic impact the Bank would have on Eastern economies, there was the task of taking back the interned staff and determining their role in the post-war world. There were readjustments relative to local staff, yet although change was essential, although 'return to normalcy' was not this time an accepted slogan, some reference to the past has first to be made.

This part of the Hongkong Bank's history covers the essential period of planning and initial implementation on which all further growth would depend. The balance sheets are less important, if indeed they are capable of interpretation. From the first Morse insisted that Head Office would return to Hong Kong. There was initial delay as problems still remained to be settled in

The Babylonian captivity

London, but eventually they were left pending, a subject for almost daily discussion by the London Manager, H. E. Muriel, and for long-distance missives from an increasingly impatient Chief Manager. Morse had a mission in the East; he could not afford to wait – 'Fast decisions. Worldwide' were best made, as of old, from Hong Kong; thus Head Office returned, the Babylonian captivity ended, and the history turns, after frustrating negotiations with Nationalist China (and with U.S. dominated SCAP), to the Bank's new tasks in an excitingly resurgent Hong Kong, in a potentially dynamic Southeast Asia.

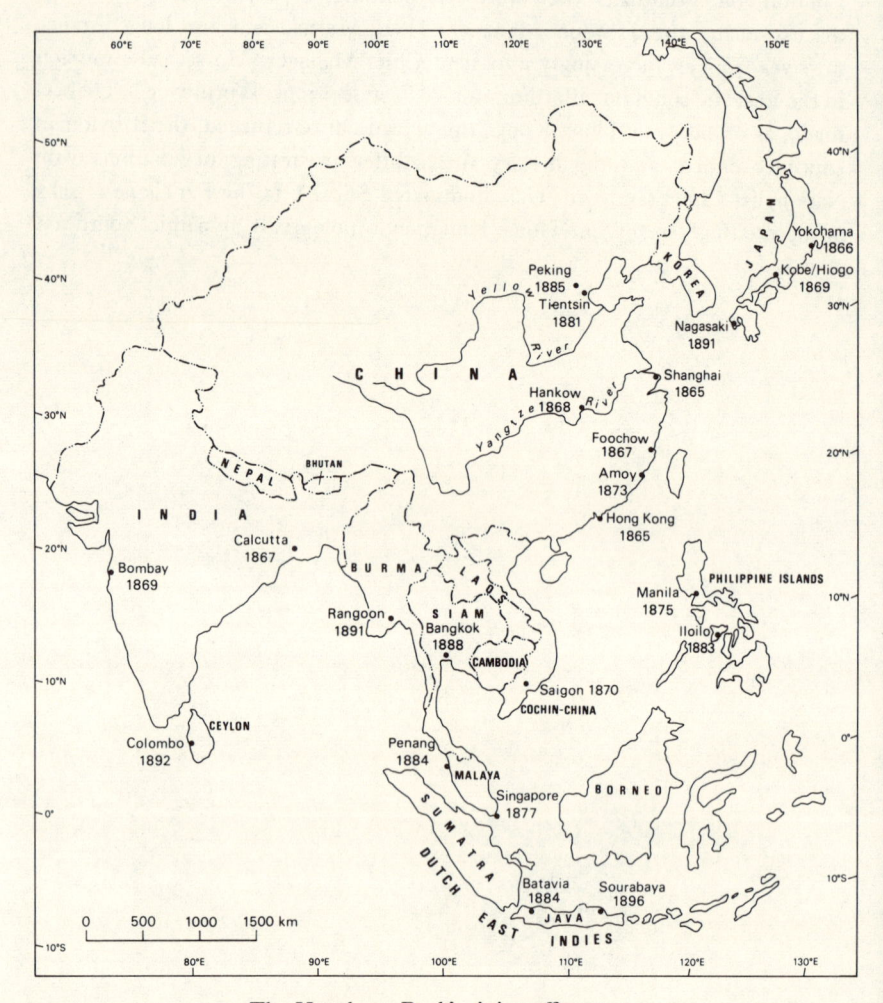

2 The Hongkong Bank's Asian offices, 1944.

1

HEAD OFFICE, LONDON: BANK OPERATIONS DURING THE PACIFIC WAR

> In accordance with Grayburn's wishes...I have taken charge.
> (Sir) Arthur Morse, December 17, 1941

As the Far Eastern situation deteriorated in late 1941, the Hongkong Bank made reluctant provisions for the transfer of its Head Office. Singapore was the first designated choice and the Bank's Chief Manager, Sir Vandeleur Grayburn, made tentative plans to leave Hong Kong should an emergency develop. These stand-by measures taken by Grayburn and approved by the Board of Directors in accordance with emergency Hong Kong legislation were never implemented. Events proved too fast moving after December 8, 1941. Instead Grayburn requested an Order in Council to enable Head Office to be established, temporarily, in London. At the same time, (Sir) Arthur Morse, the new London Manager, moved quickly to assume charge as Acting Chief Manager and thus prevent the Bank's U.S. dollar assets being frozen by the United States authorities. Although Morse took over *de facto* control of the Bank on December 17, 1941, the position was not regularized until January 1943.

Despite the Japanese sweep through Southeast Asia and the position of Hamburg and Lyons in Europe (described in Volume III), the Hongkong Bank still had Eastern branches in Bombay, Calcutta, and Colombo, American agencies in New York and San Francisco, and (from 1943) a new establishment in Chungking. The Bank, supported by its considerable sterling reserves, remained an operating bank throughout the Pacific War. Morse's first task, therefore, was to run an exchange bank in the context of the temporary corporate arrangements made in December 1941 and formalized by an Order in Council in January 1943.

The operation of the Bank would normally be accompanied by publication of balance sheets and declaration of dividends. Morse had the responsibility of attempting to piece together a balance sheet, and, in consequence of his findings and Grayburn's instructions, he recommended that no dividend be paid until the war should be successfully concluded.

The problems of the Bank's staff during the Pacific War were not a subject, as they had been inter-war, for occasional consideration at the end of a busy day dealing with exchange brokers. On the contrary, Morse spent considerable time pressing for the repatriation of Hongkong Bank Eastern staff. In this he was relatively unsuccessful. He was also responsible for transmitting funds to interned staff to the extent permitted by regulations, for approving clandestine operations for this purpose, and for dealing with staff problems in Macau. At the same time he was aware of Bank directors interned in Hong Kong, the needs of local staffs, and the casualties on active service in the European War. There were wives and dependants of interned staff to be cared for, and, eventually, the Bank had to meet the immediate needs of those released from internment as Allied forces moved towards victory.

Of all the wartime tasks the preparation for victory and for the return to the East were the most significant for the history of the Hongkong Bank. The Colonial Office had teams planning for the immediate post-war period in Malaya and Singapore and in Hong Kong. With these the Hongkong Bank cooperated, at the same time working out its own likely commitments, especially in the finance of public utilities. Extraterritoriality (extrality) ended in China in 1943 with consequent uncertainty as to the role foreign banks might be permitted to play; nevertheless, Morse's policy focus remained on the vast economic potential of China and her continued need for development financing. Hence the importance of the new link with Free China in Chungking and the planning for a return to Shanghai.

These post-war plans would be frustrated, however, if Morse failed to get officers to the East immediately after the anticipated V-J Day. With 65% of the Eastern staff interned and their health a matter of concern, with others in the armed services, and with the experience of 1919 suggesting that transport to the East would be difficult to obtain, Morse had to position his small staff at points where speedy access to Southeast Asia and the Far East would be most likely.

In addition to this positive planning designed to prepare the Bank to play an immediate role in the reconstruction of the region it had traditionally served, Morse had to face the uncertainties of Government policies relative to debtor/creditor relations and the duress note issue. On his return to Hong Kong Morse would confront further problems, but these must be left for later consideration.

THE CORPORATION – THE LONDON COMMITTEE, THE BOARD, AND MANAGEMENT

The transfer of Head Office to London

The initial Hong Kong solution

The temporary transfer of the Hongkong Bank's Head Office from Hong Kong to London was accomplished with the authority of the Board of Directors and the Chief Manager, but the full legal authority was delayed by technicalities. The first move was taken on December 2, 1941, under the terms of the Defence (Companies Temporary Transfer of Registered Office) Regulations, 1941, as amended December 2, 1941. The decisions of December 2 (i) amended Ordinance No. 6 of 1929 by in effect granting to 'Head Office' those powers stated as pertaining to the 'registered office' and by removing any relevant geographical reference to the Head Office being necessarily in Hong Kong.

Grayburn then went before the Board of Directors and obtained permission to move the Head Office to Singapore, a fact then made known to the various Hongkong Bank establishments. The essential right was the right to move; the actual place was left to Grayburn's discretion.

Emergency ad hoc *measures in London*
Once the Japanese attack on Hong Kong had developed, Grayburn himself was advised and requested not to leave; he was also unable to fulfil the technical, legal requirements of the Order permitting him to move Head Office. At this point he obtained the sanction of the Governor of Hong Kong to request that in the event of Hong Kong falling into enemy hands, the Head Office should be temporarily in London with Arthur Morse as Acting Chief Manager. Since the Hong Kong legislation and related orders had become irrelevant, Grayburn requested that any move should be regularized by an Order in Council. The Governor conveyed this with his approval to the Colonial Office on December 12 with the additional note that Grayburn would be informing Morse by cable. The last was inexplicably, but in the general confusion not surprisingly, delayed.

Morse had been alerted to developments by (Sir) Sydney Caine, formerly Treasurer, Hong Kong, and then in the Colonial Office, London. When Grayburn's cable failed to arrive and in view of the deteriorating military situation in Hong Kong, Morse had a meeting in the Colonial Office. Although it was clear that Grayburn had in mind a transfer by Order in Council only when the colony was actually in enemy hands, the Colonial Office were concerned that American regulators, anxious to deny the use of U.S. dollar funds to the enemy, might, on the assumption that the Bank was under Japanese control, call at any moment for the freezing of the Hongkong Bank's U.S. dollar assets in its agencies in New York and San Francisco. Furthermore, an Order in Council would have to be technically correct and the issues were by no means clear to London: Why, for example, were the permissions granted in Hong Kong on December 2 and confirmed by the Board on December 2 and 4 insufficient?

The result of these deliberations was an exchange between the Colonial

Office and Morse giving immediate effect to Grayburn's request pending later settlement of the legal details.

> I am directed by Lord Moyne to refer to recent discussions as to the position of the Hongkong and Shanghai Banking Corporation in view of the interruption of communication and other possible contingencies. As a result of these discussions and in accordance with the expressed wishes of the Chief Manager of the Bank, Sir Vandeleur Grayburn, as communicated by the Governor of Hong Kong, you have been authorized to assume control until further notice of all branches of the Bank outside Hong Kong and enemy occupied territory as Acting Chief Manager and it is understood that you are communicating accordingly with all such branches directing them to accept instructions from London and not from Hong Kong until further notice.
>
> 2. I am to say that it is the intention of H.M.G. to take any legal action which may be necessary eventually to validate any action which may be taken by you in pursuance of this authorization.[1]

On December 17, 1941, Morse replied formally to the above repeating its wording, especially noting H.M.G.'s intention 'to take any legal action which may be necessary eventually to validate any action which may be taken by me in pursuance of the authority contained in your letter'.[2]

Almost coincidentally, R.A. Stuart, Manager Singapore, had come to the same conclusion and cabled that Head Office should not come to Singapore but advised Morse to take over in London.

Meanwhile there had been action on three fronts. On the 16th Morse sent cables to all operating offices to the effect that

> under authorities of Government and in accordance with Grayburn's wishes received from Governor of Hong Kong as a temporary measure London Office becomes Head Office and I have taken charge as Acting Chief Manager. Re foregoing no further instructions to be taken from Hong Kong till authorized from here.[3]

On the same day the Foreign Office contacted the British Embassy in Washington informing them of the measures taken to bring the Hongkong Bank under London's control and expressing the hope that this would prove satisfactory to the American authorities. Finally, the Colonial Office cabled the beleaguered Governor of Hong Kong requesting, in the absence of any word from Grayburn, confirmation that the action being taken was in accordance with his wishes – and incidentally expressing doubts as to the terms the Order in Council should include.

Morse was correct in stating to the Government that he anticipated no trouble from the branches – there are cables of 'good luck' on file. Washington anticipated, correctly as it happened, no problems with the American banking authorities, and the Governor of Hong Kong sent London Grayburn's specific confirmation of agreement. All this was confirmed once again to Morse in more detail on December 20, and to ensure that there would be no problems in the

United States, the Foreign Office asked the Embassy to keep directly in contact with A.G. Kellogg, the Bank's Manager in New York.[a]

Arthur Morse had also thought it wise to keep the Hongkong Bank's 'clearing bank' informed and on the 16th he had visited Sir Charles Lidbury, the chief general manager of the Westminster Bank, and T.H.R. Lawman, manager of the Lombard Street branch, where the Hongkong Bank's account was kept. In his market letter of December 18, Morse expressed his appreciation to the chief manager of the Chartered Bank, W.R.M. Cockburn, and 'to many others' for offers of assistance.

Grayburn in fact sent Arthur Morse two cables on December 19. The first confirmed his request for an Order in Council and for Morse to act as Chief Manager should Hong Kong fall. It also instructed Morse to pay a dividend from the interest on sterling securities. The second was more technical. Grayburn instructed Morse (i) to transfer certain sterling investments with a face value of £515,000 from Hong Kong Office Account to a 'New Head Office' Account, (ii) to debit Hong Kong and credit the New Head Office Account (a) currency reserves of £838,935 and (b) balance of undivided profits £625,000, and (iii) credit Hong Kong and debit Head Office Account £1,113,234 Bank Premises Account.[5] Legally Morse had been covered by the Colonial Office letter of December 16; nevertheless, the actual cables from Grayburn must have come as a personal relief to the new Acting Chief Manager.

On July 31, 1942, Grayburn sent Morse a message reversing his decision on payment of dividends in view of the Bank's heavy losses, but by that time Morse had already made his own identical decision based on the realities of the accounts as seen in London.[6]

The Hong Kong Government had intended that the Hongkong Bank, should its Head Office be temporarily removed, operate under a local committee, or, if there were none, then under the London Committee. There is nothing in the correspondence suggesting that either Morse or the Colonial Office discussed this matter during these hectic days of crisis, and the authorizing letter from the Colonial Secretary refers only to Morse. Nevertheless, Morse had an existing Advisory (Consultative) Committee of which he was then the *ex officio* Chairman, and he kept them fully informed. They were not, however, directors and did not possess the authority to act as such; furthermore the minutes suggest they did not in fact pretend to act until the Order in Council was actually passed in January 1943.

---

[a] See note 4. A.G. Kellogg, whose career has been referred to in earlier volumes, was the only member of the Eastern staff who was an American citizen. He had originally joined the Bank as a local staff member in New York under A.M. Townsend but in 1903 had resigned and rejoined as a London junior. He went East in the normal way in 1906 and served in Kobe, Yokohama, Dairen, Manila, and Tokyo. He was first assigned, as a member of the Eastern staff, to the New York agency in 1930. He became Manager in 1937 and retired in 1948.

Morse concluded this initial phase by confirming in his December 18 market letter that it was the American situation that had made him act precipitately, concluding, 'These are the brief facts which led to my assuming charge and I think I can say it was the most unpleasant action that has ever had to be taken by any Officer of our Bank.'[7]

The Order in Council, 1943

Although the need to regularize the position of Morse and London Office was recognized, there proved to be difficulties. The appropriate United Kingdom authority was a Board of Trade Order under the Colonial Companies (Transfer) Order in Council, but this could not be used to effect a retroactive move.[8] The only method remaining was in fact a separate Order in Council, but the first draft, Morse reported to the Bank's London Advisory Committee (LAC), had proved inappropriate; the negotiations would prove to be lengthy.

On January 13, 1943, the Order, cited as the 'Hongkong and Shanghai Banking Corporation (Temporary Transfer) Order in Council 1943', stated that as from December 16, 1941,

the Head Office of the Bank shall be deemed to have been transferred to the United Kingdom, and all the powers, authorities and discretions vested in the Board of Directors shall be deemed to have been transferred to and to have been exercisable by the Committee in London.[9]

A legal opinion sought by the Bank confirmed that this Order made members of the London Committee *de facto* directors and that it was proper to refer to them as such.[10]

This retroactive Order does not, however, alter the fact that during the period December 1941 to February 1943 the members of the Advisory Committee were not considered as 'directors' either by the Government or by Morse and that they themselves concurred in this view. On March 26, 1942, the members of the Committee present – Sir George Macdonogh, Sir Edward Reid, A.H. Barlow, and B.D.F. Beith – agreed that 'they were prepared to act as Directors if, and when, they were required to do so'.[11] That time did not occur until the meeting of February 4 when the members of the LAC formally accepted the responsibilities of directors and then behaved as such.

Morse himself was conscious of the fact that he was operating without a Board of Directors. When R. Bruce resigned for health reasons in Simla, for example, Morse postponed assigning him retirement benefits; instead he wrote, 'There are just some things to which I do not feel justified in committing the Bank without the consent of Directors.'[12]

Regardless of the retroactive legal position, therefore, the Hongkong Bank was managed from December 16, 1941, to February 4, 1943, as if there was no

Board of Directors and with the only authority vested in Morse as Acting Chief Manager.

Morse's position as Chairman of the LAC was *ex officio* as the Senior London Manager; the Order stated that retroactively the Chairman of the Committee was, for the purposes of interpreting the powers under the Bank's Hong Kong ordinance, the Chairman of the Board of Directors, that is, the Chairman of the Bank. When the Committee met in February 1943 *as* a Board of Directors, they formally elected Morse their Chairman. Not only had their formal position changed, but the legal basis for Morse's position and indeed the whole atmosphere changed. This is reflected in the minutes.

The only other matters in the Order of particular significance here are the changes in Regulation 118, giving the new London Board the power to appoint an 'Acting Chief Manager', a post not previously mentioned in any Bank ordinance or regulation, to have all the powers of a Chief Manager as defined in the 1929 ordinance [par. 2]. This section was concluded with the provision: 'Arthur Morse, the Senior Manager of the London Office of the Bank on the 16th December, 1941, shall be deemed as from that date to have been appointed Acting Chief Manager under paragraph 2 [par. 3].'

The Schedule to the Order in Council also provided that the Chief Manager or Acting Chief Manager might be a member of the Board, thus overriding the provision in the Bank's ordinance [regulation 91(h)] that a person holding an office in the Bank was not eligible to be a director. The number of directors was revised downward – minimum five and maximum ten.

The remainder of the numerous changes detailed in the Schedule are designed to make the Regulations relevant to an English domicile. The substantive changes, to the extent they continued beyond 1946, are considered in Chapter 3.

The appointment of Morse as Chief Manager

Arthur Morse had been elected Chairman of the Board of Directors on February 4, 1943; he was Acting Chief Manager by virtue of the provisions of the Order in Council. Grayburn, interned in Hong Kong, remained the titular Chief Manager. Then, on September 23, 1943, the London Board (hereinafter referred to as 'the Board of Directors', or simply 'the Board') met to take notice of the death of Sir Vandeleur Grayburn.

Morse spoke of Grayburn's great talents, intense vitality, and dynamic force of character and concluded that his death in such heart-rending circumstances was one of the 'stark tragedies of the war'. The Board minuted:

It is with profound regret and a deep sense of loss that the Board has learned of the death of Sir Vandeleur Grayburn as a prisoner in the hands of the Japanese in Hong Kong. They wish to place on record their appreciation of his great services to the Bank, and

Table 1.1 *The Hongkong and Shanghai Banking Corporation
The directors, 1941, and their fate*

December 8, 1941		
J.J. Paterson	Jardine, Matheson and Co.	survived
C.C. Roberts	Butterfield and Swire	director, June 1946
G. Miskin	Gilman and Co.	director, June 1946
J.K. Bonsfield	Asiatic Petroleum Co.	survived
A.H. Compton	David Sassoon and Co.	director, June 1946
K.S. Morrison	Reiss, Bradley and Co.	died in captivity
S.H. Dodwell	Dodwell and Co.	survived
T.E. Pearce	J.D. Hutchison and Co.	killed in action defending Hong Kong
A.L. Shields	Shewan, Tomes and Co.	died in Stanley Camp
L.J. Davies	Gibb, Livingston and Co.	died in Bombay, May 1945

This table is designed to provide information on directors actually serving at the outbreak of the Pacific War.

their deep sympathy with his wife and family in the loss they have sustained in such tragic circumstances.[13]

Before adjourning the directors voted that Arthur Morse should succeed Sir Vandeleur Grayburn as Chief Manager.

The Board of Directors and the London Advisory Committee

The directors in Hong Kong – their fate

The last meeting of the Board of Directors in Hong Kong was December 9, 1941, at which time they noted that Grayburn with the advice and at the request of the Governor was not in fact leaving Hong Kong. They did not meet again although their legal authority remained until December 16, 1941. By the same argument as above, as neither the Hong Kong nor the British Government mentioned any change in their authority until the retroactive Order in Council of January 1943, no doubt the members of the Board considered themselves to have remained directors. Grayburn on occasion issued instructions through BAAG (British Army Advisory Group) couriers, but there is no evidence of any meeting or discussion with the interned 'directors'.

As for the fate of individual directors, T.E. 'Tam' Pearce had been killed in action defending Hong Kong, K.S. Morrison and A.L. Shields died in Stanley, and L.J. Davies died in Bombay in May 1945. When the Governor, under circumstances to be described in Chapter 2, appointed the Bank's first post-war Hong Kong directors, pending an annual meeting of shareholders, he included from the 1941 Board C.C. Roberts, G. Miskin, and A.H. Compton. The list of 1941 directors and their fate is found in Table 1.1.

The London Advisory Committee

Although E.J. Davies, then London junior Manager, had been lamenting the decline of the London Advisory (or 'Consultative' as it was generally known inter-war) Committee as early as April 1940, no action was taken during the several illnesses, retirements, and changes which occurred through November 1941. With W.W.H. Hill-Wood and Lord Ashburton concerned with war work and rarely present, it was typical that when the LAC met on December 23 to hear Morse tell the story of his appointment and the move of Head Office to London only A.H. Barlow, the retired Hongkong Bank Chief Manager, and C.A. Campbell of the Westminster Bank were present.

Morse recognized the problem and in January told Sir Charles Addis[b] he was setting about the reconstitution of the LAC in earnest.[14] The results, shown in Table 1.2, would be helpful but not dramatic. Almost immediately Lord Ashburton agreed that Sir Edward Reid, also of Baring's, should 'deputize' for him, but in fact Reid, who was related to Sir John Peter (Manager Singapore, 1911–1922), quickly became more than this; he was the confidant of Morse and remained on the Committee until 1965, giving his valued advice to a succession of London Managers back from the East and unfamiliar with the City. Matheson and Co. had been without a Committee representative since the resignation of D.G. M. Bernard in September 1939; in February 1942 B.D.F. Beith of that firm joined the Committee. But the veteran Sir George Macdonogh, who had become a member in 1923, died in July 1942.

Reid's valuable City connections supplemented A.H. Barlow's intimate knowledge of the Bank, and the Morse/Barlow correspondence indicates that Morse consulted Barlow on such matters as salaries and appointments. And with reasonable relations established with Sir Charles Addis, Morse now had support for the difficult task of managing the Bank through the war years.[15]

The Board of Directors, London

The need for a representative and credible committee became a more serious matter after the Order in Council; Morse was now trying to find directors for the Hongkong Bank. And, since directors had responsibilities to shareholders, the first task was to ask Hill-Wood of Morgan, Grenfell and Co., who had not

---

[b] Sir Charles S. Addis, KCMG (1861–1945), played a significant role in the Bank's history from his first appointment as Agent Peking in 1886 to his retirement as a director of the British and Chinese Corporation and as chairman of the British Group of the China Consortium in 1944. He was a London Joint Manager from 1905 to 1922 and Chairman of the London Consultative (Advisory) Committee until 1933. He held important positions outside the Hongkong Bank; he was, for example, a director of the Bank of England, 1918–1932, and vice-chairman, Bank for International Settlements, 1930–1932. His earlier contributions are described in the first three volumes of this history.

Table 1.2 *The Hongkong and Shanghai Banking Corporation London Advisory Committee, 1941–1946*

A. To February 4, 1943
December 16, 1941

Arthur Morse, Senior London Manager	Chairman, ex-officio	1941–46
C.A. Campbell	Westminster Bank	1919–53
Sir George Macdonogh	Director, Shell Co.	1923–42
A.H. Barlow	retired, Hongkong Bank	1927–47
Lord Ashburton (Alex Baring)	Baring Brothers and Co.	1934–42
W.W.H. Hill-Wood	Morgan, Grenfell and Co.	1939–43

Changes to February 4, 1943
Sir Edward Reid to deputize for Lord Ashburton from January 1942
B.D.F. Beith appointed, February 1942
Sir George Macdonogh died, July 10, 1942

B. February 4, 1943–June 13, 1946 (with powers of Board of Directors)
February 4, 1943

Arthur Morse (Chairman, elected)	Hongkong Bank	–1946
C.A. Campbell	Westminster Bank	–1953
A.H. Barlow	retired, Hongkong Bank	–1947
W.W.H. Hill-Wood	Morgan, Grenfell and Co.	–1943
Sir Edward Reid	Baring Brothers and Co.	–1965
B.D.F. Beith	Matheson and Co.	–1945

Changes to August 1945
W.W.H. Hill-Wood resigned, March 1943
Rt. Hon. Major General Sir Frederick Sykes, M.P. appointed, 1943
R.G. Macindoe of Maclaine, Watson and Co., appointed, 1943

August 1945

Arthur Morse (Chairman)	Hongkong Bank	–1946
C.A. Campbell	Westminster Bank	–1953
A.H. Barlow	retired, Hongkong Bank	–1947
Sir Edward Reid	Baring Brothers and Co.	–1965
B.D.F. Beith	Matheson and Co.	–1945
Sir Frederick Sykes, M.P.	retired, Governor Bombay	–1954
R.G. Macindoe	Maclaine, Watson and Co.	–1964

Changes to June 13, 1946
B.D.F. Beith resigned, January 1945
W.J. Keswick appointed
Arthur Morse left for Hongkong, March 1946; he resigned as Chairman of the Hongkong Bank.

March–June 13, 1946

Sir Edward Reid (Chairman)	Baring Brothers and Co.	–1965
C.A. Campbell	Westminster Bank	–1953
A.H. Barlow	retired, Hongkong Bank	–1947
W.J. Keswick	Matheson and Co.	–1955
Sir Frederick Sykes, M.P.	retired, Governor Bombay	–1954
R.G. Macindoe	Maclaine, Watson and Co.	–1964

When the above met on June 27, 1946, they were again without the powers of a Board of Directors: Chairman, H.E. Muriel.

attended meetings since August 1940, what his present position might be. The answer was his resignation announced at the April 1 meeting.

Morse's concept of a Board was not however the London concept. 'It seems to me', he had written to W.C. Cassels, the Bank's China specialist, in September 1942,

> that the Boards of Directors functioning in London are inclined not only to direct policy and such things but actually participate in the executive duties of the Staff. This has never been permitted in our Bank, and I hope it never will be. This difference of outlook may make it difficult to get really big men on our Board when that is formed in London, but, whatever disadvantage this may be, I feel it would be very much more if I had to tolerate interference with ordinary Banking business, and, in fact, I do not think I would ever find it possible to work on such a basis.[16]

Morse acknowledged the need for two new directors, one with the political connections of a Macdonogh and the other an East India merchant. For the former the Board elected the Rt. Hon. Major General Sir Frederick Sykes, M.P., former Governor of Bombay, for the latter R.G. Macindoe of Maclaine, Watson and Co. The main point of contact between the Bank and both Maclaine Watson and Macindoe was Java; the appointment of Sir Frederick gave the Board a contact with Indian interests at a time when the Bank's only commercially viable offices were in South Asia.

The Board/London Committee thus lost its representation from Morgan Grenfell's, renewed its contact with Matheson and Co., and retained a strong link with Baring's and the Westminster Bank. After the changes listed for 1943 and with the exception of the appointment of W.J. Keswick to replace Beith in January 1945, the Board of Directors responsible for the Hongkong Bank during the Pacific War remained unchanged until Morse's resignation as Chairman on his departure for Hong Kong in March 1946.

Arthur Morse, Chairman and Chief Manager

The significance of a Hongkong Banker as Chairman
For the first time in the history of the Bank its Chairman was a member of the staff, in fact, the Acting Chief Manager. W.H. Bell, a former member of the staff, had served on the Board and for a brief period of approximately three months, December 1929 to February 1930, had been Chairman.[c] A.H. Barlow was a former Chief Manager who, although over 70 years of age, remained when the Committee became a Board. But the position of Morse was unique.

It is tempting to read into this election some relevance to management

---

[c] There is evidence that Bell actually attended the first London meeting of shareholders and spoke in support of Morse's report, but the records are incomplete.

theory, but that would be to anticipate developments in the late 1960s. Nor would it be fair to assume that Morse's election was the consequence of his thinking as reflected in the letter to Cassels just quoted. Rather his election may be seen as a combination of respect for his competent handling of the Bank to date and recognition that an experienced Hongkong Banker needed to have the 'face' necessary to deal firmly on behalf of the Bank in the City.

Morse's position as revealed in the Cassels letter is not historically accurate if taken to refer to the period before the 1880s, but this is irrelevant. Morse spoke of the Jacksonian Bank. His opinions suggest he did not appreciate the full significance of the London custom nor foresee the type of amended corporate constitution which would permit an executive chairman and executive directors. The letter does suggest however that Morse would not keep the Head Office in London longer than necessary.

The concept of the Hongkong Bank as a 'local bank', 'almost a cooperative', managed by a staff which was merely watched over by directors as descendants, in spirit if not in fact, of the founders as representative of the Treaty Port community and their friends in London, was not a relevant consideration for a temporary wartime situation in London. Secondly, the survival of the Bank depended on an intimate knowledge of its inner reserves and long-run management plans, of its traditions and personnel, and this only a senior member of the Bank could possess. Thirdly, Morse had been effectively Chairman in the first fourteen months of the Pacific War – the vote was to ask him to remain. And finally, the Board members were either too elderly for the strain of full responsibility, Barlow for example, or otherwise preoccupied in wartime London; Campbell was the director of another bank, Sir Edward Reid was new to the Committee. There is little wonder therefore that these newcomers, knowing that Morse carried with him the recommendation of Grayburn, should have asked him to continue presiding at their meetings. It was, perhaps, the only way to meet the Bank's needs and Morse's requirements.

In doing so, however, the Board had made a further implicit decision. They had elected a man dedicated to the principle of Head Office's return to Hong Kong; the 'temporary' move to London would now prove, as far as humanly possible, to be temporary in fact. Cassels had written to Morse assuming that Head Office might have to remain in London, there being no assurance that Hong Kong would be British post-war. Morse did not even pause in his preparations for return – 'All I can say is I hope you prove wrong.'[17]

Arthur Morse, background and experience

Grayburn's chosen successor as Chief Manager was D.C. Edmondston, and he therefore had no thought that Morse might some day succeed to this position in the normal course of events. Since Grayburn did not expect Hong Kong to fall even after the Japanese attack had commenced, there is no possibility that Morse had been sent to London to be prepared for the capture of Head Office. Morse had been sent to London to beef up the management and, despite an initial but brief '*tertium quid*' status, Grayburn knew that Morse would soon be succeeding both the then London Managers, O.J. Barnes and E.J. Davies.

Born in Tipperary, April 25, 1892, the son of a banker, Morse was educated at Foyle College, Londonderry, and joined the Hongkong Bank's London Office in 1912.[18] Morse's career up to the Pacific War was not dramatic. He had never been 'on his own', that is, he had never been an Agent or Manager of even the smallest office. Beginning as a junior in Hong Kong in 1915 he moved to Tientsin in 1919 and in 1922 succeeded in convincing Sir Newton Stabb, the then London Manager, to recommend him for early marriage. Shortly afterwards an adverse inspector's report (by T.S. Baker) dealing with general slackness in the Tientsin office reached London, and Stabb pondered on the wisdom of his decision.[19] After a brief spell in Shanghai, Morse returned to Tientsin in 1924 and came down to Hong Kong in 1929. Thereafter he remained in the Hong Kong office, serving as Chief Accountant from 1932 to 1937 and as Sub-Manager Hong Kong until his departure for London in 1940.

In fact, Morse was probably better known for his handling of the 1935 Head Office building project than anything else. He was an efficient administrator.

In all Morse had served in three Eastern offices, although the Shanghai experience was negligible. This and his time in the Hong Kong office hierarchy make his career more comparable in some ways to that of Grayburn than to say that of Stephen (see Appendix Table A for comparisons). Unlike Grayburn, however, Morse had had no real experience in exchange, but in a world of controlled exchanges this was less important than in the pre-war years. In 1941 Morse had served the Bank 27 years since his first trip East. He was eleven years junior to Grayburn and his appointment certainly represents a handing-over to the next generation.

Nevertheless the fact remains that in normal times Morse's lack of experience in risk management and exchange operations would have precluded his appointment as Chief Manager to succeed Grayburn, and that, had Edmondston been appointed, age alone would have ruled Morse out from further consideration. There would have been no return from London.

When the Japanese invaded Hong Kong and Grayburn eventually accepted the need to transfer Head Office to London, he would have had little concern over Morse's ability. He obviously had confidence in his London Manager, but even he probably underestimated the flair with which Morse would take over. Morse, it would appear, had undergone a change of character, and those who knew him best had had their surprise; his success in London and afterwards was consequently seen as a fulfilment.

T.J.J. Fenwick first met Arthur Morse during the Great War in 1915; that was the year Morse came East. Fenwick came four years later and eventually succeeded Morse as Chief Accountant in Hong Kong. It was not until then that Fenwick noticed a change:

> ...around that time he started to get to know the Chinese which had never been done by anybody before, and he took on the treasurership of the University [in 1937].[d] He became mixed up in the Jockey Club. I took him out to Fanling for his first game of golf. One way and another, from being a very shy, retiring sort of chap, he blossomed out to the Arthur Morse that we all knew so well.
>
> Oh, he was very thin. He came out to the East in 1915. I don't think he would have been passed by the military people if he had tried to join the army. That's the sort of impression I got, and actually I've got an old photograph of him when he was playing for Tientsin against somebody at tennis, and it's just a cadaverous looking....
>
> I think a great deal of Arthur Morse's success was due to Margery [his wife] who was an extraordinary woman. She didn't interfere in the slightest in anything to do with the Bank, the staff or anything else like that. There wasn't any question of Margery saying so-and-so should be this and that and the other thing. She took no interest whatsoever in that. ...She encouraged Arthur to get outside himself so to speak. And there was latterly a tremendous change in him, and at that time he began to carouse and his voice changed like everything.
>
> Latterly he used to roar like a bull.
>
> He astonished me one day. He said, come on, I'm going down to talk to the Police Reserves this afternoon. ...
>
> So we went off to some place, I've forgotten where it was now, and to my astonishment...I'd never heard him do this before...he got up and made the most magnificent boosting speech to these Chinese and European – a mixed crowd – and all off the cuff. Marvelous. I didn't know he could.
>
> He made a great friend of a fellow called Duncan Sloss [the Vice-Chancellor, University of Hong Kong]. When I went down to be Chief Accountant...I found that Morse and Sloss were great friends, and I think Sloss probably encouraged him a bit, you know.[21]

Success in Hong Kong is not, however, the same as acceptance in the City. Sir Charles Addis had once again become active in the Bank's China affairs, going to the Gracechurch Street office virtually on a daily basis, and he naturally watched Morse carefully. His diary records several pleasant visits at Woodside,

---

[d] The Hongkong Bank had from the first shown an interest in the University of Hong Kong, at the University's founding by donations and then through the role of Sir Charles Addis on the University's London selection committee – Addis was awarded an Hon. LL.D. in 1922. Arthur Morse was the first executive of the Hongkong Bank to hold the post of Treasurer – and with it membership on the University Council. Morse was awarded an Hon. LL.D. by the University on his departure for London in 1940; he was succeeded as Treasurer by D.C. Edmondston; Morse took on the task again post-war.[20]

During the Pacific War Morse, as chairman of the Hong Kong University Advisory Committee in London, assisted financially, without security, faculty members and their dependants.

Addis's country home near Frant, but he was more tentative on his judgement of Morse as banker.[22] In November 1940 Addis recorded, 'Barnes says Morse has ability and I am glad to hear it for he is a windy Irishman with his interminable and irrelevant stories. He bores me.'[23]

On hearing that Morse would succeed Barnes as Senior London Manager, Addis wrote, 'He is shrewd and clever, but merely by rule of thumb. He has much to learn.'[24] But where would Morse gain a knowledge of banking other than by 'rule of thumb'? He was in fact both shrewd and clever; he learned his City banking from men like Sir Charles Addis and, later, Sir Edward Reid. When H.E. Muriel years later was writing his autobiography, he reflected along much the same lines. 'Morse', he wrote, 'knew little about technical banking, but banking is both an art and a science, and in the former he excelled. He exuded a sense of confidence, he could absorb information, formulate policy and make consistent policy decisions.'[25] Several who knew Morse commented that he worked alone or with one or two confidants – he 'held his cards close to the chest'. This was in the tradition of Hongkong Bank management, but on occasion it would cause unpopularity.

This then was the man – after all the cables from besieged Hong Kong, after all the constitutional changes and arrangements – who had to carry the Hongkong Bank through its exile in London and prepare for the return to the East.

London Office management

Throughout the war the junior London Manager was W. Park and the Sub-Manager G.M. Dalgety (see Volume III). The second Sub-Manager was G.B. Dunnett, who had joined London Office in 1907 and come East in 1910.[e] Morse also obtained the services of the highly competent C.I. Cookes (East in 1909) who had retired as Manager Manila in 1939 and now returned to the Bank as Sub-Manager London.

J.A.D. Morrison, escaped from Hong Kong, was appointed acting Chief Accountant in 1943. Also working in London Office were R.A. Stuart and J.G. Danielson, the substantive Managers of Singapore and Hamburg respectively. M.B. Lendrum had retired, but D.A. Johnston, the former Accountant and Manager-designate for Lyons, was on hand and A.S. Henchman of Shanghai attended the office regularly after his repatriation from Shanghai. And also there until his illness in April 1943, as active as ever and watching carefully for any signs of tampering with China Consortium policy, was Sir Charles Addis.

[e] Dunnett's career in its early years was entirely in Hong Kong, but, after temporary-in-charge assignments in Ipoh and Canton in 1926–1927, he had a brief attachment to London Office in 1932 and was then Acting Agent Rangoon, then Penang, and finally Agent Tokyo in 1935; he returned to London on leave in 1938 and remained in London Office from 1939.

PERFORMANCE

Despite heroic efforts on the part of interned staff and secret couriers, not all the information necessary to enable London Office to draw up complete year-end 'abstracts of accounts' was obtained, although the data available increased each year. For end-1941 no estimate was published at all, for 1942 it proved impossible to draw up a Profit and Loss Account, and even in 1946 the effects of the war were still present in the sense of doubt as to the Bank's actual position. Fortunately one of the pre-war auditors of the Bank's accounts, C.B. Brown of Peat, Marwick, Mitchell and Co., was available, and in August 1942 the Committee were informed that he 'has the work in hand'.

As new figures arrived, they were added to the balance sheet – assets unexpectedly realized on the one hand, news of additional liabilities in enemy-held offices on the other; under these circumstances each set of accounts was based in part on non-comparable information and discussion of trends or the use of the usual ratios in the usual way would have little significance. Nevertheless certain points, essential for an understanding of the history of the Hongkong Bank, can be made.

Major indicators

At the end of 1946 shareholders' funds had fallen some 17% since 1940, due mainly to the 1946 transfer of £1.1 million from published reserves to contingencies to meet anticipated war losses not otherwise covered. The decline of 4.6% shown in shareholders' funds for the years to 1945 is due almost entirely to the absence of any credit balance in the Profit and Loss Account, the whole being transferred to unappropriated contingencies to meet war losses. Any close analysis of the actual status of shareholders' funds would have to go behind the published figures, but the inadequacy of the war contingencies accounts thus built up to meet eventual requirements indicates these funds cannot be considered as free 'inner reserves'; the losses for which they were set aside were known to exist, but it was impractical to make specific assignment since neither the exact amount of loss item-by-item nor the sequence by which the specific losses would have to be met was information available in London Office (see Tables 1.3 and 1.4).

Nevertheless during the same period the Bank's total assets increased 64%, but more than half of this occurred in 1946 and was consequent on the increase in note issue and of deposits, reflecting immediate post-war developments.

The share market and a bank's losses in war

It is part of the folklore of the Bank that during the war Arthur Morse was summoned to the Bank of England and the kindly suggestion made that perhaps the Bank, with 33 of its 37 offices in enemy hands, ought to consider winding up. Morse is supposed to have placed a sheet of paper on the table showing the Bank's reserves, and the subject was dropped. Apocryphal or not, the story does focus on the question of how a business with a high proportion of its offices in enemy hands could survive a destructive war with increased assets and only a manageable drop in shareholders' funds.

That the Bank was able to perform in this way did not surprise the share market. As shown in Table 1.3 the market price/book value ratio rose from 1.42 at the end of 1940 to 1.71 at the end of 1945, with a drop only in the dark year of 1942. The favourable reception of the Bank's shares in the market was due to a number of factors, both subjective and objective which are sufficiently important to warrant consideration. This is not to say that the price rise was entirely rational. Addis had written to Morse August 1943 congratulating him on the performance of the Bank in consideration of the share prices. Morse replied that he could not explain the rise, noted that all Eastern shares were up, and suggested that 'some people will get burned'.[26]

Since the directors agreed that they could not recommend payment of dividends, those purchasing shares were obviously looking to the future; they did not wait until after the war because they expected a rise in price more than sufficient to offset any 'lost' income. It is impossible to determine why each purchaser expected bright prospects for the Bank in the East, but some general considerations may be stated. First, the British experience was opposite to that in the United States where bank shares were at a discount, because, as an American economist put it, of the Hongkong Bank's imperial status and overseas aura – the best managers and the more dynamic enterprises in Britain were those involved overseas.[27] This view is subjective, but the writer coupled this with expectations that the East would be freed of the restrictions of the past – seen mainly in terms of Japanese interference and the consequences of the Depression – and that the needs of China alone promised profitability for the Bank.

The Bank's reasonable performance in the difficult 1930s was seen as a guide to expectations as to the Bank's performance in the post-war East, when China would seek funds for reconstruction and development, and the whole area would be 'opened', this time in the context of modern-style development planning.

China, we may be sure, is destined to play a big part in the post-war world. The country waits to be laced with railways, roads and airlines. Her rivers wait to be harnessed, her towns to be rebuilt and modernized, and her minerals to be mined. In this development and that of the foreign trade your Bank will be ready and anxious to cooperate to the best of its ability.[28]

Morse was successor to a great investment tradition – the tradition exemplified by the imperial publicist and early Hong Kong Treasurer, Robert Montgomery Martin, and by Hongkong Bankers David McLean and Sir Charles Addis.

Table 1.3 *The Hongkong and Shanghai Banking Corporation
Key Indicators, 1941–1945*

(pounds sterling)

	(in millions)					(in pounds)			
December	Assets	Reserves	Net earnings	To dividend	To reserve	Dividend /share	Book value	London share price	M/B ratio
1940	77.2	7.1	0.87	0.8	0.0	5:00	53.6	76	1.42
1941[a]	—	—	—[c]	—	—	—	—	—	—
1942	84.7	7.1	—	0.0	0.0	—	52.3	67	1.28
1943	85.3	7.1	0.2[d]	0.0	0.0	—	53.6	83	1.55
1944	87.6	7.1	0.2[d]	0.0	0.0	—	53.6	82	1.53
1945	94.5	7.1	0.2[d]	0.0	0.0	—	52.3	90	1.72
1946	126.8	6.0[b]	0.6	0.5	0.0	3:00	45.9	86	1.87

Shareholders' funds (1940 Dec.) = £8,570,000 (@ $1/2\frac{7}{8}$ = $138,297,000) % change in $
Shareholders' funds (1945 Dec.) = £8,375,000 (@ $1/2\frac{7}{8}$ = $135,146,038) −2.3

[a] No balance sheet issued; figures are for the half-year from the Board minutes.
[b] After transfer of £1,125,000 from reserves to the 'contingencies reserve'.
[c] No Profit and Loss Account could be calculated.
[d] Net earnings were transferred to 'contingencies reserve' and no dividend declared or balance carried forward in Profit and Loss Account.

Note: With London as temporary Head Office, the 1942 through 1945 accounts were drawn up in sterling. There is no balance for end–1941. Share transactions on the Hong Kong Register could not be undertaken. For comparison and comment, see Volume III, Table 4.3.

Table 1.4 *The Hongkong and Shanghai Banking Corporation Balance Sheet, selected items, 1940, 1942–1946*

(millions of pounds sterling)

December 31	1940	1942	1943	1944	1945	1946
Accounts in enemy occupied territory	—	33.6	34.0	34.0	—	—
Accounts in moratorium[a]	—	—	—	—	14.1	—
+ Account liabilities[b]	—	27.2	27.5	29.7	54.0[i]	—
= Total account liabilities	55.8	60.9	61.5	63.8	68.1	93.8[c]
Net balance of drafts less remittances etc.					2.0	
Note issue	12.4	15.4	15.4	15.4	16.0	25.7
Shareholders' funds	8.6	8.4	8.4	8.4	8.4	7.4[k]
Liabilities = Assets	77.2	84.7	85.3	87.6	94.5	126.7
Cash + money at call and short notice[c]	8.8	14.2	13.8	15.3	29.3	36.8
Investments[d]	18.2	19.4	21.4	22.3	22.0	34.2
Balance of remittances and drafts in transit	12.4	2.7	1.8	0.8	—	1.7
Bank premises	1.2	1.1	1.1	1.1	1.1	1.2
HK Government Certificates of indebtedness	10.6	13.6	13.6	13.6	14.1[j]	22.9
Total advances etc.	426.1	33.7	33.5	34.4	27.8	29.9[g]
of which:						
Advances[e]		5.8	6.3	7.4	8.6	
Other assets[f]		27.8	27.2	26.9	—	
Moratorium etc.[g]		—	—	—	19.2[g]	
Profits	14.0	—	0.2	0.2	0.2	9.6
Cash/Assets ratio	0.25	0.34[h]	0.32[h]	0.33[h]	0.49[k]	0.29

[a] Accounts subject to moratorium or in offices not yet opened.
[b] Includes bills payable.
[c] Includes bills receivable, which give rise to a significant total of £3.6 million in 1946.
[d] Includes £100,000 investment in subsidiary companies (£98,958 in 1946).
[e] Advances to customers and other accounts – in unoccupied areas.
[f] Including balances of remittances and drafts in transit between enemy occupied branches and balances with branches from which no returns have been received.
[g] Advances to customers subject to moratorium and other accounts the realizable value of which cannot at present be arrived at, including losses due to war.
[h] Assets are defined as those under the control of the London Office – a rough estimate includes cash + investments + balance of remittances + advances[e].
[i] Includes contingencies. [j] Liability in occupied territory during Pacific War. [k] Including balance on Profit and Loss Account.

41

China was once again about to 'open'. The opportunities for a bank would be endless, qualified only by economic and political realities which were not critically examined. In the 1890s China was to be 'criss-crossed' with railways; now it was to be 'laced' with them. However brutal reality would prove, the judgement of the market was based on expectations, on potential.

Given this general feeling, this atmosphere of optimism, the next question was the Bank's ability to meet the financial demands of an expanding Chinese economy in the context of its wartime losses. But what were its wartime losses? To say that 'if the Bank "lost" its Eastern assets, it lost its Eastern "liabilities"' is an exaggeration, but it is a beginning. There were offsets and in victory there would be reparations.

A bank is unlike a factory. Although banks in general build themselves more impressive establishments than textile manufacturers, bankers justify this on the basis of image – a solid building for a solid financial institution. Seizing a factory may make it possible for an enemy to use it to produce – and in the end the enemy can destroy the essential tools of the enterprise, the machinery and the factory. Seizing a bank whose staff has had time to destroy unsigned notes and take its cash elsewhere does not provide the enemy either with usable assets or with the means of continuing the business – or of destroying it. The Bank as financial intermediary does not trade on its own capital but with funds deposited with it; it was the immediate rise in post-war deposits which gave the Bank the means to play an increasingly important role in post-war development – apparently the essential elements had been preserved, the Bank's credit and reputation.

The Japanese seized the Hongkong Bank's physical assets, but they had already been written down. As a consequence of the Bank's accounting policy, the value of property had been written down without regard to actual market value. The actual value of the Bank's premises in areas not in enemy hands was in consequence in excess of the total £1.11 million for all such property as published in the accounts.

The Japanese seized the staff and ledgers, but they were of use only in the task of 'liquidation', and this would be rendered invalid with the Allied victory. Under Occupation conditions, therefore, the public did not deposit funds or do business with the Bank. The most serious loss from the seizure was the loss of income, but the existence of income-earning securities in London provided the basic minimum of income, the small but growing business with South Asia supplemented it, and the Bank throughout the war operated at a 'profit'. This is not to suggest the Bank survived the war without loss; the 'profit' had to be transferred to 'contingencies against war losses' and, as noted above, it proved inadequate.

The greatest potential source of loss was a familiar one – bad loans. War conditions would make repayment or normal servicing impossible.[r] A potential loss would arise from repayment of obligations in 'banana' currency, so that assets were eliminated without a real offset. This problem of 'bad' or non-performing loans would be minimized by a moratorium, giving time for adjustment, the revival of trade making repayment eventually possible. In any case, new business would be the basis of growth, and this would depend on new deposits; losses would be offset by calling exceptionally on the Bank's reserves and contingency accounts.

An enemy can destroy physical machinery and prevent a manufacturer from operating again until he has purchased new equipment and/or built a new factory. A bank need only get its staff back in place and, provided its credit, its reputation, has not been destroyed, it can begin operations immediately. It can do this more efficiently if its books are in order, and in this the Hongkong Bank was generally fortunate. There were factors which would delay immediate full-scale operation – a subject for the next chapter – but the Bank came through the war in a position to recommence banking in the Far East. The important conclusion at this point in the history is that the share market accepted this general approach to banks and it further evaluated the Hongkong Bank as likely to surmount its problems.

The absence of a Hong Kong Share Register would limit transactions to the London Register. This may have prevented forced sale of Hongkong Bank shares on the Hong Kong Register by those who needed cash, thereby limiting the supply in the market and consequently having a favourable impact on price. But this cannot be quantified, although the legal position was one carefully investigated.

Exchange banking during the war

Arthur Morse and his London management were not then facing the question of the Bank's survival. They had both the present and a future to consider. As for the present, the main preoccupations of management in the area of bank operations were (i) to manage the remaining business of the Bank successfully and (ii) to remain liquid so that post-war needs could be met immediately, whatever form they might take.

The war-year figures in Table 1.3 reflect a Bank at rest, which is hardly fair to the activities of the staff. Nevertheless, after allowing for post V-J Day growth in 1945 and concentrating on the years of the Pacific War, there is no change in reserves, there are no dividends, no change in net earnings, little change in total assets. The Board did, however, authorize the transfer of

---

[r] The Board recorded that the Malayan Government had agreed to pay interest on local currency loans throughout the war and there may have been other cases. But in general the Board had to be more concerned with making further loans before any chance of recovering old advances.

£100,000 to the Officers Good Service Fund; this was done before publication of 'profits'. This reflects a Bank financing its swollen overheads – 'swollen' relative to actual current operations – from its interest income, making small profits on operating account which had, of necessity, to be transferred to contingencies. The Bank, thus unable in wartime to strike out in new directions and still not knowing the extent of its post-war problems, resolved to remain prepared by remaining liquid.

The last is reflected in the Cash/Assets ratios as calculated in Table 1.4. The definition is perhaps one which overstates the Bank's liquidity, but it reflects the use of funds which were at the disposition of the Bank's management. A comparison of the growth of cash and money at call in contrast to the growth of investment illustrates the point – at one time, in March 1943, the Board noted the Bank had £13.75 million lent to the market on short term. This stress on liquidity is consistent with the decline in the level of advances from £420 million in 1940 to £5.8 million in 1942. As for the ratios in the 0.33 range, these, as stated in the table, are calculated on the basis of assets of the Bank located in unoccupied territories, and, fraught with definitional problems, they are given merely for indicative purposes.

The Bank's investment policy was influenced by war considerations. During special promotions, 'Wings for Victory Week' for example, the Bank invested £250,000 in $2\frac{1}{2}$% National War Bonds; a further purchase was made in 1944 during 'Salute the Soldier Week'. And it was considered politic to lend in Chungking and underwrite a colonial loan in Colombo. On the other hand a settlement of the Brazilian bonds problem (see Volume III, Chapter 4) resulted in a sale at $76\frac{1}{2}$ and $76\frac{3}{8}$ of £50,000 worth. As the bonds had been written down since their purchase in 1937 at $86\frac{7}{8}$, the Bank's books showed a net credit of £38,144 plus £6,250 in interest. The whole sum was reinvested in Savings Bonds.

There was current business, as the growth of advances from £5.8 million outstanding at the end of 1942 to £7.4 million two years later would indicate. The increasing turnover in exchange operations is a further indication of the development of the Bank's activity in South Asia.

Profit and Loss, January 1, 1942–June 30, 1943

How the Bank operated in its truncated form may be clearer from an abstract of P&L Accounts available with the Board's minute book; it covers an 18-month period, presumably because this represented the first results of an effort to compile such accounts since Pearl Harbor.

Starting with P&L Account in Head Office Books, there is a total income of £1,126,000, all of which, except a rental income of £18,000, derives from interest on Sterling Reserve Fund investments, London Head Office investments, and branch investments.

Against this must be considered deductions for local provident funds, interest expenses, and special charges (£385,000). The consequent credit balance of £497,000 was transferred to Profit and Loss Account.

Consider next the P&L Account, Branches and Agencies. The total losses from Bombay, Calcutta, New York, Chungking, and London were £302,000. Of this £130,000 was caused by Calcutta office; the sum had been credited to Head Office Contingencies Account to provide against bills bought by Calcutta on Bangkok. A £5,000 loss in Chungking was due to the high cost of living; the exchange rate overvalued the Chinese *yuan* (or CNC dollar); it had not been readjusted to take account of inflation.

Against these losses were profits from Singapore, Calcutta, Simla (the relocated Rangoon office), San Francisco, Foochow, and London. Branches under Japanese Occupation could still earn income if they possessed earning assets in free areas.

On balance, a net debit of £178,000 was transferred to Profit and Loss Account.

The Board were at this point presented a statement of the balance of undivided profits. The balance as of December 31, 1941, was £214,000, consistent with the sum carried forward after the mid-1941 interim dividend had been deducted from P&L Account. To this was added for the eighteen months, January 1, 1942 to June 30, 1943, the net of £497,000 net income from Head Office Books and the £178,000 net loss from Branches P&L Account, say £319,000. This plus the £214,000 existing at the end of 1941 made total undivided profits of the Hongkong Bank on June 30, 1943, £533,000.

The published accounts of the Bank do not reflect this conclusion. The first wartime published P&L Account showed the profits for 1943 as £216,000. The absence of the actual balance would also seem, at first glance, to result in an understatement of shareholders' funds. The fact is that while the above compilation in one sense reflected the state of the 'operating bank', it was in another sense an accounting exercise. The major part of the Bank was not operating and large but incalculable contingencies existed; all the balances reflecting 'undivided profits' had been transferred to 'contingencies account'. And as this was to prove inadequate in the end, it is safe to conclude that the Bank's conservative policy was justified; it did not underestimate the Bank's true position. Nevertheless, the 'exercise' had to be undertaken and its results are illustrative of the means whereby the Hongkong Bank survived; Grayburn's policy of building up sterling investments had been fully vindicated.

Although Morse held the Bank together during the war and even made modest 'profits' on current operations, this is not the prime reason he is remembered as a great Chief Manager. The price of the shares was based on future expectations, and it was Morse's policy which justified these expectations as far as the Bank was concerned. Nevertheless the Bank and its staff had to survive the war; Morse's policy, as endorsed by the London Board of Directors, in connection especially with personnel, is an important element in the story.

HONGKONG BANK POLICY AND DECISIONS IN WARTIME LONDON

WARTIME POLICIES AND DECISIONS

Staff policies

The 'working Bank'
When Arthur Morse was appointed Chief Manager by the London Board in 1943 his interim salary was set at £5,000 net of tax plus a house, the latter being justified because of his need to be near the Bank in an emergency. There was no question of taking a percentage of the sums paid away to reserves and dividends – there would be none during the war. The salary was therefore identical to that awarded Sir Charles Addis when he retired from London at the end of 1921 to accept the post of Chairman of the London Committee. But in 1944 the Bank's affairs had improved – and the Chief Manager received a gross £10,000 p.a., although with wartime income tax this did not represent a great percentage improvement. Park as the junior Manager received £6,000, which was a considerable net improvement.[g]

G.L. Davidson, who had gone East in 1919, was Agent Chefoo in 1937, and retired with TB in 1939, returned to work in London Office at £10 a week; he resigned in 1944 with a gratuity of £150.

For the staff working in the East the Board had to consider the problem of cost of living allowances, with the Chungking agency creating the most serious problem as official rates remained stable while inflation was rampant. Managers, impressed with the need for conserving resources in the Bank's straitened circumstances and anxious for their operations to show a profit, were reluctant to endorse requests for cost-of-living bonuses. F.E. Nicoll, the Manager Bombay, argued, for example, that he paid out the same sum to his servant who then provided everything as before – why were his Eastern staff insisting on being paid more? In this case the explanation proved simple: his servant

---

[g] A scholarly reader has suggested that these figures be put into perspective. A professor in England would have received a salary of approximately £800 p.a. The reasons for this differential have been outlined by, among others, Adam Smith.

supplemented Nicoll's payment with his own income, the proceeds from an illicit distillery operating in the Manager's house, an arrangement which the servant did not want disturbed.[29]

Despite the Board's natural concern to conserve the Bank's resources, they were often more realistic about the need to provide for their staff than certain Managers, pressed as the latter were with the concerns of a single office. In February 1943, for example, the Board agreed to an allowance to Eastern staff in India of Rs100 p.m. (Rs220 for married staff) 'whether other banks do it or not'. This latter is interesting since there is evidence that the Eastern exchange and Indian imperial banks normally cooperated closely in such matters.

The beginnings of labour relations problems, which would be considerable post-war, were a feature particularly of the Colombo branch, and Bank Managers were by their training and experience particularly ill-suited to handling sudden demands, often politically motivated, from hitherto loyal employees, indeed from members of the Bank 'family'.

The Board took time from considering the conditions in the East to note the passing of valuable men in London Office. There was W.F. 'Fred' Wheatley, a much-respected messenger in the London Office, who died after 45 years service at the age of 63 – 'His untimely death breaks a link with the past and he will be much missed by all connected with the Bank.' At the end of the war P. Cruse, another messenger, was to retire after 37 years service with £8 p.m. pension; he dropped dead before his last day and a gratuity of £100 was paid to his widow.

By the late summer of 1944, 39 members of the staff had been bombed out – most of them since the flying bombs began – and the Board approved extended financial assistance to them.

The 'Bank interned' and the repatriates

Morse's policies relative to staff of the 'Bank interned' were formulated with recognition of the Bank's position but were at the same time touched with a humanity which was long remembered. Morse personally telephoned news as received of internees to their dependants in Britain; whenever possible he personally met returnees at the London station and sent representatives to the port. After the war he would be further involved.

In the meantime, he was concerned with every aspect of the tragedy and kept in touch with a staff and their dependants scattered world-wide in varying circumstances.

The problems of getting funds to interned members of the staff varied from normal International Red Cross arrangements to smuggling by agents, and this has been considered in Volume III. Monthly remittances to Macau for the Portuguese and Chinese staff residing there reached £1,135 p.m. of which £100 was for the Chief Clerk, X.A. Soares. The expenditure was justified on the grounds that they would be needed immediately to support the Eastern staff when Hong Kong office was reopened – and they should be in good physical shape. There is evidence that part of these funds was being passed on through agents to internees in Hong Kong.

The salaries of interned staff were to be paid in full through 1942 and thereafter on a 50% basis, the balance being pooled to meet extraordinary expenses of a compassionate or emergency nature. Payments to the Provident Fund were on the basis of full salary, and routine pay increases were allowed for. The sums due were provided for but not paid into their accounts; settlement would be made on their release.

Dependants not interned were paid on a 50% basis but with a maximum of £50 per month.

The Board resolved that the Bank would be responsible for all passages, medical and hospital fees of staff and their families on release from internment, that compassionate grants would be considered, and that uncompensated losses would be reimbursed – provided, and this was important to Morse's overall plan, that officers of less than retirement age were prepared to return to the East for duty when required to do so.[30]

In the Chairman's address at the 1944 Annual Meeting, Arthur Morse stated, 'It has been a disappointment that no more members of our foreign staff have been repatriated by means of exchange. We are continuing to do everything possible to assist those in captivity, and their dependants are being properly cared for.' This last included a Board decision to meet the expenses of Miss Grayburn's wedding before her father's death and a grant of £5,000 to each of the two children after his death was announced.

Morse had obviously been close to Grayburn; they were temperamentally attuned. The now aging Sir Charles, who in 1943 had still been active in the City and busy working with Morse on the Chairman's speech, read Morse's tribute to Grayburn delivered at the 1944 meeting and was moved to write the following comment: 'I read your Bank speech with great interest and admiration. I particularly liked your fine tribute to Grayburn. It made me regret the more that I knew him so little.'[31]

The first contingent of Bank refugees were wives, those who had made last minute escapes from places like Singapore and who usually ended their adventures in Australia, Ceylon, or South Africa. The general policy was to grant them their husband's full salary, but they were encouraged to find employment, the return from which was deducted from the amount paid by the Bank. There were wives who, having worked for several years during the war, were more than annoyed when any attempt to do so post-war was met with the cold comment from the same Chief Manager – Bank wives do not work.

Staff repatriated were usually able to reach the United Kingdom. They were put on leave at half pay (income tax paid) on a six-monthly basis, renewed until the time came for them to leave, at a moment's notice, for a post-war assignment in the East. There were exceptions to this. Morrison, as noted above, was brought to London Office as acting Chief Accountant; those with special knowledge or skills were seconded to various Government offices – Fenwick, for example, was seconded to the Colonial Office to work on post-war planning for Hong Kong, W. 'Sandy' Webster to the unit for Malaya.

In November 1943 the Indian Government relaxed its manpower controls sufficiently to permit men who had served five years or more in India to take six months' leave outside India, and the Bank was able to recall staff in poor health and send replacements.

Australian representation and the Bank of New South Wales

Australia proved to be the destination not only of staff and their wives escaping from Southeast Asia but also of a high proportion of the distressed cargoes in which the Bank had an interest. Morse early decided that the Bank needed a representative there and apparently had R.A. Stuart in mind. But Stuart had not seen his wife and children for several years and was recalled to London; the task was left to C. B. Terdre, who had gone East in 1924 and at the outbreak of the Pacific War was by chance on leave in Australia from his last post of Tientsin.

The Chartered Bank and the Mercantile Bank of India also appointed representatives. The Bank of New South Wales provided them with a large room completely furnished and with a staff of stenographers, all free of charge.

We had wives and children scattered all over Australia and it was my job to arrange finances for them and to keep in touch and pass on any news available of husbands and relatives. Besides Staff work I had to endeavour to trace cargoes in which the Bank was interested discharged from over fifty ships diverted to Australian ports, in most cases with no documents being at first available.'[h]

Terdre's job was not finished until 1947. In the post-war period he was busy getting families home or to new assignments and buying furniture for Eastern offices to replace items destroyed in the war.

Charity

As a matter of principle the Board decided that the Bank's charitable donations would be restricted to funds benefiting the Far East, and in fact the first

[h] Terdre refers specifically to the assistance of R.S. Brittain, Manager, British and Foreign Department, the Bank of New South Wales, Sydney branch, and Harold Brown of their Travel Department.[32]

Table 1.5 *The Hongkong and Shanghai Banking Corporation Certain wartime donations, 1942–1945*[a]

1942	United Aid to China Fund	£250
1943	London: Fire Service Garden Party and Fete	£5:5s
	Bombay: European Hospital Fund	£1000
	Calcutta: King of the Hellenes Greek Relief Fund	Rs500
1944	India Red Cross	Rs5000
	Chatham House, subscription	£250
	Empire Day Movement (£100 requested)	£10:10s
1945	Rangoon Church upkeep, per month	Rs50
	Calcutta Hospital Scheme	Rs15000
	India Red Cross	Rs2500
	Listed in J.R. Jones, undated	
	Far Eastern Relief Fund	
	Bengal Government Central Fund for Relief	
	National YMCA on behalf of Malaya	

[a] For donations in 1939–41, see Vol. III, Table 4.14.

serious consideration on this subject occurred in August 1942 relative to the United Aid to China Fund. The Board decided to check carefully what others were doing – Morse went to the Chartered Bank, Campbell questioned his own Westminster. The result was an unspectacular £250; at a time when shareholders were receiving no return on their investment, the Board had to be cautious about being charitable with shareholders' funds.

The Bank turned down a May 1945 request to subscribe to the British Export Trade Research Organization (BETRO); it was not in a position to be generous. Thus the list in Table 1.5 is not as impressive as in the Great War (Volume II, Table 10.2) but the reason for this has been established.

Donations of money are one problem; donations of time are quite another. The main charitable role of the Hongkong Bank came through Morse's treasurership of the Far Eastern Relief Fund, established in September 1942 for the benefit of British subjects who had lost their homes and livelihood as a result of Japanese invasion. The first donations included £50,000 from the Lord Mayor's Empire Air Raid Distress Fund and £5,000 from the Colonial Office on behalf of Malaya and Hong Kong. In some cases refugees were dependent on monthly remittances from funds which became involved in the complex question of 'Trading with the Enemy'; Morse arranged with the Colonial Office to guarantee payments pending clarification of the position. The Fund was operated from the London Office of the Hongkong Bank and payments to those needing relief totalled £301,000; administrative expenses charged by the Hongkong Bank were £357, provoking Lawrence Kadoorie to comment at the Bank's 1946 Annual Meeting, 'a striking example of the way a Relief Fund should be run'. For these services Morse was made a Commander of the British Empire in 1944.

PREPARATIONS FOR POST-WAR DEVELOPMENTS

Staff

As reports came in, Morse was becoming acutely aware that the internees would not be able to stay long in the East before being furloughed Home. Although his plans always called for the initial reopening of the branches by staff released from internment in the East, his main strategy was to have staff who were neither in the armed forces nor interned on a sort of stand-by alert. It was for this reason that the Bank granted them leave with half pay in Britain; they were not to become encumbered with other employment responsibilities. As V-J Day approached those on half pay received a letter to this effect: 'It is possible that you will be required to proceed East in the near future, so will you please make all necessary preparations and hold yourself in readiness to depart at short notice.'[33] This particular letter was sent to H.M. Cook who was in fact not sent East but was instead asked to retire.[34] Morse was uncertain of his requirements.

But having staff on stand-by was not enough; there had to be means of getting them to the East quickly. Post-Great War experience suggested this would be difficult. Morse attempted to surmount the transportation problem by (i) encouraging senior staff to be associated with post-war colonial planning boards, (ii) sending staff in excess of need to India or Colombo, or (iii) obtaining temporary positions in government in India and Ceylon. In this way Fenwick would fly in with the Hong Kong Government advance party; W. J. Hope and A. C. Kennett, who had taken positions with the Ministry of Information in India, would be that much nearer for their first assignments, Saigon and Shanghai respectively. Webster arrived in Singapore three days after the surrender and V.A. Mason, after a brief home visit with his wife and children and a time as No. 2 in Colombo, would be available for Tokyo.

One of the main problems post-war would be legal. Morse was already concerned with the implications of the duress notes, debtor-creditor relations, the absence of extrality following the 1943 Sino-British Treaty, and his choice for legal adviser fell on J.R. Jones, whose work pre-war had been with the Shanghai Municipal Council. This decision marked a breakthrough. The Hongkong Bank had used experts but had not employed them on a full-time contract basis, except the two inter-war political advisers.

Much would depend on how the war ended and whether those in the armed services could be released quickly. Apparently the Hongkong Bank's concern over staff shortages in the immediate post-war period was well enough known to prompt Barclay's Bank to ask the Hongkong Bank whether they would be interested in taking over a number of their own staff temporarily. The offer was not taken up.

The Bank's 'interned offices' were not all liberated at the same time, and this had mixed consequences for the Bank. In the first place the timing eliminated any need to take up Barclay's helpful offer. Secondly, the timing of liberation and the various military government policies caused the demand for transportation to the East to be spread out over several months (unlike the experience in 1919). Thirdly, the military could and often did facilitate access to areas under their control or to which they operated transport facilities. For a time, however, civilian requirements had to take second place. Thus the Manila staff reached the city by transport from the United States only to find their buildings destroyed with no suitable alternatives; the Bank's Eastern staff houses had been requisitioned.

Nevertheless, to the extent possible, Morse prepared the staff for the post-war takeover.

Development and financial planning

The Bank's immediate post-war activities would be dependent on several factors: (i) the terms and timing under which the Bank could return, (ii) the physical state of the office and the problems of reconstituting the accounts, and (iii) the short-term economic situation and the long-term development requirements. For British colonial territories there were planning units, and, as noted above, the Bank had representatives on both the Hong Kong and Malayan committees. The Netherlands Government-in-Exile was also planning for its East Indies territories. China was initiating new company and banking legislation and the Hongkong Bank's Chungking operations were designed to position it for post-war business.

The return to the East – timing

Although conditions were not always satisfactory the Bank was able to return to the East in reasonable time, if not with adequate staff. Morse was often frustrated by the failure of communication; in April 1945 he was still attempting to discover the terms under which the Bank would be permitted to return to Hong Kong and from time to time he had to counter impractical schemes dreamed up in the committee rooms of Whitehall. The main delays proved to be in Japan and Hamburg. The relevant problems will be considered in Chapter 2. Developments in wartime China are recounted below.

Morse's plans for returning Head Office to Hong Kong

Morse's primary focus was Hong Kong. He was concerned with the need for an ordinance, a draft of which he submitted with a comprehensive memorandum covering the opening of the Bank, the freezing of old accounts and a debt moratorium, the annulment of illegal Japanese acts, and the restriction on certain financial operations including exchange transactions. Morse was also concerned that the public utilities should operate immediately, that when plant and equipment were delivered there would be someone on the spot authorized to accept it and put it into operation, ratify the purchase, and eventually repay the Bank; he accordingly suggested an ordinance providing for emergency management. At the same time he devised accounting rules to handle the interim readjustments and yet permit immediate banking operations.[35] In essence he proposed the freezing of accounts but the establishment of a policy of interest-free advances against these accounts.

Morse ordered the preparation of two balance sheets, one as of the Japanese occupation, the other as of the date of liberation, the differences to be examined and illegal acts rectified and legitimate entries reactivated through inter-books accounts. A new set of books would be opened, and all assets which were good and collectable and all liabilities which were payable would be transferred to the new books through the medium of the inter-books accounts. There would also be inter-branch reconciliation accounts. For December 31, 1945, the final balance sheet of the Bank would consist of items still appearing on the old books representing frozen assets and liabilities, while items appearing on the new books would represent the current and free items. An abstract of this dichotomy is shown for 1945 in somewhat truncated form in Table 1.4.

Morse also gave consideration to the need for an Order in Council to remove Head Office back to Hong Kong and a revised Hongkong Bank Ordinance to take into account such matters as the duress note issue.

The complexity of these problems and the delays involved kept Morse in London until April 1946.

Government planning

The Hongkong Bank's involvement with the Malayan Planning Unit was apparently mainly remembered for the Bank's role in blocking the establishment of a Malayan Banking Agency, a sort of combined exchange bank to be operated by the Government during the initial military stages of the reoccupation. The attitudes recorded are confirmation that private sector cooperation with the Government's more incompetent projects was unlikely when choice was available. W. 'Sandy' Webster reflects a banker's position.

I had joined the American Red Cross with several of the other chaps as an auditor. It proved to be a temporary job as an Army bank was going to be formed in preparation for the reconquest of Malaya. So I was put on the Malayan Planning Unit with a pass to the War Office. It was a bloody waste of time because any question which was asked had to be referred to higher authority and never got an answer to this day. A Major General took the chair, a fellow called R.E. Turnbull, who was my immediate boss there. He was a very good chap, and he became eventually Governor of [British North Borneo]. He did very well.

You see, Mountbatten said it had to be military occupation, only people in uniform. Well, that eventually became impossible. I told Turnbull, bloody waste of time.

He said, I agree with you. I can't do anything. Can you tell Morse?

So I went to tell Morse this was the position and that Turnbull agreed. It was stupid to go out in uniform. And then Morse arranged things somehow, and we went out as civilians. ...

The Malayan Banking Agency was part of the Malayan Planning Unit. It was an Army bank, that was all. My task was preparing typewriters, books, and things like that, which never happened. Never. You indented, and that was the end of it. A chap called Columbine [Chartered Bank] was in charge of the bank with me. Just the two of us. One of the questions I asked was, who's going to handle the cash in this?

Oh, they said, we've got people to do that.

But, I said, in the Army only commissioned officers handle cash. You can't pretend to be a Captain behind the counter counting out notes, you can't do that. You need to have a system, a compradore system.

What is that?

And this was the beginning of nothing. The whole thing was cockeyed to begin with, we knew that.

They said, we could start and the other banks come and help you.

But where do you start? Do you have managers or sub-managers or accountants or what? ... no question was ever answered. We never got off the ground. We had no books, nothing. It was an absolute waste of time.[36]

In fairness a problem had arisen originally when the planners had expected that the Army would be fighting its way back into Malaya. The Government would not guarantee protection from the enemy and the banks would therefore not accept responsibility for operating a bank, hence the idea of the Banking Agency.[37] But, as Webster suggests, planning was in a vacuum and consequently the Hongkong Bank declined to assist with detailed plans; indeed it took the lead in efforts to have the scheme abandoned and in this the Bank was in the end successful.[38]

The relations with the Hong Kong Planning Unit appear to have been on a more constructive basis, but consideration of the Bank's role is better put in the context of the Bank's overall planning for the immediate post-war period.

The Bank's priorities and Hong Kong

The Hongkong Bank Board minutes refer from time to time to the result of discussions with various planning committees. The minutes make it increasingly clear that the Hongkong Bank's priorities lay first in Hong Kong and China, secondly in Malaya, the Straits, and the Philippines. In May 1945, for example, the Board resolved that the Bank would not contribute 'much' to finance commodities in Rangoon; the priority was 'further East'. In fact the

Bank contributed Rs5 million of the Rs90 million advance planned by the Burma Agricultural Products Board. For Malaya and the rehabilitation of essential rubber plantations, the Hongkong Bank joined equally with the Chartered and Mercantile banks to lend Straits $1 million each for the Malayan Public Estates Owners Company Ltd.

In the early months of the Pacific War the Hongkong Bank was investigating such legal niceties as to whether interest could be charged on overdrafts held by clients during the Occupation, but Morse's real concern was with the future, and in this context he warned the Board that the Bank needed (i) to make advances in London to keep old constituents together, even as the Bank itself was able to remain in business and (ii) to be prepared to advance large sums for rehabilitation. 'It may be necessary for the Bank to participate in the financing of supplies and/or public utilities,' Morse warned in December 1944. Earlier he had announced that a 'considerable sum of money' would have to be advanced in Hong Kong under a Government guarantee.[39]

These fears were exaggerated as the Bank found out immediately on Fenwick's arrival in the liberated Colony, but they were sufficiently real at the time to provoke Morse into his finest moment. The Government's plan for Hong Kong was based on the installation of mobile, temporary power generators. But Morse responded, 'Owing to the Bank's heavy commitments in Hong Kong it was felt it was in the Bank's interests that such companies as the Electric Company should become operative at the earliest possible date after reoccupation.'[40] What point would there be for the Hongkong Bank to advance short-term funds for long-term investments if, after taking this extraordinary risk, the loan went sour because the temporary generators broke down?

The Hong Kong Planning Unit, Fenwick reported, had obtained specific information on the requirements of China Light and Power Company soon after the Japanese Occupation in early 1942 through an engineer familiar with the situation.[41] In May 1945 Morse was able to inform the Board that a firm order had been placed by China Light and Power Company, the utility company supplying Kowloon, for a £118,000, 20,000 Kw generator and a £119,000, 200,000 lb. boiler unit. This was confirming a previous order and could therefore be filled without delay; similar facilities for the Hongkong Electric Company, the utility supplying Hong Kong Island, had just been ordered; their specific requirements had not been known earlier.

Payment had to be guaranteed and there was no officer of the utility companies available; once the equipment had been approved as part of Hong Kong's immediate rehabilitation program by the Hong Kong Planning Unit, however, the guarantee was provided by the Hongkong Bank under the signature of Arthur Morse. Hong Kong thus 'jumped the queue' for post-war orders and the basis for the Colony's recovery was established.

These two items were equivalent in value to one year's wartime profits for the Bank. The comparison is not immediately relevant except to stress that the decision, given the Bank's position and the uncertainty of conditions in the East – including the political status of Hong Kong – was a brave one. The decision was not one which was immediately appreciated by directors of the companies concerned when they were free to express their views.[42] They were not always current and were unprepared to endorse dramatic decisions made during their internment which committed them in an as yet untested world. But this served only to annoy Morse; it did not affect the course he had chosen for the Bank in the rehabilitation of Hong Kong. To the extent that, as Muriel remarked, banking is both an art and a science, Morse's decision confirms the judgement that the Bank's Chief Manager was strong on 'art', and that this is precisely what was needed at that time.

This can be contrasted with Webster's perhaps exaggerated account of how the Malayan Planning Unit handled the same problem.

Now the Malayan [Planning Unit] started getting the same for Singapore, but they didn't know whether it was AC or DC. They couldn't find that out. After the war, when I got back there, I found it was both AC and DC. Then in Hong Kong the new electrical power and everything else went beautifully, but Singapore was still back in the old stuff with breakdowns every other night.[43]

Morse also went through company files and, combining an assessment of their financial position with his banker's sense of the managerial capabilities, planned his strategy for post-war lending in Hong Kong. After all, Morse knew the taipans and had worked with them as late as 1940; several of them would be once again on the Hongkong Bank's Board of Directors. All this was but confirmation of the Hongkong Bank's key role as the local bank; Morse was acting in that tradition of assistance to local industry which had been responsible for the Bank's early successes – and losses – and for its long-term growth.

Underlying all this were two fundamental propositions. For the established companies whose reconstruction was sponsored by the Planning Unit, Morse felt that, as their bankers, the Hongkong Bank ought to finance the necessary and approved expenditures, working in cooperation with the Government. For the smaller companies, Morse felt it would be necessary to provide finance on less than a strictly business basis; he stated that there was a moral obligation to try to protect those who, through no fault of their own, had probably lost their all.[44]

To be realistic, however, most wartime planning was frustrated by the inability of suppliers to provide the goods except on a priority basis difficult to obtain. Morse worked with (Sir) William J. Keswick to set up a special loan account to finance building materials – 'if we can get priorities and shipping facilities through the Hong Kong Planning Unit'. Even an order for 88 typewriters, the number considered necessary for the Eastern branches, was held up and Fenwick was requested by the manufacturer to apply to the Directorate of Office Machinery.[45] It was not the Hongkong Bank's world.

There is little question under such circumstances as to why the Hongkong Bank remained liquid and was prepared to take advantage of this liquidity in ways which would provide a base for the Colony's industrialization. But later developments were not foreseen. Morse was anxious to restore Hong Kong as a viable, profitable, entrepôt economy – his focus was on public utilities, the port, and docks. And Morse was also looking beyond Hong Kong to China.

THE HONGKONG BANK IN FREE CHINA, 1942–1945

The Hongkong Bank opened an agency in Chungking on March 1, 1943, with foreign banking licence No. 1. On opening day vast sums of money were transferred from major Chinese banks into new accounts with Wayfoong. The following day they were taken out again. 'Face', not business, had been given, but for the Hongkong Bank face was for the time being the more important.

Morse in London and Cassels, temporarily working as commercial attaché with the British Embassy in Chungking, were both agreed that the Hongkong Bank should have an office in Free China and that, if possible, it should be a functioning agency doing banking business.[46] After this there was considerable room for discussion as to what the Bank was trying to achieve and how far they would go to achieve it. To open an office for banking business when it is clear that there is insufficient business to cover expenses suggests that one must have other than immediate commercial goals in mind.

Morse himself became a member of the China Association Committee which often met in the Hongkong Bank in Gracechurch Street.[47] Their deliberations do not appear of political consequence, although Morse was thereby enabled to keep abreast of legislative and other relevant developments in Free China.

The opening of the Chungking Agency

The most obvious principle to establish was continuity. After the initial Japanese sweep, the Bank's Foochow office was still functioning. W.C. Murray, the Penang Manager, who had escaped from Singapore, was selected by Morse to represent the Bank in Chungking. He recommended that Foochow office be evacuated and that it be reestablished in Chungking, although he recognized that this would require registration under Chinese law. For the next twelve months negotiations continued relative to the terms on which the agency should open, in the process of which the principle of reciprocity prevailed.

There was also personal tragedy. In May 1942 Murray received a cable from his twin daughters in Australia that his wife had died after an operation. She too had left Singapore at the last minute. 'I little thought', Murray wrote to Morse, 'that when I said goodbye to her on the dock, we would never meet again.' He asked to be allowed to go down to look after the teenage twins in Australia.[48] But there were enough Hongkong Bankers stranded there and Morse asked him to keep at his post. He left for health reasons only in early 1943.

Although extraterritoriality had existed, British banks had nevertheless been required to register under Chinese legislation of 1929. The problem facing the Hongkong Bank was that on January 9, 1942, the Ministry of Finance promulgated more stringent bank control measures with provisions which would require the Bank to provide all particulars of deposits and advances including the names of constituents. The American ambassador was strongly opposed to compliance and was reported to be urging Washington to resist this invasion of Treaty rights, but the British ambassador was instructed to consider the regulations appropriate for a wartime emergency and advise the Hongkong Bank to meet them as far as possible.[49]

On July 7, 1942, Murray made a formal application to the Ministry of Finance and submitted a relatively simple statement relative to the Hongkong Bank.[50]

Cassels warned Morse that certain Nationalist politicians were unsympathetic towards the British position; there was concern that Britain had not approved a £50 million line of credit. There was certainly a strong feeling that the British banks should be made to comply in full with the regulations of the Ministry, both those of 1929 and 1942.

Unfortunately even under the 1929 legislation there were provisions, previously waived for foreign banks, which made registration on this basis impractical. These included a guarantee from the local Bankers' Association, a registration fee based on the bank's capital, and the names and addresses of the shareholders. Also required were the names and addresses of the founders.

Although one could argue that the Hongkong Bank's position was unsettled – the Order in Council was still pending – and that Government delay was not therefore peculiar to China, at this point the negotiations in Chungking became more political than financial. The Chinese authorities wished to make the point that all banks were to be treated alike, Chinese and foreign, although the new regulations had not been applied to the Banque de l'Indo-Chine in Kunming. Thus an impasse was reached. E.L. Hall-Patch described the situation by cable:

Messrs [Tsuyee] Pei and K.P. Chen fully realize the unreasonableness of [the Chinese] attitude, but they can do nothing to help. They think that at some indefinite time in the future the Chinese Government may consent verbally, but probably not in writing, to some arrangement which will enable the British banks to register and open. This unsatisfactory possibility (and it is only a possibility) is the best we can hope for if we allow the question to drag on as at present. The representatives of the banks are not very happy at this prospect. They think they have already wasted enough time.[51]

The breakthrough came in September when the Wai-chiao Pu (Foreign Ministry) informed the British Embassy that compliance by foreign banks wishing to establish branches in the interior of China might be achieved by the submission of a statement, which, in the view of the Embassy, presumably after consultation with Murray, the Bank could undertake. The change of mind was the consequence of representations by Tsuyee Pei (Pei Tsu-yi) 貝祖詒 and the Bank of China following the permission granted the latter by the Indian Government to open offices in India.[52]

The wording of the Hongkong Bank's actual submission was based on instructions from Morse in London. Murray was informed that he should state the Bank's business as given in the 1929 ordinance, with the exception of the right to issue banknotes which had lapsed in July. He was further advised that the Bank did not assign capital to agencies, but that he should answer the relevant question by giving the capital for the Bank itself, which stood behind the agency. On the contentious question of details relative to loans, Morse suggested that the Bank offer to provide information in the form of totals by category or purpose, as required by New Zealand legislation.[53]

At the same time parallel instructions were being sent to the Chartered Bank's representative.[54] The British position was one which recognized China's right to regulate its banking system; the hope was that the special problems of foreign banks would be respected.

All this proved sufficient. The negotiations were successfully concluded but not before Murray had left Chungking. It was left to his successor, S.A. Gray, formerly the Calcutta branch Accountant, to actually open the first foreign bank office registered under the new regulations.

Proposals for an agency in Kunming were dropped. Expenses would prove heavy in Chungking and banking prospects in Kunming were based on expectations relative to the reopening of the Burma Road which were in the end never realized.

Foreign banks in China after the end of extrality

The Hongkong Bank opened with an Eastern staff of three – Gray, J.B. Stewart, formerly Agent Foochow, and O.P. Edwards from Swatow. Murray had obtained the services of a leading Chinese banker, K.C. Lee, about whom more will be written in the following section.

In the development of legislation to control banks, especially foreign banks, there were two contrary trends in Chinese thinking. The first stressed national controls and moved in the direction of a planned State economy, some wrote 'on Russian lines', in which foreign banks would have little role to play except on the periphery and as possible sources of foreign capital.

Against this approach were the leading Chinese bankers. Cassels, who, despite his Embassy position, kept in close touch with Morse and Hongkong Bank interests, was in frequent contact with men who, like Tsuyee Pei of the Bank of China, had great hopes of an international role for Chinese banking and understood the need for reciprocity. The Hongkong Bank, however, was also concerned with lesser matters, for example the right to continue operating savings accounts. Even granted reciprocity as a principle, there were problems of degree and detail.[55]

The legislation which evolved did not in itself curtail the Bank's post-war activities; other problems would develop.

The Hongkong Bank's wartime presence in China

But all this was for the future. Cassels saw the Hongkong Bank meanwhile losing its position in China. With only one nominally operating office, the Bank would be contrasted unfavourably with major Chinese banks, especially the Bank of China, with their growing geographical coverage. Morse had little patience with this criticism. With one branch losing money he could not afford to have others in the same position. As he pointed out, when Pei opened a new Bank of China branch overseas, he was able to take in sterling and other currencies and pay out in China in depreciating *fapi* at unrealistic rates of exchange; the Hongkong Bank would by the nature of the available business be operating the other way – taking in *fapi* and paying out in hard currency.[56]

There continued to be discussion relative to a Kunming agency; Cassels reminded Morse that it was the first important commercial town on the Burma Road (soon to be reopened it was hoped) and the first airport after the Hump, the dangerous air route over the mountains from Calcutta. These advantages were dependent on the war with Japan continuing after the end of the European War, but events moved too fast; the office was never set up.

Cassels' work with the Embassy naturally prevented him from directly representing the Hongkong Bank in any negotiation in Chungking. The Bank had sent Murray to be its representative; he had been succeeded by Gray in 1943. But this was at the working level; Cassels urged something more.

His first thought was that a 'director' should be sent out. This, not unexpectedly in view of Morse's stated opinion on the proper role of Hongkong Bank directors, was immediately turned down. Morse and Henchman, the latter having just been repatriated, then considered who among the available senior staff of the Bank scattered world-wide from Australia to Canada or in semi-retirement in Britain might be sent out at the 'representational' level. After they had studied the list they decided, without criticism of the members being so passed over, that there was no one suitable for just that type of assignment. A.S. Adamson was named, but he remained interned at Lunghwa (near Shanghai), and no one of stature outside the Bank was available; there was, Morse reminded Cassels, a war on.

There was also the problem of liaison or 'lobbying' with both business and political leaders in Chungking. Although the appointment of suitable Chinese to represent the Bank's interests was independently desirable, the importance of such a move increased when it became clear that no one would be coming out from London. But China's top men were also busy; not only was there a war, but there was considerable planning for the future. In any case the problem of selection and afterwards obtaining acceptance appeared insurmountable.

The Hongkong Bank needed one sound man, and, its 'joss' continuing to the end, it was able to secure the services of K.C. Lee 李廣釗, a banker who had served the Hongkong Committee of the Currency Stabilization Fund and who had all the right qualifications and connections. Murray, on Cassels' advice, appointed him joint Manager; he now had 'face', and the Bank had its first Chinese Manager – and access to the right authorities in Chungking.

Gray's task in Chungking was not an easy one. Although branch business was negligible, it took time and there was a frequent need to negotiate with the Central Bank of China and the Ministry of Finance on various restrictions. Gray had also to entertain and do so carefully and within the requirements of Chinese etiquette in a sensitive, overcrowded capital. With his years of Indian experience Gray was unprepared at the representational level, and, even with K.C. Lee's advice and with Cassels in the background, there would be minor storms. Nevertheless he reported contacts with Sun Fo, then president of the Legislative Yuan, and other political leaders; Gray also maintained contact with K.P. Chen, sometime chairman of the Currency Stabilization Board of China and from 1944 chairman of a committee of the Central Planning Board.

And all the time Gray was aware that the branch was operating at a loss. The lack of import finance was due to Government monopoly; export finance was limited by the paucity of exports. Gray reported that North American business would seem to be lost to the Bank of China. Current account balances in February 1944 totalled CNC$8 million, mostly British diplomatic, military, and missionary – about 100 in all after one year's working. Current accounts were mainly for the foreign community, although a leading member of the secret police opened an account – he wished to be able to engage in casual conversation with Bank staff on the whereabouts of certain Chinese whose political views were of interest. Chinese overseas inward remittances had doubled but other foreign exchange business was limited to official customers or to foreign businesses trying merely to finance their office and staff expenses.

The foreign official business reflected a 'black market' operation by which British agencies in China acquired *fapi* (CNC dollar, that is, *yuan* notes) at open market rates to cover local expenses. An agent in Kunming notified the Embassy's special operations officer, A.L.V.S. Giles (Hongkong Bank staff on military duty, grandson of H.A. Giles of Chinese dictionary fame), who then sold sterling against *fapi* through either the Hongkong Bank or Chartered Bank to Chinese businessmen building up blocked sterling accounts in London to be used for the purchase of British equipment post-war.[1]

Gray's task was to minimize his loss at a time when the Hongkong Bank was both attempting to conserve its resources and keep its name before the Chinese Government as a major international bank. This resolved itself into such cheese-paring devices as paying Eastern staff salaries in sterling in London and paying out *fapi* only to meet necessary expenses, thus minimizing the loss on exchange.

The Hongkong Bank and currency stabilization

The Hongkong Bank had rendered great service to China through its role in the Currency Stabilization Fund; it had tried to cooperate with the controversial policies of the successor Stabilization Board (see Volume III). All this must have seemed to practical politicians in Chungking long ago and far away. The Board had not been integrated into the Government structure and could be seen, somewhat unfairly no doubt, as an example of outside interference. The Hongkong Bank could expect little reward for its earlier role, except recognition from Chinese bankers who understood both the burden which had been placed on the Bank and the purpose of the old Fund. Nevertheless, until the whole scheme were wound up, the Bank would remain involved.

The declining days of the Stabilization Board have already been described by E.H. Evans Thomas, formerly Hong Kong and then Tientsin manager of the Chartered Bank and subsequently the British representative on the Board; he has written of the death of the Board's American representative, A.M. Fox, of his replacement by Solomon Adler, of the Board secretary, Ch'i Chao-t'ing 冀朝鼎, who was styled 'secretary-general', referred to H.H. Kung as 'uncle',

---

[1] A major smuggling scheme designed to provide British 'customers' in China with CNC at open market rates against blocked sterling through payments into the Hongkong Bank is described by Charles Cruikshank in his *S.O.E. in the Far East*.[57]

and had direct access to the minister, and of the consequent cliques and cabals as operations ground to a halt.[58] Before coming East with the Foreign Service, Evans Thomas, who as the Chartered Bank's manager in Hong Kong had once run afoul of Grayburn, had called on Morse to assure him that he would be working for all British interests equally; Morse was impressed and wrote accordingly to Cassels. Previous to Evans Thomas's appointment, Cassels, then a counsellor of Embassy, had been the British member (after Hall-Patch), but it would appear that neither ex-Hongkong Bank nor ex-Chartered Bank executive had real influence in the last days of the Board.

As for the 1939 Stabilization Fund, although it ceased operations as of November 29, 1941, several problems remained. First, until December 6 the Bank of China through the agency of the Hongkong Bank in Hong Kong had continued to sell sterling against Chinese National Currency (CNC) to the amount of £204,500 or CNC$20.4 million in an effort to prevent a collapse of the market. Now the Bank of China wanted compensation from the Fund. Secondly, there were problems arising from the capture of Chinese currency notes in Hong Kong and Shanghai to a total of approximately CNC$200 million (= £2.5 million) despite considerable and totally wasted efforts over the life of the Fund to devise a satisfactory destruction plan; thirdly, there were the accounts and the formal closing of the Hongkong Committee's activities to be concluded. Three meetings were in fact held in Chungking, with Murray representing the Hongkong Bank; the Hongkong Committee adjourned *sine die* on May 16, 1942, its accounts had been submitted to the Board as agreed on March 31. In July 1942 the contingency account was cleared by refunding the Bank of China for the Chinese currency bought in the last days of pre-war Hong Kong.[59]

Although the 1939 Stabilization Fund (Fund A) ceased operations, a fully audited account, the condition legally essential for its final determination, could not then be provided, and the British banks were thus not eligible to claim repayment of their contributions through a technicality; similarly the Chinese banks for the same reasons considered that their obligation to continue interest payments at $2\frac{3}{4}$% on £5 million to the British banks was unfair under these unforeseen circumstances. The accounts as available in 1942 recorded an exchange loss of £5 million resulting from purchases of CNC with sterling and holding CNC as its value fell; the assets of the Fund were, then, mainly in CNC worth £4.7 million at $\frac{31}{64}$d and the sterling held totalled £266,490 in the Bank of England with £69,000 in interest due from the Chinese banks. The British Treasury, however, could only act on its guarantee, that is pay the interest due to the Hongkong Bank and Chartered Bank by first declaring the Chinese banks in default, a solution which, for obvious reasons, the latter found unacceptable. A special vote for £5 million was eventually passed by Parliament in March

1945 enabling the Treasury to repay the principal sums as guaranteed: £3 million and £2 million to the Hongkong and Chartered Banks respectively. The Chinese Government agreed to pay the remaining interest due, and the Chinese banks were not declared in default.[60]

But all was not thus happily ended. After the war, the books were literally dug up and brought forward, the various parties made claims and counterclaims relative to several operations, sums were written off only to be reconsidered post-1949, a rather mundane and tedious ending to the heroic effort of a small group dominated by the two officers of the Hongkong Bank, Grayburn and Henchman, to stabilize the exchanges, to save the currency of an entire nation at war.

The Consortium, the British and Chinese Corporation, and merchant banking

The 1945 settlement of the Currency Stabilization Fund affair came at an opportune time for the Hongkong Bank, but the controversial and contentious winding-up procedures had taken the focus away from the Bank's positive contributions. Neither this nor its modest banking presence placed the Hongkong Bank in a strong position to influence the course of relevant events in Chungking. Its operations had of necessity to appear parsimonious and the Bank was unable to send out any big names. But then, 'top names' would probably not in those days have awed Chinese politicians, although it would be a form of declaring the Bank's respect for and recognition of China's sovereign importance; it would have given face. But the problem the Bank confronted lay deeper than this.

Within the few years since the outbreak of the European War Britain's presence in China had been overwhelmed by the all-pervading presence of the Americans – military, political, and economic. There was an inherent anti-British feeling, arising in part from the British insistence that Hong Kong, including the New Territories, should remain British after the war. Behind that were memories of the China Consortium, which, as far as the Chinese knew, still existed, and the unwillingness of the British Government to make a £50 million credit available.

Morse was not a supporter of the continued existence of the Consortium; there was official legal opinion to suggest that, with the outbreak of the Pacific War against one of the members, Japan, the Consortium had even ceased to exist. Morse's concern was with the finance of China's post-war development on a practical basis and with full Chinese agreement. He had no 'sacred cows', certainly not the Consortium, and he even saw the need for an amalgamation of the Pekin Syndicate and the British and Chinese Corporation (B&CC), with the Hongkong Bank continuing as the lead bank in the British Group, which, reconstituted and rid of its ties to the Consortium, would, he thought, provide the basis for continued British financial involvement in China.

With Cassels spelling out the possible implications of various political developments, Morse decided on the need to separate factors which should determine the Bank's China policy into two categories – those which the Bank could do nothing about and those over which the Bank had control. The former included such questions as the future of Hong Kong, which Morse assumed throughout would remain British. On the shape of China's political structure post-war, the most likely development seemed to be a return to the Nanking era, a relatively credible central Government with varying powers remaining in the provinces, but with Chiang Kai-shek and his supporters in the ascendancy. But Morse was pragmatic. From the Bank's Hong Kong base and without the need of extrality, he was prepared to react and adjust. He would do what business he could with China, but, if that were proved insufficient, there were other developing areas within the Bank's traditional region of operations where the Bank's participation would prove mutually beneficial.

This placed the focus on the Bank's organization, manpower, and the establishment of a sound financial base. This in turn confirmed Morse in the wisdom of his London policies as previously described. The Bank should remain liquid, the staff should be strategically placed and on the ready, and plans should be made for the return of Head Office to Hong Kong. To the other problems he would like to have solved before V-J Day must now be added the status of the China Consortium, the rejuvenation of the B&CC, and the reorganization of the British Group of banks interested in long-term China finance. But V-J Day came unexpectedly and Morse was still in the process of negotiations, both with regard to the Bank in China and on broader issues.

Thus he would not return to Hong Kong immediately. There would be a period of completion in London first. That period and the tasks accomplished between August 1945 and June 1946 are subjects for the following chapter.

BRANCHES IN SOUTH ASIA

The selection of operating branches for further discussion is not quite the problem it was when dealing with the inter-war period. There space limitations required recourse to sampling, and the Colombo branch was one of those chosen for detailed study; the others, selected for earlier volumes, had come under enemy control. To continue the story, therefore, the Colombo branch will now be examined with three topics in mind: (i) competition and the Bank's military business in Ceylon, (ii) the beginning of labour problems, and (iii) the general atmosphere of a branch which, while away from the war area, was nevertheless dominated by the military. Colombo, as any old hand would have agreed, had changed. In the previous section on Colombo (Volume III, Chapter 10), there was discussion of the beginning of local modern-style banking, of special purpose banks, and even the hint of regulation; these important developments were left in abeyance until after the war.

India, which for so long had been seen as outside the Hongkong Bank's region and more as a base for exchange operations than for the initiation of new business, would now perforce be examined by Morse and his colleagues in Bombay and Calcutta for its commercial banking potential. Calcutta was also a staging area; men and their families arrived from over the Hump, it was the jumping off place for those attempting to return to the Far East or to seek a way Home. One Bank officer, O.P. Edwards, even worked his passage to Liverpool on an American freighter.

As for the Chungking branch, opened in 1943 very much with the Bank's future stake in China in mind, that story has already been told.

COLOMBO BRANCH[61]

War-related business

The course to self-government and to changes in the banking system had been set before the outbreak of war. While it may be said that the Pacific War delayed the process in general, for the Hongkong Bank the actual business generated overshadowed all other developments, including the entry of yet another competitor exchange bank, Grindlays, in 1943. Although during this period the growth of the Bank of Ceylon – according to Mason, Accountant of the Hongkong Bank's Colombo branch, by accepting business at a loss – was an indicator of the future, the Hongkong Bank still held the accounts of the Command Paymaster, the Royal Naval Cashier, the Royal Netherlands Navy, and various British Government agencies. Ceylon Government accounts had, for the most part, been transferred to the Bank of Ceylon.

The Hongkong Bank handled almost all British Government-connected remittances, but, during the course of the war, the Bank gave some of this sterling business to other banks in return for part of the financing of Government rubber and tea bills. As in the Great War imports were curtailed and Ceylon's external reserves grew from Rs275 million in 1939 to Rs1,259 million in 1945; in consequence inflation, encouraged both by lack of commodities and by competition for labour, became a significant problem and an important factor in subsequent labour unrest.

The Hongkong Bank also agreed to take Rs1 million of a Rs43 million Victory Loan issued at $2\frac{1}{2}$ and 3%. The Bank was already holding Rs1 million of a previous $3\frac{1}{2}$% loan (1959/62) and Rs1 million of a 3% (1952) loan. Morse's determination of a Far Eastern priority did not preclude his approving a role, where essential and politic, in the economies of other territories served.

British Forces did not leave Ceylon immediately on the conclusion of the war and, indeed, the Bank of Ceylon only opened its Trincomalee branch, the site of the naval base, in 1946. The Naval Paymaster used this branch to pay wages, replenishing the account by paying in a cheque on the Hongkong Bank's Colombo branch on which a commission of $\frac{1}{8}$th of 1% had to be paid; since the sums involved were as much as Rs10 million a month, the commission paid the expenses of the Trincomalee branch. A commission was also charged when officers cashed their Hongkong Bank salary cheques, and, since the expectation was for exchange at par, the Navy in 1948 eventually lodged a protest with the Hongkong Bank in the course of which the Paymaster argued that, 'It is considered an honour to transact business with the Royal Navy in more enlightened parts of the world.'

The Bank of Ceylon's agent to whom the letter was referred, while confirming that he held the Royal Navy in high regard, noted the inference, which he assumed to be incorrect, that the Royal Navy considered Ceylon an unenlightened part of the world, and suggested the writer would wish to reconsider the unfortunate expression. Ceylon had just been granted 'dominion status'.

Colombo, the staff problem in a changing community

The Colombo branch of the Hongkong Bank was one of three Asian offices which survived the initial Japanese onslaught, although, as noted, a Chungking branch was established in 1943. This did not, however, mean that the operating offices were well-staffed; many officers had been interned by the Japanese, others had joined the Services, while local staff (some of whom served in the Forces) were offered higher paying jobs in newly established operations.

Colombo itself was a changed town, overrun with war-related activities, accommodation scarce and expensive, and the well-ordered routine of society disturbed. There were no compensations; indeed, on the contrary, pay would remain low and the increasing burdens, however 'war-essential', would seem but routine under worsening conditions; there was no hope of Home leave. For the Eastern staff in such circumstances a homily on how much better off they were than colleagues in Japanese internment camps would not be well-received, especially since the statement was so obviously true.

One has the impression, in other words, that the Colombo office during the war was not a happy place in which to work. If this were all there were to say, Colombo would not feature prominently in a Bank history, but, as the atmosphere affected labour relations and post-war business, the problems must be considered.

Labour relations, the beginnings of the post-war East

The initial problem, if any truly existed, was one of paternalism; it was not, for example, that the Hongkong Bank discharged elderly staff without a gratuity – the records prove otherwise – it was rather that the gratuity was just that, an *ex gratia* grant rather than a right. When a pre-war Colombo Manager reported he had fired a recently engaged clerk, Head Office instructed him to state his reasons before they would approve his action. Head Office retained its control of local staff around the world with almost the same degree of jealousy that the Board of Directors maintained its right of final decision on Eastern staff assignments, promotions, and retirement gratuities.

The Colombo Managers who faced labour disputes found it difficult, therefore, to understand them and, frustrated, blamed all on 'Communists' or, less dramatically, 'Marxists'. There can be, however, situations in which previously sound policies become, in a new environment, unacceptable, and the development of new attitudes in Colombo is reflected in the experiences of and reaction to the branch's new Accountant. Mason had been in Sourabaya when the Pacific War broke out; he escaped to Australia and there, unable to find employment, urged Acting Chief Manager Arthur Morse to give him an assignment within the truncated Bank. He was appointed Accountant Colombo. As Mason tells the story, there were shipping delays and losses, and 'since my ship was overdue and unreported I was presumed lost. Unwanted and unmet I wandered late one October evening into Colombo Office to participate in the Wake celebrating my obliteration.... A curious atmosphere of futility seemed to pervade the place – tomorrow was improbable so why take heed for it today.' Although the Manager, J.J. French, was considerably senior to Mason, he appears, as suggested earlier, to have resented the imposition of a comparatively senior Eastern staff member whose relatively high salary would be a debit in the Profit and Loss Account.

In London Morse sensed the tension and he appealed to their loyalty, once again meeting complaints by comparing their life with that of staff in Japanese prison camps. Mason caught the spirit of life in Colombo office when he wrote, 'Here discontent was bred of disorder and the climate became favourable to disgruntled opportunists and finally the staff yielded to the agitators and joined the labour union.'

Local staff and comparative efficiency

The local Colombo staff had a reputation for loyalty and many had served for periods exceeding 30 years, but they had from time to time been criticized. One Manager agreed that the Colombo Eastern staff was as large as that of the much busier Calcutta office but reminded Head Office that the local clerks needed more supervision. In 1934 in reply to C.R. Rice's lengthy defence of branch overheads Head Office came up with the following work load comparisons:

current accounts: 140 per man in Colombo: 333 in Hong Kong;
drafts issued: 7 per man in Colombo: 20 in Hong Kong;
outward bills: 20 per man in Colombo: 109 in Hong Kong and *140* in Kobe.

Mason kept a notebook in which he had written that his path should be that of a 'well-conducted firework amidst an assembly of somnolent turtles'. H.A. Greig, grandson of James Greig, the Bank's second Chief Manager, who as Manager in 1952–1954 had to face the resulting problems, commented simply, 'If that was his attitude, I don't wonder there was a strike.' Mason held a hand inspection to ensure cleanliness; he moved all the desks into one office so that work could be more closely supervised. All this proved 'favourable to disgruntled opportunists'.

It would be unfair, however, to stop an analysis of Mason's activities here. There were those who understood his role, and this dichotomy of view may explain why, in later years of labour disputes, the Bank's local staff were divided in loyalty. The differences often reflected communal backgrounds, and with the tendency of popular Governments to play to the Singhalese, the attitudes of burghers and Tamils mattered less, adding a further source of misunderstanding. The Bank's executives reacted as almost all managers have always done when confronted with what appear unfair personal accusations but which were in fact criticisms of the whole system. Paternalism and pre-war attitudes, not simply working details, were being challenged. In any case, C.G.G. Ebell, who was later to be appointed a Regional officer and who supported management throughout the troubled periods, wrote this reminiscence of Mason:

...a very strict disciplinarian and the staff were terrified by him. New entrants came in the morning, left for lunch and never came back. Those who stuck it are now among the Senior Executives and the Junior Assistants...He made a clean sweep of everything old in the office, even to the extent of buying five new typewriters...Each department was given an instruction book and junior clerks had framed specimens of how a journal was to be written, how to correct mistakes, how statements were to be addressed...

The first strike
The first strike of bank clerks lasted one day, September 1, 1944, and their complaints were referred to a retired district judge, T.A. Roberts, for arbitration. The so-called Roberts Award had more the effect of regularizing pay and conditions as far as the well-looked-after Hongkong Bank staff were concerned, but for employees of other banks the benefits were in general real and significant.

With the war over further agitation resulted in a longer strike and more serious disruption, and this will be considered in the context of other labour problems in the East.

INDIA AND THE CALCUTTA BRANCH

There were no mere rumours at the outbreak of the Pacific War which would end after the Bank – there did not have to be; the situation in Hong Kong was sufficiently serious to speak for itself. In 1914 there had been a wild but temporary concern that the Hongkong Bank was really a German bank, and there had been withdrawals in Hong Kong and, during the war, German-inspired runs on the Bank in Shanghai and Bangkok. But of December 1941, Muriel, then Manager of the Bank's Calcutta branch, has written,

> ...the only time I felt the slightest quavering in the market as to the complete ability of the Hongkong Bank to meet all its engagements, to preserve its stability and maintain its high standing, was for about 48 hours, till the announcement was made that our Head Office had been transferred to London, and that all proper steps had been taken to preserve the continuity of existence and working.[62]

The London Advisory Committee was kept informed as to Indian Government policy on the Bank, and the legal position in India was not solved as easily as the above quotation suggests. Indian legislation defined trading with the enemy in terms of the place of incorporation and thus the transfer of Head Office to London did not solve the Bank's problem; special Indian legislation proved necessary. There was no question, however, of the public's attitude.

The fall of Singapore and Rangoon seemed to open Calcutta to an attack for which the city was totally unprepared. Some 'six lacs of Indians', as Muriel put it, left, although they soon began drifting back again. The Hongkong Bank took note that its securities were in danger and eventually made arrangements through a leading jute constituent, Isphahani, for their shipment to a specially reinforced house in Lucknow; they were later returned to Calcutta with police guard in a locked van attached to the Night Express.

To avoid the controversies relative to the right to 'join up' which arose during the Great War, manpower in India was controlled by the Government and two members of the Hongkong Bank's Calcutta staff, J.N. Frost and G.O.W. Stewart, were conscripted. R.P. Edwards had already joined the Royal Navy. Then, with the development of exchange control, one banker was taken from each of the exchange banks, and Muriel, reluctant to lose a third junior, managed to have Stewart transferred to the position of civilian Assistant Exchange Controller with the Reserve Bank of India. His first assignment was in Rangoon where his duties were directed mainly at denying the enemy Burmese currency by destroying it as the Japanese advanced. Eventually he drove his car as far up a river valley as possible and walked the remaining 80 or so miles out of Burma and resumed exchange control duties in Calcutta.

One business that came within the purview of exchange control was the British clandestine attempt to obtain Chinese National Currency (CNC) at less than official rates. This was done by obtaining *fapi* against rupee deposits in Calcutta; the intervention of exchange control was designed to encourage the Chinese to transfer these deposits into blocked sterling, thus minimizing the likely demand for goods in post-war Calcutta where supply was expected to be minimal. To the extent that the *fapi* were obtained in exchange for Indian goods, Exchange Control was anxious to determine that the export of the particular commodities would not create a shortage in Bengal where the danger of inflation was ever present.

The exchange banks in Calcutta dealt with the Government through their association, of which the chairman was always the manager of the Chartered Bank of India, Australia and China. The exchanges were controlled within strict limits, consequently eliminating part of the risk usually associated with operations from India; furthermore, the demand for Indian exports was assured, disposing of another source of concern, and the Bank played an important role in the finance of the port's increasing wartime trade.

The Bank had, for example, funds locked up in the finance of gunny sacks to France at the time of the German victory there; fortunately the goods had never left India, but they had to be discovered and the deal untangled before the Bank could recover its funds.

The Hongkong Bank was in fact trying to change its image in India. Although the Bank set up its first Indian agency in Calcutta in 1867 and had registered as a 'foreign' bank in 1869, there had been little attempt to establish a locally based business; exchange operations were the key, transactions originating in other agencies or for important constituents on the China coast were important, but beyond that there was a call for caution. This is not surprising; the Hongkong Bank was born in a period of crisis in Indian banking. Over the years China-based Hongkong Bankers could look with some satisfaction at the problems they had avoided, not by being necessarily cleverer than India-focused bankers, but by staying out of the market.

And it took some of the Bank's best bankers to manage the Indian agencies even at this cautious level. Sir Thomas Jackson never served in India, but Sir Ewen Cameron made his early mark there; G.E. Noble, F. de Bovis, Sir Charles S. Addis, O.J. Barnes, were future Chief Managers or London Managers who were Agents in either Calcutta or Bombay. D.M. 'Kobe' Ross and E.J. Davies, certainly 'high fliers', were tested out there, and D.C. Edmondston had rounded out his varied experiences as Accountant in Calcutta before being called to Hong Kong. At no point was it a backwater; indeed, Addis considered training in Calcutta an important part of his education as an exchange banker – for a career, that is, on the China coast. Thus there was a prevailing attitude of running a service agency. A 'service agency' is here understood as an office working on behalf of other branches and agencies.

There were several underlying problems. First, the fear of loss by a Manager/exchange operator, apart from any control by the Chief Manager, attempting too much on a speculative market. Secondly, there was an attitude that the Hongkong Banker was too China-oriented, that he didn't understand enough about India to be able to undertake locally initiated business, even that he had a prejudice in favour of the Chinese. And thirdly, there was the opposite – the Hongkong Banker who understood India, who was left there for a considerable portion of his career. Such a man was trusted to be safe, but in being 'safe' he set the pace or the atmosphere of the Bank's Indian operations.

Such a man, for example, was W.K. Dods, who is supposed to have spent much of his time up country – he held the Indian record for the number of snipe shot with a single gun in a single day. His successor, however, the former Calcutta Accountant, H.E. Moon, attempted too much during the 1919 boom in silver, built up an uncovered position expecting higher prices and had to disengage on a falling market. Dods, like J.C. Nicholson in post-1918 Batavia, had to be recalled to salvage the Bank's position.

There was nothing unsound about the Hongkong Bank's approach to banking in India. The Chief Managers in Hong Kong had a 'feel' for banking in the Far East and that 'feel' extended to exchange operations through India. The Bank was both an exchange bank and a local bank; given the regional focus based on Hong Kong, the information flow into Head Office was inadequate for the development of the Bank's local banking operations in India. Furthermore, the Bank's capital was fully employed and its staff fully occupied. British overseas banking was regional banking, and the Hongkong Bank was best qualified east of India.

That this approach should have been challenged during World War II supports the arguments advanced. Exchange banking business in India, as in Ceylon, was to a great extent London-originated. The Bank's Indian business had been from the first Hong Kong based – but it was also Hong Kong limited. Just as in Hong Kong the taipans of leading hongs were elected year after year to the Hongkong Bank's Board of Directors, so were the London connections between the Mercantile, the Chartered, and the National Bank of India maintained with Asia-oriented businessmen who dealt mainly with South Asia. A Hongkong Bank Manager who attempted to pressure, personally, socially, the Calcutta representative of a British-based exporter might get some business; if he got too much, the representative would be instructed from London to return to the firm's regular bank.

But Morse had been sent to 'beef-up' London, and, once Head Office was there and the Indian export trade of Imperial importance in the war effort, there was an opportunity for the Hongkong Bank to search out new business in India. The opportunities were limited, and Muriel's writings indicate he was well aware of Moon's fate and of the history of the Indian branches, but there were several factors in his favour, one of which was the temporary London base of the Bank. Although Muriel found the Indian merchant difficult to deal with because of what he described as an 'inferiority complex', seeing a slight where none was intended, he searched out new business with Indian firms whose credit-worthiness he assessed as satisfactory in war conditions but which the Bank would subsequently find it difficult to assess in the long run on a continuing basis. The most obvious business available to a newly aggressive bank is that which has been rejected by other banks, but which, when reassessed, seems a reasonable risk to a manager under pressure. This can lead to sound development, provided the 'reassessment' is realistic. The Hongkong Bank's awakening in wartime Calcutta was historically understandable and from a business point of view, temporarily successful, but the Bank would find itself with problem constituents post-war.

2

THE BANK REESTABLISHED, 1945–1946

> It turned out as I thought it would.
>
> Japanese liquidator, Yokohama Specie Bank

The Head Office of The Hongkong and Shanghai Banking Corporation was reestablished in Hong Kong on June 20, 1946. The Chief Manager and Chairman, Arthur Morse, undoubtedly expressed the views of the shareholders present at the July 1946 annual meeting, the first held in the Colony since the outbreak of the Pacific War, when he said, 'I trust that never again in the lifetime of any of us here will it be necessary to move our Head Office from this site.'

This was the climax, although not the completion, of the 'return to the East', a phrase designed to refer to the reestablishment of contact with or reopening of the captured branches and agencies. For in fact the first agency to 'reopen' or to take on new business once again was Lyons, contact with which was reestablished in November 1944. Some offices never reopened, in Northeast China for example, but that was the consequence of new problems to be considered later. The longest delays were in Germany and Japan, where military occupation planners had their own priorities. The Tokyo and Hamburg branches finally reopened in 1947 and 1948 respectively.

PRELUDE TO THE POST-WAR YEARS

The first stage

The return to Hong Kong was in one sense achieved virtually on the day of the Japanese surrender when G. Lyon-Mackenzie walked down from Church House to the Bank and took over the books from the Japanese liquidators. From a business standpoint the more significant date was the arrival of T.J.J. Fenwick with the Military Government a few days later; but there would still be delays before the Hong Kong office could reopen for regular business.

This sequence was common to several branches: first the arrival of the internees, if they were nearby, who took charge and in some cases reopened for limited business; then came the relief, usually partial, by Hongkong Bankers moved from their forward bases or flown out from England; finally, the branch would reopen for business and face the complexities of meeting customer requirements while certain key questions remained unresolved – the rate of conversion of depreciated enemy currencies, the handling of accounts subject to a moratorium, the adjudication of wartime repayments in depreciated currency, the immediate impact of inflation, and the fate of the so-called 'duress notes', the unissued notes paid out by the Japanese during the Occupation.

These were among the unresolved issues which delayed the return of Head Office. Arthur Morse recognized that certain of the more contentious problems would be solved only in London and he wished to remain until decisions were reached. In this he was ultimately frustrated; the debtor/creditor ordinances in Hong Kong and Malaya were not passed until 1948 and 1949 respectively. The duress note issue question was however solved in 1946 and necessary changes in the Bank's ordinance negotiated while the terms of the appropriate Order in Council effecting the retransfer were finalized.

Wartime planning had been based of necessity on certain assumptions, both political and economic, which did not in many cases prove valid after peace had been achieved. For purely banking operations the correction was better made in the East and to this extent the delay in Morse's return might be supposed to have delayed necessary decisions. However the Bank's ability to operate was hampered not only by the very questions which were keeping Morse in London but also by a wide range of temporary problems ranging from staff difficulties to the world shortage of commodities. Local Managers did not, however, simply await the course of events. They made initial decisions in varying circumstances and through them the Bank in the East became operational.

But first the internees had to be brought home, the soldiers demobilized.

The homecoming

The reestablishment of the Hongkong Bank in the East required, *inter alia*, the return to Britain of the internees either immediately or after a brief period of assisting in the immediate reopening of an office; they then had to be sent back to the East. Neither trip resembled the imperial pre-war ritual under the house flag of the P&O.

During the war and especially in the days immediately following the Japanese surrender, communication was uncertain and Morse tried to contact next of kin directly with the relevant information – and to handle calls from distraught wives who had not heard: 'Morse was very good. He kept in touch with my mother. Whenever there was any news of us, not necessarily of me, but of all of us in Hong Kong, he would write her a letter or phone her up and give her the news. A very bluff Irishman, old Arthur.'[1] Wendy Turner was one of the distraught wives:

> ...everybody else had had telegrams to say their husbands were free, and I had had no news from him at all and was quite convinced that he was dead. And the famous Arthur Morse that I had been writing to, and who I had met in the meantime... who was a vast, very rough, raw Irishman and who was an absolute darling, but who put the fear of God into me when I met him and I realized this was the famous man I'd been writing to.
> I used to ring him up and say, I haven't got a telegram, something must have happened.
> He would say, I know Mike, he'll come out alive, don't worry about it.
> Anyway, bless his heart, when the time came for me to get a telegram, it came from Colombo, and it read, Get the boyfriends out, I'm on my way.
> So I realized then that he was obviously very much all there![2]

The general pattern was (i) eventual evacuation by ship with priority depending on conditions, (ii) the homecoming, (iii) rehabilitation and reassignment, and (iv) the return, usually by air or by a combination of air and freighter travel. The next crisis was the timing of dependants' travel; couples separated during the war years were not patient, but the question of suitable accommodation in the East was a contentious one – should the Bank stress prewar standards or accept that couples wished to be reunited at any standard.

The sources indicate variations and some accounts are more complete than others. But from this a reasonable selection can be made.

O.P. Edwards had escaped from Swatow and worked first in the Bank's Chungking office and then in Calcutta; his Home leave was long postponed. Eventually it was made conditional on his being able to find a passage. One successful applicant for a small Bank overdraft proved the key to success; he informed Edwards that an American freighter was short two crew members, and Edwards signed on as a second steward working his way back to Liverpool. He was put ashore with a virtual taxi-load of food in rationed Britain.[3]

For most, however, the voyage was on a crowded freighter and only 'freedom' and prospects of Home made the trip bearable.

Then on arrival there could be scenes of sadness and joy. Although Morse sent subordinates to meet staff at the ports, he himself was usually at the London terminal to greet returning staff. Again Wendy Turner best captures the scene:

> He eventually arrived in London... I didn't even recognize Mike as he stepped out of the train. Last time I'd seen him he was two hundred pounds. When I saw him, he was one hundred and nineteen, he looked like something out of Belsen. His hair was snowy white, [as if it] had been bleached white, and he had no teeth. He'd lost practically all his teeth in camp.
> Arthur Morse recognized him, he was standing behind me, and he said, Wendy, that's Mike, don't let him know you don't know him, for God's sake, go to him.

So I went to this strange creature and put my arms round his neck and said, it's me.

And he said, I do believe in fairies.

The moment he said that I burst into tears, and I realized it was him. Well, Arthur let us remain as we were for about five minutes, and then he came up and he tapped me very carefully on the shoulder. He said, that's enough of that.[4]

There was another reaction. Internees had lived in intimacy with each other for several years. As they made their voyage from the camp to home, one by one these associates would fall away until one day at the London station would come the final split up – and the strange feeling of being alone after so many months. Knightly felt this when he was left behind in Peiping (Peking); the Haymeses felt it as they drove off from Waterloo.[5]

Morse rented two 'reception flats' in London where returning Hongkong Bankers could remain for a week or two until they found other accommodation. He kept track of their rehabilitation and eventually made their first assignment; the arrangement of transportation back being, perhaps, one of the key tasks.

But first there was a lump sum payment – back salary (50% of the regular payment) and a further sum for any special cost, medical or otherwise, necessary for rehabilitation. In addition the returned Eastern staff member would receive full pay while on leave, additional ration coupons, and other benefits. Many used the funds carefully and wisely, but they do not make exciting history. Or perhaps it is a legitimate focus to detail the activities of the Hongkong Bank's next Chief Manager, (Sir) Michael W. Turner, and his wife, Wendy Turner.

When we were given our [£2,000], Mike said to me, are we going to rehabilitate or are we going to have fun?

I said, as far as we're concerned, we're going to have fun.

So we took ourselves a suite in the Savoy Hotel for a whole month. We hired a car, mark you, this was [just after the war], at vast expense, went out and bought ourselves all the clothes we could lay our hands on – with the coupons because we were only allowed coupons. Mike was allowed extra ones because he had to rehabilitate, re-dress himself from scratch as well.

We did theatres, we did everything. We had an absolute ball, a second honeymoon. The second morning we rang the bell to have breakfast in bed, a thing that Mike always dislikes intensely, and the beds had the most gorgeous golden quilts on them, eiderdowns, and Mike slipped his kipper which he was having for breakfast from his plate onto the golden bedcover. We were slightly mortified because we didn't know what the Savoy Hotel would think of one of their best quilts covered in kippers. So we hastily turned it over, hoping and praying that the maid would not notice it when she remade the bed!

But we did have a wonderful time with the two thousand pounds.

At the end of it all, we had nothing to show for it except a wonderful time, and we then had to rehabilitate ourselves when we went back again to Hong Kong on absolutely nothing, but it was worth it.... It really was, it was well worth it.

But everybody, when they heard afterwards, thought we were quite crazy because they'd all bought their pots and pans and their cups and saucers, and we were going back with nothing except a very good memory.[6]

The return to the East

And, finally, there would be the return to the East.

Although one plane failed to clear the Alps and returned to England, most made it through to Bombay or Calcutta, where Bank staff found themselves in transit camps and the local Bank Manager combined his ingenuity with that of the staff member involved to obtain onward transportation. One flight was manned by a Polish crew who, while they had never been East of Calcutta, had a map. They reached the China coast, but the Banker, Maurice W. Turner, could hear the pilot muttering as he flew from island to island, 'It's not this one...it's not this one'; they did finally put down in Hong Kong.[7]

THE REOPENING OF THE BANK'S OFFICES

The Hongkong Bank's offices were reopened over a period extending from 1945 to 1948, beginning with the renewal of contact with Lyons and ending with the reopening in Hamburg. Certain China branches were never reopened; some were assigned a Manager who was unable to make the office operational. The progress may be seen in Table 2.1. Meanwhile new establishments were opened and planned, but these are not considered, except perhaps in anticipation, in this chapter.

As the prospects for reopening became immediate, the following routine circular would be posted in London Office, for example, in the case of Manila:

Manila Office
If any Department has any records or stationery necessary for the reconstruction of Manila Office, they should hand them to [J.S] Watson not later than tomorrow morning, Saturday, 3rd inst, as it is quite likely that his departure will be earlier than was originally expected.

2 March 1945[8]

This was a welcome sign of future victory to a war-weary London staff.

BEFORE V-J DAY: EUROPE AND THE PHILIPPINES

Lyons and Hamburg

London Office reestablished contact with **Lyons** in late November 1944 and Morse reported to the Board that three of the local staff had died – A. Perrin, E. Riollot, and J. Carrier; financial losses of up to Fr8 million (say £33,000)

Table 2.1 *The Hongkong and Shanghai Banking Corporation Reestablishment of pre-war branches, 1945–1948*[a]

Office	1941	Pacific War	1945	1946	1947	1948
Hong Kong	×	—	×	×	×	×
Kowloon	×	—	×	×	×	×
Shanghai	×	—	×	×	×	×
Swatow	×	—	—	×	×	×
Canton	×	—	—	×	×	×
Amoy	×	—	—	×	×	×
Foochow	×	—	—	—	×	×
Chefoo	×	—	—	—	—	—
Tsingtau	×	—	—	×	×	×
Tientsin	×	—	—	×	×	×
Hankow	×	—	—	—	×	×
Peiping	×	—	—	×	×	×
Chungking	ǂ	×	×	×	×	—
Harbin	×	—	—	—	—	—
Dairen	×	—	—	—	—	—
Mukden	×	—	—	—	×	×
Saigon	×	—	—	×	×	×
Haiphong	×	—	—	—	×	×
Tokyo[b]	×	—	—	—	×	×
Kobe	×	—	—	—	—	×
Yokohama	×	—	—	—	—	×
Manila	×	—	×	×	×	×
Iloilo	×	—	×	×	×	×
Singapore	×	—	×	×	×	×
Kuala Lumpur	×	—	×	×	×	×
Ipoh	×	—	×	×	×	×
Johore	×	—	×	×	×	×
Malacca	×	—	—	×	×	×
Muar	×	—	—	×	×	×
Penang	×	—	—	×	×	×
Sungei Patani	×	—	—	×	×	×
Batavia/Djakarta	×	—	—	×	×	×
Sourabaya	×	—	—	×	×	×
Bangkok	×	—	—	×	×	×
Rangoon	×	—	×	×	×	×
Calcutta	×	×	×	×	×	×
Bombay	×	×	×	×	×	×
Colombo	×	×	×	×	×	×
New York	×	×	×	×	×	×
San Francisco	×	×	×	×	×	×
London	×	×	×	×	×	×
Hamburg	× ×	× ×	—	—	—	×
Lyons	× ×	× ×	×	×	×	×

[a] Does not include offices opened for the first time post-war.
[b] Kure, which opened in 1947, was not open pre-war.
× Operating.   × × Operating but not under Head Office control.
— Not operating.   ǂ Not established pre-war.

were anticipated. But it was not until April 1945 that the Bank was able to send in British staff; that month D.A. Johnston, the agency's former Accountant, was appointed Agent on an annual salary of £2,000 plus allowances. He remained until his retirement in 1946, at which time he was replaced by J.S. Watson (East in 1918).

There was always hanging over Lyons operations post-war the likelihood of a move to Paris, which was in fact achieved in 1953.

On August 9, 1945, Morse announced to the Board that the Bank had applied to send J.G. Danielson back to **Hamburg** but that permission was unlikely to be granted for a long time – three years as it turned out. The British Military authorities (BMG) had already made contact with the branch with the transmission of the first of an innumerable series of questionnaires. On May 30, 1945, the branch was required to inform the authorities of the number of Nazi Party members on the staff, to which F. Spandau replied 'none'. Nevertheless in June BMG instructed that Spandau was to be dismissed as a trustee and his bank account blocked. He was later tried and convicted of being a 'Nazi Class V, *Mitläfer*', which bore with it no further penalties than that he be removed from his job. The BMG then appointed E. Heuck as his successor.[9]

Spandau and his fellow procurists had displayed a continued, perhaps remarkable, loyalty to the Hongkong Bank throughout the war, sometimes under conditions of considerable hardship. They were eventually working alone; the Bank's pre-war staff of fourteen plus three messengers had been gradually reduced until by March 1943 only the three procurists – Spandau, Heuck and A. Nack – remained.[10] The Bank was required to move its offices; in one such forced move, the procurists succeeded in ensuring that the incoming company bore the cost of the Bank's move, and there were many examples of action in the interests of the Bank (see Volume III, Chapter 11). But Spandau's German Government-assigned total control of the branch, his ill-advised disposition of the Staff Provident Fund which he virtually forced on his reluctant colleagues, the pressures on Nack as a non-Party member which Spandau undoubtedly designed or encouraged and which forced Nack's temporary departure from the Bank in 1944, left him isolated at the end of the war. Under the rules of the Occupation, his dismissal was without appeal. But at this point Nack was able to return to the Bank's employ.

The Philippines

Manila

When the first contingent of the U.S. Army entered Manila on February 3, 1945, the Bank's internees were still divided between the two internment

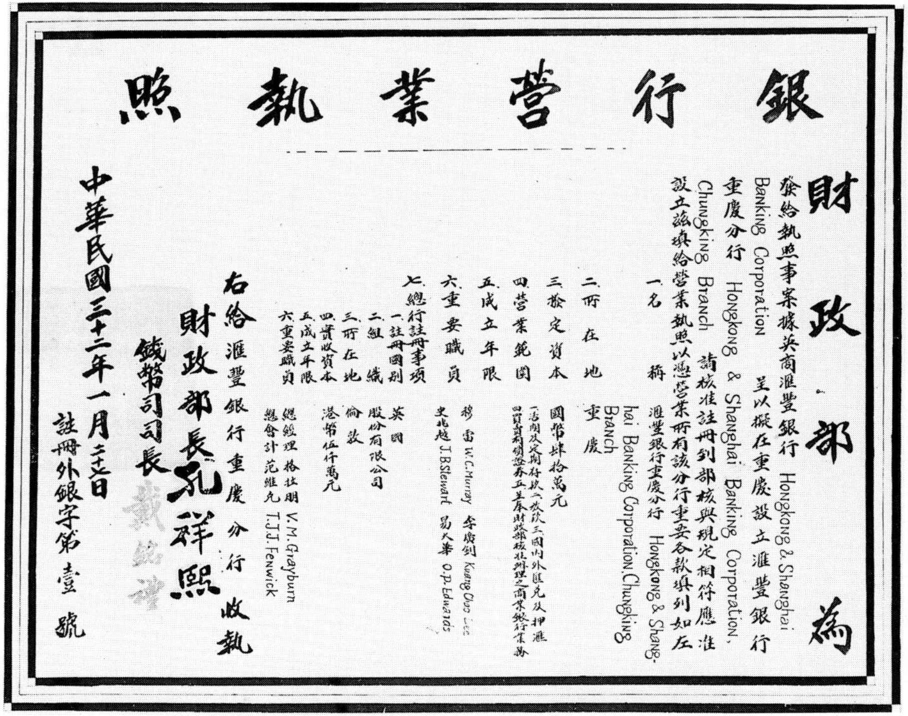

1 Hongkong Bank, Chungking branch: licence to operate, 1943.
This is the first licence (see bottom of extreme left column) to be issued to a foreign bank following the termination of extrality privileges and the promulgation of new banking regulations.

HONGKONG AND SHANGHAI BANKING CORPORATION.

THE LIABILITY OF MEMBERS IS LIMITED TO THE EXTENT AND IN MANNER PRESCRIBED BY ORDINANCE NO. 6 OF 1929 OF THE COLONY OF HONG KONG.

BALANCE SHEET AT 31ST DECEMBER, 1947.

	HK$	£		HK$	£
SHARE CAPITAL Authorised and Issued: 160,000 Shares of HK$125 each, fully paid	20,000,000	1,236,979	**CASH AT BANKERS AND IN HAND**	287,798,224	17,800,020
RESERVE LIABILITY OF MEMBERS 160,000 Shares at HK$125 per Share HK$ 20,000,000			**HONG KONG GOVERNMENT CERTIFICATES OF INDEBTEDNESS**	572,220,862	35,391,284
RESERVE FUND	97,010,526	6,000,000	**MONEY AT CALL AND SHORT NOTICE**	244,800,000	15,140,927
PROFIT AND LOSS ACCOUNT	3,421,361	211,608	**BILLS RECEIVABLE**	84,670,786	5,236,840
	HK$ 120,431,887	£ 7,448,587	**INVESTMENTS** British Government Securities HK$387,705,520 Dominion Colonial and other Securities 206,735,170	594,440,690	36,765,528
HONG KONG CURRENCY NOTES IN CIRCULATION Authorised Note Issue against Securities deposited with the Crown Agents for the Colonies HK$ 44,200,000 Excess Note Issue against Hong Kong Government Certificates of Indebtedness 571,942,086	616,142,086	38,107,746	**INVESTMENTS IN SUBSIDIARY COMPANIES** Trustee and Nominee Companies at Hong Kong, Singapore and London	2,135,735	132,080
CURRENT, DEPOSIT AND OTHER ACCOUNTS Including Provisions for Bad and Doubtful Debts and Contingencies HK$1,675,746,215			**ADVANCES TO CUSTOMERS AND OTHER ACCOUNTS** including Accounts still subject to Moratorium	572,282,798	35,395,034
PROPOSED FINAL DIVIDEND in respect of year ended 31st December, 1947	7,760,842		**BALANCE OF REMITTANCES LESS DRAFTS AND OTHER ITEMS IN TRANSIT**	42,609,698	2,635,544
	1,683,507,057	104,123,158	**BANK PREMISES** At cost less amounts written off	19,122,247	1,182,010

Notes:— 1. There are contingent liabilities in respect of bills re-discounted, confirmed credits, guarantees given and forward contracts for the purchase and sale of foreign exchange.

2. Balances in currencies in respect of which an official rate of exchange existed at 31st December, 1947 have been converted at approximately the official rate; balances in currencies in respect of which no official rate of exchange existed have been converted at approximately the bank rate ruling at 31st December, 1947 or the last rate officially quoted prior to that date.

| HK$2,420,081,030 | £149,679,491 | | HK$2,420,081,030 | £149,679,491 |

PROFIT AND LOSS ACCOUNT FOR THE YEAR ENDED 31ST DECEMBER, 1947.

	£				
To Directors' Fees £5,000 @ 1/2-27/32		HK$ 80,842	By Balance as at 31st December, 1946		HK$ 1,841,861
,, Amount written off Bank Premises		2,000,000	,, Profit for the year, after making transfers to Provisions for Contingencies, out of which accounts provision has been made for Bad and Doubtful Debts and the estimated amount of the losses arising as a result of war		16,595,079
,, Interim Dividend of £2 per Share, free of Hong Kong Corporation Profits Tax, paid 11th August, 1947 £320,000 @ 1/2-27/32		5,173,895			
,, Appropriations recommended by the Directors: Final Dividend of £3 per Share, free of Hong Kong Corporation Profits Tax, £480,000 @ 1/2-27/32 HK$7,760,842 Balance to be carried forward to next year 3,421,361		11,182,203			
		HK$18,436,940			HK$18,436,940

2 Balance sheet at December 31, 1947;
profit and loss account for the year 1947.

3 Hong Kong officers, post-war: they reopened the Bank.
Upper left, T. J. J. Fenwick, first post-war Hong Kong Manager, then chief inspector; *upper right*, A. S. Adamson, Fenwick's successor as Hong Kong Manager; (*centre*) J. R. Jones, legal adviser and unofficial Bank historian; *lower left*, a 'legend in his time', Sir Arthur and Lady Morse wave farewell to Bank staff cheering from the upper floors as the two leave the Bank for England, March 1953; *lower right* Sir Arthur Morse in London.

4 A farewell party for Sir Arthur Morse, 1953.
Left to right: (standing) I. J. O. Cruikshank, R. W. Scott, G. H. Cautherley, C. J. D. Law, F. W. Chandler, B. O'D. Paterson, (Sir) Michael W. Turner, Sir Arthur Morse, S. F. T. B. Lever, P. S. Ingham, (Sir) John Saunders, R. C. Gairdner, N. H. T. Bennett, S. J. H. Pughe, I. H. G. Thomson, P. G. A. Cantopher, F. J. Knightly, A. M. Mack, R. W. Taplin; (sitting) R. C. Olive, F. C. B. Black, O. Skinner, R. P. Moodie, G. O. W. Stewart.

centres of Santo Tomas in Manila and the campus of the University of the Philippines at Los Baños. The former were liberated by the U.S. First Cavalry Division on February 4, the latter by a daring combined operation on February 23. Tragically O.J. 'Paddy' Shannon and his wife were shot by the Japanese, who allegedly suspected their involvement with guerrilla forces, before American troops could reach Baguio; it was to prevent such a disaster on a wholesale scale that led to the dangerous but successful mission to liberate the 2,147 internees at Los Baños.

As early as February 8, 1945, Morse was able to report to the Board that the U.S. authorities had instructed the Bank to send staff to the United States for transport to Manila. T.McC. Dunlop was already working in the New York office, so Morse sent A.F. Handcock and J.S. Watson to complete the team. Within a month Morse was in contact with the Bank's Manila internees and relief funds of US$5,500 had been sent to them to meet immediate needs. By May eight Eastern staff and twelve dependants were on their way back to Britain either through the United States or Australia, and H.V. Parker and R. MacIntyre remained to wait for the new staff who had left New York on May 8. The recapture of Manila had devastated the city – General Dwight Eisenhower compared it to Warsaw – and the Bank's building had suffered heavily. The Board approved the allocation of Pesos 40,000 for its immediate rehabilitation.

The Manila branch opened for business on August 6, 1945.

The rescue at Los Baños

In early October 1944, news of successful American landings had led the internees to hold exaggerated expectations and liberation by Christmas was the general assumption. As the days passed there was a natural reaction, Max Haymes recalled that they felt 'forgotten'. But the American and Philippine forces did not reach the outskirts of Manila until late January and even in mid-February there were an estimated 8,000 to 15,000 Japanese troops within four hours' marching distance of the camp. With the capture of Manila the position of the Los Baños internees was endangered by the prospects of their camp being on the Japanese line of retreat; this forced the development of a plan designed to rescue the internees, still 50 miles within enemy lines, despite the heavy concentration of Japanese troops in the vicinity.[11]

There had been a strange 'false liberation' on January 7, 1945, when the internees awoke to find that all the Japanese guards and camp staff had disappeared overnight. This led to contact with Filipinos who kept the camp supplied with local produce while the internees took over the remaining camp food supplies. Then on January 12, Max Haymes recorded,

Well, the incredible has happened!! Last night about 2:30 a.m. the interpreter [passed along] the hallway of every barrack: 'Important Announcement. Konochi and the Commandant and his staff have returned. Keep away from all sentry boxes and fences.' It gave me a cold, sinking feeling...[12]

There was some fear of reprisals, but the main problem continued to be the food supply, which the Japanese themselves were powerless to control.

The first real intimation of rescue came in the night of February 13, when two Filipino scouts entered the camp on reconnaissance, leaving behind a few cigarettes and American coins, quarters minted in 1944. Their information, coupled with that of an escapee, gave U.S. divisional headquarters precise information of every element of the camp's physical structure and administrative routine.

The plan to liberate the internees involved a major diversionary attack which would also permit the land evacuation of those internees who could not be accommodated on the rescue vehicles of the 672nd Amphibious Track Battalion. The direct operation had three aspects: infiltration of the area by the divisional reconnaissance platoon supported by Filipino guerrilla units to mark landing sites, kill the camp sentries, and hold the area; a parachute drop by 'B' Company, 511th Parachute Infantry, to consolidate the position and take control of the camp; and a landing by amphibious vehicles to take the internees back through enemy lines by water route across Laguna de Bay.

Coordination was essential and achieved. The capture of the camp took fifteen minutes and was timed to coincide with the guards' morning physical training session; the guards were killed.

The events as they appeared to Max Haymes are as follows:

I woke up as usual about a quarter to seven. It was fine and quite cool. Just before seven when I went down the 5 to 10 yards to our cook shack behind our cubicle to make a fire and put on some hot water, I heard the sound of planes and saw 9 Dakotas in formation. When about $\frac{1}{2}$ mile from the camp as I watched I saw men dropping from them with parachutes and at the same moment there was a lot of firing near the gate opposite us and the other side of the Jap barracks....

When I looked out again I saw three American soldiers walking abreast down the earth road towards our barracks with carbines at the ready.... Then a soldier came through the barracks shouting, 'Pick up anything you can carry, we are going to get you out of here.'...

Within ten or fifteen minutes of the planes' arrival, we heard the rumble of heavy vehicles and saw a number of tanks [Amtracks]. They had drop down doors and were open on top and the internees were shuffling on to them....

When we got into the tank and rumbled off, we were told to keep down and above us were 2 50 mm machine guns which they were firing into the bush. I think this was covering fire more than at actual Japs.... After a time we heard the sound of water round us and I looked up and saw that we were in the water at the edge of the lake. It was unbelievable as of course we didn't know that such vehicles existed.[13]

By nightfall the internees, including H.V. Parker, R. MacIntyre, M.F.L. Haymes, and A.L. Snaith, had reached the safety of American lines and had had their first liberation meal. MacIntyre had been married before internment, Haymes and Parker had married in camp, and all three were accompanied in the escape by their wives.

This operation was unique. The sudden surrender of the Japanese under the personally broadcast instructions of the Emperor prevented last minute bloodshed and ensured the liberation of other internees in a relatively orderly manner.

O.J. Shannon

The Shannons as Irish citizens had been left 'outside'. They were not only responsible for easing the lot of the Bank internees but were active with a long-standing Bank constituent, Juan Elizalde, in helping the military prisoners at Cabanatuan. Elizalde, however, was arrested and executed, and the Shannons were apparently advised that it would be safer for them outside Manila. Accordingly they left with their two sons and settled in Baguio, the hill station and summer capital north of Manila.

Unfortunately the Shannons were living with a family implicated in guerrilla operations, and on February 11, 1945, the Kempeitai arrested the two elder Shannons; for many months they were listed as 'missing', but, it was subsequently learned, they had been shot in a nearby street.

The bombing of Baguio made living there unsafe, and the two Shannon children, aged nine and six, made a cross-country escape in the care of their amah, Maria Manantan, who was subsequently employed in the Bank Manager's household. They were allowed through Japanese lines because the interpreter had known the Shannons and presumably argued that the boys were citizens of a neutral country. When they reached Manila, they found that the Bank staff were still living in Santo Tomas, but by May a house had been found. For a time the boys stayed with the Parkers, who had remained behind to get the Bank in operation. Then in July MacIntyre, who had developed a severe infection due to malnutrition, was ordered home. He and his wife took the boys across the States to England, and Shannon's sister met them there for the voyage across the sea to Ireland.[14]

Meanwhile the Board of Directors had voted the boys a total £40 p.m.

Iloilo

With the Japanese defeated in the Philippines, the Hongkong Bank had to consider the fate of its Iloilo agency. The first reaction was the automatic 'return to normalcy'; the long-run future of the Bank in Iloilo would be decided not only on the basis of the opportunities for banking in the post-war Visayas but also on the alternatives possible under new legislation enacted by an independent Government. The local staff reassembled, and with them was A.I. Rabuco, the former Manager's houseboy returned from the boondocks. The Bank sent John Barnabas Stewart as the first post-war Agent. The agency was to reopen.

The first task was to open the safe, to which Rabuco had been given a duplicate set of keys by the ill-fated G.W. Garrett. As a bachelor Rabuco volunteered to open the 'vaults' in case of booby-traps, but all was well; the Japanese had apparently not even opened the safe and the books were in order. Rabuco was again talked out of going to Manila to finish his education; instead he was hired as a messenger in the Bank; he was soon promoted to clerk, and, when by 1948 the older staff had retired, the former houseboy became, as Mrs Adams had predicted, the Hongkong Bank's chief clerk. He was not yet, however, a college graduate; he would continue his post-secondary education in Iloilo under the GI Bill of Rights.[15]

Almost immediately the agency proved its temporary worth as a source of U.S. dollars to finance Hongkong Bank operations in the Philippines. The agency bought the dollars from both the U.S. and the Philippine armies for pesos remitted in some cases from Manila. The extraordinary operation was financially sensible because the Philippine Treasury had not as yet opened in Iloilo and the Bank was cut out from the more obvious source of dollars in Manila where the U.S. Army dealt directly with National City Bank. But this operation aside, a more rigorous analysis of the agency's potential would place its future in doubt.

The initial reconstruction of the accounts had been facilitated by J.F. Hulme who, after being taken off Panay in February 1944, had served for a time with the U.S. Forces in Brisbane.[16] The evidence for his field commission, referred to in Volume III, Chapter 12, was insufficient, and confirmation of his status had to await the arrival of captured Philippine records. Hulme was thus free to return to England; from there he was sent back to the Philippines by the Bank in mid-1945. His first assignment was to help to get the Iloilo agency into operation. This task completed, Hulme was ordered to Manila. He left Iloilo by military plane on November 25, 1945; the plane crashed en route and Hulme was killed.

AFTER V-J DAY: THE CHINA COAST AND SOUTHEAST ASIA

The initial contact with many offices came through the release of nearby internees; they were supplemented by new arrivals and then released for return to Britain – this was the pattern in Hong Kong, Shanghai, Peiping, Singapore, and Bangkok. But the pattern elsewhere varied. Those China branches where reopening appeared at all feasible (and this excluded the Northeast) were contacted through a Hongkong Banker being sent from either Hong Kong or Shanghai to Swatow or Hankow, for example. In Saigon conditions for civilians were such that C.A.W. Ferrier found it both necessary and practical to remain until new staff arrived; in Batavia there was a considerable lapse between the first temporary visit by an internee and the return of the first assigned staff.

The sudden surrender of the Japanese caught the Allied Forces off balance. They were not prepared to take over. Accordingly the Japanese were informed that they remained responsible for law and order; the *quid pro quo* was obviously that the internees had to continue to control themselves and restrain any desire to taunt their erstwhile captors. This was not a major problem. Despite the atrocities there was a recognition by many Hongkong Bank internees that at least part of the problem arose from cross-cultural misunderstandings and that the lack of supplies in the camp was not always the consequence of a deliberate Japanese policy.

Even after the years of suffering many Bankers were able to distinguish between the 'good' Japanese, the ex-bankers for example, those who had from the beginning questioned the wisdom of Japan's policy, and the Kempeitai who were seen to treat their own people no better than they did the internees. There was sufficient understanding of the Japanese position, short of agreement with or acceptance of their policies, to make possible this interregnum.[17]

There was, therefore, no immediate rush from the internment camps to the offices. Token take-overs occurred, but even the task of reaching the office from, say, Lunghwa (Shanghai) or Stanley (Hong Kong) camps, was not easily accomplished. Eventually the presence was made, the doors opened, the debris swept out, and a token payout of funds made to the most deserving. Some internees naturally gave a high priority to returning home, but this was not always possible. Emergency cases could be handled; others had to wait and compete for homeward berths with, one Banker recalls with a touch of impatience, Chinese students enrolled in the London School of Economics.

As already noted the Bank's books for the most part were intact. The situation varied from office to office, however, in respect to the physical condition of the building, the legal, exchange control, political, and military situation, and thus the speed with which the initial contact could be turned into a reasonably staffed operation. In all cases the first tasks were the reconstruction of the books and the physical rehabilitation of the premises, especially the safe and vaults. The very first contact with customers was usually the provision of funds on an emergency basis, regardless of the state of the books or the presence of moratoriums. The Bank's officers also cashed cheques and performed banking services for the military under terms which made the more cautious shudder.

This section deals only with the most immediate problems.

Hong Kong

The first person to reach the Hongkong Bank's building at 1, Queens Road, Central, was G. Lyon-Mackenzie. He took over the books. Meanwhile at Stanley D.C. Davis, then the senior Bank officer in camp, commandeered the Camp Commandant's car and drove into Hong Kong. He remained in the Bank, sleeping in the one Bank flat available, for at least a week; his wife, Natalie Davis, remained, as did almost all other wives, in the camp until they were evacuated – there was nowhere else. She was evacuated in October 1945, Davis in February 1946.[18]

By all reports the building, which had been used as military headquarters and by the Kempeitai, was in disorder, and it was not until the internees arrived that work could begin. F.H. King (East in 1932) had made full notes of the last transactions and had hidden the book; the Japanese did not find it, and, once recovered, it facilitated the reestablishment of many aspects of the Bank's operations. Meanwhile the Portuguese came over from Macau as pre-arranged, and Ho Wing, the Bank's compradore, reappeared with his staff. Ho Wing had been badly treated by the Japanese, and the real work devolved on T.P. Tong 唐宗保 and Peter Lee Shun Wah 李純華, Tong succeeding Ho Wing on his death in 1946; in 1953 Lee became the Bank's last Hong Kong compradore.

The first Bank officer to return to Hong Kong was T.J.J. Fenwick who left England on August 21 with officials of the Military Administration; he himself was apparently not a full member of the Administration, since he had been unable to pass the physical examination. The Hongkong Bank undertook to reimburse the War Office the price of his passage. They flew out from England, changing planes twice as they broke down en route and in consequence missing the convoy from Colombo. Two RAF Catalina Flying boats from Madras were assigned to take the group to Hong Kong, and after a non-stop flight of 30 hours Fenwick's plane landed in Hong Kong harbour; the second had got lost over Siam but arrived a few hours later. On September 26 a further group consisting of R.P. Moodie, S.H. 'Oscar' Ash, and J.A.D. Morrison, the Chief Accountant, left England by air for Hong Kong; they were split into subgroups in Calcutta, one travelling via the Hump and Kunming.

By this time Morse was able to inform the Board that Hong Kong office was open for limited business. Even without major banking operations the tasks were formidable, and Fenwick found it difficult to supervise the various requirements and at the same time meet the financial needs of small traders beginning to open up the entrepôt business once again. When G.O.W. Stewart (East in 1933) arrived from Calcutta, for example, he was assigned the task of organizing Exchange Control for the Hong Kong Government; he had spent considerable time during the war with the exchange control department of the Indian central bank and had become something of an expert. Stewart was instructed by Fenwick to operate the Control from an office in the Hongkong Bank; he was to be responsible for purely Hongkong Bank tasks when not otherwise occupied. At the same time Fenwick himself had duties relative to the Military Government and spent considerable time at meetings in Government House.

The Portuguese staff arrived from Macau in early October and were housed, ironically, in the Sun Wah Hotel where the Japanese had quartered a group of Hong Kong bankers in the first years of the Occupation. They were accompanied by Chinese staff members; at the same time Fenwick made arrangements for eight staff to come down from Shanghai, where prospects for the immediate opening of the branch were minimal.[19]

The War Office on behalf of the Military Government now contacted the Hongkong Bank and asked whether in view of the situation in Hong Kong the staff there might be asked to take a 'broader view of the Bank's functions'.[20] By this was possibly meant a 'long-run development view', that is, precisely the position the Bank had planned to undertake. This was not, therefore, the sort of comment Arthur Morse took quietly. He replied forcefully. 'I don't like to say "I told you so", but we had considerable difficulty getting Fenwick out with the Planning Unit [which had become the Military Government]. Had he not got there I shudder to think what the position might now have been.'[21] Morse, speaking on behalf of the three Hong Kong 'exchange banks', emphasized that the responsibility for the inadequate organization 'cannot be placed at the door of the banks generally'. There was, he said, a continual queue outside Fenwick's door and he had been rushed off his feet. The main problem was that the banks were operating with released internees who were not in a fit state to work.

Morse had reason to be concerned. He had faced and was continuing to face delays at all levels. He remained concerned that there was no guarantee that when machinery arrived there would be anyone in authority to receive it, guarantee payment for it, and, equally important, put it into operation. Although Fenwick had cabled Morse almost on arrival that the situation in Hong Kong was not as bad as expected, Morse was surprised when during October, with others urging the Bank to undertake further financing, the electric companies were attempting to repudiate the deals he had made for them and China Light and Power submitted a letter which purported to 'cancel' certain arrangements and modify others.[22] Morse had, however, worked in cooperation with the Planning Unit, and the utility company managers were not in full control as yet of their companies.

Nevertheless, there were bright moments. There had been a plan to overprint military yen and Central Reserve Bank notes to make them temporary legal tender in Hong Kong. However, coordinated planning, including storing notes in Cape Town, permitted the import of Hongkong Bank banknotes in time to avert this confusion which, on top of the uncertainty relative to the duress issue, might have further hindered economic recovery. The Government then agreed to guarantee repayment of Bank advances made to contractors for the payment of wages; the Bank would advance for other purposes on a normal banking basis.[23] Even before hearing from the military authorities, Morse had cabled Fenwick to help the small traders and, where necessary, obtain information on their credit-worthiness through the compradore.[24]

Problems were being overcome one by one and the Bank's unique role in the development of Hong Kong was beginning.[a] Exchange business was permitted from November 12 and in January 1946 regulations were promulgated to permit an open market and Hong Kong's finance of the entrepôt trade.

Underlying all these problems was the loss of 'joss' which the more traditionally minded believed only the restoration of the Bank building's *fengshui* could restore, and this in turn required the recovery of the Bank's lions.

In October 1945 an American sailor entered the Hong Kong office of the Bank looking in need of assistance. F.H. King approached him and heard his story. His ship had entered Tokyo Bay after V-J Day to evacuate internees of the Kawasaki Camp, and in the nearby dockyard he had seen the Hongkong Bank's two lions. As he had never been to Hong Kong he had assumed they were from Shanghai; but later, when his ship put into that port, he saw the lions had already been returned and were once again guarding the building that dominated the Bund. The sailor, after giving King detailed directions, left without stating either his name or ship. Nevertheless King immediately passed the information to Royal Naval Intelligence, then on the first floor of the Bank.[26]

In fact, the *South China Morning Post* reported, the lions had been slightly wounded in the 1941 attack and had been taken to Japan for recuperation. They were rediscovered with the statues of Sir Thomas Jackson and Queen Victoria and the lot were shipped back to Hong Kong. The lions weighing over seven tons were placed at their appointed positions guarding the Des Voeux Road

---

[a] There remained frustrations. Fenwick, writing to I.H.C. Highet (East in 1927), who after much suffering during his internment had been placed in a sanatorium in Australia, sent his sincere kind regards but added in a PS, 'I wonder if by any chance you remember the combination of the safes in the Telegram Department? We have come across all other combinations but the Telegram safes have defeated us.'[25]

entrance of the Bank during the night of October 17, 1946, in the presence, among others, of the Hon. Arthur Morse, CBE, the Chief Manager.[27] Jackson too was restored to Statue Square but with a difference. He no longer stood facing the Bank, looking sternly into the Chief Manager's office; his position was neutral, as if surveying Hong Kong as a whole. The change was symbolic. Nevertheless, with these restorations, the Bank's return to Hong Kong had been completed.

Shanghai

The internees at Lunghwa Camp were informed of the Emperor's order to surrender and that the Commandant hoped 'there would be no incidents' between the internees and the guards. Apparently there were none. As F.R. Burch put it, 'There was no personal animosity between us and the guards.'[28]

As in Hong Kong peace did not result in a mass exodus from the camp. The first to make contact with the Bank was A.S. Adamson who made the journey into Shanghai by bicycle and met the chief Yokohama Specie Bank liquidator. The Japanese themselves had no one as yet to whom they could surrender; the Chinese had to come from Chungking, flown into Shanghai by the American Air Corps.

So when we went into town, [Burch recalls] there was the same sentry in rather the same position, and the [Japanese] kept law and order until the 'vultures' as we called them, the Chungking crowd...took the Japanese surrender....

About four of our Chinese staff appeared and took myself, [I.H.] Bradford, Frances Kelly, who's now a Bank wife up in Scotland, Mrs Grant, [W.A.] Bill Stewart, and they were as thin as we were because they'd been paid off by the Yokohama Specie Bank, and their clothing wasn't much better. They took us to the nearest village out in the country there and insisted on buying rice and vegetables for us, which we said, very nice. And that was that, all very pally.

Then of course things got sorted out, but, before the office got really going, I went home.[29]

Morse had plans to send A.S. Henchman, still the titular Shanghai Manager, out to Shanghai temporarily. He had been exchanged and repatriated early in the war.[b] If this plan had gone through, he would have been a record time in the East. But Henchman felt that he was too old to fly out under the uncertain conditions of the time, and a sea passage was impractical.[30] Accordingly he resigned in December 1945, and the task of reconstruction fell to S.A. Gray, who flew down from Chungking to take over from Adamson in October. After a brief leave Adamson returned to Hong Kong in May 1946 to take over management of the Hong Kong office.

---

[b] The Bank was still able to reward its old servants. Henchman's Provident Fund after 43 years 'in the East', that is, since he first went East as a junior in 1903, was £45,307; he was granted a gratuity of £15,000.

Also in October 1945 eight internees went south to assist in Hong Kong. Adamson explained the problem, adding that after three years of being paid for no work, Hongkong Bankers should expect to do some banking, and those in Shanghai were, for the most part, still able to perform the tasks. Some were not quite up to this level of humour; others accepted that the Bank had not changed. It was the same employer who took them off the P&O and put them at their desk before they had even been to the Mess to unpack. It was good to be back.

Before leaving for Hong Kong W.A. Stewart met Saburo Yamonouchi, the Yokohama Specie Bank officer who had helped him find housing in 1942; 'It's turned out as I thought it would,' he said.[31] By coincidence, his father-in-law, Viscount Hisaakira Kano, was at that moment saying much the same to F.J. Knightly in Peiping (see below).

The Shanghai branch was now operating in Greater Shanghai, Republic of China, extrality had gone as had the old Shanghai Municipal Council and the International Settlement. The Hongkong Bank had to register and obtain a licence to operate the branch; the delays involved postponed the opening of the office until December 15, 1945, but full access to the Bank's great building would take longer. In February 1946 Morse informed the Board that the Shanghai branch had been registered with a declared capital of CNC$12 million; he also noted that the British Embassy was now pressing the Bank to establish an office in Nanking; this would be accomplished in 1947.

China – outports

Peiping

F.J. Knightly (East in 1937), who had been taken by the Japanese to the special Haiphong Road Centre, was transferred to Peiping in April 1945. His story as recorded in an oral history interview captures the mood of the time and needs no interpretation – except to note that for many, foreigner and Chinese alike, Peking by any other name was always 'Peking'.

...we'd had our usual parade, and it was so hot that everybody was outside except for my little group because we were planning, if they moved us again, to try and escape. I'd been to Peking before, I knew it roughly, and I reckoned if we got into the hills up there, we'd be safe.

We were sitting around talking this over, with a mug of tea, and this fellow [known as the 'ears and eyes of the world' for his tendency to spread rumours] came along and said, have you heard the latest?

We said, no, not again!

He said, they've quit.

We didn't believe it and told him to...

What had happened was this [Formosan] guard...said, finished, they've quit. Our cooks, if you like to call them cooks, were way down by the outer perimeter, and they remembered at twelve o'clock that day all the guards had paraded and had to stand to attention to present arms, and there was a squeaky voice that came over, and there was tremendous drama.

Of course it all fitted in then. It had been at twelve o'clock... that was when the Emperor told [the Japanese] it was all over. And the Japanese never let on one word....

And the lights of Peking we could see over there, the lights of Peking went all up.

So next morning we confronted them. We had our parade, and we stood to attention, bowed and did all the usual things, then we sent our representative, and they admitted it. They said, we've decided to shake hands with England and America.

And then the Americans came.

The Americans were very quick because they wanted to get us. The next day, in the afternoon, a plane came right over and spotted us. We lined up in a 'V' for victory, and they came very low and we waved, and they got the message. Then they parachuted down on the West Airfield at Peking which was about six miles from us. So it ended very nicely, very quickly.

There wasn't really any early contact [with the Bank] because there was no means of contacting anybody. We were able to get a message out... the Americans took one letter, a man flew them to Europe so that our people knew we were alive... to their great surprise, they hadn't heard anything about us for a long time. And then we were stuck; there was no means of getting out. Finally the Americans had a ship in Tientsin which would take them all to Shanghai, by which time a message had arrived that one man was to remain in Peking to look after, or try to get back, the Peking office of the Bank. The senior man of the Bank selected me to do that job, I suppose because I'd been to Peking before and probably knew more about it.

So one day I saw them all pile into a train and disappear, and I was left there. I had been with these fellows for three years, suddenly left all by myself in Peking. Then I just played the game myself.

The first thing was to get the building. It had been used by my friends in the Japanese Military Police, the Kempeitai, as a torture chamber. First thing was to get that back, and then try and find the records. There were instructions from the British Embassy in Chungking that we were to wait for the arrival of the Chinese Government to take over, after which we should apply to them for our properties. I thought that was rather a long wait. I decided to go ahead in spite of the instruction. I told one of my friends in the Peking Club one night, a Colonel in the American Marines, who was a liaison officer between the Japanese North China High Command and the American Sixth Marine Division.

He said, well, we have a very good Japanese attached to us.

And it turned out by a stroke of good fortune that it was Viscount Hisaakira Kano. Now Viscount Kano had been Manager of the Yokohama Specie Bank in London at the outbreak of the war and had been swapped for Henchman of the Hongkong Bank. Kano [father-in-law of Yamonouchi in Shanghai] had gone back to Tokyo, much against his will. He knew what the end of the war would be for Japan, he didn't want any part of it. He was a great admirer of [British Prime Minister Winston] Churchill whom he'd met from time to time. Anyway, I found him there in Peking as the head of the Japanese liaison between the Japanese Army and the American Marines. So I got an introduction to him through my friend in the American [Marines], and he was very helpful and so pleased that somebody from the Hongkong Bank was around, and oh, anything he could do.

So I said, well, let us have our property.

Oh, he didn't see any reason why we shouldn't. So in due course it was arranged, and there would be a handover.

Very interesting this, because I drew up a document I made the Japanese sign. I was taken in to see the inside of the premises. It was in a shocking state. Everything had been ripped out and, oh, it was terrible. So I made them sign the document eventually that they were responsible for all this, and I made the Swiss Consul, Dr Herple, witness it. So in due course, on the day, we turned up. There was a guard of honour, we walked in and sat down, and I made this Japanese Colonel put his chop on a piece of paper, and Dr Herple and I signed. Herple signed as representing H.M.G.

And so I took the building over, and then I went back to my friend Kano and said, it's in such a shocking state, I want some money to clean it up.

We'd better be quick, he said, because the currency was devaluing every day.

So he gave me twenty million local dollars. It wasn't worth a hell of a lot, still with that I got it repainted, and then I got onto missing furniture and carpets galore. We ended up with most of the carpets and typewriters, everything that was taken. They just came along and gave me everything I wanted.

Oh, coal was another thing. I said, what about coal? So they turned up with a hundred [sic] tons of coal, and other people were screaming for coal.

This was great fun, all this. And so I set up this old ramshackle building, fixed up one small room for myself, and then I found all our records. They'd been put in the vaults of one of the American banks. I eventually found them all there, and I got them out, and they were largely intact. I had to check them all, it took me a long time all by myself. Then I found some of our Chinese staff, they came drifting back. So slowly we got the job going again.

We never got back into business by the time I left because, in the first place, there was no business to be done. Peking was just sort of slowly coming back to a diplomatic set-up, but there was no trade or anything going on.

To pay the staff... I used to get money by that time. A British General turned up in a RAF plane once with an enormous paper bag of notes, and I got a message to meet him in the Peking Club. So he was sitting there at a table drinking with somebody else I knew, and he said, that's for you, it's full of notes. He said, you can sign.

I said, how much?

I don't know, just sign. So I had plenty of money to pay staff and whatnot.

...the most extraordinary thing of the lot was that no one ever queried my credentials. I just said I was the Hongkong Bank...I might not have been the Hongkong Bank, nobody ever asked me to prove. I couldn't have proved it anyway, I had no proof. You just went around and did things. I think they were just so staggered that they did what you asked them to do.

When Shanghai got to hear of this, they thought it was very irregular, and I was very naughty, that I shouldn't have done this, but there weren't any repercussions, and afterwards, of course, everybody said how smart it was. But I felt it was stupid because, with due respect to... I knew what would happen when the Chinese arrived, and they took over.[32]

The first post-war Agent was D.F.C. Cleland who returned to Peking in December 1945 but was able to open for banking only in the Autumn of 1946.

The Bank reestablished, 1945–1946

Canton

In October 1945 Fenwick sent A.C. Kennett to Canton to report on conditions there. H.J. Prata had remained on duty, but the other Portuguese had returned to Macau and the Chinese staff were scattered – five had died and others were employed by the Kwangtung Provincial Bank. Fenwick instructed Prata to authorize the compradore to find suitable Chinese assistants, to pay them to stand by, and to wait for further instructions relative to opening. The branch would open approximately one year later.

In the meantime Prata's wartime work was acknowledged and he was authorized to draw a salary of $400+15% family allowance+$180 (=$6 a day) cost of living allowance, or $640 per 30-day month in total. The compradore was to draw $430 p.m.[33]

Hankow

When the Japanese surrendered, E.C. Hutchison was in the Columbia Country Club Camp, Shanghai, and again there was a short period between the surrender and the Japanese admission that this had happened. In the interval the camp Boy Scout troop had been encouraged to climb through a transom and liberate the Japanese guards' beer supply. Reality came very quickly. As Hutchison recalls the events, the British Consul General, (Sir) Alwyne Ogden, warned the internees that Britain was in a weak position with limited resources. They must not expect much assistance.

For a few weeks Hutchison worked in Shanghai, but in October he was ordered to open the Hankow office.

The first problem was getting there.

The Ambassador was going up, and he had so many places on his plane... I was sent along and the Chartered Bank but as usual they hadn't got the places. More ambassadors and bodies were going, and we had to draw lots, and I didn't draw the right lot... Sam [A] Gray [by then Manager Shanghai]... rang up the Consul, but I didn't get up until a later plane. The Chartered Bank man had already got there...

I went up and opened the Bank. We didn't do any business. There was a great bomb hole through one side. It had gone through up to the first floor, I think. I was able to send down to Shanghai a complete set of books prior to the takeover, a complete set of books during the takover, and one as it was, and they had kept them perfectly. I was able to trace what had happened. There hadn't been much, as I said, apart from collecting interest on the Russian church's overdraft and bringing Hankow's balance up.

The Bank wasn't open, but I had to have money to be able to pay [the staff and other charges]. Shell were already up there collecting money they couldn't get down to Shanghai, so he would give me the money and I would ask Shanghai to credit them. I was able to pay my staff and live on that.[34]

Hutchison was able to obtain further funds by renting out that part of the great Bank building which had pre-war been a Naval canteen and club. But, as for regular business, he never opened the branch; he was relieved by F.C.B. Black, who had similar experiences.

He then had difficulty getting back to Shanghai; all transport was being used to move the Chungking people down to Nanking and Shanghai and the Bank was not prepared to pay the necessary black market prices for air or river transport. But LSTs with UNRRA supplies were brought up to Hankow – where they were turned over to the Chinese and sold illegally – after which a party would be thrown on board. At one of these Hutchison persuaded a captain to take him down river.[35]

Swatow

P.A. Sellars had left the Hongkong Bank to marry, but he remained on good personal terms with Arthur Morse. In 1944 Morse invited him to return to the Bank post-war, and, after being demobilized in 1945 and spending a short leave with his wife in Paris, Sellars found himself in November appointed as a Sub-Accountant, Hong Kong.

In December 1945 Sellars visited Swatow. On arrival by boat he entertained the leading Chinese officials on board and then paid courtesy calls. This for a Hongkong Banker was a new procedure; he reported that all this seemed to get the Bank off on the right foot, the merchants were glad to see the Bank returning, and Sellars himself received an enthusiastic welcome from the compradore and staff. The shroff, H.C. Liang, had lost a leg in the Allied bombing and was granted a gratuity of $200; Sellars, noting that Liang had had fifteen years service with the Bank in Harbin, Canton, and Swatow, sent him to Hong Kong at the Bank's expense to be fitted with an artificial leg.[36]

Presumably Sellars made arrangements there similar to those in Canton; that is, the Chinese staff would be hired and paid a retaining wage until the agency could reopen.

This task was also undertaken by Sellars on the instructions of A.S. Adamson (then Hong Kong Manager). The Swatow office reopened for business on October 21, 1946. The books were intact, but the staff could not open the safe; eventually holes had to be drilled all round the lock – and then Sellars had to obtain a new door from Hong Kong. Business followed the pre-war pattern except that exchange transactions were accomplished through Shanghai.

French Indo-China

Saigon

The first to arrive in Saigon was apparently W.J. Hope, who had been positioned in India for just this purpose. He found the Bank's books and securities to be safe and the office guarded by British troops. The Saigon

Manager, C.A.W. Ferrier, was interned at Mytho and was not, for reasons not recorded, released until November 6; he was thus unable to attend when the British Military Command in Saigon authorized a ceremony on September 23 at which the Japanese handed back the office to Hongkong Bank control. The office formally reopened in December and Hope was confirmed as Manager from March 1, 1946, by which time limited business was being undertaken. Ferrier returned to England and retired in France.

J.McG. Taylor had been demobbed in India and was ordered to Saigon via Hong Kong. There he picked up office supplies and proceeded on by ship, arriving to find Hope and F.W. Chandler already in possession of the office. Not all the local staff would return; operating on the local black market was too profitable. But the branch, Taylor reported, was soon operating at a profit and, most important, the Bank's French customers had returned.[37]

Haiphong

G.S. Chambers was positioned in Colombo, although he was a *budlee*, that is, a temporary replacement in an established post in the office. After V-J Day the problem was getting to Saigon; he was eventually successful in obtaining a passage on a small coal ship and for a time he was in the Saigon office while trying to find a way to reach Haiphong. Distressed cargoes were his initial problem – shipments for Saigon unloaded and sold in South Africa and how to recover the funds, etc. It was a task common to all offices.

In June 1946 Chambers headed north.

I cadged a lift to Hanoi. I was very struck by the look of animosity on the faces of the local Vietnamese because...well, it's only natural...they'd seen what had happened in Europe, and they said, why shouldn't we have independence?...The animosity was in Saigon, but, yes, I noticed it far more in the North than in the South because Ho Chi Minh was [there].

The manager of Denis frères [the Bank's Hanoi agents] kindly put me up while I was there, and I contacted my wife's parents who were living in one room in the hotel. My father-in-law had been Capitaine of the Loc du Port, he was in Haiphong before, and all administration had been taken out of the hands of the French. They were just living from hand to mouth in a small room in a hotel.

I happened to make contact with the manager of the Bank of China and told him I was trying to do this and that, and he said, well, maybe I can help you. Which he did. Whether he passed it through the Chinese diplomatic representative, or whether he contacted the Banque de Vietnam, I don't know. Anyhow he did fix up an appointment for me with Ho Chi Minh. I never expected to see Ho Chi Minh personally.

He appeared a wispy bearded old gentleman. There was nothing militant about him, nothing like that. You would have said he looked like an old country peasant.

In a very few moments he was perfectly polite. He listened, he didn't say anything. I explained that I wanted to get back to the Bank which had been there before the war, and as we were nothing to do with the French...I mean, we were British, there was no trouble between the Viet Cong and the Viet Minh and the British. They were only interested in getting the country back from the French in the same way that in India they were only interested in getting back India from the British...

Yes, you would say he was an educated country gentleman, but living in the country. Of course he had been Moscow-trained and everything. He gave me [the *laisser-passer*] at that stage. I've still got the pass signed by Ho Chi Minh, Uncle Ho.

There was no question of going down from Hanoi to Haiphong, because there were very few French military in the country at that time. They were all coming in, all the French troops came in – the British troops were the first to arrive in Indochina... So I went straight back to Saigon, bumming another lift, and there soon afterwards I found there was a Messagerie [Maritime] ship going up to Haiphong, and I managed to get a lift on that.

I went through this Vietnamese Control Post. Difficulties! There was a hell of a lot. I'd brought up a lot of ledgers and things which I thought might be needed, and they said, all right, all right. I piled them onto two or three rickshaws and then went off to the Bank, and there I found the old Chinese houseboy who had been there for years and welcomed me with open arms. I had known him from before.[38]

The agency took some time before it became operational. Fenwick, who had been down on an army plane to Saigon, was able to stop off in Haiphong for a few minutes. He recalls feeling guilty at leaving Chambers there. Shortly afterwards a case of whisky was sent from Hong Kong.

Southeast Asia

Rangoon and Bangkok

Rangoon was opened in December 1945 after relatively unimportant rehabilitation of the structurally sound office building. The Bank had bought a house known as the White Lodge, six miles outside the capital overlooking a lake on the Prome Road; it had been thoroughly looted. After considerable repair and renovation, it was leased on charity terms to the Prome Road Nursing Home Association. The problem of adequate staff housing would remain, but the Bank itself was able to participate in financing the export of rice so badly needed in Singapore and Hong Kong.

When the Japanese surrendered, G.W.E. True remained in **Bangkok** to look after the Bank's interests; other internees were repatriated as quickly as possible. The Bank of Siam staff vacated the Hongkong Bank's premises in September and True lived in the flat above the office, but official possession was not recognized until March 1946. The books were in good condition and the local staff returned to put things in order; the office was reopened as a branch by J.J. French on June 13, 1946.

Singapore – then north to Sungei Patani

As in Hong Kong the Singapore branch was first contacted by internees, although several, including the Sub-Manager, A.M. Duncan Wallace, H.C.D. Davies, Michael W. Turner, and W.T. Yoxall, were too ill to remain. Again paralleling the Hong Kong situation, the Manager, R.A. Stuart, who had been in charge of the Bank's Malayan desk at the London Head Office, came out with the Military attached to the Finance Branch; he was able to work for the Bank and undertake Government services at the same time. W. Webster flew out a few weeks later, also in a semi-official capacity, to act as Sub-Manager.

The original plan was for Stuart to be in overall charge as pre-war, but for the operation to be divided into two sections – one for Singapore and Penang, the other for the Malay States. Webster was to go to Kuala Lumpur to supervise the latter.

The political situation did not permit this development. During the prolonged period between the end of the war and the landing of a significant British force on September 5, the Malayan People's Anti-Japanese Army had come down from the hills and attempted a virtual takeover. Although they were disarmed and paid off in December, they had laid the foundation for the 'Emergency' which was to hamper the development of the Peninsula for the long period into the late 1950s, at first through politicized trade unions and then by open insurrection.

The British Government added to the confusion by decreeing, from offices in London, a political rearrangement of the area through the establishment of a 'Malayan Union' covering all the Malay States, federated and unfederated, and the Straits Settlements of Penang and Malacca; sovereignty was to be taken from the Malay rulers and vested in the British Crown while Singapore was to remain a Crown Colony. This proved wholly unacceptable to the Malays, but the ill-conceived scheme had the long-run consequence of developing Malay political awareness and thus, by encouraging their steady opposition to British rule and support of a constitutional monarchy through the Malay rulers, made possible the establishment of a viable independent Federation of Malaya in 1957.

In the consequent power struggle, the mainly Chinese leftist groups attempted unsuccessfully to cripple the economy – the Chinese merchants and entrepreneurs, who were targets of assassination and coercion, being the main sufferers. The Emergency came later but even in these first months there was considerable uncertainty, and, although the Hongkong Bank soon began to move north from Singapore and reopen its Malayan agencies, the major role designed for Kuala Lumpur had to wait for the establishment of independent Singapore in the 1960s.

In the Bank problems were also emerging. Certainly the Bank was short of funds, Singapore was short of accommodation, and needs could not all be met. R.A. Stuart was a Scot of the 'old school', reluctant, as one new junior (and former army colonel) put it, to authorize expenditure on a new pen nib. Under the circumstances he was the man Morse needed, but would he be too severe?

Before H.C.D. Davies returned to Singapore Morse had commented to him, 'Rab's a grand man to get things started', then he added in a stage whisper, 'I don't quite know what I'd do if somebody hit him' – a reference to the fate of D.M. 'Kobe' Ross.[39]

Inflation cannot be checked simply by local staff making sacrifices; army veterans of some seniority, though juniors in the Bank – and there were three ex-colonels in Singapore on their first Eastern tour – could not be told of the old days and so quiet their concern for wives waiting in England while their salary was approximately £40 a month equivalent. Since the Bank paid the cost of the Mess, there was a suggestion that the Eastern staff make up the deficiency by ordering expensive foods, but, as Sir John Saunders remarked later, you could only eat so much lobster – and, in any case, this did nothing to ease the personal cash flow problem.

Meanwhile Webster and the others recall the everyday problems of beginning again. All the books, with the exception of the Government's account, had been found safely stored in the Bank's strongrooms. But the strongrooms also contained sundry valuables deposited at the last minute for safekeeping – these items included regimental and other silver cups; the gold and precious stones had been taken by the Japanese. Piled in just before the British surrender, they were not covered by any receipt or record, and one of the first jobs was to find the owners.

The counterpart to this was finding the Bank's property. R. Beaumont, a wartime cavalry officer in the Indian Army, found himself one evening at an Army Mess dining on the Bank's china and with the Bank's silver. The next day the china and silver reappeared in the Bank Mess.

Lim Bok Kee, the Singapore compradore returned, and his staff were soon at work. The Chinese customers too returned; the Bank had not lost prestige.

The Bank's Portuguese clerks in particular suffered from the black market environment of Singapore and the corresponding prices. Wearing his best suit H.E. Cordiero, the Chief Clerk, made a formal appeal to Stuart, but this only prompted the canny Manager to comment that if he could afford to dress that well he needed no raise.[c] G.W. Stabb, the Sub-Accountant, who was in charge of local staff problems, pointed out that it was a pre-war suit carefully preserved and now brought out in respect for the Manager, and some small increase was authorized.[40]

Perhaps at the right moment, when the initial difficulties had been overcome, the internees had returned, the new men had arrived, and the old line Managers had retired, these problems could be properly considered. In 1946 Stuart retired and C.L. Edwards, recovered from his war years in Java, arrived to take

---

[c] Cordiero joined the Bank in 1909 at age 17; he retired in 1954 and died, aged 94, in 1986.

over. But a fully developed staff policy remained several years and many costly strikes away.

Arthur Morse reported to the Board in October 1945 that the Bank had reopened in Kuala Lumpur and was proceeding to reopen in Malacca, Penang, and Johore.

As for Malacca, that was reopened by G.E.B. Tytler. V-J Day found him en route from Australia to the United Kingdom; after a brief leave Morse had intended to send him to Shanghai with the prospect of reopening in Harbin. But very quickly Morse recognized the problems in China and the immediate requirements in Singapore; Tytler flew by BOAC flying boat to Calcutta and RAF Dakota to Rangoon and Singapore. R.A. Stuart assigned him to reopen the Malacca agency. 'To our surprise and pleasure we found that our current account ledgers had all been squared off, balanced and stacked in a pile in a corner of the vaults along with the securities, mainly Government bonds, neatly tied and docketed. It almost looked as though they had not expected to win the war'.[41] Or perhaps the staff of the Yokohama Specie Bank had made no prediction, it was simply that they were bankers first.

In April 1946 Tytler left Malacca and made the Bank's first post-war contact with British Borneo. This was the beginning of a significant development in the Hongkong Bank's history and will be considered in a later chapter.

J.W.L. Howard had joined London Office in 1939 – he was soon in the East, but in the Army. Nevertheless, with some diffidence he contacted the Bank in Bombay and was entertained in E.E.F. Hibberd's home; in Rangoon he visited the empty Bank building – and then returned to England for demobilization. Within days his first Hongkong Bank experience in the East began with a long and much interrupted air trip back out to Rangoon and on to Malaya. Howard was supposed to stop in Penang, but someone forgot (he says) to mention this and he continued on to Singapore.

So that was another leg in the long, long journey. In those days, and you may still do for all I know, I think you went as far as Kuala Lumpur and then spent the night there, and then went on the next day.

But a very nice man, [W.] Cardiff Murray, who was quite a character – one of these people who superficially was a very cross man, whom I got to like exceedingly later on – gave me my pep talk and asked me what I'd been doing.

I've been in the Army for the last six and a half years.

Well, you've had six and a half years of holiday at Government expense, I suppose you realize you've got to buckle down and do a day's work now![42]

Ipoh, Muar, and Sungei Patani were reopened by mid-1946.

Batavia

Not until September 29, 1945, did Allied (British) troops reach Java. With the Seaforth Highlanders in the 15th Indian Division was R.G.L. Oliphant of the Hongkong Bank. He made contact with W.H. Lydall and later with C.L. Edwards, who were on the eve of repatriation. Oliphant learned that the Hongkong Bank's Batavia books were with the Yokohama Specie Bank.

The Japanese Bank [Oliphant recalled] was not actually in my area, but I got hold of a company commander and we laid on a squad with tommy guns and we went and asked for our books, and they made no bones about it and gave us what we wanted. They had little option really. Then Lydall and Edwards got out the balances or figures that they wanted from the books, and we put them all in the safe in our office, which in fact had been used as a garage and there was oil all over the floor. It was a hell of a mess, but they went off on leave then.

[Lydall and Edwards were in pretty poor shape.] Lydall had been working in a hospital and I think he'd been able to eat some rats, but the others had been pretty short of food. In fact they both obviously needed leave, they were very thin and emaciated.[43]

The books were then locked away and the Bank building was abandoned for the time. Oliphant was demobbed in the East and assigned to Singapore. In London Morse had apparently hoped that H.A. Mabey, who was also in the area with the British Forces, would be able to go directly to the Bank, but this was considered politically unfeasible. Morse's concern, following an August 1945 meeting with Dr van Hoogstraten, Director of Economic Affairs, Netherlands Government, was that some sort of official banking scheme, Bank voor Nederlandsch-Indie, similar presumably to the abortive Malayan scheme, was being considered by the Dutch.[44] The Netherlands Indies authorities pressed the British banks to open as soon as possible on the same conditions as the Dutch banks themselves.

Before Edwards returned to Britain, the Batavia branch's Chinese constituents gave a reception to express gratitude for the Bank having given them back their balances and belongings prior to the Japanese arrival. The Hongkong Bank would appear to have been the only bank to have made these arrangements.

In the period between the Japanese surrender and the arrival of British troops, the Indonesian Republic, which the Japanese had but recently recognized, had taken hold on the political life of the area, and Dutch rule was never effectively restored. This would limit the opportunities of the Hongkong Bank, whose initial function was seen as assisting the finance of any rehabilitation of British fixed investment in Java and encouraging the growth of British trade.

The next contact with the Bank's Batavia office did not come until late February 1946 when D.A.McN. Butter was sent from Singapore to protect the Bank's interests. In April H.A. Mabey flew into Batavia with his Chartered

Bank colleague to open the agency as the first post-war Manager. The Bank building was not in a condition suitable for the immediate resumption of business. Sepoys of the 1st (Punjab) Battalion were quartered on one side of the counter in the banking hall; on the other side was a large festering pile of rubbish four feet high. The Treasury and all safes had been tampered with, pieces of metal having been forced into the keyholes.

The troops were removed through the intervention of the British Consul, but officers remained in the Mess above the banking hall while British refugees were still in Bank housing.[45]

The above account, written to Muriel, who was by then in charge of London Head Office, was dated April 18; a Board minute of April 25 states that Java would reopen in three weeks – the actual date was May 13. Mabey had made initial and fruitful contacts with the officials of de Javasche Bank and the conditions of his reopening business were outlined in a letter of April 10 from the president of the 'central bank'.

Old accounts were blocked, but limited cash payments could be made holding these as security. Similarly trade could be financed against the security of the old balances which would eventually be repaid, but not necessarily in full. New accounts could be opened in the new currency. The Bank's overbought position as of July 1940 was to be restored, and that portion considered the agency's capital account would benefit from the profits arising from the depreciation of the NEI guilder. Mabey informed London that he could not himself leave Batavia since he would be attending bankers' meetings, but he was despatching Butter to Singapore to pick up essential office supplies.[46]

The first years of the Bank's operations were ones subject to political restrictions and banking controls.

If the Indonesian authorities, including those of Dutch nationality, desire British banks to work in the country – and we are told that they do want them there – the conditions imposed on their working by the Government must be such as will allow: (a) equality of treatment with the Dutch banks, (b) a reasonable margin of profit...(c) remittance of profits from Indonesia, which is essential, especially seeing that losses have always had to be remitted.[47]

The development of the Bank's Java business was difficult and encumbered by discriminatory practices, enforced by the need to handle certain exchange transactions through the Javasche Bank.[48] In 1948 the Bank's business in Indonesia was described as 'crumbs from the rich man's table'. Nevertheless, despite these initial discouragements, the Sourabaya office of the Hongkong Bank was reopened on April 1, 1948.[49]

THE BANK IN ALLIED OCCUPIED COUNTRIES: JAPAN AND GERMANY

Wartime devastation, various political factors, and the comprehensive nature of Occupation controls delayed even the return of a Bank representative to Japan and Germany. In September 1946 the British Military in Hamburg permitted J.G. Danielson to visit the branch. On his way to the Bank's London Office Danielson had been wounded by a flying bomb with the consequent loss of an eye, and his retirement had just been authorized; it was postponed to permit this trip. The first real breakthrough in Japan did not come until mid-1947 when the Bank was invited to send a representative as financial adviser to the Commander of the British Commonwealth Occupation Forces (BCOF), Japan.

Japan: *HSBC, SCAP, BCOF, and other acronyms*

Except for a visit by Fenwick in 1946 as the personal guest of the British senior officer, there was no Hongkong Bank (HSBC) contact with Japan until mid-1947. The post-war history of the HSBC in Japan may be said to have begun with the assignment of V.A. Mason as 'officer-at-large' to British Commonwealth Occupation Forces (BCOF) Headquarters in Kure, following which Mason was assigned a room in 'Empire House', Headquarters of British Commonwealth Sub-Area, Tokyo (BRICOSAT); from August 1947 this was to be the HSBC's 'talking point'; actual banking operations to the Commonwealth Forces, the Australians in Kure, had commenced on July 1, 1947, in a sub-agency headed by H.J.S. Muriel, the son of H.E. Muriel. Its limited purpose meant that it would close with the rundown of Commonwealth troops. The HSBC had an office in Kure only from 1947 to December 31, 1949. Yokohama was reopened in February 1948.[50] W.W. Campbell was in Kobe in the Fall of 1947 facing the problem of a totally destroyed office; he was unable to open for business until April 1948. Once again there was to be an office in Osaka, although not until August 1951.[d]

Mason, by now a widower, had returned from Colombo and was en route to Canada to see his son for the first time in some eight years, when he received a message from London Office asking whether he would agree to represent the Bank in Occupied Japan. On reaching Canada Mason spent only a few days before flying back for briefing in London.

All plans were tentative as Japan was controlled through SCAP (Supreme Commander, Allied Powers), General Douglas MacArthur, son of the Arthur MacArthur who had given the HSBC trouble in the early days of the American occupation of the Philippines (see Vol. II, p. 219). Basically Mason was to be

---

[d] A Bank office was opened in Osaka in 1872 in connection with the Mint; the date of its closing has not been found, and one must assume that operations shifted almost immediately to Hiogo/Kobe, reflecting the move of the foreign community.

on hand to advise the Commonwealth Forces on their own banking requirements, SCAP on the finance of Sterling Area trade, and the HSBC on the possibilities of reentering Japan for exchange banking. SCAP through its Economic and Social Section (ESS) had discovered the importance of Japan's pre-war trade with Sterling Area countries, but its basic American orientation and expertise was of little use in redeveloping such trade, and Mason became an unofficial adviser to ESS and a confidant of its director.

Mason's introduction to the bureaucratization of Occupation came at the Tokyo airport. A fellow passenger attached to the United Kingdom Liaison Mission (UKLIM) was picked up, but the official refused to carry Mason because he was, although bound for the same billet, attached to another entity, to BRICOSAT.[51] More significantly, when ESS wanted information on Sterling Area regulations, it simplified procedures by asking Mason personally to cable the Bank's London Office, which would in turn place the query with the Bank of England or Treasury. The alternative would have been for ESS to inform SCAP, who would pass it to Washington, from there it would go to the British Embassy and finally to the Treasury in London. The HSBC shortcut worked only one way, however; the reply came back through UKLIM whose officials refused to inform Mason of its contents; he had then to wait for the message to be forwarded to SCAP and then down through the command chain to ESS, whose director would bring Mason in on the ensuing discussions. To maintain even this line of communication it was necessary to alter the arrangements from time to time, the messages coming eventually through Head Office in Hong Kong.

Morse could not know the exact position, but he was shrewd enough to give Mason a broad brief. To the latter's question, 'What am I going to do?', he replied, 'I don't know. I'm not going to ask you to do anything except arrive in Japan and look around and see what's going on.' But even Morse did not at first understand Mason's subordinate position; when Mason wrote of being 'commanded' by SCAP, Morse objected. Finally Mason explained his position by comparing MacArthur in Japan to Morse in Hong Kong; the comparison was perhaps exaggerated but Morse got the point.[52]

As for the position of the Hongkong Bank's property and accounts in Japan, it was not dissimilar to the situation elsewhere in the East except that, as the offices were by then occupied by Allies, it was more difficult to get them derequisitioned. The Bank house on the Bluff overlooking Yokohama, for example, had been requisitioned by an American general and the conservatory had been transformed into a bar with psychedelic nudes painted on the walls; the Yokohama office was 'set about with little tables with coloured tablecloths and balloons galore hanging down from the ceiling. The strongroom doors were all open and there were pastries and Coca Cola' stored there.

At this point the British Chief of Mission, Alvary Gascoigne, took Mason to meet General of the Army Douglas MacArthur.

MacArthur: You're BCOF. That's an Australian outfit, isn't it?
Mason: No, Sir, it's a Commonwealth force.
MacArthur: You know there are more people in Tokyo than in the whole of Australia?
Mason: That may be, Sir, but I'm trying to do something to reestablish Japan's trade with the Sterling Area and here is your army flying balloons in my bank and keeping coke and cake in my strongroom.[53]

Gascoigne 'probably felt in case Mason starts to attack MacArthur again we'd better go, so he made the familiar courtesies, and we trickled away'.[54]

Despite incidents of this kind, which gave Mason the reputation of being difficult in places as widely separated as the UKLIM, LON, HKG, and the inner sanctum of SCAP, he achieved a considerable reputation during the initial months which were a prelude to the issue of the necessary licences, and in late 1948 Sterling Area Payments Agreements were eventually signed.[55] He established a genuine relationship of cooperation with ESS and did much to mitigate against the American bias which was naturally expected in an operation staffed entirely by Americans with, for the vast majority, no experience except in domestic banking.

This introduces another element of Mason's character – a tendency to obfuscation. W.R. Hobbin (East in 1925), the Mercantile Bank's Manager in Tokyo, recalled that this could have advantages.

He was a chap that could talk for a quarter of an hour, and after he'd finished you wouldn't know what he had been talking about!
He was a useful man in this way.
We had three American banks, and we used to meet...the American banks and the two Dutch banks [the Foreign Banks Association]....He was Chairman, and the American banks would put forward propositions, and Mason would explain to them why it wasn't possible, and no one knew what the hell he was talking about, but it did the trick![56]

Equally important, given Mason's overall assignment as financial adviser to the Australian General Robertson, he was able to place the British Military Currency (BAFS) on a sound basis – it had been issued initially without Treasury consideration and without adequate formal cover; he also advised on the methods of paying Commonwealth troops in Japan.

And eventually Mason did obtain the release of HSBC property. First, he set up in the one room in Tokyo, liberated some cardboard boxes, and began a filing system. In December 1947 he cabled A.M. Duncan Wallace, then Junior London Manager, urging him to ask the Foreign Office to put pressure on the British Ambassador to make direct representations in turn to SCAP relative to a larger office.

Unless we can expand immediately we shall be seriously embarrassed. Hong Kong Government Open Trade Account, also resumption of Sterling Area trade in sterling, also SCAP Commercial Account, also pre-war reconstruction for all Japan Offices with resultant extensive correspondence cannot be conducted in premises at our disposal.[57]

This succeeded in annoying all those involved, but Mason did obtain more reasonable quarters.

He then turned to personnel requirements.

The Bank of Japan had taken on two of the Hongkong Bank's former clerks, and Mason took one back again to assist with the reconstruction of the books, which had been preserved, as usual, in good condition. By late 1947 it was clear that SCAP intended to open Japan to foreign trade in the near future, and Mason decided to call for assistance from Ena Coberly, his executive secretary from Hankow days, then living in the United States; she arrived in February 1948.

I [Ms Coberly] engaged all the female staff, and, fortunately for me, the women I engaged were of very high calibre. Most of them were girls of very fine, wealthy families who had come down to nothing. They were destitute, they had no money. They all went to finishing schools, they all had wonderful backgrounds.

As a matter of fact, I had one lady there, Mrs [Utako] Inoue, whose husband was the son of the Finance Minister [Junnosuke] Inoue who was assassinated, if you remember. In fact, we became such good friends, I still see them. He has just retired from the Bank of Japan. They had nothing. They had property, but their money was gone, and she had to come out to work. When I saw her, this wonderful, beautiful lady, fluent English, fluent Spanish and Japanese, I said to myself, my goodness, she will be my head girl here, and she was the head girl for two years until her husband was transferred to America.

By that time, they recognized the former bankers of Japan and the business people, and, gradually, the Japanese themselves got on their feet.[58]

Mason, meanwhile was finding a new Bank house in a country where practically everything had been requisitioned by SCAP. Eventually G-2 came up with a Japanese house in a corner of Gokokuji, a royal cemetery; this Mason took over; he named it 'Zombie Lodge'. For a servant he employed a waitress from the Marunouchi Hotel, a young lady of good family, who required that Mason be interviewed to see if he were a suitable employer.

But this was all preliminary to the reestablishment of banking in Japan, the development of Sterling Area trade, the opening of the two-way swing account between the SCAP and the HKG, but managed by HSBC, and the eventual settlement of outstanding wartime problems with the signing of a peace treaty in 1953.

Hamburg Branch

The delay in Germany cannot be blamed on American Occupation regulations as Hamburg was under British Military administration; indeed, foreign banks were reestablished in the American zone before the Hongkong Bank could reopen in Hamburg. After the Danielson visit there was a delay of more than a year before the reestablishment of Hongkong Bank control from London became a reality. At this point the history parallels that of other branches, and Hamburg's special problems are revealed.

There were difficulties in collecting debts from German firms, due partially to the absolute devastation in Germany and the lack of foreign exchange, which was even more tightly controlled than before the war. In addition Hong Kong had not been included in the Anglo-German debts agreement, and the Hongkong Bank was being considered, not unreasonably, a Hong Kong bank. This was also important in the question of the exchange rate for the new Deutsche mark, as the members of the United Nations were allowed a better rate than other nationals, and it was not clear if Hong Kong could be considered a member of the U.N. through Britain. The branch also remained in the anomalous position of having to pay interest on the Reichsmark advances made by the Deutsche Bank during the war, although the Reichsbank (or rather the Bank Deutscher Länder, which had assumed the business) was still not paying, and not allowed to pay, interest on the frozen sterling accounts, much less release them as they were blocked by the BMG's Law no. 53.[59]

In 1948 the Hamburg Branch received the necessary licence to work as an *Außenhandelsbank* (foreign trade bank). Banking conditions were much more complicated than before the war, when the Bank had required no special permits to do various types of banking, and the restrictions on 'local business' had been strictly self-imposed. For the first time the Bank was unable to accept deposits from the public, a restriction removed in 1961. Furthermore, the Bank's sphere of activity had been severely restricted by the Russian occupation of East Germany, Czechoslovakia, and Hungary, where the branch had had constituents.

In May 1948 the Landeszentralbank of the Hansestadt Hamburg wrote to the Hamburg Branch that as the Bank Supervisory Board for the City of Hamburg they formally recognized that The Hongkong and Shanghai Banking Corporation (Hamburg Branch) was the oldest foreign bank in Hamburg, and that the branch needed its old offices back in order to be able to reopen for business on July 1, 1948. This letter was to be presented to the Building Authorities in order to expedite the matter. The Board hoped this reopening would represent a kind of *Wiedergutmachung* (reconciliation) for the measures taken against the branch during the war by the Nazi regime.

But what with the new regulations and the constraints on space, conditions were so confused that it was unclear what kind of business the Bank would be able to do. The Chief Manager, Arthur Morse, visited Hamburg soon after the branch had reopened and told G.C. Moutrie, the new Manager and pre-war Accountant, 'Do what you can, and do your best – we shan't murder you!'[60]

With the move to rehabilitated offices at Monckebergstraße 27 on November 1, 1949, the branch's true post-war history may be said to have commenced.

3

POST-WAR POLICIES AND PROBLEMS: HEAD OFFICE, HONG KONG

> We do well to maintain our Head Office in the East where we can keep in touch with everyday developments and ensure flexibility in our policy.
>
> (Sir) Arthur Morse, 1946

HONGKONG BANKERS

General comments

The problems confronting the Bank at the end of World War II were similar to those of the immediate post-Great War period. In 1918 the Bank's Head Office had been in Hong Kong far from Imperial London, yet the Bank returned to normalcy with considerable efficiency. At that time, however, Sir Charles Addis was in London to look after the Bank's 'imperial' problems – negotiations with the Treasury and the Bank of England, the Colonial Office and the Foreign Office. Addis was both London Manager and a director of the Bank of England. Meanwhile, Sir Newton Stabb as Chief Manager was in Hong Kong running the Bank. Both acted with all the authority necessary, as if they had been joint Chief Managers, each in his own sphere. While this was not wholly without controversy, it worked.

In 1945 there was only Arthur Morse in London. Even if Sir Vandeleur Grayburn and D.C. Edmondston had survived internment, their health would have thwarted their desire to become immediately responsible for the affairs of the Bank. There would have been other problems.

During the Great War both the relevant Governments and the Bank continued to operate in the East. There was change, certainly, but there was also a continuity. During the Pacific War planners in London, isolated from the influences which were shaping the political thoughts of those who remained, found themselves out of step, tolerated in the East only for the brief period of rehabilitation and even that was subject in many cases to the recognition of the need for political change. This brief period over, the initiative was in the East, but by this time Morse had returned and, with him, the Head Office of the Hongkong Bank.

The fact is, however, that in the immediate post V-J period the Bank's main problems were in London; the Bank in the East could not operate properly until these were solved. Morse therefore remained where the London Board gave continuity and dealt with (i) administrative problems, mainly personnel policy and (ii) major policy questions which required Government decision. Many of these latter, whatever the constitutional position, would be solved at least tentatively in London; colonial Governments too were debilitated, their constituencies in doubt or even non-functional.

In the key Eastern branches there were also sound bankers – among them T.J.J. Fenwick and J.A.D. Morrison in Hong Kong, R.A. Stuart in Singapore, S.A. Gray in Shanghai, J. Caldwell and G.E.B. Tytler in India, and V.A. Mason in Japan. But their efforts would have been futile if Morse in London were unsuccessful in reestablishing the Bank on a sound legal and financial basis.

Post-war realities

Policy was determined, and changed, in an atmosphere of uncertainty and financial concern. This would lead to charges that the Bank, that is, Arthur Morse, was 'tight' or even small-minded and that certain decisions revealed a degree of insensitivity. There are cases which support these charges in the early post-war days, but, once the Bank had been reestablished in Hong Kong and was beginning to show signs of financial success, much was rectified. The suddenness of the Japanese surrender, the problems of the Bank's role in China even before 1949, and the delays in reopening in Japan caused much of the uncertainty which led Morse and H. E. Muriel to be first concerned with staff shortages, then aware of a staff surplus, attitudes reflected for example in the sending of a 'stand by for immediate passage East' letter followed closely by a request for the staff member's resignation on the grounds he was no longer needed at all.

There was no controversy over the contribution Lyon-MacKenzie had made in Hong Kong; nevertheless his letter of resignation dated October 7, 1945, caused Morse concern. First of all, he had bluntly asked for a gratuity and pension, something which was still *ex gratia* and within the Board's discretion. But Morse added, when asking him to submit a simple request to resign, the Bank had a problem. Morse reminded Lyon-MacKenzie that the shareholders had no dividends.[1] Morse would have preferred to wait until all internees had returned and he could judge the magnitude of the problem.

Then there was the question of the food packages sent into camps from local sources. In November 1945 Morse wrote to Fenwick, then in charge in Hong Kong, that staff must pay for the parcels – if the signature were good, Fenwick was instructed to pay the debt, debit a special account, and recover from the staff officer later.[2] The position was complicated because, for example, Selwyn-Clarke for the colonial Government had signed pro-notes to a total of eight lacs of dollars, which it was hoped the Government would pay. Furthermore some staff had been fortunate in their contacts and the prices charged had been reasonable; others had paid exorbitantly. Finally, there were certain notes which had been countersigned by a Bank official acting as such – in fact, legally, they were without authority, but the credit of the Bank was involved. The amounts involved, £7,070 in Shanghai for example, were not large, but to Morse, facing a series of contingencies of unknown magnitude, the problem of payment for parcels, though seemingly petty by present standards, was real.[3]

The London Board had agreed that internees would in principle be paid 50% of their salaries; Provident Fund contributions would be made on the basis of full salary. Some British companies were apparently more generous, and there were complaints and stern responses from Morse.

The seniors and their retirement

The Bank was aging. In 1936 only 2% of the 264 Eastern staff officers had served for 30 or more years in the East; in 1946 there were 11 such officers representing 5% of the total staff of 238. There is no full staff list for 1945, and the 1946 figures understate Morse's immediate problem.

Men like A.S. Henchman, W. Park, G. Lyon-MacKenzie had already retired. The 1946 list of those with Eastern service of 30 years or more includes Arthur Morse (East in 1915); there were also those not usually included in the 30-year 'rule' – A.G. Kellogg (East in 1906, New York), A.R.M. Blackhall (East in 1905, San Francisco), D.A. Johnston (East in 1910, Lyons), and G.B. Dunnett (East in 1910, London). But men like R.A. Stuart (East in 1912, Singapore), J.J. French (East in 1915, Bangkok, where he would die in 1947), W.C. Murray (East in 1913, Penang), A.F. Handcock (East in 1912, Manila) were still key Managers and would have to be replaced. At the same time 30% of the Eastern staff were on leave, but Morse could not be certain how many of these would eventually be in condition to return to the East, or, if they did return, what tasks they could perform and for how long.

The relative position, 1936 and 1946, can be summarized as shown in Table 3.1. From the Table it can be seen that the real problem was in the 26–30 year group. These men should long before in the normal career course have had appointments, that is, an assignment to an executive position by the Board of Directors at a rank of Sub-Manager or Accountant. Unavoidably, however, many did not; their careers had been interrupted at a key stage. Thus not only were there the usual problems of assignment arising from the relatively large percentage (18%) in this senior group – with the consequence that many were performing tasks inappropriate to their seniority – but also there was the sad fact that a combination of wartime hardships and lack of middle-level banking

Table 3.1 *The Hongkong and Shanghai Banking Corporation Seniority of members of the Eastern staff*

	Years of service				
	15 & under	16–25	26–30	Over 30	Total
A. Numbers					
1936	149	86	23	6	264
1946	98	86	43	11	238
B. Percentages					
1936	56	33	9	2	100
1946	41	36	18	5	100

experience rendered some unable to take on more senior responsibilities at this difficult time for the Bank. On the other hand there can be no generalization about individual abilities; this senior group provided the key men who perforce restarted the Bank in the East.

What Morse had to do, and do ruthlessly, was to ask for the resignation of those who could not perform. Despite the continuation of routine tasks for the juniors, there had already been a change at the top; there were no easy berths, not even Iloilo and Malacca were 'safe'. Thus despite the indications that Head Office would expand and that second-level managerial posts might be needed, despite the uncertainties of who would be in health to return from the initial post-war leave, Morse eliminated what fellow Hongkong Bankers were already referring to as 'deadwood'.

This policy did not make Morse popular. There was after all no definite rule on a 30-year service limit in the East, although that figure was one which Grayburn had used pre-war in easing out those without managerial competence. And as Grayburn had done, Morse eased the burden by recommending that the pension be made up to give the retiring staff member a parting package not less than that which he would have received had he remained the full 30 years.

The immediate post-war 'pension' policy involved a package of Provident Fund plus gratuity plus pension which would permit the purchase of an annuity providing a lifetime income equivalent to two-thirds the officer's pay. There were variations: those retiring early at the Chief Manager's request, or those who had done exceptionally well or who had suffered particular hardships. In 1946 pensions were estimated to be costing the Bank £30,000 per annum, the Officers Good Service Fund Account, which was not covered by any special trust arrangement, totalled £425,000 which at 2% gave an income of £8,500 and the balance required came from the general income of the Bank.

Morse did consider whether this was adequate, but his answer, typical for so many questions in those uncertain times, was, 'difficult to say...wait'.[4]

The move to a more formal pension scheme under a deed of trust began almost immediately, prompted by tax considerations and especially by the Finance Act of 1947; the formalities were not completed until 1950. The principles were established earlier, but the need for *ad hoc* gratuities continued throughout the early post-war period.

Financial problems of local staff

Under the leadership of Sir Arthur Morse and later Sir Michael Turner, the Hongkong Bank, while the three-tier staff system remained in place, that is, until the mid-1960s, paid particular attention to the condition of the Portuguese staff in Hong Kong. The first problem was their rehabilitation; it was a matter considered at the first meeting of the restored Hong Kong Board of Directors in June 1946. To meet initial wartime losses and post-war expenses, those with twenty years' service would receive $3,000 each; with fifteen years $2,500; with less than five years $1,000, of which half would be paid immediately and half four months later. In recognition of the role the Portuguese staff had played during the war and their loyalty to the Hongkong Bank, the Board authorized a major contribution towards the rehabilitation of the Club de Recreio of $10,000.

Inflation had destroyed the value of local staff Provident Funds in China, and the Board made *ex gratia* payments of the equivalent to local 'British staff', a term which included all locally recruited staff other than Chinese or Portuguese, and to all who contributed to a Provident Fund. 'Native' staff with long service were rewarded with a gratuity.

Comprehensive schemes were worked out by E.P. Streatfield; for example, the Shanghai package alone was estimated to cost the Bank $1.6 million and involved decisions on reemployment or dismissal with appropriate compensation in each category. The numbers involved are found in Table 3.2. For those reemployed, Portuguese staff had their Provident Fund rebuilt by a contribution of $1,000 plus $100 for every year of service over 10 years prior to 1942; Chinese clerks and the compradore's staff were granted $750 plus $75; watchmen and office boys $250 plus $25. Those who were not reemployed had their nominal Provident Fund taken at the pre-war rate of CNC$1 equals 3d and in addition were awarded compensation for loss of career equal to $200 for each year of service prior to 1942, with a minimum payment of $1,000 and a maximum of $5,000. Related scales were devised for Chinese staff.

The main problem was housing. The Bank eventually faced this by building

Table 3.2 *The Hongkong and Shanghai Banking Corporation Shanghai local staff position, November 1946*

Category	To be reemployed	Deceased	To be Retired	Unlikely to return	Others wanting reemployment
Clerks, Chinese	45	7	6	17	23
Clerks, Portuguese	31	9	12	1	36
Office boys	22	1	1	24	—
Compradore's staff	16	12	23	6	33
Coolies/watchmen	31	6	2	8	5
Workshop	122	12	—	—	1
Totals	267	47	44	56	98

flats in Hong Kong first for the Portuguese staff and then for the Chinese, but this came after the Bank was itself properly reestablished.

As for the long-serving German staff, typical of the dislocations of war was the case of the Hamburg messenger, Wilhelm Strauch, who in 1939 had retired with a pension which was almost immediately cancelled when war was declared. The pension was reinstated in November 1951 (as was that of the former Hamburg Manager, F. T. Koelle), but Strauch died aged 80 in 1952 and the Board agreed, quite exceptionallly, that the full pension (£8:10s p.m.) should be continued to the widow.

Salary and related adjustments

The basic salaries of the Eastern staff (or 'Foreign staff' as they would be known by the late 1950s) had not been reorganized since 1924, but the impact of post-war inflation was minimized for Eastern staff by the usual provision of housing in kind and by access in many places to commissary facilities. As the military withdrew or military administrations were replaced by civil authority in 1946–1947, commissary facilities were phased out and price control restricted to commodities, rice, for example, of more significance to the local population. There was consequently the need for the Bank to reconsider the salary position; alterations were made, but they were still tentative; high cost of living allowances remained. The hesitancy to adjust fully to a new price level was again in evidence, and, since a fall in price levels must have been inconceivable, the effect was to delay implementation of a sound salary scheme and, incidentally, to save on the Bank's contribution to the Staff Provident Fund.

Two problems were never satisfactorily resolved. First was the case of those who had been senior military officers and had married. As in the case of Singapore, where R. A. Stuart faced three juniors who had attained the rank of colonel, the problem was not how the 'junior' might survive in the East but how his family would survive back in England. One solution, which caused the second problem, was to press for them to be allowed East.

While the Bank was fully aware of this problem and the Board of Directors was by the Fall of 1946 approving the purchase of flats suitable for rehabilitation as family quarters, this timing would seem totally inadequate to married officers in late 1945 or in the Fall of 1946. The request was for 'now'. When the Bank was firm, Eastern staff or their wives or friends put pressure on the Colonial Office or indeed any Government department to obtain a passage. This obtained, the wife arrived and they lived, if necessary, in the bachelors' mess.

As H. E. Muriel in London wrote out to Morse, the Colonial Office is the 'real villain', giving passages directly to wives contrary to instructions.[5] Morse considered wives coming out without accommodation at their own risk and with children to be 'madness'; the rehabilitation of the Peak Mess at £3,000 had included only the minimum necessities.

Some officers considered the delays a reflection on the fact that Fenwick was a bachelor and therefore not interested. The Morses did not live in their Peak residence, which had been in any case requisitioned and was in poor condition; rather they remained in the Chief Manager's flat in the main building. And they had no children.

The policy relative to dependants was however consistent with Morse's overall approach, which recognized that the Bank would not achieve all its personnel goals at once; it did not know what funds would be available, and, even had it known, supplies and labour were in any case in short supply. To some extent the Bank's policy did show lack of imagination, that is, the concept of what constituted 'adequate' housing was pre-war; Eastern staff and their wives were willing, or, to be fair to Morse and Fenwick, *said* they were willing (which is not the same thing at all) to live under any conditions which reflected an improvement on prison camp.

The problem was compounded because juniors had married during the war without reference to the ten-year rule. Morse himself disagreed with Grayburn in the Sellars case; Mme Sellars would on occasion inform startled dinner guests, 'La Banque, I 'ate it.' For political reasons Morse would do nothing about a marriage to the daughter of a well-known Chinese, but he would not permit a marriage to a German lady in Tsingtau. The last mentioned lady had been born and raised in the East, had no connection with Germany, and feared forced repatriation. The staff member in question resigned. The Bank considered it retained some right of control over marriage, and, with the war over, the restrictions though gradually lightened were at first reimposed.[a]

Recruitment

There were several tests of the Bank's London Office recruitment tradition, but the system in its essence would remain – even the first local officers in the 1950s were sent back to London in an effort to retain the tradition. But as in the period immediately following the 1918 Armistice, the London system was in a sense nominal; all Eastern staff were interviewed and reported for initial duty in London Office, but their time there might be less than a month; the idea of a service with traditions shaped in the panelled banking halls of 9 Gracechurch Street or on the playing fields of New Beckenham had to give way to the need for juniors to reach the East.

In the period from V-J Day to August 1946 when the first post-war Eastern staff list was published, 41 juniors had come East for the first time, although all of them had been recruited before the war. This brought the total of juniors in the East and on leave, that is, the total of those with fifteen years or less Eastern service, to 98 or 41% of the total Eastern staff compared to 149 or 56% in 1936. The 1945/46 group of 41 may be compared with the 61 who came out in 1919.

Those who joined London Office for the first time in the immediate post-war period, Guy Sayer in 1946 for example, usually stayed in London less than a year. National service presented a problem and Morse had, reluctantly, to reconsider the program.

The important point here is that Morse resisted temptation on several fronts. Although he was prepared to consider the need for specialists, J. R. Jones as legal counsel, C. Slade for the trustee company, he was not ready for 'lateral transfer' into general banking. Thus he resisted pressure to accept J. D. Clague, who had been active in BAAG and in fact had met Fenwick and Morrison on their escape when some preliminary reference to the possibility of his employment was mooted. At the same time A. G. Kellogg in New York was pressing the idea of one of his local staff, who had been a senior naval officer in the Philippines, returning to work as an Eastern staff officer in the Manila office. In this case Morse stated clearly that he was concerned with the precedent; he agreed that he be offered a temporary posting. The officer concerned considered this offer, at his age and with a wife and young family, too risky a proposition.[6]

---

[a] Cost remained a key consideration. While Morse kept some control over Bank marriages, he was frustrated as Treasurer of the University of Hong Kong by those who, like myself, were married after less than two years in the East. Morse was overheard giving vent to his feelings with the comment,'...those university lecturers, up there breeding like rabbits...can't afford it, of course; can't afford it.'

Although there had been two Eastern staff taken on in the East immediately after the Great War, M.P. Langley, who applied in Shanghai, was told he must apply in London; he joined the Mercantile Bank of India instead.[7] D.A.McN. Butter was taken on in Singapore with the task of opening Batavia; he subsequently became Agent Sourabaya. Butter had, however, come East in the normal way in 1919 and resigned in 1923 to become a stockbroker in Batavia; he spoke Dutch and Malay.

Morse approved one innovation. He invited applications from the younger members of the Home staff; four applied and two eventually went East in 1946 – S.F.T.B. Lever and Maurice Walter Turner.[b] Both had attended public school and, before joining the Bank, had worked in a branch of Lloyds Bank and the National Provincial Bank respectively in Brighton. Turner was promoted to their Croydon office, but both young men had begun to consider a more exciting banking career. Turner had had an uncle on the Hongkong Bank's Home staff. He received information that there were two vacancies, the two friends applied and were accepted by the Bank in 1938. When the war came, both joined the forces.[8]

Morse's post-war decision is not difficult to explain; it is more difficult to understand why Lever and Turner had not joined the Eastern staff in the first place. Their backgrounds, attitudes, interest in sports were identical to those of Eastern staff juniors. Initially the problem may have been the Bank's need to fill the Home staff vacancies for which they had after all applied. The question of transfer was brought up, although with the outbreak of war the matter was not taken further.

Thus this 'breakthrough' was not really precedent shattering. The pre-war London junior system was confirmed. With longer waits before going East in the early 1950s the system would enjoy what proved to be an Indian summer.

TWO KEY PROBLEMS

Between December 8 and December 25, 1941, when Hong Kong was under attack, the Chief Manager of the Hongkong and Shanghai Bank failed to effect the destruction of the Bank's stock of unissued Hongkong banknotes, signed and unsigned.[c] In the period through 1943 the Japanese authorities forced members of the Bank's Eastern staff to sign those notes remaining unsigned,

---

[b] Maurice Turner's career, like Lever's, was a successful one; in 1968 he was appointed Deputy Chief Manager and then Deputy Chairman of the Hongkong Bank. Note that his initials, 'M.W.', are the same as those of Sir Michael W. Turner, the Chief Manager, hence the need to spell out the first names.

[c] Grayburn had been told by the Governor that Hong Kong would be relieved; afterwards it was too late. Burning notes was described by G.A. Leiper of the Chartered Bank as an 'unbelievably difficult task'. Leiper attempted to burn them in a furnace in a Chartered Bank house, a task fortuitously facilitated by enemy fire which turned the house into an inferno.[9]

and the total stock of unissued notes was paid out to the public through Japanese institutions in settlement of various obligations and for payment for various goods and services. This was the 'duress note issue'. The British authorities, through the British Embassy in Chungking, warned the public that the notes had been issued illegally, provided the serial numbers, and stated that they might not be honoured post-war. The total potential face value of this illegal issue was $119.8 million – of which 40% were signed and 60% unsigned. This total was equivalent to approximately £7.49 million at a time when the published sterling reserves of the Bank were £7.125 million.[10]

The Hongkong Bank maintained throughout lengthy negotiations with the British Treasury and Colonial Office that the Bank was not responsible, that the Chief Manager had had insufficient warning, and that the failure to destroy the notes could consequently not be charged to the Bank's account.

The magnitude of the sum involved and the impact of repudiation on the Bank's reputation made it essential that the question of recognition of the notes and the ultimate liability of the Bank should be resolved as soon as possible, and certainly before the Chief Manager left for Hong Kong. Despite the fact that Arthur Morse made a serious approach to the British authorities as early as May 1944, the final offer of the British Government was contained in a letter from Sydney Caine dated as late as February 28, 1946. The terms therein offered, which involved the Bank in an eventual net loss of £1 million equivalent, the London Board had no choice but to accept.[d]

This left a second basic problem unresolved, the debtor/creditor settlement, and indeed it remained outstanding in Hong Kong until early 1948. The 1945 abstract of accounts shows total advances of £27.8 million of which £19.2 million were 'advances to customers subject to moratorium and other accounts the realizable value of which cannot at present be arrived at, including losses due to war'. The reason why this position persisted was the inability of the banks and other creditors to agree on how to handle payments made during wartime in various depreciating currencies and under various conditions and degrees of individual duress.

The seriousness of this situation is readily apparent. First, the Bank's balance sheet was virtually meaningless when an item representing 20% of total liabilities and 230% of shareholders' funds should be indeterminate. A moratorium is an effective and acceptable device to cover a short period of real confusion and emergency; any temporary inconvenience can be covered by the Bank's lending against the security of the blocked accounts. But eventually the

---

[d] Shortly afterwards Caine received a knighthood. H.E. Muriel has suggested that Caine was rewarded for 'screwing the Hongkong Bank', and he noted, happily, there was to be a much deserved retribution – Muriel was referring to Sir Sydney's subsequent appointment as Director of the London School of Economics.[11]

entire economy is affected by the impasse. Both debtors and creditors are affected; the latter, not being certain of their position, are hesitant to commit themselves to projects which might be otherwise feasible.

The impasse arose partly because the Hongkong Bank, working on the basis of memorandums by J.R. Jones, took an essentially legal position. The issues had to be resolved, however, on principles of equity, taking into account the political and social impact of the decision. The Hongkong Bank and other banks were part of Government's concern, but only part.

Morse, in common with most observers, considered that the delay in passing suitable legislation on the debtor/creditor situation would impede economic recovery. The fact is that despite the uncertainty which hung over both private and business financial positions from V-J Day to November 1948, three years, reconstruction proceeded as fast as the shortage of supply of real goods and services would permit. The Bank operated as it were *de novo*; its balance sheet revealed a highly liquid position so that uses of funds could be shifted from money at call and made available for development purposes. Equally important as a source of funds was the growth of new deposits and the turnover which was achieved in the finance of the growing trade of the East.

THE DURESS NOTE ISSUE

The nature of the duress issue

'Duress' is a misleading term if the position of the Hongkong Bank is to be fully appreciated. While it is true that Bank officers signed a quantity of unsigned notes under threat, that is not the essence of the problem – after all, 40% of the total stock of unissued notes on hand when Hong Kong surrendered had been signed. Nevertheless, the problem has generally been referred to as the 'duress note' problem, and that terminology, understood to encompass both signed and unsigned notes, will be used here.

The problem confronting the Bank and Government was created therefore not by the signing under duress but by the Japanese payout of banknotes contrary to established legislation and procedures, an 'illegal issue' or 'irregular issue', depending on what legal point is being made. In consequence the status of the banknotes and therefore the effect on the Hongkong Bank's resources should these notes be paid in had to be decided, preferably by agreement between the Hongkong Bank and the Hong Kong Government. As the latter was, however, initially inoperative and then subject to military rule, the Bank found itself negotiating with interested departments of the Imperial Government in London.

Banknotes legally issued were legal tender. Their issue had been authorized by the purchase of an equivalent amount of Hong Kong Government non-interest-bearing certificates of indebtedness, the issuing bank paying in sterling funds in London. Thus the bank's liability for the notes was offset by a specific asset, the certificates of indebtedness, which were in turn a liability of the Hong Kong Government's Exchange Fund.

But there now existed Hongkong Bank notes, duly signed with the legitimate signatures of officers of the Bank apparently authorized to sign, which had been paid out and were thus in circulation. And they could be paid into the Bank for value received. If these notes were deemed to have been 'legally issued', they became legal tender. The Bank in consequence would find itself with an increase in liabilities (equal to the face value of the duress notes) against which there was no corresponding asset; there was no certificate of indebtedness. The only way this could be shown on a balance sheet would be through the corresponding write-down of shareholders' funds, the Reserve Fund for example. Unpublished reserves at this time were assigned to wartime contingency funds; transfers from inner reserves to offset the virtual elimination of published reserves was not a possibility in 1945.

The situation was the same as if the Government were to deem banknotes 'legally issued' which had been stolen from unissued stock in the Bank's vaults or which had been counterfeited. Indeed, it is this identity which might cause some to wonder what the problem was. Surely no Government would require a bank to accept as a legal issue notes which had been stolen or counterfeited; surely both Government and the note-issuing banks, for the Chartered Bank and Mercantile Bank faced the same problem in lesser amounts, would repudiate the notes and declare them so much waste paper.

This introduces the first question. Should the duress notes, the notes paid out by the Japanese from undestroyed stocks, be recognized as if they had been legally issued? The second question follows if the first is answered affirmatively. Given the initial impact of an affirmative decision on both the Exchange Fund and the bank, how is the ultimate financial burden to be shared and on what basis?

The decision to recognize the duress issue

The initial reaction was a combination of 'reserving one's rights' and objecting to any act which would give support to the enemy. The British Government therefore warned the public through Chungking that the duress notes of the Hongkong Bank might not be accepted.[e] But this was merely a holding operation.

---

[e] No mention was made then or subsequently relative to the duress notes of the Chartered Bank or of the Mercantile Bank; this was never a public problem and was solved between the banks and the Government (see below).

Whatever similarities the duress issue might appear superficially to have with a counterfeit or stolen issue, there were significant differences. First, the banknotes were not counterfeit in the accepted use of the term. There was only one way to detect that the note was not legally issued. The signatures were legitimate, the paper, printing, etc., legitimate; only the serial number could be used to identify the status of the notes. Secondly, the notes were not 'stolen' but taken by the Occupying Power and used for various purposes, some of them legitimate. Some duress notes were, for example, paid out to meet legitimate debts of the Hongkong Bank.

These difficulties could be overcome in theory. The serial numbers were published and the legitimate payments isolated, but these same remedies could, however, be negated in practice. For example, the serial numbers could be and were altered.

At this stage another level of problem arose. The banknotes issued in Hong Kong were liabilities of private banking institutions, but they were also the legal tender of the Colony; their repudiation would undermine confidence in both the Government and the banks. Whereas repudiation of stolen or counterfeit notes might be understood in ordinary times, subject to any proven charge of negligence in the normal course of law, repudiation of a large proportion of the total issue which had arisen under the conditions of the Japanese Occupation could render undue hardship to the public and have serious economic and political repercussions. The duress note issue was estimated at $119.8 million, a sum equivalent to 60% of the value of the $200.5 million total of legally issued notes as of December 31, 1940.

The decision to recognize the duress notes was not made until the conditions of that recognition were agreed by the Bank and the Government. The realities of the situation were such, however, that the decision to recognize was virtually accepted subject to negotiation of the terms. Whatever either party might threaten, both knew that almost any arrangement was preferable to outright repudiation and the confusion and recrimination which would result, not only in Hong Kong but also in China where a high percentage of Hongkong Bank notes circulated.[12] British prestige was at stake not only in a Crown Colony but in the neighbouring republic which entertained the belief that they were the rightful sovereigns of Hong Kong.

The substance of the negotiations

Starting with the fact that, with the information available in 1944, it was assumed that $119.8 million of Hongkong Bank notes were at some point to be declared legal tender by legislation and that in consequence the Bank's liabilities would increase by this amount, the negotiations were over the extent to which and the method by which the Bank's assets would be increased to cover these liabilities.

At one extreme the Government could issue 'gratis' certificates of indebtedness equivalent to the total of the duress issue, thus solving the problem entirely at Government's expense. If the Bank were, at the other extreme, to bear the entire burden, the increase in liabilities occasioned by the recognition of the duress issue would be offset by writing down shareholders' funds, including, if necessary, the capital fund of the Hongkong Bank.

The Government offered to issue certificates of indebtedness to cover the entire duress issue on payment by the Hongkong Bank of 50% of the duress issue, £3.75 million, plus any sum representing the sterling equivalent (at 1s:3d) of the value of the notes used to pay legitimate debts of the Bank. This the Bank stated it could not accept if it were to play any post-war role or even to remain solvent. The Government first offered to vary the percentage originally stated, eventually agreeing (i) to increase the Hongkong Bank's authorized issue from $30 million to $46 million (an increase of £1 million) and (ii) to issue certificates of indebtedness for the balance of the duress issue on payment to Government of £1 million plus a sum equivalent to the legitimate payouts.

This latter offer would result in an eventual net write-off of shareholders' funds equivalent to the original payout of sterling funds, that is, £1 million. The offset required for notes paid out to meet legitimate debts would be provided for in the normal way when the accounts were fully rectified.

To simplify the immediate discussion, assume that the amounts of legitimate payments have not been calculated and what follows represents the first stage. These transactions in millions of pounds sterling at £1 = $16 ($119.8 million = £7.5 million) would look as follows on the Bank's accounts:

Assets		Liabilities and Capital Accounts	
		Notes in circulation	+£7.5
		of which authorized issue	+£1.0
HK Govt c of i	+£6.5	excess issue	+£6.5
(£7.5−£1.0)			
Sterling funds	−£1.0		
		Shareholders' funds	−£2.0
Net increase	+£5.5	Net increase	+£5.5

'c of i' = certificate of indebtedness

At this stage of the negotiations the Hongkong Bank had improved its position from the original offer by the reduction of the cash payment to Government from £3.75 million to £1 million; the Government had lessened the impact on its resources by accepting a liability of less than the total duress issue. This it accomplished by dividing the duress issue into 'excess' and 'authorized' categories. Against the latter no certificates needed to be issued. This however did not relieve the Bank from the general liability created by the increase in the authorized or fiduciary issue, hence the initial impact on shareholders' funds was the total of the cash payout plus the increase in the authorized note issue – £1 million plus £1 million, or a total £2 million.

Having reduced the cash payout from £3 million to £1 million by negotiation, the Bank next tried to minimize the net impact on shareholders' funds. Morse argued that the burden on the Bank was still too heavy, and he repeated his belief that any burden was unfair and unjustified but confirmed that the Bank was willing to be reasonable.

The eventual solution was for the Government to issue further certificates of indebtedness to the Bank from time to time. This would be done until the additional certificates were equivalent in value to the increase in the authorized issue, £1 million. At that point the total cost of the duress issue to the Hongkong Bank would be reduced to £1 million.

Assets		Liabilities and Capital Accounts	
		Notes in circulation	+0
		of which authorized issue	−£1.0
HK Govt c of i	+£1.0	excess issue	+£1.0
Sterling funds	0.0		
		Shareholders' funds	+£1.0
Net increase	+£1.0	Net increase	+£1.0

The only outstanding point was to decide the basis on which the Government would give the Bank the additional certificates of indebtedness. The certificates were liabilities of the Exchange Fund, and, although they paid no interest, the Fund possessed income-earning assets.

It was agreed that a proportion of the Fund's earnings would be used to offset the issue of additional certificates to the Bank. The time involved would depend, therefore, on the income of the Fund and the proportion to be allocated to the offset. In terms of sterling the relevant annual percentage of the net income of the Exchange Fund to be used to offset certificates of indebtedness issued to the Hongkong Bank was calculated by dividing £1 million by the total duress issue less £1 million less the value of notes 'legitimately' issued. The result, as will be discussed below, was 22%, and the final tranche was paid in 1953 at which time the authorized issue of the Hongkong Bank was reduced from the temporary $46 million to the $30 million stated in the Bank's Ordinance No. 6 of 1929.

Taking the transactions in the two models already illustrated and combining them, the consequences are:

Assets		Liabilities and Capital Accounts	
		Notes in circulation	+£7.5
		of which authorized issue +£0.0	
HK Govt c of i	+£7.5	excess issue +£7.5	
Sterling funds	−£1.0		
		Shareholders' funds	−£1.0
Net increase	+£6.5	Net increase	+£6.5

The final impact on the balance sheet is exaggerated to the extent that the duress notes were 'used when first issued in discharge of any legal liability of The Hongkong and Shanghai Banking Corporation'. This proved to be approximately £1.9 million. As a simple example, assume that this had been the consequence of customers withdrawing funds from their savings accounts. The increased payout of notes would be offset by the reduction of the liability 'Savings Bank accounts'. But the notes would have been issued against already obtained certificates of indebtedness – obtained in advance under the arrangement with the Government whereby in the first instance all but $16 million of the duress notes would be covered. Now that it was discovered that the notes had been paid out to meet a legal liability of the Bank, the Bank was obligated to pay for the already issued certificates of indebtedness to the same amount.

Assets		Liabilities and Capital Accounts	
		Notes in circulation	+£7.5
		of which authorized issue +£0.0	
HK Govt c of i	+£7.5	excess issue +£7.5	
Sterling funds	−£1.0		
		Shareholders' funds	−£1.0
Sterling funds	−£1.9	Savings accounts (for example)	−£1.9
Net increase	+£4.6	Net increase	+£4.6

The course of the negotiations

Initial positions and concerns

Having stated the general substance of the negotiations using the figures then available – and in sterling since the negotiations were conducted while the Bank's Head Office was in London and its accounts published in sterling – three tasks remain: (i) to consider the course of the negotiations as illustrative of Morse at work and the Government being somewhat difficult, (ii) to restate the above calculations in Hong Kong dollars and in the precise amounts – the actual size of the duress issue was not established until 1947, and (iii) to consider the legislation which eventually embodied the results of the Government/Bank agreement on the duress note issue.

This section deals with the first task.

The Government was in a relatively weak position. The Bank could not bear the major burden and remain solvent, and the Government could not be seen as driving into liquidation a great British overseas banking institution on which so much depended. Furthermore the Government could not as practical politics wish to see the duress issue repudiated since there would be inevitable repercussions on credit, undermining confidence and threatening the pace of post-war development – at the very least the Government would in consequence be forced to take on the task of issuing the currency notes, once again at an inconvenient time. Finally, the Bank's argument that the Government alone was responsible for the non-destruction of the stock of notes was one which had potential popular support, the more so if the Governor's reassurances to Grayburn could be verified. Equally important was the Bank's position that, as the notes were paid out by the Japanese Occupation authorities, the successor Government, that is, the Hong Kong Government, was alone responsible for the consequences. These arguments were never accepted by the British authorities.

The Government itself had to be cautious in its handling of the duress note issue problem for several reasons. First, the Japanese seizure of the note stock was not the only seizure of private property, and the Government's acceptance of responsibility could be considered precedential. Secondly, the Allies had themselves taken action which might be considered comparable, and the Government did not wish to take an absolute position.

A third reason is, however, more directly concerned with the case. If the Bank's financial position was precarious, so was that of the Hong Kong Government Exchange Fund. In 1941 the cover for the Colony's note issue was 116% of the face value of the notes issued, due partly to Sir Vandeleur Grayburn's operations described in Volume III. But calculations based on the December 31, 1945, statement of the Fund's position plus the impact of the eventual agreement with the Bank – in principle as stated above – indicated that the cover had been reduced to 94%. For reasons beyond the scope of this history, the Treasury considered a 100% cover essential.[13] Because of the terms of the agreement with the Bank, the Hong Kong Government would be unable to build up the Fund to provide 100% cover until the beginning of 1950. Morse still had no reason to sympathize with the Government; the Exchange Fund's problem was not caused by the agreement with the Bank but by previous *ad hoc* grants to the Military Government of Hong Kong to an amount totalling £1.6 million made from its resources by Order in Council. Had these not been made, the Fund could have handled its agreed share of the duress issue burden while maintaining 100 + % coverage of the note issue.[14]

Official procrastination

In March 1944 Arthur Morse brought the duress note issue problem before the London Board. At that time he stressed the vital importance of honouring the notes 'not only to honour the reputation of the Bank, but as well to uphold British prestige in the East'. He took the position that the Government were responsible and should cover the issue by certificates of indebtedness.[15]

In April this position was placed before the Bank of England who advised deferring the matter. Morse wrote expressing his 'keen disappointment' as he had hoped to advise his directors prior to the reopening of the Bank in Hong Kong. A month later the Treasury agreed to discuss the problem in 'about three months' time', but in September as a result of a meeting on the 15th, the matter was again deferred until all the relevant facts could become known, and both the Treasury and the Colonial Office took the view that it was not in the public interest for the directors to inform the shareholders of the situation. Government believed the warning the Treasury had issued to the Chinese Government in 1942 was adequate to meet the existing situation.

When the Japanese surrendered, the immediate problem was to advise the Military Government as to which Hong Kong currency notes should be accepted as legal tender. The three note-issuing banks, the Hongkong Bank, the Chartered Bank, and the Mercantile Bank, agreed to advise that the proclamation should state that unlawfully issued notes of denominations of $50, $100, and $500 should not be considered legal tender; in fact only Hongkong Bank notes of these denominations were so designated. This left the position of duress notes of $10 and less unmentioned and, although this meant that the Military Administration would accept them, even their ultimate fate was unclear.

Throughout these negotiations Morse had kept the Board fully informed, and Sir Edward Reid was taking a particular interest in developments. Following the Board meeting of August 23 another exhaustive memorandum was submitted to the Colonial Office, stressing somewhat hopelessly that a decision was needed before the Bank reopened. In fact a serious political situation was developing as public reaction to the uncertain status of the duress notes came to be known. By mid-December cabled information from the Bank's office in Hong Kong, which had reopened without a decision on the duress note problem, revealed that the serial numbers, the only public guide to the status of the Bank's notes, were being altered by holders of 'duress notes'. This threatened the credibility of the Bank's entire note issue – and by extension, the currency of the Colony of Hong Kong. Other banks and utilities were threatening to refuse acceptance of the Bank's large denomination notes.

Morse again pressed for a Government decision following a Board meeting on December 13, 1945. The Colonial Office claimed it had sent an urgent cable to Hong Kong requesting full information; Fenwick cabled Morse that no such cable had been received.[16]

An unacceptable offer

The first substantive response of the Government came on December 20, some 21 months after Morse had first requested a decision. It was at this time that Sydney Caine proposed that the Bank and Government share the burden on a 50:50 basis, the Bank paying over £3.75 million. Arthur Morse informed the Colonial Office that in placing this proposal before the Board he would not be in a position to recommend its acceptance.[17]

Not surprisingly at a meeting on January 10 the London Board of the Hongkong Bank rejected the Government proposals in the face of vague threats that the Government might either force the Bank's position by legislation or, alternatively, do nothing and let the courts decide the Bank's liability. Neither threat made political sense, and the Board held that they would not be liable for a payment exceeding £1 million.

The atmosphere was becoming tense. The Board noted that Morse's plans to return to Hong Kong were being delayed pending settlement; the Government's reaction to the Board's rejection of their proposal on the one hand contained threats and on the other suggested that a further meeting might be helpful. Morse repeated once more that any unilateral action on the part of Government would be challenged and that the Bank had no responsibility to cover the duress notes by purchasing certificates of indebtedness – nevertheless, for the sake of both parties, the Bank was willing to continue the negotiations.

At this point there was a necessary respite. One of the principals, Arthur Morse, had a serious case of influenza and his doctors would not let documents past his bedroom door.[18]

The discussions continued with H. E. Muriel, who was preparing to take over London Office when Morse left for the East, Sir Edward Reid, and J. R. Jones, and it was in January during Morse's illness that the Treasury agreed the problem might be resolved by increasing the fiduciary (the 'authorized') issue of the Bank. On this basis and with the understanding that £1 million should be the sole cash obligation of the Bank significant progress was made at a meeting on February 5.[19]

The Government's final offer

The final negotiations took place in February, during which period the Bank convinced the Government to cover the increased fiduciary issue over a period of time and the full set of proposals was embodied in the Colonial Office letter of February 28, 1946, a letter written by Sir Sydney Caine in a particularly firm and formal style to facilitate, he wrote later, its acceptance by the London Board.[20]

Reviewing the events and the reasons why the notes should be recognized as legal tender, Caine again denied all Government responsibility for the failure to destroy the stock of unissued notes and then proposed:

1. Legislation would be passed in Hong Kong to make the duress notes legal tender as if they had been legally issued.
2. The Hong Kong Government would issue certificates of indebtedness to cover the entire issue less $16 million [= £1 million], equal to $103.8 million, later adjusted to $102.15 million, see below; in consideration the Bank would pay:
   (a) immediately the sum of £1 million;
   (b) a sum equivalent to the value of the duress notes actually paid out to meet legitimate obligations of the Hongkong Bank, when this amount came to be known.
3. The $16 million not covered by certificates would be considered part of the Bank's authorized (fiduciary) issue and legislation would increase the total permitted from $30 million to $46 million.
4. The fiduciary issue would be reduced year by year by the issue to the Bank of certificates of indebtedness for a sum equal to the dollar equivalent of a proportion of the net income of the Hong Kong Exchange Fund for the year in question, until the entire fiduciary issue was covered.

Caine added,

Under these proposals the Bank's liability would be clearly limited and its probable ultimate loss confined to the immediate cash payment of £1,000,000. The whole of the remaining loss involved, the amount of which is unknown, would rest with the Government through the Hong Kong Exchange Fund. Such a settlement represents, in Mr [George] Hall's view, the maximum contribution which can be expected from the Government. Should the Bank feel unable to accept this basis of settlement, the only alternative course would be to leave the status of the notes in question to be settled by legal action...

Mr Hall [the Secretary of State for the Colonies] will be glad to learn as soon as possible whether the Board of the Bank agree to action being taken on the basis of the proposals set out...[21]

The need for speed was in part dictated by the expected termination of the Military Administration and the need to ascertain the views of the Hong Kong Government. In the event the modifications proposed were not such as to affect the basic terms arrived at.

The actual figures
The first adjustment came with the discovery that certain duress notes with a face value of $950,000 were actually in circulation in exchange for valid notes which had been cancelled on February 16, 1942. This reduced the duress issue as defined from $119.8 million to $118.85 million.

The value of duress notes paid to meet legal liabilities of the Hongkong Bank proved to be $30,737,805. For the basis of the formula to determine the rate of payoff by the Exchange Fund, a further sum of $16 million had to be subtracted, giving a figure of $72,112,195. The percentage of the income of the Fund to be used to back certificates of indebtedness each year was then found by dividing the increased fiduciary issue, that is, $16 million, by $72,112,195, and the resulting percentage was 22.1876%.

This gives final 1946 and 1953 figures in millions of Hong Kong dollars as follows:

Assets		Liabilities and Capital Accounts	
		Notes in circulation:	
		authorized issue	
		1946	+16.00
		1953	−16.00
HK Govt c of i:		excess issue	
issued in 1946	+$102.85	1946	+$102.85
issued in 1947–53	+$16.00	1953	+$16.00
	+$118.85		+$118.85
Sterling funds	−$16.00		
		Shareholders' funds	−$16.00
Sterling funds	−$30.74	Legal liabilities	−$30.74
Net increase	+$72.11	Net increase	+$72.11

For comparison, the total duress issue of the Chartered Bank of India, Australia and China after the destruction described in G. A. Leiper's book was only $719,000, that of the Mercantile Bank of India $900,000; both banks had signed and unsigned stock, the latter then being signed under duress. The Colonial Office and these two banks agreed that settlement of the duress notes problem should be considered at the same time as the question of debtor/creditor relations was resolved. The problem however resolved itself; the notes had been paid out to meet legitimate liabilities of the two banks and had therefore to be covered by certificates of indebtedness in the normal way. The size of the issue was sufficiently small and the expectation of this solution was so great that no interim measure was considered necessary.[22]

The decisions enacted

The proclamations

The details of the Hongkong Bank's duress note serial numbers were first transmitted to Chungking from London in August 1942, and there followed a series of cables on the basic principles of the problem, but no definitive action was taken other than reserving of rights. Steps were considered to segregate the duress notes as they were paid in, but this proved impractical. The matter was left undetermined.

The first official public decision on the problem is contained in Proclamation No. 5 of October 12, 1945, which was then the initial post-war currency statement. First, the legal authority of the note-issuing banks which had lapsed in July 1942 was extended; legally issued notes were continued as legal tender. It then added:

> ...all bank notes of the note-issuing banks issued or reissued during the period of enemy occupation of the Colony will be treated by the Military Administration as legal tender to any amount: provided that the bank notes bearing serial numbers within the range of such numbers specified in the First Schedule hereto in relation to notes of the denominations and descriptions stated in the said Schedule will not be treated by the Military Administration as legal tender [Art. 4].[24]

The Schedule referred to listed the serial numbers, previously notified to Chungking in 1942/43, relative to Hongkong Bank notes of $50, $100, and $500 only. As noted above, those of lesser denomination and notes of the other note-issuing banks were not listed and were therefore treated by the Military Administration as if legal tender.

The proclamation also made provisions for overprinted notes of various kinds to be accepted as legal tender, but this did not prove necessary and never became effective. In the first days of peace, Japanese yen-denominated notes continued to circulate, but by September 11, 1945, the Hongkong Bank had been able to ship in notes to meet requirements, and the changeover direct from yen to Hongkong Bank notes was effected on September 13.

As a result of the negotiations detailed above, Proclamation No. 31, Currency (Amendment), cancelled the exceptions described in Schedule 1 of Proclamation No. 5, thus stating that the Military Administration would treat the higher denomination notes as if legal tender. At the same time the Hongkong Bank announced that 'as from today...it will honour and accept as legal tender all the notes bearing the name of The Hongkong and Shanghai Banking Corporation...'[25] It remained for civil legislation to make the notes legal tender.

The Hongkong Bank Ordinance, No. 8 of 1946: currency provisions
Effective June 20, 1946, the Hongkong Bank's Head Office was returned to Hong Kong and certain necessary changes in its constitution were effected simultaneously by Ordinance No. 8. This however advances the history of the Bank beyond the scope of this section, and the ordinance will be considered only to the extent that it made possible the final solution to the duress note problem.

The ordinance confirmed the provisions of No. 6 of 1929, as amended, with the additional amendment that for the authorized note issue the figure 46,000,000 should be substituted for 30,000,000. The authorized note issue reverted to the latter figure with passage in September 1953 of The Hongkong and Shanghai Banking Corporation (Amendment) Ordinance, No. 27 of 1953.

On August 15, 1946, the powers of the note-issuing banks to make, issue, reissue, and circulate notes, which had lapsed in July 1942 but reauthorized postwar by proclamation under the Military Administration, were extended by resolution of the Legislative Council to July 1947 consistent with the provisions of Ordinance No. 21 of 1939.

The Bank Notes and Certificates of Indebtedness Ordinance
The key ordinance, No. 13 of 1946, was passed without comment by the Legislative Council on August 15, 1946, and assented to by the Governor the following day. It was carefully worded.

Its purpose was to 'remove doubts concerning the legal status of certain Bank Notes' thus avoiding the question of responsibility, powers, and authorities over the relevant period. The ordinance then provided that 'notwithstanding any irregularity in the manner of issue', the notes were to be 'and be deemed to have been at all times bank notes lawfully issued'; thus once more the history of the issue and all related contentious arguments are rendered irrelevant; past payments made with the notes were rendered valid.

The balance of the ordinance recounts the provisions relative to certificates of indebtedness and the formula described above, thus making them part of the law of Hong Kong.

Consequences

The uncertainty over the eventual acceptance of the duress notes had had the inevitable consequence. Speculators purchased the notes at varying discounts, some as large as 50%. This aspect of the problem was compounded when the news that the Government would enact relevant legislation was released in Shanghai 30 minutes before release in Hong Kong, permitting those with immediate access to communications facilities an opportunity to buy up notes in Hong Kong. A letter from D.M. MacDougall, the Chief Civil Affairs Officer (and from May 1, the first post-war Colonial Secretary of Hong Kong) states that there was a strong move within the Government to buy up the duress notes secretly.

> I vetoed this at once on the grounds that physically it could not be done on any worthwhile scale, and that the secret could not in any case be kept. I also had some dim moral sense for turning down these superficially attractive proposals: I do not think we go in much for buying in articles whose price we are officially going to double within a matter of hours. Various kinds of South American governments would jump at the chance, but I do not think we can.[26]

Although the decision to recognize the duress notes did not, in MacDougall's words, create a terrific uproar or upheaval, the 'decision has given a very solid satisfaction all round...The main credit for the decision has gone inevitably to the Hongkong Bank. They are the chief gainers. I do not myself think this is at all a bad thing.'[27] In this MacDougall was proved correct. The Hongkong Bank received full credit for honouring the duress notes, thus restoring confidence in the administration of the Colony and creating a popular image of the Bank as an institution which stood above its own narrow commercial interests and was sufficiently strong financially to put the interests of the Colony's economy first.

An authoritative expression of public reaction to the solution of the duress note problem is found in the speech of D.J. Sloss, vice-chancellor of the University of Hong Kong, at the 1947 Annual Meeting of the Hongkong Bank's shareholders:

> I mention the Bank's influence, thinking not specially of its place in the commercial world, but as a social force. This influence was unquestionably enormously strengthened by the honouring of duress notes, an action which took the imagination of our Chinese neighbours. The Bank has demonstrated the wisdom of the longer view in accepting heavy immediate loss to maintain its high name. Thereby it retained its repute for equity and gained a new credit for mercy and generosity.[28]

Sloss, a personal friend of Morse, apparently got carried away. But he expressed in general a widely held view.

While nothing can alter the reality of this image, the popular picture of Morse freely handing out shareholders' funds on demand and finding fortunately that this all led to the development of Hong Kong is nowhere more ludicrous than in the history of the duress note problem. There was in Morse a combination of Chief Accountant and Chairman, of Ulster shrewdness and Irish expansiveness. He was a great Chairman and Chief Manager precisely because, although his first instincts were those of an accountant, he added to this the 'art' of banking, made his own competent assessments, decided on policies in the public interest, and then, stepping back, fought hard for the best terms available.

Morse himself summed up the duress note compromise in these terms: '...it is fortunate that, as the result of the measures taken and thanks to the aid and cooperation of the Government, the interests of the Bank and of the public have been safeguarded at not too great a cost to the shareholders while the stability and prestige of the currency are maintained unimpaired.'[29]

Morse fits the popular image of the taipan, and there is a tradition in the Hongkong Bank that the Board of Directors held little more than a watching brief. One theme of this history has been that this is a caricature of the actual situation. Morse especially was aware of the shareholder. In the duress note case Sir Edward Reid of Baring's, a member of the London Board, was particularly involved in the negotiations. Morse kept the Board fully informed and there is evidence that, if anything, they were at least as determined as Morse that the Bank should receive fair play from the Government.

From the beginning Morse and the Government knew that the duress notes would have to be honoured; from the beginning both sides were negotiating the terms, from time to time reminding each other of the consequences of failure. But the Bank held the best cards and Morse played them skilfully; the Bank's loss was cut from the original seriously suggested Government figure of £3.75 million to £1 million, and the deal went through.

The consequences were without relation to the actual sums involved. The entire community – and much of South China – was potentially affected by the duress note problem. The public saw a great banking institution, the Hongkong Bank, established by Hong Kong citizens in 1865, accepting a liability which was not necessarily theirs and accepting it in the public interest. The ordinary citizen was not concerned with the actual sums involved, with whether the Bank took all the loss or only a portion. That was Morse's concern. What they saw was an apparently disinterested act; from this the Hongkong Bank's prestige was confirmed in the community, the morality of post-war finance was provided an initial confirmation, and all concerned could turn towards the future.

DEBTOR/CREDITOR RELATIONS

Unfortunately, the euphoria expressed in the last paragraphs is somewhat premature. Morse's success with the duress note problem was not paralleled in his negotiations relative to debtor/creditor relations. It was one of the few battles which Morse was destined to lose, but typically he was outspoken and forceful throughout.

Although the relevant legislation was not passed in Hong Kong until early 1948, various compromise arrangements and official adjudication committees had been working out voluntary arrangements. The Hongkong Bank, for example, announced on July 18, 1946, that it would recognize the credit balances of depositors as of December 25, 1941. But the problem of inter-bank deposits, $13.2 million and $1.4 million for the Chartered and Mercantile banks respectively, remained. And there were other unsettled questions.

The problem stated

Put in its simplest form the basic problem was this. At the beginning of the Occupation the Bank's constituents owed it certain sums against which the Bank usually held a form of security. During the Occupation the 'liquidators' of the Bank, acting as if they were agents of the Bank, called for repayment. Some made repayment; some did not. Those who made repayment did so in various ways and under various conditions which affected the real burden to them of that repayment. For example, a debtor who repaid such a debt within a few months of the Occupation's beginning might pay in Hong Kong dollar notes; later, a debtor might pay in Occupation currency, the real value of which was very little depreciated; eventually a debtor might pay off his debt to the Bank in heavily depreciated or virtually worthless 'banana money'.

In no case would the Bank itself have been benefited, but the security would be released back to the 'discharged' debtor.

There was a second dimension. To what extent was repayment a consequence of duress? The Hongkong Bank was to claim that in Hong Kong the liquidators merely sent 'routine' notices, and that those debtors who responded did so of their own volition; they chose to repay. They did so for one or both of two reasons: either they saw that repayment in depreciated currency was in their long-run interests whichever way the war went (unless such repayment were to be repudiated as the Bank now wished) and/or they were active supporters of the Japanese regime. In an extreme form this suggests that those who made repayments were collaborators and those that did not were loyal to the British Government.

This last conclusion could be turned around. Not to repudiate Occupation payments was unfair to those who did not make such payments, to those, that is, who waited to make repayment until the true creditors returned. Such an argument would not solve the real problem in places like Shanghai where the national currency itself had depreciated. The argument was, in fact, part of the wider question of how to deal with 'collaborators' and their activities.[30]

The Hongkong Bank's position

As with the duress note problem there was more involved than the real value of the currency, but, whereas in the matter of the duress notes the Bank considered the problem in the context of broader implications, in the case of debtor/creditor relations the Bank took a particularly narrow and legalistic position based on J.R. Jones's interpretation of the relevant provisions of the Hague Convention of 1907 and of the applicable international law.

In this Jones was supported by initial rulings from courts in the Philippines.[f] These rulings were no doubt good law, but they were unacceptable politics, and after a controversial and stormy history the Philippine legislature passed a bill recognizing payments in 'Mickey Mouse' money. The bill was vetoed by President Truman in a well-argued message. The bill was then reintroduced and passed once Philippine independence had been granted. The Bank brought two test cases to court and, after winning in the local courts, lost in the Supreme Court.[32] Legalism was not a practical approach.

The Bank's strong opposition to any legislated concession to debtors, in marked contrast to its duress note position, most certainly delayed settlement of the problem by at least two to three years. And the delay was costly both to the Bank and to the community. The forcefulness with which the Bank, that is, Morse using the arguments of Jones, put its case must have surprised Sydney Caine in the Colonial Office, who in early 1946 was promising such creditors as the National City Bank of New York and other holders of clearing deposits with the Hongkong Bank that a solution could not be more than two or three months away.[33]

Arthur Morse accepted the importance of a quick settlement; at the July 1946 Meeting of Shareholders he said, 'It is a matter of urgency that His Majesty's Government should take early action to remove the moratorium and clarify in both territories the effects of enemy occupation on the relations between debtors and creditors.'[34]

The Colonial Office and the Government agreed and drew up the necessary legislation. Morse disapproved of it. The next year he stated,

At the Annual Meeting in July last year [1946] I said that it was a matter of urgency that His Majesty's Government should take early action to remove the Moratorium both in Hong Kong and Malaya, and to clarify the effects of enemy occupation on the relations between debtors and creditors.

It now appears from an announcement made on February 27 [1947] in the House of Commons by the Secretary of State for the Colonies, that the enactment of legislation is shortly to take place to deal with the value to be accorded to payments in Japanese occupation currency in respect of debts contracted before occupation.

This is a serious matter, and speaking for the Bank I must formally protest against any legislation which would have the effect of adjusting debtor-creditor relationships by the arbitrary validation to any extent of payments made in occupation currency to the

---

[f] In the case of the *Hongkong Bank v Luis Perez-Samanillo*...the decision made reference to a post U.S. Civil War case involving the Citizens Bank of Lousiana: 'But the delivery of *confederate notes in discharge of an obligation arising from a deposit of lawful money is not a payment without the consent of the creditor.*' (Emphasis added to the Archives copy by J.R. Jones.)[31]

so-called liquidators. If I understand the present proposal correctly, it is without justification either in law or in equity in its wider sense. Moreover the Bank has discharged all its obligations to depositors and other creditors but it has been precluded by the Moratorium from collecting the debts owing to it before the war.[35]

A year later, in March 1948, on the eve of the eventual passage of the debtor/creditor bill, Morse virtually admitted he was fighting a rearguard action against its expected provisions, of which he was fully aware. Enactment was now more important than content. After a well-considered plea for additional funds (from the Home Government) for the University of Hong Kong, Morse noted that despite the lapse of two and a half years since the liberation of Hong Kong and despite repeated and urgent appeals, the Moratorium was still in place. On the expected provisions, Morse commented,

...the result will be the validation against the Bank of considerable sums both in genuine and in occupation currency which the Bank never received but which were paid to agents of the Japanese Occupying Power who were appointed to liquidate the Bank and confiscated its funds in direct violation of the accepted principles of international law. Whether or not this legislation is well conceived in law or in equity the urgent concern of the public and of the banks now is that the prolonged suspense and uncertainty for which it is difficult to find any justification should be brought to an end with the utmost despatch.[36]

The Bank versus the Government

Morse was correct in supposing that the eventual solution to the debtor/creditor problem would be costly to the Hongkong Bank. Government was not particularly sympathetic, in part because of what they considered the low price the Bank had paid for recognition of the duress notes. Morse did not make the connection; he fought for the rights of the Bank in the present situation as he had for that low price in the duress note problem.

As time passed he was in an increasingly weak position.

First, whatever feelings there had been against collaborators and those who profited from payments during the Occupation, time was easing the tensions. Furthermore, the British Government had been early accused of leniency towards 'collaborators' and it would hardly be practical to reverse the position several years later.

Secondly, the Hongkong Bank was prospering in an already prospering economy. Morse no longer had the argument that the survival of the Bank was at stake or that the Bank would be unable to play the expected role in the redevelopment of Hong Kong; it was flourishing and playing that role. On the other hand Morse was fighting a losing battle on the China front; there was no sign that any of the Chinese obligations to the Hongkong Bank would be honoured. And beyond that was the threat of a new Chinese Government and a new policy. These are subjects to be considered in Chapters 4 and 9. The present discussion has already moved beyond the time frame of this chapter, but the story must be followed through to its conclusion. The resolution of the Occupation debtor/creditor controversy presented itself as an immediate post-war problem, despite the fact that this was achieved only in 1948 – and 1949 for Malaya.

Thirdly, the Bank's criticism of the Government's proposals was not always accurate. Morse claimed that those who had paid during the Occupation had done so on a virtually voluntary basis and without real cost to the debtor. The first is a matter of opinion and is political; the second was allowed for in the official proposals through the introduction of a sliding scale, taking account of depreciation and, unlike the Philippine legislation, excluding payment in depreciated currency as a full discharge of obligations.[37]

As Morse wrote to Sydney Caine in November 1946, 'I am afraid we will never see eye to eye with regard to paying off of overdrafts here.'[38]

The Debtor and Creditor (Occupation Period) Ordinance, No. 24 of 1948

The ordinance which Arthur Morse and the Hongkong Bank found unacceptable would seem, on the contrary, to be a reasonably suitable solution in the post-war political and social circumstances. The basic concession to debtors is the provision for revaluation of payments according to a scheduled scale of conversion rates which take depreciation of the Occupation currency into account. Furthermore, settlements which had been mutually arranged since the end of the Occupation were recognized and many of the Bank's constituents had in fact come to an arrangement with the Bank.

The solution might be considered inequitable for the same reason the duress note legislation was faulted. In the latter case a small group of speculators profited from the previous uncertainty and made considerable sums from the ultimate recognition of the duress notes. In the present case a small group of constituents were said to be responsible for the bulk of the payments made during the Occupation, and Morse claimed that these payments had been made with the consequences well in mind; it was unfair to those who had acted 'properly'.

The ordinance separated debts contracted before the Occupation with those contracted during the Occupation and took account of the currency in which the original debt was contracted and the currency in which it was repaid.

At this point the validity of Morse's objections became clear. The ordinance considered the burden of the payment made from the point of view of the debtor; the ordinance nowhere takes into consideration that, as Morse was continually pointing out, the Bank as creditor had received nothing from the debtor. Even if the debtor had repaid in full in Hong Kong currency, the Bank received no benefit therefrom; the Japanese liquidators had turned over the proceeds to the Occupation authorities.

Yet on the other hand the ordinance did impose obligations on the Bank relative to the accounts of its depositors [par. 6]. The liability of the Bank to a customer at the end of the Occupation period was to be:

the amount which stood to the credit of such customer on December 25, 1945, plus subsequent deposits in Hong Kong dollar currency less withdrawals during the occupation in Hong Kong dollar currency; less the excess of withdrawals made in occupation currency during the occupation over deposits in occupation currency converted into Hong Kong dollars at the rate of $4 to Military Yen 1 (the rate prescribed by the occupying power).

These provisions did not take into account the changing value of the military yen, but it is not clear that this in itself was unfair to the Bank; the real burden in this instance lay with the customer.

Conclusion

Whether on reflection Morse mellowed or whether his strong position had been merely protective of the shareholders is difficult to determine. Quite possibly the mounting repudiation of debts in China had firmed his view that the Bank could not afford to appear irresponsibly responsive to Government demands at the expense of its shareholders' legitimate interests, even though post-war recovery was well underway. In any case, his public reaction to the accomplished fact was temperate.

In Hong Kong the problem was solved on the principle that it was equitable for the Government to require the banks to make concessions from what were deemed their legal rights in order to avoid lengthy litigation and to relieve the hardship which would otherwise undoubtedly result to those who had paid their debts in good faith during the occupation.

Such a compromise which was declared by Government to be fair to all parties was achieved by the passing in June last of the Debtor and Creditor (Occupation Period) Ordinance 1948 which gave to debtors of the Bank the benefit of the full validation of all payments made to the Japanese liquidators in Hong Kong currency and partial validation of all such payments made in occupation currency. The latter is on a sliding scale based as far as possible on the true value of the Japanese military currency at the time of payment.[39]

Then too the problem was not confined to Hong Kong where the Hongkong Bank might be expected to make short-run sacrifices to assist the long-run growth in which it was bound to benefit. Similar decisions were likely to be made in the Straits and Burma. There were problems over the rates of conversion of Chinese accounts; the situation in Java was uncertain, and Morse was obviously watching developments in the Philippines. By 1949 he knew the worst; there was nothing left to protect. 'The validation in the Philippines of occupation currency coupled with the continuation of the moratorium in a modified form is calculated to preclude to a very material extent the recovery of money advanced in the Philippines before the war.'[40]

In defence Morse, as Chairman of the Bank, reminded shareholders and therefore the community at large that the Hongkong Bank 'has striven to solve the problems which resulted as a legacy of the war by practical measures which, I believe, have been of general benefit to all concerned.'[41] What the Bank had done and the consequences to the Bank are more positive and, in the context of its history, more important topics. Before considering these matters, however, the story must move back to 1946 and the Bank's Head Office must be brought to Hong Kong.

HEAD OFFICE: HONG KONG

As Arthur Morse explained to the first post-war meeting of shareholders in Hong Kong, there was never any question about the return of Head Office. The 1943 Order in Council had specifically referred to the transfer as 'temporary'. Apparently some shareholders in England, 'but not, I think, those out here', had been surprised that the Bank, once its Head Office had reached London, would really decide to return East. There were historical reasons still valid why the Bank acted as it did, and Morse, who as a junior had heard Sir Thomas Sutherland describe how he founded the Bank, decided it might be wise to remind even a Hong Kong audience that

...over eighty years ago, in 1864, the meeting held in this Colony which resulted in the establishment of this Bank was called because local merchants were dissatisfied with the existing banking arrangements. ... banks with their head offices in London were scarcely in a position to deal satisfactorily with the local trade which had become so much more extensive and varied than in former years.

I imagine that most of you agree with me that for these same reasons we do well to maintain our Head Office in the East where we can keep in close touch with everyday developments and ensure flexibility in our policy...

I trust that never again in the lifetime of any of us here will it be necessary to move our Head Office from this site.[42]

Morse had been in London long enough to recognize its importance to the Bank; long enough also to recognize that he himself belonged in the East. He began his planning early, and, after consultations with A. H. Barlow, the former Chief Manager and member of the London Board, decided to invite H. E. Muriel back to London to take over when Head Office moved to Hong Kong.[43]

Muriel was six years senior to Morse having come East to Tientsin in 1909. He had been appointed Accountant Hankow in 1925 after sixteen years in the East – the first appointment in his group had been only in 1924; half the survivors had received their first appointment with Muriel in 1925 (see Table 5.2 in Volume III). Nevertheless, the opportunities were available, and Muriel was promoted to Agent in Penang by 1931; from 1939 he was Manager in the difficult Calcutta post. Morse had never served under his London appointee, but he would have lived with Muriel at the Peak Mess in Hong Kong on his first tour from 1915 to 1919.

When Morse wrote to Muriel in 1944, the latter had already been East for 35 years and Morse stressed that the London position was a temporary one; he was then to retire without argument.[44] This was agreed and Muriel returned to England in late 1945, in time to take over temporarily during Morse's illness.

Morse left London in early April 1946, at which time Muriel was given necessary authority during the time of Morse's sea passage to Hong Kong. He did not become Acting Chief Manager in the formal sense as defined in the 1943 Order in Council. Sir Edward Reid was elected Chairman of the London Board and therefore of the Hongkong Bank. Then on June 20 the Head Office was reestablished in Hong Kong. The newly appointed Board of Directors met there the following day and elected Morse as Chairman. The members of the former London Board were appointed by the Board in Hong Kong as a London Advisory Committee once again; the Hong Kong Board of Directors also appointed Muriel as the Committee's Chairman.

How were these changes wrought?

The transfer of Head Office

The legal requirements for the move back to Hong Kong were first an Order in Council to cancel the previous Order and secondly an ordinance to confirm various changes detailed in Schedule 1 of the 1943 Order and to state other changes in the basic ordinance rendered necessary or desirable in view of experience and recent events. There does not appear to have been any controversy over either the Order or the ordinance.

The ordinance was drafted in London in consultation with Arthur Morse, agreed to by the London Board, and sent out to Hong Kong for approval.

The Order in Council

The Hongkong and Shanghai Banking Corporation (Re-transfer) Order in Council of May 16, 1946, withdrew the 'powers, authorities and discretions transferred to the Committee in London', confirming the legal point that, although it was proper to refer to the members of the Committee in this period as 'directors' and to the Committee as 'Board', it had remained the London Committee with additional authority. At the same time the new Order, in revoking the 1943 Order, noted that this revocation was 'without prejudice to anything lawfully done thereunder'.

The main provision was that the Head Office of the Bank 'shall be transferred to Hong Kong'.

The Order was to be effective by Proclamation, the latter being timed to coincide with the enactment of the appropriate ordinance.

Ordinance No. 8 of 1946

Morse arrived in Hong Kong in May. Civil Government had been renewed on May 1 and Morse was appointed to membership in the Executive Council. The Bank's ordinance, designed to revise the basic ordinance (No. 6 of 1929), was assented to by Governor Mark Young on June 20. The Bank during this interim period was run *de jure* from London, and consequently there was a temporary impasse. There were no directors in Hong Kong.

The only revision to the main provisions of the Bank's ordinance was the increase in the 'authorized' note issue from $30 million to $46 million. All other revisions were to the Bank's regulations.

The first revisions to be considered were those designed to get the Bank operating in Hong Kong. The problem of the calling of a shareholders' meeting was solved by adding a provision enabling the Governor on his own motion or that of the Chief Manager or of any shareholder to call a meeting (Reg. 57). This was, however, anticipatory of any future crisis; the existing impasse was solved in a more systematic way.

Ordinance No. 8 granted authority to the Governor, either on his own motion or on the advice of the Chief Manager or of any twenty shareholders, to fill vacancies in the Board of Directors provided that there were no directors or that their number were below the minimum and provided that there were no practical alternative way of solving the difficulty (Reg. 89). The Governor acted on this authority. At the moment of the transfer of Head Office by proclamation the London Committee members would cease acting as directors, and, unless the Governor had anticipated the situation, there would then be no directors of the Bank.

On Morse's advice the Governor appointed new directors who would then be able to meet and call an annual meeting of shareholders without the necessity of the Governor exercising his powers granted by the new Regulation 57. At this first shareholders' meeting, the appointed directors were by ordinance required to resign, but they could and did offer themselves for election.

Secondly, the ordinance considered the new situation presented by the fact that Arthur Morse was Chairman of the Hongkong Bank and had been acting as a director through his membership on the London Committee at the outbreak of the war and his *ex officio* position as that Committee's chairman, confirmed by an election in 1943 in accordance with the provisions of the Order in Council. But once the Order was withdrawn, Morse would no longer be eligible for election either as a director or as Chairman of the Bank. Nevertheless, it was clear from the role he had assumed that any 'downgrading' real or apparent was undesirable; on the other hand, an ordinance which still had 'exceptional' wartime provisions in it was also undesirable.

The solution was to make provisions for the Chief Manager's eligibility for election as a director by the shareholders or directors similar to those in the Schedule to the 1943 Order in Council (Reg. 118). This would be an exception to the rule that no officer of the Bank was eligible to be a director. A Chief Manager/director would not be subject to the rotation provisions. Thus the Board were empowered to appoint a Chief Manager; they were also empowered to elect him a director or to put his name forward at the annual meeting. A Chief Manager did not automatically become a director; he had to be elected.

Whether the Chief Manager became the Chairman of the Hongkong Bank depended therefore on (i) whether he were elected a director and (ii) whether the Board then elected him as their Chairman.

And, thirdly, the ordinance attended to other matters, some important to the history of the Bank, others merely improving or making consistent previous wordings. Several of these had been incorporated into the Schedule of the 1943 Order in Council, but this had now been cancelled; if they were to remain effective the provisions had to be reenacted.

Of the important changes, the provision in the Schedule decreasing the minimum number of directors from seven to five was confirmed (Reg. 85). Morse believed that the smaller number would operate more efficiently, and it was his intention that, although the maximum number remained twelve, only ten would in fact be elected.[45] This latter provision, found in the Schedule, was not reenacted.

The new ordinance confirmed the role of an 'Acting Chief Manager', appointable by the Board, to exercise all the functions of the Chief Manager. The usefulness of this provision was obvious from the wartime experience of Grayburn and Morse, but it would be relevant to less dramatic circumstances (Reg. 118). Before passage of this revision, an officer might act for the Chief Manager when the latter went on leave or was ill, but he did not succeed to the powers and authorities of a Chief Manager which, in an emergency, he might need to exercise. The more these latter were spelt out in the ordinance, the more there was need to refer specifically to an Acting Chief Manager. Now, for example, that the Chief Manager was eligible to be a director, the Acting Chief Manager also needed and now possessed this eligibility.

In February 1922 the Bank had responded to the Hong Kong Government's request to close the Shanghai Share Register by agreeing to act without delay but with regard to the convenience of the Bank. The status of the register is specifically noted in the 1929 Ordinance but with the implication that shares were being transferred to the principal register, Hong Kong. Apparently closing the Shanghai Register had not been a priority concern inter-war; its closing had been mentioned in the Schedule, and it was certainly existing in 1946. On this point therefore the new ordinance confirmed once again: 'The local Shanghai Register previously kept by the Bank shall be deemed to be closed and any shares registered in such local register shall on any future change of ownership thereof be transferred to the Hong Kong Register...' (Reg. 32). The loss of extrality had had its effect.

'Reconstruction of Records' Ordinance, No. 1 of 1948
The fact that the Hongkong Bank was subject to its own ordinance as amended was responsible for some duplication in Hong Kong legislation. Even routine ordinances covering incorporated companies in general did not affect the Bank. The provisions in the special ordinance (see above) enabling the Governor to appoint directors of the Hongkong Bank, for example, paralleled provisions in other emergency legislation which had already given him such authority over other companies.

Similarly there was passed in 1947 the Companies (Reconstruction of Records) Ordinance; this was not applicable to the Hongkong Bank and a parallel ordinance, No. 1 of 1948, was passed on January 15, 1948, 'to make provision for The Hongkong and Shanghai Banking Corporation analogous to...'. Both ordinances dealt with the issue of new share certificates where originals had been lost.

Chartered companies had their special privileges and their special problems.

With the assent to the ordinance 'to amend the Hongkong and Shanghai Bank Ordinance, 1929, and the Regulations thereof', and with the Governor's Proclamation giving effect to the Order in Council, the Head Office of the Bank was in Hong Kong and the Bank was operating under its new regulations.

First meetings

The Board of Directors
The new directors had been pre-designated by the Governor and with the passage of the ordinance they were able to meet immediately. This they did on June 21, and as a first item of business elected Arthur Morse Chairman and D.F. Landale of Jardine, Matheson and Co. Deputy Chairman. There were three directors from the 1941 Board, A.H. Compton, G. Miskin, and C.C.

Table 3.3 *The Hongkong and Shanghai Banking Corporation
The Board and Committee, December 1941 and June 1946*

A. The Board of Directors

December, 1941
J.J. Paterson	Jardine, Matheson and Co.	Chairman
C.C. Roberts	Butterfield and Swire	Deputy Chairman
G. Miskin	Gilman and Co.	
J.K. Bonsfield	Asiatic Petroleum Co.	
A.H. Compton	David Sassoon and Co.	
K.S. Morrison	Reiss, Bradley and Co.	
S.H. Dodwell	Dodwell and Co.	
T.E. Pearce	J.D. Hutchison and Co.	
A.L. Shields	Shewan, Tomes and Co.	
L.J. Davies	Gibb, Livingston and Co.	

June, 1946
A. Morse	Chief Manager, Hongkong Bank	Chairman
D.F. Landale	Jardine, Matheson and Co.	Deputy Chairman
C.C. Roberts	Butterfield and Swire	
G. Miskin	Gilman and Co.	
A.H. Compton	David Sassoon and Co.	
R.D. Gillespie	Imperial Chemical Industries	
H.V. Wilkinson	Gibb, Livingston and Co.	

B. London Advisory Committee

December, 1941
Arthur Morse (ex officio)	Hongkong Bank, Manager	Chairman
C.A. Campbell	Westminster Bank	
Sir George Macdonogh	Director, Shell Co.	
A.H. Barlow	retired, Hongkong Bank	
W.W.H. Hill-Wood	Morgan, Grenfell and Co.	
Lord Ashburton (Alex Baring)	Baring Brothers and Co.	

June, 1946
H.E. Muriel (appointed)	Hongkong Bank, Manager	Chairman
Sir Edward Reid	Baring Brothers and Co.	
C.A. Campbell	Westminster Bank	
A.H. Barlow	retired, Hongkong Bank	
W.J. Keswick	Matheson and Co.	
Sir Frederick Sykes, M.P.	retired, Governor Bombay	
R.G. Macindoe	Maclaine, Watson and Co.	

Note: Boldface indicates those who were not members in December 1941.

Roberts; there was one new company represented, Imperial Chemical Industries; this was probably due to the friendship between Morse and their Hong Kong taipan, R.D. Gillespie. There were only seven directors appointed, five of whom would be sufficient to form a quorum (see Table 3.3).

The Board then turned its attention to the London Advisory Committee which, by Proclamation of the previous day, had lost its powers as a 'board of directors'. The Board invited the then members to continue and appointed Muriel, the senior London Manager, as the Committee's Chairman. Their remuneration was fixed at £500 p.a., subject to tax.

The Annual Meeting to consider the 1945 accounts and hear the Chairman's report was fixed for July 12, 1946.

The Board resumed normal business. They took note of senior staff resignations and assigned the retirement gratuities and pensions; they noted the death of the compradore, Ho Wing, who had never recovered from ill-treatment under the Japanese. He was succeeded by T.P. Tong.

The Board also considered from time to time requests for contributions, often in connection with reconstruction of churches, schools, etc. A list, as compiled from the minutes is found in Table 3.4. Most of the requests were in 1947, but the list may not include smaller donations. In May 1947 the Board took up the question of 'widows and orphans' and made *ex gratia* grants to such persons as Mrs Edmondston, Mrs Garrett, Michael Hyde, Mrs Mathews, and Mrs Mills, the sons of O.J. Shannon, and the son of C.H. Howard. The total cost was £41,600.

Bangkok office was designated a 'branch'. The Peak Mess was to be rehabilitated at a cost of $250,000, and finally, and significantly, J.A.D. Morrison was awarded a gratuity of £500 for running the Head Office's exchange operations. This marked a break; it was the first time in the history of the Hongkong Bank that a senior officer in Hong Kong did not himself operate the exchanges, but Fenwick had had no experience in this field – nor had Morse. The Chief Manager had been liberated to run the Bank.

The election of Arthur Morse as (non-executive) Chairman did not change the status of either Chairman or Chief Manager. All subsequent banking decisions were made by Morse as Chief Manager; Board decisions were conveyed to the public or to Government by letters signed by Morse as Chief Manager in his capacity as *de facto* Secretary to the Board.

All that had happened, constitutionally, was that, having been elected Chairman, Morse could speak for the Bank when the occasion arose. The public were naturally aware of the commercial importance of the Chief Manager of the Bank; but at the Annual General Meetings they had been confronted with a stranger (at least in banking), who addressed them as the

Table 3.4 *The Hongkong and Shanghai Banking Corporation Charity and reconstruction, 1946–1947*

1946	
Hongkong Society for the Protection of Children	$1,000
1947	
Colombo, Joseph Fraser Memorial Nursing Home	Rs100
China Christian University Association	£250
St John's Cathedral Goodwill Offering Scheme	$1,000 p.a.
Club de Recreio, Hong Kong	$10,000
Union Church Rebuilding Fund	$10,000
SCMP Flood Relief	$10,000
St John's Cathedral Restoration Fund	$10,000
Salvation Army	$2,000
War Memorial Fund	$100,000
St John's Ambulance	$1,500
Canton Flood Relief CNC$8 million	$800
Shanghai British Community (schools, hospitals, etc.)	£5,000
Church in Malaya, Bishop of Singapore's appeal	£500
Singapore, TB Clinic	$25,000
Calcutta, St. Paul's	Rs1,000
Bengal Red Cross Appeal	Rs1,000 p.a.
Calcutta, Relief and Rehabilitation	Rs2,500
Hong Kong, Boy Scouts Association	$1,000
Hong Kong Society for the Protection of Children	$1,000
Calcutta, District Charitable Society	Rs150
British Empire Leprosy Relief Association, Bengal	Rs100

For donations during the Pacific War, see Chapter 1. See Chapter 4 for post-1947 donations.
SCMP = South China Morning Post.

Chairman of the Bank. This anomaly could now be eliminated. The man they had heard of would now be the man they heard.

There was, however, a weakness in the new system. It was neither one thing nor the other. Morse as Chief Manager had lost his independent Board, but he had not thereby gained any authority – only prestige. Morse had not become 'executive chairman'; his executive authority arose from his appointment by the Board as Chief Manager.

The ordinance had been written so that a Chief Manager might in future be neither Chairman nor even a director. The directors might agree on Morse but they were not as yet prepared to redefine the Board's role in the context of their relationship with the Bank's chief executive. Indeed, neither Turner nor Saunders, the two successors to Morse, were at first elected Chairman by their boards; Saunders' appointment as a director was the subject of discussion.

Only with the creation of an executive board of directors, made possible by shareholder-approved changes in the Bank's regulations in 1969, was the problem of the Board's role resolved.

The London Advisory Committee

On June 24, 1946, H.E. Muriel, the Hongkong Bank's senior London Manager, wrote to the former Chairman of the London Board, Sir Edward Reid, that a cable had been received from Hong Kong noting that the first directors' meeting had been held and that they had appointed the 'late London Board', with the addition of Muriel as Chairman, as the London Advisory Committee (see Table 3.3).[46]

The members met on June 27 and, after resolving to recommend to the new Board in Hong Kong recognition of the services of Arthur Morse, they dissolved themselves. Reid then left the chair and the members continued as the London Advisory Committee. Whether legally this was necessary is questionable; their powers had been withdrawn as of June 20, but the formality was appropriate to the occasion.

The Babylonian Captivity of the Hongkong Bank had ended.

POSTSCRIPT: PERFORMANCE, 1945–1946

The growth of the Hongkong Bank's balance sheet figures in the years 1945 and 1946 was dramatic, but the figures are difficult to explain with assurance. The tendency of the Bank's management to squirrel away funds into unappropriated contingency accounts makes one of the key factors, the growth of deposits, something of a composite which includes inter-bank clearing accounts, various contingency funds, Government accounts virtually at call, and private sector savings and commercial accounts. The imposition of the Moratorium forced the Bank, as it were, to operate off the top, that is, to undertake new business by making advances against the security of blocked accounts and by taking in new funds which provided the resources both for the finance of trade and for new investments. The high liquidity of the Bank's sterling resources facilitated these operations, and the lack of specificity relative to the nature of the 'deposit liabilities' gave Morse a flexibility which was essential to the type of rehabilitation he was sponsoring.

A comparison of the Bank's year-end accounts is found in Table 3.5; the figures are in sterling to provide continuity with wartime years (see Table 1.3). The 1945 accounts were drawn up in sterling while the Head Office was still in London. Analysis in later chapters will revert to the Hong Kong dollar.

The Bank did not declare a dividend until March 1947 when the Annual Meeting voted, on the basis of the end-1946 statement, a dividend of £3 per

Table 3.5 *The Hongkong and Shanghai Banking Corporation Balance sheets: end-1945 and 1946 compared*

(thousands of pounds sterling)

	1945[a]	1946[b]
Share Capital	1,250	1,237
+Reserve Fund	7,125	6,000
+P&L Account	0	114
= Shareholders' funds	8,375	7,351
HK currency notes	16,035	25,735
Total deposits	68,132	93,758
(of which = proposed dividend	0	480)
Net balance of drafts etc.	1,970	—
Liabilities = Assets	94,512	126,844
Cash	8,691	16,342
HK certificates of indebtedness	14,223	22,910
Money at call and short notice	20,000	16,901
Bills receivable	649	3,582
Investments	21,933	34,109
Subsidiary companies	100	99
Total advances	27,787	29,946
Balance of remittances less drafts and other items in transit	—	1,738
Bank premises at cost less amounts written off	1,130	1,216
[Profit	218	594]
Note issue:		
Authorized	1,875	2,845
Excess	14,160	22,886

[a] Balance sheet originally in sterling.
[b] Calculated in Hong Kong dollars and converted at $1/2\frac{27}{32}$.
Note: includes items subject to the Moratorium.

share, compared to £5 for 1940. This was done despite the transfer from published reserves of £1.125 million to, as Morse put it, wartime contingencies. But one alternative way of looking at it would be to say this latter transfer represented the cost of recognition of the duress notes plus an amount equivalent to the additional balance on year-end Profit and Loss Account.

This leads first to the question of whether the Board were justified in recommending a dividend. As the accounts are stated, current earnings more than justified the dividend; the shareholders had been without a dividend since mid-1941, and the transfer from published reserves was to meet a loss which the Bank should not have been required to bear. Furthermore so-called contingencies were being used to restore war-damaged buildings, to build up new pension funds and meet retirement demands, and to cover all possibilities on the still undecided question of debtor/creditor relations.

On the basis of a static analysis the payment of a dividend was justified. Looking at the performance of the Bank on a more dynamic basis, Morse could afford to be generous; there was no reason why the Board should not be optimistic.

To attempt to comment on the Bank's relative prosperity as between end-1944 and end-1945 would be futile; figures include assets under Head Office control, and thus the scope of coverage of the accounts varies. Then too the recovery in the East was still tentative by the end of 1945; key Eastern offices had been open at the most for three months, hardly time to provide a guide to performance (see the list in Table 2.1). In Hong Kong foreign exchange operations had begun in November and there were encouraging reports by March 1946, and it is to the 1946 accounts that one must look for indications of the future.

The first point of growth as shown in Table 3.5 is under Hong Kong currency notes which rose £9.7 million from £16 to £25.7 million. This is not wholly accounted for by taking the duress notes into the accounts for the first time; there is still a net growth of over £2 million. The significance of this must be judged with the growth of deposits by 38% from £68.1 million to £93.8 million. Even if cynically one assumes that this includes the funds transferred from published reserves, the remaining growth is highly significant.

These sources of funds had their counterpart in the increased use of funds as reflected (i) in the Bank's increase in liquid funds and (ii) by the increase in investments and advances. Investments would include subscription to ill-timed colonial Government loans which, but for the banks, and the Hongkong Bank in particular, would have failed. The total investments and advances grew during the year by 52%. The higher figure for bills receivable is also an indication of a high turnover and the growth of trade.

When Morse addressed the shareholders in March 1947 he was able to state that not only were all but seven of the pre-war offices reopened but that there were new offices in Malaya, British North Borneo, and Brunei. The Bank was still not back in Japan, and the opportunities in China seemed never to be realized. Morse's address perforce focused therefore on the performance in Hong Kong, on the growth of trade, on the opportunities which existed once rehabilitation had been completed. It is true that the future seemed still to depend on Hong Kong's infrastructure being repaired to benefit others; there would be no reason why, however, when others were busy with non-economic priorities, the infrastructure the Bank was financing should not be used for and by Hong Kong itself. And this is indeed what happened. Morse did not predict the future, but he sensed that sound overhead developments would be utilized.

Despite Morse's popular public image as a banker with a great heart, almost unlimited funds, and a willingness to advance on trust, he continued to handle the Bank's growing resources conservatively. The contingency funds he was building up would form the basis for the Bank's 'inner reserves' simply because not all the possible disasters for which contingency funds had been allocated in fact occurred. The one negative factor, the 'loss' of China, had long been written off in the accounts, the disastrous depreciation of China bonds had been written down to market on a regular basis. For the rest, it was a question of staying liquid until the opportunities for sound banking presented themselves.

The accounts reveal another fact. The confidence in the Hongkong Bank was fully restored and its role in developments immediately following V-J Day acknowledged. Morse's wartime planning, although looking forward to virtually total destruction, proved nevertheless to be relevant – staff were prepared, funds were available, offices were opened – and the duress notes were recognized. As the economies of the Far East developed, the resources of the Bank and therefore the role it could play increased. How this occurred and the limits to that increase will be considered in the following chapters.

4

THE HONGKONG BANK AND THE REPUBLIC OF CHINA, 1945–1949

> We are, Sir, first and foremost a China Bank.
> *Chairman, the First London Annual Dinner, 1908*
> We were doing absolutely no business at all.
> *F.C.B. Black, Manager, Hankow, 1947*

The Hongkong Bank was a China bank. However well it served the region's trade finance requirements in general, undertook limited internal investment, while its local managers assisted host governments with their currency and banking problems, the primary focus of the Bank's senior management in Hong Kong and London had been on its activities in China. The Bank's success had depended on a realistic evaluation of China's actual situation relative to its needs. The Bank's actual 'coverage' of the Middle Kingdom was limited; it had never attempted to compete as a 'local bank' in the Chinese domestic economy. Certainly it had served the Treaty Ports and sought Chinese retail business while working through compradores in the money markets of the China coast, but its primary role was linking China with the world through the finance of trade; the Bank provided China access to the London market and, under the right conditions and through this link, defended the creditworthiness of the Empire and Republic.

Provided that the Bank had access to funds, preferably through a continued right to obtain current and fixed deposits from the general public, it had little to fear from the termination of extrality rights *per se*. The Bank's concern would be with the general deterioration of the economy, a period during which no bank, foreign or domestic, can operate on a sound basis. When the People's Liberation Army proved successful in 1949, however, the Bank faced a revolutionary Government and found itself part of an overall criticism of capitalist exploitation; the Bank could not escape the new Government's analysis of history and of its own past role.

Not surprisingly, therefore, the Bank's role was increasingly restricted until in 1955, after an 'all-for-all' settlement, the Bank, stripped of the trappings of past grandeur, began again in China. Removed from the outports and from its great building on Shanghai's Bund, the Bank operated from a modest office managed by two Eastern and twelve local staff. The tasks it performed were those for which it had been founded – the finance of foreign trade, the providing of commercial information which bridged the gap between China and its potential trading partners.

The Hongkong and Shanghai Banking Corporation has never left China. The Shanghai branch continued to operate, although the scale was drastically limited. In this way the Bank has been removed from the context of what the Chinese authorities saw as an imperialist past. As a foreign bank it remained in Shanghai with the permission of the host Government, a presence which could be and would be developed when the appropriate time arrived.

The wisdom of the founders' decision to make Hong Kong the headquarters of their new bank was once again acknowledged. If the Bank were no longer welcome in China or its future in doubt as a physical presence in the People's Republic, it could still finance the China trade in cooperation with the Bank of China in Hong Kong. The Hongkong Bank, even in the years of most serious concern over its representation in the People's Republic itself, never ceased to be a China bank. And in Hong Kong directors and Managers could sense developments in Shanghai and react, albeit in some cases with considerable difficulty, to changing attitudes. The basic relationship, however, was never broken.

Although post-war planning relative to the Hongkong Bank's role in China was tempered by the realities of the Chungking office and its experiences, the hopes entertained by Arthur Morse and W.C. Cassels, the Bank's political adviser, seem strangely optimistic with hindsight. The sudden ending of extrality in 1943 by a treaty with inadequate safeguards – the consequence of American pressure and intended to keep Free China in the war – did not in itself discourage the Bank, although Morse was aware that China had now the power to end or modify the Bank's activities, as had any independent Government. In the end it was not the positive action of the Chinese National Government but the deterioration of the Government's economic and political position which dashed the Bank's hopes for a useful role in China's economy. The basic nature of the problem was not immediately apparent, and Arthur Morse, as Chief Manager, became engaged in a fruitless and unavoidable correspondence with the British Foreign Office in an effort to obtain redress for the losses to which the Bank and the China bondholders were subjected.

First it must be recognized that the Hongkong Bank was permitted, despite the ending of extrality in 1943, to reestablish itself in Chungking. With victory in the Pacific War, the Bank was permitted not only to reopen its pre-war offices but also to open a new branch in the capital city of Nanking. The Bank had long operated in independent countries, for example, in Japan and Siam; it was accustomed to being subject to banking controls which differed from British colonial practice, as, for example, in the United States and the Philippines; it had had experience in discrimination on the basis of nationality, as in French

Indochina and the Netherlands East Indies. The delays experienced in obtaining the 1943 licence to open in Chungking suggested that China too would be reconsidering her banking regulations but that there was as yet no effective opposition to foreign commercial banks playing a limited domestic role. This proved to be the case in the last years of the Nationalist Government.

There was, however, a less fortunate side to the Bank's China relations. Just as Morse was persistent in his demands on the Hong Kong and British Governments relative to the duress note issue and debtor/creditor relations, so too he pressed for settlement of China's pre-war obligations to both the Hongkong Bank and to the bondholders of issues in which the Bank had participated. As Morse was 'generous' with Bank funds through participation in productive projects, so he was determined in his efforts to recover the funds which would provide the basis for further loans.

The Bank's approach could be criticized for being excessively 'legalistic', but it is difficult to see how a corporation's chief executive could do otherwise than press for what was legally due. The Foreign Office was not so single-minded, and Morse's frustrations with 'China' might better be described in terms of his long-running battles with officials in London.[1] The Bank's persistence in maintaining its demands on China must be seen in the British as well as the Chinese context.

In this chapter the Bank's immediate experiences in post-war China, in Republican China, are divided into two main sections, the Bank as commercial bank operating in a context of hyperinflation and economic deterioration and the Bank as merchant bank – the end of the Consortium, the early but abortive development plans, and the frustrated attempts to settle the pre-war debts. The Bank's experiences under the Government of the People's Republic will be considered in Chapter 9.

THE BANK AS COMMERCIAL BANK IN CHINA

The economic setting[2]

To the natural dislocation of war and the destruction of productive capacity must be added, in describing immediate post-war China, the inability of the National Government to command resources through taxation and the consequent financing of expenditures through borrowing from the Government banks. The inflationary consequences were reflected in the statistics. The Shanghai workers cost of living index for January 1946 was 90,000 (1937 = 100); by mid-1948 it had risen to 57.4 million. Banknotes in circulation rose from CNC$1 million million to CNC$255 million million in the same period;

this smaller percentage increase is indicative of periods of hyperinflation, that is, of a flight from the currency. The transaction velocity of money had increased dramatically.

These adverse developments occurred despite the import surplus and the further import of goods under the United Nations Relief and Rehabilitation Administration (UNRRA). Traditionally a trade imbalance had been financed in part by the remittances of Overseas Chinese, but the overvaluation of the Chinese dollar diverted such payments to unofficial channels, as indeed the overvaluation encouraged the export of capital partly through the non-reporting of export earnings. In consequence China's official reserves declined from US$858.1 million in December 1945 to a low of $36.6 million in August 1948. Sterling reserves had been exhausted by December 1947.

The efforts of the policy makers appear to have been devoted to the task of stemming the inflation without actually touching its main cause, the Government deficit. As the problems of recovery were increased by the mounting intensity of the civil war, especially after the *de facto* breakdown of the American truce efforts by mid-1946 and the withdrawal of the American truce teams by early 1947, the Government's financial position steadily worsened, despite U.S. military and other aid.

In consequence Chinese economic control measures were designed to curb a demand which was steadily fuelled by the increased issue of banknotes; measures which would have possibly worked for a temporary period pending the implementation of real economic reform could not be expected to control inflation in a country whose citizens were becoming increasingly disenchanted with the political regime. Indeed, the measures, even if temporarily successful, would become self-defeating when people realized that real factors had not been affected.

Since real factors were untouchable, the emphasis had to be on the façade. Thus the Government was reluctant to issue banknotes of large denomination; this became a symbol of an increasingly unrealistic expectation that the inflation was temporary. When in mid-1947 the price of rice per picul had reached CNC$485,000, the Government authorized a CNC$10,000 denomination banknote for the first time – and there was panic on the money market. The Government did not try this again; instead, people traded with packets or bundles of notes, the contents of which were assumed correct. On occasion the Hongkong Bank found that this assumption was incorrect, and the system threatened to break down, endangering the money economy.[3]

One solution was again 'façade'. In the 1930s bank accounts in 'Customs Gold Units' (CGU) had been instituted to facilitate payment of duties denominated in a CGU unit of account; CGU banknotes had been issued in large denominations, mainly for interbank clearing purposes. This unit had been tied, as the name suggests, to the value of gold; its value originally fluctuated therefore in terms of CNC. With wartime controls and a fixed parity, the exchange became CNC$20.00 equals CGU1.00. The word 'gold' suggested to some, even those who in fact knew better, that these notes were gold-backed; but, for whatever reason, CGU notes commanded for a time greater confidence. The practice grew, therefore, of issuing CGU notes for retail circulation. In the period of hyperinflation, when the cost of the note issue was one of the major non-military Government foreign exchange expenditures, the practice developed of overstamping the *fapi* notes (denominated in CNC dollars) to designate them 'Customs Gold Units', thus enhancing their value by a factor of twenty in terms of the Chinese National Currency. By mid-1948 the Government authorized the issue of notes with a denomination of CGU250,000; this was the equivalent of CNC$5 million – but the price of rice per picul was by then CNC$20 million.[4]

In the control of foreign exchange operations, the Government began with an overvalued Chinese National Currency – the façade. To offset the obvious consequences of such an overvaluation, the Government instituted various programs of control, including partial buy-back of export earnings at arbitrary rates and partial open market sales, subsidized interest rates for export-producing industry, subsidized imports of essentials. These complex and often offsetting measures required a maze of regulatory orders and controls which few countries could expect to maintain free of malpractice, evasion, and corruption.

One of the more obvious consequences was the flight from the currency. In South China the Hongkong Bank's Hong Kong dollar-denominated banknotes circulated both as a store of value and for everyday transactions, if not to the exclusion of *fapi* (CNC), then certainly more commonly than the country's own legal tender. Elsewhere the U.S. dollar note and previously hoarded silver coins were important.

At the end of the Sino-Japanese War the puppet currency, Central Reserve Bank dollars, had been exchanged for CNC at the rate of 200:1; now in August 1948 *fapi* denominated in CNC dollars were replaced by notes denominated in 'gold yuan' (GY) at the rate of CNC$3 million to GY 1 (see Table 4.1). The use of the word 'gold' was unwarranted and proved not to have its hoped-for hypnotic effect on the public; the new currency was 'backed' by fixed assets unsuitable for the purpose and China's holding of gold had been reduced to US$96.6 million. At the same time people were required to surrender their stocks of foreign currency, gold and silver, and the foreign exchange statistics indicate that this indeed happened. The value of the currency stabilized for several weeks, but with a renewed offensive in the civil war prices began to rise. This is reflected in the official cost of living statistics which had been

Table 4.1 *China: currency conversion rates, 1942–1955*

6 June 1942	2 CNC = 1 CRB Central Reserve Banknote
1 November 1945	200 CRB = 1 CNC Chinese National Currency
19 August 1948	3,000,000 CNC = 1 GY Gold Yuan
28 May 1949	100,000 GY = 1 old RMB Renmenbi[a]
1 March 1955	10,000 RMB = 1 new RMB

The Shanghai resident who had CNC$1.00 in 1941 at the outbreak of the Pacific War would have, after the March 1955 conversion,
RMB 0.000,000,000,000,000,000,833.

6 June 1942	1 CNC = 0.5 CRB
1 November 1945	0.5 CRB = 0.0025 CNC
19 August 1948	0.0025 CNC = 0.000,000,000,833 GY
28 May 1949	0.000,000,000,833 GY = 0.000,000,000,000,008,33 RMB
1 March 1955	0.000,000,000,000,008,33 Old RMB = 0.000,000,000,000,000,000,833 New RMB

[a] also abbreviated 'JMP' (Wade-Giles: jen-min-pi).

doubling monthly; they show an increase of 1,486% for November compared to October.

Shanghai fell to the People's Liberation Army in May 1949. In the interim before the Nationalists were driven from the Mainland of China various monetary expedients had been attempted, including the issue of a 'silver yuan' printed to look something like a U.S. dollar note, and gold was sold back to the public, highlighting the fact of the currency depreciation which had taken place since the 'reform' of August 1948.

The chaotic monetary situation was supplemented by the destruction or disruption of transportation lines by military action. Real output was adversely affected and the economy endangered.

The role of the Hongkong Bank

At the end of the Pacific War the Bank's office in Chungking was functioning; in Shanghai A.S. Adamson struggled in from the Lunghwa Camp to take charge of the Shanghai office and elsewhere there were early adventures. Shanghai branch was officially authorized to transact business in December 1945 and by the end of 1947 all pre-war branches, with the exception of Harbin, then under Communist Party control, Chefoo, and Dairen, had reopened. But this refers to physical presence and permission to operate. It is not a statement of success in business.

In 1946 Shanghai and its agencies showed a net loss of $1.3 million; the profits of the Bank's branches world-wide returning a profit were $13.5 million, the losses of branches returning a loss were $2.0 million. The Shanghai and North China loss was turned around in 1947 and net profits were $1.4 million in 1948, but nominal losses in 1949. There were severe losses the following years, with an exceptional $4.2 million loss in 1951.

The Bank could not be accused of slighting Shanghai. S.A. Gray, the first post-war Manager, G.H. Stacey, his successor, and W.T. Yoxall, the Manager who signed the all-for-all settlement in 1955, were among the most able of the Bank's senior executives. R.P. Moodie was the Accountant and later Manager Hong Kong; Gray became a noted London Senior Manager, and Stacey, after heading the Bank's operations in Japan, moved to Head Office as Deputy Chairman, in which post he died in 1955. Yoxall, who had been through Changi (Singapore) internment, performed his last tough assignment for the Bank in Shanghai, and retired to head Sri Lanka's Development Bank.

There were 24 members of the Eastern staff assigned to Shanghai in 1947, and the total staff was 291 compared to 1941's 34 Eastern staff and 625 total. The post-war restoration was not, therefore, complete – nor was it extravagant. Morse would see to that. As for the other China agencies, with the exception of Tientsin where there were five Eastern staff, they were held down either by one officer awaiting business or at the most by two. A pattern was never established; it is difficult to tell how the Bank's business might have developed had Nationalist China's economy stabilized and then grown as the optimists had expected.

Nor was the Hongkong Bank victimized by the Nationalist authorities. The Bank received the necessary banking licences to reopen and a licence to establish *de novo* in the national capital of Nanking. Monetary policy was, of course, a matter for the Chinese Government, and the Central Bank of China, under the direction of such famous bankers as Chang Kia-ngau and Pei Tsu-yee, took back the central banking tasks which the Hongkong Bank and the Chartered Bank had been required to undertake during the Shanghai period of the Pacific War. But there was still a role for the Hongkong Bank to play.

During the period of managed flexibility relative to foreign exchange, the Government established a Foreign Exchange Stabilization Fund Committee, which operated from August 1947 to May 1948. To plan and supervise day-to-day operations, the Fund Committee had a technical committee consisting of representatives of the Fund and four leading foreign exchange banks, the Bank of China, the Bank of Communications, the National City Bank of New York, and the Hongkong and Shanghai Bank. The last mentioned was represented by G.H. Stacey, who thus found himself directly associated with China's leading financial experts on a key committee. From the Central Bank there were H.J. Shen 沈熙瑞, Cyril Rogers, and Arthur N. Young; from the Bank of China, R.C. Chen, and from the Bank of Communications, T.N. Lee.[5]

Certainly the Bank felt a long-term part of the Shanghai scene. In May 1947, when there was some cause for optimism, the Board of Directors voted £5,000 to foster British communal interests in Shanghai in the absence of extrality and the Municipal Council. The community would need hospitals and schools, towards which this sum was, given the Bank's position at the time, a generous contribution. In September the Board, in a further sign of its attitude to the Bank's China operations, approved Morse's proposal to buy the British Vice-Consul's house in Swatow for the Bank Manager.

But the failure of the August 1948 currency reform was a signal, if any non-military indicator were necessary, that development in China, if it were to come at all, must await a new Government. In April 1949, the Hongkong Bank sent up $5 million in Hongkong Bank notes on HMS *London*, to be used in Shanghai in the 'event of collapse' – it was to be held on the warship until needed but at the Hongkong Bank's expense. As Morse correctly told the Board, it was not practical to ask H.M. Government to take responsibility – it would take too long to get a decision.[6] How or under what exact circumstances the cash was

The Hongkong Bank and the Republic of China

to be employed was not specifically stated. The scheme sounds Stephenesque, another 'Last Hurrah', but it was probably innocently intended and might, if the occasion had arisen, have alleviated suffering in an interregnum. But however well-intended, such moves were now beyond the capacity of the Bank to effect, and by mid-June the Bank was facing demands from the new authorities for a deposit of capital in terms of *jen-min-pi* [JMP or *renminbi* RMB].

Mukden had already been evacuated. Before the end of 1949 Chungking, Foochow, and Nanking offices had been closed and there were plans for the closing of Canton, Hankow, and Amoy. The retreat from China had begun.

The Bank's business in China

Swatow for a brief period returned virtually to its pre-war routine; Tientsin remained an active branch to the end, but in other ports there was little business. In this section there is a sample selection, glimpses of the Bank in Hankow, Nanking, Mukden, and Shanghai.

Hankow

The Hankow branch had been reopened post-war by E.C. Hutchison; he was relieved in early 1946 by F.C.B. Black. Little business was done, and Black, in company with the few foreigners in the once flourishing Settlement, rattled around in over-sized buildings trying to recreate Treaty Port life in a China that had passed them by. The Bank's Hankow building, constructed in the context of A.G. Stephen's grand plans for expansion in central China, had been too large for the Bank's inter-war business; in 1946 it seemed somewhat ridiculous.

But for Black it was his first – and as it turned out his only – managership. After his Hankow experience he became Sub-Accountant in Shanghai and then a 'back-room' banker and eventually Chief Inspector in the Bank's Head Office. As he tells the story...

It was the first time I was in charge of anything, and, oh dear, it was a sad story....

There's a lovely bund with great big banks and buildings all along it, and the biggest building, of course, is the Hongkong Bank building with the most marvellous granite pillars I've ever seen in front of it.... Half of the ground floor was always rented out.

At the time I was there, in our half of the ground floor was a tiny little space that might have been the Cash department with the Manager's office opening off it. I sat in the Manager's office and two clerks sat in the Cash space, and the whole of the rest of the area was empty. The only thing I was thankful for was that there weren't bats flapping around in it.

Upstairs there was a most enormous Manager's flat. The first floor contained a dining room, a drawing room, a ballroom, a billiard room, a boudoir...six rooms altogether though I've forgotten what the sixth room was. And on the floor above it there were six bedrooms and bathrooms. There were enormous kitchen premises on the first floor level stuck out in an annexe at the back, and then attached was a wing which had the rest of the staff accommodation, I think four flats for the rest of the British staff.

I had to live in a room in a hotel because an American bomb had hit the top floor of our building and punctured the roof. The Japanese who had been occupying the building repaired it. The roof, I might say, was given over to a roof garden. It really *was* a roof garden with trees growing on it and soil and flower beds and shrubs. You are a long, long way from anything green in the centre of Hankow.

We were doing absolutely no business at all.

There were exactly twelve Europeans in the place, and we used to meet for lunch every day at a grimy Russian restaurant somewhere or other. At the Hankow Race Club the stands were still occupied by Japanese prisoners of war that had not yet been repatriated. There was a golf course nearby, and we had got three fairways functioning from which we played six holes, three out and three home! That was for those who were keen enough to play golf, which was about six of us. After a little while it was decided that something had to be done to revive the place, and I suggested that as we had all this space to spare above the Bank, the Hankow Club might be re-formed and rent at least one floor above the Bank. This was solemnly agreed by the twelve present, eleven of whom, I think, were ex-members of the Hankow Club and myself. And when we came out of the meeting, I discovered that, although I was not a member, I'd been elected president![a]

There was no business at all.

There was virtually no shipping, there was nothing, the only ships that were moving up and down the river were tank landing craft which were carrying UNRRA supplies to starving Chinese in the interior.[7]

But the Bank retained its social position in the British Community.

In Hong Kong the Bank was very important and all that, but *I* had been a mere junior, you see... I never realized what weight the name 'Hongkong Bank' carried in China till I arrived in Hankow. I'd only been there a week or so when the Consul General apologized to me because he'd given a dinner party, and he'd omitted to ask me, the Agent of the Hongkong Bank, to be present, and he was very sorry for the oversight.

I was really shaken by it. I mean, if he wanted to give a dinner party, that was his business.

But I began to realize then the importance of the position of being a Manager in the Hongkong Bank, even in an office that wasn't operating.[8]

Although there was no new business, the accounts had to be brought up to date and a correspondence maintained. In the course of this latter Black had the task of explaining the impact of inflation to pre-war depositors seeking remittance of their balances.

This missionary wrote from America and said that she'd left a balance in Hankow, and she'd like to have it remitted to her.

I wrote back and said that I was very sorry, but the balance wasn't worth remitting.

---

[a] Black would follow up this social victory by being elected Chairman of the Hong Kong Club; in 1985 at the age of 80 he resigned after seven years as the 'taipan' of the 'Fanlingerers', a charitable and social group of ex-Hong Kong residents who raise funds for the Scottish war-blind.

She wrote back again, very indignant, and said this was all nonsense, the balance was three or four hundred dollars to the best of her recollection and could she have a statement of her account and this, that and the other thing.

I wrote back to her and said, yes, we had a record of her balance, and I could confirm that it was three hundred and something, whatever dollars it was, but if she had any doubts about whether it was worth remitting or not, would she please have a look at the stamp on the envelope that I was sending to her... which was five hundred dollars.[9]

On the other hand there was a civil war and thus several non-banking events.

I came to the office one morning, and the verandah was occupied by a lot of soldiers, obviously ill, none of whom, I think, were actually wounded, but they were obviously ill, lying on cotton blankets, with Chinese soldiers standing by them, and they were sick and sorrowful.

I went into the office and asked one of the clerks to go out and enquire, because, of course, I didn't speak the lingo, and he came back and said that this was a regiment on its way down from Chungking to Nanking, and these men were sick.

The last thing you wanted to do after the war was to create trouble. Extraterritorial rights had gone. I rang up the Consul General, and he said, well, is there any trouble being created?

No, I'm not really doing more than just letting you know that this has happened in case there's trouble later. There's no reason why the poor devils should not have what shelter they can get.

He said, I agree with you. Just leave it at that and see.

It was all over in a day or two. They moved on.[10]

Nanking

Sir Vandeleur Grayburn, the Bank's chief executive from 1930 to 1941, had resisted pressure to open in Nanking on very sound grounds. The Nationalist Government's monetary 'capital' was Shanghai; it was not at all clear that the Hongkong Bank would be welcome in the Republic's political capital. Grayburn did, however, stipulate that he would reconsider if the British Embassy specifically requested the Bank's presence.[11] They did not.

Post-war it was different. There was no extrality; China was recognized as a major power and it was prestigious to have a branch in the nation's capital. Furthermore the Embassy did express the wish that the Bank open in Nanking. Accordingly, in August 1946, the Board of Directors approved making an application for a licence to open; in early May 1947 the new Nanking branch began banking business.

Nanking in many ways provided a marked contrast with Hankow. The office, for example, was of more appropriate size.

We got very excited about opening an office in Nanking because it was the capital of the Nationalist government.

A lot of negotiation and manoeuvring had been done in order to get this office. In point of fact, it was a little house at the end of a muddy lane by a field of cabbages, but we regarded it as a foothold.

We lived on the floor above the Bank in this little house. Little indeed it was. When we first had the safe brought in, which weighed about two tons, it went through the floor, and we had to have the floor reinforced underneath it in order to carry its weight.[12]

There was no business at first, but Colin J.D. Law, the Manager, and J.F. Marshall, the only other Eastern staff member, went on the cocktail circuit, a marketing strategy adopted on the basis of *ad hoc* analysis; neither had attended business school.

Our job was to build up a business, and so we sat through the day and chatted and had a gin every now and then, and about once every two hours a Chinese would come in and pay in ten dollars, and then in the evening our work started.

We would go round the diplomatic cocktail parties and try and persuade...no, not really persuade, but let it be known that we would be very happy to do their banking for them. And we got so professional at this that we'd go to different cocktail parties. [Law would] go to four or five, and I'd take in four or five in a different area, you see. But it didn't really amount to anything because, apart from the British Embassy, who banked with us automatically, and the Australians and the New Zealanders, Canadians perhaps, nearly all the embassies banked with Chinese banks for the sake of good relations.

The ones that we wanted to capture, like the American and the French and the Russian, banked with the Chinese banks because it indicated goodwill. We did get the personal accounts of one or two of these people by virtue of attending these parties and chatting them up and becoming very friendly with them.[13]

As a result of these efforts the branch after three months' working, in July 1947, had 40 current accounts totalling CNC$775 million (= $120,000 at the market rate of CNC$6,450 = $1.00), on which interest at 5% per month was paid. Losses for the first three months were CNC$123 million, which could have been reduced by postponing non-urgent purchases, but with prices rising at hyperinflationary rates, Law, like everyone else, was joining the flight from the currency.[b]

The cost of doing business was high. The branch cashed cheques drawn on Shanghai on demand; it therefore had to have considerable cash on hand and/or a large clearing balance with the Central Bank of China. The size of these holdings was affected by the fact that access to the Central Bank account was limited to a single daily debit which could not exceed the equivalent of one-third the bank's clearing balance. The clearing account was drawn on as described and replenished by sales on Shanghai – the Nanking branch rarely received cheques drawn on other banks. Furthermore the branch had to maintain a 'deposit reserve account' with the Central Bank equivalent to 15% of the value of its current accounts. Other liquid assets included CNC$5 million

---

[b] To prove the wisdom of this course, Law noted that the Bank's opening banquet on May 8, 1947, had cost CNC$8.5 million; he estimated that the same given on July 7, 1947, would have cost CNC$20 million.[14] In periods of hyperinflation it is therefore sound business practice to celebrate early and, presumably, often.

with the Bank of China and $5 million with the Sin Hwa Trust and Savings Bank, which, Law reported, had been very helpful to the Hongkong Bank prior to opening and maintained a reciprocal account with the branch.

These impediments to the efficient functioning of the monetary system were designed, in part at least, to slow down the velocity of circulation. Later the very task of obtaining physical cash caused delays (during which prices rose), and the public reverted to barter or the use of other monies, including, in South China especially, Hongkong Bank notes.

Another consequence of inflation was the fact that staff salaries were paid on the basis of the University of Nanking's Cost of Living Index – which, like similar indexes elsewhere, became political issues as inflation worsened and the Government sought to hold back the concurrent increase in prices.

On the positive side, the Nanking branch did handle remittances, especially between Shanghai and Nanking, and on these a commission of 4 per mille was earned – British Embassy remittances were undertaken at par. Law noted a 'few' transactions with Peiping, Tientsin, and Tsingtau. Overall profits for the first three months on account of remittances was CNC$19.5 million.

Mukden

Since the early 1930s when Japanese control of China's Northeast Provinces (Manchuria), became virtually absolute, the Bank's Manchurian branches had been isolated and unprofitable. But the Bank, true to its policy, held on. During the war under both Japanese and Russian occupation, A.T. Ostrenko had kept the Bank's properties secure, ready for the post-war return. Events made this almost impossible. The Russians retained control of Dairen, the Chinese Communist Party authorities were in Harbin, and the Bank could operate only for a brief time from Mukden.

This was another two-man post, and J.F. Marshall, being a bachelor, was sent north from time to time to assist the acting Manager, H.F. Phillips (East in 1919).

Mukden was virtually under siege. The first time I went there I went up from Tientsin by train. I remember going down to the station and seeing the engine and two flat cars in front of the engine, and I didn't like the idea of that much at all. The two flat cars were to blow up the mines before the engine reached them, you see. However, we went up, and on that trip there weren't any mines to blow up, and we got to Mukden safely, but I think that was the very last time a train got through. The only communication was by airplane.

One could climb up to the top of the Hongkong and Shanghai Bank building in Mukden, which was an eight storey building and one of the biggest and most prestigious buildings in the town, and see gun flashes at night three hundred sixty degrees all the way round.[15]

As for the business of the branch:

We were getting remittances from Shanghai in order to pay the salaries of the British Consulate. There was a British Consulate there, there was a British American Tobacco factory specially making cigarettes, there were some missionaries, and that was about it. And these people had to be kept alive, they didn't have any money, and so they were being funded from outside. We were getting remittances in, and, in order to cover the amount of cash that we had, we had to look around and get some remittances out in order to cover the other side of the book. And that's really about all we did.

We also maintained the building. We had three Russian engineers there, and we generated our own electricity. We had three huge generators making the electric current running the lifts. The three Russian engineers were very volatile characters, and to keep them pacified and on the job needed a certain amount of diplomacy. But the actual banking, there was really very little. The office most of the time was empty.[16]

As in Hankow part of the Bank's expenses were covered by renting out rooms in the large office building in which Phillips and Marshall shared a flat. And as in Nanking the Central Bank of China had an office in Mukden from which the Hongkong Bank could draw cash, but, as Marshall stressed, it was important to get 'sales on Shanghai' to cover inward remittances, and this was the main function of the Bank's compradore.

Shanghai

Pre-war the Bank had, with exceptions in New York and California, opened new agencies and branches without any required deposit of capital. Capital assigned to the branches was usually an internal bookkeeping arrangement, augmenting the free funds available to the branch Manager. The credit of the Bank was accepted by the relevant authorities as standing behind the liabilities of the Hongkong Bank's offices wherever they might be. Security might be required before Government funds could be deposited in a particular agency, but otherwise the generalization holds. It was thus relatively 'cheap' to establish a new agency, especially in the same currency area.

Post-war, banks were expected to bring in capital, and there was always the possibility that repatriation might be refused or depreciation might affect its value. This latter was possible pre-war, but the decision relative to capital was the Bank's to make. As an early example of this change, the Bank's London Board of Directors noted in February 1946 that the Shanghai branch had been granted a licence to reopen but that a capital of CNC$12 million (approx. $30,000) had been required on registration. This sum was subject to the ravages of inflation – say $4,000 twelve months later.

The impact of inflation, which was certainly not confined to depreciation in the value of the initial branch capital, was most apparent in a larger office, and Black, after his brief tour in Hankow, was in Shanghai in 1946–1948 as Sub-Accountant, a post popularly known by the staff as 'drains'. He was, that is, responsible for all matters unrelated to banking itself. But in this position he was able to note the problems of salary calculations and related matters.

The Shanghai Chamber of Commerce ran a cost of living index, and when you get really rampant inflation... and I don't mean thirteen per cent per annum, I mean thirteen per cent per week... you've got to do something about it, and they produced an index weekly.

The staff were all paid weekly.

They got one-fourth of the previous month's figure each week and then a lump sum at the end of the month to compensate according to that month's increase in the cost of living index. And this was for the local staff and the Foreign staff, too, because the Foreign staff received part of their salary in local currency and part in sterling.

It's quite a thing if you have a large office with two hundred and fifty or three hundred staff, and you have to work out all their payments and any deductions for this, that and the other thing... Some of them have loans, and you've got to deduct so much a month to repay them and all.

And then you have to do it four times a month at a different rate every time. Each thing has to be calculated out four times. You had some staff doing nothing else. And you always had people complaining that the amount of the increase wasn't enough, of course, and you had to battle with that.[17]

R.P. Moodie, the Shanghai Accountant, described the position for Eastern staff as follows:

Foreign firms had a sort of price list which consisted of whatever it was, so many catties of rice, so much of flour, so much of whatnot, so much of something else, one bottle of whisky, one bottle of gin, or something like that, you see, and on that, the price of this 'living package', they based your monthly salary, and the day on which you were told what your salary was going to be, you got on the telephone to your wife and said, Now you've got so much. Go out and spend it. Otherwise it was gone by the next week or so. So you had to buy all sorts of things.[18]

On a subject closer to banking, borrowing money for example, Black observed,

... it was the only sensible thing to do. The same thing's true in Britain today [1980]. It's better to owe money and pay it back in depreciated currency than to have cash. In fact, everybody wanted an overdraft, and as inflation got worse and worse, the Bank was in the position that it couldn't lend money to its customers because it didn't have it to lend.

I mean, nobody put money in the Bank. As soon as ever they had money, they rushed out and bought something. The oil companies had a ship that came in once a month with petrol that was supposed to last for a month.... As soon as ever they got the petrol in and sold it, they couldn't hold the cash until the next month or they wouldn't be able to afford the new price, so they would do things like buying silver bars... which was illegal... or buying corner lots where they could put up filling stations, anything to avoid holding cash. So they didn't put the cash in the bank, they got rid of it.

And people would come to us to borrow money for legitimate purposes. Shell had a tanker coming in. We'd say, all right, yes, well, we'll let you have it for three days. And the rate of interest kept rising. At the time when I left in August 1948 the inter-bank rate of interest was three hundred and sixty five per cent per annum, it was one per cent *overnight* inter-bank. So what you charged your customers over and above that was up to you.[19]

But, as Moodie pointed out, the oil companies lost out in the end – they lost their properties. Nevertheless, as far as the Bank was concerned, the earnings from short lending did provide income from which to pay staff wages. Moodie had an arrangement with the oil companies; when they had money overnight, they would inform the Bank, Moodie would then lend it out and make a turn on the rate; that, he recalls, is the only money the Bank really made in Shanghai.

You got the compradore to see what the market was.
 Shell would ring you up and say, I've got forty millions I'll lend you overnight or for two days maybe, and I want whatever rate.
 Well, if you could see that you could lend it out, as you always could, you'd say, All right, I'll give you that. Then you immediately got on the blower and lent it out at five or ten percent more.[20]

The borrowers were Chinese banks, the Chartered Bank, other companies...as Christopher Cook observed in his interview with Moodie, it appeared to be a situation in which there was a kind of inter-bank circle in which everyone was lending everybody else money and just turning it over.

'That was it?'
 'That was about it, yes.'[21]

There were, however, the occasional trade bills to finance odd shipments of Chinese produce from the interior, but this business ceased when the river was closed.

One of the practical problems was that the Central Bank of China couldn't supply notes fast enough. As Black recalled the position,

...they couldn't import them fast enough. They imported them from America, and sometimes a shipment was delayed. So they used to issue notes for five thousand Customs Gold Units rather than for one hundred thousand Chinese dollars. They tried to persuade people that inflation wasn't all that bad.
 But it didn't really matter, it got to the ridiculous stage where you got several bundles of notes from the Bank each morning, and never counted them. When you took a taxi ride, you just handed the driver a bundle of notes with a little paper band round it, and he just took it. Nobody ever bothered to count. And then some damn Chinese bank was caught cheating on this. I suppose it was one of these clever shroffs who had hefted it in his hand and decided it was a bit light and counted it and found there were fifteen notes missing. And when they started to check all the notes they got from this Chinese bank, they discovered that there were not a hundred notes in each bundle. And there was an awful 'hoohah' about that.
 On one particular end of a month, at a time when there is always a rush on cash, and at the Central Bank of China the notes hadn't arrived...the ship was delayed or something...and, well, we simply had to get means to pay our customers, and we were all sat down there, each with a book of cashier's orders, and we sat down and wrote our cashier's orders for ten thousand dollars as fast as we could go. It was illegal because in effect it was issuing notes or at least promissory notes, but they were readily accepted. A cashier's order on the Hongkong Bank for ten thousand dollars would never be questioned.[22]

This situation could not, and did not, continue. Before considering in a later chapter the transition to the new Government, however, the story turns to consider the Hongkong Bank as merchant bank in China, 1945-1949.

THE BANK AS MERCHANT BANK IN CHINA

The end of the Consortium

Sir Charles Addis, born in November 1861, died on December 12, 1945.

The following year the China Consortium was declared dissolved. Not that Sir Charles Addis could have kept it alive, but, while he lived, it survived. The concurrent endings were symbolic.

The final intervention of Sir Charles Addis
By all logical standards the Consortium should have been unable to resist the opposition of the Chinese Government at least after 1927. When the opportunity for new international loans to China came in the mid-1930s the difficulties arising from China's non-recognition of the Consortium should have affected its survival.

In fact in 1937 the British Foreign Office and in 1939 the American Group recommended its dissolution, but the time was never quite ripe, some event intervened, and Sir Charles Addis was at hand to urge 'caution' or inaction. When the American Group insisted on reducing the annual overhead payment, Addis with the connivance of Montagu Norman made up the difference from Bank of England funds.[23]

Here was a dream of 1911, reborn in 1920, surviving into World War II, its main contribution throughout being negative. But Addis had come to London Office in 1905 during the hopeful time of Europe-wide financial cooperation – and competition; he never retreated from the purposes he developed in those meetings in London, Berlin, Paris, and Brussels during which the two-party agreement between the Deutsch-Asiatische Bank and the Hongkong Bank developed into the formation of Three-, Four-, Six- and then Five-Power groups. Their purpose was to finance the development of China, but China followed another course.

And then came the Pacific War. This time the Foreign Office declared the Consortium dead, but it would not lie down. Legal advisers might state that the consortium was abrogated from the date hostilities broke out between the United Kingdom and the United States on the one hand and Japan on the other, but Sir Charles Addis made strong representations that this decision should not be announced in Washington. And Addis in 1942, at the age of 81, was still the 'Head' of the Consortium; he still represented The Hongkong and Shanghai Banking Corporation.

The Addis diaries document his continuing interest in the Consortium; talks on this subject with Montagu Norman were recorded in entries of January 5 and 9, 1942. On February 2 he learned that the Foreign Office had pronounced the Consortium abrogated; Addis earnestly protested a draft telegram informing Lord Halifax, the British Ambassador in Washington, that he should so advise the State Department. The Treasury apparently agreed; the cable was not sent.[24]

Although Addis noted that there would be more discussions later, his diary, which was becoming irregular, does not refer to them. On May 27 Addis learned, however, that Arthur Morse was attempting to free the Hongkong Bank of any association with the Consortium. Morse's very reasonable concern was to eliminate any suspicion that the Bank might be involved in an 'underhanded deal' with the Japanese. 'This,' noted the 81-year-old Addis, 'raises a question of principle which, if pressed, might force me to retire.'[25] Two days later he was at the Bank of England discussing the problem with Norman. He asked Norman to warn Morse against 'touching Consortium policy'.[26]

During 1944 Addis's current term as a director of the British and Chinese Corporation was to end and it was tactfully put to him that he might not wish to stand again. He accepted the inevitable. By mid-1944 it would be safe to conclude that Addis had at last withdrawn from effective participation in public affairs. He had been seriously ill in 1943 and he would not long survive this final retirement.

The final decisions
Arthur Morse brought the matter of the Consortium to a head on the eve of his departure for Hong Kong in April 1946. In a letter misdated 1942 and signed in the great bankers' tradition of illegibility (so that it was initially registered in the Foreign Office as from A.S. Henchman), Morse informed the Foreign Office of correspondence with Morgan, Grenfell and Co. and of the American Group's decision that either the Consortium be dissolved or the American Group should withdraw. The U.S. State Department was reported to 'contemplate this action with equanimity'.[27] Morse proposed, therefore, that the British take the initiative to announce the dissolution of the Consortium and sought Foreign Office agreement before corresponding with the French Group.

That the obvious was not approved immediately was due to the fact that no one directly concerned with China affairs could remember what the Consortium was or what it was supposed to do. To the pressing request of the Bank's London Manager, H.E. Muriel, for a decision, the Foreign Office replied that 'we were having to dig up old papers and consult other government departments and that some delay would therefore be unavoidable'.[28]

With the agreement of the Foreign Office, Muriel wrote to the Banque de l'Indo-Chine on May 28 stating (i) that the Consortium Agreement was abrogated completely from the date of hostilities but that an announcement to this effect had not seemed suitable or convenient at the time and (ii) 'we now wish to suggest that the time has come for this to be done and that the British, American and French Groups should arrange for the formal dissolution of the Consortium by mutual consent'. A similar letter was sent to J.P. Morgan and Co. Both parties agreed.

Should China be informed?
In his letter of May 28, Muriel had brought up a new problem. He assumed that the Chinese Government should be informed of the dissolution of the Consortium; the Foreign Office, however, thought otherwise. Muriel was told that neither the State Department nor the Foreign Office thought it appropriate to inform the Chinese Government on the grounds that the latter were not a party to the Agreement and had never recognized the existence of the Consortium. Muriel was afraid that, despite this, non-notification might be considered discourteous, and as a compromise the Bank was authorized to mention it to the Chinese Government informally.[29]

There being no further action to take Muriel noted that 'without further action' we will 'regard the China Consortium as being dissolved, and the Agreement of October 15th, 1920, lapsed by common consent'.[30]

Morse had given some consideration to the possibility of maintaining the existence of the British Group, despite the dissolution of the international agreement between groups, but this idea was not followed through and the British Group may be considered to have ceased its existence with the Consortium. For the first time since 1895 the Hongkong Bank stood alone.

The British and Chinese Corporation/Chinese Central Railways

Well, not quite alone.

The Hongkong Bank was still one of the two major shareholders of the British and Chinese Corporation (B&CC) and through this company of the Chinese Central Railways (CCR). Like the China Consortium these companies had long outlived their usefulness, but as they were legally incorporated and had outstanding obligations their future was to require considerable negotiation. In 1954 the CCR was dissolved, having transferred its obligations to the B&CC. The latter, being trustees for the bondholders of certain Chinese railway obligations, found no one willing to take over these responsibilities, and by a series of capital reorganizations it became a subsidiary of the Hongkong

Bank, listed as a 'dormant' company. How these changes came about is the subject of the present section.

The companies were barely tolerated in the post-Boxer 'Rights Recovery' atmosphere of Chinese railway politics in the period before the Great War, and clauses in the several agreements which called for taking over management in the case of default or of gaining title to the railways' property were recognized by the directors of the companies as inoperative. Furthermore railway reconstruction and development would be carried out by the Chinese, presumably with financial aid but certainly not on a 'concession basis'. Meanwhile the companies were incurring expenses and interest was mounting on a continuing overdraft with the Hongkong Bank. The directors had to weigh, therefore, the prospects for the repayment of outstanding obligations by the Chinese against the expense of continued existence. The impetus against letting matters drift was in fact the burden of the companies' operating expenses, which, even though at a minimum, were particularly undesirable in the immediate post-war reconstruction period.

The Chinese Central Railways

In 1905 the CCR had become a company incorporating the railway and related concessions of various competing groups of British, French, and Belgian nationality into a single British corporation, the voting power of the French and Belgian groups equalling that of the British Group but with the chairman, by agreement a British subject, having the casting vote.

The dissolution of the CCR had been proposed by the British Group in 1925, but the French Group had insisted on the company continuing and the following year agreed that the company's uncalled capital should be paid up.

With the shares of the Yangtze Valley Company, a member of the 'British Group' in the CCR, having been sold to the B&CC in September 1939, the British Group post-war consisted of the B&CC and the Pekin Syndicate, in equal amounts (although one qualifying share each of the former's allocation were actually held by the Hongkong Bank's London Manager and by a designated partner of Jardine, Matheson and Co.).[c] The smaller Belgian Group consisted of the Banque d'Outremer and the Société de Bruxelles pour la Finance et l'Industrie. Most of the 25 French shareholders were banks.[d]

In 1946 the British Group once again proposed to the French and Belgian Groups that all agreements creating the CCR be cancelled and that the

[c] The Yangtze Valley Company had gone into voluntary liquidation in 1941.[31]
[d] These included the Société Générale pour favoriser le développement du Commerce et de l'Industrie en France, Bardac N.J. & S., Comptoir National d'Escompte de Paris, Banque de Paris et des Pay Bas, Banque de l'Indo-Chine, Régie Générale de Chemins de fer et Travaux Publics, and Crédit Lyonnais.

company be dissolved, its rights and obligations to be taken over by the B&CC. The CCR's overdraft with the Hongkong Bank, which was growing by £11,474 per annum on account of interest charged at 5%, amounted to £243,412 with interest accrued – the actual original overdraft of 1927 had been £97,580 – and there was a further £23,872 debt to the B&CC. Despite cutting back of virtually all expenses, the Secretaries, Matheson and Co. for the British Group and the Banque de l'Indo-Chine for the French, were still incurring unrequited expenses. Against this the company was owed £873,967 on account of advances made under a 1913 agreement for the Pukow-Sinyang Railway.

In summary, the only purpose which the company had served for some 25 years was the continued reminding of the Chinese – with some temporary effect in the mid-1930s – that the Pu-Siang Railway advance was not repaid and that debt servicing had stopped on the public loans issued to finance the Tientsin-Pukow Railway.

That the CCR was not immediately wound-up in 1946 was in part due to the need to have the Chinese Government agree that their obligations to the CCR could be transferred to the B&CC; after 1949 this was seen to be irrelevant. In May 1953 shareholders were informed that the directors had completed an agreement between the CCR, the Hongkong Bank, and the B&CC by which (i) the company assigned to the B&CC the benefit of its claims against the Chinese Government and (ii) the Hongkong Bank released the CCR from any obligations relative to the overdraft and accumulated interest (by then £335,704), accepting instead an undertaking by the B&CC to hold upon trust any monies it might receive in respect of the claim against the Chinese Government for payment of the present outstanding debts of the CCR and the distribution of any surplus to the shareholders of the CCR.[32]

The Chinese Central Railways Company was dissolved in 1954.

The British and Chinese Corporation
Whatever arguments might have been put forward in 1945/46 for a continuation of the CCR, they could be countered by suggesting that under any likely circumstances the interests of shareholders could be better met by a single organization, the B&CC. The future course to be taken by the B&CC, however, depended on one's assessment of the company's future in China. This in turn depended in part on the company's then position.

The B&CC remained a public company for which Jardine, Matheson and Co. and the Hongkong Bank were joint agents, with each company having the right to nominate a director; Matheson and Co. were Secretaries. The major shareholders were, as always, the two agents, their shares being held in the names of the Bank's London Manager and by a designated partner of Jardine, Matheson. From his retirement from the Bank's London Committee in 1933 until his resignation from the board of the B&CC in 1944 Sir Charles Addis had been an additional 'Hongkong Bank director', although elected in the normal way. The vacancy was taken by Sir Edward Reid of Baring's, who was a member of the Hongkong Bank's London Committee. Arthur Morse and his successors and William J. Keswick (succeeding B.D.F. Beith) and his successors represented the agents; other directors in the immediate post-war period were Sir John Pratt and John D. Drummond, Viscount Strathallan.

The subscribed capital of the B&CC was £250,000 in 25,000 shares of £10 of which £5 was paid up. In 1946 a major capital restructuring was agreed: (i) £50,000 of the £100,000 in general reserve was capitalized to pay £2 per share so that £7 per share was now paid up, (ii) the £10 shares were split to make ten £1 shares with 14s:0d paid-up, (iii) there was a call for 6s:0d per share so that the company's capital was now fully paid up, and (iv) the 250,000 shares were converted into stock.[33]

These changes were designed to place the company in as strong a financial position as possible in anticipation that some progress could be made in China.

The B&CC were trustees for the bondholders of the Canton-Kowloon Railway, the Shanghai-Nanking Railway, and the Shanghai-Hangchow-Ningpo Railway (this last jointly with the China Development Finance Corporation) for which they were to receive a total of £5,750 per annum, although the last year the full amount had been paid was 1937 – nothing had been received since 1941. The B&CC were agents for the Peking-Mukden Railway at the unpaid fee of £600 p.a. The company had other rights in railways, including the nomination of engineers and members of the board, mortgages on behalf of the bondholders, and other politically impractical advantages. Through the CCR there were rights in the Tientsin-Pukow line and in miscellaneous advances.

Since its founding in 1898 the B&CC had been directly involved in the issue of China loans totalling £22.2 million of which in 1946 £17.2 million remained outstanding. Although interest had been written off in settlements made between 1935 and 1937, interest payments in arrears again had reached the high figure of £6.5 million. The problems involved in attempting a recovery of these amounts are considered in the following section. Suffice it to say at this point that the non-payment obviously affected the value of the company's assets – and their income.

The B&CC's own holdings of Chinese loans totalled £280,000, obtained at a cost of £235,000, written down to £61,000, but with a market value of £144,000. The company's income came from 'miscellaneous investments' with a market value of £110,000 yielding an income of £3,220 against an annual expenditure of £8,930.

This situation could not continue. All possible cuts in expenditures had been made and, with the end of all hope of payment from China, the Hongkong Bank in 1951 urged on Jardine's and the B&CC a scheme which would repay all capital to 'outside' shareholders, leaving the company in the hands of the founding agents with the sole purposes of paying pensions to retired employees and acting as trustees for the bondholders.

The capital required to generate the interest income needed to meet the reduced duties of the company was estimated at £75,000 and the directors in 1951 voted, subject to Court confirmation, to write down the capital of the company from £250,000 to £75,000 by paying back to shareholders 14s per £1 of stock held. At this point the issued stock would stand in units of 6s, which Matheson and Co., on behalf of themselves, Jardine, Matheson and Co., and the Hongkong Bank would acquire at 6s per unit. The total return to outside shareholders would be 20s in the pound. The offer was accepted and the Courts approved.[e]

These unusual manoeuvres were explained to shareholders as reflecting a divergence of interests between the 'outside' shareholders and the founding companies, Jardine's and the Hongkong Bank.

The Joint agents, situated as they are in the Far East, feel a special obligation to maintain the functions for the Corporation as Trustee for the Bondholders of the Chinese Railway Loans. Further, they consider that withdrawal or liquidation, even if practicable, might be prejudicial not only to their own interests but to British banking and commercial interests in the Far East in general. They thus have reasons for desiring the continuance of the Corporation which are not necessarily shared by other individual Stockholders.[35]

In fact, as Sir William Keswick stated in a letter to (Sir) John Keswick in Hong Kong, it had been the Hongkong Bank which had pressed for this particular settlement – 'The Bank, not J.M. & Co, wanted to keep face with their colleagues, the London Banks, by repaying the full par value.'[36] Furthermore, there were China loans, other than those through the B&CC and CCR, with which the Hongkong Bank was concerned. And, he was careful to point out, it was the Bank's function as the Corporation's financial agent to be responsible for matters relating to the trusteeship.

Even the developments in a dormant company need review, and on the eve of G.O.W. Stewart's retirement as the Hongkong Bank's London Manager in 1968, and thus also as director of the B&CC, the situation was reassessed. The company's paid-up capital was £75,000, realizable assets £38,000 with an income of £900 to meet requirements estimated at £400. The company's one pensioner was 88 years of age and it was even considered possible to increase

---

[e] Following acceptance by the outside shareholders, the capital was reinstated at £250,000 by the issue of 175,000 £1 shares; the £75,000 stock was converted into 75,000 shares of £1 each fully paid.[34]

her pension by £50 p.a. 'the receipt of which might make a great difference to an old lady in the autumn of her days'. The pension could be taken over by Jardine's and the Hongkong Bank, but the problem of the trusteeship remained; the Bank did not wish to take on the responsibility and the only other suggested candidate, the Council of Foreign Bondholders, appeared barred for legal reasons.[37]

Thus the impasse, which continues to affect China's ability to borrow on the London market, was reconfirmed, a living if dormant reminder of the 'Age of Imperialism' when the West built China's railways and was left with accounts unpaid and Chinese obligations unfulfilled.

The British and Chinese Corporation, which in 1898 was to be the vehicle of Britain's investment in China's development, had thus become dormant. In 1982 it would become a private company.

Debt recovery negotiations

The general position

China's foreign debt position in 1946 was intolerable and there was no possibility that an early resumption to debt servicing of loans in which the Hongkong Bank participated could be undertaken. Nevertheless the Bank made strong direct and indirect representations. To state the matter briefly, the Bank was successful in obtaining recognition of China's liability to the Bank and to other bondholders, but the Bank was totally unsuccessful in obtaining any payment of these recognized obligations.

In the period from the establishment of the National Government in Nanking to the renewed Japanese aggression in mid-1937 developments may be summarized by stating that outstanding debts had been renegotiated and new debts contracted on the security of the Boxer Indemnity payments through a Board of Trustees. By 1939 however all international debt servicing had ceased pending the end of the Pacific War.

Up to 1937 the total of foreign loans secured by the customs, salt, and other government revenues amounted to only £59 million, US$30.4 million, and Yen 3.3 million. However, in the following ten years, that is during the non-servicing of existing debt, the Chinese Government contracted further debts totalling £58 million sterling and US$541 million – totals which understate the situation as they omit certain Government credits. They had this, however, in common – they were for non-productive purposes.

When China began once again to service her debts, she focused on these later Government loans. Thus loan service in 1948 was recorded as US$50.8 million compared to US$38 million in 1936, but the former made no provision for any Hongkong Bank loan.[38] Despite, therefore, the repayment burden borne by China, neither the Hongkong Bank nor the bondholders of earlier loans benefited.

The Hongkong Bank's involvement in China's foreign debt obligations was in several categories. First, there were the old pre-1914 loans for railways, indemnities, and the Reorganization Loan of 1913, secondly, the loans secured through the Board of Trustees for the Boxer Indemnity payments, and, thirdly, the loans to the Shanghai Municipal Council, the governing body of the Shanghai International Settlement. The first were a matter of wider concern than the Hongkong Bank's; the British Council of Foreign Bondholders, whose China Committee was serviced by the Hongkong Bank's London Office at 9 Gracechurch Street, was, however, ineffective. The other two categories had been affected by the 1943 treaty which, in addition to abrogating extrality, had ended any further payments on account of the Boxer Indemnity and had renounced all British rights relative to the International Settlement of Shanghai.

Although each of these categories required a different approach and involved different legal arguments, the fate of all representations was identical – positive recognition of the debt and non-repayment. Whether the Board of Boxer Indemnity Trustees were owed indemnity payments covering the period 1939 to 1943 or not, whether the British Government had any residual responsibility with respect to Shanghai or not, all the China loans in which the Bank was involved had at least a second line of security. Arthur Morse apparently supposed – and this would appear reasonable – that if, for example, the Boxer Indemnity Board of Trustees could be shown to still be in existence and have large balances at their disposal for the purposes of debt servicing, the Chinese Government would be more inclined to see that at least some payment was made from these earmarked funds; debts on the general revenue, on the other hand, had to compete with priority demands, including the servicing of newly contracted debts to friendly Governments.

The Nationalist Government had inherited foreign debt in the late 1920s and had eventually recommenced an adjusted service of them. On August 13, 1947, at perhaps one of the brighter economic periods in the post-war Nationalist years, the Premier, Chang Chun, declared: 'China pledges her honourable intention to repay those external loans the service of which was suspended in the course of the Japanese war. In no way does the conclusion of new loans in recent years prejudice the security of these pre-war loans or vitiate the rights of holders of such bonds.'[39] This declaration, together with relevant information on the loans and the legal background, the Hongkong Bank brought before the Foreign Office in a memorandum which accompanied the covering letter of

Muriel dated September 3, 1947.[40] Morse had every reason to suppose that, provided British representation were sufficiently forceful, the Nanking Government would act consistent with this declared policy, even as they had in the mid-1930s. From this it followed that if Nanking did not pay, it must be because British representation was inadequate, and Morse wrote strong letters to the Foreign Office, replete with suggestions which were either politically impractical or legally impossible.

Loans under the Boxer Indemnity Board of Trustees
The loans in which the Boxer Indemnity Board of Trustees were involved included the £450,000 Nanking-Kiangsi Railway Materials Loan of 1936 on which interest to the amount of £703,000 had accrued by mid-1947, the Chuchow Repair Shop Loan of 1937 for £150,000 (of which only a part was advanced) on which interest of £20,000 had accrued. These were relatively small loans but with interest that totalled over £1.3 million; furthermore, they were owed directly to the Bank and Jardine, Matheson and Co. Given the Bank's circumstances in 1947, the sum involved was of considerable marginal importance to its financial position.

The £1.5 million 6% Sterling Indemnity Loan of 1934 was promulgated in July 1934 over the signatures of the contracting banks, including the Hongkong Bank, with the provision that, despite the specific security of the indemnity payments made to the Board of Trustees, it remained a charge on the Customs revenue with priority dating from the Protocol of September 7, 1901.

On the specific remedy, servicing of the debt by funds from the Board of Trustees, much depended on whether the indemnity payments which should have been made between 1939 and 1943 were still payable. The Hongkong Bank, as noted above, hoped this was the case. In June 1947 Cassels in Shanghai learned from Han Lih-wu, the Board's chairman, that the Chinese Foreign Ministry's view was that no such funds were payable. Article 3 of the 1943 Treaty contained the provision that 'the rights accorded to HM Government in the United Kingdom under that Protocol and under the Agreements supplementary thereto shall cease'; the latter phrase was said to include the 1930 Agreements relative to the funding of the Board of Trustees.[41]

The Foreign Office questioned the Chinese interpretation, but, as G.V. Kitson wrote to Muriel,

It seems to us better as a matter of tactics to press the Chinese Government generally to service the loans than to embark with them on what may be a fruitless controversy on the interpretation of the relevant article of the 1943 treaty, and we are instructing our Ambassador in Nanking accordingly. He is, however, being authorized to make the point orally to the Chinese Government at his discretion.[42]

All this had become part of a general attempt by the Foreign Office to restore specific relationships the existence or funding of which had been disrupted by the comprehensively but hastily drafted clauses of the 1943 Sino-British Treaty. In his November 1947 response to Muriel, Kitson of the Foreign Office outlined the steps being taken not only with regard to loans but also relative to the Sino-British Educational and Cultural Endowment Fund, in which the Bank was involved and which was in disarray. The British chargé d'affaires in Nanking had written personally to T.V. Soong calling his attention to various Government railway agreements and calling for the restoration of those Loan Service Committees which, in the early 1930s, had appeared the basis for international cooperation with China without the politically objectionable implications which the Chinese chose to find in the foreign-conceived China Consortium.[43]

Loans to the Shanghai Municipal Council
In the Shanghai years of the Japanese Incident, 1937–1941, the finances of the Shanghai Municipal Council had become increasingly precarious, and the Hongkong Bank had advanced, in various forms, sums totalling £445,550 on which interest to the amount of £76,221 had accrued, and US$17,857 plus interest of US$3,125.

In December 1946 the Hongkong Bank submitted, on the advice of the British Consul-General in Shanghai, the relevant claims to the Mayor of Shanghai as chairman of the Liquidation Commission. A sub-committee admitted the validity of the claims, with two minor exceptions, in April 1947; this was confirmed by the whole Commission in November 1947; indeed, like other Bank claims they never became an issue of contention *per se*, and in June 1948 the Chinese Ambassador in London confirmed to the Secretary of State that the Chinese Government were 'anxious to arrive at an early settlement of the points at issue in Shanghai [including presumably the pensions of former Council employees] and that, in particular, your Bank's claim would be settled "at the earliest date"'.[44]

Subsequently the British Embassy in Nanking was advised orally that 'owing to the heavy drain of payments on China's foreign currency holdings, it would be proposed to make payment in three instalments at reasonable intervals'.[45]

But the Chinese did not pay, Shanghai fell, and the Hongkong Bank in September 1949 turned once again to the British Government for redress, claiming that, in the particular case of Shanghai Municipal Council indebtedness, the British Government was itself responsible for repayment if, as now seemed likely, the Chinese Government failed to meet the obligations. This was a last desperate measure. The Bank knew that the Nationalist regime still had foreign currency resources; if the alternative were seen to be British Government repayment, perhaps the Foreign Office might be persuaded to apply the utmost pressure to obtain a last minute redress for the Bank.

Either that or, as it happened, the Foreign Office would focus its efforts on denying British official responsibility.

The Bank's argument was historically and constitutionally unsound; it assumed that the British Government's involvement as one of the Powers whose representatives signed the agreements bringing the International Settlement into effect made the Municipal Council a body whose authority derived from the British Government. The Bank further claimed that, by signing the 1943 Treaty, Britain had 'dissolved' the Municipal Council and, although by Treaty the continuity was provided by China, Britain by its acts remained responsible.

The Bank also urged that this link between the British Government and the Shanghai Municipal Council had led the Bank to associate the latter with British interests, broadly defined, and had accordingly lent funds to the Council at $3\frac{1}{2}\%$, an obviously advantageous rate of interest.

It may be urged that, had it not been for the close historical and traditional British interest in the establishment of the Shanghai Municipal Council and the fact that Great Britain was the treaty power principally involved and interested in its constitution and in the enforcement of claims against the Council through the Court of Consuls, it is hardly likely that the special loan at a low rate of interest of $3\frac{1}{2}\%$ would have been granted.[46]

To be on the safe side, the Hongkong Bank suggested that if Britain had no legal responsibility there was a moral one.[47]

And so, without any expectation of success, but spurred by the 'moral' implications, the British Embassy in Canton, where the National Government was then functioning, intervened once again. 'We have now heard that this *démarche* has taken place, and that the Acting Minister for Foreign Affairs frankly admitted the obligation of the Chinese Government. Unfortunately, he also made it plain that payment would not be an easy matter.'[48]

The Foreign Office then turned its attention to the Hongkong Bank's charges that the problems arose from the Treaty of 1943 and that the British Government had not taken all the steps possible to protect British interests from the adverse effects of that treaty. Further provoked by a series of letters from Arthur Morse to S.A. Gray, his new London Manager, which the latter on instructions passed to the Foreign Office, and a strong letter from Morse direct to the Foreign Office in December 1950 – signed unusually in his capacity as Chairman of the Board of Directors – the Foreign Office summed up the charges and its defence in a minute dated January 1951.

1. The Shanghai Municipal Council [SMC] was an international body not under the jurisdiction of His Majesty's Government, [which] therefore cannot be responsible for the Council's actions or obligations and liabilities;
2. Equally H.M. Government could not [as the Bank charged] 'dissolve the International Settlements' although [the Government] could and did renounce their own special rights in it.
3. [The Bank had noted that H.M. Government had failed to bring the case before the International Court of Justice], but there was no point of international law to answer. The Chinese authorities admitted the Bank's claim but evaded payment.
4. H.M. Government did not [as the Bank claimed] 'effect the transfer' of the SMC's assets to the Chinese authorities. What the Government had in fact agreed to do in the Treaty [Art. 4 ii] was to 'cooperate with the Government of the Republic of China for the reaching of any necessary agreements with the other governments concerned for the transfer to China of the administration and control of the international settlements at Shanghai and Amoy, including the official assets and the official obligations of those settlements, it being mutually understood that the Government of the Republic of China... will make provision for the assumption and discharge of the official obligations and liabilities of those settlements. In practice the Chinese moved in after the Japanese surrender and simply presented us with a *fait accompli*.[49]

Morse's final letter was regarded as petulant and accordingly all of the above was summed up by informing the Bank that the situation was the result of an Act of State for which the Secretary of State was answerable only to Parliament and that, furthermore, all had been done which could be done.[50]

What particularly frustrated Morse was the fact that the assets and revenues of the SMC had been mortgaged to the Hongkong Bank. This put the Bank in the forefront of claimants; they came close to success – and failed. But Morse had one more suggestion.

In view of the fact that the British Government was considering recognition of the new Government of China, the London assets of the Central Bank of China would be transferred to the new Government and at that time the British authorities could withhold sufficient to meet China's recognized obligations to the Hongkong Bank.

That suggestion, for which there was no legal authority, was immediately turned down. The Central Bank's assets would at no time pass through the possession of H.M. Government; they would pass directly from the control of one Chinese Government to its successor.[51] The Hongkong Bank had throughout been poorly advised. Its legal adviser, J.R. Jones, who had been a secretary to the SMC at one point and who was now working in conjunction with the enthusiastic and forceful Arthur Morse, would seem to have allowed his sentiments to carry the discussion too far.

Railway loans, negotiations relative to public issues

The British Embassy office in Shanghai estimated that of the £55 million of principal outstanding on all pre-war sterling loans (excluding the Austrian Skoda loans) some £42 million related to loans 'in the issue of which the Hongkong Bank participated'.

As with other pre-war loans, servicing had ceased by 1939 and the first task was to come to an agreement as to the terms on which such servicing would recommence. But who should negotiate with whom? The British and Chinese Corporation, in which the Hongkong Bank was one of the two major shareholders – Jardine, Matheson and Co. was the other – saw as the first step the reestablishment of the Loan Service Committees, and it seemed for a time in late 1946 that, due to the intervention of the Minister of Communications, such committees would be approved for the Shanghai-Hangchow-Ningpo Railway Loan and subsequently for the Canton-Kowloon and the Tientsin-Pukow loans.

This was seen as the first step in renegotiating renewed servicing. However, by the end of 1947 it was apparent that this approach had broken down; approvals were followed by delays and reconsideration in the context of the overall railway problem.

At another level the Chinese Bondholders Committee, working through Cassels, the Hongkong Bank's political adviser, were also pressing for the reestablishment of the Loan Committees. This approach seemed logical because the loans outstanding had been made to specific railway administrations for specific purposes and secured in the first instance on the revenues. The problem, however, had become national and, as the director of the Loans Department of the Ministry of Finance warned Cassels, nothing would in fact be gained by pressing for the restoration of the committees.

The proceeds of railway loans issued before the Japanese War had made possible the construction of the designated lines. But years of civil disturbance and abuse by the military, followed by the Pacific War, had resulted in a new situation. The railways, far from being able to generate revenue to service old debts, needed refinancing. Reestablishment of the Loan Committees would have done no more than stress this obvious fact. Repayment could only come from the general revenues of the Republic, drawing on the limited foreign exchange reserves in a time of civil war. The bondholders' case was hopeless.

According to Embassy sources, Jones, as the Bank's legal adviser, expressed the view that it was the Bank's duty to foreclose and to appoint British executive personnel. The official reaction was clearly expressed. 'Such a suggestion seems to me to be utterly impracticable, though if it could be convincingly argued that the Corporation have a legal right to do so, perhaps this might be used as a bargaining counter.'[52]

A more practical approach was attempted by Cassels through China's Inspector-General of Customs, L.K. Little. In the case of the 6% Sterling Indemnity Loan of 1934, for example, a clause in the loan agreement had stated that 'the Inspector-General of Customs has received from the Government irrevocable instructions to continue the requisite indemnity payments without interruption during the period of this loan.'[53]

Cassels was writing as 'representative of The Hongkong and Shanghai Banking Corporation, which took the lead in floating most of the Chinese Government Loans issued in London and also assisted in floating in Shanghai the 6% Indemnity Loan of 1934'. The words 'irrevocable' and 'without interruption' were not, however, magic charms; they could not change China's foreign exchange position. At best they might have provided an excuse for the servicing of one loan while discussions continued on the others, but this tactic could be, and in fact was, being attempted *ad hoc* on various of China's debts. In the end such representations could only end in confusion and recrimination.

This piecemeal, loan-by-loan approach was undertaken concurrently with direct representations to the Chinese Government by Lord Bessborough of the Chinese Bondholders Committee. The British Foreign Office had not been directly involved in the negotiations either of Lord Bessborough or of the British and Chinese Corporation. However, there had been correspondence between Muriel, the Hongkong Bank's London Manager, and the Foreign Office on the question of Foreign Office support for the negotiations. The problem was that such support could achieve very little.

...the foreign exchange position of China has seriously deteriorated during the past twelve months and we know that she is at present quite incapable of making any real attempt at debt settlement. It is also true that we have few inducements to offer (now that sterling convertibility is no more than a dream of the rather distant future). It may well be, therefore, that the view taken is that it would be idle, and would serve no useful purpose, to make any representations at this stage.[54]

Discussions continued; new stratagems were formulated. But as China was not in a position to pay, the momentary negotiating triumphs, the points temporarily gained, the possibly sincere declarations of honourable intent, while not without a certain curiosity value, form no substantial part of the history of the Hongkong Bank.

It is sufficient to note that the Hongkong Bank, through its political adviser, its representation on the boards of the British and Chinese Corporation and the Chinese Central Railways, through its advisory role to the Chinese Bondholders Committee, and through its usual high level contacts with the Bank of England, the Treasury, and the Foreign Office, as well as the informal assistance of members of its London Consultative Committee, went through all the possible steps to secure redress.

The Bank was still pressing with suggestions both realistic and fantastic when the Peoples Liberation Army moved through Shanghai and south to Canton.

Postscript

The Bank, as the financial agent of its subsidiary B&CC, could not abandon the quest for reimbursement should an opportunity arise. As Chief Manager, Michael Turner was realistic, but in 1956, with rumours that the Chinese were seeking a reopening of the Canton-Kowloon Railway to through traffic, some supposed the time had come.[f] The railway had been financed in 1907 by a £1.5 million loan of which £0.85 million of the capital and the related interest remained unpaid. Turner was pressed 'by London', despite his own misgivings, to propose that the freight charges and fares paid in Kowloon could be deposited with the Hongkong Bank for eventual payment to bondholders.[55] But the Chinese did not press for the through service.

In 1960 Turner instructed his London Manager, S.W.P. Perry-Aldworth, to determine the prices then quoted for China bonds.[56] By the end of the year the Hongkong Bank had either sold or written off the balance of its holdings.

The impact on the Hongkong Bank

For a bank which had throughout its history proclaimed itself a 'China bank' the visible impact of the adverse events in post-war China was surprisingly minimal. This fact set the tone for the Hongkong Bank's approach to the new Government; the past was virtually written off, now the Bank stood ready to help or not. If the latter, there was a final settlement to make and the Bank would have withdrawn with minimum immediate consequences from China. As it happened, nothing would be quite so simple, nor, on the other hand, quite so final. The Bank would once again, in China's time, be available for a financial and developmental role.

The failure of the Bank's China investments to cause a significant impact was due to several factors, all of historical interest.

In the first place the Hongkong Bank's financial exposure in any one territory was limited by (i) the capital assigned the branch and (ii) the funds available locally to the Manager. If the former were endangered, Head Office could take steps to write the amount down in the corporation's accounts so that, at the time of eventual catastrophe, there was no loss to record. Concern for the economic future of China was not a matter realized for the first time in 1947

---

[f] Local passenger 'British sector' trains ran from Kowloon to Lowu, and passengers for China walked across the frontier railway bridge. It was a dramatic, if somewhat inconvenient, entry for those permitted inside the Middle Kingdom.

or 1948; the Hongkong Bank's caution in action as opposed to its publicly expressed hopes can be dated to the death of Yuan Shih-k'ai in 1916. This caution was relaxed in the mid-1930s, but reimposed during the Pacific War. The Board's determination to maintain the Bank's operations in Shanghai and its prestige in China despite the danger of currency collapse after 1937 was a declaration of the Bank's faith in the ultimate development of China, but the counterpart was the continued writing down of its Chinese assets and the setting aside of special contingency accounts in London against a general loss in Shanghai.

Secondly, the major loans which were issued through the participation of the Hongkong Bank were quoted in the market and the Bank's traditional conservative policy required it to write down any holdings of such bonds to market – and, usually, not write them up again when the market became more favourable. Thus the failure to obtain Chinese agreement to post-war debt servicing made little impact on the Bank's current balance sheet.

Nor, as a third point, had the Bank had an opportunity to get reinvolved in China's post-war economy. Unlike the mid-1930s there had been no opportunity for a period of optimism and for the contracting of fresh obligations, either public or direct. Once again the Bank's losses were minimized, as in the banking disasters of 1866, by not being active at the time of crisis.

These points are similar to those raised in answer to the question as to why the Bank did not suffer greater financial losses during the Pacific War. Again it was true, for example, that the value of the Bank's real estate outside China was greater than the published Premises Account; the loss of premises in China would have no impact on the accounts.

In assessing the post-war impact of events in China on the Bank, however, the apparent ease with which the Bank absorbed the losses should not lead to the conclusion that there was, in fact, no loss. To have prepared for unspecified contingencies and thus prevent disaster is sound policy, but this does not deny the fact that there was an opportunity cost involved in holding the funds and a loss of income once they were expended for the purposes for which they had been set aside. Premises are usually productive and their existence at zero valuation raises the rate of return on the Bank's stated capital; their loss or change to non-productive uses lowers that rate of return. The actual losses, to the extent that they are theoretically calculable in money terms, cannot be determined from the figures available in the Bank's principal accounts – or could be estimated roughly only by a team of qualified auditors. But for a general history of the Bank it is sufficient, perhaps, to note that they were considerable but covered. There were however other types of loss which must be stated.

As one retiree expressed it, the Bank had trouble finding its niche after the withdrawal from China. The wartime planning had been for a return to the East, for the reconstruction of Hong Kong as an entrepôt; behind this was the assumption that the Bank would play a role in post-war China. Despite the losses the Bank sustained as a commercial bank in China in 1946 and 1948, despite the write-off to contingencies of a proportion of the Bank's overall gross operating profits throughout the period under consideration, the Bank's resources were growing beyond immediate opportunity of profitable employment in the East. Japan was not yet open, Hong Kong was still basically recovering as an entrepôt, even the growth of regional trade in the post-war boom had its limits. The fact is that the Bank was without focus.

And one might argue, despite all the developments between 1950 and 1980, despite the fact that the Bank found its niche in perhaps the most unexpected place – Hong Kong itself – it was still a China bank. In the end it never left, and, when China was ready, the Bank was invited back to play a role consistent with China's requirements as defined by China's Government.

Before considering these matters in later chapters of the history, there are details relative to the Bank's position in China in 1948–1950 to record. The Bank's losses in any area, it was stated, depended on two factors, the local capital assigned and the local funds obtained. If this were to remain true it was important that the Bank limit the funds it remitted into China to meet 'temporary' requirements. Furthermore, demands by the Government for minimum capital assignments eliminated one of the traditional discretionary roles of the Board in Hong Kong. Inflation accompanied by arbitrary official rates, demands by local unions for improved wage and other payments, the attempt to fund employees' pension schemes, and the loss of value of pre-war pension funds were among the factors leading to demands that the Bank remit funds to its Shanghai branch. These were current matters which were of continuing concern during this period and the years which followed.

Finally, and perhaps of the greatest immediate importance, was the loss of income. Pre-war, Shanghai and Hong Kong competed with each other for the status of 'most profitable' branch. In 1937, for example, Shanghai contributed one-third of the year's working profits of $13 million; in 1950 Shanghai's losses were $391,000 against gross working profits of $32.8 million. Head Office plus Hong Kong office alone contributed $16.8 million; income from the Bank's contingency and reserve accounts was more than sufficient to make up for the loss of Shanghai earnings. Nevertheless, they might have been there. The Bank was not in business to buy and keep trustee-type securities in London.

Morse might be frustrated but the Bank was never in danger. In part Morse could ascribe the China losses to 'Londonitis' on a terrible scale; the Foreign

Office had failed the Bank. Meanwhile, as Morse well knew, the main story was developing right around him. This was fortunate for Morse had always had faith in Hong Kong.

The events in the East are supposed to have had their effect on potential recruits to the Bank. The possibility of a career in the East, or particularly in Hong Kong, seemed remote to those unfamiliar with the area. The attitude of those who knew the East and the Bank was however different. Asked whether the loss of China as a banking base concerned him at the time, J.F. Marshall responded typically.

> I suppose it became obvious that we were going to lose the China theatre completely, but China had obviously got to trade somewhere, so it turned out that more and more trade was funnelled through Hong Kong.
>
> [You mean,] what the hell were we going to do if the Bank folded up under us? No, we always had confidence in the Bank. We didn't think that way, I don't think. At least I didn't.
>
> Is our career going to come to an end? Is the whole thing crumbling beneath us? Never for a moment, no.[57]

Share prices, which fell in London from £121 in 1947 to £76 in 1950, suggest that, in addition to the general average fall of 13% in the London share market, some Hongkong Bank shareholders had additional misgivings, but these proved temporary – and, as it turned out, ill-conceived.

Part II

THE CRITICAL YEARS, 1946–1961

I never granted a large loan without considering the effect on the Colony.
R. G. L. Oliphant, Manager, 1958–1964

Negotiations regarding the winding up of our affairs in China have made considerable progress during [1955]... This settlement has not been made without cost to the Bank but under the circumstances no other course was open to us.
Chairman's speech, Annual Meeting, March 1956

Table II.1 *The Hongkong Bank Group*
List of principal companies, 1961

	Date of acquisition or founding	Paid-up capital (millions)
A. SUBSIDIARY COMPANIES[a]		
Banking companies		
The Hongkong and Shanghai Banking Corporation of California, Inc.	1955[b]	US$2.0
Mercantile Bank Limited	1959	£2.94
The British Bank of the Middle East	1960	£2.0
Wayfoong Finance Limited	1960	$5.0
The British Bank of the Middle East (Morocco) S.A.	1961	—
[British and Chinese Corporation[e]	1898	dormant]
Executor and trustee companies		
Hong Kong & Shanghai Bank, Hong Kong (Trustee) Limited		
Hongkong & Shanghai Bank (Malaya) Trustee Limited [Singapore]		
Hongkong & Shanghai Bank (Trustee) Limited [London]		
Mercantile Bank (Executor & Trustee Company) Limited [London]		
Mercantile Bank (Agency) Private Limited [Calcutta]		
Mercantile Bank (Trustees) Limited [Penang]		
Nominee companies in Hong Kong, Britain, the Federation of Malaya and Singapore		
B. ASSOCIATED COMPANIES		1961 investment (millions)
The Far Eastern Economic Review, Ltd	1946	
The South China Morning Post, Ltd	1946	
Bowmaker (C.A.) (Private) Ltd	1956	$1.6[d]
Trust Corporation of the Bahamas	1959	
The Bank of Iran and the Middle East	1960	£0.58
Exporters' Refinance Corporation, Ltd	1961	£1.0[c]

Names in [ ] are not part of the legal name of the company. The names are listed as given in the Annual Reports; the variations of 'Hong Kong' for example are deliberate.

[a] Defined as companies whose accounts were consolidated in the published Group Accounts.
[b] Date of establishment.
[c] Authorized capital.
[d] South Rhodesian £100,000 = Sterling £100,218.13.5 = $1,603,498.73.
[e] The B&CC had taken over the Chinese Central Railways (see Chapter 4).

During the fifteen years from 1946 through 1961 under the chief managerships of Sir Arthur Morse and Sir Michael Turner, the Hongkong Bank took the first steps in its post-war path to multinational status. In a world of takeovers and mergers, or, more positively, of rationalization of the British overseas banking system, the Hongkong Bank had the reputation and the size to be a principal rather than a client in that process. The Bank became a holding company operating three other banks and one finance company as direct subsidiaries (see Table II.1). This set a pattern for what would soon become known, particularly in the 1960s and 1970s, as the 'Hongkong Bank Group' – today 'HongkongBank group', with the stress on the 'signature' Hongkong Bank, is preferred. 'Group' was actually a term designed to cover both the subsidiaries and the Bank qua operating bank; it described a pattern of development which permitted further acquisitions until, at the time of the offer to Marine Midland Banks in 1978, the Group was composed of 350 companies with varied activities and broad geographical distribution.

But first the Bank had problems to solve in its own region – the withdrawal from China, participation in regional development plans, the finance of Hong Kong's industrialization, adapting to American banking competition in its traditional areas, adjusting to the early requirements of newly independent states.

In this process the Hongkong Bank seemed hardly to change. Certainly the statistics, even where showing improvement, do not appear as heralds of dramatic growth. The Bank's Foreign (formerly Eastern) staff numbered no more than in the 1920s, the London Office junior system and the Peak Mess survived. The Bank's share of the market declined in such key countries as Thailand and the Philippines, total assets doubled between 1946 and 1951, then moved back and held steady until 1959. The sources of the Bank's strength and the reasons for its eventual pull-through to world financial leadership are not immediately apparent in its published balance sheets nor in other statistics. The task of the historian is made more difficult.

To fall back on a cliché, 'familiarity with the region', or with a catch-all explanation, 'head office in Hong Kong', may seem unsatisfactory, yet underlying more detailed analysis is the story of a bank which is in the region, whose executive staff come out from London to serve in the East, and whose local staff, despite post-war competition from local banking institutions, remained an essential link with the market. More prosaically, the policy of augmenting inner reserves, of maintaining a highly liquid position in a world of political and economic uncertainty, positioned the Bank to take advantage of situations created by the need for a minimal efficient size of operations. When the Mercantile Bank of India and the British Bank of the Middle East were perceived to be the potential target of takeover bids, they turned to the Hongkong

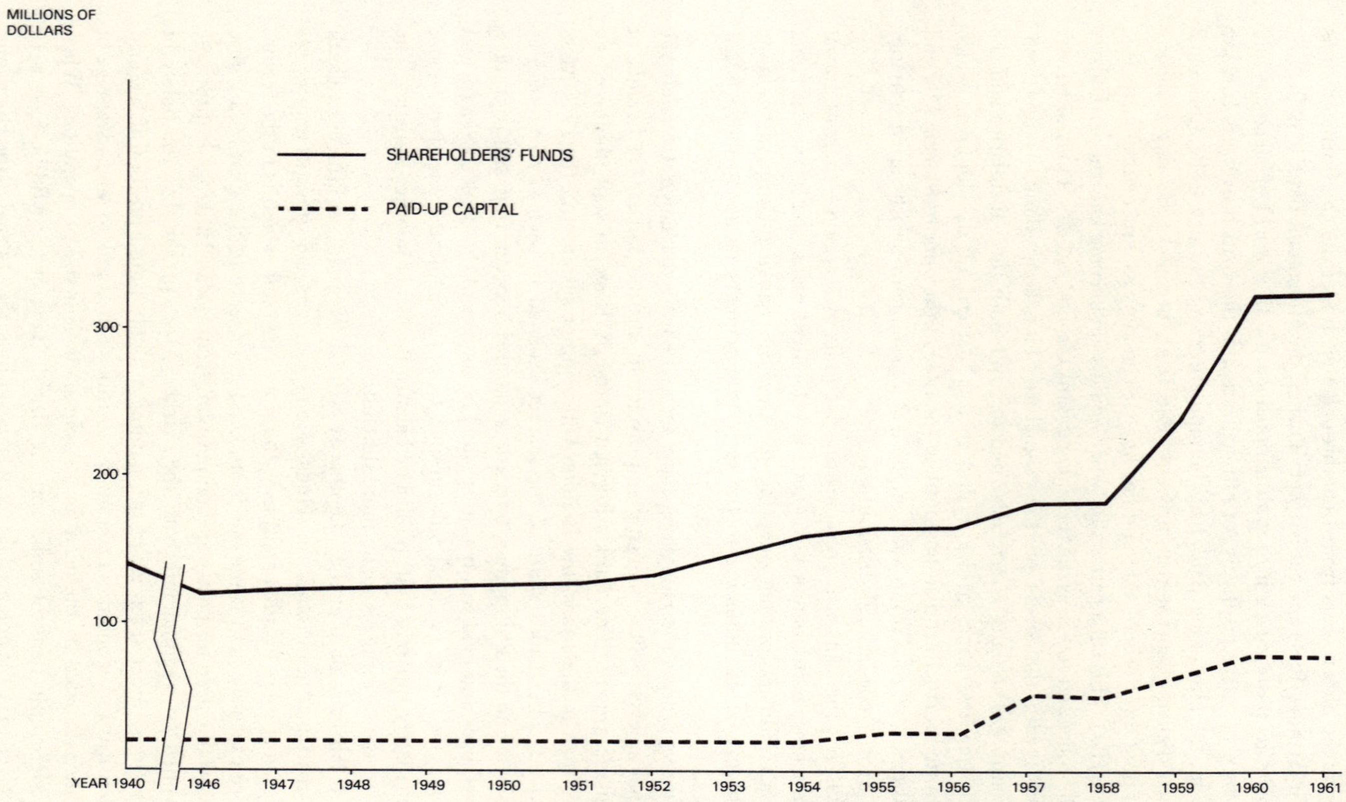

Figure 11.1 The Hongkong and Shanghai Banking Corporation Shareholders' funds and paid-up capital in dollars, 1946–1961.

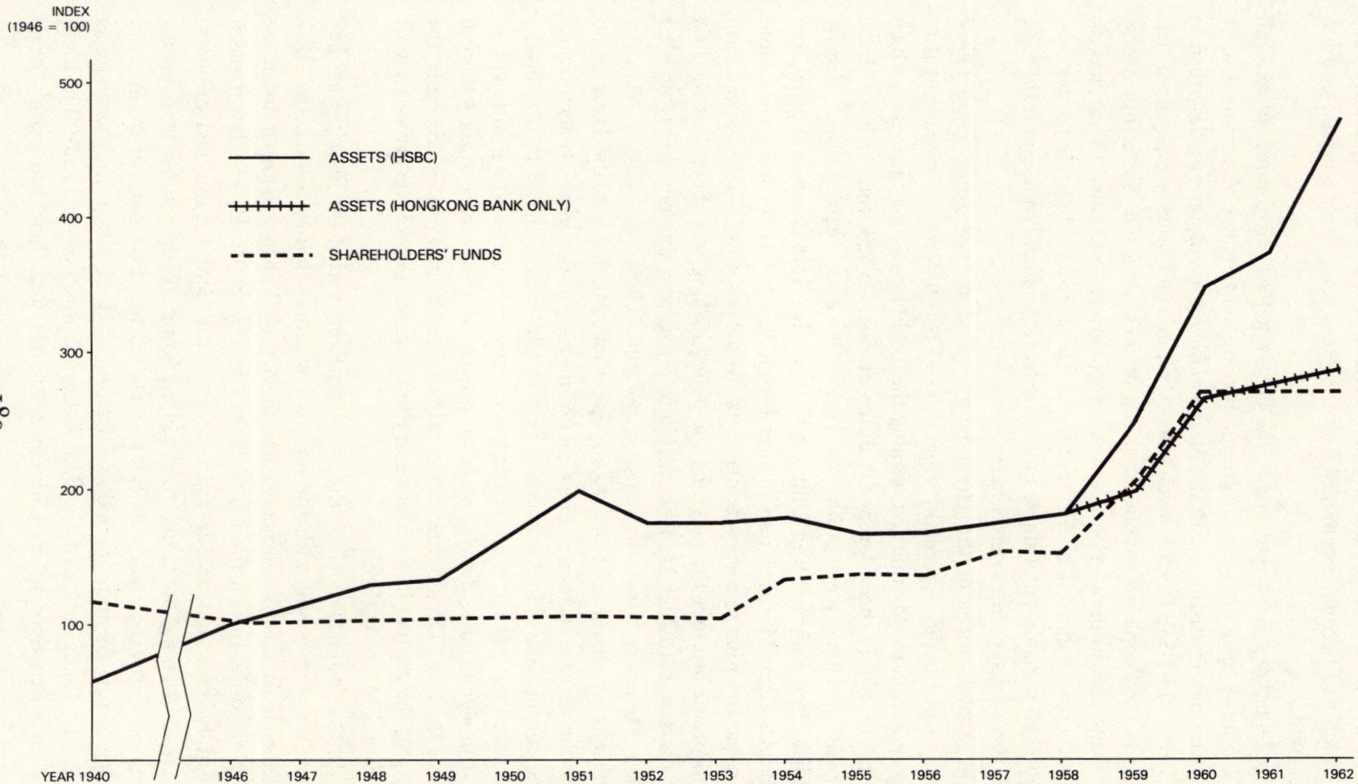

Figure II.2 The Hongkong and Shanghai Banking Corporation
Indices of assets and shareholders' funds, 1946–1962.

Bank as the more welcome partner in a rationalization which they did not seek but which had become inevitable. And the Hongkong Bank was in a position to respond.

The Hongkong Bank returned to the post-war East self-committed to a full role in China, particularly in the area of development finance. After initial years of frustrating negotiations with the National Government, already described in Chapter 4, the Bank faced a revolutionary regime and quickly recognized that its role in the People's Republic would be further restricted. Sir Arthur Morse took steps to withdraw. For years the negotiations continued. The Bank in Hong Kong financed China's trade; in China itself Michael Turner was encouraged to retain but a single link, the Shanghai office. In the meantime the Bank turned its attention elsewhere.

The establishment of the Hong Kong office in 1945 while Head Office remained in London forced the separation of two functions – management of the corporation world-wide and running the local Hong Kong business – which had never before been properly differentiated. When Sir Arthur Morse returned to Hong Kong with the Head Office in 1946, he had already established an embryo Head Office staff; over the years this would grow, and the Bank's Chief Manager, now divorced from daily exchange operations, could give some attention to corporate planning. In today's sense, such a formal term is still premature, but the potential for policy making was there. For the first time there was a Chief Manager in Hong Kong who was not simply another branch Manager, albeit the most important. There was now a Manager specifically in charge of Hong Kong operations; under him the Bank could expand in its base economy. The Chief Manager was now not only seen clearly as the corporation's chief executive, he also had time available for the task.

For time was needed even for the less dramatic decisions which, although of long-run significance, did not make an impact on the balance sheet – the full funding by Trust Deed of the staff pension schemes would be one example, the ending of the compradore system and the reorganization of the three-tier staff system would be another.

With the post-war rehabilitation of Hong Kong and of the Bank's other key Eastern economies and with the effective withdrawal from China, the Bank needed to make positive decisions. The move into Borneo was important at the time both to the British Borneo territories and to the Bank itself, but it was a move fully understandable in the context of the Bank's traditional business. More innovative was the Bank's role in Hong Kong. While continuing to finance the region's growing trade, the Bank stretched the definitions of commercial banking to participate in the industrialization of Hong Kong. Furthermore, as the need for funds increased, the Bank became a universal local bank. The Bank had always depended on its Chinese customers, but these had mainly dealt either through the compradore or, as small savers, directly with the Savings Bank. In the 1950s the Bank first set up major offices to handle the new entrepreneurs, many of them from Shanghai, where they had known and were known by the Bank, and then introduced smaller offices which would eventually reach into every corner of the potential market.

The Hongkong Bank in the early post-war years conserved its resources, transferred considerable sums to inner reserves to meet crises not all of which occurred, and remained liquid. From 1955 to 1961 the Bank, responding to various factors and developing its own policy of expansion, became a bank holding company with four major directly controlled financial subsidiaries: its own directly staffed and operated Hongkong and Shanghai Banking Corporation of California, Inc., two subsidiary banks managed through their respective boards of directors, the Mercantile Bank Limited, and the British Bank of the Middle East, and a specialist financial institution, Wayfoong Finance, which the Hongkong Bank incorporated separately in Hong Kong.

By 1961, therefore, The Hongkong and Shanghai Banking Corporation had become a very different organization. This is strangely compatible with the tentative conclusion that very little had changed; indeed, change had occurred only because its impact had been minimized through indirect control and the incorporation of the first specialized financial institution. Although, for example, the Hongkong Bank's 'Foreign' staff had changed little in nature or number over these 'critical years', the number of persons acting as executives had increased considerably – taking into account the Foreign staffs of the Mercantile and BBME, the American officers of the California subsidiary, the specialist staff of Wayfoong Finance, and the still limited role of the first local (or 'Regional') Hongkong Bank officers. Or looking at the question through the balance sheets, while it is true that the growth of the Hongkong Bank itself was limited, when the consolidated accounts of the Hongkong Bank Group, that is of the Bank and its 50% or more owned subsidiaries, are examined, the 47% growth of assets of the Bank is seen as but part of the 73% growth of assets of the corporation, that entity referred to as the 'Group' (see Figures II.1 and 2).

Successful growth depends upon appropriate management development, but the opportunity for growth does not necessarily present itself, at least in the early years, at the point when management is capable of ensuring such development. The Hongkong Bank met this problem, after its experience in San Francisco, with the indirect management which characterized the development of the Hongkong Bank Group. Integration of Group activities could then follow development of management, the introduction of suitable controls, the increase of specialized services, and therefore the logic of greater internalization – leading eventually either to total integration and eventual disappearance as in the case of the Mercantile Bank or to the move of head office from London to Hong Kong and significantly greater control from 'Group Head Office', as in the case of the BBME.

The focus of this history is on the Hongkong Bank as operating bank and on its development into a multinational bank holding company. There is no attempt to describe in detail the activities of the subsidiary or affiliated companies. Part II of this volume begins, therefore, in Chapter 5 with a survey of the Hongkong Bank's performance. In the following two chapters changes within the corporation are considered in their historical context. The provisions wisely required by the Treasury in 1865 and restated in the 1929 consolidating legislation required revision to equip the Bank to compete in a new era.

The story then turns in Chapter 8 to the Hong Kong economic 'miracle' and the role of the Bank in its financing. This offsets the story in Chapter 9 of the Bank in the People's Republic. In Volume IV perhaps even more than in the other volumes the task of describing the activities of a bank which is active in several independent economies has proved impossible. Introductory studies have been written in *Eastern Banking*, and further surveys and case studies are offered in Chapters 10 and 11. The entry into Borneo is a reminder that the Bank's ability to become multinational depended on its sound base in small, sometimes rural, but developing economies.

Only in Chapter 12 are the beginnings of today's Hongkong Bank Group considered in detail. Cautiously and even reluctantly, Michael Turner reacted to pressures which could not be safely ignored. Brought up in a context of regional banking, loyalty to a single institution, the Chief Manager and his Board of Directors were at times dealing with matters in which they had no experience – they were feeling their way. Fortunately for them, so were other bankers. But the Hongkong Bank was one of the few which succeeded.

5

THE HONGKONG BANK, POLICY AND PERFORMANCE, 1947–1961*

...the largest profits are obtained by those Public Companies which possess an interested local body of Proprietors or Shareholders, whose support naturally forms a chief element of remunerative success.

The Hongkong Bank Prospectus, 1864

A GENERAL SURVEY

Between 1946 when the Head Office was reestablished in Hong Kong and the end of 1961, the last full year of Sir Michael Turner's chief managership, the total assets of the Hongkong Bank rose 47%, those of the consolidated accounts of the Hongkong Bank Group 73%. Shareholders' funds had increased almost $2\frac{3}{4}$ times so that the 1961 published accounts show a capital/assets ratio of 6.7 and a liquidity of 37%.[a] The Hongkong Bank as holding company was responsible for four major financial subsidiaries and the Hongkong Bank Group included associated companies and other fixed and equity investments (see Table II.1 and Figures II.1 and 2, pp. 186 and 188–89). Dividends, which had been a tentative $48 (= £3) in 1946, rose immediately to $80 and had increased 1.85 times by 1960 to $150 on a comparable basis.

By the time pre-war branches had been reestablished in 1949 the Hongkong Bank was actually operating a total of 46 branches and agencies, including 2 in Hong Kong. In 1961, the Hongkong Bank itself had 63 branches and agencies (16 of them in Hong Kong), the Mercantile Bank operated a further 40, the British Bank of the Middle East 30, and the Hongkong Bank of California 3, giving a total for the Group of 136 (see Chapter 12).

In themselves the statistics indicate little more than what might have been expected – the Bank's total assets and its capital resources grew in a period of economic growth and generally increasing prices. But even a study of the list of branches will reveal that the growth occurred with a historically different geographical coverage and in conjunction with subsidiary banks. Behind this

---

* There are no end-notes to this chapter. The sources are described in a single note on p. 944.
[a] By 'capital' is meant 'shareholders' funds'. 'Liquidity' was defined in an internal managers' newsletter as the first four items on the assets side of the published balance sheet divided by the sum of deposits plus authorized note issue. The 1960 dividend assumes the 1950 shareholder retained his bonus issues and stock split; the actual dividend in 1961 was $12 per share. See Table 5.1 and discussion in Chapter 6.

are the changes in corporate structure, both legislated and determined by the Board of Directors.

The period was one of change in which, however, much remained potential and much more remained apparently unchanged, though with subtle forces already at work. These considerations of corporate structural development are subjects for Chapters 6 and 7. The present task is to state the financial performance of the corporation both as bank and as bank holding company.

From the Hongkong Bank's accounts (Tables 5.1–5.5)

During the period under review the position of the Hongkong Bank's shareholders improved visibly. Not only did dividends increase from $80.80 per share in the years 1947–1954 to $150.90 in 1961 – or doubled, $160.80, by 1962 – but the shareholder's reserved liability of $125 per share and his contingent but unlimited liability relative to the note issue had been eliminated, and the lower par value following the 5 for 1 split in 1961 added to his shares' marketability.[b] These developments were consistent with the growth of the Hongkong Bank's assets, but published profits appear to have had a three-fold increase – the figures for 1960–1962, however, include management fees from subsidiaries, dividends from the Mercantile Bank and the British Bank of the Middle East (BBME), and the income earnings from the maximum £10 million of funds deposited by subsidiaries with the Hongkong Bank for investment in British Government securities on a non-taxed basis (see Chapter 12 and Table 5.2) – this last is reflected in the increase of $164 million in the Bank's holdings of such securities during 1959 in anticipation of the acquisition of the BBME (see Table 5.4). When appropriately adjusted, all key growth indicators appear in harmony.

This approach not only disguises several inconsistencies but neglects the crucial factor of variation, the impact of local failures and successes, and minimizes the stresses of operating in an area which, at the time, appeared to many objective observers as fraught with risk. A more realistic picture emerges from an examination of Table 5.5, which states the reported income of Hongkong Bank branches, the provisions for bad debts, and the 'true' profits defined as 'profits before allocations to contingency funds'. True profits actually doubled within the shorter period from 1947 to 1951; there is a fallback in 1953–1954, a recovery followed by a relapse in 1958, and a continued rise through 1962. This pattern is consistent with other major balance sheet items.

The published profits figures are not, however, without meaning. They

---

[b] The dividends have been calculated on the assumption that the shareholder retains bonus shares and the benefits of the 1961 split, see Table 5.1.

reflect the Bank's long-run evaluation of a position dependent on conflicting political and economic factors. The plateau shown in the published profit figures from 1947 through 1953 is a consequence (i) of allocations to cover bad debts, that is, specific known or anticipated problems and (ii) of contingencies the exact nature and value of which could not be determined and which were allowed for by allocations to various contingency accounts, referred to collectively as 'inner reserves'. These former allocations are consistent with the Bank's policy throughout its history – the immediate setting aside of funds on the identification of a problem. The latter allocations proved partially justified by events in San Francisco, Calcutta, and Shanghai; to the extent that the 'inner reserves' proved excessive later in the 1950s, they were utilized to replace published reserves capitalized in the several bonus issues and in the purchase of the Mercantile Bank and the BBME.

The discussion in this chapter is focused mainly on the Hongkong Bank itself rather than on the Hongkong Bank Group, except where the two impinge as, for example, in capital accounts. There are two reasons for this procedure. First, the Group did not exist as a significant concept until the last two years of the period under consideration and, secondly, the Hongkong Bank retained its identity as an independent bank.

This last point is reinforced by consideration of management policy. Although by 1960 Turner, as the Hongkong Bank Group's Chairman, was taking an interest in specific activities of the Mercantile Bank and the BBME, his approach to the activities of the Hongkong Bank was virtually unaffected by these broader interests. The Hongkong Bank was an independent decision-making entity; when instructions were issued relative to liquidity ratios, they were sent to Hongkong Bank Managers and related to Hongkong Bank data. The public, the constituents of the Hongkong Bank, looked on it as a separate bank and judged it in this context, just as the ordinary Gulf constituents of the BBME judged their bank, as will be explained in Chapter 12, on the basis of the BBME figures, unconcerned, as yet, with what lay behind them in terms of Group resources.

Although this approach becomes increasingly unsatisfactory and will require reference to exceptions and modifications as Group integration proceeds, the Hongkong Bank retains today an identity separate from the Hongkong Bank Group, the consequence of the major operating member of the Group being also the Group's holding company.

The period under consideration was marked by significant price changes which partially account for the growth of the Bank's assets. The Hong Kong retail cost of living index, following the immediate post-war price increase, indicated a further 25% increase in the price level during the period through 1953; thereafter it was relatively stable, but in consequence and for a brief

Table 5.1 *The Hongkong and Shanghai Banking Corporation Capital and dividends, 1946–1961*

(in millions of $)

End-year	Assets	Capital resources					Shares				Dividend/share		
		Paid-up capital	Reserves[a]	P&L A/c balances[g]	Share-holders' funds[f]		Number (000)	Nominal value per share (dollars)	Book value per share (dollars)	Value of original holding[b]	as published		on original holding[b] $
											£	$	
1940	1,246.0	20.0	114.9	3.4	138.3		160.0	125.0		864.4	5:00	80.7	80.7
1946	2,050.9	20.0	97.0	1.8	118.9		160.0	125.0		742.8	3:00	48.5	48.5
1947	2,420.1	20.0	97.0	3.4	120.4		160.0	125.0		752.7	5:00	80.8	80.8
1948	2,565.1	20.0	97.0	4.3	121.3		160.0	125.0		758.1	5:00	80.8	80.8
1949	2,711.6	20.0	96.0	5.4	121.4		160.0	125.0		758.5	5:00	81.0	81.0
1950	3,456.7	20.0	96.0	6.7	122.7		160.0	125.0		766.9	5:00	80.7	80.7
1951	4,074.1	20.0	96.0	8.1	124.1		160.0	125.0		775.5	5:00	80.7	80.7
1952	3,541.4	20.0	96.0	9.5	125.5		160.0	125.0		784.3	5:00	80.7	80.7
1953	3,536.7	20.0	96.0	9.9	125.9		160.0	125.0		786.6	5:00	80.8	80.8
1954	3,571.2	20.0	128.0	10.2	158.2		160.0	125.0		988.8	5:00	80.8	80.8
1955	3,427.2	25.0	128.0	10.6	163.6		200.0	125.0	818.0	1,022.5	5:00	80.9	101.2
1956	3,430.3	25.0	128.0	11.0	164.0		200.0	125.0	820.2	1,025.2	5:00	81.0	101.3
1957	3,599.8	50.0	128.0	2.1	180.1		400.0	125.0	450.2	1,125.4	3:12½[c]	58.7[c]	106.3[c]
1958	3,643.1	50.0	128.0	2.1	180.1		400.0	125.0	450.2	1,125.5	3:00	48.6	121.5
1959	5,054.1[k]	62.3	175.2	2.1	239.6		498.5	125.0	480.7	1,201.7	3:00	48.4	120.9
1960	7,120.3[f]	79.0	240.0	2.2	321.3		632.4	125.0	508.0	1,270.0	3:15	60.3	150.6
1961	7,660.0[f]	79.0	240.0	2.3	321.4		3161.8	25.0	101.6	1,270.6	0:15	12.1	150.9
1962	9,646.1[f]	79.0	240.0	2.5	321.5		3161.8	25.0	101.7	1,271.0	0:16	12.9	160.8[h]

[a] The figure for the Reserve Fund *includes* the amount transferred at the end of the period as approved by the shareholders at the subsequent meeting; figures for 1960 and 1961 include the Share Premium Account.
[b] Assume that the owner of one share held onto bonus issues: in 1955 he would have 1.25 shares; in 1957, 2.5 shares (but see note 'c' below); and in 1961, 12.5 shares.
[c] The interim dividend of £2 was paid on the basis of 200,000 shares; the final dividend of £1:12s:6d on the basis of 400,000 shares.
[d] See note 'b'; if the holder of one share at the end of 1946 held his bonus issues, his equity would be calculated on the basis of 125 shares.
[e] The 1940 exchange rate was 1s:2⅞d.
[f] Shareholders' funds (or 'primary capital') include capital paid up+published reserves (plus Share Premium Account from 1960)+balance on P&L A/c after deduction for the final recommended dividend. [g] The amount carried forward after all allocations, including the final dividend, have been made.

196

Table 5.2 *The Hongkong and Shanghai Banking Corporation
Key indicators, 1947–1961*

(in millions of dollars)

End-year	Assets (i)	Assets (ii)	Capital[a]	Capital/assets % (i)	Capital/assets % (ii)	Capital/deposits % (i)	Capital/deposits % (ii)	Net profit (i)	Net profit (ii)	To dividends (i)	To dividends (ii)	Profit/capital[b] %	Liquidity (i) %	Liquidity (ii) %
1940	1,246.0		138.3	11.1		15.8		14.0		13.0		10.0	—	
1946	2,050.9		118.9	5.8		7.9		9.6		7.8		8.0	40.1	
1947	2,420.1		120.4	5.0		7.2		16.6		13.0		13.8	38.4	
1948	2,665.1		121.3	4.5		6.7		16.9		13.0		14.0	35.0	
1949	2,711.6		121.4	4.5		6.7		17.8		13.0		14.7	41.4	
1950	3,456.7		122.7	3.5		4.8		17.2		12.9		14.0	54.3	
1951	4,074.1		124.1	3.0		4.0		17.3		12.9		13.9	65.0	
1952	3,541.4		125.5	3.5		4.8		17.3		12.9		13.8	63.3	
1953	3,536.7		125.9	3.6		4.8		17.3		13.0		13.7	64.6	
1954	3,571.2		158.2	4.4		5.9		19.3		13.0		12.2	60.0	
1955	3,427.2		163.6	4.8		6.4		20.6		16.2		12.6	47.8	
1956	3,430.3		164.0	4.8		6.4		20.6		16.2		12.6	45.2	
1957	3,599.8		180.1	5.0		6.7		21.0		17.0		11.7	49.3	
1958	3,643.1		180.1	4.9		6.6		23.5		19.5		13.0	51.1	
1959	4,015.2	5,054.1	240.3[b]	6.0	4.8	8.4	6.0	28.1	29.4[b]	19.4[d]	28.1[c]	12.3	42.0	39.7
1960	4,418.1	7,120.3	321.3[b]	7.3	4.5	10.4	5.4	42.2	46.9[b]	24.1[d]	38.1	14.6	39.6	36.3
1961	4,774.0	7,659.6	321.4[b]	6.7	4.2	9.6	5.0	43.3	49.2[b]	24.2[d]	38.2	15.3	37.5	34.0
1962	5,823.7	9,646.1	321.5[b]	5.5	3.3	8.7	4.6	45.8	50.7[b]	25.8[d]	40.7	15.8	38.3	34.0

(i) total for Hongkong Bank only   (ii) total for Group consolidated

[a] 'Primary capital', i.e. shareholders' funds = paid-up capital + published reserves + balance on Profit and Loss Account after deducting recommended dividend.
[b] Group consolidated figures or ratios.
[c] Of which $4 million paid from inner reserves as part of purchase price of BBME.
[d] Dividend payout on 400,000 shares.

197

Table 5.3 *The Hongkong Bank*
Selected balance sheet items and ratios, 1947–1961

(in millions of dollars or percentages)

End-year	(i) Assets	(ii) Index 1929 = 100	(iii) Index 1946 = 100	(iv) Cash + Call	(v) Ratio (i)/(iv) %	(vi) Excess note issue	(vii) Total deposits	(viii) Liquidity ratio[a] %	(ix) Loans etc.	(x) Loan/deposit ratio %	(xi) Investments[f]	(xii) Trade bills discounted
1940	1,246.0	146	—	—	—	170.5	880.9		416.8	47		—
1946	2,050.9	240	100	537.5	26.2	370.1	1,508.2		484.2	32	551.5	57.9[b]
1947	2,420.1	284	118	532.6	22.0	571.9	1,675.7	35.9	572.3	34	594.4	84.7[b]
1948	2,665.1	312	130	506.7	19.0	685.4	1,807.8	31.9	696.1	39	613.4	83.1[b]
1949	2,711.6	318	132	508.8	18.8	712.9	1,820.5	35.4	700.9	39	493.8	149.8[b]
1950	3,456.7	405	169	788.0	22.8	718.6	2,558.7	54.3	770.2	30	521.2	623.2[c]
1951	4,074.1	478	199	1,234.8	30.3	721.7	3,134.1	65.0	803.1	26	414.8	823.3[c]
1952	3,541.4	415	173	1,076.0	30.4	725.3	2,639.3	63.4	699.8	27	387.4	615.9[c]
1953	3,536.7	415	172	1,119.8	31.7	725.7	2,636.5	65.3	645.7	24	388.2	622.6[d]
1954	3,571.2	419	174	907.6	25.4	645.7	2,672.6	60.0	829.5	31	406.8	494.7[e]
1955	3,427.2	402	167	450.0	13.2	645.7	2,557.4	47.8	1,069.7	42	415.3	560.7
1956	3,430.3	402	167	351.0	10.2	645.7	2,564.3	45.2	1,213.5	47	349.1	600.0
1957	3,599.8	422	176	430.3	12.0	661.7	2,695.2	49.4	1,186.0	44	342.0	490.2
1958	3,643.1	427	178	539.5	14.8	677.7	2,726.3	51.1	1,096.0	40	408.9	437.3
1959	4,015.2	471	196	450.6	11.2	741.7	2,857.8	42.0	1,308.1	46	570.5	538.2
1960	4,418.1	518	215	402.7	16.7	805.8	3,075.7	39.6	1,560.5	51	559.4	529.4
1961	4,774.0	560	233	415.5	15.7	837.8	3,363.1	37.5	1,804.0	54	540.3	655.5
1962	5,823.7	683	284	476.5	8.2	925.8	3,684.0	38.3	1,941.8	53	572.8	761.3

[a] (Cash in hand and balances with other banks+money at call and short notice+British and other Government bills+trade bills discounted) ÷ (current, deposit and other accounts incl. inner reserves+authorized note issue) × 100; for adjustments, see Table 5.7. The definition differs according to the figures available; in early years, for example, it included 'items in transit'.
[b] Bills receivable.
[c] Bills receivable, in hand and in transit.
[d] Bills receivable including Government Treasury bills.
[e] Excluding Treasury bills of $208.2 million.

198

Table 5.4 *The Hongkong Bank Investments (at under market values)*

(in millions of dollars)

End-year	(i)	(ii)	(iii)	(iv)	(v)	(vi)	(vii)
1946	551.5				551.5		
1947	594.4				594.4		
1948	613.4				613.4		
1949	256.9	228.8	1.6	6.5	493.8		
1950	319.5	190.9	1.5	9.2	521.2		
1951	294.9	104.8	1.7	13.4	414.8		
1952	274.5	98.6	1.2	13.2	387.4		
1953	276.9	96.2	0.3	14.8	388.2		
1954	280.0	96.3	15.7	14.7	406.8		
1955	281.9	99.8	19.7	14.0	415.3		
1956	211.3	105.7	18.1	13.9	349.1		
1957	190.7	112.4	27.2	11.8	342.0		
1958	229.5	130.7	35.0	13.8	408.9		
1959	393.1	144.3	26.7	6.4	570.5		
1960	363.0	139.5	46.8	10.2	559.4		
1961	350.6	130.5	45.1	14.1	540.3	19.5	37.8
1962	383.8	128.7	49.8	10.4	572.8	30.2	38.6

(i) British, Colonial and other Government securities, quoted in Great Britain.
(ii) British, Colonial and other Government securities, quoted outside Great Britain.
(iii) Other investments, quoted in Great Britain.
(iv) Other investments, quoted outside Great Britain.
(v) Total quoted investments.
(vi) Unquoted investments, less amounts written off.
(vii) (Total liquid assets + quoted investments)/deposits
[Liquid assets = cash at bankers and in hand + money at call short notice + British Government and other Government Treasury bills + trade bills discounted].
Source: Balance sheets as published by the Hongkong Bank.

period dividends did not maintain their real value.[c] The price of primary commodities was similarly affected by the events of 1949–1952 – the Liberation or accession of the People's Government in China, the Korean War, and the various embargoes – but the course was more erratic than the cost of living index; there was, for example, a temporary fall in commodity prices in 1958.

The accounts provide evidence that both Sir Arthur Morse and Sir Michael Turner were primarily concerned with (i) asset (as opposed to liability) management and (ii) liquidity, reinforced by a cautious dividend policy and a

[c] The mean annual inflation rate in Hong Kong as measured by the Consumer Price Index was 2.6% for the years 1947–1959, 1.9% for the years 1960–1969.

Table 5.5 *The Hongkong Bank*
'True' profit estimates, 1947–1961*

(in millions of dollars)

Year	HK Bank branches (gross)	Less: bad debt etc. provisions[a]	'True' net profits (estimates)	To various reserves (gross)[a]	'Profits'	To premises	To dividends
1947	25.0	3.9	19.1	2.5	16.6	2.0	13.0
1948	29.3	9.9	18.8	2.0	16.9	3.0	13.0
1949	33.2	7.6	23.4	3.5	17.8	3.0	13.0
1950	36.3	4.0	30.9	11.4	17.2	3.0	12.9
1951	49.1	4.8	41.9	24.6	17.3	3.0	12.9
1952	58.6	11.2	44.9	26.7	17.3	3.0	12.9
1953	48.3	na	42.3	25.0	17.3	4.0	13.0
1954	43.6	na	40.6	21.3	19.3	6.0	13.0
1955	60.1	5.5	51.6	31.0	20.6	4.0	16.2
1956	67.8	13.7	46.7	26.0	20.6	4.0	16.2
1957	66.9	11.8	51.7	30.6	21.0	4.0	17.0
1958	51.0	9.0	40.0	16.2	23.5	4.0	19.5
1959	64.3	16.5	45.8	17.2	29.4	4.0	28.1[b]
1960	69.1	na	80.2[c]	38.0	42.2	4.0	38.1
1961	59.7	na	67.7[c]	24.3	43.3	5.0	38.2

* This table should be considered as indicative only; changing definitions exist; it cannot be used for calculation of 'inner' reserves. For example, contingency accounts, staff contingency accounts, high cost of living, but does not include payments out of such accounts for purposes designated; does not include transfers from inner to published reserves. Hence figure is gross and not accumulative.
[a] Of which $4 million from inner reserves; payment of dividend to former shareholders of BBME before receipt of dividends from BBME considered part of purchase price.
[b] Including dividends from MBLD and BBME of $11.1 million (1960) and $18.4 million (1961).
[c] The criteria for determination of amounts to be subtracted from gross earnings before 'true' profits is not consistent; in general, sums for specific known bad debts are subtracted either at the branch level before reporting branch gross profits or after reporting and before statement of 'true' profits.

preference for increasing hidden rather than published reserves. This is consistent with a conservative banking strategy reflecting the Chief Managers' concerns with the uncertainties in the Bank's area of operations. An indirect benefit of this policy was the Bank's ability to take advantage of the circumstances which made the Mercantile Bank and the BBME available for acquisition.

Turner's declared policy was to maintain a high liquidity ratio of 50%. In this he was only partially successful in the face of pressures not only in Hong Kong itself but from virtually every branch Manager who saw opportunities escaping the Bank for want of local funds and of facilities in London. Despite the positive role that the Bank played in several of the territories in which it operated, and especially in Hong Kong, its market share in each constituency area declined, but, given the Bank's resources and the nature of the competition from American and local banks, this was unavoidable and there would be long-run favourable consequences.

Although the published accounts confirm the Bank's basically conservative approach, for several reasons they understate it. In the first place the Bank's banknote issue distorts the picture. The $600–$700 million excess note issue was covered under the provisions of the Bank's ordinance by 100% in Hong Kong Government non-interest bearing certificates of indebtedness; to compare the Hongkong Bank with a non-note-issuing commercial bank, the value of the excess note issue and of the certificates ought to be deducted; this would add a percentage point to the capital/assets ratio. The second distortion arises from the fact that a large amount of shareholders' funds, that is, of hidden reserves, appears on the balance sheet as 'current, deposit and other accounts', thereby understating the liquidity ratio as defined (see notes to Table 5.3; see also Table 5.7). Furthermore, the Bank's practice of quoting Government investments at below market, although necessitating a considerable drain on inner reserves ($9 million in 1962) to offset the depreciation of British Government securities, ensured that there was a further line of defence which could be used in an emergency with little fear of additional capital loss (Table 5.4).

The restraint shown by the Bank in its lending policies is reflected in the loan/deposit ratio; the Bank was certainly not loaned up. However, deposits were potentially volatile and the Bank's account ratios appear at their soundest during the period when transient funds had been deposited, particularly in the years 1950 and 1951, when the cash/assets ratio was also abnormally high. The favourable liquidity ratio in 1958, on the other hand, was the result of a trade slump and consequent slowdown in economic activity generally – another index of this is found in the value of trade bills discounted (Table 5.3).

Part of the Bank's liquidity was the consequence of its considerable investment in British Government Treasury Bills, first separately listed on the published balance sheets for 1954. These assets, valued on the average at approximately $220 million equivalent, but topping $400 million in the depression year of 1958, yielded a relatively high tax-free income and thus served two important functions.

This much is revealed from the accounts, but the analysis is only a background to a consideration of the Bank's actual operations in a changing East.

The Bank in its region

The dramatic events in China which eventually led to the Bank's physical withdrawal from all but a small office in Shanghai (see Chapter 9) had an impact throughout the region, more especially in Hong Kong. Arthur Morse had been pleasantly surprised at the condition of post-war Hong Kong, and the Bank had played a key role in financing its rehabilitation. Following this, there was the growth of trade in which the Bank, through the administration of the swing account with Japan (see Chapter 10) and through its contacts with local banks operating in the Hong Kong Open Market for U.S. dollars, played its traditional role. But even before 1949 there had been discussions with Nationalist China about financing industrial growth, and new equipment ordered by Chinese entrepreneurs was already reaching Hong Kong prior to an onward shipment which, in many cases, never occurred. The Shanghai industrialists and Shanghai workers were to come to Hong Kong; the Bank would finance them and others in investments which by 1961 would provide Hong Kong with an industrial base from which the territory would develop in the 1960s.

The dramatic rise in Hong Kong's entrepôt trade caused by the Korean War, the dislocation and redirection of intra-regional trade caused by the American freezing of China-controlled dollar assets and subsequently by the United Nations embargo placed a burden on a Colony then overwhelmed by the influx of refugees. When Morse retired and turned over the chief managership of the Bank to Michael Turner in 1953 the process of Hong Kong's industrialization was just beginning. It was never a proclaimed or directed activity, nor did the Bank ever set out to finance 'industrial development'. The Hongkong Bankers, trained in commercial banking, in the concept of the self-liquidating loan and the principle of rapid turnover of funds, nevertheless discerned an obvious need and adjusted sufficiently to enable Hong Kong's new entrepreneurs to begin the all-pervading change.

The situation was similar to that confronting the Bank in the days of (Sir) Ewen Cameron and the young (Sir) Charles Addis in the mid-1880s. Then Imperial China had needed modest financial support; the China-coast bankers with David McLean in London felt their way, learning as they progressed; they eventually became sufficiently skilled to lead the various European consortiums in the financing of China's railways. But the Bank's system was unable to provide their successors – these were specialists from 'outside'.

In Hong Kong the new Mongkok branch was located north along Nathan Road from the long-established but poorly located (for industrial lending) Kowloon office in the prestigious Peninsula Hotel. Its successive Managers, held in check by the responsible Sub-Manager in the main Hong Kong office, felt their way in the jungle of small enterprises struggling to grow and whose owners possessed little but a problematic know-how which had to be identified and watched. But when a more stable and affluent middle class sought finance for consumer durables, automobiles especially, the Hongkong Bank founded a specialized company, Wayfoong Finance, to handle a specialized type of banking. The typical Hongkong Banker remained a generalist at a time when varied experiences at all levels of banking would be particularly important. Again, in the early 1970s, when the more successful of the enterprises decided to go public, when mergers increased the stakes and multinationals sought off-shore financing, the Hongkong Bank created its wholly owned subsidiary, Wardley Ltd, and staffed it with experienced investment bankers.

These changes were significant, and yet the major banking changes in the East did not come until the very end or, in the majority of cases, until after the period now being considered. The countries in the traditional area of the Bank's operations became independent, and central banks were established. New policies were instituted; they had two major consequences (i) the withdrawal of official and semi-official funds from the Bank and (ii) restrictions relative to the use of foreign exchange. Both impeded the Bank's activities as a financial intermediary and limited the role it could play, especially in the context of the new Governments' encouragement of local banks, in financing of development plans. Nevertheless, the countries remained in the Sterling Area or, in the case of the Philippines, with a secure link to the former metropolitan currency, the U.S. dollar. Furthermore, although the Bank's branches were cut off from certain obvious sources of funds, they were not as yet faced everywhere with restrictions on establishing new offices nor were their loan portfolios subject to detailed management by a central bank in favour of specific country development or political/social goals. The position varied from country to country, but in 1961 the banking scene would remain surprisingly familiar to those whose careers had begun in the inter-war period or earlier.

Familiarity can, however, be more apparent than real. There were significant new elements, the most positive of which were the development plans, the new Government industrial banks, and the pressures on foreign banks to prove beneficial participation in the economy – which in the 1960s would change to legislated or regulatory direction. After World War II the still colonial Governments had attempted to issue development loans, but the exchange banks as underwriters found themselves holding at least initially the bulk of the bonds. In subsequent flotations the foreign banks were under some pressure to make substantial subscriptions. In several instances this suited the Hongkong Bank's portfolio requirements, but the pressure was there; the Bank was accordingly cautious at first in its response to World Bank invitations to participate in their development loans to, for example, the Federation of Malaya.

Hesitantly it seemed the Hongkong Bank sent G.O.W. Stewart to the IMF/World Bank meeting in Delhi, but almost immediately, as if the World Bank and the Hongkong Bank had at last discovered each other, the latter agreed to direct participations – the Bank was entering the world financial scene once again.

Inheriting sterling reserves, which survived and indeed increased during World War II, Arthur Morse continued a policy of allocating funds to sterling, U.S. dollar, and Hong Kong dollar contingency funds. The income from these sources and from current operations provided pools from which Managers, with insufficient funds of their own, might draw – subject to Head Office agreement and control. This provided the flexibility the Bank required; only Hong Kong, Singapore, and Malaya – and to a more limited extent the Philippine and the Borneo offices – had their own sources of funds. Borneo had limited funds and limited opportunities. Hong Kong's needs knew no quantitative limit, but Turner particularly was convinced that over-exposure to, for example, the textile industry could be dangerous and, as a matter of policy, the Bank passed significant opportunities by while building up liquid earning assets in London and New York.

The Bank's financial policy results were summarized by Michael Turner at a Managers' conference in November 1960.

The need to supply funds for development and expansion elsewhere [than Hong Kong] had not, however, been overlooked and funds had been provided to capitalize Incorporated [HSBC of California = HBC] and Wayfoong Finance; to acquire the issued share capital of the BBME and Mercantile Bank Limited; to purchase shares in Bowmaker (Central Africa) Limited, the Trust Corporation of the Bahamas, Theo. H. Davies and Co. Ltd, and Finance Corporations in India and Ceylon; to subscribe to World Bank loans connected with such projects as the Cameron Highlands Hydro Electric Scheme.

Loans had recently been granted abroad to two Japanese Banks and as a quid-pro-quo these banks have lent our Tokyo Office Yen funds at favourable rates of interest which have enabled our Offices in Japan to compete for the first time for Japanese business of a profitable nature.[d] A similar type of proposition had been approved in

[d] In 1879 there was a similar event when the Japanese Government deposited much needed funds in the Hongkong Bank in return for services relative to the popularization of the silver yen.

principle in Bombay while in Rangoon a Sterling Loan to Ava Bank, which is a subsidiary of the Defence Services Institute, had also been approved.

In addition many branches have been granted overdraft facilities in London and New York whilst other branches have facilities available for use in an emergency. Managers would appreciate, however, that investment was not attractive in areas where penal rates of taxation were in force or where political or economic conditions were so unstable that payment of interest or capital was in doubt.

The upheaval of 1949 and after excepted, the course of events through 1961 in the Bank's region of operations proved remarkably sympathetic to Western-influenced financial intermediation. This was not preordained; there was always the threat of discriminatory action against foreign banks; it was perhaps that socialist speeches did not yet form the basis of banking legislation.[e]

Nevertheless political discord within the newly independent countries was reflected in the Bank's labour relations, and serious strikes in Colombo, India, Singapore, and Japan had an impact on the Bank at various levels. Pre-war the Bank had been for the most part shielded from labour problems by the non-competitive nature of the labour market, by the role of a paternalistic Government, and through the existence of the compradore as an intermediary. For its part the Bank had, as stated in previous volumes of this history, established a traditional master/servant relationship, making provisions in times of personal and individual hardships through decisions made on occasion at Board of Directors level – although it might be argued, unkindly, that the directors had little else with which to concern themselves. Post-war the Hongkong Bank's Managers were as inexperienced in labour relations as they were experienced in virtually all other aspects of banking. Although they recognized that they lived in a new post-colonial era and Morse prided himself that the Bank had adjusted itself to the new environment faster than many other European institutions in the East, labour activism still came as a surprise, the more so because Managers saw loyal employees apparently 'duped' or 'forced' to participate in strikes designed primarily for political ends unconnected with terms of employment in the Hongkong Bank.

At still another level there were threats from insurgents, especially in Malaya and the Philippines, although by the late 1950s both countries would enjoy relative political stability. In 1960 the Burmese leaders U Nu and U Ba Swe told Turner frankly that Burma would like to be without foreign banks, but, they added, Burma cannot do without such banks for another ten to twenty years. These leaders were, however, not in power when three years later foreign banks in Rangoon were nationalized.

[e] In 1954 on his retirement as Manager Colombo, Hugh Greig and his successor (A.M. Kennedy) were called to Government House where the Governor-General, Sir Oliver Goonetilleke, said, '...tell them [in London] not to worry about the Ceylonization of banking, it's all so many words'. What happened next is described in Chapter 10.

The Bank would also leave and return to Indonesia, be forced to evacuate Cambodia and Vietnam, and suffer restrictions in virtually all other territories, but in the period during which Morse and Turner were Chief Managers, the Hongkong Bank had time to reestablish itself, reorient its approach within the limitations of existing staff and existing banking practices. However, the pressures were mounting not only within the corporate structure as described in Chapter 6, but also in the territories the Bank was serving.

The pressures for change

Michael Turner has been described as the last traditional Hongkong Bank Chief Manager. It is more accurate to describe him as one who used a vocabulary which deprecated the changes he determined to see through. Confronted with George Marden and his holding of Mercantile Bank shares (see Chapter 12), Turner attempted to find an alternative to acquisition; the Hongkong Bank didn't acquire banks – but when that course forced itself on him, Turner pursued it with determination. The Bank did not move outside its region of expertise – Turner would have agreed with the point of view characterized in the 1880s by David McLean's terse comment, 'Colombo not required for China business'. Nevertheless it was under Turner that the Bank became responsible for operations in the Middle East, moved into hire purchase financing, and established its first functional department, the Industrial Relations Unit in Mongkok. Significantly, however, Turner's Hongkong Bank did not venture into insurance; it did not acquire equity to any great extent in non-financial companies. The banker, Turner is reported to have commented, sticks to his last.

These developments are an extension of Turner's agreement to innovations in banking more narrowly conceived. When Turner became Chief Manager in 1953 the Bank had only two branch offices in Hong Kong – Kowloon and Mongkok; in 1961 there were sixteen. There was limited branch expansion in Singapore and Malaya; the Bank remained hesitant about extending operations in India – and those it did attempt proved costly; elsewhere the Bank's efforts to branch were checked by regulation (as in the Philippines) or by the self-restricted nature of the Bank's business (as in Thailand and Burma). The underlying reason for the decision to branch bank was the need to garner funds; a bank which is seeking to participate in the financing of industrialization cannot depend on the countervailing deposits of trade customers, the casual deposits of constituents' employees, or the venturesome worker who braves the marble halls to make his small savings deposit. Turner, though he disapproved of advertising, nevertheless supported Godfrey Oliphant, his Hong Kong

Manager, in his branching policy; the Bank recognized the need for an ever-expanding source of funds.

In this even Iloilo played a role. When in 1957 the Manila Manager suggested closing the agency and obtaining permission to substitute an office in the Port Area, Turner noted the illiquid position of the Philippine operation and the real role Iloilo-garnered funds were playing – an office in the Port Area would not provide the Hongkong Bank with funds. For a time Iloilo remained a key link in the Philippine operations.

Chapter 6 will outline the pressures for change within the corporate structure while at the same time noting the real adjustments which were made pending those changes. Other chapters relate the pressures on the Bank to change its concept of banking; nevertheless, the Hongkong Bank through to the 1980s eschewed the extreme concepts of liability management. In the 1950s, however, the Bank experimented with industrial banking, moved into hire purchase, and began branch banking and customer-oriented retail banking within Hong Kong; at the same time tentative steps were made to improve office efficiency with the introduction of postronic equipment after study of new methods in the United States.

Chapter 5 remains the story of the Hongkong Bank as traditionally known; it is not as yet the history of the Hongkong Bank Group. Despite this, the Group intrudes into the accounts; it has an impact on the capital structure of the corporation and on the profitability of the Hongkong Bank qua bank. The first task therefore is to look more closely at the accounts and the story they relate – together with the position of the subsidiary and acquired companies. The history will then return to the Hongkong Bank itself and consider developments in Hong Kong and in the several major territories, including case studies.

THE ACCOUNTS AND THE CHAIRMAN'S STATEMENTS

EXPLANATION AND INTERPRETATION

The annual presentation

The Hongkong Bank's balance sheets, originally referred to as 'abstracts' of the accounts, have been subject to criticism from an early time (see Volume I). In 1949 the Bank, having an office in the United Kingdom, became subject to the relevant provisions of the Companies Act as to presentation of annual accounts to the Bank of England; the directors resolved to offer these revised accounts to the shareholders. Not until the 1959 accounts, when there is a Group consolidation, are explanatory notes appended. A major development beginning with the 1957 accounts, however, was the increased attractiveness of the presentation, a combined 'Report of the Directors and Accounts' being produced on glossy paper with pictures.[f] A Federal Reserve Board official unkindly commented that the amount of information provided by the Hongkong Bank varied inversely with the attractiveness of the presentation – and in the 1970s the Bank, turning in this as in other activities away from a reliance on the generalist to the engagement of the specialist, obtained the services of Henry Steiner Associates; the Bank's annual report was winning prizes for the artistic quality of the presentation, but not for its analytical content.

The Bank's annual report was divided into four sections: (i) the formal report of the directors, including recommendations for the appropriation of funds from the Profit and Loss Account, (ii) the minutes of the Annual Meeting, including the Chairman's usually helpful explanation of various items in the accounts, (iii) the December 31 balance sheet of the Hongkong Bank, the consolidated balance sheet of The Hongkong and Shanghai Banking Corporation, that is of the Hongkong Bank Group (from 1959), and the balance sheets of major subsidiaries, and (iv) the Chairman's statement.

This last was a comprehensive review of the economic and political situation in the Far East as seen from the reports of Managers to Head Office and from a survey of published reports. This review had originally formed a brief portion of the Chairman's remarks to the then semi-annual meetings of proprietors, but with the contributions of Charles Addis from London, and, after him, of the Bank's political advisers in the East, the statement had lengthened into an authoritative exposition of the Eastern scene as seen by the Hongkong Bank's management and directors.

The preparation of the statement was, in consequence, taken seriously by the Chief Manager and by the Board. The annual meeting provided the Chairman, as the representative of the Bank, with a forum; the Chairman's Statement was thus a very public comment on key issues as they affected the Bank and its constituents – and the economies the Bank served.

During the 1950s the newly established post of 'adviser' in Head Office, a post filled first in 1956 by G.O.W. Stewart, was the locus for the final compilation of the draft Statement. In a sense he took over from the Bank's former 'political adviser', W.C. Cassells in 1956, but Cassells had been recruited from the Foreign Service and was not a career banker. Stewart was

---

[f] Sir Vandeleur Grayburn (Chief Manager, 1930–1943) reportedly refused suggestions from London that his picture appear with the Bank's annual report. He considered it incomprehensible that such an embellishment had any legitimate role to play in the public's understanding of a financial statement.

a full member of the Foreign staff and his role was consequently not only more comprehensive but also different in kind – it had a direct impact on the Bank's banking decisions.

After Stewart's appointment as Deputy Chief Manager, N.E. Clark (East in 1936), was brought from his post as Manager Kuala Lumpur in 1959 to act as 'adviser to the Board', and the Chairman's Statement accordingly became one of his responsibilities. The Bank also employed a specialist, S. Olver, for a brief period each year; he came out from England to complete the final draft. At this time the Bank had no research or economics department; the statement was prepared on the basis of information collected by Clark, written up by a specialist, and vetted and made the Bank's by the modifications and revisions of the Chief Manager and the Board. It was a unique statement of the leading Eastern exchange bank, and was awaited as such; but, typically, it was a generalist's statement; it was not the product of a service department staffed by professional economists or political scientists, and the Hongkong Bank – and probably the Bank's shareholders – still wanted it that way.

The balance sheet – adjustments and comparability

Although the existence of inner reserves and the failure to state 'true profits' make an analysis of the Hongkong Bank's performance, based on its annual accounts, a task subject to a range of error, the problem can be partially met through an understanding of how at the Board level the published accounts were determined. There had been little change in procedure since the nineteenth century.

The Chief Manager presented the Board with the net profits as reported from each branch; these figures incorporated those of the agencies reporting to the particular branch, for example, Manila included Iloilo, Singapore included all agencies in Singapore and the Federation of Malaya until Kuala Lumpur was established as an independent branch in 1959. Although in earlier days branches had closed their books some months before the end of the year, improvements in communications made this unnecessary; the books were closed on December 31. The branch statement of profits was, as is normal practice, net of amounts set aside against bad debts, but there is evidence that sums might also have been set aside against unspecified contingencies, a practice which came close to permitting a branch its own inner reserves.

From this total figure the Board made pre-publication allocations. Certain of these were actually expenses of running the Bank but had remained discretionary with the Board by long-established custom – directors' and auditors' fees, bonuses to Managers and Agents, and any additional payment to the Bank's staff, high cost of living allowances for example. At this point a

Table 5.6 *The Hongkong Bank
Annual accounts, 1951*

(in millions of dollars)

Branches with net profit			Allocations		
Head Office	3.7[a]		US$ contingency account	3.984	
Hong Kong and agencies	18.0		HO contingency account	0.240	
Singapore and agencies	10.8		HO sterling cont. a/c	0.081	
Manila and agency	1.6		Branches cont. account	0.580	
Bombay	0.8		10% HCL	1.600	
Calcutta	1.2		To directors	0.081	
Colombo	0.4		To auditors	0.040	
New York	1.4		To Chief Manager	0.235	
Bangkok	2.4		To Managers/Agents	0.404	7.2
London	2.9				
Saigon	2.4		'True' Profit		41.9
Jakarta	0.7				
Tokyo and agencies	4.5		To contingencies, reserves, etc.		
Rangoon	0.7		HO investments account	16.0	
Lyons	0.2		HK$ cont. for Shanghai	0.6	
Hamburg	0.2		Future expenses, Shanghai	4.0	
Jesselton and agencies	0.5	53.5	HO sterling cont. a/c	4.0	24.6
Branches with net losses			**Published profits**		17.3
Shanghai and agencies	4.2		To premises account	3.0	
San Francisco	0.1	4.3	To dividends	12.9	
			To profit and loss a/c	1.4	
Gross income from branches		49.2	**Total allocations**		49.2

HCL = high cost of living, cont. = contingency.
Jesselton is now Kota Kinabalu, Sabah, Federation of Malaysia.
[a] After allocations to charity of $60,000 for 1950.
Source: Hongkong Bank Board of Directors, Minutes, Group Archives

difficulty of interpretation arises: certain contingency funds were deducted before the profit line, some afterwards. Theoretically the former should be for 'bad debts' or for contingencies with a high probability factor, the latter for general contingencies or 'inner reserves'. The practice appears inconsistent and to this extent the 'true profit' figures as shown in Table 5.6 (and those in Table 5.5) are inexact. The value of the Chief Manager's additional remuneration indicates that all such allocations are considered sums transferred 'to reserves' as defined in his contract.

These deductions made, the resulting figure was reported as 'profit' and published for the benefit of shareholders as an addition to the Profit and Loss

Account. The consequence of this procedure was that, during troubled times, for example 1948–1953, reported profits could be made to stand still, while any addition to true profits could be placed into contingency funds. One purpose of reserve funds had been, as described in the Bank's charter, the equalization of dividends; this was never accepted by the shareholding public, but inner reserves could serve the same purpose. As a matter of fact, the inner reserves performed a one-way function; they were used to prevent (i) the buildup of published reserves and, thus, (ii) pressure for an increase in dividends, but post-war inner reserves were never used to pay the dividend.[g]

One difficulty with these policies is that prudential ratios are understated and the Bank could eventually appear to have inadequate capital, to be illiquid, and to be over-loaned. To correct this, transfers have to be made from time to time from inner reserves to published reserves; published reserves can be and were capitalized, thus correcting the image of the Bank as seen from a reading of the published accounts. In 1953 inner reserves were well in excess of published shareholders' funds; this had a serious impact not only on actual shareholders' funds but also on the item 'Deposits...' and thus all ratios expressed in Tables 5.2 and 5.3 would need significant revision. In defence of this practice, one could note that the growth of business overlying a growth of inner reserves outweighed the contingency factor, and that a portion of 'inner reserves' was no longer legitimately part of a contingency account. Their transfer to published reserves was, therefore, justified as a visible support for the expanded business of the Bank.

Another problem in interpretation, or comparability with the accounts of other commercial banks, is, as noted above, the position of the note issue. If the Bank had to wind up, bearers of the Bank's banknotes would be paid off immediately and in full – paid off in what is another question, presumably, in the unlikely situation posited, in a new Government note issue. This would affect the balance sheet by the reduction of both assets and liabilities by the value of the note issue; the affected assets would be Hong Kong Government certificates of indebtedness and British Government securities earmarked for this purpose and so noted in the published accounts. From this it follows that for comparability in analysis, there is an argument for making the adjustment before calculation of operating ratios.

A third adjustment involves 'Acceptances' which are now listed on both sides of the balance sheet, being both a Bank liability and a customer liability to the Bank. That the Bank's shareholders and constituents should be aware of the value of 'Acceptances' is obvious, since risk is involved, but risk is also

---

[g] An exception occurred in 1959 when former BBME shareholders had to be paid a dividend from Hongkong Bank funds before the Bank had received dividends from the BBME; this, however, was considered as being part of the purchase price rather than a true dividend.

Table 5.7 *The Hongkong Bank 1953 accounts and ratios adjusted*

(in millions of dollars)

			Ratios (%)
1. Assets		3,536.7	
– note issue	755.7		
– acceptances	10.6	2,770.4	
(Cash+money at call)÷assets			
(1,119.8÷2,770.4)			40.4 not 31.7
2. Deposits etc.		2,636.5	
– inner reserves (say) 125.9[a]		2,510.6	
liquidity ratio			67.8 not 65.3
3. Capital (shareholders' funds)		125.9	
+inner reserves 125.9[a]		251.8	
Capital/assets (251.8/2770.4)			9.1 not 3.6
Capital/deposits (251.8/2510.6)			10.0 not 4.8
4. Profit		17.3	
'True profit'		42.3	
Profit/capital (42.3/251.8)			16.8 not 13.7

For unadjusted figures and ratios, see Tables 5.1–3 and 5.5
[a] Inner reserves were actually substantially in excess of this amount.

involved in other items which, although included in the notes to the accounts, are not part of the balance sheet.

In this history, the decision has been made to base analysis on the published figures, since restatement of the accounts on a consistent basis would require a team of auditors to redo the work of a hundred years. On the other hand, knowledge of the problems involved can assist in consideration of particular periods of crisis; *ad hoc* adjustments for a particular purpose can be useful. The magnitude of the problem is illustrated for a randomly chosen year, say 1953, and calculated on the arbitrary assumption that inner reserves were equal to shareholders' funds (see Table 5.7).

Reserves

Inner reserves – their size, purpose, and uses

Despite the fact that it was always possible to make adjustments to the accounts, the Bank, as has been stressed before, had to stand on its balance sheet. Inadequacy of ratios could not be explained by stating there was something extra available – as far as the public was concerned, those extras were of unknown quantity and designed for unusual exigencies; and in the 1950s not even regulatory agencies were aware of the true position.

The true position was, however, known to the Bank's auditors and there is considerable evidence in the Bank's internal correspondence that management was influenced by auditors' 'advice' on the handling of these reserves. Allocations, that is, had to be compatible with definitions acceptable to the auditors, who were conscious of the Bank's need to formulate its accounts in a form acceptable to the Bank of England under the British 1948 Companies Act. This gave assurance to shareholders that, although amounts were not stated, the allocations referred to in the Chairman's speech or by direct reference in the accounts had indeed taken place. Funds were placed in inner reserves for such published requirements as, for example in the 1960 accounts, 'provision for diminution in value of assets' – and it was certainly no secret that such a diminution must have taken place. To this the Chairman added at the Shareholders Meeting in March, 1961, '...and for all known doubtful debts and contingencies'.

From time to time the Chairman would announce that this or that transaction in the annual accounts had been the consequence of a 'transfer from inner reserves' – like a magician pulling a rabbit out of a hat – and yet there was consistency even here.

To appreciate this point, note in Table 5.1 the failure of the published Reserve Fund to increase. The unadjusted capital/assets ratio, with 'capital' defined as shareholders' funds, had declined to 3.0% in 1951, admittedly an exceptional year with the sudden increase in deposits. This situation combined with lack of immediate investment opportunities in troubled times caused a high liquidity ratio – at year-end it was 69%. The decline in the value of assets the following year resulted in an improved capital/assets ratio (as defined for this analysis on the basis of published figures – but see Table 5.7) of 3.5%. The ratio was not, however, significantly improved until 1954, when the Board of Directors approved a transfer of $32 million from inner reserves – the end-year ratio was then 4.4%.

Post-war not only was the regular transfer to reserves achieved by the transfer of large sums from 'true profits' to inner reserves before publication of the P&L Account, but the surplus on published P&L Account was not transferred to published reserves; it was allowed to accumulate. Thus despite the buildup of total shareholders' funds throughout, the published Reserve Fund stagnated. This was a new Bank practice, but it was not critical to the analysis; capital ratios take account of the surplus on P&L Account.

The Hongkong Bank's policy of heavy transfers to inner reserves – due to a combination of factors, the wartime practice, the tendency of Sir Arthur Morse to secrecy, the very real concerns caused by the revolution in China, and the uncertain economic future of Hong Kong, handicapped by the trade restrictions in the United Nations embargo – while undoubtedly sound to those with implicit faith in the directors, neglected the shop window. The directors could not continue to disregard the resulting ratios. The transfers out of inner reserves became therefore the topping up of published reserves almost, it would seem, reluctantly, driven by the need to reassure the public of the Bank's respectability.

The pre-war practice had been to transfer funds from current P&L Account to published reserves. Transfer from inner reserves, which in the 1930s had become necessary in some years to meet dividends, was effected before publishing the P&L Account. Such a transfer affected net profits and, therefore, the sum available for distribution to shareholders. Post-war transfers from inner reserves were undertaken to correct the visible ratios, to reassure shareholders and constituents who studied the annual balance sheet.

A historical note

Traditional Hongkong Bank policy was to transfer annually some appropriate amount from current published profits to the published Reserve Fund. In the early years of Sir Thomas Jackson's management (1876–1886, 1888–1889, 1890–1891, 1893–1902), Jackson had set himself – and therefore the Bank – the goal of a Reserve Fund equal to paid-up capital. With the fall of silver the problem of location became one of equal importance with amounts, but the overall policy of building up reserves whenever possible continued. At the same time there were inner reserves, and Jackson left the Bank with a third line of defence; inner reserves were virtually equivalent to published reserves.

By the 1930s a general policy of overproviding for various specified contingencies had resulted in the creation of several unpublished contingency accounts, not only in Head Office books but also in the branches. Inner reserves were also created by providing funds when securities depreciated or the exchanges went against sterling and then leaving the assets undervalued in their own particular accounts when their dollar value once again improved – the difference between the improved market value and the written down book value became a 'contingency account'. The tendency to transfer to unappropriated contingencies to meet general losses in an era of considerable political uncertainty of an equally general nature paralleled the transfer from published profits to published reserves.

The establishment of the Hong Kong Exchange Fund in 1936 and related factors in what would become the Sterling Area minimized the exchange risk and eliminated the location problem for the time being. But also in the 1930s inner reserves had to be drawn on to pay dividends, although Grayburn had probably restored them by the outbreak of the war.

During the war Arthur Morse understandably built up the inner reserves of the Bank in preparation for the total losses anticipated under circumstances which never occurred. Nevertheless the first Hong Kong Annual Meeting in March 1947 confirmed the 1946 transfer of £1.125 million equivalent from published reserves to increase wartime contingency funds – the sum being slightly in excess of the cost of recognizing the 'duress issue' of the Hongkong Bank. With that transfer the published Reserve Fund of the Hongkong Bank stood at $96 million (£6 million) as compared with the pre-war figure of $114.9 million (£7.1 million) for December 1940 (see Table 5.1).

Reserves policy, 1946–1961

After 1946 the Bank's policy relative to reserves took a new course. Pre-war, for example, although the balance carried forward on Profit and Loss Account varied, it was never permitted to accumulate to the point where it constituted a significant percentage of shareholders' funds. Or the difference might be put this way: before the war sums in P&L Account not paid out in dividends or used for other published purposes were regularly transferred to reserves; postwar they were not. Although amounts varying from $2 million to (exceptionally) $6 million (see Table 5.5) were transferred to write down the book value of Bank Premises, there were no transfers to reserves, and the balance was allowed to accumulate until at the end of 1956 there was a credit balance of $11 million. Meanwhile the Reserve Fund continued to stand at the reduced amount of $96 million.

Morse was, in fact, building up inner reserves which at the end of 1952 had reached a sum substantially in excess of the Bank's published capital. Of these only a third were in sterling, a third were in dollars, and the balance was unspecified – but undoubtedly a high proportion was in U.S. dollars. The problem of exchange control and the need to conserve U.S. dollar resources led to the policy of retaining U.S. dollar profits in the United States, partly as an inner reserve. The relationship between the Hong Kong dollar and the pound sterling remained fixed, but the question of location of reserves had taken a new dimension; with London no longer preeminent in world finance and, with the developing complexity of Hong Kong's worldwide trade connections, there came the need to diversify.

The first post-war increase in published reserves came at the end of 1954 by a transfer of £2 million ($32 million) from inner reserves. The following year the capital accounts of the Bank were again adjusted to better reflect the true position by a further transfer from inner reserves of $5 million to capitalize a 'bonus' issue of one new paid-up share for four held.

The doubling of the Hongkong Bank's paid-up capital authorized in August 1957 was financed by the transfer of $16 million (£1 million) from inner reserves and the draw-down of the balance on P&L Account by $9 million, bringing the latter to a more usual total.

Further increases in published reserves during the period through end-1961 were achieved by including the Share Premium Account, consequent to the acquisition of the Mercantile Bank and the British Bank of the Middle East. The Share Premium Account originated from the difference between the par value of the new shares and their equivalent cash value under the terms of the respective offers, less the excess of cost of the investment in the two banks over the total of their capital, published reserves, and balance of P&L account at the end of 1958 and 1959 respectively.

In 1960 the Reserve Fund of the Hongkong Bank itself increased by $64.8 million to $240 million, equivalent to £15 million. This was due partly to the increase in the share surplus but also to the transfer of $20.5 million from inner reserves – another 'topping-up'; the policy of building up inner reserves from 'true profits' and transferring to published reserves periodically as required by the growth of business continued.

The reserves of the Hongkong Bank Group, as far as the consolidated accounts are concerned, are those of the Hongkong Bank itself. However, as will be explained in Chapter 12, the acquired banks had their own reserves, both published and inner.

Other interpretational problems

The first set of changes occurred in 1949 as a result of requirements of the United Kingdom Companies Act. The Bank, having an office in London, had to submit reports to the Bank of England with the accounts in the form prescribed; the Board decided that the accounts submitted to shareholders should be compatible.

Changes required by the United Kingdom Companies Act
The 1949 accounts can be compared only with difficulty with the 1948 accounts. Consider first the item (in millions of dollars):

	1948	1949
Current, deposit and other accounts	1,807.8	1,820.5

This appeared as a small increase during a year when funds, due to the unsettled conditions in China, were flowing into Hong Kong. The small print explained that in 1948 this item included provisions for bad and doubtful debts; in 1949 these were no longer listed as part of the Bank's liabilities but were rather subtracted from 'Advances to customers'. In 1949 the sum for 'provisions' was subtracted from both sides of the balance sheet, causing an understatement of the size of and growth in deposits, advances, and total footings.

The second change in 'current, deposit and other accounts' was the non-inclusion in 1949 of 'acceptances on behalf of customers', which was listed separately as $8.5 million. On the assets side the counter-item 'Liabilities of customers for acceptances as per contra' was now listed separately, instead of being included in 'Advances to customers and other accounts'. This change did not affect total footings.

A third change was the separate listing from 1949 and after of 'amounts due to subsidiary companies', which although only $270,451 in 1949 became of great importance after 1954.

From 1948 to 1949 it would seem at first glance that account liabilities had increased by $12.7 million. In fact to this sum must be added (i) the (unspecified) 1948 provision for bad and doubtful debts, (ii) the total acceptances outstanding in 1949 ($8.5 million), and (iii) the amounts due subsidiaries ($0.27 million). But both years include the figure for inner reserves and clearing house and interbank deposits. Thus the total increase in current deposits and other accounts held by the non-banking public between 1948 and 1949 was: $12.7 as shown in the accounts plus acceptances = $21.2 million plus the increase in provisions for bad and doubtful debts less the increase in inner reserves and interbank deposits and in the provisions for taxation.

Consider another item:

	1948	1949
Advances to customers and other accounts	696.1	700.9

This increase of $4.8 million must be adjusted by adding (i) 'liabilities of customers for acceptances' ($8.5 million) and (ii) the provisions for bad and doubtful debts which had been subtracted from the 1949 figure.

The Profit and Loss Account had also to be changed to conform to the provisions of the British Finance Act.

In the 1948 accounts profits were shown as being allocated in part to directors' fees, set at £5,000, or $80,842, distributed among the directors at the discretion of the Board itself. This did not include the remuneration of Arthur Morse as Chief Manager, nor did it include the fees paid to the London Committee. These were supposed to be listed separately (see Sec. 149(4) of the Companies Act), but in doing so, Morse argued in a 1949 letter to the Board of Trade, London, his salary, and his salary alone, would be revealed. On the eve of the age of revelations, Morse claimed this was contrary to English tradition.

With only one executive on the Board, it would be impossible to disclose 'special administrative expenses' without virtually revealing the remuneration of the Hongkong Bank's Chief Manager. In the 1951 P&L Account, this new item, 'Special Administrative Expenses, including Chairman's emoluments as Chief Manager, directors' fees and London Committee fees' totalled $770,505. Assuming that the members of the London Committee received the same fees as the directors, the only item left, the Chairman's emoluments as Chief Manager, could be seen by any observer to have been approximately $474,000 (= £29,600) for the year 1951.

In subsequent years Special Administrative Expenses were not included in the published P&L Accounts, but were deducted as a cost of operating the Bank, similar to Managers' bonuses. Nevertheless to meet the requirements of the Companies Act, these expenses were stated in a note to the accounts.

Later changes

In the 1950 accounts the category 'Balance of Remittances, drafts and other items in transit' was omitted as a separate entry on the assets side. This was a net figure, and in 1950 the assets section, that is, 'items in transit' was included with 'Cash and bills receivable'; the Bank's liability for 'drafts in transit' was added to 'Current, deposit and other accounts', making that item even less useful for analysis.

There was a slight increase in current, deposit and other accounts in 1956, from $2,557 million to $2,564 million. The Chairman informed the Annual Meeting, however, that account should be taken of the transfer of all Staff Retirement Scheme funds from this item to the Hongkong Bank's trustee companies. This is the first time that the main pension schemes of the Hongkong Bank had been covered by a full deed of trust. On the assets side the consequent transfer of £3.5 million ($56 million) of investments to the Trustee Company was one of several reasons for the decline in the total value of the Bank's investments.

THE IMPACT OF SUBSIDIARY COMPANIES ON CAPITAL STRUCTURE

The next major change in the Hongkong Bank's capital structure came with the measures necessary to acquire 100% of the shares of the Mercantile Bank Limited (MBLD) and the British Bank of the Middle East (BBME), by an offer which, in both cases, provided those who found the basic offer of Hongkong Bank shares unacceptable a cash alternative; the Bank was in effect underwriting its own acquisitions (see Chapter 12). But before consideration of the implications of these changes, note must be taken of the formation of the Hongkong and Shanghai Banking Corporation of California, Incorporated (HBC), in August 1955.[h]

[h] For obvious reasons, there was an immediate internal Bank need for an abbreviated name – 'Inc' was the solution.

The relevant figures and company names are found in Table 5.8; the company names are in Table II.1.

The incorporation of 'Inc.'

The Bank's wholly owned California subsidiary was capitalized initially by the issue of 10,000 shares, with a par value of US$100, at US$150, giving it US$1 million plus a US$250,000 surplus – the minimum capital funds required by the State Banking Department. The subsidiary, HBC, was established on August 15, 1955, and undivided profits for the rest of the year totalled US$1,489, so that on December 31, 1955, shareholders' funds were US$1,251,489.

California law required a minimum of five directors, each of whom had to hold five qualifying shares. The Hongkong Bank did not, therefore, own 100% of HBC's capital. The directors' 25 qualifying shares with an issued value of US$3,125 had to be owned by them free of lien; they were financed by an interest-free loan from the Bank's New York office. Directors, however, had to sign an agreement that, on retirement or transfer from San Francisco, they would offer their shares at cost to the Hongkong Bank, thereby assuring that the shares and their voting rights would never be alienated from the parent company's control.

During 1956 the HBC's capital was increased by the issue of 5,000 shares at US$125. At the end of the year the subsidiary's authorized and issued capital stock was US$1.5 million and the surplus 'paid in by stockholders' was US$375,000. A further increase in capital was accomplished in 1960 by the issue of 5,000 fully paid-up shares at US$125, so that at the end of the period considered in this chapter, that is, end-1961, the capital of HBC was US$2 million and the surplus US$500,000. Retained profits of US$55,710 resulted in total shareholders' funds of US$2,555,710. The Hongkong Bank's fixed investment in its subsidiary was $14,285,714.

Mercantile Bank Limited

At the commencement of the final successful negotiations for the acquisition of the Mercantile Bank in October 1958 the Hongkong Bank already held a block of Mercantile shares – about 19% of the total. On December 23, 1958, the Hongkong Bank offered to acquire the balance of the outstanding shares at the rate of twenty Mercantile shares for one Hongkong Bank share; for those who preferred a cash alternative, the Bank offered to buy the shares at the rate of 44s (ex final 1958 dividend). The offer was circulated to the Mercantile's shareholders on January 23, 1959, and was conditional on the acquisition in this manner of 90% (or some other percentage agreeable to the Hongkong Bank)

Table 5.8 *The Hongkong Bank Group*
Consolidated accounts: assets and reserves, 1946–1962

(in millions of dollars)[a]

End-year	Assets	Capital	Share premium a/c[b]	Reserves[c]	Assets of subsidiaries[a]				
					HSBC	HBC	MBLD	BBME[e]	Wayfoong Finance
1940	1,246.0	20.0	—	114.9	1,246.0	—	—	—	—
1946	2,050.9	20.0	—	97.0	2,050.9	—	—	—	—
1954	3,571.2	20.0	—	128.0	3,571.2	—	—	—	—
1955	3,427.2	25.0	—	128.0	3,427.2	39.1	—	—	—
1956	3,430.3	25.0	—	128.0	3,430.3	54.8	—	—	—
1957	3,599.8	50.0	—	128.0	3,599.8	86.6	—	—	—
1958	3,643.1	50.0	—	128.0	3,643.1	104.9	—	—	—
1959	5,054.1	62.3	47.2	175.2	4,015.2	110.9	1,137.3	—	—
1960	7,120.3	79.0	91.5	240.0	4,418.1	134.9	1,169.9	1,782.3	20.9
1961	7,659.6	79.0	91.5	240.0	4,774.0	132.0	1,392.4	1,749.7	41.2
1962	9,646.1	79.0	91.5	240.0	5,823.7	129.7	1,746.2	2,333.4	41.2

[a] Exchange rates used: £1 = $16; $1 = 1s:3d; US$1.00 = $5.70; $1.00 = US$0.175.

[b] The Share Premium Account represents the difference between the par value of the new shares and their equivalent cash value under the terms of the respective offers, less the excess of cost of the investment in the two banks over the total of their capital, published reserves and balance of P&L Account at the end of 1958 and 1959 respectively.

[c] The figure for the Reserve Fund *includes* the amount transferred at the end of the period as approved by the shareholders at the subsequent meeting; figures include the Share Premium Account.

[d] Main banking and financial subsidiaries of the Hongkong Bank qua bank; for a list of other subsidiaries see Table II.1. HSBC Hongkong Bank, qua bank; HBC Hongkong and Shanghai Banking Corporation of California; MBLD Mercantile Bank Ltd; BBME British Bank of the Middle East; Wayfoong Finance, Ltd.

[e] For information on the BBME prior to their acquisition by the Hongkong Bank, see the history by Geoffrey Jones.

of the shares not then owned by the Hongkong Bank. The offer, which was to expire on or before February 16 was extended to March 6, at which time the Bank held 97.5% of the total issued capital. Under the terms of the British Companies Act, the balance was compulsorily acquired.

Acceptances for shares totalled 1,902,020, and consequently the Hongkong Bank issued 95,101 (plus 3,390 for late acceptances) new shares in exchange. The final figure of 98,491 is reflected in Table 5.1. By the closing date there had been acceptances for cash totalling 406,142 shares, or 18% of the total number of shares involved, costing the Hongkong Bank £0.89 million.

The book value of Mercantile shares was approximately $29.24 at a time when Hongkong Bank shares had a book value of $450.20; thus using published figures at the ratio of 1 to 20, the sum of $450.20 acquired shares with a total book value of $584.80. This was the basis of the Hongkong Bank's Share Premium Account (added to its published reserves) of $47.2 million representing the premium arising on the issue of the new shares (as shown in the difference in book value) less the excess of the cost of the investment in Mercantile Bank over the total of the issued share capital, published reserves, and undistributed profits of that bank at December 31, 1958. This is shown in Table 5.8; the increase in reserves is from $128 million to $175.2 million.

The increase in the book value of the Hongkong Bank's shares in consequence was from $1,125 to $1,202, or $77 per share (× 400,000 = $30.8 million.

The Hongkong Bank's shareholders' funds had increased by the smaller sum of $59.6 million reflecting the fact that the Hongkong Bank (i) had already owned 19% of Mercantile shares and (ii) had to pay out cash for over 406,000 shares at 44s = approximately $13.5 million, which together totalled $73.1 million. The balance represented the value of the already acquired shares on the Hongkong Bank's books.

No action by the Hongkong Bank was possible, however, without the approval by shareholders of an increase in the authorized capital of the Bank. Accordingly an extraordinary general meeting was called for February 18, 1959, at which the authorized capital of the corporation was doubled from $50 million to $100 million by the creation of 400,000 shares of $125. This no longer required the prior consent of the Governor.

These shares would be on the London Register of the Bank, and the Bank's offer was further conditional on the Committee of the Stock Exchange granting permission to deal in a quotation for the new shares.

The shareholders approved and the Stock Exchange granted the requested permission.

The Chief Manager, Michael Turner, on behalf of the Board of Directors, explained to shareholders on January 23, 1959, that the Board intended to issue only sufficient of these new shares to effect the purchase of the Mercantile Bank. But he added, 'Whilst your directors have no present intention of issuing the balance of the new shares, they consider that it is of advantage to have unissued shares available.'

They could be used, for example, to buy another bank.

The British Bank of the Middle East

Acquisition of the British Bank of the Middle East (BBME), which would put the Hongkong Bank into the Middle East for the first time, was achieved through a similar offer of shares, with a cash alternative for those dissatisfied with the basic offer.

The offer, which was unconditional as of December 31, 1959, was inclusive of the final dividend. This cost the Hongkong Bank $4 million which was paid from inner reserves, the last time in the history of the Bank that a dividend was so paid. The problem was that the BBME's year closed on March 31, and the Hongkong Bank had received no income from its new subsidiary from which to make the payment; the Hongkong Bank's current earnings did not in the view of the Board justify the payment, which must be considered therefore as a capital payment, an increase in the total price paid for the BBME, although calculated on a different basis.

At the March 1960 Shareholders Meeting the Chairman, Michael Turner, announced that by the issue of 133,307 shares the Bank had acquired 99% of the outstanding shares of the BBME. Too late the Hongkong Bank realized that, as it was a chartered bank, the BBME was not subject to the relevant provisions of the Companies Act and there was no procedure for compulsory acquisition of the balance. However the BBME, after some hesitation and considerable legal advice, was henceforth treated as if wholly owned, which it was not in fact until the death of one shareholder holdout in 1972.

By the end of 1960 the Hongkong Bank had acquired 99.67% of the shares and the Bank's issued capital had in consequence increased by 133,878 shares with a par value of $16.7 million; the Share Premium Account was $91.5 million on account of both of the acquired banks and this sum was included in the published reserves of $240 million. The total issued and paid-up capital of the Bank was $79,046,125 in 632,369 shares of $125. With authorized capital standing at $100,000 the Board still had a margin of $20 million without recourse to an extraordinary meeting, but at this point the question of management and 'absorption' of the two new banks was the more important problem.

A final adjustment

Although the book value of the Hongkong Bank's shares in December 1960 was $507.90, the market price was over $1,000 (or, for example, £62:10s). The shareholders were informed at the March 1961 meeting that this was a considerably higher price than that for most other bank shares. Behind this statement was the knowledge that the high price per unit and the alleged impact on marketability had been a factor in the less favourable 20:1 ratio for Mercantile Bank shares actually obtained, when the Hongkong Bank had unsuccessfully insisted, literally to the last minute, on a 22:1 ratio.

This was not intended as a comment on earnings or other performance ratios, that is on the desirability of purchasing Bank shares. It was simply a statement that other things being equal the size, as it were, of the unit was too large and therefore cut out many potential investors from the market. Given that shares were selling in London in 1928 at £143 when the real value of the pound sterling was higher, this is an interesting comment on a changed attitude to investment. The Board did not suggest any lack of demand, or that the market price was lower than it should be by some objective measurement, rather they argued, as a point in favour of the change, that with a lower price the shares would be more widely held. The small investor was being encouraged; previously such a person, if he bought at all, had obtained one or two shares and held them as a long-term investment; now it was thought that he should have more flexibility and ready access to the market.

The Board scheduled an Extraordinary General Meeting to follow the March 1961 Ordinary Meeting; shareholders were asked to approve the subdivision of each $125 share into five $25 shares and to increase the maximum number of shares any one shareholder could possess, without the permission of the Board, from 10,000 to 50,000. Approval was given and consequently the number of issued and paid-up shares increased to 3,161,845; the book value became $101.70.

The change was possible at the practical administrative level as a consequence of resolutions passed at an Extraordinary Meeting in July 1960 which amended the regulations as stated in the Hongkong Bank's ordinance to (i) dispense with distinguishing numbers on share certificates, (ii) use the common type of share transfer form, and (iii) permit the use of mechanically applied signatures. These changes had already been necessitated by the increase in shares consequent to the acquisition of the Mercantile Bank and the BBME; they paved the way, as the Chairman put it, for the proposal to subdivide the shares and thereby certainly increase the volume of share transactions.

THE GROUP ACCOUNTS

The path to consolidation

Until the publication of the Hongkong Bank's 1959 accounts, the Hongkong Bank's year-end published balance sheet was not a consolidated statement of the Bank and its subsidiaries. Capital investment in subsidiaries – that is, in the Bank's nominee and trustee companies – had been shown as a separate item valued at $2.1 million under 'fixed assets'. Other permanent equity investments were less than 50% and the relevant company's accounts were not consolidated with those of the Bank. Furthermore, the Bank's investment in, for example, the British and Chinese Corporation, remained in the form of shares in the name of the London Managers.

This procedure was consistent with standard practices given the nature of the Bank's subsidiary companies, but, with the incorporation of 'Inc', the Hongkong and Shanghai Banking Corporation of California, Inc., the accounts of a major income-producing financial subsidiary had to be considered. The Bank still did not consolidate its accounts, however; the Bank's profit and loss statement excluded the profits of subsidiaries – the profits of HBC remained undistributed. The Bank simply added the value of the HBC's total shareholders' funds, including undistributed profits, at first as a separate item under 'fixed assets' and then as a combined total.

The Bank's investment of a third of the capital of Bowmaker (C.A.) in 1956 is shown in the accounts under 'Fixed Assets: investment in Associated Company, at cost $1,603,499.' As the investment was less than 50% of the total capital, the accounts were not consolidated.

The acquisition of Mercantile Bank required further consideration as far as the 1959 accounts were concerned, especially as, by this time, the acquisition of the BBME was virtually assured.

The Board decided to continue to provide the balance sheet of the Hongkong Bank almost as before, that is, with fixed investments and amounts due to and from subsidiaries. At the same time the Board agreed to provide a 'Group Consolidated Balance Sheet' and a 'Group Consolidated Profit and Loss Account.' These 'Group' accounts were really the statement of The Hongkong and Shanghai Banking Corporation qua corporation; the older format stated the position of the Hongkong Bank qua bank before taking into account the activities of subsidiaries, defined as companies owned 50% or more. In the Group accounts the fixed investment in subsidiaries cancelled out the capital of the subsidiaries to the extent the capital was owned by the corporation; similarly amounts owed by or to subsidiaries cancelled out with counter-entries in the accounts of the subsidiaries. Group profits exceeded Bank profits to the extent that the profits of subsidiaries were retained by the subsidiaries and thus had not been taken into account by the Bank.

The use of the term 'Group', to stress the point, merely made it possible to retain the heading 'Hongkong and Shanghai Banking Corporation' for the traditionally defined balance sheet of the Bank qua bank; the Group account was the consolidated account of The Hongkong and Shanghai Banking Corporation qua corporation, that is, qua legally recognized entity comprising (i) the Bank as 'holding company', (ii) the Bank qua bank, (iii) the subsidiaries of the Bank qua holding company, and (iv) the subsidiaries of the subsidiary companies; to all this, if total assets are to be understood, must be added the fixed investment in affiliated companies by both the Bank (qua bank) and the subsidiaries.

On the Bank's end-1959 balance sheet the Bank's fixed investment in the Mercantile Bank was shown as $85.9 million (see Table 5.9). The Mercantile placed nearly £5 million or $80 million equivalent of its own funds on deposit with the Hongkong Bank (for reasons to be considered in Chapter 12); this is the major part of the item on the Bank's balance sheet: amounts due to subsidiary companies. Similarly, the Hongkong Bank had US$794,000 on deposit with the HBC in San Francisco; this is part of the item 'amounts due by subsidiary companies' in the Bank's accounts. These disappear in the Group Consolidated Accounts.

The consequence of consolidation may be seen by comparing the assets figures for the Bank as shown in Table 5.1 (for example, $4,015 million end-1959, $4,774 million end-1961) with the assets of the Group as shown in Table 5.9 ($5,054 million and $7,660 million respectively). The 1961 Group total reflects factors to be considered in the following section.

The impact of later additions

The companies

The Hongkong Bank's fixed investment in the BBME as stated in the end-1960 accounts as $71.6 million, equivalent to that bank's adjusted shareholders' funds. The BBME held 49% of the shares of the Bank of Iran and the Middle East; this was, therefore, an associated rather than a subsidiary company, and the BBME's investment therein was listed as such on its own year-end statement; the accounts of associated companies are not consolidated.

The 1960 year-end Group accounts reflect the completion of the acquisition of the BBME, but the Hongkong Bank had by then established a fourth financial subsidiary, Wayfoong Finance, with a capital of $5 million and Head Office in Hong Kong. The Hongkong Bank had been developing hire purchase financing through its North Point branch, but business had grown in this specialized field to such an extent that a subsidiary specially staffed and organized to handle it was required – the Manager, however, was a Foreign staff officer, D.P.G. Learmond. Licenced as a bank, Wayfoong Finance could accept deposits from the public, but in fact it was depending mainly on deposits of $19.5 million from the parent company. Profits were retained.

The pooling of Group funds

The growth of net funds due to subsidiaries, shown in Table 5.9 as reaching $140.5 million by the end of 1961, is an illustration of the coordination in the sources and uses of funds which came with the development of the Hongkong Bank Group. The gross figures are more important – and more relevant: for end-1961 there were (i) amounts due to subsidiary companies $165.4 million or 5% of total Hongkong Bank deposits and (ii) amounts due from subsidiary companies $24.9 million – equivalent to 2.7% of the total HBC deposits plus 55% of total Wayfoong Finance deposits.

The Mercantile Bank and the British Bank of the Middle East were depositing surplus funds in the London branch of the Hongkong Bank. This branch, being the office of a bank domiciled overseas, was able to invest in certain securities at a tax advantage. At the same time the Hongkong Bank was depositing its surplus U.S. funds in part in the HBC, San Francisco, and also its Hong Kong funds, for the initial period, with Wayfoong Finance, providing a source of funds for these two subsidiaries until their own resources could be built up.

These movements, which represent one of the key potential advantages of the creation of the Group, are stated here only in connection with the Hongkong Bank's accounts – they obviously net out in the Group Consolidated Accounts. The policy implications will be considered in Chapter 12.

This consideration of the Bank's performance and the comments on its accounts suggest that The Hongkong and Shanghai Banking Corporation had been undergoing years of considerable change. With this chapter as a quantitative background, the history now turns to an examination of change and development in all its variety in these 'critical years'.

Table 5.9 *The Hongkong Bank Group*
Consolidated accounts: capital of subsidiaries, 1955–1961

(in millions of dollars)[a]

	Hongkong Bank Group		The Hongkong Bank			Subsidiaries: shareholders' funds			
End-year	Paid-up Capital	Shareholders' funds	Fixed investment[b]	Due from[c]	Total investment[a]	HBC	MBL	BBME	Wayfoong Finance
1955	25.0	163.6	7.1	9.7	17.2	7.1	—	—	—
1956	25.0	164.0	9.3	5.1	12.7	7.2	—	—	—
1957	50.0	180.1	12.8	7.8	19.0	10.8	—	—	—
1958	50.0	180.1	12.8	2.5	13.8	10.9	—	—	—
1959	62.3	240.3	96.6	−72.8	23.8	11.0	86.0	—	—
1960	79.0	321.2	176.8	−120.1	56.7	14.6[e]	86.0	76.4	5.2
1961	79.0	321.4	176.8	−140.5	36.3	14.6	86.2	78.9	5.8
1962	79.0	321.5	176.8	−132.3	44.5	14.7	86.2	87.0[e]	6.6

Exchange rates used: £1 = $16; $1 = 1s:3d: US$1.00 = $5.70; $1.00 = US$0.175.

[a] 'Fixed investment in subsidiaries' is the total of fixed investment in the four financial companies listed in this table and excludes investment in nominee and trustee companies of $2.1 million.

[c] 'Due from subsidiaries' is a net figure; the negative figure is due to deposits first of the Mercantile Bank and then increased by deposits from Wayfoong Finance with the Hongkong Bank.

[d] 'Total investment in subsidiaries' is the total of fixed investment plus net balances as listed in the published accounts.

[e] The increase from the previous year represents an increase in paid-up capital.

227

6

THE CORPORATION, 1946–1962

> This is a banking establishment, not a gambling hall. The rule is you cover for exchange.
>
> Maurice W. Turner, 1951

Stability and change – What's in a name?
In the years of dramatic post-war change, 1946 to 1961, the Bank in some significant sense did not 'really' change. Its name was 'virtually' as it had been first stated in 1864 as the 'Hongkong and Shanghae Banking Company, Limited'. The 'Hongkong' and 'Shanghai' would remain. In 1866 the 'Company' became 'Corporation', reflecting the change in the Bank's status. Thereafter the name was variously written – 'and' or '&', no definite article or 'The', Shanghai or Shanghae, even Hong Kong or Hongkong. But the usual form as decreed by the Court of Directors and found both in general use and in subsequent legislation was 'Hongkong and Shanghai Banking Corporation'.

Since the mid-1930s, however, the Government had been tending to use the form 'Hong Kong', as for example in the 1943 Order in Council. Sir Arthur Morse, moreover, had strong views on the inclusion of 'The' as part of the legal name of the Bank.

The qualifications 'really' and 'virtually' are necessary therefore, because Morse, in Ordinance No. 37 of 1950, forced through a standardization. The Bank was formally declared to be 'The Hongkong and Shanghai Banking Corporation', and beginning with Part II of this Volume, grammatical conventions notwithstanding, the 'The' will be capitalized when citing the Bank's *full* name.

Even the corporate image exercise of 1980, although adding such linguistically extraordinary combinations as 'HongkongBank' (and thus the advertiser's 'HongkongBank on it'), left the full name of the corporation intact. While some major firms have denied their heritage in favour of initials, the Bank has remained faithful to its early base cities, even during the period when 'and Shanghai' was not everywhere appreciated.

That the Bank should remain 'Hongkong and Shanghai' is not as obvious a decision as it may seem. The Mercantile Bank of India dropped the 'of India' in 1957 – at the 'intimation' of the Indian Government; the Chartered Bank of India, Australia and China became simply the 'Chartered Bank' in 1956.

The Corporation, 1946–1962

These banks were London based; they were neither 'of India' nor 'of India, Australia and China'.

The Hongkong Bank, however, could still claim to be 'of Hong Kong'. This was implicit in the move back in 1946. The significance of this is greater than a discussion about names; behind the name was a banking base, a community with which the Bank was identified, which it financed, and from which it drew its funds, its corporate life, and, to an extent, its political support.

The 'and Shanghai' is more difficult.

Certainly the Bank had post-war expectations; they were frustrated on two occasions. But the Bank never left Shanghai, and by the early 1980s it was again in a position to assist in the development of China. There was certainly some popular misunderstanding in the emotional 1950s over business with a bank which, for all the name implied, might be subject to the People's Government in Peking. This was one factor in the Bank's California subsidiary's change of name from the very long 'Hongkong and Shanghai Banking Corporation of California' to the 'Hongkong Bank of California, Inc'.

Sir Arthur Morse and Sir Michael Turner had been brought up with the full name and its tradition; this was the corporate image they wished to retain.

As there was a positive reason for retaining 'Hongkong' and a long-run hope in retaining 'Shanghai', so there was a positive reason for changing. The traditional wisdom of the Hongkong Bank was challenged. The very purpose of the original, geographically descriptive name seemed to some outdated. When the Bank had been founded the Treasury intended that British overseas and colonial banks should be geographically confined, and 'Hongkong and Shanghai' suggested China and the Treaty Ports with, perhaps, agencies on the edge of other regions to finance trade with this basic area. With the establishment of its own agency in Singapore in 1877, the Bank's name had already become outdated – or misleading. In 1942 V.A. Mason, just escaped from Java, reported that in Australia bankers he questioned specifically on this subject informed him they gave their Hong Kong and China business to the Hongkong and Shanghai Bank, their Indian business to banks with India in their name. He suggested to Morse, then Acting Chief Manager in wartime London, that the Bank's name be changed to something short – 'Wardley', the Bank's Hong Kong telegraphic address, for example. His suggestion was undeniably neutral; no one would know what it meant. Morse replied on the only rational grounds possible, '...the Hongkong and Shanghai Bank is sufficiently well known throughout the world and no alteration of the name is really necessary.' The position is unchanged today.

One theme of Part II is that the changes which occurred in the Hongkong Bank over the period covered by the administrations of Sir Arthur Morse and of his successor, Sir Michael Turner, took place in a Bank soundly based on

Hong Kong and flourishing within its traditional region. It was this strength in its traditional region, ironically, which made it possible for the Bank to absorb the Mercantile Bank and to reach out and acquire the British Bank of the Middle East, thereby moving for the first time into a new region.

Even then the Bank retained its image; it became both an operating bank, with its old name in its old region, and a bank holding company, operating in a new region under the name of the acquired bank. The Bank as holding company was given the popular title 'Hongkong Bank Group', a term without legal status which functioned (again except in legal or formal situations) as if it were the actual title of an overall holding company. A modification of this concept occurred after 1980 (see Chapter 18).

This solution to the corporate-image problem was not totally satisfactory, but it reflected the *de facto* situation. The Hongkong Bank's major extra-regional subsidiaries and associated companies were operating as a group.

Furthermore, the subsidiaries which operated directly under the Hongkong Bank's own management and in its traditional area were named in the tradition of the Bank – the Hongkong and Shanghai Banking Corporation of California and, for the Hong Kong based finance company, Wayfoong Finance, Ltd, 'Wayfoong' being the popular Cantonese 'romanization' of the Bank's Chinese name. There would eventually be other subsidiaries with names like 'Wayhong', 'Waylee', 'Wardley', and 'Carlingford', even 'Gracechurch [Street]' – all identified with the Bank's history.[a]

A major change had indeed occurred in the Bank's development, but it was accomplished in a way which caused least change in the Bank's Eastern image, the staff, the procedures, or even with the Hongkong Bank's constituents. Nevertheless by 1962 the Hongkong Bank, whether bank or 'group', had become an inter-regional banking institution.

Examples of change – the capital structure

During the remaining post-war years of the chief managership of Morse and first two years of Turner's administration, the Hongkong Bank retained a capital

---

[a] 'Wayhong' or 'Hui-hang' uses the Hongkong Bank's first character 'hui', which can mean (*inter alia*) 'to advance money'; 'hang' is 'firm' or 'company'; Waylee or 'Hui-li' ('high principled') was an early alternate Chinese name of the Bank, still used to the end in Tientsin (see Volume I, Chapter 2). 'Wardley House' was the name of the Bank's first office building; 'Wardley' was also the Head Office telegraphic address. 'Carlingford' is less obvious. Head Office instructed N.H.T. Bennett, then London Manager, to register a company in the United Kingdom under the name 'Wardley', but there were already two companies with this name on the company register; Bennett, requested to choose a title, selected the name of the house he had occupied in 1963/64 as Manager Bangkok. The company remained dormant until Head Office, looking for a suitable vehicle to take over the Bank's various insurance interests, decided to use it for this purpose. From the many possible examples, the following, selected at random, must suffice: Wayfoong (Bahamas), Wayhong Finance, Waylee Investments, Wardley Marine International Investment Managers, Carlingford Swire Assurance (Bermuda), and Gracechurch Holdings.

structure based on the original ordinance of 1866, the amounts having been augmented by rights issues in 1883, 1890, 1907, and 1921. With the first capitalization of reserves through a 1955 bonus issue, a number of changes were initiated, each of them in a sense independent of the other (and thus to some extent unforeseen), which were the consequence of several diverse factors – the capitalization of reserves, the elimination of shareholders' reserved liability, the acquisition by purchase of 100% of the share capital of two smaller but flourishing banks, and the decision to divide the nominal or par value of the by then 'top-heavy' shares by five during 1961.

This last change was undertaken reluctantly. Michael Turner held tenaciously to a vision of the Bank as a Far Eastern bank whose interests were those of both shareholders and constituents, who, ideally, would be identical. It was not quite a romantic reversion to the Bank as a Hong Kong cooperative, but the concept of a bank owned by people who knew the Bank and were interested in its long-run development was certainly part of his thinking.

This romantic view, however, was never quite accurate; David McLean and the great TJ (Sir Thomas Jackson) himself had speculated in Bank shares, and in boom times even shares at $125 par could be used as, to employ Turner's phrase, 'gambling counters'.[1] Even before new shares had been issued in London for the acquisition of the Mercantile Bank in 1959, 220,000 of the 400,000 shares were on the London register; in 1960 after the acquisition of the British Bank of the Middle East, there were 452,369 in London and the same 180,000 in Hong Kong.

Turner had tried to avoid these developments by insisting on a cash offer to the Mercantile Bank, but this proved impractical (see Chapters 5 and 12). Once shares were held by people to whom the Hongkong Bank was unknown, what would be the consequences? With his hand forced in the matter of the takeover offers, Turner was all the more insistent that the par value of the shares should not be changed. But here again he was frustrated. Hongkong Bank shares were being quoted in London at £70 – other bank shares were quoted in shillings, the Westminster at 61s for example; dividends were 64% of the par value of the Hongkong Bank shares. Share brokers wrote of the expectations of their customers, some of them former shareholders in the acquired banks; comparison with other banks' shares suggested the Hongkong Bank's position was unusual, and in 1961 Turner surrendered – the $125 shares were divided into five shares of $25 each.[2]

Quite naturally Turner's misgivings were not reflected in his speech as Chairman of the Bank at the March 1961 Annual Meeting:

For some time past our shares have been considerably higher in price than those of most banking companies and it has been suggested that this results in many small investors being discouraged from buying them. Although there has been no sign of any lack of demand, I think it is very likely that a lower-priced share would be more widely held. Your directors therefore decided that the time had come to divide the shares into smaller units and you will be asked to approve that the existing shares of $125 be subdivided into shares of $25 each and that the maximum individual shareholding should be increased from 10,000 to 50,000 shares.

Despite Turner's concern that this change was part of a series of events robbing the Hongkong Bank of its historical characteristics and thereby possibly endangering its future, the Bank was able to minimize the impact of any forced change until management was able to adjust to the new challenge. The methods were often defensive, but they bought time; the full impact of events in the 1950s was not fully absorbed until the mid 1970s during the chief managership of Guy Sayer.

The events referred to above were accompanied by changes in the Bank's constitution, its basic ordinance, and in the bank regulatory environment of the Bank's base city state, Hong Kong – although even more significant changes would come during the chief managership/executive chairmanship of Sir John Saunders.

The Hongkong Bank was apparently the last bank incorporated under the terms of the old Colonial Banking Regulations, but it was no longer part of a colonial banking 'system' regulated by the Colonial Office on Treasury advice.[b] In Chapter 3 there were instances noted where the special status of the Bank was an anachronism, simply a nuisance – for any desired general change two ordinances were needed, one for the Bank and one for everyone else. With the passage of the Banking Ordinance of 1949 the Hongkong Bank, while remaining a 'note-issuing bank', was also designated as a 'licenced bank', and as such was subject to the broader legislation which for the first time gave the Government certain specific powers over the banking sector. For the time these were minimal; as far as the Hongkong Bank was concerned, the Government already had the powers it required. Only with the 1964 ordinance, which contained provisions through which monetary policy might be implemented, did the Hongkong Bank enter a new regulatory era in Hong Kong.

The timing of these changes depended on such diverse factors as the attitude of the Hong Kong Government to the Bank, the reaction of investors to the Bank's extraordinary published reserves/paid-up capital ratio, and the changing attitudes of the Bank's management under diverse pressures. Certain of these problems will be considered in the context of the particular feature at issue.

With the acquisition of two operating banks, the Mercantile Bank and the

---

[b] Other British banks were subsequently established on the basis of a Royal Charter, including the Imperial Bank of Persia (later BBME), but there were special factors involved, unrelated to normal British or colonial banking considerations. The Imperial Bank, for example, was to operate in non-British territories, with a head office in Persia, subject to the conditions of concessions from the Shah; it was to be the state bank of Persia.

Royally chartered British Bank of the Middle East in 1959 and 1960 respectively, and with the existence of financial subsidiary companies – in addition to nominee and trustee companies – there had appeared what was to be known as the Hongkong Bank Group, which was, as stated above, merely The Hongkong and Shanghai Banking Corporation as a bank holding company – the name giving stress to the parts rather than to the whole. The accounts of the operating Hongkong Bank could be, and indeed were, published separately. Thus the Bank can continue to be studied from published sources in the context of its history. But there would now also be consolidated accounts – that is, accounts of the Group – which could also quite legitimately be termed 'The Hongkong and Shanghai Banking Corporation'. Shareholders held shares in the Hongkong Bank qua Group, and thus the capital accounts for the Bank qua bank holding company and the Bank qua operating bank are identical, but other items differ and the two will need to be distinguished.

This chapter deals with the Hongkong and Shanghai Bank as a corporation, noting changes in its legal status, capital position, its Board of Directors, and its London Committee. The succession of Chief Managers and their relation to the Board and the continued but qualified existence of the three-tier staff system are examined in Chapter 7.

LEGISLATED CHANGE

THE HONG KONG NOTE ISSUE

For the Hongkong Banker the most important development in the Bank's note issue was the end of hand-signing. Post-war the notes were shipped East with two printed signatures. There remained, however, other routine tasks to test the dedication of young Bankers. Printed banknote signatures did not herald the immediate arrival of computerized banking.

The Hong Kong Exchange Fund

A fixed par of exchange
Hongkong Bankers are generally agreed that post-war banking did not involve exchange banking. In a world of exchange controls and Government monopolies of foreign exchange transactions, international banks were virtually passive operators. A great many assumptions are made in such statements and they need clarification.

One of the principles of exchange banking pre-war was that the sound banker did not take a position. Yet this is precisely what the exchange banks had to do in the age of silver, that is, before 1936. The individual Bank 'agent' did not speculate on silver, but the managers of the major branches took positions which were based on their estimation of need and their expectation as to the trend of the market. Funds had to be in place, for example, for the tea buying season; they could not always be covered.

Thus there were two sources of profit (or loss) from exchange: (i) taking a position and therefore taking the consequences resulting from an uncovered position being affected by a change in the rate of exchange and (ii) turnover of funds and the profit arising from the difference between the buying and selling rate at any given level of exchange. This second source of profit can be replaced by or increased by a 'commission' depending on the methods of doing business in the particular port.

When Bankers spoke of the absence of exchange operations post-war, they were referring to the taking of a position. The banks continued to buy and sell foreign exchange but their profit was based on turnover and arose from the second factor mentioned above. Exchange rates in the world of the International Monetary Fund (IMF) were allowed to fluctuate within a narrow margin, and thus there remained the opportunity of making a small profit by taking a position – if such were permitted by the relevant authorities, but relatively this was a minor issue. As the post-war currency arrangements came under strain, the positioning of assets would again be a matter of major policy concern. But that was later.

The British Colonial currencies, the Straits dollar for example, operating under their own Currency Board, had, however, a fixed par of exchange; the Board dealt with the banks and public at this rate, charging a commission; the banks dealt with the public in similar fashion. The Hong Kong Government's Exchange Fund still operated with a spread of $\frac{5}{8}$ths of 1% (0.625%) around a par of 1s:$2\frac{29}{32}$d (£0.06211) – which the Colonial Office considered an 'inconvenient figure'. The Colonial Office, encouraged by Sir Sydney Caine, were anxious to eliminate this, set the par at 1s:3d (£0.06250), and operated the Fund exactly as if it were a Colonial Currency Board.

The change was practical. The note-issuing banks had agreed with the Exchange Fund that they would operate with the public at an additional margin which effectively increased the potential spread of the dollar from 1s:$2\frac{25}{32}$d to 1s:$\frac{31}{32}$d. The banks were, however, actually operating at the high end of the range with a difference of only $\frac{1}{16}$d between their buying and selling rates. From this point of view the time was ideal for effecting the 'reform'.[3]

Arthur Morse was opposed on several grounds. First, the change marked a slight appreciation of the dollar. At the time the Exchange Fund could not provide 100% cover for the note issue, and the change would aggravate the position, consequently Morse advised waiting until the Fund's income had

The Corporation, 1946–1962

built up the reserves to 100% of the note issue. Morse was also concerned that no measure be taken to change the dollar at a critical political time.[4] The change would also eliminate the small profit the Hongkong Bank obtained from taking a position within the range permitted.

The Colonial Office decided to effect its reform when the Exchange Fund cover reached 100%, but these considerations and the problems referred to below were among those which led in 1950 to a further consideration of the whole question of a Government note issue.[5]

The British Treasury informed the International Monetary Fund that the par value of the dollar was 1s:3d, and at this rate Hong Kong Government accounts were kept. The Exchange Fund, however, in order to earn from a spread between buying and selling rates, sold certificates of indebtedness to the note-issuing banks, that is, in the interbank market, against the deposit of 1s:3d per $1.00 and bought at 1s:2$\frac{7}{8}$d; thus the actual central rate around which the dollar moved was not 1s:3d but 1s:2$\frac{15}{16}$d. Under the same circumstances the other banks requiring to increase their dollar assets would sell sterling to the note-issuing banks at 1s:3$\frac{1}{32}$d per $1.00; the public rate would be 1s:3$\frac{11}{16}$d.

If, however, the net demand were for sterling, the Exchange Fund was prepared to sell sterling to the note-issuing banks at 1s:2$\frac{7}{8}$d for each dollar received. Other banks would receive 1s:2$\frac{27}{32}$d and the public 1s:2$\frac{13}{16}$d. The overall spread between the rates to the public for buying and selling sterling was therefore between 1s:3$\frac{1}{16}$d and 1s:2$\frac{13}{16}$d, a spread of $\frac{1}{4}$ of a point or $\frac{8}{32}$ of a point; the usual margin between the Bank's buying and selling rates was $\frac{3}{32}$ of a point, thus allowing a minimal movement of the exchanges which was within the 1% allowed by the IMF (provided the par is calculated at the central rate and not at the official rate of 1s:3d).[6]

And within these constraints the Hongkong Bank remained an 'exchange bank' in the pre-war sense. To the extent that these changes in the exchange were accepted as a signal to the market, they had a significant impact. The Hongkong Bank could, therefore, make an exchange profit or loss in addition to the income from the 'turn'; its privilege of access to the Exchange Fund, which it shared with the Chartered Bank and the Mercantile Bank, was a further source of income against which it had to offset the cost of handling clearing accounts and the unrequited cost of the note issue.

Exchange operations – a digression

Despite the world of 'fixed' exchanges, the Hongkong Bank remained an exchange bank. J. Caldwell (East 1920) was Manager Calcutta, 1945–1952, and had seen the great A.G. Stephen and A.S. Henchman at work.

When I did become senior enough to run my own exchange in Calcutta, of course silver trading was out of the question. None of that there, and it was just a matter of fixing your dates and trying to marry your contracts in so many months' time so that they all came to fruition together, paid off and balanced out. That's the interesting part, especially when you have quite a big office. It's like running a huge book. You have got positions on all different currencies, and, depending on world affairs and world markets, you vary your different currencies accordingly.[7]

H.A. Mabey was one of the few Hongkong Bank Managers mentioned in oral histories as being interested in the instruction of juniors – Occy Paterson and John Howard were others. As a first-tour junior, Norman H.T. Bennett recalls Mabey as Acting Manager Calcutta in 1948. 'Mabey used to send little notes out saying, if I'm in Brazil and I want to sell some cruzeros forward and cover them through Paris, what rate should I quote in sterling? This was absolutely mystifying for us, but I mean this was marvellous training.'[8]

The 'positions' referred to by Caldwell are working positions; normally they would not remain 'uncovered' on the basis of expectations relative to a 'devaluation'. Bennett was reminded of this in no uncertain terms.

I remember Maurice [W.] Turner when he was head of Books Office when he was in Hong Kong which would be in 1951 or '52, and I was in the Drafts Department having some business with Pakistan. I said to Maurice that I thought the Pakistan rupee was going to be devalued, and I didn't see any point in covering for the exchange. This had just been done.

Maurice, in very sort of sombre manner, said, this is a banking establishment, Bennett, not a gambling hall. The rule is you cover for the exchange.

We covered for the exchange, and we lost money. But this is the difference between doing it the correct way and taking a flyer on what you thought was going to happen in a week or so's time on the Pakistan rupee. Maurice was quite right, but he wasn't going to have any departmental head taking a position which was his responsibility anyway.[9]

Transferability of certificates of indebtedness

A second problem relative to the Hong Kong Exchange Fund arose from the fact that the Colony's legal tender consisted of the note issue of three commercial banks; the notes they issued were designed to be readily identifiable as the liability of a specific bank and thus had potentially separate demand schedules and, consequently, 'price', that is, the discount or premium relative to par. This would seem to be contrary to their status as legal tender, but this conclusion is in error for two reasons.

First, the bulk of the Colony's note issue circulated in South China until at least 1950, and there the notes were not legal tender (indeed, quite the contrary). The Hongkong Bank's note issue was at least ten times that of the Chartered's, but, for whatever reason, Hongkong Bank banknotes were more readily acceptable in China and the Chartered's notes passed at a 10% discount. Therefore, when remittances from Malaya were received by the Chartered Bank in Hong Kong and paid out in large denomination notes (usually $500) to the payee who intended to smuggle them into China, he would first pay them in to the Hongkong Bank for Hongkong Bank notes.[c]

This in itself would have created no problem if the Hongkong Bank had been willing to pay out Chartered or Mercantile Bank notes across its counters. In the immediate post-war period the note-issuing banks did in fact pay out each other's notes as supply required. One day, however, Morse sent the office messenger down for cash; he returned with Chartered Bank notes. This, one observer reported, resulted in an explosion. As a consequence this convenient practice ceased.

The Hongkong Bank, which would no longer pay out the notes of another bank, held a large stock of Chartered Bank notes – on December 13, 1947, it held $14.5 million of the Chartered's notes – which it had to pass over to the Chartered Bank for payment. This was to be effected at first by drawing down the Chartered's clearing account with the Hongkong Bank. At some point, however, this account became exhausted and had to be replenished by the Chartered Bank selling sterling to the Hongkong Bank. This the latter could use to buy certificates of indebtedness to cover its increased note issue. In January 1948, for example, the Hongkong Bank reduced its holdings of Chartered Bank notes to $6.9 million and the latter sold the sterling equivalent to the Hongkong Bank.[10]

In effect these transactions could be looked at in the following way – although the sequence is not necessarily exact.

The Chartered Bank sold sterling to the Exchange Fund for certificates of indebtedness against which it increased its note issue to enable it to pay out remittances from Malaya. These notes could not be kept in circulation but were returned to the Chartered Bank which, assume for this exposition, withdrew them from circulation, selling certificates of indebtedness back to the Exchange Fund, and selling the resulting sterling over to the Hongkong Bank for a dollar credit to its clearing account with the Hongkong Bank. The Hongkong Bank then bought certificates of indebtedness to cover the increased Hongkong Bank note issue resulting from the inability of the Chartered Bank to keep its notes in circulation, a situation resulting, as described, from the payee of the Malayan remittances substituting Hongkong Bank for Chartered Bank notes.

Each step cost the Chartered Bank a marginal amount. And the solution was obvious. Instead of redeeming certificates for sterling to sell to the Hongkong Bank to credit the Chartered's dollar account, the Chartered Bank could have acted at an earlier stage and cut out all the expensive operations by simply transferring certificates of indebtedness to the Hongkong Bank in return for a credit to its clearing account. The Chartered Bank had sold sterling for

[c] Pre-war the remittances were more often made directly to agencies in South China and the problem did not arise in this form.

certificates of indebtedness to enable it to increase its note issue; the public wanted an increase in the note issue but in the form of Hongkong Bank notes; therefore, the Chartered would take back its unwanted notes and transfer its consequently unwanted certificates of indebtedness to the Hongkong Bank.

The certificates were, however, non-transferable.

The second force at work was the very size of the Hongkong Bank and the fact that it handled the accounts of the major public utilities. Thus a large number of Chartered Bank notes were paid into the utility companies which in turn deposited them with the Hongkong Bank. Again the Hongkong Bank's stock of Chartered Bank notes increased. Granted that there were offsets, for example, a general increase in the note issue with the Chartered Bank's share being met by the returned notes from the Hongkong Bank; the system worked against the Chartered Bank.

Not surprisingly the General Manager of the Chartered Bank, W.R.M. Cockburn, proposed that the certificates be made transferable; also not surprisingly, Arthur Morse objected. As Morse pointed out, by arbitrage transactions the Chartered Bank could make a small profit; it could also have the advantage of a note issue without the cost of managing it, shifting that to the Hongkong Bank whenever it suited them. Following the 1948/49 controversy, the then Financial Secretary in Hong Kong had obtained a compromise agreement between the two banks that some $2 million would be made transferable.[11] When the reforms mentioned above, a par of 1s:3d fixed and operations at a stated commission on either side of par, were effected, the financial objections to the transferability of certificates of indebtedness would in fact be removed.

A government note issue revisited

The controversies considered in the preceding section indicate that there was a conflict of interest. The Hong Kong Government consistently took the position when considering 'property rights' that the note issue was the concern of three commercial banks, the notes were their property, and their responsibility. It was not a position that could be sustained. Once the note issue had become of any magnitude, its soundness had been a matter of public concern; once it had become legal tender, its management involved the Government which had, after all, agreed to meet a high proportion of the cost of issue. Where the banks' policy as commercial institutions conflicted with the Government's currency policy, the Government did not hesitate to interfere and the banks did not hesitate to resist.

The above controversies came to a head in the period 1948–1950, which, considering the revolution in China, was not a time to undermine confidence in the Hong Kong currency. Therefore, although the Government was again pressed by the Colonial Office to consider their own note issue, the local authorities resisted. In consequence the requirements of the note-issuing banks had to be taken into consideration; where these were in conflict, the Hongkong Bank had to be shown some special consideration.

The Government was naturally not anxious to admit publicly to any special consideration, but the fact was that the Government depended on the Bank for the note issue and for financial support. 'Indeed, we must face the fact that it would not be practical politics to float a loan locally unless we had the Hongkong Bank behind it,' the Financial Secretary wrote to Sir Sydney Caine in February 1948.[12] A $50 million public loan had been supported indeed by both the Chartered and the Hongkong Banks, but in the end public response had been so poor that the Hongkong Bank had to take up over $20 million – the Chartered Bank only $5 million.[d]

Furthermore, the Hongkong Bank issued 90% of the banknotes; only the Bank was equipped to administer this major portion of the issue. Once again it was a choice of dealing quietly with the Bank or of taking over the issue.

Dealing quietly did not, however, mean losing the argument. The par rate was fixed at 1s:3d and the range narrowed so that the Fund operated like a Currency Board; $2 million of the certificates of indebtedness were made interchangeable. The Hongkong Bank had more important problems under consideration.

The responsibility for unissued notes

The question of the responsibility for unissued notes was somewhat broader than the problem of the 'duress notes'. The latter involved the illegal issue under specific historical conditions of printed 'pieces of paper', which were consequently not a 'legal tender'. The problem now was broader in that any agreement had to consider a range of possible events and even include certain legally issued banknotes – which were an admitted liability of the Bank – constituting the Bank's 'cash in hand' and which had thus not as yet been issued to other banks or to the non-banking public. Furthermore a conflict of interest was involved.

When the Japanese attack on Hong Kong Island appeared inevitable, the Financial Secretary had given reluctant 'permission' for part of the unissued notes to be burnt, but quietly so as to avoid panic. This would always be the case. In a time of threatened political crisis the public wishes to be liquid; this could develop into a run on the banks if the public thought that, in addition

---

[d] This discouraged the Government from further issues, thus obtaining for the Hong Kong Government a reputation for sound and conservative financial policy. The event stressed the dependence of the Government on the Bank.[13]

to the external risk, the banks were taking actions which would render themselves less liquid. If, however, the issuing banks are responsible for their notes in their possession, it would be in their interest to destroy or ship out of possible harm's way as many notes as possible.

During 1949 and into 1950 with refugees coming into Hong Kong, banknotes previously held in South China were being brought back to the Colony and deposited. As the banks were responsible for these notes, their safest policy would have been to cancel them and ship out the cancelled notes without notice – difficult when the public would be likely to learn through the leaking of the contents of cargo manifests. On the other hand, when conditions are uncertain banks ought to have cash in hand.

Morse took a simple but clear position; he assumed that sound banking required remaining liquid, this required keeping large stocks of notes on hand and that therefore the Government should be responsible for the Bank's loss in the event the notes were seized. The duress issue had cost the Bank £1 million; it had cost the Government considerably more, but Morse assumed that the obvious principle of responsibility had been accepted.

Morse's position led to great concern in the Colonial Office and apparent near hysteria in the Treasury. A Colonial Office minute states that Norman Young of the Treasury insisted the Colonial Office send, that night, a cable 'peremptorily ordering the Governor [Alexander Grantham of Hong Kong] to summon Mr Morse and tell him where he got off' – the Treasury had apparently been subjected to high-level pressure on behalf of the Hongkong Bank by the Bank of England.[14]

Mr Young's suggestion, in the form in which he made it, was of course ludicrous. I told him that if we communicated with the Governor in the terms suggested, and, if the Governor for some reason felt unable to comply, he would have no alternative but to resign on the spot.

At the same time the attitude of the Hongkong and Shanghai Bank on this matter is undoubtedly unsatisfactory, and moreover we have already asked the Governor to make the position clear to them, although it is doubtful whether he has done so.[15]

Why the Bank's obvious position was 'undoubtedly unsatisfactory' is not convincingly stated. The Government's position, on the other hand, was untenable, and eight years of desultory negotiations later the Government was forced to give ground.

The public had no access to the Exchange Fund. The public demand for sterling purchased by the pay-in of banknotes did not automatically affect the position of the Exchange Fund; whether the note-issuing banks, the only persons who could deal with the Fund chose to cancel the paid-in notes and redeem certificates was a matter for these banks to decide – the transaction in itself involved the banks in a loss and would therefore be undertaken only if the

A general view of Macau, May 29, 1839, by Auguste Borget
—from the Hongkong Bank's collection.

Sir ARTHUR MORSE, KBE (1892–1967).
Chairman and chief executive
The Hongkong and Shanghai Building Corporation, 1941–1953
—a portrait by Simon Elwes.

Chinese Imperial Railway 5% Gold Loan of 1899, a £100 bond.
This loan, with a face value of £2.3 million, was issued for the British and Chinese Corporation at 97 for 45 years to finance past advances and new developments on the line from Tientsin to Mukden (see Volume II). Although service of the loan had been continued by the Japanese until 1942 (see Volume III), as with the bulk of China's foreign debt, payments of both capital and interest were in default post-war.

Hongkong Bank lions – types and uses.
One of the two bronze lions (*above*) which guard the Bank's head office; a model in butter serves as a banquet centrepiece for the opening of the new Butterworth office, 1980 (*upper far right*); the 'friendly lion' is a symbol of retail service (*upper right*); and, *immediately above*, the bronze lions are featured on a recent $100 Hongkong Bank banknote.

The Hongkong Bank/Marine Midland Banks definitive agreement, at the signing in Buffalo, New York, 1979.
Left to right: John R. Petty, President, and Edward W. Duffy, Chairman, MMBI, with (Sir) M. G. R. Sandberg, Chairman, and I. H. Macdonald, Executive Director, the Hongkong Bank.

The Hongkong Bank's 1982 Board of Directors.

Left to right: T. J. Bedford, D. R. Y. Bluck, E. W. Duffy, I. H. Macdonald, (Sir) Q. W. Lee, D. K. Newbigging, P. E. Hutson, P. G. Williams, (Sir) Yue-Kong Pao, (Sir) Michael Sandberg, P. E. Hammond, J. L. Marden, Hui Sai Fun, N. S. Thompson, Li Ka-shing, R. W. Hubner, J. F. Holmes, R. V. Munden, (Dame) L. S. Dunn, (Sir) John Archer (see Table 15.2). The caricature is by Circle Lo.

'At Home', Carlingford, the Bangkok Manager's residence
—*Living in Thailand* (April 1979).

This house 'where tradition lingers' is located on a valuable 21 *rai* Sathorn Road site, originally purchased in 1909 before restrictive land-holding regulations were enacted. The Managers entertained as befitted the doyen of foreign banks, but such activities are now differently assessed. The house was sold and the remaining property developed for modern staff accommodation, a pattern followed by the Hongkong Bank in Singapore, Tokyo, and elsewhere.
The name 'Carlingford' has been taken to designate the Hongkong Bank Group's several insurance companies.

Hong Kong, Central, from the southeast, a 1986 view.
The completed Foster Associates hi-tech Hongkong Bank head office building is clearly visible.

banks decided that their holdings of notes would remain excessive for some period of time, that the interest forgone would be less than the loss of exchange. As a matter of practice, however, the decision to redeem certificates of indebtedness was a matter of negotiation with the Financial Secretary; sudden redemption could force the sale of the Fund's securities, possibly at an inconvenient time.

The note-issuing banks' willingness to negotiate, a process which could result in an agreement to hold more notes than the banks considered safe, would be affected by the question of who was responsible for the ultimate security of the notes as physical entities, that is, who was responsible in the event of the notes being seized and issued by an invading force.

The Government's final proposals, after Sir Norman Young had retired, were contained in a mutually agreed Memorandum of June 13, 1958, which reached the Board for approval the following day; Michael Turner, by then the Chief Manager, informed the Board he considered them less than satisfactory but the best which could be obtained.

The unissued banknotes, that is, the banknotes which were still 'pieces of paper' issued neither to the Bank nor to the public, were to remain the property of the Bank and the Bank would continue to be responsible for their security. However, if the Bank would agree to follow certain general rules and accept peremptory orders in periods of emergency, the Government would accept responsibility for any adverse consequences not due to negligence.

The Bank agreed that its stock of unissued notes, of which only 50% was to be physically stored in Hong Kong, would not exceed 100% of the notes issued. Value was one problem; bulk another. The Bank therefore also agreed that unissued notes of denominations of $100 or less held in Hong Kong should not exceed 25% of the total face value of the notes of these dominations in circulation, etc. The Bank would require prior Government approval for the printing of notes and for their import into Hong Kong. More generally, the Bank agreed to follow Government instructions as to storage, destruction etc., the costs being shared by the Bank and Government according to the then prevailing formula for sharing overall note-issuing costs.

Currency legislation in Hong Kong

Cancellation of the right to the increased fiduciary issue, 1953

Changes in the Bank's capital structure were coincident with changes in its ordinance of incorporation which eroded the peculiar provisions the importance of which had become by this time almost anachronistic. The first legislated change occurred in 1953 and, although unimportant in itself, was illustrative of the Bank's historical relationship to Government. The Hongkong and Shanghai

Banking Corporation (Amendment) Ordinance, No. 27 of 1953, referred to in Chapter 3, terminated the temporary increase from $30 million to $46 million of the Bank's authorized banknote issue.

There are several historical points which can be made. First, the survival of the Hongkong Bank's note issue was the consequence of a series of chances which have no parallel. Every serious governmental consideration of taking over the note issue, including the rethinking referred to above in the 1948–50 period, came at a time either of financial difficulty or economic crisis, but the Treasury and the Colonial Office regarded these setbacks as temporary.

The Bank's basic 1929 ordinance took away the Bank's note issuing rights effective 1939, but the Government was careful to write in an escape clause – the Bank's rights could be extended by legislation. And they were. Over the same period the relative benefits of the note issue to the Bank – other than as an advertisement – became less obvious; as successive Chief Managers had argued, it was a costly process. The size of the 'authorized issue', against which cash or securities could be deposited as security and from which the Bank might be said to earn income directly from its right to issue notes, became an increasingly smaller percentage of the Bank's total liabilities. As for the 'fiduciary' issue, that portion of the note issue against which neither certificates of indebtedness nor securities had to be deposited, its potential total value was less than 1% of the Bank's liabilities. Indeed, advantage was no longer taken of the privilege; the securities deposited covered the entire authorized issue.

Nevertheless, this is what the ordinance of 1953 was all about. The fiduciary part of the authorized issue had been increased in 1946 by $16 million and the Bank, by agreement, had been gradually covering it with certificates of indebtedness as they were issued, without charge, by the Exchange Fund. In 1953 the right to the extra fiduciary issue had thereupon been extinguished by the full formality of an amending ordinance, a precaution which in the mid-nineteenth century would have been of the utmost significance but which was now, from a practical point of view, meaningless. In any case, the position was returned *de jure* to the *status quo ante*.

The note issue after the ordinance of 1957

In the context of a major revision of the Bank's ordinance (No. 36 of 1957) to be considered below, the right of the Bank to issue banknotes – in Hong Kong, but not elsewhere – was reinserted into the Bank's charter, the ordinance of 1929. The right was subject, as it always had been, to existing regulations and to cancellation by the Government. Nor was the Bank to issue notes for less than $5.00 in value beyond limits prescribed by the Government; some traditions would seem never to die, but in this case the Government now had a one-dollar issue of its own (par. 5, amending sec. 10). Nevertheless, despite these conditions – all of which made sense when put in historical context – the change did eliminate the need for parallel currency legislation and gave an impression of permanence; the Government, while reserving its rights, had given up any pretence that it would take over the note issue.

The ordinance, as part of an agreement to end the Hongkong Bank shareholders' double liability, ended the right to the small fiduciary issue. Henceforth the authorized note issue of $30 million had to be covered entirely by approved securities; the excess issue, by certificates of indebtedness.

CAPITAL STRUCTURE AND RELATED CHANGES, 1951–1961

The emergency transfer of Head Office

Morse was not concerned only for the safety of unissued notes. In the years following the appearance of the People's Liberation Army on the Hong Kong frontier and the establishment of the People's Republic in China, Hong Kong appeared vulnerable, and the question of the physical security of the Colony was one of considerable concern. Morse's responsibility was to protect the Hongkong Bank and its shareholders; being caught unprepared in 1941 might be excused, being caught only ten years later would appear negligent. The British in Hong Kong were either those caught in the East when the Pacific War broke out or those who were aware of sufferings still bitterly remembered. There was a general nervousness; no one wished to be 'in the bag' twice.

Accordingly in 1951 Morse entered into negotiations with the Hong Kong Government and through them with the Secretary of State for the Colonies. The latter agreed that a draft Order in Council, modelled after the 1943 Order, should be drawn up, together with a draft resolution for the Board of Directors which would remove Head Office to London and make the London Advisory Committee the Board of Directors, with the specific authority to appoint a Chief Manager. The Order provided that the Bank would immediately lose the right of note issue.

The drafts were approved in Hong Kong in December 1952 and in London in 1954. However subsequent discussions included the thought that in an atomic war, London might be less safe than, for example, Australia – or the Bank might prefer to remove to Bermuda. This would require appropriate enabling legislation in the specified political territory, but the matter was not further pursued.[16]

The Chief Manager and the Board could however rest assured that, provided there were time for the Board to meet and pass the draft resolution, the Bank had prior British Government approval for its Head Office to be removed to London at a moment of physical emergency.

The 'bonus' share issue of 1955

At an extraordinary meeting in March 1955 shareholders approved a proposal for a 'bonus' issue, that is, a capitalization issue, on the basis of one share for every four held, thereby increasing the number of shares outstanding from 160,000 to 200,000 and the paid-up capital from $20 million to $25 million, as shown in Table 5.1 above. The annual accounts show published reserves unchanged; the bonus issue was financed by capitalizing $5 million of inner reserves. Since inner reserves are included in the published accounts with 'Current, deposit and other accounts', the transfer from inner reserves to capital account explains the decline in these 'deposits' during an apparently prosperous year (from $2.67 to $2.56 million; see Chapter 5).

Since the Pacific War the Bank had built up the Profit and Loss Account and inner reserves. The Bank was in an undoubtedly strong position but (i) shareholders were not benefiting directly through improved dividends and (ii) the ratios, consequent to the Bank's policy, were extraordinary. On this last point, published reserves (including P&L Account) reached 554% of paid-up capital, compared to a more usual 134% for the Mercantile Bank or 118% for the Westminster. Furthermore, the dividend as a percentage of paid-up capital was extraordinarily high – over 80%.

The Hongkong Bank might claim to be *sui generis*, but, as it became more closely involved in takeover bids and brought in shareholders unused to the traditions of the East, it was under pressure to change. More important in this case, however, was the dividend issue. The bonus issue was a first step towards structural conformity.

The shareholders' decision had come within the scope of par. 7 of the 1929 ordinance which, after stating that the capital of the Bank was $20 million divided into 160,000 shares of $125 each, gave shareholders the right, subject to the consent of the Governor previously obtained and notified in the *Government Gazette*, to vote an increase of capital up to a limit of $50 million. The directors' notification of the meeting stated, therefore, that the Governor's consent had been given. These restrictions would not apply to other licenced Hong Kong incorporated banks; the Hongkong Bank was still subject to its heritage, still required to meet formal requirements established to protect (i) the public in the matter of the note issue and (ii) the Government in the matter of public funds held by the Bank. On this latter, the Bank was obligated by other jurisdictions to put up security where it had been entrusted with public funds independent of British, charter, or Hong Kong Government requirements. The provisions of the Bank's charter, however, required procedures which were increasingly anachronistic.

Ordinance No. 36 of 1957

Traditionally, the Hongkong Bank's ultimate regulator, in common with other British overseas banks, had been the British Treasury. The burden which this placed on the Treasury was one factor leading to the ending of the chartered banking system after the reports of the 1880s (see Volume I). Nevertheless, until 1948 Hong Kong was, for historical reasons, without a general banking ordinance. In that year and under the provisions of this ordinance the Hongkong Bank became a 'licenced bank', the first time its unique Hong Kong status had been compromised.

Furthermore, it was during the years from 1948 to 1964 that the Bank underwent legislated changes which removed certain particular characteristics inherited from and peculiar to the colonial chartered banking system. The Bank faced the new regulations of 1964 and the Commissioner of Banking without these unusual, but historically understandable, features. Although retaining their *de jure* authority, the Treasury were interested only in the note issue; the Government of Hong Kong was not yet prepared to take up the regulatory task. One could argue, therefore, that in these interim years the Bank was *de facto* without an effective 'regulator', despite surviving provisions in the Bank's own ordinance to the contrary.

Elimination of double liability and related changes

In very small print on every Hongkong Bank letterhead readers were informed that 'the liability of Members is limited to the extent and in the manner prescribed in Chapter 70 of the Laws of Hong Kong'. This mystifying message from the East was necessary because the Hongkong Bank's shareholders had 'double liability' plus unlimited liability for the note issue as carefully defined in the ordinances. This could not be described as 'limited liability' as ordinarily understood; hence the need for the notice of an anachronism.

The dramatic changes which occurred during 1957 were in part effected under previous legislation, in part through the provisions of the Hongkong and Shanghai Banking Corporation (Amendment) Ordinance 1957. In brief the capital of the Bank was raised to $50 million, the limit permitted by the 1929 ordinance, by the issue of one bonus share for each share held, a doubling of the Bank's paid-up capital. This was financed by debiting the Profit and Loss Account, swollen by untouched 'carry-forwards', by $9 million, and by transferring $16 million from inner reserves, thereby leaving published reserves unchanged at $128 million.

This was approved at an Extraordinary Meeting held in August 1957, anticipating passage of the ordinance in early September – assented to by the Governor, Sir Alexander Grantham, on September 25. The timing of this decision meant that the interim dividend was paid on 200,000 shares, the final dividend on 400,000 with the arithmetical consequences stated in Table 5.1.

The decision to double the capital was connected with the desire to eliminate the double liability provision which was complicating the Hongkong Bank's negotiations relative to equity participations and acquisitions (par. 7 amending sec. 12). The cost of achieving this was (i) doubling capital and (ii) elimination of the fiduciary issue (par. 6 amending sec. 11). This second condition meant that the authorized issue of $30 million had now to be covered 100% by approved securities lodged with the authorities, but, as noted above, the Bank had been doing this in any case. The excess issue was covered 100% by certificates of indebtedness issued by the Exchange Fund on payment of the equivalent in sterling.

This and other matters relating to the note issue have been considered in the previous section.

The ordinance restated the Bank's capital in its most recent amount – $50 million in 400,000 shares of $125 each. At the same time it eliminated another nineteenth-century requirement — the shareholders of the Bank would now be able to increase the capital of the Bank without limit by a resolution of shareholders without obtaining the consent of the Governor (par. 3 amending sec. 7).

Further flexibility was given the shareholders in that their right to capitalize reserves was confirmed, and they were additionally given the right to vary the normal or par value of shares by converting any paid-up shares into stock and reconverting that stock into paid-up shares of any amount (par. 4 amending sec. 8).

'Reserved liability'

There are two historical contexts for the additional liability of bank shareholders: (i) the colonial chartered banks operating under the Colonial Banking Regulations and (ii) the early limited liability legislation following the failure of the City of Glasgow Bank in 1878. Those unfamiliar with the colonial tradition thought in terms of the Reserved Liability Act of 1879, and indeed the Hongkong Bank, in arguing its case, referred both to the Letters Patent whereby the Chartered Bank had ended the double liability of its shareholders in 1956 and to the precedent of British joint-stock banks, for example Lloyds Bank in 1920 and more recently the National Provincial, which with others had ended the reserved liability of their shareholders.[17]

The Hongkong Bank's proposals were, therefore, well timed.

The question of management

In a wholly unconnected matter the opportunity was taken to register the fact that a dramatic change in the Bank's management had occurred since 1875; it had been partly recognized in 1929 by the specific references to a 'chief manager'; now the full reality was noted in an apparently inconsequential amendment: Section 5 (of the 1929 ordinance) is amended by the deletion in subsection (i) of the words 'under the management of the directors' (par. 2 amending Sec. 5 (i)).

The section thus referred to stated that the objects of the Bank shall be the carrying on of the business of banking (elsewhere defined) under the management of the directors. The 1957 amendment confirmed the objects of the Bank but left unspecified who would carry them out, confirming, in effect, the fact that the Board might be non-executive and that the objects of the Bank might be carried on under the management of the Chief Manager. The amendment did not, by the manner of its wording, rule out a change back to an executive board.

The timing of this amendment was not unconnected with the Bank's 1955 experience in incorporating its California subsidiary, the Hongkong and Shanghai Banking Corporation of California. The Articles of the subsidiary had to take into account that as a subsidiary of the Bank it had to be 'under the management' of the Hongkong Bank's Board of Directors. Even though the parent board could delegate its authority, this provision was seen to affect the independence of the Board of Directors in San Francisco and this in turn had an impact on its composition. Looking far ahead, the management provision of the 1929 ordinance would have made the Bank's offer to the board of Marine Midland Banks, Inc. particularly unacceptable, but there would have been problems with the boards of the Mercantile Bank and the British Bank of the Middle East – the Bank was already negotiating with the former.

THE BOARD OF DIRECTORS AND THE LONDON ADVISORY COMMITTEE

THE PROBLEMS OF A NON-EXECUTIVE BOARD

There had been several reasons why informed observers expected that, sooner or later, the Head Office of the Hongkong Bank would remove to London. First, London was the financial capital of the world and, as the Bank grew in importance, it could not afford to be so far from the centre. This was most serious in the period of the indemnity and railway loans, say 1895–1914 (see Volume II); it was countered by an impressive London management operating with the advice of a convincing London Advisory (or, as it was known interwar, 'Consultative') Committee.

Second, Hong Kong was too small to provide an effective Board of Directors. This comment was divided into questions relative to (i) conflict of interest and (ii) qualifications and ability. Both questions were resolved *de facto* by delegating the actual running of the Bank to the Chief Manager. Nevertheless, even then there were critics who felt that at least the Chairman of the Board should be a person of high quality, but, consistent with the non-executive character of the Board, the chairmanship had been, with exceptions, virtually rotated on a seniority basis. The man who really represented the Bank was the executive secretary to the Board, the Chief Manager.

Post-war the problems remained but the traditional solution became increasingly unsatisfactory.

The Chief Manager and his role were understood in Hong Kong, but even here his status was confused by the fact that the pre-war separation of Board and management had been broken by Sir Arthur Morse. Overseas it would be Morse the Chairman that mattered; when he retired his successor seemed to be Cedric Blaker of Gilman's rather than Michael W. Turner of the Hongkong Bank. If as in pre-war days both Blaker and Turner had remained in Hong Kong for five-year tours, perhaps this would not have mattered. But taipans began to travel, not only in the region, but back to England, to the United States, and to various meetings. The International Monetary Fund invited the chairman, not just a bank manager, even if he were 'chief manager', whatever that might mean.

The image of the Bank was in danger if a non-executive director were, through no fault of his own, (i) Chairman of the Bank and (ii) innocent of any knowledge of banking.

The problem as seen by both Morse and Turner was, however, more serious. Morse had little regard for the calibre of the directors before the Pacific War; he was less impressed by Hong Kong taipans post-war. Morse had worked in the City with City leaders. Blaker was acceptable, but the Deputy Chairman was the aging H.D. Benham of Sassoon's; Morse and Turner were agreed that, despite his expectations, he should never be Chairman. This particular problem ended with Sassoon's withdrawal from Hong Kong in 1956. On a more general problem, Turner recognized that with the new transport and communications facilities, Hong Kong taipans were likely to be more subject to the wishes of their London friends.

The conflict of interest also remained. In the 1900s the Bank's silver position was of vital competitive importance and had to be held secret from the directors – with their agreement. Post-war planned changes in the Bank's credit policy, for example, could not be revealed; a tightening of credit during the Hong Kong stock market boom of 1955 could be expected to raise interest rates and force down share prices. On at least one occasion a director, Benham,

The Corporation, 1946–1962

strongly objected to being kept uninformed of so important a policy change, but Turner suspected he had intended to 'unload' had he been given any hint of the Bank's intentions.[18]

All this forced Morse and Turner to face a major crisis in the Bank's structure. At a time when the chief executive needed Board support for major policy changes, for example, the founding of the Bank's California subsidiary in 1955, both were agreed that the Board, as with the London Advisory Committee, should be told as little as possible.[19]

Neither Turner nor his London Manager, S.A. Gray, were comfortable with this policy. When Sir Edward Reid came out to Hong Kong in 1954 as a guest of the Bank, he attended a Board meeting. The agenda, Turner wrote, was embarrassingly thin – a list of Foreign staff retirements and other staff information and details of the purchase of a new house in Tokyo for the Manager (the No. 1 House on the Bluff in Yokohama being too distant) – and that was it. The situation would be partially remedied when the Bank began consideration of major new policies which, by their nature, had to be brought before the Board. Turner would soon have information from China and political/economic intelligence of importance to the Bank which would also legitimately concern the directors, and this formed a regular part of most Board meetings, but the late 1950s were particularly difficult years of transition.

At a time when leadership was needed, the Chairman at least should have been a banker. If one could not change the general level of competence of the Board, one could at least expect an experienced Chairman. But the only experienced bank chairman in Hong Kong in 1952 was Morse; in 1961 it was Turner. Turner, however, would succeed Morse as Chief Manager but not as Chairman, and this for three reasons. First, only the Chief Manager attended the Board meetings, albeit as Chairman; Turner, not having attended a meeting (except 'in attendance' during Morse's absence) could not as a practical matter move in and take over; secondly, even if he felt competent to do so, there was evidence that the Board would not tolerate it – even the new Chief Manager's appointment as a director was a matter to be decided by the Board alone; and thirdly, the fact that the Chairman and the chief executive officer had been the same person – even when that person were Morse – had brought criticism on the Bank in the City of London.[20] It was not done.

Two obvious solutions, (i) a move of Head Office to London and (ii) an executive board, were never even considered. In the past the need for a head office in Hong Kong, the rationale for the Bank's very founding, remained an unshakable reason. If post-war this seemed less an argument, a new problem, taxation, would be a determining factor. The Bank could not afford to move to London. But this was only mentioned in passing – the tax position might affect every other decision, but the location of the Hongkong Bank's head office had to be Hong Kong for banking reasons; the decision makers must be resident in the fast moving East and see the Bank's problems in the perspective only Eastern residence could provide.

Morse and Turner themselves had, therefore, no solution to suggest, except to state their determination that the chairmanship should remain in the hands of a non-banker for as short a time as possible.[21]

Having stated their views in confidence to each other, Morse and Turner then had to return to reality and cope with the situation at hand. This they did by carrying the Board with them; Turner particularly needed their full support and, indeed, advice as he moved the Bank in new directions. In part the criticism levelled against the directors was unfair; they were non-executive; they were elected for what they could bring to the Bank; no one, least of all the directors, considered them bankers. They were placed in an impossible position and judged by impossible standards.

The retirement of the non-banking Chairman seemed an appropriate time; accordingly the Chairman's position was not rotated, but remained with C. Blaker until he retired in 1958, at which time the Board duly elected Turner. The same problem would arise with the succession in 1962.

As the discussion below will indicate, relations proved much easier than anticipated in the early Morse/Turner correspondence. One might go further; the successful cooperation between the Board and their Chief Manager brought the Board into a closer involvement with the policy of the Bank than ever before. This does not negate the problems stated; it merely proves the obvious usefulness of non-executive, outside directors. What was needed was the professionalism of the bankers and the contribution of the non-bankers, a conclusion which can hardly claim originality. This solution would not prove possible in Hong Kong, however, until 1969 when the then Chief Manager and 'non-executive' Chairman, J.A.H. Saunders, obtained the necessary revisions to the Bank's regulations and inaugurated an executive Board with himself as executive Chairman.

THE BOARD OF DIRECTORS

The Board minutes – a comparison

By 1902, the end of the Jackson Era, management of the Bank's banking activities was under the firm control of the Chief Manager. Until 1962 this arrangement was unwritten but fully understood. The 'minutes' of the Board's inter-war meetings are virtually of no interest in the history of banking – the qualification, 'minutes', is important because the record of true profits and related matters was attached (precariously) every six months and these constitute a basic record. The minutes themselves deal with staff – retirement gratuities, appointments, special happenings – buildings, charities, matters often wholly routine requiring the use of the corporate seal or the Board's signature, records of appreciation, and lists of documents laid on the table but not attached to the Minute Books.

The Minute Books provide a record without which the full history of the corporation could not be written, but, with possibly one exception, they contain nothing of basic concern to banking, narrowly defined. The one exception, the authority for the Shanghai Manager, A.S. Henchman, to continue active and prominent in Shanghai banking given the known risks, is significant (see Volume III). The Chief Manager had come to the Board for a policy decision when purely banking considerations had dictated a policy of withdrawal.

The interest of the Minute Book depends in part on the Chief Manager, since he personally wrote the minutes. During and immediately following the war the proceedings of the London Advisory Committee both before and after its designation as a Board of Directors are of interest because Arthur Morse included informational items and because the non-banking decisions were of importance.

Once settled back in Hong Kong the minutes for a time return to the routine of non-banking. There are however new interests – the list of charities expands to more like modern corporation proportions, the property program is, as it was in A.G. Stephen's time, a matter of primary concern, and the regularization of retirement gratuities with the eventual establishment of a Trust is the inevitable conclusion to years of thoughtful but relatively *ad hoc* thinking on this important subject.

From the mid-1950s the Board's involvement appears to increase. First, Sir Arthur Morse had retired and Michael Turner was not immediately elected Chairman; secondly, the equity investment in, for example, Bowmaker (C.A.) of Salisbury, Southern Rhodesia, involved policy – as indeed did the many decisions relative to expansion, the question of withdrawal from China, the acquisition of the Mercantile Bank and the British Bank of the Middle East. When Turner was elected Chairman in 1958, he kept the Board informed of the negotiations with the Mercantile and BBME, obtaining their authority for the Hongkong Bank's offer price and related matters.

This may be seen in a sense as a new relationship, but yet it was historically consistent. The Board had throughout remained responsible to the shareholders not only for the non-banking operations of the corporation but also for its successful banking – this was statutory whatever arrangements the directors may have come to with their Chief Manager. By the late 1950s the Board of Directors were confronting a fast changing situation in which the future of the Bank was involved and in which irrevocable policy decisions were necessary. The Board participated in the policy making and approved the final policy, however carefully they might be brought to the point by the usual educational process of management.

Then with the retirement of Turner and the succession of the 'new generation' imminent, the Board formalized its relationship with the Chief Manager. By doing so it introduced an element of concern to management which would lead in 1969 to the transformation of the Board.

For these reasons a study of the Board of Directors post-war takes on new importance. However, their role relative to 'expansion' and acquisitions will be considered in Chapter 12.

Composition

In accordance with Sir Arthur Morse's preference, the Board was kept down to eight members until 1957 – by 1962 the total had risen to ten, as shown in Table 6.1. For the most part the directors came from firms long represented on the Board of the Hongkong Bank. Only one new post-war firm was 'represented' – Imperial Chemical Industries from 1946.

In 1956 David Sassoon and Co. withdrew from Hong Kong and their representative on the Board resigned. This marked a break; Sassoon's had been the only firm represented on the Board of Directors (the war years excepted) without a break since that first August meeting of the Bank's Provisional Committee in 1864. Gilman and Co. were now the last survivors of the original committee.

From time to time the Board had invited leading businessmen whose personal impact in the Colony was greater, perhaps, than any one affiliation. Douglas Lapraik of the Provisional Committee or H.R. Belilios of the Board were examples of such men. In 1957 the Board invited Lawrence Kadoorie (now Lord Kadoorie) to the Board, and, although his role with China Light and Power was undoubtedly a major factor in the decision, his interests and his contribution to the Board were far more broadly based. For this reason he has been listed under his basic affiliation with Sir Elly Kadoorie and Sons.

In the fast moving post-war business world of Hong Kong various long-standing hongs would be taken over or amalgamated, and this accounts for the non-appearance of formerly familiar names – for example, Shewan, Tomes and Co., the British successor to the interests of the pioneer American hong of Russell and Co. Similarly the close relationship between Mackinnon Mackenzie, representing the Inchcape interests, whose local taipan was also Chairman of Gibb, Livingston and Co., required making a choice for the listings in Table 6.1. The close connection of this latter hong with Hongkong Electric Company should also be noted. J.D. Clague had mapped out an aggressive policy for John D. Hutchison and Co., which returned to the Board

Table 6.1 *The Hongkong and Shanghai Banking Corporation*
The Board of Directors, 1946–1962

June, 1946 (appointed by the Governor of Hong Kong)
A. Morse	Chief Manager, Hongkong Bank	Chairman
D.F. Landale	Jardine, Matheson and Co.	Deputy Chairman
C.C. Roberts	Butterfield and Swire	
G. Miskin	Gilman and Co.	
A.H. Compton	David Sassoon and Co.	
R.D. Gillespie	Imperial Chemical Industries	
H.V. Wilkinson	Gibb, Livingston and Co.	

The above were confirmed by the Meeting of Shareholders, 12 July 1946.

March, 1947
A. Morse	Chief Manager, Hongkong Bank	Chairman
D.F. Landale	Jardine, Matheson and Co.	Deputy Chairman
C.C. Roberts	Butterfield and Swire	
G. Miskin	Gilman and Co.	
R.D. Gillespie	Imperial Chemical Industries	
N.O.C. Marsh	Gibb, Livingston and Co.	
S.H. Dodwell	Dodwell and Co.	
H.D. Benham	David Sassoon and Co.	

March, 1948
A. Morse	Chief Manager, Hongkong Bank	Chairman
D.F. Landale	Jardine, Matheson and Co.	Deputy Chairman
C.C. Roberts	Butterfield and Swire	
H.D. Benham	David Sassoon and Co.	
R.D. Gillespie	Imperial Chemical Industries	
N.O.C. Marsh	Gibb, Livingston and Co.	
S.H. Dodwell	Dodwell and Co.	
C. Blaker	Gilman and Co.	

March, 1949
A. Morse	Chief Manager, Hongkong Bank	Chairman
D.F. Landale	Jardine, Matheson and Co.	Deputy Chairman
C. Blaker	Gilman and Co.	
H.D. Benham	David Sassoon and Co.	
N.O.C. Marsh	Gibb, Livingston and Co.	
E.R. Hill	Dodwell and Co.	
H.J. Collar	Imperial Chemical Industries	
E.G. Price	Butterfield and Swire	

March, 1950
Sir Arthur Morse	Chief Manager, Hongkong Bank	Chairman
D.F. Landale	Jardine, Matheson and Co.	Deputy Chairman
C. Blaker	Gilman and Co.	
H.D. Benham	David Sassoon and Co.	
E.R. Hill	Dodwell and Co.	
H.J. Collar	Imperial Chemical Industries	
C.C. Roberts	Butterfield and Swire	
J.D. Alexander	Gibb, Livingston and Co.	

Table 6.1 (*cont.*)

March, 1951
Sir Arthur Morse	Chief Manager, Hongkong Bank	Chairman
D.F. Landale	Jardine, Matheson and Co.	Deputy Chairman

(resigned and replaced on Board by J.H. Keswick in June)

C.C. Roberts	Butterfield and Swire (from June)	Deputy Chairman
C. Blaker	Gilman and Co.	
H.D. Benham	David Sassoon and Co.	
E.R. Hill	Dodwell and Co.	
H.J. Collar	Imperial Chemical Industries	
J.D. Alexander	Gibb, Livingston and Co.	

(replaced, June–November, by J.W. Hay-Edie)

March, 1952
Sir Arthur Morse	Chief Manager, Hongkong Bank	Chairman
C. Blaker	Gilman and Co.	Deputy Chairman
H.D. Benham	David Sassoon and Co.	
E.R. Hill	Dodwell and Co.	
H.J. Collar	Imperial Chemical Industries	
J.D. Alexander	Gibb, Livingston and Co.	
J.H. Keswick	Jardine, Matheson and Co.	
J.A. Blackwood	Butterfield and Swire	

March, 1953
Sir Arthur Morse	Chief Manager, Hongkong Bank	Chairman
C. Blaker	Gilman and Co.	Deputy Chairman
H.D. Benham	David Sassoon and Co.	
E.R. Hill	Dodwell and Co.	
H.J. Collar	Imperial Chemical Industries	
J.D. Alexander	Gibb, Livingston and Co.	
J.H. Keswick	Jardine, Matheson and Co.	
J.A. Blackwood	Butterfield and Swire	

March, 1954
C. Blaker	Gilman and Co.	Chairman
H.D. Benham	David Sassoon and Co.	Deputy Chairman
J.A. Blackwood	Butterfield and Swire	
B.T. Flanagan	Gibb, Livingston and Co.	
A.V. Farmer	Imperial Chemical Industries	
J.H. Hamm	Dodwell and Co.	
R. Gordon	Jardine, Matheson and Co.	
Michael W. Turner	Chief Manager, Hongkong Bank	

March, 1955
C. Blaker	Gilman and Co.	Chairman
H.D. Benham	David Sassoon and Co.	Deputy Chairman
J.A. Blackwood	Butterfield and Swire	
B.T. Flanagan	Gibb, Livingston and Co.	
C.B. Cook	Imperial Chemical Industries	
J.H. Hamm	Dodwell and Co.	
R. Gordon	Jardine, Matheson and Co.	
Michael W. Turner	Chief Manager, Hongkong Bank	

Table 6.1 (cont.)

March, 1956
C. Blaker	Gilman and Co.	Chairman
H.D. Benham	David Sassoon and Co.	Deputy Chairman
J.A. Blackwood	Butterfield and Swire	
B.T. Flanagan	Gibb, Livingston and Co.	
R.J. Sheppard	Imperial Chemical Industries	
H.D.M. Barton	Jardine, Matheson and Co.	
Michael W. Turner	Chief Manager, Hongkong Bank	
J.F. Macgregor	Caldbeck, Macgregor and Co.	

March, 1957
C. Blaker	Gilman and Co.	Chairman
J.A. Blackwood	Butterfield and Swire	Deputy Chairman
B.T. Flanagan	Gibb, Livingston and Co.	
R.J. Sheppard	Imperial Chemical Industries	
H.D.M. Barton	Jardine, Matheson and Co.	
Michael W. Turner	Chief Manager, Hongkong Bank	
J.F. Macgregor	Caldbeck, Macgregor and Co.	
L. Kadoorie	Sir Elly Kadoorie and Sons	
L.B. Stone	Asiatic Petroleum	

March, 1958
C. Blaker	Gilman and Co.	Chairman
B.T. Flanagan	Gibb, Livingston and Co.	
R.J. Sheppard	Imperial Chemical Industries	
H.D.M. Barton	Jardine, Matheson and Co.	
Michael W. Turner	Chief Manager, Hongkong Bank	
J.F. Macgregor	Caldbeck, Macgregor and Co.	
L. Kadoorie	Sir Elly Kadoorie and Sons	
L.B. Stone	Asiatic Petroleum	
W.C.G. Knowles	Butterfield and Swire	
G.M. Goldsack	Dodwell and Co.	

March, 1959
Michael W. Turner	Chief Manager, Hongkong Bank	Chairman
B.T. Flanagan	Gibb, Livingston and Co.	Deputy Chairman
R.J. Sheppard	Imperial Chemical Industries	
H.D.M. Barton	Jardine, Matheson and Co.	
J.F. Macgregor	Caldbeck, Macgregor and Co.	
L. Kadoorie	Sir Elly Kadoorie and Sons	
L.B. Stone	Asiatic Petroleum	
W.C.G. Knowles	Butterfield and Swire	
G.M. Goldsack	Dodwell and Co.	
S.J. Cooke	Gilman and Co.	

March, 1960
Michael W. Turner	Chief Manager, Hongkong Bank	Chairman
H.D.M. Barton	Jardine, Matheson and Co.	Deputy Chairman
J.F. Macgregor	Caldbeck, Macgregor and Co.	
L. Kadoorie	Sir Elly Kadoorie and Sons	
W.C.G. Knowles	Butterfield and Swire	

Table 6.1 (*cont.*)

G.M. Goldsack	Dodwell and Co.	
S.J. Cooke	Gilman and Co.	
C.A. Wright	Imperial Chemical Industries	
G.T. Tagg	Gibb, Livingston and Co.	

March, 1961

Michael W. Turner	Chief Manager, Hongkong Bank	Chairman
H.D.M. Barton	Jardine, Matheson and Co.	Deputy Chairman
J.F. Macgregor	Caldbeck, Macgregor and Co.	
L. Kadoorie	Sir Elly Kadoorie and Sons	
W.C.G. Knowles	Butterfield and Swire	
G.M. Goldsack	Dodwell and Co.	
S.J. Cooke	Gilman and Co.	
C.A. Wright	Imperial Chemical Industries	
G.T. Tagg	Gibb, Livingston and Co.	
J.D. Clague	J.D. Hutchison and Co.	

March [16], 1962 (at the Annual Meeting)

Michael W. Turner	Chief Manager, Hongkong Bank	Chairman
H.D.M. Barton	Jardine, Matheson and Co.	Deputy Chairman
W.C.G. Knowles	Butterfield and Swire	
G.M. Goldsack	Dodwell and Co.	
J.F. Macgregor	Caldbeck, Macgregor and Co.	
L. Kadoorie	Sir Elly Kadoorie and Sons	
S.J. Cooke	Gilman and Co.	
G.T. Tagg	Gibb, Livingston and Co.	
J.D. Clague	J.D. Hutchison and Co.	
J. Hackney	Imperial Chemical Industries	

(changes at first Board meeting after the Annual Meeting, March 20)

Resigned:

Michael W. Turner	Chief Manager, Hongkong Bank
G.M. Goldsack	Dodwell and Co.

Elected:

G.G.D. Carter	Dodwell and Co.
J.A.H. Saunders[a]	Chief Manager, Hongkong Bank

[a] Turner retired March 16; Saunders attended the March 20 meeting as Chief Manager; he was elected a director during the meeting.
Bold face indicates a new member.

in 1960; Clague would move Hutchison's into increasing prominence, in part through merger with well-established local companies.

In consequence of these changes, the information in Tables 6.1 and 6.2 requires supplementing with the details in the Appendix to this chapter. There are two problems. First, the director himself was more than the taipan of the firm listed in the tables; his affiliations, directorships, social contributions, etc.

Table 6.2 *The Hongkong and Shanghai Banking Corporation Companies represented on the Board of Directors, 1946–1962*[a]

	1st Year[b]		1946–1962	
Butterfield and Swire	1914	1946–		1962
David Sassoon and Co.	1864[c]	1946–	1956	
Gibb, Livingston and Co.[d]	1869	1946–		1962
Gilman and Co.	1864	1946–		1962
Hongkong and Shanghai Bank	1941	1946–		1962
Imperial Chemical Industries	1946	1946–		1962
Jardine, Matheson and Co.	1877	1946–		1962
Dodwell and Co.[d]	1896	1947–		1962
Caldbeck, Macgregor and Co.	1956		1956–	1962
Sir Elly Kadoorie and Sons	1957		1957–	1962
Asiatic Petroleum Co.	1924		1957– 1959	
J.D. Hutchison and Co.	1930			1961–1962

[a] This does not preclude the fact that a director may have been elected for reasons other than the primary affiliation listed.
[b] First year company was represented on Board, not necessarily continuously.
[c] Only founding company with virtually continuous representation (World War II years excluded) to 1956.
[d] Inchcape Group

are many and explain what he could bring to the increasingly important deliberations of the Board of the Hongkong Bank. Secondly, even to the extent that his one affiliation is mentioned, the position is understated from a banking point of view. Each one of the companies 'represented' on the Board held agencies, some for over 100 other companies for whose products or activities they had an agreement and whose business might be expected, therefore, to come, at least in major part, to the Hongkong Bank.

The Board, the Chief Manager, and the Chairman

Their respective roles – changes over time
After the failure of Dent and Co. in 1867 the chairmanship of the Hongkong Bank's Board of Directors was, where possible, changed annually on the basis of seniority. This strict rotation did not continue throughout, but the principle was roughly adhered to, with exceptions mentioned in previous chapters, until 1941. The Order in Council, 1943, retroactively appointed the Chairman of the London Committee as Chairman of the Bank, and that put Arthur Morse, an

Table 6.3 *The Hongkong and Shanghai Banking Corporation Charitable donations as listed in minutes, 1949*

Aberdeen Industrial School	$1,000.00
Alice Memorial and Affiliated Hospitals	2,500.00
The Boys' and Girls' Clubs Association	2,000.00
The Boy Scouts' Association, Hongkong Branch	2,000.00
Christian Mission to Chinese Seamen	1,000.00
Diocesan Boys' School and Orphanage	2,000.00
Diocesan Girls' School and Orphanage	2,000.00
Hongkong Social Welfare Council	2,000.00
Hongkong Society for the Prevention of Cruelty to Animals	1,000.00
Hongkong Society for the Protection of Children	2,500.00
Little Sisters of the Poor	2,000.00
Provisional Council for the Deaf and Hongkong School for the Deaf	2,000.00
Remembrance Day Fund	2,500.00
Sailors' and Soldiers' Home	2,500.00
Sailors' Home and Missions to Seamen (General Funds)	2,500.00
The Salvation Army	5,000.00
Society of St Vincent de Paul	2,000.00
St John's Ambulance Association and Brigade	1,000.00
St John's Cathedral Goodwill Offering	5,000.00
St Louis Industrial School (Third Street)	1,000.00
Stanley Camp	1,000.00
Tung Wah Hospital	2,000.00
Union Church	5,000.00
	$51,500.00

employee of the Bank, in this important position. This was confirmed when the London Committee met in 1943 as 'directors' and again in June 1946 when the newly appointed Board in Hong Kong elected Morse as Chairman. A new dimension had appeared.

The Governor had appointed Morse a director under emergency authority; the shareholders confirmed the Governor's decision in the July 1946 meeting. But had the Governor appointed Morse or the Chief Manager as director; had the other directors elected Morse or the Chief Manager as their Chairman? Or, put more generally, had precedents been established?

The dominant personality of Morse and the dominant role he played, matching his personality, made the question necessary. The answer came in 1953 when Sir Arthur Morse resigned and returned to England. The Board appointed Michael Turner Morse's successor as Chief Manager and they elected him a director of the Bank, but they elected Cedric Blaker of Gilman and Co., previously the Deputy Chairman, as their Chairman. The transition was smooth, but whatever competence Turner might have, it was hidden from the public. There was only one Chief Manager; he dominated the public's conception of the Bank, just as in other ports the Manager was the Bank. Turner had to be brought out gradually – in the United States the company president is not necessarily the chairman of the board; the situation here was not an exact parallel, but the comment is not irrelevant.

Morse had been a community leader, a confidant of the much respected Governor, Sir Alexander Grantham, an architect of the Colony's post-war recovery. Freed from the tyranny of exchange operations and the immediate demands of exchange brokers, Morse was the first 'liberated' Manager of the Bank, the first who was master of the use of his time. The prominent role Hongkong Bank Chief Managers have played as members of the Executive Council was a post-war phenomenon. A.G. Stephen was an exception, but generally pre-war Chief Managers had played only occasional or limited community roles, except in matters of their banking expertise. They were valued honorary treasurers of charitable organizations; they were members of special committees but rarely of the main Government councils (see Appendix Table A and the discussion in Volume II, Chapter 3). There was no tradition, therefore, which insisted a Chief Manager should be, as Stephen and Morse were, leaders of the community. If the task of the Chairman were to present the Bank's public image and that of the Chief Manager to run the Bank, the two tasks need not be performed by the same person. Whether Turner would prove another Morse could not be known while Morse, overshadowing all, was in Hong Kong.

Turner, as it happened, grew with the job and, with the departure from Hong Kong of Blaker in 1958, he was naturally elected Chairman of the Board. He had been Chief Manager for four years; he would remain for another four.

In September 1960 Michael Turner informed the Board that he intended to retire after the Annual Meeting in 1962; J.A.H. Saunders was approved as his successor, in principle. In November 1961 with the retirement from the East of G.O.W. Stewart to become the London Manager, Saunders was appointed Deputy Chief Manager. He was now publicly known as the Bank's next Chief Manager. At the time of his taking up the post he would have been in the East only seventeen years, less than any former Chief Manager since Jackson and comparable to the eighteen years of François de Bovis. Saunders' seniority, however, dated from 1940 and, but for the war, he would have been 22 years in the East or slightly more than J.R.M. Smith and Sir Newton Stabb (see Appendix Table A).

At this point the Board for the first time in the Bank's history formalized the arrangement between the Board and the Chief Manager.

It is intended by the Board that the Chief Manager should have complete authority to manage the business of the Bank.

In so doing he is expected to consult the Board and secure their support on all matters of policy affecting the Bank, its Branches and subsidiaries, always bearing in mind that the final authority and responsibility under the ordinance for the conduct of the Bank's affairs rests with the Board of Directors.

This authority shall be subject to confirmation at the first Board Meeting that is held after each Annual General Meeting unless previously revoked under Art. 117.

This minute records on the one hand a very sound and obvious decision but on the other a thought-provoking departure from past practice. The first sentence presents no problem. As the Bank's activities expanded and vast sums were at stake world-wide, many more previously unwritten understandings were being formalized and if such previously *ad hoc* matters as pensions now warranted a Trust Deed then surely the basic authority of the Chief Manager required specific recording.

The second sentence, however, arouses speculation. After all, Sir Michael Turner had been pushing the Board hard, and G.O.W. Stewart at one point requested the approval of the Board for the acquisition of a banking subsidiary, the BBME, in circulation. He had been refused; a meeting was accordingly scheduled. The new Chief Manager, a former lieutenant-colonel, was known to possess a forceful personality. Perhaps the Board, having accepted the need for further expansion, wished to ensure their control of the probable developments.

Whatever the intention, the wording made the Board more closely involved in the business of the Bank than at any time since the recovery after 1875. 'In so doing' is the key phrase. The business of banking was undergoing change which might well be described as policy change. This phrase would, therefore, bring all but routine (broadly defined) banking (narrowly defined) matters before the Board. But was this a change or was it that pre-war there had been only routine matters? The latter is more nearly true, but that does not alter the impact of the Board's resolution.

The resolution was to be amplified by the Deputy Chairman (and Chairman-designate) H.D.M. Barton in discussions with Turner, who undertook to take the matter up with the incoming Chief Manager. This confirms that the Board considered it impossible for a major international bank to be run by a Chief Manager, a 'servant of the company', in isolation. The relationship had to be redefined, but the full extent of the Board's mood had not yet been realized.

The 1962 succession problem

The Board had now to return to the question of precedent. In 1953 they had established in the case of Michael Turner that the immediate election of Arthur Morse as Chairman had not been precedential. Turner had, however, been elected a director to coincide with his assumption of the position of Chief

Manager. Some members of the Board apparently balked at the immediate election of Saunders; the immediate elections of Morse and Turner to the Board were not to be considered precedential.

Turner and Morse were once again in correspondence. Turner correctly predicted and Saunders accepted that the new Chief Manager could not walk in as Chairman, but Morse, Turner, and Saunders agreed that tenure by a non-banker should somehow be minimized. One alternative was direction from London, but that would endanger the Bank's tax position; the possibility of Turner remaining until the centenary was not acceptable to Turner and even then a solution might not be to hand. Perhaps, Morse speculated, Turner could remain as Chairman, but having the former Chief Manager looking over the shoulder of the new chief was unacceptable.[e] Equally impractical was his suggestion that Turner continue to be Chairman of the Bank, residing in England and returning for a few months in the year until such time as Saunders could take the chair.[22]

Certainly every solution – except the eventual one – was fully considered. The problem was complicated because Morse at least was opposed to Hugh Barton of Jardine's becoming Chairman, possibly because Barton held strong views as to the need for a positive role for the Chairman. Turner, however, recognized that practical politics dictated the Chairman could be no one else – Barton had, after all, been Deputy Chairman since 1960. Then too there was the question as to whether Barton would be acceptable to the Bank of England, but that question was quickly resolved in Barton's favour.[23] Kadoorie, as a prominent member of Hong Kong's Jewish community, could not be Chairman of the Bank which had acquired the British Bank of the Middle East – the choice was narrowing. In any case, the basic problem appeared to be without solution; Turner fell back on the hope, with some misgivings, that when Barton retired Saunders would take over without controversy.

Consequently when the Board met for the first time after Sir Michael Turner's departure in March 1962, Saunders attended as Chief Manager, but he was not a director of the Hongkong Bank. The situation had become impossible. The Board, totally non-executive and without a single member with banking experience, were to be involved in virtually every new development and expansion decision of the Bank with their Chief Manager 'in attendance' – by invitation and not by right, it might be added.

The Board were partly correct; they sensed that the Bank was the responsibility of the directors and that the directors had, therefore, to be more

---

[e] The statue of Sir Thomas Jackson had been placed *facing* the Bank, virtually looking over the shoulder of his successors. The returned Jackson statue was placed post-war in a more neutral position in the Bank's public garden in Statue Square; Morse liked to play his cards close to his chest. A live ex-Chief Manager in taipan-oriented Hong Kong would be intolerable.

closely involved, given the rapidly changing situation. The ultimate question was, however, not the role of the Board but its composition, and this question was not resolved until 1969, when obviously Saunders' experience in 1962 would reinforce his resolve to effect reform. When informal understandings are 'formalized', latent problems are revealed, the solution to which may involve a total reconsideration.

Saunders attended his first meeting as Chief Manager only, but he left a director. The Board elected him on March 20, 1962, with the extraordinary proviso that this too was not to be considered a precedent. This resolution alone confirmed the need for restructuring the Board.

When all key issues fell within the scope of the Chief Manager's 'complete authority to manage the business of the Bank', when, that is, there was nothing of importance for the Board to discuss, a non-director Chief Manager could 'come to' the Board for advice and support. But the Board's supposition that the Chief Executive of the Hongkong Bank need not necessarily be a member of the Bank's Board of Directors created an intolerable situation. It was as untenable as his directorship would have been pre-war – only twenty years previously. Saunders made that clear. Later he would ensure that his successor did not have to fight the same battle on an individual basis.

The remuneration of the Chief Manager – from profit sharing to salary
The remuneration of the Chief Manager was also placed on a more normal basis during this period, but for reasons at first glance quite different from the forces at work in the matters considered in the previous section. From 1949 the Chief Manager received £15,000 per annum plus $\frac{1}{2}$ of 1% of the profits, the latter defined as profits arising each year at Head Office, branch offices, and agencies after providing for such amounts as needed for tax, bad and doubtful debts, and provision for contingent losses arising from the year's profits. The $\frac{1}{2}$ of 1% is of a remainder rather than being positively defined as of the amounts paid away in dividends and to the reserves. Under Morse's reserves policy this latter would have been impractical; there were no transfers from published P&L Account to published Reserve Fund. The transfers to contingencies before publication 'fudged' the definition of contingency and reserve funds.

Turner's initial remuneration remained as in Morse's time, but the definition of profit became 'current net earnings' exclusive of 'capital gains or exchange appreciation as defined by the auditors'.

The next change came in 1959 and was again definitional. The Hongkong Bank would soon be responsible for three other banks – the Hongkong and Shanghai Banking Corporation of California, the Mercantile Bank, and the British Bank of the Middle East. If the Chief Manager's remuneration depended on the profits of the Hongkong Bank, he could be involved in a conflict of interest since it was in his interest to maximize that profit by, possibly, instructing the subsidiary banks to pay higher dividends than sound policy would recommend – or even to have business diverted from subsidiaries to the Hongkong Bank. He was therefore to be paid on the basis of the total profits of the Bank and all subsidiaries.

The complexities introduced into the scheme by refinements in definition and by the problem of conflict of interest led Turner to recommend to the Board that his remuneration be changed to a salary of £30,000 p.a. tax free. Once the Chief Manager was on a straight salary, however, the Board faced the question of benefits and allowances – as with all employees. The Board at the same time, therefore, reviewed the Chief Manager's obligations and authorized the Bank to pay certain business entertaining expenses hitherto met from his own remuneration, for example the annual staff party; the Bank agreed that one car with running expenses should be provided the Chief Manager as an expense; the Bank would also pay for his 9th floor flat in the Bank's Head Office building (in addition to the house on the Peak); it would also include him in with the rest of the staff on leave passages and children's educational allowances – but he would not be entitled to special payments or bonuses awarded Managers. Turner was to pay 10% of his salary (and the Bank a further 20%) to the Provident Fund.

The Board agreed that if this worked out at less than he would have received under the old scheme, he would receive a lump sum payment on retirement. The Board also agreed that the straight salary decision was a precedent for Turner's successor.

With the appointment of J.A.H. Saunders the above arrangements were confirmed, but in keeping with the Board's policy at the time, the contract was considerably more detailed.

This change marks the end of an historical evolution. Initially the Bank's Chief Manager simply received a higher salary than any other company servant, but the differential was only marginal. As a disgruntled shareholder, H. Kingsmill, reminded the Board at the February 1875 meeting, the Chief Manager was only the manager of a joint-stock company, not a partner (see Volume I, Chapter 7). This was sound so long as the directors ran the Bank through the Chief Manager as executive secretary of the Board. In Hong Kong the directors' remuneration came from their fees, from their dividends, but also from the benefits reaped by their companies by the existence of a well-managed banking institution designed to meet their requirements. The Bank, as has been said before, was almost a cooperative venture.

When, however, the directors divorced themselves from management and asked the Chief Manager to handle their risks for them, they had, in effect, to ask him to share in the results of his sound handling. Thus with Jackson a profit sharing element was added to an ample salary.

There were limits to the profit sharing, however. The Board reverted to the payment of a straight salary, but the 'risk' element remained – not the Chief Manager's risk, certainly, but the risk he managed for the shareholders – and for which, so long as the Board had no executive directors, he managed alone. The directors, who could not escape their ultimate responsibility as defined in the ordinance and laws of the various territories in which the Bank operated, were largely in his hands. Hence his salary was some five times that of the next highest paid member of staff.

The role of the Board of Directors

The resolutions passed on the eve of Sir Michael Turner's departure only reflect the relationship between Board and Chief Manager which existed, in principle at least, from 1941 onwards. To give substance to this statement, a review of the type of subject brought to the Board follows – certain of the more important items will be considered in some detail in subsequent chapters.

By 1949 the traditional charitable decisions of the Board needed some rationalization. The first step would appear to have been an attempt to present the Board with an annual list, at least of the regular Hong Kong donations. This totalled $51,500 (see Table 6.3) and by 1961 had increased to over $110,000. But this did not remove the *ad hoc* element – there were emergencies and regular requests from the Bank's Managers overseas, as the second part of the table reveals. Nevertheless, the Bank was beginning to accept a new definition of its community role in societies which understood the personality of a corporation not only in a strictly legal sense. The climax of the trend would be the formation of the Hongkong Bank Foundation, but that would be in 1980.

In the early 1950s the Bank's rebuilding program had increased the value of fixed investment in premises in the range of $21–22 million despite write-offs which had increased from $3 million to $4 million per annum. Another surge of building resulted in such fixed investment reaching a peak for this period of $25.3 million, with write-offs at the rate of $5 million per annum. This as always was a matter for the Board.

The stimulus for regularization of the pension scheme may have been British legislation as it affected the staff of London Office, but by 1951 several schemes, covering most of the Bank's staff, both Foreign and local, had been approved, although the funding was not properly under a Trust Deed for Foreign staff until 1957. Several revisions had to be considered: (i) the scheme proved inequitable to widows, (ii) allowance had to be made for a rise in the cost of living, (iii) consideration had to be given to those who retired early at the request of the Bank, and (iv) provision had to be made for others to join the scheme, despite seniority or affiliation, for example, specialists transferring to the Hongkong Bank with seniority or members of affiliated companies, including the Mercantile Bank, when Hongkong Bank retirement schemes were more favourable.

As with charitable contributions, the Board still found it impossible to avoid dealing with special cases, obviously including those who had retired before the scheme had become effective. In 1954 they were informed, however, that in view of his health, J.D. Taylor had been granted an unusual 'joint' pension – it would carry on to the widow, presumably in expectation of his early demise. The arrangement had been approved in 1911; now 93 years of age and the oldest pensioner, Taylor passed on, and the pension was paid to the widow without a further Board decision.

At each meeting specified accounts were laid on the table. Each half-year more detailed accounts revealing true profits were written into the minutes; at this time the allocations were made on the vote of the Board to inner reserves, Managers' bonuses, contingency accounts, and the subsequently published decisions relative to write-off of Premises Account and dividends. The Board also considered the matters discussed earlier in this chapter: capital policy, reserves policy, legislative matters, changes in the Bank's regulations, and matters relative to the Bank's relations with Government. There is nothing new in this list, but the frequency of their occurrence was cumulative in its impact on the Board's relations with management.

Perhaps the most important development on the Board's agenda was the item headed 'expansion'. The Board's role in the formation of the Hongkong Bank Group is not entirely clear, but that is because the formation of the Group was not a clearly defined prior goal. The Board were presented with this development on a case-by-case basis; neither they nor management could be certain of the outcome. However, with the need to consider the acquisition of the Mercantile Bank from 1957, involved as it was with the possibility of combinations which included the British Bank of the Middle East and National and Grindlays Bank, the Board began not only to consider the case presented but also the long-run 'expansion' policies which acquisition implied. That their discussions were often overtaken by events and therefore their decisions rendered inoperative does not detract from the importance of this development on the Board of Directors.

At another level the Board concerned itself with arrangements for the forthcoming centenary celebrations. The directors resolved to commission two Bank histories, one a presentation volume, the preparation of which was assigned to Maurice Collis, and the second a 'solid history written by an economist'. The first was completed on time; the second involved negotiations with academics and was consequently delayed, then forgotten, and then reconsidered. The final product is before you, some quarter of a century after the Board's first resolution.

From the records it has been impossible to determine what information the pre-war Chief Managers provided the members of the Board in oral summaries or what subjects were quietly discussed with the Chairman but not presented at meetings. Occasionally there is a mention of a major change in investments and information is reported which, one might suppose, came within the Chief Manager's terms of reference.

Post-war the informal content of the Board meetings remains impossible to determine, but minuted information is more consistent and detailed. For example, the Board was kept relatively fully informed of developments in China from 1948 to 1955, and it was the Board which agreed in 1953 to a final 'all-for-all' settlement which was eventually accepted by the Chinese authorities in 1955 (see Chapter 9). The concern over deteriorating labour relations is also apparent with the strikes in Colombo, Singapore, and Japan fully reported; the Board generally supported the strong line taken by the Bank's Manager in the field.

The Board was kept informed of new developments, especially those relative to investment in associated and subsidiary companies. The Chief Manager does not appear, however, to have been consistent in his timing; there would appear to be little correlation between the importance of the item and whether it was submitted for information or for approval, for long-run consideration or for immediate agreement. This suggests a possible reason for the Board's decision to specify the information they required to be brought before them and to formalize the relationship between the Board and their Chief Manager.

LONDON AND THE LONDON ADVISORY COMMITTEE

The role of the Committee

The importance of the London Advisory Committee in the period 1946 to 1961 is particularly difficult to assess. Certainly it had been 'up-graded' and was composed of prominent City men and key persons retired from the East. This applied not only to those appointed during the war when the Committee acted as the Bank's Board of Directors, but to their replacements. The problem is that the minutes of their meetings are pro forma, suggesting only that they kept abreast of the Bank's London investments, were informed of the movements of key Hongkong Bank executives, of the Far Eastern political situation, and, as with the Board in Hong Kong, provided with useful pieces of general information relative to events in the East.

This agenda was not often queried, but C.A. Campbell of the Westminster Bank and R.G. Macindoe of Maclaine, Watson and Co. complained that, for example, they should have been told in advance of Morse's intention to nominate Turner as his successor; Campbell even suggested that the London Committee should play a role in the selection. As Morse pointed out, both these members had been on the Committee when it was the Board of Directors; they possibly resented the minor role they were now playing.[24] The role Morse and Gray had assigned the Committee was, however, well within the Hongkong Bank's tradition.

Perhaps the wrong question is being asked. The contribution of the Committee as a whole might be only routine, but the contribution by individual members, available as they would be for immediate consultation on specific matters, is really the key to the Committee's importance. It provided the Bank with a body of experts which it could consult formally or informally, the importance of the latter being certain but difficult to quantify.

This conclusion is consistent with the roles played in London by Sir Edward Reid and by Sir Arthur Morse. Reid represented Baring Bros and Co. on the Committee, but he became the confidant of Morse during the war and gave much appreciated assistance to the several senior London Managers – and eventually to Sir Michael Turner when he returned to London. Reid's role is apparent throughout the period from 1957 when the Bank was negotiating first with the Mercantile Bank and then with the British Bank of the Middle East, negotiations which also involved the Bank of England and the Treasury.

There is always the feeling that Sir Thomas Jackson, despite his directorships and his chairmanship of the Imperial Bank of Persia, was never really at home in the City – or, equally, that the City while regarding his Eastern abilities highly, never accepted him as one of them. Morse would glory in his non-conformity to the City mould; nevertheless, he made his success initially in London. When in 1953 he returned triumphant to the City, he was not a stranger. But his ability to contribute to the Hongkong Bank's position in Britain was facilitated by the continued close relations he retained with Michael Turner, his successor as Chief Manager in Hong Kong.

During the negotiations with the Mercantile and the BBME the Board in Hongkong delegated certain responsibilities to a sub-committee of the London Advisory Committee. Significantly, this sub-committee comprised Morse, Reid, and the London Manager, S.W.P. Perry-Aldworth. The delegation had not been all-embracing. Nevertheless a much more important role was being played by the Committee than in later years when, for example, the Bank was negotiating with the Royal Bank of Scotland Group.

Underlying all this was the basic factor which led to the formation of the Committee in the first place. The Hongkong Bank was a major British overseas banking institution with its head office outside the United Kingdom. It somehow still needed more than a senior manager in London; there had to be a committee, even if its functions, beyond the routine vetting of the Bank's City investments, were never clearly defined.

The composition of the Committee

The London Advisory Committee in 1946, just after the departure of Arthur Morse for Hong Kong, has a familiar look (see Table 6.4). The Chairman was the senior London Manager, H.E. Muriel. When he retired in 1948, he was replaced as Chairman by the new London Manager, S.A. Gray. The return of Sir Arthur Morse to London recreated the Jackson situation; he became the 'permanent' Chairman, but, as with Jackson, the power balance between Hong Kong and London was in no way affected. Morse did not attempt to second-guess Turner.

With the latter's retirement from Hong Kong in 1962, the suggestion was made by the Board that Turner should replace Morse, but Turner advised against this. He recommended to the Board that he join the London Committee as an ordinary member on the grounds that 'Nothing must be done to give the authorities the impression that the direction of the Bank is being moved away from Hong Kong.' This is an interesting comment, since the Board had shown itself particularly possessive in 1962 and a move from Hong Kong was less likely then than at any time in its history. The reference must, therefore, be related to the tax concessions Inland Revenue had approved relative to the Bank's London investments from £10 million of deposits received from its London-based subsidiaries. The details of this are discussed in Chapter 12, but the basis for the concessions was the overseas direction of the Hongkong Bank. Perhaps Turner was concerned that any excuse might be used to reopen the recently concluded negotiations; any other interpretation appears difficult.

Unlike the days of Sir Thomas Jackson's and Sir Charles Addis's chairmanship of the Committee, the London Manager remained a member in addition to Morse. In fact this relationship was stressed when in 1957 S.W.P. Perry-Aldworth was designated as the Committee's 'Deputy Chairman'.

The second Hongkong Bank member was A.H. Barlow who had joined London Office in 1888 as a junior; he came East in 1891 and served as Manager Bangkok and as Sub-Manager and then the first Manager Hong Kong. Scheduled to be Manager Shanghai in 1924 he was asked to act as Chief Manager during A.G. Stephen's leave; when Stephen died, Barlow became Chief Manager. Barlow retired from the East in 1927, but he would serve the Hongkong Bank for another twenty years. After six months as a travelling inspector, he joined the London Committee on which he served until his final retirement in 1947. During the war years he had acted as a director of the Bank;

Table 6.4 *The Hongkong and Shanghai Banking Corporation
The London Advisory Committee, 1946–1961*

June, 1946		
H.E. Muriel (Chairman, appointed)	Hongkong Bank, Manager	1946–48
Sir Edward Reid	Baring Brothers and Co.	1942–66
C.A. Campbell	Westminster Bank	1919–53
A.H. Barlow	retired, Hongkong Bank	1928–47
Sir William J. Keswick	Matheson and Co.	1945–55
Sir Frederick Sykes, MP	retired, Governor Bombay	1943–54
R.G. Macindoe	Maclaine, Watson and Co.	1943–65
July, 1948		
S.A. Gray (Chairman, appointed)	Hongkong Bank, Manager	1948–55
Sir Edward Reid	Baring Brothers and Co.	1942–66
C.A. Campbell	Westminster Bank	1919–53
Sir William J. Keswick	Matheson and Co.	1945–55
Sir Frederick Sykes, MP	retired, Governor Bombay	1943–54
R.G. Macindoe	Maclaine, Watson and Co.	1943–65
E.C.H. Charlwood	Blyth, Green, Jourdaine and Co.	1947–58
December, 1953		
Sir Arthur Morse (Chairman)	Hongkong Bank, retired	1953–67
S.A. Gray	Hongkong Bank, Manager	1948–55
Sir Edward Reid	Baring Brothers and Co.	1942–66
J.A.F. Binny	Westminster Bank	1953–81
Sir William J. Keswick	Matheson and Co.	1945–55
Sir Frederick Sykes, MP	retired, Governor Bombay	1943–54
R.G. Macindoe	Maclaine, Watson and Co.	1943–65
E.C.H. Charlwood	Blyth, Greene, Jourdaine and Co.	1947–58
December, 1955		
Sir Arthur Morse (Chairman)	Hongkong Bank, retired	1953–67
S.W.P. Perry-Aldworth	Hongkong Bank, Manager	1955–61
Sir Edward Reid	Baring Brothers and Co.	1942–66
J.A.F. Binny	Westminster Bank	1953–81
R.G. Macindoe	Maclaine, Watson and Co.	1943–65
E.C.H. Charlwood	Blyth, Greene, Jourdaine and Co.	1947–58
Sir John Nicoll	retired, Governor Singapore	1955–63
New members, 1956–58		
G.R. Roper-Caldbeck	Boustead and Co.	1957–70
F.H. Atkinson (vice Charlwood)	Blyth, Greene, Jourdaine and Co.	1958–67
(S.W.P. Perry-Aldworth appointed Deputy Chairman, 1957)		
May, 1958		
Sir Arthur Morse (Chairman)	Hongkong Bank, retired	1953–67
S.W.P. Perry-Aldworth (Deputy Chairman)	Hongkong Bank, Manager	1955–61
Sir Edward Reid	Baring Brothers and Co.	1942–66
R.G. Macindoe	Maclaine, Watson and Co.	1943–65
J.A.F. Binny	Westminster Bank	1953–81

Table 6.4 (cont.)

Sir John Nicoll	retired, Governor Singapore	1955–63
G.R. Roper-Caldbeck	Boustead and Co.	1957–70
F.H. Atkinson	Blyth, Greene, Jourdaine and Co.	1958–67

May, 1959

Sir Arthur Morse (Chairman)	Hongkong Bank, retired	1953–67
S.W.P. Perry-Aldworth (Deputy Chairman)	Hongkong Bank, Manager	1955–61
Sir Edward Reid	Baring Brothers and Co.	1942–66
R.G. Macindoe	Maclaine, Watson and Co.	1943–65
J.A.F. Binny	Westminster Bank	1953–81
Sir John Nicoll	retired, Governor Singapore	1955–63
G.R. Roper-Caldbeck	Boustead and Co.	1957–70
F.H. Atkinson	Blyth, Greene, Jourdaine and Co.	1958–67
Cyril E. Jones	Board, Mercantile Bank	1959–66
Sir Kenneth W. Mealing	Board, Mercantile Bank	1959–66

May, 1960

Sir Arthur Morse (Chairman)	Hongkong Bank, retired	1953–67
S.W.P. Perry-Aldworth (Deputy Chairman)	Hongkong Bank, Manager	1955–61
Sir Edward Reid	Baring Brothers and Co.	1942–66
R.G. Macindoe	Maclaine, Watson and Co.	1943–65
J.A.F. Binny	Westminster Bank	1953–81
Sir John Nicoll	retired, Governor Singapore	1955–63
G.R. Roper-Caldbeck	Boustead and Co.	1957–70
F.H. Atkinson	Blyth, Greene, Jourdaine and Co.	1958–67
Cyril E. Jones	Board, Mercantile Bank	1959–66
Sir Kenneth W. Mealing	Board, Mercantile Bank	1959–66
Sir Dallas G.M. Bernard	Board, BBME	[a]1960–64
Sir Alec Kirkbride	Board, BBME	1960–69

May 1961

Sir Arthur Morse (Chairman)	Hongkong Bank, retired	1953–67
G.O.W. Stewart (Deputy Chairman)	Hongkong Bank, Manager	1961–69
Sir Edward Reid	Baring Brothers and Co.	1942–66
R.G. Macindoe	Maclaine, Watson and Co.	1943–65
J.A.F. Binny	Westminster Bank	1953–81
Sir John Nicoll	retired, Governor Singapore	1955–63
G.R. Roper-Caldbeck	Boustead and Co.	1957–70
F.H. Atkinson	Blyth, Greene, Jourdaine and Co.	1958–67
Sir Cyril E. Jones	Board, Mercantile Bank	1959–66
Sir Kenneth W. Mealing	Board, Mercantile Bank	1959–66
Sir Dallas G.M. Bernard	Board, BBME	[a]1960–64
Sir Alec Kirkbride	Board, BBME	1960–69

[a] Previous service on the Committee, 1929–1939 (see Volume III).
Bold face indicates new members.

Morse had consulted him on personnel matters, and H.E. Muriel was proud to record in his autobiography that Barlow had commended him on his management of London Office. As Muriel correctly stated, Barlow did not give praise easily.

In all Barlow had served the Hongkong Bank for 59 years – he had passed the age of 70 without controversy. During his final illness in Southern Rhodesia these years of strain took their toll; he suffered from the impression that he had to go to the Bank to work. His wife appealed to the Bank, and the Chief Manager wrote a kind letter expressing appreciation for his services and suggesting that he need not concern himself about the office but should relax and recover. This letter put him at ease and he died shortly thereafter in July 1960 in Salisbury, Rhodesia.

The Hongkong Bank's 'clearing bank', the London and County Bank, had first been represented when the Committee was founded in 1875; through mergers the bank had become the Westminster Bank and continued to be represented, in 1946 by C.A. Campbell, from 1953 by J.A.F. Binny. Jardine, Matheson and Co. were represented at first by Sir William Keswick, but he retired in 1955 and the appointment of a successor was postponed, pending the return of his brother, Sir John H. Keswick, from Hong Kong. There was no representative from Morgan, Grenfell and Co. but with the acquisition of the Mercantile Bank the connection was renewed through the interest of Morgan Grenfell in Yule, Catto and Co., which had been in turn closely associated with the Mercantile Bank for many years.

New companies with members on the Committee included Blyth, Greene, Jourdain and Co. and Boustead and Co. The former is generally associated with Mauritius and the Mercantile Bank, but their representative, E.C.H. Charlwood had been many years in Malaya with Harper, Gilfillan and Co. As pre-war the Bank appointed prominent retired civil servants from the East. Sir Frederick Sykes, retired Governor of Bombay, served to 1954; the following year Sir John Nicoll, sometime Colonial Secretary, Hong Kong, and retired as Governor of Singapore, was appointed.

In 1959 with the acquisition of the Mercantile Bank, the Hongkong Bank's Board of Directors invited two members of the Mercantile's Board to be members of the London Committee – Sir Kenneth Mealing and Cyril Jones accepted. This was thought to stress the 'merger' as opposed to the 'takeover' concept, and it reassured those directly concerned with the Mercantile, including their constituents, that continuity was planned for the time being. The acquisition the following year of the BBME led to the Board's invitation to Sir Dallas Bernard, a former Chairman of the Hongkong Bank and a son-in-law of Sir Charles Addis, to rejoin the London Committee in his capacity as

Chairman of the BBME. He was joined by another BBME director, Sir Alec Kirkbride.

The Committee was now composed of twelve members; Morse himself preferred small committees and this had become unwieldy. Morse consoled himself with the thought that not all would attend and, indeed, once two members had been invited from the Mercantile, the Bank's hand was forced. The fact is, however, that the Committee had become, despite the spurt of activity during the acquisitions, an important contact with the City – and very little more. But this was enough. Such contacts were essential to management and for a new London Manager, the goodwill of the Committee was of considerable importance.

APPENDIX TO CHAPTER 6

COMPANIES WITH CONNECTIONS TO MEMBERS OF THE HONGKONG BANK'S BOARD OF DIRECTORS, A SAMPLE LIST

J.D. Alexander
Gibb, Livingston; Partner, Mackinnon Mackenzie; chairman HK Electric; director, Dairy Farm, Ice and Cold Storage, HK and Kowloon Wharf and Godown, HK Tramways, Star Ferry, Union Insurance Society of Canton; consultant, Douglas Steamship, committee, St Andrew's Society.

Hugh David MacEwen Barton
Chairman and managing director, Jardine, Matheson; member, Legislative Council, Court of Hong Kong University; chairman, Henry Waugh; alternate chairman, HK Aircraft Engineering; director, HK Telephone, HK Electric, Cathay Pacific Airways, Shek-O Development, Far Eastern Economic Review, HK Land Investment and Agency, HK Tramways, Indo-China Steam Navigation, HK and Kowloon Wharf and Godown, Jardine Engineering, Star Ferry, Lombard Insurance, HK Fire Insurance, South China Morning Post; general committee, Sailors' Home and Missions to Seamen; HK General Chamber of Commerce; steward, HK Jockey Club.

Harold Dudley Benham
Manager, David Sassoon; director and manager, Australian Leathers (Hongkong); director, China Light and Power; HK and Kowloon Wharf and Godown, Star Ferry, HK Land Investment and Agency, HK Tramways, Malabar investment Trust, Nepean Investment Trust, Trans-World Commodities; committee, HK Fire Insurance.

J.A. Blackwood
Manager, Butterfield and Swire; chairman, Cathay Pacific Airways, Swire and Maclaine HK, Taikoo Sugar Refining, Duro Paint Manufacturing; board of governors of Matilda and War Memorial Hospital; unofficial JP; committee, St Andrew's Society.

Cedric Blaker
Director, Gilman (HK), South China Morning Post, HK General Chamber of Commerce, Union Insurance Society of Canton, Wheelock Marden, Textile Corp. of HK, Nanyang Cotton Mill, HK Realty and Trust, Multitrade Corp, Humphreys

Estates and Finance, HK and China Gas, Eastern Asia Navigation, Moutrie (HK); chairman, Rediffusion; member, Executive and Legislative Councils; Hon. Consul, Sweden and Greece; unofficial JP; president, Society of St George; committee, Diocesan Boys' School.

G.G.D. Carter
Director, Dodwell, Engineering Equipment, Dodwell Motors, Great China Hardware, Hibiscus Shipping, Lincoln International; member, Trade and Industry Advisory Board, Commerce and Industry Dept; council, HK Management Assoc.

John Douglas Clague
Chairman, John D. Hutchison, General Chamber of Commerce, A.S. Watson, British Oxygen (HK); deputy chairman, Federation of HK Industries Working Party; managing director, Dunbar; director, Wheelock Marden, Lombard Insurance, Dairy Farm, Ice and Cold Storage, Textile Corp. of HK, HK Realty and Trust, Harriman Realty, American Lloyd Travel Service, Blair, F.E. Skinner (HK), Liddell Bros (HK), Oriental Mortgage and Finance Corp., Reiss Bradley, Far Eastern Motors, Marine Navigation, Cameron Shipping, Vanguard Shipping, Cornes, Eastern Asia Navigation, Far Eastern Prospecting and Development Corp., Far East Flying Training School, Far East Aviation; member, Legislative and Urban Council; president, HK Family Welfare Society; chairman, HK Housing Society; member, HK War Memorial Fund Committee, Grantham Scholarship Fund Committee.

H.J. Collar
Vice-chairman, ICI (China); director, HK Anti-TB Assoc.

Stanley Jack Cooke
Director, Gilman, Moutrie (HK), Multitrade Corp., Paris Glove; unofficial JP.

Brian Thomas Flanagan
Governing director, Gibb, Livingston; managing director, Mackinnon Mackenzie of HK; chairman, HK Electric; director, British Trader's Insurance, Union Insurance of Canton, North Pacific Insurance, HK Tramways, Cathay Pacific Airways, HK and Kowloon Wharf and Godown, Indo-China Steam Navigation, HK Rope Manufacturing, Star Ferry, Dairy Farm, Ice and Cold Storage; committee, St Patrick's Society of HK.

G.M. Goldsack
Dodwell; Chairman, Great China Hardware, HK and Kowloon Wharf and Godown, HK and Whampoa Dock, Union Insurance Society of Canton, Nanyang Cotton Mill, Holme Ringer, HK Telephone, HK Electric, Dairy Farm, Ice and Cold Storage, Dodwell Motors, Union Waterboat, Engineering Equipment, Lincoln International, G. Herring (HK), British Trader's Insurance, North Pacific Insurance; committee, HK General Chamber of Commerce; trustee, Zetland Hall Trustees.

R. Gordon
Director, (Private Office) Jardine, Matheson, Jardine Engineering Corp.; committee, St Andrew's Society.

J.H. Hamm
Resident director, Dodwell, Dodwell Motors; director, HK and Whampoa Dock, Great China Hardware, HK Electric, HK and Kowloon Wharf and Godown, Engineering Equipment; unofficial JP.

E.R. Hill
Director, Dodwell, Union Insurance Society of Canton, HK Telephone, Engineering Equipment, HK Electric, Dairy Farm, Ice and Cold Storage, HK and Kowloon Wharf and Godown, Marsman Hong Kong China, HK and Whampoa Dock; unofficial JP.

Lawrence Kadoorie
Partner, Sir Elly Kadoorie and Sons; chairman, China Light and Power; director, Acrow Engineers (Asia), HK Engineering and Construction, HK Carpet Manufacturers, Major Contractors, Nanyang Cotton Mill, Far East Commodities, HK and Whampoa Dock, HK Fire Insurance, Lombard Insurance, Oriental Marine Products, Rubber Trust, Shanghai Land Investment; president and trustee, Ohel Leah Synagogue; cofounder, Kadoorie Agricultural Aid Association.

John Keswick
Managing director, (Private Office) Jardine, Matheson; chairman, Jardine Engineering Corp.; chairman and managing director, HK Land Investment and Agency; chairman, Indo-China Steam Navigation, Canton Insurance Office, HK Fire Insurance; director, Shek O Development, HK Electric, HK and Kowloon Wharf and Godown, Star Ferry; committee, St Andrew's Society.

W.C.G. Knowles
Manager, Butterfield and Swire; chairman, Taikoo Dockyard and Engineering; Taikoo Sugar Refining, Duro Paint Manufacturing, Swire and Maclaine, Cathay Pacific Airways; director, HK Aircraft Engineering; chairman, HK Tourist Assoc.; Council of HK University.

John Farrar Macgregor
Chairman, Caldbeck, Macgregor; Macgregors, Union Insurance Society of Canton; director, Amalgamated Rubber Estates, Shek-O Development; steward, Jockey Club; president, HKSPCA; ex-chieftain, St Andrew's Society (HK and Shanghai).

C.C. Roberts
Manager, Butterfield and Swire; chairman, Swire and Maclaine; chairman and director, Cathay Pacific Airways; committee, Society of Yorkshiremen in HK; past-pres., St George's Society; committee, HK Club; unofficial JP.

R.J. Sheppard
Chairman, ICI.

L.B. Stone
General manager, Union Insurance Society of Canton, North Pacific Insurance; president, St George's Society; committee, HK General Chamber of Commerce.

G.T. Tagg
Chairman, HK Electric; managing director, Mackinnon Mackenzie of HK; director, Mackinnon Mackenzie of Japan, HK Tramways, Dairy Farm, Ice and Cold Storage, Union Insurance Society of Canton, British Traders' Insurance, North Pacific Insurance, Star Ferry, HK and Kowloon Wharf and Godown, Cathay Pacific Airways, Indo-China Steam Navigation, HK Rope Manufacturing; local chairman, Far Eastern Freight Conference.

C.A. Wright
Chairman and managing director, ICI; committee, Employers' Federation of HK.

[*Sources*: Hongkong Album, Hongkong Who's Who, Hongkong ($) Directory]

7

HONGKONG BANKERS AND THE EMERGENCE OF HEAD OFFICE

> It is the wish of the directors to afford to the Corporation's servants every chance of encouragement and promotion.
>
> Minutes, Court of Directors, 1867

Perhaps in no other aspect of the Hongkong Bank's early post-war history is the theme of creative tension within the traditional system better illustrated than in personnel policy. The Bank's pamphlet, 'Conditions of Service on the Foreign Staff', dated January 1961, did not differ materially from the identically entitled mimeographed pages dated 1951. The London Office apprenticeship and the emphasis on sports on the playing fields of New Beckenham remained an essential part of the program, and the Foreign staff, almost without exception Sixth Form graduates, came East without a written contract of service to perform in too many cases fifteen years of 'operations' duties before a Board 'appointment'.

And yet nothing was really the same. Early post-war juniors had been senior service officers, as in 1919 their London service was nominal but now they came to an East which was visibly changing. If there were attempts to restore the Empire, even the more conservative 'old hands' gave at least lip service to the possibility of eventual local political independence. The need for economic restoration delayed political implementation, but it did not change the atmosphere. This was not a post-Great War 'return to normalcy', and the Bank juniors not only accepted the challenge, they were part of it. While conforming to a point, they were pushing the limits of the system.

There were indeed modifications in the system of Foreign staff leave, emoluments, fringe benefits, and marriage rules, but the system remained intact. The paternalistic role of the Board of Directors remained. And yet the very modifications called logically for further change, and paternalism could be accepted only if the actual decisions for Foreign staff took account of statutory and contractual measures common in the United Kingdom.

Local staff were promoted and permitted to sign for the Bank; it is true that the numbers by 1961 were still limited and the actual role restricted, but the change had been made and in the context of political independence would eventually take on greater significance.

Even the planning and execution of these changes suggest the need for a greater administrative overhead. The need had been seen inter-war, but there had been no formal differentiation of tasks and thus the potential for specialization had been limited. The change in the years to 1961 was quantitatively insignificant, but the emergence of a recognized 'head office', separate and distinct from the 'Hong Kong office' was the essential first step. There was immediately a locus for administrative development, however simple it might seem to those looking back from the 1980s. The Inspectors, the Legal Adviser, the Deputy Chairman, the Inspector (personnel) proved the essential base for the Bank's subsequent growth.

The two themes move together – the Hongkong Banker and the emergence of Head Office.

It could be argued in 1961 that nothing had 'really' changed, but the adjustments which might have seemed but part of the system were to prove the basis of significant development. This is not to suggest that the position in 1961 would be subject to immediate and revolutionary reform. But as changes in banking practices, the growth of competition, the expectations of young Foreign staff and Local staff alike in an era of national independence strained the limits set by the early post-war adjustments, yet another 'essential' aspect of the traditional Bank would be forced to yield. By 1981 after the acquisition of Marine Midland Banks it is legitimate to ask what relevance the Bank's history has to its present operations? The young waiter in the Hong Kong Club's Jackson Room was showing commendable initiative in asking to be told something of Sir Thomas Jackson, but when a very competent junior Bank officer, commenting on Jackson's statue, asked with surprise, 'Oh, did he work for us?', the consequences of post-war changes become sadly apparent.

This chapter covers the first tentative steps from regional bank to a multinational financial services corporation in two key areas – personnel and corporate organization.

CHIEF MANAGERS: THE SUCCESSION

With the exception of a reference to William Kaye as a successor to James Greig (see Volume I, Chapter 7), there is no suggestion in the records that the Board of Directors ever considered the appointment of an 'outsider' as Chief Manager of the Hongkong Bank. And post-war, as in 1867, it remained 'the wish of the directors to afford to the Corporation's servants every chance of encouragement and promotion'. This policy was not challenged; no search was made for bankers with a good 'track record' who might be brought in at senior levels or who might even be appointed directly as the Bank's chief executive. The directors were but reconfirming the 'strong opinion' expressed by their predecessors in 1876 that 'in future all clerks joining the service of the

Bank should go through the London Office, save under very exceptional circumstances...'.

And, since the chief executive officer of the Hongkong Bank, the Chief Manager, had exceptional authority and must set the tone of the Bank's subsequent policies, the first task in this chapter is to consider the self-defined problem of the internal succession.

General considerations

As personnel matters were part of the responsibility of the Chief Manager, although formal appointments were brought before the Board and made in the name of the Board, the *de facto* power to select a successor rested with the Chief Manager. An analysis of Foreign staff executives whose seniority ranked between Morse and Turner suggests that in 1952, at the time the Board were considering Morse's successor, there was only one practical choice, Michael W. Turner. The reason for this rested in large part on the fact that Morse had pre-selected Turner and placed him in position.

This conclusion relates only to the moment of final selection. It forces the analysis to shift back to the point where the initial positioning takes place. In any case, there can be pitfalls along the way; as the 'interregnum' of the early 1890s (see Volume I, Chapter 12) illustrates, plans can be upset by health, apparently capable executives can begin their chief managership at an unfortunate time; as the 1902 succession suggests, whatever the plans of Sir Thomas Jackson, the Chief Manager, to favour V.A. Caesar Hawkins the Board had exceptionally detected more than one qualified candidate and had made their own selection (J.R.M. Smith). Sir Arthur Morse knew, none better, that the succession can be forced by events.

In the period 1946–1961 there were two successions agreed – from Morse to Turner and from Turner to Saunders. Each occurred as planned and both were successful. No documents would appear to have survived whereby the incumbent Chief Manager's or the directors' views have been explained, and the following discussion is therefore based on consideration of the careers of potential candidates and their known relationship to the incumbent.

Even under the new Bank regulations, a new Chief Manager would not necessarily and certainly not immediately be elected Chairman, nor, in the Board's view, was it necessary he should be a director. In the developing circumstances of the 1950s and early 1960s this position became untenable, but it was based in part, at least, on several relevant factors.

First, and perhaps not directly relevant to the present discussion, the Board wished to be in control.

Secondly, there was little opportunity, given the hierarchical structure both of the Bank and of Hong Kong society, for a potential chief manager to create an independent public image for himself. Directors, as constituents of the Bank, would have met the nominee as Chief Accountant or Manager Hong Kong, and thus have a shrewd estimate of his ability as a banker and, indeed, of his overall potential. This in turn suggests that a new Chief Manager would virtually have to have sound Hong Kong experience, and his early promotion within the Hong Kong office would be an indication of his possible future. But it was still difficult to really 'know' the new Chief Manager.

Thirdly, the Board's desire to 'vet' the new Chief Manager was the offset, as it were, to the unspoken agreement that the new Chief Manager would be selected only from the Foreign staff of the Hongkong Bank.

Provided the Chief Manager recommended as his successor the man who had been 'positioned', there was little role for the Board to play at the moment of decision. They had in fact sanctioned the positioning; appointments were, after all, made only with the sanction of the Board. Therefore to conclude that the Board was without a role in the selection of the Chief Manager would be to disregard its continuing watching brief; to suggest that the Board, at one moment in time, would choose a new Chief Manager from a list they themselves compiled for the occasion is unrealistic. The Board both played a role and accepted the recommendation of the retiring Chief Manager. Should the system have failed, the Board retained the final decision.

From Sir Arthur Morse to Michael Turner

About Turner – Morse said, What do you think about this fellow?
Oh, a very good chap, Sir.
Prepared to work under him?
Any time.
Morse said, I see.
That was that.

G.W. Stabb, London Office: a wartime conversation[1]

Sir Arthur and Lady Morse actually lived in the 9th Floor Flat of the Bank's Head Office building, 1, Queen's Road, Central. The Bank House on the Peak had suffered damage during the war and had been requisitioned afterwards. The Board-approved rebuilding was being completed towards the end of 1952 when Morse sent his Hong Kong Manager to make weekly inspections. Turner, accompanied by his wife, duly made his reports, drawing up a list of the deficiencies and recommending alterations, to which Morse responded, 'I don't know what on earth you're worrying about because you're not going to live in it.'

Morse invited Turner to move his desk from the Manager's office into his office. No reason was given at all because, as Wendy, Lady Turner, put it,

'Arthur's sense of humour was a very warped sense of humour.' Sir Michael put it more bluntly, 'He was a real bugger, he could just as easily have told us because he made so many mistakes in that house we couldn't remedy, but he didn't tell us. No, no, he was as close as an oyster.'

Two days after Turner had moved into Morse's office – so that he could learn how hard the Chief Manager had to work – Morse informed him that he had been approved by the Board as the next Chief Manager. The decision, the Turners insist came as a surprise, but, even if the Turners had been unwilling to admit it to themselves, the decision had been made earlier and there had been signs, apparent to close observers, that this was so. And after the event others, like Stabb in the quotation above, would remember casually dropped queries. As Sir Michael said, Morse was as close as an oyster in this and many matters concerning the Bank.

The years 1947–1949 were crucial. Both R.P. Moodie (East in 1925) and Michael Turner (East in 1930) were 'juniors' in Hong Kong office. In 1947 Moodie was moved from Hong Kong office to Head Office, but in 1948 he was transferred to be Accountant Shanghai. Turner was called to replace him in the Inspectorate and in 1949 was appointed acting Chief Accountant. To some observers this had been the moment of decision – or, perhaps, of expectation, because Morse's argument for not informing Turner earlier of his plans would be a very reasonable one: until the time came there was always a chance that he would be forced to change his opinion. Turner was not the appointed successor until he was actually appointed and any premature indication is dangerous and probably unfair.

This analysis is based on several assumptions which need consideration. First, the argument appears to be concluded when Turner is appointed Chief Accountant as if, barring an error in judgement by Morse, this position were the key. As has been stated in Volume III, in the early history of the Bank the assumption that the Chief Accountant would become Chief Manager is invalid. A.C. Hynes, Vandeleur Grayburn, and Arthur Morse, had all been Chief Accountant, but Morse certainly and Hynes probably became Chief Manager for extraneous reasons. Furthermore D.C. Edmondston, intended as the successor to Grayburn, had not been Chief Accountant. As a guide to the succession, and barring exceptional events, the post depended on the importance of Hong Kong; post-war the importance of the experience in Hong Kong was accentuated. Those with sound field experience might be assigned to the vital managerial posts of Singapore, Tokyo, Calcutta, Bombay and, as yet, Shanghai. Therefore Turner's appointment was, in the post-war Bank, a turning point in his career, confirmed by his succession of promotions, first to Hong Kong office Sub-Manager under A.S. Adamson in 1950 and then to Hong Kong Manager as Adamson's successor in 1951. There would have to be considerable reason not to promote under these circumstances the Manager Hong Kong to the Chief Managership – his age, health, personality, and wife (not necessarily in that order) being acceptable.

When Morse began to consider the name of his successor, he could easily determine that there was no 'A.G. Stephen' in waiting, anxious to take over the Chief Managership despite his seniority.[a] Of Morse's own general seniority there had been J.J. French, but he died in harness in Bangkok. Adamson, a nephew of Sir Charles Addis, had a great reputation as a banker; T.J.J. Fenwick had been the first post-war Hong Kong office Manager and had shaped the new Inspectorate, but, able as he was, he disliked social protocol and would not have sought the most senior post. S.A. Gray (East in 1919) in Shanghai was active and would soon take over London Office, but there was no question of his remaining in the East into the late '50s. All these officers retired from the East before Morse.

Probably no decision as to 'generations' was consciously made. There was no effective choice; it was just obvious that the Chief Managership should be passed on to the next generation. If this is defined, on the basis of the 'normal' occupancy of the post, as ten years, then there were at the time of Turner's appointment some 37 officers senior to him, that is Foreign staff with seniority dating from 1925. There were five junior to Turner who had also come East in 1930.

Turner had been interned in Singapore throughout the war, but his recovery was reasonably complete and did not interfere with his career. In this he was fortunate; many of his seniors were physically incapacitated for long careers in the East, others could no longer accept the necessary responsibilities. Other seniors suffered from lack of career planning and, through no failing of their own, lacked the breadth of experience necessary for the more important managerial posts. A.L.V.S. Giles (East in 1930), for example, although of the same seniority as Turner, had been provided experience almost entirely in current accounts; only in the mid-1950s was he given an opportunity to prove himself, successfully, as Accountant in Penang and Bangkok, and eventually Manager first in Kuala Lumpur and then in Colombo.

Still others were considered, indeed considered themselves, 'back-room' bankers in the Fenwick tradition, F.C.B. Black (East in 1929) and A.M. Mack (East in 1930), for example. They made a vital and new contribution to the development of the Hongkong Bank, but they were not competitors for the post of Chief Manager. There were those who had satisfactory careers as senior Managers in important branches or were known for their specific area

---

[a] Stephen had come East in 1885. When, at the age of 58 with 35 years seniority, he was appointed Chief Manager in succession to Sir Newton Stabb in 1920, he had already established himself as a community leader in Shanghai (see Vols. II and III).

expertise – S.W.P. Perry-Aldworth (East in 1925) was Manager Bangkok, then Tokyo, and then, under Michael Turner, London at the time of the acquisition of the Mercantile Bank and the British Bank of the Middle East; H.V. Parker (East in 1925) moved from Manager Manila to Manager Tokyo and then to Paris, retiring in 1962 after 37 years as a member of the 'Foreign' staff. Among the area specialists might be included B.P. Massey (East in 1928), who succeeded the very senior A.G. Kellogg (East in 1906) to the management of the New York agency in 1949, and G.S. Chambers (East in 1929) who became Manager Saigon in 1954.

Without, therefore, examining each career in detail in this history, the list of reasonably eligible and positioned Foreign staff officers narrows. At this point there must be a personal element. Michael Turner had been the immediate assistant to Morse in 1932 when the latter was Chief Accountant; Turner was dedicated to the Bank and was noted for his great attention to detail, qualities which would have endeared him to Morse. When in the early post-war years the new Inspectorate was the subject of debate in the Bank, Moodie had his doubts and expressed them forcefully. For whatever reason he was sent to Shanghai as Accountant, a post of great importance and therefore a logical assignment without reference to the succession; had China developed otherwise, the assignment might have led to a Shanghai career. As it was, Moodie returned to Hong Kong and, under Turner, became Manager Hong Kong and in 1958, before his retirement, Deputy Chief Manager.

The importance of Moodie's Shanghai assignment is that it cleared the way for Turner, subject always to his own ability. He proved himself and Morse moved him forward until, two days before the event, Turner moved into Morse's office.

Turner's seniority was 1930, he had come East some fifteen years after Sir Arthur Morse. On appointment Turner had had 23 years in the East, including wartime internment; by comparison de Bovis had had eighteen years, J.R.M. Smith and Newton Stabb twenty years. Stephen, Barlow, and Hynes were exceptions with seniority of 30 years or over; Grayburn had been 26 years in the East, Morse 27. Turner's experience had been confined, however, like that of Grayburn and Morse, to the main offices. In fact, his Singapore banking experience was so brief as to be discountable; Turner had effectively served only in Shanghai and Hong Kong. Unlike his predecessors, however, he would be able to make up for the deficiency while in office; developments in transportation and communication would make it possible for the Chief Manager to tour all the branches and agencies of the Hongkong Bank.

In June 1961 he became Sir Michael Turner, and the Board of Directors referred to the contribution he and Lady Turner had made.

Sir Michael Turner to J.A.H. Saunders

The war years had an impact on the range of choice and the time for positioning the next Chief Manager. Turner might have stayed as Chief Manager beyond 1962; he retired after only eight years. But he had in a sense made his contribution; it was for others to reorder the Bank to accommodate the changes he had achieved. Furthermore Turner was looking to the 1965 centennial; he thought it right either to remain through that celebration or to leave early enough to permit his successor time to prepare. And four more years in the East was too long.

The first question was, as always, should the succession be passed to the next generation or should a near contemporary be given the opportunity in what would of necessity be an interim or short-term appointment. There would be two reasons for the latter move: (i) courtesy to an able colleague and (ii) lack of anyone in the right age range to take over.

Saunders in 1962 had been in the East only seventeen years, but his seniority was 1940. Thus looking at it on a generation basis, that is on age, it is the latter date that is relevant – appointing anyone senior to Saunders would not be passing on a generation. Two near contemporaries (as defined for present purposes) to Turner come to mind – G.O.W. Stewart (East in 1933) and R.G.L. Oliphant (East in 1934), the former was Deputy Chief Manager from 1958 when R.P. Moodie retired, the latter was Manager Hong Kong in 1962. Stewart preferred to return Home as the London Manager. Now, for the first time since Sir Newton Stabb (during the tenures of Stephen, Barlow, Hynes, and Grayburn as Chief Manager), there would be a London Manager under whom the Chief Manager had served in the East (see Volume III, Table 1.3). Oliphant had moved up too slowly for full consideration, but he concluded his career as Manager Hong Kong and the Deputy Chief Manager in the centennial year of 1965. I.J.O. Cruickshank (East in 1935) had been Saunders' Manager in Singapore, but he too returned to London – as junior Manager. J.S. Dunnett (East in 1935) was on the American track, moving from Manager Manila to President of the Hongkong Bank of California; he retired in 1969.

Two outstanding bankers of 1937 seniority should be noted, but they fell, as it were, in between – they were hardly contemporaries of Turner yet neither were they sufficiently junior to be considered the 'next generation' – M.G. Carruthers was Manager Tokyo in 1962 and he retired in 1967 as Deputy Chief Manager; F.J. Knightly retired a year later, but before retirement he had become, as Acting Chief Manager, a director of the Bank; he would be reappointed after his retirement.

When Saunders was first appointed Chief Manager in 1962 there were 61 members of the Foreign staff junior to Turner but senior to Saunders, of these sixteen had seniority dating, like Saunders', from 1940. There is little reason, therefore, to consider those junior to Saunders; they would not have had time to be recognized.

Of these sixteen officers three in particular would seem, from the bare record, to require consideration. First, there was G.P. Stubbs, who was Manager Singapore in 1962 and later moved to London as Manager for Europe, retiring in 1972. A University graduate, the son of a former Governor of Hong Kong, Sir Reginald Edward Stubbs (1919–1925), young Stubbs ran afoul of Arthur Morse and was transferred to Manila; he rose quickly to become Manager Tawau, Accountant Colombo, Manager Orchard Road (Singapore), and, by 1962, Manager Singapore, but he never returned to Hong Kong. The second was *Maurice* W. Turner, sent down to Singapore in 1953, returned briefly to Hong Kong in the late 1950s; he had become Manager Jesselton by 1962. Turner returned to Hong Kong to become Controller of Overseas Operations and Deputy Chief Manager. The third was S.F.T.B. Lever, who, with Maurice Turner, had transferred at the end of the war from the Home to the Foreign staff. He began in Singapore with Saunders and had risen to Manager Calcutta in 1962; he then took charge in New York during a crucial period, returning to the East to head the Singapore and Malaysian operations of the Bank, retiring with the new rank of General Manager in 1971.

In the last two years of the Morse administration, Maurice Turner, Lever, and Saunders were juniors in Hong Kong. They had all three been senior officers during the war; they are remembered by retirees for their activities under R.A. Stuart in the immediate post-war days in Singapore. By 1954 only Saunders remained in Hong Kong, and in 1955 he succeeded G.O.W. Stewart as Chief Accountant.

The conclusion drawn by the historian is that at this point a selection had been made; the selection may still have been tentative – as with Michael Turner, Morse was willing to the last day to reassess – but it was nevertheless a selection. In 1958 Saunders returned to Singapore as Assistant Manager; he then came back to Hong Kong as Assistant Manager under Oliphant; when Oliphant went on leave in 1960, Saunders became Manager Hong Kong. Shortly thereafter, in September 1960, he was accepted by the Board as the successor to Michael Turner – there would be no cliff-hanger decision this time – Sir Michael's sense of humour lacked the edge of Sir Arthur's.

In the capacity of Inspector and Chief Manager designate, Saunders toured the branches; on his return in November 1961 he became Deputy Chief Manager, again in succession to Stewart, and in March 1962 was Chief

Manager. His election as Chairman of the Board occurred in 1967, and he became Executive Chairman of the reorganized Board from 1969 to his retirement in 1972.

HEAD OFFICE: THE CHIEF MANAGER AND MANAGEMENT

The Bank's Executive Chairman in early 1986 was Sir Michael Sandberg. He had served under Sir Arthur Morse and Morse had heard the Bank's founder, Sir Thomas Sutherland, recall the events of 1864–1866.

The Bank Sandberg entered in 1949 and the Bank Sir Michael Turner left in 1962 would have been recognizable to pre-war Chief Managers to a point. The task of this section is to describe how, given the apparent continuity, the Bank was actually in the process of dramatic change through developments in Head Office. While the last of the pre-war Bankers played out their traditional role, they were setting the stage for the new banking world of the mid-1960s and beyond. The emergence of Head Office was on the one hand nothing more than the logical differentiation Grayburn would no doubt have undertaken had he (i) seen the need or been willing to delegate, (ii) had the time to set about it, (iii) been able to justify the cost of the additional personnel, and (iv) had the funds to manage it. Once Head Office was seen as separate from Hong Kong office and identifiable as such further developments occurred beyond the thought of earlier Bankers.

The Hongkong Bank depended throughout this period on the generalist banker, the young Foreign staff officer who was virtually apprenticed, undertook menial and routine banking tasks, moved from department to department, and finally reached a senior position with a broad background of banking experience. Pre-war there had been one or two 'experts' – the political advisers. Post-war there was an increasing need for specialists, but, as before, they could be bought on the market; Bank generalists monitored the development of trustee business pre-war and undertook the initial management, but the actual formation of a Trustee Company required – and the Bank recruited – a specialist. The pre-war specialists had not been perceived as part of the Bank family; post-war there had to be some better relationship established; sheer numbers would force a restructuring of personnel thinking and policy.

Although apparently new departures could be matched against some pre-war precedent, the number of these post-war 'departures' or adjustments would force the more fundamental structural changes which were made after 1961. From the point of view of timing, the fact is that the technical changes did not begin to have an impact until late in the 1946–1961 period. The Hongkong Bank itself, as measured by the number of major branches and Foreign staff, grew only moderately; the Bank narrowly defined was still shielded from impact of the growth of the corporation, that is, of the Hongkong Bank Group; there was growth through fixed equity investments and acquisitions, but the staffs of these firms were left in place.

Pre-war the Bank had been free of committees. But this was more fact than policy: who would have sat on the committees? Everyone had a single task which he performed; advice, if not provided by the Portuguese assistant, came from one's superior – it was all 'on line'. A pre-war committee comprised of all staff members interested in a particular problem would have consisted of the Chief Manager (or the Hong Kong Manager if the matter had been temporarily delegated) plus the officer responsible. How this changed is described best from inside the Chief Manager's office – and the evidence of Miss C.M. Goldney on this subject is provided below. Once there is a separate Head Office, a Staff Officer, and a Chief Inspector, there is the nucleus of a committee. Or, less formally expressed, the Chief Manager may need to call in more than one man to discuss certain problems.

Foreign staff assignments and accomplishments

Although in the question of the succession from Morse to Turner the group closest to Morse in seniority, those with 1919 and 1920 seniority (or earlier), had to be ruled out, Morse's success in the immediate post-war period was nevertheless due to the ability of these men, who were then serving their last years in the East. With Adamson managing Hong Kong, Gray in Shanghai, Stuart in Singapore, W.J. Hope in Saigon, J. Caldwell in Calcutta, G.E.B. Tytler in Bombay, W. Webster in Manila, and the veteran Kellogg in New York, the redevelopment of the Bank was in sound hands. Morse had left H.E. Muriel (East in 1909) behind as senior Manager in London with A.M. Duncan Wallace (East in 1919) and Muriel's old London Office and Shanghai musical partner M. W. Wood (East in 1911).

By 1951 the next group, many of whose names appear in Volume III and whose seniority is dated mainly in the mid-1920s, had taken over major branches – with Morse on Home leave Adamson (East in 1919) was Acting Chief Manager, and Gray (East in 1919) had replaced Muriel in London, but Michael Turner (East in 1930) had taken over in Hong Kong, W.T. Yoxall (East in 1922) was in Shanghai where in 1955 he would make the 'all-for-all' settlement, Perry-Aldworth (East in 1925) in Bangkok on the death of French (East in 1915), G.H. Stacey (East in 1920) transferred to Tokyo, H.V. Parker (East in 1925) in Manila, M.D. Scott (East in 1925) in Kuala Lumpur, J.McG. Taylor (East in 1925, son of J.D. Taylor) in Jakarta, J.H. Raikes (East in 1921) in New York; and officers from the late 1920s and early 1930s were showing up as Managers of smaller agencies, for example M.F.L. Haymes (East in 1931) Orchard Road (Singapore), R.A. Jardine (East in 1926) in Haiphong, and S.J.H. Fox (East in 1928) trapped in the non-operating office in Swatow. G.C. Moutrie (East in 1925) was in Hamburg and D.C. Davis (East in 1921) was soon to move his office from Lyons to Paris.

These and many others maintained the traditions of the Bank and bridged the gap between Eastern exchange banking and the changes which were beginning even in the 1950s. Just as Morse heard Sir Thomas Sutherland speak of the Bank's founding, so too post-war juniors, while admitting that Morse was truly a 'legend in his own time', would admire in him the best of the old traditions while questioning the future; those who would eventually lead the Hongkong Bank – and the Hongkong Bank Group – in the late 1970s in a new world of banking were already on hand some years before Sir Arthur Morse retired. In 1951 G. M. Sayer (East in 1947) was on leave after a tour in Tientsin. B.J.N. Ogden was then in Hong Kong with Maurice Turner, Lever, and Saunders. Among others who came East in 1949 were, for example, J.L. Boyer in Rangoon, P.E. Hammond in Ipoh, M.G.R. Sandberg in Tokyo under the watchful eye of P.A. Sellars, soon to be Staff Controller.

Sandberg had served under the Chief Managership of Morse, Morse of Sir Newton Stabb, Stabb of Sir Thomas Jackson, and Jackson of Victor Kresser.

Head Office

Size and impact

The Board of Directors and their Chief Manager, Sir Vandeleur Grayburn, recognized the distinction between 'head office type' and 'Hong Kong office type' functions. The Staff List however did not differentiate; the Foreign staff located in the main office building of the Colony are listed under 'Hongkong'. Grayburn operated the exchange, a Hong Kong office function, and made investment decisions – either in Head Office or in Hong Kong office, depending on which books the investments were listed in; he was also interested in personnel – a Head Office function. Edmondston was the Manager Hong Kong, but important taipans might and often did demand to see the Chief Manager, a practice which continued into the 1960s at least. When a head office is in the same city as the local office, the latter has trouble retaining the same sovereignty a more distant branch might possess, but the pre-war constituent might be forgiven for pressing to see Grayburn; the Bank had not even set down the demarcation lines for its own internal purposes.

Pre-war there had been Head Office accounts which recognized investments and other items not related specifically to Hong Kong operations. To the extent they included sterling investments, they might have continued to be on London

Table 7.1 *The Hongkong Bank*[a]
Managers, posts, and Foreign Staff, 1950–1962

Year	Establishments	Managers	Gazetted posts	Eastern staff
1936	39 + 3[b]	40 + n.a.[b]	63 + n.a.[b]	264
1950	43 + 3	43 + 4	71 + 6	241
1951	42 + 3	42 + 4	68 + 7	243
1952	41 + 3	41 + 4	71 + 8	242
1953	41 + 3	41 + 5	68 + 9	243
1954	40 + 3	41 + 5	70 + 9	251
1955	38 + 3	38 + 6	66 + 11	253
1956	40 + 3	40 + 4	76 + 8	256
1957	41 + 3	41 + 4	78 + 8	266
1958	45 + 3	45 + 4	80 + 9	272
1959	45 + 3	45 + 4	82 + 10	273
1960	47 + 3	47 + 4	79 + 10	269
1961	51 + 3	51 + 6	81 + 11	271
1962	48 + 3	48 + 5	79 + 9	270

[a] The term 'Hongkong Bank' as opposed to the usual 'Hongkong and Shanghai Banking Corporation' is designed to differentiate between the Hongkong Bank qua bank and the Hongkong Bank Group, which latter includes subsidiary companies especially the MBLD and the BBME.
[b] London, Hamburg, and Lyons/Paris.

Office books but for the fact that there were tax advantages for the head office of any overseas bank. Then too London Office 'serviced' the Bank, and these costs, to the extent they could be specifically identified, for example, a junior's first passage East, had to be separated. (Subsequent passages would be charged against the office for which he had last worked.) The impetus for a separate Head Office accounting came from overseas, not from an organizational design originating in Hong Kong.

As suggested previously, two factors facilitated the post-war differentiation, (i) the initial different geographical location of the two offices, London and Hong Kong and (ii) the relative freedom of action which Arthur Morse possessed once free from the exchange desk. When Head Office returned to Hong Kong in 1946, the new Staff List shows four senior staff in 'HEAD OFFICE' and two senior and 31 junior staff under 'HONGKONG' with a sub-head for 'Kowloon' with one senior and one junior.

In February 1962 there were thirteen in Head Office, and five senior staff and 43 'juniors' in Hong Kong office. The growth of Head Office is however deceptive; it includes Saunders as 'inspector', but this was merely a temporary assignment prior to his becoming Chief Manager; there was another officer seconded to operate the Hong Kong Government's Exchange Control Department, and four were temporarily attached. The real net increase had been only two senior staff members, a Deputy Chief Manager and an adviser – for the rest the assigned functions had remained virtually unchanged.

Nevertheless, what had been done was important despite numbers; the separately acknowledged existence of Head Office was the key to a change in thinking and operating which cannot be quantified. This development must be seen in the context of a broadening hierarchy throughout the Bank. As shown in Table 7.1, there had been 40 Managers out of a total 63 gazetted posts in the 1936 Bank; in 1950, when the post-war establishment had been regularized, there were 43 Managers but 71 gazetted posts; in 1959 the figures were 45 and 82; in 1962, 48 and 79 respectively. These figures do not include the Managers in London and Europe, but their inclusion does not require reinterpretation. The on-line simplicity of the pre-war Bank was changing even in the 1950s, and the existence of a Head Office provided the pattern.

Composition and functions

The Head Office in 1946 consisted of the Chief Manager, the Inspectorate, and the Inspector (Staff). Growth depended on additional support for these functions. The Inspectorate increased, the Staff Inspector was assigned an assistant. For the Chief Manager senior assistance was also long in coming. G.H. Stacey, who had been Manager Tokyo until 1954, was brought down to Hong Kong as Deputy (in effect, 'acting') Chief Manager during Turner's leave; when Turner returned, he remained as Deputy; he died in office in May 1955. Moodie acted for Turner in 1958 again during a period of leave, but returned to head the Hong Kong office. From 1956, however, G.O.W. Stewart, who had been Chief Accountant before Saunders, was assigned to Head Office first as adviser and then, from 1959 to 1961, as Deputy Chief Manager.[b] Turner described him as his 'right-hand man'; there had been no designated post similar to it in the previous history of the Bank. There is a significant progression from a pre-war Hong Kong Manager who might deputize as requested to a specifically designated post of 'deputy'. The Chief Manager had

[b] Reference has been made to the 'Deputy Chief Manager', but this title was at first used post-war as a substitute for 'Acting Chief Manager' when the Chief Manager was on leave. The latter term had been defined in the revision to the Bank's ordinance (No. 8 of 1946) to fit the role Morse played from 1941 until the death of Sir Vandeleur Grayburn; an 'Acting Chief Manager' took over all the functions and responsibilities of the Chief Manager as assigned by the Board, something not necessary in the post-war world of improved communications. Hence, when the Chief went on leave he deputized a substitute with the Board's agreement. Stacey's appointment was intended to continue on Turner's return, but as noted he died; with the appointment of Stewart in 1959 the Deputy Chief Manager became, as the title suggests, the Chief Manager's deputy.

been further liberated; now an additional senior Foreign staff member was free to undertake special assignments, and Stewart's role in negotiating with the Mercantile Bank and the BBME, either direct or in correspondence with Perry-Aldworth, the London Manager, is a major example of his tasks.

When Stewart became Deputy Chief Manager, N.E. Clark was brought in from his post as Manager Kuala Lumpur to be Adviser to the Board, assigned to Head Office. Clark had had Head Office experience in 1950–1952, and he had also a considerable Malaysia/British Borneo expertise. He brought managerial and field experience to the Head Office.

This then was Head Office in the key years of Sir Michael Turner's management: the Chief Manager, the Deputy Chief Manager, the Adviser, the Inspectorate, and the Staff Inspectorate. It would meet the requirements until Saunders' restructuring in the late 1960s.

The Inspectorate

From this it is possible to suppose the Chief Manager lent heavily on his Chief Inspector – Fenwick (1946–1951), O. Skinner (1951–1956), Black (1956–1960), and Mack (1960–1962). Indeed, from this it is also possible to suppose that there would arise the basic conflict between the man-on-the-spot and the man-in-Head-Office. Moodie had been particularly outspoken and had the added problem of being Manager Hong Kong; the Inspectors were both on the spot and in Head Office. His solution was to deny them ready access to Hong Kong office, and there is some evidence that the balance could otherwise have been upset. Nevertheless, in the classic conflict between bank manager and bank inspector, the inspector will win, or more accurately, the principle of inspection from a head office will win if the company is to survive. There is no point in arguing, as Moodie did, that the Inspectors had never been Managers and therefore lacked the necessary understanding and qualifications. The objection was cogent, nevertheless. But when circumstances permit, former Managers can be and would be appointed as 'Inspectors' – or later to similar posts with expanded functions.

The change was significant in a bank in which the Managers had always operated with virtual independence. Although the Inspectors were unable to stop major losses in Calcutta and San Francisco, they undoubtedly brought system to the Bank and permitted the imposition of more formal controls, including lending limits for Managers, before the Hongkong Bank had wholly outgrown the traditional system of control through 'knowing' the other chap, through being of the same 'service'. Formal controls would facilitate the integration of the local officer, of the Mercantile and BBME officers into the system, and it would make feasible the growth of the branch system which began in Hong Kong under the Hong Kong Manager, Oliphant, in the late 1950s.

Fenwick was a class in himself. A long-time friend and colleague of Sir Arthur Morse's, his only independent managerial experience had been in Hong Kong from 1945 to 1946, but he was not, by his own account, a front office man. As the Chief Accountant pre-war, Fenwick had noted the contribution of the embryo inspectorate – two officers in the Hong Kong office, the only 'true' Head Office. Although his service had been almost entirely in Shanghai and Hong Kong – he had first had a tour in Singapore and Malacca – Fenwick's service in London and his role as Chief Accountant had made him the ideal choice for the 'founder' of the reestablished Inspectorate. Morse certainly consulted him on a wide range of subjects, but Fenwick, in common with others, found that Morse revealed nothing in these discussions; suddenly the decision was made.

The Hongkong Bank's internal correspondence in the 1950s begins to reveal a breadth in top management which suggests the new role being played by men like Skinner and Black. And they in turn trained a new type of Hongkong Banker, men like F.J. Knightly who, with very brief tours elsewhere, virtually made their careers in Head Office; Knightly joined the Head Office staff in 1952 – he had earlier been one of Fenwick's protégés; by 1962 he was Chief Inspector in succession to Mack, moving from there to Deputy Chief Manager in 1965; he was a director of the Bank in 1967 and retired as a Director and Adviser to the Board. As the task grew so did the Inspector move up from his role of 'ticker-upper' of branch returns to become a Bank executive of key importance.

Personnel

Early post-war personnel policy was hampered by the uncertainty of the Bank's basic financial position, and this was not resolved until the nature of the post-war rehabilitation problem was known and more specifically until the 1946 solution of the 'duress note' issue and the passage of the 1948 debtor/creditor ordinance. Partly for this reason, partly because of his insistence on keeping matters close, and partly because there is evidence of a 'mean' streak – a reversion to the penny-pinching attitudes of the pre-war Depression as the Accountant in him overcame, however temporarily, his vision as a banker and community leader – Morse does not get full credit for innovations which he initiated but which saw fulfilment under Michael Turner.

The first senior officer assigned to handle personnel problems was E.P. Streatfield. He served after his partial recovery from internment in Hong Kong – he would seem never to have fully recovered – until 1950, when he retired. His official designation was 'Inspector (Staff)' and as such he came under Fenwick.

Streatfield's tasks included matching the pre-war 'service'-type salaries with the realities of the post-war world – both as to necessary adjustments to meet the 'temporarily' high cost of living and to increments to meet new expectations. He had also to consider such problems as gratuities for those retiring early, to take advice on a new pension scheme to meet British requirements and put the Hongkong Bank's own plans in order. But his brief was not all-encompassing; such matters as construction of new buildings for staff, employment of local officers, that is, questions involving expenditure of considerable funds and matters of basic policy, Morse retained to himself.

Following Streatfield's retirement there was an interregnum until Turner brought P.A. Sellars down from Tokyo. Turner had noted Sellars' administrative qualities in his first post-war assignment in Hong Kong, and in 1954 appointed him 'Inspector (Staff)' in Head Office. Not until 1961 with the appointment of R.C. Gairdner did Sellars have an assistant.

Sellars was not a professional personnel expert; the Bank continued to operate with generalists, but the 'expert' posts were created in this period and would eventually be the province of specialists. Nor did Sellars change the system in any radical sense; it was just that some attention was being paid to a problem which, pre-war, Grayburn had had to consider himself, after banking hours. There was an attempt at career planning, but not in consultation with the officer involved; as Sellars put it, 'We planned his career for him.' And officers were still expected to go when and where directed; complaints were noted with promises of a better assignment next time. On the other hand Turner insisted that juniors come first to Hong Kong – or at least at some point in their (shortened) first tour – so that they could be looked at. There was much room for improvement in career planning, and Sellars had begun the task of reform.

Recruitment of Foreign staff was left to London because, as Sellars explained, the Bank was satisfied with the job London Office was doing. There had to be minor age limit adjustments due to the existence of national service, but the principles remained unchanged – preference was given to public school leavers, or to a type considered suitable for the East. This proved more difficult than in the days of Empire and Depression; the East had lost its attraction, the shutdown of the China offices suggested to some that a career in the East was uncertain. The Bank departed from precedent and contacted schools and even took out discreet no-name advertisements – even as the Mercantile Bank and others were forced to do.

Sellars' task – indeed the task of the Head Office Inspectorate as a whole –

was facilitated by the holding of annual Managers Conferences in Hong Kong. There Sellars would discuss personnel problems and get first-hand reports from Managers – looking for 'high flyers' for example:

> I remember Jock Morrison, who was Manager in Singapore, coming up for a Managers Conference, and he came into my office to discuss staff. We looked down the staff in Singapore office, and he looked at Mike Sandberg, and he said, you can put three stars against that one.
> So he was beginning to show already.[c]

On a more routine basis, Managers' confidential reports were submitted annually on each member of their Foreign staff. The best and worst of these were sent by Sellars to Turner, and in some cases a letter was sent to those whose careers were in danger advising them of the problem. The staff members were not, however, as in the British forces, shown adverse reports, and Turner still had to depend a great deal on his knowledge of the Manager writing it. Top appointments were made by Turner himself, and, in Sellars' opinion, he was let down only once or twice. A personnel survey made in 1977 revealed that over 90% of these Foreign staff officer reports provided only one word responses to standard questions, for example, conduct towards constituents, correct relations with local staff, good conduct outside the office, health, knowledge of foreign languages – the format appears as early as 1905.

In this tradition Sandberg's 1955 Singapore report, with its series of 'good' or 'correct', does not seem particularly helpful. But additional comments were on occasion offered. For Sandberg, Morrison, as Singapore Manager, wrote (1956), 'A man of distinct ability and intelligence, well in excess of his years who stands out amongst those of similar seniority. He has a pleasant and efficient manner which has been favourably commented on by constituents during the period in securities where he has done an excellent job.' In an earlier report (1955) Morrison had added, 'Head Office should watch him carefully and I am quite sure he is a man for the future.'

The Bank had not yet reached the size where individual officers could not be noticed in the old-fashioned way. Turner knew Morrison well enough to be able to interpret and accept his comments. Even then the opportunities might not be available and the young man held back too long. Sandberg was able; he was also fortunate.

Head Office – a second perspective

There were four lady members of Head Office staff employed on 'expatriate' terms, and at least two of these were considered members of the 'Foreign staff', although not so listed in the Foreign Staff List.

[c] No date for this was given, but M.G.R. Sandberg served under J.A.D. Morrison 1954–1957.[2]

Also not listed (and not employed) was another lady, Wendy Turner, who made a voluntary though professional-style contribution to staff affairs, a contribution which would now be undertaken by personnel, property, and other specialist departments. The role of the Chief Manager's wife depended on the social structure of the time, the personality of the wife, and the presence of opportunities. The 1950s, for example, were the earliest period during which organized visits to the several branches, other than those on the route to and from the East, were practical; it was also a period before the advent of service departments in the Bank. Lady Turner was not the first to take an interest in staff matters; during World War II, Lady Stabb, the widow of Sir Newton, had, in keeping with her long-noted concern, demanded to know if Arthur Morse were treating the staff with appropriate and sympathetic generosity – much against his preference for secrecy; in this great tradition Lady Turner acted. She worked closely with Sir Michael Turner; underlying a dramatic romance there was an enduring partnership, acceptable in its time (although not without comment), bridging a gap in staff relations and amenities until the new demands and complexities of modern commercial life overseas could be handled by a more formal and specialist establishment.

If her role were unique in its scope, this is no criticism of those wives of Managers who played a role, though less dramatic or visible, in the welfare of the staff. Nor is it a criticism of those wives who played no public role, considering their main task to be that of keeping their own family in a condition to render service to the Bank. Thus without criticism of others there is a record of Lady Turner's contribution.

This section is about style of management. It is also about the Bank as family.

The spirit of Sir Arthur
When Miss Margaret Goldney, private secretary/personal assistant to three Chief Managers/Executive Chairmen – Michael Turner, J.A.H. Saunders, and G.M. Sayer – from 1958 to 1977, stated that the Executive Chairman was not so central a figure in the Bank as the Chief Manager had been earlier, she was speaking not of the constitutional position or ultimate degree of authority but of the 'presence'. Despite the beginnings of specialization, despite the very significant distinction between Head Office and Hong Kong office, the Chief Manager was involved in 'everything'.

Certainly Turner and probably Saunders in the early years of his administration read every semi-official letter leaving both Head Office and Hong Kong office and all inter-branch S/O's. All reminiscences of Morse postwar recall his 'presence', his large figure walking through the office, 'bellowing', making an impact which lasted through the Turner administration as an immediate memory. Turner himself recalls the atmosphere at a time when he was Chief Accountant and therefore an officer of some considerable responsibility.

Arthur didn't really trust me not to upset the running of the office. Arthur was the person who'd originally been given the job of building that new office, and it hadn't been built large enough. There were many mistakes in it, and eventually one had to keep moving counters and moving this, that and the other, and I used to go up with Fenwick, who was then the Chief Inspector. I'd say to Fenwick, we've got to get Arthur to pull himself together, allow me to move this...

So Fen used to get Arthur to come out, and we'd walk round the aisle, and he'd say, Mike wants to do this....

And eventually Arthur would turn round to me and say, well, if you want to go mess up the office, go mess it up! [That, at least, was the gist of what he said.]

Then I was allowed to do it, but Arthur was like that. He couldn't believe that anything could be as good as the office he'd done originally.[3]

As a side issue, it is interesting to note that Adamson, as Manager Hong Kong, was not involved in the discussion. The banking hall was still the Chief Manager's immediate concern.

Sir Arthur's spirit continued to influence the Bank in Turner's time. As Miss Goldney explained,

I never worked for Arthur Morse, but Arthur Morse's hand was still very much there. People talked of Uncle Arthur with enormous respect, I think because he had done such a lot to resurrect the Bank and resurrect Hong Kong after the war. He was a big man, I think, in all respects, and people who had served him had a very great respect for him.

Mike still consulted Arthur. He went to see him when he was in England, and he would ask the London Manager to get Arthur's views if there was something they weren't sure about. He lived in Arlington House in Piccadilly, very central in London. His views were very much considered in my early days in the Bank. As I say, I think his hand was still there.[4]

But the tradition would change later:

[Sir John Saunders had] never served in the same way under Arthur, you see, and Jake was much more sort of independent. I think he always rather wanted to do things his way. He never looked back to Mike Turner's reign in the same way that Mike looked back to Arthur Morse's. I think, having had quite a distinguished war service, he was determined to make his own decisions. He'd grown up making decisions in the Forces, and he was determined to make them.[5]

The working of Head Office – a personal viewpoint

Miss Goldney came to the Hongkong Bank in 1958 after a term as private secretary to the Vice-Chancellor of the University of Hong Kong, Sir Lindsay Ride. Although she had met Turner frequently in his capacity as Treasurer of the University, it was Wendy Turner who learned of her availability – and it was Sellars who employed her on expatriate terms as a member of the Foreign staff.

She was not the first lady to invade the offices of the Hongkong Bank. The initial role of ladies during the Great War has been told (Volume II), and, as their seniority had increased, so the importance of their positions in London Office increased. In the East there had been lady secretaries in both the Hong Kong and Shanghai offices, on terms which would appear to have included passages. When Miss Goldney arrived at the Bank she found Miss Audrey Unthank in charge of the vital Correspondence Department, and Miss Mary Mackintosh, who had worked first in London Office and had then been sent out as adviser on U.K. taxation. In addition there were four ladies who performed secretarial and filing work. Ladies not designated 'Foreign staff' were on the 'Expat Women's staff'.

The Chief Manager had, I suppose, the most central office in the Bank when it was built, and the Chief Manager was really in those days a bigger figure than the Chairman became later because everything was smaller, everything in Hong Kong was smaller, and the Chief Manager of the Bank was a very big figure indeed. He had this office with marble walls.

...you are walking in the 1, Queen's Road entrance, you walk right through the banking hall and there were stairs up from the Des Voeux Road side, and then there were these glass doors, and you walked through and then there was a sort of lobby and the Chief Accountant's Department even in those days was away to the left, and the Chairman's office was behind where the office boys sat, and then I had a little office which had really been made, I think, by walling in what had originally been hall.

There was quite a temporary partition, and the lamps were those bronze ones and there was a hole in mine that had been made during the fighting in the war, and Mike Turner would never have it changed. He wouldn't have the holes in the marble and the hole in my lamp repaired because he said it was a bit of war history! But it was just sort of walled off really, and I usually had the door open so I could see what was happening.

Then the Hong Kong Manager was next door, and the Chief Accountant went somewhere down the corridor because Jake Saunders was Chief Accountant for a lot of the time, and he had very military shoes, and he would march up and down. I always knew that he was walking past because of his heels.

I had an ancient Imperial typewriter. All the Bank typewriters were Imperials, and one didn't have really any of the sort of modern equipment that came later. There were no photocopiers in those days. Confidential papers had to be burnt, there was no other way, paper shredders hadn't come in. Mike (Turner) had a tin can in his Chief Manager's lavatory at the back of his office and occasionally burnt secret papers in there. People used to come in and say, is something on fire? I used to have a sack, and if there were some (draft copies of) confidential business or confidential Board papers or something, then I had to make arrangements and go down to where they burnt the banknotes in the basement. I used to go down with an escort, one of the office boys would come down with me with the sack, and we set fire to these in the boiler and that's how we disposed of confidential waste.[6]

As for communications within the office, Turner would on occasion ask Miss Goldney to summon some member of the staff by the telephone.

Most people tended to come down to his office. ...He walked about occasionally, but people did come down. There was a very primitive sort of intercom, I think, a thing with buttons. I'm not sure that was there in Mike's day, it certainly was in Jake's.

Of course there weren't that number of people within the Bank to come and see you because the Hong Kong Manager was next door and the Chief Accountant was down the passage, so that was Hong Kong business really taken care of.

Then upstairs there was the Staff Controller, who was Philip Sellars, and he had a secretary, and I don't think there was anybody else in the Staff Department. I think they more or less managed. ... And the local staff, you see, the Portuguese were Wayfoong Staff Association. They didn't exactly run themselves, but they were sort of an entity of their own and very much responsible for the Portuguese staff. Then you had the Chinese staff who were all bonded to the compradore, and the compradore brought them in. So the local staff personnel department didn't exist at all. It came into being afterwards.

[There was a Hong Kong Sub-Manager and Assistant Sub-Manager, but] they dealt with R.P. Moodie. They didn't have much occasion to come, and the same with Head Office. I mean 'Titch' Black came down, and ... [Mack] was his Number Two in those days, [he] was there. They came down for conferences if something was happening somewhere.[7]

Miss Goldney too had contact with the redoubtable Moodie – brief Head Office/Hong Kong office conflicts at a different level.

Moodie was very outspoken at times, and then he had a great habit of hiding things in his safe, and I used to have to go in and say, this file is missing, are you sure it isn't in your safe?

He'd glare at you and say, of course not, and then he'd go and open the safe and there it always was![8]

Those who look back to simpler days recall that the Hongkong Bank had a reputation for no committee meetings.

Really, I don't think we did have meetings much. People came to see the Chief Manager, but they usually came on their own.

If there was perhaps a crisis in some place, well then it's possible that 'Titch' Black would come and they'd have Philip Sellars in because they might be having to think who they could possibly move round and send there. But nothing like ... I'm told now that there's nothing but committees in the Bank. Ever since I've been out here this time [for a visit in 1984], I've been told this by several people that they spend their entire life having meetings. In those days they just didn't. People came to see the Chief Manager, but it wasn't really a meeting round the table.[9]

The improvement in air transport caused a great worldwide movement of bank presidents and chairmen who, for whatever reason – tax deduction, curiosity, or even business – would want to call on the Hongkong Bank's Chief Manager personally. This began to take up an increasing amount of Turner's time. Miss Goldney had to sort out the visitors and direct some to lesser personages, a task made more difficult by the fact that at the same time the senior staff 'Newsletter' was instructing branch Managers not to waste time writing letters of introduction – just say the Chief Manager's door is always open.

There was, however, another area in which the Hongkong Bank changed but little during the Morse/Turner administrations – the Chief Manager's relations with the Board. Earlier in this volume the gradually increasing involvement of the Board in the overall policy of the Bank has been noted. Miss Goldney saw it reflected in the increased information the Deputy Chairman, Hugh Barton of Jardine's, began to require for meetings – this was one of the several tasks of the Chief Manager's Adviser, N.E. Clark. On the other hand it remained true that no member of the Bank's staff, other than Chief Manager, attended the Board meetings; the Bank's top executive officers had no contact with the Board, no knowledge of their thinking or policy. Several retired senior officers report that they had never seen a Board minute. For them the Bank continued to reach up only to the Chief Manager like schoolboys unaware that there was authority beyond the headmaster. Legends of the Board's impotence continued, even in the years when basic policy was under discussion and, therefore, Board involvement in matters affecting the Bank was increasing.

This exclusion policy extended to Miss Goldney even though her duties included preparing the agenda and relevant papers and, interestingly, writing from notes the draft version of the minutes of meetings she had not attended.

The role of Lady Turner
This is not the place to discuss the role of corporation wives as a sociological phenomenon, although it is fair to point out that in the East there were certain special considerations at work. First, there had been, and continued to be in modified form, restrictions on marriage; there were thus a few senior officers married and a large number of bachelors in a mess or 'chummery' situation – organized by the Bank or by the individuals. This would be particularly true in Hong Kong itself. The branch Manager was primarily a banker; he was also a landlord with his Foreign staff as 'captive' tenants. His mind was rarely on this latter task. 'Compound living' with its closeness, its occasional pettiness, and its obvious hierarchy is a subject in itself. The responsibility of the senior lady in the absence of the many present-day corporate services was real, and her status had therefore to be equal to it. Where the wife relieved her husband-Manager of non-banking responsibilities, she was in fact performing a task now undertaken by support services.

Some did it well; others did not. Some focused on the services they could render, some on their position. The dog of the Manager's wife ranked over all other pets... but this is the stuff of novels, fascinating perhaps, but beyond my competence to relate. To the young wife of a junior officer, Lady Turner could be formidable and the eccentricities of others have been remembered.

The role of Lady Turner, however, went beyond the traditional 'maternal' image of the chief lady on the post. Her interest was systematic and verged on the professional; the consequences of her involvement, typed out and specified, became the basis of Bank administrative action. Had she been paid as Staff Relations Officer with the ear of the Chief Executive, her role would not call for comment; in the absence of such an appointment it is necessary to recall that absence and to suggest that, on the whole, the Bank as family continued for a longer time than the post-war world would expect due to Wendy Turner's abilities. The 1950s might be described as a period in which individual problems were ably met but system changes put on hold; Wendy Turner bridged an important gap.

Miss Goldney, who dealt with Lady Turner's reports, put it this way:

Wendy's hobby was, and I think it still is, people really. She had an enormous interest in people and their lives and their children. She kept a card index of all the Bank children, she remembered birthdays, all sorts of things. She was incredible over that. So when [Sir Michael and Lady Turner] went on these visits, she sort of asked to meet the wives and talk to the wives and find out their problems and how they were living and if anybody had a sick child or anything, Wendy did a tremendous amount to help them in getting the right sort of doctoring. All sorts of things.

The Bank was so much of a family in those days, and of course the Turner's children were away at school, so she wasn't away from that sort of thing when she was [on tour]. On the whole, the way things were done in those days it was an advantage because somebody did know a great deal. I mean, she used to come back and produce some notes about things she'd been told about difficulties that were being encountered perhaps in areas where medical treatment wasn't good, food supplies were perhaps lacking, and the Bank sometimes used to send stuff to areas that just couldn't get things.

I think Wendy did find out a tremendous lot of things... In a way she did a lot of work that probably later was done by correspondence with the Staff Department, but in those days it wasn't.

The [material she collected] used to be her little notes. Sometimes I typed up what she'd said about them, and some of it used to be very confidential. She'd comment on which wives were being the greatest help to the place. They met other people at receptions, and I suppose she had her ear to the ground. I can remember comments on which of the wives were obvious value as backups, and which were less so!

Nowadays I'm quite sure this wouldn't [be accepted], but in those days I think it was the way people looked at things.

You have to take things in their period, and the Bank was looked upon much more as a family, and you were sort of reporting how the family members were doing in a way.[10]

Wendy Turner's own account is a combination of compassion and shrewd business sense. In a system under strain she, with others who broke through traditional parameters, was one who made it work. As for the part she played, Sir Michael Turner explained,

Oh, an incalculable part, I should say, it made a tremendous difference. I suggest I don't think I could have got on without it. She was tremendously useful in this question of going round these various branches and finding out bits and pieces behind the scenes. ...she was tremendous value, and everybody liked her, and she had a tremendous capacity for knowing who was who, knowing the names of their children, their interests generally, and keeping her finger on the pulse of the wives, you might say, because we had some very difficult wives. Luckily, I wasn't married to them, that was just as well.

She had the privilege of meeting most of them, and she would get a bit of the slanging from the background, what a miserable blighter her husband was, you see, but we survived.

I was the first Chief Manager who'd ever done a series of tours round all the branches to try and see what things were like on the spot, and I could not have done it without a wife. At least I couldn't have done it anything like as well. And so Wendy, who liked travelling and she doesn't mind doing the packing... I'm no bloody good at packing... so we toiled around the whole blooming lot.

It was the first time the Chief Manager had been to a lot of branches, and certainly the first time a wife had been to a lot of them either. Oh no, it made all the difference in the world, and I think she knew it, too. All the people who knew her had the highest admiration for her.[11]

This is naturally a slightly exaggerated assessment. Managers who resented the interference of Head Office Inspectors in matters of banking might be expected to resent the involvement of the Chief Manager's wife in non-banking affairs in their territory. One at least played King of Hearts, following behind the entourage countermanding Lady Turner's recommendations. Even then she had at least made the point; it undoubtedly had some impact even where resisted.

Signs of change

First of all Miss Goldney convinced the Chief Manager of the need for a shredder.

I had a great battle, I got the first paper-shredder in the Bank. They were coming in, and I had a great battle, and nobody would really believe that somebody wasn't going to piece...!

Mike Turner had one or two, I'd better not say who they were, but there were one or two people whom he'd known in the old days in China, and he was always sure they paid the rubbish collectors to collect confidential waste of the Bank to the benefit of certain other firms. It was a great thing about this. ...Occasionally when we had something very secret, we burnt the shreddings, but basically that was the first piece of modern equipment I had, I think.

I can't remember the exact dates, but there was a big change in the banking hall when the old clattering machines went out. When I first worked for the Bank, the banking hall sounded like a weaving shed, clackity-clackity-clackity-clack.[12]

Some would have said these clattering machines were progress personified. Until the early 1950s the Hongkong Bank had ledgers.

This in turn had an impact on staffing, affecting at last the three-tier system which had been basic to the Bank's policy since the earliest days.

HONGKONG BANKERS – THE THREE TIERS

The system reviewed

The three-tier system had existed virtually since the beginning of the Bank. This was not at first obvious; the diary of C.J. Gonsalves (see Volume I, Chapter 7) suggests that he was surprised as a form of discrimination became evident; the Portuguese were not to be the equals of the British expatriate. This separation between the Portuguese and the 'Foreign staff' (or 'Eastern staff' as it was then known) had been formalized by 1876 when the Board confirmed that only those coming through as London Office juniors would be eligible for executive posts. The impact of this fell, it is true, not only on the Portuguese but also on the few local Europeans; the Shanghai office had a 'local British' staff, foreigners who had not come through London and were thus not eligible to be considered as or transferred to the 'Eastern staff'.

The system was not the invention of the Hongkong Bank. On its founding the Bank had taken its buildings, furniture, ledger books, and staff from immediately available sources. And yet within a period of fifteen to twenty years the few non-British on the Eastern staff had been dropped or become in effect 'local' by continuous assignment in their own country. Local recruitment for the 'Eastern staff' virtually ended. With the exception of Kellogg and Koelle, both of whom went through London, the non-British subsequently employed were on 'local' terms, however much respected. This was consistent with the preferences of David McLean, the first Shanghai Manager; it was also consistent with practices on the China coast.

If the anti-foreign feeling was never so forcibly expressed in the Hongkong Bank as it had been in the Imperial Bank of Persia, that is perhaps because no non-English British subject, no Joseph Rabino (the Imperial's first chief executive), remained long in top executive authority. Victor Kresser resigned as Chief Manager in 1870 before the staff system had been formalized; François de Bovis did not remain at the helm long – and, although severely criticized in private correspondence by Charles Addis, his French background was never as such commented on in derogatory terms (Volume I, Chapter 15). Nevertheless, it is interesting that disaffection on racial grounds in the Imperial Bank would be reported to their board by an ex-Hongkong Bank officer and then member of the Imperial Bank board of directors, V.A. Caesar Hawkins, a man known to be close to the chairman, who was none other than Sir Thomas Jackson himself.[13]

Whatever McLean's initial role had been in encouraging a British staff in opposition to the necessary opportunism of Kresser and the weak administration of James Greig, Jackson was not in disagreement with it. By the time

McLean had retired from the management of the Bank's London office in 1888 he had formalized the recruitment system; it would remain virtually unchanged until after the personnel review of 1977. And McLean too became a director of the Imperial Bank.

The Chinese role in the Hongkong Bank was similar to their role in the merchant hongs of the period, from which example the Bank developed its policy. Reasonably, it might have been argued at the time – and considering the hongs were partnerships with unlimited liability and were relatively small – a British merchant firm should have only British staff in a British colony. The difficulty of undertaking business directly with Chinese merchants and the problems of handling the currency, however, required Chinese cooperation. This in turn suggests, as it did in India, a local, that is, a Chinese, partner. That such intercultural partnerships occurred elsewhere in the East, that the Hongkong Bank had Parsee promoters and directors, and that the Bank's early Managers had apparently close or at least friendly intercourse with their Chinese associates may cause surprise given the absence of Chinese partners or directors in the formal business sense. Apparently, the tradition of the compradoric system was too strong; this had been the organizational basis of business cooperation on the China coast in pre-Treaty relationships; it was established and could not be shaken. The compradore provided the contacts with the local markets, despite patterns successful elsewhere. The communities on the China coast were particularly separate, usually by mutual desire, and the compradoric system met the needs of the times; unfortunately, the system outlived the times.

Thus the Hongkong Bank, as with other foreign firms, grafted on Chinese 'agents' and their staffs in each office; there was formal adherence to the compradoric system. This fixed the role to be played by the Chinese in the Bank, although one of the Bank's original declared purposes was the elimination of the 'compradoric system'.

In non-Chinese ports, the Hongkong Bank still maintained a three-tier system. The second-tier in Colombo, for example, were 'burghers' instead of 'Portuguese'; in the third-tier the 'guarantee shroff' enacted the role of the 'compradore'.

As already noted, the three-tier system was not without its exceptions. In Hamburg local employees had been given joint powers of attorney and had managed the office during two world wars. In New York and San Francisco, as in London, there were local officers. A local Swiss employee ran the Savings Bank in the Shanghai of the 1930s; Webster was taken on for the Foreign staff in Shanghai immediately after the Great War; Butter, a former Foreign staff member, was appointed 'special staff' to manage the post-Pacific War Sourabaya office until his retirement (and the closing of the office) in 1958.

The key to the entire structure was the narrow gate of the London Office and admission as a Foreign staff junior. Transfer from local 'Home' staff was as exceptional in London as it was in Shanghai. This point is made to stress that the London gate was not designed as a racial barrier, as a way of preventing local pressure for the appointment of 'native' officers; the Board would not have considered appointing a 'native officer' in the nineteenth century. Their London rule was designed (i) to prevent pressure from locally based constituents in favour of the claims of a young European adrift in the East, and more positively (ii) to build up the service through the common years together in London and New Beckenham, and (iii) to assist adherence to the Board's policy of promotion from within.

So strong were the positive factors in the London decision that the first local officers to be appointed went to London for training before taking up their new assignments.

At the close of the Pacific War in 1945 the Hongkong Bank staffs reassembled; the three-tier system was reestablished. Arthur Morse had a new block of flats built for the Portuguese staff; Turner built for both the Chinese shroffs and separately for the lower grades at a time when housing was at a considerable premium in Hong Kong. The system must have appeared irreplaceable.

Change: factors for and against

By the end of 1962 there were 114 regional officers and 270 Foreign staff as originally defined. There had been factors, therefore, which had forced change. But, as with other changes in the Hongkong Bank, as the pressures mounted in the 1950s, thought was given to the problems and tentative solutions introduced, but the major breakthroughs came in the 1960s and later. Before considering the fate of each of the three tiers in this period, it would be useful to consider the problem of locally appointed officers in its early context – given the historical background reviewed above.

As the Bank's demand for executive officers increased, especially in the latter years of Turner's administration, the immediate situation forced a reevaluation; this was reinforced by pressures from the immigration authorities of newly independent territories. But pressures do not in themselves offer solutions, nor would agreement to employ local officers necessarily suggest agreement as to what duties they should in fact perform.

To the extent that a local staff member would merely be given authority to pass on his own or his subordinates' traditional work without necessity of the signature of a member of the Foreign staff, the Bank was dismantling the first stage of its supervisory system before it had thought through a full substitute. But this step did have the effect of releasing a member of the Foreign staff for work more appropriate to his expectations. By the mid-1950s senior Portuguese clerks had been designated supervisors, the impact of which is described below.

The recruitment of well-educated young local citizens into a category which would lead one day to branch Manager presented additional problems. First, the Bank had previously recruited a 'type' and implanted concepts of service in London Office. The recruitment of a local executive officer was not seen, therefore, as a process of simply making arrangements for local University Employment Service interviews or enlisting the service of the compradore to nominate qualified young officers as he had in the past found and guaranteed shroffs. In the end the Bank did both of these, but the decision was more difficult, more profound than simply finding a young man with appropriate academic qualifications. This local politicians found difficult to accept.

Second, what would be the local officer's expectations?

What, first of all, were Foreign staff expectations? There is no way to generalize, but there were some impractically romantic views of life in the East. James Caldwell (joined London Office, 1919), for example, had early expectations of a life of adventure in the East.[14] There were others who thought more about being 'in charge' and ordering a lot of natives about. Dreams, all of them, quickly shattered by the reality of the first assignment at the 'chopping desk' and the realization that managership came after many years of the routine. Juniors recruited inter-war either accepted this or resigned, usually in their London years. Even post-war recruits with several years of military leadership experience behind them accepted the routine tentatively; their seniors wanted to be sure they went through the initiation and became general bankers before specialization.

The first local officers recruited post-war in India were less amenable. One such attempt has been described by Caldwell, then Manager Calcutta (1945–1952).

> I had a case where I took six men from Calcutta University thinking I would train them up to have them as departmental managers. It didn't work out because they didn't want to work. They expected to have a battery of telephones in front of them, that's what they had seen in the movies. I said, you can't be in charge of twenty or thirty clerks. You have got to be better than they are! So you have got to start at the bottom, the same as we all had to do and learn as you go up. They wouldn't have this, so they resigned one by one, and then I found out they had gone to these new Indian banks and told them they had been trained in the Hongkong Bank. They were put as managers of small offices, but of course there was no big business for them. It was just current account business, but it was very amusing.[15]

Ian Bradford, who was in Calcutta at the time, spoke of the resentment such direct appointments caused among the senior clerks – as it would, indeed, in Hong Kong among the Portuguese.[16] The more successful early appointments came from within the clerical ranks.

There was another side to 'expectations'. What of the customer who had chosen to deal with a foreign bank? As one American bank manager ('Red' Newall of National City Bank) put it in 1953, a customer chooses our bank because he wants to deal with Americans – there are plenty of good Chinese banks in Singapore; a customer would not, therefore, wish to open the manager's office door and see a Chinese behind the desk. This seemed reasonable; it was accepted opinion.

And beyond this would it ever be possible for the officer recruited in Singapore, for example, to be sent as an officer to Manila. What, in other words, would be his role in an international bank? Would not the 'Foreign staff', that is, the London-recruited officer, still have a major role to play; if so, the continuity of this category needed to be given priority.

These were all reasons, sound by pre-war standards, for hesitation. But just as a contemporary British, Bombay-based Hongkong Bank executive studied the history of Indian cricket and discussed the topic authoritatively with local constituents as a prelude to business, so the shock of seeing a Chinese in the Manager's chair could be overcome in a few minutes of suitable preliminary conversation. The Chinese officer was not the pre-war shroff with new duties; he was, for example, a Singaporean citizen with sound educational background and business training, fully qualified to deal with the requirements of a Western constituent. Furthermore, his posting to a top position was not immediate; by the time he reached the inner office, both he and the business world around him would have changed dramatically.

All this was difficult to foresee in the early 1950s. The entire organizational structure of the foreign firms was being challenged, the cultural preconceptions of several decades had to be overcome while the future of one's business was still in the post-war balance.

Nor was it always true that potential local officers wanted to join foreign banks. Not every qualified young Chinese would want to commit himself to a life of Western food – nor would he feel assured that his future promotion was clear. Much was still experimental; would he be part of the team or the 'token' native? Could prowess in other sports – basketball in the Philippines – be substituted for the previously almost universal 'rugger'? Against the complexities of family and clan relationships in the local business firm the young Nanyang Chinese had to set the possibly limited and certainly untested opportunities of working for a foreign firm.

The assumption sometimes is that the Bank and other firms were always turning away willing and qualified local applicants in favour of even younger and less qualified Britons. But this is a backward look. The Britons were not by definition less qualified in the task they had traditionally fulfilled, the task of being British and being seen to sign for the firm. That this was thought an anachronism or worse was not immediately recognized. When it was recognized, alternatives took time to work out. The problem was more complex than sometimes portrayed and hesitations worked both ways.

The first local officers came in the majority, therefore, from within the Bank; the first to be given assignments previously reserved for Foreign staff were those most recently recruited. Not only were the majority of the older local clerks set in a certain social and work pattern but in the East they had suffered through the Occupation. In the same way as acceptance of responsibility came with difficulty to many of the older Foreign staff who had had pre-war expectations, for many of the older Portuguese the change was coming too late. The younger ones had entered the Bank post-war but on the old three-tier terms; many of these men proved sufficiently competent to adjust to meet new demands as that system broke down. Other adjustments were made within the Bank. Not all early officers proved capable of promotion, but many eventually moved to managerial positions. As the system was regularized, direct local officer recruitment became feasible.

By 1985 there was a local officer in control of the Hongkong Bank's operations in Sri Lanka; the Hamburg Manager was a German citizen for the first time since 1920. The majority of the Bank's branches and sub-branches were managed by Regional officers. Major branches and other top management positions were, with only a few exceptions, in the hands of the 'International staff' (vice 'Foreign staff'), that is, of the young career executive British officers recruited through London, those transferred from the Regional officer status, and those brought in as specialists (see Chapter 18).

The second tier – the Portuguese

The role of the Portuguese clerical staff – or, more generally, the second or clerical tier – was crucial to the functioning of the Bank. But this second tier was vulnerable on two fronts, (i) as a minority community the Portuguese and Sri Lanka's 'burghers' could suffer from the growth of local nationalism and (ii) as the male clerical staff they would be the first subject to replacement as new accounting equipment was installed.

The rise of nationalism put pressure on the various Portuguese communities or their counterparts to associate more closely with the major national groups – if that were possible or permitted – or, somehow, to emigrate. The revolution in China gave many hundreds the status of refugees; they came initially to Macau and Hong Kong, but that was a stepping-stone to Australia and North America. The burghers looked also to Australia; the local Russian staff in China's Northeast Provinces, Manchuria, were granted the opportunity of repatriation to the Soviet Union in the mid-1950s. Some of the Hongkong Bank's Russian employees who did not accept were assisted by the Bank in their often successful attempt to emigrate to Australia and North America (see Chapter 9). By the later 1950s the Hong Kong Portuguese community was beginning to reconsider their future and many left the Colony.

The China-coast Portuguese diaspora affected Hong Kong last and, by comparison with other ports, least. Hence the Portuguese staff attempted to retain their traditional monopoly on the clerical posts in the Bank. In the Great War they had successfully opposed the introduction of women to these positions; in the Pacific War they had proved their loyalty to the Bank, and their immediate availability when Japan surrendered had made possible the speedy reopening of the Hong Kong office. By the late 1950s, however, the situation was affected by the introduction of new machinery requiring less physical stamina and thus, it was argued, suitable for female staff, by the first promotions of Portuguese to the rank of officer, and by the beginning of the 'Portuguese' exodus and the consequent pressure to permit the employment of both Chinese clerical staff and women.

The case of A.M. Prado will illustrate the change and pressures. Born in Macau in 1931, Prado received his secondary education in Hong Kong, joined the Bank in 1948, spent most of his middle career in the Exports Department, was appointed the Hongkong Bank's first Manager Macau, in 1972, and became the Hongkong Bank Group's representative in São Paulo, Brazil, in 1975. After duty in Head Office, he retired to Brazil on contract as the Bank's representative in 1983.

Even in 1948, however, many young Portuguese were looking overseas for the first time, not always with success. Prado had matriculated but could not obtain entrance into crowded North American universities.

While waiting, one day I came to Central, and I walked through the Bank from Des Voeux Road. Crossing the banking hall I met a former classmate of mine, and I asked him what he was doing there.

He said, I am working here in the Hongkong Bank.

I said, how much do you get paid?

Three hundred Hong Kong dollars.

Three hundred, that's a fortune! What do you do to get in?

He said, Oh, very simple, do you want to get in? And right there and then he informed the Chief Clerk, who was Mr [F.X.] Soares.

Mr Soares was a severe looking man, and he came out and said, young man, you want to join the Bank?

I said, yes.

He said, are you healthy?

I said, I think so.

He said, write out a letter of application – five lines. We are needing one more.

So at the counter I wrote this application out. He looked at it. Okay, now you go and see Dr To – or somebody, I forget – for an X-ray and come back to see me tomorrow morning.

And I was in![17]

In-depth recruitment interviews were not the Hongkong Bank's strong point either in London or Hong Kong.

In fact, Prado admits, Soares did ask him one or two further questions. He was anxious, significantly, to establish that Prado, coming from Macau and being unknown to him, was in fact Portuguese. There was also the question of schooling.

F.X. Soares himself celebrated the completion of fifty years service with the Hongkong Bank on April 16, 1956. Sir Arthur Morse sent a telegram through Michael Turner; Soares had fulfilled a life-long ambition.

Prado began as a ledgerkeeper in current accounts – with G.A. Stewart in charge; Prado thus had the potential, by making an error, of keeping the staff of the Bank in until midnight on balancing day; for a youngster it was an awesome responsibility. But the outlook was traditional; the highest aspiration was promotion to chief clerk, social life was in the Portuguese community, the social and sports club, the Church, the schools. When the local Portuguese intermarried with the China-coast refugees and families split as some emigrated – often to jobs in banks overseas, including the Hongkong and Shanghai Banking Corporation of California – the system was shaken. As the Hong Kong economy expanded, many left the Bank to found their own firms or to face new opportunities. And Prado remembers the day the first Chinese clerk was employed.

The major shock to the system was a positive one.

[The Bank] then created a supervisory grade. The supervisors were given certain responsibilities which in those days probably some of them spent sleepless nights under this tremendous change.

They could put their initial on a voucher, which was a great thing because until then it was only the Foreign staff who could do that.

Clerks would write everything out, but somebody else would put his initial. When I say initial, it was equivalent to a full signature today because in those days... one lives and learns of course, an initial is very dangerous, unless you have a full signature you don't know about the authenticity... but in those days, the good old days, an initial was sufficient to effect a transaction. So the supervisors were given the authority to initial a voucher.

Then that was further refined to junior supervisors and senior supervisors. Obviously changes had to be made, you couldn't sit still too long in that situation, and it was recognized that some more senior Portuguese in the Bank should be promoted to officer rank, and that was more or less done... I'm not criticizing... on the basis that you had so many years' service, you were Number One of the local staff in the department, you became an officer. So right away a cross-section of fifteen of the more senior members were promoted to officer rank.

Having done that and removed perhaps the obstacle it was then decided to see what we had in the way of bright lads at lower levels, and that is when Joe Xavier and Vickers Souza were also promoted to officer rank.

They went to London for training.

I had been identified at that stage as possible officer material, and in fact I had been informed by certain people who were in a position to know that as soon as Vickers and Joe returned that I and somebody else would be the next two to go to London.[18]

In fact Prado was promoted but he never went to London. Was there an adverse report on London Office training?

Not really an adverse report. I think they thoroughly enjoyed their stay in London as I would have I am sure, but they thought that they really didn't learn very much. Of course, there is no point in sending people at great expense to London to train when they could come back and say that they learned nothing.[19]

Someone had missed the point.

The Hongkong Bank Group's senior executive in Sri Lanka, R. Thambiah, underwent London training with the Mercantile Bank; to hear him tell the story he learned very little about banking but a great deal about the 'service', which is what London Office was all about. Serious-minded Portuguese and other future local officers might expect more, and today London has all the facilities for modern-style 'training'; if so, it isn't 'London' any more; someone has failed to read his Wodehouse (see Volume II, Chapter 3, and Volume III, Chapter 6).

Dramatic change, and yet not so.

Once the Portuguese had been given signing responsibility, the printed slips which bore the notice 'Not Valid unless signed by a member of the European Staff', the key announcement which separated the foreign exchange banks from the modern-style Chinese and other local banks, had to go. Yet the next step came only in the late 1960s. For what, after all, had happened? The Portuguese clerk who had previously written up a receipt and then handed it to a Foreign staff member to initial, now initialled it himself; he did not perform a different task, despite the additional responsibility. Again Prado illustrates the situation.

...when I was in Exports Department and Roy Munden was Number One, he found it a bit strange that the department was made up of various sections. There was one section that advised Letters of Credit, there was one section that would make out all the payments, there was one section that would look after all the things that had gone wrong, what we called 'the snags' section, a section that would check all the export documents. Roy found it a bit strange that certain of those positions as section heads were 'reserved' so to speak to English staff whereas Portuguese staff were performing as section heads certain jobs like checking documents, and there was no interchange.

So he said, why?

I said, I don't know why, I don't think it's for me to ask why can't I do that job? He said, there is no reason. You do that job.

So I was moved from a job that was traditionally done by a Portuguese lad to a job that had traditionally not been done by a Portuguese lad.[20]

And Prado added, 'I always consider that that decision by Munden actually changed my professional life.'

He may be underestimating the importance of Munden's decision. When the

Portuguese were made officers and given certain authority, this was for the older men a very traumatic situation, but the type of work they did was little changed; Prado has described the next step – as an officer he was for the first time assigned a task which was not simply an extension of responsibility in an area traditionally reserved for Portuguese; his move to a European desk brought the staff one step further to functional integration, but the step came ten years later, in the 1960s – and beyond the period covered in this chapter.

The Chinese staff

The term 'Compradore' is regarded as an anachronism and will no longer be used.

R.G.L. Oliphant, Manager, 23 November 1960

In July 1955 Sir Robert Ho Tung, the great man behind the Bank's Hong Kong compradores, asked for an appointment with the Chief Manager. Michael Turner recalls,

I said, no, Sir Robert, you've now reached the age of ninety, I'll come up and see you.

All he wanted was for me to promise that when he died we would fly the Bank's flag at half mast. ...that was old Sir Robert's wish.[d]

The Board duly minuted that 'in view of his long connection with the Bank', which, as Sir Robert had reminded Turner, extended from the time of Sir Thomas Jackson, the flag would indeed be lowered.

And half an hour after he died [in 1956] his secretary rang through to my office and said, you've promised Sir Robert... well, Sir Robert died half an hour ago.

So we duly did it, and I had the whole Board standing outside the door of the Bank [with senior members of the Bank's staff] watching old Sir Robert go by. He was a great man in our earlier life. He'd been the compradore or guarantor for all our Chinese staff. He'd made money out of it, yes, and he was a difficult man to get money out of, but he was a figurehead at that time in Hong Kong.[22]

Lady Ho Tung's message of appreciation was recorded in the Board's minutes for May 8, 1956.

The act had been symbolic. The death of Sir Robert Ho Tung occurred as the compradoric system itself, a system in which his family had played so significant a part, was dying.

Ho Wing, the Bank's wartime compradore, the fifth in Hong Kong, was the nephew and adopted son of Sir Robert. He died in 1946, never having recovered from his treatment at the hands of the Japanese. His successor was T.P. Tong; born in Hong Kong in 1885 and educated at Queen's College, he

---

[d] Apparently when Turner called on Sir Robert he was handed a letter – it mentioned that the flag had been lowered when T.P. Tong had died.[21]

had first been joint compradore with Ho Wing in 1927. But Tong died in 1953 to be succeeded by the seventh and last Hong Kong compradore, Peter Lee Shun Wah. The Board minuted his appointment and his deposit of security totalling $120,000; this would be supplemented by the deposit of commissions until the total reached $300,000. Even this was relatively little for the sums involved and the Board noted that the compradore was, as usual, guaranteeing every member of his staff. The Board therefore increased the Bank's insurance against defalcations – it was a small but symbolic eroding of the system.

In 1960 Peter Lee's title was changed from 'compradore' to 'Chinese Manager', but the guarantee and commission system, in modified form, remained until his retirement in 1965, at which point it may be said that the compradoric system which the Bank had been founded to help abolish had died, not because of the Bank but because the Chinese business world had changed around it. Elsewhere the very term 'compradore' had fallen, unfairly in so many cases, under social and political criticism as something reminiscent of the 'unequal treaties' and the days of Treaty Port China. This was probably not a factor relevant in Hong Kong, but certainly the time had come for a change. The task to be done had changed.

The Hongkong Bank's involvement with Chinese constituents was itself changing. First, there was the influx of old Shanghai customers, well-known to the Bank, but little known to the Hong Kong compradore and speaking a different dialect and dealing in different commodities. Secondly, there was the growth of industrial finance, especially from the Bank's Mongkok office. In this growing risk area, the Bank needed not so much a financial guarantee which would, from the nature of the amount involved, curtail business, but a knowledge that funds lent were being utilized as agreed. This required on-site investigations by Chinese trained with industrial knowledge, and a special unit was established. Thirdly, the Bank's local retail expansion required additional Chinese staff, and, with the breaking of the Portuguese staff monopoly on clerical work, the intrusion of Chinese into all offices of the Bank, beyond the traditional jurisdiction of the compradore.

These new Chinese staff were usually Western business oriented, like the new Bank constituents – they could do business together without the intervention of a compradore. Furthermore, the new staff were employed directly by the Bank; under the compradore's agreement they were still technically guaranteed by Peter Lee. Again the Bank had taken the initial steps in the 1950s, but the situation created was unstable, unfinished; the rationalization would be completed, as with the position of the Portuguese staff, in the mid-1960s.

The Hongkong Bank's last compradore, however, remained an important and prestigious member of the Colony's business community. In the Bank, he employed experienced bankers to train the young Chinese officers, the future Managers of the Bank's expanding Hong Kong branch network. The need was urgent. Oliphant, who was then Manager Hong Kong, had embarked on a farseeing policy of opening small sub-branches managed entirely by Chinese officers. At the time, 1958–1963, O.P. Edwards was in charge of branches, and as such he negotiated new relationships with the compradore and took over the main responsibility for the necessary training programs. His background knowledge of China and the Chinese stood him and the Bank well at this time.

The tasks of a senior Chinese did not cease with the termination of the compradoric system as traditionally understood. Working in the Chinese business community, Lee found that the newcomers from the China coast were obviously not all known to the Bank, not all capable of dealing directly with the Foreign staff manager; they had to be introduced. There were new Chinese banks to work with, and Peter Lee developed important contacts with the fast-developing Hang Seng Bank with its surprisingly close relations with the U.S. dollar open market and Irving Trust Company of New York. Peter Lee was also chairman of the Chinese Banking Association, a member of the Tenancy Tribunals, and chairman of the New Territories Agricultural Association.

The last compradore was in the grand tradition.

And after him there would be a succession of senior Chinese advisers and managers undertaking new and vital tasks.

And the 'Foreign staff'

En route by P&O –
The two overwhelmingly decent young men going out for the first time to the Hongkong Shanghai Bank, one of whom has carried his father's gift of a book on elephants about for days and days...
Patrick Anderson, *Snake Wine*[23]

By the end of 1961 only two branches, Suapah Road (Bangkok) and Beaufort, British North Borneo (Sabah), were managed by local officers. The Bank's 'Newsletter' to Managers in May 1960 admitted that the integration of local staff into a system designed for Foreign staff was still presenting difficulties. As the Chief Inspector, Black, commented, there is obviously no point in having a local officer check and initial a document only to have a Foreign staff officer recheck; the local officer (or Regional officer, to use a later term) should do what he had always done but he should now *check it* himself; the Foreign staff officer's work would be virtually unchanged.

Once again the period to 1961 proved to be one in which problems developed, many of which were correctly identified, but the solutions proved impossible of proper implementation piecemeal. The system had to be changed, once sufficient pressure had been built up, not only in the Hongkong Bank but in other Eastern firms and, indeed, throughout British business. What Addis attempted to do out of historical context in the years before the Great War would be accomplished in the 1960s.

This is not to say that Hongkong Bankers, trained during and by their careers, did not become highly qualified bankers before retirement. As they left the Bank in their mid or early 50s, many who had survived internment and become Managers of, for example, small Borneo branches retired quietly. Others, however, accepted senior positions with new development agencies and banks – for example, R.A. Jardine went to Nepal, G.C. Moutrie to Mauritius, W.T. Yoxall to Sri Lanka, A.L. Snaith to the Philippines, and B.P. Massey to the World Bank; others were recruited to the London offices of foreign banks – for example, R. Stilliard to Continental Illinois National Bank and Trust Company of Chicago; still others were employed in senior capacities in America. I.H. Bradford returned to San Francisco, where he had been Manager in 1954, and worked with the United California Bank. A.M. 'Fuji' Ford had met many young Japanese from Keio University during his earlier tours in Japan; one rose to become chief executive of the Bank of Tokyo's California subsidiary, California First Bank; he employed Ford as the senior training officer in San Francisco.[e] With the development of the Hongkong Bank Group, certain retired Foreign staff took management positions in subsidiary or associated companies – although this was a later development. As an example, J.W.L. Howard served as executive director, Antony Gibbs and Sons, 1972–1981.

There was, however, rationalization in the 1950s. Pensions were funded, and the necessary assets transferred to the Bank's Trustee Company in 1956. This did not avoid *ad hoc* decisions entirely; there were those who had long since retired and whose income needed adjusting; there were those caught in between the systems; and there was an unexpected increase in the cost of living which required adjustments to the basic system in 1958. As Morse wrote in 1952, a general policy relative to the Bank's existing pensioners was impossible; 'no two men retired on exactly the same basis'.[24]

In 1958 pensions were revised, with an upper limit set at £2,112:1s:1d p.a., the maximum which British tax authorities would permit free of surtax. Turner, as Stabb and Stephen in 1919, was anxious to assist retirees; he was equally anxious to keep Bank funds from the Chancellor of the Exchequer. Bank widows found their pensions raised to £750 in 1960.

Meanwhile the Hongkong Bank's serving Foreign staff remained apparently unchanged.

[e] The dates for first assignment in the East and retirement for these executives are: Jardine 1926–1957, Moutrie 1925–1959, Yoxall 1922–1955, Snaith 1937–1969, Massey 1928–1960, Stilliard 1931–1961, Bradford 1928–1962, and Ford 1936–1964.

Prospective Hongkong Bank juniors approached London Office for the *ad hoc* interview and the examination of doubtful purpose; they remained to experience the on-the-job training and the life at New Beckenham. After seeing his team defeated by the Hongkong Bank juniors, a National Bank of India manager commented to Gray on the Bank's 'team spirit' – he wondered how it was achieved. In a letter to Morse, Gray commented, 'I could have answered – your senior manager isn't even present and he is the host.' To which Morse replied that when the juniors played Jardine's, Hongkong Bank senior management showed up; Jardine's did not – and critical comments were passed.[25] Morse and Turner after him thought it worthwhile to maintain these traditions, from New Beckenham with its annual subsidy of £2,000, to the shipboard adventures on the P&O East for a first assignment under conditions little changed since the inter-war years, to the life in the then Spartan Hong Kong junior mess on the Peak.

The father/son and two brothers rule had become, to use Turner's term, 'obsolete'. S.A. Gray's two sons indicated an interest in joining the Bank and Turner wrote approvingly, noting however that only one could become Chief Manager.[26] Only J.M. Gray actually joined; he had become an executive director – a status unknown to Turner – by 1986.[f]

There had to be minor adjustments, but none challenged the system. The time in London was shorter, given the requirements in the East; Jim Coles retired at New Beckenham to be replaced by his son Stan in 1950; the P&O became less formal, and the officer needed 'immediately' took the airplane rather than the Trans-Siberian route. Morse, however, viewed the gradual transition to the East, the shipboard experience, the meetings with Hongkong Bankers at the ports en route, and the gradual realization of the new life as an essential first experience. Too soon it would become a luxury the Bank would not afford, a decade later the ships themselves ceased their monthly schedule. Since the mid-1950s the junior has been flying to Hong Kong.

The Bank, however, still insisted that a first-tour junior be unattached. Turner once complained to Gray in reference to a new junior who had just reached Hong Kong, 'When you sent this young man out, you exported not only the gentleman himself but also his father, his mother, his maternal grandmother, and his fiancée – a conglomeration *très formidable* – to put it mildly.'[27] They expected appropriate housing. Gray replied that he had discovered the departure of the family only too late. He had meant to warn Head Office, but the matter had slipped his mind. As for the young man, on being told that his family were not welcome in the East, he resigned on the spot,

---

[f] The elder son, David Gray, had joined the Chartered Bank before his national service; understandably he decided not to move. What had upset Arthur Morse, however, was that with David Gray's rugger ability the Chartered Bank team was able to defeat the Hongkong Bank. The father/son rule was declared obsolete.

Table 7.2 *The Hongkong Bank[a]*
Eastern or 'Foreign' staff, 1946–1962

Year[b]	Number	Juniors to the East	Senior
1900 June	156		Sir Thomas Jackson
1914 July	214		J.P. Wade Gard'ner[c]
1918	183		J.P. Wade Gard'ner
1925	274	20	G.H. Stitt
1941	249	0	A.S. Henchman
1946	238[d] [4]	45[e]	A.G. Kellogg[c]
1947 April	226 [5]	8	A.G. Kellogg
1948 April	225 [5]	26	A.G. Kellogg
1949	242 [5]	14	Sir Arthur Morse[f]
1950	241 [6]	22	Sir Arthur Morse
1951	243 [7]	12	Sir Arthur Morse
1952	242 [8]	13	Sir Arthur Morse
1953	243 [9]	17	A.M.D. Wallace[g]
1954	251 [9]	19	A.M.D. Wallace
1955	253 [11]	16	A.M.D. Wallace
1956	256 [9]	20	A.G. Cameron[g]
1957	266 [9]	15	A.G. Cameron
1958	272 [9]	19	S.W.P. Perry-Aldworth[g]
1959	273 [10]	8	S.W.P. Perry-Aldworth
1960	269 [10]	21	S.W.P. Perry-Aldworth
1961	271 [11]	11	S.W.P. Perry-Aldworth
1962	270 [10]	12	H.V. Parker[h]

[a] See note *a*, Table 7.1.
[b] August, unless otherwise stated.
[c] Manager, New York.
[d] From 1946 includes [*x*] assigned to London, Hamburg, and Paris who would have been excluded from the list above.
[e] Made up of 1, 1939; 10, 1940; 11, 1941; 9, 1942; 4, 1946 who had not been East before the War – these last had only a 1946 seniority, however.
[f] Chief Manager.
[g] Manager London.
[h] Manager Paris.

and the Bank found itself paying the return transportation costs for the entire family.

There were, however, some concessions. The tours were shorter. Marriage rules were relaxed both as to time in the East and as to choice; the first marriage to a Chinese lady had occurred during the war.

The opportunities for early appointment, however, were not improved. The Foreign staff reached a peak in 1925 with 274 (see Volume III, Table 5.1); in

Table 7.3 *The Hongkong Bank*[a]
Seniority distribution of the Foreign staff, 1946–1961

Year	15 & under	16–25	26–30	Over 30	Total
	\multicolumn{4}{c}{Years in the East}	
1920	178	49	14	18	259
1936	149	86	23	6	264
1946	98	86	43	11	238
1947	94	81	45	6	226
1948	99	77	46	3	225
1949	121	72	46	3	242
1950	130	68	31	12	241
1951	139	56	36	12	243
1952	144	57	30	11	242
1953	146	60	25	12	243
1954	148	65	25	13	251
1955	158	56	32	7	253
1956	150	68	30	8	256
1957	157	69	30	10	266
1958	164	69	30	9	272
1959	172	60	32	9	273
1960	177	58	23	11	269
1961	188	53	20	10	271
1962	195	49	19	7	270

[a] See note *a*, Table 7.1, p. 287.

the period through 1962, as shown in Table 7.2, the maximum occurred in 1959 with 273 actually in the East (or on leave).[g] Table 7.1 notes that the number of gazetted posts in the East had increased from 63 in 1936 to 82 in the peak year of 1959. Despite this increase, the seniority distribution of Foreign staff (based on length of service in the East with allowance for war service), as shown in Table 7.3, indicates that if one assumes all those with 26 or more years of service had appointments, only a proportion of the 16–25 year group could also have appointments, consequently leaving none available for the most junior

[g] Pre-1945 Foreign staff figures excluded those permanently assigned to London, Lyons, and Hamburg offices – although, inconsistently, they included those assigned to New York and San Francisco. Post-1945 Foreign staff figures include those assigned to all the above named offices. In 1959, for example, in addition to the 273 in the East and America, there were ten in London, Lyons, and Hamburg. Pre-war there were usually a total of seven Foreign staff posts in London, Hamburg, and Lyons. Postings in Europe tended to extend an officer's service, hence their exclusion permits one to focus on those in the competition during a normal period of service with the Hongkong Bank.

Table 7.4 *The Hongkong Bank*
Offices and their Managers, 1946 and 1961

Office	1946 Manager Date appointed	1961 Manager Date appointed	Date first went East		Years East	HK[a]
Hong Kong	A.S. Adamson (1945)	R.G.L. Oliphant (1958)	1919		27	—
Kowloon	G. Travers (1945)		1919	1934	27	++
					27	—
Mongkok		A.W. Helbling (1961)		1938	23	+
North Point		I.H. Bradford (1956)		1932	29	++
Tsuen Wan		I.T. Townend (1959)		1948	13	+
Yuen Long		P.M. Ryan (1961)		1948	13	++
		C.A. Odling (1961)		1953	8	+
Shanghai	S.A. Gray (1945)		1919		27	—
		E.C. Hutchison (1961)		1931	30	—
Chungking	J.T. Edkins (1946)		1930		16	+
Swatow	P.A. Sellars (1946)		1927		19	—
Canton	C.M. Jamieson (1946)		1919		27	##
Foochow	J.B. Stewart (1947)[b]		1919		27	##
Amoy	L.G. Robertson (1946)		1925		21	+
Tsingtau	J.C. Sutherland (1946)		1920		26	##
Tientsin	A.H. Matthews (1946)		1919		27	##
Peiping	D.F.C. Cleland (1946)		1924		22	—
Mukden	W.G. Turnbull (1946) nyo[c]		1922		24	##
Hankow	J.S. Davenport (1946) nyo		1920		26	+
Tokyo	V.A. Mason[d]		1919		27	+
Kobe	L.G. Robertson[e]	M.G. Carruthers (1961)	1925	1937	24	+
					21	+
Yokohama	H.J.S. Muriel[e]	R.G. Ouseley (1961)	1946	1946	15+6[f]	+
					15+6	+
Osaka		A.D.M. Ford (1960)		1936	25	—
		A. Robertson (1961)		1932	29	—
Manila	A.F. Handcock (1945)		1912		34	##

316

Location			Year	Count	
Saigon		H.L. Pierce (1961)	1948	13	+
	W.J. Hope (1946)	A.L. Murray (1960)	1920	26	+
Haiphong	G.S. Chambers (1946)		1929	26	#
Phnom Penh	J.J. French (1946)	F.W. Chandler (1961)	1934	17	–
Bangkok		W.A. Stewart (1961)	1915	27	–
		Nibhavisn Krairiksh (1959)	1933	31	+
Suapah Rd	R.A. Stuart (1939)		local	28	na
Singapore		I.J.O. Cruickshank (1959)	1912	na	–
Orchard Rd		J.H.P. Young (1961)	1935	34	–
Tanglin		S.J.H. Pughe (1961)	1946	26	#
Kuala Lumpur	C.H. Eldridge (1945)		1946	15+5	–
Bukit Terendak			1919	15+5	–
Ipoh	J.A. Clark (1945)	M.J. Bond (1961)		27	
Johore	J.W.R. McPhail (1945)	P.B. Tay (1960)	1919	9	+
			1919	27	+
Malacca	G.E.B. Tytler (1945)	P.H. Scoones (1960)	1919	23	–
	T.W. Doyle (1946)		1918	27	+
Muar	L.H. Thorn (1946)	D.G. Day (1960)	1923	27	+
Penang	W.C. Murray (1938)	I.L.G. Wheeler (1959)	1913	28	–
		R.W. Mills (1960)	1933	23	+
		B.C. Rogers (1961)	1954	23	+
Petaling Jaya	P.A. MacDougall (1946)	R.W. Scott (1960)	1920	30	#
Sungei Patani				33	#
Teluk Anson	G.W. Stabb (1946)		1930	28	#
Cameron Highlands		G.P. Cross (1961)	1946	7	–
Jesselton		R.C. Beauclerk (1961)	1947	26	–
Beaufort		Maurice W. Turner (1961)	1946	21	+
Brunei		B. Chung (1961)	local staff	16	#
Kuala Belait		P.G.A. Cantopher (1960)	1939	15	–
		J.M. Beazley (1960)	1940	14	+
Kuching		G.N.B. Haynes (1961)	1946	15+6	–
			na	22	na
				21	+
				15+6	+

317

Table 7.4 (cont.)

Office	1946 Manager Date appointed	1961 Manager Date appointed	Date first went East	Years East	HK[a]
Labuan		C.J. Campbell (1959)	1950	11	+
Sandakan		A.K. Forsyth (1959)	1929	32	+
Seria		R.R. Clarke (1961)	1955	6	+
Sibu		M.J.S. Figg (1960)	1949	12	−
Tawau		J.F. Marshall (1959)	1946	15+6	+
Batavia	H.A. Mabey (1946)		1920	26	+
Sourabaya	W.W. Rae (1946)	T.G. Mead (1961)	1920	15+5	+
Rangoon	J. Campbell (1945)		1919	27	≠
Calcutta	J. Caldwell (1945)	A.M. Kennedy (1960)	1920	25	+
Bombay	G.E.B. Tytler (1946)	S.F.T.B. Lever (1959)	1946	26	+
Colombo	J.C.G. Fergusson (1946)	B O'D Paterson (1960)	1919	15+8	−
New York	A.G. Kellogg (1937)		1937	27	−
San Francisco	A.R.M. Blackhall (1938)	R.P. Edwards (1961)	1911	24	+
London	H.E. Muriel (1945)	H.C. Peterson (1960)	1906	35	+
	A.M.D. Wallace (1946)		1916	40	≠
Hamburg	G.C. Moutrie (1948)[e]	S.W.P. Perry-Aldworth (1955)	1931	30	+
		G.O.W. Stewart (1961)	1929	22	≠
Lyons/Paris	D.A. Johnston (1944)	D.B. Soul (1959)	1925	32	+
			1919	37	+
			1925	36	+
			1933	28	−
			1932	21	−
		H.V. Parker (1958)	1910	29	−
			1925	36	≠
				36	+

The term 'Hongkong Bank' as opposed to the usual 'Hongkong and Shanghai Banking Corporation' is designed to differentiate between the Hongkong Bank qua bank and the Hongkong Bank Group, which latter includes subsidiary companies, especially the MBLD and the BBME.

[a] + = in Hong Kong first tour; − = in Hong Kong after first tour; ≠ = never in Hong Kong.

group. A new junior of the immediate post-war period had still to expect a wait of more than fifteen years before his first appointment.

Table 7.4, which admittedly deals only with managerial posts however junior they might be to, for example, a Sub-Manager in Head Office, reveals exceptions to the above generalization relative to the junior group, but many of these disappear if years in the East are adjusted for the war years, an adjustment applicable for those who were actually accepted in London Office (whether they served or not) before or during the war. Exceptions remain. These can be shown to relate to small sub-agencies, for example, Petaling Jaya and Teluk Anson in Malaya and Tsuen Wan and Yuen Long in Hong Kong's New Territories. There was also the small military banking facility in Bukit Terandak. The office in the Cameron Highlands was partly bank and partly rest home; it too was an exception. Perhaps the appointment of H.L. Pierce to Iloilo after only thirteen years' Eastern service should be noted; his career switched in the 1960s, however, to specialization in technical services.

This list suggests that the Bank had at last opened the smaller branches which not only extended its deposit and service coverage but which also, like the Mercantile Bank's East Coast Malayan branches, provided opportunities to test younger officers. Although a more comprehensive discussion of the Bank's branches is reserved for Chapter 10, at this point one should note several problems with this optimistic analysis. First, the number of Bank offices showed a 23% increase from 1936; the openings in Borneo and the Malay Peninsula were partially offset by closings in China. Secondly, there were many senior officers anxious for appointments. Thirdly, although young men were accommodated in the new offices, the Bank's freedom of assignment was soon limited by increasingly restrictive immigration rules designed to encourage localization through appointment of local citizens as Bank officers.

Fenwick held that the junior not seen early in Hong Kong suffered a career disadvantage. The evidence in Table 7.4 is inconclusive. Some nineteen of the managerial appointments listed were of Foreign staff who had never been assigned to Hong Kong and a further 29 had not been assigned here during their first five-year tour. Those who despite this impediment were appointed Managers had careers which defy generalization; there were those who served almost entirely in Southeast Asia, others with French language competence served long periods in French Indo-China, others with Chinese were based in North China and then moved straight to South or Southeast Asian posts when promotion opportunity was lacking in their preferred area.

Regardless of the statistical verdict, Fenwick's recommendation that juniors be assigned to Hong Kong first was sound, if only to allow the young man the experience of work in the Bank's home base. In this Fenwick was able to convince Morse – subject to the emergency needs of what was still a small service. The statistics indicate relative success; certainly juniors coming East after 1959 were assigned to Hong Kong within their first two years of service.

As for the Hongkong Banker some 30 years in the East who had never seen Head Office, he was unusual even in unplanned days.

Despite the great attention paid to staff affairs post-war, the task of assignment remained a difficult one. The turnover in the various branches suggests that leave patterns and the desire to promote long-serving officers, health, and other extraneous matters could take priority over policy.

The Bank still stressed on-the-job training. Often after quite senior military responsibility and command assignments the 'junior' found himself undertaking the same routine tasks which characterized the pre-war Bank. There was still no mechanization and there were at first no local staff officers. New accounting equipment had been introduced by 1961, but it made little difference to the life of a junior. There was still banknote counting and cancellation; only banknote signing had been eliminated by allowing two printed signatures. Indeed, when the local staffs went on strike in offices as far separated as Colombo and Tokyo, the Foreign staff were competent to handle all aspects of the work and could keep the Bank operating, albeit under siege. This was a comforting thought, but there were offsetting disadvantages.

First, there was a significant drop-out rate. Several explanations have been tendered for this, but juniors were not systematically interviewed on resignation. It is reasonable to suppose that men out of the Forces and seeking a career might choose hastily or on the basis of insufficient knowledge; others with experience of wartime captivity would be sensitive to the exposed position of Hong Kong. Above all there was the existence of a routine which might prove unacceptable to the post-war generation.

This last point has a counterpart, providing a second disadvantage to the traditional system. Whereas the Bank continued to insist that juniors perform routine, clerical tasks, the increased costs of an expatriate officer arising from his higher expectations, earlier marriage, more frequent leaves – to mention a few items, made it essential that his product consist of something more objectively determined than his integrity and consequent aura which induced local people to leave their funds with a British bank. However much this had been a factor pre-war, the post-war citizen of an independent country, witness to the defeat of the European, had revised criteria in banking.

The specifics: 1951, 1954, and 1961 compared[28]

> The Chief Manager's salary is in a class by itself.
> 1954 'Conditions of Service' brochure

In 1951 the Hongkong Bank was accepting 'a limited number of youths under the age of 18' for London Office as trainees prior to their military service at £180 p.a. Foreign staff juniors were young men, maximum age 23 or 24, who had completed their military service and were taken on for training prior to overseas assignment at a rate of £310 p.a. – net take-home pay was accordingly £22 p.m. After six months' probation the stipend rose to £360 p.a. Lunch was provided five days a week.

An outfit allowance of £200 was payable on first assignment to the East, which was expected within a two-year period.

The basic salary on joining the 'Foreign staff', that is, arriving in the East, was £540, but gross salary, inclusive of all Hong Kong allowances was £790 (= $12,636 @ 1s:3d) p.a. (Regular increments were awarded, regardless of merit, at two-yearly intervals for fourteen years.) After ten years' service the junior was promised a basic salary of £1,040 or £1,810 with allowances (= $26,566). Free accommodation (including fuel and servants) in the Junior Mess is not included in these figures; more senior staff received rent-free accommodation and utilities or a housing allowance.

Juniors were informed that *basic* salaries as high as £4,000 p.a. were attainable. The Chief Manager's salary with high cost of living was £11,430 p.a., his total remuneration for 1949/50, including honorarium, director's fee, utilities, and tax paid, was £26,380 (= $422,080). This the brochure did not detail.

Leave with full passages, first class P&O, was granted for eight months on full *basic* pay (plus high cost of living allowance of 30%) after four years in the East.

Retirement benefits were specified in detail and included a non-contributory Pension Fund payable when the officer reached the normal retirement age of 55, after at least 25 years of Eastern service, or the date on which the officer completed 30 years of Eastern service, whichever came first. There was a contributory Officers' Provident Fund to which officers contributed 5% and the Bank 10% of *basic* salaries. On retirement the individual would receive at least £8,000 from the combined contributions plus interest.

These early post-war information sheets did not include information on marriage or on passages, etc. for dependants.

By 1954 the format had improved and there were pictures of the Junior Mess, senior managers' homes in the East, the athletic grounds at New Beckenham, and the first and most recent rugby teams. The messes and homes, which all dated back to the early 1920s, spoke of the expansiveness of the pre-air-conditioned East and of the grand style of living which the junior might someday achieve. For the present the brochure stressed the facilities at New Beckenham.

The actual conditions of service had, however, varied little. The London salaries had been slightly adjusted to take account of age at the beginning of service. The free lunch continued, with good reason, to be stressed. The outfit allowance remained at £200. The basic salaries in the East remained as before, although more detail on marriage allowances was included and the fact that the Bank paid income tax on staff salaries was noted.

The major addition to the information provided related to passages and, by inference, to the marriage rule. A Foreign staff officer could marry after completion of his first four years of Eastern service, that is, during his first leave. If, however, he married, with permission, while in the East and on the eve of his first leave, the officer 'will not normally have his wife's homeward passage paid'. For young men who had served in the Korean War and who had joined the Bank at the upper age limit of 24, even a four-year limit was difficult to accept. It could be 'fudged'. Michael Turner faced the problem in 1958 and proposed solving it by, exceptionally, shortening the young man's tour to $3\frac{1}{2}$ years – and adding, 'I know very well how you feel, as I was up against the same difficulty years ago, but I was battling against a ten-year rule whilst you and your contemporaries only have to cope with a four-year rule... try and hang on.' This special arrangement required considerable negotiation and it is clear that Turner had received good reports of the junior involved. The Bank was in fact successful in retaining the services of William Purves.

Once the young man was married provision had to be made for dependants' travel. In 1954 passages for wives were paid once a tour. Additionally the officer with children in school in the United Kingdom had the choice of his wife returning at Bank expense once during the tour or of bringing out the children for one holiday. The advantages of air travel were being incorporated into the conditions of service for the first time.

The 1961 brochure had been little changed – the messes and houses were the same, the rugger teams and New Beckenham featured prominently. London salaries had however increased, and a beginner received from £360 to £450 p.a. depending on age. The Bank was still recruiting at 'about the age of 18' with the upper limit at 22 years of age but, taking notice of University graduates, extended the limits, presumably to 24 years of age. Salaries in the East began with a basic £750 and might eventually reach £6,000. Intending juniors were again reminded that 'The Chief Manager's emolument is in a class by itself'.

In view of high British taxation, the Bank considered it wise to remind juniors that the salaries were tax paid and compared favourably with others in Hong Kong.

The four-year marriage rule remained intact. Leave with passages still came after four years' Eastern service. Children's passages were paid once a tour; the assumption was that, if they were being educated in England, the father would bring them out for a holiday. If his place of work were unsuitable for children, however, he could apply for permission to send his wife for a visit to England.

While there is no question but that these terms were in general more favourable than those prevailing before the Pacific War, the categories are unchanged. The concessions made in the years to 1961 were very real, but they were of degree, not kind. The life of the expatriate in the post-war East was structurally unchanged, and much of the discussion in previous volumes remains relevant.

These comments would all seem capable of separation into two components: the first, that the system was unchanged; the second, that the system had within it pressures which the Bank could not long withstand. The resolution, however, came after 1961.

By 1961 the Hongkong Bank was also a holding company with two subsidiary banks, the Mercantile Bank and the British Bank of the Middle East. Their personnel policy is, however, still a subject for their own history, not for that of the Hongkong Bank. There were three sets of Foreign staff; in 1961 a history of the Hongkong Bank need deal only with its own, noting, however, that the other two staffs were in the same *tradition* as to selection, training, promotion, marriage, leaves, and gratuities. This would not necessarily make them easy to merge, but that problem too does not arise in the period now under discussion.

8

THE HONGKONG BANK IN HONG KONG, 1947–1962*

> When I was Manager in Hong Kong [1958–1964], I never granted a large loan without considering the effect on the Colony...the future prosperity of the Colony was always in mind. [This attitude] always existed, and, I hope, it always will. The Bank long ago reached an influential position, which allowed it to enjoy a number of privileges, but we never forgot that privileges carry responsibilities.
>
> R.G.L. Oliphant, 1985

The role of the Bank in Hong Kong in the post-war years to 1961 is consistent with the theme of Part II of this volume. New policy departures were initiated the full impact of which came after 1961; the Bank in 1961 would seem recognizable to a returned Old China Hand, but the tensions and potential had moved to the point where change was virtually inevitable. If this hidden element were a particular characteristic of the terms of service for the Foreign staff, just reviewed in Chapter 7, the efforts of the Bank in Hong Kong were relatively visible, even though the days of investment banking subsidiaries, equity investment, and specialized subsidiaries were still at least a decade away. The Bank in financing Hong Kong industry made pragmatic adjustments to traditional exchange banking but in doing so undertook changes in internal organization and banking practices which formed the basis for major developments to come.

The development of the Hong Kong economy was interrupted by several crises of confidence and in this sense was far from continuous; it was never inevitable. However 1962 is not the year that an economic historian would choose as his breaking point – unless his focus were on the role of the Hongkong Bank. The change of Chief Managers in 1962 affected all levels of senior management and Managers who had felt the impact of industrial financial requirements at branch levels were promoted. This would affect the Bank's policies. By the mid-1960s statistics are available for analysis, both at the Bank and Government level. The story of the Bank in post-war Hong Kong must, therefore, be split. The beginnings only are related here.

* All references for this chapter have been summarized in a bibliographical essay in lieu of endnotes, see pp. 945–46.

A SURVEY OF HONG KONG'S GROWTH

The manufacturing sector accounted for 31% of Hong Kong's 1970 Gross Domestic Product (GDP) at factor cost; by 1980 this had declined to 25%, reflecting the comparative growth of the financial services sector. Hong Kong had become the world's third financial centre, but manufacturing remained vital, constituting 65% by value of the territory's total 1980 exports worth $161,000 million. Preliminary estimates for 1984 indicated a GDP at market prices of $249,000 million. The money supply, narrowly defined (M1), was $36,800 million, and the territory's total bank deposits from customers was $296,000 million, excluding those in other deposit-taking companies. The Hongkong Bank's total assets in 1984 were $206,000 million and its deposit liabilities $166,000 million – the consolidated Group balance sheet states $482,000 million and $422,000 million respectively.

The essential point about the period under present consideration is that Hong Kong and the Hongkong Bank then presented a totally different image. Unfortunately neither banking statistics before 1964 nor GDP statistics before 1966 are adequate for relevant analysis, but estimates of varying accuracy indicate for 1950 a GDP of $2,800 million, total exports of $3,715 million with no estimate for the proportion of Hong Kong origin, but with a small manufacturing sector comprising 1,752 establishments, employing 92,000 workers. The Mainland of China had just witnessed the victory of the People's Liberation Army which now stood on the threshold of Hong Kong, a city crowded with refugees with uncertain prospects in an economy with the necessary overheads, docks and shipyards, banks, and world wide communications geared for the development of a flourishing entrepôt trade, soon to be curtailed by embargoes.

Although this was a moment of new crisis, it could also be said that the Hongkong Bank had just recovered from the period of post-war readjustment, with a fall during 1949 of its investments against an increase in trade bills discounted (see Table 5.3). The Bank was once again financing the growing trade of the East; it was a time to look back – the future was uncertain. Perhaps in this context the 'seconding' speech at the March 1950 meeting of shareholders was most appropriate: J.H. Ruttonjee, after reviewing the favourable trade statistics and the profitable year which the Bank had enjoyed, turned to an event of 1897, recalling the first time as a young apprentice in his father's firm he had tried to do business in the Bank, had become totally confused, and had been assisted by a kindly but elderly gentleman who had been watching him sympathetically – it was the great TJ himself. No one of the Bank staff hearing the speech could claim to have known TJ as Chief Manager, although Morse could recall the old man as Chairman of the London Advisory

Committee. But there were many in the Indian and Chinese communities in Hong Kong who still remembered; the Bank's past was not far away.

It was, then, the old Bank, the 'British exchange bank', which faced the new decade, a decade which would not so much achieve inevitable change in the Hong Kong economy as it would prepare the foundations for that change – the resources of the entrepôt would be diverted to support industry; after the 1950s Hong Kong would never be the same. But that was not apparent in the early years, and Ruttonjee's backward glance at the Jackson Era can be understood; not until after the Korean Armistice in 1953 did the Colony really begin to regain its self-confidence. Morse, and Turner after him, acted as he had done during the war when Hong Kong's future status as a British territory was under question – he carried on with the resources available to meet the problems which confronted the Bank without comprehensive plan, indeed not with all the Bank's Managers moving in the same direction. In this Morse, Turner, and their Managers reflected the pragmatic approach of Government and of the entrepreneurs, the Chinese especially, who, beyond hope, began the industrial revolution which would flower in the next decade, in the 1960s, and beyond.

Hong Kong was but one of the several Eastern economies in which the Bank operated, but a history of the Hongkong Bank cannot include all the details of these early developing years. Fortunately there are studies at several levels to which one can turn. Hong Kong, however, was the site of the Hongkong Bank's Head Office, and an examination of the rough figures presented in Table 8.1 suggests the importance of its Hong Kong operations in the overall performance of the Bank, with up to 46% of gross profits originating in the territory. However, a true estimate of relative importance should include the figures for Head Office; Hong Kong was a communications and transport centre, and, although it was not then the financial centre it would become say 25 years later, even in 1950 global planning for the Bank could be successful only in the free atmosphere of the British colony. One could go further: the attribution of profits among Head Office, Hong Kong office, and London, although not arbitrary, were linked. Put this way, Table 8.1 shows the central nucleus of the Bank against the peripheral offices, which no matter how important – for profits or, in the case of San Francisco, Shanghai, and India, for losses – had a marginal quantitative impact on the aggregate profit figures. But without the offices in, for example, Rangoon, Jakarta, Colombo, and Jesselton (not included in the table) the Bank would not have had the necessary coverage to service the regional operations on which its success was based. To finance industrial growth in Hong Kong without the ability to finance the import of the raw materials and the export of the finished product would have been impossible;

Table 8.1 *The Hongkong Bank*
Branch profits as reported 1947–1961*

(in millions of dollars)

Year	Hongkong Bank branches	Head Office	Hong Kong	London	Singapore	Manila	India	Bangkok	Japan	San Francisco	New York
1947	25.0	6.7	5.0	—	3.7	2.7	3.5	1.4	—	—	—
1948	29.3	6.7	6.2	—	4.0	4.4	2.5	2.7	—	—	—
1949	33.2	6.7	10.2	—	3.3	3.0	1.9	3.4	1.8	—	—
1950	36.3	4.3	14.1	—	6.2	2.0	1.8	2.1	2.7	—	—
1951	49.1	3.7	18.0	2.9	10.8	1.6	2.0	2.4	4.5	(0.1)	1.4
1952	58.6	4.8	14.8	16.4	7.3	2.0	3.1	2.2	2.5	0.4	1.2
1953	48.3	5.1	11.2	13.7	4.2	1.4	1.3	2.0	—	1.0	2.4
1954	43.6	5.4	12.6	13.3	2.7	2.2	—	1.4	1.1	0.6	0.9
1955	60.1	6.5	15.5	22.7	0.4	2.9	1.0[b]	1.0	—	1.2	2.9
1956	67.8	6.7	16.7	23.2	10.9	4.9	(0.2)[b]	0.7	1.1	(1.1)	1.8
1957	66.9	5.8	19.8	18.3	11.0	5.3	(0.5)[b]	1.0	1.4	0.6	1.9
1958	51.0	7.5	19.0	14.7	6.4	3.2	(2.1)[b]	0.8	0.6	(0.7)[c]	1.2
1959	64.3	13.2	29.4	13.5	4.4[a]	3.4	(1.0)[b]	(0.4)	—	(0.4)[c]	0.9
1960	69.1	14.2	27.1	17.4	6.9[a]	2.7	(3.0)[b]	—	—	(0.4)[c]	1.6
1961	59.7	14.0	12.9	16.5	6.1[a]	3.3	2.1	1.1	—	0.4	2.2

* This table should be considered as indicative only; '—' indicates marginal profits only; ( ) enclose negative amounts; definitions may change from year to year.
Singapore = Singapore and Federation agencies; Manila = +Iloilo; Hong Kong includes South China agencies; other agencies show marginal profits; Rangoon shows steady, small profits; Shanghai heavy losses.
[a] Singapore and the Federation of Malaya are separately listed in the sources.
[b] Does not allow for bad debts of Calcutta office totalling $38.6 million.
[c] Losses due to arbitrarily high agency fee charged by 'Inc.' to affect its profits.

Source: Board of Directors Minutes, Group Archives.

for every tie-up of funds in factory finance there had to be a compensating turnover in trade finance related to it.

In this the Bank was not innovating; Eastern exchange banks had always been willing to undertake longer term financing – even underwriting loans for China's railways and mines – provided always that the purpose was a growth in international trade. What was innovative was the Hongkong Bank's methods as it felt out a rational approach to new problems. A historian might have compared the dangers to those faced by the first Chief Manager, Victor Kresser, when he and his directors moved uncritically into the finance of admittedly needed undertakings which nevertheless proved to be, to use the contemporary term, 'bug-bears'.

At the beginning of the 1950s the Bank in Hong Kong was managed by officers who had first come East between the Great War and 1929. The Manager Hong Kong was A.S. Adamson (East in 1919), succeeded by Michael Turner and R.P. Moodie (East in 1926). The key office in Mongkok on the Kowloon peninsula was established only in 1948; in 1950 G.H. Cautherley (East in 1926) was Manager – he was to see the beginning of the change, but he was in poor health and was transferred. By the mid-1950s Hong Kong was led by the next generation – R.G.L. Oliphant (East in 1934) in Mongkok and then Manager Hong Kong; I.H. Bradford (East in 1932) returned from San Francisco to take over Mongkok. While Sir Michael Turner and G.O.W. Stewart (East in 1933) watched major developments in London and Oz Skinner and F.C.B. Black as successive Chief Inspectors kept watch of the various branches, as North Point office (established 1956) turned to specialize in consumer finance, Oliphant and his Hong Kong colleagues initiated the changes which were to be vital to the growth of the Bank in the next quarter-century; they convinced Turner of the need for branch banking on what was then considered a major scale.

The Hongkong Bank began the 1950s in a strong position. Morse had held down dividends, indeed the uncertainties of the time made argument with this policy difficult; shareholders were aware that inner reserves were being built up. Morse and the Bank were already known for their key role in the initial rebuilding of Hong Kong; they were now looked to for leadership in a time of new problems. Despite these strengths and the positive role the Bank played throughout, by the end of the decade its market-share in Hong Kong banking and the proportion of 'industrial' lending originated by the Bank had declined. In Hong Kong as elsewhere in the East, the Bank grew, but competition developed. The Bank had its limitations and in this section it is appropriate to ask what in fact was the role of the Bank in Hong Kong during the period from the establishment of the People's Government in Peking (Beijing) to the end of 1961.

THE ROLE OF THE BANK

THE BANK, THE GOVERNMENT, AND RESPONSIBILITY

A view to the sea – a cautionary tale

Between the Hongkong Bank's Head Office building at 1, Queen's Road Central and Connaught Road there is an open area, immediately beyond which was the sea; the area is known as Statue Square (see Figure 8.1). It is a symbol to many of the apparently undoubted and allegedly unbridled power exercised by the Bank as the premier financial institution in this most money conscious of all territories. Despite the value of land in the Central District, the Bank has been sufficiently influential to enforce its right to a 'view to the sea'; its Chief Manager, the great TJ, could once look across Des Voeux Road, when it was but a path on the edge of the harbour, and see the ships passing; when the land beyond was reclaimed, he insisted on the right to continue to gaze at the shipping unimpeded. And when he left the Colony, his statue was placed across the street, which became known as 'Statue Square' – how appropriate, one visiting journalist noted, that the only statue in Statue Square should be that of Hong Kong's premier banker and that it should be placed in a public park – these facts said something about Hong Kong.

Those familiar with the pre-British history of the area are aware of a flourishing Chinese folklore. But for those dependent on post-1842 Hong Kong, 'The view to the sea' story must make do, for it is pure legend. Whether it is true or not may appear immaterial to any analysis of the Hong Kong polity, but this would be an error. Behind the story is the mistaken belief that the Hongkong Bank is all-powerful; the story supposedly provides the visual evidence of that hidden authority.

This is the same Hongkong Bank which was the victim of another myth – that it was the Far Eastern agent of an alleged 'British financial imperialism'. Major sections of this history have recorded the Bank's controversies with Government, including the Bank's efforts over a period of its first twenty years to prove its existence outside Hong Kong. A climax of a kind came when (Sir) Norman Young of H.M. Treasury urged that Sir Alexander Grantham, the Governor of Hong Kong, be ordered to summon Morse to tell him 'where he got off' (see Chapter 6). Morse didn't need to be told; he had won some battles with Government but had lost several more.

Having demolished the substance of the myth, the history must demolish the symbol.

The origins of the open area now fronting the Bank's Head Office building date back to the Praya Reclamation of the late nineteenth century and stem from the 1901 agreement made on the initiative of the Government that the

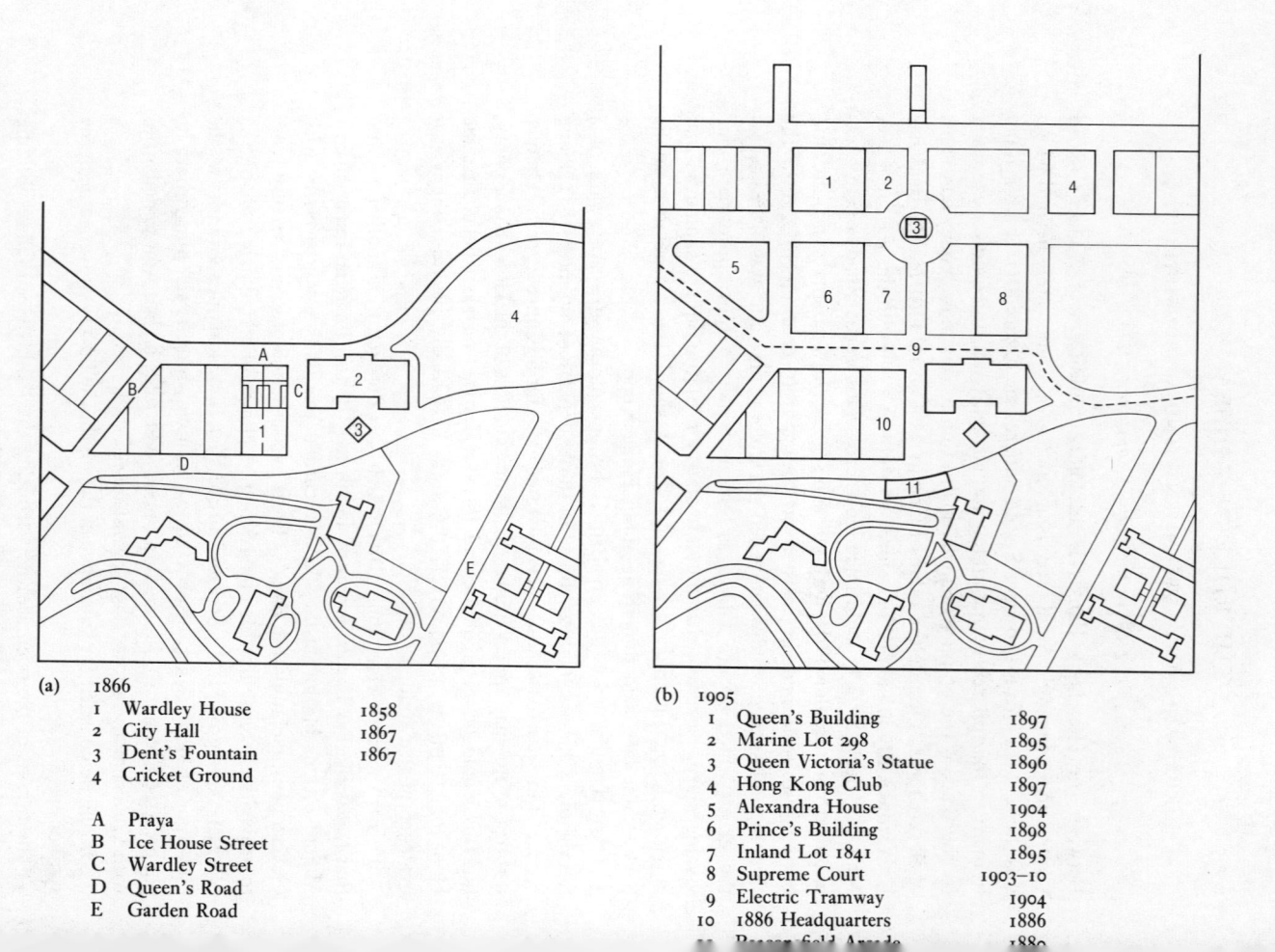

(a) 1866
1 Wardley House 1858
2 City Hall 1867
3 Dent's Fountain 1867
4 Cricket Ground

A Praya
B Ice House Street
C Wardley Street
D Queen's Road
E Garden Road

(b) 1905
1 Queen's Building 1897
2 Marine Lot 298 1895
3 Queen Victoria's Statue 1896
4 Hong Kong Club 1897
5 Alexandra House 1904
6 Prince's Building 1898
7 Inland Lot 1841 1895
8 Supreme Court 1903–10
9 Electric Tramway 1904
10 1886 Headquarters 1886

330

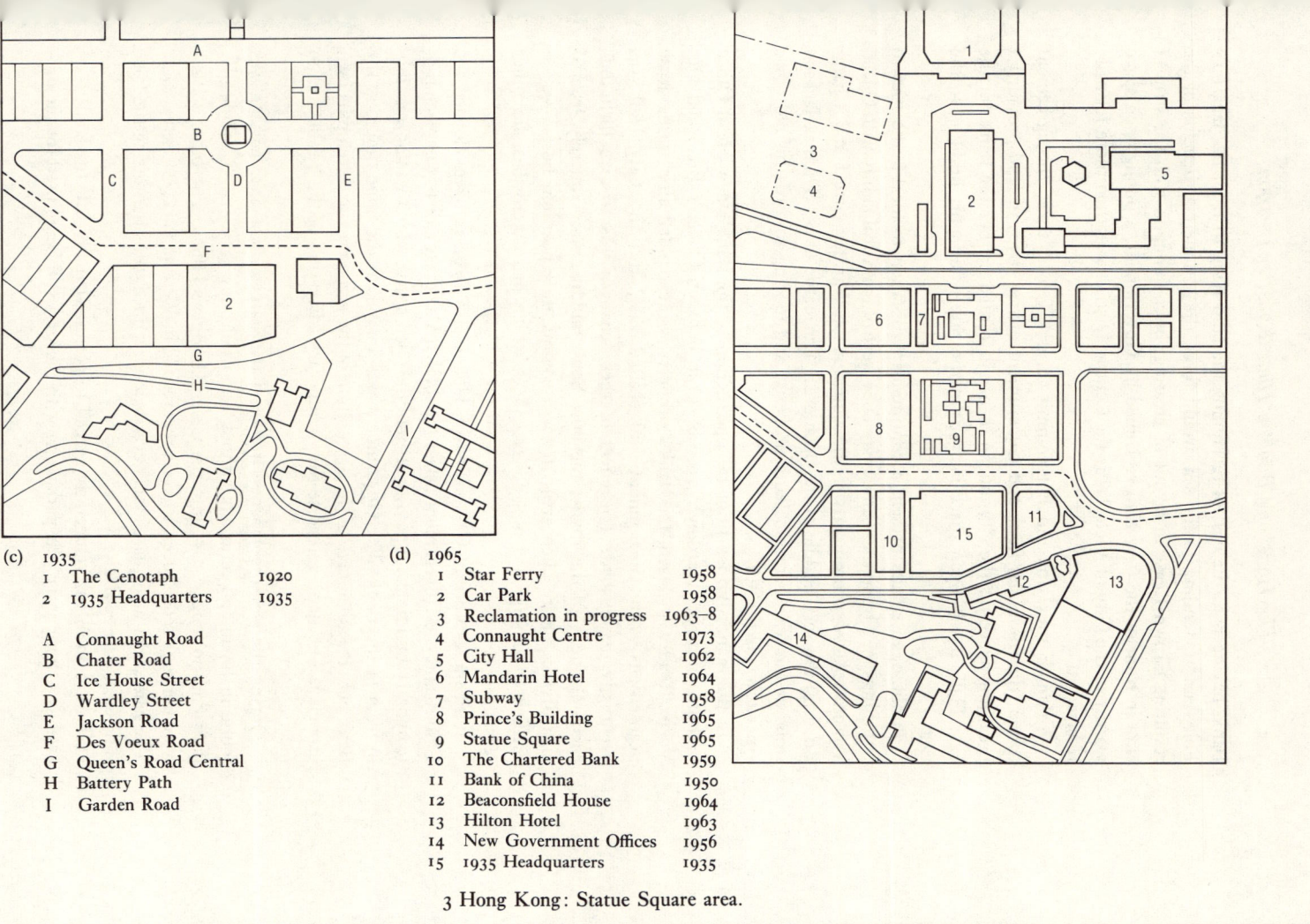

(c) 1935

1 The Cenotaph 1920
2 1935 Headquarters 1935

A Connaught Road
B Chater Road
C Ice House Street
D Wardley Street
E Jackson Road
F Des Voeux Road
G Queen's Road Central
H Battery Path
I Garden Road

(d) 1965

1 Star Ferry 1958
2 Car Park 1958
3 Reclamation in progress 1963–8
4 Connaught Centre 1973
5 City Hall 1962
6 Mandarin Hotel 1964
7 Subway 1958
8 Prince's Building 1965
9 Statue Square 1965
10 The Chartered Bank 1959
11 Bank of China 1950
12 Beaconsfield House 1964
13 Hilton Hotel 1963
14 New Government Offices 1956
15 1935 Headquarters 1935

3 Hong Kong: Statue Square area.

Bank, having paid the cost of reclaiming the land lying in front of 'Jackson's Folly' and extending to the sea, would forgo the commercial benefits of the resulting Crown Lease in favour of creating, in conjunction with the strip of land in front of the City Hall reclaimed by Government, a public open space worthy of the City of Victoria, as the Central District was then more formally referred to.

Although the Bank did not commit future Boards, there the agreement rested; the combined Bank and Government-owned strips of land provided a breathing space for the city, but in theory it fronted neither the Bank nor the City Hall; it was open space in front of the Supreme Court building to the east.

Public open spaces present a continuous temptation to local authorities to put things in. The statues came first. They were of the Royal family with Queen Victoria placed prominently at the junction of Wardley Street and Chater Road, in the very middle of the open area. The statue of Sir Thomas Jackson stood at the periphery, on Bank property, and looking towards his old office – not towards the sea.

In the manoeuvrings prior to construction of the Bank's new Head Office building of 1935, Wardley Street as it ran between Queen's Road and Des Voeux Road was closed, the Bank's property was expanded after formal lease negotiations with Government and shifted east, and the City Hall was eventually demolished. The effect of these changes was to give fortuitous encouragement to the myth; the new Bank building now squarely fronted virtually the entire open area; it was a commanding position, but it was an accidental consequence of land exchanges which had taken place for other reasons.

With the capture of Canton by the Japanese in 1939, refugees flooded the Colony and the Government asked for the Bank's agreement to the placing of temporary buildings on its own strip of the open space, which was now mainly in front of the Bank. The Government was anxious at the same time that the Bank not take advantage of the desecration of the green area to develop its own property. The Bank agreed to this 'temporary' diversion of the public area to meet a crisis.

During the war the Japanese removed the statues. Post-war, Jackson was found in Japan and returned, although he would now face east. Symbolically, he would no longer stare into the Chief Manager's Office. The other statues were not replaced; Queen Victoria was resited in Victoria Park, Causeway Bay. The name 'Statue Square' was nevertheless retained, thus permitting the false conclusions to be drawn.

In 1950 the Bank reluctantly agreed to permit virtually half the land to be used as a 'temporary' car park along with the strip still being used for the pre-war 'temporary' buildings. Five years later the Chief Manager, Michael Turner, apparently woke up to the fact that not only was the car park still in place but the temporary buildings were still there – they were housing a recreation club for minor staff.

Turner now tried to pressure the Government into removing the offending activities and replanting the ground so that the land could be rededicated to public use. So strong was his letter withdrawing Bank approval for the temporary uses of the open space that he took the unusual course of securing specific Board approval for the letter itself. The Governor was indignant; the right of the private car owner to leave his car in Central District was being challenged; the rights of junior staff to a club were being trampled. Nevertheless, the offending facilities were removed, the Governor unconvincingly threatening to replace the car park where the temporary buildings had been if any traffic problem should develop.

Meanwhile the land north of Connaught Road was being reclaimed; it was to include the site of a new multi-story car park, and, as a consequence of the Bank's pressure for the removal of the Statue Square car park, some priority was given the scheme. However, it was built to contain only three storeys of parking, and this has led some in Hong Kong to believe that the Bank, while apparently agreeing to a limited facility, had prevented its being higher because the Chief Manager still had the right to a view to the sea. Since even three storeys would block the view, there is little logic to the argument; on the other hand, the view from the Chief Manager's ninth-floor flat would remain unobstructed either way. In fact the height was determined by a Public Works Department cost/benefit analysis, which concluded that a five-storey building (the other alternative considered) would require stronger foundations and consequently be too costly in relation to the additional space provided.

The Bank, relying solely on its property rights and the agreement of 1901, had successfully protected the public's open space in Central against the inevitable urge of officials to undermine the purposes for which the area was created.

In 1957 the Board agreed to 'renew' the agreement of 1901 but with an exchange of land; the Bank at the request of Government, surrendered half its strip (Marine Lot 298) in exchange for approximately 14,800 square feet on the southeast corner of Statue Square; in effect, the Bank exchanged the northern half of its strip for the southern part of the Government's strip; the Bank now had the lease of the land immediately in front of the Bank, but only as far as Chater Road. The Bank no longer had the lease of land down to where the sea had been; meanwhile the sea had been pushed back beyond Connaught Road. At its centenary the Bank dedicated its land to the Urban Council and the whole area is now an integrated park, although sporadic attempts by

Government to use parts for this or that purpose continue to be monitored. In 1985, however, the Bank lost a round; a new entrance to Hong Kong's underground railway, the Mass Transit Railway (MTR), was opened on Bank land near Sir Thomas Jackson's statue.

Eternal vigilance, not the secret financial power of bankers, would appear the price of success if open spaces are to remain open. The park provides evidence of the Bank's concern for the community, as the Bank's major contribution to the environment; it is ironical, therefore, how the park's history has been interpreted. The story is, as suggested at the beginning, cautionary, and with that thought the history turns to the more important question of the Hongkong Bank as central bank. It may not have the power to force a view to the sea, but what of its role in the Hong Kong economy?

The central bank issue

The Hongkong Bank is one of the two banks in Hong Kong that are authorized by the Hong Kong Government to issue Hong Kong currency. It is principal banker to the Hong Kong Government but has no central bank role.

I.H. Macdonald, Executive Director, HSBC[a]

There are two basic questions: (i) what was the role of the Hongkong Bank in the Hong Kong economy and (ii) was the Hongkong Bank Hong Kong's central bank? The second question has to be qualified. If a central bank is conceived of as a bank owned by or constitutionally controlled by the state, then the Hongkong Bank, being owned by some 80,000 shareholders, is not a central bank. The Hongkong Bank's role may, however, lead to the conclusion that it acts as a central bank; therefore the second question should read, 'Was the Hongkong Bank Hong Kong's *de facto* central bank?'

The first is obviously important. Once the Bank's role has been described and perhaps judged, however, what difference does it make whether or not it is Hong Kong's *de facto* central bank?

However defined, the term 'central bank' implies an accepted subjection to the authorities which incorporated the bank, in this case, the Government of Hong Kong. If the bank operates outside its own territory of incorporation, the host Government may wish to know to what extent the bank reacts to normal banking criteria, to what extent it will operate to meet its Government's political policy, to what extent does it have responsibilities in its home economy which make it unsafe as a bank in the host country – or affect its role there?

These are legitimate concerns.

---

[a] Taken from his testimony given on June 25, 1980, before the Subcommittee on Commerce, Consumer and Monetary Affairs of the House Committee on Government Operations, U.S. Congress.

Whether a commercial bank is a *de facto* central bank would also appear to be a vital political question in the bank's home territory. This is partly because, like a national airline or an integrated steel mill, a central bank is a status symbol of sovereignty; the exercise of central bank functions by a commercial bank consequently appears to some as usurpation. From this it follows that if the commercial bank is acting as a central bank, whatever that may be, perhaps it should be made to stop.

Such a position may, however, be the consequence of (i) a misunderstanding of the role of central banks and (ii) an assumption that monetary policy cannot be determined and monitored by, or that banks cannot be supervised by a regular department of Government – despite the example provided by the coexistence at the Federal level in the United States of the Federal Reserve System *and* the Treasury, of the Office of the Comptroller of the Currency and the Federal Deposit Insurance Corporation.

Indeed, the subject is fraught with misconceptions and in the case of the Hongkong Bank certainly requires full consideration.

With the growing importance of the financial sector in Hong Kong's economy, the absence of a publicly owned central bank is then a legitimate subject for comment. On the assumption that a complex economy must, almost by definition, have a central bank, it is also reasonable to ask who, in the absence of a central bank, is performing its apparently essential functions. Following this line of reasoning, many conclude that the Hongkong Bank is Hong Kong's *de facto* central bank; some would go further and suggest, not entirely in jest and with some disagreement over the order of importance, that the Bank had been part of an 'inner government' – along with Jardine Matheson and the Jockey Club.

This attitude came in part from a misreading of history. Appendix Table A indicates that the Chief Manager's political role pre-war was limited. How could it be otherwise when the Board of Directors were responsible for the Bank's operations and the Chief Manager was the corporation's servant, whatever internal arrangements may have made mockery of such a statement. The Bank's servants played their part on specialized committees and as expert witnesses and advisers. Post-war, however, Morse was not only on the Board, he was Chairman; he was both in charge and servant. At another level it is clear that a major bank must take a responsible position relative to the stability of the banking sector. This is clear from Cleveland and Huertas' history of Citibank, when the National City Bank of New York played a major and responsible role in the solution of New York's banking crises prior to the inauguration in 1913 of the Federal Reserve System. It is clear from the shocked reaction of the Hongkong Bank's Manager when irresponsible jingoists suggested it encourage a run on the Russo-Asiatic Bank. More positively, the

Bank took a leading part in restoring confidence after the 1910 banking crisis in Shanghai.

A Government which has for some one hundred years actively avoided becoming responsible for the physical task of issuing the territory's paper currency might not be expected to promote plans for a central bank. There are several levels of argument. In the 1950s it was claimed, incorrectly, that, as Hong Kong was an entrepôt and its money supply externally determined, there could be no monetary policy and consequently no need for an especially created institution to implement it. Another argument at the technical level was, and is, based on the virtual absence of Government debt; there is a characteristic budget surplus; there was no money market function for a central bank to perform – at the end of 1955, for example, with post-1949 conditions virtually normalized, the Colony's public debt was $56 million and the accumulated budget surplus $263 million.

Central banks, it was more cogently noted, are expensive; they are staffed with highly paid experts – and in some third world countries central bank staff are paid outside the civil service rates to perform statistical and planning exercises which were, at least through the 1960s, considered unnecessary in Hong Kong.

Central banks were associated with controls and planning, and with central bankers experienced in European banking. Hong Kong did not need the former; as for the latter the Hongkong Bank feared the imposition of textbook standards on its pragmatic approach to banking, an approach which seemed appropriate in the East. Hong Kong Government officials feared the imposition of British economic policies which were unsuccessful in Britain and which, it was thought, would prove disastrous in Hong Kong.

The cogency of the arguments is actually irrelevant. The future of Hong Kong's economy was seen to depend in the first instance on a simple premise: no one without Hong Kong experience should meddle in Hong Kong's economy. A central bank was assumed to involve such meddling.[b]

Then as now the absence of a central bank in Hong Kong is consequent to the prevailing view that a central bank is as expensive as it is unnecessary. Its policy functions can be handled by appropriate Government departments, its technical banking implementation by the Government's commercial bankers.

The Hong Kong Government could not, however, avoid responsibility for

---

[b] Although central banking did not become universal in the region until the 1960s (except, significantly, in Singapore and Hong Kong), by 1952 there were already central banks in India, the Philippines, and Sri Lanka. The exchange banks were, in Morse's phrase, 'at loggerheads' with at least Sri Lanka's central bank. On the other hand Morse accepted that 'the times have changed and that in countries like Ceylon we can no longer be dogmatical or dictatorial'. (Morse to Gray, 1952.) Nevertheless, there was an attitude among Hongkong Bankers that the banking system would do well without them – especially in Hong Kong and Singapore.

the banking sector nor could it successfully maintain the argument that there was no scope for monetary policy in Hong Kong – if only because the retention of a system which allegedly made such a policy impractical was itself the consequence of a monetary policy decision. Policy of a complexity which has increased in the past thirty years can, however, be established by the executive and administered in a Government department, the Finance Branch; the actual banking implementation can still be performed, on instruction, by The Hongkong and Shanghai Banking Corporation as the principal Government bankers and by other banks as instructed by the authorities.

As the banking industry grew in importance the need for regulation became obvious; this was handled through the enactment of increasingly detailed legislation beginning in 1964 and through the appointment the following year of a Commissioner of Banking supported by his own staff. In a sense the Government was bringing to the territory the modern counterparts of those Colonial and Treasury officials who in earlier days had overseen the Colony's money and banking problems from London and directed affairs by correspondence with more or, usually, less relevance.

In all this the Hongkong Bank played a significant role, but does this make it the *de facto* central bank?

The confusion arises from focusing on the functions performed rather than on the nature of the institution's responsibility. A bank having a major market share in any economy will, if successful, be managed by senior bankers who have knowledge and skills; they sense the policy problems in the process of daily business; they will most likely be consulted by Government. Macdonald and Oliphant, quoted above, were not making incompatible statements.

The role of the Hongkong Bank has varied consistent with the overall situation. In the small pre-war Colony of Hong Kong, expertise was limited; the Governor sought bankers' advice and on occasion invited the Bank's Chief Manager (or the Chartered Bank's manager, T.H. Whitehead, in the late 1890s) to membership on his Councils.[c] Not all Chief Managers accepted – Sir Newton Stabb, for example, did not. If the Governor were naive and his local banker provided self-interested advice, there was in the old days a Treasury back-up; money and banking were reserved subjects. Post-war the Governor had official opinion even closer to hand.

Government officers professed sympathy with 'laissez-faire' principles, but their understanding of economic affairs did not, in those early days of post-war development, always permit them to judge the consequence of actions they

[c] According to Compton Mackenzie's account in *Realms of Silver* (p. 181), Whitehead's appointment to Hong Kong's Legislative Council not only met with the opposition of Sir Thomas Jackson but was also criticized by the Chartered Bank's board of directors. The board expressed the typical reaction – Whitehead's official duties would clash with the bank's interests. But Whitehead successfully held out.

considered economically neutral. A banker may not consciously espouse any economic philosophy, but he will feel consequences.

In 1955, for example, the Financial Secretary, A.G. Clarke, had moved surplus Government funds to London, thereby decreasing the base on which an increase in the money supply could be made, creating a tightness in the market which was detrimental to an expansion of credit commensurate with the growth of trade and industry. The Hongkong Bank sensed the problem at an early stage; the location of the Government's surplus should have been determined in the context of the Colony's need for an expanding money supply, instead it had been determined solely on the basis of obtaining a maximum return through investment in British Government securities. Through failure to recognize the policy potential of Hong Kong's monetary system, Clarke found himself faced with a tight credit market at a time when the obvious remedy, the repatriation of the surplus, was difficult. The gilt-edged securites he had purchased were depreciating and their sale would be impossible without a capital loss.

Turner informed Morse in London that he had made representations to the Financial Secretary to bring back the funds, that is to sell sterling to the exchange banks in return for Hong Kong dollar deposits, a process which would lead to the possibility of multiple credit expansion. He did this in the context of a banker unable to meet the legitimate credit requirements of his constituents, not as a 'central bank' adviser, not necessarily even as a member of the Executive Council. Nevertheless, Turner's intervention must have been received with the knowledge that he was Chief Manager of the territory's leading commercial bank and that he was a member of the Executive Council. The question of the Hongkong Bank's role cannot, therefore, be avoided.

The Hongkong Bank issued some 90% of the paper currency of Hong Kong, a task usually performed by a Government agency if not by the central bank. The issue in itself was, however, non-discretionary; the Bank performed a job for the Government and was in part reimbursed for it – whether sufficiently reimbursed was a matter for occasional acrimonious debate.[d] The Bank was the Government's principal (but not sole) banker, it also managed the clearing. The Bank was a member of the Exchange Banks Association, but in this period the Hongkong Bank's Hong Kong Manager was not the chairman – the Chartered Bank is the older of the two note-issuing banks in Hong Kong. (In the mid-

[d] The Bank was reimbursed for a percentage of the actual cost of the physical note issue and its transportation, the percentage being related to the proportion the excess issue bore to the total issue, see discussions in Volume III. The Bank was not reimbursed for the cost of such financial operations as providing the additional currency required, often for a period of a few days, during Chinese New Year. The resulting loss in exchange caused by the difference in the buying and selling rates for certificates of indebtedness was, in 1967 for example, £100,000.

1970s, at the instigation of the Bank's Deputy Chairman, M.G.R. Sandberg, the chair would alternate between the two note-issuing banks.)

The Hongkong Bank was concerned with the terms on which it did business and therefore made policy recommendations on such diverse matters as Sterling Area regulations, the operation of the open market, and the United Nations embargo; these representations were often made in the context of the welfare of Hong Kong – what is good for Hong Kong is good for the Hongkong Bank. Finally, there would be instances during banking crises when the Hongkong Bank acted *as if it were* a bank of last resort – but it did not always do so. Whether it acted or not was the consequence of case by case commercial assessment. Furthermore in serious crises the Chartered Bank cooperated or was on occasion independently involved.

There can be no doubt that, as the largest bank in the Colony, the Hongkong Bank was interested in policy and concerned with the soundness of the banking system; as the Government's banker it performed tasks which, had there been a central bank, would probably have been assigned to the central bank. But none of this made the Hongkong Bank itself even a *de facto* central bank.

The essential question is one of responsibility.

The Hongkong Bank is responsible to its constituents and to its shareholders but especially and specifically to the latter through an elected Board of Directors. A central bank is ultimately responsible to the public as determined by its constitution, which should state the manner and degree of its subordination to the Government of the day.

Although there is considerable coincidence in the interests of the shareholders of a major bank and the public of the economy in which it operates, there are times of divergence, especially in the matter of lender of last resort. The question of responsibility is then not a quibble, it is key. To return to the original questions, the term '*de facto* central bank', though useful at times, involves for a commercial bank a logical contradiction.

In the interests of shareholders there were risks which were unacceptable, there were limits beyond which the Bank could not go even in the interests of the banking system itself.

The Hongkong Bank was the banking system's clearing bank. There were 25 banks clearing through it; these themselves cleared for a total 37 non-member banks – accounting for 63 of a total 85 licenced banks in 1961. Two major share issues caused problems as the public transferred funds to the Hongkong Bank in depositing subscriptions for an oversubscribed issue. The Hongkong Bank, as the clearing bank or the bankers' bank, was virtually forced to feed out substantial inter-bank call loans – but at increasing rates. A second share issue for Jardine Matheson was 56 times oversubscribed, draining the banking system of funds; to save one 'native' bank the Hongkong Bank – after all-night deliberations and in coordination with the Chartered Bank – agreed to advance funds to meet its requirements.

When in 1965, however, the Bank felt that it would be unsound to offer further assistance to the Hang Seng Bank without a majority control through acquisition, the Hang Seng's board of directors had little choice but to accept this condition (see Chapter 15).[e] There have been many instances in the history of the Bank in Shanghai and Hong Kong when, alone or in cooperation with other major banks, the Hongkong Bank has made funds available to prevent the collapse of the native banking system. In the more serious cases, however, Government was induced to participate in the risk.

Since the 1950s in Hong Kong it has been the Government, not the commercial banks, which has accepted whatever public responsibility existed for the banking system. The Government, however, chose not to actively pursue its responsibilities in the banking sector; the principal commercial banks, led by the Hongkong Bank with the Chartered Bank and the 'Mainland Group' of Chinese banks, did indeed play at times a more significant role in the working of the system, with or without consultations, with or without instructions from Government, than might have been expected in a post-war economy.

Responsibility and loyalty – the broader context

The Hongkong Bank operates in territories throughout the East; newly sovereign Governments were particularly anxious that foreign banks licenced to provide banking services within a particular national jurisdiction should not instead act as the agents of a foreign authority or be constitutionally subject to foreign political interests. The Federation of Malaya would prove particularly sensitive, especially in view of the presence and potential political role of the state-owned Bank of China; the Hongkong Bank was at pains to insist on its private sector status. This would again be an issue in 1979 when the Bank sought to acquire Marine Midland Banks; the American banking authorities wished to ascertain whether the Hongkong Bank was tied to the interests of a foreign Government or whether it would operate in the interests of its

---

[e] The Hongkong Bank has in crises come to the rescue of local banks, put in management at Government request or, as in the case of Hang Seng, acquired a controlling interest. These are not necessarily central bank functions. The Bank's 1890 assistance to Baring's was at the request of the Bank of England, the takeover of Hang Seng was at the request of their board with the acquiescence of the relevant department of Government; in California the HBC was on occasion requested to consider acquiring a bank in trouble, and in 1970 it took over the Republic National Bank and Trust Company of Beverly Hills (see Chapter 13); in New York in 1985 the Bank acquired the business of Golden Pacific National Bank with the approval of the banking authorities. The Bank's decisions were based on both business assessment and sense of public responsibility in varying degrees in virtually each case.

shareholders as a private commercial bank. Satisfied that the latter was true, one American concern was removed.

The Hongkong Bank played (and continues to play) an active role in Hong Kong's economy; its chief executive and his deputies advised Governments; a Bank officer was seconded to manage the Exchange Control; the Bank issued the currency and handled the Government's banking business; but it was not nor was it expected to act as Hong Kong's central bank. There are limits beyond which it is imprudent for a commercial institution to act solely at the request of Government. As Grayburn had complained before the Pacific War, the Bank was on occasion expected to respond to a Government request and yet take the consequent banking risk; this risk successive chief executives continued to resist.

Sufficient evidence has been presented in this history to support the claim of an underlying distrust of the 'public' role of the Bank; the suggestion that the Bank were actually allowed or encouraged in such a role would be particularly resented.[f] An individual Bank Chief Manager might be nominated to the Executive Council, but that was a choice within the constitution; he might be consulted in matters of his expertise, but the Government did that on a wide scale without commitment. A governor, depending on his personal style, might call in a Chief Manager, as Grantham did, for a non-committal discussion. Nevertheless the Bank's senior Managers sensed suspicion of the Bank's motives and resentment – or, as one Manager expressed it, 'jealousy' – of its business strength, its 'power' in the banking sector. This was especially true in the 1960s during the period when Sir John Cowperthwaite was Financial Secretary. The gap was not as clearly defined as in India where the banker or 'box wallah' knew (or thought he knew) precisely how he was regarded by the Indian Civil Service, the 'Heaven born', but it was there, as it was in so many of the relationships between members of the Colonial civil service and the Foreign Service on the one hand and the business community on the other.

Cynical or presumptuous, there were nevertheless limits to the dictates of the profit motive, narrowly defined for the short run. The Hongkong Bank was a British overseas bank, it was subject to Sterling Area constraints, IMF prohibitions relative to gold trading, and UN embargoes. Anxious to serve the

---

[f] Specific instances come to mind: the attitude of the Treasury relative to the 'extraterritorial' position of the Bank; the comments passed over the attempt of the Bank to operate a Hong Kong Savings Bank; Governor Frank Swettenham's condescending attitude to the Bank's apparent issue of excess notes; Sir Sydney Caine's running battles with Grayburn and Morse. The method of expression used by Young may have been exceptional but the sentiments were not. The Bank had, however, been better appreciated in Hong Kong itself, and Morse had great respect for Sir Sydney, who, Turner hoped, might be induced to be the Bank's first economic expert, possibly succeeding Cassells. The mutual confidence of Bank and Government in Hong Kong perhaps climaxed in the relationship between Morse and Sir Alexander Grantham. There was a strongly felt reaction in the days of J.A.H. Saunders.

countries in which it operated, the Bank could be confronted with the problem of meeting conflicting national interests.

In such a situation, Sir Arthur Morse wrote to his London Manager, S.A. Gray, in 1952, 'It has always been our policy to conform to the wishes of H.M. Treasury.' On the specific question which prompted this comment, the financing of a shipment of natural rubber from Sri Lanka to China, such financing would have pleased both countries, but overriding this was the fact that the Treasury had asked British banks, in compliance with the provisions of the embargo, not to finance such shipments. 'I feel', wrote Morse, 'it is incumbent upon us to allow such business to pass us by.'[g]

The question of conflicting loyalty was particularly vexed because it was a new experience for the Hongkong Bank as an interregional corporation. Pre-war the interests of the imperial territories had been in the last analysis centrally determined; the Hongkong Bank could resolve conflicts as between British territories through accepted advice or instructions from authorities which were ultimately responsible to the Treasury; in others – with the exception of China and, perhaps, the Philippines – it played but a marginal role. In the Philippines its role in the American period was defined by regulations. As for China, the Hongkong Bank considered its loyalty to China, rightly or wrongly, as consistent with its British status. Underlying all these arguments was the fact that the banks were not subject to post-war type national expectations as to their role; they were service institutions designed primarily for the benefit of their shareholders and constituents, including Governments, and Governments established the rules of play. The concomitant of non-regulation was non-expectation; where pre-war Governments did not hold such views, they instituted the necessary constraining legislation.

Realization of the magnitude of the problem came slowly, in part because the newly independent territories were, at first, permitting considerable continuity of behaviour. When that realization came, the impact on the Bank's decision-making process was mitigated by the increasing role being played by central banks, national banking departments or their equivalent, and the appropriate restrictive legislation. Bank managers did not have to be loyal, they had only to be law-abiding – if that were possible and if pressures for 'political donations' could be avoided.

The confusions of the 1950s can be illustrated by Michael Turner's 1958 letter informing his senior Singapore Foreign staff – all British subjects – that as likely long-term residents the Board of Directors had agreed it would be

---

[g] This must have been particularly upsetting for the Hongkong Bank in view of the fact that China, apparently dissatisfied with the Bank of Ceylon, was attempting to shift the business to the British banks. The Chartered Bank of India, Australia and China, the Mercantile Bank of India, and the National Bank of India similarly declined the business which was consequently offered once again to the Bank of Ceylon.

perfectly all right for them to become Singapore citizens. There was the opinion that not to take out citizenship might even be interpreted as a slight. That Turner's recommendation was a gesture of goodwill to the newly self-governing city-state of Singapore, a gesture of faith in its future is undeniable, but it neglects the Koelle factor.[h] Admittedly the cases were not identical since under Commonwealth citizenship laws the possibility of dual nationality was foreseen and, at that time, accepted.

Only a few months later the Board was informed that the Bank was under pressure from the Governor of Singapore to support the candidacy of Lim Yew Hock, presumably to block the 'inevitable' victory of the People's Action Party (PAP); the Board refused to sanction a contribution. If the Bank's British officers had become Singapore citizens, the problem would have been even more confused.

As local nationalism developed, local attitudes to dual citizenship would change, together with concepts of a sovereign monetary policy; the two developments were not unrelated.

In several territories the Hongkong Bank has performed tasks which, in other economies and in more recent times, are performed by the central bank. Nowhere is this more obvious than in Hong Kong. The Bank in performing these tasks in the absence of a central bank treats them as a commercial operation tempered (i) by a recognition of the public responsibility which banks, perhaps unique in the private sector, have always borne, (ii) by an acceptance of the principle that as a British overseas bank it must be responsive to the policies of H.M. Treasury and the Bank of England, and (iii) a coincident recognition that, subject to this overriding factor, the Bank must be sensitive to the requirements of and be obedient to the regulations promulgated by the several national banking authorities in its area of operation – including those in Hong Kong.

Although the above comments have taken the discussion beyond Hong Kong and the related issue of central banking, the Bank's concept of its responsibilities in Hong Kong are but a special case, which may be better appreciated in a more general context. Indeed, it is in both the general and the specific contexts that

---

[h] F.T. Koelle (East in 1894) was born in Constantinople (Istanbul) of a German missionary father serving with the Church of England and a British mother; he was educated at Marlborough and emigrated to Canada. He returned to England on hearing that his earlier application to the Hongkong Bank had been successful, and he entered London Office in 1890, served in the East, and was appointed Accountant Hamburg in 1903. At this time he was apparently stateless, not having resided a sufficient period in a British territory since his majority to be eligible for British naturalization. He enquired and was informed that his decision to become a German citizen would not affect his career in the Bank; in 1906 he was confirmed Manager Hamburg; in 1920 he was forced to resign from the Bank's service on the grounds he was a German citizen (see Volumes II and III).

the question of the Bank's role in Hong Kong's industrial development should now be considered.

THE BANK AND HONG KONG'S INDUSTRIAL DEVELOPMENT

Nowhere in the Bank's Archives or in its leaders' statements can one find any self-conscious grandiose design to industrialize Hong Kong.
– Y.C. Jao, 'Financing Hong Kong's Industrialization'

General background

Factors favourable to Hong Kong's industrial growth
Hong Kong's traditional role had been that of an entrepôt and legal and military base for British activities in the Far East. There had been manufacturing in Hong Kong before – none knew this better than the Hongkong Bank which had financed it to the Bank's early cost (see Volume I) – but with China's tariff autonomy, there was an advantage to being located within the Republic; with the establishment of Imperial Preference in the 1930s, this advantage was only partially offset. Furthermore, the entrepôt trade required some industrial support, for example, dockyard-related operations and shipbuilding.

There was industry in Hong Kong before the influx of Shanghai refugees from 1948–1951, but inadequate statistics make any quantification difficult. One series estimates on an assumed percentage of total exports that Hong Kong's domestic exports for 1950 were valued at $420 million; if so, then between 1950 and 1966, when domestic exports totalled $5,730 million, their growth had been at the compound annual rate of 17.7% (approximately the same both at current prices and in real terms). As the bulk of Hong Kong manufactured products were exported, these figures provide some indication of the magnitude of growth in the manufacturing sector. Since the best estimates indicate a growth rate for GDP of 8.3% in current prices over the same period, there must have been a significant increase in the proportionate importance of the manufacturing sector. This is consistent with the figures (probably underestimated) for 1950 of 1,752 registered factories with a workforce of 91,986 compared to 1966 – 10,413 industrial undertakings and 424,155 workers.

Although the actual causes of successful growth are always difficult to ascertain, the factors which were objectively favourable to manufacturing and its development in Hong Kong are not. New equipment for China's industries reached Hong Kong in years of doubt; the machines remained in the Colony, and China's Shanghai entrepreneurs, many of them known to the Hongkong Bankers, left China. In Hong Kong they met both their capital and their labour supply; the former fishing village of Tsuen Wan became a virtual Shanghai dialect speaking enclave. Planned joint ventures for industry on the mainland of China with foreign capital did not materialize, but the funds for investment were available in Hong Kong; the trading hongs, long experienced in the management of associated companies with diverse activities, including manufacturing, were prepared to invest in new industry.

The facilities developed for an entrepôt are, to a point, similar to those necessary for an industrial development which must be, given the size of the domestic market, almost entirely export-oriented – shipping services, international business contacts, and international banking facilities. Furthermore in developing Hong Kong's post-war trade, payment arrangements had been made which were equally beneficial to an export industry. Perhaps the most important of these was toleration of an open market in foreign exchange, despite the fact that Hong Kong had been incorporated into the Sterling Area.

The Hong Kong open market

> I don't know anything about exchange control, Bennett, but when you get a question asked you, say to yourself, is it good for Hong Kong? If so, say yes. Is it bad for Hong Kong? If so, say no.
> – Sir Alexander Grantham, 1955[1]

The purpose of the open market was to permit the coexistence within Hong Kong of Sterling Area regulations and a free exchange of certain currencies, to permit the finance of intra-Sterling Area trade without adverse impact on the Far Eastern entrepôt activities of the port. This was done through two virtually separate banking groups (at least as far as U.S. dollar exchange is concerned), the Authorized Foreign Exchange Banks, a group including the Hongkong Bank, and the unauthorized. The former dealt with foreign exchange at official rates subject to Sterling Area constraints; the latter dealt on the open market at rates which varied with supply and demand. At its simplest, this meant that a Hong Kong resident with a current account in the Hongkong Bank who desired U.S. dollars for, say, the import of commodities which did not qualify for an allocation of official exchange would transfer funds to an unauthorized bank, for example, the Hongkong Bank's friends, the Hang Seng Bank, and purchase U.S. dollars on the open market at the open market rate. Alternatively, the customer might cross the banking hall and deal separately with the compradore.

---

[1] The Hongkong Bank supplied the Government with an officer to run the exchange control; when seconded that Bank officer became a civil servant and as such would be introduced to the Governor. The Governor's instructions to N.H.T. Bennett as recalled in the latter's oral history are recorded. Bennett, as a banker, was often able to advise bankers and merchants on how to present a case in ways which permitted him to say, 'Yes.'

The Hongkong Bank could still handle the financing of the imports if the customer supplied the Bank with the U.S. dollars he had thus purchased.

One purpose of the exchange controls was to prevent dollars earned by Sterling Area residents from being exchanged on Hong Kong's open market; physical controls prevented cargo shunting designed to achieve the same purpose. The advantage to Hong Kong of the combined system was that a Hong Kong resident could on the one hand request official U.S. dollar exchange, but if he were refused by Exchange Control – and official exchange was granted on a more restricted basis than in the United Kingdom – he could purchase his U.S. dollars on the open market.

The supply of open market dollars on visible account arose from the fact that, with certain exceptions, exchange earned from the shipment to the dollar area of goods which had originated in Hong Kong, China, Macau, the Republic of Korea, or Taiwan did not have to be sold to one of the twenty-eight Hong Kong authorized banks at official rates but could be sold on the open market. The trade-originated demand for U.S. dollars arose from the need of the Hong Kong importer to finance his shipment from the dollar area – provided it were destined for Hong Kong or the territories listed above – with U.S. dollars purchased on the open market.

The financing of invisibles, including capital movements, was also handled on the open market, but lack of balance of payments statistics for Hong Kong makes this difficult to analyse. In concluding that Hong Kong was not a drain out of the Sterling Area, but was a net recipient of funds, Leslie Pressnell noted that of the £10 million sterling remitted to Hong Kong in 1959 perhaps 40% were overseas Chinese remittances which went to local or mainland families, 20% were involved in switch sterling operations, and the balance was used for investment in real estate, in shares, or in speculation.

Resident sterling might be converted indirectly through the open market as a consequence of securities sales; depending on New York rates, switch sterling transactions, that is, sterling obtained by the sale of sterling securities owned by non-residents of the Sterling Area, might be profitably effected in Hong Kong. A variety of capital operations effected their exchange through Hong Kong, and although the authorized banks, including the Hongkong Bank, were not involved at the point of Hong Kong dollar/U.S. dollar open market exchange, they might be involved at all other stages, providing the background for the later development of international operations which would develop in the next decade and after.

The advantages of the open market were also enjoyed, although on a more regulated basis, by territories of the Malayan Currency Union, that is, by Singapore, the Federation of Malaya, British North Borneo, Sarawak, and the State of Brunei. The arrangements whereby these transactions were allowed facilitated Singapore's role as a Southeast Asian entrepôt; they were limited by the capacity of the Hong Kong open market to provide U.S. dollars at acceptable rates.

Other factors
Underlying any investment decision was the concern that Hong Kong might not survive; peaceful India seized Goa and international opinion did not favour the survival of colonial enclaves. All that can be said on this factor is that (i) the concern was real, (ii) significant investment however did take place, and (iii) Hong Kong remained a British territory.

The problem was not China itself but its role in the Korean War and the subsequent American embargo on the shipment of strategic goods to China, America's freezing of China's dollar assets in December 1950, and the imposition of a U.N. embargo in May 1951. These measures affected Hong Kong because the American authorities made assumptions relative to the actual ownership of Hong Kong registered U.S. dollar assets and on the Chinese origins of Hong Kong domestic exports. Sir Arthur Morse commented on the earlier developments at the March 1951 meeting of shareholders:

The sudden application of these measures without warning led to the disruption of contracts already made and a good deal of uncertainty and chaos. It also upset the industry of the Colony by depriving it of cotton and other raw materials essential for its own needs and for its exports to markets outside China, and it jeopardized the livelihood of its workers and the indispensable functions served by this great port... We have endeavoured to the best of our ability and with the utmost frankness to comply with the strict terms of these regulations.
I trust, however, that I shall not be deemed lacking in appreciation of the urgent motives which impelled our American friends to apply these measures if I stress the vital danger of undermining confidence in the absolute obligation and ability of banks to honour their commitments under commercial credits on which the whole vast system of the world's trade has been built. To plunge the sword into the delicate texture of international trade and finance may cause irreparable injury and shatter faith in the sanctity of contract.
We cannot therefore see eye to eye with the United States Authorities in regard to the embargo or freeze.

Despite this strong view expressed by Morse as Chairman, Bank correspondence suggests very strongly that the Bank was careful to keep the relevant provisions while negotiating for the release of funds which were not in fact China Mainland connected.

Hong Kong's population, swollen by refugees to 1.6 million just prior to the Pacific War, was only 600,000 in 1945; by 1948 there were an estimated 1.8 million in the territory and, with the flood of refugees in the years immediately following, the population probably reached 2.5 million in 1954. This placed a considerable burden on the Colony's services, but the overcrowding probably did not affect the efficiency of services directly connected with or serving industry. Investment in electricity kept capacity in line with growing demand; between 1948 and 1956 consumption had more than quadrupled and reached a total 650 million kwh.

By 1961 statistics would show that over 25% of Hong Kong's population had arrived since the People's Army reached Canton in 1949. These included the skilled workers who were to play so important an initial role in Hong Kong's industrialization. Population growth was sudden, disruptive, costly, but an essential part of the process which transformed the economy.

Given Hong Kong's apparently insecure position, the disruption caused by the freeze and embargoes, and the existence of an open market, one might reasonably assume a significant capital outflow and minimal domestic investment. Undoubtedly funds moved to North America, but the open market rates suggest this export of capital could not have been overwhelming. The fact is that there were factors favourable to investment and these improved dramatically after 1953 when the Korean Armistice was in effect.

First of all, Hong Kong itself, internally, was well-governed and policed; there was stability of a kind which did not exist everywhere in Southeast Asia, and any outflow of capital was, as noted above, more than offset by an inflow from Overseas Chinese and others who had links with Hong Kong.

Secondly, although the Government of Hong Kong was British, there was a Chinese overtone to it, an Asian flavour – the open market for example was a blatant example of the multiple exchange rate practices the IMF was anxious to eliminate. Hong Kong chose to see it as a dual banking system 'suitable for Hong Kong' – a phrase much used 'to explain' to outside economic experts and central bankers that regulations suitable for the rest of the world were inapplicable here; little surprise that the Hong Kong Government and the bankers did not encourage calculation of comparative national income and balance of payments statistics, suspected experts and central banks, and found in the catch-phrase, '*laissez-faire*', a useful and somewhat flexible 'explanation'.

Thirdly, those able to emigrate, once having secured their right of unrestricted reentry to the safe haven of their choice, could safely return to Hong Kong. It was in Hong Kong, after all, that the skilled labour remained and in which initial business contacts had been made before the flight from the Mainland. In Hong Kong there existed a unique combination of British law – and British banking – and a Chinese approach. And for these entrepreneurs, Hong Kong was still, after all, 'China'.

Finally, the impediments imposed by the American authorities and the United Nations were relaxed or abandoned after 1953. In the shipment of U.S. dollar notes in open market dealings, for example, the Americans, except where

Mainland interests were obvious, took a surprisingly lenient position; industrial exports of Hong Kong products came to be covered by Government-issued comprehensive certificates of origin, which were accepted worldwide as evidence that no Mainland economic interest existed.

The entrepreneur decided to remain and invest. He had know-how, access to skilled labour, a cooperative Government relative to land and labour policy. He lacked adequate financing. Financing, therefore, is the subject of the following section.

The Bank's historical policies and their modification

There would seem to have been several impediments to industrial finance in Hong Kong by the Hongkong Bank, if the clichés of pre-war banking prevailed. First, there was the prohibition against Managers' lending to the movie industry, for shipping, or for airplanes; the Hongkong Bank did not take an equity interest or become involved in management. There had been exceptions, many of them unfortunate. Then too, the Bank dealt with Chinese customers through the compradore because members of the Foreign staff were unqualified to judge the merits of the proposition as put forward. The Chinese businessman was in many cases unable to speak English, to present an acceptable balance sheet, or to offer security the worth of which could be determined without compradorial interpretation. Furthermore, the Bank was an exchange bank and its profitability and indeed its solvency depended on a turnover of funds based on transactions secured by marketable property on a margin sufficient to cover the Bank's involvement. Security in the form of goods, 'pawn-broking' as some referred to old-style banking, made particular sense in a business society in which bankers did not visit their clients; what the local Club failed to supplement in the way of business information had to come through the office. This was a real limiting factor. Only in a time of crisis could certain of these impediments be overcome through the intervention, for example, of the Chinese Chamber of Commerce, as in the Shanghai crisis of 1910 (see Volume II, Chapter 8).

Post-war these impediments remained, but their implications were reexamined and methods devised which in many cases permitted loans otherwise beyond the scope of exchange banking. Morse pressed by the Hong Kong Government to consider loans for movie productions which would be politically neutral declined to consider the risk, although shortly afterwards loans to Singapore's film industry were made. Shipping and airplane loans were made, but not by branch Managers; Chief Managers may modify the standing instructions. And not all the innovations proposed by branch Managers in Mongkok and other industrial areas were immediately accepted; risks were being taken and, on occasion, reconsidered by the Hong Kong Manager, especially in the days of R.P. Moodie.

Although it has been said in a general way that the compradore became unnecessary not so much when foreigners became more proficient in Chinese as when the Chinese adopted Western business methods, this is, in many specific cases, an exaggeration of the change. The Bank, in its industrial lending, did ask for balance sheets, and, on occasion, the Chinese firm produced them, although often after the loan had been made. The fact is that 'pawnbroking' could not be entirely dispensed with; once the Bank Manager was willing to visit the customer, he could assess at several levels; the lien of property or a mortgage was still seen as a wise back-up to the Manager's assessment.

The change came most obviously in the matter of assessment. Pre-war the foreign bank manager knew local businessmen only through the compradore; he had no independent source of information – with exceptions, as the partially successful efforts relative to chettiars and local trading firms by the Colombo Manager suggest (see Volume II, Chapter 2). Post-war the separation of the communities was nowhere so great; eventually British banker and Chinese customer might belong to the same social club, the Junior Chamber of Commerce, or one of the other service clubs. In Hong Kong and in the newly independent countries, the new relationships, which were just being hinted at pre-war, have facilitated the obtaining of business information across communal lines. The compradore was first reinstated, a reflex return to normalcy; he then faded away, so that no one seems quite to remember when the system effectively 'ended'. The fact is, it didn't 'end'; it changed often imperceptibly until some Manager, wondering perhaps what a compradore did, changed the name with or without fanfare, with or without a change of person. Oliphant's circular, quoted in Chapter 7, gave recognition to what had happened.

And if banker and customer still didn't speak the same language, the banker or the customer brought an interpreter with him.

Although the Hongkong Bank had lent to industry before – to Hong Kong's 'bug-bears' in the 1870s, to Shanghai textile mills in the 1880s, to Li Hung-chang's modernization efforts and to compradore Wu Mao-ting's projects in Tientsin in the 1890s – this was not 'precedential' information; its use, if any, would have been marginal and against those who said, 'The Bank *never* lends for...', but the proposer still had to make his case.

In the early days of Hong Kong's post-war industrialization, in 1948–1953, all was still tentative; it is therefore not surprising that loans to these early factories took a form as familiar as possible to an 'exchange bank' and were rationalized with familiar arguments. All this would be regularized eventually, beginning under Oliphant as Manager Hong Kong and O.P. Edwards in

The Hongkong Bank in Hong Kong, 1947–1962

Mongkok. By the mid-1950s there were responsible Managers asking pointed questions about equity investment; firms helped on their way by the Hongkong Bank were prospering, but the Bank was left only with its interest revenue.[j] Moodie pressed a particular case; Turner refused consideration; Moodie recalls that this was just as well, his candidate went bankrupt in a few years. Equity investment too had been known in the Bank's history, and Oliphant with Manchurian experience would remember Tschurin's department store, fully owned and managed by the Hongkong Bank – but the choice had not been the Bank's. Tschurin's, heavily financed by the Bank, had defaulted. The equity question was not resolved in the period to 1961.

The overall situation, 1948–1953

The story begins not with the refugees but with post-war economic and political instability in China; the first textile mills were of Shanghai origin, and the decisions were made in the main office by Adamson as the Hong Kong Manager. As he recalls it:

It was about the year 1948 that the Bank was first called on to help with the financing of cotton mills in Hong Kong. The industry was new to the Colony and no one could say for certain that it would prove successful. There were serious drawbacks since Hong Kong provided no raw materials, no basic home market for the finished products, and very little in the way of skilled labour. Moreover an adequate supply of water and of power was not assured, to begin with at least.

On the other hand the men who were proposing to set up the mills had wide experience of the industry which they had gained in Shanghai, no easy school, and they knew what they were about. They were men of substance, too. Many of them had ordered and paid for new machinery from England during or immediately after the war [in part from CNC sold against blocked sterling]. It was now coming forward and in those days of scarcity was worth its weight in gold.

It had originally been intended for the owners' mills in Shanghai or other Chinese cities, but owing to the political insecurity in China since the surrender of the Settlements the British Colony seemed a much safer place in which to establish it. There was no difficulty experienced in bringing a nucleus of skilled labour from Shanghai to start things off.

Sites for the mills had to be acquired, buildings to house the machinery and the workers had to be erected, and there were many incidental expenses. Usually all that was asked of the Bank in the first place was to advance the cost, or a substantial part of the cost, of the land and buildings against a general debenture over the whole undertaking. The owners put up the rest of the capital, and theirs was the first risk. This was a reasonable proposition from the Bank's point of view, provided the Bank could be persuaded that there were good prospects of success for the venture and this the mill

---

[j] The Hongkong Bank had equity investment in the British and Chinese Corporation, but that was a holdover from the particular circumstances of Bank/Jardine relations in 1898. Since the war the Bank had acquired an interest in the South China Morning Post, Ltd, and the Far Eastern Economic Review, Ltd, but in this period the Bank did not consider these as 'investments' in the accounts. These companies also had a special history, for which see Chapter 12.

owners, after many lengthy discussions, were able to do with the result that the necessary finance was forthcoming.

The atmosphere of the time is caught by G.M. Sayer, Chief Manager 1972–1977, who returned to Hong Kong after four years in Tianjin (Tientsin). His account is important because it confirms (i) the beginning of the breakdown of the compradoric system pre-war and (ii) the impact of the Shanghai industrialist on the system in Hong Kong post-war. The old Crown Colony of Hong Kong had its pre-war manufacturing, but this was not sufficient to change the colony's 'backwater' image relative to the International Settlement of Shanghai or to the complexity of the Greater Shanghai economy.

The Hongkong Bank traditionally didn't deal directly with the Chinese. It had only started about 1950. In fact one's trading, even in the early 1950s, was still through the compradore. The majority of Chinese business came through the compradore, including particularly business from Chinese banks who put business through us because we had the machinery to process import and export bills, etc. But there were many Chinese who started to deal with us directly. Most of them were in fact not Cantonese; they were Shanghai people.

In Shanghai, and I suppose to some extent in Tientsin, the direct dealing between the Chinese and the Bank had started just before the war and had been cultivated since then. So the Shanghai people were generally more sophisticated and better educated and so on, and certainly more commercially knowledgeable. Being Shanghai people they didn't want to go through a Cantonese compradore, who took a cut on everything they did. So they started to go direct, and the Bank was prepared at that time to do this. This was a crucial change, and it was without any particular direction from the management who tended to take a pre-war view on things.

Hong Kong was expanding at a rapid rate and the compradore really couldn't physically handle the business. He was not really qualified to either because a completely new type of business was going on. Vast imports of pharmaceuticals and smuggling, and goodness knows what else. Secondly, [as noted], the Shanghai people didn't necessarily want to deal through a Cantonese compradore. I mean, everything was nicely parcelled out in pre-war Hong Kong like it tends to be in any society. There was big rapid change going on, and this was reflected in Hong Kong...

And this is where it started.

The Chinese clients, and they were Shanghai clients, started to go directly to the Bank and dealing with the officers of the Bank. At that time we were all Foreign staff officers...

...doing business with the Chinese is not all that different from doing business with anybody else. There are set, fixed commercial methods. You required a little bit of adaptability here and there because their English was not all that good and so on and so forth. Their written English, particularly, was not good. And sometimes they had to employ their own clerks whom they couldn't necessarily trust. But again, you built up a mutual relationship. You help them when they're in need and the Chinese won't forget.

One talks about the Chinese being clever, and they are clever, and, whether he's your best friend or your worst enemy, he's still trying to make money out of you. Make no mistake about that. On the other hand, if you do a man a favour, and you help him or anything like that in his struggle, he will play the game. He won't try to take advantage of you.

I think the Bank's always blown with the wind a little bit, and times were changing in Hong Kong, and this was nothing new. I think people always talk about the wonderful, new Industrial Revolution in Hong Kong, but a lot of it was brought on by the circumstances of the region, and every banker has to move with the way things are, as they are presented to him in running his business.... you can't afford not to take advantage of the opportunities that present themselves.

This is how the Chinese saw it. Hong Kong had the machinery and the expertise, they got the people here. It's an environment here where we're not subject to petty officialdom or exchange controls or anything like that. It looked good, and they started on that. The Bank understood this, and we took risks as well in sponsoring and financing this.

Hong Kong just made the best of the circumstances that were prevailing at that time. They were still difficult times in Hong Kong... very difficult and uncertain times... and the Bank couldn't do anything else but make the best of circumstances, but they did very well in this.

This has been the history of the Bank, to be practical about things and do the best you can. I think at the time I continued to be very much influenced by what had taken place in China, realizing this was a major revolution by any standards in any period of history. And it was having its impact on this little place, Hong Kong. Hong Kong itself was in a good position.

The limitation of risk – and market share

Adamson's experience confirmed the need for the Bank to assess not only the Hong Kong operation but also the relevant world markets and the manufacturers' relations thereto. This in turn suggested that a branch Manager, usually Mongkok (see below), would never be in a position to assess the Bank's exposure; he would on occasion be frustrated by the main Hong Kong office despite the particular merits of a case.

Later when operations were under way the Bank was required to open confirmed credits for imports of raw cotton and from time to time had to make advances against cotton stocks at the mills and against cotton yarn waiting to be sold and shipped. Prices for both commodities fluctuated a good deal, exposing the mills to losses, and before long serious difficulties were encountered in disposing of the yarn, which strained the mills' finances and in some cases got them into deep water with the Bank.

As Oliphant, then Mongkok Manager, confessed,

I think probably I was trying to lend more than they wanted to lend. I could see the opportunities, but they could see the overall picture better because I was concerned purely with Mongkok. This was the centre of the newly arising manufacturing industry in Hong Kong, of all kinds. It was the centre of it – the factories were going up round about...

Eventually, in the mid-1950s, overexposure to the textile industry at a time of tight money when the Bank's liquidity ratio had fallen below 50% worried the Chief Manager, Michael Turner. But cutting back, though necessary, could have long-run implications and account for the Hongkong Bank's loss of market share. To effect a cutback was, as Moodie put it, 'very simple'.

All you had to do was the next time the manager of the cotton mill came in and said, I want another five lacs, you would say, all right, it will cost you whatever the percentage was, call it six or seven percent, anyway something above the best rate. He would then say, oh, no, far too much, and you'd say, well, I'm very sorry, I can't do better.

Whereupon he took his request away to some other bank.

Some of them [then took all of their business away. But] we were up to our necks.

I think it was Mike actually who brought the problem up, and he said, you don't think we're getting too overladen with cotton mills? Some time later he said, I think we'd better pull our horns in a bit.

And just shortly after that [an important textile company] came, and they wanted an extra whatever it was. I said, well, the best I can do was whatever it was, three percent. And they said, oh, that's no good, it will have to be better than that. And I said, well, I'm sorry. He went away to [another] bank, lock, stock and barrel. Well, we didn't really mind. I mean, there might have been a time when we were sorry afterwards. That situation might have arisen, but as it was we then had more than we wanted anyhow.

Early experiences of Oliphant in Mongkok

Top-level encounters with larger manufacturers would always be part of the Hong Kong scene; the more exciting story, however, developed at the branch level. Furthermore, when Oliphant went to Mongkok in 1952, it was his first managerial assignment.

...I was very lucky in that the Korean War had started, and this really was the generation of industry in Hong Kong. A number of enamelware factories had been set up, and the cotton spinners, and weavers to some extent, were there – the whole thing was beginning. There'd been this awful setback when trade with China was suddenly stopped by the United Nations, a number of firms were in difficulties, but Mongkok was the new centre of industry, and the place was growing fast at the time I was there. The industry was really bursting forth, and I was very lucky to be there at the time.

I don't think that I was given any particular instructions regarding [my assignment], but it seemed to me there was an opportunity to really get in on the ground floor, there was so much to be done. There were so many firms either starting up, or expanding, and it was a question of sorting out which were most likely to repay what we lent them. I was told later, by a Chinese, that I was known amongst them as 'The Father of Hong Kong Industry', but that, of course, is greatly overstating the case.

[I was prepared to lend to] anything that had a good prospect of success. Enamelware was doing well at the time and there were ten or a dozen enamel factories, but the local population very much tended to jump on the band-wagon and within a short time there were thirty or more factories.

Well, then one had to look out for overproduction.

[There were] enamelware, and spinning, weaving, cotton and wool, which was only just beginning – I think there was only one woollen mill at that time, Pacific. But it began with enamelware and then it spread out from there into rubber shoes, leather shoes, gloves. Different things kept coming up. Pearl buttons, later plastic buttons, there was a great spread of industry and one garment manufacturer we financed wanted buttons which he could not get, so he started pearl button factories, and, as the fashion, or the cost, of pearl buttons became too high, then he went into plastic buttons. And you might get a conglomerate all under single ownership or you might get different people starting different industries independently.

Many people would rent premises, they would get their machinery on hire purchase, they would possibly not put enough of their own money into a project, and one had to beware of them. One went rather carefully into the structure of each company and, if they had a reasonably good market and they were making, as I say, a reasonable quality of goods, they could be worth supporting. But I kept a very keen eye on the market side of what they were producing. And a lot of it was going to African countries which were not the best payers, and many Indian firms were involved which again proved to be unreliable, and there were certainly problems.

The cotton spinning and weaving industry was progressing. They started off by making fairly coarse cotton and then they got to the thinner and thinner, the higher grade stuff, and, as the materials improved, the markets began to change. To begin with, they were going to the developing countries which wanted cheap goods and later on when Taiwan came in, they came in at the bottom and Hong Kong moved up market a bit.

When the reclamation at Tsuen Wan began, Government built a seawall and they sold off strips of water which had to be filled in and built on within a certain time, having provided no facilities in the way of roads, electricity, drains, water, anything. And, as it was built piecemeal, there were certainly problems, but we financed quite a number of factories there.

As the danger of overproduction became apparent, Oliphant attempted to go beyond Hong Kong to determine the situation, and not necessarily through Head Office.

We tried to get reports from banks in the market areas as to what the potential was. How far it was being fulfilled. In certain countries enamelware was used purely for ornamentation hung on walls. In another country it was used as kitchen utensils or whatever. One tried to gain an impression of what things were used for and the possible market trends in each country, which might be quite different.

We could write direct to banks abroad. We didn't go through [Hong Kong Office]. There were arrangements with correspondent banks or there were banks to whom we'd been selling bills of exchange, or who had opened letters of credit to us. And we followed it up through business connections.

Like other Hongkong Bankers, Oliphant had not been trained in industry; he was a generalist. Yet in Mongkok he was making his own decisions on technical matters.

Obviously, you've got to learn as you go along. I used to try and go out to visit the factories and gain an impression of general cleanliness – how many machines were working. You would see in a spinning mill that so many machines were stopped, or in a weaving mill that there was too much waste lying around. There was a steel rolling mill, you could see what sort of stocks he carried and what sort of finished goods were lying around. It wasn't difficult to gain a general impression of his operation.

I don't think any great expert knowledge was required unless you were going fairly deeply into quality, this was, say, harder for the inexperienced chap to judge. But, if you got some idea of his operation, you knew his financial position, and you could find out a certain amount about his markets, what the reputation of firms in that country were as regards payment and what were the prospects of selling what he made, you came to an opinion as to whether he was worth supporting.

And then you had to judge the man himself.

You try to get to know the chap – he entertains you and you entertain him. But you meet him as often as you can and you see how he works, how he treats other people, and now and then you may get information from other people about him – if he's highly regarded. I think you can always form some impression of what a chap is likely to do.

At the same time, the Hong Kong main office through the Sub-Manager in charge of branches, then C.J.D. Law, kept a close watch. Oliphant's lending limits were low – 'probably $50,000. I think I expected that,' he said, 'I was very new to managership and this was the first time I'd done it. Obviously I needed some guidance.'

There were other limitations. Mongkok was supposed to use its own funds 'We were supposed to balance our own book as it were, and we did have a great deal of Savings Bank money. The Savings Bank business grew enormously in Mongkok, and this was a source of funds and one which later gave me ideas of expansion, but we were dependent on roughly our own deposits.' This limitation could not be sustained unless all project proposals of any size were to bypass the relevant branch Manager and be brought directly to Hong Kong's main office. Later Managers confirmed this by noting that main office kept them covered, thereby implying that at branch level at least there had to be liability management.

Banking problems

Borrowing short, lending long
This introduced the 'classic banking dilemma' – borrowing short and lending long. If there were any obvious problem relative to industrial lending this was surely the basis, especially in the context of the operations of an exchange bank.

We never lent for very long term – three to four years was the absolute maximum and within that time you could expect somebody to build a factory building and repay. Things turned over pretty quickly then. I think all land had a building covenant, that was a limited term within which you had to build expending $10 per square foot or whatever it was, and we found that people were making considerable profits and could repay within a short time. So we had no long-term loans, nothing five years or more.

All our loans were, of course, repayable on demand, this was part of the agreement. We never intended to call them in suddenly if it could possibly be avoided, and as it worked out we never had to.

But there were bad debts in Mongkok.

Nothing of any size – no. We had small ones, yes. I think that's bound to happen. One of the rolling mills was not a limited company and we had a bill of sale over their assets, and we may have lost a bit on that, but there was nothing of any size. I think that this was largely due to the fact that virtually everybody was doing well, and business was going ahead.

Security
On the question of acceptable security, Oliphant noted,

Unlimited companies might give a bill of sale over assets, or the proprietors had authority to mortgage property. This, of course, was the first choice – if they could mortgage the land or the buildings.

You could take a debenture over their assets if they were a limited company, but then, of course, you were dependent on seeing that they didn't shift the assets just as you needed them.

No, I think the mortgage was the first choice, but we would take anything. Occasionally we had goods in our godown or a neutral one, but this was obviously dependent on market conditions; was there a demand for those goods and were they easily saleable?

I think that one just assessed the situation. I remember once turning down one which the chap wanted to set up a factory for making foam rubber mattresses. As there was a new hospital going up, he was going to sell so many hundreds to them, and he thought he had a good market, but his idea was to borrow from us the money required to rent premises, buy the machinery, buy his raw materials, and he was going to supply the idea. This didn't seem to be a fair distribution of the risk, and one judged it rather like that. Was he taking a fair proportion, and was he really financially involved? If a chap was prepared to put his own money in on a generous scale then you had more confidence in him.

Balance sheets
And on the question of balance sheets:

We [did request them], yes. But I think they were always of fairly limited value because there were different balance sheets for different purposes, i.e. tax, partners, banks.

And also there was the question of banks. An Indian came in to me one time asking for facilities, and he produced a balance sheet showing that he already had eighteen different bankers. Well, that doesn't give you the same confidence as if you are the sole banker, and balance sheets, although they might be, and usually were, audited, were not what they might be in [England].

Bradford, who was Manager from 1956, added,

It just was very foreign to the Chinese. It seemed to be the general way of the Chinese doing business that they didn't have balance sheets. They kept their accounts, but things like a properly drawn up balance sheet or a financial statement were rather foreign to them. They didn't understand it. I don't think they were suspicious, they just couldn't understand it, and we didn't insist on it all the time because I thought it just wasn't very practical. I know from banking over here [in California] the length of time it takes to get a financial statement, and these Chinese wanted a decision on the spot. So you had to take a chance and hope that perhaps sometime during the year they would produce some statement. As a result they were quite happy. I don't think they were offended about being asked.

By the time Sayer became Manager Mongkok in 1965, industry had developed an accounting sophistication, but problems naturally remained.

We liked to see balance sheets, but some of them didn't mean very much. Basically you'd look for a mortgage against the property which you knew was all right. It was always going to go up in value. Sometimes you'd take a charge on the machinery, or you could take a formal debenture and list the machinery as a specific charge. Sometimes a personal guarantee from a proprietor would do as well... he'd put his house up. He may have, for example, letters of credit and, provided he manufactured, he's bound to get his money back. That's a case of taking a little more risk and making sure the chap was manufacturing and not just closing down his factory and spending your advances in Macau or something.

Packing credits

When the first small factory owners sought financing for materials in process, the Bank turned to the precedent of its already overworked 'packing credit' facility. As Adamson, then Hong Kong Manager, recalled,

Oh, yes, we did. But then that was again to help exports.

A chap got a letter of credit and you gave him an advance to buy raw materials and took it back out of the proceeds of the shipment which must be covered by a letter of credit. You only gave packing credit where a letter of credit was concerned. So it was an extra form of finance but very commonly used to reliable people and I think justified. But it worked very smoothly.

The problem was that 'packing credits' developed into 'industrial loans', especially where the exporter was also the manufacturer. This was confirmed by Moodie who described the situation this way:

There were also packing credits. [The manufacturer] could give you letters of credit for shipments of cotton goods... Well, everything you can think of on a packing credit basis. I mean, Jardine's, Gibb Livingston's, Dodwell's, Hutchison's, they all had lines whereby they were shipping these blasted plastic flowers, all sorts of junk, toys, clothing, socks and shoes and everything, you see, under letters of credit. If they could produce a homeside letter of credit for so many hundreds and hundreds of bales of shoes or something, they could get an advance against it. What was known as a 'packing credit'.

Nevertheless, as this type of financing became increasingly important, it also became necessary to differentiate – packing credits and trust receipts were risky even in normal trade finance, when they disguised industrial lending the risk increased.

...one of the major mistakes made by people in Hong Kong... they talked about a thing called 'packing credit'. Now a packing credit was an advance of money to a producer or to a packer, if you like, of rice or peanuts, and it could be applied to factory-made goods, I suppose...

This cost us a lot of money and caused a lot of trouble because the money lent to these industrial firms was not packing credit at all, they were advances to manufacturers, and whereas a packing credit was supposed to buy peanuts for packing and shipment, a manufacturing advance was entirely different. It involved the buying of textiles perhaps to be cut up into garments, stitched up and then packed and exported, and there were more chances of slips. The things could be cut, and the supposed security, the textiles, were useless until somebody made them up. Now this never got into the heads of people in Hong Kong in my time. They all knew better.

It was Titch Black who in Head Office got very angry on one occasion and said, these aren't packing credits at all, they're advances to manufacturers. Head Office were entitled to take an interest in the agencies' returns within Hong Kong, but Hong Kong office itself never made any returns, you see. I insisted when I got onto the Sub-Manager's job [1960] that they stop talking about 'packing credits'. I insisted that they call them 'advances to manufacturers'. Many people understood, but it was very difficult to get into the heads of some of them the difference between the one thing and the other.

This was typical of our 'amateur banking approach', to use Mike Turner's phrase. Some of our people were just babes in the wood, and we were dependent entirely on the integrity plus the ability of the people to whom we were lending. In many cases it paid off handsomely. Look at Hong Kong today. But we got caught right, left and centre when a lot of the time we didn't need to be.

Despite the problems, the 'packing credit' remained. Sayer was recalling various types of advances to manufacturers:

We had different types of advances for manufacturers... 'packing credit advances'... basically, you give a chap money to enable him to pack up his goods to sell. We would go a little deeper than this. We were lending the money to buy materials in the first place, and then the process would go on. You'd manufacture, then package, and then ship under a letter of credit. Sometimes they shipped them without a letter of credit. We'd buy bills, and, hopefully, if they were selling to somebody who was a good regular buyer, you felt pretty safe. There was an element of risk. It was all a question of judgement.

Other adaptations

The packing credit is an example of adaptation, however its merits might be viewed. Behind this and similar adaptations was the attempt to lend short (to more closely match the borrowing) on a long-term project, justifying this by dividing the process into component parts. The difficulty is that although the process may indeed be divisible into discrete observable sections, the banker is concerned only with the point at which repayment becomes a feasible proposition. Unless repayment is based on repayment feasibility, the banker is provided only with a legal right which cannot, in normal circumstances, be usefully exercised – and the evidence is that it was not. In the case of 'packing credits', finance was being given for goods which had no value while in process of production, whereas the packing credit concept had been for credit against goods which retained whatever value they had while in the process of actual local transport and packing.

A more obvious example of this sectional approach is found in the financing of factory construction, where funds were lent on completion of each stage as certified by, for example, the architect. Or, in an opposite case, shipbreaking, an early Hong Kong business, could be financed as the break-up reached predetermined points, perhaps actually marked by the Bank's representative on the ship.

These adaptations, while unsatisfactory as a basis for repayment, were important for purposes of controlling the use of borrowed funds. The project might in the end go sour, but in the process of construction (or destruction) the Bank would be in control of the decision to commit further funds; it would not grant additional credit until its past funds had been certified as properly utilized.

Although the Bank and, indeed, on occasion the local branch Manager often acted alone, the Hong Kong Government was becoming involved. The very process of allocation of land involved the Government in determining end-use and, to this extent, controlling land prices and thus forcing the would-be purchaser to make some declaration of intention of use to the lending bank. The mechanization of the fishing fleet, for example, was based on credit to owners of craft on the basis of credit ratings determined by the Department of Agriculture and Fisheries, the suitability of the engines was also vetted by Government, and repayment was guaranteed by the owner through his cooperative fish marketing organization, which held the monopoly on wholesale transactions.

The early days of Hong Kong's industrialization were days of trial, of success and failure, and of only tentative intrusions by Government – except in the matter of land. A more professional, fully cooperative development would not come until the late 1960s.

'Opinions'

The information necessary to enable the Bank to make a loan decision had to be formalized and expanded to be useful to those who wished to do business with the manufacturer or perhaps enter into a joint venture. At the same time part of a manufacturer's credit-worthiness depended on that of his supplier and buyer. At the main Hong Kong office, Oliphant developed the traditional 'opinions' file into a functional department, run initially by Mrs. Webster, specially hired for the purpose – this was the origin of the Bank's first Commercial Credit Department.

Inspection

The combination of Shanghai origins and specialized credit requirements of Mongkok's new customers suggested that the compradore would be bypassed, and this development, while not unique to Mongkok, confirmed a trend. From the first, Cautherley insists, he dealt directly with the Chinese industrial customer. Inspection of customer installations was hardly a post-war development; juniors had often been sent to godowns and vegetable oil tanks to assure themselves that goods hypothecated to the Bank were there – and the young Bankers were on occasion misled. Factories would seem to present more complex problems, although, unlike storage facilities, they can be judged on the basis of a performance which is more difficult to disguise. Nevertheless, the burden of the task – and the language problem which still existed – led to the development of a factory inspection unit and the employment of Chinese staff especially for this task.

The basic role of the compradore as responsible for handling cash and for the management of the local staff remained until the task merged into that of the Chinese office manager, but the significant developments, the Industrial Banking Department (IBD), the appointment of Business Promotion Officials (BPO), later renamed Business Representatives (BR), came in the 1960s.

But earlier, in 1952 and after, Oliphant, as Manager Mongkok, did not remain at his office desk. He visited the factories...

...in Mongkok it might be a couple of afternoons a week. But not necessarily the same day, I mean, as opportunity came. I would like to – and I did, in fact – visit factories quite frequently. It wasn't a question of going once and never again, but so that one could compare one visit with another. I would go every few months to those whom we were lending money, just to see what they were doing with it. You got some impression from the bills and the letters of credit and so on, but the actual operation was important.

By the time Bradford had been Manager in Mongkok for some three years, the size of the operation called for, as noted above, a more formal inspection system.

[The Chinese manufacturers] were very open, and they didn't mind [my visits] at all. They rather welcomed anybody who showed an interest in what they were doing. [In 1959] I even set up what I called a Factory Inspection Department. I had three or four Chinese clerks in Mongkok office who did nothing else but go around looking at the factories and seeing that they were operating well, that the money which had been advanced to people to buy merchandise was being used properly, because every month these people we gave advances to had to sign a letter indicating what it was that they had purchased to make the garment. It was a little risky to make these advances unless you had somebody going around all the time watching because we were virtually dependent on the companies' and the managers' morality.

Bradford's inspection unit was reorganized by O.P. Edwards as the IBD in 1962; its principal function was to provide back-up services for senior management in the area of industrial lending. Although administratively IBD was under the control of Mongkok office, it served all offices and branches of the Bank on a colony-wide basis; in this it could compare with the Bank's hire-purchase operations which were centred on its North Point branch. The IBD, however, can claim to be the first functional department of its kind ever to be set up in any bank in Hong Kong.

THE MONGKOK OFFICE BUILDINGS TO 1961

In the period to 1961 the Hongkong Bank may have appeared to the outside observer to be handling its embryo industrial financing activities strictly within a traditional framework. Indeed, the most visible development was the establishment of the Mongkok office in 1948 at a time when the first Shanghai spinning mills were setting up in Hong Kong. The agency showed a loss for the first three years of its operations, but by 1952 the branch's business volume had grown to such an extent that it was decided to build a new eight-storey building to accommodate the expansion; this was completed in 1954.

The Mongkok office was in fact rebuilt on two occasions. From its initial year of operations in 1948 to Oliphant's arrival in 1952, current accounts had increased ten times and the number and amounts of saving accounts more than five times. A new office was overdue. In 1954, a new eight-storey building with a total floor area of 27,700 square feet was opened. Oliphant recalled the events.

[The building had been] acquired from Henry G. Leong, who was a big landowner at that time, and it was next door to a cinema on the south side of Nathan Road. It was a one-storey building with a corrugated iron roof and it was pretty cramped. Well, by the time I got there the new office was not completed; it was going up fast. We did find that we had to replan the ground floor particularly because we needed more counter space for the public, and when we moved in we put the Savings Bank up on the 2nd floor. There was no lift working and people had to walk up and we were afraid this would discourage them, but not in the least, the Savings Bank went ahead at a tremendous rate. So people were longing to deposit money with us. Well, this made the whole operation easier.

'Mongkok' itself means 'busy corner' and it certainly was. It was in the right place, so far as business was concerned, but as regards the opening date – yes, we did [consult a *feng-shui* expert]. We always went to the compradore who selected the right day and also we had to have the firecrackers. Well, it was a multi-storey building and the firecrackers from the ground to the roof took fifteen to twenty minutes to go off, and the place was littered with red paper which then caught fire and there was a terrific blaze as it were. All traffic in Nathan Road was diverted whilst the opening took place.

We originally had three Foreign staff and about thirty locals. Within a couple of years there were five Foreign staff and something over a hundred locals because the business warranted it.

The activities of the branch had recalled to top management the Bank's heritage, and the Chief Manager, Michael Turner, in a speech opening the new building, took the opportunity to confirm that the Bank would act consistent with its traditions, broadly defined.

The opening of this new office may be looked upon as an act of faith on the part of the Bank – in the first place in what the industry of the Chinese people, in conjunction with other elements in our cosmopolitan community, can accomplish under conditions of good Government and the rule of law and, secondly, faith in the future of Hong Kong.

Hong Kong is the Bank's home; the Bank has its roots and its Head Office here and it was originally sponsored by local merchants representing nearly every firm and individual trading in the Colony, so it is, in its origin, the Hong Kong merchants' own bank, and possibly because of that it has been a cardinal point of the Bank's policy not to be content with profit on mercantile transactions but to assist in the development of the Colony to the best of its ability.

This new office is designed to provide the people of Mongkok with all banking facilities, including a safe deposit department and a Savings Bank. Should any hesitate to bring their small savings to the Bank or be afraid to bother it with small transactions, I would remind them of the assurance given by one of my predecessors [Sir Thomas Jackson] a long time ago: There is nothing too small for the Hongkong Bank and so far we have found nothing too big.

Mongkok was not the only branch to make industrial loans, but until the establishment of branches in the industrial townships of Taipo and Tsuen Wan in 1960, the main rival was the main Colony Office at 1, Queen's Road, Central. Subsequently, other important industrial areas such as Aberdeen, Sham Shui Po, Shaukiwan, San Po Kong, Kwun Tong, and Hung Hom were also covered. By 1966, the Bank had established a network of forty-eight branches and sub-branches all over Hong Kong, Kowloon, and the New Territories (see below). Mongkok, however, continued to grow; by 1966 it had become necessary to build another skyscraper, which was completed two years later, to house the branch. Couched in terms of *feng-shui* the relative lack of success of a rival bank across the main intersection is apparently consistent with the theory that the latter's location violated certain accepted principles of geomancy.

In 1960 the Industrial Bank Committee concluded in its Report that there was no need for an industrial bank in Hong Kong. There was evidence that the Hongkong Bank – despite disclaimers of Managers, which seemed more appropriate to the technical legal status of their loan portfolios than the actual practical situation – had been lending consistent with the conclusion that 'a substantial proportion of bank loans have been outstanding for five years and some have continued for ten years and more' (p. 8).

But 1960 was only the beginning. A further study of the Bank's role will be made for the period to 1970 (see Chapter 14).

BRANCHING IN HONG KONG – TO 1961[k]

Factors for and against Hong Kong branching

To suppose seriously that a Chinese, his life savings lost in a hyperinflation, his assets shrunken to a few U.S. dollar bills and some hidden gold, his income limited to his wages or salary in the politically precarious British colony of Hong Kong, would put what little he had left over after paying the landlord into a savings account with the Hongkong Bank – or any bank – was surely quite ridiculous. It was a 'known fact' that the Chinese did not trust banks; they kept their money in mattresses or bought gold and ornamented their teeth therewith. Or to suppose that the Chinese businessman who had any regard whatsoever for 'face' would deal with other than the main office of his bank was almost equally preposterous. That was why so many who had their principal operations on the Kowloon side kept a tiny office on the Island to have ready access to the Bank at 1, Queen's Road, Central.

Indeed, there were more cogent arguments to show that branches not only would be under-utilized but that they would be uneconomical and, given the staff available, totally impractical. The Hongkong Bank's Foreign staff in the 1950s never exceeded its 1925 peak (see Table 7.1); nothing the Bank did was valid without the signature of a member of the Foreign staff, and he could sign nothing without the work of the Portuguese clerks and ledger-keepers at a time when the Portuguese were beginning to emigrate.

There was, therefore, a practical element to the arguments against branching. Before establishing a branch there ought to be a specific and proven trade-related reason for doing so. In the days of Exchange Control and when Government certificates of origin were virtually essential for domestic exports, the firm had to deal with Government offices on the Island – and why not have one's bank account there too? There were many Chinese who indeed had little to deposit, but there were evidently a large number of Chinese near the Mongkok branch who revealed the true situation, providing business sufficient to justify the Bank in constructing a larger office.

Furthermore, with liquidity ratios (based on published figures) running from 54% to 65% in the crucial years 1950–1955, it would be difficult for anyone – other than the Manager Japan and the Manager Mongkok – to argue that more funds were needed. And yet this very comment is self-contradictory. The sudden rise in liquidity in 1949–1950 can be clearly ascribed to the increase in deposits; the Hong Kong Chinese were changing their attitudes to

---

[k] Branch expansion after 1961 is covered in Chapter 13. Tables 13.1 through 13.3 include the figures for Hong Kong branches, to which readers are referred.

Year	No. of licensed banks	No. of offices	Total offices[a]	Banking density[b]	Savings deposit/ total deposit	Annual % growth of deposit	Average real term per capita deposit growth
1954	94	3	97	0.42	9.45		
1955	91	3	94	0.40	11.69	9.9	(4.9)
1956	86	4	90	0.36	13.10		
1957	83	5	88	0.33	13.45		
1958	81	8	89	0.32	15.41		
1959	82	13	95	0.33	17.94		
1960	86	38	124	0.42	20.02		
1961	85	101	186	0.58	19.69	36.1	(26.1)
1962	92	121	213	0.64	20.38		
1963	87	144	231	0.66	21.10		
1964	88	204	292	0.81	23.15		
1965	86	215	301	0.82	22.34		
1966	76	242	318	0.85	23.58	6.1	(4.2)
1967	75	256	331	0.86	26.70		
1968	75	274	349	0.89	26.90		
1969	73	289	362	0.94	27.30		
1970	73	326	399	1.01	28.23	16.8	(15.9)
1971	73	358	431	1.06	32.34		
1972	74	404	478	1.17	33.74		
1973	74	469	543	1.27	29.06		
1974	74	557	631	1.44	27.86	17.0	(15.2)
1975	74	629	703	1.59	35.23		
1976	74	685	759	1.70	36.20		
1977	74	719	803	1.76	37.17		
1978	88	790	878	1.86	41.46	16.7	(12.0)
1979	105	906	1,011	2.02	49.20		
1980	113	1,032	1,145	2.22	48.38		

[a] No. of branches plus head offices.
[b] No. of banking offices per 10,000 population.
Source: Y.C. Jao, Banking and Currency in Hong Kong (London 1974), pp. 19–27; HK Annual Reports.

Table 8.3 *Hong Kong*
The branching networks of the major local bank groups, 1954–1981

Bank Group	1954	1961	1966	1971	1976	1981
Hongkong Bank	3	16 (8.5)	46 (14.8)	68 (15.4)	143 (18.6)	250 (21.5)
Chartered Bank	2	6 (3.2)	18 (5.8)	33 (7.5)	72 (9.4)	86 (7.4)
Hang Seng Bank	1	3 (1.6)	11 (3.5)	17 (3.9)	30 (3.9)	45 (3.9)
13 'Leftist' banks	13	37 (19.6)	55 (17.7)	74 (16.8)	125 (16.3)	189 (16.3)
Others	75	128 (67.2)	180 (58.1)	246 (56.2)	398 (51.8)	591 (50.9)
Total	94	190 (100.0)	310 (100.0)	438 (100.0)	768 (100.0)	1,161 (100.0)

Figures refer to total bank offices; figures in parenthesis are percentages of Hong Kong total.
Source: Economic Reporter, *Hong Kong Annual Review*, various dates.

Table 8.4 *The Hongkong and Shanghai Banking Corporation Spatial pattern of branching in Hong Kong, 1961–1981*

Census districts	1961 and before	1962–1971	1972–1981	Total	% set up after 1971
Central	1	1	9	11	82[a]
Sheung Wan	0	2	6[a]	8	75[a]
Wanchai	1	3	7	11	64
Tai Hang	0	4	6	10	60
North Point	1	2	10	13	77[a]
Shaukiwan	1	1	5	7	71
West	2	2	2[a]	6	33
Mid-Levels	0	0	4	4	100[a]
Aberdeen	1	0	6	7	86[a]
Peak	0	0	1	1	100[a]
South	0	1	2[a]	3	67
Island subtotal	7	16	58	81	72
Tsim Sha Tsui	1	1	10	12	83[a]
Yau Ma Tei	1	2	9	12	75[a]
Mongkok	0	1	4[a]	5	80[a]
Homantin	0	3	4[a]	7	57
Hung Hom	0	2	9	11	82[a]
Kowloon subtotal	2	9	36	47	76
Cheung Sha Wan	1	4	13[a]	18	72
Shek Kip Mei	0	2	3[a]	5	60
Kowloon Tong	0	0	0	0	0
Kai Tak	0	5	13[a]	18	72
Ngau Tau Kok	0	4	7[a]	11	64
Lei Yue Mun	0	2	9	11	82[a]
New Kowloon subtotal	1	17	45	63	71
Tsuen Wan New Town	2	3	21	26	81[a]
Rest of Mainland NT	4	3	22	29	76[a]
Islands	0	0	4	4	100[a]
New Territories total	6	6	47	59	80
Hong Kong total	16	48	186	250	74

[a] Rate of growth equal to or exceeding Colony total.
Source: Computed from unpublished data of the Bank by Victor Sit.

the use of banks; many, including some of the recent arrivals from the Mainland, were using bank accounts.

Underlying the arguments against branch banking, however, was the survival of a pre-war attitude or preconception relative to the purpose of a commercial bank. Banking then was not for the masses. The Hongkong Bank ran a savings department pre-war, but it was called the 'Hong Kong Savings Bank' and its origins were to be found in an aborted Post Office Savings Bank – a heritage of Victorian concepts of self-help for the poor (see Volume I, Chapter 10). The Savings Bank was, then, a public service.

Traditional wisdom was to be proved mistaken. In 1977 the Hongkong Bank had 150 branches in Hong Kong; Hang Seng Bank had 33. By the end of 1984 there were 411 Hongkong Bank Group commercial banking offices in the territory. But this was a development over time; the facts do not contradict the proposition that there was a risk in establishing branches with the principal purpose of collecting funds in the early 1950s; given the general situation and the low cost of funds, they might have been impractical and uneconomical. Furthermore, the Bank lacked staff, technology, and organizational back-up.

As for 'face' and the insistence on dealing with Head Office, this argument was less satisfactory; the evidence of Mongkok was there to refute it. Nevertheless, the success of this one branch would not support a policy of extensive branching; for example, the North Point branch, established in 1956, was not immediately profitable.

An analysis of the Bank's branch development in Hong Kong has been undertaken by a Hong Kong University economic geographer, Victor F.S. Sit.[1] His approach confirms the aggressive policy adopted in the search for funds to meet the demand created by an equally aggressive policy towards the securing of industrial customers – subject to the availability of funds. The Hongkong Bank was competitively oriented, but it was never seriously threatened and competition in the sense of 'fear' cannot have been a major factor in the Bank's policies. Oliphant as Hong Kong Manager was aware of the loss of market share and concerned about it. The situation could not, however, be immediately remedied. The loss of market share came not from a lack of competitiveness but from a narrow range of opportunities and a lack of funds. The response to the latter was branch banking.

Victor Sit quotes an American financial journalist, L. Kraar, writing in *Fortune*, who described the Bank as passive in response to local business demands.

The gentlemanly Hongkong Bank managers tend to sit in their air-conditioned offices and wait for old customers to call. These officers are well-grounded in handling the short-term financing of trade, but lack the more sophisticated skills required to evaluate the long-term industrial loans that are now much in demand.

Although it is true that the Hongkong Bank's Shanghai Manager during China's Cultural Revolution (see Chapter 13) would perforce stick close to his

---

[1] See his 'Branching of The Hongkong and Shanghai Banking Corporation in Hong Kong: a Spatial Analysis' in King, ed. *Eastern Banking* (London, 1983), pp. 629–54. The present discussion profits from Sit's findings.

desk, Kraar's Bank does not sound like the Bank of Kresser, McLean, Jackson, Addis, or Grayburn, to mention but a few. More important, it is a particularly inept description of the post-war Bank. While journalists sat interviewing the chief executive in his admittedly air-conditioned office, the Foreign and local staffs were out searching for new business. Branching made this practical.

The impact of branching policy on Hong Kong's banking structure is shown in Tables 8.2 through 8.4 taken from Victor Sit's study which refers also to the basic work of Y.C. Jao.

Early developments

By the late 1950s the Hong Kong scene had changed. There was an expectation of medium-term political stability, the refugees were becoming integrated into a new society, people were saving – others were investing. The shortage of funds was to be felt throughout the Bank's branches; in some cases it could be remedied by branching within the territory, in other cases there were impediments. The Manager Japan, for example, felt the shortage of funds, but had he obtained the funds required there would have been other problems. Each overseas branch has its own history.

In Hong Kong, recognition of the need to secure the Bank's sources of funds – and not simply consider the provision of savings accounts as a public service – came first in a small way in the Mongkok branch, but fortunately the Manager who had experienced the problem, R.G.L. Oliphant, became Manager Hong Kong at a crucial time. Money was tight, liquidity was low; the Bank was passing business by. The Bank needed additional funds. Those in favour of small branches were beginning to have the weight of argument on their side.

The first breakthrough was chance. Lawrence Kadoorie of China Light and Power Company faced the practical problem of handling electricity consumer retail payments in the New Territories. If the Bank were to collect the payments, he stated his willingness to rent office space at $1.00 a year, and the Bank could begin its branching quite economically – and without capital commitment.

The first tentative and temporary offices proved that funds were available; by 1961 the Bank had set up in New Territories towns such as Sheung Shui, Taipo, Tsuen Wan (2), and Yuen Long. There were offices on Hong Kong Island (moving clockwise from southwest to the northeast) in Aberdeen, Kennedy Town, Sai Ying Pun, Wanchai, North Point, and Shaukiwan; in the Kowloon urban area, the Bank set up in Sham Shui Po and San Hui, in addition to the earlier Kowloon and Mongkok offices. These were dual purpose – garnering funds and supplementing Mongkok's industrial financing efforts. The growth was not spectacular even then: in 1962 a further three branches were set up; in 1963 four, in 1964 eight, in 1965 fourteen. From then until 1973 when seventeen branches were added the pace slackened. But it was to be one of the characteristics of branch banking in Hong Kong that apparently, no matter how many offices were set up, funds would be forthcoming – and not at the expense of an existing office.

However enthusiastic management might be over this new program of branch banking in Hong Kong, the annual additions were not at first particularly noteworthy when compared to the 55 offices opened in 1979. There are many reasons why this was so, and the problems were not always 'banking' – the task of finding suitable sites in crowded Hong Kong where site preparation is a major element of cost would prove one of the more intractable. But the limited early growth reflects again the fact that major changes cannot occur by themselves; they require supporting developments which may also be the restraining factor.

Developments, 1958–1962 and afterwards

The first banking impediment to branching was the lack of Foreign staff. By the late 1950s, however, the fact of local officers had been accepted; the next task was to convince the compradore. He was at first opposed, supposing, quite rightly, that the Bank would recruit, *inter alios*, his best shroffs. He also understood that, although he would still be asked to recommend dependable people, the Chinese element in the Bank would no longer be under his control. The Chinese staff would be independent of the compradore, trained to modern banking, and dealing across the counter with other Chinese. All this was sufficient to doom the compradoric system. There was, however, no alternative; nor would society defend or protect the role of the compradore. On the other hand, there were Chinese in the Bank's employ and young Chinese waiting to be recruited who were capable of handling an all-Chinese staffed small branch. All now awaited the decision.

The decision was made by Oliphant as Hong Kong Manager. As Sir Michael Turner was to write Oliphant after the centenary celebrations in March 1965,

The opening of these subsidiary offices, both in Hong Kong and Kowloon, was your idea, and the credit for their success should therefore go to you, and, though other people will forget that, I won't. Granted the big offices were opened, or conceived, in Arthur [Morse's] time, but the hole-in-the-corner banking was your idea, and it has proved an unqualified success...

To follow the development briefly – the actual training and related organization was undertaken in the mid-1960s by O.P. Edwards, the Sub-Manager in the Main Office in charge of branches. Edwards had knowledge of

Chinese and was otherwise temperamentally suited to prepare the breakthrough. Edwards also coordinated the search for sites, working with the Property Manager and the Sub-Accountant in such matters as furnishing and staffing of the new smaller offices. By the 1970s the operation had become virtually standardized, with equipment installed almost as a routine, but when all was ready a lucky day was selected, some official of the Bank or public was asked to open the office, by which was meant dotting the eyes of the guardian dragon. This done, there would be a dragon dance – and on at least one occasion the Manager Branches was observed looking at his watch to make sure the dragon dancers performed for the agreed period – in Hong Kong tradition merges with the commercial. By the time the doors were to be officially opened, the noise of the drums keeping rhythm for the dragon dancers would have aroused the neighbourhood. In fact, workers on the construction site opposite would already be downing tools and preparing a rush to be the first to open an account or deposit funds and so obtain 'joss'.

Once inside, officials and early depositors alike find a modest buffet set out with sufficient champagne to create a festive atmosphere. For whether this is branch no. 140 or 200, it is the first for the new Manager. Other Hongkong Bank Managers from nearby offices come to extend their good wishes to him – or her (for the barrier is down). Flowers come from major customers who plan to open a new account in this, presumably, more convenient office; all the while an increasing number of people push their way past the guests, fortunately ignoring the smoked salmon sandwiches, to begin immediate business. There is a brief write-up in the staff magazine with pictures and the Hongkong Bank has another Hong Kong deposit-garnering operation on line.

This small office will now operate with other such offices under a major branch, for example, Mongkok or North Point.

The development of a branch network, necessary as it might be to get close to traditionally minded customers who did not wish to come to Central and to service them either as a source of funds or in connection with industrial loans, created problems of its own. One of the first was the consequence of success; how is the cash to be moved from the Bank's central treasury to and from – and among – the smaller offices. This required a security service, another of Edwards' tasks; eventually the Bank established a security firm subsidiary. In the New Territories the Bank tried to reach the more rural areas with a mobile bank, but the local people (and who could blame them?) did not feel comfortable with using a bank which appeared – and then disappeared with their funds. The only solution was to extend the branch network to the New Territories.

In Chapter 13 brief consideration will be given to the technical developments, but it is obvious that the increased number of branches and their geographical concentration favoured the use of a real-time, on-line computer system, and, once the banking habit had become more familiar, the idea of cash dispensers, credit cards, and other retail banking facilities. As money became more expensive, many savers even in the smaller offices objected to the low rates of savings accounts and demanded access to the Bank's deposit-taking finance company subsidiary. This meant, however, that the local branch lost the profit on the account, and the Manager might be discouraging. If he were, he would eventually lose the account; in the end special places at the counters were set aside for such depositors.

Even though the compradoric system for a time remained in place, by 1961 it was clear that the Hongkong Bank had become the bank, not just for expatriate firms and employees, for Chinese firms willing to deal through the compradore, and for the public willing to brave the grandeur of the main banking hall, but to all in the territory. And furthermore, if they would not come to the Bank, the Hongkong Bank would go to them.

9

THE HONGKONG BANK IN CHINA, 1949–1962*

[Make] every effort facilitate matters for Chinese Government...
1894 cable to Hongkong Bank, Tientsin

Pursue an active role.
Advice of the Bank of China, 1954

Transition

There was an exodus from Shanghai as the People's Liberation Army (PLA) approached the city, partly, it is true, because of the fear that there might be street-to-street fighting rather than of political concern. The Hongkong Bank was overstaffed for the business it was then doing; it seemed sound to move some staff from China – in case problems should develop. J.F. Marshall's orders to leave Shanghai were sudden.

I was at the Shanghai Country Club playing tennis, and I received a telephone call about eight o'clock in the evening to say would I pack ten pounds of luggage and be prepared to leave from Lunghwa airport at six o'clock the following morning. A telegram had come in from Hong Kong to say that I and about eight others were to leave immediately and about four were going to be left behind.

There was a curfew in Shanghai at nine o'clock, and this was eight o'clock. I had to get myself home and prepare for this rather surprising denouement, which I wasn't expecting for a moment.

I had a dog and a motor car. The motor car was only one of those little tiny Fiat Ballilas. I got rid of the dog by breaking through the fence into the house next door – to one of the chaps who wasn't going away – and saying, here, you've got a dog. I left all my belongings in the hands of my houseboy, who was a very good chap. I said, pack them up in your own time and deliver them to the Bank.

I flew out on one of those short Sunderland flying boats with I suppose fifty or sixty other people. The plane was very much overloaded. There was nowhere to sit, we just stood hanging on like in a bus. This lot was mainly people with British passports, Chinese who'd been born in Hong Kong. Most of them were English-speaking, but not English-born people going out at this time.[1]

R.P. Moodie, the Shanghai Accountant, remained behind.

---

* Although the official romanization known as '*pinyin*' was not in fact used for foreign purposes until the early 1980s, Chinese names are hereafter rendered in this system, unsuitable though it is for English-language purposes. Exceptions are made for (i) Peking, (ii) Hong Kong names, which are in Cantonese, (iii) names in Taiwan, and (iv) names of people who rose to prominence before 1949. The last two categories are rendered either in Wade-Giles or in the version common or preferred at the time.

Plans were made for evacuation, but of course the plan depended on the HMS *London* being available. The idea was that *London* was going to come up to the docks and tie up there. Shanghai was divided into areas, and those in charge of each one had to collect all their foreigners and get them down to a point on the river where a launch from the *London* would take them away. Well, as it happened, of course, *London* got holed on its way up to try and rescue the *Amethyst*, you see, so she trickled down to Hong Kong and that was the end of the plan.

After that the Consulate issued a broadcast on the radio saying, when the Communists take the city, people will stay put in their houses for forty-eight hours.

They came in overnight. I went over [to Yoxall's house], that was right on the Bubbling Well Road, and in the middle of the night I heard this pitter patter, pitter pat of the Communist troops coming down on either side of the road in plimsoles. Quite a strange noise. I peeked through the window to see them.

The next day one stayed put. But the following day, as I say, we walked down in the afternoon to the Country Club. The strangest thing was that whereas before all the roads were covered with Nationalist flags, this time they were all Communist flags.[2]

Moodie returned to the Bank after two or three days.

Down in Hong Kong there had been anxious watching. Head Office kept in touch with Shanghai by a daily scheduled telephone call. The day before the PLA arrived, Stacey notified Hong Kong that they would probably enter the city the next day. As Hong Kong hung up, they wished him good luck. The next morning the operator announced, 'Shanghai on the line'. G.H. Stacey, the Shanghai Manager, came in clear and cheerful. Nothing had changed.

Not yet.

Strike

There had in fact been a change. Moodie's office boy came in with his hat on – he was the Union leader. The position in the Hongkong Bank would be better than in many firms; the Foreign staff were locked in only on one or two occasions.

I don't know quite why we were locked in, but the workers decided they wanted something, and none of the Foreign staff were allowed to go out, except the girls were hustled out by O.P. Edwards. He was working in the Books office, and he collected the girls and let them out through the window which was only about five feet above the ground, and they managed to clamber down.

The rest of us had to stay put that day, but we were allowed home by nightfall.

Our biggest trouble there was that we had a very large engineering staff who were very bolshy. You see, we had engineers for the heating and the cooling and the water and all the rest of it.[3]

On another occasion the Manager was confronted by the engineering staff and called in Moodie, who, as Accountant, was responsible for staff affairs.

The Engineers were in fact at that time in his office, and [Stacey] sent for me, and he said, get these people out of here.

Easier said than done, however I managed to arrange that we would have a meeting in the Chinese compradore's department. And that was the only time that I really had trouble. Somebody took a swipe at me when I was addressing the meeting, but that really was the only time that I felt endangered.

Of course you really didn't have a leg to stand on. The one thing you had to do was to avoid getting into any trouble at all with the staff. The head of our staff was my office boy. He dictated the terms for all the others with the compradore and K.C. Lee (the Chinese Manager) as sort of go-betweens.[4]

The events had a social impact. The Hongkong Bank's engineering staff was headed by a local Briton, E.W.A. Clements. As O.P. Edwards put it, he would not normally have been considered 'one of us', not being on the Foreign Staff List.[5] But he ran the operations excellently and would later provide the Shanghai office the practical advice it needed. On leaving China in 1955 he was awarded a gratuity of £5,000 in lieu of his Provident Fund, made worthless by inflation, and he was pensioned at £500 p.a. Edwards noted that Clem ('as we called him') was also invited to Bank parties; in the days of the People's Republic he was socially one of the Hongkong Bankers.

Business resumed

The changes were neither sudden – the episode of the office boy's hat excepted – nor dramatic. There was no entry of troops into the banking hall or disturbance of foreigners in the streets. Since the Pacific War the Hongkong Bank had operated without extrality and had received regulatory instructions through the Bank of China and the Central Bank of China, with both of which it had long had good relations, especially in the early post-war days when Tsuyee Pei was Governor of the Central Bank.

Regulations continued to be received through these channels, the compradore and K.C. Lee, the Chinese Manager, acting as intermediaries.

The immediate impact was negative. There was little business. There was a curfew and recreational clubs were eventually shut down. There would be renewed problems with local staff and the Bank's business was seen as being permanently curtailed and many became redundant, but that was later. There was little to do; there was boredom. On the other hand, the Chinese authorities were anxious to develop the export trade and business might develop at any time. This was the period of transition.

Edwards was the Shanghai branch exchange dealer at the time; he met an old friend.

...it wasn't very long before the threads were picked up, and, as the exchange dealer, I was off to the Bank of China every morning where I sat, as representative of the Hongkong Bank, buying or selling such exchange as we were permitted to buy. This was when they'd worked out their arrangements.

The chairman of this meeting was a man called Ch'i Chao-t'ing, whom I'd known in Chungking, and at whom, when we put on a big rioting performance in aid of charity, I threw my hat, and it hit him. He was rather amused. Ch'i was chairman, and he knew me very very well, but he was wearing by then what I call 'coolie blues' which all respectable Communists wore, distinguishable from the others only by his beautiful English-made shoes which he still wore whenever he could get away with it. No one thought down there, as it were, but his other clothes had to be like everyone else. He never said a word to me from start to finish, and we sat sometimes as close as I am to you, never so much as looked at me. He knew me because he'd been [the Secretary-General] of the Stabilization Board in Chungking and went over to the Communists at a certain point about 1948.[6]

Edwards was in fact at the Bank of China on one occasion when the rest of the Hongkong Bank Foreign staff were locked in by the union negotiators; he set up a temporary office in Jardine's and operated in exchange from there.

The new Government did not so much take positive action as make the position obvious by what did not happen. Without business the Bank had no purpose. With staff troubles and increasing costs, the Bank would make its own decision to withdraw. At that point the authorities intervened. There were outstanding issues to be settled before the relations of the Bank with the People's Republic were stabilized.

INITIAL ADJUSTMENT PROBLEMS AND POLICY

Sir Arthur Morse was a 'legend in his own time'; he was the man who planned and financed the recovery of Hong Kong, who stood up to London officialdom, who safeguarded the Bank's resources and launched it once again as the leading British bank in the East. When he left Hong Kong his car was drawn by Bank officers down to Blake Pier; he was gone, but memories and stories about Morse, his booming voice, his outgoing generosity, or, on a more practical level, his ability to sense a sound proposition and finance it – all these are part of his heritage.

Foreign staff discontent

There is, however, a discordant note. Was Morse unreasonably optimistic about the Bank's opportunities in the People's Republic? Did he abandon the Foreign staff to years of boredom and consequent loss of career development? Among those who remained in China during the period to 1955 there are those who are highly critical of Morse. In the past many Hongkong Bankers would have preferred some other assignment or cursed their luck at missing some opportunity, but these sentiments were usually expressed in terms of membership in a 'service', of 'taking the good with the bad'. Addis, for example, recorded his refusal on several occasions to formally express a preference over his own assignments, despite his strong personal expectations. Others have stated that on the whole the system worked out fairly.

The Hongkong Bank in China, 1949–1962

Discordant notes relative to China assignments, therefore, merit consideration.

In a letter to A.S. Adamson in September 1951 Morse wrote, 'I feel that the sooner we can cut down our whole staff in China the better.' In the following January he wrote to W.R.M. Cockburn, Chief General Manager of the Chartered Bank, that they were in agreement, 'the general policy was to get out of China as quickly as possible'.[7] These are unofficial statements of general intent; their implementation has to take place in the context of the laws of the People's Republic and the long-term interests of the banks, their constituents, and their shareholders.

The statistics

There is no question of serious mistreatment of Hongkong Bankers in post-Liberation China. Negotiations were often tough, at times unfriendly especially in the early years, but this was not the basis of complaint.

Life was boring, there was little to do, and there was always the possibility of an incident. Simply put, the problem was this: too many of the Foreign staff had been interned during the Pacific War. They were particularly sensitive about being 'caught' again. Any delay in processing an exit permit, any delay by the Bank's Manager in Shanghai or the Chief Manager in Hong Kong in ordering their transfer once the permit had been granted was judged in this context. The staff were 'on edge'. If a promised transfer were not effected exactly on schedule, there was no margin of tolerance; someone in Hong Kong, it would be thought, didn't realize the situation, or perhaps the replacement was stalling, or perhaps Morse was purposely holding them in China to be ready for a resurgence of business which would never come.

In context this is all understandable. Several in Hong Kong were nervous. T.J.J. Fenwick had planned to retire in Hong Kong but left for South Africa. The experience of internment camp hung heavy in the memory.

The charges of insensitivity were directed at Morse, but it is fair to note that, once the situation had been fully assessed, replacements were either 'volunteers' or those who had specifically expressed a willingness to be assigned in China. The problem was confined to those on duty in China at the time of Liberation and to those sent in immediately afterwards, who were promised a shorter assignment than in the event proved practical – and all this happened when Morse was Chief Manager of the Bank. The cold statistics put the problem in perspective without denying that some were aggrieved. Morse had a reputation for shrewdness which will not so easily be overturned.

In August 1949 there were 29 Foreign staff assigned to offices in China. This number was reduced each year: there were 26 in China in August 1950, only eleven in 1951, seven in 1952 and 1953, and four in 1954. After the 'all-for-all' settlement in April 1955, only two Foreign staff officers were assigned to Shanghai; there were none elsewhere. By mid-1952 all those assigned to China in August 1949 had left the country. Only three staff members had had long tours, say three to four years in China, at the time of their departure.

These China-wide statistics do not quite tell the story. Juniors in the Shanghai and Tianjin (Tientsin) offices could be moved out or replaced after some delay but in the meantime they at least remained with their colleagues. The authorities were, however, more concerned with retaining the 'responsible person' under their control, and thus obtaining an exit permit for S.J.H. Fox, the Manager Shantou (Swatow), for example, was a more prolonged problem – and he was alone with no work to be done. Eventually the Bank appointed H.A. Thalberg, a foreign resident of Shantou, as local agent, thus obtaining a 'responsible person' and making Fox available for repatriation. The failure to close down Shantou was not a failure of Morse's or the Bank's Board of Directors' to assess the situation properly; it was a delay caused by the Chinese authorities with jurisdiction in the particular region.

Shanghai, however, was a special case. This was the main branch for China and there was considerable work to be done once the authorities had decided on their policy towards the Hongkong Bank. Furthermore, the Chinese wished to ensure (i) that sufficient staff were on hand to fulfil the requirements and (ii) that there be an acceptable 'responsible person' available for contact. Despite these restrictions, the Shanghai Foreign staff declined from seventeen in mid-1949 to fifteen in mid-1950; the big drop came the following year with only seven in mid-1951, then four and three and finally, in 1955, there were, as previously noted, only two left.

Nor was there any question of holding a particular Manager 'hostage'. Stacey (East in 1920) was Manager through 1950; he was replaced by W.T. Yoxall and, although the latter retired only after the agreement with the Chinese authorities had been reached in April 1955, his replacement, D. Buchan (East in 1925), had already been accepted as the 'responsible person'. In Hong Kong the problem was viewed as one causing temporary disruption to complex personnel transfer programs; in China some Hongkong Bankers judged events more harshly.

There is no evidence that Morse was unaware of the hardship involved in serving a long tour in China at the time. But Morse was no more able to operate an ideal personnel policy, satisfactory to all, than his predecessors. The situation in China added a new dimension to an already complex problem. They were not forgotten men; it is nevertheless true that they felt forgotten.

Both Morse and the Board took the problem seriously. Morse did his best to minimize operations and transfer unneeded staff from China. But there were impediments: on occasion a member of the staff might be able to leave only if a replacement were sent and Morse was reluctant to send new staff in – he simply wanted the long-serving members out. By 1951, as the statistics show, he had begun to make a net impact.

From time to time in the history of the Bank, the Board had authorized additional pay, for example in Saigon, for unhealthy posts, or awarded honorariums for specific situations – the Siege of the Legations during the Boxer Uprising. For those who had to remain in China, for men like H.L. Pierce and Edwards, both of whom were familiar with the Chinese language and who spent six and four years respectively in Shanghai, it seemed as if the Bank had forgotten them, that Morse did not understand. Nevertheless, Morse had secured Board recognition that this was a hardship post, and Morse accordingly awarded, with Board approval, an honorarium of £1,000 for four years and £500 for each further year spent in China. For Managers there was an additional bonus.

Personal stories

H.L. 'Peter' Pierce (East in 1948) had studied Chinese at the School of Oriental and African Studies, London, and, after a brief tour in Hong Kong, was assigned to the Bank's Chungking office in 1949. When that office closed later in the year he returned briefly to Hong Kong and then left for Shanghai via Tianjin where he stayed the night with G.M. Sayer and learned that the branch was then doing 'foreign trade finance and general banking'. The trip south to Shanghai, which he reached in October 1950, was by train.

[I lived in Shanghai] at Haig Court [now, 1985, the Jing'an Hotel] which was where most people were living then, apart from the Bank compound in Bubbling Well Road which was still going at that time, and the Accountant's house on Avenue Haig. There were four chauffeur-driven Chevrolets and a bus to take us to and from the office and to the Bank garden at Hungjao on Sundays.

There were still a number of clubs at that time. The British Country Club was still going. When that closed down, we then moved to the French Club...then the Italian Club. But the Golf Club kept going until the time of the Coronation in 1953, and the RAF Association, which was in the dome of the Bank, kept going most, if not all of the time I was there [Pierce left in September 1954]. The Shanghai Amateur Dramatic Society was still operating at the Lyceum Theatre, and we were allowed to put on plays periodically, subject to censorship. The last night club closed in 1954. I also did a lot of riding out at Hungjao most mornings. I kept two horses which were very cheap, at the rate of exchange which we used, about seventy Hong Kong dollars a month.[8]

During Pierce's period in Shanghai, the authorities waged several programs of re-education, including the famous five-anti's (*wu-fan*) campaign.

...it was a little frightening hearing the police jeeps going round with their sirens in the dead of night, and you wondered who they were going to pick up next, and this included one of the people living below me in Haig Court. In one of the other campaigns when people were dropping off roofs of buildings and jumping into the river, we had one jump off the roof of the Bank into the courtyard. The watchman was reprimanded by Yoxall, the Manager at that time, for allowing a man to go up on the roof. Somebody else under interrogation jumped out of a lavatory window and partly through the glass roof of the banking hall.[9]

When one of the Bank's staff, D.C. Williams, was imprisoned, Pierce went along with food and blankets and, using his knowledge of '*putunghua*' and smattering of Shanghai dialect, tried to find out what had gone wrong. As the officer in charge of branch affairs Pierce would also learn that A.C. Groves was being held in Canton because he was the surviving member of the Canton Club, hence the 'responsible person', and there was some question that the Club had smuggled in liquor. Meanwhile D.F.C. Cleland (East in 1924), who had left the Bank in 1946 to go into the antiques business in Peking, was rehired with instructions to undertake a 'caretaker' job until the branch could be officially closed. As Adamson told Morse, '[Cleland] is determined not to leave Peking and he would never let us down'.[10]

F.R. Burch had joined London Office in 1926, come East in 1929, and after serving in Hong Kong, Calcutta, and Shanghai was interned by the Japanese in Lunghwa Camp. He served as Accountant in Shanghai from 1950 to 1954. As the officer responsible for both local and Foreign staff matters, he had considerable experience both with the union and with those of his colleagues who felt abandoned by Morse – 'the forgotten men', who were particularly angered by a letter from Morse in effect saying that he was sending in no more replacements – he was working only for a net decrease. The immediate result was longer tours for those still in Shanghai.[11]

Despite the general austerity, there were some recreational outlets remaining, although they closed, as Pierce has related, one by one over the period. The foreign community, dwindling in numbers, made the best of it – not without the cooperation at times of the Shanghai authorities. And at the end there was a final ball, a last farewell to the days of Treaty Port China and the gaiety of the great international city that Shanghai had once been.

[Social life was] much more lively, particularly when we first went up there, than it had been in the past.

Everybody was in the same boat, there was not this rather rigid taipan/junior, you know, and the Country Club and putting on your correct tie and all that sort of thing....

And we had the British School still. The firms [including the Hongkong Bank] all built a big new building there after the war called Britannia House. Imported umpteen teachers for various grades on home contracts, some of whom were still there. The last class of the British School was held in the Bank house we were living in, in the attic with our two children and four others! Anyway, we closed the British School down, and Leach, a man who's dead now, did negotiations. He had nothing else to do.

The Golf Club only went in '53, Hung Jao Golf Club. That became and is a People's

Park, a lovely park, of course. There again, they paid us for our tractor and our little club house until we had enough to pay off all the staff. We had that luxury called a fore caddy because there was a lot of water about. Everybody was happy.

[Eventually] the only club we could use was the French Club which had an enormous ballroom with a sprung floor and everything [and which is now, in 1985, the Jin Jiang Club for foreigners in Shanghai]. The Chinese had said they didn't want it. The Club was only kept open because the staff said, pay your taxes, pay your utilities, and divide the rest among us and anything above, below, still owing, put it in the book and perhaps pay one day. So the Club ticked over with what foreign community was left.

And then they said, we're going to requisition your building! That was that. The first thing was that they found that the French Club had rented from the French Municipal Council for a dollar a year, a great big area, right in the city it was by that time. Oh, they said, this has got to stop... we want it for a People's Art Gallery, or something... I've forgotten. So, knowing all the ploys, we got one of our blokes, he was our Bank engineer, Clements... of course he knew a lot about property... to go and see the Bureau.

They said, we want it on the twentieth of December.

And so he, being a wise fellow, said we were going to use it for some our celebrations at Christmas, you know, it's a big feast.

All right.

Then we said, New Year is coming...

All right, we'll take you over officially, signed away on the twentieth December. You may use the club till two a.m. on the first of January.

And so at two a.m. on the first of January, having had our last 'toot' there, all in dinner jackets, all with our cars and chauffeurs outside, we trooped out with our silk scarves, ladies all in their dresses, and the little boys in blue walked in and put up pictures and things ready for opening next day!

Absolutely mad.[12]

'After the break of morn' – the Bank's initial policy in the People's Republic

The Hongkong Bank did not lightly give up its heritage or turn away from the business which Arthur Morse and his associates were certain must exist for a bank involved in the finance of foreign trade. Initial indications were favourable; business continued after Tianjin had been liberated, and Morse advocated an early recognition of the People's Government. With the involvement of China in the Korean War relations became strained and the Bank was involved in difficulties, especially after December 1951 following the U.S. decision to freeze all Chinese 'Mainland'-controlled assets. Morse was determined that the potential losses involved should not be borne by the Bank at that particular stage of its post-war resurgence. There was no point in remaining unless the Chinese authorities wished it. One reading of the situation was that the Chinese did not wish the Hongkong Bank in China; this was to prove incorrect, but in 1950 it was a reasonable conclusion for Morse to make.

As already noted, by the end of January 1950 the Board had been informed that Xiamen (Amoy), Guangzhou (Canton), Chongqing (Chungking), Hankou

Table 9.1 *The Hongkong and Shanghai Banking Corporation Closure and reopening of China offices, 1949–1985*[a]

	opened	closed	reopened/opened (after 1949)
Shanghai	1865		
Hongkew	1909	1939[b]	
Foochow	1867	1949	
Hankow	1868	1949	Wuhan 1985[d]
Amoy	1873	1950	Xiamen 1984[e]
Tientsin	1881	1954	[Tianjin 1986[e]]
Peking	1885[c]	1955	1980[e]
Canton	1909	1949	Guangzhou 1979[d]
Taipei[g]	1909	1930	1984
Tsingtau	1914	1951	
Harbin	1915	1941[b]	
Dairen	1922	1941[b]	
Mukden	1926	1949	
Chefoo	1926	1941[b]	
Swatow	1937	1953	
Chungking	1943	1949	
Nanking	1947	1949	
			Shenzhen 1982[f]

[a] For dates of closure during and after the Pacific War, see Table 2.1.
[b] Not reopened after the Pacific War.
[c] Date of actual opening, not of the later legal acknowledgement.
[d] Subordinate representative office.
[e] Representative office. For Tianjin see Plate 17.
[f] Representative office upgraded in 1985 to a branch.
[g] Agency during period of Japanese rule; branch opened in 1984.

Note: Original opening date is the year a Bank-staffed agency was opened for business; a Bank staff member may have been assigned previously to work in the Bank's merchant agency in the port.

(Hankow), and Nanjing (Nanking) had closed down (see Table 9.1). In Shantou the Bank did not move fast enough; the branch was required to remain open until 1953 while the Manager resisted demands of the local authorities and until permission was obtained from the Bank of China for the foreign liabilities of his branch to be transferred to Shanghai. The Board of Directors confirmed (i) in August 1950 that they were prepared to undertake in China only such business as was remunerative and (ii) in 1952 that all steps necessary to close down Shanghai office were being taken. These were historic decisions.

The first was not a decision to leave China but a recognition that its presence in China could only be justified on a commercial basis. The Bank was not the financial agent of the British Empire; it had no business maintaining a purposeless 'prestige' at shareholders' expense. The 1952 decision was recognition that the authorities were apparently not prepared to permit the Shanghai branch to remain on a profitable basis.

So much from the Board minutes. But lingering always was the feeling that this was surely not the end. It might be China's wish in the aftermath of the revolution. If China modified her intentions the Bank was always willing to cooperate because, whatever present reality dictated, the Hongkong Bank could not escape its heritage as understood by its directors, its Managers, and its juniors. The Hongkong Bank was a China bank.

TO AN 'ALL-FOR-ALL' SETTLEMENT

Whatever China's original intentions had been relative to The Hongkong and Shanghai Banking Corporation the intervention of China in the Korean War, the American embargo, the various measures authorized by the United Nations – including their failure to recognize the Government in Peking as the Government of China – and the existence in the world of two Bank of Chinas made real cooperation in Shanghai particularly difficult. Arthur Morse was able to secure the exit and the closure of only one branch – Qingdao (Tsingtau) in May 1951, albeit at a price in the form of compensation to employees; Tianjin was closed after considerable problems in 1954. The Chinese claims against these and branches closed on the eve of Liberation were shifted to Shanghai.

The main Shanghai branch faced the need to meet tax liabilities, increased labour compensation, and, subsequently, revalued pre-Liberation account liabilities. The branch had, however, insufficient income to meet the Chinese claims. Between 1950 and 1954 inclusive, Head Office had to remit funds to Shanghai to cover losses of approximately $10 million; furthermore, the Bank assigned $18 million to contingency accounts, before published profits, specifically to cover staff payoffs and other expenses expected in any eventual China settlement. This drain of Bank's resources had to be stopped.

On May 27, 1952, the Board, as previously stated, authorized the Chief Manager to take all steps necessary to close down the Shanghai office, noting that the three British banks in China had informed the Chinese authorities of their intention. This was the goal Morse and later Turner were striving to achieve. To speed the process and cut short the lengthy negotiations on minutiae, Morse and the Board of Directors minuted agreement to the concept of an 'all-for-all' settlement – all the Bank's assets in China were to be given up in return for cancellation of all the Bank's liabilities or their assumption by some Chinese organization. This would be the prelude to a full withdrawal.

In March 1955 the final negotiations relative to the settlement were all but completed and the Chinese authorities seemed surprised that the Bank was considering closing its Shanghai branch and abandoning China. The settlement itself was never complete; the Bank's foreign exchange liabilities could not be settled given the U.S. Treasury's Foreign Assets Control regulations at the time. Accordingly the Bank could not follow through on its closure plan. Instead, with the cooperation of the Bank of China, the Hongkong Bank's Shanghai branch moved from the Bund to occupy two floors of a building on Yuan Ming Yuan Road overlooking the then British Consulate-General compound. From this new base the branch was operated by two members of the Foreign staff – in the mid-1960s reduced to one. In the words of the post-war advertisement of Soho's Windmill Theatre, 'We never closed.' Sufficient business was undertaken so that costs were in the main fully covered, a nucleus of a local staff, assisted eventually by an officer seconded from the Bank of China, kept the office functioning, and the Hongkong Bank awaited the turn of events.

Developments in the Shanghai branch

Revaluation of pre-Liberation accounts

The initial approach of the People's Republic of China to monetary questions was one of pure nominalism; that is, the authorities set the rate of exchange between the old and the new currency and ordered debts discharged in the new currency accordingly. The consequences of this approach may be determined from an examination of Table 4.1; this shows that a debt of CNC$1.00 contracted prior to the outbreak of the Pacific War could be repaid by tender of RMB 0.000,000,000,000,008,33. At first glance such a situation might be seen by revolutionary authorities as one favouring the small debtor; he could repay the money-lender in currency depreciated to the point of worthlessness. However, some poor people were creditors, they held savings accounts with banks, and the People's Courts began to examine the problem in terms of equity.

An attractive political argument can be based on the assumption that, for example, a small saver before 1936 could have tendered his silver coins or bullion to the Hongkong Bank Savings Department in return for a credit entered in his passbook; this the Hongkong Bank, acting in accord with public law as promulgated by the various authorities to which it had been subject over the years, now informed the customer was worthless. Stated thus, it seemed unfair, even though pre-war accounts had already been revalued in accordance with National Government regulations; it seemed the type of abuse which a People's Government had been established to remedy, which was precisely the reaction of the Courts in Shanghai.

Once again, financial institutions in China, including the Hongkong Bank, were required, therefore, to revalue their pre-Liberation liabilities according to a scale established not on the basis of a nominalist theory of money (as shown in Table 4.1), but on a basis of equity involving various formulas depending on the amounts involved, the time of the initial deposit, the cost of a package of commodities, and whether the deposit were a fixed or current account, as shown in Table 9.2.[a] As the recalculations required were arithmetically complex and time-consuming and as the Shanghai branch's depleted Foreign staff was inadequate to handle it, the work was done, virtually unsupervised, by the local staff, which had remained at the pre-Liberation level and had little or nothing to do except to calculate its own remuneration by various formulas.

In consequence of these revaluations the Hongkong Bank's China liabilities were increased but the Bank was without local funds to pay. Protests by British overseas banks that the regulations were inequitable were lodged with the Foreign Affairs Department of the Shanghai Military Control Commission, but to no avail.[13] Pressure was put on the Bank to remit funds in; after initial compliance Head Office resisted and the resulting impasse was only resolved by the overall settlement of April 1955. The Bank attempted to sell off its assets on an *ad hoc* basis as funds were needed, but, although the Bank did sell its Bubbling Well Road housing property (including eight residences) in 1950 and its Peking office building to the Indian Embassy for RMB2,196 million in 1954, the Chinese authorities refused to facilitate such sales. They chose to regard the revaluation of deposits and the sale of property as two separate issues.[14]

To express the situation this simply is to ignore the potential problems and the nervous tensions which Foreign staff worked under. They knew, for example, that Robin Gordon of Jardine's, Chairman of Ewo Brewery, had been imprisoned while pressure was put on their Hong Kong office to send in funds. That problem was resolved by the Hongkong Bank making available funds deposited by a foreign-owned chemical factory, which was still in profitable business.

Such happenings, and this was not an isolated case, offset for the most part the pleasures of the last days of the Shanghai clubs. There was a tension from which all suffered, although the treatment of the Hongkong Bank and its staff by the Shanghai authorities was satisfactory by revolutionary standards.

---

[a] Only a portion of any amount so calculated was to be paid over in cash; the balance would be credited to a savings account with the People's Bank. Deposits in Japanese and puppet Government banks were not included, and there were other conditions which are not relevant to this history.

Table 9.2 *China: 1951 conversion rates for pre-Liberation deposits*

STEP I:

(i) Year of deposit	(ii) price index	(iii) real value of the Chinese dollar as a percentage of 1937	(iv) CNC$1.00 converts to RMB (renminbi)
1937	100	100	12500
1938	131	76.34	9543
1939	220	45.45	5681
1940	513	19.49	2436
1941	1296	7.72	965
1942	3900	2.56	320
1943	12936	0.77	96.25
1944	43197	0.23	28.75
1945	163160	0.06	7.50
1946	379600	0.026	3.25
1947	2710750	0.0037	0.46
1948[a]	126932224	0.00008	0.01

STEP II (e.g. for deposits made in **1939**):

amount of fixed deposit[b]	CNC$[d]	× standard of repayment	repayable ×% rate of payment	= RMB[b]
1–200[c]	200	5681 = 1136200	100 =	1,136,200
201–300	100	5681 = 568100	90 =	511,290
301–400	100	5681 = 568100	80 =	454,480
401–500	100	5681 = 568100	70 =	397,670
501–600	100	5681 = 568100	60 =	340,860
601–700	100	5681 = 568100	50 =	284,050
701–1000	300	5681 = 1704300	40 =	681,720
1001–2000	1000	5681 = 5681000	30 =	1,704,300
2001–5000	3000	5681 = 17043000	20 =	3,408,600
over 5000	X–5000	5681 = 28405000	10 =	2,840,500

where X is the amount of the deposit, say CNC$10,000.

[a] August. After August gold yuan debts were calculated in RMB at rates established at Liberation by the Shanghai Regulations.
[b] Current accounts and demand savings deposits repayable at 80% of amounts shown.
[c] Only CNC$200 equivalent paid in cash, the balance in time deposit certificates, etc.
[d] Of the amount deposited, the amount below available for conversion.

Source: 'Regulations of the Government Administrative Council of the Central People's Government regarding the repayment of unpaid sums deposited with financial enterprises before Liberation', in *Chin-jung fa-kuei hui-pien* (Collection of financial laws and regulations; Peking, People's Bank of China, 1953), pp. 117–19, translated in Appendix to Affidavit of Stanley Lubman in the case of *S.A. Judah v Delaware Trust Co. and Shanghai Power Co.*, No. 79. 1974, in the Supreme Court of the State of Delaware.

Seconds of exchange

There were other demands on the Bank.

As told in Volume III, pre-war Hamburg Branch had sold dollar drafts to Chinese seamen, issuing them with both the first and second of exchange. Burch, as Accountant in Shanghai, was confronted with the results.

Hamburg before the war, by German exchange control, could only sell something like twenty Chinese dollars to every applicant. Well, every Chinese seaman in Hamburg invented six names at least and went in and got six drafts, and the idiots in Hamburg issued them with duplicates.

Really the amount, twenty dollars! I mean this is valuable security printing. Absolutely mad.

And lots of these had come and been paid, and the seconds were kept. The Chinese don't like throwing things away, and these kept coming along. To cut a long story short... this is more than one occasion... the second of exchange usually arrived shaped like a foot. They had cut that nice beautiful thick paper to the shape of their slipper, and it was in their insole, and then they fished it out when they heard they could get some money for it.

Of course we paid out very, very little really [the first of exchange having been paid].[15]

Labour relations

The Bank had rationalized its post-war staff and paid off local staff who had been found redundant (see Chapter 3). These now brought a case against the Hongkong Bank in the People's Court for wrongful dismissal claiming back pay. And so F.R. Burch, the Shanghai Accountant and therefore in charge of staff matters, found himself before the Chinese assessor. Fortunately Burch had three factors in his favour: (i) the able Bank interpreter – a former Straits Chinese who had been working with UNRRA – had been unable to leave and needed employment pending receipt of an exit permit, (ii) a bag full of old receipts signed by the complaining ex-employees, and (iii) a fair hearing by the Chinese court.

The Hongkong Bank won the case; it was brought back to the Court on new grounds and the Bank again was successful. The assessor had been satisfied that the Bank had made the payments and that the subsequent inflation was not the Bank's responsibility. This would appear to contradict the equity position referred to above, but the case was different; in the previous instance the liability had remained on the books of the Bank, in the case of the redundant workers the liability had long ago been equitably discharged.[16]

A high proportion of the time spent in labour negotiations was still on the question of redundancy, and the Bank was unsuccessful in further reducing its staff until the settlement of 1955. The Bank by 1953 had, however, reached the position that it could approximately cover its overheads – with the exception of coal for the winter – from rents on its China-wide property holdings and the small amount of business it was permitted to undertake.

There were matters of less importance which nevertheless took time. Discussions were lengthy, but decisions could not be reached at the discussions; the union members had to refer to higher authorities and come back with the new position. Among the problems which arose were: (i) outside messengers were issued with Bank umbrellas, but now the entire local staff demanded umbrellas – eventual outcome: they were issued and (ii) local staff resented the fact that the English 'Wayfoong' was on their uniform in addition to the relevant Chinese characters – outcome: the English was removed.[17]

The Bank agreed to provide new uniforms for the staff and thus, when Yoxall found he had insufficient local funds to cover the cost, he requested and obtained an exceptional remittance of funds totalling $41,000 for the purpose. 'I regret having to ask you for remittances for this item,' he wrote, 'but think you will agree that the Hongkong Bank must abide by its contracts.'[18]

By agreement Burch had succeeded in having the discussions end at 7:00 p.m. each evening, at which time he would leave in style by chauffeur-driven car.

There was none of this locking you in and that sort of thing, or assault for that matter, which happened in the past to some people. You couldn't have union meetings in production time, so I said, well, look here, there's nothing going on now is there in the office?
No.
I said, well, let's start the meeting at half past three and finish at seven. And usually they agreed to seven o'clock. One waited for whatever was being discussed to finish, and I asked them the time, stood up, and there was never any trouble. I just walked out and they walked out.
You resumed again next day. I don't know how many hours one spent.
We had four cars, there were three of us. We couldn't get rid of the car, couldn't sack the chauffeurs, driven home by a chauffeur in real imperialistic style saying, thank heavens, that's over for a moment.[19]

The Board of Directors' policy for settlement and withdrawal

The experience gained from foreign business contacts with China over a period of two hundred years suggested to 'old China hands' that the new Government would be initially difficult to deal with and hard bargaining would be required. But, the conventional wisdom was that in the end a reasonable deal would be made. Hongkong Bankers in Tianjin, for example, who had early experience of the People's Government in the north, were concerned that the full extent of the revolution had not been understood further south – especially in Hong Kong. But the stakes in China are high, and the risk generally considered worth taking, no matter what words of caution are offered.

The policy stated

Both Morse and the Board of Directors had very early taken a pragmatic view of the Bank's China position. As it became apparent that the main occupation of the Shanghai staff was the negotiation of and calculations for an apparent continuing series of demands, Morse pressed for a final solution and for the repatriation of the Foreign staff. In 1953 the Board minuted certain basic principles and authorized Yoxall to negotiate on that basis.

The Board laid down as a general principle that the Bank should not remit funds to China after December 31, 1953. This was agreed by all three British exchange banks. The Foreign Office informed the banks that the British Embassy in Peking had been instructed to support the policy. Until this date funds would be remitted (i) to cover overheads, (ii) to pay off claims totalling £40,000 equivalent registered under the pre-Liberation deposit regulations, and (iii) £10,000 to give the Foreign staff a little hard cash.

Up to mid-1953 negotiations in Shanghai had been on an *ad hoc* basis, taking each problem as it was brought to the Bank on the assumption of continuity. Now the Board instructed Yoxall, the new Shanghai Manager, that he was to negotiate on the basis of a final settlement. At the time Shanghai branch had still to contend with the problems of caretakers in the various offices around China, with repairs, rents, and local disputes. The Board therefore recommended to the Chinese authorities a 'clean' all assets against all liabilities settlement, contingent on the Foreign staff being free to leave the People's Republic. The Board also instructed that Yoxall should inform the authorities that the Bank had done its utmost to obtain release of frozen U.S. dollar assets; in this the Bank was unsuccessful.

The changing atmosphere

In March 1954 there was some progress. A.D.M. Ford and S.J.H. Fox had left China and P.G. Rynd, the Manager Tianjin, noted that if the Bank were to remit in salaries to March 31, 1954, the staff would resign content with that and with the payment of the previously remitted severance allowances – all other matters to be included in the overall settlement. To this the Board agreed, and Rynd left Tianjin on December 16 with the branch closed.

The Chinese authorities also approved an entry permit for W.A. Stewart after some months delay. There had been a question as to whether, in view of his life-style and work during the Pacific War in Shanghai and Lunghwa, his approach was too 'missionary'; he didn't (and doesn't) fit the textbook image of an imperialist. Stewart, who would later serve two tours as Manager Shanghai, was ideal for an assignment in the People's Republic. He was a practical man, who, after calling for assistance to fix the drain, would be discovered down the manhole attempting to cope with it himself when the comrade workers arrived. They appreciated his 'correct attitude'.

By this time Yoxall had been in Shanghai for over three years of tough bargaining and the new Chief Manager, Michael Turner, turned to D. Buchan, then the Manager of the small Malayan branch of Muar, to ask whether, in view of the increased salary and prestige, he would be willing to relieve Yoxall. By the time the change of management was affected, the settlement had been reached and Buchan had the task of implementation, which he conducted in such a way as to suggest that Turner had been aware that Buchan's abilities had been hitherto underutilized.

In this same period overall relations at the national level were improving, a factor which may have played a role in the final settlement. A British trade mission was mounted in London with – much to the annoyance of the Hongkong Bank – a Chartered Bank general manager, W.G. Pullen, as chairman; the Bank's nominee, F.C.B. Black, was deputy. Thus while there was shouting and fist thumping on the negotiating table in Shanghai, there were diplomatic parties in Peking.[20] The improved atmosphere was nevertheless felt in Shanghai.

Shanghai branch was technically open for new business, but Hong Kong did not encourage its development. New business meant the possibility of new controversy. Although the Bank's circulars on the subject were 'hedged', the message was clear; the focus was on settlement and withdrawal. Business with China could be better done in Hong Kong.

This took the argument one step further than the Chinese wished. Shanghai branch as a historical symbol might be harassed, but a Shanghai branch for current purposes might be useful. If the harassment could be terminated by an overall settlement, a new basis for its continued presence might be established. Alternatively, if the Chinese Government were not immediately prepared to take advantage of a 'new' Shanghai branch, arrangements could be made whereby the Hongkong Bank would be willing to put its Shanghai operation on hold.

In August 1954 Yoxall reported that he had been invited to a reception for a British mission hosted by the Indian Consul-General in Shanghai and that, at the party, he had had an 'unprecedented' discussion with the head of the Foreign Affairs Bureau in the English language. Toasts had been drunk to improved Indian, British, and Chinese relations.

At a garden party Yoxall gave for a Labour Party delegation headed by Clement Atlee, Aneurin Bevan informed him that Chinese in Peking had stated they would not hold the representatives of a company because of an outstanding controversy with that company.[21]

THE HONGKONG BANK LEAVES THE BUND
China policy restated

'You, strange to relate,' Michael Turner wrote to Sir Arthur Morse in October 1954, 'never had a positive policy over China. You left me the China problem as a legacy with no suggestions as to how to deal with it and I have dealt with it as I thought best.'[22]

This is the tough Chief Manager Turner sometimes revealed in the correspondence. The criticism is unfair, but what had provoked Turner was Morse's criticism of the Hongkong Bank's planned participation in a forthcoming, China Association organized trade mission to Peking. Turner saw it as an opportunity to open a dialogue and he was determined to talk to the authorities in China's capital. Unlike the 1930s, Shanghai was not the location of the key financial institutions; the Bank of China's head office – and its true policy headquarters – was in the capital; the Shanghai Manager was unable to fill the essential liaison role.

But what was Turner's policy?

Turner's first priority was the early closure of all the Hongkong Bank's offices in China and the granting of exit permits for its Foreign staff. He then sought the acceptance by the Chinese authorities of the broad principle that all the Bank's assets in China should be accepted as an offset to all the Bank's liabilities, and that a Chinese bank should be appointed to facilitate the final closure.[23] On this last, although the Bank of China assisted the Hongkong Bank whenever this was appropriate, the eventual agreement was signed with a specially created entity known as the Ta Hwa Enterprises Company.

Turner also had a positive policy. The Hongkong Bank desired to set up a form of representation in China for the purposes of furthering foreign trade. Turner wished, in other words, to set up a 'post-closure' agency, entirely divorced from all problems arising from the Bank's 90-year history in China. He was even willing to set up the 'post-closure' liaison office before the closure was final.

The Bank of China had throughout cooperated with the Hongkong Bank in the finance of the China trade, mainly in Hong Kong. The Bank of China was anxious to extend this cooperation to banking in China; they accordingly asked, on the assumption that the Hongkong Bank wished to do business with them 'later', that is, after 'closure', why was it not possible to begin immediately. Turner's suggested response as communicated to Yoxall was that the Bank's Shanghai staff were busy with the calculations required by the repayment of pre-Liberation deposits and other administrative requirements, that, in the then atmosphere of suspicion, the Bank was unable to get members of its

Foreign staff either into or out of China, but that the Hongkong Bank was willing to consider ways of undertaking further business.[24]

This dual policy of closure and reopening, logical as it seemed to the Bank, was impractical. From the first, negotiations relative to the Bank's liabilities had to exclude consideration of U.S. dollar liabilities in view of the apparently unshakable position of the American Government relative to frozen assets.[b] A true 'all-for-all' settlement, although the eventual Ta Hwa agreement continued to be referred to in this way, was consequently impossible.

The 1954 trade mission

The Shanghai negotiations were making little progress, and Turner was anxious, as were the East India Company merchants of the eighteenth-century or the Shanghai Manager of the 1880s, to contact Peking, to enter into a dialogue in the capital. He saw the trade mission, whatever its other drawbacks and organizational problems, as an opportunity, and he appointed Black, the Chief Inspector, as the Bank's representative. It was in this context that Turner wrote so sharply to Morse.

By the time the mission actually left London, much had indeed gone wrong in petty but annoying ways. The China Association's secretary, Hugh Collar, had learned that the Bank's representative, Black, would join the group in Hong Kong; the organizers thereupon chose the Chartered Bank to chair the mission on the grounds that the briefings would be held in London and the senior delegate ought to be present. In the event the briefings were held in Hong Kong, and Collar apologized to G.H. Stacey, then Turner's deputy in Hong Kong.

Then the Association, which banked with the Hongkong Bank, issued a circular advising mission members to do their personal financial travel arrangements through the Chartered Bank; S.A. Gray, the Hongkong Bank's London Manager, was angry; they might at least have consulted their own bankers, he wrote. This time Collar wrote apologetically to Turner and issued a revised circular, placing the Hongkong Bank's name first – but with Black's name listed incorrectly.[26]

Once in Peking Black received a cool but not hostile reception from the Vice-Minister of Foreign Affairs, Chang Han Fu, who was concerned, significantly, with the problem of the frozen dollar assets.[c] From the Bank of China, Black

---

[b] The only relevant exceptions made by the U.S. Government were in cases where the release of the assets would secure the exit permit of an American bank employee or merchant from China. These exceptions, coupled with the unwillingness of the American Treasury to grant licences when British nationals were involved, quite naturally annoyed the Hongkong Bank.[25]

[c] The Trade Mission were accompanied by an interpreter from the British Embassy, (Sir) Edward Youde, later Governor of Hong Kong.

received 'friendly advice' – 'Pursue an active role.'²⁷ The Bank of China's policy, the general manager asserted, had been consistent throughout; it had been encouraging and there had been good relations.

At this point Black stood back and reflected. He had to agree with the Bank of China's claim; relations with the Bank of China had been as described. Black's eventual conclusions would parallel Turner's; there had been no basic policy, only reactions. The Hongkong Bank's draw down in China had preceded the Liberation; with the Bank's domestic role fading in the immediate post-war period, a policy of retrenchment was called for. After Liberation there had been a brief period of optimism, killed by the growth of barter trade, the preference for the Bank of China to deal in Hong Kong, and the burden of the pre-Liberation Deposits Regulations. He took the opportunity to urge the assistance of the Bank of China, especially in connection with the sale of assets in China to offset the expense of meeting 'closure' requirements and until the 'all-for-all' settlement were reached.

At the same time Black began negotiations for a new correspondent banking arrangement with the Bank of China, based on back-to-back financing. This offer was followed up immediately from Hong Kong, and indeed negotiated successfully during March and April 1955 while the last weeks of discussion were being held in Shanghai on the Ta Hwa agreement.²⁸

There was a final irony in all this. Turner, then in London, in agreeing to the correspondent relationships added in his cabled instructions to Head Office, '... but I do feel we should stress the need of their cooperation in order to enable us to get our final *closure* completed [emphasis added].'

This appeared in the Bank's official letter of acceptance as '... the negotiations between the Ta Hwa Enterprises Company and our Shanghai Office have continued in a mutually satisfactory manner but have not yet reached completion, and we would once again bespeak your help in bringing these negotiations to a rapid conclusion.'

As previously noted the Ta Hwa Agreement was not the path to final closure; it was not the 'all-for-all' settlement the Bank had hoped for; it excluded the U.S. frozen assets, which no amount of discussion at Peking had solved.ᵈ The Chinese asked for a 'concrete proposal'; the Hongkong Bank, in common with the others represented, had none to give. The Ta Hwa Agreement could, therefore, be ratified only if a Manager remained behind in China. The Hongkong Bank should withdraw its application, filed in 1952, to close its Shanghai office.

ᵈ In 1960 G.O.W. Stewart estimated that the Hongkong Bank's liability was approximately US$4 million but that other banks were even more exposed, for example, the French Bank US$15–25 million and the Banque Belge US$12 million. Their managers were not permitted to leave China.²⁹

Aware that the Chartered Bank had already acted, the Hongkong Bank on May 10, 1955, withdrew its application to close Shanghai; it would remain.[30] There was some concern in Hong Kong, however, that perhaps the Bank would be wiser to establish a representative in Peking. Turner agreed to consult K.C. Jay 謝啟儔, the Bank of China's Hong Kong manager, but in the end the Shanghai office was retained; Peking would come later.

The agreement and its impact

The agreement signed

On the eve of Yoxall's turnover of the Shanghai branch to Buchan the final steps were taken for an agreement in the context of the Board's 1953 policy recommendation. It would be an 'all-for-all' settlement but with foreign liabilities excluded; all the Bank's China properties would be traded for all domestic claims against the Hongkong Bank. The settlement, therefore, despite its importance in the Bank's history, only partially fulfilled the Bank's original expectations.

The final negotiations were detailed and intense. The Hongkong Bank wanted to be certain that the agreement was in fact a final settlement, with 'unknown' items being allowed for at least to an amount in excess of reasonable expectations. There was always the hope that perhaps special provision might be made for such outstandings as the Shanghai Municipal Council (SMC) debt or the sums owed the Bank by the old Stabilization Board for exchange sold but not reimbursed. These concessions by their nature were never realized. On the other side the Chinese negotiators, operating as the Ta Hwa Enterprises Company, needed to be assured that they were not agreeing to give up People's rights without full knowledge and agreement at all levels.

The final negotiations also resolved a potentially contentious situation arising from the claim that the Shanghai Manager was personally liable as trustee for the debts of the SMC. This had first arisen in 1951 over attempts by former Russian SMC employees to have the authorities admit that the trust agreement had made the Manager personally liable for the pension and superannuation funds of the SMC.[31] The Bank claimed that Yoxall was a 'holding Trustee' only, and that the original Deed of Trust, designed to protect the SMC's assets against political confiscation or misuse, was effective only if the Manager agreed to act. The use of the 'unknown' liabilities clause in the agreement, within which this claim was now included, permitted this problem to be passed over.

In February 1954 the draft agreement had been approved by Michael Turner, albeit without reference to the Bank of England, an omission which had to be squared later through the good offices of Sir Edward Reid. But, as

Turner noted, the matter had to be handled on a day-to-day basis on the spot; the opportunity could not be missed and only those in China knew the actual potential for manoeuvre.

Yoxall noted that the Mercantile Bank, which eventually did close its Shanghai branch, had signed its agreement with Ta Hwa on February 28, 1955. Agreement with the Chartered Bank was apparently not far off; hopes were running high. Expectations were not disappointed; the Hongkong Bank/Ta Hwa Agreement was signed April 26, 1955, and three copies transmitted to Head Office in Hong Kong.

The terms

The agreement, known officially in translation as 'Deed of Properties Transfer signed between the British Hongkong and Shanghai Banking Corporation (Transferor) and Ta Hwa Enterprises Company (Transferee)', is simple in its exposition.[32]

The Preamble recites the fact that the Hongkong Bank, 'in consideration of its huge organization in China which needs adjustment, also of its various debts and obligations which need to be settled, has decided to adjust its organization and transfer all its properties in China to settle its debts in China.'

Paragraph One states that the Bank of its own accord transfers to the Ta Hwa Enterprises all its properties, and these are then enumerated by geographical location and by category – the complete list was to be attached. Paragraph Two states that Ta Hwa agrees to undertake payment of the Hongkong Bank's debts and obligations in China; these are enumerated and include taxes and pre-Liberation deposits not paid out, obligations to staff members, obligations regarding unredeemed China-issued banknotes, and other concrete items agreed to. Debts which are not listed but are discovered later are covered to a total of (new) RMB50,000.

The remaining paragraphs deal with implementation.

The agreement did not cover the frozen U.S. dollar assets. This made a final clean cut with the past impossible; it also reopened the question of the Bank's continued operation in China.

Yoxall leaves the Bund

The Ta Hwa Agreement might be supposed the virtual end of the history of the Hongkong Bank in China. In consequence, W.T. Yoxall, the man who had signed over the Bank's heritage to the People's Government, left the great Shanghai office building, the very building A.G. Stephen had ordered built to dominate the Bund. This building, built, as a contemporary Chinese journalist wrote, with the blood and sweat of the Chinese people, was finally handed over to the Chinese people.

People still remember vividly the scene in which the last manager, Yoxall, left the bank building. With a bulky briefcase under his arm, he came out of the main entrance in low spirits. Down the stone staircase, step by step, he walked and then stopped for more than once, turned his head around to look attentively at the building.

His eyes fell on the pair of bronze lions, from one to the other, and was reluctant to leave the place.

Only after a long while did he move on again. After a few paces he turned round again and made a deep bow to the building, murmuring inaudibly. He moved on again and looked back once, a second time...

How reluctant he must have felt to take leave of this building – a symbol of colonialism and imperialism![33]

This was high drama. And yet, surprising as it may seem, the key question remained unanswered: what was to be the Hongkong Bank's role in the People's Republic of China?

To remain or not?

The Bank as symbol had to be removed; the Bank as bank had to be retained. For its part the Bank could never shed its interest in China business; the only question was where to base that business. Grayburn had hesitated to force the Bank on Nationalist Nanking; now Turner questioned the wisdom of a Bank presence in Shanghai. Furthermore, the Bank's relations with the Bank of China and especially with the China Resources Company in Hong Kong were excellent. The Bank was heavily involved in financing the China trade through the Bank of China's Hong Kong office, facilitating the export of key commodities to, among others, the United States.[e]

This relationship with the Bank of China seemed to Turner the basis for the Bank's new China policy. The events in Peking in November 1954 seemed to confirm this – Black had initiated successful negotiations for a new comprehensive correspondent relationship with the Bank of China. With the Ta Hwa Agreement signed, the Hongkong Bank would close in Shanghai, but this is not what happened. Turner had considered as an alternative the opening of a 'post-closure' office, divorced from the past. But this is not what happened either. The continued existence of the U.S. dollar liabilities required the Shanghai branch to remain open; it was this office which would constitute the Bank's visible presence in China throughout the difficult years to come. The historical continuity was not, after all, to be broken.

---

[e] The United States required, for example, bristles and duck feathers – the products of the once despised 'muck and truck' trade. In view of the embargo, these goods had to be routed via Japan and/or Singapore, a costly process facilitated by the Bank – and by the American customs authorities.

First post-agreement, post-mission consequences

The change in atmosphere became of considerable concern to the Hongkong Bank. Having made a settlement, to what extent could it afford to redevelop in Shanghai, to what extent could business be expected to cover any increased overheads and staff salaries? Buchan, as the Shanghai Manager, advised Head Office that the Bank of China had asked the Bank to remove the note 'not operating', which appeared in its circulars advising on its branch network. Later he would write, 'For some peculiar reason they are adopting a most friendly attitude towards us at present, even to the extent of offering us business on a platter, despite existing Agency arrangements.'[34] And even these had been extended; on July 20, 1955, the Bank of China's general manager in Peking wrote (as translated):

...we should like from now on to entrust directly to your branches in Japan banking business in connection with Sino-Japanese trade. Meanwhile, we shall be glad to be entrusted with such business by your branches in Japan.

The above mentioned banking business, however, shall be restricted to irrevocable letters of credit opened by either of our two banks, to the exclusion of advising of letters of credit opened by other banks in China or Japan without confirmation being added by either of our two banks.[35]

The Bank of China also wanted advice on its new export drive to Canada.

The Hongkong Bank naturally welcomed these opportunities; the Bank's problem was solely with the possible overburdening of its Shanghai office, that is, with business to be handled by Shanghai branch given the new conditions and the minimal staff retained. After consideration, the Bank issued a circular from London Office, dated November 18, 1955, in which the Bank's agents and correspondents were notified that, as an amendment to circulars of March 1952 and November 1953,

We are happy to advise you that the situation has since improved to the extent that our *Shanghai* Office is now able to deal with mail and telegraphic transfers directed to it, but that for the time being it is not equipped to handle letter of credit or documentary bill business because of the small representation at present maintained there. It will also be glad at all times to help with information or advice on local firms or conditions.

As for Tianjin, Peking, and Shantou, the circular noted, these had been closed and 'it is not our present intention to reopen them'.

Earlier however Buchan, the Shanghai Manager, had asked that Head Office notify correspondents, 'We are now in a position to receive and advise credits as well as negotiate documents under them.'

Moodie, by then the Hong Kong Manager, was less sanguine. He considered dealing with the Bank of China in Hong Kong would be easier; he asked pointedly whether, given that Chinese was the official language, Buchan could

Table 9.3 *The Hongkong and Shanghai Banking Corporation Shanghai branch: business, 1957, 1958*

(values in pounds sterling)

	June 1957	December 1957	June 1958
Bills negotiated			
numbers	57	83	129
value	106,603	162,500	415,500
Letters of credit advised (HSBC)			
numbers	45	49	72
value	92,800	185,800	256,400
Letters of credit advised (other banks)			
numbers	12	11	11
value	15,500	49,500	12,270
Inward remittances			
numbers	53	68	53
value	42,400	59,750	60,500

Source: Shanghai file, Head Office, Hongkong Bank

guarantee the translation of documents. The decision to stay was being questioned. Finally in May 1956 Buchan put the issue squarely once again to Moodie. Do we stay or not?

The response came from the Chief Manager, Michael Turner, in August. He confirmed that the Bank would remain in Shanghai as long as permitted by the Chinese authorities.

Uncertainty remains

Despite this favourable response, the problem of China's frozen foreign exchange assets remained. The Hongkong Bank, as well as other banks, had made representations in Washington, but to no avail. Until the assets were released, or until times had changed to make the issue of less significance, the situation, although vastly improved, was potentially unsettled.

Turner was writing as late as June 1957, 'I am not an optimist about either trade with China or our share in it.' He authorized Perry-Aldworth, then as London Manager about to embark on a tour to visit correspondents in Scandinavia, to inform them, contrary to the circular cited above, that business from agencies and correspondents with Shanghai was being diverted at the Hongkong Bank's instigation through the Bank of China – the Hongkong Bank's Shanghai office had retained insufficient staff to handle any but direct Hongkong

The Hongkong Bank in China, 1949-1962

Bank branch business. Turner also confirmed that a full settlement remained the priority and determination of subsequent relations was secondary.[36]

That, however, was not the way the Chinese authorities wished to proceed. The foreign exchange problem remained unresolved, and it was for the Chinese to determine developments.

Business did increase, and the problem would be how to handle it (see Table 9.3). This was really Turner's dilemma; how much could the Bank do without being over-committed at a time when not all outstanding problems had been resolved? For a time the Bank decided to retain a second member of the Foreign staff in Shanghai. Even then the annual losses on Shanghai's Profit and Loss Account were reduced to some $300,000; furthermore the losses had disappeared by 1959. Shanghai was very close to paying its own way, even though profits could not be remitted.

More satisfactory, the basic decision to remain had not been reversed and the Bank was learning to settle down in the New China, work with the Bank of China in developing Chinese exports, and retain a simple, waiting presence. Political issues would arise from time to time – during the Rectification Campaign in 1958, for example, the local staff were not available until 10:45 a.m. Other problems will be considered in Part III, but the Hongkong Bank's presence remained. This would prove very important to the Bank and, in the end, useful to both parties.

THE POST-AGREEMENT BANK AND CHINA

New problems

Moving to new premises

Although it was obvious that the Hongkong Bank's Shanghai branch could hardly expect to occupy the building on the Bund, Yoxall had hoped that he might be able to rent a small portion of it. This, he reported to Head Office, was impossible. The building was to become the offices of the People's Council of Shanghai; there was no room for a bank. However, quarters were found on the fifth and sixth floors of a building on Yuan Ming Yuan Road, with space totalling approximately 3,716 sq. metres; additional space was found in an adjoining godown for some 400 large crates of the Bank's records.[f] The Chartered Bank occupied a floor in the same building immediately below the Hongkong Bank.

---

[f] By the time the Mercantile Bank closed its office in Shanghai it was already wholly owned by the Hongkong Bank. One of the first consequences of this acquisition was the willingness of the Bank to hold the Shanghai records of the Mercantile. With the very helpful permission of the various authorities, the Bank was able to ship the bulk of this material for preservation and consultation in its Archives in Hong Kong.

A Shanghai journalist has been quoted on the departure of the Bank's Shanghai Manager from its building on the Bund. Yoxall carried a 'bulky briefcase'. W.A. Stewart, however, was responsible for the removal of everything else, and his story follows. First, however, it is well to record that the occupation of the building had not really been that practical even before the settlement of 1955.

> The thing I do remember about that [time] most of all is the bitter cold in the winter time. We had no heating in the old building... marble floors, marble pillars, bronze gates and bronze counter grilles and so forth, and we wore our overcoats and hats and gloves in the office. Of course, Shanghai is bitterly cold in the winter time, but to be in that marble-faced hall was really dreadful. Sometimes we used to get up from our chairs and stamp our feet on the marble floors to bring back circulation.
> When I was there, it was decided that these one hundred fifty clerks, except for a dozen, be paid off, and that we should move out of our building on the Bund... a truly magnificent bank building... to quarters which the authorities found for us behind the British Consulate compound.
> I had an awful job then of moving the records. We didn't take them all with us, but I had to pack, with the help of a few clerks, about four hundred crates of records, which was quite a lot, and move them over by hand trolleys to a godown adjacent to our present quarters in Yuan Ming Yuan Road. This took quite some time.
> Another job I had there was parcelling up and recording details of former customers' securities, which were very numerous, bearer bonds and share certificates and whatnot, labelling them with the customer's name and lodging them with one of the Chinese banks for safe custody, where I presume they lie to this day.[37]

Local staff

As late as April 1955 one of the Hongkong Bank's chief concerns remained unresolved. All parties had agreed that the local staff would be reduced from some 150 to about twelve, 'including menials', but it was not clear how the twelve were to be selected or by whom. The Bank was naturally anxious that the selection not be arbitrary or come from a Union pool. Once again the authorities were cooperative; the Bank was permitted to submit a list of preferences, and the list was honoured. The Bank was fully satisfied with the selection in which the Manager had been permitted a major role. Those remaining were referred to as 'hard-working and loyal'. Included among them was Zee Tsung Yung who had been told by Connie Martin in 1938, 'Stick with the Bank. It will never close or let you down.'[38]

On a technical point, however, the Bank was permitted to 'retain' rather than 're-employ' the staff. The Chinese authorities were, in the 'all-for-all' settlement, responsible for the severance and all other staff benefits of those leaving the Bank's service. This, then, would not include those remaining; the Bank would have to treat them, relative to benefits, as old staff rather than as newly employed. As Buchan pointed out, the additional responsibility, while hardly negligible, should be accepted under the circumstances. Given the fact that the Bank's nominees had been agreed to by the Chinese for continued service with the Shanghai branch, the Chinese position was logical.

As for Mrs Martin herself, she chose to remain in Shanghai to care for her many cats and there was always work to be done. When secretarial work had fallen to a minimum, the new Manager in 1961, E.C. Hutchison, at the instigation of J.R. Jones, asked her to type out key documents from the files to assist in the collection of material for the Bank's centenary history.[g] During the Cultural Revolution this activity was considered with suspicion; Mrs Martin was confined for a period and after release left China for retirement in London, the last of the Bank's local British employees in Shanghai.

Lions and Russians
The Chinese authorities had assured the Labour Party delegation that they would not retain British staff in China because of disagreement with the corporation. They said nothing about lions or Russians.

In a dramatic article entitled, 'What the Bronze Lions Saw and Heard', a Shanghai journalist described the historical events which had occurred along the Bund.[39] They were a landmark, and Yoxall wrote, 'Old customs survive even in changing times. The paws get more wear and tear from stroking by passers-by than ever.'[40] As in the days of Stitt, Lowson, and Henchman (Shanghai Managers, 1920–1926, 1926–1931, and 1931–1945 respectively), there remained the hope that the joss might rub off.

The lions had served the Hongkong Bank well, and, following the 'all-for-all' settlement, the Chief Manager sought permission for them to be shipped to Hong Kong. The first Chinese response was that the building would look 'barren' without them.[41] Furthermore the export of bronze required special authority and this was never forthcoming, even though Turner in an April 1956 letter to the British Consul in Shanghai requested his assistance and noted that Bank would make payment in foreign exchange.

And then the lions disappeared.[h]

The Russians in China had not enjoyed extrality since the early 1920s. Descendants, for the most part, of White Russian *émigrés*, they remained in exile, mainly in the north and in Shanghai, during the inter-war period. But with the Liberation of 1949 the role of the resident foreigner had come to an end, and the Russians were in a difficult position. Many in Manchuria had taken Soviet passports in the period immediately following World War II and were

---

[g] Even though the main files were, with the permission of the authorities, shipped to Hong Kong after 1979, the 'Hutchison file' (like the 'F.H. King file' from London) has proved of great value in the writing of this history.

[h] Although lost to public view, they were later seen in a photograph. In the 1980s negotiations were again undertaken for their release, this time on the initiative of the Bank's Chairman, Michael Sandberg.

offered repatriation to the Soviet Union in the mid-1950s. Many, however, including some who had become Soviet citizens, did not wish to go to Russia; they sought permission to emigrate to Australia and to North America.

The Hongkong Bank employed White Russians as guards and engineers and, especially in the Northeast, as the 'second tier', that is, as clerks. The Russians in Shanghai sought increased benefits in the immediate post-Liberation days but more were taken care of eventually by repatriation.

One Russian in particular has a place in any history of the Hongkong Bank. Alexander Triphonovich Ostrenko was born in Dneprpetrovsk, Russia, in 1894, and moved to Harbin in 1904 – his father was employed by the railway. Educated in Harbin, Ostrenko went to Petrograd where he joined the Russian Army and became a prisoner of war in Germany; he later served with White Russian forces in Ha'erbin (Harbin). After working as an accountant and bank clerk, he joined the Hongkong Bank in 1923 and served continuously until his death in 1957. Ostrenko is named in several written and oral memoirs of Foreign staff; during the Pacific War he preserved the Bank's property and kept a successful watch over the Bank's investment in I.I. Tschurin's department store and related properties. In this way he served through Japanese, Russian, and Communist Party occupation of Ha'erbin; post-war he was again in communication with the Bank in Shanghai.

The Bank never reopened in Ha'erbin, although it was slow to give up the hope that this might be possible. Accordingly Ostrenko was given the option of remaining in a caretaker position or of being assisted through the Hong Kong office of the U.N. High Commissioner for Refugees should he wish to emigrate. At first he decided to remain; then in 1953, recognizing that the Bank would not soon return to Ha'erbin, he stated his intention of emigrating, and R.W. Taplin, then in charge of personnel matters in Head Office, took an interest in the case, especially after a retiree, H.F. Phillips, who had known Ostrenko from his Shenyang (Mukden) assignment, wrote, 'I know you will help...[he is] a fine sort of chap.'

The size of the file on this case – possibly even the amount of executive time committed – seems to rival the Bank's involvement with the 'all-for-all' settlement. Between 1953 and 1954 the Bank wrote letters to the Bank of New South Wales to ask their advice on what might be considered a fair pension acceptable as self-supporting by the Immigration Department, to the Australian Trade Commissioner in Hong Kong, to the UN High Commissioner, to the Hong Kong authorities to obtain transit visas for Ostrenko, his wife, and son, to various medical authorities, and to the British Consulate in Ha'erbin. When these preliminaries had been completed, the Bank wrote letters of appreciation to all involved.

The Bank apparently still believed that, as Sir Thomas Jackson had put it, nothing was too big and nothing too small for the Hongkong Bank.

Ostrenko however now held a Soviet passport and the Chinese authorities were unwilling to grant him an exit permit while the Soviet Consulate were processing repatriation requests. At this point Ostrenko's son decided to return to the Soviet Union, thus making the family a less self-supporting unit in Australia. The delay into 1956 resulted in all the visas and other permissions becoming out of date; and, on learning that Ostrenko still planned to emigrate and that the Soviet offer had been closed, the Hongkong Bank wrote again to all concerned and had the visas and permissions reissued.

In January 1957 Ostrenko's wife became ill. The pressures, the hopes, and the delays were proving too much for him. On May 12 he wrote to the Bank, expressing his appreciation for their help, urging their assistance to his wife, and stating, 'I have decided to take my life!' Written in pencil at the bottom of the letter was the note, 'My husband died 24 June.'

The Hongkong Bank had been prepared to pay Ostrenko a gratuity of £2,500 plus £100 p.a. pension. They were, however, willing to use at least part of these funds for related purposes. They accordingly paid for a funeral, and a wreath was provided; the Chief Manager wrote a letter of condolence. More practically, the Bank began another round of correspondence with the authorities to get Mrs Ostrenko to Australia. She, however, died in early 1958. At this point the Ostrenkos' Russian housekeeper had been commended to the attention of the Bank. The Bank immediately wrote the housekeeper offering assistance 'before she has to ask for it first'. She had made the last days of the Ostrenkos bearable and with minimal remuneration; she was now destitute and asked to be assisted to emigrate. The Bank accordingly made successful arrangements for her to leave Ha'erbin for Australia through Hong Kong.

A June 1957 minute by the Board of Directors took note of Ostrenko's death and valuable service. It also noted the assistance the Bank was giving to other Russians, referred to as the 'Manchurian Staff'. G. Yasheroff, a guard who had joined the Bank in 1934, had passed through Hong Kong for Australia under the Bank's patronage; at his age no further problems were anticipated. A widow recently arrived in Australia with Bank assistance reported her son was in technical college and that she was looking for work; a gratuity of $1,000 each had been given to I. and N. Cherepanoff, guards at Shenyang, in addition to the Bank's assistance in their voyage south.

Corners of foreign fields
There were Foreign staff who would, however, in some sense remain forever in China. In a series of instructions dating from 1957 to 1958 P.A. Sellars

(Inspector, staff) set out the Bank's policy with reference to overseas graves, and Bank Managers were responsible for locating them and ensuring that flowers were laid on the graves at least once, preferably twice a year. E.G. Hillier's grave was found in Peking and a new tombstone erected; graves in Shanghai's Bubbling Well cemetery had been removed to a location farther from the city, but the removals had been fully documented and the Chinese authorities cooperated with the Shanghai and Peking Managers in these gestures to past servants of the Hongkong Bank.

This was apparently part of a general program. In early 1958 the Board of Directors were informed that the Bank had located 55 Foreign staff graves, put them in good order, and ordered flowers to be placed on the graves at Christmas-tide.

As far as China is concerned, all this was further evidence of another transition, a transition indeed which is not yet completed. In 1984, for example, the Shanghai branch was once again able to accept deposits from overseas customers and new representative offices were being opened to serve China's financial requirements as her modernization programs developed. China's forbearance with a capitalist enterprise and the Bank's underlying feeling that its destiny must always depend in large part on China made possible the continuing relationship during difficult times. For both sides there would be benefit.

THE SHANGHAI BRANCH AND ITS MANAGERS, 1958–1966

The Managers

W.A. Stewart (East in 1933) first served in Shanghai in 1933–1935 and again from 1939 until caught by the outbreak of the Pacific War. He returned as Accountant in 1954 but left Shanghai in 1956. Then after a year in Hong Kong and a further year as Manager of the Suapah Road branch in Bangkok, Stewart returned to Shanghai as Manager in 1958. He remained until 1961 in which year he was appointed the Manager Bangkok. After a tour in Head Office he again returned to Shanghai, serving as Manager from 1963 to 1966 and leaving some two weeks after the Cultural Revolution may be said to have commenced.

During these periods the Shanghai branch made a small profit; remittance of profit was limited as funds needed to be built up against possible reassessment of tax liabilities. Business was basically the financing of China's exports, dealing with China's export corporations – 'bicycles to Pakistan and rosaries to Italy, pianos to Iceland' was the way Stewart described the variety. Banking business was discussed with the Bank of China, the responsible institution, and there were periodic visits from their liaison officer.[42] Day-to-day contact was made by telephone between the Hongkong Bank's Chinese staff and the appropriate 'opposite numbers' in the Bank of China.

E.C. Hutchison had come East first in 1931 and served in Shanghai through 1936. He was interned in Shanghai and served there immediately post-war, although he was also sent to reopen Hankow office. After serving as Manager of the Kobe, Kowloon, and Singapore's Orchard Road branches, he relieved Stewart as Manager Shanghai in 1961.

The following vignettes of the life of the Hongkong Bank's Shanghai Managers between the post-1955 rebirth of business and the Cultural Revolution are a measure of the Bank's commitment to China and its resolve, as expressed in 1956 by Michael Turner, to remain in Shanghai while the authorities permitted the Bank to do so. Business and social life can hardly be separated; it was a total experience.

The Shanghai branch at work

Stewart must have been aware of some of the problems of life in Shanghai. The question was whether he was reluctant to go back?

> I was due to retire in '63. No, especially as I was going back [to Shanghai in 1958] as Manager, I rather looked forward to it. And I thought, well, here's a chance. I haven't got all that longer to go. I had no reason to refuse it. I'd no objection, and I knew the house where I would live. It's a beautiful house with extensive grounds, of course, so I didn't mind at all.[43]

On business
On profit and remittance, W.A. Stewart recalls:

> Our profit was very much controlled by the Bank of China, who could raise the profit or lower the profit by allowing us business or not. We advised letters of credit to the exporting corporations. Now these letters of credit...the bills under them negotiated when the goods were shipped...can be either brought to us or brought to the Bank of China. If it were a big amount, it was usually taken to the Bank of China because they then got the exchange and any commission on it. They could give us exactly what they wanted. So in that way they could control very accurately what we made...
>
> The profits had to remain in Shanghai and you built up a fund. I can't remember whether we ever remitted out or not. I think there were profits, small profits. But, of course, there was taxation also. You were never given a discharge for the taxation. They could come back in, say, three years' time and say, we're going to raise the rates retroactive for three years by ten percent, and then you'd have to pay, say, three years' increases. So there was always this danger, and I think a balance was always kept in Shanghai in our name at that time.[44]

This is consistent with assurances given by the Bank of China to G.O.W. Stewart, when he visited Peking in 1958, that sufficient business would be directed to the Hongkong Bank so that the Shanghai expenses would be covered.

Business developed further under Hutchison's management in 1962.

...the Bank there could do no domestic banking. You had to hand over your foreign exchange to the Bank of China every night and telegraph London, pay Bank of China. They gave you local currency equivalent that you used to pay yourself and your staff. But I will say in fairness to them, of the letters of credit opened... you see, again they're dependent on Bank agency arrangements... on the letters of credit opened with them, they gave us seventy-five percent.[45]

There were two difficult moments in the routine of business. The first involved a visit from Bank of China inspectors who required to be shown the Semi-official correspondence...

which of course are private letters from one Manager to another Manager and not letters which go into the general filing system. [This] rather put me in a difficult and embarrassing position. They were very pressing, and they said that in future they would want to see all semi-official letters, in and out.

So I wrote to Head Office and explained this to them; they were always very understanding. Without my saying too much they understood exactly what was wanted. I remember going home that night with great files and wading through letters going back quite a bit, just to see whether there was anything really objectionable in them, or to which objection might be taken, but there was nothing out of the ordinary, and I felt I was quite lucky.

Another problem I had once was verbal guarantees covering negotiation of documents, where there were discrepancies between the documents themselves and the terms of the letter of credit. We formerly would get a written guarantee from the exporter in case the bill was unpaid at the other end, when we could claim refund from the exporter. Well, for some years we had taken verbal guarantees, which were normally not permitted.

Anyway in Shanghai, at that time, you had to do business as best you could.

We usually noted the name of the official in the Export Corporation who was speaking to us on the phone. If there were any troubles at the other end when it came to paying the bill, we could come back on the official and say, oh, well, you told us that if the bill were unpaid because of this or that, you would see us put right. For a long time this worked very well, they never once failed to honour the verbal guarantee, they kept their word, and we never lost out on anything until one day when there was a large export shipment. We paid the exporter, but the bill was unpaid at the other end. When we came back on the exporter, they more or less refused to honour their verbal guarantee. So I was somewhat annoyed at this. I remember at the time saying that in future we must get something in writing each time from the Export Corporation under which we could claim a refund in the event of the relative bill being unpaid by the drawee. I must say, they made no objection at all, and from that time on we got some initial on a letter or something of that sort. That was the second incident I can remember.[46]

On labour relations

Relations with the local staff were generally on a sound basis, but there could be misunderstandings. The chairman of the union covering the staff of the two foreign banks was a Hongkong Bank clerk, formerly an office boy. Before the Pacific War he had fallen ill and W.A. Stewart had gone to see him in hospital...

...a dreadful hospital, not well kept at all. He'd got malaria I think.

Anyway I think he always remembered it, and I found him not too exacting. But, of course, he had to support the Union, and I remember him once coming down to me with the office interpreter. This chairman could speak quite good English himself, but when he appeared with the interpreter, you knew there was trouble!

He sat down at my desk in my room, and there was a silence for a few seconds, and then he said, through the interpreter... which was very strange because normally we spoke English between ourselves directly... he said he had a matter to make a complaint about.

I'm sorry to hear that.

He said that the Accountant had come up the previous day at lunch time or near lunch time and spoken roughly to the staff.

I'm surprised to hear that, how did it come about?

He was calling some figures with Mr So and So, and we were talking amongst ourselves in the same room some distance away, and he told us to keep quiet because he couldn't hear what was being said by the clerk.

Well, I said, of course, naturally if the noise was disturbing him, he probably would ask them to keep quiet.

This man hates the Chinese.

I don't think so at all.

You look at his face, he hates us.

I wouldn't have thought that at all.

Anyway, this Union representative said, Would you speak to him and explain to him about our complaint?

I said, all right, I'll have a word with him, and they went off. This sort of thing. So it was difficult at times.

On the other hand I got praised sometimes. One day the messenger went out, the Bank messenger, on his rounds during the floods in his bare feet, and I just happened to see him coming back. Walking in his bare feet... I walked in my bare feet home in Shanghai myself during the floods pre-war, but I said to the chief clerk, Specky [Yang San Lin 楊三驎], hasn't Yung [Zse Tsung] 徐春榮 got a pair of boots for the wet weather?

He said, no.

I said, you must get him a pair of boots, Bank account... which he did, and the following week or two, I don't know how it arose, but this clerk came to me and said, the Union were very gratified that I considered the clerk's feet and ordered the boots, it showed the right attitude and so on and so on.

I said, Oh, well, anyway that's that.[47]

On life in Shanghai

The clubs had closed, most foreigners had left – there were some 24 when Hutchison took over Shanghai office in 1961 – but the British Consulate was still there in the great compound facing the Bund and foreigners still had their houses with gardens. In the earlier period Stewart recalls:

We had a very large garden and a bowling green in the garden, a grass green, and I had two pianos in the house in the drawing room. Weekdays, of course, you went home and either visited a friend...there was a Bank car...or listened in to the radio or music or wrote letters or did something in the house. It was a quiet life. There were no entertainments, no. There were cinemas, but they were all propaganda films in Chinese. And at weekends I always had all the foreign community and some Chinese round to play bowls on the lawn. There was a lady who came round and we used to practice duets together on the two pianos.

I had a number of dinners in the house, quite good dinners at a huge table and maybe twenty to thirty guests. Of course, there weren't all that many foreigners so it became possible at last to invite members of our junior staff, of course including Chinese members.[48]

The pace did not change during Hutchison's managership, but official entertaining was also required. When Hutchison arrived to take over from Stewart, representative members of the export corporations came to a Bank cocktail party.

There could be occasional trouble with the police – especially over non-registered societies.

Chartered Bank were going to hold a dinner on St Andrew's night, and they invited as many guests as they knew. The manager asked me would I like to share in expenses. I said, sure. So we arranged it all and sent out invitations to a St Andrew's Day dinner.

On the day of the dinner we both received telephone calls from the local police station, and we went to the station in the afternoon and met there. I thought, funny...we were always very worried about these summonses. I couldn't think why we were there, I had no idea that it was anything to do with the party.

We were taken to the back room of the station, and the policeman had his hat on, which meant he's on official business. He said to my colleague, what is St Andrew's Society? Then it dawned on me what the trouble was! My colleague said, it's a loose collection of Scotsmen who gather together on this day to commemorate St Andrew and so on and so on.

[The police official replied,] this Society is not registered with us at all; the party must be cancelled, and you must both write letters of apology to us. So we went back to our offices and wrote letters of apology, and then he rang up all these people he'd invited and said, very sorry, it can't be held. So that was a result of having our dinner on St Andrew's night![49]

Several years later the Society was registered under provisions for minority groups.

Miscellaneous comments

The problem of reference matter
Reading material sent in from Hong Kong could cause problems. In one instance the Hong Kong Government's annual report was confiscated because it referred to China and to Taiwan, suggesting the latter was not part of the former. The reason for another confiscation was not quite so obvious – at least not to Stewart.

I wanted an office atlas. The atlas we were using was about 1890, a *Times* atlas, much out of date, especially Africa. We often got calls from the export corporation asking us where was the capital of Zaire or some other place, and, of course, the atlas was completely out of date. So I wrote to Head Office and said, would they please send us an atlas? And eventually the atlas was posted in. Next thing was I got a letter from the post office customs summoning me to the post office at ten-fifteen the next day, room number so and so. I thought, oh, dear, what's gone wrong now?

So I went along with an interpreter, Mr Meng, and we were invited to a room upstairs and sat on big horsehair easy chairs, and eventually an elderly man came in dressed in a boiler suit, carrying an opened parcel.

He said to the interpreter, is this Mr Stewart?

And the interpreter said, yes.

Is he the Hongkong Bank Manager?

Yes.

He opened the parcel and there was the atlas! He said, did he ask for this atlas to be sent in? Meng spoke to me.

I said, no, I asked for *an* atlas to be sent in.

Did you specify what name?

No, I don't know any names of atlases... I didn't specify anything, I just said an atlas and left it open to Head Office to choose.

Why do you want it? I explained why I wanted it.

It went on like this for a long time, then he opened the atlas at page sixty-seven or something and said, handing it to me, do you see this map?

I said, yes, it's a map of India and the Himalayas and Tibet and that part of the world.

Do you see anything wrong with it?

I looked at it and said, I'm not sufficiently knowledgeable to know whether it's all correct or not.

He said, there's a grave error here.

Where is it?

Do you see that line?

There was a line... not more than half an inch, maybe less than half an inch. I said, I see it, yes.

Don't you see anything wrong with it?

No, it seems all right to me.

Mmmm, he said, it shows Mount Everest in India.

I said, is that wrong?

This atlas, he said, is disseminating false knowledge. And he went on like that for a long time about disseminating false knowledge... this is a very grave error, the book is confiscated.

Well, I said, if you say so, that must be true. So I got up and came out and went back to my office.

About four months later I said to Meng, do you think that atlas has really been confiscated? He said, well, no harm in writing again.

So I wrote a letter to the post office customs asking them would they reconsider the matter of the atlas, if it was still in their possession, and gave it to Meng to put into Chinese because you could only write in Chinese as the official language. Meng came down about five or ten minutes later and said, you can't say this.

Can't say what?

He said, this line is too strong.

Well, I replied, you water it down a bit, what would you say?... So he wrote a letter and sent it off. Next morning we got a telephone call from the post office customs, would

Mr Stewart and his interpreter attend the post office now. It was really a command, not an invitation!

So we put on our coats and hats and went down to the post office customs again, the main post office, in fact to the same room, and the same man appeared carrying the same parcel, the brown paper was still on it. He sat down in silence for a bit, then he opened it up and produced the letter I'd written the previous day, and he said through the interpreter that he'd received the letter, that it was couched in the proper language. In view of the statements contained therein they had reconsidered the matter, and it had been decided to release the atlas to us. So I nodded my head in appreciation. Then he said, moreover the offending page will not be torn out, neither will the offending boundary be expunged. These were the words that the interpreter used.

...and furthermore there would be no charge for storage!

He became quite friendly, and he said, well, would you go back to the office now and write out a receipt for the atlas and send it to us with your messenger tomorrow morning.

I said, I'll do that...and we got our atlas. It took us nearly five months.[50]

Surveillance

The movements of foreigners were a matter of routine police reporting. This was neither surprising nor disturbing – in fact, Hutchison felt better if he were assured his activities were fully known and, equally important, understood. The Bank Manager had, of course, servants, and Hutchison described their relationship.

...We also had the Lane Committee which used to meet in my house, which I thought was probably a good thing. That's how they had complete surveillance. They had a Committee of Fifty under the Lane Committee, then there'd be a Street Committee above them, there'd be an Area Committee, until you get right up to the top.

...I'd rather they knew exactly what I did. I mean, your chauffeur would tell them if they wanted to know. No, I don't think the Lane Committee would have a ticket to spy upon us. I think they liked our kitchen, and they probably got a bit of our food or something. And they kept the locals from stealing all our stuff. They did steal all our bamboo fence, poor things, for fuel I suppose. An enormous big bamboo fence – it all disappeared, and the authorities built us a brick wall in its place.

Yes, we were quite [friendly with the servants]...Ah Tu, yes. We had a boy, a cook, and an amah. We had two boys, one young boy. We were quite friendly with them, yes. The chauffeur was quite pleasant. I mean, he knew where we went. As I said, my thing was, the more they know about me, the happier I am.[51]

Hospitality in Peking

Both Hutchison and Stewart took weekend trips, especially to Hangzhou (Hangchow). Both also went to Peking – Stewart on several occasions. It was at times like this that the Bank of China spontaneously displayed its store of goodwill for the Hongkong Bank and its managers. Hutchison recalls:

We went up and stayed there for about a week. The Bank of China entertained us. They took us to the theatre, they took us round this great hall where they were trying all these people. They've got a museum there as well. We wandered around the Forbidden City and the Chinese Summer Palace ourselves. One of the Vice-Consuls took us out to the Ming tombs. The Bank of China were very pleasant, gave us a dinner. Very funny, we were sitting in the theatre, and there was a whole row behind us of really 'by gum' Lancashire cotton mill people. They weren't very keen on us turning round and talking to them though somehow.[52]

During Stewart's second tour, his last trip to Peking occurred at the outbreak of the Cultural Revolution.

I also managed to put in about half a dozen visits to Peking from Shanghai, business combined with pleasure. The first time I was turned down...this was in the 1950s...for no particular reason. In those days many people were turned down, but in the future I was quite successful. The last time I went to Peking my relief had already arrived in Shanghai, this was in 1966, and I thought I really must make one more visit to Peking.

It is a wonderful city.

So I thought hard of what to put on the application form, of course, you have to apply in writing on a special form. So I put down that I wished to complete my sightseeing of the capital and say farewell to the Bank of China, and the application was granted straightaway, so off I went.

Each time I visited Peking I was very hospitably received by the Bank of China, and I always called on them and they regaled me with dinners and so forth. On the last occasion I was given two guides to take me sightseeing. Then, when I left Peking, the plane departed at some very early hour in the morning, something like six o'clock, they even sent a car with another official to see me off at the airport, which was quite a long distance from Peking city. So my visits to Peking each time, apart from sightseeing, were very pleasant indeed from the point of view of the Bank's relationship with the Bank of China. My China interlude was extremely interesting.[53]

Exit from China – the Bank remains

Before a Hongkong Bank Manager could leave China two documents had to be obtained. The first was the authorization to turn over the management of the business to one's successor and the second was the exit permit. The successor had to be in China before the serving Manager was permitted to leave. In 1966 W.A. Stewart was succeeded by D.N.H. Self; Stewart left China and retired from the Bank, becoming Secretary to the Matilda and War Memorial Hospital; in 1971 he retired to his country home on Lan Tao Island in Hong Kong's New Territories.

The pattern of business had been set. In the next few years there were interruptions, but the Cultural Revolution and its aftermath is a story for the summary chapters which follow in the third part of this volume. The history has to turn now to the areas in which the Bank developed actively through its regional branch network.

10

THE COMMERCIAL BANKING BRANCHES, 1947–1962*

> As circumstances render it advisable, the Bank will establish branches at other places.
>
> *The Hongkong Bank Prospectus, 1864*

This and the following chapter are concerned with the various commercial banking offices of The Hongkong and Shanghai Banking Corporation outside Hong Kong and China, their location and function, and, to a lesser extent, their size and organization.

In previous chapters on the Bank's branches there was considerable discussion concerning the difference between a branch, an agency, and a sub-agency; this was paralleled by discussions as to whether the Banker-in-charge was a Manager, Agent, or Sub-Agent. In at least one case, Yokohama, the Bank's agency was headed, against all custom, by a Manager.

At first the distinction between 'branch' and 'agency' was related to the note-issuing privilege and to the distinction made in the Bank's ordinance of incorporation – a 'sub-agency' was an office subordinated to an agency. In the period now being considered, the Bank could only issue banknotes in Hong Kong; the various other distinctions, though useful, had been confused by exceptions for local usage, and in 1956, with the approval of the Board of Directors, all commercial banking offices, with the exception of those legally designated otherwise by a foreign Government, for example, in the United States, became 'branches' and the officers in charge 'managers'.

There were important distinctions between the branches relevant to the internal management of the Hongkong Bank. The major office in each territory might have offices reporting to its Manager and the accounts consolidated before being forwarded to Head Office. There had long been a procedure whereby certain agencies had not carried an exchange position but had based their rates on those quoted by the senior branch. As branching within a city developed, certain offices were expected to perform fewer functions; there were 'mini-banks', offices operating merely for the receipt and payout of savings and perhaps current accounts, but their Managers had direct communication with a full-service branch and a customer could be referred. Between the mini-bank and the full-service branch there would be several variations.

---

* There are no end-notes in this chapter. Readers are referred to the bibliographical note on pp. 947–48.

For these reasons it is sometimes easier to refer to the separate units of the Bank as simply 'offices'.

There are at least three ways, appropriate to the post-war years, of looking at the offices of the corporation. First, one may, as in previous chapters, be concerned with their location by territory as a measure of the geographical coverage of the services provided by the Bank, noting, for example, the withdrawal from Rangoon and Burma or the new extension of the Bank to Chile. Secondly, one may look at 'branching' within a service area – both the coverage of the territory itself and the coverage of a particular city; these are different and yet there are factors common to both. Thirdly, one may be concerned with function. Chapter 8 provided examples in the Mongkok and North Point offices in Hong Kong, noting also that at first the geographical role of the office as local branch and the functional role of the office as industrial bank and in personal finance respectively were not mutually exclusive concepts in the days of early post-war development.

These two chapters are mainly concerned with the first two approaches. The functional offices can best be considered when discussing the functions they perform, for which, and to the extent that the subject deals with post-1961 events, see Chapters 13–15. This procedure will lead to the omission of certain cities – even of territories – in which the Bank had an office for purposes other than commercial banking, for example, trustee service companies in Gibraltar, the Isle of Man, and St Peter's Port, Guernsey.[a]

In the early days the Bank transacted its business in a China-coast port through a merchant house acting as 'agent'. Indeed, this continued to be the role of Harrisons and Crosfield in the British Borneo territories until immediately after the Pacific War. As business increased, the Bank took back responsibility and established its own Bank-staffed office or 'agency'.

The history of post-war Representative Offices is not quite parallel, but these were in some instances precursors of the Bank's own operating branch. More accurately, however, these offices signify either the need for representation even in a country where either the Bank does not, at least at first, need its own agents or agency or the inability to open such an office due to local regulations. The Hongkong Bank could conduct commercial banking through a correspondent bank but might need a representative for the Group's other financial activities in the country – the Seoul office in the Republic of Korea is a good example. The Hongkong Bank had an equity interest in the Korea International Merchant Bank, then in 1982 opened a branch in Busan (Pusan), and more recently (1985) was permitted to convert the Representative Office in Seoul into a second operating branch.

[a] The Hongkong Bank and Trust Company, Ltd, Hongkong and Shanghai Trustees (Isle of Man), Ltd, and Hongkong and Shanghai Trustee (Guernsey), Ltd respectively. See Table II.1 for a list of principal subsidiary and associated companies as of the end of 1961.

Inclusion of these Representative Offices broadens the geographic coverage of the Hongkong Bank Group; their omission does not distort the picture until the late 1970s and they also will be dealt with separately in Chapter 13.

These chapters are not concerned with the problems presented by the increasing complexity of the Hongkong Bank Group. That is a post-1962 problem. The discussion can be limited, with occasional exceptions, to the commercial banking branches of the Hongkong Bank, the Mercantile Bank, and the Hongkong Bank of California (HBC – to use the shortened title approved by the State authorities in 1970). Non-banking subsidiaries are excluded because 'functional' offices are not being considered. The British Bank of the Middle East (BBME) and its subsidiaries and its changing list of associated banks are excluded because, as there is no overlap except in London and Bombay, the policy of the Hongkong Bank was not in this period affected by its existence.

The HBC was a bank in its own right, but it was founded because the Hongkong Bank could not branch in California. In New York where the Bank can operate several branches, it did so. As Chapter 12 will explain, Sir Michael Turner was concerned with rationalization of Hongkong Bank and Mercantile Bank branches from the first; this became increasingly significant after the move of the latter's Head Office to Hong Kong in 1966. In consequence, this chapter deals primarily with the branches of the Hongkong Bank as far as 1961; thereafter the branches of the Hongkong Bank, the HBC, and the Mercantile must be included, the offices of other subsidiary banks operating with reference to these banks will also be noted.

Put positively, this chapter describes the history of The Hongkong and Shanghai Banking Corporation's commercial banking offices for the Hongkong Bank itself and for those subsidiary banks whose branching policy was closely related to and determined by the Hongkong Bank, that is, the HBC after its founding in 1955 and the Mercantile Bank after its acquisition in 1959. The story is continued in Chapter 11 with particular reference to the Bank's operations in the three British territories in Borneo.

The present chapter deals first with the international spread of the banks' branches and the reasons for the observed changes. Branches within Hong Kong were considered in Chapter 8, but there is a survey of selected other branches. This chapter then continues the history of the Colombo and Iolilo offices, stories commenced in Volume II and followed through in Volume III.

THE BRANCH NETWORKS: THE HONGKONG BANK, 1947–1961

The initial development

There was a continuity in Hongkong Bank policy through 1961. Although at the end of 1985 the Hongkong Bank Group was advertising service from its 1,000 offices in 54 countries, in 1946, with funds scarce and the focus on reconstruction in the immediate post-war period, the Board had little choice but to echo an historical attitude, though, significantly, in both 1879 and 1946 the concern expressed immediately preceded an agreed expansion – in 1880 to New York, in 1947 to British Borneo. As will be described in Chapter 11, by 1959 general geographical expansion was actively pursued, but the policy could not be immediately implemented. The acquisition of BBME excepted, nothing dramatic occurred in the Bank's policy relative to geographical coverage through 1961.

That is not to say there were no dramatic changes. A comparison of three tables, Table 9.1 (Volume III) for 1941, Table 10.1 for 1947, and Table 10.4 for 1961, confirms that the judgement 'little had changed' must except the extension into Borneo and the closure of the China branches, the latter a consequence of overwhelming events and not the Bank's own policy initiative.

The early move into Borneo may appear surprising; it was not, as some have thought, a reaction to the 'loss of China'; the timing makes this clear. Senior London staff had been involved with post-war colonial planning and, although preoccupied with plans for the reconstruction of Hong Kong and the redeployment of Bank staff in China, Morse was aware of the virtual destruction of the economy of northern, that is, 'British', Borneo. It was in this context that the Bank considered opening in Borneo, operating from its Singapore branch. The move was delayed, however, by a misunderstanding; the Colonial Office claimed that the Bank had agreed to give the Chartered Bank priority. This and related matters are considered in Chapter 11.

The various years of openings can be followed in Tables 10.2 and 10.3; details of these and related Borneo developments are told in the concluding section in this chapter.

The initial misunderstanding relative to British North Borneo meant that the honour for the first post-war opening of a new Bank office rests with Peninsular Malaya, with the little one Foreign staff office of Teluk Anson. This was followed in 1947 by an equally unexciting expansion, at least from the banking point of view – the opening of the Cameron Highlands office. The Bank had owned holiday property in this pleasant Malayan Hill Station pre-war and there had long been discussion of a sub-agency being established. Post-war the Bank

Table 10.1 *The Hongkong and Shanghai Banking Corporation Branches, 1947*

HONG KONG	PENINSULAR MALAYA	BURMA
Hong Kong	Kuala Lumpur	Rangoon
Kowloon	Cameron Highlands	
	Ipoh	INDIA
CHINA	Johore	Bombay
Shanghai	Malacca	Calcutta
Swatow	Muar	
Canton	Penang	CEYLON
Amoy	Sungei Patani	Colombo
Foochow	Teluk Anson	
Tsingtau		UNITED STATES
Tientsin	SINGAPORE	New York
Hankow	Singapore	San Francisco
Peiping		
Chungking	BRUNEI	UNITED KINGDOM
Nanking	Brunei Town	London
Mukden	Kuala Belait	
		GERMANY
VIETNAM	BRITISH NORTH	Hamburg (nyo)
Saigon	BORNEO	
Haiphong	Jesselton	FRANCE
	Sandakan	Lyons
JAPAN	Tawau	
Tokyo		
Kobe (nyo)	INDONESIA	
Yokohama (nyo)	Batavia	
	Sourabaya (nyo)	
PHILIPPINES		
Manila	THAILAND	
Iloilo	Bangkok	

nyo = not yet reopened

was able to combine rehabilitation of staff with banking as a sort of occupational therapy. G.W. Stabb spent two years there after an unhappy time physically as Agent in charge at Kuala Belait; after four years in Calcutta G.P. Stubbs (East in 1947), his health broken, was sent there on a brief assignment as Agent in 1956. Presumably the Bank expected a growing European (and Chinese) patronage of this hill station, but, although there were no incidents there, the assassination in 1949 of Sir Henry Gurney, the High Commissioner, while en route to Fraser's Hill, another though smaller hill station, and the events of the 'Emergency' in general undoubtedly discouraged potential visitors.

Table 10.2 *The Hongkong Bank Branches, 1946–1961*[a]

Year	Branches opened[b]	Branches closed[c]
1946	Teluk Anson	
1947	Brunei Town	
	Kuala Belait	
	Jesselton	
	Tawau	
	Cameron Highlands	
	Sandakan	
1948	Mongkok, Hong Kong	
	Kure, Japan	
1949	Orchard Rd, Singapore	Canton
		Foochow
		Chungking
		Nanking
		Hankow
		Mukden
1950		Amoy
		Kure
1951		Tsingtau
1952	Osaka	
1953	Paris	Lyons
		Swatow
1954		Tientsin
1955	Phnom-Penh	Haiphong
	San Francisco (HBC)	Peking
1956	North Point, Hong Kong	
	Suapah Rd, Bangkok	
1957	Labuan	
	Los Angeles (HBC)	
1958	Kuching	Sourabaya
	Seria	
1959	Tanglin, Singapore	
	Sibu	
1960	Sheung Shui, Hong Kong	
	Taipo, Hong Kong	
	Tsuen Wan, Hong Kong	
1961	Sham Shui Po, Hong Kong	
	San Hui, Hong Kong	
	Yuen Long, Hong Kong	
	Aberdeen, Hong Kong	
	Sai Ying Pun, Hong Kong	
	Wan Chai, Hong Kong	
	Chung On Street, Hong Kong	
	Bukit Terandak	
	Petaling Jaya	
	Beaufort	
	Papar	

[a] For developments from 1926 to 1941, see Table 9.1 (Vol. III); from 1962–1985, see Table 13.1 below.
[b] New branches only; for reopenings following the Pacific War, see Table 4.1.
[c] Dates refer to year of legal closing, not to the cessation of business. The location of branches by country is shown in Tables 10.1 and 10.3. In this table, country names are added if they were not listed in 1947 or 1951. Where a second office is established in a city or in Hong Kong or Singapore, the city or territory is also named.

Table 10.3 *The Hongkong Bank Branches, 1946–1962*

Office	1941	1946	1947	1948	1949	1950	1951	1952	1953	1954	1955	1956	1957	1958	1959	1960	1961	1962
Hong Kong	×																	
Kowloon	×																	
Mongkok																		
North Point																		
Sheung Shui																		
Taipo																		
Tsuen Wan																		
Sham Shui Po																		
San Hui																		
Yuen Long																		
Aberdeen																		
Sai Ying Pun																		
Wan Chai																		
Chung On Street																		
Kennedy Town																		
Shaukiwan																		

Shanghai
Swatow
Canton
Amoy
Foochow
Chefoo
Tsingtau
Tientsin
Hankow
Peking
Chungking
Nanking
Harbin
Dairen
Mukden
Saigon
Haiphong
Phnom Penh
Tokyo
Kobe
Yokohama
Kure
Osaka
Manila
Iloilo

Table 10.3 (cont.)

Office	1941	1946	1947	1948	1949	1950	1951	1952	1953	1954	1955	1956	1957	1958	1959	1960	1961	1962
Singapore	×																	
Orchard Road																		
Tanglin														——	— —			
Kuala Lumpur	×																	
Bukit Terandak																		
Cameron Highlands																		
Petaling Jaya																		
Ipoh		×	×															
Johore		×	×	×														
Malacca		×	×	×														
Muar		×	×															
Penang		×	×															
Sungei Patani																		
Teluk Anson																		
Jesselton																		
Beaufort																		
Papar																		
Brunei Town																		
Kuala Belait																		

420

Kuching
Labuan
Sandakan
Seria
Sibu
Tawau
Batavia
Sourabaya
Bangkok
Suapah Road
Rangoon
Calcutta
Bombay
Colombo
New York
San Francisco
Los Angeles
London
Hamburg
Lyons
Paris

This chart marks the years in which the branch was open; it does not indicate specific months. '×' and bold face indicates the branch was open before the Pacific War; ——— indicates the branch was not open for business.

Table 10.4 Hongkong Bank Group Branches, 1961, the Hongkong Bank and Mercantile Bank

BORNEO
 Colony of British North
  Borneo
 Jesselton
 Beaufort
 Labuan
 Papar
 Sandakan
 Tawau

 State of Brunei
 Brunei Town
 Kuala Belait
 Seria

 Colony of Sarawak
 Kuching
 Sibu

BURMA
 Rangoon + MBLD

CAMBODIA
 Phnom-Penh

CEYLON
 Colombo + MBLD
 Pettah, Colombo, MBLD
 Galle, MBLD
 Jaffna, MBLD
 Kandy, MBLD

CHINA
 Shanghai

FRANCE
 Paris

GERMANY
 Hamburg

HONG KONG
 Hong Kong + MBLD
 Aberdeen
 Kennedy Town
 Kowloon
 Mongkok
 North Point
 Sai Ying Pun
 San Hui
 Sham Shui Po
 Shaukiwan
 Sheung Shui
 Taipo
 Tsuen Wan
 Chung On St.,
  Tsuen Wan
 Wanchai
 Yuen Long

INDIA
 Bombay + MBLD
  (+ BBME)
 Calcutta + MBLD
 Delhi, MBLD
 Gandhidham, MBLD
 Howrah, MBLD
 Madras, MBLD
 Sowcarpet, MBLD
 New Delhi, MBLD

INDONESIA
 Djakarta

JAPAN
 Tokyo + MBLD
 Kobe
 Osaka + MBLD
 Semba, Osaka, MBLD
 Yokohama

FEDERATION OF
MALAYA
 Kuala Lumpur + MBLD
 Bentong, MBLD, 1961
 Bukit Terendak
 Cameron Highlands
 Ipoh + MBLD
 Johore Bahru
 Kota Bharu, MBLD
 Kuala Lipis, MBLD
 Kuala Trengganu, MBLD
 Kuantan, MBLD
 Malacca
 Mentakab, MBLD, 1961
 Muar
 Penang + MBLD
 Petaling Jaya
 Raub, MBLD, 1961
 Seremban, MBLD, 1959
 Sungei Patani
 Taiping, MBLD, 1959
 Teluk Anson
 Temerloh, MBLD

MAURITIUS
 Port Louis, MBLD

PAKISTAN
 Chittagong, MBLD
 Karachi, MBLD
 Khulna, MBLD

PHILIPPINES
 Manila
 Iloilo

SINGAPORE
 Collyer Quay
 Orchard Road
 Tanglin
 Raffles Place, MBLD
 Beach Rd, MBLD, 1959

THAILAND
 Bangkok + MBLD
 Suapah Road,
 Rajawongse Road,
  MBLD

UNITED KINGDOM
 London + MBLD (+ BBME)
 Pall Mall, London, MBLD

U.S.A.
 New York
 San Francisco (+ HBC)
 (Los Angeles HBC)

VIETNAM
 Saigon

BBME (British Bank of the Middle East) branches are shown only in those locations where Hongkong Bank and/or MBLD offices are also located

Indeed, the outbreak of insurgency in the Peninsula delayed further developments, and the Bank's next new office there did not open until 1961.

Perhaps the most significant addition to the Hongkong Bank's network was Osaka in 1952. As reported in Chapter 3, SCAP was slow to permit British banks to reopen in Occupied Japan, and the first breakthrough, other than the Representative Office in Tokyo, was the Kure military facility in 1947 – closed in 1950.

In 1953 the Bank decided to open an office in Paris but, under French regulations at the time, this meant the closing of the historic Lyons branch.

Back in the Far East Haiphong was closed, but in the same year of 1955 the Bank moved for the first time into Cambodia opening in the capital, Phnom-Penh. Also in 1955 the Peking office was closed, marking the completion of the 'all-for-all' settlement and the events described in Chapter 9. The geographical position in China would remain unchanged until the opening of a Representative Office in Guangzhou (Canton) in 1979 and the return to Peking the following year (see Table 9.1).

The adjustments consequent to events in China and Annam (North Vietnam) are seen in the historical context of successful Communist Party led revolution. The first instance of purely anti-colonial reaction to 'neo-colonialism' was witnessed in Indonesia. The Bank had always had problems in Java; its role had in any case been marginal, but in 1958 Turner, very reluctantly – 'I hate to see a branch closed' – agreed that, with the retirement of D.A. McN. Butter, the Sourabaya office should be put in a 'care and maintenance' status, but by the end of the year the Board of Directors had agreed to its closure.[b]

In 1956 and 1958 the first 'second office' developments occurred outside Hong Kong with the establishment of the Suapah Road and the Tanglin offices in Bangkok and Singapore respectively. The Hong Kong branch development program was underway in 1960 and 1961. Mongkok, North Point, and Tanglin offices were initially in response to a perceived demand for full banking services; they were not seen as primarily designed to increase sources of funds. By 1960 pressures on the Bank's liquidity combined with the traditional assets management approach to banking policy encouraged the Hong Kong Manager, R.G.L. Oliphant, into a program of establishing smaller branches for varying purposes, but particularly to garner additional funds; the consequences of this may be followed in Tables 8.2 and 8.4.

At the end of Sir Michael Turner's last full year as Chief Manager the list

---

[b] Butter came East in 1919 and was assigned to Batavia. He resigned from the Bank in 1923 and settled in Sourabaya; he spoke Dutch and Malay. In March 1946 the Bank asked him to assist with the Batavia branch reopening and in 1948 he was taken on to be the 'Agent' Sourabaya as 'special staff'.

of Hongkong Bank offices reflected (i) the departure from China, (ii) the move into all three 'British Borneo' territories, (iii) minor readjustments in Asia, France, and the United States, and (iv) the first results of the Bank's new policy to branching as a source of funds (see Table 10.4). Only the last would have surprised members of the Bank's nineteenth-century senior management and directors.

Policy and finance

Foreign staff policy and the branches

Despite the greater post-war concern with personnel policy, assignments to branches were made to a very considerable extent on an *ad hoc* basis, depending on leaves, illnesses, and general availability. At the Bankers' Association dinner given when N.H.T. Bennett left Bangkok in 1964, his friend, J.H. Delacour, the Chartered Bank manager, began his presentation – 'I'm very pleased to say that Norman Bennett is the seventh Hongkong Bank Manager to whom I've said goodbye.' And yet the records as reflected in Tables 10.5 and 10.6 show a mixed record for the Bangkok branch: J.J. French was there three years until his death in office, S.W.P. Perry-Aldworth six years, and J.E.B. Thomson five years – the others, not so long. The extended terms of W.J. Hope and G.S. Chambers as Managers in Saigon, nine and five years respectively, reflect the Bank's recognition of their ability to operate in a French-speaking area; Butter's eleven years in Sourabaya was a special case already discussed, and the traditionally longer assignments in Europe and North America are evidenced.

J.S. Dunnett (East in 1936) was sent to San Francisco because of his knowledge of American business practices from his term as Manager Manila.

In major branches some effort was made to provide continuity, although there might be short-term interim appointments. The largest turnovers were in the smaller offices – twelve in the restful Cameron Highlands in the period 1948–1961, eleven in Teluk Anson, ten in Muar, but only five in Singapore; nine in Iloilo, but five in Manila.

The question of long or short tours of duty as Manager in a main branch depends, in theory, on whether policy is to stress knowledge of the local scene or experience in banking. In pre-war days, part of the task of learning about the local situation was facilitated by the input of the compradore or guarantee shroff. The exchange banker was considered a 'bird of passage' in the small and settled foreign communities in Asian port cities, but, to the extent that there was a basic list of relatively loyal customers, even a newcomer could carry on while feeling his way on the fringes. He competed, certainly, but much competition was on marginal turns in the exchange; here a Manager could build up an expertise with experience.

Table 10.5 *The Hong Kong and Shanghai Banking Corporation Managers who served five years or more at one post, 1946–1961*

Name	Establishment	Number of years
A.S. Adamson	Hong Kong	5
R.P. Moodie	Hong Kong	6
I.H. Bradford	Mongkok	6
W.J. Hope	Saigon	9
G.S. Chambers	Saigon	5
S.W.P. Perry-Aldworth	Bangkok	6
J.E.B. Thomson	Bangkok	5
C.L. Edwards	Singapore	5
N.E. Clark	Kuala Lumpur	5
P.S.M. Dew	Penang	5
H.E. Foy	Jesselton	5
M.F.L. Haymes	Jesselton	6
J.McG. Taylor	Batavia/Djakarta	5
D.A.McN. Butter	Sourabaya (Special Staff)	11
E.E.F. Hibberd	Rangoon	5
J. Caldwell	Calcutta	6
G.E.B. Tytler	Bombay	5
J.D. McClatchie	Colombo	5
J.H. Raikes	New York	5
B.P. Massey	New York	7
S.J.H. Fox	San Francisco	5
W.R. McCutcheon	Los Angeles	5
S.A. Gray	London	8
A.M.D. Wallace	London	8
H.A. Mabey	London	5
S.W.P. Perry-Aldworth	London	7
M.D. Scott	London	6
G.C. Moutrie	Hamburg	12
D.C. Davis	Lyons/Paris	5

Post-war the pattern changed, but particularly at the end of the period now being considered. Nevertheless, the changing political scene, the varied opportunities for uses of funds, and the beginning of a new technology were already making a knowledge of banking development more important than being the doyen of the bankers in the city. A banker left too long in a less developed economy would lose contact with developments in banking. In Japan, Germany, and Thailand the Hongkong Bank's pioneering role was courteously acknowledged, even honoured, but, as for business, the Bank and its Manager were on their own.

Table 10.6 *The Hongkong Bank
Branches, agencies, and their Managers, 1946–1961*

Establishment	No. of Managers
Hong Kong A.S. Adamson 5; M.W. Turner 1; R.P. Moodie 6; R.G.L. Oliphant 4 (+3 AM)	4
Kowloon G. Travers 4; H.F. Phillips 2; G.H. Cautherley 3; E.C. Hutchison 1; G.G. Waller 3; W.H.B. Rigg 2; A.W. Helbling 1	7
Mongkok (1948–) G.H. Cautherley 3; J.M. Beazley 1; R.G.L. Oliphant 2; R.E.H. Nelson 1; I.H. Bradford 6 (+2 AM)	5*
North Point (1956–) J.M. Pattinson 2; J.F. Marshall 1; D.P.G. Learmond 1; I.T. Townend 2	4*
Tsuen Wan (1960–) R.B. Moore 1; P.M. Ryan 1	2*
Yuen Long (1961) C.A. Odling	1*
Amoy (1947–1950) L.G. Robertson 1; R.W. Lee 1; H.F. Phillips 1+1 no	3*
Canton (–1950) A.C. Meredith 1 nyo; C.M. Jamieson 2; A.C. Groves 1+1 no	3*
Chungking (–1949) J.T. Edkins 2; H.E. Foy 1	2*
Foochow (1947–1950) J.B. Stewart 2; G.G. Ralston 1+1 no	2*
Hankow (1947–1949) G.G. Ralston 1; W.W. Rae 1; F.J. Bond 1 no	3*
Mukden (1947–1948) H.F. Phillips 2	1*
Nanking (1947–1949) C.J.D. Law 1; D.A. Cumming 2+1 no	2*
Peiping/Peking (1947–1954) E.M. Moffatt 2; P.G. Rynd 2; D.F.C. Cleland 4	3*
Shanghai S.A. Gray 2; G.H. Stacey 3; W.T. Yoxall 4; D. Buchan 2; W.F. Curwen 2; W.A. Stewart 2; E.C. Hutchison 1	7
Swatow (1947–1953) P.A. Sellars 2; S.J.H. Fox 2+3 no	2*
Tientsin (–1954) A.H. Matthews 2; H.L. Pickford 2; G.S. Dunkley 1; P.G. Rynd 4	4*
Tsingtau (–1951) J.C. Sutherland 4; P.A. Sellars 1+1 no	2*
Tokyo (1947–) V.A. Mason 1; J.McI. Brown and V.A. Mason 2; G.H. Stacey 4; H.V. Parker 3; A.H.R. Butcher 3; M.G. Carruthers 1 (+1 AM)	6*

The commercial banking branches, 1947–1962 427

Table 10.6 (*cont.*)

Establishment	No. of Managers
Kobe (1948–)	9*
L.G. Robertson 1; G.G. Waller 1; W.J. Sutherland 1; D.L. Milne-Day 1; A.H.R. Butcher 2; E.C. Hutchison 1; M.G. Carruthers 1; A. Robertson 2; Carruthers 2; A. Robertson 1; R.G. Ouseley 1	
Kure (1948–1950)	2*
H.J.S. Muriel 1; P.F. Hutton 1	
Osaka (1952–)	4*
G.G. Waller 1 no+4; M.G. Carruthers 2; D. Pike 3; A. Robertson 1 (+1 AM)	
Yokohama (1949–)	8*
H.J.S. Muriel 1; A.F. Judd 1; D.A. Cumming 1; E.C. Hutchison 1; A. Robertson 1; L.E.V. Rumble 3; I.L.G. Wheeler 2; Robertson 1; A.D.M. Ford 2	
Manila	5
A.F. Handcock 1; W. Webster 4; H.V. Parker 3; R. Macintyre 4; J.S. Dunnett 4 (+1 AM)	
Iloilo	9
J.B. Stewart 1; A.B. Kelly 2; G.W.E. True 4; R.P. Edwards 1; J.H.W. Marshall 3; D.A. Cumming 1; R.H. Lloyd 1; A.D.A.G. Mosley 2; H.L. Pierce 1	
Saigon	3
W.J. Hope 9; G.S. Chambers 5; A.L. Murray 2 (+2 AM)	
Haiphong (1947–1954)	4*
G.S. Chambers 2; B.C. Allan 2; R.A. Jardine 2; I.L.G. Wheeler 2	
Phnom Penh (1955–)	3*
A.L. Murray 4; B.C. Allan 2; F.W. Chandler 1	
Bangkok	5
J.J. French 3; S.W.P. Perry-Aldworth 6; J.E.B. Thomson 5; J.H.W. Marshall 1; W.A. Stewart 1 (+1 AM)	
Suapah Road (1956–)	4*
K.D. Robertson 1; W.A. Stewart 1; D.A. Cumming 1; Nibhavisn Krairiksh 3	
Singapore	5
R.A. Stuart (7)+1; C.L. Edwards 5; J.A.D. Morrison 4; W.H. Lydall 3; I.J.O. Cruickshank 3 (+3 AM)	
Orchard Road (1949–)	7*
J. Kindness 2; M.F.L. Haymes 2; B.C. Allan 2; D. Pike 2; E.C. Hutchison 3; G.P. Stubbs 1; J.H.P. Young 1	
Tanglin (1958–)	3*
G.N.B. Haynes 1 no+1; R.E.H. Nelson 1; S.J.H. Pughe 1	
Kuala Lumpur	6
C.H. Eldridge 3; H.E. Foy 1; M.D. Scott 2; J. Kindness 2; N.E. Clark 5; A.L. Snaith 2; Clark 1 (+2 AM)	
Bukit Terendak (1961)	1*
M.J. Bond 1	

Table 10.6 (*cont.*)

Establishment	No. of Managers
Ipoh J.A. Clarke 4; W.F. Curwen 2; J. Wilkie 2; W.H.B. Rigg 2; R. Stilliard 1; B.C. Allan 2; B.G.D. Miller 1; P.B. Tay 2	8
Johore J.W.R. McPhail 3; R.A. Fawcett 4; H.A. Browning 1; D. Pike 1; A. Robertson 1; A.K. Forsyth 3; A.W. Helbling 1; P.H. Scoones 2 (+ 1 AM)	8
Malacca G.E.B. Tytler; T.W. Doyle 4; A. Chalmers 1; P.S.M. Dew 2; W.F. Curwen 4; F.W. Chandler 1; R.E.H. Nelson 1; D.A. Cumming 1; D.G. Day 2	9
Muar L.H. Thorn 2; T.S.B. Nicoll 2; R.W. Lee 1; J.N. Frost 1; G.G. Ralston 1; L.G. Robertson 1; H.R. McGilchrist 2; T.G. Mead 2; A.W. Helbling 1; I.L.G. Wheeler 3	10
Penang W.C. Murray 1; J. Hall 4; A. Chalmers 2; R. Stilliard 1; J. Kindness 1; P.S.M. Dew 5; R.W. Mills 2 (+ 1 AM)	7
Petaling Jaya (1961) B.C. Rogers 1	1*
Sungei Patani P.A. MacDougall 2; R.A. Fawcett 1; H.W. Brady 2; A.K. Forsyth 3; F.M. Thompson 2; F.H.F. Swayne 1; R.G. Ouseley 2; R.B. Moore 1; R.W. Scott 2	9
Teluk Anson G.W. Stabb 1; W.J. McConnell 2; G.G. Ralston 2; R.H.D. Wade 2; D.A. Cumming 1; J.M. Beazley 1; I.L.G. Wheeler 2; H.R. McGilchrist 2; R.W. Scott 1; R.C. Beauclerk 1; G.P. Cross 1	11*
Cameron Highlands (1947–) L.H. Thorn 1; H.C.D. Davies 1; A.L. Murray 1; R.W. Lee 2; R.H.D. Wade 1; G.W. Stabb 2; G.P. Stubbs 1; A.W. Levett 1; D.P.G. Learmond 1; R.G. Ouseley 1; A.D. Morrison 1; R.C. Beauclerk 1	12*
Jesselton (1947–) G.G. Thomson 2; C.M. Jamieson 1; H.E. Foy 5; M.F.L. Haymes 6; Maurice W. Turner 1 (+ 1 AM)	5*
Beaufort (1961–) B. Chung 1	1*
Brunei (1947–) A.D.M. Ford 1; G.W. Stabb 1; N.E. Clark 2; S.H. Ash 4; P.H. Scoones 1; H.A. Browning 3; A. Woollcombe 2; P.G.A. Cantopher 2	7*
Kuala Belait (1948–) H.C.D. Davies 1; L.H. Thorn 1; L.G. Robertson 3; G.W. Stabb 1; P.H. Scoones 2; G.H. Cautherley 4; J.M. Beazley 2 (+1 AM)	7*
Kuching (1958–) A.R. Petrie 1; G.G. Aitkenhead 2; G.N.B. Haynes 1	3*
Labuan (1957–) H.J.S. Muriel 2; C.J. Campbell 3	2*

Table 10.6 (*cont.*)

Establishment	No. of Managers
Sandakan (1947–)	7*
G.G. Aitkenhead 1; I.L.G. Wheeler 2; B.C. Allan 1; I.H. Bradford 2; A.K. Forsyth 1; A.W. Helbling 2; J.H.W. Marshall 2; Forsyth 3	
Seria (1958–)	4*
C.A. Odling 1; T. Welsh 1; A.I. Donaldson 1; R.R. Clarke 1	
Sibu (1959–)	2*
C.A. Odling 1; M.J.S. Figg 2	
Tawau (1947–)	9*
M.McD. Holmden 1; A.W. Helbling 1; L.H. Thorn 3; A.L. Harman 1; R.C. Beauclerk 2; D.R. Reid 1; G.P. Stubbs 1; G.G. Aitkenhead 1; J.F. Marshall 3	
Batavia/Djakarta	5
H.A. Mabey 2; J.McG. Taylor 5; H.C. Peterson 5; F.H. King 3; T.G. Mead 1 (+ 2 AM)	
Surabaja (Sourabaya; –1958)	2*
W.W. Rae 1; D.A.McN Butter 11 (+2 AM)	
Rangoon	6
J. Campbell 3; E.M. Moffatt 2; H.C. Peterson 1; D.L. Milne-Day 3; E.E.F. Hibberd 5; A.M. Kennedy 2 (+3 AM)	
Calcutta	6
J. Caldwell 6; C.B. Terdre 4; D.L. Milne-Day 3; D.B. Soul 1; S.F.T.B. Lever 1; J.W.L. Howard 1	
Bombay	6
G.E.B. Tytler 5; A.F. Judd 2; G.A. Stewart 4; C.J.D. Law 1; F.R. Burch 2; B.O'D. Paterson 2 (+ 1 AM)	
Colombo	6
J.C.G. Fergusson 2; J.D. McClatchie 5; H.A. Greig 2; F.R. Burch 2; R.C. Gairdner 1; A.L.V.S. Giles 4	
New York	4
A.G. Kellogg (9)+3; J.H. Raikes 5; B.P. Massey 7; R.P. Edwards 1	
San Francisco	7
A.R.M. Blackhall (8)+1; W.J. Clerk 1; C.J.D. Law 4; P.H. Scoones 2; I.H. Bradford 1; S.J.H. Fox 5; H.C. Peterson 2	
(Los Angeles (1957–) HBC)	1
W.R. McCutcheon 5	
London (Two and sometimes three London Managers at a time)	8
S.A. Gray 8; A.M.D. Wallace 8; H.A. Mabey 5; S.W.P. Perry-Aldworth 7; M.D. Scott 6; G.O.W. Stewart 1; G.A. Stewart 1; W.H. Lydall 1	
Hamburg (1948–)	2*
G.C. Moutrie 12; D.B. Soul 2	
Lyons (–1953) Paris (1953–)	5
D.A. Johnston 1; J.S. Watson 4; D.C. Davies 3/2; R.A. Jardine 2; H.V. Parker 4	

* = not open for the whole period
AM = Acting Manager
no = not operating
()+ = years as Manager in that office before 1946

Finance and the branches

The Hongkong Bank did not suffer from competition so much as from lack of funds. There were also limits to its lending set by the availability of Foreign staff. The Bank might have successfully financed a high proportion of the available international trade, had the funds been available, but innovative lending was already stretching managerial capacity – as the record of serious losses suggests.

Since the 1950s was a time of loss of market share for the Hongkong Bank, the statements above need explanation and context. The branch Manager, using an assets management approach, began with a consideration of his sources of funds. The most obvious was local deposits. These were unlikely to grow commensurate with the growth of international trade, despite the growth of the banking sector, because the Hongkong Bank had become in this context (except in Hong Kong) a foreign bank. There were restrictions on branching; the local banking sector developed and, through branching, took up the slack. Where central bank regulations set rates, the Bank could not compete; furthermore, local banks could risk, in France for example, giving 'backhanders'.

The Manager would then consider his own 'capitalization', that is, the funds made available to him by Head Office on a 'permanent' basis. This would depend on pre-war decisions and on availability of funds at Head Office. The latter would not usually be interested in assignment of funds to branches operating in countries with a high rate of income tax. The risk was already there; the high taxes were discouraging. To overcome this reluctance a central bank might be given the authority to determine the amount of funds a foreign bank must 'bring in' before it could continue to operate. In Thailand, the Hongkong Bank met this problem, which arose first in 1963, by revaluing its land up to market – and the Bank held valuable land in Bangkok. This satisfied the Bank of Thailand for a short time, but did not provide the Manager with loanable funds.

One solution was for a branch to borrow from London or New York with the permission of Head Office. Borrowing from the former was restricted if the country, Thailand for example, were outside the Sterling Area. This moves the problem back a stage.

Although its reserves were primarily in sterling, it is clear that the Bank also had an increasing U.S. dollar reserve, the uses of which were restricted by Sterling Area regulations, to which the Hongkong Bank was, to a great extent, subject. New York funds in excess of the Bank's requirements had, in principle, to be surrendered to the control of the Bank of England, but the Hongkong Bank could use any surplus and any further borrowings to expand its financing of international trade and to subscribe to U.S. dollar issues of bonds designed for Commonwealth purposes and for World Bank loans.

The Hongkong Bank's New York office became the centre for Hongkong Bank Group U.S. dollar finance, working with Bankers Trust and Morgan Guaranty. The Mercantile Bank had been close to the Chase Bank. The Hongkong Bank used its available funds primarily for short-term trading advances, but the Manager, R.P. Edwards, was authorized to subscribe to such loans as the Port of Calcutta, the IBRD loans for the Thai State Railways, and a 1961 loan to Sri Lanka. The Mercantile Bank also participated, although not necessarily in U.S. funds; the decision of the Chartered Bank was also a factor in the Hongkong Bank's decision. Turner was anxious about liquidity; he was also concerned to participate on an equal basis in development loans, at least to the extent of rivals. In 1960, for example, he authorized New York office to participate up to US$2 million in the US$3.4 million offered by a Chase-led syndicate to finance Qantas, the Australian airline, in its purchase of new aircraft.

The cost of New York overdrafts to branches – and the Philippine overdraft facility was increased to US$4 million in 1961 – was $\frac{1}{2}$ of 1% over prime when prime was low. The rate was designed, however, to be profitable to New York yet low enough to permit authorized branches to use the facilities on a profitable basis. Despite the size of New York's operations, Turner did not approve the New York office, then in New York State banking terms an 'agency', becoming a 'branch', a change which would have enabled the Bank to accept deposits directly. No reason has been found; presumably the availability of the Hongkong Bank of California was considered sufficient for the Group's customers. The change to branch status by New York law was made in 1973.

The principles on which the allocation of available funds would be made was not a matter set out in a single policy document. Head Office had to be convinced that local sources of funds had been exploited; it was not thought 'fair' for a Manager to depend on a London surplus which had been built up by Head Office 'sacrifices', that is, Head Office might have used them itself. While this is true, it is not necessarily sound, and presumably the Chief Manager agreed. Hong Kong too was losing its market share, but only partly through lack of finance, the sacrifice of access to funds. The industrial loan market was biased to textiles and the Bank considered itself overcommitted in this industry – to cite but one example.

Given that funds were available in London and New York, on what further principles, once Managers had proved that they had exhausted local sources, would funds be allocated? The annual reports contained the Chairman's address, evidence that the Bank had been assessing national economic prospects throughout the region. Countries with high taxation, high political risk, possibilities of exchange depreciation, and other impediments would obviously rank low as potential recipients of the Bank's 'imperial' funds. These assessments might change suddenly as a Chief Manager became 'concerned'. They might also be overridden by specific events such as unexpected defalcation or, at the other extreme, a particularly sound proposal.

This last factor suggests that branch Managers had to seek out business positively and then defend their consequent proposals when either exceeding their limit and/or their available loanable funds against any Head Office concern relative to regulatory changes, political disturbance, taxation, labour problems, etc. to which the branch was subjected.

The first reference by a Chief Manager to 'Euromoney' may have been as late as 1961 – by Turner. The Bank was not operating in the Eurodollar market until 1963, and the flexibility this market provided had no impact on the Bank's branch financing in the period through 1961.

CASE STUDIES

Not every branch can be covered, and some are considered in more functional contexts, as, for example, San Francisco in Chapter 12 and London in Chapter 6, although there is more to consider in the case of London. A geographical survey of branch development has been made earlier in this chapter. The comments made below are selective and designed to illustrate the policy and role of the Bank in its more important areas of operation.

JAPAN

Early staff problems
Despite the delays in reopening in Japan, the eccentric character of the Bank's first post-war Manager, V.A. Mason, and the predominance of National City and Chase Banks under an American dominated SCAP, Japan played a not insignificant role in the history of the post-war Hongkong Bank – although the profits reported from Japan to Head Office as shown in Table 8.1 were not spectacular, moving to a high for the period of $4.5 million in 1951 and declining to a notional amount in 1959.

As a foreign bank the Hongkong Bank in Japan would, in any case, have had a limited role. Arthur Morse and his successor, Michael Turner, may have further restricted the Bank's role by being unwilling to commit, as they did for certain other branches, a portion of the Head Office's London or New York reserves. Funding would have to wait for the Bank's discovery of the Eurodollar market. Nevertheless the branch's history was eventful.

The Bank initially had Foreign staff problems in its main Japan office of Tokyo. Mason, always an enigma, spent most of his time explaining banking to SCAP officials; since by all accounts Mason was difficult to understand, this took time. Morse accordingly sent up J.McI. Brown (East in 1919) as joint Manager. No specific reason for this has been found, but the London situation, where one senior Manager was 'outward' and the other 'inward' oriented, may have been the model. Whatever the reason, it proved disastrous; Brown, whose career was beginning to develop by 1937 when he was appointed Accountant Singapore, was interned in Singapore during the war. He was noted for his prison camp lectures on banking, but the experience had apparently broken him. He could not stand up to Mason, and he reportedly kept his telephone in his desk drawer where it could not be heard. No one seemed to know who was in charge.

By 1951 G.H. Stacey was Manager and both Mason and Brown had retired. A sound banker Stacey too had problems with the Foreign staff, being either cordially disliked or unwillingly respected by the juniors and there was friction at the top. One junior to observe this was Michael G.R. Sandberg (East in 1949), on his first assignment after a few months in Head Office; another bank junior in the great city of Tokyo was Peter A. Graham, a friend of Sandberg's who had originally applied to the Hongkong Bank, but in the event joined the Chartered Bank, where in 1977 he became their Group managing director.

In 1955 the new Manager, H.V. Parker, was confronted by the bank union in an apparently bitter strike by the local employees, which nevertheless proved not to have engendered lasting ill-will.

One problem, difficult to assess, was the fact that the post-war Managers, Mason excepted, had been through internment; Mason himself had proved particularly anti-Japanese when Manager in Hankow and chairman of the Chamber of Commerce before the Pacific War. Even when M.G. Carruthers was assigned to Japan in 1954, he and his wife had thought it wise to discuss their attitudes, reminding each other that it had all been a long time ago; as Carruthers put it later, they agreed that they bore no resentment then; in retirement they would look back on their experience in Japan and conclude, 'I must say we thoroughly enjoyed it.' Of course, they had told themselves, they would be dealing with entirely different people.

Japanese bonds and 'face'
This, interestingly, was not entirely accurate. Nobutane Kiuchi had been the first Yokohama Specie Bank supervisor of the Hongkong Bank in Japanese-occupied Shanghai; by 1951 he had become the head of the Foreign Exchange Control Board (FECB, abolished in 1952) with cabinet rank, and he and Stacey, who had been interned in Shanghai, established a sound relationship.

In 1952 Kiuchi, accompanied by Michitaka Kondo, the assistant chief, Banking Section, Ministry of Finance, decided to take an important step by visiting Hong Kong and London in preparation for Japan's post-SCAP, post-Treaty days. Arthur Morse noted that, 'When the Japanese call they will receive every courtesy. However, I am afraid I have not completely forgotten the past and it is at times hard not to remember some of our friends who suffered so much.'

Morse in fact went out of his way to accommodate the mission by rearranging the vacant flat in the Bank's Head Office building so that there were private rooms for each member of the delegation. Kiuchi asked if it were safe for them to go out on the streets and was answered in the affirmative, but the fact is that Japanese had not been seen in Hong Kong since the war; the very presence of Japanese was very much a subject for comment, not only in Hong Kong, but anywhere in Southeast Asia. Morse took them to the races at Happy Valley, but they stayed close in the Chairman's Box.

There followed an event which cannot be unrelated. The Japanese Government had, contrary to cynical expectation, decided to honour its pre-war debt, including bonds floated by syndicates of which the Hongkong Bank had been a prominent participant in the heady days before the Great War of 1914. The funds were held in several British banks to the credit of the FECB and had to be transferred to the Bank of England. The FECB under Kiuchi, however, transferred the funds first to the Hongkong Bank in London. The Bank then wrote a £20 million cheque payable to the Bank of England as a first instalment of Japan's repayment.

This would seem to have served no banking purpose, but it gave 'face' to the Bank. It was a typically Japanese gesture, which Morse understood and appreciated. One practical aspect would be that the Bank's £200,000 (nominal value) holdings of the bonds, which the Bank had written off, were sold over the next few years at a premium over 100; the proceeds went into inner reserves.

The changing pattern of business

In the first years after Mason's entry into Japan in 1947, the Hongkong Bank was key to the development of limited Japan/Sterling Area trade. The capacity of Hong Kong to absorb an increasing value of Japanese imports and the exchange control restraints under which Japan operated led to the creation of a bilateral trade financed by a Hong Kong Government 'swing' account, managed by the Hongkong Bank, in which the balance moved to agreed limits either way. That is, the account provided for credit to be extended to the party with the import surplus within the limit; from the first the balance was in favour of Japan. The Tokyo office also financed wool imports direct from Australia.

The commercial banking branches, 1947–1962

The growth of this specialized Japan/Hong Kong trade led to the establishment in Hong Kong office of a Japanese Trade Department, managed by a relative junior, for example, J.W.L. Howard (East in 1946) and N.H.T. Bennett (East in 1949), after approximately five years experience; the Department handled both sides of the operation, both inward and outward bills. Even after the end of the special arrangements, the Bank found it useful to retain the department in view of the various specialized problems with which the Bank was now familiar.

The department also financed the Japan/China trade. In view of various embargoes, which did not affect Hong Kong law, the goods had to be routed indirectly, sometimes via Rotterdam, and brought back to China after some nine months on the water. This rerouting was also true of Chinese goods exported to the United States. Since the trade was not financed with U.S. dollars, American prohibitory regulations were unavailing.

In the early 1950s the basis of Japanese trade broadened, but Japanese banks had no credit rating overseas. The Hongkong Bank was granted a licence to open in Osaka in late 1951, and much of the business was in import and export bills. At that time the Japanese banks had no overseas branches or even agency arrangements; they brought in the bills, asked for them to be examined and, if in order, requested to be paid immediately; the Bank for these services paid at a discount. This actively employed a staff of eight and continued until the Japanese had trained their own staffs and had set up overseas; from the mid-1950s this business declined and its scope narrowed.

In Kobe the Bank serviced its traditional customers, especially those with Hong Kong connections. The export trade involved shipments by middlemen who bought from factories, packaged and marketed the products, the export of which the Hongkong Bank, among others, financed.

The Japan offices operated under Tokyo, and it was in the Tokyo office that the exchange was handled, rates set, and accounts squared with the branches in order to avoid dealing with and thus losing on the differential between buying and selling rates set by the Bank of Japan. Japanese banks were not equipped to deal effectively with foreign customers, and many came to the Hongkong Bank, among them a small group of Jewish merchants, expelled from Northeast China and then from China itself, who had become resident in Japan and managed small factories which manufactured for export.

Although by the mid-1950s Japanese banks had overseas offices in London and interbank deposits were consequently being withdrawn from foreign banks, including the Hongkong Bank, the Japanese in Southeast Asia retained a low profile. The Bank's Japan Managers became increasingly concerned that Hong Kong was unaware of the potential industrial developments about to break through and that the Bank would 'miss the boat' in Japan. As already noted,

Morse and Turner would not assign additional funds to the Japan offices; back-to-back lending – although the Bank may have undertaken a limited amount – was contrary to Bank of Japan regulations, and the branches were thus limited in the business they could undertake.

Even rationalization of the Bank's property and housing position in and around Tokyo was delayed. The Yokohama operation had become minimal, but the Bank still had housing on the Bluff overlooking the port city near the cemetery where eight Hongkong Bankers had over the years been buried.[c] What eventually happened was the sale of such irrelevant property and the use of the remaining land held in Tokyo for the replacement of a single house by an apartment block; the solution was typical of later developments elsewhere, notably in Bangkok and Singapore.

The 1955 strike

The Hongkong Bank had no experience in labour relations. That is not to say that there was no employee dissatisfaction pre-war or that the Bank had not suffered from political strikes affecting an entire community. In this latter the question of 'relations' did not arise; there was nothing the Bank could do but wait it out. In general, however, the Bank had not been a leader in setting wages; in the early years terms of service were taken basically from other institutions, especially from major constituents who, after all, might be represented on the Board of Directors. The Chief Manager often, however, had secured favourable amendments sufficiently generous to be the subject of comment. The compradore had served as a buffer between the Manager and the local staff; individual cases of hardship were tempered by an accepted paternalism and handled, as they were handled for the Foreign staff, *ad hoc* directly by the Board of Directors.

The demise of the compradoric system, the post-war inflation coupled with political and overall economic demands, and the rise of politically oriented trade unions in the East were all factors suggesting that this industrial peace would end. The Bank was hit first in Ceylon and India; there were politically oriented troubles in Singapore; and there was the Japan strike of 1955. In India the Bank was part of the overall banking scene, in Singapore and Japan the Bank was first precisely because it was a leader in the foreign banking sector. It could be argued that, in this present history, all the strikes should be considered in a single section; they were characteristic of the post-war East. Each strike, however, arose in such different circumstances that they had little specific in common – except, perhaps, the inexperience of the Hongkong Bankers facing the problem.

[c] These with year of death are: D. Moncur 1873, A.L. Turner 1878, E. Morriss 1890, A. Veitch 1893, H.E. Harries 1898, D. Jackson 1903, I.C. Morrison 1923, and J.S. Lee 1944.

M.G. Carruthers was in Kobe during the strike; it begun when his sons arrived on holiday and was ended virtually when the boys returned to England; he hardly saw them the entire time. In Hong Kong the Chief Manager, Michael Turner, had set the pattern by refusing even to undertake official entertaining on weekends during vacation periods when the children were home, but during the strike in Kobe the Foreign staff kept the office open; four or five staff were doing the work of forty-five – for a time. The Hongkong Bank had been used as the first target by the Union; fortunately the Bank was fully supported by the Chartered Bank and Carruthers was able to obtain sound advice from the manager of the Bank of Tokyo who had himself been involved in the Indian bank strike. The strikers permitted the Foreign staff and Japanese Manager access to the office and there was no violence.

The story was different in the larger Tokyo and Osaka offices, where the Managers were not particularly popular, and the Board of Directors in Hong Kong were kept in touch with developments at every meeting. The senior Manager in Japan, H.V. Parker, was told to hold firm and advised not to argue; representations were made through the Embassy to the Japanese Government and eventually a settlement, on September 27, 1955, was reached which fell far short of the Union's demands. There was no victimization; at least one of the strike leaders was hired by the Bank and became the Chief Personnel Officer. Many striking Bank staff were embarrassed by the affair and apologized privately to members of the junior staff; the latter had been offered an opportunity to transfer if they considered that the event had caused them to lose face, but only one Foreign staff member asked to be transferred. At the same time the Board voted them and the Japanese Manager, S. Hayashi, bonuses.

The success in keeping open during the strike was used as an argument in support of the then system of Foreign staff training. All such staff could, as a result of having started on routine tasks, actually perform the work done by clerks. They had not moved in at the top. As it happened, it was fortunate the officers had received such training, but it was hardly a sound argument for the continuation of the system.

In fact, it is an exaggeration to suggest that the Foreign staff as then constituted in Japan kept the operation going. The Bank had to fly in additional staff; they entered the country on tourist visas. They did not go to the Bank itself but remained in their Tokyo hotels; work was smuggled out from the Bank office; the officer had to shake off his Union tail, reach the hotel undetected, deliver the work to be done, and return later to collect it.

The ramifications of the Bank's Japan business were world-wide and were particularly significant to London Office.

THE EUROPEAN OFFICES

London

Any discussion of the London Office should be read in conjunction with the relationship with the London Advisory Committee, a subject considered in Chapter 6. There are several categories of subjects: the ordinary banking work of the London Office, the representational aspect of the office, its relations with Head Office, with the Bank of England, with the Advisory Committee, and with the Bank's subsidiary companies. This last is not new; it was a problem in the pre-war period when the Bank had two associated companies, the British and Chinese Corporation and the Chinese Central Railways.

There is no question but that Morse and Turner sent highly qualified officers to head the London Office as senior Manager – H.E. Muriel, S.A. Gray, S.W.P. Perry-Aldworth, and G.O.W. Stewart. In Table 1.3 (Volume III) the question was answered as to which Chief Managers had served under their London Manager. Between 1931, when Stabb died, and 1962 when Saunders became Chief Manager, the Bank's Chief Managers had not actually served under their London Manager, although Muriel was senior in the service to Morse, Gray and Perry-Aldworth to Turner. The problem, however, is to assess the relationships in terms of new activities and new communications facilities.

As Perry-Aldworth described his position in 1960, his only connection with the routine of the London Office was his handling of Head Office investments, call money, and Treasury bills. Like Sir Charles Addis, his main preoccupation was with the Bank's subsidiary companies, for Perry-Aldworth was on the boards of the British and Chinese Corporation, the Trust Corporation of the Bahamas, and Bowmaker, and of the Mercantile Bank and the British Bank of the Middle East; he was on the committees of the various regional associations – the Malayan Commercial Association, the India, Pakistan and Burma Association, the Philippine Society, the Indonesian Association, the China Association, and the Japan Association; a Hong Kong Association was being formed. He was a member of the committee of the British Overseas Banks Association and as such testified before the Radcliffe Committee (Committee on the Working of the Monetary System, 1959).

He was the Deputy Chairman of the Bank's London Advisory Committee but he was not its Chairman. The criticisms of Grayburn remained valid; the London Manager did not have easy access to the Committee since the Chairman was Sir Arthur Morse, who held the inner line of communication to Turner in Hong Kong. The Turner/Morse relationship was more closely parallel to that of Barlow/Stabb than Grayburn/Barnes (see Volume III) or

Saunders/Turner. Sir Edward Reid, a member of the Committee, was one of the Hongkong Bank's greatest friends and his contribution to the success of the Bank in London was undoubted. But he too had inner lines both to Morse and to Turner, and several things happened behind Perry-Aldworth. This had little personal impact on Perry-Aldworth until the point of his retirement when, as previously noted, he did not become Chairman of the Committee nor was he kept on the boards of the subsidiary banks.

The consequence of all this was that the position of London Office was growing weaker at a time when it seemed to be most active. As long as the boards of the subsidiary banks were in London, as long as the Bank's reserves were largely in sterling, London would continue to be important. But the removal of these props, the isolation of the Committee from any real function, and the development of alternative lines of communication would have an impact on the Bank's position in the City. This is a theme that will be continued in Chapters 14 and 18.

The Hongkong Bank held considerable funds for local Asian banks, but with their development would come the eventual recognition that money could be obtained on the London Call Market, and they withdrew their deposits from the Hongkong Bank – most dramatic was the loss in 1956 when the Bank of China withdrew the bulk of its funds. Although competition from London branches of Japanese banks was foreseen as early as 1952, in 1956 London Office was still rediscounting their paper to the extent of £11 million. Nevertheless by the end of the decade, the growth of the direct Japanese London business through their own branches had had a net negative impact on the profits of London Office.

Meanwhile, at a lower level, there were officers in the East questioning the efficiency and accuracy of London Office operations. The Securities Department was particularly singled out; the files were sufficient for Turner to note that such a reform had been needed in 1937; had he gone back further, he would have discovered records of the department's problems immediately following the Great War. But this was all evidence – to Hong Kong at least – of inevitable 'Londonitis'.

Hamburg

With the passing of H.A. Siebs of Siemssen and Company in 1950, the last of the German directors of the Hongkong Bank (1908–1914) was gone (see Volume II); G.C. Moutrie attended his funeral on behalf of the Bank and a special message from Morse in Hong Kong applauded this gesture and noted the Bank's good relations with Siemssen's. In 1954 A. Nack resigned after 47 years of service; he had been the Hamburg Branch Chief Clerk since 1939 and a procurator during World War II. In addition to a pension initially of DM600

(£50) p.m. and a gratuity of DM35,000 (£3,000), he and his wife were brought to England and invited to the Bank's annual dinner. Anxiously he asked if he would be required to give a speech; Morse reassured him – but several drinks later Morse changed his mind, and Nack suddenly found himself addressing the assembled company. Nack's retirement benefits and pension and those of other retiring Germans came, as in the old days, before the Board of Directors for approval. This would include F.T. Koelle's reinstated pension; Koelle went East in 1884, resigned in 1920, and died in 1958 (see note 'h', p. 343).

The inability of the branch in this period to accept local deposits limited its scope of operations. There is nothing to add therefore to the comments to be found in Chapter 2.

Lyons/Paris

The Hongkong Bank's 1951 decision to remove from its traditional French base in Lyons was made reluctantly. The evidence, however, was in favour of the move. The silk trade with the East had dwindled, the Bank's French customers were more widely based than a purely Lyons operation justified, the French economy had become increasingly centralized, and the money market was in Paris. The Bank would have preferred to remain in Lyons and open a new office in Paris; this the French authorities would not permit. There had been a rationalization in French banking, offices had been closed; it would not then be politically practical to permit a foreign bank to open a second office. When examining the situation in 1960, W.H. Lydall would conclude that a second office was not practical from the Bank's point of view.

The last Lyons Manager was D.C. Davis (East in 1922), who had served in the Bank's Vladivostok branch and had been four years in Haiphong. He had served as Manager in Hong Kong before this last assignment, and he was responsible for the actual move and for the location of suitable property in the prestigious Place Vendôme. Too prestigious, perhaps. When the Bank was faced with the need for an opening party, a junior was told to fix up the catering with a neighbouring restaurant. He did, and the Ritz just across the square did it well but not cheaply. Thus began a life-style which Head Office did not appreciate; it was one of the factors which would encourage a move to another location – and to a less suitable office for banking. In 1979 the Bank would return once again to the neighbourhood on the Rue de la Paix.

In 1954 Davis found that the committee controlling the square would not allow him to put up a sign advertising the Hongkong Bank without the permission of the Minister des Beaux-Arts, which was impossible to obtain. In 1960, however, the then Manager, H.V. Parker, accepted an invitation to become a member of the committee controlling the Place Vendôme; Perry-Aldworth informed Turner that Parker had accepted. It is prestigious, he said, 'Parker was right to accept.'

Meanwhile back in Lyons, the Bank's premises were sold to the Banque Française du Commerce Extérieure, and a small office was rented in the business district for J. Palisson, the agency's *sous-directeur* and then the Bank's temporary representative in Lyons. He wound up the business or saw it transferred to Paris; he then retired in 1954 with his Provident Fund and a gratuity. Younger employees were invited to transfer to Paris, and several did.

In the late 1950s the Paris branch was showing a loss and Turner urged Parker to consider financing local advances from locally raised funds. He was anxious that Parker not become dependent on an increasing overdraft in London. Turner suggested cutting back on expenses. Parker's predecessor, R.A. Jardine (East in 1926), had tried to solve the problem by recommending the establishment of an office in Monte Carlo. His argument actually was that a good number of people from Indochina, who knew the Bank, retired there; they were presumably a source of funds.[d] Turner had replied, 'My first reaction is not altogether enthusiastic', but he authorized an investigation, about which nothing further has been located.

THE PHILIPPINES AND ILOILO

> Please let [the Hongkong Bank] know that I value very highly their confidence in the future of my country.
>
> President Manuel A. Roxas, 1946

The Bank in the Philippines

In 1946 President Manuel A. Roxas in commenting on the role played by the Hongkong Bank, told Colonel Hodsoll of Warner, Barnes and Co. that he valued very highly their confidence in the future of the Philippines. This confidence, however, had proved expensive.

The Hongkong Bank might have played an even greater role, but there were impediments: (i) a debtor/creditor dispute was settled by the Supreme Court in favour of those debtors who had paid in Japanese wartime 'Mickey Mouse' currency, (ii) the Bank did not profit from any post-war rehabilitation legislation, (iii) the possibility of nationalization or other discriminatory enactment was an ever present threat, and (iv) the Bank's own U.S. dollar funding limitations were an initial adverse factor.

The Bank took a strong public position on the debtor/creditor issue at least partly because Arthur Morse was arguing the issue with the British authorities and did not wish to weaken his case. As a practical matter, however, the Manila Manager, W. Webster (East in 1919), did business with firms which had taken

---

[d] Among them, in due course, the successive Hongkong Bank Saigon Managers W.J. Hope and G.S. Chambers.

advantage of the wartime currency payments, and, after advising Morse of the problems, received no further criticism from Head Office. Furthermore the possibility of adverse banking legislation was always tempered by the reciprocity clauses of the various Philippine/U.S. treaties. The General Banking Act of 1948 indeed set out new regulations for foreign banks, but the existing four foreign banks were 'grandfathered'.[e] The Bank's U.S. dollar resources could be supplemented by borrowing in New York, and at one time Webster recalls that he was US$22.5 million overdrawn, until Morse ordered him to cut back. He had preempted virtually the entire U.S. dollar credit of the Hongkong Bank, and the Federal Reserve were becoming concerned at the Bank's position.

Traditionally, the Hongkong Bank had done the bulk of its Philippine business with a small group of major customers. These were in need of rehabilitation, and, in at least one case, the Bank could not provide the funds necessary, driving a major old time constituent to other banks for finance. But, as the Central Bank of the Philippines noted, acknowledging the foreign banks' efforts in its first annual report:

Branches of foreign banks established here in the Philippines were primarily concerned before the war with foreign trade and foreign exchange transactions. As a consequence, a feeling existed then in local business circles that foreign banks did not use their resources, derived in large measure from local deposits, to promote the growth of the national economy. However, when these banks commenced operation after liberation, they made a number of sizeable rehabilitation loans to local interests, a policy which greatly contributed to the development of the national economy.

This was a gracious statement, but the underlying assumption that finance of foreign trade did not promote the growth of the national economy might have been a warning that Central Bank regulations would be biased in favour of development financing and that the foreign banks' contributions would be measured in this way, despite their primary interests as exchange banks.

By 1948 the Manila branch's profits, including Iloilo's were $4.4 million, greater, that is, than those of Singapore (with Malaya). This would appear to be owing primarily to an extraordinary series of gold financing operations, legal under the then laws of the Philippines and based upon apparently 100% advances – 'apparently' because the Bank valued the gold at its official price, whereas it was destined to be sold at open market prices. The gold came in from Mexico, was stored in the Bank's vaults, and then placed on an amphibious plane which appeared from the direction of the China coast; it was presumably

---

[e] The four banks were: the Hongkong Bank, the Chartered Bank, the National City Bank of New York, and the Nederlandsch Indische Handelsbank. The last mentioned was bought by the Bank of America. The new regulations (in Republic Act 337) prevented foreign banks from accepting deposits, unless they in fact formed a subsidiary in which 60% of the shares were held by Filipino citizens.

from Macau. When the IMF were successful in pressuring Mexico into stopping these exports, the trade moved to Peru; the IMF struck again, but as there was no prohibition against the export of religious images, the gold began to appear in this shape – it was known, inevitably, as 'Virgin gold'. Eventually, the Philippine Government forbade gold exports, catching the Hongkong Bank with considerable gold in its vaults awaiting the plane. Arrangements were made, costly arrangements; the prohibition was lifted to enable a final shipment, and the trade was for the time being ended. By 1951 Manila's profits were down to a low of $1.5 million (see Table 8.1).

The relative position of the Hongkong Bank in the Philippines declined during the next decade. In the period 1949 through 1959, the loan portfolio of the Bank expanded by 44%; the Philippine banking system's by 200%; the Hongkong Bank's market share accordingly dropped from 5.4% to 2.6%. This is consistent with the development of the local banking sector and the general decline of foreign banks; it also reflects the relative strength of domestic lending as opposed to the finance of foreign trade.

The calls for Filipinization of the banking system were not stilled by the 1948 Act. There were during the 1950s general calls for the Filipinization of all businesses, and anti-Chinese as well as anti-foreign legislation was considered; some measures, for example, limiting the remission of profits to 40% (1950) and the nationalization of the retail trade (1954), were enacted. But in defending itself, the Hongkong Bank came up with statistics which reflected its own reorientation in the now developing economy; in 1954 74% of the Bank's deposits came from foreign groups or foreign-controlled domestic corporations but 67% of the Bank's loan portfolio went to Filipino borrowers.

The various enactments and Central Bank regulations led in the Philippines, as elsewhere, to (i) centralization, (ii) increased opportunities for corruption, and (iii) nationalism in economic policy and enforcement. The first would affect the business of the Iloilo agency, whose consequent sole purpose was as a source of funds for Manila operations. Throughout the period, Morse and Turner were reluctant to commit further funds to the Philippines from the Bank's central reserves.

Nevertheless, the Hongkong Bank continued to play a role in the economy of the Philippines. In the present chapter the discussion is confined to the history of the Iloilo agency, continuing a story begun in Chapter 2 of Volume II.

Iloilo, 1946–1965

The post-war business of the Iloilo agency

In January 1947 A.B. Kelly then Agent in Iloilo wrote, 'I note to start a policy of gradually closing down Iloilo.' A month later the Chief Manager, Sir Arthur

Morse, wrote to Webster, then Manager in Manila, of a 'tendency to construe what I have said to you about closing down Iloilo by degrees into advocating an operation to be commenced immediately and carried on with utmost speed'. This is not what Morse had had in mind, but the Iloilo agency might be thought of just a size that required the officer in charge to either close it or operate it. The agency's fate was nicely balanced between events in Iloilo itself and the overall Philippine banking scene as it affected the Hongkong Bank, and the agency was not in fact closed until 1981.

As noted in Chapter 2, Iloilo proved its temporary worth in late 1945 as a source of U.S. dollars bought from both the U.S. and Philippine armies for pesos remitted in some cases from Manila. The extraordinary operation was financially sound because the Philippine Treasury was not as yet open and the U.S. Army in Manila dealt directly with the National City Bank, cutting out the Hongkong Bank from a cheap source of dollars.

But pleased as the former Manila Manager, A.F. Handcock, had been at the time, a more long-run analysis was necessary. Kelly reported that Iloilo as a sugar port was moribund, that the port facilities had depreciated, the sugar godowns were damaged, and labour problems, if anything, were worse. He predicted that trade would continue to shift to Cebu and he noted that Negros sugar would be shipped direct and not via Iloilo, while imports would be routed via Manila where exchange was settled. Indeed there were no facilities for bulk loading in Iloilo and a sugar-loading terminal would soon be built on an island in the strait between Panay and Negros permitting shipments to bypass the port. 'As much as I would like to note some factors on the credit side of the book, I am afraid I simply cannot and be truthful.' With this Handcock's successor, Webster, concurred.

The Hongkong Bank now faced a decision – to close Iloilo and deal only in Manila or to expand into Cebu and possibly to Bacolod in Negros. Morse, however, was procrastinating for two reasons: (i) the Bank's continued presence in the Philippines was in doubt given the possibility of anti-foreign banking legislation which, now that the Islands were independent, might actually pass the Philippine Congress and be signed into law and (ii) as noted above, Morse considered the settlement of the 'Mickey Mouse' occupation currency payment argument to have a significant bearing on the Hongkong Bank's future plans.

By 1953 Iloilo had found a new role. '[Its] chief value to us', wrote H.V. Parker, the new Manila Manager, after a visit of inspection, 'is the extent of funds it can accumulate. We never have much difficulty in putting them to good use here.' Iloilo was justified then as a deposit base, gathering peso funds for use mainly in Manila, although a small loan business was continued by the agency (or 'branch' as it would soon be properly referred to). There might be

Table 10.7 *The Hongkong Bank: Iloilo branch:*
Profit and Loss Accounts, 1962–1964
For six months periods ending June (i) *1962,* (ii) *1963,* (iii) *1964*
(thousands of pesos)

	(i)	(ii)	(iii)
Expenditure:			
Deposit interest	1.3	2.2	10.8
Savings Bank interest	56.9	77.5	104.8
Taxation	2.8	3.4	4.6
Charges	91.9	120.5	127.0
Income:			
Adjustment between Branches	68.9	95.0	132.3
Commission	22.2	23.8	33.2
Interest and discount	31.6	39.1	53.9
Notes purchased	0.6	1.2	1.2
Profits in exchange	1.5	2.8	4.6
Net loss	34.8	47.0	29.3

For years in the 1900s see Volume II, Table 2.2; for the 1930s, Volume III, Table 10.2.

better locations, but there were two hesitations – could one be sure, given uncertain political conditions, and would the Central Bank permit the Hongkong Bank's Iloilo licence to be transferred? The Bank seriously considered moving to Bacolod in 1955 but eventually decided to hold on to Iloilo.

Savings accounts in the Iloilo agency began with G.W.E. True in 1950 when the office was moved from its original site on the river to a busy intersection near the shopping district where buses disgorged the people from up-country barrios. By September 1953 there were 1,709 accounts, a year later 2,150. Reactions to Iloilo were again positive – 'I feel that, all things being equal, we shall see enough improvement to justify the maintenance of the Iloilo office.' By 1957 with 3,000 savings accounts, mechanization was being considered, and so to 1980 when, during negotiations for the sale of the branch, the Bank could point to 25,000 depositors. Head Office watched the early growth with approval, as concerned as was True that money was being switched back and forth between current and savings accounts, not, noted F.C.B. Black, 'in keeping with the objects of a Savings Account' – and he sent copies of the rules of the Hong Kong Savings Bank for information. Black added, 'It may suit you of course to have everything you can lay hands on in the Savings Bank, and we should like to have your views on the subject.' It was the beginning of the

Table 10.8 *The Hongkong Bank: Iloilo branch Calculation of theoretical profit*[a]

(thousands of pesos)

Manila, their a/c	4541.0	
Less: statutory deposits	441.0	
	4100.0 at net interest of 6% =	102.5
	less 5% tax on gross	5.1
	less 30% tax on net	29.2
	plus Manila profits on:	
	Iloilo inland exchange	8.6
	Bacolod inland exchange	4.4
	plus adjustment in exchange	
	commission	5.4
		86.6
	less Iloilo's Loss on P&L A/c	31.1
	Estimated theoretical profit	**55.5**

[a] for six months ending December 1962

escalation or post-war sophistication of the small saver encouraged by higher interest rates – banks were indeed soon to seek everything they could lay their hands on and count themselves lucky if they could keep it at no higher cost than payment of interest at savings account rates.

It was a new world, and the obvious questions for Iloilo are: who were the depositors and why did they deposit in the Hongkong Bank?

The two questions are not unrelated to the extent that the growth can be accounted for by those receiving a pension in the form of U.S. Treasury warrants, which the Hongkong Bank would process immediately despite the fact that there was no time limit within which the Treasury could have recourse against the Bank for incorrect payment.

In addition to this objective factor there were several factors less easy to evaluate. The Iloilo agency sponsored real (as opposed to tombstone) advertisements, and the Chief Manager, Michael Turner, was apparently not pleased to note on his drive in from the airport a series of signs marking the distance from the city centre *and* a branch of The Hongkong and Shanghai Banking Corporation where you could open a savings account. In the 1960s Robin Campbell advertised the Bank as a giant, 'ho-ho-hoing' suitably during commercials; leaflets were dropped on the barrios; an agency, operated by Warner, Barnes and Co. (and managed by Jack Grieve, a grandson of the Hongkong Bank's first Manila Manager) was established in Bacolod; the Bank's

Manila basketball team came down to play – every effort was made to get the Bank known.

Other explanations for the growth in the number of depositors were that the Bank was foreign and some considered it safer and that, unlike the Chartered Bank, it still had a foreign Manager – two reasons particularly difficult to evaluate. The fact is that in the face of growing competition from up to 26 other banks in the community and despite the decline in pensions paid in Treasury warrants, the Hongkong Bank's savings accounts continued to grow throughout the post-war period under the control of cautious predictions from Managers anxious, not unreasonably, that Head Office not be over-expectant.

The bottom line in the Profit and Loss Account statements in the 1930s read 'Profit', and the losses were specifically marked as such. More realistically, the post-war account just labelled the footings, as above, 'Net Loss'. Were the advantages of Iloilo sufficiently great as to warrant these continual losses? Had the advantages been confined to such non-quantifiable items as 'convenience to Manila customers' or 'information on the South' etc., Iloilo might have been closed before other arrangements for an office had been finalized (see Table 10.7). But when the Chief Manager, J.A.H. Saunders, wrote to the Iloilo Manager, C.P.B. Mathews, 'I see your deposits continue to increase, with the result that your office makes a useful contribution to the Bank even though you do not show a profit', he had specific figures in mind. Given, for example, a loss for the half-year ending December 31, 1962, of Pesos 31,100, a profit of Pesos 55,500 can be calculated as in Table 10.8.

The question of 'profit' was one of constant concern in Iloilo, because it was apparent that if Manila permitted a higher rate of interest on interbank deposits, the main source of Iloilo's income, in the first place, the nice adjustments would perhaps not be necessary, and the branch would show a profit. Staff morale was a factor. On the other hand the calculations do not include such items as Head Office overhead allocation and possibly other items, which suggests that determining this sort of 'estimated theoretical profit' is mainly an exercise where the important factor is uniformity, thus providing a consistent standard to assist Head Office management in making global allocations of the corporation's resources.

Thus far the existence of the post-war Iloilo branch has been justified entirely in terms of the funds it gathered for use in Manila. But could the branch have used them in Iloilo City itself, that is, could the branch have acted as a normal domestic, retail bank?

The Hongkong Bank operated with certain advantages and certain handicaps. It had been long-established in Iloilo and had made important contacts, but the Bank could not easily exploit this: (i) for large operations it was limited by ratios governing the size of a loan to any one customer and then, too, major decision-making had been transferred by the Bank's larger customers to Manila and (ii) loans against land and fish ponds were restricted by the problems which might arise on foreclosure, the Bank being unable to own real estate. With the growth of sound domestic banks, the Hongkong Bank's branch limitation also became relevant; most commercial customers would have to have a second bank, and eventually accounts and business were shifted. While the branch did lend to local merchants to finance stocks and, according to H.L. Pierce, opened a few import letters of credit and financed customers in Bacolod through Warner Barnes, for larger matters the Hongkong Bank became, in the frank reports of former customers, something of a handy standby. Should the manager of, for example, the Philippine National Bank (PNB) be unable to provide accommodation for some reason, or if the delays were too great, then there was always the Hongkong Bank.

In keeping with post-war trends, the Republic of the Philippines quite naturally became involved in development planning and, with that planning, the control of resources including foreign exchange. Allocations were made in Manila and prudence suggested to many importers that they deal with Government in Manila, importing through that port. Although many customers from the Chinese community remained loyal to the Bank, the Chinese naturally sought to integrate as citizens of the Republic, and another obvious source of business declined. Regulations are subject to interpretation and often a domestic bank can cut them finer than would be appropriate for a foreign institution; the Hongkong Bank sometimes felt that the growing competition in Iloilo did not always follow the rules. In some instances it was unwise to press, thus while the PNB as an agent of the Central Bank had to undertake to remit funds to Manila at par, the Iloilo Agent advised Warner Barnes in Bacolod not to offend the PNB by attempting too zealously to take away their customers in favour of the Hongkong Bank.

Not that the Hongkong Bank was passive.

A.I. Rabuco especially recalls that George True, not by chance the secretary of the Golf Club, sought out small borrowers – although some of these were later described as 'pawn shop' loans and allowed to run off. But particularly he recalls the stress on service – all we have to sell is service – and the boast that the Hongkong Bank handled its business more efficiently than the others. Interviews with former customers support the view that the Bank tried to maintain its position through fast decisions, but this would be no help at all in such overriding situations as the monopoly financing of sugar by the PNB or the decision of the Manila branch that crop loans, except to Warner, Barnes and Co., were not an appropriate activity for the branch. In keeping with the realities of the situation N.A. Keith was in 1967 for the first time given 'limits' for the express purpose of improving service to clients: Pesos 30,000 secured,

Pesos 6,000 unsecured. He was also advised to attempt to meet fine cutting of inland remittance rates by omitting any commission on transfers between Hongkong Bank branches and by forgoing reimbursement for postal or cable expenses... and by offering 'first class, friendly service'.

The expense account comes to Iloilo
Post-war every action of the Bank had a significant tax aspect, whether it be the pension scheme, the profitability of an acquisition in the context of a series of holding companies, or the expense account. This last was the consequence of the increased tax on personal income which made it impractical for the Bank to pay its Managers sufficient to cover their representational expenses. Indeed, in London this had been true even before the Pacific War; Morse was as London Manager sent with a lower salary than his predecessor – but with an expense account.

Each office had, however, a Charges Account. This was primarily established to handle expenditures on essential business items and for wages. The Manager had always been provided with a Bank house or with an equivalent allowance and with transportation – a cart in Peking, a horse and carriage in the tropics, and later, a motor car. The Bank also paid for his servants. Beyond this the Manager's position was quite clear; except for the most unusual circumstances he was expected to entertain within his salary. Permission to debit the account for unusual entertaining, charity, and other non-business items had to be sought from the Chief Manager, who frequently referred to the Board.

The salary of the Iloilo Agent had always been modest, and an unusual expenditure was the more likely, therefore, to arise. A series of Iloilo incidents from 1934 to the mid-1960s provide an insight into the pre-war stringency and difficulties and illustrate a not unusual course which leads eventually to the more modern concept of business entertainment.

In a plaintive letter the Bank's Iloilo Agent, H.A. Courtney, notified Manila in 1934 that HBM's Honorary Vice-Consul had requested the British community to entertain the officers and men of a visiting British cruiser. In the past, the Agent noted, the port had been visited by smaller vessels which the British community, consisting of about 25 persons, mostly juniors, could handle... 'Usually they send us a submarine or perhaps two submarines, which we managed to entertain without doing anything elaborate, but a cruiser is a different matter and I wonder if you will authorize me to debit Charges with say pesos 50 on this account.' The subsequent year he took it upon himself to debit 'Charges' 18 pesos to buy a Union Jack to fly over the agency, but this was perhaps excusable in the King's Jubilee year, and he subsequently requested additional authorization for the actual celebrations.

Post-war the honour of being Honorary Vice-Consul in Iloilo fell from time to time on the Agent of the Hongkong Bank, who in 1947 was instructed by the British Ambassador to entertain yet another visiting cruiser and to 'Please report any costs incurred for settlement in Manila'. But when A.B. Kelly, then Agent, in fact reported expenses totalling 1,285 pesos, he was informed by the Ambassador that no public funds were available and that 'one must expect the British communities who undertake such entertainment to do so at their own expense' – this at a time when Iloilo counted but six British subjects, three of them juniors. Sandy Webster, the Manager in Manila, felt unable to justify a debit to Charges and Kelly appealed to Head Office, where Sir Arthur Morse informed Webster that 'in spite of Kelly's stupidity, you must meet their bill'. Neither the Manila Manager nor Morse (nor HBM's Ambassador) offered to provide an alternative interpretation to the instruction 'report any costs incurred for settlement in Manila'.

H.L. Pierce, the Manager in 1960–1961, reported that Royal Navy minesweepers had visited the port, but presumably they were of an entertainable size. Between 1967 and 1971 the position was to change on both fronts. The Iloilo Manager in his role as Honorary British Vice-Consul was informed by the Embassy itself that he would be provided an allowance of £40 for the Queen's Birthday and £20 whenever a British naval vessel called – the latter provision being perhaps less useful in practice since authorization coincided with (i) the silting up of the port and (ii) the lack of British warships available for entertaining, and anyway with C.R. Rowe's departure in 1974 the post itself was discontinued. Indeed from the Bank's point of view, this proved just as well, as the anti-British demonstrations during the Sabah confrontation had led to picketing of the Bank, although on this occasion without any serious long-run consequences. As it remained unlikely that British prestige could be maintained on £40 and as there were now but two British subjects resident in the area, the Manager was authorized by the Bank to debit 'any' excess expenditure to Charges account. But when in 1971 the Iloilo Manager, D.H. Livesey, was advised by Ian Sutherland, then Manila Manager, to 'make it a point to take your selected customers to lunch at the hotel at least once a week... the expense is negligible and the results can be worthwhile' and with the clear inference that it was in order **to debit the cost to Charges account**, it may be truly said that modern banking had reached the Western Visayas and that the expense account had come to Iloilo.

Hongkong Bankers, the Bank, and the community
The Hongkong Bank 'is very highly thought of in Iloilo' reported one Inspector to Head Office – almost in surprise. In 1955 another Bank visitor wrote, 'I was most impressed by the complimentary remarks made about the Hongkong Bank both in Iloilo and Bacolod.' The Bank had been part of a small community for nearly 100 years and its Agents and staff had contributed

accordingly. If savings accounts were first thought of as practically a charity service, their usefulness to the small depositor was not the less because these deposits were now seen to be of basic importance to the Bank in the Philippines. With 25,000 accounts in a community of perhaps 300,000, a goodly percentage of those who banked came to the Hongkong Bank's Iloilo branch.

But just as the branch's banking activities changed with the economy and with the new laws and regulations, so the Bank's staffing and community role changed with the great social upheavals which followed the Pacific War.

Pre-war it was not uncommon for an expatriate Foreign staff officer to remain in Iloilo for four years or more, but, aside from any question of decline in the type of business requiring such an officer, there was already the question of career development – the needs of the customers for continuity had to be balanced against the career of the officer. There had been a change as career planning developed: the first 'Agent' (or Manager), in the late nineteenth century, remained for perhaps ten years or more and might develop into what the local press referred to as a 'long-established resident', sometimes into a 'well-known character'; in the inter-war years the assignment might last one tour (or possibly a little less); but by the 1950s it was seen that two years was probably the maximum.

The alternative was a Filipino Manager. On the eve of closing the branch, the Bank did in fact install Roberto E. Paredes as the first local Manager, but in the interim there had been reservations. Paralleling the policy of military commanders who consider it essential that every officer be familiar with the rifle even if his duties involve him solely in computerized war-gaming, senior Bank management inclined to the somewhat romantic concern that juniors were being deprived by localization schemes of experience in small offices where they did everything from wait on customers at the counters to the books – it was such experience, surely, that enabled the Bank to keep open during staff strikes in the post-war period. There was also the view that a customer felt reassured by the presence of an expatriate or, to put it in a more reasonable context, that given the presence of up to 265 banks in Iloilo, one reason for choosing the Hongkong Bank would be the foreign Manager.

But even if you decided on a local officer, there was the problem of selection. Iloilo was a provincial city and it was clear that senior officers from Manila would be unwilling to transfer – even if the unions were not to object. The Bank had then to turn to its own Iloilo local staff and engineer the change over time.

With the departure and death of Hulme, Iloilo was for a time staffed by only one officer, and he, of course, an expatriate. The practical problems this policy provoked, the problems of the 'one-man' office, were partly overcome by flying down an officer from Manila for one week a month to free the Agent temporarily from the office routine. By 1954 however the growth of business required the Bank to take action. A foreign woman could handle the savings accounts (it was never considered whether a foreign woman could handle the Bank itself), but none was to be found. As the other Iloilo expatriate Managers retired, they were replaced by Filipinos; the Clubs, except the Golf Club, closed or were never reopened after the war – the situation was well summarized by a Filipino surgeon who commented to the Manager, A.D.A.G. Mosely, as he was going under, 'You're the first white man I've operated on in twenty years.' But the Bank's solution was against the trend: from 1954 to 1963 there was a second Foreign staff officer assigned to the branch despite pressures for localization and increasing immigration restrictions.

The older staff had retired in the years following the Japanese surrender and in 1953 Parker said of their replacements, 'a young and inexperienced staff which one could weld into quite a good team'; Rabuco was marked as a chief clerk who would, with the routine gradually removed from him, supply the need for a local supervisor. But there were hesitations about a local officer.

In 1963 however Rabuco became the No. 2 in the branch, effectively replacing the second expatriate; he became a Regional Officer in 1967. But in the local community he was the 'assistant manager' of the Hongkong Bank – his studies in the local university and degree in finance, his years from the village to houseboy, guerrilla fighter, messenger, chief clerk, had reached a climax that typified the development of the post-independence Philippines. Rabuco retired in 1975.

Parades, the first Filipino Manager of the Hongkong Bank in Iloilo, came to the Bank after a temporary position with Caltex in 1956. The son of a widowed schoolteacher, he was, in the great Filipino/American tradition, working his way through college. But Caltex had no permanent opening and Paredes asked the manager, W. Prichet, for assistance.

> Then he asked me one question which I cannot forget. 'Are you willing to work at any company, at any place, if I recommend you?' Anyway, I agree. And so he gave me a card (that was usual in those days) and instructions...
> He didn't tip you the name of the company?
> No, he didn't. He didn't tell me the name of the company. I was very excited, so I made a personal investigation and then I saw it was the Hongkong Bank. Oh my, I said, it's a bank. And of course I was still an undergraduate and I was nervous that I could not be taken in, but I went to see Mr [J.H.W.] Marshall, gave him Mr Prichet's card with my name on the reverse side. After having a few words...you know just sitting down...and trying to find out what's with me, the next thing I knew he said, 'Report first working day next month', which happened to fall on April 2nd, 1956. So that's when I joined the Bank...

...as janitor. Paredes commented, 'I'd never done so much physical work in my life then, you see. I'd been spoilt probably in the family.' When he completed his BSc in Commerce he was promoted to office boy and was soon himself teaching part-time at the Central Philippine University; he was then promoted to clerk. His opportunity, however, came during the great fire of 1966 – but that story is told in its proper place, together with the events leading to the closing of the Bank's Iloilo branch.

THE COLOMBO BRANCH, 1945–1965

Like the Iloilo branch, the Colombo agency/branch has been the focus of a specific case study, and the following history follows on the discussion of wartime Colombo in Chapter 1.

The immediate post-war period was marked by the Bank's first labour troubles, but generally the Bank found the post-independence Government anxious for continuity, subject to certain adjustments. The fate of foreign banks in Sri Lanka, however, became increasingly uncertain; as with many Governments, certain contributions made by the exchange banks were acknowledged, but the Government was not prepared to assure the means whereby the banks might efficiently continue those contributions. Sri Lanka, as many other independent countries, saw the banks as a source of foreign capital; the banks saw themselves as financial intermediaries, including a role, even a restricted role, in the domestic banking scene.

Events in Sri Lanka were complicated by the fact that the Mercantile Bank with its up-country offices became part of the Hongkong Bank Group, and consideration of the Hongkong Bank's role had to take the Group interests into account.

But despite difficulties, the Hongkong Bank was reluctant to close, and in the end it did not.

The Bank's labour relations
The first strike of bank clerks lasted one day, September 1, 1944, and their complaints were referred to a retired district judge, T.A. Roberts, for arbitration. The so-called Roberts Award had more the effect of regularizing pay and conditions as far as Hongkong Bank staff were concerned, but the benefits were in general real and significant.

With the war over, further agitation resulted in a longer strike and more serious disruption. Under the leadership of Labour Party leader A.E. Gooneshinha, then president of the Bank Clerks Union and already a man with a formidable record of strike organization, a strike was called for November 1, 1945, on the grounds that many of the benefits of the Roberts Award had not been implemented, that there were other significant grievances, and that the workers had lost faith in tribunals and arbitrators.

Management was represented by J.G. Scroggie of the National Bank of India, who claimed that the position of the banks and the terms of the Roberts Award had been misrepresented to the bank clerks and that they were in any case better off than Government clerks. To which Gooneshinha replied that Government employees were not driven like slaves and had fringe benefits. It should be added that Gooneshinha was a dynamic speaker, the atmosphere was ripe for a general strike, and that the political situation was tense. Given the changed social, political, and economic environment, it was no longer possible for adjustments to be made in an atmosphere of paternalistic concern either in Ceylon or in Singapore, Japan (when their time came), or apparently elsewhere in Asia. And in fairness, given the straitened circumstances of a bank attempting to rebuild, one can wonder whether anything short of extreme pressure could have led to improved conditions. To them the response may be that in Colombo, at least, the Hongkong Bank's clerks gained very little if anything in terms of immediate compensation from the strike as their terms of service very largely met the union's demands.

This time the strike lasted for over a week. In 1946 there was a more serious strike over the discharge of two clerks which lasted 65 days. Not all joined in, and several senior clerks of the Hongkong Bank, men with long service like Brohier, Colette, Ebell, Dias, Massillamany, and Van Geyzel, came to work at the risk of being manhandled. V.A. Mason, who was then still awaiting permission to enter Japan, recalls,

> I visited one of the office staff [Colette] in hospital who'd run into some trouble. The rabble had put wires across a road knowing that these boys were going to cycle that way home. And in the dark these wires would catch a man under the chin and throw him backwards... Finally Dr Wignaraja wanted me to live on the bank premises... didn't like me to leave the office at night time.

The terms of the settlement included:
(i) implementation of the Roberts Award relative to annual increments and promotions;
(ii) supervisors and local assistants should be paid an initial salary of Rs300 rising to Rs400 by increments of Rs12.50 [Hongkong Bank salaries for clerks in 1934 ranged from Rs50 to Rs400 a month];
(iii) pensions to be two-thirds of the last salary after 30 years service – although this was not necessary for Hongkong Bank employees as the Bank made a 20% contribution to a Provident Fund, but this rate should apply to all future employees of the Bank by agreement;
(iv) overtime at an hourly rate equal to 1.5 times 1/240th of the monthly pay;
(v) the right to a leave of 14 days plus casual leave of seven days, and sick leave as supported by medical certificates; and
(vi) dearness allowance as detailed in the agreement.

Whatever the social impact on the Bank's Foreign staff may have been – and it appears to have been, as already indicated, one of incomprehension, especially in view of the small gains their own staff received – such events, while never routine, became less 'personal', less a 'challenge' and were seen as part of the adjustment process which a foreign bank, as a guest in the economy, must come to expect. But if the strike did not cost the Bank by the terms of its settlement, there were other considerations. The work of the Bank continued throughout, partly through the loyalty to the Bank (or disloyalty to the labour movement) of the senior clerks and partly because the Foreign staff were all competent, thanks to apprenticeship in other British banks, to early 'training' in the London office, and to their continued learning on the job experience as juniors, to handle the routine clerical tasks of banking. They were thus able to keep the office open.

On the other hand the Bank of Ceylon clerks, whose manager had promised to award them any benefit won by the strikers, did not go on strike, which thus appeared to be directed against the *foreign* banks, although the issues were industry-wide. Many customers accordingly made conclusions about the future and transferred part or all their business to the Bank of Ceylon, whose growth, uninhibited by certain of the original restrictions, for example, on exchange dealings, had already been considerable.

Another major disturbance, in 1956, settled by the Thalgodapitiya Award was mainly concerned with the provisions of the various provident funds. In this case the Hongkong Bank's fund contributions were so far in excess of those of other banks that the Tribunal specifically stated they could not be expected to match them and even recommended that the Hongkong Bank, whose staff had participated in the disturbances, should reduce its benefits. The Bank did not act on this recommendation but in the 1960s did come into line with an overall agreement.

The Hongkong Bank's Manager A.L.V.S. Giles was in a position to deal with the prolonged 1961 strike since he had successfully urged Head Office to make several additional appointments of clerks to local officer status on condition that they leave the union. This they were willing (perhaps pleased) to do as there had been intimidation and union loyalty was as yet undeveloped. In consequence the Hongkong Bank was again able to operate throughout.

In all these various labour troubles, therefore, certain Hongkong Bank clerks and local officers continued to show up daily for work and the Bank, as has been stated, stayed open. Their loyalty was acknowledged, as, for example in this letter of May 25, 1961:

Dear Mr Brohier,
    I have just read a full report on how Colombo Office carried on during the recent strike. I am told that you were of the greatest assistance in every way and I write to thank you for your loyalty and hard work during what must have been a very difficult time.
    Yours sincerely, [signed] Michael W. Turner [Chief Manager]

Similar letters went to all non-strikers. This would cause problems later.

The Hongkong Bank's policy was apparently picked up by other foreign banks and in 1964 the union specifically moved against the practice by which a staff member was required to resign from the union when appointed an officer; this practice had not been proved until the Hongkong Bank by oversight and before determining the opinions of the staff member involved actually put the requirement in a letter offering appointment. The practice, which was contrary to conditions for membership in the United Kingdom's National Union of Bank Employees and to those imposed by the Bank of Ceylon and the new People's Bank, as well as being contrary to ILO convention 87, was discontinued, although bank managers were permitted to encourage their new officers to leave the union of their own accord.

The Hongkong Bank had been caught.

Previously its policy of creating local officers who would, with the older staff, keep the Bank open, had been successful – one customer even commenting that service was better during a strike due to shortcuts in procedure! It chose to contest the particular issue, at first with the support, quietly stated, of other banks. Perhaps the Manager, H.L. Pierce, had been used to methods of confrontation prevalent in India. In any case, the Bank had to concede, thereby losing some support from those who had remained loyal and endangering future relations. So who must be blamed? That question would seem a *non sequitur*; this was a period of adjustment and adjustment takes considerable time.

This was not the end of the Bank's labour problems, which is hardly surprising, considering that a high proportion of the staff were unsympathetic to the union while the rest, which included the national union's president, were strong supporters. In 1966 for example, there were two strikes, the first for pay and the second, lasting over three months, dealt with the right of the union to involvement in matters of promotion. The latter was sufficiently serious for the Prime Minister, Dudley Senanayake, to take notice with a reported encouragement for a settlement in favour of the union.

To conclude this section on a more positive note, this was also the period in which, originally for more positive reasons, the first local officers were appointed. The Mercantile Bank had appointed a Ceylonese officer in 1944 and the Hongkong Bank now followed with its first local appointment. The Ceylon Banking Commission of 1934 had asked pointedly (knowing the answer) whether there were local officers and had been informed that this was a Head Office matter. This issue first came before the Hongkong Bank's Board of Directors in 1893 with relation to a query from Iloilo and the Board 'declined to do so [that is, make a local man an officer of the Bank] for him or any other not trained in London'. And the policy was only partly changed in the 1950's in that the intention was to send those recruited directly to London for training while there would also be direct appointment of long-serving and qualified clerks – a battlefield commission as it were. The Mercantile Bank of India had appointed its first officers in Calcutta before World War II, and it cannot be said that the Hongkong Bank was a pioneer or, on the other hand, that they acted only under the pressure of localization demands – these were to set a faster pace beginning in the 1960s. In the early 1950s it seemed in any case sound policy; Foreign staff were in short supply, the senior clerks tried and able; there seemed no reason why young Sri Lankans should not be sent to London and the already qualified directly appointed.

In 1951 the first senior clerks were appointed executives – H.A. Colette and C.G.G. Ebell. Of the two first direct recruits one found the strain of London too much while the other, C.S. Fonseka, completed his training and remained in an executive position for several years. The list does not however include R. Thambiah, the first Sri Lankan to be appointed Manager of the Hongkong Bank's operations in Colombo; he was, until 1974, with the Mercantile Bank.

Adjustments in banking
Adjustments are of many kinds and the Pacific War postponed rather than assisted the changes necessary for work in an independent Sri Lanka. The economic importance of and the social continuity provided by the continued existence of British defence establishments may have been misleading and even postponed further adjustments both in attitudes and business. The Hongkong Bank was East Asia oriented and the reactions of Managers trained in China were unpredictable. On the one hand there might be a reaction similar to that of Mason who focused on the local staff and compared efficiency. On the other hand a reaction like that of Giles, who, looking at the survival of the British community as late as 1960, could remark on its 'colonial attitude' and the negative impact this must have on business relationships with the Sri Lankans. But important as all this must be to success in business, this section deals with changes considered part of banking more narrowly defined.

The war ended with a flourishing Bank of Ceylon; there was also the Ceylon State Mortgage Bank (est. 1932) which lent on the security of agricultural land and house property and was financed by monies raised from the public sale of debentures. Indian banks operating in the immediate post-war period were the Bank of Chettinad, the Indian Overseas Bank, and the Indian Bank. The Hatton Bank was mainly up-country and it, in 1974, as the Hatton National Bank, had developed sufficiently to purchase the Sri Lankan offices of the Hongkong Bank Group's Mercantile Bank. The banking business of Thomas Cook had already (in 1943) been taken over by Grindlays Bank, and in 1958 this latter became the National Overseas and Grindlays Bank on amalgamation with the National Bank of India – in 1975 and after further changes it again became known as Grindlays Bank Ltd. The Sri Lankan Government established the People's Bank in 1961 to take over cooperative society banking, while the Bank of Ceylon itself was nationalized. The Eastern Bank, a foreign 'exchange bank', was taken over by the newly established Commercial Bank of Ceylon in 1969, the year which also saw the development and rationalization of savings banks under Government jurisdiction. International banking developments in the 1970s will be noted below.

But the most significant change was the establishment of the Central Bank of Ceylon in 1950 with a capital of Rs15 million and responsibility for the administration and regulation of the monetary and banking system of the country. The Hongkong Bank was unused to close central bank supervision, and Manager H.A. Greig, for example, when asked by an examiner in 1954 to provide the balance sheets of his customers argued that they were the property of the borrower and it was not within his authority to provide them to the Central Bank. Twenty-four hours of consideration later, Greig provided the information requested.[f]

Reflecting past complaints, the Central Bank required banks to maintain records of rejected advances and the reasons therefor, and advances had also to be classified as to the communal status of the borrower – Sri Lankan or non-Sri Lankan. As with Federal regulatory concern over 'red-lining' in the United States, the banking authorities in Sri Lanka wished to ensure there was no discrimination unjustified by banking criteria.

The Central Bank was responsible for implementation of controls relevant to the pursuit of Government monetary policy, for example, with the foreign exchange position. Banks were permitted to hold only small working balances, selling any excess to the Central Bank. There was also a requirement that a rupee deposit equal to a stated percentage of liabilities had to be maintained with the Central Bank, and F.R. Burch, the Hongkong Bank's Manager 1955–1957, recalls that he was often short and had to borrow interbank to meet the reserve requirement, reflecting an inadequate deposit base. As long as interbank borrowing was possible and reasonably priced, this was cheaper than establishing small sub-branches, but, as the Mercantile Bank was to discover in India, when the need to enlarge the deposit base was recognized, banking regulations had already been imposed to prevent or delay such expansion. Nor was it desirable to sell sterling since rupee funds acquired in this manner could not necessarily be reconverted. In any case, the Central Bank's requirement that sterling balances of the branch be minimal would have forced Colombo

---

[f] This information is not from the Hongkong Bank archives but from Selvaratnam's report on the history of the Ceylon branch. He was a central bank examiner at the time; the story sounds autobiographical. Greig was the grandson of James Greig, the Bank's second Chief Manager.

into intrabank borrowing at a time when there were higher priorities for the sterling funds involved.

These regulations were a subject for complaint if only because they appeared new and complex and interfered with the private business of banking. In fact the 'good old days' were ill-remembered. The Imperial Bank of India, for example, had tried to insist that the Hongkong Bank maintain an interest-free deposit of Rs5 lacs as the price of acting as clearer, and the Hongkong Bank had complained about the level of the commission on remittances to and from India. Nor had the currency system worked smoothly in the interests of exchange banks; indeed the Hongkong Bank's business problems in Sri Lanka bore a close real resemblance, despite terminology, to those of pre-war Colonial (and British) Ceylon. The most that could be said against the new and soon-to-come regulations and restrictions was that they prevented the foreign banks from keeping their percentage share of growing business and that there was a period when they would come very close to preventing any domestic banking by the old exchange banks. Some would argue that the regulations, as measures to promote the economic development of Sri Lanka, were counterproductive; it may be so in part, but the argumentation required would take us too far afield to pursue in this history.

Meanwhile the Hongkong Bank in Sri Lanka continued to service its old customers, both foreign and Sri Lankan, and to play a role in the financing of development projects. British Government accounts with the Bank declined as the Forces left the island; Sri Lankan Government deposits, never large, were phased out by transfer to the Central Bank between 1953 and 1959, a surprisingly late date. The Hongkong Bank extended facilities to those, N.S.O. Mendis, for example, who were attempting to purchase the foreign-owned plantations, and the Bank's initiative in this did not sit well with the more traditionally oriented expatriate community.

There was considerable political argumentation in favour of financing the export of rubber and especially tea through Government channels and the Bank of Ceylon. The close connection among the estates, the agency houses, the British parent companies, and the customary bank finance were vital, and the banks, including the Hongkong Bank, kept the bulk of their accounts – among them Rowley Davies, Ceylon Trading Company, Harrisons and Crosfield, Heath and Co., and Dodwell's. When the change in financing came in the early 1960s, predictions of catastrophe proved incorrect because the structure of the industry, including the holding of tea auctions in Sri Lanka and the changing pattern of trade, had made the British links less important, while the acquisition by Sri Lankans, either Government or private entrepreneurs, of many of the estates was also a significant factor. The exchange banks obtained some new business from foreign companies establishing in Sri Lanka, but, if these companies intended setting up a local subsidiary (with a required Sri Lankan director), the account had to be established with the Hongkong Bank before the formation of the subsidiary – if this were done, the account could be kept.

In 1948 the Hongkong Bank became involved in the financing of the *Times of Ceylon*, with the Colombo Manager on the board of directors. The advances to the company were secured, but there were continual problems which did not end with the nationalization of the newspaper in 1971. The Bank continued to lend to Sri Lankans, but the percentage at some 57% in 1954 was not significantly different from the pre-war maximum, and the Bank continued to have problems with traders speculating on movements in the price of leading export commodities, problems which were not fully covered by the guarantee shroff.

While profits remained minimal, especially given the size of the establishment, the problem of income tax early became a matter of concern which increased as socialist policies were enacted. The Hongkong Bank's original solution had been to pay a low salary while the officer was in a high tax country and make a lump-sum payment when he left on transfer or retirement, a procedure which was determined illegal; the Bank amended its policy accordingly.

The need for large-scale public works or development projects had been urged as long ago as 1864 by the Mercantile Bank's H.D. Andree, but their finance was never considered a responsibility of the exchange banks. The Banking Commission of 1934 had stated,

Cheap and efficient mechanical power is another factor indispensable for industrial progress...Hydro Electric energy is however available but the source of power has not been tapped yet on an extensive scale...and Government should accept the initial responsibility of providing the cheap means of motive power...it is not an exaggeration to say that for the general economic welfare of the country the Hydro Electric Scheme cannot be completed a day too soon.

When the scheme was eventually contracted for, the successful firm, the French Alsthom, kept its account with the Hongkong Bank – as did another French firm, Socoman, contractors for the Kalatuwewa Reservoir Scheme.

As part of the country's development plan the Development Finance Corporation of Ceylon was established with both Government and private sector finance – the Hongkong Bank purchased 4,000 shares of the 71,178 allocated the private sector @ Rs100. The Central Bank enquired of the Bank's Colombo Manager about the suitability of W.T. Yoxall to lead the new corporation, and Burch had to confess that, well, he was an ex-Hongkong Bank man! The Bank's retired Shanghai Manager took on the assignment; the Hongkong Bank would continue to serve Sri Lanka one way or another. Yoxall's reorganization of Elephant Lite Corporation, with which the Hongkong Bank was heavily involved financially, proved fortunate for all.

Restrictions and new opportunities, 1956–1965

With the election of the People's United Front under the leadership of Prime Minister Bandaranaike a socialist program was pledged and the six-year development plan passed in 1955 was scrapped, while various *ad hoc* control programs, exchange restrictions, nationalization, subsidies, and taxes were imposed, and labour unrest continued. The 1956 'Sinhala-Only Act' aroused the fears of the Tamils while the burghers looked to Australia as a place of settlement.

The Hongkong Bank was affected by the 1957 Banks' Debits Tax Act, which levied a charge of 0.1 % every month on the total debits to current account – interbank and intrabank accounts were exempted. The Act, which discouraged the development of the banking habit, was not enforced in the period 1965–1970 and was replaced by a stamp duty on cheques by the new Government in 1977.

In 1959 the Hongkong Bank acquired the Mercantile Bank, which became the senior representative of the Hongkong Bank Group in Sri Lanka until the sale of the Mercantile's business to the Hatton National Bank in 1974. J.M. Gregoire, destined to be the Mercantile's last General Manager in London, was then Colombo manager with L.G. Atterbury, the Mercantile's last Colombo manager, his sub-manager. The two banks remained separate throughout, conducting their own business, but coordinating on a 'friendly basis'.

The most serious intervention came with the Finance Act of 1961. With the nationalization of the Bank of Ceylon came the provision that foreign banks could not accept new deposits or an increase in present deposits from Sri Lankan citizens (unless they were employees of the bank in question) or from Sri Lankan companies, the latter defined as those with at least one Sri Lankan director. Unfortunately the Mercantile Bank asked formally whether a renewal of a fixed deposit was a 'new' deposit under the Act, a point which had not been clearly defined; it was then so defined. It is hardly surprising that between 1963 and 1968, for example, the percentage of deposits held by British banks declined from 32% to 23%, although the absolute value declined but little – from Rs412 million to 409 million, with a peak of Rs431 million in 1965. While the number of offices remained unchanged at twelve for British banks, the total for the system rose from 83 to 141 in this same period. Clearly the restrictive provisions were turning domestic banking over to the local banks; the foreign (British) banks were barely tolerated and then mainly in connection with foreign trade. Indeed, this must follow. Being cut off from a deposit base, the exchange banks could now only increase their investments in the country by interbank borrowing or by selling sterling to the Central Bank, acts which, given other demands on Bank (or Group) funds and the political situation, would have been unsound.

These were discouraging years for the Group. With fixed deposits falling, imports (and their finance) restricted, and competition from the Government's Bank of Ceylon on the financing of exports, there was no possibility of expansion and profits were reduced. There was a threat that the Hongkong Bank would have to sell off its overbought position in sterling to the Central Bank and there were other restrictions. Salaries over Rs2,000 per month had to be deposited with the Government's Savings Bank, although departing foreign employees were permitted to withdraw their balances and convert them into foreign exchange.

Indeed, the question might be asked, why remain? To this the Hongkong Bank's Manager, F.R. Burch, based on experience almost a decade earlier, could only reply,

> We did a certain amount of business, I suppose, on account of other branches, but we had our own exchange accounts and had our own exchange profits on which we were taxed. I have stated that Hong Kong didn't really care two hoots whether we made a small loss or a big or small profit, so you ask, 'Why be there?' Having got there I suppose...prestige.

But by 1963 the question might no longer be one of choice. The Hongkong Bank was concerned not only with the poor business prospects but also with the real possibility of nationalization. When H.L. Pierce was sent as Accountant he was almost immediately designated as Manager – the managerial post had, however, been downgraded within the Bank's internal classification in anticipation of this development.

Given Colombo's position in the Hongkong Bank Group's overall branch network, there seems to be little other explanation when considered in the short run. 'Prestige' can, however, be interpreted in several ways; it can mean a reputation for staying with the country and being known to assist the economy to the extent permitted. It can mean being ready to increase that restricted role from a long-term historical base when the opportunities arise again. The Hongkong Bank left Indonesia; it was later to return. The Bank never left Sri Lanka (see Chapter 18).

11

PIONEERING IN BORNEO – BRITISH NORTH BORNEO AND SARAWAK*

> Oh, it was a wide open country... I mean, anything went.
> F.J. Knightly, Manager, British North Borneo (Sabah)

THE IMMEDIATE POST-WAR SITUATION

Of the three British Borneo territories, British North Borneo, the State of Brunei, and Sarawak, the largest in size and population in 1947 was Sarawak with just over half a million people in an area of 47,000 square miles. But the Hongkong Bank did not invade this Chartered Bank territory until 1958. Brunei was the smallest territory with 2,226 square miles and a population nearing 50,000, but it had potential growth from oil revenues. The worst hit by the war and the poorest economically, despite the potential of its forests, was British North Borneo with a population of nearly 350,000 living in 28,400 square miles. The percentages of the population of Chinese origin ranged between 28% for Sarawak and 20% for Brunei.

The three territories although referred to as 'British' had different political backgrounds: British North Borneo had been governed by a Chartered Company, the Raj of Sarawak was a British protected state, and Brunei was a Sultanate, also a British protectorate. The first two would become British Crown Colonies with the surrender of the charter and the abdication of the third Rajah Brooke; as such they would 'open up' and would require banking facilities. Brunei, as noted, had oil; it too would need a bank. This much was agreed.

Alfred Dent, the founder of the Chartered Company which had sovereignty in British North Borneo until 1946, had consulted David McLean, the Hongkong Bank's London Manager in the 1880s, over the establishment of a small bank in the territory. H.E.R. Hunter had made a survey of the banking possibilities in 1889. Although there appears to have been a small company-run bank for some time before the Pacific War, banking was on a merchant agency basis in all territories. This is not surprising; it is rather the post-war banking 'boom' which requires comment.

---

* The sources for this chapter are from Group Archives and are summarized in a bibliographical note found on p. 949.

At the time the surprise was not that the Hongkong Bank established itself in Brunei and British North Borneo in 1947 but that it had waited so long after V-J day to do so. In fact, in 1946 Morse authorized Harrisons and Crosfield, the Bank's pre-war Borneo agents, to open a branch for the Bank in the former Chartered Company capital of Sandakan. Permission was refused by the Colonial authorities; the Chartered Bank was to be given priority on the basis, the Colonial Office claimed, of a mutual understanding between the Government, the Chartered Bank, and the Hongkong Bank. This Morse angrily denied. The Government and the Chartered Bank were embarrassed by the misunderstanding, but the Government asked Morse to hold back.

The Hongkong Bank established its first Borneo branch in the capital of Brunei, in what is now known as Bandar Seri Begawan, but was then referred to as 'Brunei Town'; the date was April 1947. There was subsequently expansion to serve the oil company areas of Brunei in Kuala Belait.

In July 1947 the Hongkong Bank opened in Jesselton (now Kota Kinabalu), the town to which the capital of British North Borneo, previously in Sandakan, had moved. The Bank established its Tawau and Sandakan offices late in 1947 but opened for business in January 1948. The Chartered Bank remained the only British exchange bank in Sarawak until the Hongkong Bank opened in that colony's capital of Kuching in 1958. Later expansion can be seen by reference to Tables 10.2 and 10.3.

Although no policy document has been located, it is obvious from the existence of a misunderstanding that the subject of Borneo banking was discussed by Morse with the Colonial Office in the context of post-war planning. The new colonial Government and the British advisers in Brunei would need banking facilities and financial advice; there would be the possibility of Government-guaranteed loans for rehabilitation and development; in addition the Bank would take back the account of Harrisons and Crosfield and the business they had developed, on payment of a severance fee. Small English-owned estates and rubber smallholders (*kebun*) needed advances and there would be a growing export-barter trade, legal in North Borneo but not necessarily legal in the other country. The situation only partially paralleled that on the East Coast of Malaya, where the Mercantile Bank had agreed to open as an encouragement to trade but on the understanding that they would become the Government's bankers. The Chartered Bank held the small Government account in Jesselton and Sarawak; the Hongkong Bank operated for the Sultan and his government in Brunei Town.

Income would at first be small, but so too would costs. British Borneo was part of the Malayan Currency Area, the note issue, identical with that of Singapore and Peninsular Malaya, being the responsibility of the Commissioners of the Currency in Singapore. Communications and transport focused on Singapore, and the Hongkong Bank's Singapore branch would manage the area's exchange position; the Singapore Manager would at first be the immediate senior to the Borneo Manager in Jesselton. The Bank would not have to commit 'permanent capital' to the Borneo offices; its first source of funds would be Government accounts and there was the expectation that Chinese merchants would ultimately deal with the Bank. As for initial uses of funds, these would be small shop loans and export financing, the former guaranteed by the Government. The cost of new offices would be minimal in the 'land below the wind'; a small hut would do at first. Finally, Foreign staff salaries were not at today's levels (in comparative real terms) while the opportunity cost of local staff would be minimal.

The small offices, most of them requiring in the early years – Jesselton excepted – one, or at the most, two Foreign staff, provided a final assignment for those who came East in 1919 and the early 1920s or a testing place for those coming East in the early 1930s. Today such offices are entirely staffed by local officers; even if immigration controls permitted, senior Foreign staff could not be afforded for such posts and those not qualified for the most important managerial posts in the Bank can now be assigned to highly responsible tasks coping with the enlarged activities of the major branches. The Borneo offices can still serve as a limited training area for new members of the Foreign staff, however, since 'trainees' are not subject to the same immigration restrictions, they must not 'sign' or act as 'officers'; they cannot be permitted if there is a suggestion they make unnecessary the employment of additional local citizens.

A note on Brunei

The total revenue of British North Borneo was less than the Brunei Government's S$88 million surplus for 1956, yet there were pioneering aspects to banking in the Sultanate; Brunei Town office, opened by A.D.M. Ford, certainly did not handle the State's investments. Ford was fortunate in employing Daniel Yap Siong Lin as his compradore. Yap had been working in Sarawak; he was Hokkien and a descendant of the Hongkong Bank's Amoy (Xiamen) compradores (see I, 516–17).

The Bank also opened in Kuala Belait on the Sarawak border near the Seria oilfields, and later at Seria itself (see Table 10.4). There was no road connection between Seria and Brunei Town, although it was possible to run a jeep along the shore at low tide. The oil company itself dealt also with the Chartered Bank in Miri, a town beyond Kuala Belait in Sarawak.

These offices provided experience for young Bankers and a service to a major industry. This chapter is focused, however, on the two British colonies, and to their story, based to a large extent on oral history interviews, this history now turns.

BRITISH NORTH BORNEO

Jesselton, 1947

Although in 1947 G.G. Thomson (East in 1919) was in overall charge of Borneo offices, the Jesselton 'temporary in charge' was F.J. Knightly (East in 1937). Asked whether such an assignment was an indication of failure or an opportunity for advancement, Knightly's reaction is typical: 'Initially I thought, what the hell's happening to me? Am I banished forever? And then I suddenly realized it was such a great chance to get something moving, and I enjoyed every moment of it...and in the small community I knew everybody there; I was sorry to leave...'

Back in Hong Kong Arthur Morse was not expecting immediate profits from Borneo; this was a development opportunity. There were many who expected Borneo to develop sufficient for banking to be profitable; none who anticipated the growth which actually occurred. As Knightly recalls, the Bank began in a very small way, with small loans, sufficiently small indeed that, with a few exceptions, they did not have to be referred to Singapore for approval. They might be queried by the inspectors in Hong Kong – why hasn't this rubber loan been paid for some two to three months? To which a typical answer might be, 'the borrower has just married off his daughter and consequently cannot pay for a few months yet'.

The Jesselton office was initially a wooden shack with a palm leaf (*atap*) roof built on land assigned to the Bank on a Temporary Occupation Licence. The strong room was concrete; there was a safe inside, but the door was of locally made iron with a Chubb padlock. The advances to smallholders were made on the basis of local credit information and the land was mortgaged to the Bank, a procedure only requiring a Land Office stamp on the title deed. Repayment was made monthly, except during months in which the rubber trees were 'wintered', this is, not tapped. The quality was far short of RSS No. 1, but the trade was profitable, and savings were deposited in the Hongkong Bank – a growing source of funds. Some of these early borrowers eventually bought out Japanese timber concessions and were in business in a big way, but that was years away. Knightly has stated that there were a few bad debts and these were often caused by a rubber shipper buying at a high price and finding the Singapore market had fallen when the rubber arrived; then, instead of reporting immediately to the Bank for consideration, the customer might gamble, and perhaps go bankrupt.

The territory's total international trade in 1947 (including reexports) was only S$37.5 million; this had increased to S$139 million by 1950; it was S$435 million in 1961. The growth was, at least in part, the consequence of

Colonial Development Corporation projects, in the finance of which the Hongkong Bank participated. There were exports of rubber, lumber, and copra (some of this last being a reexport of Philippine copra); there was a significant trade in cigarettes and other dutiable goods designed for the Philippines and Indonesia, where they were smuggled in. These last mentioned goods were sold in exchange for copra which had entered North Borneo legally but presumably smuggled out from the neighbouring territories. The trade was encouraged by the British Administration because, as the Governor, Lord Twining, explained, there was both an import and an export tax, and revenue was needed. The Bank financed this business, especially from Tawau (see below).

Describing trade, Knightly said,

[The people of North Borneo would] have to smoke about a million cigarettes a year to justify the imports, and all went out in *kumpits*. A *kumpit* is a fast native boat with a great big outboard at the back which could go faster than anything else. They used to come in with their copra, fill it up with cigarettes, and off they went.

And of course piracy, as it goes on today, that was another thing... oh, they're a tough crowd down there, very tough. I've seen the old harbour in Tawau with the fast sailing skiffs come in from the Celebes and these other chaps from the Philippines with their fast outboard motors. We recognized it. I mean, [Governor] Twining made it quite clear. He said, as far as we're concerned, all we're doing is, they're bringing in copra which we reexport to Europe. We take an export duty on it, so that's the money for us, and they take our cigarettes, so it's money for us both ways, coming and going. And whether their taking it into the Philippines or Indonesia is illegal, that's up to them, not up to us.

When Knightly returned to Borneo on an inspection trip and chided an old customer in Tawau for being slow on repayment, he argued that he had security and took Knightly to see his battered old safe, which was practically stuffed with Filipino currency and gold bars. The latter were illegal and Knightly was forced to turn his head away. '...the bars lying around there. Oh, it was wide open country. The Governor used to say, well, this is like the Wild West frontier in the old days in America. I mean, anything went. You had to be sure you weren't kidnapped or picked up.' On the other hand, '...if our friend had wanted to do anything illegal with gold, we would have said, no, no way. But copra and cigarettes and all that were all quite legitimate. But if he'd played around with anything that was [illegal]...there was no suspicion, at least I never saw anything about drugs – we never touched anything.'

Tawau

Opening and early business

Thomson had supervised the opening of Jesselton, with Knightly, and of Sandakan, with G.G. Aitkenhead (East in 1938), when he was informed that the Chartered Bank manager had gone off along the coast to survey other possible places for a bank office.

Thomson promptly chartered a launch, loaded a table, chair, and typewriter on board, and steamed off in pursuit. After two days' voyage [D.] MacGregor of the Chartered reached Tawau, inspected the place, and decided to have a look at Tarakan further south in the Netherlands East Indies. As MacGregor disappeared over the horizon to the south Thomson came foaming round the headland into Tawau. Leaping ashore, he rented the Chinese Ping Pong Club (a wooden hut on the edge of the Padang), signed on the only two English-speaking Chinese Clerks in the place, and set up our shingle. When MacGregor returned, he found the H&SBC installed and ready for business. It was ten years before the Chartered again set foot in Tawau.

Thomson had cabled Singapore to obtain authority from the Manager, C.L. Edwards, to open the office. The latter's immediate reaction was, 'How the hell do I know what he should do?' Turning to J.A.H. Saunders, then a Singapore 'junior', he said, 'Go out and buy me a map so that I can find out where he's talking about.' This Saunders duly did. But once Edwards got Tawau located on the map, he wasn't much further forward. So he cabled Thomson permission to open.

Thomson then wired Singapore to rush someone out while he held the fort, and the choice fell on B.C. Allan (East in 1933). But 'rush' was not feasible in 1947, and Thomson remained for a time waiting. Allan recalls:

I proceeded with the utmost despatch, but it took me seventeen days to get there. The R.A.F. ran a weekly flying-boat service to Jesselton, but to go further one had to wait for the fortnightly boat from Singapore. I eventually took the old Straits Steamship Company's 'Marudu' and eventually arrived at Sandakan. The voyage included a stop of four days at Labuan loading old stocks of Army flour... At Sandakan I transferred to the 'Serudom', a tubby motor-vessel of some 200 tons which had been mass-produced at Goole two years before.

Allan eventually arrived, releasing Thomson to return to Jesselton to sit in his little wooden office reading, as Knightly recalls, the *Elgin Times* with a thermos flask of brandy and water ready against the regular visits of the Governor, who might need help on his way back to his residence on the hill.

Meanwhile in Tawau the task was to find customers.

Business was rather slow at first as none of the locals had ever seen a bank or a cheque before in their lives.

We obtained the account of a leading Chinese merchant in rather an unusual manner. The back door was on the beach and at very high tides the floor was covered with wet sand washed under the door. One morning the peaceful atmosphere was shattered by the Malay tamby leaping into life, seizing a broom, and dashing through the back door. He came back with a large monitor lizard which had been strolling past along the beach. The Chinese merchant was passing at the time, and our cashier called him in and offered the lizard for lunch. He was so delighted that he opened an account then and there.

To handle this business Allan bought a bicycle to be used during office hours by the tamby and in the evening by the Manager. Further business success forced the Bank to acquire a small godown to store the goods which were the security for loans. To keep down the rats Allen bought a python, listed in the books as 'Rodent Controller'; there were consequently regular debits of petty charges under the title 'milk for the Bank python'.

Allan's dash to Tawau had been for a temporary assignment. He was replaced by M.McD. Holden, then A.W. Helbling – both of 1938 seniority – and by L.H. Thorn who had come East in 1923.[a] Unfortunately, if Michael Turner's information were correct, the Foreign staff officer who became 'Sub-Agent' in 1953 apparently alienated several customers, who were urging the Chartered Bank to transform the banking scene from a monopoly to a duopoly.[b] The Chartered Bank was reported to have accepted the invitation. Turner in Hong Kong wrote an urgent letter to Arthur Morse in London asking him to contact the Chartered Bank's (Sir) William Cockburn, the chief general manager. If they open in Tawau, Turner wrote, no one will make a profit. 'Try and get them not to come, but the fault is ours for opening wide the doors.'

They did not come – not yet. And business was growing so that a new building was required; indeed by the time G.P. Stubbs took over for a brief period in 1956/57, the branch was thriving. While Stubbs was in Tawau, a second Foreign staff officer had to be assigned.

The port town's prosperity depended on a Colonial Development Corporation agricultural policy, exploitation of Bombay Burmah's timber concession, and smuggling out of and into the Philippines and Indonesia. The business leaders were Chinese and, therefore, the Bank was fortunate in its Chinese Manager, Charlie Wong. According to Stubbs, he was liked by everybody.

The Government had embarked on a program of trying to increase the size of shophouses in various towns in Borneo and had agreed to guarantee the finance put up by banks to build shophouses. A shophouse was basically a shop on the ground floor with living accommodation above. We had a large number of shophouse loans in our books, and the last day of every month an instalment would be paid to reduce the loan. Every month Charlie Wong and I would go round the shophouses, not all of them, but at random to see that the business was going on normally and that the stocks were there. It was very casual, and they were making so much money that there was no difficulty about the loans.

[a] Thorn's career is not dissimilar to others interrupted by internment. After a first tour in Shanghai, Thorn had been in Bangkok and then served from 1935 to 1938 as 'temporary in charge' at Sungei Patani. This was a relatively important appointment for one of his seniority. After internment in Shanghai, however, there is evidence that his health had deteriorated. He first became Sub-Agent in Muar and then moved, significantly, to the Cameron Highlands. After approximately two years there he was transferred to Kuala Belait and then to his final assignment as Sub-Agent in Tawau. He retired in 1953 after 30 years in the East.
[b] A.L. Harman had a distinguished career representing the Hongkong Bank in Australia from 1965. In 1970 he became the Managing Director there of the Bank's subsidiary, Hongkong Finance Limited; he retired the following year.

I was absolutely astonished. I remember saying to Charlie Wong one day that I'd never been in a branch where on the repayment date of each month every single instalment was always paid on its loan.

And he smiled and said, this is exceptional, is it?

I said, yes, it is.

I only discovered afterwards that of course the ones who couldn't pay would ring Charlie Wong up, and his account would be debited and he would pay the instalment for them. But also I was told on fairly good authority by a number of Chinese that Charlie Wong never charged them anything extra for this, he did it out of a kindness to them and that he never tried to make money out of it. And so when I got to know of it, I never stopped it in fact.

The Bank had a thriving business in export bills. Small boats from Indonesia and the Philippines would crowd the harbour, and the Chinese merchants would buy their small cargoes of copra and gum copal. These would be held until a shipment large enough to send to Singapore had been collected. The Bank financed the merchants.

Some of those bringing in the goods were based on Tawau. Stubbs recalled one old Chinese constituent particularly well – 'a very pleasant rogue ... '.

I had amusing incidents with [him]. He was a difficult man. He had been successful. He'd started life after the war, so I was always told, as a deck hand on some little smuggling boat and then decided he'd go into business on his own. By the time I got to Tawau he was a very wealthy man indeed and bought a lot of property, plantations not just in Tawau but further up the coast as well. The trouble was that he was never liquid; he never had any cash at all. His business was smuggling. He used to get into difficulties. He had to pay bribes to the Indonesian authorities to try and keep them from enquiring too much into his affairs.

He came in and was talking to me through Charlie Wong interpreting one day, saying that he was having a very bad time because the Indonesians had arrested three or four of his captains of his little smuggling boats recently, the captain being the only man who knew anything about navigation on board the craft. The Indonesians had realized this and that, if they took off the captain and put him in jail, [our constituent] could be held to ransom to get him out again.

I suggested that the obvious way of dealing with this was to take on one extra coolie deck hand and, when they saw an Indonesian Navy vessel coming in sight, strip the captain of his cap and put it on the coolie so that he'd be the chap who was arrested.

And he nearly fell off his chair laughing and thought this was a most excellent idea.

He told me he [tried it out], but I think that the trouble was that it would be so easy for the Indonesians to discover that the man they were dealing with was a dolt who didn't know anything about navigation that you probably couldn't do it more than two or three times.

Even then there were limits to banking excitement in Tawau. While Stubbs never referred to Jesselton for authority to lend, this was because the lending was for such small sums on appropriate security that there was never an occasion to refer. Interest rates were set by Jesselton; exchange rates were based on those set in Singapore. If the agency ran short of loanable funds, Stubbs had lent to a Bank agreed loan/deposit ratio, he could request funds on overdraft from Jesselton. The growth of savings usually meant that Borneo had a credit balance in Singapore, so Stubbs did not see availability of funds as a problem.

The coming of competition
The increasing business activity in Tawau generated income; this led to deposits in the Bank and to its ability to act, as it should, as a financial intermediary. This, however, inevitably raised the question of whether the Bank were showing favouritism, whether, with a second bank, lending practices would be more flexible. Stubbs sensed that once again there was talk of inviting in the Chartered Bank. When such a situation develops, there is little use in arguing that business is insufficient or that the Hongkong Bank was too strong. The day would come.

Meanwhile the Bank was financing a new Tawau Club.

The Tawau Club was an interesting place in that it was open to all nationalities, and you had Indonesians and Chinese and British and Polish, Swiss, American, German members. It was an extraordinary club. The staff consisted of one extremely efficient Indonesian steward who more or less ran the club. You could get good meals there, and you could get any amount of booze that you wanted there. In fact, the longest party I've ever been to in my life was at the Tawau Club...

In 1959 when J.F. Marshall (East in 1936) came from Hong Kong's North Point branch to Tawau, luck ran out. The Chartered Bank came in with a manager noted for his aggressive competitiveness. Furthermore, pirates were moving in on the smugglers and the situation was becoming dangerous. While Turner in Hong Kong was busy acquiring the Mercantile Bank and considering a dividend which would meet the Bank's requirements in its negotiations with the British Bank of the Middle East, all in another world from a banking point of view, problems were being resolved in Tawau.

The first problem was offset at least in part by the growth of business; the Hongkong Bank could not keep its (100%) share of the market, but it could keep its overall figures improving slightly. The second problem was eased by the surprise conviction of the pirates – due to their surprise pleading of 'Guilty' – and their removal from Tawau by submarine to a more secure jail near Jesselton.

Marshall recalls that the Chartered Bank came in after he had been in Tawau for some six months and set up some twenty yards away from the Hongkong Bank.

...and I must say he caused me a great deal of problems.... Tawau consisted of three rows of shops, and they all had their accounts with the Hongkong Bank, and they all borrowed money from the Hongkong Bank, the basis of their security being the stock in trade. I walked once a week down one street and up the other one, and I looked in here and there, and I said how do you do to the chap and looked round to see that his stock was up to scratch. There was no need for detailed stock-taking or anything like that. I'd just glance around and say to myself, oh well, my loan here is adequately covered.

But this was very vulnerable for raiding from the opposition. Indeed, when the Chartered opened their branch there, [their manager] went down the rows of shops, and he said, how much does the Hongkong Bank lend you against this? Now here's a Chartered Bank signature card, just sign this up, and I will make your facilities up half as much again.

Really there isn't much defence against this sort of thing unless you're going to go down yourself and make it double. And so in six months I had lost a great deal of the Hongkong Bank's business, and I wasn't really very happy about this situation.

Worse still was the fact that he was going to work on these mounds of copra which were piled up on the foreshore. They were pledged to me because I would lend money to the towkay – the Chinese merchant/trader – who'd paid [for the import of] copra, and he would give me a letter of lien against the mound of copra. In due course the copra would be loaded on board ship for export. In the meantime a letter of credit would arrive in the towkay's favour and I would hold the letter of credit, and then when the copra was shipped, I would negotiate a bill under the letter of credit and the overdraft would be wiped out.

That's how it worked in theory, but I knew perfectly well that when the letter of credit for it came through that the Chartered Bank would then issue another overdraft on another letter of lien, all against this same copra piled on the foreshore. The pile was in fact being pledged to both banks, and there was nothing I could do about it except either create a bloody fuss, in which case all the business would go next door, or pretend I didn't know about it, in which case I'd at least get half of it. Every now and then I would say to the towkay, you know, I've got this overdraft, when is this copra going to be shipped? And he'd pretend he hadn't already promised it to the Chartered. It was tricky business.

However, tricky businesses are what we are born to cope with, and we did cope with it.

Fortunately, at this time the business in general in that part of Borneo was increasing at an enormous rate, and, although I was losing half the business at the port, my figures more or less maintained their previous value, and my half yearly returns of profit didn't fall off significantly. In fact, they might even have had marginal increases from year to year.

The problem was fully understood in Jesselton by the Manager, Max Haymes. Very nice chap. He was a tremendous help to me, and he fully understood exactly what was going on, and he more or less, as far as he could, countersigned my policies of looking the other way, but it's not the best way to run a situation. I think you've got to run a situation of that nature that way, but eventually you've got to bring it down so that a letter of lien means what it says, and it's not just a piece of paper to keep Head Office quiet.

Marshall was not, however, acting rashly. He held the 'principal security', the mortgage on the towkay's property, which underlay, as it were, the trade finance and justified the original overdraft without which the towkay could not have purchased the imports. Haymes, for his part, kept Head Office in Hong

Kong fully informed. A turn in prices would endanger the Chartered Bank's whole position.

At the same time this competition was going on, the Chartered Bank kept writing Marshall to obtain confidential credit ratings on the Bank's Tawau customers, presumably to see if they were worth poaching. Marshall held him off by regretting lack of time. It was, as Marshall claims, 'a difficult period. It always is when somebody muscles in on your territory.' But it would only be a year later (1958) that the Hongkong Bank, with Angus R. Petrie in charge, moved in on the Chartered Bank in Kuching.

Chief Office, Borneo territories

Max Haymes in Jesselton

M.F.L. Haymes had the reputation in the Bank as something of a 'loner'. Although he had played team sports, he preferred to walk alone in the hills or go yachting. Michael Turner, the Chief Manager, knew this. He and Haymes had been juniors together in London; they had, with their wives, shared a house in Stanley soon after their return in 1946. And, although by 1954 Haymes was beginning to become acquainted in Yokohama, where he had been Manager for a little over a year, Turner knew that his heart was in Southeast Asia. As a junior he had been in Bangkok, going out into the countryside on the weekends, learning a little Siamese, talking with the local people. He had served post-war in Saigon and Singapore, but if he were to be promoted he had to be willing to move to unfamiliar territory.

Then Turner made one of those assignments which a whole department of personnel experts could not have bettered. In 1954 he sent Haymes to Jesselton as Accountant in anticipation of the retirement of the Manager, H.E. Foy (East in 1925). Haymes (East in 1931) in fact succeeded Foy in May 1955 and remained Manager Borneo until 1961, when he in turn retired. During that time he served on the British North Borneo Legislative and Executive Councils.[c] He was also on the boards of various Government financial operations, and was the key unofficial responsible for the setting aside of the wilderness area which is now Mt Kinabalu National Park. As a banker he was responsible for the expansion of the Hongkong Bank's activities in Borneo, opening offices in Labuan, the important North Borneo island at the entrance

---

[c] There was no opposition to his accepting these positions from Head Office or the Board of Directors. He was, in fact, sent congratulations. This is in contrast to the very difficult position they took in the pre-Great War period (see Volume II, Chapter 1). On the other hand, except in Hong Kong, there would not appear to have been any other case of so senior a political appointment post-war. Different periods of the Bank's history have different problems, which, though at one time considered of great importance, become matters for virtually routine comment.

to the Sungei Brunei (the river up to Brunei Town), Papar, and Beaufort, in Seria and in Kuching and Sibu (see Table 10.4). He was responsible for the appointment of the first local officer as a branch Manager – when Beaufort was opened in 1961.

As Haymes put it, 'I wouldn't have exchanged my job in Borneo for any other job in the Bank – including the Chief Manager's – if I'd been offered it!'

When Haymes arrived in Jesselton as Accountant, the branch had five Foreign staff positions; its main business was the finance of rubber. It was the year the Bank moved from its hut with an *atap* roof into its new office – the only building in Jesselton with a lift and therefore a considerable 'tourist' attraction. The office was ceremoniously opened by the new Governor, R.E. Turnbull:

We had about seven hundred people, and there weren't enough glasses in the town. We had to get flowers and all that sort of thing over from Singapore. The champagne got upset on the beautiful black marble counter, polished to the Nth degree, and of course it's like putting vinegar on it. It marks it and eats into it, and we couldn't get it out, no matter what we did. We called in the marble experts...

Haymes learned sufficient Malay for business purposes – but not for political conversations. Although most of the business was with Chinese, their preferred second language was often Malay rather than English, and Haymes was therefore able to deal direct both with Chinese and Dusun constituents. A typical story of business in Borneo involves Haymes and the Bank's favoured Tawau customer, already described in the account by Stubbs (see above).

...A real old rogue, but a likeable rogue. I first met him when I first went over to Tawau in the process of taking over from Foy, by way of running that branch for a couple of weeks on my own so I knew what went on there. I wanted to buy a crocodile skin and our customer was the man. So I was directed to his house which was on piles over the sea, along a narrow causeway about a hundred yards long and then a little hut, and there he was.
I said I'd like a crocodile skin.
Yes. And he brought out a skin and laid it on the floor, quite a sizeable crocodile, about six or eight feet long, laid it out on the little causeway.
Well, is it very expensive? How much?
He quoted me a price... two dollars an inch.
What! two dollars an inch?
Oh, he said, when you're buying a crocodile skin, you don't measure it lengthways, it's across the width of the belly. So we just struck up a good acquaintance there, a good friendship.
He was always playing us off against the Chartered, the one against the other, but he came up to Jesselton only on rare occasions. He was there one Sunday morning, and he said he'd like to meet me in a Chinese coffee shop, so I went along. We didn't go into the coffee shop itself with all the tables, we went upstairs, and there was a room seething with kids screaming and running around all over the place. All hell let loose up there.

We had a bottle of warm beer, and, if I remember rightly, he wanted a loan of about a million [Straits] dollars or something against property and God knows what. I mean, he already was a good customer of ours, but in this case it was question of extracting as much security as one could get, which I did, and we did the deal in Malay in this coffee shop on a Sunday morning.

As Haymes saw it, the danger in North Borneo was the narrow base of the credit structure, all depending on a reasonable price for natural rubber. The Jesselton shopkeeper borrowed from the Bank; the up-country shopkeeper came into town to obtain stocks for his smaller shop and ran up an account with the Jesselton towkay; he then returned up-country and sold goods to smallholders and rubber tappers on credit. To pay off such borrowing, rubber had to be sold – and at a reasonable price. In a farewell speech to the Chinese Chamber of Commerce Haymes warned of the problem.

There were others.

If a local shopkeeper failed to pay off his obligations to the Bank and if it were apparent that his stock, the Bank's secondary security, had nevertheless been sold, the Bank might close up the shop and auction off the remaining movables.

It was sad. It's something which, you know, worries me at times whenever I think of it.

This was the case of the Number One shop in Jesselton with a very good reputation, and it was a place where all the Europeans went. It was obvious that things were not going right there, and every time we went in we noticed there was less stock, and something was wrong. We told the old boy that we had noticed this, and he had better do something about it, and nothing appeared to be done, and it seemed to be getting worse. We went round one day to see this chap in his house and read the Riot Act, and said, the time has come that if you don't do something, I'll close you up.

And next day, the old boy shot himself, which upset me a lot.

It turned out that he had ... somebody who was running off with the stuff, and I think the old chap just couldn't face the loss of the place. But of course I had no idea that that was going to be the result, and it was a sad thing to have happened.

Haymes did not inspect shops himself because, unlike the situation in Tawau, the towkays were afraid that the presence of the Bank Manager would suggest a serious problem to customers and rivals. Haymes depended on his compradore, Wong Tau Sem, who would become an important businessman in Sabah after it became a state in the Federation of Malaysia. The compradore secured business and was the Manager's eyes and ears, he found staff and guaranteed the cash, but he did not guarantee business as in the old days.

Being responsible for North Borneo and later Sarawak, Haymes visited each office once or twice a year. When the Bank's security was in land, crops, or equipment up-country, in the *ulu*, inspection could too easily be neglected. In the case of a coconut plantation up-river from Sandakan, for example, Haymes found that it had not been visited for some five years.

I said, well, we'll see it.

Oh, it's very difficult to arrange a boat. The compradore was edgy.

You just get me a boat.

We went up to this place way, way up the river about twenty miles, and these Chinese kept plying me or trying to get me to have a few drinks, but I wasn't having that one. I knew this. They got rather quiet as they got up, and we got on this little jetty and went off straight into this coconut estate which we were advancing against, partly against the crop and partly against the property. There wasn't a coconut on the trees. They'd subcontracted it all out and sold off all our security.

I jumped hard on them because I closed them up bang, just like that. But then, that was the Manager's job, whoever he was at the time, to have gone out and inspected these places for himself because when I went over the advances, I said, when did you last see this?

On another occasion the situation proved more satisfactory.

There was one man in a very out-of-the-way place up in the North, up towards Kudat. He was a one-man band to whom advances had been made before my time, and Hong Kong were getting rather restive about him. He was miles away, right out in the *ulu*... and not a place one could get to at all from Jesselton. I had been in correspondence with him, and he seemed to have reasonable answers and this sort of thing. I was up on a trip round near Kudat at one time inspecting a rubber estate, and I found myself not too far away from this chap, about six or seven miles, so I hired a bicycle and I rode across the paddy fields, along bunds and things, without telling him I was coming.

I thought, oh, well, he'll have a native wife, you know, doodling along.

He was a Scotsman, and he had a very nice Scots wife, and there they were, working like beavers with all his machinery. He was trying to plant tobacco, and he'd worked up the land and worked like a slave himself. But he was one of these people who expected to get the same amount of work out of his men as he was doing himself, and of course they didn't like this. It only transpired that he was having a lot of labour trouble. His machinery and all that stuff was in good nick, and I was satisfied.

I said, well, you've got to try and work along with these people. Otherwise obviously you're not going to get any returns.

He said, oh, I'll manage.

I managed to persuade Hong Kong from foreclosing on him, and he turned up trumps, and we didn't lose any money. I suppose he had come down to Jessleton and put his case, and he'd put the land and his machinery as security, and well, it was land which had once grown tobacco, and then it had failed and gone to ruin, and then he'd taken it on again.

This story is also a reminder that Jesselton was watched by the inspectors in Hong Kong. A.L. Harman, who after leaving Tawau had been assigned as Inspector in Head Office, apparently tried to control rubber lending, but Haymes had his way; a more understanding and experienced F.J. Knightly, although critical, was helpful in this.

Expansion

As for branch expansion Haymes was watching developments closely in Lahad Datu, a small coastal town near Tawau. He concluded that a branch would not be worthwhile until barter trade were opened with the Celebes; from his membership on the Executive Council he knew that this would be soon, but he could not act for the Bank on this insider information. In consequence he was annoyed to learn that the Chartered Bank had opened, and there was only one explanation. The Governor reportedly had leaked the information to Malcolm Hannah, the Chartered Bank manager. The explanation given Haymes was that the Hongkong Bank had been first in Tawau and it was now the Chartered Bank's turn. As the Hongkong Bank's 'first' in Tawau had not been on the basis of Government information, the comparison was irrelevant; Haymes made an official protest through the Colonial Secretary.

In Beaufort, the Hongkong Bank was more successful. Haymes was after the business of Chung Chao Lung, a prosperous timber merchant, based on Beaufort and banking with the Chartered in Jesselton. But his nephew, Chung En Loi, worked as chief clerk in the Hongkong Bank's Bill Department. Haymes decided to open in Beaufort with the young nephew as Manager. The branch was opened two weeks before Haymes retired, Chung became the first Asian Manager in Borneo – he was later sent to London for training – and the Beaufort branch succeeded, its new building subsequently opened by Michael Sandberg, the Bank's Chairman.

Maurice W. Turner, Manager, 1961–1963

The Hongkong Bank had not, however, financed an industrial revolution in British Borneo. Trade had developed, plantations had been improved, timber exploited, and shophouses financed on a Government-guaranteed basis – Tawau had been burned to the ground and rebuilt on the same basis. Haymes had seen through the finance and construction of a Yacht Club. But Turner's initial reaction was not much different from Knightly's some fourteen years before.

...the place was very sleepy, and nothing much was happening. It was just starting to open up in my day, I suppose. It was a little colonial backwater, but it had prospects. It was a wonderful job, if you liked an easy life, Manager of Jesselton, with all these little branches around the countryside. You got on a ship, and you went away for a fortnight calling in at all the little ports, visiting people. Everybody lived in such a placid, relaxed way. There were never any problems, you know. Nobody ever locked their doors at night in Borneo. You'd leave the windows open. No crime. Nothing at all.

Turner particularly recalls the Bank house, the sunsets, the Somerset Maugham existence:

...the fortnightly ship that turned up from Singapore. It wandered round the coast. It had some fascinating people on it...wandering round, looking for something to write about...People who'd come to look at the birds or climb up the mountain, and wherever you went people came out of the interior. Old planters came to have a good meal on the ship, or a bath, and then go back again. They were great characters, the people that lived there. You go up into the interior of Borneo, and you found people who had been living there for donkey's years, Europeans, living with native girls – some of them married them. They would never go anywhere else. Those funny little clubs, tin huts, called, for example, the Papar Club, which were the centre of life. Odd planters came out of the jungle and drank themselves stupid in those places and then went back into the jungle again.

A little railway runs through the interior up to Tenom, and it's a single line track. It had the most enormous Hornby engine, beautiful looking machine, burned wood, would stop frequently to take it on, and off it would go again. You can't believe all this, but it is perfectly true. If you wanted to go and visit one of our little offices on the railway line, you rang up the station master and said, I want to go to Papar, can I have a train? And he would say, yes, sir, what time would you like to go? So you said, well, I think I'll go at ten, please. Would you mind putting a few drinks on board? And you'd get a little private railcar with a driver, and off you went. It didn't cost very much. You did your business and back you came on your train.

The local airline was fascinating. It was called Borneo Airways in those days. The planes were driven by mostly Australian pilots, some British, and they were little Twin Rapides and later on Twin Pioneers. They used to plod around like taxis. They were always breaking down, but didn't have any crashes.

Turner also played a public role as member of the North Borneo Development Board.

This was a Government organization which advanced to the very small men who wanted to buy a new canoe or an engine to put in the back of it, buy a few more pigs, that sort of thing. It was run by the Financial Secretary, and I was on the Board, and so was the Chartered Manager. We used to sit there solemnly in the Sports Club, decide to advance fifty dollars to some chap to buy a large pig...unbelievable really...and to a chap who probably couldn't speak any known language. It was just a gesture by Government to try and get the small man set up in business.

In summary, Turner stated, 'I think we did what we could down there with such very limited opportunities.'

And then the idyll ended. Sir William Goode departed on a destroyer, the people wept, and North Borneo became Sabah; Jesselton, Kota Kinabalu. And Turner himself departed. Originally London 'Home staff' he had come East in 1946; he served the Bank well in Borneo but, unlike Max Haymes, this was not his paradise. By 1964 he had become Controller, Overseas Operations, in 1968, Deputy Chief Manager, and the following year an executive director and Deputy Chairman of the Hongkong Bank. Jake Saunders had brought him in from the cold.

SARAWAK, THE OPENING AND FIRST OPERATIONS

It all began quite innocently with Max Haymes going down to Kuching to stay with the Chief Justice, an old Hong Kong friend. The Chartered Bank had been in Sarawak's capital, Kuching, since 1924 when they had come at the request of the Rajah, Sir Charles Vyner Brooke; now the Hongkong Bank appeared to be challenging their position. They did not hold a monopoly; there was the important Oversea-Chinese Banking Corporation (OCBC), with a Singapore head office and connections with the Hokkien community; there were also smaller Chinese trading banks. Haymes was able to reassure the Chartered Bank.

On his return to Jesselton, Haymes wrote to Hong Kong advocating the establishment of offices in Sarawak subject to confirmation as a result of an official survey visit. He liked what he had seen unofficially; he would now revisit Kuching as Manager Borneo. The visit was successful and Haymes was able to bid away the able Ong Yen Jin from the OCBC to be the Hongkong Bank's compradore; he would later become Manager of Business Development for the Bank in Sarawak.

The Chartered Bank had Kuching very well covered, so in 1958 Haymes established the Hongkong Bank's first office on the road to the Port, where new developments were expected. A second office was opened in the main area of Kuching in 1966.

There were more immediate prospects, however, in Sibu on the Rajang River. This was the centre of both logging and the illipe nut marketing; the first was normal banking, the latter had a special Borneo atmosphere to it. Illipe nuts, used for making chocolate, were gathered in the rain forests by Dayaks, who brought them down river, sold the nuts, and disappeared up the river again with cash figured in the hundreds of thousands of Straits dollars. From time to time the Dayaks would return with the cash to purchase items which, due to the lack of electricity, they couldn't in fact use in the villages. It would be much better, Haymes thought, if they would deposit their funds in a Hongkong Bank savings account.

Sibu branch (established in 1959) bought a fast long-boat with an outboard motor for moving along the rivers looking at property pledged as security for loans and searching for Dayak villagers who wanted to open a savings account. Actually, Haymes was more organized than this; the Bank had commission agents who picked up the money and kept their own books; the funds were brought back to Sibu and credited, not to the agent, but to the Dayak depositor; the pass book was made out in the owner's name and kept up-to-date on the information of the agent.

By minimizing the use of cash and the large shipments into and out of Sibu from Kuching, the savings accounts were a great boon both to the Bank and to the Government departments involved.

When Maurice Turner succeeded Haymes he visited Sibu and travelled up-river to inspect a sawmill which the Bank was financing. The Manager, M.J.S. Figg (East in 1949), reputedly drove the Bank's boat as he did his own Jaguar, very fast. The boat hit a sandbank and Turner waded ashore...

...climbed up the mangroves, it was most unpleasant. I hate snakes anywhere. And blow me, about half a dozen men carrying spears came out of a tree, and they looked at us, and we looked at them. Of course, nobody spoke a word, and Mike Figg held out a ten dollar note. They recognized that all right. We eventually got them to push us off the sandbank.

Well, we got a bit further down the river, and Mike wasn't quite sure, because there were dozens of little tributaries, which one to turn into. Anyhow he said, we turn left here. And then we had to turn right again and so on deeper into the jungle. It got narrower and narrower. Suddenly, we came to the end. We couldn't go any further. We were deep in the jungle at the end of a bit of water which had just run out!

I really thought the end had come, I didn't think we'd ever see civilization again. And blow me, out of the jungle again came a group of women...and they came and looked at us. We sort of waved, and they all went away again...not surprising.

Anyhow we eventually got them to come out again, and I sat in the boat, and the rest of them waded around and pushed us down through the creeks...I thought [one] was going to give birth, and it was getting dark, and the flies and the mosquitoes and the noises of the jungle were all rather grim. We eventually came out into the river again, and after I suppose about another two hours, when it was pitch dark, we were picked up, floating miles away from where we were going, by a police boat...not looking for us, mind you, just happened to be coming up that way. They took us then to the sawmill eventually. But it really was rather a frightening experience.

Obviously there were people in the rain forest, people who might help expand the Hongkong Bank's deposit base. Turner's story is evidence that they had ten dollars at least; there was further evidence that they had considerably more. The illipe nuts remained economically important. The plan was to go up to the villages and set up displays with pictures of the Bank, savings boxes made in the shape of Head Office building, trying all ways to obtain savings accounts – all sorts of schemes, which, Turner considered, 'were not unsuccessful'. But the Bank did not forget its impecunious inter-war days. The little savings banks sold for a dollar; the Bank made two cents on each sale.

But North Borneo and Sarawak were underpopulated. The great resource, timber, was still too expensive to exploit successfully on a large scale, although heavy equipment was being brought in at high risk. All too soon successful techniques would be developed and the forests destroyed without adequate replanting, threatening the ecology of tropical and insular Southeast Asia.

Did the Hongkong Bank help finance the initial development of British Borneo? That question now would seem difficult to answer. The Bank financed what happened; whether it was development (in the sense of 'progress' or a 'good thing') or not is for others to answer.

Meanwhile there were other Hongkong Bankers in Hong Kong, Singapore, London, and elsewhere operating on a different level. While Managers hiked through the virgin jungle, others were negotiating the acquisition of the British Bank of the Middle East. As the years passed the difference would be accentuated, but, while Sandberg was concerned with the position of the Federal Reserve Board, the Congress of the United States, and other regulatory agencies relative to the Bank's offer to Marine Midland Banks, the local Borneo Managers continued their concern for the small saver and for the borrower in the *ulu*.

12

THE HONGKONG BANK'S NEW SUBSIDIARIES, 1955–1961, AND THE ORIGINS OF THE HONGKONG BANK GROUP*

Sir Michael Turner: I'm a humble banker.
H.M. the Queen: I don't think you're so humble. Otherwise you wouldn't be here.

> At the Investiture, Buckingham Palace

GENERAL CONSIDERATIONS

The impact of the Bank's first subsidiaries

Not until 1955, with the establishment of a wholly owned California subsidiary with head office in San Francisco, did The Hongkong and Shanghai Banking Corporation become a bank holding company. Nor, until 1959, had the Hongkong Bank acquired another bank; its experience with the Mercantile Bank and subsequently with the British Bank of the Middle East was something totally new in the Bank's history, carrying an impact which, although not wholly unforeseen, was all-pervasive in its final consequences.

The Hongkong Bank's great rival, the Chartered Bank, had acquired the P&O Bank pre-war and would acquire the Eastern Bank and the Cyprus branches of the Ionian Bank in 1957; even the smaller Mercantile Bank of India itself had acquired the Bank of Calcutta in 1906 and the Bank of Mauritius in 1916. The British Bank of the Middle East had perforce established an affiliated bank, the Bank of Iran and the Middle East with a 49% interest – as the Chartered Bank obtained a 35% investment in the Irano British Bank in 1959.

Aside from its trustee and nominee companies and its ventures into publishing, the Hongkong Bank remained innocent of such corporate complexities.

Exceptionally, in the peculiar circumstances of post-war Hong Kong, the

---
* There are no end-notes to this chapter. The sources are described in a single note on p. 949.

Bank had acquired a controlling interest – 40% of the equity capital – in the South China Morning Post, Ltd. and joined with Jardine's and the Kadoories, on the instigation of K. Weiss, to found the Far Eastern Economic Review, Ltd., in 1946, with J.R. Jones as chairman of the board.

The growth of the Hongkong Bank had depended on its secure Hong Kong base, its finance of trade from key 'hub' branches – Shanghai and the Treaty Ports, Yokohama or Kobe, Manila, and Singapore – from which a series of agencies emanated, its exchange links with India, London, and the United States, and at times its pre-eminence in the London capital market in matters related to the Far East.

The control of these almost independent decision-making centres was formally achieved through the over-riding authority of the Chief Manager, by the various regulations issued by Head Office, by the exchange of 'semi-official' and private letters among senior management – all of which were read by the Chief Manager – and by the occasional visits of a single Inspector of Branches whose work was supplemented, on an *ad hoc* basis, by chance or emergency visits of senior officers. Branches operated, apart from limited capital assigned by the Board of Directors in Hong Kong, on their own resources. 'Internalization' existed but its greatest impact was felt in facilitating the exchange operations of the branches through India to London and with the United States. To this should be added the provision of access to the London money market through the facilities of the London Office. The Hongkong Bank, as previously suggested, retained into the post-war period many of its earliest attributes as if it were, in the words of a nineteenth-century Treasury official, 'a collection of several banks' operating with a single capital under a single Board.

Although the Shanghai compradore had not been unreasonable in his exclamation, 'Surely joss protect this bank!', there was a more prosaic explanation for the Bank's survival than the undoubtedly excellent *feng-shui* provided by the locational attributes of Head Office and the additional joss consequent to the positioning of the guardian lions. Grayburn's management saw the Bank through the 1930s, but his ability at Head Office would have been of little use if his Managers in the branches and out-port agencies had been incompetent, overly adventuresome, or, worse, corrupt. But Grayburn knew they were none of these, and he could dismiss such concerns. He could not be in communication with them in today's sense, but he knew what they were thinking; if he heard of a problem with sugar, he could sense how the Manila or Batavia Managers would react to it. Grayburn was also aware of what his Managers did not know, and thus in anticipation of a devaluation of the tical he could send recommendations to the Manager Bangkok.

Although London Office training was the basis for a homogeneity which made possible control and operation of a successful bank, it was only the most important aspect of a total system. Before going to London the juniors had felt the same atmosphere, with English, Irish, or Scottish overtones, which, despite the diversity of traditions, was part of 'British' banking. They did not learn from theoretical models but absorbed banking custom and studied banking law and practice. When they later showed initiative, it was within the system; when they later deviated from the model, they did so aware that it was a deviation and therefore did so within acceptable limits or after checking with the next senior in their hierarchy.

Furthermore Managers knew their contemporaries and, at least to some extent, could judge their subordinate officers on assumptions sensible in the context of similar experiences in London and as juniors in the East. Bringing all this together was a sense of a 'service', of loyalty to and pride in the Hongkong Bank. There were personal failures, there were, unfortunately, decisions which were not corrected in time; these have been part of the history of the Bank. The balance, however, was in favour of the system, the control remained personal, and the bank prospered. But the system was specific to the Hongkong Bank; the socialization had taken place within a single organization. These attributes could not be transferred.

Not surprisingly, therefore, the Bank's first bank subsidiary, the Hongkong and Shanghai Banking Corporation of California (HBC), was seen at first as merely a branch specially organized to meet the requirements of California law. The subsidiary would be managed by Hongkong Bank Foreign staff, and they and their local assistants, some of whom were given signing power and designated (as who is not?) 'Vice President', would handle the traditional trade-related and investment activities of the San Francisco agency.

Many of the Hongkong Bank's more serious crises had been caused by the defalcation of compradores or guarantee shroffs. This was not the consequence of any original criminal intent; on the contrary, the compradore usually suffered, in a proportionate sense, more heavily than the Bank. These problems arose from the delegation of control by the Bank in matters relating to the local economy. The system worked well and was appreciated in normal times; even during financial crises the compradore's experience might shield the Hongkong Bank for a time, and recovery was often possible with minimal loss. The compradore was a key to the system.

In the Hongkong Bank of California the parent bank had set up a subsidiary through which it became involved in a local economy. The Foreign staff officers who managed the California bank faced problems similar to those confronting the pre-war Managers on the China coast and elsewhere in the East. They faced, that is, an economy for which they had no feel beyond its foreign trade, a banking system with which they were unfamiliar, and a language which, while deceptively similar, was dangerously different. The HBC's President had no American equivalent to a compradore; the Hongkong Bank of California's performance would soon be less than satisfactory.

The experience with this wholly controlled subsidiary was one of several factors which forced the Bank to reconsider its overall organization and indeed its entire management system. The same problem was faced in the East itself where the compradore system could not survive in changing political and social conditions; in the East the solution, part desired, part required by newly independent Governments, was to recruit local staff to executive and eventually senior management positions. But the East was the area of the Bank's own expertise; the Foreign staff could supervise this new development and evolve the system over time. In California the Foreign staff, with no formal banking education, lacked the basic experience to achieve this. Eventually another – and radical – solution had to be found.

The acquisition of the Mercantile Bank Limited provoked a policy discussion at Board level which was in a sense interrupted by, in a sense fulfilled by a second major acquisition, that of the British Bank of the Middle East. From these events were formulated policies which came to change the Hongkong Bank; more objectively, they proved the origins of the Hongkong Bank Group with its 500 + subsidiary and affiliated companies (see list of 1986 in Appendix Table B).

The total assets of the Mercantile Bank (£72.6 million) and the British Bank of the Middle East (£111.4 million) were £184.0 million, that is, at end-1960 they were almost exactly two-thirds the total assets of the Hongkong Bank. The Bank's California subsidiary began at the minimum capitalization permitted by local law, but, within a period of four years, the Hongkong Bank was acquiring two banks – assets, liabilities, staff, branch offices, two London head offices, two boards of directors, pensioners (and widows) – and being responsible for the consequences. The implications were so obvious that the Hongkong Bank's Chief Manager, Michael Turner, and his adviser (and deputy), G.O.W. Stewart, never considered an alternative solution. The two banks would have to remain separate identities – at least for the time being. Both Turner and Stewart were particularly careful not to tie their successors.

There would now be three banks with three 'services' responsible to three boards of directors – but to one body of shareholders who looked only to one of the three boards, the Board of the Hongkong Bank, as responsible. The position was impossible; it could not safely be left unchanged, but it could not safely be changed until management had devised systems alternative to 'tradition' and 'service'. The need for change was quickly recognized and minor but useful exchanges and improvements took place almost immediately, but complex liaison and control through a London-based board was not the channel for major revisions. The determination to integrate the Mercantile Bank into the Hongkong Bank for operational purposes with the head office of the former moved to Hong Kong coincided with the need to revise management in the context of developments in the banking industry, especially in the late 1960s.

When Sir Michael Turner left Hong Kong in March 1962, the Hongkong Bank was both changed and unchanged. The capital structure had changed, the Bank's acquisitions had had an impact on the accounts and on profitability, and the existence of the 'Hongkong Bank Group' had already suggested greater internalization; within the Hongkong Bank itself there had developed a formal separation between Head Office and Hong Kong office; each had an awareness of its particular role.

Nevertheless the historians of each bank are also overwhelmed with the sense of continuity. In 1961 attitudes and practices and loyalties had not changed. The junior system was intact – in each bank – and retirees visiting the several London offices, which remained in place, would have found nothing startling.

Under pressure of the consequences of these 1959/60 acquisitions and the great growth of the decade, that is by the end of Sir John Saunders' term as executive Chairman of the Bank in 1972, the Hongkong Bank had changed dramatically; during the period of Guy Sayer's administration these changes were solidified. By 1977 the Hongkong Bank was ready to form a partnership by the purchase of 51% of the shares of America's twelfth largest bank through its holding company, Marine Midland Banks, Inc., and this time the Chairman, Michael Sandberg, knew exactly what he – and the Bank – were doing. In planning a major move in the United States, Sandberg reverted to the solution of partnership. The HBC model was seen to be inapplicable. The experience with the British Bank of the Middle East also contained warnings.

These considerations go far beyond the scope of this chapter. The point being made here is that when the Bank formed its California subsidiary, when the Bank acquired two already flourishing subsidiaries in the late 1950s, either change or crisis became inevitable. By 1962 this change was latent; it would be unnoticed by the visitor or possibly even by the constituent, but it was already sensed by most of those directly involved. The Hongkong Bank as described in the preceding chapters, as indeed it existed through 1961, would never have survived, but now it was subjected to the pressures which would force change and thereby ensure survival.

Policy or chance?

The Hongkong Bank's approach to Marine Midland Bank in 1979 was the consequence of several years of intense and careful planning. The timing was excellent; the board of Marine Midland had become convinced that its capital requirements could best be met, or could only be met, by partnership with another bank, probably an overseas bank. To expect this sort of development in the 1950s would be ahistorical. The fundamental principles of British overseas banking had not been rethought; there was only the sense of those familiar with the City that certain changes had occurred which made the survival of small, regionally specialized banks uncertain, that there existed foreign, especially American, competition, and that, as the Bank of England firmly believed, rationalization of British overseas banking – if it were to remain British – was essential.

Recognition of this need at the intellectual level does not necessarily guarantee implementation. The board of the Mercantile Bank (no less than the board of Marine Midland) were justifiably proud of their bank, of its history and performance; the directors had spent considerable time on ensuring its survival. They were reluctant to suppose that the need for rationalization applied specifically to them. And yet the general recognition of the fact led to discussion, and discussion meant that when an offer came it was on the one hand unwelcome and yet on the other seen as a means to bargain for survival, if possible in 'partnership'.

The combinations resulting were not necessarily inevitable but were often the consequence of special circumstances, chance friendships, old relationships revived and amended. Nor was timing necessarily in the hands of financial experts. 'Take-overs', defined as the acquisition of a company against the wishes or advice of the directors, too often resulted in asset stripping and the end of the corporation taken over. Directors were therefore aware of the dangers, but they remained reluctant. In this they were not necessarily personally selfish; their concern was for the staff and the constituents of the bank. In their desire for survival they were torn between holding out for independence or moving quickly for what appeared the 'best deal'. Much was determined by size and by events in the areas in which the bank operated.

The Hongkong Bank was in a unique position. It was large enough in the 1950s not to be itself an immediate target, especially in view of the limitation on beneficial holding of its shares, a limitation written into the statutory regulations. The Hongkong Bank's Hong Kong base gave it the hope for growth and to many a reasonable degree of assurance that it would not be suddenly confronted with a situation beyond its control. The East was not without risk, but the risk was diversified. If there were concern for the Bank's future in China, there was new development in Borneo; if the Bank were losing in Phnom Penh, it was participating in the revival of Japan. The problems in Vietnam were offset by the growth of the Bank in the increasingly politically stable Federation of Malaya and in Singapore. The Hongkong Bank's approach to these problems and indeed to the challenges of industrialization in Hong Kong was dynamic. As the Bank's constituents expanded their operations they looked to America and made relevant banking demands on the Hongkong Bank. Michael Turner, frustrated by restrictions on a foreign bank agency in California, was willing to advise his Board of a new departure – the establishment of a subsidiary.

None of this meant, however, that, with the exception of a perceived need for a presence in Switzerland, the Hongkong Bank was searching out targets for acquisition. But with a determined Turner in Hong Kong and a still very active Sir Arthur Morse as Chairman of the London Committee, with S.A. Gray (1949–1955), S.W.P. Perry-Aldworth (1955–1961), and G.O.W. Stewart (1961–1968) as senior London Managers, the Hongkong Bank was well informed of banking trends and problems. The Bank faced American competition in Japan; they had seen the Chase Bank leave Hong Kong – and the East (except Japan) – at the time of the apparent threat of Chinese invasion in 1949. The Hongkong Bank was still expanding in these areas and they did not wish for renewed American competition. If the smaller banks could not survive, bankers like Michael Turner would consider a proposition. Once the proposition had been favourably considered, he would press hard for successful completion of the deal.

The Hongkong Bank's policy was one of examining the potential of new business. F.J. Knightly had been sent to southern Africa in 1957 and reported negatively; P.A. Sellars had visited Australia and New Zealand and built up contacts, and there were other surveys. Thus when George Marden telephoned Michael Turner his news relative to the Mercantile Bank, Turner put him on hold, examined the position, and eventually acquired the Mercantile Bank. The Bank considered other propositions but were aware of their limited capacity for 'absorbing' other banks; Turner, after much consideration, did accept the need to acquire the British Bank of the Middle East. The management limitations rather than the financial position then dominated decision making.

This chapter will first examine the formation of the Hongkong and Shanghai Banking Corporation of California, Incorporated, and then the acquisition of the Mercantile Bank Limited. These events provide practical examples of expansion, indeed of two different types of expansion. Nevertheless there was a basic similarity; in both cases external circumstances pressed on the Bank and encouraged the decision – the former through the limits set by California banking regulations, the latter by Marden's possession of a block of Mercantile shares, the implications of which the Bank could not ignore.

At this point the chapter turns to a discussion, even as the Bank itself did, of the consequences of its tentative and opportunistic expansionist activities, moving from this to the debate at Board level to determine the policy which would state the basis for the rationale of expansion.

There is then an interruption – the approach of the British Bank of the Middle East. This chapter recounts the Bank's positive decision to acquire 100% of its share capital – and the consequences of that decision. In conclusion there is consideration of the immediate impact of these acquisitions and of other equity investments on the Hongkong Bank, that is, on the emergence of the Hongkong Bank Group.

THE FOUNDING AND EARLY HISTORY OF THE CALIFORNIA SUBSIDIARY

THE FOUNDING

Agency or branch?

The Hongkong Bank first established its own staffed agency in San Francisco in 1875, primarily to handle the finance of silver shipments. In 1936 with China off silver Vandeleur Grayburn, as Chief Manager, decided that, although the usefulness of the agency was greatly diminished, it ought to be retained, perhaps on a more economical basis. As late as September 1947 Arthur Morse was questioning the wisdom of that decision but withheld a final judgement on the grounds that it was too soon after the war to determine the agency's potential. When Morse visited San Francisco soon after this, he apparently resolved the question in favour of the agency.

C.J.D. Law (East in 1928), who had been the San Francisco Agent since 1948, used his office as a base for obtaining business along the Pacific coast. The Bank's presence was still modest – the Hongkong Bank celebrated its 75th anniversary in San Francisco with a cocktail party at a Head Office approved cost of $500 – but Law began to investigate the possibilities of a larger role for the Bank in California. He quickly realized that if the Bank wanted a 'branch' it would have to establish a wholly owned 'in-house' bank incorporated in the State of California as a member either of the State or the Federal banking system. Correspondence dating from July 1951 indicates an exchange of information on these subjects between Law in San Francisco and O. Skinner, Chief Inspector, in Head Office.

The optimism generated by this correspondence was confirmed in 1953 by G.H. Stacey, who, in his Inspector's report, noted that business was increasing but that, as the agency could not accept deposits from U.S. residents, it was entirely dependent on Far East customers. He saw California industry developing, he sensed the impending growth of the State, and he encouraged the establishment of a subsidiary to enable the Hongkong Bank to seize the opportunity to secure a proportion of the financing of the foreign trade these developments would engender.

By the time I.H. Bradford had become Agent in April 1954, Head Office had become interested but hesitant. After a visit to various Pacific ports in September, Bradford discussed the problem with C.I. Cookes, former Manager Manila and wartime Sub-Manager in London, who had retired to Vancouver and had considerable North American experience. Bradford, with his support, advocated a branch in San Francisco and some presence in Canada. The latter was limited until 1983 by the nature of Canadian banking legislation, but in October 1954 Michael Turner wrote to Bradford stating that he was willing to reconsider the San Francisco subsidiary.

The senior local officer of the agency, R.M. Roche, gave a less enthusiastic report when he visited Hong Kong in December; he was concerned at the capital cost and at the reaction of American banks. Head Office nevertheless determined to move ahead.

The establishment of HBC

Turner's basic policy was for the establishment of a wholly owned and totally controlled subsidiary which would exist together with the agency, each handling business which was appropriate to itself. The details were worked out in the first five months of 1955 and application for incorporation was filed with the State Banking Department on June 8 and approved within the month. There was a last minute argument with the Secretary of State for California over the name of the subsidiary – the name as finally approved was 'The Hongkong and Shanghai Banking Corporation of California' – and the Bank opened for business on August 15, 1955, with Bradford as Chairman of the Board of Directors and S.J.H. Fox, the new San Francisco Agent, as the first President.[a]

The most obvious advantage of a locally incorporated subsidiary was the right to accept deposits from the public. This meant that, on the assumption that constituents granted advances would deposit at least a portion for a time in the Bank, this free money would lower the average cost of funds and so render the operation more profitable. Uses of funds would include investment in U.S. Government securities to ensure a flow of income, but the main source of new income – and the greatest potential for losses, realized later – would be the greater scope for advances.

[a] The disapproved version was 'The Hongkong and Shanghai Banking Corporation (California)', which the California Secretary of State thought confusing to potential customers. They would not know whether they were dealing with the parent or the subsidiary. On being informed that there was a precedent, he replied that he was not bound by bad precedents. In 1970 the name was simplified to 'The Hongkong Bank of California'.

Bradford recommended that the subsidiary should become a State bank, membership in the Federal Reserve System seems never to have been considered, and Bradford advised that membership in the Federal Deposit Insurance Corporation (FDIC) was unnecessary. In this last he was mistaken. The Canadian bank subsidiaries he used as models had been incorporated before the FDIC had been established; the State Banking Department quite sensibly insisted on membership and a representative of the Bank called on the FDIC in May 1955. The FDIC had never heard of the Hongkong Bank but were interested; in the event they rushed their report, which was favourable.

California law required the Bank to have five directors, each of whom would hold five shares free of lien. This was solved by the granting of interest-free loans to the designated directors by the New York agency of the Hongkong Bank. Control was assured by the fact that the director would be an employee of the Hongkong Bank or its subsidiary and that he undertook to sell back to the parent bank his five shares on ceasing for any reason to be a director. The operating quorum was three; this enabled the Board to include the chief executive of the parent Hongkong Bank as Chairman and the New York Agent of the Bank, B.P. Massey, as a member.

Head Office, in the person of J.R. Jones, remained concerned. What if two of the three directors were somehow to vote contrary to Head Office policy? Various schemes were suggested but in the end the lawyers had to bow before the reasonable position in California law that directors must stand on their own feet. This would not prove to be the Bank's main problem.

The unitary tax was not then the threat which would in any case have forced eventual reconsideration of the subsidiary. When that issue was raised, the Hongkong Bank was particularly vulnerable as any burden imposed could not be offset, as would have been the case of a London-based bank, by provisions for relief in cases of double taxation. In 1955 the tax position was seen as favourable. California would recognize that, as the subsidiary's activities would be supervised by Head Office in Hong Kong, the parent company was entitled to levy a management fee which could significantly reduce taxable income.

After the Hongkong Bank filed its application on June 9, 1955, Bradford was able to report that he received telephone calls or letters from competitors wishing the new bank good luck. 'These sincere expressions of friendliness from our American competitors have really been most gratifying,' he wrote to Hong Kong.

In the application the Bank stated that the proposed bank was established

to provide complete banking (commercial and savings) facilities for present customers of the San Francisco agency of The Hongkong and Shanghai Banking Corporation and to provide more direct banking facilities in California, and particularly in San Francisco, for persons having financial transactions between California and the various places throughout the world served by The Hongkong and Shanghai Banking Corporation.

The stress was clearly on international trade finance; this would too soon be forgotten. As the agency and the bank would operate with the same (as enlarged) staff in the same building, questions as to how the proposed bank would operate were easily answered. There had, however, to be a formula developed to apportion costs.

Directors and management

The only hitch came with the requirement that, if Michael Turner were to be a founding director, he should file full financial information; this he was reluctant to do, and Head Office considered the appointment of Skinner or F.C.B. Black instead. The reporting requirements were subsequently modified, but in the event B.P. Massey in New York became a director and was invited to be present at the opening; Bradford, who after working through the preliminary stages would be transferred back to Hong Kong, was temporarily Chairman. When Bradford resigned his directorship on departure, Turner was elected a director and voted Chairman.

The Hongkong Bank's first subsidiary bank had been established with a minimum of trouble, with goodwill expressed on all sides, and with a modest brief to expand the traditional business of the agency on a more efficient basis. But almost from the beginning there would be problems.

Bradford left San Francisco in September 1955 and Fox was in charge.

Fox (East in 1928) was actually four years senior to Bradford, and he had a background which at first suggested success. Educated in a village school he was not a public school product, but being Scots he had established his ability in an apprenticeship with the National Bank of Scotland and been recruited in the normal way through London Office. From 1934 to 1938 he had served in the New York agency. He was then assigned to Shanghai where, presumably, his ability was not unnoticed by fellow 'juniors' including Michael Turner.

His career then stood still. He was interned by the Japanese in Shanghai during the Pacific War. In 1946 he returned to China and was there, without leave from 1947 to 1954, at first in Shanghai. His ability had been recognized in 1949 when he was appointed Agent Shantou (Swatow), but the agency was virtually inoperative then, and he was little more than a prisoner at large after the establishment of the People's Government.

Even the interlude in Shanghai office would not have given Fox normal banking experience; it was the period of China's hyperinflation. Thus he had been out of the mainstream since 1940; he no longer had the background to take over a major operation, much less develop a new bank in California.

Furthermore, almost on the morrow of the HBC's opening, a new note appears in the correspondence. The HBC must stand on its own feet, it must

Table 12.1 *The Hongkong and Shanghai Banking Corporation of California, Inc. Balance sheets, 1955–1961 – selected items*

	1955	1956	1957	1958	1959	1960	1961
(in millions of U.S. dollars)							
Shareholders' funds	1.25	1.26	1.89[a]	1.92	1.92	2.56[a]	2.56
Total deposits	4.98	4.67	11.83	14.66	15.66	19.01	20.38
of which: HSBC deposits	1.77	0.90	1.08	0.64	0.79	0.38	0.55
Acceptances and LCs	0.61[b]	3.63	1.35	1.67	1.66	2.06	0.17[b]
Total assets	6.87	9.62	15.19	18.41	19.45	23.67	23.17
(in thousands of U.S. dollars)							
Profit for the year	1.49	4.23	10.63	26.75	6.17	6.45	9.71

[a] 5,000 additional shares @ US$100 plus surplus.
[b] Letters of Credit (LCs) not included.

make its own agency arrangements, it must be considered a separate entity. The extension of this approach meant that the HBC must go beyond the simple purposes stated in the application for incorporation and become not simply a *de facto* branch of the Hongkong Bank but a local bank – eventually a local retail bank with several but always insufficient branches located here and there, virtually at random, throughout the State of California. The need was there; it might have worked, but it didn't.

INITIAL OPERATIONS, EXPANSION PLANS, AND SETBACK

Performance, 1955–1961
The total assets of the Hongkong and Shanghai Banking Corporation of California (HBC) increased almost 3.5 times between its founding in 1955 and the end of 1961, and the paid-up capital was increased in both 1957 and 1960. Total deposits, excluding deposits of the parent company (the Hongkong Bank) increased sevenfold in the same period (see Table 12.1). These figures, despite the inconsistent handling of 'Acceptances and Letters of Credit' would suggest a sound initial performance on the part of the Bank's first banking subsidiary.

The profit figures even as stated suggest caution. In fact, they are overstated. The San Francisco agency used the facilities and staff of the HBC and the latter was reimbursed by an agency fee. This agency fee was arbitrary and could be and was varied to change published 'profit figures' as desired – a loss could be covered by the fee and charged to the Hongkong Bank's account with its New York agency. As far as the consolidated Group accounts are concerned, the final aggregates will be unchanged, but, for those interested in an analysis of the HBC alone, this practice creates problems.

The 1960 results, for example, showed a loss of US$4,000 for HBC, but the agency fee of US$15,000 gave a tax paid profit of US$6,000. In 1961 the fee was raised to US$50,000 for the specific purpose of showing an increased HBC profit for the year.

Whatever profit figures were published, the fact is that HBC had run into difficulties which reflected on the Hongkong Bank's ability to manage a subsidiary and which understandably affected their plans relative to the Mercantile Bank and the British Bank of the Middle East immediately following their acquisition in 1959 and 1960. Turner had also to consider what to do with the management of the California subsidiary itself. His solutions would be only temporarily effective.

Initial 'success' and plans for expansion
Following notification of HBC's 1957 results, Turner sent a congratulatory cable to Fox. Not that Turner considered all was well. He had been worried as early as October 1957 that the original purpose of HBC was being forgotten. In a letter to Fox he noted that, although deposits had grown, they were small accounts and, therefore, costly. More important was the fact that Fox was fully loaned up to the limit of 70% of assets and that none of the loans appeared to be in connection with the finance of foreign trade. We are an exchange bank, Turner reminded him, and HBC was set up primarily to get new customers for trade finance. While admitting that such customers were hard to get, if one were now to appear, Turner pointed out, Fox would be unable to extend a line of credit without borrowing from New York or Head Office reserves. These remarks were not intended as a criticism, but Fox was advised to 'look it over'.

This sort of comment from Head Office, made in the face of balance sheet success, is evidence of the work of the Bank's Inspectors. Fox, along with other Managers, would reassure himself that these Inspectors had never managed a branch and were unaware of the situation which only the experienced man on the scene could evaluate. There were many fellow emigrants from 'Mainland China' in San Francisco, some with schemes requiring finance, and Fox was apparently insufficiently critical. In any case Fox was locked in; he could only make the best of it.

Accordingly he wrote back optimistically in terms of expansion. A Los Angeles branch had been opened (together with a Hongkong Bank agency) in

1956, Fox now wrote recommending an office in San Francisco's Chinatown to obtain the remittance and foreign exchange business. He also thought it worthwhile to consider opening in Sacramento, the developing State capital – 'no longer the sleepy town it was pre-war' – and to search for a small loan association suitable for purchase.

On a broader front there was the question of acquiring and operating banks in Alaska and Hawaii. The 1956 Bank Holding Company Act effectively checked the Hongkong Bank's plans to acquire additional financial institutions. Turner was himself about to commit the Hongkong Bank with Baring Bros to the acquisition of a block of shares of the 52% British-owned Honolulu and Manila based company, Theo H. Davies, Ltd. These shares, which had come into the market from the company's pension fund and from retiring directors, would be made over to HBC and would give the California subsidiary a toehold in the finance of the San Francisco/Honolulu trade and might eventually result in the opening of a banking office in Hawaii. Here again Turner learned of the 1956 Bank Holding Company Act too late and was advised to sell off part of the shares acquired. The Hongkong Bank was not yet used to operating in America, despite its long but highly specialized presence, nor was it always careful to check the growing list of regulations. Nevertheless, through March 1958 Turner's attitude to HBC and the American operation was positive.

On March 1, 1958, Turner again wrote to Fox of his concern that HBC had no new foreign trade customers. But then the news broke of a major loan disaster which forced Head Office to cable Fox specific instructions. These were not followed, and Turner wrote in April:

Never before have I met such circumstances...

The Bank gives wider authority and greater discretion to its manager than any other organization, but the corollary to this wide responsibility is that general policy and specific instructions from Head Office should be conscientiously carried out. It is always open to Managers to question or ask for review of policies both general and particular, and I am very ready to listen to such pleas – though the final decision must rest here.

In the matter of (these) affairs, you have over the past two months had definite instructions which you did not question and yet which you did not carry out.

Fox acknowledged his error but took the position that he had got the Bank into the trouble and he saw a way on his own to correct the situation.

HBC's success was on paper only. The new bank had taken over a local staff inexperienced in general banking and had been sent as President a Foreign staff officer who, by all accounts, was a most personable banker, but who had, through no fault of his own, no management experience. O.P. Edwards, who was sent to set up the operating systems, stirred up the staff and was not returned after his leave; instead he was replaced by F.M. Thompson (East in 1937), whose most recent experience had been in Rangoon and then for two years as Sub-Agent Sungei Patani. The reason usually ascribed for this strange assignment was personal. There would later be internal irregularities in the San Francisco office, but, at this point the story returns to the bad loans of 1957/58.

Consequences

The HBC's lending policy drew adverse comments from the FDIC inspectors, and in October 1958 Turner reacted.

First, he cancelled all consideration of expansion until the present business of the subsidiary were on a 'sound footing'. He then issued Fox specific instructions. Reminding him that the Hongkong Bank was very new to commercial banking in California and that the State Banking Department had been enthusiastic in issuing HBC's 1955 banking licence under the impression that the California subsidiary would focus on the finance of international trade, Turner warned Fox to spread his risks and not to allow the profit motive to lead him into taking undue risks or extending large loans to a few customers. The Bank was being tempted in California as it had been in the Philippines; furthermore, the Bank had come late and was picking up marginal business. Do not lose sight, Turner urged, of our original function – the finance of international trade.

Meanwhile a major loan had been made on a clean basis to a customer who had borrowed elsewhere on a secured basis.

This led Turner to increase the HBC's Board from five to eight members with instructions to meet every two weeks – it had been meeting once a month. From this strengthened Board was to be formed a loan committee – a major decision, since the Hongkong Bank had traditionally avoided management by committee; Fox himself was limited to granting loans of up to US$10,000; beyond this and up to US$100,000 on a clean basis (or US$200,000 if secured), Fox had to refer to the loan committee. Loans in excess of these latter limits would be referred to the Head Office.

But the damage had been done. The price of having neither developed a sound management plan nor of having selected the staff carefully was a loss in excess of $10 million by the end of 1959. By December 1961 the Bank's fixed investment (= shareholders' funds) in HBC had nevertheless increased to US$2.6 million (= $14.8 million); amounts due to the Hongkong Bank by HBC were US$553,000 (= $3.2 million).

Turner was making plans to retire Fox. In 1958, with Thompson now Vice President of HBC, a junior, D.H. Leach (East in 1948), who would be appointed Manager New York in 1974, was sent to assist the work in the agency. Then in 1959, a year after matters had gone sour, Turner sent H.C. Peterson (East in 1929) as Executive Vice President with the expectation of replacing Fox. His reception was hostile, and it was some days before a desk

5 Chief executives: Sir Michael Turner, CBE, 1953–1962.

THE HONGKONG AND SHANGHAI BANKING CORPORATION
GROUP CONSOLIDATED BALANCE SHEET AT 31st DECEMBER, 1961

1960 Hong Kong Dollars		Hong Kong Dollars	Sterling Equivalent		1960 Hong Kong Dollars		Hong Kong Dollars	Sterling Equivalent
	Share Capital				$307,889,397	Cash in Hand and Balances with other Banks	$421,865,545	£ 26,366,597
$100,000,000	Authorised: 4,000,000 Shares of HK$25 each	$100,000,000	£ 6,250,000		341,225,636	Money at Call and Short Notice	326,345,988	20,396,624
79,046,125	Issued: 3,161,845 Shares of HK$25 each, fully paid	$79,046,125	£ 4,940,383		472,655,185	British and Other Government Treasury Bills	295,514,424	18,469,651
240,000,000	Reserve Fund (including Share Premium Account $91,530,549)	240,000,000	15,000,000		944,140,312	Trade Bills Discounted	1,140,115,470	71,257,217
2,206,181	Profit and Loss Account	2,340,534	146,283		815,300,000	Hong Kong Government Certificates of Indebtedness	837,300,000	52,362,500
321,252,306		$321,386,659	£ 20,086,666			Quoted Investments, at under market values:		
839,101,648	Hong Kong Currency Notes in Circulation	871,397,296	54,462,331			BRITISH AND OTHER GOVERNMENT SECURITIES:		
5,901,151,712	**Current, Deposit and Other Accounts,** including Inner Reserves and Provisions	$8,401,926,402			1,005,194,462	Quoted in Great Britain	$981,194,472	
					236,316,673	Quoted outside Great Britain	212,458,073	
33,432,015	Acceptances on Behalf of Customers	39,563,175				OTHER INVESTMENTS:		
25,400,596	Proposed Final Dividend	25,400,596			46,766,206	Quoted in Great Britain	45,079,600	
					12,984,111	Quoted outside Great Britain	17,994,795	80,551,684
		6,460,820,173	404,176,686				1,288,826,940	1,840,635
					20,951,935	Unquoted Investments at cost, less amounts written off	29,450,160	199,415,645
					2,729,650,079	Advances to Customers and Other Accounts	3,190,650,312	2,479,507
					27,423,268	Balance of Remittances, Drafts, etc. in transit between Offices	39,672,115	2,468,948
					33,432,015	Liabilities of Customers for Acceptances	39,563,175	
						Fixed Assets		
					13,983,600	INVESTMENTS IN ASSOCIATED COMPANIES, AT COST	$14,783,600	
					31,608,998	BANK PREMISES AT COST, LESS AMOUNTS WRITTEN OFF	25,606,399	
							40,389,999	3,116,875
$7,120,338,277		$7,659,614,128	£478,725,883		$7,120,338,277		$7,659,614,128	£478,725,883

MICHAEL W. TURNER
Chief Manager.

N. H. T. BENNETT
Chief Accountant.

H. D. M. BARTON
W. C. G. KNOWLES } *Directors.*
J. D. CLAGUE

The annexed Notes form an integral part of these Accounts.

6 Group Consolidated Balance Sheet at December 31, 1961
—from the 1961 *Annual Report*.

7 Bank buildings—a study in contrasts.
Upper left, Hankow office ('Stephen's folly') at night; *upper right*, Haiphong, French Indochina; *lower left*, Seria, Brunei, (abandoned temporary office); *lower right*, the 1970s Mongkok office.

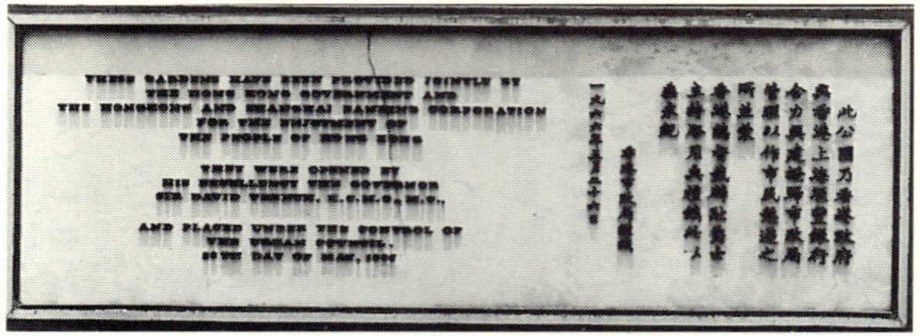

12 Statue Square.
(i) a 1972 view to the sea.
Note the statue of Sir Thomas Jackson; the plaque is on the south wall of the square, opposite the Bank's head office.
(ii) a 1972 view from the sea with the 1935 head office building.

could be found for him in the office; he had difficulty securing the cooperation of the staff. Fox was retired and Peterson succeeded as President; Thompson resigned shortly thereafter.

In Los Angeles the HBC's Vice President was W.R. McCutcheon (East in 1936); he was without American experience. In 1960 he was assisted by D.G. Lachlan (East in 1948). Lachlan had at least visited America on an inspection trip with F.J. Knightly and had studied new banking office machinery both with the manufacturers and in the using banks. While in Los Angeles Lachlan studied American banking practices at night school, but his North American tour was too short to have any impact, and he never returned.

The limitations of the system
In a post-1958 policy letter, Turner commented in passing that the President of the HBC would always be a member of the Foreign staff. This limited the type of American banker who could be induced to join the HBC and was a further but perhaps unavoidable impediment to sound management. At a lower level, the HBC was having technical difficulties introducing the Hongkong Bank's own routine operations into an American situation. Here there was one bright spot: as the operations of the HBC developed, new staff were recruited from former Portuguese employees of the Hongkong Bank, newly immigrated to California from Shanghai and Hong Kong.

Only an exceptional executive officer who had learned banking on the job in the East in the 1920s and 1930s might have succeeded in the new California environment. In his study, 'Lombard Street on the Riviera', Geoffrey Jones has described sound British bankers doing strange things once they had crossed the Channel. It is dangerous to generalize, but the conclusion appears obvious. Sir Charles Addis had been correct – if the Bank were ever to attempt something new, the Foreign staff had to be selected from candidates who had had a fuller post-secondary educational experience. Now half a century later this should have been accepted, but there would still be opposition to change. Nor could the change take place immediately. Fortunately the Bank had post-war officers of a 'new breed'; they were capable of bridging the gap through self-education or specialized short-term training, as in the case of Lachlan – and Learmond with Bowmakers (see below).

Although successive Chief Managers of the Hongkong Bank were never quite able to cope with the HBC, they were acutely aware of the problem. The experience in California must have influenced Turner's approach to expansion; the first San Francisco crisis came only the year before the final negotiations for the acquisition of the Mercantile Bank Limited. Pleas that the Hongkong Bank needed time to 'digest' a previous expansion or promises that the staffs of acquired banks would be left in place were not empty expressions of false modesty. The Bank's hesitations relative to expansion were due partly to its reluctance to break loose from traditional practices which had caused its undoubted success, but another important factor was the overwhelming evidence that managing another bank in another area presented problems which the Head Office in Hong Kong were not, in the late 1950s and early 1960s, capable of supervising. The Bank most certainly had executives who would have performed more wisely in California, but, even if they could have been identified, they were needed elsewhere.

THE ACQUISITION OF MERCANTILE BANK LIMITED

In the early days of the Japanese occupation of Shanghai George Marden, a Shanghai merchant, urged the three British banks to pool their resources and to issue joint cash pay-outs, referred to as 'dividends'. This procedure would have favoured those who held deposits in the Mercantile Bank of India, the least liquid of the three. The Hongkong Bank and the Chartered Bank appear to have had no objections, but J.R. Huxter, manager of the Mercantile, refused to cooperate. As L.C. Blanks, the Mercantile Bank's Accountant, recalls it:

I remember [George Marden]...going in and seeing Huxter – and coming out again with a flea in his ear. He was furious; as he walked out of the office he said,
'Bloody impossible man! I'll buy this bloody bank one day.'

In 1954 George Marden telephoned Michael Turner, the Chief Manager of the Hongkong Bank, to tell him he had bought 5% of the Mercantile Bank's shares, was Turner interested? G.H. Stacey and G.O.W. Stewart were, as it happened, in Turner's office; they heard him turn Marden down.

In 1957 George Marden again telephoned Michael Turner. This time he had shares with over 14% of the voting rights and this time Turner was interested.

The Hongkong and Shanghai Banking Corporation did not want to acquire the Mercantile Bank of India. During these years the Bank was disengaging itself from China and actively seeking investment elsewhere. The Mercantile Bank was not an obstacle to this; on the other hand it had little to contribute. Certainly it was efficient and competent, but it was small; it had its own loyal customers, and its presence in India was not seen by the Hongkong Bank as either a threat or a potential instrument to facilitate implementation of its own development plans. Turner in particular would have been content to let the Mercantile stand as it was.

This was now impossible.

Although Marden may have been influenced by Shanghai memories, his own

The new subsidiaries, 1955–1961

account is stated in business terms. He began buying Mercantile shares in 1953 when the price was low; his plan had been simply to sell to the Hongkong Bank at a higher price. When Turner rejected the offer in 1954, Marden turned to the Bank of America. His 5% holding was obviously far from a controlling interest and the Bank of America was not interested.

At this point Marden turned to Samuel Montagu with the intent to buy control. On the assumption that the Mercantile Bank would not remain a viable corporate entity in the post-war banking world, Marden, who had no thought of management, planned with Samuel Montagu to sell off parts of the bank to other banks.

The Bank of England was opposed to such a sell-off, and Montagu backed off. This left Marden with (i) 14% of the shares – and still buying – and (ii) a reluctant Hongkong Bank. It was becoming obvious that he must at some point sell and if not to the Hongkong Bank then to whom? From the Hongkong Bank's point of view, the continued separate existence of the Mercantile Bank of India was acceptable, often convenient. The competition of the capably staffed branches of the Mercantile with the resources of a larger international bank was quite another matter. Furthermore, that larger bank might be American and the Hongkong Bank had enough American competition with the Bank of America and the Chase Bank encroaching in its traditional region.

Turner went to London in early 1957 and discussed the problem with R.H. Vivian-Smith, Lord Bicester, who was a director of both the Bank of England and the Mercantile Bank of India, and Sir Edward Reid of Baring's, a member of the Hongkong Bank's London Committee. Turner still did not want to acquire the Mercantile; his recommendation was that Bicester on behalf of the Mercantile organize a consortium of investors to buy Marden out and hold the shares under conditions which would prevent their alienation. But Marden quite naturally would only sell at a price considerably above the market; under this condition Bicester, suffering in Turner's irreverent view from mental constipation, was not interested, and Turner, after consulting the Bank of England and receiving their informal support, returned to Hong Kong to deal first with his Board and then, if they approved, with Marden.

The Hongkong Bank would buy the shares.

The first approach, April–July 1957

In March 1957 Michael Turner as Chief Manager informed the Board of Directors that George Marden had acquired 14% of the shares of the Mercantile Bank of India, and the directors agreed that the Bank should buy these shares 'if only to prevent Mercantile being sold elsewhere'. The Board also stipulated that Marden agree to stop buying on his own account and that the Bank should not be obliged to enter into any partnership with him in the matter of the Mercantile.

The decision was made in the context of a discussion on the Hongkong Bank's 'expansion', under which heading minutes on the unfolding drama of the Mercantile's acquisition were for a time included. A Bermuda banking subsidiary was considered and rejected. The Board agreed that a presence in Geneva was desirable, and they decided (as who did not?) to acquire a small, well-established Swiss bank. The potential of West Africa, where banking had been reported as inadequate by one member of the Board, was recommended to a sceptical Chief Manager for consideration.

By the end of April Marden and the Bank had come to an agreement and the beneficial ownership of Marden's shares, which had been bought quietly by his broker dealing through the Bank's London nominee company, was transferred to the Hongkong Bank. Marden and the Bank continued to buy shares at market, but for the Bank the point being that, if the Bank wished to reverse itself, it held an option to do so until September 15, 1957. The shares being purchased in the meantime by Marden were included in the agreement.

Although the Board's March minute is not precise on the subject, it is clear that Turner at least had decided that the agreement with Marden was a preliminary to acquiring the entire capital of the Mercantile Bank. Should this prove to be undesirable, on the basis of an examination of the accounts, Turner could cancel the agreement with Marden at any time before mid-September.

Turner was associated in the discussions and subsequent negotiations primarily with Perry-Aldworth, then London Manager, G.O.W. Stewart, Turner's adviser and from April 1959 the Deputy Chief Manager, and Sir Edward Reid. Sir Arthur Morse was kept informed. During the six weeks between the agreement with Marden and the end of May, the first contacts had been made and assessed. The Board of the Mercantile had authorized Lord Bicester to negotiate with Stewart, Perry-Aldworth, and Reid.

The first disagreement was over the Hongkong Bank's preference for making an entirely cash offer; this would in fact prove the final stumbling block in the first round of negotiations. In their early meetings Bicester made it clear that he did not favour a cash offer because of the considerable inner reserves the Mercantile possessed and the difficulty his Board would have in recommending a cash offer without revealing the size of those reserves.

Unfortunately the Hongkong Bank's position hardened on this aspect. The Bank's three London negotiators agreed that a share offer would have to include a cash alternative. This led them to a *non sequitur*: if a cash alternative had in any case to be part of the offer, there could be no objection to making a solely cash offer. Turner would seem to have been reluctant at that time to increase the subscribed capital of the Bank and broaden the shareholder base; one remarkable feature of the Bank's capital structure was the fact that, in 1957, published reserves were more than $2\frac{1}{2}$ times paid-up capital.

To this underlying reluctance to broaden the capital base, the negotiators added specific arguments to support positively the Bank's preference for a cash offer. Morse and Perry-Aldworth in particular were concerned with the impact on the price of Hongkong Bank shares if a high proportion of Mercantile Bank shareholders should opt for cash. They argued that the shareholders of the two banks were in quite different categories: Hongkong Bank shareholders were mainly non-residents of Britain wanting a British-tax free investment; Mercantile Bank shareholders were mainly insurance companies wanting dividends on which British tax had been paid. The latter were unfamiliar with the Far East (as opposed to India), and an unfavourable event could cause those who had chosen the share option to panic sell.

By June the Hongkong Bank had control of nearly 20% of the voting power of the Mercantile Bank.

When Turner again brought up the matter with his Board on June 11, he had firmed his view on the need for a cash offer and had news to report on other relevant problems. From the earliest stages Turner and his colleagues had been concerned as to the future development of the Mercantile if they should be successful in acquiring 100% of its capital. Stewart was instructed to consult the Bank of England as to whether the head office might be removed to Hong Kong; he reported that the Bank of England approved and that other authorities, while not committing themselves finally, wrote supportive of the proposal. Turner also informed the Board that auditors from the two banks had met for discussion, they were now at work and that their conclusions would not take long to reach.

While the auditors were examining the accounts, the board of the Mercantile had also become concerned with the future of their bank. What did the Hongkong Bank intend, especially with reference to the fate of the staff? The Hongkong Bank was at the same time considering several scenarios, but on one point all parties became agreed: they believed, rightly or wrongly, that the handling of staff problems, when the P&O Bank had been 100% acquired in 1939 by the Chartered Bank, had been highly unfavourable to staff of the former bank. The Hongkong Bank, while keeping its long-run options open on all other subjects, was firm in its assurance that the Foreign staff of the Mercantile would receive equal consideration with its own and that where integration of the two banks' operations caused redundancy in local staffs the latter would be compensated either according to the local law or by similar formulas where no such law existed.

The Hongkong Bank's plans, however, were very much subject to tax and other legal considerations. On the assumption that British tax regulations would virtually force the move of the Mercantile's head office to Hong Kong, the Hongkong Bank variously planned to establish a 'Mercantile Bank (Hong Kong) Limited', a shadow head office in Hong Kong preparatory to a later move, a token board in London, etc. Turner did learn that dismissal of the London directors would require, by City custom, payment of three years' stipends, totalling some £34,000, and he did consider a London Committee for the Mercantile as a 'face saver'. But all these plans were aborted by the breakdown of negotiations in July. When negotiations began again sixteen months later, in November 1958, more developed plans in a changed tax situation were on offer.

In June it was becoming clear that, whatever the logic of the Mercantile's situation, the directors were in angry disagreement over the idea of a 'take-over', a concept, as popularly understood, in considerable disrepute in the City. Lord Bicester and the Mercantile Bank's management had failed to prepare the other board members for the possibility. Sir John Hay of Guthries, for example, had spent years in Malaya dealing satisfactorily with the Mercantile; why should the banks 'merge' now?

On June 18, 1957, the first meeting with Mercantile board members other than Bicester began inauspiciously; the Mercantile Chairman, Sir Kenneth Mealing, informed Reid, Perry-Aldworth, Stewart, and the Hongkong Bank's London junior Manager, M.D. Scott, that the Mercantile's board had come to the conclusion that they had either to deal with Marden or with the Hongkong Bank and that they would prefer to deal with the latter. Mealing then handed over a 'list of conditions'.[b]

Marden was still buying shares and Mealing threatened that, if this did not stop, he would advise his shareholders not to sell. The Hongkong Bank countered by stating that, as they had as yet received no confidential information, there was no reason why they should be restrained from buying; they promised however to put pressure on Marden to hold up until July 1. A second condition was that information on the Mercantile was for the Hongkong Bank Board only; third, the board had contractual and moral obligations to its staff which would need to be covered; and finally, an independent expert would have to be involved.

By July 12 Turner had decided to acquire the Mercantile Bank with an offer of £4.5 million, equivalent to just over three times its paid-up capital. On July 16 the board of the Mercantile rejected the offer, which the Hongkong Bank then withdrew. The offer would have given the shareholders a higher than market price for their shares, but the board felt they were unable to recommend

---

[b] Sir Kenneth Mealing was not a 'City man'; he had, in fact, spent most of his career in India with Yule, Catto and Co. Ltd, reflecting the interests of Sir David Yule and his later companies, together with Morgan, Grenfell and Co.

a cash offer unless the Hongkong Bank either (i) offered the 'break-up' price of the Mercantile Bank or (ii) permitted the board to reveal the inner reserves and the true earning power of the bank. The former was too expensive, especially since the Hongkong Bank intended to continue the bank's operations and required the inner reserves as such. The latter would have been unacceptable in the City and would have served little purpose.

This information was conveyed to the Hongkong Bank's Board on July 23. Turner advised the Board that the only alternative would have been to approach the shareholders directly, that is, without the Mercantile Bank board's approval, an unthinkable proposition at that time in either the City or, more especially, in banking. Turner also disclosed that the Hongkong Bank had nevertheless bought Marden's shares and that Marden himself would no longer be buying; the Hongkong Bank on the other hand would continue to buy quietly on the market.

By September 1957 the Hongkong Bank owned 18% of the capital and 21% of the voting rights of the Mercantile Bank of India, Ltd.

Interim: August 1957–September 1958

Despite the agreement reached between the Hongkong Bank and George Marden, the situation remained unstable. As Turner told his Board, there were no present prospects of obtaining a majority interest. The Mercantile Bank of India survived as an independent concern but with a large block of its shares owned by a bank unrepresented on the board; it still appeared a suitable target for some form of take-over, merger, or 'partnership'. In fact it was the approach of Chase Manhattan Bank from New York which precipitated the Hongkong Bank's second and successful round of negotiations in late 1958. The period from August 1957 to November 1958 was a sort of unsatisfactory interim, during which, however, the Mercantile Bank continued to perform well as a bank, justifying the pride with which its board and staff viewed it.

The September meeting

The unsatisfactory nature of the relationship between the Mercantile and the Hongkong Bank was revealed at a meeting between Mealing, Sir Cyril Jones, and Bicester for the former and Turner, Reid, and Perry-Aldworth for the latter.

Turner first made clear that in his opinion the directors had been ill-advised by their consultants and hasty in their assessment of the Bank's offer; they should have given their shareholders the opportunity of making their own decision. Secondly, Turner was annoyed that he should be asked for a 'snap' decision on whether to support the Mercantile's proposed reorganization of their capital. The plans had been under consideration by the board for two months; the Hongkong Bank was then asked to support the proposals virtually at a single meeting, although its voting rights would be adversely affected thereby.

This led to the crucial issue. What would the relationship be between the two banks? If this could not be resolved, the Hongkong Bank stood ready to sell back the shares to the Mercantile's nominee, if approved by the Hongkong Bank, at a price which would obviously not be approved by the Mercantile Bank. Turner, for example, demanded a seat on the board for the Bank's nominee; Mealing countered by arguing that, while this was acceptable in principle, he was unwilling to recommend election of a senior executive of the Hongkong Bank. His alternative suggestion was the election to the board of a member, presumably as inactive as possible, of the Bank's London Committee. This alternative and the underlying concern of conflict of interest Turner rejected outright; he wanted his senior London Manager on the Mercantile board on the understanding that he would not sit on the loan committee or examine into the details of the bank's business – he would act, perhaps, like a Hongkong Bank director.

From this meeting Turner's position became clear. Annoyed at the Mercantile board's unwillingness to face reality, Turner was seeking as close a position as possible to keep up the pressure; in this context he reserved the Hongkong Bank's right to continue buying shares in the market. His attitude was stern and aggressive. While he didn't accuse the directors specifically of 'Londonitis', he came very close.[c]

Confronted with Mealing's disapproval of his proposal relative to the election of a director, Turner agreed to hold off for a period but insisted on some form of close cooperation between his senior London Manager and the chief manager of the Mercantile Bank. To this Mealing promptly agreed. The proposal was on hindsight so obviously unworkable that there is temptation to suppose it part of an overall strategy to reopen the question of an acquisition. Perry-Aldworth and the Mercantile's R.N. Drake did have meetings, but it was never clear what the chief executives of two rival banks were supposed to agree to. Once this was made obvious to the Mercantile board, it would have an easing effect on later negotiations.

To apparently sweeten relationships while purposely achieving the opposite Turner then offered to sell the shares to the Mercantile's nominee. Mealing took the bait and asked for a price. Turner, noting that as his offer of £7:10s per share (on which £2:10s was paid up) had not been considered 'good

[c] Grayburn used the term 'Londonitis' (see Volume III) to describe a state of mind typical of what he considered the inept ways of the City as opposed to the dynamism of the East, of Hong Kong especially, and of the Hongkong Bank in the East most especially.

Table 12.2 *The Mercantile Bank of India Ltd. Capital structure, 1957*

(pounds sterling)

Authorized	
150,000 'A' shares of £5 each	750,000
150,000 'B' shares of £5 each	750,000
1,500,000 'C' shares of £1 each	1,500,000
	3,000,000
Issued	
150,000 'A' shares, £2:10s paid	375,000
150,000 'B' shares, £2:10s paid	375,000
720,000 'C' shares, £1 paid	720,000
	1,470,000
As rationalized	
Authorized: 4,000,000 shares of £1 each	4,000,000
Issued: 2,940,000 shares fully paid	2,940,000

Source: High Court of Justice, Chancery Division, in the matter of the Mercantile Bank of India, and in the matter of the Companies Act, 1948, No. 00729 of 1957.

enough', argued that Mealing should not be surprised if he suggested £8:10s. This brought the discussion back to point one – Mealing countered that he had never argued that the Hongkong Bank's offer was insufficient but rather that his board could not recommend it without also revealing the inner reserves.

'Mr Turner, I think, left you in no doubt as to his reaction to this statement', Perry-Aldworth wrote Mealing in summarizing the unsatisfactory meeting.

The restructuring of the Mercantile Bank's capital
A reading of the Mercantile Bank's proposals for capital restructuring suggests that Michael Turner may have been a little unfair. The Mercantile's capital was, like that of the Hongkong Bank, the product of its history and, established as it had been following the crisis year of 1892 as a reorganization of the Chartered Mercantile Bank of India, London, and China, it retained elements of the colonial banking system plus features which suggested a natural hesitation on the part of the first subscribers. The problems the board confronted were formidable and apparently took time to work out.

The Mercantile Bank had three categories of ordinary shares, referred to as 'A', 'B', and 'C'; all three of which had been targets of George Marden's buying program. The first two, issued in 1892, were of the same nominal value, but 'A' was entitled to a fixed cumulative preferential dividend of 5%;

thereafter 5% was to be paid on 'B' shares – and after their issue in 1920 on 'C' shares – any remaining dividend was to be paid on all shares *pari passu*. The 'A' and 'B' shares had a nominal value of £5 of which £2:10s was paid up, that is, shareholders had a liability equivalent to the unpaid capital of £2:10s per share, although £1:5s of this could only be called up on the dissolution of the company. The 'C' shares, first issued in 1920 with a nominal value of £5 at £10 (with a £5 premium), ranked relative to the dividend *pari passu* with 'B' shares; in 1954 with the existing 'C' shares split into five, a further 420,000 were issued at £1 fully paid.[d]

Voting rights were assigned in proportion to the nominal value of shares, that is, one vote for each 'A' or 'B' share held, one vote for each five 'C' shares held. This last provision was a consequence of an article providing that when the 'C' shares were split their holders would not thereby obtain increased voting rights.

The existence of issued capital not fully paid-up and thus resulting in uncalled and reserve liabilities to the shareholder, although not unusual in the early days of limited liability, suggests both the vestigial provisions of the old imperial charter and the Reserved Liability Act of 1879; the preferential element suggests the uncertainty of the time.

The capital structure is shown in Table 12.2.

The purposes of the proposed restructuring were (i) to simplify the capital by combining the three classes into one with equal rights, (ii) to eliminate the uncalled and reserve liabilities of shareholders of 'A' and 'B' shares, and (iii) to enlarge the capital by capitalizing a part of the reserves.

The simplification was done on the basis of capital paid up per share; the various privileges were disregarded on the grounds that they were either irrelevant or off-setting. Thus with large inner reserves and a sound record, shareholders in fact lost nothing by cancellation of preferential rights, a judgement supported by Stock Exchange quotations for the various shares, and by the agreement of the shareholders. On the same basis the reserved liability entered into no current calculation, but, as with the Hongkong Bank, it could become an impediment when accountants attempted to agree on recommendations for mergers or take-overs.

The increased capitalization would be accompanied by replacement of published reserves from inner reserves. This paralleled changes then being

[d] The 'B' shares had been issued to former shareholders of the former Chartered Mercantile Bank of India, London and China; the 'A' shares represented new capital and, under the circumstances of 1892, had to be offered with a preference. The 5% minimum was paid on both 'A' and 'B' shares for the first time in 1903. The issue of 'A' shares was increased in 1919; 60,000 'C' shares originally with a par value of £5 were issued at £10 in 1920, the premium being set aside in a 'share premium account'; they were split into five shares of £1 fully paid and a further 420,000 issued in 1954 giving a total of 720,000.

made by the Hongkong Bank. The ending of the reserve liability, although differently stated in the two banks, would in both cases be offset by doubling the paid-up capital.

Stated simply, what the board of the Mercantile Bank proposed and what was accepted by shareholders was the accomplishment of the above in roughly the following steps: (i) the reduction of all shares on a simple arithmetical basis to 10s shares fully paid up, (ii) the issue of an equal number of 10s shares to shareholders on a one for one basis, fully paid by capitalization of reserves, (iii) the transfer of an equivalent sum from inner reserves to exactly replace capitalized published reserves, (iv) the consolidation of the consequences of these moves by halving the number and doubling their par value to £1 fully paid, and (v) the raising of the authorized capital from the resulting £3 million to £4 million.

This together with a proposal to change the name of the bank to 'Mercantile Bank Limited' was put before a November 1957 meeting of shareholders and approved. In consequence the capital structure was: authorized 4,000,000 ordinary shares of £1 each; issued, 2,940,000 ordinary shares of £1 each fully paid, that is £2,940,000. The Reserve Fund stood at £2.2 million.

These moves had been preceded by an increase in the dividend. Taken together the increased dividend, the stronger capital position, and the deliberate re-creation of unissued but authorized capital suggested to analysts that the Mercantile Bank was preparing to face up to potential bidders or perhaps even to enter the merger field itself. Although this proved correct, it was also true that the increased dividend resulted in part from pressure by the Hongkong Bank which wanted a higher return on its troublesome investment. In February 1958 rumours were published that the aggressor was the Hongkong Bank, but at that time both boards were able to deny the story with very clear consciences.

The Hongkong Bank had originally offered £7:10s for the 'A' or 'B' shares; this was the equivalent to 30s per reorganized ordinary share and the market in February 1958 had settled to 28s, which Stewart considered too high. The Hongkong Bank therefore withdrew from the market for a time, but it was clear that, if negotiations were ever restarted, the Bank's offer would have to be considerably higher than the aborted cash offer of July 1957.

The successful negotiations

An approach by Chase and the immediate consequences
Over the previous years the American business of the Mercantile Bank had brought it close to the Chase Manhattan Bank of New York. There was nothing surprising therefore when in September 1958 Chase's London manager

telephoned the acting deputy chief manager, C.F. Pow, to say that David Rockefeller, the Chase President, would like to meet Sir Kenneth Mealing. And the interview was held.

They sat there politely biting their nails, with nothing happening. I [Pow] started off therefore by saying, 'I find it curious, Mr Rockefeller, that you haven't got a branch between Tokyo and Beirut.

And he said, 'Well, that's just what I've come to talk to you about.' He was very relieved.

This preliminary discussion was followed on September 16 by a visit from John L. McCloy, the chairman of the Chase Bank. This would be a key interview and the Mercantile Bank was anxious that everything should be properly managed. Pow faced two major problems. As the guests were American Mealing felt it essential to provide bourbon; as there should be no leaks relative to such a meeting and as anyone seeing bourbon brought into the dining room of a British bank would quite rightly suspect something unusual was afoot, Pow had to smuggle the bottle in unnoticed. He put it in a dark corner of the bar, where, as far as he knows, it remains. Americans, he would learn, are quite happy with Scotch.[e]

As forces of the People's Liberation Army moved south from Canton in 1949 certain foreign investors panicked. It was at that time that Chase pulled out of Hong Kong. The Governor, Sir Alexander Grantham, is reported to have told them that if they deserted then they would not be granted a licence to return. He and his successors were true to their word. Chase Manhattan eventually came back to Hong Kong through purchase of the Hong Kong (Bangkok and Singapore) branches of the Nationale Handelsbank, a subsidiary of Rotterdamsche Bank, in 1963.

What Chase was apparently attempting was reentry into the East through a partnership with the Mercantile Bank. Initially share acquisition would be limited to say 20%, but, as Perry-Aldworth reminded Turner, the precedent of National City Bank and the International Banking Corporation earlier in the century was sufficient warning that, after a period, total acquisition might be forced. Nevertheless Perry-Aldworth recommended considering some sort of tri-partite accommodation, and Turner told himself that he must react as a shareholder; the role of even a major shareholder was different from that of a banker with 100% of the shares.

By mid-October events had taken a serious turn. McCloy had expressed the view to the Bank of England that Chase was interested in helping British

---

[e] Similar thinking during the Marine Midland negotiations led the London Office of the Hongkong Bank, as yet unaware of New York State's own production, to stock up on California wine. Several bottles came eventually to the personal attention of the Bank's American historian. They have been liberated.

banking in the East; this was seen, fairly or unfairly, as bare-faced hypocrisy and the Bank of England become seriously concerned. Despite McCloy's assurances to the Mercantile Bank board that the Bank of England had no objections to his approaching them, the hope was that the meeting would not be successful; the Governor and his colleagues were very much concerned.[f] Hints were dropped to Sir Arthur Morse and others at chance social meetings that the Mercantile should remain British, and Sir David Eccles of the Board of Trade was interpreted as suggesting to Morse at a luncheon meeting of the British Travel Association (of which Morse was chairman) that Chase's real target was the Hongkong Bank. Whatever the truth of this might be, given the limitation on shareholding embodied in the Bank's regulations, the Hongkong Bank had come perilously close to cooperating in a plan which would at the least have brought Mercantile, the Hongkong Bank, and Chase into an uneasy grouping, with Chase the richest participant. The time had now come for decisive action.

Apparently the Bank of England thought so, too. Perry-Aldworth reported the Morse/Eccles conversation to C.F. Cobbold, the Governor of the Bank of England. As he told it to Turner in a key letter dated October 24, 1958,

Cobbold got a bit excited and said, 'For goodness' sake, keep all this on a business basis.'
The inference must be drawn that Cobbold considers that anything to do with Eccles could mean that politics might enter the field and God knows what might happen then. If Trinidad Petroleum is anything to go by, I think we could find ourselves being sold down the river by the politicians for a handful of dollars to tide over a balance of payments crisis.

There were several factors which favoured a new approach by the Hongkong Bank. First, as noted, the Bank of England was taking a stronger interest and would perhaps be positively supportive as opposed to 'encouraging'. Secondly, the basis of the tax assessment on the Hongkong Bank's London earnings had been changed radically; the tax saving from bringing Mercantile's head office to Hong Kong was no longer the *sine qua non* of an agreement, and this would make negotiations with the Mercantile's board a more pleasant undertaking. Thirdly, both banks had eliminated the historical peculiarities of their capital structure. And finally, other make-shift cooperative arrangements between the two banks could be seen to be non-productive. Interestingly, however, Turner still started out with the intention of making a cash offer, but he too had learned much since July 1957.

On the other hand there would be a temporary complication and a negative

[f] According to J.D. Wilson in his history of the Chase (p. 100), the Chase's approach to the Bank of England was later considered a 'tactical error', and McCloy would express the view that had he been 'a little more aggressive and acted a little more promptly', the deal could have been accomplished. These statements verge on the ludicrous.

development. On November 15, two months after Chase Manhattan had made its September contact with the Mercantile, the deputy chairman of the British Bank of the Middle East (BBME), Sir Geoffrey Eley, came in with a proposal for a merger, but Mealing was not particularly interested in a Middle East involvement. Eley, who was also a director of the Bank of England, then called on Sir Edward Reid. For a brief period in early November 1958 all three banks – Mercantile, BBME, and the Hongkong Bank – with the intermediation of Reid and the strong encouragement of the Governor of the Bank of England, considered the possibility of a tri-partite merger, but complications relative to the BBME forced the Hongkong Bank to focus entirely on the Mercantile Bank problem which was, after all, immediate. The development of the Hongkong Bank's attitude to the BBME will be told in the following section.

The negative factor was the Hongkong Bank's 1958 performance. Although Turner himself was apparently still focusing on a cash offer, the exchange of shares was no longer impossible, and certainly the Bank's London negotiators were thinking in these latter terms. For the latter the ratio would be determined both by the underlying figures which would not be released to the public and by the comparison made by the public on the basis of published figures and performance. The acceptability in the market of any Hongkong Bank offer would depend, *inter alia*, on the Bank's performance as reflected in its dividends. The timing of the negotiations made it essential that the Hongkong Bank announce its year-end dividend as soon as possible and, more to the point, make it as generous as possible. Gross earnings were down; losses in San Francisco and Calcutta continued high; Turner had in fact been thinking of an improved dividend, but in view of the increased capital which would result from a share exchange he was loathe to commit himself. It was not the time to be generous, but the Bank's hand was forced.

The Hongkong Bank's second offer
These developments provided the Hongkong Bank with a basis for approaching the Mercantile Bank formally with the suggestion that they reopen negotiations with a view to the former's acquisition of the remainder of the Mercantile's outstanding shares.

Accordingly on October 23 the Hongkong Bank returned to the offensive; led by Perry-Aldworth, Sir Edward Reid, and Sir Arthur Morse – the last being included 'in order to show we really meant business' – the Bank again talked with Sir Kenneth Mealing. Their main points were: (i) the Hongkong Bank was prepared to make a share offer, as neither capital had uncalled liabilities, but that an alternative cash offer would be made, (ii) the Mercantile Bank would be retained as a separate entity, that the move to Hong Kong was in the future, but that the present intention was for head office to remain in

London with Hongkong Bank representatives on the board, and (iii) previous promises relative to the staff remained valid.

On October 28 Mealing wrote to Sir Edward Reid that the Mercantile's board had informed Chase that 'as our principal stockholder is not prepared to cooperate in the proposals, we assume they will agree that this really closes the matter'. Chase accepted Mealing's reasoning; this proved the breakthrough.

Then the Hongkong Bank was informed that the Mercantile board were discussing an investment in an Australian bank. Turner was not amused; it seemed as if the board were deliberately trying to avoid reality during a dangerous period. This the Mercantile was told on November 14; the Australian proposition was quickly withdrawn.

Meanwhile Perry-Aldworth had come up with tentative figures. The Mercantile's paid-up capital and published reserves were £5,040,000 and its inner reserves £2,475,000 or 50% of published shareholders' funds. On the assumption that the Hongkong Bank's inner reserves were approximately of the same order, an assumption later confirmed, Perry-Aldworth came to the conclusion that the ratio of shares should be one Hongkong Bank share on the London Register for 21 Mercantile or a cash alternative of 40s per Mercantile share (= to £10 for the old £2:10s share, which compares with the Bank's previous offer of £7.10s) against the then market price of 32s:6d. Hongkong Bank shares were at £42.

The Hongkong Bank's advisers recommended 1:24, but, for reasons which will be considered as the process of negotiation unfolds, the Bank was eventually beaten back to 1:20 or an alternative of 44s per share.

The course of the negotiations

The Hongkong Bank's Board of Directors was officially informed of the new developments on November 25, 1958 – this is the first reference in the minutes since the breakdown following rejection of the original offer in July 1957. The Board specifically authorized the Chief Manager to resume negotiations.

Turner telephoned Perry-Aldworth in London and authorized the announcement in terms of an exchange of shares; the announcement was made on November 28:

The Board of Directors of the Mercantile Bank Limited announce discussions are in progress with The Hongkong and Shanghai Banking Corporation with regard to a possible share exchange offer to be made by The Hongkong and Shanghai Banking Corporation for the whole share capital of the Mercantile Bank Limited. Shareholders will be informed in due course upon the outcome of such discussions.

Between November 25 and December 2 Turner came to a decision on the final dividend and on the latter date his Board met again to approve the recommendation of £1:17s:6d 'in view of the proposed merger'. With the interim dividend of £1:2s:6d this represented a pay-out per share of £3 on 400,000 shares, compared with the previous year's dividend of £3:12d:6s, partly on 200,000 and partly on 400,000 (see Table 5.1). Thus on the assumption that the shareholder kept his bonus shares, he would receive, for each share he held at the beginning of 1957, a dividend payout of £5:5s in 1957 and £6:00 in 1958, representing an increase of 14%. Or, expressed another way on the part share basis, the dividend in 1956 had been at the rate of 9.7% of book value; in 1958 the dividend was 10.8%, an 11% increase.

This increase had been made, despite the Hongkong Bank's fall in true gross earnings, (i) to match the sharp increase in the Mercantile Bank's dividends as announced in 1957 following the breakdown in the initial negotiations (but kept at an unchanged rate of 6.25% in 1958) and (ii) to conform to the custom that an increase in the interim dividend, unless otherwise stated at the time, implies an increased final dividend. When Turner recommended the increased interim 1958 dividend, the new negotiations with the Mercantile had not been contemplated; when these occurred Turner was faced with an implied undertaking but on an increased capital. It might be argued that the dividends which would be payable from the Mercantile to the Hongkong Bank would compensate, but on December 2 it was too early to be certain. Nevertheless, as Sir Edward Reid had advised and urged, the Hongkong Bank had raised its dividend and was now in a stronger position to bargain with the Mercantile Bank on the ratio for the share exchange.

Shares on the London Stock market had earlier been £47 for the Hongkong Bank and 47s for the Mercantile. Once more the signs were for a 1:20 exchange, giving, on the basis of the dividend figures stated above, an income advantage to the Mercantile Bank shareholders. On the eve of the press announcement, however, Mercantile Bank shares had been at £1:18s:6d and thus twenty would be valued at £38:10s compared to the Hongkong Bank's one share valued at £43:10s; the twenty Mercantile shares paid a dividend of £2:10s compared to the Hongkong Bank's £3. A 20:1 ratio would be favourable to the Mercantile Bank, a good bargain for the Hongkong Bank, and would provide just that premium necessary to ensure the success of the offer.

Although, with auditors' approval, the Board gave authority to the London negotiators – a Board-appointed sub-committee of the London Committee composed of Morse, Perry-Aldworth, and Reid – to close as low as 20:1 if necessary, there was reason to suppose that opening at 24:1 might be successful with 22:1 likely. This last figure did for a time appear agreed, but two factors intervened.

First, the Mercantile Bank's auditors were not impressed with the trend in the Hongkong Bank's earnings and Turner had to cable figures adjusted for the fact that profits from previous years were included in the profit figures supplied; the adjusted figures showed an improved trend, but the damage had been done. Secondly, the Mercantile board were advised that the Hongkong Bank's shares were 'top-heavy', that is, expensive per unit; Turner refused to consider splitting them, and the question of marketability arose. This tipped the balance and the Mercantile held out for 20:1. As Perry-Aldworth cabled Turner on December 16, the market expected 20:1; if the ratio were set at 22:1 there would be a collapse in the price of Mercantile shares. At the same time he warned Mealing not to be too difficult.

On December 17 Turner replied that he would agree to 20:1, but this was as low as the Hongkong Bank would go. At the same time he agreed to a cash alternative of 44s to offset the effects of 'top-heaviness' and the consequent questioning of the marketability of Hongkong Bank shares.

With this authority Perry-Aldworth wrote to the Mercantile Bank board setting out the proposed offer and the related conditions. The 20:1 exchange was ex-dividend, the Mercantile Bank to pay its own shareholders the last dividend from Mercantile Bank funds. The offer was for an exchange of shares, therefore the Mercantile Bank directors must agree (i) not to reveal inner reserves, (ii) to recommend the offer, and (iii) to accept publicly the offer for their own personal shareholdings. The cash alternative, Perry-Aldworth explained, 'is intended merely as a "stop-loss" for those shareholders of the Mercantile Bank who cannot or feel unable to become shareholders of the Hongkong Bank'.

The status of the cash offer also overcame the concern of the Hongkong Bank's solicitors that offering Mercantile shareholders either Hongkong Bank shares or cash as equal offers might cause the Bank to be disqualified from taking advantage of Section 209 of the Companies Act. The relevant section provided for compulsory acquisition of shares once 90% had been obtained – the Act referred to 'an offer' in the singular and there were no relevant precedents. As the offer was now stated, the Bank was in effect underwriting its own share issue.

At a formal meeting on December 22 the necessary basics were agreed; the Mercantile board indicated their willingness to accept and a formal press announcement was issued to state that the two boards had reached an agreement 'in principle, subject to a formal contract', and setting out the terms described above.

The formal announcement to shareholders was dated January 23, 1959, and the Hongkong Bank's offer was made unconditional on February 16, subject only to the approval of its own shareholders of the necessary increase in the authorized capital of the Bank at an extraordinary meeting scheduled for February 18. Mercantile Bank shareholders had until March 31, 1959, to accept the offer.

In a summary which included the 13,292 Mercantile Bank shares acquired compulsorily under Section 209 (3) of the Companies Act 1948 (0.4% of the total issued), the figures indicated that the Hongkong Bank had issued 98,491 shares on the London Register for 1,969,820 shares of the Mercantile and paid £903,911:16s for 410,869 shares of the Mercantile belonging to those who chose the cash alternative of 44s a share. The investment was listed under the Hongkong Bank's assets as the equivalent of £5,371,407 (= shareholders' funds); on the opposite side share capital was increased by £771,300 (for 98,727 new shares at par) and the share premium account (included in published reserves) was increased by the difference between par and £44 per share or £3,572,688.

Mercantile Bank's shareholders' funds were listed as of December 31, 1958, as £5.4 million. The Hongkong Bank had issued new shares worth, at £44, a total £4.3 million; the Bank had previously bought 559,319 shares on the market at £0.6 million; and it paid out in the cash alternative £0.9 million. The total cost to the Hongkong Bank was £5,969,804, that is £598,397 above the value of shareholders' funds, an amount offset in the accounts by a transfer from the Hongkong Bank's inner reserves.

Under the agreement inner reserves were not revealed, but, as noted above, they were in rough proportion. The Hongkong Bank, not unexpectedly, had had to pay a premium to ensure the success of the offer. Still to be answered was the question as to whether the deal had been sound for the Hongkong Bank and the shareholders.

The immediate consequences

In his statement to Mercantile Bank shareholders, Sir Kenneth Mealing had said,

It is intended that the change in control shall not affect the management, staff, relationship with constituents, or business progress of the Bank. The Head Office and board will continue in London as hitherto, and the Board believe that an association or merger of ownership such as this will strengthen the resources and provide opportunity for the progress of both Banks in the future which should prove beneficial to their constituents throughout the world.

The Mercantile Bank as an operating subsidiary of the Hongkong Bank survived until 1984, but it is not intended to recount that history here. A more immediate date would be the inevitable transfer of the Mercantile's head office to Hong Kong in 1966, perhaps sooner than Mealing had hoped, but long enough for the older members of the board to recognize power was slipping past them. In March 1959 Morse and Perry-Aldworth were elected to the board; pressure from Morse brought the Mercantile's chief manager, C.R. 'Towkay' Wardle, onto the board. Policies of concern to the Hongkong Bank would be passed to Wardle, who would inform his chairman; policy could thus be influenced even before consideration by a board on which two representatives of the Hongkong Bank were members.

Early in 1959 Wardle toured the branches of the Mercantile reassuring them. L.G. Atterbury (East in 1944) recalls his manager in Karachi calling the Foreign staff officers to his house; there Wardle told them, 'You needn't be afraid of big figures now.' In the context Wardle meant that the Mercantile could call on reserves; it was not, Atterbury explained, that the Hongkong Bank was going to put money into any of these countries, but that they were now part of a much larger organization and could therefore take on larger commitments. The Mercantile still sensed the impact of the events of 1892.

With prospects of staff salaries being raised to meet Hongkong Bank levels, pensions increased, and, in particular, widows' benefits improved (the Hongkong Bank had itself just made the necessary improvements for its own widows), the immediate reactions were all favourable. Indeed, the Hongkong Bank accepted the Mercantile virtually as a senior partner in India. In response to a query as to whether the Hongkong Bank objected to the opening of a second office, a sub-agency, in Madras, G.O.W. Stewart, by then Deputy Chief Manager, advised the Mercantile Bank that the Hongkong Bank would be guided by their experience, if it didn't cost too much. A new building was completed in Kuala Lumpur, new offices would be opened in India, Mauritius, and Japan, new staff recruited; it seemed as if the promise of continued parallel development would be fulfilled. In February 1959, for example, Michael Turner, as the Chief Manager of the Hongkong Bank, after full consideration of the situation in Kuala Lumpur gave specific instructions that the proposed Mercantile Bank building there should be completed. Turner considered and specifically rejected the obvious suggestion that both banks be housed in a single building. Rather he planned to move into the Mercantile Bank's old quarters while the Hongkong Bank built a new prestigious headquarters for its own Federation of Malaya operations. By the early 1970s the existence of these two Hongkong Bank Group buildings, almost side-by-side, would be used as an example of the cost of failing to integrate the two banks at an earlier date.

There were indications almost from the first that integration would some day occur. The Hongkong Bank in its negotiations was careful not to commit its future course. In 1957 a move of Mercantile Bank's head office had been assumed; only changes in the tax position made London tenable, and the balance was marginal. Early discussions within the Hongkong Bank had focused on ways to rationalize operations, not by integration but by division of territory, as indeed was done in India when the Hongkong Bank first turned over its offices to the Mercantile and then, on the eve of the dissolution of the Mercantile as an operating bank, took back all Group offices, except the

Bombay branch of the British Bank of the Middle East. Behind the thinking was the question of staff integration and supposed country expertise.

The concept of two relatively small banks operating in specialized areas seems now to have been the heritage of an earlier period of banking, when banks were supposed, sometimes by the terms of their charter required, to confine their activities geographically. In this case, although efforts were made to differentiate, there were agreed overlaps – in Kuala Lumpur, for example, in Japan, Thailand, and Singapore. Both banks would be nationalized in Burma, neither bank considered it profitable to operate in Pakistan. The areas of specialization were insufficient to offset the growing arguments for integration.

And these were from the first encouraged by measures taken for other purposes. For example, the apparently unrelated question of staff pensions and widows' benefits. The Hongkong Bank's terms were superior and Turner considered it appropriate for the staffs of both banks to enjoy equal benefits. For operational and legal reasons this was best achieved not by improving the Mercantile's arrangements but by offering the staff of the Mercantile participation in the Hongkong Bank scheme on condition they renounced their own. This they did. The assets of their trust were then run down to pay certain Mercantile pension expenses, but thereafter it was the Hongkong Bank who accepted responsibility for the Mercantile Bank staff.

There were several points on which the Mercantile had operational practices of use to the Hongkong Bank. A Hongkong Bank officer – the first being W.H. Lydall, a personal friend of Wardle's – sat in 15 Gracechurch Street, the Mercantile's head office, to learn about the new acquisition and how it worked. Lydall reported, for example, that a saving could be obtained by Hongkong Bank branches printing their forms, stationery, etc. in-house and noted that almost all Mercantile offices had small printers for this purpose. This was useful, but it could hardly be a factor in the timing of the Mercantile's inevitable absorption into the Hongkong Bank.

The basis for this came early. The arrangements made with the Inland Revenue authorities in Britain in May 1959 not only permitted the Bank to consider other acquisitions but with hindsight marked the end of the Mercantile as an independently operating bank within a 'partnership'. The deposit of up to £4 million of surplus funds at $1\frac{1}{2}$% with the Hongkong Bank for tax reasons cut the Mercantile's profit; the payment of a large 'management fee' prevented any accumulation of reserves. Deprived of growth through retained earnings the Mercantile Bank had little hope for expansion; it was too dependent on its parent bank. Potential recruits to the Foreign staff saw it as the junior partner and were attracted first to the Hongkong Bank; when the Mercantile stopped recruiting and the staff were 'interchangeable', that is, virtually one service, the Mercantile Bank became a 'name' of significance to loyal constituents and to the regulatory agencies which had assigned it a banking licence, a historical link to the past in the field of British overseas banking, but operationally very much a part of the Hongkong Bank Group.

THE HONGKONG BANK'S POLICY OF EXPANSION

A background survey

Despite the oft-professed need to 'digest' the acquisition of the Mercantile Bank, the fact is that by the end of 1959 the Hongkong Bank had virtually acquired a second major financial subsidiary, the British Bank of the Middle East (BBME). The development of the Bank's San Francisco office from agency to subsidiary California bank plus agency can be explained by the particular provisions of California banking law; the acquisition of the Mercantile Bank, to the fact of George Marden's purchase of a significant block of shares which the Hongkong Bank could not ignore. But to explain the acquisition of the BBME in terms of chance or because their chairman approached Turner is to leave too much for 'chance' in history to explain. The initial impetus may have been caused by a chance factor, but the Hongkong Bank's pursuit of the Mercantile and its subsequent acquisition of the BBME suggests, correctly, that behind these developments was a policy of expansion – or at least an acceptance of expansion – which permitted Turner to act with considerable force, knowing his Board was supportive.

'Policy' and 'chance' are not necessarily opposites. The Bank's policy of expansion could take concrete form only where the opportunity was made or arose, and the former was not always within the power of the Bank nor was the latter predictable. Given the restraints in banking, aggressive policy has its limits; to decide as a policy on diversification is sound, but the policy may not be capable of implementation unless the chance, such as the BBME, presents itself.

Turner's policy was to maintain a liquidity ratio of 50%; in this he was not always successful, but it suggests an awareness of political risk which events in China had demonstrated. Inheriting a Bank with a high liquidity ratio and substantial inner reserves, Turner could depend on an income from investments, but this is not banking. During the 1950s the Hongkong Bank witnessed its position in its traditional strongholds being eroded; the intervention of American banks pointed to the financial strength they derived from their base in the United States. Their incursions into Eastern finance partly in connection with American industrial development, aid, and military programs, partly in support of local development plans could not be directly challenged with resources from the Hongkong Bank's base of Hong Kong. It is true that Hong Kong provided a basis for growth of a type the Mercantile Bank lacked from its Indian branches; the Hongkong Bank also received income from its growing reserves. Neither were sufficient to challenge the American banks – not yet.

Nevertheless the Bank's resources were of sufficient magnitude to require diversification and to permit the thought of equity investment and acquisition. There were funds at the disposal of the Board on the advice of the Chief Manager.

In the 1950s the Hongkong Bank was, apparently, the same Bank that had survived the 1930s. The Foreign staff, trained on the job, were prepared to run an exchange bank in the tradition of British overseas banking, but they were not trained in corporate take-overs, nor, if Sir Charles Addis had been correct in his evaluation of the importance of university education, did they have that familiarity with principles which would lead to a new conceptualization of the Bank's role. James Hall had retired in 1949; this left Michael Turner and G.P. Stubbs as the Bank's only university graduates. Turner needed and wanted to force the Bank's way out of the limitations of the exchange bank mould, but it was not obvious how he should proceed. He felt his way and he was not always successful. He worked with a relatively few key men; he needed reassurance from Sir Arthur Morse and investment banking guidance from Sir Edward Reid; in the Hongkong Bank itself only his immediate deputy and the senior London Manager were involved. As for the rest of the staff, in the period to 1962 they might be involved in some plan which affected their office but otherwise they carried on much as before in an exchange bank which, as far as could be seen, was itself operating very much as before.

Turner however brought his Board closer into partnership; his plans involved basic policy; they needed Board support.

The trouble with a Hong Kong head office, it had been argued at least since the early years of the century, was that the Bank's directors had to be Hong Kong based; they were China oriented, they were unfamiliar with opportunities elsewhere. The Hongkong Bank in the days of Empire had links with the world through London; thus it had been able to lose money in Brazilian investments without incurring the additional expense of actually having an office in Brazil. Investment success depended on the London Manager and the advice of the London Committee with the organizational dangers this involved. Now it seemed London was no longer the key to world-wide investment success (or danger); New York was alien, despite the Hongkong Bank's long presence there; in the 1950s when the Bank sought world-wide connections it appeared more Hong Kong bound than ever.

This analysis underrates both Hong Kong and London. In the Appendix to Chapter 6, changes in the company representation on the Bank's Board were described; the merchants of Hong Kong like their Bank were thinking first of Hong Kong's development but they too were contemplating diversification; they too were looking beyond their traditional region. They would be sympathetic to a Chief Manager with similar thoughts.

As for London, with the departure of Morse in 1946, the London Manager took over the chairmanship of the London Advisory Committee *ex officio*, even as O.J. Barnes had done in Grayburn's time. On his retirement from the East, however, Sir Arthur Morse became Chairman of the Committee – as in the days of Sir Thomas Jackson and Sir Charles Addis. There were, however, significant differences. The Hongkong Bank was not again to be 'two banks'; neither Morse nor Turner wished the London Committee to play a major role. It is important, therefore, to recognize that this policy is not contradicted by the role of the London Committee sub-committee in negotiating the acquisition of the Mercantile Bank and the BBME. The sub-committee did not report to the main committee but straight back to Turner in Hong Kong. The role of Sir Edward Reid was virtually that of personal adviser to Morse and Perry-Aldworth. The sub-committee was very much an extension of the Bank's Head Office. And yet it was undeniably a sub-committee of the London Committee; the City would understand, or think it understood, the exact position of the negotiators. At the same time the existence of the London Committee was vindicated; the Bank was using it for legitimate purposes without the danger of a London challenge to the management in Hong Kong.

When action in the City was needed, Turner not only depended on his London Manager and on Sir Edward Reid, but on the continued cooperation of Sir Arthur Morse – a Chief Manager who had originally made his reputation in London. When the Board in Hong Kong needed full professional support in London they not only had the London Committee and its 'sub-committee', but the Bank could also call on the Bank's long-trusted solicitors, brokers, and other City connections built up over the years. And Reid kept them in appropriate close contact with the Bank of England and its Governor.

The Hongkong Bank was not at that time considering expansion in Britain itself; the importance of London in the Bank's expansion policy was due to the fact that British overseas banks were, with few exceptions, incorporated in England and needed to be considered in the context of British law and the Government's and the Bank of England's concern for the fate of British overseas banking.

It is not surprising, therefore, that the weak point in the Bank's expansion policy was not Africa, which the Hongkong Bank virtually rejected, nor Australia nor Canada where the opportunities were restricted by regulation, nor Europe where the opportunities seemed non-existent; it was the United States. The Bank's experience in New York and San Francisco, its links through the

Philippines, its finance of America's Eastern trade – all these were apparently irrelevant to involvement in America's domestic banking industry. But it was here that the Hongkong Bank chose to begin its diversification, and it was here that it was most firmly checked. There would be virtually another quarter of a century before the Hongkong Bank was sufficiently prepared to move decisively in North America; when it did, with the acquisition of Marine Midland Banks, Inc., it proved the value of its preparation.

In this context the expansion policy of the Hongkong Bank may be examined.

Developments to 1959

The Hongkong and Shanghai Banking Corporation of California (HBC) was conceived for the purpose of offering to constituents normal branch facilities beyond those which a California-based agency had the regulatory authority to grant. Almost immediately it was treated as a bank in its own right, as indeed legally it was. With an inexperienced management it was soon in trouble, and the losses incurred in 1958 and 1959 – they would not be the last – forced Turner to explain the position to the Board. The Bank, he said, had been used to dealing with the honest Chinese; it now faced Californians. The Board was sympathetic but more encouraged by the report that the HBC's Board had been significantly strengthened and now included people familiar with the natives.

Turner faced the initial crisis at a time when he was attempting, with Board support, to develop a long-term strategy and solve the immediate problem of the Mercantile Bank.

In July 1956 the Hongkong Bank became involved with Bowmaker Ltd and Tozer Kemsley and Millbourn Ltd in an equity investment in their hire purchase business, Bowmaker (CA) (Private) Ltd, established only in May 1956 in Salisbury, Southern Rhodesia, Central African Federation. The two founding companies had invested in a total of 100,000 shares, par value Southern Rhodesian £1.00, of an authorized capital of £500,000 in 500,000 shares. The Hongkong Bank agreed to make an initial investment by subscription to 100,000 fully paid ordinary shares, with the right to nominate two directors to the board. An investment of $1.6 million equivalent, which, despite hesitations about African investment following F.J. Knightly's 1957 African tour, would be increased as the business expanded with branches in Ndola and Bulawayo in the period under consideration.

The initiative for this investment came from Sir Arthur Morse, who was chairman of the parent Bowmaker Company, suggesting once again that the Bank had need for and was endangered by the lack of a development policy. Nevertheless, despite the *ad hoc* selection of this venture, judged on purely business terms, the correspondence reveals that the Bank in Hong Kong was provided with substantial data on the problems and techniques of a hire-purchase organization, which, as Perry-Aldworth pointed out to Turner, would prove useful in the implementation of the Bank's own hire-purchase plans then in an early stage of development. A member of the Bank's Foreign staff, D.P.G. Learmond (East in 1945), was seconded to Bowmaker's; he would be the first Manager of the Hongkong Bank's subsidiary, Wayfoong Finance.

The first reference in the Board minutes to what might be termed development policy – as opposed to the discussion of specific development proposals made by the Chief Manager – was in March 1957. The occasion was an approach by two shipping companies regarding banking opportunities in Bermuda, but the Board saw the cost as prohibitive. At this point the new Board member, Lawrence Kadoorie (later, Lord Kadoorie), recommended that the Bank consider acquiring a small Swiss bank in Geneva, setting Turner on a search which would not end until after his retirement. Then, as Chairman of the BBME, Turner was able to establish a branch of that bank in Geneva, apparently contrary to all advisory expectations. Even more important was the general instruction to the Chief Manager to consider carefully the merits of a move into West Africa.

It was in June of 1957, in the context of the Mercantile Bank offer, that Stewart began negotiations with United Kingdom authorities which would lead to the tax concessions necessary for profitable investment by the Hongkong Bank in overseas banks with British head offices.

With the Mercantile Bank negotiations apparently permanently terminated, a meeting of Hongkong Bank branch Managers in Hong Kong – in itself an important development – considered future planning. They came to a significant conclusion: within the Hongkong Bank's traditional region opportunity for expansion existed only in British Borneo. The move of the Chartered Bank into Brunei seemed to the Hongkong Bank a challenge; they would now move into the previously exclusively Chartered Bank area of Sarawak.

The Managers concluded that in other countries either the Bank was not permitted to expand, for example, the Philippines, Thailand, Burma, and Sri Lanka, or there was no business justification for expanding. In this last the Managers may have been correct at the time; funds could be acquired relatively cheaply on the local interbank markets, but the position would change when such funds became expensive. When conditions in fact changed, the authorities were usually unwilling to permit the Bank to establish new sub-agencies.

The conclusion of the Managers confirmed Turner in the conviction that he must look elsewhere. But the search would prove frustrating.

In November 1957 the Board were informed that a potentially suitable Swiss bank had been identified, but this initiative would soon be dropped. A suggestion both at a Board meeting and also independently from Leo

D'Almeda that the Bank open in Macau was frustrated until the early 1970s by regulations in that neighbouring Portuguese territory. In early 1958 the Bank acquired 12,000 shares of a Honolulu agency house, Theo H. Davies and Co., to be held by the San Francisco agency, the capital of which was accordingly increased. The Board also turned its attention to the loss of its capital investment in Hong Kong's Far Eastern Economic Review. E. Halpern's management had proved unsuccessful and, as relations between Karl Weiss, the founder and one of the first directors of the company, and Halpern, who may have initiated the idea for such a journal, soured, the company's financial position deteriorated. Turner advised the Board that a further $100,000 was being invested, of which the Bank's portion was $20,000, and its partners, Jardine Matheson, the Kadoories, and the South China Morning Post, Ltd. – in which last the Bank also had an interest – made up the balance. Dick Wilson was appointed editor, and the journal began its rise to journalistic acclaim for coverage of the Far East in dynamic times.

Towards the end of this inconclusive year the Hongkong Bank returned to the problem of negotiating with the Mercantile Bank, simultaneously considering for the first time entry into the Middle East and, through National and Grindlays Bank, into Africa. This will be considered in the following section.

The Bank had again identified a possible acquisition in Switzerland, but was advised of aspects unsatisfactory as far as the Hongkong Bank's requirements were concerned, unless 100% of the shares could be obtained. This proved impossible.

The one positive development was the Hongkong Bank's investment in the Trust Corporation of the Bahamas, Ltd, the principal shareholders being the Royal Bank of Canada, Montreal Trust Company, and Morgan, Grenfell and Co. The shares were tightly held but 300 at £28:5s (= £8,475 = $135,600) had been made available by these companies for the Hongkong Bank. Turner explained this development to the Board in terms of the possible need to transfer trust accounts handled by the Bank's own Hong Kong trust company should future conditions warrant it. The Board authorized a further investment as shares became available to a total of £250,000; Perry-Aldworth became a director of the company.

Policy discussions in 1959

Several factors conjoined in the first half of 1959 to encourage long-run thinking. First, with the successful completion of negotiations relative to the Mercantile Bank, the Hongkong Bank had broken with its tradition; an inhibition, perhaps, had been overcome. What the Bank would achieve in the future would not be achieved alone but in conjunction with another financial institution with a tradition equal to its own. There was still a real concern for 'digestion' of the first acquisition to be complete, but such caution would be effective only until the Board were confronted with another opportunity. Secondly, there was motivation: the Philippine legislature were engaged once again in an attack on foreign banks and there was a possibility, which in the event did not materialize, that foreign banks would be prohibited from accepting local deposits. This reinforced the need to consider extra-regional expansion. Thirdly, such expansion was facilitated by the announcement to the Board in May of tax concessions in Britain, which meant a saving, at the then current rates of interest, of £90,000 per annum in taxes on the Mercantile Bank's income and made it practical to consider further investments in British financial institutions. The overshadowing question of the BBME was a further stimulant to discussion, but the Board moved beyond the immediate situation to consider general questions.

In June the Board agreed unanimously that efforts should be made to diversify after the 'digestion' of the Mercantile – but as suggested above this qualification can be ignored. Once diversification is agreed, the danger of opportunities missed is realized. The element of chance takes no account of a bank's digestive time schedule.

Having agreed on the principle, the Board asked itself quite simply, Where? Directors recognized that sound banking opportunities were most likely to be found in developed countries requiring further development; they also were aware of the problems involved – the news from San Francisco continued to be discouraging. If the Bank entered a developed area *de novo*, its California experience suggested that it was likely to receive only 'left over' business; there appeared very little chance of acquiring control of any well-established bank. If the Bank entered a developed area either *de novo* or through buying control, it ran the risk of losing the profitable correspondent banking business with the target area which it then held.

The directors concluded that, despite the risks, expansion would most likely be in other undeveloped areas, the most obvious of which was, given past approaches, the Middle East.

At this point 'digestion' did play a role. The Board was aware of discussions relative to a tripartite merger involving the BBME, Grindlays, and the Hongkong Bank. This they saw as premature and they were particularly worried over the prospect of further investment in the Indian sub-continent where Grindlays was particularly strong. They suggested, as an alternative, that the Hongkong Bank consider underwriting the merger of the BBME and Grindlays.

But once again the Board was not master of the situation. The BBME rejected an alliance which would have a strong Indian overtone and approached the Hongkong Bank directly. Turner warned the Board on June 30, 1959, that to protect itself from corporate predators the board of the BBME intended, if the Hongkong Bank were unwilling to enter into discussions, to call up capital, increase its published reserves, and increase its overall dividend. The Hongkong Bank's Board was now confronted with a proposal which could never be repeated in its present form. They were better informed and experienced than they had been two years previously when the Mercantile Bank negotiations were first cut off.

The directors' consideration of long-run policy had now to be focused on an existing situation. Except for the timing the importuning of the BBME's directors was consistent with the Hongkong Bank's goals as agreed only three weeks previously. Not surprisingly they minuted that, if the price were right, 'such a merger would give the Bank a stake in an area where we are not at present represented and would cause very few integration problems as the two banks overlap only in London and Bombay.'

Accordingly, the Board of the Hongkong Bank agreed (i) to postpone indefinitely discussions with Grindlays and to so inform their chairman, (ii) to begin negotiations with the Inland Revenue relative to tax concessions similar to those agreed relative to the Mercantile Bank, and (iii) to appoint a subcommittee of the London Committee – Morse, Sir Edward Reid, and Perry-Aldworth – to negotiate with the board of the British Bank of the Middle East. Once again the Hongkong Bank's hand had been forced.

Frustrated expansion – the Bank's planning efforts

Before turning to the dramatic events which led the Hongkong Bank to acquire the British Bank of the Middle East, before considering the problems of the embryo Hongkong Bank Group which were a consequence of the Bank's success, this history must record the Bank's frustrations as it sought opportunities for sound and legitimate expansion. 'Expansion' and 'diversification' can become catchwords; there comes a time when these are obvious things to do. The problem is illustrated in a brief 1959 conversation with a senior Bank Inspector; it was recalled by the 'junior':

JUNIOR: Why doesn't the Hongkong Bank take over another bank to expand our area of operation?
KNIGHTLY: Well, what bank do you suggest?
JUNIOR: I hadn't really got as far as thinking about what bank.

While the Bank's search for areas suitable for expansion were not systematically planned, Michael Turner did from time to time encourage tours and surveys which, by 1961, had covered much of the world; they revealed that opportunities for expansion were indeed limited. This is one reason why the Bank's successful moves may appear opportunistic. This is unfair. Turner had to react to opportunities since his own surveys suggested that an aggressive interventionist policy, given the Bank's personnel and financial resources, would be unsuccessful or even dangerous.

Europe
The Bank had been in the United States for some 75 years, but this did not guarantee success in California. As Congressman Benjamin Rosenthal told the Bank's representative, I.H. Macdonald, at a 1980 hearing relative to the Marine Midland Bank acquisition, 'Yes, but nobody ever heard of you.' The Bank's presence had been specialized.

The story in Europe was similar. The Hongkong Bank, as a British overseas bank, pioneered in Lyons and Hamburg, but was it, as Fivel-Démoret commented in the title of his essay, 'Busy, but too discreet?' In 1951 in an effort to be better placed for an increase in the Bank's French business, the Board authorized a move from Lyons to Paris, but little else was changed. In the 1950s the Hamburg Branch was even more limited in its operations than in the inter-war period. Nevertheless consideration had been given to a more active Bank role in Europe. After the Great War Hamburg Branch had taken the initiative, but nothing had been approved. After the Pacific War Muriel had encouraged a survey of Scandinavian countries, but banking regulations had prevented any further development at that time. Indeed, by 1954 Gray was able to inform Turner that, with the exception of Switzerland and Spain, 'all continental countries' had been visited – he did not define 'continental country'. Gray now intended to send M.D. Scott (East in 1925) on another round on his being assigned to London Office.

By 1960 there had been no innovation in the Bank's relations with the Continent and a more formal plan for investigation of opportunities was devised by Turner. This was to be undertaken by Lydall, whose French and German were considered adequate for the task and who was in a sense supernumerary in the London Office since he had been assigned there primarily to liaise with the newly acquired Mercantile Bank and particularly with Pow, its new Chief Manager. In July 1960, Turner asked Perry-Aldworth specifically:

(i) What business is it we want to do in Europe?
(ii) What methods are we going to adopt to get this business?
(iii) Who are we going to get to do it?

Turner noted that the Bank was already financing 'goods-on-the-water' business to Asia and, therefore, to expand in Europe meant undertaking some new task, for example, financing Continental trade with the United Kingdom or with North America, exchange arbitrage or commodity shunting, or financial participation in development projects. If any new ideas proved practical, would the Bank's present branches prove adequate or should the Bank open in, for example, Rotterdam, Brussels, Zurich, Geneva, or Frankfurt?

Turner added, significantly, that the Bank's experience 'elsewhere' suggested that, if the Bank were to buy an existing institution, the staff should be included in the transaction.

Accordingly Lydall set out. His reports were not encouraging.

Looking first at France and Germany where the Bank already had branches, Lydall concluded, for somewhat different reasons, that expansion was not practical. To finance British trade with the Continent would place the Hongkong Bank in competition with the clearing banks. In Germany bankers were on the boards of exporting manufacturers; these bankers were agents of the clearing banks and the conclusion was obvious. To enter into domestic banking would not be possible under existing German regulations; in France it would mean establishing a new bank at a time when trained French banking staff was scarce. Furthermore, interbank agreements and regulatory decrees limited the range of competition; to compete successfully in France would mean therefore following (or out-doing) the French custom of 'backhanders', a dangerous activity for a foreign bank.

Returning from the Netherlands Lydall reported that there was only one foreign bank doing local business – the Banque de Paris et des Pays-Bas, and that had been established before the Great War. Lydall reminded Perry-Aldworth of Dutch nationalism, citing the Bank's experience in Batavia. Competition would be limited as rates were controlled by the Central Bank, correspondent banking business would be lost, there were shortages of qualified bank staff and of housing, and, in view of the language difficulty, a Dutchman would have to be employed at a high salary.

These views were not challenged, but Stewart had reservations relative to Lydall's negative view of possibilities in Switzerland. Lydall argued that Gulf leaders already had unnumbered accounts in Swiss banks and that the Swiss Government was discouraging the opening of new accounts; he concluded that a Hongkong Bank branch would not receive deposits. Stewart noted, however, that the Group was 'giving Swiss banks more than they give us', and Musker, as manager of the BBME, argued that if the Group went in, the BBME should undertake the task. This in the end is what happened.

The Hongkong Bank negotiated in November 1960 with a Geneva bank, but the controlling interest was Jewish and the Hongkong Bank was beginning to recognize limitations to its policy initiative in view of its ownership of BBME. When Stewart took over in London he was able to assure Head Office that establishing a branch would not be that difficult, consideration of acquisition was dropped, and, with Turner as chairman, the BBME set up in Geneva.

Lydall concluded that the Hongkong Bank should for the time being concentrate on developing its traditional business. This recommendation was accepted. He also advised that there should be a European head office, based on the Continent, either at Paris or Hamburg. With this senior management disagreed, and it was carried no further.

Given these discouraging reports, the Bank focused on further development of its Asian trade finance.

Africa

If expansion in developed countries proved difficult, expansion in the Third World would be even less encouraging. In the Hongkong Bank's traditional region of operations, expansion was possible in the normal way, subject, however, to new regulatory restrictions. 'Expansion' as defined for the present discussion refers to new geographical areas, and one obvious potential was Africa. This was viewed by the Hongkong Bank in two contexts: (i) in consideration of acquiring British overseas banks with African business, for example, National and Grindlays and (ii) *de novo*. The Bank also separated North Africa, as being within the area of the BBME, and East Africa, as being within the orbit of other British overseas banks, from the balance of the continent. The Bank considered Southern Africa, Central Africa, and West Africa.

The Hongkong Bank had become involved with Bowmaker through Sir Arthur Morse; it therefore found itself in Central Africa, but the experience did not encourage further exposure, especially in view of the strong position of well-established British banks in the area and the discouraging view of the Central Bank as to the Hongkong Bank's opportunities there, a view confirmed by Knightly. Knightly's 1957 report stated two major obstacles to business in South Africa: (i) apartheid, which promised trouble for the future and (ii), in his opinion, the inefficiency of the average [white] South African – 'only a country possessing South Africa's natural riches could afford to maintain a people as inefficient.'

Turner sent Oliphant to Nigeria in early 1960 for a view of West Africa. There were already Dutch and American banks in the area, but Oliphant ascribed the presence of the former to the specialized nature of Dutch trade with the region and the latter to political motives. He noted that taxation was as high as in the United Kingdom, that there was a strong program of nationalization of staff but a complete lack of qualified local replacements, and that new local banks would be encouraged at the expense of foreign banks. The rampant corruption which would soon characterize the area was apparently not as yet the determining factor, but Oliphant did note the fact that established foreign banks had lent to local concerns on the same basis as to foreign firms – 'This', he wrote, 'proved expensive.'

With these negative reports it is not surprising that Turner proved unreceptive to a proposal from Hongkong Bank director Lawrence Kadoorie relative to a participation in an international consortium of banks to finance African development projects. Perry-Aldworth warned Turner that if the Bank went into African investment it would have to rely on the banks already there, on the Standard Bank and on Barclays, and that in any case the projects were more suitable for Government-to-Government financing.

Elsewhere

Despite the historical link through Macau with Brazil – or the fact of an early merchant agent in Chile (see Volume I) – the Hongkong Bank would not appear to have considered involvement in Latin America at this time. Its experience with Brazilian sterling bonds in the 1930s had been disastrous, but this would not have been a relevant factor. The North American position had been considered in the context of expansion of the HBC. The fact is, however, that there were limits to the Bank's resources; had Turner found a major opportunity it is not certain to what extent the Bank would have been in a position to exploit it.

This is exemplified by the Bank's approach to Australia. The Bank had obvious regional banking links with Australia, but that country's regulations prevented the establishment of an agency or branch there. This rule was of long standing and had indeed prevented the Chartered Bank from fulfilling the promise of its title 'of India, Australia and China'. However London-based banks had been established in the Australian colonies in the 1830s; some had failed, others had merged; three remained. In May 1961 rumours were circulating in the City that the Hongkong Bank might acquire an interest in the English, Scottish and Australian Bank, Ltd. The matter was in fact considered by the Board, but the idea was rejected in May 1961; it was, the Board decided, too much to digest.

The analysis had been sound. The Hongkong Bank was correct in supposing that its future lay in product and geographical diversification. Certainly it made sense to expand and to acquire suitable banks. What was not so certain was how these goals were to be achieved in the absence of any opportunity to implement the policy. Thus when, fortuitously, opportunity presented itself, the Bank reacted; policy must combine with chance to be effective. Even then there would be limits set by both finances and staff capacity, and clearly the Australian possibility had come too late. The Hongkong Bank had acquired the BBME, and the Hongkong Bank Group was faced with controversy; it was in need of an agreed 'imperial' policy.

The history now turns to a consideration of these positive developments and the problems they created.

THE ACQUISITION OF THE BRITISH BANK OF THE MIDDLE EAST

Regarding the British Bank of the Middle East, I know 'sweet nothing' about it.
Michael Turner, Chief Manager, the Hongkong Bank, 1954

Background

The rationalization of British Eastern banking
The Hongkong Bank's acquisition of the British Bank of the Middle East was not a replay of the Mercantile Bank take-over. It is true that price alone made George Marden's steady buying of Mercantile shares a sound investment – whether or not his angry Shanghai threat played a role in his actual decision – but once the shares were acquired and on offer the situation took on a special feature which was unique. Nevertheless, there were common factors at work which made the Hongkong Bank's decision consistent with the requirements of the late 1950s and consistent also with its subsequent decision to negotiate with the British Bank of the Middle East.

Size in banking was already a key factor. The several British Eastern banks, the BBME, the Ionian Bank, the Eastern, the National Bank of India, Grindlays, the Mercantile Bank of India, and even the larger banks – the Chartered Bank and the Hongkong Bank – needed to consider a major reorganization and rationalization. Not that the chairmen could be expected to sit down together and work it out or that the Bank of England would make unsolicited, formal recommendations; as in the case of the Hongkong Bank and the Mercantile there had to be an element of chance and timing, with the Bank of England encouraging with a greater or less sense of urgency. Their main goal was to maintain a British banking presence, and in this they were successful.

The shake-out took place between 1957 and 1960: in 1957 the Chartered had taken over the Eastern Bank and the Cyprus branches of the Ionian, Grindlay's had merged with the National to form the National and Grindlays; in 1958 the weakened Ionian Bank disappeared; in 1959 the Hongkong Bank had acquired the Mercantile and in 1960 the BBME; in 1960 Lloyds Bank sold its India and Pakistan branches to the National and Grindlays and took back a 25% interest.

In 1958 the BBME, liquid and profitable, despite potential political troubles in the Middle East, stood alone. It had for some years been the subject of City take-over rumours, on occasion these were connected with the Hongkong Bank. Furthermore at that time Grindlays was not then out of danger.

As Geoffrey Jones relates in his history of the British Bank of the Middle East (formerly the Imperial Bank of Persia), the BBME board had not been unaware of its endangered position. In 1954 the BBME chairman had attempted to engineer a merger with the Chartered Bank but had been thwarted by H. Musker, the General Manager, who had been concerned, *inter alia*, for the fate of the staff; Musker succeeded in obtaining an adverse vote by his directors. There were rumours in the City that the Hongkong Bank was the aggressor; the Bank's files reveal only one 1954 reference to the BBME in this context – the Turner quote cited above.

In 1956 Morse reported that the BBME's chairman, Sir Dallas Bernard, was apparently considering approaching the Chartered Bank a second time. In a letter to Turner he wondered why Bernard had not turned to the Hongkong Bank and he asked for Turner's reaction. Turner wrote to Morse a frank negative. In 1957 there were further rumours that the Hongkong Bank was seeking a merger, but this was false and the Bank had once again to deny its interest. The real test of its intentions came in late 1958 when the Hongkong Bank had committed itself to serious and eventually successful negotiations with the Mercantile Bank.

To avoid a take-over by a financial group primarily seeking the BBME's assets, the BBME considered a merger with Grindlays, a tripartite arrangement with both Grindlays and the Hongkong Bank, and further defensive action in an effort to remain independent. In the end the BBME and the Hongkong Bank came together. How this happened is the subject of the present section.

The Hongkong Bank and the Imperial Bank of Persia/BBME in history
There had been throughout the history of the Imperial Bank of Persia/BBME various levels of relations with the Hongkong Bank, not the least of which (and certainly the least sentimental) was the fact that the Hongkong Bank did the bulk of its Middle East business through the BBME.

Other relationships have been mentioned from time to time in this history (see especially Volume I), but to recapitulate: the founding of the BBME as the Imperial Bank of Persia had come in 1889 at a time of Eastern promotions including the ill-fated Trust and Loan Company of China, Japan and the Straits. The Imperial Bank's first chairman, William Keswick, was also chairman of the Trust and Loan Company; he had previously served as Chairman of the Hongkong Bank. The Hongkong Bank's former London Manager, David McLean, was also a member of the Imperial Bank's board of directors from its founding to 1903. When Sir Thomas Jackson returned from the East in 1902 he was elected a director and later became the chairman of the Imperial Bank of Persia (1908–1915). Undoubtedly it was Jackson who brought the retired V.A. Caesar Hawkins, whose last appointment had been as the Hongkong Bank's Yokohama Manager, onto the Imperial's board; he remained until 1939. In 1916 H.E.R. Hunter, the Bank's former Shanghai Manager, also became an Imperial director.

The new subsidiaries, 1955–1961   531

Since the Imperial Bank operated in the area from which the Sassoon family originated before its move to Bombay early in the nineteenth century, it is not surprising that their interests, represented on the Hongkong Bank from the founding of the provisional committee in 1864 to 1956, were also on the board of the Imperial Bank. At least two of the early Imperial Sassoon directors had previously served on the Hongkong Bank's Board.

The two banks had done business with each other in the normal way. However from 1906 to 1919 the Hongkong Bank was the BBME's Bombay agent when the latter had no branch there. In 1933 the BBME decided once again to close its Bombay branch and asked whether the Hongkong Bank would take over the agency; after much negotiation, the BBME decided however to deal with Lloyds Bank which, through its acquisition of Cox and Co., had offices 'in other towns in India'.

And now, in 1958 the BBME chairman – since 1955 when Lord Kennet resigned – was Sir Dallas Bernard. When he had been Jardine's taipan in Hong Kong he had served as a director of the Hongkong Bank from 1921–1928 and was Chairman for two difficult years, 1926–1928. Once returned to London he became a member of the London Committee on which he served from 1929 until war duties forced his resignation in 1939.[g] In 1932 he had protested vigorously to V.M. Grayburn over the enforced retirement of Sir Charles Addis, his father-in-law, ostensibly on grounds of age; now he was proving the validity of his arguments. Addis had been 70 when he retired; Sir Dallas Bernard, approaching 80, remained chairman of an important British overseas bank and, on the basis of the events to be recounted, there is no doubt Bernard remained more than capable. Ironically it was another son-in-law of Sir Charles Addis, Alexander Geddes, who would be an unsuccessful protagonist in the story.

These facts are interesting relative to the history of the overseas banking community in the City; they were undoubtedly factors in promoting good-will. They would appear, however, to have been of no practical concern to those involved in determining the fate of the BBME in the crucial years 1958–1960.

The events to June 1959

'Funnily enough', the Hongkong Bank's Paris Manager, H.V. Parker, wrote to his Chief Manager on November 28, 1958, Alexander Geddes, son-in-law of Sir Charles Addis, had been in the office two days previously sounding him out on an extraordinary proposal. The Lombard Banking Group, referred to as

---

[g] To put this into perspective – Michael Turner, the Hongkong Bank's Chief Manager during the BBME negotiations, joined London Office in 1926 when Bernard was Chairman of the Bank. By the time Turner came East in 1929 Bernard had already retired from the East and had just become a member of the London Advisory Committee.

'West End financiers', allegedly had a plan to make a £5 million take-over bid for the British Bank of the Middle East, strip its liquid assets, and then offer the empty branches to the Hongkong Bank to operate. Geddes wondered if the Bank would be interested; Parker suggested that perhaps, if it were, the interest would be shown elsewhere than in the Paris office.

The threat to the BBME was real enough and Sir Edward Reid had already alerted Michael Turner in Hong Kong. But he had dealt with the financial aspects; the Lombard Banking Group had no bank behind them and they needed funds. The idea of turning over the physical shell, 'for free' as it were, to the Hongkong Bank to facilitate their expansion into an area, possibly rehiring the abandoned BBME staff, was a new twist to the affair and was presumably designed to minimize the already apparent and not unexpected opposition of the Bank of England.

Apparently [Parker wrote] one of the many reasons given for refusal of the official blessing was that the Bank of England naturally would not approve of a take-over of the shares which would result in liquidation of the bank for the sake of the cash surplus which would accrue.

Geddes had the gall to say in effect that he and his West End friends, however, could collar the profit with a clear conscience since they would be able to state that they had 'arranged' for another bank to continue to operate the branches of the Bank of the Middle East.

It would be up to the Hongkong Bank.

This particular scheme had already caused rumours in the City. On November 11, two weeks before the conversation in the Paris office, Bernard, as chairman of the BBME, had acted defensively but decisively by raising the interim dividend (to be announced that evening) from 4% to $7\frac{1}{2}$%; at the same time he announced that the final dividend would be similarly increased – the BBME's fiscal year ended March 31. Obviously this had not proved sufficient to stop the manoeuvrings, despite Reid's assurances to Turner on November 14, although it had apparently checked the likelihood of their success.

As previously noted, the BBME deputy chairman, Sir Geoffrey Eley, had approached the Mercantile Bank in October; the Mercantile Board in effect rejected the offer in favour of a merger with the Hongkong Bank. There was some attraction, however, in a tripartite combination and Mealing certainly brought the BBME's approaches to the attention of Sir Edward Reid, the latter in turn sounded out Cobbold, the Governor of the Bank of England, who was much in favour. The Chartered Bank's acquisition of the Cyprus offices of the Ionian Bank had been coupled with the sale of the latter's Greek branches to the Commercial Bank of Greece; this was a loss to British overseas banking, and Cobbold was apparently anxious that there be no further eroding of Britain's financial position in the area.

When, however, negotiations began formally between the Hongkong Bank and the Mercantile, one of the Mercantile directors, E.J. Bunbury, insisted that the Hongkong Bank drop the BBME angle. As the Mercantile had already virtually rejected the idea on the grounds of the political uncertainty of the Middle East – just as early in 1959 the BBME was to reject overtures from Grindlays on the grounds of uncertainty in India – he was concerned that the Mercantile board might be unable to recommend a Hongkong Bank offer to its shareholders if the BBME were involved.

Sir Edward Reid, writing to Turner on November 20, had other reservations. He was concerned that two blocks of BBME shares might be in undesirable hands. There was no time for an investigation.

The impact of all this was therefore sufficient to cause the Hongkong Bank to postpone any further consideration of a relationship with the BBME.

There the matter rested until on January 28, 1959, a new tripartite combination was mooted in a conversation with Morse by the chairman of the National and Grindlays Bank, supported by Bernard with whom the latter had been in touch for some months. The initiative had been that of Grindlays, and it had been the BBME's chairman who recommended bringing in the Hongkong Bank. The actual position of the Hongkong Bank is difficult to assess, especially because in the end it was Bernard who in a sense broke with Grindlays and turned to deal solely with the Hongkong Bank in June.

The Bank of England supported the tripartite merger as solving the general British exchange banking problem; Cobbold specifically acknowledged however that any commercial banking decision was the responsibility of the several banks' directors acting on their responsibilities to shareholders. This dichotomy of approach was in a sense reflected by the initially favourable response by Perry-Aldworth in London, who advised Turner to 'think big', and in the subsequent reevaluation. The layman too senses the attractiveness of a comprehensive solution, but as the discussions proceeded practical problems of a 'commercial banking' nature intervened.

There would appear to have been several hesitations; some have been previously noted. First, the question of tax relief for the Mercantile Bank's income was not resolved until mid-May; secondly, the Hongkong Bank's Board were hesitant about any further acquisition until the Mercantile had been digested – a position which was quickly reversed in June and may therefore be considered from a practical viewpoint as inoperative; and thirdly, the Board was specifically hesitant about investment 'in and around' the Indian subcontinent and in East Africa.

One of the tasks of management is to educate their board of directors. The minutes show clearly that Turner was more enthusiastic about the tripartite deal than his fellow-directors, once the tax situation had been clarified. Against the 'digestion' policy there was the need for immediate consideration of diversification, with the apparently adverse Philippine and Indonesian developments particularly relevant. Nevertheless in June, following a discussion on the general expansion policy of the Bank described above, the Board agreed that the time was not ripe to go ahead with the tripartite plan.

There are several related decisions which suggest the cause of the Board's reluctance, especially in view of their decision that the Bank's expansion must come in less developed areas, was Grindlays. After all, when Sir Edward Reid reported in May that a client had been offered 25% of the shares of BBME at a time when those involved were wary of 'another Marden', the Board agreed that the Bank should attempt to purchase them – although not as the preliminary to a 'take-over'. The 25% offer did not in fact materialize, but the Board's reaction is significant; they were concerned with the fate of British Eastern exchange banking. The Board's policy discussions between April and June and the eventual decision to negotiate with the BBME, once Grindlays had been excluded from consideration, confirm the conclusion that the Board, while committed to expansion, were genuinely concerned about Grindlays' geographical coverage – Grindlays had 30 branches in India and Pakistan and 44 in East Africa, whereas the Hongkong Bank needed, it then thought, no more in the Indian sub-continent and none in East Africa.

In late June 1959 Stewart, who was acting Chief Manager during Turner's Home leave, informed the Board that the BBME had called off any tie with Grindlays and would welcome merger talks. He unwisely, given the importance and controversial nature of the subject, asked the directors for their agreement by circulation. Lawrence Kadoorie requested a meeting. At the June 30, 1959, meeting the Board of Directors, after considerable discussion, agreed to an acquisition, 'if the price were right'. The BBME's concern had also been with Grindlays' Indian connections. The geographical expertise which had once been the basis for British overseas banking was becoming the barrier to necessary merger considerations; the political risks in the 'other' area were seen as serious; each board assumed its shareholders would be hesitant to approve mergers which subjected them to these 'other' presumably more dangerous risks, although, unless this were to happen, no significant merger could take place and the rationalization of British overseas banking would not be accomplished.

Given this attitude, how are the Hongkong Bank's decisions explained? With regard to the Mercantile Bank, its Indian image and expertise should not be confused with the source of its income; this, the Hongkong Bank had early learned, came primarily from its activities outside India. The same might be said of the Hongkong Bank and China – but not, significantly, of the Hongkong Bank and Hong Kong. The Bank's acceptance of a merger with the Mercantile and its rejection of Grindlays were, therefore, consistent – with the added concern over Africa in its consideration of the latter.

The acquisition of the Mercantile Bank involved questions of rationalization of branch operations and eventual integration of staff serving in the same general region. Acquisition of Grindlays, whether or not part of some package deal, would intensify the problem. The attraction of the BBME to the Hongkong Bank's Board was therefore precisely because its operations were in an area where the Bank was not then represented – fulfilling the expansion policy requirements – and for this very reason would also cause 'very few integration problems', overriding the concern about digesting the Mercantile first.

In informing the Board of the new BBME development, Stewart also presented a warning. If the Hongkong Bank did not accept their invitation to discuss a merger, the BBME would at their annual meeting on July 14 recommend to the shareholders the call-up of £500,000 of capital, an increase in their published reserves, and an overall increase in their dividend. Such a visibly stronger position would affect the price of the BBME's shares. The Hongkong Bank's Board were impressed; they voted to negotiate and again appointed a sub-committee of the London Committee – Morse, Reid, and Perry-Aldworth – for the purpose.

The negotiations, July–December 1959

Tax relief and the preliminary negotiations

The BBME's threat to raise the overall dividend was double-edged. While it encouraged the Hongkong Bank to negotiate, it also gave an indication that bargaining on the ratio of the share exchange would be based on the knowledge that the BBME could and would, if negotiations failed, raise the dividend rate; the Hongkong Bank had to more than match that prospect. On the other hand the very feature of the BBME which had attracted the Board at its meeting of decision on June 30, 1959, seemed afterwards to require tough bargaining over the price. Although the lack of overlap (except in London and Bombay) made the BBME attractive because of the few 'integration problems', there would be in consequence no savings due to rationalization of the branch network.

Overriding these considerations, however, was the fact that the BBME was in a sound, liquid position, its investments almost entirely in sterling and in London, and its prospects in the developing Gulf something which offset specific political uncertainties in a politically uncertain world. On top of this, two major tax concessions were secured. First, double taxation relief for those on the London Register and subject to United Kingdom income tax was obtained to the extent of 2s:2d in the pound. Second, in November 1959 the

Hongkong Bank negotiated successfully with the Inland Revenue for an arrangement, similar to that with the Mercantile, whereby £6 million of BBME funds might be deposited at the nominal interest rate of $1\frac{1}{2}$% for tax-free investment in designated British securities; alternatively, the Hongkong Bank could work on the figure of £10 million from both banks, dividing the sum as they considered appropriate. This flexibility was particularly welcome.

The two parties first met formally on July 9 at which time Sir Dallas Bernard explained to Perry-Aldworth that, as the BBME was a Royally chartered bank, there were certain special features which had to be taken into account. The head office, for example, had to be in England and the bank's identity retained. Unfortunately neither Bernard nor the legal advisers were as familiar with the charter as they supposed; the problem was not what the charter contained but what it did not contain; however, no one discovered that until it was too late.

The auditors were then given a difficult task – to determine a fair share exchange ratio while each party kept back some of the 'inner' figures despite their favourable content. The Hongkong Bank's auditor, W.R.T. Whatmore of Peat, Marwick, Mitchell and Co., had been especially selected to work with the Bank on the Mercantile acquisition on the grounds of his hard-headed approach; he had done well and looked with equal caution at the accounts of the BBME. Not unexpectedly no agreement could be reached and, on October 8, Perry-Aldworth expressed the view to Bernard that there was 'nothing to be gained by continuing the discussions any further'. At this point the BBME released its 'true' profits to Perry-Aldworth, who cabled them to Hong Kong, where they caused an immediate reaction and change of position.

By October 13 it was clear that although the gap between the two banks' auditors remained surprisingly great – the Hongkong Bank's advisers recommending a 19:1 ratio, the BBME's a 12:1 ratio – the Hongkong Bank Board were informed that anything less favourable than 12:1 was unlikely to be accepted in view of the BBME's high income and intended dividend increase. The Hongkong Bank Board authorized the London sub-committee to offer 15:1 and in the next two weeks the BBME conceded up to 14:1. At that position they stuck and the Hongkong Bank Board minuted that it would be a pity if negotiations broke down when the difference between them was so narrow.

Once this view has been expressed in acquisition negotiations the task is greatly simplified. The basic question is, Do you want this to happen? Accounting is an art; the accountants therefore returned to the figures and found that, after all and considering one thing and another, the higher price was more than justified; in this case 14:1 was not only justified but also, the Hongkong Bank's auditors suddenly concluded, 'a damn good buy'.

The new subsidiaries, 1955–1961

The terms of the final agreement

The Hongkong and Shanghai Banking Corporation on November 26, 1959, wrote to the directors of the British Bank of the Middle East offering to exchange 100% of the ordinary shares of the bank, £1 par value, for shares of the Hongkong Bank, $125 par value, both fully paid, at the ratio of fourteen of the former for one of the latter. As an alternative to this, the Hongkong Bank would be willing to pay 77s:6d per share to those who did not wish to accept the primary offer. The BBME Board accepted and an agreed announcement was made to shareholders on December 3, 1959, the offer to close on December 28 – or a later date up to January 19, 1960. The offer was ex-interim dividend.

The basis for the ratio expressed in the agreement was a letter from Whatmore dated November 2 in which he worked out, on the basis of the BBME's true profits, the market price of the Hongkong Bank's shares, and the likely tax agreement with the Treasury that, if total assets of the BBME were £7.5 million (they were just over £8 million), then (i) the ratio of 14:1 was correct on the basis of the post-merger market price of the Hongkong Bank shares assuming a pro-rata decline, (ii) the Hongkong Bank could afford to pay a 25% dividend on the new shares created subject to the Treasury permitting a tax-free fund of £5.5 million (£6 million was agreed on January 21, 1961) calculated to earn a net £123,750.[h]

Given the auditor's calculation of 79s per share for BBME, he recommended a cash alternative offer of 77s (subsequently agreed at 77s:6d), to encourage acceptance of the basic share offer.

Other conditions of the offer had become standard: for example, the BBME would not disclose its inner reserve position; there must be acceptances for 90% of the shares (or less if the Hongkong Bank agreed) by the closing date. This last reveals that the Bank, once it had obtained acceptances of 90%, intended to exercise its rights under the Companies Act 1948 to acquire the balance compulsorily at the rates stipulated in the offer. The day after the offer was posted, however, Perry-Aldworth had to write Turner, 'I regret to have to inform you that the lawyers on both sides have slipped up badly...'. The BBME had been incorporated by Royal charter; the relevant provisions of the Companies Act (Section 209) did not apply. Turner gives the credit for this discovery to the BBME general manager's private secretary, Miss Hilary

---

[h] The market value of Hongkong Bank shares was £60 or 1200s, of BBME shares 58s (× 14 = 812s); on this basis the post-acquisition value of the Hongkong Bank share would be reduced to 1110s, which divided by 14 is equal to 79s. But this was Whatmore's valuation of the BBME share assuming a 25% dividend and the £60 value of the Hongkong Bank share. BBME, with profits at £1.6 million (gross) or, say, £0.8 million (net), could afford to pay a dividend of 25% less tax, absorbing £306,000. 'If this dividend is put on a yield basis equivalent to that of the Hongkong Bank, the market value of the shares of the BBME should be approximately 79s.'

McCormick. The Hongkong Bank should have recalled from its own experience that a general ordinance dealing with Hong Kong companies would not affect the Hongkong Bank under its special ordinance – there had been cases recounted, see Chapter 3, of a parallel ordinance having to be passed just for the Bank. The position was the same in England. The Hongkong Bank had no right to acquire the last 10% of outstanding shares under compulsion.

The inability of the Bank to force 100% acceptance made Perry-Aldworth and his London associates naturally concerned over a series of press articles which criticized the deal on the basis of failure to reveal inner reserves. The Bank's stipulation that inner reserves not be revealed – it was one of the conditions of the offer – led some journalists to conclude that there was something underhanded going on. The hidden wealth of the BBME was probably being bought at a bargain price by the Bank, otherwise why would there be objection to BBME shareholders being told what their bank was worth. Indeed, if they were not told, how could they decide whether to accept the offer?

The *Investor's Chronicle* wrote that the clause calling for non-disclosure of inner reserves '...is certain to bewilder the shareholder and make it difficult for him to judge the merits of the proposed merger even though it carries the recommendation of his directors [December 11, 1959]'. The articles in the *Sunday Despatch* and the *Sunday Express*, December 13, 1959, were stronger.

These articles, written against a background of questionable take-overs and reports critical of the concept of inner reserves, neglected the exception on this subject relative to banks, shipping, and insurance companies. Also neglected was the offer letter's well-publicized opinion of the auditors – there was a veiled suggestion that auditors were in a position to be in on such a deal. The attacks were directed against the BBME board, including specifically Bernard and Eley; the Hongkong Bank itself was not criticized.

Perry-Aldworth noted (i) that the Mercantile Bank deal had not been questioned on these grounds, but that (ii) an independent assessor had been brought in by the Mercantile to give his advice. When contacted by the *Daily Telegraph*, he put the position with sufficient clarity as to obtain a fair assessment the following day. On December 15, the *Telegraph*'s account reported on the work of the auditors, explained that revelation of the BBME's reserves would not facilitate assessment of the offer without revelation of the Hongkong Bank's reserves, commented critically on the principle of inner reserves but accepted that it was part of the system under which the banks operated and could not be changed suddenly for this specific case.

In follow-up letters to reluctant BBME shareholders in February the Hongkong Bank pointed out that if, for example, a shareholder had 200 BBME shares his 1959 dividend had been £18:17s:6d net of tax at the standard rate of 7s:9d in the pound. If these 200 shares were exchanged for fourteen Hongkong Bank shares (+cash for the $\frac{4}{14}$ths share due) the net dividend would be £29:5s, assuming the current rates and relief from double taxation (giving an effective standard rate of 5s:5d in the pound). There seemed little need to know about inner reserves.

The atmosphere was, however, in danger of becoming unfriendly and one shareholder who had accepted the offer asked to withdraw. Perry-Aldworth was at first inclined to agree, but on legal advice he refused; such an acceptance could have encouraged a sufficient number of withdrawals to endanger the success of the offer. For the same reason the Bank decided they would declare the offer unconditional when some 75% of the shares had accepted. This would protect those who had accepted and prove the Bank's determination to acquire the bank. The percentage of 75% was decided on the grounds that the Treasury's tax concession would probably be operative provided the Bank owned at least this percentage of the issued capital.

In fact the Bank made the offer unconditional on December 30, 1959, with $82\frac{1}{2}$% acceptances of which 10% were for cash.

By the latest date stipulated in the offer, January 19, 1960, the Hongkong Bank had received acceptances for 97% of the issued shares of the BBME. In the correspondence complex schemes were dreamed up for bringing the bank within the Companies Act and then taking it out again or of revising the charter, etc., but as time went by all this seemed as unnecessary as it was impractical. With so few shares held by the public, they could no longer be quoted on the Stock Exchange; the bank could and eventually did suspend payment of dividends, albeit for tax reasons unrelated to the minority shareholder. On March 10, 1960, the Hongkong Bank wrote the remaining shareholders that the original offer had lapsed but renewed the offer on adjusted terms, as the offer was now ex-dividend an additional payment of 1s:6d would be made per BBME share acquired. Eventually this general offer too was withdrawn.

Slowly the remaining shareholders were being contacted personally; for the next two years the Hongkong Bank waited for estates to be settled and beneficiaries to be located. And then it was down to a single Yorkshireman with 62 shares. The Bank wrote, attempted to engineer a chance meeting at the local pub, but suddenly withdrew the pressure; what if the shareholder in his annoyance provided in his Will that the shares were not to be sold? The Bank waited as bonus share issues increased his holding to 86. Then in 1972 he passed on. After negotiations with his executors, it was July 1973 before the BBME became at last a wholly owned subsidiary of the Hongkong Bank.

IDENTITY AND THE IMPERIAL VIEW

> I was extremely glad to hear that four of the BBME's staff took part in this year's production.
>
> Michael Turner, Chief Manager, the Hongkong Bank

Even small signs of cooperation were appreciated. Answering an appeal from the London Office's dramatics society in June 1961, Turner approved a donation of £100; his further comment is quoted above.

'There is a subtle difference', Perry-Aldworth wrote to Michael Turner in April 1960, between 'We shall continue to operate,' and his amended form, 'We are continuing to operate.' Thus in the BBME Chairman's first post-acquisition speech, a possible conflict was placed in focus. The initial working out of the role of the various subsidiary banks in the Hongkong Bank Group is the subject of this section.

GROUP FINANCES

The conflict stated

The directors and Chief Manager of The Hongkong and Shanghai Banking Corporation as a bank holding company were now responsible to their shareholders, to their constituents, and to various regulatory bodies for the operation of four banks: The Hongkong and Shanghai Banking Corporation, qua bank, the Hongkong and Shanghai Banking Corporation of California, the Mercantile Bank Limited, and the British Bank of the Middle East. This was the embryo 'Hongkong Bank Group' which, some might have supposed, could now be rationalized to meet the convenience of the senior board and the shareholders to whom they were responsible. There were however special factors and in some cases overriding constraints which in effect limited the Hongkong Bank Board's range of manoeuvre; the consequence was partial rationalization and the continuation of anomalies which would render the organizational structure unstable into the 1980s.

Working on the assumption that total integration was the most profitable solution in the abstract, the Board were faced with insuperable management and control factors. Simply put, the executive staff of the other banks had not been through the Hongkong Bank's London Office. This brought about a historical change in Hongkong Bank procedures. At a later stage, for example, lending limits were placed on the Group's Managers; previously Hongkong Bank Managers had been limited only by their own branch funds and by standard regulations as to the acceptable uses of funds. The change did not come, however, as a Hongkong Bank innovation forced for the occasion, it had

The new subsidiaries, 1955–1961

been standard practice in the Mercantile Bank and was adopted for the Group.

There were absolute restraints on the Board independent of the question of the Hongkong Bank's capabilities. The California subsidiary had been formed because the functions it was required to perform could not be undertaken by a branch. The British Bank of the Middle East would successfully urge that its independence as a bank was the *sine qua non* of its business in the Gulf.

Each bank, therefore, required a particular solution and followed a different course of development. As for the California bank, since it had to remain separate and since management by a Foreign staff officer who was virtually nothing more than a 'branch manager' under Head Office control had already proved ineffective, Turner, as previously noted, upgraded that bank's Board of Directors in an attempt to improve its image as an independent operation.

Decisions on the Mercantile and BBME were affected by the issue of taxation. While management problems might suggest for a time the independence of the banks, the tax savings to be achieved by moving the maximum of earning assets to the Hongkong Bank would maximize the net income of the Group, that is, the 'imperial' or corporation-wide view. But banks require reserves and the preservation of various ratios, including capital/assets; on the other hand the Group's reserves stood behind the subsidiary banks.

The Hongkong Bank's Chairman would find that it was virtually self-contradictory to attempt to retain the independent organization of a subsidiary if, in fact, holding company control was so all-pervasive that the subsidiary's balance sheet made no sense by itself and if its board of directors lacked the authority appropriate to highly qualified bank directors. Yet, at first, the continued goodwill of the several sets of directors was essential; through them came the very important goodwill of the constituents.

This contradictory situation was even more apparent once the executive staff became interchangeable.

Consequently it is not surprising to find that the Mercantile Bank became more quickly integrated; it was in the same area, rationalization was accepted by constituents, the close connection between the Mercantile and the Hongkong Bank well-known and understood in an area where the Hongkong Bank itself was a leading financial institution. For these reasons the Hongkong Bank could 'drain' the Mercantile of its earnings. The Mercantile would show some initial growth but by the mid-1960s could be seen to be an 'auxiliary' of the parent institution.

On the other hand the Hongkong Bank accepted that the Middle East was not its area. The BBME needed to be preserved as a credible bank; it had, the Hongkong Bank's Chief Manager conceded with some reluctance, to have a self-explanatory balance sheet, and its staff, with their experience in the region, had, for the time at least, to remain separate.

Taking these factors into account, similar financial analysis would lead to totally different organizational decisions. For a time implementation of the 'imperial view', while accepted even by Sir Dallas Bernard in principle and in part, was subordinated to the continuing need for the separate identities of the several members of the Hongkong Bank Group.

In the story which follows, the principal focus is on the BBME; it succeeded in retaining its funds and its 'face'. This is contrasted with the fate of the Mercantile Bank, a fate which was understood by its directors and staff as inevitable, though in sentimental terms regretted. A typical staff reaction would be that of L.G. Atterbury whose career involved eighteen years with the Mercantile Bank before acquisition, fifteen years (to 1974) with the Hongkong Bank in the East, followed by a further four years as Hongkong Bank Manager, Manchester.

My feelings are not for having worked for the Mercantile Bank, but for working with the Hongkong Bank. I've long since lost my sole dedication to the Mercantile Bank, transferred it totally to the Hongkong Bank, and if I had the same choice of career to make all over again, my choice would be exactly the same.

The first calculations

The two acquired banks had been bought by issuing new shares and by paying out cash. The former ranked *pari passu* with the old shares for dividends and the latter involved an opportunity cost, the loss of interest on the sum paid out. Offsetting these new 'costs' were the dividends paid by the subsidiary banks to the parent corporation now holding 100% of their share capital. Overall the Group Accounts might show a gain, but the holding company was also an operating bank, and the acquisitions must not be allowed to show as unprofitable on the Hongkong Bank's own banking accounts.

The first task is to examine the overall contribution of the acquisitions.

The Mercantile Bank
The calculations arising from the agreement with Inland Revenue relative to the deposit of £4 million at $1\frac{1}{2}$% are shown in Table 12.3 as £173,000. But the dividends for 1960 paid by the Mercantile Bank to the Hongkong Bank totalled only £225,000 against 'costs' to the Hongkong Bank of £377,000. The solution to this problem will be considered below.

Table 12.3 *The Hongkong and Shanghai Banking Corporation*
Impact of tax concessions relative to the Mercantile Bank
(pounds sterling)

Revenue (net adjusted profits)	570,000[c]
Cost in additional HSBC dividends 295,473[a]	
Loss of interest on cash purchases 81,300[b]	377,000
Net gain to the Hongkong Bank	173,000

[a] On 98,491 shares
[b] Cash cost of £1,626,000 @ 5%
[c] Profits after adding back the £140,000 income lost by the transfer to the 'tax-free' fund.

Table 12.4 *The Hongkong and Shanghai Banking Corporation*
Impact of tax concessions relative to the BBME
(pounds sterling)

£6 million at 1½% on which HSBC earned 5% net gain =	210,000
9 months revenue pro rated to one year	989,497
Revenue:	1,199,497
Cost of shares obtained for cash = £656,000	
Loss of income at 5% on £656,000	32,800
Cost of HSBC dividend on additional shares	501,373
Net gain = Revenue less loss of income and cost	665,324

The British Bank of the Middle East

The Hongkong Bank made the offer firm on December 30, 1959. Despite the fact that the BBME had not become a wholly owned subsidiary the Bank decided to act, to the extent possible, as if it were. Calculations for 1960 indicated that the deal had in fact been sound – the net gain to the Hongkong and Shanghai Bank for the nine months following the close of the BBME's financial year was £665,324, including £210,000 in interest differential in consequence of the £6 million 1½% deposit permitted by the Treasury, as shown in Table 12.4. This compares with the Mercantile Bank's contribution on similar calculations of £326,000.

At the time these calculations were made the Hongkong Bank had been represented on the board of BBME by Morse and Perry-Aldworth for some nine months. Two members of the BBME board joined the London Committee, Bernard, who had previously served from 1929 to 1939, and Sir Alec Kirkbride. There were now twelve members on the Committee, which Turner (and probably Morse) considered too many, but there was no alternative given the precedent of the Mercantile Bank and, as Perry-Aldworth hopefully observed, they probably would not all attend.

The British Bank of the Middle East was now a member of the Hongkong Bank Group, a 99+% owned subsidiary of the Hongkong Bank. What role would it play?

The imperial view vs the status of the BBME in the Gulf

The imperial view might be said to include two separate issues, (i) financial and (ii) all others. In the second category would be coordination and rationalization of business, mutual recommendations to constituents, and similar terms of service and pensions. As for terms of service and related matters, the Hongkong Bank had advantages; there could be no objection from the subsidiaries to standardization on Hongkong Bank terms. Rationalization of business caused more concern to the Mercantile Bank than to the British Bank of the Middle East; the former overlapped in key areas with the Hongkong Bank, the latter did not. This was, in any case, a matter requiring full consideration and long-term solutions.

The imperial problem arose in a more immediate form in the financial category and involved the 'image' of the BBME in the Gulf. Ironically, Sir Edward Reid when first writing about the BBME had seen it possibly merging with the Mercantile under the Hongkong Bank; he had commented that, as it had changed its name several times in the past decade, it was not, like the Mercantile, a household word. But virtually from its arrival in the Gulf it had been the BBME, and there it was a household word, and there it mattered very much.

The figures provided above show a net gain to The Hongkong and Shanghai Banking Corporation, qua corporation, of approximately £700,000 after offsetting the additional cost of the dividends on shares issued to acquire the BBME. The annual dividend of the BBME, however, 99+% payable to the Hongkong Bank, would be, say, £200,000, that is, less than the £500,000 required to pay the dividends on shares issued to acquire the BBME. Thus the Hongkong Bank, qua bank, would be paying dividends for which it had an inadequate income offset. This would appear satisfactorily in the Group Consolidated Accounts but, given the public focus on the Hongkong Bank's own performance, might prove unsatisfactory.

A more substantive imperial problem arose from the fact that funds with the Hongkong Bank, qua bank, could earn a higher return than funds left with a subsidiary with head office in Britain. The obvious solution was to devise methods by which the funds of the subsidiaries could be transferred. The most profitable way would be to transfer before U.K. income tax, but the Treasury limited this to the deposit of £6 million (in the case of the BBME) with the Hongkong Bank; the BBME earned $1\frac{1}{2}\%$ on which it paid tax, the Hongkong Bank earned 5% on which it paid no U.K. tax. The terms of the tax concession stated the net amount which could be transferred under this arrangement. There was however no Treasury, tax-related restriction on the transfer of funds from the subsidiaries if U.K. tax had been paid on the funds to be transferred; the advantage then came from future earnings on the funds transferred.

These additional funds could be transferred in the form of dividends, but this was thought at first to be limited by the fact that the BBME was not a wholly owned subsidiary and the minority shareholders, few as they were, would benefit. The Mercantile's board had agreed to pay a 'management fee', a device originally brought to the Hongkong Bank's attention when it was planning its California subsidiary; the Hongkong Bank expected the BBME to do the same.

In achieving the imperial goal of maximizing income from Group funds, the funds normally available for the development of the subsidiary had been transferred. The funds deposited with the Hongkong Bank under the terms of the tax concession were still on the subsidiary's books, but funds paid as a management fee or paid in dividends were not. Carried to the extreme there would be no growth of published reserves, no increases in capital. If the subsidiary's business were growing, this would affect the capital/assets and other ratios by which the soundness of a bank is judged; the failure of shareholders' funds to grow with the business would be a factor the ordinary constituent, even the savings bank depositor, would notice.

The Hongkong Bank could not order such transfers except through the board of directors of the subsidiary. Even if, as with the Mercantile, the Hongkong Bank held 100% of the shares, the directors were seen legally as independent; they were there to act in the best interest of the subsidiary as a separate entity. Were that not so, there would be no point to an independent bank, carrying on its business under a well-known name. If the Hongkong Bank did not own 100% of the shares, as in the case of the BBME, the situation seemed even more difficult; minority shareholders could, in theory, sue the directors for failing to manage the affairs of the bank in their interest. The payment of a management fee was particularly contentious. Indeed, it was for this reason that Section 209 of the Companies Act existed (see above); it was for this reason that its inapplicability in the case of the Royally chartered BBME was taken so seriously. By the time the outside shareholder numbered but one, however, the Hongkong Bank's management had in reality a free hand.

The attempts of the Hongkong Bank to manage its subsidiaries as if they were 'in-house' branches would be fraught with frustration. The bank holding company cannot override the responsibility of the directors of the operating banks who serve not only the shareholders, in this case the holding company, but also the constituents – and are responsible for adherence to any regulatory requirements established by the various national jurisdictions. The holding company can absorb the subsidiary and operate it or it can leave it as an independent bank with a responsible board of directors; it cannot do both. If the members of the board have had a long association with their bank, if they are experienced in dealing with their particular business, they are not likely to be totally controlled by two directors appointed to represent the interests of the Hongkong Bank on the board. The Hongkong Bank should have learned that lesson in California.

This general point is further supported by the existence of minority shareholders, even if they represent but a fraction of 1% of the total – at the end of June 1960 there were 6,120 of two million shares in minority possession. Nevertheless, exhaustive legal and accounting analysis led to the conclusion that (i) the BBME under a Royal charter could undertake anything it wished, subject to revocation of the charter, (ii) the Companies Act empowered the authorities to investigate but did not permit the usual remedies, and (iii) therefore, although shareholders could sue the directors for damages or appeal for revocation of the charter, neither course was likely – if only because most of the minority shareholders were dead and their estates merely in the process of being wound up. Even then, there remained doubts, and the Hongkong Bank acted cautiously until the minority was reduced to the single Yorkshireman; nor did it agree to an increase in the capital of the BBME until the minority shareholders had been virtually eliminated (1962).

To these general considerations must be added the particular position of the BBME in the Gulf. Assuming that the BBME had, because of transfers to the Hongkong Bank, failed to build up its reserves and then faced difficulties, the Hongkong Bank would come to the aid of its 'wholly owned' subsidiary. But, as the BBME Chairman, Sir Dallas Bernard, pointed out, this was not enough. The man in the Gulf did not know the Hongkong Bank and did not study its balance sheet; nor would he understand that his deposit in one bank was somehow guaranteed by another bank. The BBME's income was greatly enhanced by exclusive banking concessions, especially in Kuwait, where the Ruler was under political pressure to cancel or modify the arrangements. There had to be, as Bernard put it, sufficient in the shop-window to convince customers that the BBME remained a vital, growing, and liquid banking institution.

Thus the Hongkong Bank's expectation that the BBME directors should recognize that what was good for the Group was good for the BBME was bound to be frustrated. The Hongkong Bank had agreed that the BBME should operate its own branches with its own staff under its own directors. This being so, there was a limit to what the Hongkong Bank's representatives on the BBME board could and should be able to dictate. Against the imperial income advantage through tax differentials which suggested transfer of funds, the proper management of the BBME qua separately incorporated bank required adequate growth through retention of sufficient earnings to permit an increase in both capital and published reserves.

But establishing the principle did not determine the amount.

The specific BBME proposals

Sir Dallas Bernard acknowledged that, in round figures, the additional dividend pay-out to former shareholders in the BBME was costing the Hongkong Bank £500,000 p.a. but that the BBME dividends were only £200,000. It did not follow from this that the balance (net of the deposit of £6 million into the Group's tax-free fund) should be paid over to the Hongkong Bank in the 'imperial' interests. Bernard reminded his colleagues that the BBME's capital/assets ratio was declining and that the Kuwaiti authorities, whose deposits accounted for close to half the total deposits of the bank, were reportedly being pressed by the First National City Bank of New York to place their funds in a bank with larger resources. Had the acquisition by the Hongkong Bank not taken place, the directors had planned a rights issue at a premium sufficient to increase capital by £500,000 with the premium augmenting published reserves to the extent of £400/£500,000. The acquisition did not affect the need to effect an increase in published shareholders' funds of a similar amount.

The BBME as a subsidiary of the Hongkong Bank could in theory borrow from the Hongkong Bank in a crisis. Given its business focus on the Gulf, this was not a practical proposition. The BBME had either to stand on its own feet or withdraw from business. To the directors who understood the traditions in the Gulf this conclusion seemed incontrovertible.

This position was embodied in Bernard's notes dated July 17, 1961, for presentation to his board. These views were well-known to Perry-Aldworth who had been conducting a lengthy correspondence both with Michael Turner and with G.O.W. Stewart, his Deputy Chief Manager, who would soon be coming to London to replace Perry-Aldworth on the latter's retirement. Turner was never fully convinced, but, as stated above, if the BBME were to operate as a bank with a separate identity, its board of directors made the decisions.[i]

---

[i] Perry-Aldworth was having trouble even getting Musker, the BBME's General Manager, on his own board – it was contrary to City practice. But the BBME, Turner argued, was an overseas trading bank, an exchange bank. Eventually, with the forceful support of Sir Arthur Morse, Musker came on the board. This, however, was typical of the early frustrations. It was a repeat of the story of Wardle and the Mercantile Bank board.

Specifically Bernard, on the assumption that 1961's available after-tax profit would be £1 million (in contrast to earlier predictions during acquisition of £0.8 million), recommended a transfer from inner reserves of £400,000 plus the appropriation of £100,000 from the bank's Share Premium Account to finance a bonus issue and increase paid-up capital from £2 million to £2.5 million. He also recommended that the £1 million profits be appropriated as follows:

Transfer to Reserve	£100,000
Write off Premises	£50,000
Dividend	£200,000
Service Fee to Hongkong Bank	£300,000
Contingency Account (inner reserves)	£350,000+

From 1961 and 1962 the Hongkong Bank would receive from BBME:

	1961	1962
Dividend	£200,000	£250,000
Service Fee	£300,000	£300,000
Interest on deposit	£250,000	£250,000
	£750,000	£800,000

This would more than cover the cost of the additional dividends and Bernard saw his recommendations as a compromise; the Hongkong Bank did not. Nevertheless there was force behind Bernard's arguments. Aside from the basic point of the need for the BBME to develop as if it were an independent bank, there was once again the tax question. Anything paid to the Hongkong Bank as a service fee would lose its status as a tax-paid sum so far as providing for losses was concerned, and, if the Hongkong Bank were obliged to refund the service fee because the BBME had insufficient reserves to meet bad debts, such amounts refunded would have the status of ordinary income of the BBME.

As far as the published accounts were concerned, these are shown for the relevant years in Table 12.5, from which it can be seen that Bernard's goals were accomplished, although one year later. The delay was due in major part to the problems created by the existence of minority shareholders and to the time involved in the procedures for the bonus issue once the legal opinions had been evaluated.

As early October 1961 a draft had been prepared for the necessary motion to be introduced at the 73rd Annual General Meeting of the British Bank of the Middle East, March 13, 1962. It called for the capitalization of £500,000 by the pro-rata allotment of 500,000 shares of £1 each, fully paid. Of this sum £400,000 would be from Reserves and £100,000 from the Share Premium Account; the Reserves were reinstated by transfer from unpublished

Table 12.5 *The British Bank of the Middle East Shareholders' funds, 1960–1962*
(in millions of pounds sterling)

	March 30	December 31		
	1960[a]	1960[a]	1961	1962
	Actual	Actual	Bernard[b] Actual	Actual
Capital				
Authorized	2.5	2.5	2.5 2.5	2.5
Paid-up	2.0	2.0	2.5 2.0	2.5
Share Premium Account	1.0	1.0	0.0 1.0	0.0
Reserves	2.2	2.5	2.6 2.6	2.7
Profit and Loss Account	0.17	0.17	na 0.23	0.24
Shareholders' funds[c]	4.5	4.8	na 4.9	5.4

[a] Note the nine month period as the BBME changed its reporting date.
[b] As recommended by the BBME Chairman, Sir Dallas Bernard.
[c] As published.
Source: Hongkong Bank or BBME Annual Reports and D.G.M. Bernard, 'Notes by the Chairman for Directors', July 17, 1961.

contingency funds, that is, from inner reserves. At the same time transfers were being made to published and inner reserves.

In 1961 the BBME acquired 100% of the shares of Société Chérifienne de Gérance et de Banque and re-launched it as the British Bank of the Middle East (Morocco) S.A. The Hongkong Bank also accepted that the BBME had 49% of the shares of the British Bank of Iran and the Middle East, for which, if anything went seriously wrong, it would be responsible.

The British Bank of the Middle East would then continue as a bank in its own right with capital and reserve growth and sufficient contingencies to counter likely disasters. Both the shop-window and contingencies would be provided for, but the Hongkong Bank would hold the Group's true inner reserves; Bernard had convinced the Hongkong Bank that in international banking a simplistic interpretation of the 'imperial interest' was not practical; the Hongkong Bank had established its own central authority.

THE QUESTION OF BRANCHES

One of the advantages of a 'Group' would be rationalization and thus economies of operation. The most visible aspect of any effective policy would be the question of 'branches'. This can be considered at various levels – who is the final authority for the opening, closing, or developing of a branch, the particular bank's board of directors or the Hongkong Bank's Chief Manager? Was there to be absolute rationalization in the sense that only one member of the Group would have an office in any one city or country, or was rationalization to be based on individual office profitability, that is, if more than one office in a town were profitable, more than one office could be justified.

At still another level, branch policy could be considered a 'test' of the Hongkong Bank's sincerity relative to permitting the acquired banks to continue as viable, aggressive entities. Approached in this way, the issue was sensitive, and it was not always handled sensitively by the Hongkong Bank's London officers who had direct contact with Mercantile Bank's management. As far as the BBME was concerned, the branch problem was not significant; the Hongkong Bank accepted the need for their office in Bombay and obviously for a head office in London. The two banks did not overlap elsewhere.

The branch policy should not have been an issue with the Mercantile Bank. From the first Turner had approved the Mercantile's new office building in Kuala Lumpur. Turner had also, reluctantly, agreed to the closure of the Hongkong Bank's agency in Sourabaya in 1958. Furthermore, the Hongkong Bank had brought the question of a branch in the Seychelles to the Mercantile's attention; they did not act, and Barclays went in – with quite favourable consequences. But when Turner in February 1960 issued instructions through Lydall to Wardle for the closure of the Mercantile's sub-agency on Rajawongse Road, Bangkok, a minor emotional crisis developed.

There were four Hongkong Bank Group offices in Bangkok, the principal branches of the Hongkong Bank and the Mercantile respectively, and two sub-agencies – the Hongkong's on Suapah Road, the Mercantile's on Rajawongse Road. The last mentioned was not profitable and Turner wrote Lydall to discuss closure with Wardle, adding significantly, 'I should have preferred to close one of our own first.' That should have been received as a signal for delicate handling, instead there is evidence that the two sides met head on in London.

At first Wardle asked for time. Turner agreed to await developments at the half year, but when these proved unprofitable, he instructed Wardle to close down. Wardle, apparently accepting that he had had his chance, then went to his board with a recommendation to close. The board proved stubborn. While, in view of the Hongkong Bank's position, they agreed to closure, they requested 'compensation'. As the business of the Rajawongse Road sub-agency might be transferred to the Hongkong Bank's Suapah Road sub-agency (which was already profitable), the Mercantile board asked that a portion of the Hongkong Bank's profits be transferred to the Mercantile. Turner saw this as a complete misunderstanding of the relationship between the two banks and a failure to understand the imperial position.

Sir Edward Reid complained of the way in which the Hongkong Bank's representative on the board, Perry-Aldworth, had discussed the matter. Sir Arthur Morse suggested to Turner that he be briefed before the meeting and that he would then discuss the matter with Mealing as the board chairman. Instead Turner had been instructing Wardle – another bank's chief manager – through Lydall; Wardle had brought up these matters for approval to his board but with the underlying implication that, although introduced from 'below', the board had to accept because they had been ordered from 'above'.

Turner's insistence on dealing through Wardle, though a practical solution, made the Mercantile board's position very difficult. They might have been more willing to accept Wardle's 'recommendation' had not the Hongkong Bank's representative at the same time made it impossible for them not to realize that the 'recommendation' was in fact an 'order'. The controversy was a factor which obviated Perry-Aldworth's post-retirement position on the board, forcing the retention of Morse until Turner had returned to London and Stewart was in place.

The matter of the Rajawongse Road office was not quickly resolved because a new factor entered the discussion. An agency once closed was lost forever, but it was possible that, under pending Thai banking legislation, if the office still existed it might be transferred to Haadyai, an important market town in the southern rubber district. In November 1960 Turner agreed that implementation of the decision to close might be delayed until passage of the legislation. In the event, the Thai decision was negative, and the agency did in fact close.

There was never, in all this, a question of who ultimately was in charge. Nor was the issue in itself a question about the future of the Mercantile Bank. Turner's decision had been made, reluctantly, with that one sub-agency and its profitability in mind. Once again, however, the issue was seen to be about the limits within which the holding bank could instruct management of a subsidiary bank over the heads of its own responsible directors. Since there was no satisfactory solution, the ultimate consequence was the eventual effectual merging of the Mercantile into the Hongkong Bank, its head office moved to Hong Kong, and its board composed of Hongkong Bank Board members.

POSTSCRIPT: THE HONGKONG BANK GROUP

With the acquisition of the British Bank of the Middle East the Hongkong Bank had confirmed its role as a bank holding company under the generally accepted but legally undefined designation 'Hongkong Bank Group' (see Table II.1). The policies the holding company pursued relative to its subsidiaries would vary to meet developments which could not be foreseen from the first. The BBME's claim to separate identity has proved valid and has been (as of 1985) retained. The specialized in-house finance subsidiaries, Wayfoong Finance founded in 1960, for example, were an indication of the development of 'department store banking', and their separate identity was recognition of their specialized functions and need for specially qualified staff.

The fate of the Hongkong Bank of California, as it came to be called in 1970, requires examination in the context of the Bank's American strategy. The contrasting development of the Mercantile Bank compared to the BBME is a reflection on the ability of two similar banks, operating in roughly the same areas, to integrate. The Mercantile's shareholders' funds remained stagnant throughout the period. By 1965, for example, BBME's capital and reserves had risen 22% from an end-1960 figure of £4.6 million to an end-1965 figure of £5.6 million; for the same dates the figures for the Mercantile were unchanged at £5.14 million. Lacking the strong arguments in favour of independence which BBME successfully maintained, the Mercantile's resources failed to grow – the 'imperial interest' prevailed. Nor was there any excuse for failure to rationalize.

The Hongkong Bank's Board of Directors had in a sense been correct – it did take time to digest the Mercantile. The ability of the Bank to expand despite this fact was consequent on its adopting administrative controls which were not dependent on direct supervision and management. But this was done at the cost of some possibly unnecessary frustration on the part of senior management.

The formation of the 'Group', therefore, permitted the expansion of the Hongkong Bank without undue strain on its organization and staff abilities. Without the acquisition of the subsidiary banks and the formation of the in-house financial companies, expansion in the period 1957–1961 would have been impractical. The Hongkong Bank's Foreign staff was no larger than it had been in the 1920s; it had been recruited and trained in the old traditions, although with innovations, pressures, and opportunities which subtly changed the approach of those pressing for development and expansion. Nor was the Hongkong Bank yet prepared to depend on its recently appointed local officers; the system had not been adapted.

The original declarations made both by the Hongkong Bank and the boards of the acquired banks were not merely 'face saving'. The 'inevitability' of greater control was not then so obvious, and the actual initial relationships were, after all, determined after examination of many alternatives.

Two reminders need, therefore, to be stated. First, the initial declarations of continuity of directors, staff, and (hopefully) constituents were genuine, even though they were always hedged as to the future. Secondly, the Hongkong Bank made a symbolic statement of its sincerity by inviting two directors from the board of each acquired bank to become members of the Hongkong Bank's own London Advisory Committee, which was then – if not always – playing a significant role.

As Sir Michael Turner and G.O.W. Stewart were later to admit, they knew little about mergers and acquisitions at the time, they learned as they progressed, and they made mistakes along the way. A plan which later develops problems which require change is not necessarily a plan which, when first implemented, was unsound, nor would it be fair to conclude that a practical alternative existed. Given the restraints under which the Hongkong Bank's Board of Directors were operating, the compromises reached in 1958–1960 would appear to have solved the immediate problems to the satisfaction of most of those involved.

Building on the recovery engineered by Sir Arthur Morse, Sir Michael Turner had pioneered the Bank's organizational expansion from its sound Hong Kong base, even as its directors were, in their own businesses, contemplating similar developments. When Turner retired in 1962, however, the Hongkong Bank was structurally little changed; the pressures were there, the ideas were under discussion, the Managers' meetings, the new technology – all were factors suggesting that major developments were on stream. To bring this potential to organizational reality and establish a banking group capable of facing the new banking of the 1970s was the task of (Sir) John Saunders and his successors.

PART III

CHANGE, GROWTH, AND THE AMERICAN STRATEGY, 1962–1984

The Hongkong and Shanghai Banking Corporation is one of the great institutions of British commercial and colonial history. In its present manifestation it is one of the great banking empires of the modern commercial world. Based in Hong Kong, it is in most senses still a very British enterprise.

The Times, April 9, 1981

The accounts of the Hongkong Bank over the years 1949 to 1961 do not appear those of a bank which by 1984 would be the fourteenth largest in the free world as measured by shareholders' funds. The *consolidated* accounts of the Hongkong Bank Group, that is, of The Hongkong and Shanghai Banking Corporation as a bank holding company and an operating bank, over the same years suggest, but do not as yet ensure, a brighter future. In these consolidated accounts some use of the hidden reserves is revealed: they were in part capitalized as new shares to buy 100% of the Mercantile Bank and, eventually, of the British Bank of the Middle East. Given the impact of leverage, the growth of assets in consequence of these purchases was considerable. If December 1948 were taken as 100, then total Hongkong Bank assets at the end of 1961 would equal 176, but consolidated assets would equal 287 (see Table 5.2 and Figure II.2).

These consolidated data are not, however, the only guide to the future of the corporation. Although HSBC had acquired two banks, had established a California subsidiary and a finance company in Hong Kong, its record in California was poor, its finance company was as yet untried; Sir Michael Turner had recognized the position by agreeing that the management of the two newly acquired subsidiaries should remain subject to their own boards of directors – for the present. Size and location rather than management had been their problems.

Furthermore, although the Bank had been successful in spreading its risks, the growth and performance, but not necessarily the survival, of HSBC would remain heavily influenced by the prosperity and growth of Hong Kong itself; this was true even post-1979 when Marine Midland Banks had become a partner in the Hongkong Bank Group.

The encouraging performance of HSBC was in part due to the capabilities of its Foreign staff in changing times. While they are due full credit, they had as yet been unable to steer the Bank through critical years and, at the same time, to effect fundamental changes in management structure and geographical distribution. The Hongkong Bank still possessed the traditional characteristics of a colonially chartered bank. Sir Michael Turner and his deputy, freed from day-to-day management of Head Office's exchange position and in touch through London Office with Sir Arthur Morse and the London Advisory Committee, could, however, make decisions which ran counter to their own vocabulary, to their own professed philosophy of banking.

Indeed, their decisions were consistent with the changed world view of the Hong Kong expatriate business community to which they belonged. But the administrations of Sir Arthur Morse and Sir Michael Turner are more clearly seen as years in which pressures mounted within the Bank, pressures which were in a few cases partially met but which in general were left unresolved. Yet the success of HSBC depended on their resolution.

To list the pressures both external and internal is virtually to summarize Part II of this volume. How they were eventually met is to go far in the explanation of the events described in Part III.

The most serious problem was personnel. HSBC was still relying on three Foreign staffs – that is of the Hongkong Bank, the Mercantile Bank, and the British Bank of the Middle East; the Hongkong Bank's own Foreign staff was, as already stated, no larger than it had been in the 1920s. The problem had only been partially solved by the breakdown in the traditional three-tier system; the new regional officers were not as yet given tasks which significantly relieved the Foreign staff of the routine. The banking industry would soon be subjected to revolutionary change; HSBC had to meet this challenge, together with the obvious problem of growth, with an inadequate Foreign staff, the members of which had had no formal professional training. The problem was resolved by (i) the integration of the three 'foreign staffs' into an International staff and the consequent elimination of duplication (or triplication) of functions – the integration 'threw up' senior officers for reassignment, (ii) the up-grading of regional officers to positions of significant responsibility, (iii) the employment of specialists within the Bank and the acquisition or formation of service companies, and (iv) the initiation of formal training programs.

Pressures on the structure of the corporation were resolved by (i) the integration, as previously noted, of the staffs of the three 'similar' banks, the Hongkong Bank, the Mercantile Bank, and the British Bank of the Middle East, (ii) the development of the holding company structure with an increasing complexity to handle (a) tax considerations, (b) specialist and technical services, (c) banking and financial subsidiaries better handled through independent management, for example, Hang Seng Bank and Wardley Limited, (iii) broadening of Head Office and the differentiation of functions and establishment of Group-wide services overriding the virtual absolute autonomy of the branch Manager, for example, HS Property Management Company, and (iv) the development of a technology to handle these changes.

The relationship between the Board of Directors and the Chief Executive had become increasingly unsatisfactory, despite the fact that, like so many other corporate relationships under strain, the relationship had worked, at least until the question of (Sir) John Saunders' position as Chief Manager and Board member became serious. Fortunately, the directors and their world view were also changing, facilitating the eventual resolution of the problem by an amendment in the Bank's regulations: the Board would become executive, the Chairman would be an executive director in the service of the Bank, and other senior Bank officers were eligible for election as executive directors.

Where the Bank's colonial charter hindered its development, the provisions were changed. Where the Bank's colonial charter ran counter to statutory banking controls, the latter prevailed. The Bank was shedding its past; the process by which this was achieved is one theme which follows through Part III.

The Bank's concerns relative to growing nationalism had not been fully justified in the 1950s, but the potential for disruption was there and the question of ultimate loyalty had already been raised. By the 1960s the 'honeymoon' was over; the Rangoon branches of both the Hongkong Bank and the Mercantile Bank were nationalized in 1963. Soon HSBC would recognize that it would not receive 'national treatment' in such matters as branching, but that it would nevertheless be expected to cooperate with the new central banking authorities in the execution of national plans as they affected the banking sector. Despite such restraints and, in some countries, high taxation, 'HongkongBank', that is, the Hongkong Bank Group, was able to work with the authorities and, in most cases, continue to serve the several economies, even though, as in Saudi Arabia, for example, the Bank operated through an associated, locally incorporated bank in which it held less than 50% of the equity capital.

The events immediately following 1949 and the growth, albeit at an uneven pace, through 1961 had resulted in an increase in funds which the Hongkong Bank could not safely reinvest to the full extent in Hong Kong. At the same time the Bank was facing international competition. The early solution was found in the 1960s – the sharing of markets and the consequent spreading of risks both geographically and by industry. At first, this was done reluctantly; the Bank had been Hong Kong based and regionally oriented from its founding. There were local observers carefully watching for 'defection', for 'loss of confidence' in the economy of Hong Kong or whatever territory was involved; indeed, there were senior Managers who were equally concerned – 'the banker sticks to his last', 'banks do not acquire other banks', 'our area is the East', etc. But events forced Sir Michael Turner to deny all these traditional, and not particularly accurate, clichés.

As noted above, despite the dramatic decisions Turner made in 1959 and 1960, HSBC's dependence on Hong Kong remained. However, Hong Kong's economy grew with some diversification; it would have its dramatic booms and setbacks, but the Bank's established business seemed sufficient to protect it while the several internal corporate 'reforms' took place over a period of almost twenty years. The fortuitous acquisition of the dynamic Hang Seng Bank in 1965 would be one factor in the success of the Hongkong Bank Group, otherwise growth came from developments mainly within the Hongkong Bank, the BBME, and Wardley Limited. The increasing importance of investment banking, for example, led to initial development within the commercial banking framework; at first a 'desk' in the Hong Kong main office, it followed (Sir)

Michael Sandberg when he moved to head all Colony operations; in 1974 the operation became a separate and increasingly profitable subsidiary, Wardley Limited. At virtually the same time (1973) the Hongkong Bank invested in Antony Gibbs (Holdings) in London.

The special nature of banking had made it subject to regulation even in those territories in which the Government claimed a policy of '*laissez-faire*'. A bank did certain things; a bank did not do other things, despite the fact that the Hongkong Bank's actual ordinance and regulations permit a wide range of activities. Bankers were increasingly concerned, however, that non-banking financial institutions were encroaching on traditional banking fields, whereas banks could not, in many jurisdictions, counter by moving into other financial activities. The preconceptions relative to the 'proper' activities of banks had to be broken down even as the geographical preconceptions had been abandoned a few years earlier. This could be done, where legislation permitted, through the creation of a holding company and the establishment of financial subsidiaries whose activities were coordinated even if legislation and/or sound business practice required that actual transactions be on an 'arm's length' basis.

The Hongkong Bank had responded with the founding of a finance company, Wayfoong Finance Limited, which, as a Hong Kong deposit-taking company, was free of certain regulations directed at commercial, full-service banks. This became the precedential response to pressures in the financial industry, but the breakthroughs occurred at intervals, sometimes in response to changing legislation; insurance and leasing came in the early 1970s but the other main developments, for example, the 1986 acquisition of James Capel and Co. (stockbrokers), came after the acquisition of Marine Midland Banks. The growth of the network is yet another major theme in Part III.

The Hongkong Bank Group remained, however, a very conservative banking group. This may be measured by its liquidity, the absence of gearing, and the buildup of significant inner reserves. The focus of Head Office was on 'asset management'; not until 1985 did HSBC itself buy-in capital funds in the form of long-term borrowing, a measure designed to affect favourably the capital/assets ratio. Consequently, the Bank was spared certain problems, especially when interest rates rose in the 1970s, but it was faced with other pressures, specifically those on its capital/assets ratio and on the need to expand its sources of funds. These problems had been apparent in the 1950s; they would increase in severity during the period to 1984; they are reflected (i) in the capitalization of reserves to improve published ratios and (ii) the new positive policy to branching. Unfortunately this latter came at a time when many Governments were deciding to limit branch banking by overseas banks.

The acquisition of the Mercantile Bank began with a telephone call from

George Marden; BBME was consequent to approaches from several quarters; the founding of the Hongkong Bank of California was intended as the establishment of an ordinary branch on terms which would meet local regulatory requirements; Wayfoong Finance was a consequence of local banking constraints. This was perhaps satisfactory for a beginning, but at some point planning would become necessary.

The Hongkong Bank's traditional attitude was one of suspicion of purely academic qualifications, specialization, and planning – although traditionally the Bank had relied on all these from time to time. Planning in Hong Kong would be regarded with particular suspicion. Nevertheless, HSBC's breakthrough, its 1980 acquisition of Marine Midland Banks, was the consequence of very careful planning; subsequently the Bank formally acknowledged the planning function, and the financial broadening of the Group was rationalized. Plans could still go awry; the Royal Bank of Scotland Group was not acquired, but the fault was not with HSBC.

This is not to suggest that *ad hoc* moves were eliminated after 1961. The acquisition of Hang Seng was not premeditated. More to the point, the Bank's equity investments in non-financial activities could be characterized as 'random', even though they developed from long-standing associations which originated in commercial banking. The Hongkong Bank's investment in shipping and in the local Hong Kong airline were almost opportunistic; they caused a maximum amount of discussion and introduced a minimum growth element into the Group. Their relative unimportance was publicly demonstrated at U.S. Congressional hearings in 1980. Much would be made then of the American separation of financial from non-financial activities in opposition to Continental practices, but the Hongkong Bank's equity involvements would hardly qualify it to rank in this regard with a major German bank. HSBC remained in the British tradition but with gestures to prove its independence of action.

Hong Kong remained of importance to the Hongkong Bank, and the Hongkong Bank was the largest bank in Hong Kong. While it never became a 'central bank', it remained the principal banker to the Government and, as the largest bank, had a direct impact on the prosperity of the banking sector. The Bank also continued to issue, on a back-to-back basis, banknotes which were legal tender in the territory. Its relations with the Hong Kong Government were, however, uneven, although its advice was sought and usually valued; there were times when its cooperation was essential. Thus in banking crises and share market heights or depths, the Bank was expected to intervene in the interests of the economy, but it was also expected to coordinate or at least discuss these interventions with Government. Equally important are the Bank's integration into the several local banking systems and the growth of local banking regulation – especially in Hong Kong itself. These are further themes to be developed.

The Hongkong Bank Group played a major role in the financing of the territory's Mass Transit Railway system; the Bank was a channel through which sterling reserves were moved at an appropriate pace through the open market into other currencies; the Bank from time to time and often in cooperation with the Chartered Bank (as the Standard Chartered Group continued to be known in the East) 'guaranteed' to support a particular local bank for a specified period. This was only done, however, if that bank were solvent, its problems arising from lack of liquidity and/or unjustified rumours. The consequences of such interventions were positive on the banking system and, therefore, on the major members of that system and can be justified in terms of 'enlightened self-interest', even though the Bank received encouragement or, on occasion, guarantees from the Government for so acting. The scope of the banking problems in 1983 and afterwards show the limits of this private sector approach. The Hongkong Bank did supply management to a bank taken over by the Government; it did assist others. But the problem did not disappear and the Hongkong Bank's contribution had its limits.

Through Wardley Limited and then through its other investment and merchant banking subsidiaries and associates, the Hongkong Bank came to play an increasing role in the world of syndicated loans, especially those designed for the East. On occasion Wardley was lead manager, but the Hongkong Bank's role never comprehended any particular area in both finance and policy; it was a leading merchant bank among many large merchant banks. Its rise to prominence in the 1970s, its move into the list of the largest financial institutions, did in many ways resemble its first breakout into world prominence during the indemnity loans of 1896 and 1898 and the various railway, reorganization, and other loans of the years to 1914.

If the Hongkong Bank could no longer dominate what was once referred to as 'exchange banking' in the East, this was offset by its greater global role; members of the Group were interested in Africa (the Equator Bank), in wholly owned commercial banks established in Canada and Australia, and in overseas commercial bank branches as distant as New York City and Chile. A global role was assured above all through partnership with Marine Midland Banks.

In the years 1949–1961 the Bank had moved successfully from problem to problem, but pressures mounted; some of them had been correctly assessed and partially answered. From 1962 through 1977 further resolution of problems came through the structural changes and by other policies instituted by J.A.H. Saunders and G.M. Sayer. From the mid-1970s the successful development of an American strategy was a foretaste of a more professional approach to corporate planning. Structural and personnel policy changes

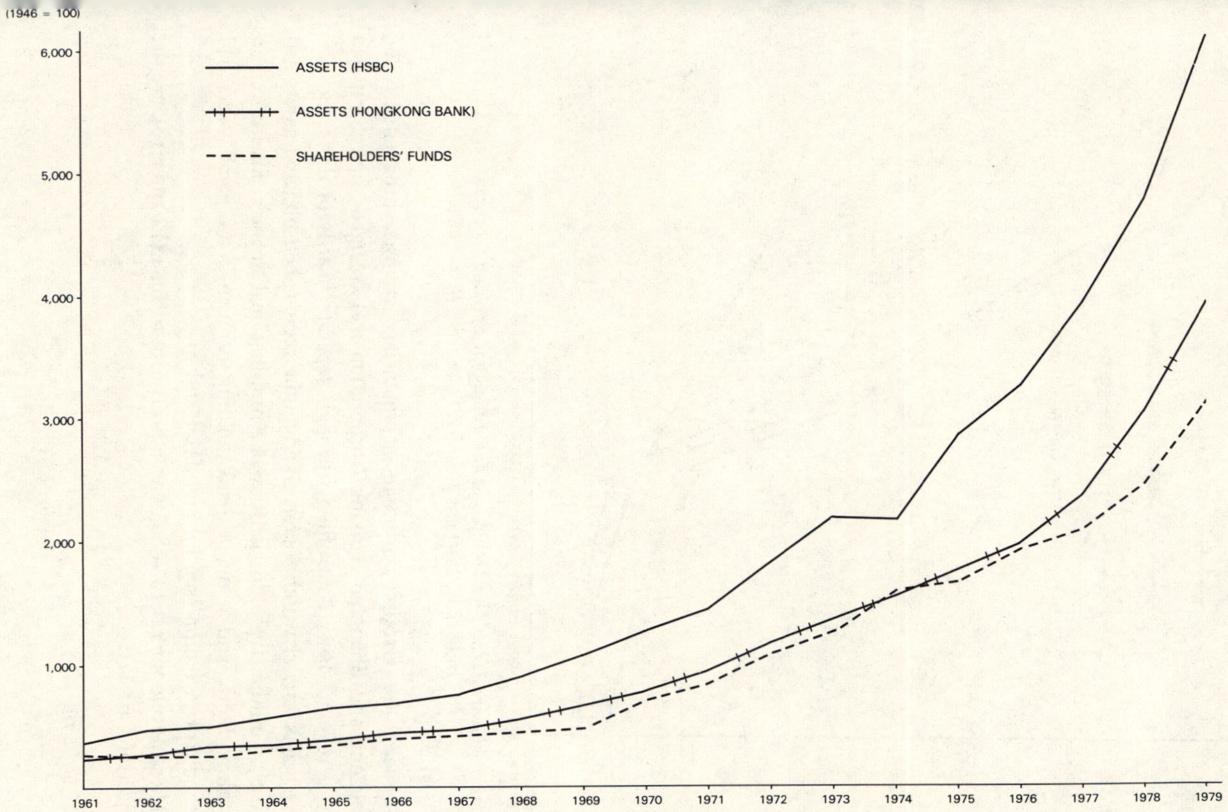

Figure III.1 The Hongkong and Shanghai Banking Corporation
Indices of assets and shareholders' funds, 1961–1979

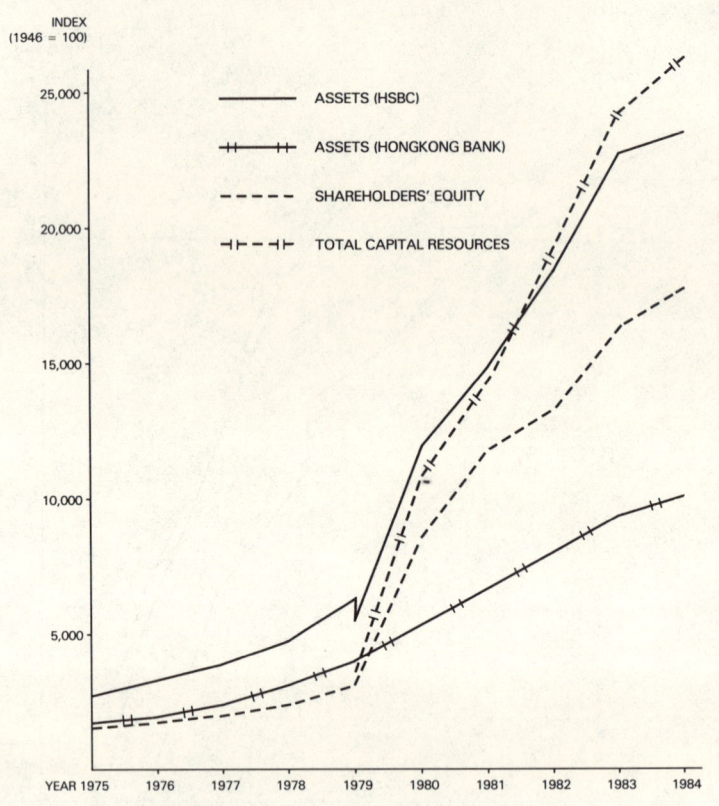

Figure III.2 The Hongkong and Shanghai Banking Corporation
Indices of assets and capital resources, 1975–1984

continued; the Group's coverage of financial activities broadened. The Hongkong and Shanghai Banking Corporation had changed; in 1961 it had been a regional bank controlling, through separate boards of directors, two other banks, one of which was in an adjoining region; consolidated assets had been $7.7 billion. By 1980 HSBC was a multinational financial institution, an operating Bank, and a major bank holding company; the total assets had reached $481.6 billion (see Figures III.1 and 2).

These developments to 1980, with a postscript to 1984 (Chapter 18), are the subject of Part III.

13

THE HONGKONG BANK GROUP, 1962–1980, I. STRUCTURE AND GROWTH*

> My Lords have, as you are aware, been careful to divest themselves of interference in the affairs of Banking Companies.
>
> Treasury to Colonial Office, 1890

SHEDDING A STRUCTURAL HERITAGE

The Hongkong Bank is incorporated under its own separate ordinance and the 'regulations' under which it operates can be changed or amended only with the approval of the Governor of Hong Kong and after publication in the *Hong Kong Government Gazette*. The evolution of this arrangement has been detailed in previous volumes of this history and in Chapter 7 above. In 1983 both the provisions of the Bank's ordinance and the regulations were printed as Chapter 70 of the *Laws of Hong Kong* and extracts have been appended in this volume. In brief, the Bank's original incorporation was under the Companies Ordinance of 1865, subsequently disallowed; it was then incorporated under its own ordinance in 1866, but the provisions failed to meet the requirements of the Treasury. This was corrected by the shareholders' agreeing to a Deed of Settlement (the regulations) which incorporated the required provisions and which in consequence could not be changed except with the permission of the Governor.

The first comprehensive restatement of the provisions of the Bank's incorporation came in 1929. The major amendments in the intervening period had dealt with the problem of colonial extraterritorial jurisdiction and the note issue and its security. The first major restructuring came in 1957 and has been considered in Chapter 7. From the mid-1960s the Bank's corporate structure evolved through the further removal of historical provisions and in the context of new general banking and companies legislation. The Treasury had abandoned direct regulatory responsibility on terms first conceived in the 1830s as the Government of Hong Kong accepted the task consistent with the development of the territory into a world financial centre.[a]

---

* There are no end-notes to this chapter. Readers are referred to the bibliographical note on pp. 949–50.

[a] There is an anachronistic, residual reference to the Treasury in Regulation 150 referring to the Bank's yearly statements: '...such returns to be made to such persons, and published in such manner as the Treasury shall direct...'.

The changes in the legal corporate structure were accompanied by internal changes necessitated by the requirements of a bank not only in changed times but with a changed vision. As the Bank dropped traditions and practices which had served it well for some 100 years, there arose the legitimate question as to the extent it remained what staff, constituents, and shareholders had known as 'the Bank'; in other words, how relevant was its history? As the Bank has been successful in moving from regional to multinational status, the evolutionary transition period, the period of preparation before a major U.S. acquisition, takes on particular importance. The purpose of this and the following chapters is to recount the history of the Bank and the Group with this question of heritage in mind; the dimensions of the subject are set out in the following section.

THE HERITAGE OF THE COLONIAL BANKING REGULATIONS

The Hongkong and Shanghai Banking Corporation began operating under a Hong Kong ordinance incorporating the provisions of the Colonial Banking Regulations in December 1866. As a 'chartered' bank it became part of a network of British overseas banks or exchange banks whose ultimate regulatory authority was the British Treasury. Although the Bank was incorporated in Hong Kong, money and banking were 'reserved' subjects and the Governor referred (when he remembered) substantive Bank matters, whether a change in the ordinance or in the Bank's regulations – which latter also required the Governor's approval – back to the Colonial Office, who in turn consulted with the Treasury.

Thereafter there were several divergent trends. The Treasury's insistence that provision for the incorporation of banks with limited liability be excluded from the Colony's 1865 general companies ordinance left Hong Kong without effective general banking legislation. Tentative measures to prevent abuses were introduced, but banking legislation with any effective regulatory provision (as opposed to registration *per se*) was not enacted until 1964. In the meantime the imperial banking system of chartered banks had been made irrelevant by the enactment of local legislation in self-governing territories, and charters were not issued after the 1860s, except in unusual circumstances, for example, the Imperial Bank of Persia. This meant, *de facto*, that, in the case of the Hongkong Bank, the Treasury was actually deciding on issues which affected that bank alone, or that bank with the Chartered Bank of India, Australia and China; the Treasury no longer had an imperial role, and the problems might be left to regular legislative and regulatory procedures, if this were possible.

The purpose of chartering banks subject to imperially determined provisions was to permit their operation in more than one colonial territory without upsetting the right of a single colony with an elected legislature (thus not including Hong Kong) to incorporate banks *ad hoc* for operation within their own territory. But the charters were not intended to override local legislation and thus their usefulness diminished as colonial territories established their own note issue or independent territories set up their own banking systems and central banks. Indeed, it was argued that the only current advantage to a Royal charter was just that, its distinctiveness. There was the argument that, if the charter were revoked, it would be taken as an adverse comment on the bank's operations. The Chartered Mercantile Bank, for example was obliged to surrender its charter during its difficulties in 1892.

In the immediate post-war years the Hongkong Bank resisted the implication that it would be subject to the provisions of a general Hong Kong banking ordinance and, as noted in Chapter 2, special ordinances were passed to make decisions for which general legislation had already been enacted applicable to the Hongkong Bank. By the 1960s, however, this duality was recognized as impractical; the Hongkong Bank was part of the Hong Kong banking system and that system was in need of regulatory legislation. Indeed, the Bank's senior officers, especially R.G.L. Oliphant, were active in formulating the recommendations which were considered by H.J. Tomkins in his 1962 report on the banking system and which became the basis for the 1964 legislation. The Bank's earlier claim to be treated separately was purely 'bluff'. Morse was in the grand tradition of the pre-war Bank; he did not approve of being regulated. J.A.H. Saunders, among others, recognized the new problems, and there were in any case provisions in the Bank's ordinance sufficient to require it to conform; the only issue remaining was, as is so often the case, prestige.

Prestige is, however, bought at a price. The Bank had, it is true, been able to abandon certain special provisions of its ordinance, but it was in the potentially contradictory position of attempting to obtain normal corporate rights at the same time as it was determined to retain its 'special position', that is, its own independent ordinance. The Bank accepted the terms of supervisory legislation in Hong Kong as it had long done overseas. This was not the issue. The ordinance did not in any case protect or exempt it from the impact of general banking legislation but it did impose a certain formality and potential rigidity to its structure – the regulations of this private-sector corporation were very much a public affair; they had to be agreed to by the Governor and published in the *Gazette*. One provision, for example, requires that the Bank's Head Office be situate in Hong Kong.

This is consistent with the position taken in Part II of this volume. There were pressures building within the Bank which would force change. For the most part these came after 1961.

The trend to conformity

Changes in the regulations – general

In the 1950s the Bank's ordinance was amended to end the double liability of its shareholders and the Bank gained the right to increase its authorized capital without reference to the Governor. In 1957 certain changes were made in the ordinance to recognize the problems of managing subsidiaries, but the major changes affecting structure came with the Governor's approval of amendments agreed by shareholders in an Extraordinary Meeting in March 1969, as published in the *Hong Kong Government Gazette* of May 9.

These provided, *inter alia*, for the appointment of a corporation secretary to replace the Chief Manager as the officer handling the seal and matters relating to shares, the removal of the prohibition against officers of the Bank other than the Chief Manager becoming directors, and the concept of an 'executive director', a director who is also an officer of the Bank. The most significant of these changes provided that the Board-elected Chairman must be an officer of the Bank. From this it does not follow, however, that the Chairman of the Board must be the chief executive officer of the Bank or that the chief executive need be a *previously* employed officer of the Bank; there is the potential of inviting in a chief executive. A provision stating that the Board can only delegate its banking responsibilities to the Chairman or Executive Deputy Chairman thus corrected the position which so concerned Turner – and Saunders after him.[b]

The changes incidentally brought about an end to the historic titles 'Chief Manager' and 'Chief Accountant'. The implications of this and related consequences will be considered separately below.

The current position

By 1986 the Hongkong Bank was subject in Hong Kong to (i) the Banking Ordinance, (ii) its own ordinance, with the proviso that the provisions of the Banking Ordinance shall prevail where they conflict or are inconsistent with the HSBC ordinance, (iii) through the Banking Ordinance to the Companies Ordinance with respect to the audit of accounts, (iv) the Securities (Stock Exchange Listing) Rules 1986, and (v) the Stock Exchange of Hong Kong 'Exchange Listing Rules'. These ordinances may, in turn, refer to others, to the relevant provisions of which the Bank is accordingly subject.

During the 1950s the impact of United Kingdom legislation on the Hongkong Bank as an overseas company became increasingly apparent. This

---

[b] When Michael Sandberg announced in January 1986 that he was resigning as chief executive officer and would be succeeded by William Purves, the executive Deputy Chairman, he was able to remain as Chairman of the Board.

was particularly true relative to the statement of accounts, although modifications can be granted by statutory instrument (see 1984, No. 134, Art. 37). The provisions of these several acts developed into the Companies Act 1985, especially Part XXIII and s. 700. As in Hong Kong, the Bank is also bound by the London Stock Exchange's 'Admission of Securities to Listing' as negotiated for the special circumstances of the Bank.

The situation would be made particularly complex in the United States by the Bank's acquisition of Marine Midland Banks (see Chapters 16 and 17), and indeed by the requirements of the more than 40 jurisdictions in which the Bank operates. However economic policy and controls in Hong Kong may be judged, the locally incorporated Hongkong Bank has become subject world-wide to normal banking controls and its position is fully disclosed to key regulatory authorities.

Shares and dividends

Originally the Hongkong Bank maintained share registers not only in Hong Kong and Shanghai, but also in other major offices, including Calcutta. By 1875 there were three registers – Hong Kong, Shanghai, and London. In 1922, the Board agreed to give up the Shanghai register in return for favourable consideration of its application for an amendment of the Bank's ordinance; the register was not actually closed until the 1930s.

Post-war there had been an increasing discrepancy between prices on the two surviving registers, with profitable arbitrage operations possible. Shares could be and, in the pre-war period, actually were, transferred between registers in blocks, but differing tax and other regulations made this difficult if not impossible post-war. With the development of communications, the ending of the practice whereby dividends were quoted in sterling, the desire to place the Bank's London operations on a more normal branch footing, and the increasingly strict disclosure requirements, the need for a separate London register ceased. Shares would soon have a par value of $2.50; the concept of share ownership mainly in the hands of taipan-constituents with the inherent danger of a forced transfer of Head Office to London were both problems of the past. The majority of the shareholders now appeared to be ordinary investors, probably British subjects, and probably resident in Hong Kong.

The London share register was closed in 1974, at which time 70% of the shares were on the London register. All shares were transferred to a single register in Hong Kong. By mid-1982 73% of the shares were held by shareholders with registered addresses in Hong Kong. Shares continued to be quoted on the London market, however, and the Bank continued to be involved in lengthy discussions relative to disclosure regulations. In 1973, for example, over the Board's objections, the Bank was required to list major loans to directors. The Bank argued that, as management was entirely in the hands of the chief executive and loans were not referred to the Board, the provision was unnecessary. The special circumstances of Hong Kong were not, however, permitted to prevail.

Since 1957 the shareholders had enjoyed 'single' liability, that is, they were responsible in the case of the company being wound up for an additional payment equal to any unpaid portion of the shares held (par. 12). The complex voting provisions which were first introduced in 1865 were abandoned under the terms of a 1969 change (reg. 73). All shareholders are now entitled to one vote per share.

The practice of quoting dividends in sterling ended in 1972, coincident with the break in the link between the dollar and sterling. The origins of this anomaly are described in Volume I, but in brief, the Bank's dividends were quoted in one unit of account (sterling) and its capital in another (the Hong Kong dollar then on silver) because the Hongkong Bank was thought to have fixed the exchange rate between Hong Kong dollars and sterling for its own capital purposes at the originally prevailing rate of $1 = 4s:6d; this rate had been printed on the Bank's scrip issued in London. As the dollar was depreciating in terms of sterling, the 'official' rate was higher than the market rate; if dividends were declared in dollars they would have to be converted, it was thought, at the 'official' rate. This would result in a London Register shareholder receiving more sterling than the then market rate for sterling warranted. To prevent this the dividend had been quoted in sterling. The Bank subsequently (1900s) received legal advice that this procedure was now unnecessary (if indeed it ever had been) since new scrip no longer stated the exchange rate; the actual change was made in 1972.

Exceptions to conformity

In 1964 the Board wished to introduce certain minor changes in the ordinance, specifically in par. 9 (1) dealing with reorganization of capital. It became clear, however, that the Governor, on advice and acting as 'gatekeeper', would not approve amendments unless the Bank agreed to a Government requested change in the Regulations to provide that the Bank make its register of shareholders available to the public in conformity with Hong Kong company practice. In October the Board resolved to refuse and consequently withdrew its own request. The Bank-requested amendment in fact went through in 1965, yet the list of shareholders remains unavailable, but clearly there were to be limits to conformity.

General intent and an exception

The purpose of these changes had been to give back to the Bank's shareholders and Board of Directors powers normal to a corporation, but at the same time subjecting them to the control of the local banking authorities in Hong Kong, in the same way that they were already subject in other territories of operation. The note issue, though exceptional and considered below, had become so hedged in with restrictions that the issue was in total government control. The Bank had by 1970 virtually returned *de facto* to its original position in 1865–1866 before its formal incorporation by special ordinance. To this generalization there remained, however, an important exception.

Regulation 6 remains as contained in the 1929 edition, that the 'Bank shall always be provided with some house or office in the Colony, which shall be its head office or principal place of business'. As the Bank cannot amend this (or any other regulation) without the approval of the Governor and publication in the *Gazette*, the regulation was one factor affecting the Bank's decision relative to creation of a separate holding company, that is, the decision relative to separating the corporation as operating bank from its role as the holding company with a controlling interest in subsidiary companies. The Board sensed a public feeling that a holding company could easily be registered elsewhere without affecting the location of management; the need to bring sensitive matters to the Governor and have them considered as public issues made the Bank hesitate. One could argue that a bank with ambitions to become a multinational financial institution had in any case limited options; the domicile of its holding company would have to be a jurisdiction with credible banking controls. But this line of thought is premature; the initial hesitation was Hong Kong oriented. The only course therefore was for the corporation to be both holding company and operating bank.[c]

Maximum share holdings

There had always been a provision in the Bank's Deed of Settlement and subsequent regulations limiting the number of shares which could be beneficially held by a single shareholder. Although there is no correspondence on the subject, it would seem that the provision is consistent with (i) the original idea of the Bank as serving the Treaty Port community rather than a

---

[c] As a general political issue, the fact is that the Bank, a company in the private sector, could not alter its own regulations as agreed by shareholders without bringing them into the political arena and discussion in public by non-shareholders. In the context of imperial banking control this had been reasonable, but time and perceptions had changed. A comparison which, though different in content was the same in context, would be that of the Church of England's need (unlike that of any other religious body in the United Kingdom) to have Prayer Book changes approved by a secular Parliament and the latter's failure to do so in 1928. In the case of the Church, the 1928 revisions came into general use notwithstanding, but banks cannot appeal to a higher Regulator.

few dominant shareholder/constituents and (ii) the later concern to frustrate attempts to move the Bank's Head Office to London. The maximum figure had been revised upward when the shares were revalued at $25 and again in 1973 when the shares were set at $2.50 – in the latter case to 3,000,000 or 1.3% of the total then issued. In 1979 the Board reverted to a fixed 1% of the capital then issued (Reg. 19). Exceptions can be made at the discretion of the Board, and this has been done on rare occasions, for example when the excess shares to be owned stems from the Bank's having bought a subsidiary with newly issued shares. In 1985 the directors of the Bank were still able to report: 'There are no substantial shareholdings in the share capital of the Bank.'

Disclosure

Throughout this period the Hongkong Bank retained its practice of non-disclosure of 'true profits' and its retention of inner reserves, the two policies being directly related. The Bank's argument for this remained unchanged; banks operating in exceptional risk areas without access to assistance from a Government agency require a cushion to absorb unexpected losses or gains which arise from situations beyond the control of any bank or which are exceptional in nature. The legal authority rests in the regulations which provide that 'No shareholder shall be entitled to require discovery of or any information respecting any detail of the bank's trading or banking business... if in the opinion of the board it is inexpedient in the general interests of the shareholders to give the information required' (Reg. 157). The right of the Governor (or any person he appoints for the purpose) to all details of the Bank's operations is clearly reserved in Regulation 151.

The most significant challenge to this position, albeit indirect, came in the early 1970s when British clearing banks themselves made public their inner reserves. The Chairman, G.M. Sayer, commenting at the 1974 Annual Meeting, expressed the view that although the Bank would review its position relative to disclosure, he was of the opinion that the interest of shareholders was best served by retaining inner reserves. Sayer virtually invited comments from shareholders; there were none.

Bank regulators have accepted this position with varying degrees of enthusiasm, and the Hongkong Bank has revealed its true position to authorities where the confidentiality of this information is protected by law. Bank examinations in the United States, for example, are excluded from the provisions of the Freedom of Information Act. The U.S. Securities and Exchange Commission is not similarly protected, and the consequent problems which developed in clearing the Hongkong Bank's offer for the shares of Marine Midland Banks are discussed in Chapter 17.

The purpose of inner reserves is sometimes described as one of dividend equalization. Post-war the Bank's published profits have not, as a matter of policy, included transfers *from* inner reserves, and more recently the Bank has stated its intention of maintaining such a policy. It is presumably in consequence of such an understanding that foreign regulatory authorities have not insisted on full public disclosure, at least while the Bank's own regulatory authority, the Hong Kong Government, publicly supports a contrary policy.

One consequence of these structural changes is that the Bank, it could be argued, should give up its special ordinance and accept ordinary incorporation. The Bank's note issue could become, as it was after the 1929 Ordinance, a matter for Government decision through separate legislation. The Bank is already subject to various company act provisions in Hong Kong and in the countries in which it operates; thus regulation *per se* is not an issue in the question of the special ordinance.

As a statement in logic such urging has much to commend it. However, the Hongkong Bank remains the creature of its history, despite the changes witnessed since 1946 and especially since 1962. Just as there is no compelling reason to retain the special ordinance, so there is none to discard it, and there the matter rests.

The note issue

Considering the years of Treasury and Colonial Office encouragement to Hong Kong, urging a Government note issue, the survival of a commercial banknote issue in the Colony is remarkable. Originally considered an essential source of funds if an overseas bank were to be profitable, the note issue is no longer a source of profit. But it remains 'profitable' as a statement of status.

The 1984 figures for the Colony's money supply vary between $33,351 million and $388,301 million, depending on definition. The legal tender note issue of the two authorized private-sector, commercial banks totalled $14,246 million or 40% of the smaller figure for the money supply (legal tender in the hands of the non-banking public plus demand deposits in licensed banks adjusted to add back legal tender in banks). Of this note issue, $11,754 million (or 82.5%) was issued by the Hongkong Bank.

The Government note issue in Hong Kong is confined to the one-cent notes; the Government one-dollar notes issued first in 1936 have been withdrawn in favour of coins. The Government is responsible for less than 10% of the territory's legal tender currency supply, and even this includes $274 million worth of $1,000 gold coins which are not in general circulation.

The Scottish system comes to mind; this is not, for reasons stated earlier in this history, a useful comparison. The survival of the territory's private banknote issue and the predominance of the Hongkong Bank are consequences rather of colonial history and a unique combination of circumstances which can be more usefully contrasted with currency developments in Ceylon and the Straits Settlements – and in the independent Kingdom of Siam (see discussions in previous volumes).

A historical survey of banknotes in Hong Kong

The banknote issue in Hong Kong has passed through several clearly defined stages. In the first stage, the early issues were those of the Royally chartered banks with London head offices; these can be directly related to factors in colonial monetary history. The opening of the Hongkong Bank in 1865 and its subsequent incorporation by the Hong Kong Legislature on terms agreeable to the British Treasury and consistent with the Colonial Banking Regulations resulted in further banknote issues consistent with the established system.

The second stage, which might be described as a sub-stage of the first, began with the failure of the Oriental Bank Corporation in 1884. The events surrounding this failure, especially the pledge given by the Government of Ceylon to redeem the 'private' issue, led to a changed Treasury position relative to the private vs Government note issue controversy, and the Hong Kong Government with its preference for a continued private note issue found itself consequently on the defensive. Regulations governing the security or the backing for the banknotes were tightened, but there was no immediate change in the essential features of the Hong Kong system.

As the use of banknotes became increasingly popular, however, pressures mounted; the issuing banks were reaching their authorized limits. Temporary measures were necessary by 1898 and enacted on an annual basis. The stage was set for a change in the system.

The third stage, roughly from 1898 to 1935, marked a departure from colonial tradition. The note-issuing banks had reached the limits permitted by their constitutions and yet the Hong Kong Government was not prepared to take over responsibility for the issue. The solution was found in a legislated 'excess issue' against 100% deposit of silver coin or bullion. This was, however, a half-measure. With a tax of 1% on the note issue and a required 100% specie backing of the 'excess', an increased note issue was no longer at the margin a source of profit to the banks. The decision to expand the issue – and therefore the size of the money supply – was discretionary with the banks, and there were times when this expansion was refused. The practical consequence of this was that Hong Kong went off the silver standard, narrowly defined, and exchange (Hong Kong on London) was quoted in terms of 'bank money', both notes and demand deposits, which often showed a premium against the rate based on calculations of relative but adjusted gold/silver bullion prices.

I. Structure and growth

The very success of the Hong Kong banknote issue both in the Colony and in China, where some 70% of the total Hong Kong issue was at one time circulating, made its take-over by the Government a formidable physical and administrative task. The official position was put quite frankly: the banks were doing a good job, the Government did not have the facilities, and the Government did not want to do it. As these protests came at times when the Government faced some sort of financial crisis, the Colonial Office (and behind them the Treasury) did not insist.

The fourth stage began with the 1935 decision by China to go off silver and the subsequent decision of the Hong Kong Government to follow, in general terms, China's lead. The Government once again refused to consider an immediate Government issue (other than one-dollar notes) but instead made the banknotes of the authorized banks for the first time in their history a legal tender. This had the consequence of forcing the note-issuing banks to issue on demand. Working in the context of a Government-operated Exchange Fund, these three banks – the Hongkong, the Chartered, and the Mercantile banks – became, in a sense, agents of the Government for the note issue. To the very limited extent that discretionary monetary policy was feasible in an entrepôt economy, the Government, which had virtually but unwittingly abdicated in the interim period, was once again in control.

The position of the Hongkong Bank

The Hongkong Bank quickly came to dominate the issue of banknotes in Hong Kong. Several rival note-issuing banks failed. The Chartered Mercantile Bank surrendered its charter in 1892; its successor, the Mercantile Bank of India, did not have the right of note issue in Hong Kong until 1911 legislation specifically granted it; the bank was not aggressive and its note issue remained small. Only the Chartered Bank of India, Australia and China maintained its banknote issue throughout, although the size of that issue was limited by its relative banking position in the territory.

The right of the Hongkong Bank to issue banknotes was first removed by the provisions of the 1929 ordinance, but the note-issuing banks continued to issue notes in Hong Kong by virtue of special enabling legislation; the right was then reestablished in the 1957 ordinance but for Hong Kong only (Cap. 70, par. 10). With the acceptance by Government of the responsibility for the safety of the note issue and by the Bank of the regulations which had led to this acceptance, the Bank had become even more an agent of the Government.

This surrender was not without adverse consequences, since the Government, anxious not to be caught with potential duress notes, set the maximum number of printed but unissued notes permitted in storage, which number almost proved inadequate in two banking crises. In the first, in 1965, sterling

Bank of England notes were shipped for issue in Hong Kong and regulations were issued by which the amount of cash which could be withdrawn from the banks each day was severely limited. Fortunately, the Bank of England notes did not have to be issued, the crisis passed, and the restrictions were withdrawn within a week. Although lessons were learned and more printed notes were stored in England, the banks were caught short again during the Left-wing disturbances in 1967; this time the Hongkong Bank notes were flown out from England and brought to the Bank under police escort just moments after demonstrators had moved away from the area in front of the Bank itself. The notes arrived on a Saturday; on Monday morning they were paid out – a close run affair.

The Hongkong Bank had not, however, freed itself from all responsibility relative to the note issue. Exceptional fluctuations in the size of the issue, for example, at Chinese New Year or during banking crises, had to be met and could be costly, with any increase being financed by the sale of sterling at 1s:3d and any decrease by the purchase of sterling at 1s:2$\frac{7}{8}$d. In 1963 the Bank's issue increased $152 million at Chinese New Year, a time when debts are traditionally paid and a high liquidity required, and then fell by $128 million within the next two weeks. During the 1967 disturbances the note issue increased by $600 million, of which $240 million had been retired by the end of the year. Notes issued to meet such a crisis could, however, by arrangement with the Government be redeemed at 'even rates'. This is just as well; the 1967 New Year's increase had already cost the Bank $1.6 million in exchange loss.

The position in 1983 was covered by pars. 10 and 11 of the Bank's ordinance as revised. The historical concern with the issue of small denomination notes, defined (as in the nineteenth century) as notes with a face value of $5.00 or below, remained intact [par. 10(2)]. The distinction between the original 'authorized' and the 'excess' issues also remained (par. 11). As for the authorized issue, since 1907 its size had ceased to be stated in terms of the Bank's paid-up capital; in 1953 the issue had been fixed at $30 million. In 1978 the Bank was granted the right to assume the relevant rights of its wholly owned subsidiary, the Mercantile Bank, whose note issue at the end of 1977 had been $29.1 million. This decision increased the Hongkong Bank's authorized issue to $60 million out of a total Bank end-1978 issue of $5,854 million. Against the authorized issue the Bank deposited approved interest bearing securities – the right to a proportional fiduciary issue had ceased in 1957 in return for an amendment to the Bank's ordinance eliminating shareholders' unlimited liability for the note issue; against the excess issue the Bank continued to hold Hong Kong Government certificates of indebtedness. And once again the size of the excess issue was affected by the situation in China; a 1985 Reuters report stated that some 28% of the issue of the two Hong Kong note-issuing banks was once again circulating across the border.

Changes in the standard

The *de facto* fixed rate with sterling was broken in 1967 when Hong Kong first followed the full 14.3% devaluation and then revalued by 10% from $16 = £1, but remained pegged to sterling at the new rate of $14.55. In December 1971 both sterling and the dollar appreciated 8.57% against the U.S. dollar. When sterling was floated in July 1972, the dollar was pegged for the first time to the U.S. dollar at $5.65 = US$1.00 = SDR 0.92; in 1973 when the U.S. dollar was devalued, the dollar did not follow, but kept its SDR value (SDR 1.00 = $6.134) and was repegged to the U.S. dollar. Then in November 1974 the dollar was allowed to float – with Exchange Fund intervention – until 1983 when the dollar was again linked to the U.S. dollar at the depreciated par rate of US$1.00 = $7.80.

During the 1970s the Exchange Fund became the repository of virtually all of the territory's official foreign exchange. But for the purposes of this section, only its functions relative to the currency are stated. Before 1973 the Fund issued certificates of indebtedness against deposit by the note-issuing banks of sterling at 'fixed' though alterable exchange rates. From 1973 to 1983 payments for the certificates were made in dollars, with inflationary consequences. The link rate since that date has been US$1 = $7.80; the Exchange Fund still deals only with the note-issuing banks, and the actual rates to the public vary within a margin, the upper limit of which is $7.84.

The Government's *Annual Report* succinctly states, 'The Exchange Fund bears the costs of maintaining the note issue apart from that proportion of costs which relates to the (authorized) issues'. This is not quite the situation, but at least arguments which once filled the files are reduced to a single sentence.

The impact these changes and the various Government guarantees had on the Hongkong Bank's accounts is considered in Chapter 15.

There is no central bank in Hong Kong. Policy and prudential functions are performed by various Government departments, especially the Monetary Affairs Branch, and assigned for implementation to commercial banks, usually the note-issuing banks and, because of its relative size, usually the Hongkong Bank. This remains the position, banking ordinances notwithstanding; but, when the issue of loyalty – to a Government or to the shareholders/public – came up during a U.S. Congressional consideration of the Bank's acquisition of America's Marine Midland Banks, Inc., the Hongkong Bank's witness was able to deny that it had any central banking *responsibilities* (as opposed to *operations*). Holding the bulk of the territory's clearing balances, however, provides the Bank with the potential for controlling the system's liquidity and, therefore (*inter alia*), the interbank interest rate. A government seeking to implement monetary policy has traditionally the power of 'moral suasion' and the Bank has reacted in the tradition stated by Oliphant (p. 185). More recently the Bank has come to consider itself the major bank within a banking system and has repeatedly denied central bank responsibilities – but it cannot deny its ability to impact on the system. Thus the Bank could be faced with a conflict of interest. Should the Hong Kong Government ever undertake an active monetary policy, it would need, therefore, to resolve this conflict by appropriate modifications in the system; only thus would the Bank's position as a private sector corporation responsible to its shareholders and depositors be protected. Meanwhile the Hongkong Bank and the Chartered Bank carry out banking in Hong Kong. It does, like the Chartered Bank, carry out banking instructions that it accepts from Government, one of the most important of which relates to the territory's legal tender note issue.

CHANGES IN CORPORATE ORGANIZATION

The historical tradition

Consistent with the nineteenth-century approach that a joint-stock bank with branches was in some real sense a collection of banks using a common capital and subject to the same board of directors, the pre-war Hongkong and Shanghai Banking Corporation's local branch Managers had considerable autonomy over their own sources and uses of funds. The Bank then had a relatively small Eastern staff and economized by a strictly hierarchical relationship which minimized overlapping of responsibility and the need for lateral consultation – it was all on line from Chief Manager as chief executive officer to branch Managers to department heads. Only the Accountant – and/or the Sub-Manager – had duties which were part of the Manager's responsibilities and were therefore in a sense delegated, for example, the administrative operation of the office, the discipline of junior staff, and, in some cases, the overseeing of credit advances.

In Head Office this delegation of the Manager's responsibilities involved senior officers. The 'chief' Manager originally implied that, of all the Bank's Managers in Hong Kong, Shanghai, Yokohama, Singapore, the Manager Hong Kong was the 'chief'. This interpretation is reinforced by the fact that, when the Board offered David McLean, then Shanghai Manager, the 'chief managership' of the Bank in 1870, he considered accepting it on the condition that he be allowed to remain as Manager Shanghai, that is, he acted as if he believed the Chief Manager need not be the most senior Manager in Hong Kong (see Volume I).

I. Structure and growth

This concept of the Chief Manager as merely the Bank's Hong Kong Manager with seniority over other branch Managers could not last; there had to be a Chief Manager *and* a Manager Hong Kong, but as late as the early years of the administration of J.A.H. Saunders, the distinction was never complete because of the total authority of the Chief Manager. An important constituent like (Sir) Y.K. Pao could always ask to have his case considered by the Chief Manager, but if he were a Hong Kong constituent the move past the 'Manager' appeared, unwisely no doubt, little more than going to the top 'locally'. If such a request came through, for example, the Singapore Manager, the 'Chief' would be much less ready to override the Manager on the scene and so undermine his position in Singapore. The confusion in Hong Kong could not be easily overcome while the 'on-line' structure remained unchanged; the differentiation of functions was uncertain. To retain normal branch autonomy, the Hong Kong Manager had to exaggerate his independence; R.P. Moodie, for example, made a point of not 'permitting' Head Office inspectors access (without comment) to the affairs of his office. Although this assisted in differentiating a growing 'Group' Head Office from a distinct Hong Kong office, it did so at the expense of full application of the sound supervisory measures which Head Office was developing. When G.M. Sayer interposed a level of General Managers (as opposed to non-executive advisers) between himself and any operating Manager the differentiation was fully recognized.

This lack of job differentiation had apparently first proved a problem in London Office. When Thomas Jackson and Ewen Cameron were both in London Office (1890–1893), and the latter, with his successful Shanghai management behind him, requested authority to be referred to as 'Manager', the Board agreed and created two London Managers whose relative seniority had to be understood and whose duties had to be agreed.[d] This peculiar situation brought about a further anomaly when Sir Ewen Cameron, the senior Manager, became ill in 1904 and Charles Addis, then on leave in London, was brought in as the junior London Manager with instructions to undertake a high proportion of Cameron's responsibilities, that is, the former duties of the senior Manager. Until Addis himself became senior Manager in 1912, the duties of junior and senior were practically reversed. Furthermore the existence in London Office of Eastern staff executives and Home staff executives, of local employees and juniors training for overseas assignment, forced the need to define tasks and responsibilities which were not altogether dictated by the nature of the banking business narrowly defined.

Pre-war the role of specialists had been limited. In London Office there were

---

[d] Previously D. McLean had been Manager, W. Kaye Sub-Manager, London (1875–1889), and the former had undertaken the representational responsibilities; his character and background obviated the necessity of formal delineation of functions (see Volume I).

Home staff who had developed a special expertise, for example, in the handling of the routine of the China loans; they had become in a sense 'experts'. But at a higher level, the Bank never went beyond the appointment of a political adviser. When the new Head Office was under construction in 1935, Grayburn had a management expert sent out to devise a new filing and records handling system and to supervise the physical layout and the training of the clerical staff. There was, however, no legal adviser on the staff until Morse first employed J.R. Jones in London during the Pacific War.

During the 1950s there was recognition of the specialist problem. There was correspondence dealing with the appointment of an economist as adviser, but, as Sir Sydney Caine was the expert Morse had in mind, the post should be viewed as a continuation of the political adviser with modified terms of reference. The first internal auditors came from the Bank's Eastern staff, the first consideration of the use of computers was undertaken by an in-house team. The ability of Bank officers to become fully qualified in these specializations is not the question; the generalists' recognition and preliminary description of the problem often forced a more professional investigation followed by the employment of specialists in the Bank or in a subsidiary, on occasion supervised by a Bank officer.

The increasing complexity of tasks, the activities of specialist departments and subsidiary companies, and the need for control of these developments as well as the several acquired or specially established financial subsidiaries required a more complex management structure.

These changes occurred (i) between the Board and the executive officers of the Bank, (ii) between both the Board and the executives on the one hand and the subsidiary company management on the other, and (iii) within the Bank itself. In the next section, changes within the Bank itself will be considered.

Changes within the Hongkong Bank

Background

In the pre-war Hongkong Bank the basis of control was the effective socialization of the Eastern staff, the integrity of the Portuguese as a community, and the hold on local staff through the guarantee of the compradore. By the late 1930s there were inspectors in Head Office but the Board still depended on the external auditors supplemented by irregular visits by a Bank officer appointed for a term or for a voyage as 'Inspector of Branches'.

Managers held the Bank's power of attorney. The framework of their activities was established by the Bank's regulations but within this they had virtually absolute discretion in banking matters – charity and assistance to local staff and local retirees being referred to Hong Kong, usually reaching the underworked Board of Directors itself. Managers were not bound by 'limits', although the appropriate percentage of their sources of funds would provide a practical limit beyond which they could not go without recourse to Head Office.

Supplementing this were the semi-official letters, copies of which circulated to the main branches, the private (confidential business) letters of the Managers and Chief Manager, the monthly position statements, and the various accounts required by Head Office. The basis for complex management arrangements was, therefore, present; until the mid-1930s the Chief Manager, however, had no structured assistance in his task of control. Grayburn and Saunders read the semi-official letter files and personally kept track of developments in the several branches; branch Managers were more closely involved with the agencies and sub-agencies which reported to them.

The growth of the Bank was ultimately limited to the capacity of one man to comprehend the task. This had not been true in the period to 1932 when Cameron and then Addis sat on the boards of associated London-based China companies, while successive Chief Managers, A.G. Stephen excepted, showed almost total lack of detailed interest. But the consequence of all this was that, eventually, in the 1920s the Chief Manager lost not only interest in but also contact with London events; the relevant files were not even available in Hong Kong. Grayburn's reaction in 1932, and the retirement of Sir Charles Addis in 1933, though abrupt, was in part a consequence of his need to regain full knowledge and control in a very dangerous period for the Bank as exchange bank.

There were changes in the 1950s. Special responsibilities of Head Office were recognized and officers assigned to them were specifically so designated, just as in routine banking officers working on current accounts or inward bills were differentiated. Managers were called to Hong Kong for regional meetings; the Chief Manager himself travelled extensively. The first postronics equipment was installed. But the system was demonstrably inadequate; banks could be established or acquired but the subsidiary Hongkong Bank of California could not be managed successfully, the acquired banks could not be integrated. The point may again be made that pressures had grown; change was essential if the Bank were to hold its own; change had to be basic if the Bank were to expand further.

Change – and what to preserve

And yet there was a reluctance to change based not only on natural sentiment but on the objective consideration that the Bank, with its then existing system, had been successful. The problem was to separate out the factors which were essential to the Bank's underlying success.

First was the Bank's Hong Kong base. This remained fundamental, previous arguments being reinforced by increasingly important tax considerations. Secondly, there was a reluctance to move to a committee-dominated system which Bank officers associated with American banking. The Bank had always operated on-line with full responsibility in the field; this made for fast decisions, although these were, on occasion, influenced by a Manager's particular prejudice. Hongkong Bankers were generalists, they understood a wide range of banking and were thus better suited for the management of a bank which operated as an exchange bank, a local bank, and a merchant bank; they had a 'feel' for the region that was partly their own, partly inherited from tales retold, casual comments made in passing, living and working in the East. Finally, there were the team/career, common background aspects which facilitated interpersonal communication, minimized the need for formal structures and controls, in a sense making possible all the other benefits of the Bank's traditional system.

The practicality of old traditions in the post-war world might continue because of supportive developments. The improvements in transport and communications, for example, retained the practicality of the Hongkong Bank's Hong Kong Head Office.

The other factors had all to be balanced against new requirements and specific compromises reached in each case. Thus Managers had to retain their ability to make fast decisions, but this had to be tempered by the establishment of lending 'limits', a hindrance offset by the promise of an equally fast and sympathetic response from Head Office. Furthermore, Managers were still expected to make their decisions and either act on them within the limits or refer them to Head Office; improved communications were not to make 'delegates' of branch Managers, there were to be no preliminary telephone conversations which in effect put the management task on the Head Office desk officer. The Manager must continue to manage.

If the key service were to remain general, then all officers could not be generalists; the homogeneity of the service had to be sacrificed by specialist requirements, but these newcomers had to be accepted on the team – the 'we' and 'they' attitude needed to be played down for the system to work. The positive aspects of paternalism acceptable in the pre-war service had to be retained in a staff system based on contracts and comparability of terms of service (but with advantages) with other major hongs – this last had indeed always been the case.

These crucial adjustments were made in two major stages. The first, within the traditional 'on-line' system, originated in Turner's administration but developed under Saunders. The second was even more severe; it began at one level with the Saunders inspired changes in the Bank's regulations in 1969 and continued with the interposition of General Managers under Guy Sayer and

I. Structure and growth

with the implementation of the staff report of 1977. The essential recommendations of the latter report had been agreed before Sandberg's departure for Buffalo (see Chapter 16).

The structuring of Head Office

Developments in the 1960s

In 1961 Head Office consisted of the Chief Manager, his deputy, and a chief inspector, his assistant, and up to four temporary assistants. This is what S.G. Redding has referred to as the Bank's 'strategic apex'.[e] The support staff consisted of an 'Inspector (staff)' and his assistant. There was, in addition, an 'adviser' to the Board, a post which in itself suggested there was something lacking in the Head Office structure. Although not at first shown on the Foreign staff list, which was still very traditionally composed, there were a legal adviser and a tax consultant.

The strategic apex. By October 1963 there were seven inspectors and an embryo of the technostructure with the assignment of an inspector to Internal Audit. The support staff were now listed to include the tax consultant and legal adviser, changes more in attitude than numbers, and therefore significant. In 1964, the first clear identification of line roles was given in the use of the title 'Controller Overseas Operations'. This definition of a key line area was to remain in use until 1980. In 1964 also, the word 'Inspector' was dropped from Head Office titles and replaced by 'Controller'. In 1967, the technostructure took its first major step towards growth with the assignment to it of a Methods Research function, containing a Controller, Assistant Controller, and four EDP (Electronic Data Processing) specialists. Other additions at the time (already on the staff but, as with the tax consultant, etc, not previously listed) were two Chief Manager's assistants and a senior Personal Assistant – Miss Margaret Goldney. The Deputy Chief Manager, F.J. Knightly, when Acting Chief Manager, became a member of the Bank's Board of Directors. Further significant changes came in 1969. The implications for internal structural change consequent to the establishment of executive directors were for the future.

The Secretary. The most immediate change was the appointment of a Corporation Secretary, B.J.N. Ogden, to take over certain responsibilities from the chief executive, especially those related to the issue of shares, and the post

[e] This section is heavily dependent on the analysis by Redding in his 'Organizational and Structural Change in The Hongkong and Shanghai Banking Corporation, 1950–1980', in King, ed. *Eastern Banking* (London, 1983), pp. 601–28. Redding's analytical framework was based on H. Mintzberg's model, for which see references in the bibliographical notes.

of 'chief manager' then disappeared. N.E. Clark had been 'adviser to the Board', a position misnamed; he had been something of a corporation secretary without legal status, and someone had to perform the miscellaneous tasks for which he had become responsible. At virtually the same time Saunders had been advised by the legal adviser, E.R. Udal, that a Secretary was legally necessary; accordingly, the post was added in the new regulations. Saunders himself, however, was not interested in a major role for the Secretary, who, he insisted, was not even to be present at meetings of the Board. Saunders was not yet ready to change corporate practice; he sought flexibility and a sounder structural relationship with the Board of Directors, but he was still at heart a 'chief manager', anxious to restrict access to the Board, to keep the Board at arm's length, and thus preserve his role as sole interpreter of policy, as the sole source of the authority of the executive. This is consistent with his apparent decision not to develop the potentials of the London Advisory Committee or to inform it of the Bank's policies.

Alternatively, there is a pragmatic explanation. Board papers did not circulate, the chief executive or some other executive director would have command of the information required for consideration of any issue, and Board discussions were not, with few exceptions, matters for record – the minutes were virtually the agenda reworded as decisions. There was apparently no function for a Secretary to perform at Board meetings.

Sayer, as Saunders' successor, took the same position. When the new legal adviser, F.R. Frame, assumed the additional role of Secretary in 1980, there was no vacancy on the Board, but M.G.R. Sandberg, the Chairman, considered that Frame's contributions on increasingly important legal questions would prove essential, and he was thus the first Secretary to be invited to attend meetings of the Board of Directors.

Despite Saunders' original intention that the Secretary's Office be narrowly defined, certain support activities, for example public relations, archives, the corporation's 'library', were from time to time attached. In the several reorganizations these might develop into departments and be reassigned, and thus Ogden's office served as an initial administrative basis for several corporate developments, including the Bank history project, in the period to 1980. With the shift of share operations to the Bank's 50% owned subsidiary (with Jardine, Matheson and Co.) Central Registration HK Ltd, the Secretary's Office was allowed to fold into the Legal Department with Frame as Group Legal Adviser and Corporation Secretary.

Head Office and the subsidiaries
Of significance to the structure during the mid-sixties onwards was the merging of the Mercantile Bank, which in the first years had been left only loosely

attached. An important watershed was the decision in 1964 not to recruit any further juniors into the Mercantile as such, but it was to be some time before the merging of the Mercantile and BBME into the main structure was complete.

Upon the acquisition of the Mercantile Bank Turner had sent a Hongkong Bank officer, the first being W.H. Lydall, to that bank's head office, then in London, as liaison; this practice continued even when the Mercantile Bank's head office was in Hong Kong. The growth of the Hongkong Bank Group, however, required a formal overall control system. The chief executive and his colleagues charged with controlling the policy of the subsidiaries, especially the BBME, continued to run against the problem of attempting to dictate to an entrenched board and their chief executive officer.

Saunders expected to act through a Hongkong Bank officer, the Manager Europe, who was a member of the subsidiary banks' boards of directors. The Manager was, however, but one of several directors, and directors do not vote with the authority of proxies. A bank may have but one shareholder; that shareholder can elect the board, but once elected the members of the board are responsible not only to the shareholder but also to the bank's depositors and to the Government as required by law or custom. The one shareholder can dismiss the board, but where would he find suitable new directors? He can dismiss the board but what of the constituents they represent? Saunders and Baldwin Maull, the chief executive of Marine Midland Banks, were, be it noted, having the same problem at the same time (see p. 785).

Developments in the 1970s

In 1970 Saunders appointed Guy Sayer as General Manager in charge of subsidiaries; he was aware that any mistake eventually came to rest with the parent company in Hong Kong. From his new position Sayer took the view that, in a fast moving world, it was easy to become badly exposed. There had to be more information, and information of better quality, flowing into the centre in order that proper vigilance could be maintained and improved. This required restructuring of the management control system.

The emergence of the new Head Office structure by 1973 indicates, for the first time, the emergence of a small caucus of very senior executives surrounding the Chairman, with a Deputy Chairman and two Directors/ General Managers. Monitoring of overseas operations was now via two Controllers, a Senior Assistant Manager, and six Assistant Managers. Moving Mercantile Bank's head office to Hong Kong had been but a first step; in 1973 the post of General Manager of the Mercantile Bank disappeared. This with parallel measures, the integration of the staff, for example, made full integration operationally complete.

Control can be seen in the negative sense of the ability to override decisions in the field; control can also be seen in the context of positive management of resources. By 1973 certain functions, performed in the head office since the early days of the Bank, for example, 'books', had come specifically into Head Office organization charts subsumed in Group Finances. Head Office had almost completed the change from being simply the extension of a Chief Manager who depends for operations entirely on his branch Managers, to a 'central bank' for the Hongkong Bank Group, where the sources and uses of funds overall are studied and where positive plans are initiated for branches and subsidiaries to accomplish.

As Redding observed, management control, in terms of the monitoring of financial performances, had become increasingly evident and specialized in the late Sixties. It was represented in the 1973 structure by an Assistant Manager Group Finances and two Assistant Managers Head Office Books. Internal Audit had now grown to five officers. 'Electronic Data Processing' (EDP) and Methods Research had divided and would remain, as EDP would continue expanding and subdividing.

The 'final' pattern as Guy Sayer had envisaged it did not, however, emerge until the creation of new General Manager posts in 1974. By 1976 the key subdivisions, which have remained largely unchanged since, crystallized out.

Guy Sayer's view was that the restructuring of Head Office should leave him with the ability to delegate to this caucus of senior people, each of whom would have at his fingertips the critical information related to one area or function. Access to the informed judgements of this team would allow him to take on the growing responsibilities associated with the mushrooming complexity he oversaw. In the event, the subdivision of responsibilities left a General Manager in charge of Group Finances, another in charge of Overseas Operations, another for general administration, one for the Hong Kong operations, and an executive in charge of the fast-growing Wardley operations.

By 1976 line control under the General Manager, Overseas Operations, had further developed; in three years the executive staff had increased from nine to fourteen with a doubling of Assistant Managers. The group under the General Manager, Administration, now included Property, as well as Training and a proliferating Staff Department. Within the technostructure, Group Finances were under a General Manager and now formed an eight office unit. Both Internal Audit and Methods Research had increased in strength. The growing EDP now came under an Assistant General Manager, Management Services.

Following 1976, increasingly specialized functions continued to be added to both the support staff and the technostructure. The key activities of Overseas Operations and Group Finances continued to be subdivided, both of them displaying significant size increases in 1978, from 11 to 17 and 32 to 41 respectively. In 1978, Management Services for both Group Head Office and Hong Kong were brought under one General Manager, Central Services.

Technological change
In the early days of the Hongkong Bank applicants for the Eastern staff might be asked during the interview to add a column of figures. There are many later reminiscences of hours spent tracing the error preventing a balance in the several accounts. Acceptance of machines came slowly. Perhaps typical of the old attitude was that of F.T. Koelle, the Hamburg Manager, who kept the first adding machine in his office for weeks, testing it against his own calculations before permitting its general use.[f]

In early 1964 the Bank accepted that the postronics system installed in the 1950s was inadequate. The Bank's percentage market share in Hong Kong was declining and any attempt to recover would eventually probably require computerization. O.P. Edwards' first report, recommending the establishment of an Electronic Data Processing Department, was reconsidered by a team headed by M.W. Bond, a Foreign staff officer, but including R.L. Barrington, an expert from Peat, Marwick, and Mitchell's consulting service, and another Bank officer, L.V.S. Laville. In October volunteers for training courses were sought and the following year aptitude tests for computer work were administered and courses instituted. Meanwhile Bond and others had attended IBM courses, visited banks in the United States and Japan, and, together with N.H.T. Bennett, then Controller, Special Duties, had submitted reports which led to a Board-approved decision to install a duplex IBM 360/30 on-line system.

By 1967 with the installation of the IBM 360 the Hongkong Bank had created the basis for one of the largest on-line, real time systems in the banking world. The concentration of business and high-rise residences was ideal for such a development. The Bankers Clearing House, operated by the Bank, was handling 300,000 cheques a day when, in 1973, a paperless, electronically recorded system using magnetic tape was introduced. Paralleling these innovations was the development of informational systems facilitating management control.

The telex complemented the capabilities of the computer; at its simplest the telex eliminated the time between cable and bank offices – and the possibility, on occasion realized, of someone reading the message en route. In a short time 'conversational' telex became the normal method for long-distance operations in foreign exchange, for deposits, and for inter-bank messages. Increased use

---

[f] A story told to Koelle's son, Dr. W. Koelle, by A. Nack, who joined Hamburg Branch in 1907. Nack was interviewed by D.J.S. King in 1981 when the former was 92 years of age and the story is retold in King's report (Group Archives).

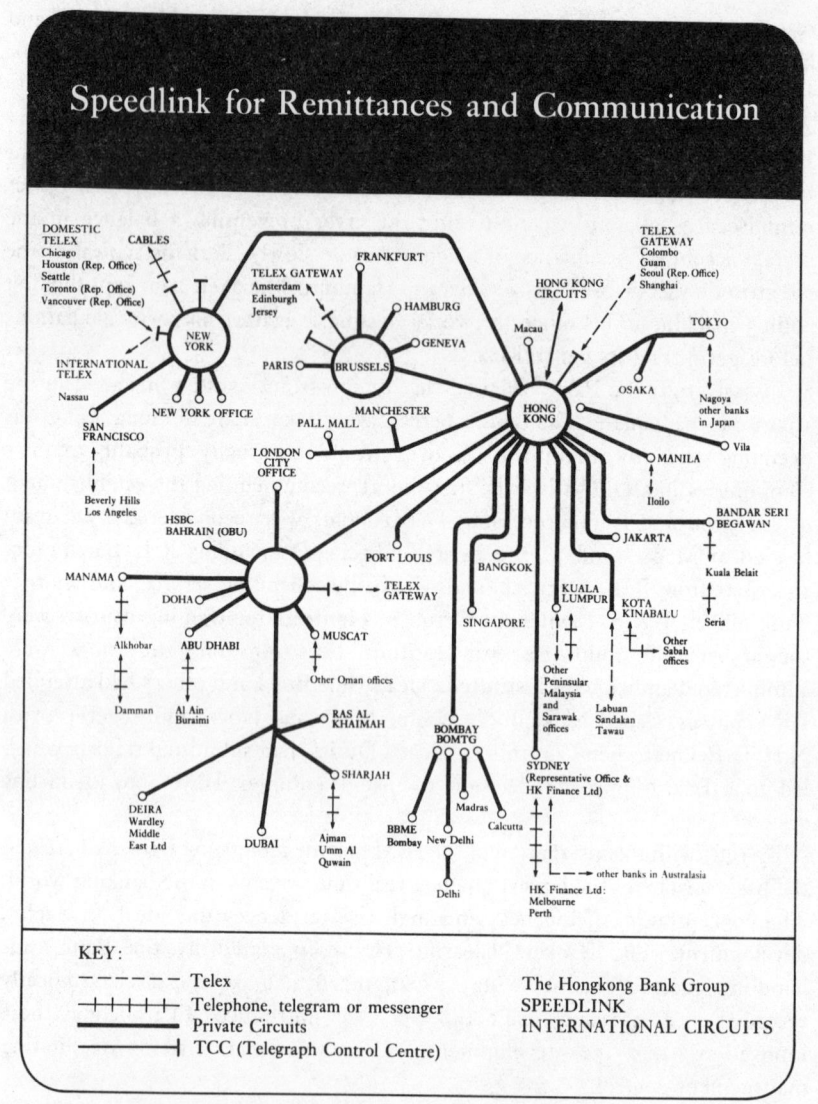

Figure 13.1 Speedlink for remittances and communication

coincided with decreased cost while postal charges increased faster than postal efficiency. The next stage was leased circuits, linking branches with Head Office. A breakthrough came in 1971 with the availability of computerized message switching facilities, and in 1975 the various circuits were joined into a Group network to be known as SPEEDLINK, incorporated as a wholly owned Belgian subsidiary. By 1977 the system had 70 stations, of which 27 were

I. Structure and growth

in Hong Kong (see Figure 13.1). Efficient handling required a message switching centre in Hong Kong itself with subsidiary switches at Bahrain, New York, and in Europe, where Brussels offered better facilities than London itself.

Head Office and branch management

The broadening of the management hierarchy in Head Office had further significant policy implications. Two aspects of the Bank's organization appeared unsatisfactory to men like Sandberg: (i) inspectors/desk officers in Head Office being totally 'soft-end' bankers without branch management experience but nevertheless commenting to Managers in the field on their operations and (ii) the tendency to reserve the best men for Hong Kong and the consequence, on occasion, that an officer might be sent to manage a branch on the wrong grounds, proximity to retirement, for example – let him do his last years out there and retire with a pension based on a higher final salary base. The fact is that major overseas offices would be best served by highly qualified Bankers in mid-career.

The solution was possible primarily because of the changes in Head Office. The 'on-line', one level one man system, when combined with the promotion pattern, suggested that appointment as a Manager was the last appointment. Once a member of the Foreign staff had sufficient seniority to be appointed Manager of one of the more important branches, he would be too old for consideration as Chief Manager, and no other post in Head Office (except latterly Manager Hong Kong) would represent even the equivalent of a lateral transfer, much less a promotion.

Interestingly, the Mercantile Bank of India had had a solution not available to the Hongkong Bank. After 30 years service in the East, further service in London, with the later retirement age there, had proved a useful pattern.[g] The Eastern staff officer could be asked to serve as a regional desk officer or even Chief Manager of the Mercantile Bank in London. A Hongkong Bank Foreign staff officer could also serve in London, but only in the few posts reserved for Foreign staff in London Office. Even a Chief Manager, Sir Newton Stabb, would as London Manager be junior to the new chief executive in Hong Kong. Now it was in effect the Mercantile system which Sandberg wanted for the Hongkong Bank, but with an important difference – Head Office was in Hong Kong.

The ideal career pattern became, in consequence, an earlier managerial

---

[g] Climate and other health factors suggested an early Eastern retirement. The 1935 Hongkong Bank Head Office was air conditioned, but this was unusual; air-conditioning and consequently improved working conditions became general in the mid-1950s. The extension of Eastern service was not, however, practical without either unusual company growth or, alternatively, considerable disturbance to career expectations.

assignment which, if successful, would result in the Manager's recall to Hong Kong for promotion in the Head Office hierarchy, including regional supervision based on knowledge gained in the field. With a total career plan in mind, this policy suggests that only the best should be sent to such overseas posts, that such an assignment was neither exile nor necessarily a final posting. The result would be a stronger Head Office and a sounder control of the branches.

The 'cost' of this policy was the necessity of relatively brief postings in an overseas branch – brief in the context of the pre-war terms of ten or more years. But then other aspects of the problem had changed. The shorter postings suggested the need for highly qualified and senior 'local' officers. This created a further problem. If the Bank were operating only one or possibly two offices in a particular country, could a bright local career-oriented banker be attracted or retained? The more recent answer has been to bring such an officer on secondment to work in Hong Kong, in a relatively senior position. This has proved the beginning of a truly international 'International staff' (vice 'Foreign', vice 'Eastern staff').

One of the arguments for long-term last appointments for a Manager in the outports was, pre-war at least, the nature of outport business and social life. This was no longer relevant. Even if the old foreign firms survived, their managers were by the mid-1970s local citizens. The foreign communities had dwindled. Nor, with few exceptions (mainly in the Middle East) could the Bank put Foreign staff juniors in small branches – visas were limited and expatriates had become expensive.

What the major branches needed was a middle-career, competent banker, straight from Head Office with the latest developments and ideas, to inspire an operation increasingly dependent on the ability of its local officers and staff. Having undertaken this task successfully, the 'International staff' officer could move on to another major branch or return to a senior management position in Hong Kong. For the system to work, however, the existence of such a senior management position was crucial.

The impact – is this the Hongkong Bank?

First of all, 'Is *what* the Hongkong Bank?'

Certainly not its associated company Cathay Pacific Airways nor the subsidiary, Speedlink. These companies, and others like them in the Hongkong Bank Group, have their own purposes, staffs, morale, and contributions; they have their own independent management. Their being part of a larger financial group suggests that certain group mutual benefits were intended to be derived from such 'membership', but their separateness is, in some sense, an indication that they are not and ought not to be the 'Hongkong Bank' of the question.

The Hongkong Bank historically had certain characteristics which, because they were particularistic, could not be shared as the immediate consequence of a financial acquisition. The changing structure of Head Office was designed to permit centralized monitoring of all Hongkong Bank Group companies, especially of the planning and supervisory control of the financial companies and the direct management control of selected companies and activities. The existence of the Hongkong Bank Group concept is evidence that complete integration was not intended. Even with the financial companies, it was obvious that only a few had a background sufficiently similar to that of the Hongkong Bank's to be integrated.

Hang Seng Bank, acquired in 1965 (see Chapter 14), was a Chinese bank and its continued success depended on its continued separate management; Marine Midland Bank as an American bank was seen as a partner; the Hongkong Bank put their own directors on the relevant boards, the very solution which, in the case of the Mercantile and BBME, had proved insufficient for Group purposes of total control. In these cases, however, the measure was suited to the purpose; the Group's Head Office did not want total control.

The other Group companies were, where possible, organized as it were around 'hubs', represented by holding companies, and the extent of management control depended on the nature of the enterprise, the extent of the Hongkong Bank's ability to make an input, the extent of the Bank's equity involvement, the ability to 'down-stream' dividends, and local regulatory requirements.

The question, 'Is this (still) the Hongkong Bank?' now relates to the Hongkong Bank as operating bank, the Hongkong Bank as Head Office for the Group and the integrated operations of the Mercantile Bank and the British Bank of the Middle East.

A successful bank has on the one hand an executive staff capable of handling a highly structuralized procedure and of innovation and initiative on the lending side of banking. The parallel with team sports is and has long been obvious – the initiative within the constraint of pre-determined and set rules. The addition of specialists who rationalize the rules and facilitate the initiative with EDP, Methods Research, and Speedlink do not in themselves alter the Hongkong Bank if the focus of its historical success is placed on the general bankers. Thus the question narrows itself once again to the impact of change on the core – the bankers among the members of the executive staff.

This in turn suggests two sub-problems, concerning (i) the London-recruited International staff and (ii) the locally recruited officer serving in a single country.

Certainly, as the question has been narrowed down, the significant changes which occurred between 1961 and 1979 take on a less dramatic image. The focus on university graduates, necessary from the Bank's point of view, coincided with the tendency of the traditional Bank junior opting for university before seeking career employment. The shorter London Office period, the substitution of brief 'Outward Bound' training for the years at New Beckenham in the socialization process does affect a Hongkong Banker's self-image in part because the self-image necessary in a new age for banking leadership has itself changed. Senior Managers of the Hongkong Bank had from time to time considered change in this or that aspect of staff policy, but they operated in a total social context and were consequently frustrated. In some cases, for example, the long voyage East, a virtue was wisely made of necessity, and the voyage East by P&O was itself part of the expatriate's total experience of the East, but the P&O regular service has long been discontinued.

The Bank can no longer afford to recruit solely from a particular type within a particular social group and let the 'cream rise to the top', as A.G. Stephen put it in opposing Addis's pre-1914 recommendations for 'up-grading' the staff (see Volume II). The self-selection that took place in a junior's first fifteen years is too expensive to tolerate in days of annual leaves and early marriage, dependants' education allowances, family transportation, etc. These factors alone necessitated the review of policy in 1977 (see discussion in Chapter 15) with consequences which were already apparent in the early 1980s. The carefully selected young executive finds himself in a small, 'elite' service in which personal contact remains possible, where banking continues to be that difficult combination of strict attention to regulations and procedures coupled with innovation and initiative. He will after all still have London training, he will serve a general banking apprenticeship in the East, and he will be associated with his colleagues socially. He will, with the assistance of these four volumes, still be able to identify with the Bank, its traditions and its folklore, even as did the rugby-playing junior of the inter-war and early post-war periods.

Part of the concern for the Bank's continued identity arises from a natural idealization of the past; it was, after all, a successful past – on the whole. But, as Muriel's autobiographical writings indicate, the Hongkong Bank family had family problems; certain senior officers could not work together and had to be separated; certain Managers were saved from disaster only because of the routine nature of the business they would undertake and because of what the Shanghai compradore had long ago recognized as 'joss'. Joss is an integral part of banking, but it is unwise to depend heavily on its continuation, with or without lions well-placed, with or without good *feng-shui*.

Although the breakdown of the 'three-tier' system was in a sense forced by

I. Structure and growth

the emigration of the Portuguese and the expansion of the business, the pace was dictated by the change in society itself as well as by the regulations of several Governments. From a business sense the change permitted rationalization of assignments, economical use of expensive Foreign staff, increased marketing potential, and closer management control of local lending. This last may seem a contradiction. The local loan officers are now locally recruited and may be supposed, incorrectly, to lack the socialization necessary for controlled initiative in lending. However, lending to the local market had previously been through an intermediary, the compradore or equivalent, whose guarantee was insufficient in a crisis and whose contacts might well be limited for clan, dialect, or other reasons.

After structural reforms, the essence of the Hongkong Bank remains. Whether this essence is sufficient to ensure success is perhaps the most interesting of questions. It falls, however, outside the scope of a history.

BRANCHES AND GEOGRAPHICAL EXPANSION

The discussion of branches in Chapter 10 dealt almost entirely with those of the Hongkong Bank itself. With the development of the Hongkong Bank Group the problem becomes more complex. The obvious continuity is found in those offices of the Group which are in fact branches of the Hongkong Bank as an operating commercial bank. The Hang Seng Bank did not open an office outside Hong Kong before 1983. The British Bank of the Middle East and its subsidiary and associated banks varied their coverage as permitted, operating under their own boards of directors.

The Hongkong Bank's own ability to branch was severely limited or even prohibited. In most cases a minimum local capital requirement was instituted; this, however, could usually be met by revaluation of locally held property to a reasonable market price. But the Bank's overall country operations depended on garnering local funds, and without branches these had to be bought in at an increasingly high price. For a bank with ambitions beyond the traditional port or capital city areas, beyond trade finance, branches, including small offices or minibanks, had become essential in difficult political times.

This section describes the history of the commercial banking offices of the Hongkong Bank and of those subsidiary banks whose branching policy is closely related to and determined by the Hongkong Bank, that is, the Mercantile Bank and the Hongkong Bank of California.

Having made this decision, two problems remain. The Hongkong Bank was in some countries prevented from undertaking full commercial banking operations, but its interests were of sufficient importance to warrant, where permitted, a 'representative office': in 1965 Sydney, 1970 Vancouver, 1972

Table 13.1 *The Hongkong Bank Group
Commercial bank branches, 1962–1984
Hongkong Bank, Mercantile Bank, Hongkong Bank of California*[a]

Year	Branches opened[b]	Branches closed
1962	+3 branches, Hong Kong	[New York rep, MBLD[c]]
1963	+4 branches, Hong Kong	Djakarta
	Queenstown, Singapore	Rangoon
	Nagoya, MBLD	Rangoon, MBLD
	Butterworth, MBLD	Tokyo, MBLD[c]
	Curepipe, Mauritius, MBLD	
1964	+8 branches, Hong Kong	Phnom-Penh
	Padungen Rd, Kuching	
	Visakhapatnam, MBLD	
1965	+14 branches, Hong Kong	
	Bukit Bintong Rd, Kuala Lumpur	
	Ipoh Rd, Kuala Lumpur	
	Jurong, Singapore	
	Serangoon Gardens, Singapore	
	Bukit Panjong, Singapore, MBLD	
1966	+4 branches, Hong Kong	Osaka, MBLD[c]
	Rock Rd, Kuching	Semba, Osaka, MBLD[c]
	Kowloon, MBLD	
	Tardeo Road, Bombay, MBLD	
	Vile Parle, Bombay, MBLD	
	Gariahat Road, Calcutta, MBLD	
	New Alipore, Calcutta, MBLD	
	Sealdah, Calcutta, MBLD	
	Dacca, MBLD	
1967	+4 branches, Hong Kong	Head Office, London, MBLD
	Head Office, Hong Kong, MBLD	
	Cameron Rd, Kowloon, MBLD	
	Chembur, Bombay, MBLD	
	Quatre Bornes, Mauritius, MBLD	
	Rose Hill, Mauritius, MBLD	
	High Street, Singapore, MBLD	
	Chinatown, San Francisco, HBC	
1968	+6 branches, Hong Kong	
	Robinson Rd, Singapore	
	Djakarta	
	Bandra, Bombay, MBLD	
	Kadamtala, Calcutta, MBLD	
	Shakespeare Sarani, Calcutta,	
	Sacramento, HBC	
	[BBME: Geneva][d]	
1969	+2 branches, Hong Kong	Chittagong, MBLD
	Andheri, Bombay, MBLD	Dacca, MBLD
	Nimtollah Ghat, Calcutta, MBLD	Karachi, MBLD
		Khulna, MBLD

I. Structure and growth

Table 13.1 (cont.)

Year	Branches opened[b]	Branches closed
1970	+5 branches, Hong Kong Pall Mall, London[e] Lumut, Brunei North Point, Hong Kong, MBLD Asoke Lane, Bangkok, MBLD[f] Beverly Hills, Los Angeles(2) North Hollywood, Encino, Carson, HBC	Sowcarpet, Madras, MBLD Pall Mall, London, MBLD[e] Rajawongse Rd, Bangkok, MBLD[f]
1971	+2 branches, Hong Kong Wanchai, Hong Kong, MBLD Lai Min, Port Louis, MBLD Beau Bassin, Mauritius, MBLD San Jose, HBC	Lumut, Brunei
1972	+7 branches, Hong Kong Kota, Djakarta Macau Port Vila, New Hebrides [Vanuatu] Vir Nariman Rd, Bombay, MBLD Dalhousie Square, Calcutta, MBLD	Bombay[g] Calcutta[g]

1973	+17 branches, Hong Kong
	Honiara, Guadalcanal,
	  [British] Solomon Islands
	Frankfurt
	Mahebourg, Mauritius, MBLD
	Singapore[c]: Raffles Place,
	  Beach Road, Bukit Panjang,
	  High Street
	Malaysia[c]: Kuala Lumpur, Khota
	  Bahru, Kuala Trengganu,
	  Seremban, Taiping, Bentong,
	  Butterworth, Ipoh, Kuala
	  Lipis, Kuantan, Mentakab,
	  Penang, Raub, Temerloh
		Yokohama
		Kobe
		Galle, MBLD
		Jaffna, MBLD
		Kandy, MBLD
		Singapore[c]: Raffles Pl.
		  Beach Road, Bukit
		  Panjang, High St, MBLD
		Malaysia[c]: Kuala Lumpur,
		  Khota Bahru, Kuala
		  Trengganu, Seremban,
		  Taiping, Bentong,
		  Butterworth, Ipoh,
		  Kuala Lipis, Kuantan,
		  Mentakab, Penang, Raub,
		  Temerloh, MBLD

1974	+19 branches, Hong Kong Manchester Seattle (Washington)	Colombo & Pettah, MBLD
1975	+18 branches, Hong Kong Chicago (Illinois) Agana, Guam, HBC	Saigon San Jose, HBC
1976	+17 branches in Hong Kong Manama, Bahrain (OBU) St Helier, Jersey, CI Chinatown, New York one branch in Malaysia	London, MBLD[c] Kowloon, MBLD[c] Wanchai, MBLD[c]

Table 13.1 (cont.)

Year	Branches opened[b]	Branches closed
1977	+6 branches in Hong Kong Chinatown, London Nassau, Bahamas (OBU) Amsterdam Edinburgh Flacq, Mauritius, MBLD	Los Angeles (1), HBC North Hollywood, HBC
1978	+15 branches, Hong Kong Agana (Guam) Burra Bazaar, Calcutta, MBLD Goodlands, Mauritius, MBLD Vacoas, Mauritius, MBLD Port Vila, New Hebrides, MBLD	New Alipore, Calcutta, MBLD Agana (1), HBC Encino, HBC
1979	+55 branches, Hong Kong Dublin (Irish Republic) Borivli, Bombay, MBLD Plaine Verte, Mauritius, MBLD	San Francisco+1, Los Angeles, Beverly Hills, Carson, Sacramento, HBC
1980	Portland (Oregon) Zurich (Switzerland) Brompton Rd, London [BBME] Washington, D.C. (Rep Office)	
1981	Pasig, Manila (Philippines)[f] Fukuoka (Rep Office)	Iloilo (Philippines)[f]
1982	Muara (Brunei) Seri Complex (Brunei) Santiago (Chile) India[c]: Bombay+6, Calcutta +8, Delhi, Madras, New Delhi, Visakhapatnam Madras Milan (Italy) Busan (Korea) Karachi (Pakistan)	Nagoya, MBLD India[c]: Bombay+6 Calcutta+8, Delhi, Madras, New Delhi, Visakhapatnam
1983	Mauritius[c]: Port Louis+1 Beau Bassin, Curepipe, Flacq, Goodlands, Mahebourg, Plaine Verte, Quatre Bornes, Rose Hills, Vacoas Milan Fukuoka Nagoya Osaka Birmingham Leeds +4 branches, Macau Flushing, New York Valparaiso	Mauritius[c]: Port Louis +1, Beau Bassin, Curepipe, Flacq, Goodlands, Mahebourg, Plaine Verte, Quatre Bornes, Rose Hill, Vacoas, MBLD Port Vila, MBLD

I. Structure and growth

Table 13.1 (cont.)

Year	Branches opened[b]	Branches closed
1984	Taipei Stockholm (Representative Office)	

BBME British Bank of the Middle East.
HBC Hongkong and Shanghai Banking Corporation of California, Inc. (in 1970 and after Hongkong Bank of California, Inc.).
MBLD Mercantile Bank Ltd (the name was sold in 1984).
OBU Offshore Banking Unit.
The location of branches by country is shown in Tables 13.2 and 13.3. In this table, countries are given only if the branch did not exist in 1971 or 1977. Where a second office is established in a city or in Hong Kong or Singapore, the city or territory is also named.

[a] Branches are Hongkong Bank unless otherwise indicated. For developments from 1926 to 1941, see Tables 2.4 and 9.1 (Vol. III); from 1946–1961, see Table 10.2.
[b] New branches only; for reopenings following the Pacific War, see Table 2.1.
[c] Rationalization: transfer from MBLD to the Hongkong Bank.
[d] Rationalization: BBME branch as a Group facility.
[e] Transfer of MBLD's Pall Mall branch (West End branch) to Hongkong Bank.
[f] Transfer of a banking licence from one location to another.
[g] Rationalization: Hongkong Bank's Indian branches to MBLD.

Toronto, 1974 Seoul, 1975 São Paulo, Brazil, 1978 Houston, Texas – and in 1980 Peking. This is taken into consideration in the discussion. However, neither the tables nor the text follow the geographical development of non-commercial banking companies of the Group.

THE HONGKONG BANK AND MERCANTILE BANK, 1962–1971

During the period 1962–1971 when Saunders was Chief Manager and then Chairman of The Hongkong and Shanghai Banking Corporation, the overall branching policy had to take into consideration the position of the wholly owned banking subsidiaries, the Mercantile Bank and the British Bank of the Middle East. As the relevant part of Table 13.1 indicates, there was considerable activity and it would be stretching the point to suggest that the Hongkong Bank, taken by itself, would provide no surprises to pre-war Eastern staff; with the Mercantile Bank the picture is even more complex. However, some generalizations can be made to assist in the interpretation of Table 13.1 and in the comparison with the tables in Chapter 10.

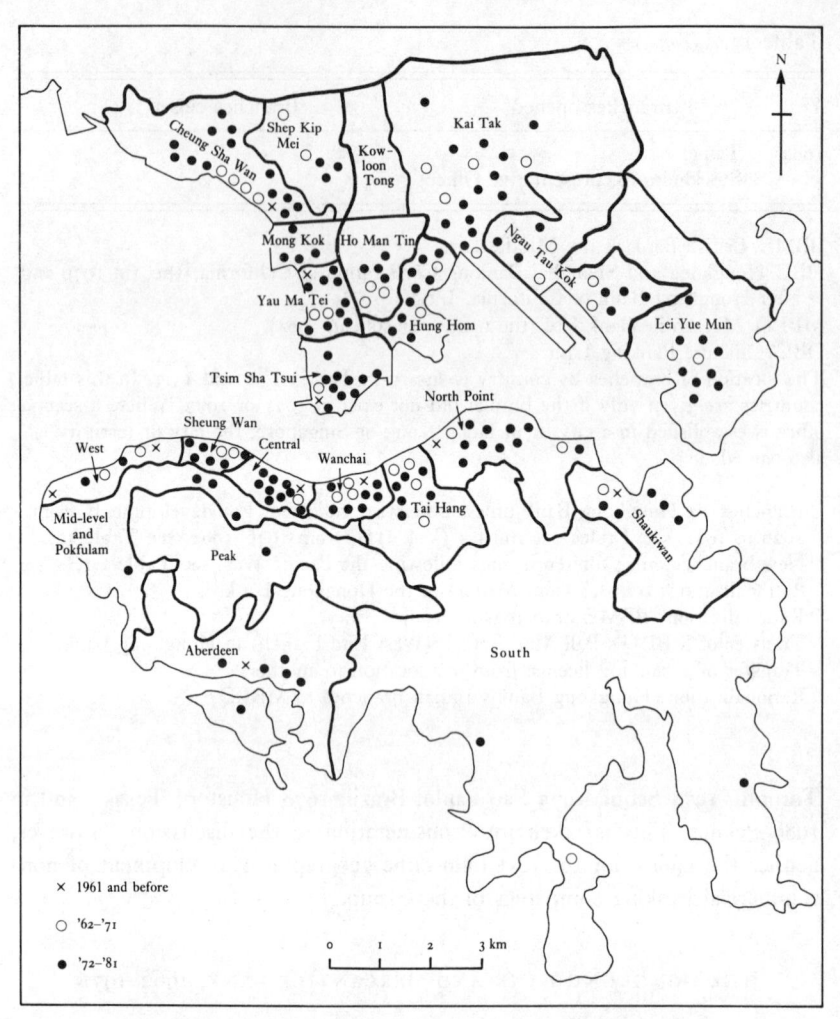

4 Hong Kong: the 1980 branch network of the Hongkong Bank:
(A) Urban area

Small branch policies

Perhaps the most obvious point to make is that the establishing of small branches primarily to garner funds was accelerated as funds became more expensive and as the development of local banks made competition on the interbank markets more intense. The Hongkong Bank had 68 offices in Hong Kong alone by the end of 1971, the Mercantile had four, and Hang Seng Bank two. For the situation at the end of the decade, see Maps 4A and B. This growth policy was also implemented in Singapore and in India, where Group policy

I. Structure and growth

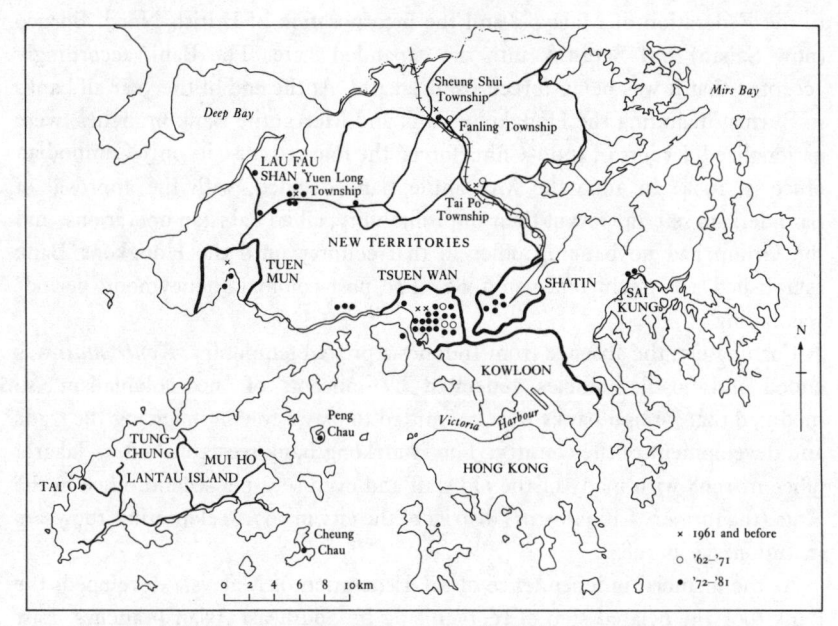

4 Hong Kong: the 1980 branch network of the Hongkong Bank:
(B) the New Territories
from Victor F.S. Sit, 'Branching...'

was coordinated by the Manager India. In 1964 the Reserve Bank of India first approved additional offices which had, however, to be located in cities in which the Mercantile Bank was already established. In consequence, the number of Mercantile Bank Indian offices increased from eight to eighteen, mainly because of smaller offices opened in Bombay and Calcutta.

The Mercantile Bank began an expansion policy in Mauritius, setting up a second office in the capital, Port Louis, and also in the smaller towns. The tables in Chapter 10 provide evidence that Sir Michael Turner's policy relative to the Mercantile's Rajawongse Road office in Bangkok had never been intended to prevent the development of the Mercantile Bank. Indeed the Rajawongse office itself, the one which had caused such heartaches in 1961 (see Chapter 12), lasted to 1970 and was moved, with Thai approval, to Asoke Lane, Bangkok.

Changes in regional coverage

There was significant change in geographical coverage within the Far Eastern region – and some in the United States and Europe.

In 1963 the Hongkong Bank decided that it could no longer operate in the hostile atmosphere engendered by *Konfrontasi*, Indonesia's policy of opposition to the Federation of Malaysia and the incorporation of British North Borneo (now Sabah) and Sarawak into the expanded state. The Bank accordingly accepted that it was being forced from Jakarta. At the end of the year all banks in Burma, including the Hongkong Bank and Mercantile Bank branches, were nationalized. Events in Indo-China forced the Bank to close its only Cambodian office in 1964. In 1969 the Mercantile Bank decided, with the approval of Saunders, to sell, in view of their unprofitability, all its Pakistan operations, and the Group had no banking office in that country until the Hongkong Bank established a Karachi office in 1982. The post-colonial 'honeymoon period' was fading.

Fortunately, the absence from Indonesia proved temporary. *Konfrontasi* was ended and hostile policies generated by concepts of 'neo-colonialism' so modified that foreign banks were permitted to play a role in financing the trade and development of the country. The Hongkong Bank reestablished its Jakarta office in 1968 with many of the old staff and even set up a second office in the Kota (the former 'Chinatown') district of the city in 1972, celebrating 100 years in Indonesia in 1984.

As the financial independence of the Federation of Malaysia developed, the Bank took the belated step of reorganizing its Southeast Asian branches. East Malaysian (Sabah and Sarawak) offices already reported through Kota Kinabalu (Jesselton) directly to Hong Kong. Brunei also reported directly. By 1960 offices in Peninsular Malaysia came under Kuala Lumpur, and the branch in the capital was directly subject to Head Office. (For the Malaysian branches, see Map 5.) Singapore branch dealt with increasingly complex Singapore business only.

In the United States the extension of the Hongkong Bank of California to include branches in San Francisco's Chinatown and the State capital of Sacramento, originally discussed in 1957 before the bank's setbacks, were accomplished in 1967 and 1968 respectively. Dunnett, the California subsidiary's President, advised Saunders that he could not expect to expand his share of California-originated Eastern trade finance due to the competition of the Bank of America and Crocker National Bank. He advised further investment in local banking; this policy was implemented after his retirement. In 1970 HBC acquired the questionable assets and undoubted liabilities of the Republic National Bank and Trust Company of Beverly Hills, California, adding five offices in the Los Angeles region. In 1971 the bank opened in San Jose in anticipation of an urban redevelopment which was never undertaken. Its location in a particularly seedy part of town between pornographic bookshops was unfortunate. The decision to encourage new customers by handing out free book bags was inspired, one would like to suppose, by the proximity of San Jose State University.

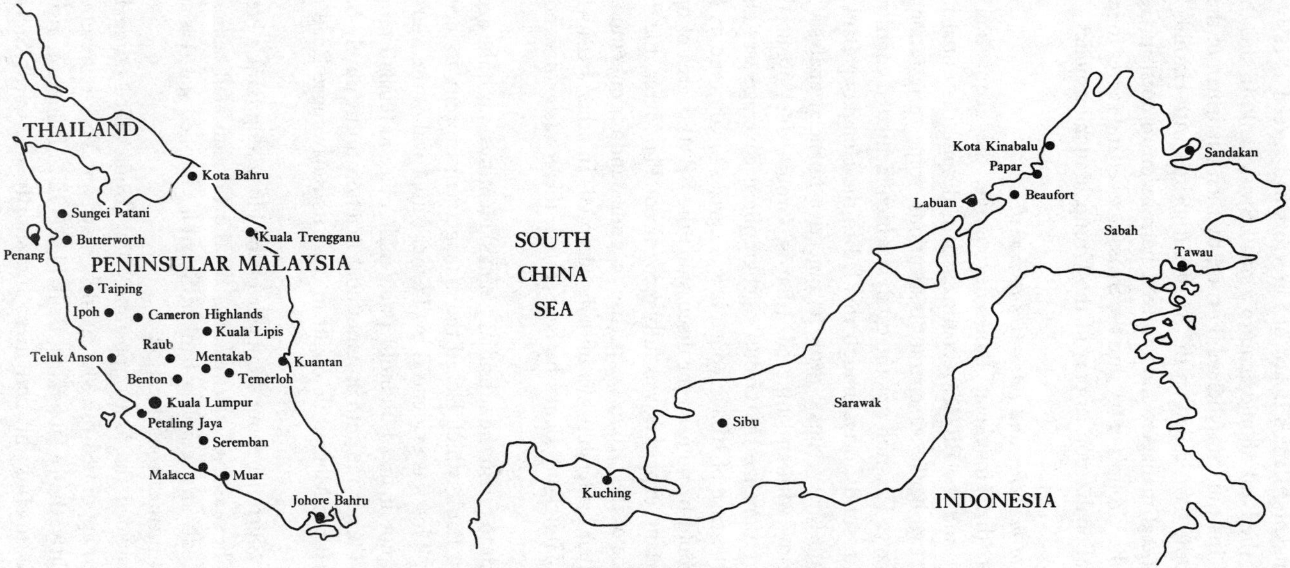

5 Malaysia: the Hongkong Bank's branches, 1980.
From Chee Peng Lim et al, in *Eastern Banking*

On the assumption that it would be difficult to obtain permission to open a branch, the Hongkong Bank's Board of Directors had agreed as early as 1958 that, if possible, the Bank should acquire a small Swiss bank. In this the Board were frustrated. Instead, Sir Michael Turner, by then Chairman of the British Bank of the Middle East, called on the Swiss authorities with Harold Musker, the BBME's general manager, and received permission to open in Geneva in 1968. This was the Group's entry into the Swiss market and serves to introduce the subject of rationalization as part of the Group branching policy.

Rationalization of branches and intra-Group transfers
The officers of the Hongkong Bank negotiating the acquisition of the Mercantile Bank and the BBME recognized that, despite the initial intention of retaining the two banks as separate institutions, some early rationalization would be necessary. Taxation was the catalyst which facilitated coordination in the use of surplus funds, even though this led to the Hongkong Bank's being arbiter of the subsidiary banks' growth; objective financial analysis made it impossible to argue with an 'imperial' (that is, Group-wide) financial plan.

The need to rationalize the Group's geographical coverage was also early recognized. In the case of BBME, once it was agreed to continue its Bombay branch, there would be no need for discussion; the BBME's area of operation and, more important, expertise, was fully recognized. The Mercantile Bank was seen as the source of the Group's expertise on India, and for operations on the sub-continent their leadership was initially accepted. In other areas where the Mercantile and Hongkong Banks both operated, there was at first no overall decision.

The agreement to retain the subsidiary banks' identities was quite acceptable to the Hongkong Bank, which lacked the management capacity to incorporate their operations. This was evidenced by Turner's approval of the Mercantile's 1959 plans, then not finalized, to build a new main office in Kuala Lumpur. On the other hand Turner ran into an emotional reaction to his purely business-level decision that the Mercantile ought to close its Rajawongse Road office in Bangkok.

When J.R.N. Shirreff became Manager of the Hongkong Bank's New York branch in 1963 he was No. 250 (of 262) on the Foreign staff seniority list. Although admittedly an exemplary banker, Shirreff's implied status as an 'early starter' requires further consideration.

New York provided the first opportunity for Group office rationalization. Shirreff had been appointed the Mercantile's first New York representative in 1960; F.J. Knightly, then a Hongkong Bank Head Office Inspector, visited him on two occasions to study his activities; and shortly afterwards Shirreff was instructed to move his office into the Hongkong Bank branch. R. Beaumont, the Hongkong Bank's No. 2 (in New York), initially put him in a back room by the mail clerks, but the Manager, R.P. 'Scar' Edwards, brought him into the front office – for which Shirreff was grateful. So far the change had been one of saving rent; Shirreff was still representing the Mercantile Bank.

In 1962, however, the Mercantile 'closed' its representative office in New York, and Shirreff came onto the staff of the Hongkong Bank as No. 2, with seniority dating from April 1962.[h] In late 1965 he became the Manager New York and a third officer, seconded – not transferred – from the BBME was brought in. The New York office, which had also been handling the BBME's requirements since 1960, was a Hongkong Bank branch but it was also a Group facility.

Early discussion focused on the unprofitability of continuing two Rangoon branches, but Saunders was spared the need to make a decision; in 1963 both branches were nationalized. In Thailand there was the hope that one of the Mercantile Bank offices might be transferred to the south. In both Singapore and Malaya the Hongkong Bank and the Mercantile Bank expanded; in the Federation there was already a long-standing rough division of operations, despite the two main Kuala Lumpur offices – the Mercantile Bank had the virtual monopoly of banking business on the economically less developed East Coast.

In Japan, where expenses were high and opportunities for competition with the now fully reestablished Japanese banks were limited, it was sensible for the Mercantile Bank to close its Tokyo branch in 1963, where the Hongkong Bank was represented, and open in Nagoya where the Group had had no licence. The choice of the Mercantile Bank for this latter was partly the consequence of pressures from the Bank of Japan, favouring the smaller foreign bank, and partly for tax reasons – the sale of the Mercantile's Tokyo office had led to a capital gain which would have been heavily taxed had it not been reinvested in a bank building. As Saunders, the new Chief Manager, put it at the 1963 annual meeting, 'This will give the Group wider coverage in Japan and enable us to give better service to our customers trading with that country.'

The Mercantile Bank made a 'net' closure in 1966 with the withdrawal of its two Osaka offices. This move was probably unwise in the short run since the Group lost sound Indian customers and soured labour relations in Japan while leaving regulatory authorities concerned about the Group's ultimate intentions. The Hongkong Bank would nevertheless have preferred to see a complete Mercantile withdrawal in the 'imperial interest', but the Japanese authorities

---

[h] This suggests that the Bank's personnel practices would require reconsideration before integration of Foreign staffs. Shirreff (b. 1909) joined the London Office of the Mercantile Bank of India in 1926, came East to Calcutta in 1930, and served as agent in Galle, Kandy, and Jaffna and as manager in Colombo and Bombay; he retired in 1966.

proved reluctant to transfer the Nagoya licence from the Mercantile to the Hongkong Bank. This was eventually effected in 1982, thus permitting the termination of the Mercantile as an operating bank and its sale as a corporate shell to Citibank in 1985.

The most important rationalization was the actual transfer of the Mercantile Bank's head office to Hong Kong, the end of separate recruiting, and the joining of the two Foreign staffs for common assignments (see below). This resulted in the end of the Mercantile Bank's retail business in London, and in 1970 the Hongkong Bank took over the Mercantile's West End office on Pall Mall – where there had also been branch management problems.

A history of the main impact of the acquisition on the future of the Mercantile Bank, therefore, lies outside the scope of this chapter. Certainly in the period to 1971 the Mercantile closed branches, but only three (plus a representative office) on the basis of Group rationalization; on balance the number of Mercantile offices showed a net gain.

To some, full integration would appear to have been inevitable; such persons may ask, therefore, why branch rationalization was so slow. The short answer is to be found in the time taken to integrate the staff – there was, for example, a certain lack of policy imagination in a 'lateral transfer' which resulted in a veteran Mercantile Banker like Shirreff being ranked below many Hongkong Bank juniors. Furthermore, as long as the Mercantile's important customers retained a strong loyalty to the bank, as long as the Mercantile's ascendancy in India were continued, as long as the rough separation of West/East coast Malaya were considered sufficient, there was not much more the Hongkong Bank's Head Office could achieve. The Group needed additional funds; the Mercantile moved out to the small savers, as did the Hongkong Bank, in many new small branches. The Mercantile's continued growth was in the interests of the Hongkong Bank Group.

Before Saunders retired, the Hongkong Bank Group had representative offices in Australia (1965) and Canada (1970 and 1972), the main function of which was to coordinate the Group's activities, which did not then include a Hongkong Bank commercial banking office or a local subsidiary. The position as of December 1971 is shown in Table 13.2.

THE COMMERCIAL BANKING BRANCHES OF THE HONGKONG BANK AND MERCANTILE BANK, 1972–1979

Relatively speaking the period beginning with the appointment of G.M. Sayer as the executive Chairman of The Hongkong and Shanghai Banking Corporation and ending on the eve of the successful negotiations for the acquisition of

Table 13.2 *Hongkong Bank Group: Branches, 1971*
Hongkong Bank, Mercantile Bank, Hongkong Bank of California, Hang Seng

BRUNEI
Hongkong Bank, Bandar Seri Begawan, Kuala Belait, Seria

CEYLON/SRI LANKA
Hongkong Bank: Colombo
Mercantile Bank: Colombo (Main Office) and Pettah; Galle, Jaffna, Kandy

CHINA
Hongkong Bank: Shanghai

FRANCE
Hongkong Bank: Paris

GERMANY
Hongkong Bank: Hamburg

HONG KONG
Hongkong Bank: (Main Office), Kowloon, Kwun Tong, Mongkok, North Point, Tsuen Wan + 62
Mercantile Bank: (Main Office) + 3
Hang Seng Bank: Head Office + 11

INDIA
Hongkong Bank: Bombay, Calcutta
Mercantile Bank: Bombay + 5; Calcutta + 7; Delhi, Madras, New Delhi, Visakhapatnam
[and BBME: Bombay]

INDONESIA
Hongkong Bank: Jakarta

JAPAN
Hongkong Bank: Tokyo, Kobe, Osaka, Yokohama
Mercantile Bank: Nagoya

FEDERATION OF MALYSIA (East Malaysia)
Hongkong Bank: Kota Kinabalu, Beaufort, Kuching + 1; Labuan, Paper, Sandakan, Sibu, Tawau

FEDERATION OF MALAYSIA (West Malaysia)
Hongkong Bank: Kuala Lumpur + 2; Bukit Terendak, Cameron Highlands, Ipoh, Johore Bahru, Malacca, Muar, Penang, Petaling Jaya, Sungei Patani, Teluk Anson
Mercantile Bank: Kuala Lumpur, Bentong, Butterworth, Ipoh, Kota Bahru, Kuala Lipis, Kuala Trengganu, Kuantan, Mentakab, Penang, Raub, Seremban, Taiping, Temerloh

MAURITIUS
Mercantile Bank: Port Louis + 1 Beau Bassin, Curepipe, Rose Hill, Quatres Bornes

PHILIPPINES
Hongkong Bank: Manila, Iloilo

SINGAPORE
Hongkong Bank: Collyer Quay + 6
Mercantile Bank: Raffles Place + 3

THAILAND
Hongkong Bank: Bangkok + 1
Mercantile Bank: Bangkok + 1

UNITED KINGDOM
Hongkong Bank: London, City + Pall Mall
Mercantile Bank: London
[and BBME: London]

UNITED STATES OF AMERICA
Hongkong Bank: New York, San Francisco
Hongkong Bank of California: Northern Calif: San Francisco + 1, Sacramento, San Jose Southern Calif: Beverly Hills, Los Angeles (2), North Hollywood, Encino, Carson

VIETNAM
Hongkong Bank: Saigon

[SWITZERLAND – BBME: Geneva]

Table 13.3 *Hongkong Bank Group: Branches, 1977*
Hongkong Bank, Mercantile Bank, Hongkong Bank of California, Hang Seng

BAHAMAS
Hongkong Bank: Nassau

BAHRAIN
Hongkong Bank: Manama (OBU)
[and BBME]

BRUNEI [Negara Brunei Darussalam]
Hongkong Bank: Bandar Seri Begawan
+2, Kuala Belait, Seria

CHINA
Hongkong Bank: Shanghai

FRANCE
Hongkong Bank: Paris

GERMANY, Federal Republic of
Hongkong Bank: Hamburg, Frankfurt

HONG KONG
Hongkong Bank: (Main Office) +150
Mercantile Bank: Head Office +1
Hang Seng Bank: Head Office +33

INDIA
Mercantile Bank: Bombay +6,
Calcutta +8, Delhi, Madras, New
Delhi, Visakhapatnam
[and BBME: Bombay]

INDONESIA
Hongkong Bank: Djakarta +1

JAPAN
Hongkong Bank: Tokyo, Osaka
Mercantile Bank: Nagoya

MACAU
Hongkong Bank: Macau

MALAYSIA, Federation of
Peninsular Malaysia
Hongkong Bank: Kuala Lumpur +2
Bentong, Butterworth, Cameron Highlands, Ipoh +2, Johore Bahru, Kota Bahru, Kuala Lipis, Kuala Trengganu, Kuantan, Malacca +1, Mentakab, Muar, Penang +1, Petaling Jaya, Raub, Seremban, Sungei Patani, Taiping, Teluk Anson, Temerloh

Sabah
Hongkong Bank: Kota Kinabalu, Beaufort, Labuan, Papar, Sandakan, Tawau
Sarawak
Hongkong Bank: Kuching +1, Sibu

MAURITIUS
Mercantile Bank: Port Louis +1,
Beau Bassin, Curepipe, Flacq,
Mahebourg, Quatre Bornes, Rose Hill

NETHERLANDS
Hongkong Bank: Amsterdam

NEW HEBRIDES [Vanuata]
Hongkong Bank: Port Vila

PHILIPPINES
Hongkong Bank: Manila, Iloilo

SINGAPORE
Hongkong Bank: Collyer Quay +9

SOLOMON ISLANDS
Hongkong Bank: Honiara

SRI LANKA
Hongkong Bank: Colombo

THAILAND
Hongkong Bank: Bangkok +1
Mercantile Bank: Bangkok +1

UNITED KINGDOM
Hongkong Bank: London +2,
Manchester, Edinburgh
[and BBME: London]

CHANNEL ISLANDS
Hongkong Bank: St Helier
(Jersey)

UNITED STATES OF AMERICA
Hongkong Bank: New York +1
Chicago, Seattle
Hongkong Bank of California:
San Francisco +1, Sacramento,
Los Angeles +1, Carson, North
Hollywood, Encino, Agana (Guam)

[SWITZERLAND – BBME: Geneva]

Marine Midland Banks, Inc., was one of extraordinary development and change both for the corporation and for the Hongkong Bank itself. Although Table 13.3 states the position in the year of Michael Sandberg's taking over from Sayer, a longer period has proved more suitable for purposes of considering the scope of the changes (see Table 13.1).

The changing position of the Mercantile Bank

'Rationalization' in this period would be a euphemism as applied to the history of the Mercantile Bank. The fact is that its operations were being phased out. That the final stages occurred only in 1982 and 1983 is a consequence of the banking licence problem, the need to obtain local regulatory permission to transfer the physical office and the business from one bank to another, from the Mercantile Bank to the Hongkong Bank. The two main office buildings in Kuala Lumpur had by now come to be seen as a symbol of past pussyfooting; rationalization was insufficient, integration was essential. By the early 1970s these comments had become valid.

The period began with an unexpected setback. Sayer determined that operations should be shifted, as soon as practicable, from the Mercantile to the Hongkong Bank. With this in mind the Bank's representative approached the head of India's central bank, beginning his presentation by stressing the need for integrated services. Before he was able to come to the concluding remark, the central bank chairman expressed his pleasure that a bank with a name so well-known in India was being permitted to act for the Group – the Mercantile Bank in its new role would be most welcome. Hence in 1972 there was indeed 'rationalization' rather than 'integration'; the two new branches of the Mercantile Bank in Bombay and Calcutta respectively were transferred *from* the Hongkong Bank.

The following year there was, however, an unequivocal development. The Mercantile Bank ceased trading in Singapore and the Federation of Malaysia and its offices were transferred to the Hongkong Bank.

The Mercantile's closure in Sri Lanka was dictated by a complex of events which first suggested a trade off – the up-country branches for the permission to continue operating in the country. Then, as conditions temporarily became more difficult for foreign banks, it was clear that one Group office would be enough; in 1974 the Mercantile closed its two offices in Colombo. The first local officer to take over country responsibilities, however, would be a former Mercantile Bank staff member, R. Thambiah, in his new role as Manager Colombo, for the Hongkong Bank.

The process continued. In 1976 the Mercantile ceased its operations in London and began closing its smaller offices in Hong Kong. Where the

Mercantile Bank did not close down, however, it continued the Group's policy of expansion, for example, in Mauritius. As shown in Table 13.1 the final transfers came in 1982 and 1983; the Mercantile Bank had become a corporate shell; the Hongkong Bank was its operating successor.

Geographic coverage

The shutdown of the Mercantile brought the Hongkong Bank name into new areas, but it wasn't the same bank; it had inherited the staff and background of the Mercantile – the integration had been accomplished.

Macau

The Hongkong Bank had been banking correspondents for the Provincial Macau authorities from time to time and in the 1950s the gold trade, banned in Hong Kong due to British adherence to the IMF, was conducted from Macau, with related exchange business handled in Hong Kong. Except for the brief agency managed by Sir Charles Addis's friend, (Sir) Gershom Stewart, in 1887 (see Volume I), however, there had been no office in the territory.

In the period 1962–1972, the Hongkong Bank's own expansion, if it may be put that way, began with the establishment of a branch in this Portuguese Province of Macau across the Pearl River Estuary from Hong Kong. The Board had considered a suggestion relative to a Macau branch as early as July 1957, but the negotiations proved lengthy, and it was not until 1972 that, with the final permission granted, the Hongkong Bank opened in Macau – its initial capital was Patacas 5 million. The first Manager was the Macau born but Hong Kong educated Portuguese, A.M. Prado, who would later be the Bank's first representative in São Paulo, Brazil. A local 'board' was established in accordance with Macau law; its members were Michael Sandberg (Chairman), J.F.G. Tait, E.R. Udal, P.H. Lobo, Y.C. Liang, and H.T. Ho, with unlimited authority to negotiate and make final settlement with the State and with private individuals in the Province. In 1979 the Bank agreed to increase its capital in Macau to Patacas 10 million in return for permission to have a total of six offices in the territory; at that time, however, the Bank planned to open only a second and third office.

New banking, new departures

This same year the Bank opened in Port Vila, the capital of the New Hebrides (now Vanuatu), a historic departure, but consistent with the new demands of international banking. The Hongkong and Shanghai Banking Corporation would establish itself in territories with banking policies friendly to multinational banks. In some cases the Corporation's office would not be

I. Structure and growth

concerned with commercial banking; it would be represented by a non-banking subsidiary and therefore is not covered in this chapter. In Port Vila, however, the Bank established a commercial banking office.

In 1973 the Bank opened an office in Honiara, Guadalcanal, the capital of the (British) Solomon Islands.

In 1976, in line with these developments were the entry of the Bank into the Channel Islands, with a branch at St Helier on Jersey, and the opening of an Offshore Banking Unit (OBU) in Bahrain, where the BBME was fully established as a commercial bank.

Although Turner had agreed that banking in the Netherlands would not prove profitable to the Hongkong Bank, the Bank's new financial activities and the protection of its trade finance (estimated at one-quarter of the Netherlands' Hong Kong trade) required that all previous reports be reviewed; in consequence the Bank opened in Amsterdam in 1977. Indeed, the Bank had been frustrated in the 1950s; Turner would have been willing to expand in Europe had he been advised of a profitable purpose and a way of accomplishing it. Developments in the decade from 1965 to 1975 had revolutionized the banking industry, and in 1973 the Bank opened in Frankfurt, a second office in the Federal Republic of Germany and better suited for operations in foreign exchange and the Euro-currency markets. This policy was furthered in 1979 by the opening of the Hongkong Bank's own Swiss branch in Zurich, approval for which had originally been sought in 1972. The application, although acknowledging the usual limitations, had been held in suspense until the reciprocity question had been answered by the Hong Kong Government's lifting of the new banking licence moratorium.[1] The Zurich office supplemented the Group facilities in the BBME Geneva office.

The British Isles and Chinatowns

Reversing a long-standing policy in the United Kingdom, in 1974 the Hongkong Bank sent M.P. Langley, originally with the Mercantile Bank, to open an office in Manchester. He was succeeded almost immediately by L.G. Atterbury, who had just retired but who was taken back on contract. Atterbury, who had formerly served as manager, Mercantile Bank, Colombo, brought in L.Y. Wickremeratne, a former Mercantile local officer, who remained to become a successful Sub-Manager of the new Manchester office. In 1977 the Hongkong Bank returned to Edinburgh – there had apparently

---

[1] In negotiating for permission to open in Zurich the Hongkong Bank had agreed to (i) omit business conflicting with the credit and monetary policy of the Swiss National Bank, (ii) abide by agreements made between the Swiss National Bank and Swiss banks of the relevant category, (iii) lend at rates not more favourable than those requested for monetary policy reasons, (iv) notify any change of business, and (v) offer no objection to examination by agents of the Swiss Federal Banking Commission.

been a short-lived office there in 1874; there had certainly been an agent (not a Bank employee) who operated for the Bank until 1882, mainly for the purposes of obtaining sterling funds to finance the London end of the Eastern trade.

The Bank opened in Jersey in 1976 after the purchase of Wyte Gass. As the company had operated in Alderney, Guernsey, and Jersey, legal advice indicated the Hongkong Bank would have the same rights, but this proved an error. The licence, granted by the States of Jersey, was valid for that jurisdiction only.

These new United Kingdom offices, whatever their original purpose, also attracted the retail business of local Overseas Chinese. The Hongkong Bank, in fact, made a point of opening in Chinatowns – on San Francisco's Grant Avenue in 1967, in New York's Chinatown in 1975 (from 1976 at 50, Bowery Street), and in London's new Soho Chinatown in 1977. As a retail bank, the Hongkong Bank could not provide the network of services provided by domestic banks and could not, therefore, compete. Exceptionally, Chinese would come to and use the services of the Bank despite some inconvenience.

The Bank opened its first office in the Republic of Ireland in 1979 – in Dublin. In accordance with Central Bank of Ireland regulations, an Irish Advisory Committee was appointed with P.E. Hutson, the Executive Director for Europe, as Chairman.

Developments in the United States

The Hongkong Bank's earlier development in the United States was overshadowed by its 1978 offer to acquire 51% of the shares of Marine Midland Banks (see Chapter 16), although negotiations were continuing through 1979, the end of the period being presently considered. The Bank Holding Company Act and the International Banking Act operated so that The Hongkong and Shanghai Banking Corporation as a bank holding company would be unable to own commercial banking subsidiaries in more than one State. The successful completion of negotiations to acquire MMBI would consequently require the Corporation to have already divested itself of its California subsidiary, the Hongkong Bank of California. This did not prevent the Corporation as an operating bank from continuing to operate branches in one designated 'Home' State and also in other States in which the Corporation was already established subject to State laws, any prohibitions to the contrary in the new legislation being 'grandfathered' – a term indicating the right to go on doing what you are already doing.

Except for the opening of a Representative Office in Houston in 1978, the history of the HSBC's geographical presence in the United States during the period 1972–1979 is the history of the wind-down of the HBC and the establishment of new Hongkong Bank offices where permitted. In 1974, however, the first of the HBC's two Guam branches was established.

The sale of two Southern California HBC offices – to the American Pacific State Bank and the Los Angeles National Bank respectively – was actually undertaken in 1977 before the question of divestiture arose; in 1978 the HBC's trust business was sold to the Trust Company of California and the Encino office to the First State Bank of Encino. One Guam office was closed but the main Guam operation was transferred to the Hongkong Bank.

The final event was Central Bank of Oakland's 'merger with and into' the Hongkong Bank of California in February 1979.

The HSBC's presence in California was not thus ended, however. There remained the 'agencies' of the Hongkong Bank in San Francisco and Los Angeles, still able to carry on foreign business as in the days before 'Inc.' in 1955.

As for the lions, they were taken from the front of the San Francisco office and others and placed in the small garden at the mezzanine floor level, which took on the aspect of a cage for bronze and stone lions; they were available for the new offices about to be established.

The story of the Hongkong Bank must move back to 1974 when the Bank's presence on the Pacific Coast was reinforced by a Seattle branch. Illinois laws permitted the establishment of foreign banks within a designated area of Chicago; accordingly the Hongkong Bank, after considering a Representative Office (to avoid adverse reaction from local bankers), established a branch in 1975. The Bank's official American banking home was, and is, New York State, where, as noted above, a Chinatown office was established in 1975. The Bank that same year moved into prestigious quarters at the new World Trade Center, complete with a ground floor retail office and the traditional lions guarding the entrance. New Yorkers stroked them – as the Chinese had done in Shanghai and as they still do in Hong Kong. Before the International Banking Act became effective in 1978, the Hongkong Bank secured a licence to establish a branch in Portland, Oregon; the branch was opened in 1980.

With the acquisition of MMBI the Bank's role in the United States changed completely. The story is summarized, together with an account of other developments in the Americas, in Chapters 16 and 17.

Korea and Brazil

The Hongkong Bank had never established an office of its own in Korea, although it had authorized merchant agents who opened current accounts on behalf of the Nagasaki branch (see Volume II). After the Pacific War the Bank was at first content to be represented in the **Republic of Korea** by the Bank of Seoul. In November 1974 however the Hongkong Bank opened a representative office in the capital, Seoul; contacts developed and by 1985 the Bank had equity investment in the Korea International Merchant Bank and two Hongkong Bank branches – one in Busan (Pusan) and the other in Seoul.

In 1975 the HSBC opened a Representative Office in São Paulo, **Brazil**, with Prado as the first Bank representative. The office was incorporated as 'Hong Kong Bank Serviços' and was to be one of several approaches to financial participation in South America – HSBC already had a presence on the continent through Antony Gibbs, in 1980 Marine Midland would provide a second base, and the Hongkong Bank's own branches in Chile, the first of which was established in Santiago in 1982, would provide a third. The major purpose of this latter focus was the finance of Pacific Rim trade. Supervision came from an Executive Director for the Americas operating from New York.

China

The Shanghai branch remained open throughout the period, but its business was limited and it could not accept deposits from the public. Head Office expectations varied with the change in the political climate, but the Bank of China's frozen U.S. dollar account was still a problem; when senior Hongkong Bank officials met socially with the chief manager of the Bank of China in Hong Kong in 1962 the question proved of such importance that it was not discussed. In 1963, however, the Board were informed that the Shanghai branch had been permitted to remit $16,000, a portion of its operating profits, to Hong Kong; the principle rather than the amount was significant. Then in April 1965 the Board authorized payment of $16 million, including $1 million *ex gratia* in lieu of interest, to the Bank of China to discharge all outstanding foreign currency liabilities in China, excluding only those related to the Stabilization Board.

There were naturally expectations to developing business, but with the outbreak of the Cultural Revolution a particular strain was placed on the Shanghai Manager, who, as an involuntary witness to revolutionary events, was in constant danger of arrest. At one time he remained the only foreign banker not in a Shanghai prison. In 1967, 1968, and again in the early 1970s the Bank made efforts to close the branch and renewed consideration was given to the idea of a representative office in Peking; the Chinese did not respond and the evidence now is that the authorities wished the Bank to provide continuity.

In 1968 D.N.H. Self, the Shanghai Manager, was not granted an exit permit, and the Board noted that the branch had been fined $125,000 for an alleged Customs violation. The arrest of Mrs Connie Martin (aged 70) in 1969 gave the Board further concern; she had retired but was helping with secretarial work, including, earlier in the decade, the typing out of key letters, referred to as the 'Hutchison letters' (see Bibliography), in the Shanghai archives for use by Maurice Collis, the author of the Hongkong Bank's centennial history.

I. Structure and growth

Furthermore, although Self had been permitted to leave China, the Board were now anxious about the fate of D.G. Lachlan, the new Manager. Working through a Hong Kong Chinese broker, whom the Board knew to be close to Premier Chou En-lai, they secured the release of Connie Martin and the assurance that Lachlan was not in danger. This latter information could not, however, be passed to Lachlan. After several applications, he received an exit permit in 1970. Responding to questioning as to his reasons for wishing to leave the People's Republic, Lachlan informed the officials that he was unmarried and that he had to return before it was too late to find a bride, a task which he duly had no intention of fulfilling. Something must, however, have occurred outside the scope of this history; he married on his return to the United Kingdom. As the Chinese authorities would not permit the exit of a Manager before his replacement had arrived, Saunders appealed successfully for volunteers.

With the changing political scene in China J.W.L. Howard and Michael Sandberg were invited to China and the Board noted that the question of closing the Shanghai branch was no longer being pressed. It was not until after the overthrow of the 'Gang of Four' in 1976, however, that significant changes occurred. The Hongkong Bank was once again able to send representatives to the Guangzhou (Canton) Trade Fair. High-level contacts were reestablished by visits to Peking and in 1978 the Bank set up a 'China Desk' in Head Office to study developments and be prepared to meet customers' needs in Hong Kong.

The contacts in Guangzhou resulted in early 1979 in the unofficial opening of a liaison office in the Dung Fang Hotel – official recognition came only in February 1982. The Bank's representative was available to assist joint venture customers. As Hong Kong business generated additional work for Shanghai, the Hongkong Bank's long-standing request to burn its archives to make room for further branch activity was approved by the responsible authorities in 1980; the Bank had by this time commissioned a history and therefore requested permission to transfer the archival material to Hong Kong. The authorities acceded to the Bank's request; without their consideration, this history, which draws heavily on Shanghai material, would have been severely restricted.

In October 1980 the Hongkong Bank opened a Representative Office in Peking with M.P. Langley as the first Group Representative.[j] The Hongkong Bank was, after all, still a China bank.

---

[j] Langley applied to join the Hongkong Bank in Shanghai in 1947 but was advised to go to London; the Mercantile Bank of India accepted him in Shanghai. He served as the Hongkong Bank's Manager, Main Office, Hong Kong, 1978–1979. In 1983 he retired to London and became Consultant Manager, China, in the London Office.

14

THE HONGKONG BANK GROUP, 1962–1980, II. CASE STUDIES: HONG KONG, LONDON, ILOILO, AND COLOMBO*

The greatest asset of all will be good service.

Sir Vandeleur Grayburn, 1938

HONG KONG

Despite developments within the region and within the Group, The Hongkong and Shanghai Banking Corporation's principal operations remained in Hong Kong. Furthermore, despite the increasing role of the Government in monetary policy and banking regulation through its Monetary Affairs Branch under the Financial Secretary, the Hongkong Bank, as the largest bank in the territory, remained the principal bankers to the Government and continued to be the visible instrument in the execution of official policy. In this chapter of case studies, therefore, there is reason to begin with Hong Kong. First, there is an example of the Bank's role in the banking system, secondly, some notes on the centennial, thirdly, glimpses through 'oral history' interviews at the working of two new-type Hong Kong branches, and, finally, a continuation of Y.C. Jao's important study of industrial finance. These should be read as a continuation of Chapter 8 and in conjunction with the general discussions in Chapters 13 and 15.

DEVELOPMENT AND POLICY

'Central banking'

Smaller banks were often heavily involved in lending against property and were consequently in danger of becoming illiquid, especially during a crisis in the property market. This was basically the problem of the Liu Chong Hing Bank in 1960–1961, and the Hongkong Bank came to their assistance with funds lent against mortgages. While this appears to be 'lender of last resort' central bank business, it should rather be considered as a commercial bank operation given particular priority because of the potential damage to the banking system and therefore to the system's largest bank.

* There are no end-notes in this chapter. Readers are referred to the bibliographical note on pp. 949–50.

II. Case studies

R.G.L. Oliphant, who, as Manager Hong Kong, was responsible for the decision at the banking level, was also a member of the Government Banking Advisory Committee. In this capacity he urged the formulation of adequate banking legislation and, although supported by unofficial members, found the Government's response excessively slow. This typical official reaction has been labeled, incorrectly, as if it were an expression of an economic philosophy described by the now virtually meaningless catch-phrase, '*laissez-faire*' – and, therefore, excusable. Oliphant, however, was not satisfied with the current legislation, and he, with A.M. Mack, then a Hongkong Bank Inspector, drew up a series of proposed reforms, which, as a member of the Committee, he submitted to Government. This in turn provoked Government to call out H.J. Tomkins from the Bank of England, leading eventually to the first significant banking act (1964) in the territory.

Banks turned naturally to the Hongkong Bank when they were in difficulty (i) because it was not a central bank, that is, it was not part of the official world and (ii) because it had the funds to lend. On occasion the Bank took risks; if these appeared unsound commercially, the Bank turned to the Government for approval and, if necessary, a guarantee. There were instances where the Bank sent in its own manager or management team; there were other instances in which the Bank considered the case too serious for private-sector assistance. One problem with intervention is that of withdrawal. In the case of the Liu Chong Hing Bank, the problem was rectified by the Liu family managers themselves. In other cases a foreign bank, seeking a foothold in Hong Kong, would take over the Hongkong Bank's (or the Chartered Bank's) responsibilities. In the case of Hang Seng Bank, the Hongkong Bank actually bought a controlling interest (see Chapter 15). In the early 1980s, however, when serious problems developed in the banking sector, the role of the Government was public and considerable; the Hongkong Bank on occasion injected funds and provided management, but Government sponsorship was visible throughout.

The centenary

In 1965, the Hongkong Bank marked its centenary by increasing its authorized capital to $200 million in connection with a 1:1 capitalization issue. Special grants to charity included $200,000 to the Community Relief Trust Fund (in lieu of a cocktail party for constituents) and capital grants to the University of Hong Kong and the Chinese University of Hong Kong designed to generate $50,000 for four scholarships in each university.

The Hong Kong Government approved the conversion of the whole of Statue Square, that is, both the Government's and the Bank's land, to a public garden at cost of $1.1 million to the Bank for the southern half (for which the

Bank has the leasehold); the Government took responsibility for the $800,000 necessary for the northern part. The open space appeared guaranteed for the future and the Bank had its 'view to the sea' provided one went high enough to see over the three-level car park on the newly reclaimed land beyond Connaught Road. The Bank had also proposed that, in view of the absence of statues (other than that of 'TJ'), the name of the square be changed to 'Wayfoong'; the Government suggested 'Victoria'; the Bank pointed out that, as the place was known colloquially in Chinese as 'Queen's Statue Square', there was really no need after all to make a change. In the meantime the Bank gave 1,000 Bauhinia trees to the Royal Hong Kong Golf Club and the 'Wayfoong Centenary Cup' to its good constituent the Royal Hong Kong Jockey Club. The first of the Bank's two histories, Maurice Collis's *Wayfoong, The Hongkong and Shanghai Banking Corporation*, was published.

Two new branches

The general expansion of Hong Kong branch banking has been considered in Chapter 8 and related tables. The establishment of branches with functional specialities, Mongkok and North Point for example, almost suggested that the Bank was carrying out limited experiments in new-style banking outside the precincts of Head Office, but the locational importance of the branch was in fact a principal factor. Mongkok had already been expanded and yet there remained untouched opportunities in Kowloon, hence the establishment of Kwun Tong branch in the industrial area reclaimed in the late 1950s. North Point branch, on the other hand, was set up to be close to new industrial estates on Hong Kong Island, and also to automobile sales and hire purchase customers.[a]

Kwun Tong branch
The Kwun Tong branch was established in 1963 with B.J.N. Ogden as the first Manager. He was assisted by a No. 2, Vickers de Souza, and a Business Promotion Officer, John Loch. This was witness of the end of the 'three-tier' system. Superficially, the set-up appeared unchanged; the management team running the office was still a Foreign staff officer, a Portuguese officer, and a Chinese, but their status and responsibilities had a modern definition; the Portuguese was no longer a clerk, but a 'local officer' with signing rights; and the Chinese was not the compradore's man tied to the handling of cash, but employed in his own right as a staff member of a modern bank.

The branch was located in a particularly suitable industrial area newly

---

[a] J.F. Marshall was Manager North Point, 1957–1959, and his problems with the early hire-purchase business are frankly recounted in his *Whereon the Wild Thyme Blows* (Grayshott, England, 1986), Chapter 10, 'Hong Kong and Disaster'.

II. Case studies

established at Kwun Tong, on filled-in land between Hong Kong's international airport of Kai Tak and Lei U Mun (Lyemun Pass). This meant, however, that the branch would make loans to new industry before it could collect savings from newly employed factory workers; the gap was covered by borrowing from Head Office at an internal rate of interest which meant a loss – an anticipated loss – for the new office.

To obtain new business John Loch pioneered the ground and at an appropriate time brought the Chinese-speaking Ogden along. In some cases the owner of the new factory was already banking with another branch; there was some inter-branch jealousy and the matter had to be handled delicately. The fact was, however, that Mongkok was again 'bulging at the seams'; business had to come to Kwun Tong and it had to be handled within that office. The Manager's limits were low, say $25,000 clean and $100,000 against security. But this was not the main problem; the Manager could always call Hong Kong – J.N. Frost was Sub-Manager and M.G. Carruthers the Manager Hong Kong – and secure a ruling within 24 hours, if all the relevant information were provided.

The main problem was to offer the service and ensure that potential customers knew the service existed. To achieve this Ogden was permitted an advertising campaign, something very new in the Bank. Banks traditionally did not advertise beyond the formal, dull announcement type of 'box' in a newspaper. In addition to the more serious approaches to industrialists and major customers, there were many little things a Manager could do to establish an atmosphere. As Ogden recalls:

We were the first branch to sell Jockey Club Sweep tickets... We kept a record of the numbers we sold, so that if any of our tickets won, we put up its number outside the booths with the notice, 'This number won a first prize last week...'. We became known as a lucky place for buying sweep tickets.

To encourage children to come in we used to give away horrible sorts of lollipop things. When a child started screaming, some unsmiling teller would lean over and hand it a sweet.

Ogden designed a scheme to collect savings at source, that is, within the factories as the workers were paid. Although the scheme had initial problems, as Ogden explained:

The idea was to encourage the factories' staffs to open savings accounts into which the factory itself would pay a cheque once a month instead of having to draw money, pay it out, and risk a payroll robbery. The idea was to get the staff to open savings accounts, so we used to send a team up to the factory, taking savings bank books and everything and explain to the workers in the factory what to do and get them to open accounts there with a few dollars each or even one dollar. The factory would then pay a cheque in to us and the workers' salaries and wages would be credited from the proceeds.

It worked, but it didn't work as well as I had hoped it would, but it did encourage some people – and now, of course, we've got the autopay system which does the whole thing so much better.

The increase in the total value of savings accounts on the scale required to fund branch lending operations could not be limited to the collection of personal 'savings' narrowly defined. Savings accounts were no longer to be simply a service to the deserving poor, encouraging them to save for their old age. Savings accounts had to develop as a facility for increasingly well-paid factory workers who were willing to bank and who required from their bank everything but the cheque-drawing facility. This development began in such branches as Kwun Tong. By the early 1970s cash could be withdrawn from one's savings account at any office in the Colony or from the cash dispensers. With autopay, regular bills could be handled automatically. Other transactions, for example, the remittance of funds, could be made at the counter in any full service branch (or through the Manager of one's own smaller office) – and if the complexity of the operation bothered the unsophisticated, there was no need to hope for the ghost of TJ to appear with friendly advice; special assistants were assigned for this purpose.

North Point branch in 1965
Like Kwun Tong, the North Point office was a full service branch. By the time Donald Lachlan took over in 1965 the branch had responsibility for the satellite or sub-branches on Hong Kong Island which were less than full service. Lachlan himself reported to the Sub-Manager Branches in the main Hong Kong office. By the mid-1960s the preconceptions of the early 1950s had disappeared; the Chinese would use banks. The problem was to find a suitable site for a new office – near a bus stop, a market, a corner – and then to give the office an atmosphere suitable for the neighbourhood. Even then Managers did not sit back and wait for business. As far as industrial customers were concerned, Lachlan recalled,

I used to go round and see the companies opening up there and say, whether you bank with our main office or the Chartered or whomever, we are right here, and we can offer a full banking service. Anything you want.
I took them out to a good lunch. I had a small fridge in my office, and there were pre-chilled martinis and beer and anything else you can think of. I would say, come round at half past twelve. They used to come round, and we'd have a few snifters at the office, and I was on the telephone if anyone wanted me. Then we would go out for a good Chinese chow, discuss this, that and the other, and I'd enlarge upon it. I'd say, look, notwithstanding the fact that you have the loan from Hong Kong office why not get them to transfer it down to here, and we'll do your full banking?
So they would transfer the whole lot down, Head Office would hold me covered, and I would lend them the money, which was much more convenient for them there in Watson's Estate and around there, and then I would do their full banking for them.
On the other hand I used to go and visit companies in the North Point area and say,

II. Case studies

is there anything we can do for you, wherever your banking is? Maybe we can help or offer better banking and cheaper rates, more convenient. It's a sales operation, it's a service. You have to chat people up and see what you can do. At Hong Kong office Peter Hutson, who was the Chief Accountant there, always helped me and gave me as much backing as he could.

There were a lot of what they call 'flatted factories' in Hong Kong. They would have heavy lifts and machinery to lift up cargoes...If a chap were in a small way of business, he would take one quarter of a factory flat...if it was very big, he'd take three or four floors, and you were financing people in mortgages to buy. They were expanding, you were handling their exports, imports of whatever products they were manufacturing.

There was a chap who was doing dolls, [trade marked] dolls I think and various other dolls, I put a lot of money in, and he was expanding all the time, and he was doing a very good business. But it used to frighten me because he was the brains in the organization, and all the chaps that he trusted were his relatives. I used to be very frightened in case he died and the whole edifice would come crumbling down, but he has done well, and he has got on well.

There were wig factories and toy factories and all sorts of things like that, apart from the larger firms like Otis elevators and the European firms. Also the [British Forces] Command Cashier kept his account with us, and all sorts of business like that.

On his responsibilities towards the sub-branches, Lachlan was concerned both with control and with furthering their business.

All the sub-branches were mainly a limited banking facility, and there was no reason for a Foreign staff to be there because you were dealing with local Chinese. If there were any advances or loans or any problems, then it was referred back to North Point. I used to visit each branch once or twice a month because I had to balance the current accounts and the books there myself; my Number Two in North Point every six months had to balance all the savings accounts. So we were in close contact with them. At any time, if they wanted to ring up, they could ring me up, or I could go down. I wanted all the time to make them feel free to ring me up about any problems they had.

[As for incentives to find new business] they had tremendous incentives on their own part because they were very interested in their profits. They got an interest factor on the deposits they brought in which was the profit on their office.

I used to tell them all, if you want it, every two months you can have a first-class Chinese chow on the Bank with a table of twelve and bring in any local businessmen or notables you want. I will come or not come as you wish. You may wish an all-Chinese chow, in which case I'd be an embarrassment, or you may want me to come down and add a spot of face if you feel that's required, but do what you want and you let me know what you want.

City offices in other territories – a digression

To conclude that branching in other cities followed a similar pattern would be to over-generalize, but there were the same factors favouring similar banking development. The Orchard Road branch in 1949 would be Singapore's 'Kowloon' office, a location in a secondary business area for the convenience of customers. Suapah Road (1956) similarly took the burden off a Bangkok office sited on the river and therefore inconvenient in a city which had taken to the roads with increasing traffic chaos. In Indonesia, Kota office (1972) in 'Chinatown' relieved the main Jakarta branch; in the Philippines, once the decision to close Iloilo had been made in conjunction with permission to transfer the licence, Pasig office (1981), located in a new industrial estate near the factories of a main customer, supplemented the main Manila office, which itself had moved to the new business centre in Makati.

The Bank opened two small offices in Kuala Lumpur, the capital city of the Federation of Malaya (later, Malaysia). A third office situated in Petaling Jaya (1961) is, however, a somewhat different case, as it was located in a new satellite town and was originally intended to be virtually complete in itself. Nevertheless, organizationally, in the sense of being closely subordinate to the main office, it was a second office for the capital area. The Kuala Lumpur Manager, N.E. Clark, had been on the town's Development Board until his departure in 1959 – he was replaced by an additional Malay member – and this may account for the permission granted the Bank to open this last new office in Peninsular Malaysia.

The similarities continue, where they are permitted. The Jurong branch in Singapore was situated in what was designed to become a major industrial complex, and there were smaller offices there and in Kuala Lumpur set up over the same period and for the same purposes as in Hong Kong. The Mercantile Bank's policy was not dissimilar, even setting up small offices in Hong Kong but also in Bombay and Calcutta, in Malaysia, and in Thailand.

By the mid-1960s banking regulations restricted branching. The Hongkong Bank had no problems in Hong Kong obtaining the necessary licence when this became required after 1968, but elsewhere the problems were mounting at just the time when funds became particularly expensive and small, deposit-gathering branches would have been particularly helpful.

FINANCING HONG KONG'S INDUSTRIAL DEVELOPMENT

In 1981 Y.C. Jao of the University of Hong Kong undertook the first analysis of the Hongkong Bank's role, based on the Bank's own archival material, in the finance of the territory's early industrialists, a period which covered roughly the years 1950 to 1966 with a continuation to 1972.[b] In the resulting article he detailed the statistical gaps, both in the Bank's records and in the files of

[b] 'Financing Hong Kong's Early Post-war Industrialization: the role of The Hongkong and Shanghai Banking Corporation', in King, ed. *Eastern Banking* (London, 1983), pp. 545–74. Jao placed his analysis against the findings of Alexander Gerschenkron with useful results, which are not considered here. Readers are also referred to Jao for further sources. Nevertheless this section is heavily dependent on Jao's work, including also his major study, *Banking and Currency in Hong Kong: a Study of Post-war Financial Development* (London, 1974).

II. Case studies

Government, which prevented a quantitative approach and prevented a definitive statement of the percentage role the Bank had played in the growth of industrial output. He was nevertheless able to identify the techniques utilized to reconcile banking in the British tradition with industrial finance and to summarize these together with case studies. Certain of this material has been presented in Chapter 8, together with a survey of Hong Kong branch expansion through the period now under consideration. What follows is a continuation of the story against this background.

The statistics and the Bank's share of the market

In 1961 the Hongkong Bank agreed to finance half the cost of a £10,000 survey of Hong Kong's industrialization by the Economist Intelligence Unit (EIU). Even with this sponsorship and the cooperation which went with it, the EIU was unable to quantify the Bank's relevant share of the market. The report, published in 1962, merely stated that 'so far as we could discover, The Hongkong and Shanghai Banking Corporation and the Chartered Bank are responsible for at least three quarters of advances to industry, possibly more' (p. 17). J.A.H. Saunders, writing as Executive Chairman of the Bank in 1970, estimated that 'at one time it was thought that well over half of all industrial advances in Hong Kong were provided by the Hongkong Bank Group'.

The results of various archival searches by Jao are summarized in Tables 14.1 and 14.2, the former presenting the Hongkong Bank's loans and advances by category for five quarters between June 1966 and March 1980. During that period, loans and advances to the manufacturing sector increased by 7%, while the Bank's total loans and advances grew by 37.1%. The relative share of the manufacturing sector in the total loan portfolio therefore dropped from 33.5% to 26.1%. However, manufacturing still accounted on the average for over 30% of the Bank's loan portfolio and remained the largest sector in terms of credit allocated, leading other major sectors like transport, building and construction, and general commerce. Within the manufacturing sector itself, textiles used to account for well over half of the loans and advances, but by March 1970 their share had declined to 28%. Reflecting the changing industrial structure and diversification, other industries, like wearing apparel and electrical and electronic, had grown in importance both absolutely and relatively as the recipients of bank credit.

An even more important indicator of the Hongkong Bank's role in financing post-war industrialization is the Bank's relative share in loans and advances emanating from the whole banking system. Details about this indicator for the five quarters concerned are presented in Table 14.2.

Table 14.1 Hong Kong: The Hongkong Bank's loans and advances by category

(in millions of dollars)

	Quarter Ended					
	June 1966	September 1966	March 1968	March 1969	March 1970	
1. Manufacturing	534	533	516	535	581	
(a) textiles	284	264	246	255	163	
(b) footwear and wearing apparel	46	48	43	53	107	
(c) metal products and engineering	52	51	51	44	55	
(d) rubber, plastics and chemicals	30	28	21	18	34	
(e) shipbuilding and repair	9	9	11	7	12	
(f) electrical and electronic	4	6	7	8	42	
(g) food	2	2	0.4	0.4	6	
(h) beverages and tobacco	26	19	27	26	28	
(i) printing and publishing	2	1	1	2	10	
(j) miscellaneous	90	105	108	123	123	
2. Agriculture and fisheries	23	18	34	0.2	0.8	
3. Transport and transport equipment	36	31	42	43	429	
4. Electricity, gas and telephone	37	25	126	101	75	
5. Building and construction	267	286	309	279	315	
6. General Commerce	255	259	317	334	371	
(a) import, export and wholesale trade	240	242	300	311	319	
(b) retail	15	17	17	23	52	
7. Mining and quarrying	1	1	0.6	0.2	0.4	
8. Miscellaneous	459	456	424	481	443	
(a) hotels, boarding houses and catering	50	48	38	49	28	
(b) financial concerns including banks	74	71	48	33	115	
(c) stockbrokers	19	15	15	16	23	
(d) professional and private individuals	80	81	85	94	89	
(e) others	239	241	238	239	187	
Total Loans and Advances	1,612	1,610	1,769	1,773	2,215	

Table 14.2 Hong Kong: The Hongkong Bank's share in loans and advances of all banks

(per cent)

	Quarter Ended					
	June 1966	September 1966	March 1968	March 1969	March 1970	
1. Manufacturing	48.3	47.5	46.6	41.7	35.6	
(a) textiles	54.1	52.8	51.2	44.6	32.2	
(b) footwear and wearing apparel	38.0	41.0	35.4	29.1	36.0	
(c) metal products and engineering	55.9	55.7	45.3	43.4	40.2	
(d) rubber, plastics and chemicals	38.0	36.9	28.5	23.1	29.7	
(e) shipbuilding and repair	53.4	55.1	72.4	47.9	71.0	
(f) electrical and electronic	9.9	13.2	13.2	11.6	21.1	
(g) food	5.9	5.9	1.4	2.1	16.2	
(h) beverages and tobacco	83.0	75.5	79.5	77.7	73.0	
(i) printing and publishing	5.0	4.2	3.8	4.9	19.4	
(j) miscellaneous	58.5	57.9	68.0	68.6	55.6	
2. Agriculture and fisheries	59.9	55.6	1.0	15.5	47.3	
3. Transport and transport equipment	18.9	16.5	18.2	12.0	48.4	
4. Electricity, gas and telephone	90.7	96.6	86.0	85.2	85.0	
5. Building and construction	28.5	30.5	34.3	35.1	40.8	
6. General Commerce	15.4	15.0	17.8	14.0	12.8	
(a) import, export and wholesale trade	15.6	14.9	17.9	15.5	11.8	
(b) retail trade	13.4	15.9	15.9	17.5	26.7	
7. Mining and quarrying	23.3	27.7	18.9	16.4	12.4	
8. Miscellaneous	34.9	33.9	30.5	29.5	21.0	
(a) hotels, boarding houses and catering	57.8	55.1	45.5	54.1	32.0	
(b) financial concerns including banks	40.0	41.0	31.3	23.3	38.1	
(c) stockbrokers	45.1	42.5	53.2	41.4	30.4	
(d) professional and private individuals	12.5	12.0	11.8	11.1	8.0	
(e) others	65.1	63.5	58.9	56.5	35.9	
Total Loans and Advances	30.6	29.9	31.1	28.0	26.5	

Sources: HSBC and Banking Commissioner's Office from Y.C. Jao in Eastern Banking.

The Hongkong Bank provided as much as 48.3% of total bank finance to the manufacturing sector in June 1966, though this share gradually declined to 35.6% in March 1970. Within the sector itself, there were certain industries such as textiles, metal products and engineering, rubber, plastics and chemicals, and beverages and tobacco, for which the Bank's market shares were extremely high initially but then followed a falling trend. Shipbuilding and repair was an exception: the Bank's share showed both a high and rising trend. For others, such as electrical and electronic, food, and printing and publishing, the Bank accounted for a modest but rising proportion of total bank finance. In footwear and wearing apparel, and other unclassified miscellaneous industries, the Bank had a solidly entrenched and generally stable position, probably consequent to its earliest financing from Mongkok.

As regards the non-manufacturing sectors, the Bank had all but monopolized loans to the public utilities (electricity, gas, and telephone). It also had strong positions in building and construction, and miscellaneous sectors like hostels, financial concerns, and stockbrokers. However, its market share in general commerce was surprisingly small.

In his study, cited above, Jao has concluded that:

> It can be inferred with confidence that the Bank accounted for more than half of all bank loans and advances to the manufacturing industries. Its leading position was particularly strong in such industries as textiles and clothing, metal products and engineering, plastics and chemicals, shipbuilding and repair, and beverages and tobacco. For other non-manufacturing sectors, the Bank consistently provided more than eighty-five per cent of total bank finance to the public utilities, which constitute the infrastructure for industrial growth, until the end of the Sixties.

The Bank's share in total loans and advances of all banks in Hong Kong declined from 30.6% to 26.5% during the period considered in the tables. This declining trend is also confirmed by the figures for 1959 to 1969 extracted from the files of the Bank's Treasury Department and is consistent with what is known about the Bank's market share in other national markets; it is also consistent with the Bank's policies relative to use of funds, especially its priority relative to liquidity and, at the other extreme, its obligations relative to official and World Bank (IBRD) lending. A Hong Kong market share of 26.5% is still significant, but it does not support the popular image of the Bank's supposedly overwhelming role – the fact is that in 1970 the Hongkong Bank was one of 73 banks in Hong Kong; these banks operated 399 offices in the Colony, of which the Hongkong Bank had 66 or 16.5%.

For an understanding of the Bank's role in Hong Kong it is the absolute rather than the relative figures which are explanatory. The market grew faster than it was safe for the Hongkong Bank to follow – even if the possibility had presented itself. Indeed, the heavy bias of the territory's industrialization towards a few industries, especially textiles, forced the Bank to focus not so much on market share as on portfolio balance. There were instances of the Bank deliberately letting business pass it by when a conservative management across on Hong Kong Island balanced their natural concern over the loss of market share against the total 'uses-of-funds' approach necessary to hold in check the specific enthusiasms of the Manager on the spot in Mongkok.

As Manager Hong Kong, R.G.L. Oliphant, was aware that the Bank's market share was declining; he was also aware that the Bank's branch Managers took an active position in soliciting business. Nevertheless, on one occasion Oliphant formally solicited applications for loans up to $100,000 for small operators through the Chinese Manufacturers Association. The response, including some 130 applications, was minimal and the CMA proved reluctant to vet the applications before forwarding.

In fact the response was probably appropriate given the availability of loanable funds. The policy of a 50% liquidity ratio restricted the Bank's lending ability, but it had an important positive consequence – the motivation for the new branching policy effective from 1960 was the obvious need for additional funds.

Tables 14.1 and 14.2 do not include the relevant data of the Bank's subsidiaries. By adding the loan figures of Wayfoong Finance Limited (as from 1960) and Hang Seng Bank (as from 1965) and making suitable adjustments, the figures for the Hongkong Bank Group in total bank loans and advances declined from around 41% at the end of 1966 to 36% at the end of 1969. This proportion, too, is hardly overwhelming.

One inference that may be reasonably drawn, however, is that the Bank's position in the earlier period must have been more dominant. Thus, if in June 1966 the Bank accounted for 48.3% of total bank loans and advances to the manufacturing industries, and the share was still falling, then the same must have been much higher in the early 1950s, even though there is no documentary evidence to prove this proposition. This is consistent with Saunders' estimate, quoted above, that '... well over half of all industrial advances in Hong Kong were provided by the Hongkong Bank Group.'

Lending practices

Jao's summary of lending practices is based upon case studies of twenty firms, summarized in the Appendix to his paper in *Eastern Banking*, and on the basis of which general comments on the Bank's lending practices as they developed up to the mid-1960s can be made.

1. The Bank expected full information from its client concerning his business and financial position. The procedure as it eventually developed was, briefly: a new client was required to fill in an elaborate form, providing not only details about the firm's latest balance sheet and net worth, but also names of partners and directors, nature of business, facilities required and their purpose, security offered, turnover during the past twelve months, foreign exchange business generated through various documentary credits (L/C, T/R, D/A, D/P, etc.), and, last but not least, facilities received from any other bank or financial institution.[c] The branch Manager or lending officer in receipt of the request then made his recommendation for approval by senior management, usually a Manager or Sub-Manager in Hong Kong Office. Before repayment was due, another form, developed along similar lines, was completed for internal review as to whether loans/advances should be renewed or terminated. Again the branch Manager/lending officer made his recommendation on the basis of the client's past performance, for the approval of senior management.

2. As a rule, loans and advances for financing working capital were granted for a period of one year (though cases of six months are not unknown) subject to annual review. However, unless the borrower was obviously a bad credit risk, renewal was normally granted. Quite often a request for additional facilities was approved along with renewal of existing facilities, provided the client's performance was satisfactory and business expanding. Formally, the Bank in its letter approving a request for loans and advances reserved 'its overriding right to repayment on demand', though this was seldom if ever exercised.

3. For working capital the most convenient form of finance was the Manufacturing Advance (M/A), sometimes also called Packing Credit (P/C), which might be extended up to 80% of the face value of the Letter of Credit or confirmed order the manufacturer had received.[d] The purpose of this loan was to enable the manufacturer to buy raw materials, pay wages and overheads so as to facilitate the manufacture and delivery of goods. For the manufacturer who had to import raw materials or intermediate inputs from abroad, an important facility was the Trust Receipt (T/R), which was often used in connection with an L/C opened by the Bank on behalf of the manufacturer,

---

[c] Letters of Credit, Trust Receipts, Documents against Acceptance, and Documents against Payment.

[d] Strictly speaking, Manufacturing Advances are loans extended to the manufacturer to finance the initial stage of production, while a Packing Credit is a loan to the exporter for packing finished products for shipment; the exporter in turn may finance the manufacturer. Where the manufacturer and the exporter are one and the same party, there is of course no distinction between the two kinds of loans. However, in Hong Kong the term 'packing credit' is often used to cover both cases, see Chapter 8.

often with little or no margin, provided the latter's credit standing were good. The manufacturer could take delivery of the goods even before the bills were retired by signing a T/R in favour of the Bank. As the name implies, the granting of a T/R facility indicated a high degree of trust in the borrower.

4. For financing fixed capital on a medium- or longer-term basis, the most important facilities were those for the construction of factory buildings and the purchase and installation of machinery and equipment. As soon as the manufacturing firm had purchased a piece of land, whether in cash or by instalments, the Bank was, as a rule, prepared to finance the greater part of the cost of upperstructure, on the understanding that it was to be used for industrial purposes only. Repayment normally started after the building had been completed or occupation permit had been issued, over a period of three years or more. For smaller firms which lacked the resources to construct factories of their own but wished simply to purchase a floor or several floors of a multi-storey building hire-purchase terms were available. Similarly, bank credit was available for the purchase and installation of machinery and equipment, with repayment spread over a number of years. But this form of finance was usually handled by the Bank's wholly owned subsidiary, Wayfoong Finance Limited.

5. An acceptable collateral was required from the borrower in the form of real property, debenture over the assets of the firm (in the case of an incorporated company) or Bill of Sale (in the case of an unincorporated company, marketable securities, time deposits, inventory, personal guarantee by the firm's owner or chairman or guarantee by another reputable firm. However, in exceptional cases unsecured loans and advances might be granted, if the facilities were of a self-liquidating nature (for example, export and import trade) and the credit standing, future prospects, and cash-flow position of the borrowing firm were beyond doubt. For the secured loans the average ratio of banking facilities to collateral offered was 51.5%.

6. The lending rates charged on loans and advances varied with the type of facilities and the credit standing of the borrower. Generally speaking, the rate on import and export bills was closest to the best lending rate; the rate on Manufacturing Advances or overdrafts was somewhat higher by between 0.5% and 1%, while the rate on building and machinery loans was higher by another 0.5% to 1%. (During the period under review, the best lending rate of the Bank varied between 6% and 7.5%.) In theory, the lending rate was subject to 'fluctuation without notice', but since interest rates in those days were remarkably stable, the impact of rate changes was minimal.

7. In considering or reviewing a loan proposal, the Bank not only carefully scrutinized a client's financial statements and used a conservative method of estimating assets, but also carried out periodic inspections of the client's factory premises to assess the current state of production and to make sure that bank credit was properly used.[e]

8. While the past and current performance in honouring obligations, financial position, and business prospects were obviously the overriding criteria for the approval or rejection of a loan request, there were other considerations as well. An important one was the foreign exchange turnover generated by the client's business and, in the great exchange bank tradition, his willingness to give a major, if not exclusive, share of this turnover to the Bank, since the spread between the buying and selling rates of foreign exchange was one of the most lucrative sources of bank profit in Hong Kong. Indeed, the Bank sometimes stipulated exclusive control of exchange business as a condition for granting loans. The Bank was also sensitive about competition from other banks, although attempts to ensure that the customer was confining his banking business to the Hongkong Bank could have been for purposes of credit control. This view is supported by the fact that on occasion the Bank noted, 'While we do not stand to gain much by the way of exchange business by granting the required accommodation, we will be assisting local industry.' Jao lists this as a specific basis for lending – 'though perhaps somewhat residual'. The difficulty is that such phrases can be used simply to cover less defined but complex reasons for making a particular exception in the case being considered.

9. Consequently, an unsatisfactory balance sheet or lack of financial information, poor business prospects, overlapping in loan requests (for example, a subsidiary asking for a loan when 'umbrella' facilities have already been arranged with the parent company), unwillingness on the client's part to switch business from other banks, and suspected improper use of banking facilities were the most often cited reasons for refusal.[f]

The behaviour pattern that emerged from these observations is stated by Jao in the following summary: the Hongkong Bank adopted a very hard-headed,

[e] The Bank used a concept called 'Estimated Conservative Asset Value' in appraising a customer's net worth, which heavily discounts non-cash and non-liquid assets, for example, buildings, machinery, fixtures and furniture, receivables, and investments.

[f] See Cases 7, 8, 13 in *Eastern Banking*, pp. 570–71. Concerning Case 7, Hong Kong office's 1963 decision was stated as follows: 'The visible profits would not enable them to pay a rent of $25,000 a month and I do not wish to take a chance on the market for factory property in a year or so. However, the main reason is that there is something indefinably wrong with the whole matter and I do not wish to be involved in it.' The file reveals that the client also refused to divert all its business from another bank.

prudent, and shrewd lending policy towards Hong Kong's manufacturing industries, tempered, however, with flexibility, pragmatism, and a general desire to assist local industrial development.

Internal organizational changes

Mongkok and other branches
In the period to 1961 the Hongkong Bank appeared to be handling its industrial financing activities strictly within the traditional framework. The most visible development was the establishment of the Mongkok office itself in 1948 at a time when the first Shanghai spinning mills moved into Hong Kong. This however was made within the context of a conservative branching policy; there was no anticipation either of the great economic changes to come or of a major change in the Bank's branching policy – a subject to be discussed in the next section. Indeed, the branch showed a loss for the first three years of its operations, but by 1952 the branch's business volume had grown to such an extent that it was decided to build a new ten-storey building to accommodate the expansion; it was completed in 1954.

Mongkok was not the only branch to make industrial loans, but, until the establishment of branches in the industrial townships of Taipo and Tsuen Wan in 1960, the main rival was the main Colony office at 1 Queen's Road, Central. Subsequently, other important industrial areas such as Aberdeen, Sham Shui Po, Shaukiwan, San Po Kong, Kwun Tong, and Hung Hom were also covered. By 1966, the Bank had established a network of forty-eight branches and sub-branches all over Hong Kong, Kowloon, and the New Territories. Mongkok, however, continued to grow; by 1966 it had become necessary to build another high-rise, which was completed two years later, to house the branch.[g] The traditional explanation for this success was couched in terms of *feng-shui*, and the relative lack of success of a rival bank across the main intersection is apparently consistent with the theory that the latter's location violated certain accepted principles of geomancy. Reasons better understood in business schools could also be advanced to explain the situation.

The compradore, the new Business Representatives, and the first Chinese Manager
The combination of Shanghai origins and specialized credit requirements of Mongkok's new customers suggested that the compradore would be by-passed, and this development, while not unique to Mongkok, confirmed a trend. From

[g] In 1965 the Mongkok office was given the authority to exercise business operational control over thirty branches and offices in Kowloon. During the credit squeeze following the banking crisis, however, this authority temporarily reverted to Hong Kong office.

the first the then Manager, G.H. Cautherley, dealt directly with the Chinese industrial customers. Inspection of customer installations was hardly a post-war development; juniors had often been sent to godowns and vegetable oil tanks to assure themselves that goods hypothecated to the Bank were there – and the young Bankers were on occasion misled. Factories would seem to present more complex problems, although, unlike storage facilities, they can be judged on the basis of a performance which is more difficult to disguise. Nevertheless, the burden of the task – and the language problem which still existed – led to the development of a factory inspection unit and the employment of Chinese staff especially for this task.

The basic role of the compradore as responsible for handling cash and for the management of the local staff remained until the task merged into that of the Chinese Office Manager.

Some innovations in the staffing system, initiated during the period, should also be briefly mentioned. In 1962, at approximately the time the Bank created an Industial Banking Department (IBD), Michael Sandberg, the head of the Inward Bills Department, decided that the 'bill collectors', with their knowledge of the Hong Kong market, could be put to a more constructive use as Business Promotion Officers. The first, in 1959, were Horace Lo and Dennis Lo; John Loch joined them the following year. They were soon renamed 'Business Representatives', charged with the task of keeping existing clients happy while attracting new clients whenever possible. Some of them were assigned to Mongkok to specialize in liaising with industrial firms in close cooperation with IBD. The advantage of appointing these officials was that effective communication between the Bank and its clients was enhanced through more personal contacts and the elimination of the language barrier.

In January 1964, the Bank attracted wide publicity by the appointment of H.J. Shen as a Joint Manager in Hong Kong office on the initiative of M.G. Carruthers and with the full support of Saunders, then the Chief Manager. Shen, a former ranking central banker in Nanking and Shanghai under the Nationalist Government, came to Hong Kong in 1950 and subsequently became a prominent businessman and industrialist. Before he joined the Bank, he had been managing director of East Sun Textiles Company Ltd. Thus the Bank's links with the industrial community were further strengthened through Shen's intimate ties with the Shanghai-born industrialists. His appointment was also important in that it was the first time in the Bank's history that a Chinese was appointed to a senior managerial position, an appointment consistent with the demise of the old compradoric system.

II. Case studies

Industrial inspection

Another important development was the establishment by I.H. Bradford of a factory inspection unit under Mongkok office in 1959. This unit was later reorganized by O.P. Edwards as the Industrial Banking Department in 1962, whose principal function was to provide back-up services for senior management in the area of industrial lending. Although administratively IBD was under the control of Mongkok office, it served all offices and branches of the Bank on a Colony-wide basis; in this it could compare with the Bank's hire-purchase operations which were centred on its North Point branch. The IBD, however, can claim to be the first functional department of its kind ever to be set up in any bank in Hong Kong.

Initially, IBD concentrated on the manufacturing sector, but, as banking business expanded, its work also became much more complex and diversified. By the mid-'60s, IBD's functions, as summarized by Jao from the annual reports of the officers in charge, had expanded to include the following:

1. Factory Inspection: the main objectives of a factory inspection were to observe the operations of a manufacturing business so as to assess its production capacity and level of utilization, management efficiency, financial position and business prospects.

2. Stock Inspection/Valuation: the purpose of this job was to check the inventory list and appraise the current market value of stocks in the factory.

3. Machinery Inspection/Valuation: the objective of this function was two-fold – to appraise the realizable value of the machinery under specific charge to the Bank and to check whether the right kind of machinery and equipment was in use for a given manufacturing activity.

4. Property Valuation: this refers to the appraisal of real properties offered as collateral for industrial loans. Generally, IBD used a conservative approach that emphasized the 'quick sale' value of the property rather than its market value.

5. Feasibility Study: in considering factory building loans, the IBD was often asked to look into the viability of the proposed project with respect to its date of completion, cash-flow prospects, and amortization plan.

6. Financial Analysis: as a follow-up of inspection and valuation, it was IBD's job to examine the manufacturing client's financial statements, in order to assess the firm's profitability, liquidity, and managerial efficiency. The more relevant accounting ratios were prepared on both a cross-section and time series basis for the management.

7. Investigation: IBD may be required by the management to investigate a doubtful client's business affairs, which may involve a full auditing of the firm's financial accounts.

8. Information and Advice: although these functions were somewhat peripheral, IBD regularly collected business information and market data through a variety of sources, including direct enquiries to and interviews with customers. It also provided advice to clients on matters relating to prospects in local manufacturing industries and industrial property development.

9. Miscellaneous Duties: in carrying out its main functions, it was essential for IBD to conduct searches at the Business Registration Office, Companies Registry, Land Offices, and law courts. While the tasks were trivial in themselves, they were extremely time-

consuming. A considerable amount of translation work was also handled by IBD, as the accounts and correspondence of many manufacturing concerns, especially the smaller ones, were done in Chinese.

IBD started with one Resident Officer in charge and one or two Industrial Assistants, but by 1965 its staff had expanded to one Resident Officer and nine Industrial Assistants. Even so, the department was always hard-pressed in coping with the mounting pressure of work, since requests for inspection and other jobs came not only from Mongkok, but from other branches as well. The frequency of inspection was variable and at the discretion of the management; roughly speaking, industrial concerns whose credit was beyond doubt were inspected annually; those with lesser standing were inspected quarterly, while the doubtful or marginal cases were inspected monthly or even weekly. The latter 'emergency cases' created the most pressure for the department, particularly during the recession of 1964 and the aftermath of the 1965 banking crisis.

The IBD was a first though important step. It survived in the Bank, characterized by growing specialization and expertise, until June 1981, when most of its functions were transferred to other departments; factory inspection and financial analysis were taken over by the Credit Department, property valuation was absorbed by a wholly owned subsidiary firm of professional surveyors, and trade information and market survey were transferred to the Market Research Department. The IBD played a valuable role as an effective link between the Bank and the industrial community; its constant contacts with the manufacturing industries at the grass-roots level acted as a conduit through which the industrialists' problems and difficulties could be relayed to the Bank. There was thus a valuable exchange of information of mutual interest in the period to the late 1960s when such statutory bodies as the Hong Kong Trade Development Council, the Hong Kong Export Credit Insurance Corporation, and the Hong Kong Productivity Centre were established. Through the IBD and Mongkok the smaller industrialists were linked into the Hongkong Bank's international network; they received services and information which would only later be provided by Government and Government-related agencies.

LONDON AND THE INTEGRATION OF TWO BANKS

'Londonitis' revisited

The continuing problem

Relations between the British resident in the Crown Colony of Hong Kong and those who worked in the City of London changed dramatically as the dynamic development of an industrial Hong Kong was placed against the perceived

II. Case studies

problems of the British welfare state. What remained a factor throughout was the Hongkong Bank's love-hate relationship between its Head Office and its London Office; in the 1960s and 1970s the trend was to emphasize the areas of misunderstanding, which ranged from questions of office efficiency to the management of the Bank's two major banking subsidiaries, the Mercantile Bank and the BBME. Whatever differences may be found in the management techniques of Saunders and Sayer, they were together in their often stated intention to straighten out London (Office) – or, more accurately, their intention to have someone else go to London to do it. When the unspecified reforms did not take place, Hong Kong's concern was that their lieutenant had joined the enemy or was himself suffering an attack of 'Londonitis', and Head Office determination to reduce overheads and control the two subsidiaries in ways unspecified through agents inadequately empowered was consequently renewed. In the process Head Office virtually withdrew The Hongkong and Shanghai Banking Corporation from visibility in the City of London. In 1981 Sandberg attempted a dramatic reversal; he made an offer for the Royal Bank of Scotland Group and was unsuccessful. Although some visibility was most certainly restored and the sympathy of the City was seen to be with the Hongkong Bank, it is still fair to ask whether past policies, which had resulted in the loss of continuity of contact, had impacted negatively on the Government decision. This question would be asked anew in 1987 in the light of the purchase of 14.9% of outstanding Midland Bank shares.

The underlying problem was that London Office was in London. London Office is located in the capital of the British Empire and the Hongkong Bank is a British overseas bank. The Hongkong Bank had been chartered under terms approved by the British Treasury, as communicated by the British Colonial Office; the Bank declared its dividends in sterling; the Bank had a London Advisory Committee of leading City merchants and bankers virtually as an alternative to moving its head office to the world-important City. The Bank had to operate in London and raise gold funds through London, thus, although silver-based, it remained 'on an even keel'. Consequently the Bank was subjected to certain London and British Government controls. Thus a succession of Boards and Chief Managers determined on policies designed to prevent Head Office being pulled to London. To prevent such an event the Hongkong Bank was willing to do much. But the consequent relationship was never easy; the ways of the City were not the ways of the British in the East. This would be appreciated more in up-State New York than, quite naturally, in the City itself.

By the 1930s Grayburn felt an unease; there was something wrong with the Bank's London operations. He downgraded the Bank's presence in London ironically at the same time that he effectively made the Hongkong Bank a sterling bank, with its reserves moved to London after China and Hong Kong went off silver.

During the Pacific War Sir Arthur Morse was quickly wearied of arguing with Colonial Office officials. He left to get on with the reconstruction of the Bank and of Hong Kong, leaving behind his Manager, H.E. Muriel, who would soon complain that he was kept virtually in the dark as to the Bank's plans. During the years that Sir Edward Reid was a member of the London Advisory Committee, at least until his retirement in 1966, successive London Managers had a counsellor who was also respected in Hong Kong. The process of acquisition of the Mercantile Bank and the BBME brought Hongkong Bank officers in London and Hong Kong together to achieve an objective also desired by the Bank of England and which had at least the sympathy of the British Government.

Changes in the 1960s

During the 1960s, however, the factors underlying attitudes changed on several levels. There was a loss of sympathy between London and Hong Kong itself. The latter appeared a success story consequent to the policies of a Government which understood the necessity of capitalist enterprise and was able to provide the economic and social overheads at low rates of taxation. Their success was possible, Hong Kong 'belongers' told themselves, not only because of the favourable environment but also because the people of Hong Kong worked hard; it was almost that simple. In contrast, 'stop-go' economic policies, high rates of taxation, poor performance, and general interference seemed characteristic of a British Government and a City which, though still vital in world finance, no longer overawed. Then in 1968, as if to confirm their views, sterling was devalued.

The argument at this level was as much between the two Governments as between the Hongkong Bank and its London office. Indeed, one Bank of England official said frankly to a Hongkong Banker after both he and Saunders had lost their tempers at a meeting, it was a toss up as to who was the more unpopular visitor, Cowperthwaite of the Hong Kong Government or Saunders of the Bank.

There were four specific categories of problems as seen by the Hongkong Bank's chief executives: (i) the fact that the Bank held its reserves in sterling during a period when their assessment of Britain's economic policies was negative, (ii) the increasing amount of information sought by British Government departments, by the Stock Exchange Market Committee, and by the Bank of England, (iii) the cost of the London Office and by implication the inefficiency of its operations and staff, and (iv) the control of the Bank's subsidiary banks. The first two can be elaborated immediately.

II. Case studies

The Hongkong Bank was a Sterling Area bank operating within the exchange controls as exercised by the relevant Governments. Saunders, as were many others, was aware of the real possibility of devaluation, but until it came he could not prove his point. The Bank's sale of sterling assets during the early 1970s removed one area of frustration, but only after it had paid at least part of the price Saunders had sought to totally avoid (see Chapter 15). As a consequence of the Bank's diversification of its reserves, London seemed even less important and the cost of London Office overheads even more unnecessary.

The difficulties in Hong Kong/London relations must not, however, be exaggerated. Business continued, but the problems flared up with surprising and inconclusive frequency.

The London Managers cooperated with the Bank of England and in return received immediate assistance. A run on the BBME in Beirut undermined confidence in that bank, for example, and the Bank of England through the Federal Reserve Bank of New York guaranteed facilities in favour of the BBME's Beirut branch. Despite disagreements on fundamental policy matters, which were the direct concern of neither the particular Government nor the Bank of England officer nor the Hongkong Banker, at the practical level there was mutual assistance and appreciation. Successive London Managers have commented in oral history interviews on the helpful attitude of the officials with whom they dealt.

These underlying political differences might not need to be recorded in a purely business history were it not for the 'spill-over' into inter-office attitudes which affected the operation of the corporation. The internally contradictory nature of the above discussion is but a reflection of the irrational approach to London Office displayed from Hong Kong.

London Office – senior management and their role

London's several roles

London Office had in its history played many roles; it was one branch among many Hongkong Bank branches world-wide, it was the Bank's contact with the City and with the British Government, it was a training centre for juniors and a social point in the City where Eastern constituents on leave came in almost, as it were, to feel at home. The London Office handled the 'overheads' for the Bank in the East, and they were expensive – even if certain costs were charged directly to Head Office.[h] London Office was for a time a virtually independent merchant bank under its 'own' committee (see Volume II) and as such made

---

[h] An example would be the costing of Geoffrey Jones's BBME history project. In submitting the preliminary budget I failed, that is, never gave a thought, to make allowance for the imputed rent for floor space at 99 Bishopsgate. Head Office (i) had the project moved to a less expensive building and (ii) paid London Office from a budget devised by skilled bankers.

the Hongkong Bank Britain's lead bank for China, Philippine Islands, and Siam issues.

The London Office Manager was the Manager of a branch of the Hongkong Bank called upon to act with and hold his own against chief executive officers of other overseas exchange banks. He was subject to a Chief Manager in Hong Kong but responsible, as the senior resident representative of a British exchange bank, for responding to requests or requirements of the Bank of England and the British Government.

The London Office Manager capable of these tasks was also capable in such a heady atmosphere of taking decisions unpopular in Hong Kong, either because he was compelled to do so by the authorities or because of his own loss of contact with the reality of Hong Kong. Either way he was in trouble. At the same time the Bank's chief executive was not certain how to cope with the problem. If he had a Manager senior (in terms of years in the East) to himself and/or if he acceded to his London Manager's requests for some new status, he was in danger of reinforcing London's tendency to independence; if he placed a less senior man as the London Manager, that Manager might, for example, have even greater difficulty enforcing Head Office policy on the chief executive officers of the subsidiary banks and, as in the 1930s, the London Manager would lose credibility with senior British and Bank of England officials.

The lack of relative status was felt by G.O.W. Stewart when he became London Manager in 1961; he had been Deputy Chief Manager and was as such received by chief executives at meetings of the IMF. Saunders asked him to represent him once again – but as a branch Manager? Stewart was unsure of his reception.

Since the days of Jackson and Cameron there had been two London 'managers', one to 'represent' the Bank and one to manage London Office – although the duties were never entirely separated in so clean-cut a fashion. The policy problem was to somehow elevate the representational Manager without thereby losing effective policy control from Hong Kong. Sir Charles Addis had tried to rationalize his position as both 'representative' and 'branch manager' by in effect creating a third post, or, more accurately, by changing the role of the Chairman of the London Advisory Committee. Placing Addis, as an active member of the Bank's executive staff, as Chairman of the Committee with the responsibility for representing the Bank as head of the New China Consortium and as the Bank's representative on the boards of the then active British and Chinese Corporation and the Chinese Central Railways would certainly have undermined the position of Head Office itself. Instead, the new Chief Manager, A.G. Stephen, moved Addis to a salaried chairmanship, but as a retiree, and he secured the agreement of his predecessor, Sir Newton Stabb, to accepting an

II. Case studies 637

appointment as senior London Manager, effectively neutralizing Addis while giving him the status he desired.

The problems of the Managers

By 1961 the London senior Manager had become, like Addis, much involved with the 'representational' role. There was a difference. Sir Ewen Cameron and Sir Charles Addis had, in effect, created the subsidiaries on which they represented the Bank; in the 1950s the London Manager had not played so key a role. Either Turner personally or such Head Office deputies as Stewart had been at least as much involved. Furthermore S.W.P. Perry-Aldworth found himself in the shadow of Sir Arthur Morse, who, as Chairman of the London Committee, played a role similar to but more active than that of the retired Sir Thomas Jackson. The potential conflicts here were muffled by the degree of understanding between Turner and Morse and by Morse's overwhelming personality. If Jackson in the eyes of admiring juniors had made the Bank, Morse was universally acclaimed as having resurrected it and, more important, financed the reconstruction of Hong Kong.

Sir Arthur Morse was ailing; he died in 1967. In the 1960s the Morse/Turner relationship found no counterpart under J.A.H. Saunders as Chief Manager, although Turner did become the Chairman of the BBME. The first London Office reorganization came in 1963 with, in effect, the Addis solution – the senior post was retitled, 'Senior Manager and Manager for Europe', and the junior post was eventually designated 'Manager London'. G.O.W. Stewart was the first senior Manager to receive the new title; G.P. Stubbs and N.H.T. Bennett succeeded after serving a period of familiarization as Manager London.

This change, though rational and useful, did not solve the senior London officer's problems. He was still by rank a 'manager' and the problem of a branch or even an area Manager controlling chief executives of subsidiary banks, although eased in 1965 when the Mercantile Bank's head office moved to Hong Kong, became increasingly difficult relative to the BBME on the retirement of Angus Macqueen and the appointment of G.A. Calver. Bennett's appeal to be at least designated a 'general manager' of the Hongkong Bank was never acceded to by the new chief executive, G.M. Sayer.

There was, moreover, a new dimension in the Hong Kong/London relationship. Pre-war Chief Managers had to and until 1932 did recognize that, whatever they thought of London, major negotiations were handled there by the London Managers; the Chief Manager in Hong Kong could not effectively intervene once policy had been established in London – or indeed in the affairs of other branches. Grayburn's personality was such that even *his* first choice of London Manager, O.J. Barnes, although perhaps insufficiently independent of the cables from Head Office, was judged in London on the basis of his independence and ability to influence Bank policy. After the Pacific War the situation was 'fudged' by the role of Sir Arthur Morse. Nevertheless the precedent was set for the direct involvement in London of the chief executive in the Bank, either by his coming to London in person or acting through Sir Edward Reid or Sir Arthur Morse. Similarly, as the Treasury had discovered in the late 1930s – once they had reassured themselves that the Head Office of the Bank was actually in Hong Kong – it was possible to deal directly with Hong Kong and bypass London Office. Thus here was another confusion in points of contact and policy relationships.

London Office – the new building

Discussion of the Bank's new London Office building at this point is not quite the digression it may seem. The move from Gracechurch Street to 99, Bishopsgate was the physical manifestation of a forced Group rationalization; the Mercantile Bank's London office had moved in with the Hongkong Bank at 9 Gracechurch Street, but the BBME was still inadequately accommodated in its old quarters in Abchurch Lane. G.M. Sayer's eventual solution was the lease of the lower thirteen floors of the new but inappropriate Barclay's/ Hambro building, a deal somewhat improved eventually by the Bank's ability to secure the 125-year head lease for £32 million against the £50 million originally asked. Sayer saw the building, which was actually purchased by a Vila subsidiary, 99 Bishopsgate, Ltd, as a potential fall back office should an emergency occur in Hong Kong; in the process, however, he sold the freehold in Gracechurch Street.

The Mercantile Bank began integration of its London branch in 1970. There was still customer loyalty, but, although several expressed disappointment, only two notified the manager that they were withdrawing their accounts. The task completed, P.T. Lamb, the last Mercantile London Manager, became a Manager in the Hongkong Bank's office; he retired in 1973 but was retained on contract to supervise the banks' move to Bishopsgate.[1] As there were now two banks, it apparently seemed sensible that the new office building should have two banking halls, one done in Chinese-style red and gold for the Hongkong Bank and the other for the BBME. But back in Hong Kong, just before the move in May 1976, Head Office had been examining the impact of United Kingdom taxation and determined that the high overheads of retail banking should be borne as far as possible by the BBME. The shift, it may seem

---

[1] While London Manager, Lamb (East for the Mercantile in 1945) compiled a survey history of his bank from its founding as the Chartered Mercantile Bank of India, London, and China up to its *de facto* integration and the year 1970. See reference in the Bibliography.

paradoxical, meant that the Hongkong Bank would withdraw from retail banking in the United Kingdom – its Pall Mall (London, West End), Manchester, and new (1977) Edinburgh branches excepted.

Now on the ground floor both banking halls were to be for the BBME, while on the thirteenth floor, the BBME's Secretary, J.L.A. Francis, was busy laying out a Head Office complex suitable for the entertainment of its major Gulf customers. On the question of the Hongkong Bank's loss of face there could be no debate.

The Hongkong Bank had a long history of retail banking in the City; many of its Eastern constituents kept their current accounts there; those retired from the East would resent being presented with the cheque-book of a bank they had never heard of; some Jewish customers would protest. Quick thinkers instructed that their accounts be moved to the Pall Mall office, which was still Hongkong Bank, but that office reached capacity, even though Bank staff were not permitted to transfer their accounts. Those experts who were aware of the tax situation, including the Bank of England, fully understood the Bank's decision at the business level. Nevertheless, the Hongkong Bank had removed, as it were, its window from the City; it had become less visible, and it had disturbed relations with customers.

None of this made the position of the Bank's Manager for London and Europe any the easier. He was now operating in what was, to the public at least, the head office building of the BBME; the prestige had been shifted and was focused on the suddenly very visible subsidiary bank.

The representational role – the initial resolution

The Hongkong Bank had one new card to play, the executive director. Sandberg as Deputy Chairman had been disturbed by the downgrading of the Hongkong Bank in the still important financial centre of London. He had opposed both the sale of the freehold site in Gracechurch Street and the withdrawal of the Hongkong Bank (in favour of BBME) from the City. To counter this, he persuaded Sayer to appoint the senior man in London an executive director, thus at least giving the executive in charge the status that in a sense the Bank itself had lost. The first partial resolution of the London problem came, therefore, in 1976 with the appointment of P.E. Hutson as the resident executive director in London and the representative of the Hongkong Bank Group – he would also be appointed to the board of the BBME.

This achieved not quite the duality of Marine Midland with its Buffalo and New York head offices, but at least it put an enclave (with virtual extraterritorial rights) into the London Office building. The line of communication from Head Office to the Bank of England and other authorities had become direct. It was a solution to a long-standing problem which had become possible only when transportation enabled a director to live outside Hong Kong and yet be able to attend a minimum four Board meetings a year. The role of 'Head Office in London' was enhanced by the presence from 1973 of F.I.C. Herridge as the Chairman's representative. He had returned from Hong Kong where he had been the last separate chief executive of the Mercantile Bank. In similar circumstances, Kenneth Bradford would return from Hong Kong after transferring the BBME head office from London; he too would be given the title of Chairman's Representative.

But this is to anticipate. Bennett remained for a short period as senior Manager of the Hongkong Bank, but he retired in 1976. Hutson became a member of the board of the BBME and found Calver very much in control at 99 Bishopsgate; Hutson himself had no day-to-day banking responsibilities, not even, as in the past, some duty relative to the Bank's sterling investments – these had ceased to be important. But he did still find the Group with three banks in London and a 40% stake in Antony Gibbs.

The first task was the integration of the Home staffs of the BBME, Mercantile Bank, and Hongkong Bank into a coordinated operation. The next task was policy control. When the much respected Angus Macqueen retired as chairman of the BBME, he was replaced in 1979 by Hutson. Hutson's new role coincided with a change in the British Government and the removal of exchange controls, making the transfer of BMME's head office to Hong Kong a feasible proposition. Sandberg pressed the issue; the Governor of the Bank of England, Gordon Richardson, was entirely sympathetic, and negotiations with various governmental bodies, including the Treasury, were accordingly successful. The move, which had the support of the BBME's new general manager, Kenneth Bradford, was concluded in early 1980 with the granting of a Royal Supplementary Charter.

At this point the Group's retail operations returned to the Hongkong Bank, and Hutson's replacement, Tom Welsh, who had been sent by Sandberg with the task of restructuring the Bank in the United Kingdom, was an executive director of the Hongkong Bank, the Chief Executive London, and responsible for the U.K. operations of the Bank, now to be focused on wholesale banking, and of the Group. European branches operated under Head Office in Hong Kong. The position of London Office had been rationalized; the front bank was the Hongkong Bank, although the BBME retained two branches in the West End for its own customers; the Mercantile retained nothing but a non-operating 'registered office', and the former representational aspects of the senior London Manager became the responsibility of the Executive Director of the Hongkong Bank resident in London and of the Chairman's Representatives.

There remained the problem of the Bank's investment in Antony Gibbs. In

1981 the question of the Hongkong Bank's bid for the Royal Bank of Scotland was a dominating issue; the Bank's relations with London and its functions in Britain had not been resolved, but its organizational rationalization at 99 Bishopsgate would for a time prove stable.

The London Office – efficiency

While the Hongkong Bank's successive chief executives were tackling the problem of London Managers, their status, and the role of London in the coordination of Hongkong Bank Group activities, Head Office was also concerned with the efficiency of the office itself.

When Sayer sent Bennett to London with instructions to 'sort them out', he was acting in the grand tradition. Grayburn had sent E.J. Davies in 1937, who reported that one important account hadn't been balanced since before the 1914–1918 war. But Davies was not in good health; Grayburn then sent Morse to put life into the job. In his time Saunders sent A.M. Mack to London in 1962, and he, according to O.P. Edwards, had been unable to 'scratch the surface'; Edwards went to London in 1965 to undertake an internal audit; at the request of Saunders he also compiled a full report on the working of London Office. Although management would agree that the majority of his points were well taken, it so shook up the London staff that G.O.W. Stewart spent considerable time defending his colleagues. Bennett, who described the Edwards Report as a 'document for tearing an office into pieces' was sent two years later to write a more temperate report with more realistic time limits for correction.

In 1971 Bennett became London Manager and attempted to effect reforms, but a new stage was reached with the planning for the move to 99 Bishopsgate. Physical integration was expected to reveal surplus staff who would then be offered attractive retirement packages, made even more attractive on the basis of representations made in concert by both Calver for the BBME and Bennett for the Hongkong Bank. London's overheads, it was thought, would accordingly be cut. Bennett argued, however, that moving into a larger office with an expanding business would eventually mean an increase of staff, but he was overruled. Accordingly, almost all the experienced, senior Home staff resigned; very soon the staff shortage was felt and recruiting began. According to Bennett,

Sayer had achieved his main object of breaking down what he saw as the resistance of London Office staff to Hong Kong. The fact that we lost many able men of long service, who took early retirement, did not seem to worry him. Nor was he too concerned that the BBME soon had to recruit two or three staff to replace each man lost. The BBME in London had replaced the HSBC London Office and hopefully the problems would go away. It was a forlorn hope.

This was vigorously denied by Sayer; he remained convinced of the need for a shake-up and of the success of the new team. Underlying both positions, however, was the incompatibility of London and Hong Kong attitudes.

The role of the London Advisory Committee

Briefly stated, the Hongkong Bank's London Committee played a minor role during the years under consideration. In the 1950s a sub-committee had been involved in negotiations relative to the acquisition of the Mercantile Bank and BBME, but this activity was deceptive. Although nominally a sub-committee, its members – Morse, Reid, and Perry-Aldworth – had in fact been appointed by Turner for reasons independent of their status on the main committee. The Committee were consulted about the terms of the lease of 99 Bishopsgate, but that, Lord Catto recalls, was the only substantive matter brought before them. Sayer recalls that members were asked their views on the Bank's intended investment in Antony Gibbs – the Committee had been in favour; during the early 1970s, when the Bank was running down its holdings of sterling securities, questions were asked of the Committee about the trend of gilt-edged prices, but the Committee – no more than Stubbs as London Manager – were told of the Bank's underlying change in investment policy. This would be consistent with Saunders' policy as chief executive; later as Committee Chairman he would not appear to have advocated a more active Committee. Furthermore, with Saunders as Chairman the relationship of the Committee with the London Manager was cut once again, suggesting an inconsistent view of both London management and the Advisory Committee.

This lack of formal consultation did not render its existence pointless. the Bank needed contacts in the City and the members provided this; the committee had become, in a sense, a formal acknowledgement of this assistance. Then, too, Hong Kong did not at that time feel politically secure – certainly not during the Red Guard troubles – and the London Committee remained, potentially, the emergency fall-back board of directors. This last was apparently to both Saunders and Sayer its only real function qua committee.

The very reasons for the Committee's first establishment in 1875 were against it. The Hongkong Bank, recovering from the 1874 crisis and wishing a recognized position in London without a resident board, had reluctantly to find a substitute, but David McLean, then the London Manager, decided from the first not to provide the resulting committee full information. The Committee, despite its key role at least between 1895 and 1914, was a symbol of London's apparent challenge to Head Office. Yet it was comforting to the Bank to know that they were there and available for consultation and in a crisis. The problem therefore was to tell them very little, but to keep them as happy as possible.

II. Case studies

Table 14.3 *The Hongkong and Shanghai Banking Corporation London Advisory Committee, 1962–1985*

March 1963
Sir Arthur Morse (Chairman)	Hongkong Bank, retired	1953–67
G.O.W. Stewart (Deputy Chairman)	Hongkong Bank, Manager	1961–69
F.H. Atkinson	Blyth, Greene, Jourdain and Co.	1958–67
Sir Dallas Bernard[a]	Board, BBME	1960–64
J.A.F. Binny	Westminster Bank	1953–81
Sir Cyril E. Jones	Board, Mercantile Bank	1959–66
J.H. Keswick	Matheson and Co.	1962–70
Sir Alec Kirkbride	Board, BBME	1960–69
R.G. Macindoe	Maclaine, Watson and Co.	1943–65
Sir Kenneth W. Mealing	Board, Mercantile Bank	1959–66
Sir John Nicoll	Governor, Singapore (ret.)	1955–63
Sir Edward Reid	Baring Brothers and Co.	1942–66
G.R. Roper-Caldbeck	Boustead and Co.	1957–70
Sir Michael Turner	Hongkong Bank, retired	1962–80

New Members, 1964–71
[G.O.W. Stewart appointed Chairman, 1964]
G.E. Marden	Wheelock, Marden and Co.	1964–66
N.C. Ballingal	Maclaine, Watson and Co.	1965–71
K.M.G. Anderson	Guthrie and Co.	1966–78
A.H. Carnwath	Baring Bros	1966–74
Lord Catto of Cairncatto	Morgan, Grenfell and Co.	1966–81
W.H.C. Bailey	Blyth, Greene, Jourdain and Co.	1967–68
C.E. Loombe	Board, BBME	1967–74
G.P. Stubbs	Hongkong Bank, Manager	1967–73

[G.P. Stubbs appointed Chairman, 1969]
H.J. Jourdain	Blyth, Greene, Jourdain and Co.	1968–73
F.C. Rowan	Vavassuers	1969–73
J.A. Swire	John Swire and Sons	1969–
M.A.R. Young-Herries	Jardine, Matheson and Co.	1970–75

March, 1972
G.P. Stubbs (Chairman)	Hongkong Bank, Manager	1967–72
K.M.G. Anderson	Guthrie and Co.	1966–77
N.H.T. Bennett	Hongkong Bank, Manager	1971–76
J.A.F. Binny	Westminster Bank	1953–81
A.H. Carnwath	Baring Bros	1966–74
Lord Catto of Cairncatto	Morgan, Grenfell and Co.	1966–81
M.A.R. Young-Herries	Jardine, Matheson and Co.	1970–75
H.J. Jourdain	Blyth, Greene, Jourdain and Co.	1968 72
C.E. Loombe	Board, BBME	1967–74
F.C. Rowan	Vavassuers	1969–72
J.A.H. Saunders	Hongkong Bank, retired	1971–
J.A. Swire	John Swire and Sons	1969–
Sir Michael Turner	Hongkong Bank, retired	1962–80

New members, 1972–1976
[Sir John Saunders, Chairman, 1972–1976]
J.M. Blyth Currie	Blyth, Greene, Jourdain and Co.	1973–80

Table 14.3 (cont.)

Sir Philip de Zulueta	Antony Gibbs and Sons	1973–
R.J. Dent	Baring Bros	1974–
A. Macqueen	BBME	1974–78
H.N.L. Keswick	Jardine, Matheson and Co.	1975–
P.E. Hutson	HSBC, Executive Director	1976–82
April 1978 (Year ending December 1977)		
P.E. Hutson (Chairman from 1976)	HSBC, Executive Director	1977–82
J.A.F. Binny	Westminster Bank	1953–81
Lord Catto of Cairncatto	Morgan, Grenfell and Co.	1966–81
J.M. Blyth Currie	Blyth, Greene, Jourdain and Co.	1973–80
R.J. Dent	Baring Bros	1974–81
M.J. Gent	Guthrie and Co.	1977–82
H.N.L. Keswick	Jardine, Matheson and Co	1975–
A. Macqueen	BBME	1974–78
Sir John Saunders	Hongkong Bank, retired	1971–
J.A. Swire	John Swire and Sons	1969–
Sir Michael Turner	Hongkong Bank, retired	1962–80
Sir Philip de Zulueta	Antony Gibbs and Sons	1973–
New Members, 1978–1984		
Sir John Addis[b]	Diplomatic service (ret.)	1978–83
K. Bradford	BBME	1978–81
E.P. Heath	Inchcape and Co.	1978–80
G.M. Sayer	Hongkong Bank, retired	1978–
Sir Geoffrey Arthur	Diplomatic service (ret.)	1980–84
G.A. Calver	BBME	1980–84
Lord Denham	BBME	1980–
H.P. Foxon	Inchcape and Co.	1980–84
Viscount Weir	The Weir Group, PLC	1980–
J.L. Boyer	HSBC, Antony Gibbs	1981–82
Sir Donald Hawley	Diplomatic service (ret.)	1981–
P.F.H. Mason	BBME	1981–
T. Welsh, Chairman	HSBC, Executive Director	1982–85
Lord Rawlinson of Ewell	former Attorney-General	1983–
Sir James Craig	Diplomatic service (ret.)	1984–
D.F.K. Heathcote	James Capel and Co.	1984–
G.H. Turnbull	Inchcape, PLC	1984–

[a] Sir Dallas Bernard, a son-in-law of Sir Charles Addis, had served as a director of the Hongkong Bank, 1925–1929; he was Chairman for an exceptional two years, 1926–1928. From 1929–1939 he was a member of the London Committee, representing Jardine, Matheson and Co.

[b] Sir John Addis (1914–1983), the son of Sir Charles Addis, had served as HBM's Ambassador to the Philippines and to China.

II. Case studies

The membership of the Committee and the several changes can be seen in Table 14.3. The establishment of a Mercantile Bank Advisory Committee in 1965 was responsible for certain movements – Sir Kenneth Mealing and Cyril Jones, for example, were transferred. The Westminster Bank and several of the traditional firms continued to be represented, but there was new representation from retired political experts. Earlier the Bank had failed to obtain permission for Sir Alexander Grantham and Sir David Trench, former Hong Kong Governors, to join the Committee, but by 1980 advisers from the East and Middle East were members. With the transfer of head offices to Hong Kong, the Mercantile Bank Committee was joined with that of the Hongkong Bank, selected members of the BBME board were invited to join the Committee, and a representative from Antony Gibbs was appointed.

As for the chairmanship, it moved back and forth from retired Chief Managers, Morse and Saunders, to senior London Managers, Stewart and Stubbs. The original plan for Turner to take over from Morse ran into the problem of Morse's reluctance to retire; when he did, G.O.W. Stewart as Manager Europe was appointed. Hutson and his successors, as the resident executive directors, were, for the time, a sensible choice.

The question of control and the transfer of head offices

The location and indeed the continued existence of the Mercantile Bank had from the first been partly a question of taxation and British Treasury authority to move the bank's head office, partly a question of maintaining sound relations with valued constituents, and partly a matter of Group rationalization and control. Turner sent W.H. Lydall to coordinate policy; Saunders sent A.M. Mack, previously the Chief Inspector in Head Office. Lydall was sent to smooth over the problems of transfer; Mack was sent as one of a series of officers instructed to do something – he was told, 'There has to be a change.'

The fact is that a façade of independence had nevertheless to be retained until the Mercantile board of directors accepted the futility of its own position and agreed to retire without recrimination. Nevertheless, when the time came there would be sadness.

Preliminary talks were held with Sir Kenneth Mealing, the Mercantile Bank's chairman in late 1964, British Treasury authority to move the head office of the Mercantile Bank was obtained in 1965, and the move was effected at the end of March 1966. Saunders had neither consulted with nor informed the Mercantile's board or its chief executive, C.F. Pow, as to the exact timing; to both it came as a surprise. The reasoning, tax and control, was however accepted. The former board members were formed into the Mercantile Bank consultative committee with fees of £500 p.a., and Pow, as the last London Chief Manager, retired. In Hong Kong F.I.C. Herridge (East for the Mercantile in 1945) became General Manager under an executive committee composed at first of Saunders, F.J. Knightly, and Herridge. In effect he ran the Mercantile Bank; eventually he became a member of the Mercantile Bank board of directors. The coordination of financial resources of the two banks was assured; Herridge considered himself both Mercantile Bank and Hongkong Bank Group.

The two head offices were merged at the end of 1971, but Herridge, now both chief executive officer and chairman of the Mercantile Bank, remained in Hong Kong to 'allay concern'. In 1973 he returned, as noted above, to London as the Chairman's Representative. His brief, as usual, was not specific, but Sayer instructed him to go and have a good look at the BBME. Herridge found, what others had already discovered, as the Hongkong Bank's Board minuted, that the BBME were reluctant to follow Hongkong Bank advice especially in the area of merchant banking. Calver, the General Manager, was carrying out a policy he considered sound for the BBME, whether this was consistent with Hongkong Bank Head Office wishes or not; this, from the Hongkong Bank's point of view was described by Herridge, by Bennett, and by many others as 'obstructive'. In 1974 the Board took note of Sayer's efforts to gain control, including standardized accounting and terms of service, compatible operating systems, and integration in London, to all of which the BBME's board eventually agreed. At the same time Calver was ultimately responsible for running BBME, thus once again the Hongkong Bank was trying to operate a bank with its own board through the fact of its 100% shareholding. This Sandberg found unacceptable.

The foreign staff of the Mercantile were assigned to Hongkong Bank posts, or vice versa, initially by 'secondment'. The two staffs were integrated in 1972 and 'wore the hat' appropriate to the sign outside the branch in which they worked. J.W.L. Howard (East in 1946), General Manager for Overseas Operations in 1969, put it this way:

For quite a number of years the Hongkong Bank/Mercantile Bank staff were not identifiable as such except in the minds of those idiots who kept on saying, oh, well, of course he's a Mercantile Bank man, in a sense that he's an inferior citizen – which is not really the way to go about it.

G.M. Sayer, referring to his first years as Chairman, was even more outspoken on the issue. 'There are still people in the Bank who say, he's ex-Mercantile, he's ex-Hongkong, he's ex-BBME, but basically they're people like us. Some people say that their people are sub-standard. I don't believe that. I found it was the other way round, if anything.' New officers were recruited to the Group, which not being a legal entity, meant *de jure* to the Hongkong Bank as holding company. By the end of 1980 control of the three banks under integrated management in Hong Kong had been achieved and the separate identities had no operating significance.

This left Antony Gibbs, and it was not performing satisfactorily. The original acquisition of 20% of the equity was in itself a consequence of Gibbs's problems, with which the Bank of England had been acquainted. Their new chairman, Sir Philip de Zulueta, attempted a turnaround, but it was incomplete.

Nevertheless, Gibbs was English, and the Hongkong Bank, confronted with the necessities of the BBME, had seen no other opportunity to move into wholesale banking in London. With 40% the Hongkong Bank had 'control', but the problems remained unresolved. The Hongkong Bank's solution was eventually to obtain 100% equity, but its preoccupation with the acquisition of Marine Midland delayed negotiations.

THE PHILIPPINES AND SRI LANKA

THE PHILIPPINES: MANILA AND ILOILO

General developments

As stated in Chapter 10, the Hongkong Bank continued to play a significant role in the foreign banking sector of the Philippine economy despite unfavourable legislation and, on occasion, deteriorating economic conditions. Critics of Filipino policy might be answered by noting, correctly, that the Hongkong Bank was able to make and to remit profits. The Bank in 1970 assigned a permanent capital to the Manila branch of one million pesos; at this time Manila's assets had been Pesos 166.8 million equivalent to 1.4% of the Pesos 12,000 million combined resources of the banking system. The Hongkong Bank was in any case turning to wholesale banking, and in 1975, with the Bank of America, led a US$80 million loan to the copper mining firm, Atlas Consolidated Mining. The Bank then became involved with financing for an ASEAN (Association of Southeast Asian Nations) telecommunications network, the first phase of which required stand-by credits of US$40 million for eight years.

The Hongkong Bank took a minority interest in the Private Development Corporation of the Philippines and made other equity investments, in 1977, in the Malayan Insurance Group through a 20% equity in Mico Equities. The Bank and Wardley, the latter being the Hongkong Bank Group's investment bank, took 25% each of the equity of State Investment House. In the late 1970s the Hongkong Bank became involved in offshore banking through the newly authorized offshore banking units and the foreign currency deposit units.

In 1971 the Hongkong Bank transferred its main office from the old city site to the new business and financial hub district of Makati. In 1975 the Bank had been 100 years in the Philippines, an anniversary celebrated with a special Philippine postage stamp issue, and the then Chairman, G.M. Sayer, with the Duchess of Gloucester was present at the related festivities. In 1981 the Bank's new Manila office in the Bank-supported Ortigas commercial development in the Mandaluyong (Pasig) area was opened. But this was the consequence of a transfer of licence and the consequent need to close the Iloilo office after 97 years of service.

Iloilo office, the story concluded[j]

The Iloilo fire of 1966

Fires are not unusual in the wood-built shopping centres of Philippine towns, and Iloilo was not spared.

ILOILO OFFICE DESTROYED BY FIRE 7TH FEBRUARY AND TEMPORARILY NOT FUNCTIONING ALL CORRESPONDENCE AND BUSINESS TO BE DIRECTED TO MANILA UNTIL FURTHER NOTICE

The Manager, Robin W. Cambell (East in 1954), was apparently too busy to notice that a fire had broken out close to the Hongkong Bank office. His wife, Angela, reported the danger and an hour or so later she called again to remark that smoke was coming out from under the Hongkong Bank sign. Within approximately two hours Campbell, with the assistance of the staff, had removed the cash to the Chartered Bank and, in the absence by this time of any other transport, had packed the essentials – including the 32 NCR (National Cash Register) transfer book machines, 3 NCR Savings Bank/Current Account posting machines, the Agent's small Mosler safe containing the telegram books, foreign currency notes, etc. and a small supply of travellers cheques – into his car, which was so heavily laden in the back that the driver couldn't steer. Mrs Campbell had to sit on the bonnet (hood), and, as they drove through the streets, people cheered – a Banker's wife was responsible for the balance.

En route Campbell met B.J. Wall, manager of Warner Barnes, who made his showroom available as a temporary office. Although three members of the staff had lost their homes in the fire, they reported to Campbell's house early and all arrangements were made to open on time, with the money laid out on the desks in the great tradition of A.P. Giannini after the San Francisco fire. The Chief of Police assigned four guards, although, as one of the staff reported, they themselves had on the average about one and a half guns apiece which they kept in their desk drawers.

The Bank advertised its new location on the radio and posted signs in the

---

[j] The Iloilo branch has been made a small office case study; its history was begun in Chapter 2, Volume II, and continued in Chapters 10 and 12 of Volume III, and Chapters 2 and 10 of Volume IV.

now totally gutted old site, and customers naturally were anxious. As A.I. Rabuco tells it:

> The crowd was so big and they demanded their money. Well, as soon as they came to me, because I signed, I did the savings accounts, when they found out that all the records are safe, they said never mind, we just wanted to know whether our money was safe. And from that time, they believed that the Hongkong Bank was really a bank of integrity.

During all this Campbell was able to obtain authorization from Saunders to give a donation of Pesos 10,000 to the relief fund for fire victims, both the sum and the speed with which it was granted were well received in the community.

This was a time when the local staff showed the full range of their loyalty and initiative, and the records refer specifically to Rabuco's role in running the office during the Agent's absence. At the same time R. Paredes was assigned especially responsible accounting tasks and in the aftermath was informed that he was being recommended for appointment as an officer. A year later he was sent to London for training.

The Iloilo agency moved from the Warner Barnes showroom to the second floor of the Philippine Development Bank building, which could not be a permanent home. Campbell found a new central site and supervised the construction. As a 1967 inspection report states:

> The new office is really excellent, and reflects great credit on all concerned. There is plenty of space and light and the layout is very convenient...The building, although small, is one of the showpieces of Iloilo and many people apparently use it as a meeting place. However, new savings accounts are being opened at the rate of over 10 a day and the total is now over 12,000, amounting to nearly Pesos 10 million.

A 1975 report confirmed the suitability of the building and noted the availability of limited parking facilities. By this time deposits totaled Pesos 25 million, mainly from the 21,000 savings accounts, of which Pesos 20 million was lent to Manila, with advances in Iloilo at the not surprisingly low figure of Pesos 4–5 million. Yet the agency made a bookkeeping loss of some Pesos 300,000, given the nominal 8.5% rate of interest paid by the Manila branch – it would have taken a not unreasonable 9.5% for the agency to break even.

The last years: Iloilo to 1981
The appointment in 1979 of Roberto Paredes as the first Filipino Manager of the Hongkong Bank agency in Iloilo was, for him, bittersweet; at the same time he was informed the agency would close – he was also to be the last.

While it was reassuring that, as a 1978 report stated, 'our prestige here is considerable', and that the growth of deposits continued beyond all predictions of earlier years, this but made the departure a greater historical break and focused criticism on the regulation which prevented the Bank from retaining

Iloilo while pursuing a corporate policy more in keeping with its potentials in wholesale banking. Despite the information provided the Bank's Board of Directors that the agency had long been operating at a loss, it was known that the meaning of such a statement is subject to varying interpretations and that Iloilo's contribution was positive. The real issue was both the amount and the type of loss set against the fact that the Hongkong Bank had found in 1978 and the Central Bank of the Philippines had in March 1980 finally approved a new site in MetroManila, in Pasig, close to industrial developments to the finance of which the Bank had sound reason for believing it could contribute.

Accordingly the Bank set about divesting itself of the Iloilo agency, and of the two bids it received accepted the Pesos 3 million of the Allied Banking Corporation, the largest of the Philippine private domestic banks. The negotiations concluded, the Hongkong Bank had to inform its customers and a press release was made: 'After almost a century of service to the people of Iloilo... The Hongkong and Shanghai Banking Corporation takes this opportunity to express its gratitude for the trust and confidence its Iloilo customers have reported for so many years...' The take-over day was set, a grand opening of the new Allied Bank branch was planned, the customers appeared satisfied, and the Hongkong Bank was prepared for a peaceful withdrawal. But the ties were not so easily, or so happily, broken.

An inspection of the Iloilo agency had revealed that it was 'grossly overstaffed' and it was hardly surprising that the Allied Bank agreed to take over only 50% of the local staff. In any event a former union leader, rejected in a recent election, was able to convince the local staff to accept neither employment with Allied nor relocation in Manila, but rather to strike... presumably to force the Hongkong Bank to remain, or at least to improve its severance package.

News of a possible strike was leaked to Paredes, and the Manila Deputy Manager, W.E. Young, flew down to stand by. The strike came at the busiest time, when the veterans were cashing or depositing their U.S. warrants – one after another of the staff called in sick and the agency was expected to close by noon. However Paredes had recently employed two temporary typists who were not members of the union, and his available staff consisted of Young, a second staff officer, the two typists, the gardener, and Mrs Paredes. The gardener, who was part-time, was reported quite capable of helping 'inside', an interesting fact which suggests something about the banking profession or the general educational level of Filipino gardeners, or, probably, both. In any case, the Bank remained open.

The staff were successful in obtaining an injunction which was to prevent the 'Hongkong Bank' opening in Iloilo on the Monday morning, the Monday following the take-over by Allied and the first day of Allied's business. In this

II. Case studies

confusion the Hongkong Bank turned to its lawyer, a classmate of the Minister of Defense, who in turn routed out the Minister of Labor at midnight, had the injunction suspended and the order to open flown down to Iloilo. Naturally the signature was challenged but a telephone call confirmed its authenticity and the Allied Bank, with police in the background, opened for business. As the former Hongkong Bank staff had refused to remove their property from their desks they now entered the Allied Bank and were given permission to retrieve it; instead they dumped the contents on the floor and swept the opening-day chocolates and other items off the counters. The case was then referred successfully for the Bank to the Supreme Court of the Philippines.

Former major customers were naturally less demonstrative, but they felt themselves deserted. 'The Hongkong Bank is part of the Iloilo community and it was its duty to remain here unless prevented by law from so doing.' Paredes, who was left behind as representative until the several problems were resolved, felt the mood, but the irony was that in one sense the Bank was 'prevented by law'; the limitations on branch banking had forced the Bank to make a choice. It had been not only an exchange bank, but a retail 'main street' (high street) bank in the many areas it had served, and this had been especially true in the Philippines 'Queen City' of Iloilo. But in one way or another, by limitations, local incorporation, immigration restrictions or outright prohibition, the Bank had been forced to reevaluate its main street role. In the Philippines the decision had been to focus on wholesale banking, to which, given no other alternative, the Iloilo agency had been a useful supplement. But when the alternative came, the Hongkong Bank seized the opportunity, and a new agency stands in an industrial development area of MetroManila. Behind in Iloilo there is history – not the least of which is the fine museum to which the Bank contributed as a charter member. The Allied Banking Corporation must now care for the Hongkong Bank's customers, and, as part of the take-over agreement, for two graves which remain in the American cemetery of the nearby and ancient town of Jaro.[k]

---

[k] H.W. Stedman came East in 1903, was assigned to the Iloilo office on his first tour, and died there in 1904. G.W. Garrett joined London Office in 1909, came East in 1912. After service in Shanghai, Tsingtau, Tokyo, and Hong Kong, he was Agent or acting Agent in Saigon, Hankow, and Rangoon. He came to Iloilo as Agent in 1941 and was killed in March 1942; the story of his last days is told in Volume III. Both Hongkong Bankers are buried in the American cemetery.

SRI LANKA AND COLOMBO

The Hongkong Bank Group and Colombo office[1]

1965–1977

After nine years of rule by the socialist Sri Lanka Freedom Party, the foreign banks received a respite under the more conservative Government of Dudley Senananyake between 1965 and 1970, although at a cost. Not only was the threat of some form of closure averted but also the law preventing the exchange banks from taking new deposits from Ceylonese was repealed and the tax on debits to accounts *de facto* suspended. The cost to the Hongkong Bank Group fell primarily on the Mercantile Bank who, as part of an overall 'package deal' between banks and Government, sold their sub-branches in Jaffna and Kandy to the Commercial Bank, which, as stated above, took over the Sri Lanka business of the Eastern Bank, a subsidiary of the Chartered Bank. In the same way the 'out-station' branches of the former National Bank of India (then Grindlays) were sold to the indigenous Hatton National Bank.

The main contribution of the exchange banks however was in the provision of foreign exchange during a particularly difficult period. In 1965 the Hongkong Bank, for example, agreed to provide up to £1 million sterling outstanding at any one time from a special sterling loan account in London, the purpose being to finance imports into Sri Lanka.

The account would be used for bills drawn under the Hongkong Bank Ceylon branch's letters of credit and for bills received on a collection basis. The sterling amount of £1 million was to cover the outstanding sterling loan granted in London for the purpose of settling import bills plus payments under the total outstanding import letters of credit established by the Hongkong Bank's Colombo office... The rupee equivalents paid over to the Central Bank would be regarded for purposes of the Bank's exchange position as deliveries by the Bank of sterling equivalents. The Central Bank which was acting on behalf of the Government was to keep the exchange positions of the Bank covered.

Interest was to be at $\frac{1}{2}$ of 1% over Bank (of England) rate. The Hongkong Bank was also responsible for arranging lines of credit in U.S. dollars and Canadian dollars for Ceylon.

This set the stage for negotiations which began in 1969 and resulted in the repeal of the law preventing the growth of Ceylonese deposits in the foreign banks. The sale of outstanding branches was part of the understanding and has been described above. The second part was a further extension in 1971 of credit to finance imports, for which the Hongkong Bank Group put up £3 million at $\frac{1}{2}$ of 1% over Bank of England rate. The Bank also agreed to train

[1] The Colombo office has been presented in this history as a case study of the Bank's operations in South Asia. For earlier sections see Chapter 2, Volume II; Chapter 10, Volume III; and Chapters 1 and 10, Volume IV.

II. Case studies

Ceylonese and to reduce the number of expatriates and to invest approximately Rs10 million in debentures of the State Mortgage Bank or the Agricultural and Industrial Credit Corporation and in National Housing debentures. L.G. Atterbury, then manager of the Mercantile Bank, together with H.J.S. Muriel (son of H.E. Muriel) of the Hongkong Bank, negotiated with the Central Bank and, after further discussions with Ian Herridge, the Mercantile's general manager in Hong Kong, came to an agreement for £2 million presumably for both banks, but the Central Bank assumed the Group was committed for £4 million, that is for £2 million from each bank. By the time this had been renegotiated, other exchange banks had reached their own agreements and were already capturing Ceylonese deposits. However, the records show that Group deposits in the period immediately following these arrangements also expanded significantly.

With the change of Government and the establishment of the Republic of Sri Lanka in 1972 a further program of socialism was promised under a coalition Government headed by Sirimavo Bandaranaike, and the Business Undertakings (Acquisition) Act of 1971 seemed to doom foreign investment and bring into question once again the viability of foreign banking in Sri Lanka. With taxes on profits of 83%, only 17% could be remitted, and, as the Bank's advances in the country were largely unsecured or unrealistically secured by property, there were dangers of substantial capital losses. There were also potential problems with loans made to enable Sri Lankans to buy up former foreign-owned estates and which might now come under the 1971 Acquisitions Act.

In this atmosphere the question of nationalization or voluntary withdrawal again arose. Atterbury wrote to the Mercantile Bank's head office in Hong Kong recommending that both the Hongkong Bank and the Mercantile Bank withdraw. The immediate response was that, as both banks were profitable in Colombo, they should remain. But shortly afterwards, on the initiative of the Hongkong Bank, Atterbury was called to Hong Kong and a Head Office committee, which included A.D.A.G. Mosley, decided that the risks were not worth the potential return and accordingly recommended withdrawal. This however would not be easy; first, because it would be difficult to find a suitable buyer with adequate funds and, secondly, for more technical reasons, for example, that neither bank had funded their pension schemes, which they would have to do before any sale, probably at a cost of Rs8 million for the Mercantile alone.

The Hongkong Bank's executive Chairman, Guy Sayer, took a very decided position when he read the final recommendation – you may sell Mercantile if you like, he told Herridge, but I'm not going to sell the Hongkong Bank. And that put an end to the discussion.

The sale of the Mercantile Bank is part of the history of that bank, but it should be recorded that it was not a popular decision in Sri Lanka. While Atterbury was successful in finding positions for his staff, mostly in Hatton National, the executives were not happy there, and all have since resigned. In fact R. Thambiah, who became a covenanted officer in the Mercantile in 1959 and had been trained in their normal London program, joined the Hongkong Bank in 1975, becoming its first Sri Lankan Manager in 1981.

By 1975 some 90% of the Sri Lanka banking system, measured by equity, was already controlled by the Government, while the eight branches of the seven foreign banks were responsible for no more than 5–10% of foreign trade finance. The Hongkong Bank, now the sole representative of the Group, came to the conclusion that, unless political pressures were irresistible, the foreign banks would not be nationalized.

The prediction proved correct, but for a complex of reasons consequent to events which kept the Bank on the defensive throughout. Despite this, funds raised and employed in 1974 actually increased, while in 1975 there were steady profits despite the nationalization of estates and plantations and the expected diversion of business to Government banks. The upward trend was renewed in 1976 and the first half of 1977, the height of a nationalization threat. In the latter period, working profits increased by 27% as the additional funds available coincided with better lending opportunities at higher rates.

The improvement in the branch's business and the increased threat of nationalization were not unrelated. With the Finance Ministry in the hands of N.M. Perera of the Trotskyist Lanka Sama Samaja Party (LSSP), nationalization of the banking industry was always a declared goal, but the Government was a coalition with the Sri Lanka Freedom Party of Mrs Bandaranaike, and those officials more aware of international financial and aid problems were still able to restrain the Minister. Indeed when the leftist Government came to power in 1972 they found themselves bound by the agreements made with the foreign banks making it difficult to act against them until the Government loans, referred to in Chapter 10, had been fully repaid.

But the expectation of Government was that, with further nationalization of plantations and estates, the business of the foreign banks would simply wither away; they would close down of their own accord without the need of nationalization. When on the contrary their fortunes were seen to improve, positive action, coinciding with the repayment of the loans in December 1975, became a political probability.

The Government inherited a banking system with a truncated foreign sector, which lacked out-station branches but which had considerable domestic business and significant international connections protected at least temporarily by agreements and loans. Perera's first solution was to insist on local incorporation with a minimum 55% of the shares held by Sri Lankans. But local incorporation in Sri Lanka would result in (i) the diminished credit standing of the resultant entity, restricting the foreign business it could undertake, (ii) an adverse comparison of Sri Lankan financial policy with that in other Southeast Asian countries, and (iii) no real likelihood that the banks, as part of the local incorporation process, would actually bring in new capital – it was more likely they would close down. Local incorporation was unattractive to the Hongkong Bank for two further reasons: (i) with control vested in local directors, the name of the Group could be used in ways which management in Hong Kong might disapprove and (ii) the ultimate goal of nationalization had not been abandoned and might indeed be facilitated. The Bank was aware that local incorporation as a potential solution to the foreign bank problem was not confined to Sri Lanka, and its reactions to events there were not unrelated to its general position on this subject. The Bank had nothing to gain by compliance and less to gain by defiance. The Manager accordingly maintained a low profile, arguing an exemption in the legislation, provoking the Finance Minister to proposals for positive action which failed to receive support in the Cabinet. In September 1975 the coalition broke up and the more radical LSSP joined the opposition.

With the appointment as Finance Minister of Felix Dias Bandaranaike, a nephew of the Prime Minister, the Bank was for a short time optimistic, but in fact the role of the foreign banks had not been resolved. Indeed by January 1977 Felix Dias was publicly insisting on the nationalization of the foreign banks, from which they were saved only by the defeat of the Government in the July national elections. What had gone wrong with the Bank's expectations?

Felix Dias had spoken in favour of foreign banks, even suggesting that new banks should be invited to Sri Lanka, but he had advocated this policy in the context of the introduction of foreign capital. In November 1975 he addressed the National State Assembly in the following terms:

What we now require of the foreign banking sector is not merely mobilization of domestic resources and channelling out to the traditional forms of investment. What we do require is the infusion of new external capital from private sources to be used in the establishment of new enterprises in this country to provide new employment...

Thus the new Finance Minister's policy was in fact a direct threat to the traditional role of the Hongkong Bank in Sri Lanka, and it very shortly came to be seen as such. Whatever the Hongkong Bank might, under such a policy, have undertaken in the future, it would have had first to *de facto* give up its existing business, including its deposit base, and then, in effect, have returned to Sri Lanka *de novo*, as any international bank might have done had the new policy become effective.

There were several possible courses of action and the foreign banks were not in agreement. The Chartered Bank with its equity stake in the Commercial

Bank of Ceylon may have felt it would continue to have access to local funds. The Hongkong Bank's position was that its business had been eroded and that there was little benefit, in the sense of overall Group profits and policy, from staying in Sri Lanka. Taking a passive position the Bank on the one hand waited quietly for nationalization and on the other decided not to assist the process in any way – indeed, funds available and profitability improved throughout. Nevertheless the Bank did analyse its position in Colombo on the basis of value by a willing seller to a willing buyer as of year-end 1976 and found, *inter alia*, that maintainable profits were Rs1.3 million, net tangible assets Rs4.2 million with an expected rate of return as a percentage of capital employed estimated at 21%.

During 1976 complex political manoeuvrings made analysis difficult; on the one hand the Finance Minister seemed determined to change the role of the foreign banks, by nationalization if necessary, while on the other the Government seemed to consider the small political profits from such nationalization outweighed by the local and international results of such action. There is evidence that Felix Diaz did not always conduct his campaign with adroitness, but, with early elections inevitable, the political arguments came to outweigh the Cabinet's doubts and a nationalization bill was declared constitutional (in advance of its passage) in April 1977. The Hongkong Bank meanwhile had limited itself publicly to a modest statement:

After our efforts over so many years to provide services to the people of Sri Lanka and to assist in the finance of local and Government business, we are most distressed to be faced with nationalization particularly when we have voluntarily reduced our interest in the country through our sale of our wholly owned subsidiary, the Mercantile Bank Ltd.

The apparently inevitable process was stopped by the preparations for a mid-year election. In June 1977 the manifesto of the Sri Lanka Freedom Party demanded the nationalization of the three British Banks. But a pre-election interview with the opposition leader Jayawardene led P.M. Ryan, the Hongkong Bank's Colombo Manager, to report that his policy was more in line with that of Singapore and that the banks would not be nationalized – if he were successful. If the United National Party proved the winner as expected, Ryan urged, there would be keen banking competition; Wardley should be on the doorstep, prepared for a loan of US$15 million.

1977–1980

In the course of post-independence legislation, many new nations, including Sri Lanka, seemed determined to ensure that the old exchange banks were forced by regulation to adhere to their historical but inaccurate image, that they only financed trade. This is not intended as a criticism of the determination to

II. Case studies

Table 14.4 *The Hongkong Bank: Colombo branch Examination results*[a]
(millions of rupees)

	1974	1976	1978
Total assets	91	86	162
Total advances	73	67	118
Total deposits	66	72	144

[a] January of selected years

build an indigenous domestic banking system or to control banking and monetary policy through a central bank, which are basic prerogatives of government – as are making errors in policy and implementation. But the foreign banks wanted to play the role they had been earlier criticized for not playing – and which they often, in some perverse way, had denied they were playing. On the other hand the exchange banks themselves were slow to change their approach, and the on-the-job training bankers received in the pre-war period did not make the transition easier. Tradition is not without respect in Asia, and the fact that the Mercantile had served Ceylon since 1854 and that the Hongkong Bank had been active since 1892 carried some weight, but it took more than this to justify their activity in an era of increasing nationalism. In 1977 the forces liberated by the new conservative Government under the United National Party of Junius Richard Jayawardene provided the foreign banks their opportunity at a time when their executive staff and their international connections permitted them to take full advantage.

The new Government undertook reforms which rationalized the system of subsidies, controls, and restrictions (mainly by eliminating them), which had been built up over the years of ineffective socialism. The rate of exchange was unified and import regulations liberalized. In the context of a mixed economy, certain undertakings nationalized under the 1971 legislation were returned to their original owners. The banks were freed of the debit tax and their assistance sought in the finance of the accelerated Mahaweli Development Scheme, the Free Trade Zone, while foreign currency banking units were authorized.

The immediate impact on the Hongkong Bank can be seen in part from the comparative figures quoted below and in part from Table 14.4. Net profit after taxes rose from Rs534,000 in 1974 to Rs702,000 in 1976 and Rs1.8 million in 1977 when the new laws were already in effect. Interest on advances and profits on exchange was 52% and 48% respectively of income in 1977, virtually the same as in 1974. But as might be expected interest paid on deposits increased significantly in 1977, from Rs2.6 million to Rs4.7 million in a single year. These figures alone justified Paddy Ryan's recommendations and Guy Sayer's decision. The policy, put simply, is to be there when it happens.

The Hongkong Bank supported the Free Trade Zone; John Boyer, Deputy Chairman of the Bank, went to Colombo to attend a seminar on the purposes and opportunities of the zone.

In early 1977 there had been in all eleven banks, of which four were indigenous, four Indian or Pakistani, and three British. Under the new policy several international banks established branches, including the Bank of America, Citibank, three European banks, and several from the Middle East, from which area inward remittances increased to some Rs1,000 million due to the presence of Sri Lankan professionals there. There is, in fact, a special counter at the Hongkong Bank to cope with this business.

One indication of the Hongkong Bank's confidence in its future in Sri Lanka was the decision to move ahead with refurbishing the branch offices at a total cost of Rs10 million, although largely financed by blocked rupees and with the danger of a strike as employees argued on the amount of inconvenience pay. But there were limits; the role of foreign banks in a sovereign nation is not only a debate between Left and Right.

The basic difference of approach shown by the new Government was in its tolerance of a continued traditional and domestic role by the existing banks. But what of expansion? Apparently the Hongkong Bank had high hopes and sought to reestablish the larger geographical constituency the Group had lost when it sold the Mercantile branches, under the previous UNP adminstration, surely a historical warning. The Bank nevertheless conducted feasibility studies and determined first on reopening in Jaffna, perhaps influenced by Thambiah's knowledge of the area and its people; indeed with its intention to appoint a Tamil as Manager, the Bank may have seen itself as possibly acting as a local bank through its Sri Lankan management without the necessity of local incorporation. But the Hongkong Bank was to be disappointed. The Bank of Ceylon and the People's Bank had a total of 667 branches spread now over the country, and the Central Bank in January 1979 ruled that Jaffna was overbanked – unless the Hongkong Bank wished to introduce a new service, loans to the fishing industry, for example. The risk was high, however, and the Bank had no expertise, so the possibility was not further explored.

The Hongkong Bank after considering Kandy and other locations decided to focus on a branch in the Colombo metropolitan area, the FTZ, and possibly in an area nearby where deposits could be obtained, for it was believed, probably correctly, that there were still funds which were not reaching the banking system. In June 1979 the Bank accordingly applied for a branch in Ratmalana and in May the following year was again rebuffed. The Government had meanwhile formulated a policy restricting foreign banks to a main branch and one other, presumably in the FTZ, while the Hongkong Bank still hoped that this restriction would not apply to the three established British banks. That the Government remained flexible is evidenced by the permission granted to the State Bank of India to open a branch with the understanding they would assist in agricultural development in rural areas.

The Bank's expectations were thus still frustrated and with uncertainties developing in the FTZ, the Bank in 1981 was hesitating. The basic problem remained, indeed was accentuated by the Government's liberal policies in other economic matters: the increase in the Bank's Sri Lankan business required a broadened deposit base and a consequent increase in resources to meet customer requirements for funds while at the same time providing other banking services to the public. On occasion, the branch's liquidity position precluded any consideration of rupee financing. The alternative was to bring in additional capital with no guarantee of the right of repatriation over the long run. Meanwhile the Bank took full advantage of the Foreign Currency Banking Unit (FCBU) opportunity, competition requiring the subscription from 1981 of US$3,000 a month to a Reuters monitoring service – the Bank had been losing out on bids for FCBU deposits; the service would also provide the branch with information to enable it to quote more competitive rates for export finance.

Traditionally, the exchange banks financed peak trade periods by large overdrafts in London and New York, but this did not meet the requirements of a base for funding local enterprise, and although foreign funds might be utilized to finance the foreign exchange costs of major projects, it was still sound banking to expect to mobilize local funds for local costs. It was precisely on this point, however, that the conservative Government wavered, and the Hongkong Bank, prepared to move substantially in Sri Lanka, hesitated.

When all the factors are weighed, the consequence of the Government's policy was to force a pattern of business which remained traditional. If the charges of discrimination were unproved throughout the Bank's history in Colombo, that it focused on trade was always a fair assessment. Although in the two years from 1978 through 1980 the total assets of the Bank's Colombo branch had doubled to Rs360 million, including Rs6 million (to be capitalized subsequently) for refurnishing the building, advances, which accounted for the bulk of the growth, remained almost entirely in trade finance. Deposits too had grown, but not as fast, as the Bank had to borrow to finance a portion of the advances. Indeed, this was an obvious answer to queries about loan diversification – this and the lack of geographical spread, which hindered the Bank in handling developmental loans outside the well-banked capital city.

In many ways the long wait was over – business developed from many forms

Banking History in the making...

The Hon. Minister of Finance and Planning
Mr. Ronnie De Mel
will ceremonially declare open
Sri Lanka's First
Electronic Teller Card machines
today at 4.30pm. at
The Hongkong and Shanghai Banking Corporation

I must congratulate the HongkongBank for introducing Electronic Teller Card machines to this country. Though it is a common feature in other countries, Sri Lanka has been deprived of this facility all these years.

Ever since it established a Branch Office in Sri Lanka in 1892, the HongkongBank has been a major force in banking in this country. Concentrating initially on financing the tea trade, it has gradually diversified its activities over the years, to cater to all types of Bank business and to customers from all walks of life.

Sri Lanka's banking truly steps into the electronic age today with the commissioning of HongkongBank's Electronic Teller Card machines; the first of their kind in Sri Lanka.

HongkongBank, one of the oldest banks in Sri Lanka, continues to lead the way in providing the newest in banking developments and innovations for Sri Lanka and her people. HongkongBank was also the first to introduce computerised consumer banking to Sri Lanka.

With the introduction of the E.T.C. machines, the holder of an Electronic Teller Card, can now withdraw or deposit cash, check bank balances, order a fresh cheque book or a statement, transfer funds to any other account in the Bank, or even deposit written instructions to be acted upon by the Bank the next working day

And because the Electronic Teller Card machines are installed through the wall of the Bank, you don't even have to enter the building to transact your business.

Its virtually like having your favourite bank open both day and night — every day of the week!

HongkongBank on it!

It is more than a century since The Hongkong and Shanghai Banking Corporation first came to Sri Lanka to assist in the island's export trade in tea and coffee. I think we can be proud of the part which our Bank has played in Sri Lanka's economic development since those days.

A key factor in the growth of The Hongkong and Shanghai Bank has been its pioneering role in banking technology. It has gained an international reputation for its advanced communications systems and for the services it provides electronically to its customers throughout Asia. The increasing computerisation of our operations has already brought benefits to

The HongkongBank has always been in the forefront in the introduction of new technology to streamline banking services. A few years ago it spent over Rs.20 million on refurbishing and systems development to give a better and more efficient service to its customers. In keeping with this tradition, it has today introduced Electronic Teller Card machines for the first time in Sri Lanka. These machines will revolutionise retail banking by providing the bank's customers with round the clock access to their accounts every day of the week.

If Colombo is to become an important financial centre in Asia, it is essential that the Banking Sector keeps up with the times, and introduces modern technology when and wherever it is feasible to do so. I am happy that the HongkongBank has given the lead in the introduction of ETC machines. I have no doubt that other banks will follow suit and that in the not too distant future Colombo can boast of an efficient, modern banking service equal to the best in Asia.

Ronnie de Mel
Minister of Finance & Planning

It gives me great pleasure to contribute this message on the occasion of the ceremonial opening of Sri Lanka's very first Electronic Teller Card machines.

HonkongBank is proud to add this to the list of "firsts" in Banking Technology in Sri Lanka, having been the first bank to computerise its customer operations and the first to introduce Online Teller Terminals at its counters.

This is in keeping with HongkongBank's worldwide philosophy of applying the best of modern technology towards streamlining and enhancing banking services.

Of course, all this would not have been possible without the ready assistance we have received from our Head Office in Hongkong, from the Ministry of Finance and the Central Bank of Sri Lanka, which we gratefully acknowledge.

R. Thambiah
Manager — Sri Lanka
The Hongkong and Shanghai Banking Corporation

I also wish to add a personal word of thanks to all our staff, without whom our march towards providing a better service to our customers would not have been made possible.

The assistance of the engineers from Philips (Singapore), who installed the ETC machines, the contractors and architects who undertook a daunting exercise in preparing the site (and completed it to our utmost satisfaction), is also gratefully acknowledged.

Looking to the future, the Bank expects to install a Universal Banking Package in all its small and medium sized branches over the next three years which will be linked by telecommunication lines/satellite to the Bank's Global Data Network. HongkongBank's local constituents will then benefit from one of the most up-to-date electronic banking systems in the world.

I wish to congratulate HongkongBank for introducing fast moving new technology into banking operations in Sri Lanka. By installing these Electronic Teller Card (ETC) machines HongkongBank not only provides a convenient service to the customers but also allows them to withdraw any amount of money with a maximum limit and deposit cash and/or cheques any day at any time. This type of machine should become popular among the banking public and would be well suited to large offices as it will not only increase the banking habit among the employees but also cut-down the time taken by them to cash cheques. Banks in turn will have less customers at their counters and could devote more of their time to other operational activities. These Electronic Teller machines have been installed by every leading bank in all developed countries and have been extremely popular with the customers.

Dr. Warnasena Rasaputra
Governor, Central Bank of Sri Lanka

HongkongBank expects to make this facility free of charge. Technology in banking has been marching forward and it is most gratifying to note that necessary steps to go with the present trends. It is, therefore, important to provide customers with a speedy withdrawal of their money and efficiency in banking operations. The computerisation of banking offers this opportunity and takes a heavy load out of bank officials in dealing with the public. I wish this project every success.

The opening of our Electronic Teller Card machines, the first to be installed in Sri Lanka, is the latest example of this. They will enable our customers to carry out a number of routine banking activities with the maximum speed and convenience. I have no doubt that the ETC machines will become a valued part of the ever-increasing range of banking services which we provide to Sri Lanka.

Technology can never replace the traditional relationships which a bank builds up with its customers over many years. Technology does, however, allow us to improve our efficiency and the quality of our services.

Sir Michael Sandberg CBE
Chairman
The Hongkong and Shanghai Banking Corporation

Insert your card into the slot as shown on the sign. This raises the Protective Screen.

When instruction appears on the display screen, key in your secret Personal Identity Number (PIN)

Follow the instructions appearing on the display screen to complete your transaction.

Select the transaction you wish to perform by pressing the button alongside.

Remove your card and your printed record of the transaction.

HongkongBank ◆

The Hongkong and Shanghai Banking Corporation
24, Sir Baron Jayatilaka Mawatha, Colombo 1, Sri Lanka.

of liberalization (but with competition also increased), and the greater flexibility permitted banks though FCBU's, which at end-1979 were dealing in eight major international currencies with total assets of US$39 million (Rs602 million), to operate under conditions hardly expected a few years previously. The Hongkong Bank's Sri Lanka Manager, R. Thambiah, was in 1981 representing the commercial banks on a committee established by the Central Bank to advise on the then current bank credit restrictions. He was also looking beyond Sri Lanka to the Republic of the Maldives. The banking scene in Sri Lanka had changed dramatically, but impediments remained to the full restoration of the Hongkong Bank Group's role. The Bank was nevertheless positioned, while not forgetting its long record of service to the economy, to take advantage of the new opportunities afforded in the 1980s.

These proved marred by communal violence, which Thambiah experienced personally. Both he and the Bank nevertheless continued to develop the business positively. Indeed the Hongkong Bank pioneered once again; in 1986 it was the first to introduce an automatic teller machine system into Sri Lanka. The occasion was taken to remind Sri Lankans of the Bank's long history in their country (see Figure 14.1).

15

THE HONGKONG BANK GROUP, 1962–1980, III. POLICY, DEVELOPMENT, AND PERFORMANCE*

We are now in the process of trying to achieve steady and sustainable growth rates without excessive inflation.
　　　　　　　　　(Sir) Michael Sandberg, Chairman, 1978 annual meeting

BANKERS AND DIRECTORS

PERSONNEL: STATISTICS AND POLICY

With the acquisition of the Mercantile Bank and the British Bank of the Middle East, The Hongkong and Shanghai Banking Corporation began the significant corporate development which saw a ten-fold increase in total assets for the 'Group', from $7,660 million in December 1961 to $80,479 million in December 1977, the year in which the major personnel policy study was undertaken. In 1961 the total Foreign staff, traditionally defined as (i) those who were employed by the Hongkong and Shanghai Bank in Head Office and *Hongkong Bank* offices and (ii) those who had entered through the London 'gate', was 278. This figure would appear (definitional problems notwithstanding) to have declined to 268 by 1970. Even if this latter number is increased to allow for the integration of the 79 expatriate 'convenanted' Mercantile Bank officers when the staffs were combined (coincident with the merger of the Head Offices) in 1972, the total is only 378; thereafter there is a decline to 341 (307 excluding those seconded to the as yet non-integrated BBME staff) by mid-1977.

These figures do not require refinement to convey an obvious message. The corporation's personnel policy must certainly have changed; no matter how many of the Foreign staff had been relieved of operational routine and placed earlier in executive positions, the number stated could not have managed the enlarged Group. And yet the fact of a major policy study and the consequent changes in 1977–1979 is indicative that the changes, however significant they had proved to be, had still not touched all key areas. The first fifteen years of the post-war period witnessed the tentative introduction of Regional officers – there were five in 1957 and 114 in 1962; in other ways the system as described

---

* There are no end-notes for this chapter. Readers are referred to the bibliographical notes, pp. 949–50.

in Chapter 7 bore close resemblance to the inter-war approach to staff. The second period now under consideration, that is, from 1960 to 1977, was one of changed proportion, changed requirements which were met by necessity rather than consistently thought out policy. From 1977 personnel policy was in the hands of professionals; the changes which had already occurred *ad hoc* and their consequences were rationalized and combined with new policies which substantially modified personnel policy in an effort to keep it in line with the changes in the corporation's requirements. The structural changes which had occurred in the corporation between 1969 and 1977 had their counterpart in personnel mainly in the years after 1977. By 1984 a different pattern had emerged, although there were hints of the past and the Hong Kong junior mess, in a re-rebuilt (1986) Cloudlands, would survive.

One possible reason for delay in implementing thorough policy revision was the expectation that rationalization of the two major acquired banks, especially of their head offices, would throw up senior, qualified officers. Integration proved a slower process than expected, especially due to the BBME's claim of unique skills in the Middle East and the need for a continued separate identity. Furthermore, growth outpaced the potentials to be reasonably expected from the merger of Foreign staffs.

This discussion is limited to those areas of the corporation the management of which was controlled directly by Group Head Office. This excludes the British Bank of the Middle East, the Hang Seng Bank, and the many specialized non-financial companies; it includes the Hongkong Bank itself, the Mercantile Bank, the Hongkong Bank of California, Wardley (the investment bank), and the trustee companies. For purposes of comparability, the main analysis, however, is further restricted; it deals with only Group Head Office and the Hongkong Bank (including the Mercantile) as operating bank.

Statistical profile

The obvious explanation as to how the management of the enlarged corporation was accomplished is found in the significant increase in Regional officers and specialists. Thus to the mid-1977 figure of 341 Foreign staff must be added 498 Regional officers and 75 contract executives. For the Group Head Office (GHO) and the Bank the numbers were 71 (GHO) and 184 (Bank) Foreign staff, plus 20 and 439 Regional officers and 10 and 21 contract executives respectively.

Table 15.1 takes the explanation a step further. There had been a shift in the use of Foreign staff from the field to GHO and Hong Kong office where in 1977 57% of all Foreign staff were serving (compared to 33% in 1962). This shift was consequent to a positive policy by the Bank, responding, *inter alia* to both

III. Policy, development, and performance

Table 15.1 *The Hongkong Bank
HSBC Foreign staff, 1962 and 1977
HSBC Regional staff, 1977*

	Foreign 1962	Foreign 1977	Regional
Group Head Office	13	71	20
Hongkong Bank	229	184	439
of which:			
Hong Kong	67	95	96
Brunei	7	7	6
India	10	7	42
Indonesia	3	7	5
Japan	17	6	15
Malaysia	47[a]	12	138
Philippines	9	6	9
Singapore	27	12	44
Sri Lanka	6	1	4
Thailand	7	7	10
United Kingdom	5	3	13
U.S.A.	4	7	11
Other	18	13	23
Hongkong Bank of California	2	1	23

Total 1977 GHO + Hongkong Bank staff: 11,577

[a] includes British North Borneo and Sarawak.
Source: Staff lists and P.A. Management Consultants Ltd report.

immigration restrictions and the need to up-grade the tasks performed by the Foreign staff, whose cost was estimated at between 1.5 and three times that of equivalent Regional officers. By restricting the figures to Hongkong Bankers in 1962, however, the table understates the change. The Mercantile Bank was particularly strong in India and Malaysia and, if the base year of 1972 is taken, then the number of Foreign staff in the HSBC/Mercantile dropped from 280 to 184, with the most significant being in India (36 to 7), Malaysia (30 to 12), Sri Lanka (9 to 1), and Hong Kong (125 to 95).

Despite the fact that the Hongkong Bank was as yet making little or no concession to graduates, 12% of the Foreign staff had their first degree. That this was a growing trend is illustrated by the fact that 56% of the Foreign staff with less than five years' service had degrees. This, however, was the vulnerable group – half of the few who resigned voluntarily did so in their first four years and a higher proportion were graduates rather than non-graduates. These figures would seem to suggest the changing pattern of availability of suitable Foreign officer recruits on the one hand and the unwillingness of many graduates to accept the integrated life-style still prevailing and/or the routine of operational duties. Even a graduate would still require fourteen or more years in the East before an 'appointment', that is, an assignment to a significant executive responsibility.[a] As the recognized need for graduates increased, so the pressure for a more developed personnel policy, giving priority to career development and professional training, eventually caused the 1977 review from which this data has been taken.

The most significant figures are those which state the growth in the number of Regional officers – from 5 in 1957 to 114 in 1962 and then by 50% every five years (after allowing for the inclusion of Mercantile Bank officers from 1967) to the 1977 level of 498. Since 1967, the greatest increases outside Hong Kong were in India, Malaysia, and Singapore. In contrast to the Foreign staff, all of whom (the chief executive's assistant and two or three Head Office specialists excepted) were male, Regional officers were recruited from both sexes (and, in many locations, two months' maternity leave was granted). In GHO 20% of the Regional officers were women, in Hong Kong 15%, Malaysia and Singapore 5% each, and in the California subsidiary, 13%. But there was other 'discrimination': not surprisingly 78% of the resident Malaysian officers were non-bumiputra (and, therefore, mostly of the Chinese community); in the United States an interesting 17% were not of the 'main indigenous race', the designation of which is not, however, vouchsafed.

One of the post-war complaints against colonial regimes was that less qualified English (or French) were brought out as civil servants while local graduates were passed over. Of all the Regional officers, 40% or 197 had degrees, and of these nearly 20% (or 38) were from European, North American, or Australian universities. The percentage had been rising, indicating the change from the early policy of promoting existing staff to active recruiting from the local universities. In 1977 58% of all Regional officer trainees were graduates.

[a] Most of the Bank's policies had a historical explanation. The insistence, contrary to American practice, of requiring thorough operational experience originated in the nature of the pre-war social structure, whereby the young expatriate banker was employed for his integrity – for his signature; executive jobs were few, and he therefore performed this routine but essential 'signing' role until a vacancy became available on a strict seniority basis. Secondly, the Bank's post-war experience with strikes proved the value, the magnitude of which was exaggerated in the telling, of having all senior staff conversant with all details of essential operations. Such points would be argued in favour of retention of established practices.

III. Policy, development, and performance

Policy: Foreign staff

The increasing importance of Regional officers should suggest a focus on personnel policy as related to their recruitment, training, etc. However, the unique feature of the Hongkong Bank has been the Eastern or Foreign staff, and this section is particularly interested in the course of historical change. The Mercantile Bank had stopped London recruitment in 1964 and its junior requirements had been met by secondment from the Hongkong Bank. The following discussion relates, therefore, to the Hongkong Bank with the integrated Mercantile Bank included.

Recruitment

Although the pattern remained unchanged, elements of professionalism were becoming apparent, a trend which the 1977 review would reinforce. The Bank was still recruiting for a career of 30 years in the East, with entry age into London Office now dependent upon educational background. School leavers with 'A' levels (minimum of two passes) were expected to apply before the candidate reached twenty years of age; graduates in subjects giving exemption from some Institute of Bankers' examinations were admitted up to the maximum age of 24. And the Bank, continuing a post-war practice, advertised; in 1976/77 there were 800 applicants, of which the Bank interviewed the 'best' 25%. In contrast to pre-war days, when two years' experience with another firm was virtually an essential prerequisite, very few of those recruited had had any banking or other employment experience.

There were, however, a few exceptions. Older officers were recruited and, perhaps after an initial contract, were transferred to the Foreign staff in specialist positions, especially in Group Head Office.

Separate recruitment for the BBME continued to mid-1975. Thereafter Foreign staff joined The Hongkong and Shanghai Banking Corporation; if and when they were assigned to a Middle East office, they became for that period staff of the BBME. This completed the task of Foreign staff integration.

In 1977 the Bank's new chief executive, Michael Sandberg, could still look back to the traditional recruitment system as manifest in 1948. Through his father he met B.C. Lambert, once with the Hongkong Bank in Vladivostok and who had retired as Agent Saigon in 1926; this interested Sandberg in the Bank and provided an introduction. Then for the interview with A.M. Duncan-Wallace – but the Manager was suffering from one of his periodic bouts of TB, and Sandberg unexpectedly appeared before A.G. 'Sandy' Cameron. This executive could think of nothing better than, according to Sandberg, taking him out to lunch, feeding him pink gins, and waiting to see if he survived while being questioned as to his interests in rugger and cricket. He survived, admitted to playing the games, and was in. But, as chief executive, he was willing to acknowledge that there must be another way of operating.

The change was indeed underway as Sandberg took over. Each candidate was receiving two interviews of approximately 30 minutes each. The task of the interviewer was clearly stated: (i) 'eliminate any obviously weak candidates in terms of personality, appearance, intelligence or general suitability' and (ii) 'try to identify those who will be sociable, self-reliant, conformist and who are likely to give the Bank a life-long commitment with complete integrity'. There were no suggestions as to how these goals were to be achieved, except a note that no formal intelligence, aptitude, or psychological tests were used. The interviewer was also to answer the candidates' questions about the Bank.

London and New Beckenham

Those recruited in the immediate post-war period had little time in London. Even then, Sandberg recalled his weekends at New Beckenham and the socialization the experience provided. This brief period was too often followed by an air passage East. Sir Arthur Morse reinstated the slower P&O passage as soon as it was practical; he too was looking back to earlier days. By 1970 the P&O had discontinued its regular monthly service to Hong Kong; senior management would have no choice but to fly the young men out. But in other matters Sandberg and his colleagues would be reluctant to formalize the changes which were already taking place; they nevertheless in part did so.

The London experience could be as long as two years for school leavers, but the impecunious continuation of public school life *à la* Wodehouse in London was no longer acceptable, partly because (i) public schools themselves were changing and (ii) likely young men were proceeding to University, after which they would have higher expectations. Despite the fact that London Office itself had changed (see Chapter 14) and could no longer afford to entertain half-serious juniors as they learned banking 'on the job', little improvement in training practices had in fact been made. There were no formal courses and the personnel consultants stated bluntly that the Bank failed in its efforts to provide juniors a basic knowledge of banking and of the Group, about life overseas, or a foretaste of the work they would do in the first few years of their career. Specifically the report noted that the juniors were given no lecture on the history of the Hongkong Bank.[b]

But perhaps developments at New Beckenham provide signs of change. The Hongkong Bank Sports Club had in the past been handled informally, promoted by 'keen' members of the Home staff and effectively managed by

---

[b] It is not surprising, therefore, when a group of young executives drew me aside to ask, on a confidential basis, whether or not the Bank ever financed the opium trade. I referred them, as I would readers of this volume, to Volumes I and II of the history.

young juniors, including, for example, (Sir) Vandeleur Grayburn. In 1950 Stan Coles succeeded his father as Groundsman (see Volume III) and carried on in the same tradition, the first important change coming with the introduction of soccer, a consequence of the acquisition of the BBME. As Coles remembers this remarkable event:

Mr [N.H.T.] Bennett, who was London Manager, said, we've taken over the British Bank of the Middle East, and they are soccer players mostly in their bank. Would it be possible to accommodate them at the ground? They were playing at Eltham at the time, and the facilities were very, very poor.

Since Bennett did not become London Manager until 1971, even integration at the grounds level apparently took considerable time. Coles took them in but also took the opportunity to have the facilities expanded. In fact soccer flourished and the Bank was able to turn out two soccer sides and but one rugger XV, due, Coles stated, to the fact that the Eastern staff were mostly rugger players, the Home staff soccer – the former remained in London for shorter periods, 'and of course messengers are allowed to play for the Bank now, which at one time they weren't.'

Terms of service
The members of the Hongkong Bank's Foreign staff had served traditionally without written contracts or legally acknowledged terms of service. This remained the position throughout the period under discussion – and there has as yet been no change.

Housing. The Bank's 1965 recruiting booklet still featured pictures of the first Rugby Football XV (1887) and views of the still existing pre-war housing, the latter indicating that Colonial-style living remained apparently intact. The new recruit might yet have dinner in traditional style, but, by the time he reached a managerial position, the old houses would be gone. By the 1970s the great Managers' residences and their spacious grounds were in process of change; excess land was sold, the remaining space was redeveloped to meet expected demand for less pretentious Foreign staff housing. Lots on Yokohama's Bluff were sold in 1972 for Yen188.4 million as the staff moved into Tokyo, where the Manager's house in Roppongi (with its land worth an estimated Yen 263 million) became a block of flats.[c] In 1973 Mt. Echo was redeveloped; 35 of the 40 acres were sold for Singapore $38.9 million, and flats for staff were constructed. Carlingford, the great house at Bangkok, was eventually sold to the Japanese Embassy and the remaining site developed, just as the imposing river

[c] This was part of a major Japanese property redevelopment, which also involved the Bank in Kobe and Osaka. The various moves were coordinated to comply with Japanese capital gains tax legislation, thereby increasing the surplus remitted to Hong Kong.

front Bank building was replaced by a five-star joint-venture hotel. The loss of traditional-type prestige was accepted; in some cases the Bank's high property profile had in fact been resented and no analysis could justify the opportunity cost then involved.

Marriage. More realistically, the prospective applicant was warned that he could not marry until he had completed four years' (one tour) Eastern service. But most young men who wish to marry, wish to do so coincident with the recognition of their wish; nor did the post-war world possess a sufficient number of chaperones to protect a long engagement. It was therefore little comfort to a young man in 1980 to know that some twenty years earlier Turner had written Purves about the even earlier, pre-war, ten-year rule or that, as the first tour had been shortened even since the mid-1950s, so had the period of waiting. Senior management wrote as sympathetically as ever, urging the junior to wait until the first tour were over and he had reached the age of 22 years 10 months. Once it had been 27, and before that officers lived enforced bachelor lives into their early 30s. The Bank, however, was not and is not prepared to permit marriage and the resulting administrative problems and costs during the first tour. The tour itself has been shortened; air travel makes visits by a fiancée possible, but the restriction remains.

Length of tours. As passenger planes became larger, cultural life in the East was enriched; only with the coming of the 747 could one reasonably transport a full symphony orchestra, and still there could be empty seats. Then came the age of charter flights, student fares, cabotage rates from Hong Kong to London, and accordingly, more generous provisions for dependent children's visits; the great question of 'class', however, was introduced – at what level would first-class fares be granted and, more recently, at what level business class? In 1965 the dependent child came out once during a tour of two years, twice in three years – or the wife could visit Home. The 1977 report indicates the growing complexity of the arrangements, but since 1970 an officer of sufficient seniority had been permitted to bring out two children twice a year during tours which last (except for the longer first tour) from two years three months to two years nine months.

Remuneration. In 1961 there had been a consolidation of cost-of-living and most other allowances, nevertheless the salary structure remained complex, reflecting the ultimate need to show United Kingdom comparability while allowing for the realities of life in various posts in the East.[d] First there was a 'basic sterling

---

[d] Among the continuing allowances was one for dependent children's education; at the end of 1964 this was set at £250 p.a., costing the Bank an estimated £20,000 p.a. All relevant conditions and payments have been continuously adjusted.

salary', used mainly as the basis for Home leave pay, provident fund contributions, and pensions. A first tour junior received £2,600 p.a. – the equivalent of a U.K. pre-tax income of £5,400; an officer on first appointment to a senior position received £7,350 (= pre-tax £28,000); General Managers might receive as high as £17,250 (= pre-tax £100,000). These figures were translated by various and changing formulas to Hong Kong dollar salaries. For those elsewhere in the East, salaries were adjusted to provide a rough equivalent to the level of living enjoyed in Hong Kong, although there was nowhere else in the East where a Hong Kong level of living could be enjoyed at any salary level. Consistent with the statement in earlier brochures that the Chief Manager's salary was in a class by itself, in 1972 the Board had voted Sayer, as the new executive Chairman, a tax-paid salary of £40,000 p.a., with fringe benefits including a motor car, servants, and entertainment expenses. This compared with £15,000 for the executive directors. All were subject to a biennial review and there were increments before 1977 when the personnel material was compiled.

Fringe benefits and amenities. Expatriate life with major hongs in the East depends on other payments and fringe benefits, even as it had in the late nineteenth century (see Chapter 15, Volume I). Foreign staff still received an annual bonus, their income taxes were paid, housing was provided or an allowance granted, medical cover guaranteed, certain fees in one business and/ or sports club paid, and special loan facilities were available for purchase of homes and cars. Travel on 'local leave', which sometimes included a trip to Hong Kong, was financed on varying scales, depending on the country. The Bank paid the equivalent of 50% of basic salary into a non-contributory pension fund designed to provide a pension equal to one-half the final basic salary; there was also a Provident Fund to which both the officer and the Bank contributed.

Especially important in crowded Hong Kong is the provision of amenities. Major club waiting lists had become so lengthy that admission might take more than two years; the territory has been listed, by some authorities, as a hardship post. The possession of corporate debentures or corporate-owned facilities was and remains a major factor in staff morale. Launches and weekend bungalows rank high in the order of priority and they are often available to both International and Regional officers on a 'sign-up' and seniority basis.

Training

At least from the later 1950s the Hongkong Bank's Japan operations had been hampered by lack of funds. There existed the opportunity to finance those Japanese exports handled by foreign firms, but the Bank's Japan branches had an inadequate deposit base, and Tokyo office was forced to borrow from a reluctant Hong Kong or limited London Office. When in 1963 Donald Lachlan was Accountant Tokyo, he recalls, '... we had a telex from a French bank asking what would we quote for Eurodollars, and we hadn't really heard about them before.' Meanwhile other foreign banks, including an Indian bank, had been financing their Japanese operations by borrowing in the Eurodollar market. The Tokyo Manager B.O'D. Paterson flew down to Hong Kong to talk to Head Office about it. With Head Office approval the Hongkong Bank in Tokyo began with borrowing US$10 million, and the operation thrived.

Today this is not the sort of information the Hongkong Bankers can afford to learn about on-the-job; a young banker is expected to know about Eurodollars and to be abreast of current developments. This requires a background education in finance with formal updating. The changes recommended in 1977 were designed to achieve this, but formal training began in the period under review and the Bank developed a Training Department which by 1977 had a Manager and five teaching staff. Annual expenditures totalled $3 million. The scope of their efforts could not include the basics of such important subjects as investment management and merchant banking; for this the corporation had to go outside the Hongkong Bank, as the development of Wardley indicates (see below).

Regional officers, initial training

While the London training of Foreign staff trainees continued much on traditional lines with consequences already described, the training of Regional officers could be planned without the burden of precedents. The training period lasted some two years and included on-the-job training in departments, a period in some country other than their own, and a period in London. Regional officers attended a Junior Executive Course of a kind not then provided to the Foreign staff, and, of their six to twelve weeks in London, part was devoted to formal management and English language courses – and there was time for 'outings'.

The London experience was not designed to replicate the Wodehouse world of the pre-war London Office; this concept had had mixed success in the 1950s, but in any case 'moods' or atmosphere cannot be re-created and London had changed. Rather the purpose was to acquaint potential overseas officers with European customs and business practices and, significantly, spouses were encouraged to accompany the trainees – the London visit was primarily for 'face'. Furthermore, some concept of socialization remained.

Other training
The recognition by newly arrived Foreign staff that they were unprepared for a banking career led to changes first in the East and then in London itself. The recognition by senior bankers that they needed an expert input from specialist consultants led to the acceptance that training of executive staff was justified; the consultants were expensive and changes in the banking profession were continuous. The cynical attitude to formal courses was gradually eroded.

Nevertheless executive staff filled only 238 places in internal courses and 157 places in external courses in 1976/77 (the latter at a cost of $500,000), an average of only three to four days a year, although weighted towards the more junior executives. This however marked a significant improvement from the beginnings in 1972 and refers, as do the other statistics, only to the Hongkong Bank and the Mercantile Bank. Most of the teaching was done in Hong Kong and Regional officers were sent to Head Office for training.

The developments immediately following the 1977 report, however, were sufficient as evidence that in the area of personnel policy also the Bank's senior management had recognized the need for restructuring preparatory for its declared intention of major expansion by acquisition.

In the Hongkong Bank's new Kuala Lumpur office, the headquarters of the Bank's Malaysian operations, a young-looking senior executive sat confidently in his modern office; he was a citizen of the Federation and he was of Chinese descent. 'I entered the Bank', he said, 'twenty years ago as a schoolboy, a messenger in open shirt and short trousers. Since then I have risen to one of the most senior posts...' Suddenly he paused; it was if a spasm of pain induced by memory was passing, then as suddenly he continued, quietly: '...the pace was forced, it had to be, and there were some very difficult times.' In 1961 there had been 44 Foreign staff in the present Federation of Malaysia area; in 1980, despite the fact that new offices had been set up and the Kuala Lumpur main branch expanded, only five working visas were granted. The pace of localization was forced and, since Malaysians tend to take a serious attitude to economic life, the task for those who reached the higher position sometimes involved intense study and personal sacrifice.

Pre-war attitudes had changed. The failure of the first Indian recruitment exercise would give way to the discovery of excellence and the transfer from time to time of Indian Regional officers to the new International staff. But this and other developments would come; they will be touched on briefly in the concluding chapter. The pressures of the period to the mid-1970s provoked revisions in policy which are themselves the subject of continuing study and change.

THE BOARD OF DIRECTORS AND SENIOR MANAGEMENT – THE
HONGKONG BANK

The Board of Directors

Until 1969 the Board operated very much as it had in the 1950s. The new Chief Manager, J.A.H. Saunders, did not necessarily expect to be Chairman the first year, but he did expect to be a director. The Board had apparently resisted, Sir Michael Turner had not insisted, and Saunders went to the Chairman-designate, H.D.M. Barton of Jardine Matheson, to state simply he would not accept the responsibilities of the chief managership without Board membership. He was elected, however, only in the course of his first Board meeting as Chief Manager. The Board then delegated the management of the Bank to him as chief executive officer with the traditional title of 'Chief Manager', but, for the first time in the history of the Bank, the agreement was specific and in writing. In 1964 the Board formally minuted that the Chief Manager was to consult the Board in all matters of policy affecting the Bank, its branches, and its subsidiaries, reminding itself that under the ordinance the final authority and responsibility for the conduct of the Bank rested with the Board of Directors. The concept of an irrelevant Board had never been valid, even in a period when policy was relatively set and pure banking the only concern of the chief executive. From the mid-1950s, however, this had not been the case, and the role of the Board had to be restated and reinforced to avoid misunderstanding by a forceful Chief Manager. The initiative, however, remained with management.

The details of Board membership are found in Table 15.2, but several points should be made in the narrative. Barton was succeeded as Chairman by W.C.G. Knowles, despite Turner's earlier concern that he would be too subject to instructions from Swire's. Knowles, who also served as Vice-Chancellor of the University of Hong Kong from 1964 until his untimely death in 1965, was then succeeded by Saunders himself.

In 1967 F.J. Knightly, as Acting Chief Manager, was elected a director; it was the first time the Bank had had two staff members on the Board, but Saunders felt he needed support. Then in 1969 the regulations were changed and the Chairman had to be an executive of the Hongkong Bank; obviously Saunders was elected and he brought on Maurice W. Turner as executive Deputy Chairman (succeeded by M. Curran). The non-executive Deputy Chairman was J.D. Clague of Hutchison's. Many informed observers were convinced that the move to change the regulations had been designed – or at least timed – to prevent Clague's becoming Chairman of the Bank during the

Table 15.2 *The Hongkong and Shanghai Banking Corporation*
The Board of Directors, 1962–1985

March 20, 1962 – Annual Meeting 1963
H.D.M. Barton	Jardine, Matheson and Co.	Chairman
W.C.G. Knowles	Butterfield and Swire	Deputy Chairman
G.G.D. Carter	Dodwell and Co.	
J.D. Clague	J.D. Hutchison and Co.	
S.J. Cooke	Gilman and Co.	
J. Hackney	Imperial Chemical Industries	
L. Kadoorie	Sir Elly Kadoorie & Sons	
J.F. Macgregor	Caldbeck, Macgregor and Co.	
J.A.H. Saunders	Chief Manager, Hongkong Bank	
G.T. Tagg	Mackinnon, Mackenzie & Co. of HK	

At the close of Annual Meeting

March 1963
H.D.M. Barton	Jardine, Matheson and Co.	Chairman
W.C.G. Knowles	Butterfield and Swire	Deputy Chairman
G.G.D. Carter	Dodwell and Co.	
J.D. Clague	J.D. Hutchison and Co.	
S.J. Cooke	Gilman and Co.	
J. Hackney	Imperial Chemical Industries	
L. Kadoorie	Sir Elly Kadoorie & Sons	
J.F. Macgregor	Caldbeck, Macgregor and Co.	
J.A.H. Saunders	Chief Manager, Hongkong Bank	
G.T. Tagg	Mackinnon, Mackenzie & Co. of HK	

March 1964
W.C.G. Knowles	Butterfield and Swire	Chairman
J.A.H. Saunders	Chief Manager, Hongkong Bank	Deputy Chairman
G.G.D. Carter	Dodwell and Co.	
J.D. Clague	J.D. Hutchison and Co.	
S.J. Cooke	Gilman and Co.	
L. Kadoorie	Sir Elly Kadoorie & Sons	
I.H. Kendall	Imperial Chemical Industries	
J.F. Macgregor	Caldbeck, Macgregor and Co.	
G.M.B. Salmon	Mackinnon, Mackenzie & Co. of HK	
M.A.R. Young-Herries	Jardine, Matheson and Co.	

March 1965
J.A.H. Saunders	Chief Manager, Hongkong Bank	Chairman
S.J. Cooke	Gilman and Co.	Deputy Chairman
H.J.C. Browne	Butterfield and Swire	
J.D. Clague	J.D. Hutchison and Co.	
L. Kadoorie	Sir Elly Kadoorie & Sons	
I.H. Kendall	Imperial Chemical Industries	
J.F. Macgregor	Caldbeck, Macgregor and Co.	
G.M.B. Salmon	Mackinnon, Mackenzie & Co. of HK	
P.G. Williams	Dodwell and Co.	
M.A.R. Young-Herries	Jardine, Matheson and Co.	

Table 15.2 (*cont.*)

March 1966
J.A.H. Saunders	Chief Manager, Hongkong Bank	Chairman
S.J. Cooke	Gilman and Co.	Deputy Chairman
H.J.C. Browne	Butterfield and Swire	
J.D. Clague	J.D. Hutchison and Co.	
L. Kadoorie	Sir Elly Kadoorie & Sons	
I.H. Kendall	Imperial Chemical Industries	
J. Dickson Leach	Union Insurance Society of Canton	
G.M.B. Salmon	Mackinnon, Mackenzie & Co. of HK	
P.G. Williams	Dodwell and Co.	
M.A.R. Young-Herries	Jardine, Matheson and Co.	

March 1967
J.A.H. Saunders	Chief Manager, Hongkong Bank	Chairman
S.J. Cooke	Gilman and Co.	Deputy Chairman
F.J. Knightly	Hongkong Bank	
H.J.C. Browne	Butterfield and Swire	
J.D. Clague	J.D. Hutchison and Co.	
L. Kadoorie	Sir Elly Kadoorie & Sons	
I.H. Kendall	Imperial Chemical Industries	
J. Dickson Leach	Union Insurance Society of Canton	
G.M.B. Salmon	Mackinnon, Mackenzie & Co. of HK	
P.G. Williams	Dodwell and Co.	
M.A.R. Young-Herries	Jardine, Matheson and Co.	

March 1968
J.A.H. Saunders	Chief Manager, Hongkong Bank	Chairman
S.J. Cooke	Gilman and Co.	Deputy Chairman
F.J. Knightly	Hongkong Bank	
H.J.C. Browne	Butterfield and Swire	
J.D. Clague	J.D. Hutchison and Co.	
I.H. Kendall	Imperial Chemical Industries	
J. Dickson Leach	Union Insurance Society of Canton	
G.M.B. Salmon	Mackinnon, Mackenzie & Co. of HK	
P.G. Williams	Dodwell and Co.	
M.A.R. Young-Herries	Jardine, Matheson and Co.	

March 1969
J.A.H. Saunders	Chief Manager, Hongkong Bank	Chairman
D.J.R. Blaker	Gilman and Co.	Deputy Chairman
F.J. Knightly	Hongkong Bank	
H.J.C. Browne	Butterfield and Swire	
J.D. Clague	J.D. Hutchison and Co.	
I.H. Kendall	Imperial Chemical Industries	
G.R. Ross	Deacon & Co.	
G.M.B. Salmon	Mackinnon, Mackenzie & Co. of HK	
P.G. Williams	Dodwell and Co.	
M.A.R. Young-Herries	Jardine, Matheson and Co.	

Table 15.2 (*cont.*)

March 1970
J.A.H. Saunders	Hongkong Bank, chief executive	Chairman
Maurice W. Turner	Hongkong Bank	executive Deputy Chairman
then **M. Curran**	Hongkong Bank	executive Deputy Chairman
F.J. Knightly	Hongkong Bank	
J.D. Clague	J.D. Hutchison and Co.	Deputy Chairman
D.J.R. Blaker	Gilman and Co.	
H.J.C. Browne	Butterfield and Swire	
I.H. Kendall	Imperial Chemical Industries	
G.R. Ross	Deacon & Co.	
G.M.B. Salmon	Mackinnon, Mackenzie & Co. of HK	
W.S. Stocks		
P.G. Williams	Dodwell and Co.	
M.A.R. Young-Herries	Jardine, Matheson and Co.	

March 1971
J.A.H. Saunders	Hongkong Bank, chief executive	Chairman
G.M. Sayer	Hongkong Bank	executive Deputy Chairman
J.D. Clague	J.D. Hutchison and Co.	Deputy Chairman
J.W.L. Howard	Hongkong Bank	executive director
H.J.C. Browne	Butterfield and Swire	
H.P. Foxon	Gilman and Co.	
G.R. Kenderdine	Imperial Chemical Industries	
H.N.L. Keswick	Jardine, Matheson and Co.	
G.R. Ross	Deacon & Co.	
G.M.B. Salmon	Mackinnon, Mackenzie & Co. of HK	
W.S. Stocks		
P.G. Williams	Dodwell and Co.	

March 1972
J.A.H. Saunders	Hongkong Bank, chief executive	Chairman
G.M. Sayer	Hongkong Bank	executive Deputy Chairman
Sir Douglas Clague	J.D. Hutchison and Co.	Deputy Chairman
J.W.L. Howard	Hongkong Bank	executive director
H.J.C. Browne	Butterfield and Swire	
H.P. Foxon	Gilman and Co.	
G.R. Kenderdine	Imperial Chemical Industries	
H.N.L. Keswick	Jardine, Matheson and Co.	
J.L. Marden	Wheelock Marden & Co.	
Pao Yue-Kong	World Wide Shipping Group	
G.R. Ross	Deacon & Co.	
G.M.B. Salmon	Mackinnon, Mackenzie & Co. of HK	
W.S. Stocks		
P.G. Williams	Dodwell and Co.	

March 1973
G.M. Sayer	Hongkong Bank, chief executive	Chairman
J.W.L. Howard	Hongkong Bank	executive Deputy Chairman
Sir Douglas Clague	J.D. Hutchison and Co.	Deputy Chairman

Table 15.2 (cont.)

P.E. Hutson	Hongkong Bank	executive director
A.D.A.G. Mosley	Hongkong Bank	executive director
M.G.R. Sandberg	Hongkong Bank	executive director
H.J.C. Browne	Butterfield and Swire	
H.P. Foxon	Gilman and Co.	
G.R. Kenderdine	Imperial Chemical Industries	
H.N.L. Keswick	Jardine, Matheson and Co.	
J.L. Marden	Wheelock Marden & Co.	
Pao Yue-Kong	World Wide Shipping Group	
G.R. Ross	Deacon & Co.	
G.M.B. Salmon	Mackinnon, Mackenzie & Co. of HK	
W.S. Stocks		
P.G. Williams	Dodwell and Co.	

March 1974

G.M. Sayer	Hongkong Bank, chief executive	Chairman
M.G.R. Sandberg	Hongkong Bank	executive Deputy Chairman
Sir Douglas Clague	J.D. Hutchison and Co.	Deputy Chairman
P.E. Hutson	Hongkong Bank	executive director
A.D.A.G. Mosley	Hongkong Bank	executive director
E.R. Udal	Hongkong Bank	executive director
J.H. Bremridge	Swire Group	
H.P. Foxon	Gilman and Co.	
Hui Sai Fun	Central Development	
G.R. Kenderdine	Imperial Chemical Industries	
H.N.L. Keswick	Jardine, Matheson and Co.	
J.L. Marden	Wheelock Marden & Co.	
Pao Yue-Kong	World Wide Shipping Group	
G.R. Ross	Deacon and Co.	
W.S. Stocks		
P.G. Williams	Dodwell and Co.	

March 1975

G.M. Sayer	Hongkong Bank, chief executive	Chairman
M.G.R. Sandberg	Hongkong Bank	executive Deputy Chairman
Sir Douglas Clague	J.D. Hutchison and Co.	Deputy Chairman[a]
P.G. Williams	Dodwell and Co.	Deputy Chairman[a]
P.E. Hutson	Hongkong Bank	executive director
A.D.A.G. Mosley	Hongkong Bank	executive director
E.R. Udal	Hongkong Bank	executive director
J.H. Bremridge	Swire Group	
H.P. Foxon	Gilman and Co.	
Hui Sai Fun	Central Development	
H.N.L. Keswick	Jardine, Matheson and Co.	
F.J. Knightly	Hongkong Bank, retired	
J.L. Marden	Wheelock Marden & Co.	
Pao Yue-Kong	World Wide Shipping Group	
Sir Albert Rodrigues		
G.R. Ross	Deacon and Co.	
W.S. Stocks		

Table 15.2 (*cont.*)

March 1976
G.M. Sayer	Hongkong Bank, chief executive	Chairman
M.G.R. Sandberg	Hongkong Bank	executive Deputy Chairman
P.G. Williams	Dodwell and Co.	Deputy Chairman
P.E. Hutson	Hongkong Bank	executive director
A.D.A.G. Mosley	Hongkong Bank	executive director
E.R. Udal	Hongkong Bank	executive director
J.H. Bremridge	Swire Group	
H.P. Foxon	Gilman and Co.	
Hui Sai Fun	Central Development	
F.J. Knightly		
J.L. Marden	Wheelock Marden & Co.	
D.K. Newbigging	Jardine, Matheson and Co.	
Pao Yue-Kong	World Wide Shipping Group	
Sir Albert Rodrigues		
G.R. Ross	Deacon and Co.	
W.S. Stocks		
Sir Douglas Clague	J.D. Hutchison and Co.	

April 1977
G.M. Sayer	Hongkong Bank, chief executive	Chairman
M.G.R. Sandberg	Hongkong Bank	executive Deputy Chairman
P.G. Williams	Dodwell and Co.	Deputy Chairman
P.E. Hutson	Hongkong Bank	resident executive director, London
A.D.A.G. Mosley	Hongkong Bank	executive director
E.R. Udal	Hongkong Bank	executive director
J.H. Bremridge	Swire Group	
H.P. Foxon	Gilman and Co.	
Hui Sai Fun	Central Development	
F.J. Knightly		
J.L. Marden	Wheelock Marden & Co.	
D.K. Newbigging	Jardine, Matheson and Co.	
Pao Yue-Kong	World Wide Shipping Group	
Sir Albert Rodrigues		
G.R. Ross	Deacon and Co.	
W.S. Stocks		

April 1978
M.G.R. Sandberg	Hongkong Bank, chief executive	Chairman
J.L. Boyer	Hongkong Bank	executive Deputy Chairman
P.G. Williams	Dodwell and Co.	Deputy Chairman
P.E. Hutson	Hongkong Bank	resident executive director, London
A.D.A.G. Mosley	Hongkong Bank	executive director
J.H. Bremridge	Swire Group	
Hui Sai Fun	Central Development	
F.J. Knightly	Hongkong Bank, retired	
J.L. Marden	Wheelock Marden & Co.	
D.K. Newbigging	Jardine, Matheson and Co.	
Pao Yue-Kong	World Wide Shipping Group	

Table 15.2 (*cont.*)

G.R. Ross	Deacon and Co.	
W.S. Stocks		
[Sir Albert Rodrigues, Consultant to the Board]		

April 1979

M.G.R. Sandberg	Hongkong Bank, chief executive	Chairman
J.L. Boyer	Hongkong Bank	executive Deputy Chairman
P.G. Williams	Dodwell and Co./Inchcape (HK)	Deputy Chairman
P.E. Hutson	Hongkong Bank	resident executive director, London
A.D.A.G. Mosley	Hongkong Bank	executive director
(Sir) Q.W. Lee	Hang Seng Bank, chief executive	
J.H. Bremridge	Swire Group	
Hui Sai Fun	Central Development	
F.J. Knightly		
J.L. Marden	Wheelock Marden & Co.	
D.K. Newbigging	Jardine, Matheson and Co.	
Sir Yue-Kong Pao	World Wide Shipping Group	
G.R. Ross	Deacon & Co.	
W.S. Stocks		
N.S. Thompson	Mass Transit Railway Corp.	

As of Chairman's Statement:

March 1980

M.G.R. Sandberg	Hongkong Bank, chief executive	Chairman
J.L. Boyer	Hongkong Bank	executive Deputy Chairman
Sir Yue-Kong Pao	World Wide Shipping Group	Deputy Chairman
P.E. Hammond	Hongkong Bank	executive director
P.E. Hutson	Hongkong Bank	resident executive director, London
I.H. Macdonald	Hongkong Bank	resident executive director, New York
A.D.A.G. Mosley	Hongkong Bank	executive director
Q.W. Lee	Hang Seng Bank, chief executive	
E.W. Duffy	Chairman, Marine Midland Banks	
R.W. Hubner	Director, Marine Midland Banks	
J.R. Petty	President, Marine Midland Banks	
J.H. Bremridge	Swire Group	
J.F. Holmes	Inchcape (HK)	
Hui Sai Fun	Central Development	
Li Ka Shing	Cheung Kong (Holdings)	
J.L. Marden	Wheelock Marden & Co.	
D.K. Newbigging	Jardine, Matheson and Co.	
G.R. Ross	Deacon and Co.	
N.S. Thompson	MTR Corp.	
P.G. Williams	Hong Kong Electric	

March 1981

M.G.R. Sandberg	Hongkong Bank, chief executive	Chairman
J.L. Boyer	Hongkong Bank	executive Deputy Chairman
Sir Yue-Kong Pao	World Wide Shipping Group	Deputy Chairman
P.E. Hammond	Hongkong Bank	executive director

III. Policy, development, and performance 681

Table 15.2 (*cont.*)

P.E. Hutson	Hongkong Bank	resident executive director, London
I.H. Macdonald	Hongkong Bank	resident executive director, New York
Q.W. Lee	Hang Seng Bank, chief executive	
E.W. Duffy	Chairman, MMBI	
R.W. Hubner	Director, MMBI	
J.R. Petty	President, MMBI	
D.R.Y. Bluck	Chairman, Swire Group	
J.F. Holmes	Inchcape (HK)	
Hui Sai Fun	Central Development	
Li Ka Shing	Cheung Kong (Holdings)	
J.L. Marden	Wheelock Marden & Co.	
D.K. Newbigging	Jardine, Matheson and Co.	
N.S. Thompson	MTR Corp	
P.G. Williams		

March 1982

M.G.R. Sandberg	Hongkong Bank, chief executive	Chairman
P.E. Hammond	Hongkong Bank	executive Deputy Chairman
Sir Yue-Kong Pao	World Wide Shipping Group	Deputy Chairman
P.E. Hutson	Hongkong Bank	resident executive director, London
I.H. Macdonald	Hongkong Bank	resident executive director
R.V. Munden	Hongkong Bank	executive director
Q.W. Lee	Hang Seng Bank, chief executive	
E.W. Duffy	Chairman, MMBI	
R.W. Hubner	Director, MMBI	
J.R. Petty	President, MMBI	
Sir John Archer	Royal Hong Kong Jockey Club	
T.J. Bedford	Hong Kong Land	
D.R.Y. Bluck	Chairman, Swire Group	
L.S. Dunn	John Swire & Sons HK	
J.F. Holmes	Inchcape (HK)	
Hui Sai Fun	Central Development	
Li Ka Shing	Cheung Kong (Holdings)	
J.L. Marden	Wheelock Marden & Co.	
D.K. Newbigging	Jardine, Matheson and Co.	
N.S. Thompson	MTR Corp.	
P.G. Williams		

March 1983

M.G.R. Sandberg	Hongkong Bank, chief executive	Chairman
P.E. Hammond	Hongkong Bank	executive Deputy Chairman
Sir Yue-Kong Pao	World Wide Shipping Group	Deputy Chairman
R.V. Munden	Hongkong Bank	executive director
A.R. Petrie	Hongkong Bank	resident executive director, New York
W. Purves	Hongkong Bank	executive director
T. Welsh	Hongkong Bank	resident executive director, London
Q.W. Lee	Hang Seng Bank, chief executive	
E.W. Duffy	Chairman, MMBI	
R.W. Hubner	Director, MMBI	

Table 15.2 (*cont.*)

J.R. Petty	President, MMBI
Sir John Archer	Royal Hong Kong Jockey Club
T.J. Bedford	Hong Kong Land Co.
D.R.Y. Bluck	Chairman, Swire Group
L.S. Dunn	John Swire & Sons HK
J.F. Holmes	Inchcape (HK)
Hui Sai Fun	Central Development
Li Ka Shing	Cheung Kong (Holdings)
J.L. Marden	Wheelock Marden & Co.
D.K. Newbigging	Jardine, Matheson and Co.
N.S. Thompson	MTR Corp.

March 1984

M.G.R. Sandberg	Hongkong Bank, chief executive Chairman
P.E. Hammond	Hongkong Bank executive Deputy Chairman
Sir Yue-Kong Pao	World Wide Shipping Group Deputy Chairman
R.V. Munden	Hongkong Bank executive director
A.R. Petrie	Hongkong Bank resident executive director, New York
W. Purves	Hongkong Bank executive director
T. Welsh	Hongkong Bank resident executive director, London
Q.W. Lee	Hang Seng Bank, chief executive
E.W. Duffy	Chairman, MMBI
J.W. McKee, Jr	Director, MMBI
J.R. Petty	President, MMBI
Sir John Archer	Royal Hong Kong Jockey Club
T.J. Bedford	
D.R.Y. Bluck	Chairman, Swire Group
P.C.S. Deveson	Inchcape (HK)
L.S. Dunn	John Swire & Sons HK
Hui Sai Fun	Central Development
S.L. Keswick	Jardine, Matheson and Co.
Li Ka Shing	Cheung Kong (Holdings)
J.L. Marden	Wheelock Marden & Co.
N.S. Thompson	MTR Corp.

March 1985

M.G.R. Sandberg	Hongkong Bank, chief executive Chairman
W. Purves	Hongkong Bank executive Deputy Chairman
Hui Sai Fun	Central Development Deputy Chairman
R.C. Farrell	Hongkong Bank executive director
R.V. Munden	Hongkong Bank executive director
A.R. Petrie	Hongkong Bank resident executive director, New York
T. Welsh	Hongkong Bank resident executive director, London
E.W. Duffy	Chairman, Executive Committee, MMBI
J.W. McKee, Jr	Director, MMBI
J.R. Petty	Chairman, MMBI
Sir John Archer	Royal Hong Kong Jockey Club
T.J. Bedford	
P.C.S. Deveson	Inchcape (HK)

Table 15.2 (cont.)

L.S. Dunn	John Swire & Sons HK
S.L. Keswick	Jardine, Matheson and Co.
Li Ka Shing	Cheung Kong (Holdings)
H.M.P. Miles	Swire Group
H. Sohmen	World International (Holdings)
J.C.C. Tang	South Sea Manufacturing Co.
N.S. Thompson	MTR Corp.

Bold face indicates a new member.
Those listed without affiliation were elected *primarily* for reasons other than company affiliation.
[a] Clague was Deputy Chairman to October 1975 and resigned from the Board effective the end of March, 1976.

'interim' period in which a new Chief Manager becomes familiar with his tasks and with the Board. Saunders himself has denied the proposition outright, but there was more involved than personalities.

In fact Saunders and indeed other Bank executives considered it was now time for an executive board with a Hongkong Banker as chairman. The complex affairs of a multinational bank could no longer be the responsibility of the traditional board composed solely of leading Hong Kong taipans. Although Morse, Turner, and Saunders—the latter two after an interim period—had been elected chairman in turn, these precedents fell far short of the reforms Saunders and his colleagues had in mind. To prevent any misunderstanding, precedent had now to be more fully defined and institutionalized. This is compatible with Saunders' own explanation: he (i) deplored the interim period under any circumstance and (ii) saw no alternative to such a period if a new Chief Manager were appointed without Board experience. And, at a different level, Saunders appreciated that the term 'chief manager' was an anomaly outside Hong Kong. The change in the regulations, discussed in Chapter 13, solved the structural problem; it also solved the particular concerns of senior Hongkong Bankers.

In 1970/71 position papers were developed suggesting that, in line with these 1969 changes, an opportunity might be taken to broaden the geographical base of the Board. One memorandum recommended three directors from outside Hong Kong, preferably from London, who would attend four meetings a year; another proposal, assuming the enlargement (effected in 1972) of the Board, would have added directors from Australia and North America. This latter proposal would have been an immediate statement of the Bank's international intentions and solved the London question (see Chapter 14), but the proposals were premature. Neither Saunders nor Sayer had as yet solved the question of Board membership at the executive director level.

In 1973, however, the Board, on the recommendation of the Chairman, elected certain of the Bank's General Managers as executive directors, and in 1974 the Bank's legal adviser, E.R. Udal, was elected. Hongkong Bank Group representation was broadened in 1979 with the election of (Sir) Q.W. Lee, the chief executive officer of Hang Seng Bank, and the following year, with U.S. regulatory approval of the Bank's acquisition of Marine Midland Banks (MMBI), three of their directors joined the Hongkong Bank Board; two were MMBI executive directors, E.W. Duffy and J.R. Petty, and one was a non-executive director, R.W. Hubner. Included in the Bank's own representation were the executive directors resident in London and New York respectively.

Table 15.3 indicates the companies represented on the Board. The list is a combination of old and new. As to the former, Gilman and Co., first represented on the Provisional Committee in 1864, was on the Board in 1985, but now under the Inchcape umbrella.[e] Gibb Livingston, Dodwell's and/or Mackinnon Mackenzie appeared under Inchcape. Caldbeck, Macgregor and Co. was not a Board member of long-standing, but the founding Macgregor had opened his company's first account with the Bank in 1865; it was lost to the Bank during Inchcape's renegotiation of the banking relationship following their acquisition of the company.

Jardine's continued their support throughout. The firm of Elly Kadoorie and Co. had come on the Board in 1956 when one of the Bank's founding firms, David Sassoon and Co., closed in Hong Kong. In 1967 there was a serious run on the Beirut branch of the BBME, which required the support of the Bank of England. The fear in 1960 had been that Arab customers would be unaware of the Hongkong Bank's role as holding company – this was in the context of financial support. Activists however became clearly aware of the Hongkong Bank; they learned that a Jew sat on the Board of the BBME's parent corporation. There were allegations in the Egyptian press that the Hongkong Bank was in an unsound condition. The Board reacted unanimously by asking Lawrence Kadoorie (now Lord Kadoorie), one of the Bank's real supporters and major constituents and a leading Hong Kong citizen, to resign. The Board considered the situation 'deplorable'; it was not a happy decision.

Deacon and Co. is another old Hong Kong firm, founded by a tea taster in the employ of the founding firm of Augustine Heard and Co. The appointment of G.R. Ross, however, was more a recognition of his personal contribution to Hong Kong's development, especially his role on the General Chamber of Commerce. Turner had been unwilling to consider Marden as a Bank director,

---

[e] Gilman's had a particularly difficult history, but, as revealed in the recent history of the Inchcape Group, 'the backing of The Hongkong and Shanghai Banking Corporation enabled the company to prosper and expand' through the inter-war period. See Stephanie Jones, *Two Centuries of Overseas Trading: the Origins and Growth of the Inchcape Group* (London, 1986), p. 186.

Table 15.3 *The Hongkong and Shanghai Banking Corporation Principal companies represented on the Board of Directors, 1962–1985[a]*

	1st year[b]	1962–1985			
Swire Group					
Butterfield and Swire	1914	1962–	1974		
John Swire & Sons			1974–		1985
Inchcape (HK)[c]					
Gilman and Co.	1864	1962–			1985
Dodwell and Co.	1895	1962–			1985
Mackinnon, Mackenzie	1929	1962–	1973		
Jardine, Matheson	1877	1962–			1985
Imperial Chemical Industries	1946	1962–	1974		
Caldbeck, Macgregor	1956	1962–1965			
Sir Elly Kadoorie & Sons	1957	1962– 1967			
John D. Hutchison	1930	1962–	1976[d]		
Union Insurance Society of Canton	1966	1966– 1968			
Hongkong Bank	1941	1962–			1985
Deacon and Co.	1969		1969–	1980	
Wheelock Marden & Co.	1972		1972–	1984	
World Wide Shipping	1972		1972–		1985
Central Development	1974				1985
Mass Transit Railway	1979			1979–	1985
Hang Seng Bank	1979			1979–	1985
Marine Midland Banks	1980			1980	1985
Cheung Kong (Holdings)	1980			1980–	1985
Hong Kong Electric	1980			1982	
Gibb, Livingston & Co.	1869	[See Inchcape (HK)]			

[a] This does not deny that a director may have been elected for reasons other than the primary affiliation listed.
[b] First year company was represented on Board, not necessarily continuously.
[c] Inchcape's representatives on the Board were at first primarily identified with the familiar company names; this policy has now changed.
[d] Became a subsidiary of Cheung Kong (Holdings), q.v.

but the continued development of Wheelock Marden and the Bank's increasing association with George Marden, for example, in connection with Harbour Tunnel Company (in which the Bank had a 10% equity investment from 1966), suggested Board representation. However George Marden left for London where he became a member of the London Committee; his son, J.L. Marden, succeeded him in Hong Kong and was represented on the Board from 1972. The disappearance of Hutchison's is consequent to its overextension, financed in the main by Bank support, and the consequent reorganization which first put the Bank in control and resulted eventually in the sale of the Bank's Hutchison shares to Cheung Kong (Holdings).

The two elections which received particular public attention, however, were those of (Sir) Y.K. Pao in 1972, the first Chinese on the Board, and of L.S. Dunn of the Swire Group in 1982, the first woman on the Board. Both had specific qualifications, but, if the Board were waiting for the right man and the right woman to break precedent, their decisions were correct. In 1972 the Board by a vote of the shareholders had been potentially increased from a maximum of fifteen to a maximum of twenty. This would permit a better community representation on the Board, but it would also make possible a further increase in the number of executive directors. With the officers responsible for running the Bank actually on the Board, the broadening of its non-executive base followed normal bank board custom.

Despite the continued presence of old firms, by 1982 the newcomers, the executive directors, and the Marine Midland directors had given the Board a totally new look.

Chief executives: the succession

Historical background
When Sir Thomas Jackson retired in 1902, the successor could be seen as one of two men, V.A. Caesar Hawkins or J.R.M. Smith; the selection was made by the Board of Directors meeting virtually in camera and without Jackson. This is the last time the Board were confronted with a choice. Either by accident or design, there was always an heir apparent. Setting aside the successions caused by accident, Newton Stabb on the sudden resignation of Smith for health reasons, A.H. Barlow on Stephen's death, Arthur Morse on the Fall of Hong Kong, the Chief Manager was always able to pick out a successor and bring him to Hong Kong, or alternatively, as the Head Office/Hong Kong office hierarchy developed, the Chief Manager could watch a young Banker's progress and decide not to send him away permanently to the branches.

Morse had sent R.P. Moodie to Shanghai and kept Michael W. Turner; Turner noted J.A.H. Saunders and sent him for independent assessment in Singapore, designating him as successor only after G.O.W. Stewart had been approached.

Indeed, this was typical of another hazard; the first choice might prove at the last minute to be unavailable. The prospect might refuse formally or informally, as did David McLean, Ewen Cameron, John Walter, Charles S. Addis, and G.O.W. Stewart, they might prove surprisingly unsuitable, for example, D.M. 'Kobe' Ross, or for no objective reasons displease the chief

Table 15.4 *The Hongkong and Shanghai Banking Corporation Chief executives from 1876*

Year as chief executive	Name	Seniority	Years East when appointed	Branches served
1876–1886	(Sir) Thomas Jackson	1866	11[b]	4
1886–1887	John Walter	1868	18[b]	5
1887–1889	(Sir) Thomas Jackson			
1889–1890	G.E. Noble	1866	23[b]	4
1890–1891	(Sir) Thomas Jackson			
1891–1893	F. de Bovis	1872	19	6
1893–1902	Sir Thomas Jackson			
1902–1910	J.R.M. Smith	1882	20	5
1910–1920	Sir Newton J. Stabb	1891	19	5
1920–1924	A.G. Stephen	1885	35	9
1924–1927	A.H. Barlow	1891	33	7
1927–1930	A.C. Hynes	1897	29	6
1930–1941[a]	Sir Vandeleur M. Grayburn	1904	25	3
1941–1953[a]	Sir Arthur Morse	1915	26	3
1953–1962	Sir Michael W. Turner	1930	23	3
1962–1972	Sir John A.H. Saunders	1940[c]	(6+)16	3
1972–1977	G.M. Sayer	1947	24	6
1977–1986	Sir Michael G.R. Sandberg	1949	28	3
1986–	W. Purves	1955	30	6

[a] 1941–43 Grayburn was interned and Morse was acting.
[b] Years in the Hongkong Bank in the East.
[c] East in 1946.
Seniority is based on the number of years 'in the East', defined as years after leaving London Office (but including war service).

executive, as may have been the case with D.C. Edmondston.[f] It is also wise to remember that not everyone wanted to be Chief Manager.

Since A.H. Barlow the chief executive officer has, with one exception, risen through the Hong Kong office hierarchy under the observation of the then chief. Even Morse, who became Chief Manager under exceptional circumstances, had been promoted to a London managership in consequence of his excellent work in Hong Kong. Those on the scene detected that with Moodie sent to Shanghai, the line was clear for Turner to become Chief Manager, that with Stewart set for London, the return of Saunders to Hong Kong indicated his selection. Furthermore it followed from the Hong Kong emphasis that, with the exception of Barlow, the chief executives would have had little experience

[f] Edmondston had been selected as Grayburn's successor, and the growing crisis was reason enough for Grayburn to stay on (see Volume III, Chapter 4).

outside Hong Kong. This was shown in Table 4.11 (Volume III), reproduced here as Table 15.4 (see also Appendix Table A, pp. 923–24).

The table also indicates clearly that Saunders' successor, G.M. Sayer, does not fit the pattern – he had served in six branches; a study of his career shows however that, before his appointment as chief executive, he had spent some thirteen of his 26 years in the East in Hong Kong, including a term as Manager of the important Mongkok branch. Nevertheless contemporaries did not identify him at an early stage in his middle career partly because his appointments in Rangoon and Osaka did not fit the pattern and partly because there appeared to be more obvious contenders.

– *Saunders to Sayer*

With the accession of Saunders in 1962 it was natural that men compatible with his style of management would be brought into Head Office. Saunders inherited and made good use of R.G.L. Oliphant and he had, in common with many others, an admiration for the abilities of M.G. Carruthers and F.J. Knightly; he also brought in men of the calibre of, *inter alios*, J.W.L. Howard and Maurice W. Turner, but it apparently took a certain type of man to 'stand up' to Saunders in matters where views differed.

Among those who were particularly able at handling this sort of situation was M. Curran (East in 1946), who had served with Saunders at the beginning of the war and who had also been with him during the first post-war assignment in Singapore. Curran had been appointed Accountant Penang in 1957, eleven years after coming East, and had served also as Accountant Jesselton – where Max Haymes requested his removal (but later admitted this was a misjudgement) – and Accountant Osaka before being brought back to Hong Kong as Sub-Manager in 1963. He then served as Manager Mongkok for two years and in 1966 began his move up the Hong Kong hierarchy, first to become Colony Manager and then to Deputy Chief Manager, then Director and General Manager.

Saunders obviously did not bring all his capable officers to Hong Kong. As one example, he held J.S. Dunnett in high regard, but Dunnett (East in 1935) went to Manila in 1950 and spent the next eleven years there; the branch did well, and Saunders sent him to become President of the Hongkong Bank of California, where, despite the questionable logic of the appointment (that Manila banking was good preparation for American banking), he brought some light into the history of the Hongkong Bank's problem subsidiary.

These were all Bankers who would retire just before or with Saunders; they formed from time to time key elements in his 'team', but they did not answer the question of the succession.

Reflecting on this period G.M. Sayer (East in 1947) considered that there

III. Policy, development, and performance

must have been three main contenders for the position to which he was, in the event, appointed – P.E. Hutson (East in 1948), Michael Sandberg (East in 1949), and A.D.A.G. Mosley (East in 1950), and, since all chief executives since Barlow had been Chief Accountants, it is important to note that Hutson held the post 1965–1967, Sandberg 1968–1969, and Mosley 1969; Sayer had not been Chief Accountant. There had also been accidental events, including death, which removed likely juniors and possible contenders – or those identified as such by contemporaries – from the running.

Other able officers would be ruled out on the basis of timing. N.H.T. Bennett, for example, had been Chief Accountant, 1961–1963, but the Hong Kong Managers were in place and Saunders had only just become chief executive. In 1963 Bennett went to Bangkok as Manager, and, although he returned to important positions in Hong Kong, it was clear that, like Morse before him, when an able man was required in London, if Bennett were ever to occupy a senior executive position, 1970 was the time and London the place. He left Hong Kong.

Contemporary observers playing the usual corporate game of 'cross him off' tended to favour Hutson's chances. This being so there was no point to moving to a consideration of Sandberg, who was one year junior and who succeeded to Hutson's post as Accountant Singapore when the latter was appointed Chief Accountant, and, for the reasons stated, they can be excused for not calculating on Sayer. In 1968 the wisdom of this approach was confirmed when Hutson was appointed Manager, Main Office, Hong Kong, and was again succeeded by Sandberg, this time as Chief Accountant. A year later the picture had changed; Hutson had become the Chairman's Assistant, a post without specified duties, and this time Sandberg's succession to Hutson's managership of the Main Office had a new significance. Much would depend on when Saunders decided to retire.

This was not the time for conventional wisdom. Saunders was watching Sayer, with whom he had successfully worked on several occasions in Hong Kong, and brought him back from Osaka in 1965 to run the difficult Mongkok operation. After Sayer's initial success in this post, Saunders advised him, 'Don't build a wall around yourself here, I may need you in Head Office.' He brought Sayer to Head Office as Staff Controller in 1968; Sayer became General Manager in charge of subsidiaries and overseas operations in 1970. That same year Saunders informed Sayer that he would recommend him to the Board of Directors as his successor if Sayer agreed; after considerable deliberation, Sayer did agree. His appointment as Deputy Chairman was part of the public acknowledgement of the fact, leaving Saunders free to retire from the chairmanship in 1972.

On the appointment of Sayer, the Board conferred on him the responsibility for the day-to-day running of the Bank and its subsidiaries, with the authority to sub-delegate. This was made subject to the restriction that any change in general policy, whether by sale or alteration in structure of existing subsidiary companies, any new acquisitions, or the establishment of new ventures, whether alone or in conjunction with others, whether by way of incorporation of new companies or otherwise should be subject to the prior approval of the Board.

– Sayer to Sandberg

Sayer became chief executive of the Hongkong Bank as Chairman of the Board in 1972. By that time Sandberg had become Manager Hong Kong. He became an executive director in 1972 but he did not come to Head Office until 1974; in the meantime Hutson and Mosley, both General Managers and directors, were on Sayer's Head Office team, but with duties still not clearly defined. When Sandberg eventually came to Head Office, however, he came as Deputy Chairman. For the first time he had become senior to Hutson; furthermore Sayer informed Sandberg from the beginning that he would be serving but one five-year term and that Sandberg was to be recommended as his successor.

As Sayer himself described the selection, he looked round at the available material and decided on Sandberg. To the question, 'Why?', he replied, 'Well, he is likeable, he's a very good banker, and he's got a quick brain. He gets on well with the Board, and he's decisive. Are there any more qualities you need?' But having made the selection, Sayer then exposed Sandberg to all aspects of the task, including deputizing at international meetings. The succession occurred without further discussion in 1977.

Chief Accountants and the succession – careers compared

One key to potential Chief Manager status is said to have been appointment as Chief Accountant, even though this judgement would prove inapplicable in the days before the Great War and the post was abolished in 1974 soon after W. Purves left to be Manager Tokyo. Sandberg has stressed that, whether it were the stepping-stone to the top or not, the very visible post of Chief Accountant was a legitimate mid-career goal and, undeniably, an indicator of potential.

Hutton, Chief Accountant (CA) from 1959, was by all reports a very able banker, but he resigned in 1961. Clout (CA 1963–1964) had had a specialized career, but neither Hutton, Bennett (CA 1961–1963), nor Clout could move to chief executive if Saunders were to remain a normal nine to ten year period. Conventional wisdom, based on the Chief Accountant theory, is therefore correct in focusing on Hutson (CA 1965–1967) as the successor to Saunders. When this did not work out Saunders had three alternatives: (i) moving to

III. Policy, development, and performance

someone much younger, for example, Purves, (ii) moving ahead to the next ex-Chief Accountant (1968–1969), Sandberg, or (iii) moving back. Purves had become Chief Accountant only in 1970 at the instigation of Sandberg, and he did not yet have the depth of experience necessary. There was no particular reason for not moving ahead to choose Sandberg, but perhaps Saunders felt that was too close. Saunders had in fact to look outside the Chief Accountant succession, and he found Sayer.

This is not a historical judgement on the persons appointed or not appointed. It is an *ex-post* analysis and test of the 'chief accountant as stepping-stone' theory.

With the eventual appointment of Sandberg there had been a return to the pattern; Sandberg had served only briefly in Tokyo as a junior and in Singapore as Accountant; like several other chief executives he was a three-branch man; he had also been Chief Accountant and come up successfully through several levels in Hong Kong. His ability to work with Curran, for whom he had considerable respect, would have endeared him to Saunders; his authoritative handling of the Hong Kong operation, now larger than the Bank itself had been but a few years previously, and his 'founding' and chairmanship of the Bank's merchant bank, Wardley Limited, would have been a sure measure of his ability to succeed eventually as the Bank's chief executive.

THE HONGKONG BANK GROUP – THE COMPANIES

THE GROWING COMPLEXITY, 1962–1979

Chapters 13 through 15 deal primarily with the Hongkong Bank in its historical continuity, that is, with the Hongkong Bank qua bank. The Bank and Group cannot, however, be sensibly separated. Indeed, in 1968 the Board recorded its intention that 'as with all subsidiaries, the bank will in case of need give unlimited support and assume financial and other liabilities'. In effect, the history must recount the development of the Hongkong Bank Group, but it need not, given the restriction stated, deal in detail with the history of even the main subsidiaries.

The growth of the Group in this section refers primarily to the increase in the number of the Hongkong Bank's subsidiary and associated companies, defined as a minimum 50% or 20% owned respectively. The ultimate list is that provided by the Bank to a Congressional Committee and is accurate as of December 31, 1979 (see Table 15.12). If this list is compared to that in Table II.1 above, the magnitude and complexity of the changes can be readily seen; their interpretation, however, is quite another matter. Furthermore, interpretation is essential if the growth of the corporation is to make historical sense or bear any resemblance to rational development.

The situation was complex at the end of 1979. In 1980 the Hongkong Bank acquired Marine Midland Banks, which is sufficient reason for dividing this post-1961 summary of the history in the year before the acquisition can impact on the Bank's organization and fortunes.

A survey and explanation, 1962–1979

The period is well-chosen. The impact of the acquisitions made under Sir Michael Turner in his last years as Chief Manager forced the Hongkong Bank's Board and senior management to consider something larger than the Bank as traditionally conceived. There were several policy courses theoretically available. The acquired banks could have been immediately merged, but, for reasons already considered, this was impractical; furthermore such a solution was in no way suitable for certain of the corporation's later acquisitions. The corporation could have adopted a structure involving a separate holding company, but this would prove a politically insensitive course and was not further considered. The result was for The Hongkong and Shanghai Banking Corporation to be both an operating bank and a holding company. The name 'Hongkong Bank' attached itself, not surprisingly, to the corporation as operating bank. How then could the acquired banks, the subsidiaries, and associated companies soon to be held by the corporation state their own relationship to the parent company without confusion? The solution was in a sense to act as if a separate holding company actually existed and to refer to the Hongkong Bank, the BBME, the Mercantile, and others as if they were comparable in the corporation structure and all organizationally subordinate to something called 'the Hongkong Bank Group'.

This was useful but had no legal basis. The Group was not comparable to, for example, the Royal Bank of Scotland Group, which is a corporate entity. It was merely a collective name used for purposes of identification and given reality by referring to that part of the corporation's management responsible for global operations as 'Group Head Office' – and the archives as 'Group Archives'. In the corporate identity exercise of 1980, the Board concluded that confusion nevertheless existed, and the 'Group' name was downplayed (but not eliminated); a single corporate symbol and the signature 'HongkongBank' (with the full name of the corporation surviving in small print by way of legal explanation) appeared to be a more appropriate solution. The year 1980, perhaps by coincidence, is also the year in which the final consolidation of the early acquisitions was achieved, Head Office control rationalized, and a new partnership negotiated with Marine Midland Banks.

III. Policy, development, and performance

The corporation's assets increased from $7,660 million at the end of 1961 to $125,292 million at the end of 1979, in which year the Group was composed of some 396 subsidiary and associated companies. This development was certainly not planned in the formal sense. Neither the Board nor the executives of 1962 could have conceived of the organizational changes required to achieve the growth actually accomplished; nor, it is probably reasonable to say, would they have wanted it. Throughout the 1960s the corporation's total profit was attributable primarily (42% to 57%) to the Hong Kong operations; if Head Office's contribution were added, the percentage would be a maximum 70%. The Board were anxious that on the one hand the Bank should flourish and grow; on the other hand they and the Chief Manager were concerned with control, with the fear of leaving traditional regions or challenging traditional but partially self-imposed restraints.

The first fully planned, Hongkong Bank initiated acquisition was probably that of Marine Midland Banks. One of the most profitable of the Hongkong Bank's acquisitions, Hang Seng Bank in 1965, was consequent to an emergency development. But the Board recognized that the Bank could not continue to reinvest its increasing funds wholly in Hong Kong, especially given the imbalance of industry and the consequent over-exposure in textiles. There was, therefore, a tendency to see one problem at a time and to solve each without an overall plan. In consequence there were small investments in this or that finance company, often on the invitation of other participants, and too often turning sour. In Hong Kong itself the Bank supported new major investments by token share purchases, as in the case of the Cross Harbour Tunnel Company; it also invested in the equity of companies with which it otherwise had considerable dealings, as in Cathay Pacific and (Sir) Y.K. Pao's shipping companies.

Even these investments brought the Bank out of its region, out of its traditional thinking, and prepared it for a later multinational status. The corporate structure was revised (see Chapter 13), and this was a continuing process. Then in the 1970s a more aggressive approach became apparent. The growth of the Bank's merchant banking activities not only forced reorganization within the corporation, it also led to an awareness that acquisition in London was a necessary course, and this in turn led to the relationship with Antony Gibbs and Sons. Despite this, the Bank was not using its paper at a time when its market price was above 'true' (as opposed to the lesser 'published') book value. If opportunities were not to be missed, some planning, some active search was obligatory. The Bank was, however, unfortunate on two counts. First, the first planning officer, appointed from outside the Bank, had the problems of an outsider and his contribution was therefore seriously restricted. Secondly, Saunders' successor, Guy Sayer, opted for one tour as chief executive; he was not prepared to push through projects for which he could not subsequently take responsibility. Even after the need for an American strategy had been recognized, there were hesitations and delay. These would not in the end hinder the American acquisition, but that delay could well have been responsible for the Bank's failure to identify the European target bank in time (see Chapter 18).

To a Hongkong Banker of the 1950s, however, the corporation's position in 1979 would be seen as nothing short of 'unbelievable'. Despite the limitations described above there was significant growth of the Group in a form which, despite the apparent *ad hoc* content of the list of companies, can for the most part be rationalized. The next task is to describe the situation in 1979 and then to recount major developments.

The position in 1979

There were 396 subsidiary and associated companies (defined *for this purpose* as a holding of 25%) held by The Hongkong and Shanghai Banking Corporation or held through these companies in similar proportions. This can be narrowed down by noting that the Bank had only 47 directly owned subsidiaries, a figure which both overstates and understates the situation: overstates because four companies were dormant and several more were 'merely' holding companies; understates for precisely this latter reason – several of the Bank's operating subsidiaries were held through holding companies. These operating subsidiaries were, probably without exception, the management responsibility of the direct subsidiary, for example, Wardley Investment Services was 100% owned by Wardley which in turn was 100% owned by HSBC, but the management of Wardley Investment Services was the responsibility of Wardley. In addition there are only ten associated companies whose shares were held directly by the Bank.

Several of the companies have names which excite curiosity – the Disappearance Project Company, Spartan Enterprises, Carnation Shipping Company, Liberian Tulip Transports, and Perpetual Publicity. There are others whose names come from Hongkong Bank (or at least from Hong Kong) history – 99 Bishopsgate (the address of the present Hongkong Bank London Office), Carlingford (the name of the Bank Manager's house in Bangkok – and a town in Ireland) Holdings, companies beginning with 'Hong Kong' and 'Shanghai' variously spelt and spaced, Kellett (one of the hills in Hong Kong's Peak District) Investments, Lion Corporate Services, Wayfoong Finance, Wayhong Holdings, and Wardley.

This approach tends to confuse; indeed, it succeeded in raising questions in the U.S. Congress as to whether the Hongkong Bank was in fact primarily a

III. Policy, development, and performance

financial institution and therefore eligible to become an American bank holding company. This latter issue will be considered in Chapter 17, but the confusion is reasonable and should be resolved here.

The policy of the HSBC was to broaden the scope of financial operations both in content and geographically. This policy, when combined first with management limitations, resulted not in absorption but in a form of control which preserved the name and status of the acquired company, as in the case of the Mercantile Bank and British Bank of the Middle East, considered in Chapter 12. More recently the policy would account for the retention of the name of Antony Gibbs – at least until 1980. Such companies would generate their own list of subsidiaries and associates, for reasons identical to those relevant to the parent company. The geographical spread of the corporation had the consequence that many operations had by local law to be separately incorporated in each territory, accounting, for example, for the proliferation of nominee and trustee companies – and for the Hongkong Bank of California itself.[g]

In some jurisdictions separate incorporation of a separate 100% owned subsidiary would be necessary and sufficient to satisfy local legislation. Alternatively, unless a foreign bank incorporated locally its activities were restricted. In consequence under the British Bank of the Middle East, for example, are listed the Bank of Iran and the Middle East and the Saudi British Bank.

The grouping of operations for control or tax purposes led to the establishment of holding companies, of which Wayhong, NH, is a good example. Through this and a second tier wholly owned holding company, Wayhong Investment, the HSBC controlled certain of its non-financial operations. Insurance at this time was grouped mainly under Wayhong Holdings. Grouping would also be a useful technique for geographical control: Wardley Australia (Holdings) controlled Wardley Australia and its subsidiaries; Wardley Investments Canada performed the same function in that country.

The existence of dormant companies was a consequence of history in each case; they were preserved for specific reasons, the British and Chinese Corporation, for example, because of residual responsibilities which it was powerless either to execute or abandon, Carlingford Investments because the name might prove useful later – the HSBC would in fact bring its insurance operations under this title – or Bowmaker (CA), the unresolved remains of what became an unsuccessful Central African operation.

Another significant factor in the proliferation of companies was HSBC's adherence to a management trend of creating single-purpose subsidiaries for

---

[g] As this bank had been sold earlier in 1979, it does not appear on the list.

specialized functions ancillary to but supportive of the corporation's main activities. At one end of the scale there is Wardley Limited, designed to be the merchant bank of the Group and perform functions which had previously been undertaken within the Hongkong Bank itself. At the other end would be Lion Corporate Services and Guardforce, the former 100% owned by HSBC and the latter 51% owned through the 100% owned holding company.

Property holding and property companies are another important example of the tendency to incorporate ancillary activities in separate companies, Gatechurch Property Management, for example. In the case of property, there is also the assumption that banks *per se* should not hold real estate beyond their own office and housing requirements. Although not absolute under the Bank's ordinance, this was a factor in the decision.

The Bank's decision to take an equity position in certain companies as a deliberate policy rather than only as an emergency rescue operation explains the existence of further groups of companies, many of them held, as noted above, through Wayhong Investment. This company leads to Cathay Pacific Airways and through them to service companies such as HK Aircraft Engineering and Securair. The HSBC's decision to invest in Y.K. Pao's shipping group through Wayhong Investment and WHS Investments, World Maritime Ltd (Bermuda), and World Shipping and Investment Company (Hong Kong) is alone responsible for 100 companies or 28% of those on the end-1979 list. The reason for this is straightforward: each ship was incorporated as a separate company.

Having explained the bulk of the list as the consequence of deliberate policy, there remain companies which were the result of particular circumstances. In some cases the HSBC planned to retain ownership, in others, the rescue having been completed, the Bank sold off its holdings. In the former category the most dramatic and successful acquisition was that of Hang Seng Bank in 1965; in the latter category, the Bank's rescue of Hutchison in 1975 and its sale in 1979 (and therefore its absence from the list) is a good example. The Hongkong Bank had been involved in such rescue investments before, for example, the I.I. Tschurin department store in Manchuria or certain Macau public utilities companies in the inter-war period, but the inclusion of such companies post-war in what purported to be a financial group raised questions.

The list of companies belonging to the Hongkong Bank Group can therefore be rationalized, but the list remains formidable. For purposes of analysis, however, it can be abridged by restricting consideration to those companies listed in the Annual Reports as 'principal subsidiaries' and 'major associated companies'. These, as they existed in 1979, are basically those in bold face in Table 15.12; they include nine subsidiaries and two associated companies. From 396 the list has been brought down to 11; discussion of the Hongkong Bank Group is manageable once again.

III. Policy, development, and performance

But is the HSBC and its subsidiary and associated companies a financial Group?

The HSBC's own analysis as presented by executive director I.H. Macdonald before a sub-committee of the House Committee on Government Operations, began with a definition of 'financial' consistent with that in the U.S. 1978 International Bank Act: commercial banking, merchant banking, insurance, leasing, property management and holding, holdings of non-controlled investments, and various services used in banking, for example, data processing, secretarial services, and communications.

By this definition only three of the 59 companies in which the HSBC owned directly 25% or more shares were non-financial: (i) SDC International Ltd, a Canadian investment holding company with timber and brewing interests, (ii) South China Morning Post Ltd, with seven subsidiaries including the Far Eastern Economic Review, and (iii) Wayhong NH, with significant holdings mainly in shipping, but also in Cathay Pacific Airlines. These equity investments were explained in the context of the corporation's long standing interest in communications and transportation. Saunders as the Bank's chief executive officer and the Board of Directors accepted the principle that commercial banks were properly entitled to make equity investments, and Saunders' apparently well-placed faith in the abilities of Y.K. Pao rather than any historical consideration was a deciding factor, once the more routine analysis had proved positive.

These and the odd additional non-financial company totalled 1.35% of the Hongkong Bank Group's 1979 consolidated assets and accounted for 10.18% of the Group's profit. Wayhong alone accounted for 1.29% and 9.1% respectively. Macdonald conceded that there were many ways of defining 'financial' and 'non-financial', but, he added, 'We know of no method which would increase the non-financial assets above 5% or the non-financial net income above 15% of the comparable consolidated figures of HSBC.'

DEVELOPMENTS, 1962–1971

Expansion and frustration

Under the management of Saunders, the corporation moved into two Commonwealth territories which had historically been reluctant to accept the presence of 'foreign' banks – Australia and Canada. Other significant changes were the Hongkong Bank's participation in the London-based International Commercial Bank, the investment in RoyWest Banking Corporation in the Bahamas, the equity investments referred to above, and the withdrawal from former British Central Africa with the virtual failure of Bowmaker (C.A.) and its associated companies. The most profitable and fortuitous investment was,

Table 15.5 *The Hongkong Bank Group*
List of principal companies, 1962

A. Subsidiary companies
The Hongkong and Shanghai Banking Corporation
The Hongkong and Shanghai Banking Corporation of California, Inc.
Mercantile Bank Limited
The British Bank of the Middle East
The British Bank of the Middle East (Morocco)
Wayfoong Finance Limited
[British and Chinese Corporation, dormant]

B. Associated companies
The Far Eastern Economic Review
The South China Morning Post
Bowmaker (C A) (Pvt) Limited
Trust Corporation of the Bahamas Limited
The Bank of Iran and the Middle East
Exporters' Refinance Corporation Limited

however, HSBC's purchase of 51% of the shares of Hang Seng Bank, a subject to be discussed separately below. The course of these changes can be seen in Tables 15.5 and 15.6 which deal with the situation in 1962 and in 1971/72 with chronological notes on the main events.

The first new subsidiary actually referred to in the Chairman's annual statement was the Wardley Corporation, a 100% owned subsidiary of the Hongkong Bank of California created for the purpose of owning and financing the erection of a seventeen-storey building in San Francisco, ultimately to house the Bank. This is an illustration of company-formation for specialized purposes and of the use of names historically associated with the Hongkong Bank. Otherwise it is of no particular significance.

By contrast the move into Australia in 1964 was of importance, leading ultimately (and when laws had been amended) to the formation of the Hongkong Bank of Australia in 1986. First the HSBC purchased a 40% interest in Mercantile Credits of Sydney, described by the Bank's Chairman as 'a well-known and old established finance house'. Saunders had, however, moved on several fronts. He had incorporated Wardley Australia, Pty, as a holding company for Mercantile Credits under which he also placed a second subsidiary, Hongkong Finance, Pty. To oversee these activities, Saunders secured permission for the HSBC to open a representative office in Sydney. Eventually there would be problems, but this was a substantial beginning. In 1965 the capital of Wardley Australia was increased to A$2 million, and it became a public company able to accept deposits from the public.

III. Policy, development, and performance

Table 15.6 *The Hongkong Bank Group*
List of principal companies, 1972 (March)

A. **Subsidiary companies**
The Hongkong and Shanghai Banking Corporation [sic]
The Hongkong Bank of California
Mercantile Bank Limited
The British Bank of the Middle East
The British Bank of the Middle East (Morocco), Casablanca
Wayfoong Finance Limited, Hong Kong
Malaysian Australian Finance Company Berhad, Kuala Lumpur
Wardley Corporation, San Francisco
Wardley Australia Pty Limited, Sydney
Hongkong Finance Limited, Sydney
Wardley Investments Canada Ltd, Vancouver
Wayhong Investment Ltd, Hong Kong
British Acceptance Corporation Ltd, Vancouver
Wardley Investments (NZ) Ltd
Wardley Finance (Thailand) Ltd
Hang Seng Bank Limited, Hong Kong

B. **Associated companies**
Mercantile Credits Limited, Sydney, Australia
International Commercial Bank Ltd, London
Exporters' Refinance Corporation Limited, London
Roy West Banking Corporation Limited, Nassau, Bahamas
Trust Corporation of Bahamas Limited
The Bank of Iran and the Middle East, Iran
World Maritime Bahamas Ltd
Cathay Pacific Airways Ltd, Hong Kong
Melanesia International Trust Co. Ltd
The New Zealand Investment Mortgage and Deposit Co. Ltd

Source: 1971 *Annual Report*, March 1972.

Meanwhile the Trust Corporation of the Bahamas had become an operating subsidiary of RoyWest Banking Corporation, a consortium bank of which the Hongkong Bank was a member. The Exporters Refinance Corporation in London had increased its capital to £1 million with the entry of Lloyds Bank to the owning group, which included HSBC, Charterhouse, Japhet and Thomasson, and National and Grindlays Bank – each with a 25% share of the equity. The understanding was that as capital was increased further, Lloyds' percentage share in the equity would increase; Lloyds was in competition with Barclays Bank. In 1966 capital was increased by £2 million and Lloyds' share to 40%.

In London the Hongkong Bank's Manager G.O.W. Stewart was obviously abreast of the latest banking trends. The International Commercial Bank

(ICB) was the first of the new-type, London-based consortium banks specializing in medium-term finance; it was founded in 1967 by the First National Bank of Chicago, Irving Trust Company, Westminister Bank, Commerzbank (of West Germany), and the Hongkong Bank; it was geared with equity capital of £3.15 million and subordinated loans of over £6.8 million. The capital was increased by £2.5 million in 1970, the HSBC's share being subscribed by the BBME for tax reasons. In 1971 confusion reigned when the National Westminster Bank, a merger of the National Provincial and the Westminster, noted a conflict of interest through the former's equity investment in Orion; the National Westminister withdrew from the ICB, and new partners (Banco di Roma and Crédit Lyonnais) were found to join with Commerzbank to form a 'Continental Group' with 34% of the shares; the Hongkong Bank and the two American banks held equal shares of the balance.

As part of a policy of 'following the Bank's customers', Saunders sent F.J. Knightly and J.S. Dunnett, the latter was then President of the Hongkong Bank of California, to seek a Canadian base, if possible in Vancouver, British Columbia. They identified the British Acceptance Corporation, which had been established in 1960 as a subsidiary of the British Wagon Company of England for automobile finance and had developed into commercial and industrial lending. Accordingly, in 1969 HSBC acquired 75% of the equity and Hastings West Investment held the remaining 25% until 1978 when they sold out to the HSBC. Following the Australian precedent, Saunders sought permission from the Federal authorities to open a Bank representative office in Vancouver; this was granted in 1970 and the office established.

These developments were followed by the acquisition in August 1970 of the Alberta financing division of Avco-Delta Corporation Canada, a subsidiary of Avco, a U.S. company; the HSBC-owned British Acceptance Corporation moved into Alberta; by 1971 the company had an office in Toronto and the name eventually changed to Wardley Canada.

At the 1971 Annual Meeting, Saunders presented to shareholders the background of HSBC's equity investment in shipping. In 1964 the Hongkong Bank, World Wide (Shipping), and Wheelock Marden and Co. formed World Maritime Bahamas, in which the HSBC's investment was 40%. Y.K. Pao was chairman, and the new company was operating with a fleet of approximately 1.2 million tons, which would be expanded to 3.6 million deadweight tons by 1974.

New Zealand was another former British colonial territory reluctant to accept 'foreign' banking, and the Hongkong Bank moved cautiously into the country with a $24\frac{1}{2}$% share (in association with the New Zealand Investment Co.) in the New Zealand Investment Mortgage and Deposit Co.

III. Policy, development, and performance

This summary, taken together with earlier comments, generally covers the developments which led to the list found in Table 15.6. Equally significant to the history of the Hongkong Bank Group was the move of Mercantile Bank's head office to Hong Kong, but this together with a summary of other banking developments is reserved for consideration in connection with a discussion of the Hongkong Bank's own growth during the period. In the present context, the acquisition of Hang Seng Bank was of particular importance, and to this the history now turns.

The acquisition of Hang Seng Bank

Background

The Hang Seng Ngan Ho (evergrowing native bank) was founded in 1933 by B.Y. Lam and S.H. Ho with a capital of $100,000 and was from the first active in the gold market and the remittance business. The bank closed during the Japanese Occupation, but reopened in November 1945 and was immediately active in the gold bullion trade, while S.H. Ho's many trading activities brought sound business to the bank. There then began a most remarkable change in the bank's outlook. Based on knowledge gained by world-wide investigative trips undertaken by S.H. Ho and the newly joined Q.W. Lee and with the advice of their banking friends, in particular The Hongkong and Shanghai Banking Corporation, the partners made the decision to incorporate. Hang Seng Ngan Ho became a bank as defined in the 1948 banking ordinance on December 5, 1952, with a paid-up capital of $5 million.

Hang Seng Bank was not an 'authorized' bank in the exchange control context; it operated therefore – and very successfully – on the open market, developing its friendly relations with the Hongkong Bank in the process. By stressing an educational policy designed to attract depositors, Hang Seng built up a retail business with a sound deposit base. In 1959 its paid-up capital was increased to $15 million, in 1960 Hang Seng admitted its new modern approach by changing its designation of 'Ngan Ho' (native bank) to 'Yin Hong' (modern bank), and by 1962 the bank had moved to its new 22-storey head office building at 77 Des Voeux Road in Central District. Furthermore, Hang Seng had established branches in Yaumati, Mongkok (1960), Tsimshatsui, Shamshuipo (1963), Causeway Bay, Tsuen Wan, and Kowloon City (1964), by which time its paid-up capital was $22.5 million.[h]

This success was in part the consequence of a highly active policy, including heavy loans to the property sector, high interest rates to attract deposits, and a liquidity ratio which declined from 60% in the mid-1950s to 40% in 1964 (the Hongkong Bank's ratio at the time was only 32.5%). Other

---

[h] For a more detailed account, see Y.P. Ngan, 'Hang Seng Bank Limited: a Brief History', in King, ed. *Eastern Banking* (London, 1983), pp. 709–16.

local banks had followed similar practices, the Hang Seng being differentiated from them by the soundness of its lending policies, subject only to the proviso that confidence in the local banking sector in general and in Hang Seng in particular be not undermined.

The banking crisis of February 1965

Unfortunately in January 1965 the Ming Tak Bank closed its doors and was found on examination to be not only illiquid but also insolvent. On February 6, 1965, there was a run on the Canton Trust and Commercial Bank's Aberdeen branch; the Hongkong Bank was understood to have offered unlimited support, but this proved premature and conditional. The Hongkong Bank sent in its internal audit team and its findings led to a denial of assistance; the bank then closed its doors. There followed runs on leading local banks including Hang Seng.

The runs continued and emergency Bank Control Regulations (9 February 1965) were issued, Bank of England notes declared a legal tender (but Bank of England notes did not in fact have to be issued), and cash withdrawals limited. The Hongkong Bank, based on its knowledge of Hang Seng's long-run position and its immediate problems as revealed in the clearings, was able to pledge publicly full and unlimited support to Hang Seng; Saunders informed Lee, Hang Seng's deputy general manager, that he could safely make the pledge without examining the bank's books. The Government was equally anxious that Hang Seng remain open and had quietly informed the Hongkong Bank they would counter-guarantee their aid. Then, together with the Chartered Bank, the Hongkong Bank undertook to support several specified local banks facing a similar liquidity crisis.[1] By February 16 the more obvious manifestations of this crisis were over and the emergency regulations withdrawn.

One of the important factors in the restoration of confidence had been the Hongkong Bank's pledge of assistance not only to Hang Seng but also to the Far East Bank and to Wing Lung Bank. Responsibility for the Far East Bank was taken over by Citibank in 1969. Meanwhile, the Chartered Bank had pledged similar support to the Dao Heng and Kwong On banks. The history of Hang Seng was, however, to take a peculiar turn.

The April crisis

For the Hang Seng Bank the crisis was continuing – quietly. As Q.W. Lee put it, '...in March slowly, slowly we felt that we were losing blood, drop, drop, every drop.' By April the bank had lost $250 million of its $500 million deposits. But the drain continued. There were hundreds of depositors, their

---

[1] An account of the several banking crises is found in Y.C. Jao, *Banking and Currency in Hong Kong, a Study of Postwar Financial Development* (London, 1974), Chapter 9.

fears fanned by rumours the origins of which a subsequent police investigation was unable to identify definitively, standing quietly in queues which extended along Des Voeux Road almost to the Hong Kong Club on the east side of the Statue Square area. Lee came to R.G.L. Oliphant, then Deputy (and acting) Chief Manager of the Hongkong Bank, with property deeds worth $100 million; the Bank advanced funds against this security. A Hongkong Bank officer sat in Hang Seng's main banking hall as visible evidence that funds were being made available. Furthermore the Hongkong Bank received full media support in advertising its determination to assist Hang Seng. But both sides knew that this represented the last assistance which could be offered on a routine, commercial basis.

As the crisis continued the bankers met again, but it was becoming increasingly clear to Oliphant that, as Hang Seng's negotiable assets became pledged, the next step was the acquisition of a majority of Hang Seng's equity.

Despite the Hongkong and Chartered Banks' actions, the banking system was not in a position to weather another shock. The failure of two badly managed and under-capitalized local banks had sent the system into crisis; the failure of a leading local bank, which had been known generally for its sound management and which was in fact both solvent and reasonably liquid, would, bankers then felt, have undermined the whole system and endangered the economy. Both the Hongkong Bank and Hang Seng were operating with this in mind; they also knew that once depositors had lost confidence and were determined to remove their funds, no liquidity ratio short of 100% was adequate.

Hang Seng's decision

The Hongkong Bank's reiterated statements failed to reassure depositors. On April 5, Hang Seng lost $80 million. The Hang Seng directors reassessed their position. They had received a cable from Chase Bank in New York offering assistance – on unstated conditions. But it was known that Chase, who had left Hong Kong precipitously in 1949, wanted back now that the economy was developing. With the banking licence moratorium in effect, Chase could come back only by buying into or taking over a bank already operating in the Colony. Hang Seng could therefore accept Chase's unspecified offer, close their doors, or ask the Hongkong Bank to take them over. On April 7, after a series of discussions, the directors agreed to (i) calm themselves down, (ii) sleep well, and (iii) decide quietly very early the next day.

On April 8 the directors rejected Chase as an American bank, refused to close the doors of their bank as an irretrievable loss of face, and determined, subject to Government approval, to offer their bank to the Hongkong Bank, because, as Q.W. Lee has put it, it was the Bank of Hong Kong.

In the morning of April 9, after speaking to the Financial Secretary, (Sir)

John Cowperthwaite, who gave his blessing to the proposal, Lee went to Oliphant with an offer from Hang Seng's directors for the Hongkong Bank to acquire a majority interest in Hang Seng.

There were now only two questions to settle: (i) the proportion of the equity to be acquired and (ii) the price. On both points there were, however, serious differences of opinion. Oliphant for the Hongkong Bank insisted on acquiring 76% of the equity capital and he valued Hang Seng at $67 million. Hang Seng insisted they would only sell 51% and that the Bank should be valued at $100 million. Hang Seng won both points.

The equity question was important because the Hongkong Bank wanted to be able to change the articles of association to ensure that management was clearly vested in the seven managing directors. This required favourable votes representing 76% of the shares. Ho surmounted this problem by authorizing the Hongkong Bank to vote the additional shares without actually purchasing them.

The second question could have held up the deal; one day is not long to resolve such differences had not the stakes been high and the circumstances fortuitous. Oliphant argued that if the Hongkong Bank did not take over Hang Seng, the latter would be worth much less than even the $67 million being offered by the Bank; Lee countered that if Hang Seng went under, the whole banking system, including the Hongkong Bank, would be endangered. This exchange of challenges was rationalized by an appeal to the accountants, an appeal facilitated by the fact that both banks employed the same auditors and Hang Seng had been recently audited. The real difference in Oliphant's and Lee's assessments was revealed in part as a difference in dates, with the Hang Seng's auditor team successfully arguing Lee's position.

Discussions in fact continued to nearly midnight, but that night an agreement for the Bank's acquisition of a majority interest was reached in principle. The Government's information office had been kept open; the press release was run off and by morning the problem as it concerned the banking public had evaporated.

Saunders' objections and the outcome
As it happened the Chief Manager of the Hongkong Bank was away from Hong Kong, and Oliphant, having cleared the decision with each of the Bank's directors, contacted Saunders by telephone; he was strongly opposed to any proposal to take over a 'Chinese bank'. There were several factors in Saunders' thinking: (i) despite the modern approach of the Hang Seng's management, its success had depended on its being Chinese, and Saunders felt that the Hongkong Bank could not manage a Chinese bank, (ii) Hang Seng was closely involved with Macau and the gold market, which, at some point, might reveal

China Mainland contacts sufficient to provoke American authorities to act against Hang Seng and, if the acquisition went through, the Hongkong Bank, and (iii) the success of Hang Seng had made it a formidable competitor of the Hongkong Bank; its acquisition would be seen as the act of a competitor taking unfair advantage in an emergency situation.

Despite the cogency of his objections, he was faced with the unanimous contrary views of his deputies in Hong Kong, with the approval of the Bank's Board, and with the agreement of the Financial Secretary; the transaction was effective on April 12, 1965.

Saunders did not argue his position fully on the telephone. He merely expressed his surprise at developments, his dislike of the action proposed, and his agreement that the officer on the scene must make the decision. As Knightly reported the conversation,

...he was absolutely shaken to the core. He'd heard there was a run on the Hang Seng Bank, but the idea that we should make a bid for it shook him to the core, and he was very doubtful about all this.
We said, it's the only thing to do.
He said, well, if you characters are certain that this is the only way to save the day, all right; it's on your head, you do it.

Saunders' first objection was in fact easily handled. The Hongkong Bank didn't have to run a Chinese bank; they only agreed to the take-over because they had faith in the ability of the Hang Seng management. Instead, they appointed nominees to the Board and then, after the initial few weeks, refrained from interfering. The initial post-acquisition board consisted of the seven managing directors—S.H. Ho, Ho Tim, (Sir) Q.W. Lee, Knightly, Carruthers, Maurice W. Turner, and Hutson—and the eleven other then existing directors. The Board subsequently invited two Chinese businessmen, Lau Chan Kwok and Hui Sai Fun, to broaden the representation. They were resolute in their determination to manage Hang Seng Bank, to restore the bank's position and to forge ahead. It was S.H. Ho who had had the courage to 'think the unthinkable' and recommend the offer to the Hongkong Bank. To realize the opportunities for the future which he had, through the Hongkong Bank, now secured, Ho chaired a meeting of all his staff members on April 12 at which he successfully encouraged them to continue their support.

The second problem never arose.

The third was correctly foreseen by Saunders; naturally adverse comments on the Hongkong Bank's actions would be made, and although ill-informed and irrelevant they were sufficient to suggest that Hongkong Bankers' skins were not as thick as they pretended. Certainly events were to prove that the Bank had made a profitable investment; Hang Seng's published profits rose from $38 million in 1970 to $437 million in 1980. Hang Seng went public in 1972 with a capitalization and a rights issue (to which the Hongkong Bank subscribed). Although Hang Seng originally planned to place only 5% of the issued capital, Sayer insisted on 10%. His consequent offer to make a market proved unnecessary—the issue was 29 times over-subscribed. By 1979 the Hongkong Bank had acquired an additional 11% of Hang Seng's shares privately. This accomplished two purposes: (i) the Bank prevented a large shareholding from coming onto a particularly weak market and (ii) persistent but ill-founded speculation that the Bank might sell its controlling interest in Hang Seng was abandoned. Hang Seng's estimated contribution to total consolidated Hongkong Bank Group's profits on this basis was 17.6% (in contrast to the Hongkong Bank's 46.3%).

The acquisition decision and the price had been reached, however, in different circumstances in April 1965.

DEVELOPMENTS, 1972–1979

A survey

The five years of Guy Sayer's leadership were ones of consolidation. Following the appointment of Michael Sandberg as Chairman of The Hongkong and Shanghai Banking Corporation in 1977, certain developments, planned in some cases earlier, become operational. The story of the Hongkong Bank Group is therefore taken in this section to the eve of the acquisition of Marine Midland Banks, Inc. (MMBI). The chronological changes are explained below bringing the story up to Sayer's retirement in 1977; the position in that year is found in Table 15.7, and the few changes from then through 1979 are then described. The actual position at the end of 1979 is found in Table 15.12, and reference to this table will facilitate understanding of the details which follow.

The existence of identifiable 'groups', either functional (Wardley Limited) or geographical (Wardley Canada), suggest that in this context an examination of the Hongkong Bank Group through these 'groups' is preferable to the chronological approach – although one or two companies will perforce be neglected.

One new factor in the proliferation of companies within the Hongkong Bank Group was consequent to the requirement not only that financial institutions be locally incorporated but also that a certain proportion of the shares, usually 50% or more, be owned by local citizens. This could result in the main bank (Hongkong Bank, Mercantile Bank, or BBME) continuing to operate under restrictions but with a management contract to assist in the development of a new local commercial bank organized as an associated company. This explains, for example, the 1970 establishment of the Bank of Kuwait and the Middle East

III. Policy, development, and performance

at the end of the BBME's exclusive banking arrangement with Kuwait, and, in 1978, of the Saudi British Bank, 40% owned by the British Bank of the Middle East (BBME).[j]

Another factor to note is the use of holding companies. This can be an effective way of grouping several specialized companies of the same type, insurance, for example. In certain countries HSBC might have a finance company and a branch of the Hongkong Bank. By subordinating the finance company to a separate holding company, Kellett Investments Ltd, for example, the activities of the two operating offices could be kept separate; this might be useful for tax purposes. The 'downstreaming' of dividends through holding companies is useful for holding profits in low tax jurisdictions or for diluting the taxable proportion of income received. In some cases such arrangements make the entire operation feasible; they are in fact the essential element in the profitability of an acquisition. In the 1950s tax considerations, as agreed with the relevant authorities, were important factors in the determination of the terms and circumstances relative to the acquisition of the Mercantile Bank and the BBME; such factors became even more important in subsequent years.

A study of the lists in the several tables will reveal 'drop-outs'. Some of the early associations, which seemed significant mainly for their signalling a new role for the Group, did not flourish. Bowmaker (C.A.) paid no dividend after 1967 and only ten years later was the Bank able to be rid of the problem but with a probable loss of $3 million. In 1974 the Bank initiated attempts to sell its interest in RoyWest Banking Corporation; a year later it did so. The Exporters Refinance Corporation (over 75% now held by Lloyds) turned sour in mid-1971 as the Bank, with only an 8.125% equity holding, was planning to sell out; the eventual cost to the Bank was £852,000. Other companies (or names) dropped from the list as a consequence of reorganization or as the Bank's interests changed.

There were other factors causing changes in the characteristics and composition of the Hongkong Bank Group. For example, the ICB became a public company to meet German requirements prior to obtaining long-term Deutschmark financing at a fixed rate of interest. The small investment in the Dutch bank Hope and Co. became insignificant when that bank merged first to become part of the Mees and Hope Group and then with the Algemene Bank; the HSBC eventually sold its 0.45% of the equity. The Bank of Iran and the Middle East, an associated company of the BBME and HSBC (17.5% plus 17.5%), was nationalized in June 1979. There were also changes in the names

---

[j] The time sequence might be reversed, as in the case of Hongkong Bank Group activities in Australia and Canada, where commercial banking had to await legislative changes. Or the Group might take an equity position in a new merchant bank, for example, Korea International Merchant Bank, and later decide to operate a commercial banking office if the laws permitted – the Hongkong Bank opened two branches in the Republic of Korea: Busan in 1983 and in Seoul (where the Hongkong Bank already had a Representative Office) in 1985.

of several companies, usually for purposes of Group identification consistency, for example, in May 1979 'Far East Data Services' was renamed 'Wardley Data Services' – the company was, after all, a 100% subsidiary of Wardley Limited.

Selected principal developments are covered in outline below.

Hutchison International

One dramatic development was the Hongkong Bank's purchase in 1975 of 150 million new shares at par of $0.20 thus obtaining the basis for the Bank's maximum involvement of 33.65% and a controlling stake in its long-standing constituent, Hutchison International. The company had been developed through the 1960s by the dynamic Col Douglas Clague, sometime Deputy Chairman of the Hongkong Bank. Clague was one of the more colourful figures of post-war Hong Kong industrialization; Hutchison's was a major debtor of the Bank, and there had been considerable internal criticism within both Head Office and Hong Kong office of the piecemeal methods by which Hutchison's credit-worthiness was being assessed. Expansion immediately following the 1966 disturbances proved random and opportunistic, and in the 1974/75 slump the conglomerate faced a negative cash flow and a consequent inability to service its debts. By mid-1975 the Hongkong Bank recognized the urgent need to protect its interests.

An obvious solution appeared to be a rights issue advised by Wardley, but at the last moment Wardley were unable to clear the prospectus; they encountered unexplained problems. Furthermore, although this would have solved the financial position for a time, Hutchison's problems stemmed from a management which would have been left virtually in place. Hutchison's, the Governor of Hong Kong confirmed to the Bank, was too important a company to let go at such a time, and the Bank determined to mount a Bank-controlled rescue operation. The Bank would in effect buy the shares which would have been offered as a public rights issue, thus turning debt to equity and at the same time obtaining control on terms which eventually included the provision that Clague step down from the chairmanship of his own board. Over the continued opposition of Clague, who understandably sought to retain ultimate control and who was seeking alternative sources of finance on terms which Sayer considered would have endangered the Bank's position as major creditor, the Bank moved firmly and, with Hutchison shareholder approval, the new shares were issued and bought, the alternative and still potential rights issue was disapproved, and the Bank's nominee, W. Wyllie, subsequently installed. Clague's behaviour had worried Sayer and in October Clague, under pressure, stepped down as Deputy Chairman of the Bank and declared his intention of retiring from the Board

Table 15.7 *The Hongkong Bank Group*
List of principal companies, 1977

A. Subsidiary companies:
The British Bank of the Middle East
Mercantile Bank Limited
The Hongkong Bank of California
Hang Seng Bank Limited
Mortgage And Finance (Malaysia) Berhad
Wardley Australia Limited
Wardley Limited
Wayfoong Finance Limited
Wayfoong Mortgage and Finance (Singapore) Limited
Wayhong Investment Limited
BC Facilities Limited, United Kingdom
99 Bishopsgate Limited, New Hebrides
The British Bank of the Lebanon, SAL
Carlingford Investments Limited, United Kingdom
Carlingford NH Limited
Far East Data Services Limited, Hong Kong
Gatechurch Property Management Limited, United Kingdom
Hang Seng Finance Limited, Hong Kong
Hang Tung Travel Service Limited, Hong Kong
Hongkong Bank Serviços Limitada, Brazil
Hongkong Finance Limited, Australia
The Hongkong and Shanghai Banking Corporation (CI) Limited
Hong Kong Middle East Holdings Limited, Hong Kong
Kellett (New Hebrides) Limited
Kellett Investments Limited, Hong Kong
MetWay Limited, Hong Kong
The Middle East Finance Company Limited, Dubai
Mortgage And Finance Limited, Brunei
Mortgage And Finance (Malaysia) Berhad
Perpetual Publicity Limited, Hong Kong
Pittencrieff Investments Limited, Hong Kong
Société Immobilière Atlas, Switzerland
Stanbridge Limited, New Hebrides
Wardley Australia Limited
Wardley Canada Limited
The Wardley Corporation, USA
Wardley (Exchange) Limited, Hong Kong
Wardley Finance (Thailand) Limited
Wardley Gibbs Limited, Hong Kong
Wardley Gibbs Agencies Limited, Hong Kong
Wardley Insurance Company Limited, Hong Kong
Wardley International Management Limited, Hong Kong
Wardley Investment Services Limited, Hong Kong
Wardley Investments Canada Limited
Wardley Investments Limited, New Hebrides
Wardley Investments (NZ) Limited

Table 15.7 (*cont.*)

Subsidiary companies: (continued)
Wardley Limited, Hong Kong
Wardley Middle East Limited
Wardley Securities Limited, Hong Kong
Wardley Services (New Hebrides) Limited
Wardley (Vila) Limited
Wayfoong Credit Limited, Hong Kong
Wayfoong Finance Limited, Hong Kong
Wayfoong Investments Limited, Hong Kong
Wayfoong Mortgage and Finance (Singapore) Limited
Wayhong Holdings Limited, New Hebrides
Wayhong Investment Limited, Hong Kong
Wayhong NH Limited, New Hebrides
Wayhong Properties Limited, New Hebrides

B. **Associated companies:**
Associated Bankers Insurance Company Limited, Hong Kong
The Bank of Iran and the Middle East
Banking Computer Services Private Limited, Singapore
Benteng Redevelopment Sdn Bhd, Malaysia
Cannae Limited, Hong Kong
Cathay Pacific Airways Limited, Hong Kong
Central Registration Hong Kong Limited
Commercial Discount Company Limited, Singapore
Cross Harbour Tunnel Company Limited, Hong Kong
Eastern Asia Navigation Company Limited
Antony Gibbs Holdings Limited, United Kingdom
Hongkong Fintracon Limited
Hongkong & New Zealand Properties Limited, New Hebrides
Hongkong and Shanghai Thomas Cook Limited
Hutchison International Limited, Hong Kong
International Commercial Bank Limited, United Kingdom
Mercantile Credits Limited, Australia
NZI Financial Corporation Limited, New Zealand
Ocean Properties Private Limited, Singapore
Ormskirk Company Limited, Hong Kong
Real Property Leases Limited, Australia
Sharps Pixley Wardley Limited, Hong Kong
South China Morning Post Limited, Hong Kong
UDA Merchant Bankers Berhad, Malaysia
Wardley Nikko Management Limited, Hong Kong
Wardley Swire Assurance Limited, Hong Kong
WHS Investments Limited, Hong Kong
Woodhall Company Limited, Hong Kong
World Finance International Limited, Bermuda
World Maritime Limited, Bermuda
World Shipping and Investment Limited, Hong Kong

Source: 1976 *Annual Report*, March 1977.

effective at the next general annual meeting. Nevertheless at the March 1976 meeting Sayer was able to stress the positive and give credit to Clague's 'very valuable contribution...during a period of great change...and not the least for the interest he has shown in the well-being of the staff'. Later he would comment, 'I like old Duggie Clague; he was a buccaneer.'

Wyllie was successful in achieving a turn-around. In a 1977 merger with a subsidiary, Hong Kong and Whampoa Dock Company, Hutchison's became 'Hutchison Whampoa', and the Bank's shareholding was in consequence diluted to 22%. Then in 1979 the Bank sold its 90 million ordinary shares to a wholly owned subsidiary of Li Ka Shing's Cheung Kong (Holdings) Ltd for a consideration of $639 million, a price criticized at the time for being less than their true worth. The sale nevertheless resulted in a profit to the Hongkong Bank of $517.6 million, the whole of which was transferred, as an extraordinary profit, to inner reserves.

These events, although of great importance in Hong Kong, were not part of the long-run growth of the Group. The equity investment had been temporary, in the tradition of previous Bank rescue operations.

Merchant banking

Wardley Limited
Of greater long-term importance was the creation in 1973 of a separate 100% owned subsidiary merchant bank, Wardley Limited, with Michael Sandberg as the first Chairman and R.H.L. Bacon as Managing Director. The Hongkong Bank had traditionally operated as both a commercial and a merchant bank, its role in the management of China, Japan, Philippine, and Siamese bond issues having been discussed in Volumes II and III of this history. In 1961, during a brief period of new public issues in Hong Kong, the Bank had played its normal dual role; this was renewed as activity developed following the 'Red Guard depression'.

In the early 1970s the Bank, however, now faced rivals.

Surprisingly, the first formal Hong Kong-based competition came from Jardine's with the formation of a joint-venture merchant bank, Jardine Fleming. Despite the apparent conflict of interest consequent to this development and Saunders' warning of the consequences, H.N.L. Keswick, Jardine's representative on the Bank's Board of Directors, was not asked to resign, presumably because Jardine's participation on the commercial level was considered a sufficient offset. This decision reflects Hong Kong's interlocking interests better than it does the theory of business principles; in a dynamic economy, old loyalties were bound to be strained, but pragmatism remained dominant.

The Hongkong Bank responded to an increased activity in Hong Kong company formation with the development of a specialized section within Hong Kong Main Office, that is, within the principal commercial banking office in the territory (as distinct from Hong Kong office, now differentiated as the management office for all commercial banking offices in the territory); this 'group' was transferred with Sandberg when he became Manager Hong Kong; it became a separate department within Hong Kong office.

The position was studied by Derek McLennon, a managing director of Baring Bros; Bacon and others worked with McLennon developing the Hongkong Bank's expertise. An internal department did not meet the Bank's needs. Separate companies were required for separate financial activities, and Wardley Limited was accordingly incorporated with a paid-up capital of $100 million; at the end of 1974 shareholders' funds were $105 million, total assets $1,081 million, and net profit for the year $773,000. Wardley's capital was increased by $59 million in 1975. Hongkong Bankers were still not in command of investment portfolio management techniques, nor could they acquire the expertise with sufficient speed; consequently Wardley formed Wardley Vickers Ltd, with Vickers, da Costa and Co. holding 40% of the equity. Bacon was again involved, this time with A.C.R. Chappell and K.A. Miller.

As a Hong Kong 'deposit-taking' company, Wardley Limited's main source of funds was customers' deposits. Uses of funds were varied: in 1975 Wardley organized the first syndicated Hong Kong dollar facility for the Mass Transit Railway for $500 million for seven years; for the same customer Wardley acted as manager of the first bond issue offered to the public in Hong Kong dollars – a ten-year issue of $400 million, thus being instrumental in the establishment of a visible market for fixed income securities denominated in the local currency. Other firsts for the Group's Hong Kong merchant bank are (i) a syndicated loan for US$55 million in the name of the Republic of Indonesia, (ii) the first syndicated loan for a Burmese borrower – the Myanma Oil Corporation of US$38.75 million co-managed by Chase Manhattan Asia, Ltd, and (iii) the first Eurodollar loan in which the Government of India was directly involved – US$50 million in 1977 for the Oil and Natural Gas Commission. In 1979 Wardley Limited pioneered with the issuance of the first certificates of deposit denominated in Hong Kong dollars; this should be considered a step in the path to Hong Kong's developing status as a major world financial centre.

At the end of 1979 Wardley Limited's total sources of funds were $5,515 million, of which 85% were from 'Customers' Deposits and other accounts'. During the year issued and paid-up capital was increased from $125 million to $250 million; the new shares were sold to the parent company, the HSBC, at a 60% premium. Wardley Limited was particularly liquid (58%), indicating inadequate loan margins during the year and the consequent difficulty in placing the new funds received; uses of funds included 'Loans, Advances and other accounts' of $2,054 million (37%). In 1980 Wardley Limited accounted for 7.2% of the Group's consolidated profits.

Wardley Limited had direct equity investment in and control of 20 subsidiary and one associated company and through these in a further 27 companies. This number reflects the decision to create separate companies (i) in each of several countries, (ii) for specific functions, for example, bullion dealing (Sharps Pixley Wardley)[k], (iii) for investment funds managed by Wardley Investment Services, (iv) service companies, for example, Wardley Data Services, and (v) holding and dormant companies.

Wardley was established originally in Hong Kong to serve as the Hongkong Bank's merchant bank, but the need for merchant banking services and their separation from commercial banking operations developed elsewhere. Consequently there were three categories of development: (i) through Wardley Limited's own expansion, (ii) through the formation of a company not subsidiary to Wardley Limited – with or without 'Wardley' in the name, for example, Wardley Investments (NZ), Resources and Investment Finance – or (iii) through acquisition of a company which either was itself a merchant bank or which had a merchant bank subsidiary, for example, Antony Gibbs. Wardley's itself established subsidiaries, for example the Wardley International Bank Ltd in the Bahamas, or associates, the State Investment House of the Philippines (25% through Wardley [Vila]),[1] branches or representative offices (Manila, for example) overseas; Wardley's also had a management involvement in HSBC's two directly held merchant bank joint ventures (associated companies), in South Korea, 1978, the Korea International Merchant Bank (30%, with the Korea Exchange Bank 40%, Commerzbank AG 20%, and Korea Development Bank 10%) and in Papua New Guinea, Resources and Investment Finance (33.3%).

Wardley Canada and Antony Gibbs

Although after 1977 Sandberg as the HSBC's new chief executive officer was beginning a policy of a more centralized control and in 1979 had authorized Wardley Limited's acquisition of Wardley Australia, the process was far from complete; the Hongkong Bank Group's merchant banking activities were not under the single leadership of Wardley Limited, even though, as noted, the

---

[k] This joint venture of the Hongkong Bank, Hang Seng, and Wardley with the Kleinwort Benson Group was established in 1976. In 1983 Sharps Pixley bought back the 49% HSBC investment and became Sharps Pixley Pacific Ltd.

[1] This company itself established a Hong Kong branch in 1978 as a Hong Kong registered 100% subsidiary, under which in turn operated SIH (Vila) and State Leasing; Tenix was a 100% Hong Kong registered subsidiary of SIH (Vila).

name 'Wardley' was in some cases nevertheless used in the company title. The reasons for this were partly historical, as in the case of the particular development of the Group's investments in Canada, and partly necessitated by circumstances, as in the case of Antony Gibbs, a long-established merchant bank in which the Hongkong Bank Group at this time still held but 40% of the equity. The BBME had continued to operate under its own London board; its merchant bank, although entitled 'Wardley Middle East', was a 20% associate of the BBME and an 80% directly held subsidiary of HSBC – a situation reflecting the reluctance of BBME management to move into merchant banking; this was one factor in the frustration existing in the relations between the holding company, HSBC, and the operating bank, BBME.

Wardley Investments Canada was a 100% owned subsidiary of HSBC acting as the holding company for the Hongkong Bank Group's Canadian activities through Wardley Canada, which had replaced the now dormant 'British Acceptance Corporation' as the operating company. This is in contrast to the troublesome Australian situation, where in 1979 Wardley Australia (Holdings) became a 100% owned subsidiary of Wardley Limited, and Hongkong Finance Limited became the main subsidiary operating company under the name of 'Wardley Australia' after the 1978 sale of the Group's interest in Mercantile Credits.

Furthermore and as noted above, at the end of 1979 the HSBC held a 40% interest in Antony Gibbs Holdings and through this an involvement in 78 directly or indirectly held subsidiary and associated companies (fifteen of which were dormant or in liquidation). This was one collection which required Macdonald's explanation before the Congressional sub-committee; it included project companies far removed from financial activities, for example, movies, which were consequent to investment problems but which appeared to confirm accusations of *ad hoc* acquisition.

The Antony Gibbs Group

As the Hongkong Bank's chief executive learned in the late 1950s the desire to diversify may be frustrated by the lack of opportunity to diversify. Timing is often the issue; an appropriate company must be ready for acquisition (or lesser degree of association) when the Hongkong Bank is in a position to take advantage of the opportunity. Thus when Antony Gibbs Holdings Ltd, the principal firm of a Group which can trace its history back through Antony Gibbs and Sons at least to 1808, went public in 1972 and family-held shares became available, Sayer sent Sandberg, then responsible for the Hong Kong office's merchant banking department, Eric Udal, the legal adviser, and John Bray, Director of Internal Audit, to report on the prospects. They recommended involvement and the Bank of England permitted the Hongkong

Bank, as a British overseas bank, to invest beyond the then limitation of 15% for 'non-British' banks; at the time this was seen as an indication of the Bank's status in the City. In June 1973 HSBC had 20% and by 1974 40% of the shares of Antony Gibbs Holdings financed through newly issued Hongkong Bank shares. The Bank was at last using its premium-priced paper to acquire new assets.

The investment did not prove trouble-free. When a merchant bank goes public, it is time to be careful. Antony Gibbs had been in trouble, the Bank of England were concerned and advised new management; accordingly Sir Philip de Zulueta became the chief executive and the Hongkong Bank came in hoping to help 'turn it around'. Sandberg was soon to learn that this would be difficult. Neither the customers nor the staff were there to achieve the Bank's purpose. For a time the banking side was managed by J.W.L. Howard, retired executive Deputy Chairman of the Hongkong Bank. But in the end there would be but one solution; in 1980 HSBC acquired the entire equity of the company prior to a thorough reorganization in which the very name 'Antony Gibbs' was lost.

The Hongkong Bank had needed a merchant banking presence in London. In Hong Kong merchant banking could no longer be contained within the Bank's own Hong Kong office. Even in the days when Sir Ewen Cameron and Sir Charles Addis operated as career executives of the Eastern staff within London Office and Julius Brüssel assisted from Hamburg, the large bonuses voted these 'merchant bankers' suggested that the tasks lay outside the usual expertise of commercial and exchange bankers. In Hong Kong the Bank had brought out an adviser from Baring's and developed in-house with Sandberg and Bacon. In London to begin *de novo* was impractical.

And yet the task of finding a suitable London associate was not an easy one. The Bank's BBME connection ruled out Jewish-dominated houses. Antony Gibbs was seen as an old and respected name; it was willing to grant an equity participation without reciprocity; it would cooperate with the Hongkong Bank Group without intrusion into the Bank's Eastern affairs; the independent status of Antony Gibbs would leave intact the Bank's existing business relationships; and the chief executive, Sir Philip de Zulueta, was highly recommended. These factors led the Board to approve Sayer's recommendation to accept the report of his appraisal team; the equity participation was authorized.

Many of the advantages Sandberg predicted seem realized. Furthermore in the initial agreement, Antony Gibbs agreed to provide training facilities for Hongkong Bankers. It was not their performance or the quality of their management which had been the sole consideration. The Antony Gibbs Group would, it was hoped, provide the Hongkong Bank Group 'presence' and 'access'. The price, however, proved high.

The holding company itself had maintained more of the traditional merchanting activities than most Accepting Houses; it was a member in London of both the Accepting Houses Committee and the Issuing Houses Association. Through the wholly owned subsidiary Antony Gibbs and Sons, Limited, the HSBC found itself with a fully operating merchant bank in all the traditions of the City – and with an international network of associations based on London. Thus it complemented rather than competed with the HSBC's expanding merchant bank operations centred on Hong Kong.

The relationship with Antony Gibbs was also the Hongkong Bank Group's first international contact with an interestingly neglected financial activity, insurance – Hang Seng already had insurance contacts (see below). Antony Gibbs, Sage Limited – an existing amalgamation of Antony Gibbs & Sons (Insurance) Ltd and Lionel Sage and Co. Ltd – brought the Hongkong Bank Group, through its broker at Lloyd's, into the world insurance market. Gibbs Nathaniel Ltd, a merging of long-established dealing and broking houses, held seats in many of the world's leading commodity markets; sugar, coffee, cocoa, and metals were traded in London, Paris, and New York. From this base the firm had branched out with a food division which handled food imports and repackaging for export.

Antony Gibbs also provided geographical access. Its important presence in Australia was through Gibbs Bright Holdings Pty Ltd, and through that to various projects, especially in timber. In Latin America, Gibbs y Cia S.A.C. Representaciones, was a merchant house, an insurance agent for Lloyd's and several insurance companies, and had industrial interests all based in Chile. Through this company there was access to Bolivia and the 50% owned Gibbs Williamson (Bolivia). In Canada the Antony Gibbs Group operated through Gibbs Nathaniel (Canada). In the important Swiss financial market, Antony Gibbs Holdings (with Electra Investment Trust and the Hongkong Bank's long-time friends, Panmure Gordon and Co.) had a joint interest in the Société Financière Privée, a Geneva portfolio management company specializing in investment monitoring services. Antony Gibbs was itself involved in financial investment through Antony Gibbs Unit Trust Managers.

The relationship of these various enterprises as they affected the Hongkong Bank Group can be seen in Table 15.12. There would be rationalization and eventual take-over, but during the formative 1970s the Antony Gibbs Group provided a broad though imperfect instrument whereby the regional image of the Hongkong Bank Group was modified; it provided a window to both Britain and Latin America.

Insurance

The concept of the Hongkong Bank as the creature of the Hong Kong merchant hongs was slow in dying. In 1864 there were hongs reluctant to give up banking to a Hong Kong based bank; in the early days of the China loans, members of the Board of Directors were in direct though ineffective competition with the Bank, and even after joining the Bank's Board of Directors Jardine's continued to aspire to a merchant banking role on the China coast. These same hongs were also involved in shipping and insurance. When in 1964 the Hongkong Bank took an equity interest in Y.K. Pao's operations, there would seem to have been no objection; the suggestion that the Bank should move into insurance was, however, another matter. Jardine Matheson's representative on the Board was opposed; the Bank which the merchants had created seemed to be competing with those very merchants for business.

This was a wholly unacceptable position in the early 1970s; the Bank had outgrown the tutelege of its founders long ago. If it had not been a competitive threat before, it was because, as Turner had put it, a banker sticks to his last. But then Turner was involved with problems enough. With the acceptance of specialized companies and specialized Bank officers, of a broader definition in most jurisdictions of the legitimate activities of a bank or bank holding company to include the whole spectrum of financial services, the Hongkong Bank's hesitancy in entering into insurance was inconsistent with its declared intention of diversification of financial product and area. The restraining hand of Jardine's, meriting attention only in Hong Kong's historical context, could not long remain effective, once a real opportunity arose.

The HSBC were in fact in insurance through Hang Seng's 20% held associated company, Associated Bankers Insurance, and through the various insurance activities of Antony Gibbs. But this was passive participation in the activities of companies over which the Hongkong Bank did not then attempt to exercise any direct management control. In 1973 the Board agreed that the Bank should have its own insurance company, but with the understanding that reinsurance would be effected through those companies with which the Bank was then doing business. When virtually within months insurance became an integral part of the Hongkong Bank Group's activities, the business expanded rapidly and the line of control moved through one or more of the following: (i) Hang Seng, (ii) Antony Gibbs Holdings, (iii) Mico Equities Inc., as well as through (iv) the Hongkong Bank's own holding companies (see Figure 15.1).

The number of Hongkong Bank Group insurance companies reflects in part the corporation's passive entrance into this particular activity and the attempt to rationalize through holding companies, the need once again for incorporation

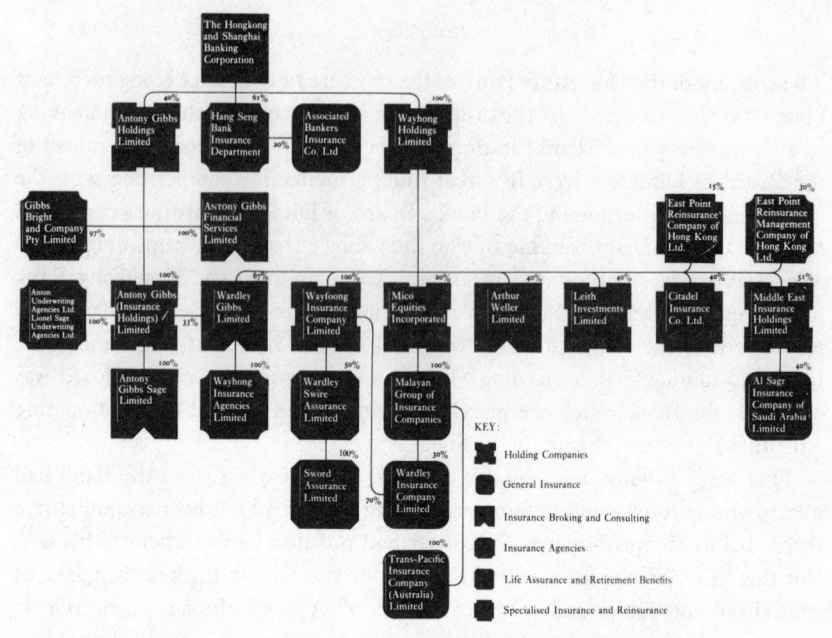

Figure 15.1 The Hongkong and Shanghai Banking Corporation
Family tree of insurance interests

by country, and the separate categories within the insurance business – brokers, life assurance, reinsurance, etc. – which reinforced the tendency to specialization by company.

The first insurance company directly under the control of HSBC was Wardley Gibbs Ltd, insurance consultants and brokers, in 1975. In the 1980s the Hongkong Bank Group has used the name 'Carlingford' to designate insurance, as 'Wardley' now refers to merchant banking. In the 1970s names were not used consistently. 'Wardley Gibbs' itself is an example, but there were others. The HSBC operated its insurance companies through Wayhong Holdings, a 100% subsidiary, directly to Wardley Gibbs (67%); another line of control moved to Antony Gibbs Holdings (40%), to a second-tier holding company, Antony Gibbs (Insurance Holdings) (100%), and then to Wardley Gibbs (33%).

In 1976 HSBC joined with the Swire Group to form Wardley Swire Assurance (now Carlingford Swire), which provides life assurance systems for funding retirement benefits for Hong Kong employers. This was also held through Wayhong Holdings then through a second-tier holding company, Wayfoong Insurance, to Wardley Swire. The picture was further complicated

III. Policy, development, and performance

– but virtually completed – when in 1977 HSBC obtained a 20% interest in a Malayan Group of companies, through Mico Equities Inc., incorporated in the Philippines. There were then two links to a new company, Wardley Insurance, which issued all types of policies, other than life insurance. The line came down from HSBC to Wayhong Holdings and then split: (i) through Wayfoong Insurance (100%) to Wardley Insurance (70%) and (ii) through Mico Equities (20%) to the Malayan Group (100%) to Wardley Insurance (30%). The corporation's insurance activities in Australia were handled through Wayhong Holdings to Arthur Weller (40%), to Arthur Weller Holdings NV and Arthur Weller Australia Pty.

At the end of 1978 this structure was in place and the Bank's direct investment in insurance ventures provided services in the open market to an extent of $42.7 million.

The final developments in the 1970s included the development of reinsurance through Wayhong Holdings' equity involvement in East Point Reinsurance Company of Hong Kong (with, as the name implies, Jardine Matheson) (15%) and related companies, and entry into the Middle East through Wayhong Holdings, Middle East Insurance Holdings (51%), and Al Sagr Insurance Company of Saudi Arabia (40%).

Finance companies – the Wayfoong Finance Group

The founding of Wayfoong Finance in 1960 was designed primarily to finance hire-purchase and the company was incorporated as a bank, subject to the interest rate rules of the Hong Kong Association of Banks. The legal question was raised as to whether a bank could be involved in hire-purchase; for this and other reasons, a subsidiary of Wayfoong Finance was formed in 1973 and named 'Wayfoong Credit'. This was a 'deposit-taking company', that is, it was not legally a bank, could not use 'bank' in its name, and could not accept current or savings accounts. It could, however, carry out all other banking business except that deposits from the public were limited to a minimum of $50,000, but were consequently not subject to the interbank agreements relative to interest rates.

The principal operating company of the Group became Wayfoong Credit, which moved into home mortgages in addition to taking over Wayfoong Finance's hire-purchase business. The Group finances leasing, factoring, and the discounting of post-dated cheques. This last requires an explanation. Goods sold on credit terms may be paid for on receipt by tender of a cheque dated for the day the credit term ends; it is these cheques which the seller, requiring immediate funds, can discount. Leasing was not particularly popular in Hong Kong, and factoring, which appeared at first as merely an expensive alternative to bill financing, had to be 'sold' to Hong Kong merchants on the basis of its combination of credit service and financing of accounts receivable.

Metway financed the sale of motor vehicles for the Inchcape Group; Fortway, another subsidiary, the sales of household electrical goods in the Fortress stores.

In 1980 this 'mini-group' contributed 3% of the Hongkong Bank Group's consolidated profits. There were, however, other consumer financing companies, separately incorporated for legal and geographical reasons: Wayfoong Mortgage And Finance (Singapore); Middle East Finance Company, a Dubai subsidiary (90%) of the BBME; Concorde Finance SA, incorporated in France and a subsidiary of Concord International (Curaçao) NV through Euro-Concord Finance BV and Concorde Equipement SA; and, avoiding the Chinese 'Wayfoong' name, Mortgage And Finance Company, incorporated in the State of Brunei, and Mortgage And Finance (Malaysia).

Other companies

Leasing

The HSBC's first venture into a leasing associate was in 1972 with its participation in the founding, with the World Wide Group and the Industrial Bank of Japan, of World Finance International, through Wayhong NH (see below).

At the end of 1979 the HSBC also owned 37.64% of the equity of Concord International (Curaçao) NV, a holding company incorporated in the Netherlands Antilles. Through a second-tier holding company, the Bank thus acquired an equity interest in another 'mini-group' of some nine companies. Concord International, a multinational equipment leasing and financing group, was established in 1972 by a group of international banks which was joined by The Hongkong and Shanghai Banking Corporation in 1978 and which in 1980 became the majority shareholder with 51% of the equity. In this venture the HSBC was associated primarily with the Philadelphia National Bank (through its subsidiary, Philadelphia International Investment Corporation), Arbuthnot Latham and Co., Banque Worms, and Nedbank.

Wayhong Investment

The Hongkong Bank Group's non-financial activities were placed, for the most part, under Wayhong Investment.

The Hongkong Bank's equity investments in transportation were concentrated in Wayhong Investment, which was held indirectly through Wayhong NH, an off-shore holding company registered in the New Hebrides. The two principal groups also remained (i) Cathay Pacific Airways, which was held, together with its eleven specialized subsidiaries and associated companies, by the Bank, the Swire Group, British Airways, and other interests and (ii) Pao's World Wide shipping enterprises.

The Bank was legally obligated to disclose loans outstanding in excess of 1% of total loans and advances made to companies in which a director had a material interest. At the end of 1975 the list was confined to loans to the Pao-managed operations through two holding companies – the Bermuda registered World Maritime ($222.3 million) and the Hong Kong registered World Shipping and Investment Company ($232.7 million). With total Hongkong Bank loans outstanding at $8,747 million, this represented 5.2% of the total. This was particularly high because 1975 was a depression year in which the Bank's loans had been cut back 16% from the peak in 1973.

The Hongkong Bank Group's equity interest in these latter two companies was 50% of US$30.2 million for World Maritime and 45% of US$40.7 million for World Shipping and Investment, that is, $74.7 million and $90.7 million respectively, through Wayhong Investment and Wayhong NH.

Despite these significant figures and the fact that by the end of the decade Wayhong Investment contributed 8.8% of total Group profits, the testimony of I.H. Macdonald before the Congressional sub-committee must be recalled (see above) – this was the only significant non-financial operation of The Hongkong and Shanghai Banking Corporation.

Nevertheless, shipping particularly was risky enterprise. Saunders had first followed Pao's development when Chief Accountant in the mid-1950s; as Chief Manager Saunders had virtually dealt with Pao personally, since the latter would appeal to Saunders against adverse decisions of subordinates. It was not shipping in general that attracted Saunders; he was lending and investing on the basis of his estimate of the ability of Pao. His judgement proved correct; for many years Pao surmounted the problems of the shipping industry; the Bank's investments continued sound.

Indeed, in his annual statement the Hongkong Bank Chairman would appear to offset his reporting of the adverse results of the Hongkong Bank of California with favourable news from the World Wide Shipping Group. In 1975 Sayer reported: '...the results of the Hongkong Bank of California remain disappointing but were affected by a decision to accept a capital loss on disposal of low yielding Government Bonds...Wayhong Investment...also benefited from a substantial increase in dividends on its shares in the World Wide Shipping Group...', and when in 1976 Sayer was able to report favourably on the Hongkong Bank of California, he had to hedge the statement with news of the California State tax claim based on the Hongkong Bank's worldwide profits, adding quickly news of substantial improvement in the results of Wayhong Investment – the dividend had been increased from $59.9 million to $73.7

million, 'mainly as a result of increased dividends received from companies of the World Wide Group'. Sandberg's first annual statement as Chairman made similar paired comments; in 1979 he was able to report, however, that arrangements to sell 'Inc', the Hongkong Bank of California, had been concluded.

Guardforce

The origin of Guardforce was as the security department of Hong Kong L.P. Gas Company which was subsequently organized as a separate company of high professional standards in 1977. The Hongkong Bank took 51% of the equity through Oroton Investments, a 100% owned subsidiary, in 1979; its holding was increased to 86.83% by 1986.

The company's largest customer was China Light and Power Company, and the Hongkong Bank does not automatically give this 'in-house' firm its business unless the price is right. But Guardforce with its 24 armoured cars moves the Bank's cash; it also secured the contracts to advise on security for the Bank's new building at 1 Queen's Road, Central and to act as agents to supply the vault doors for the building's safe-deposit centre and cash vault.

When the Hongkong Bank began developing its local branch network, the secure moving of cash was one of the first problems to be faced by R.G.L. Oliphant and O.P. Edwards. They solved it – for a time. But characteristic of the forces causing the proliferation of companies in the Hongkong Bank Group was the need at some point to turn to professional advice, in computers, communications – and security. Cathay Pacific took the same course in the establishment of Securair (50%) and Securair International.

This summary has covered the principal companies in the Group as they existed at the end of 1979, with the exception of property companies. Any activity which requires specialized management, which may require separate legal handling, or which for tax reasons ought to be separately incorporated in the same or some other jurisdiction is an activity which may properly be considered for a separate incorporation. Property acquisition and management fulfils these requirements, and it is not surprising, therefore, to find listed 99 Bishopsgate (New Hebrides), Collyer Quay Properties (Pte), Gracechurch Property Management, etc. The role of such companies may be passive, that is, the holding of property for the use of the Bank itself, or active, the holding of property for development or speculation. The Group's property companies were of both types.

The Hongkong Bank and its subsidiaries remain keen supporters of their employees' athletic efforts. Professional organization is certainly available, but as of 1985 the Bank had refrained from the separate incorporation of any of its

III. Policy, development, and performance 723

teams. Charity on the other hand is rationalized by the Hongkong Bank Foundation, founded in 1979 (see Chapter 18).

BANK AND GROUP: PERFORMANCE AND CHRONOLOGY, 1962-1979

General comments

Performance defined

The total assets of the Hongkong Bank Group increased more than sixteen times, that of the Hongkong Bank over 24 times between 1962 and 1979 inclusive, while shareholders' funds increased 11.6 times in the same period. By any measure the Hongkong Bank Group performed well, although adjustments are needed to consider real growth in an inflationary situation.

One obvious deflator to the performance is, in fact, just that. Group Assets between 1966 and 1979 increased 8.8 times but this is decreased to 3.2 times if the Hong Kong GDP deflator is applied to express the total assets in terms of constant 1980 prices. Price increases varied in the several territories in which the Bank operated; changing exchange rates make comparability in real terms difficult. Nevertheless, in terms of Hong Kong, it should be recalled, when dealing with the current price figures in the tables, that price changes were erratic, and the significant upward trend, the inflation, began only after 1975.[m]

The accounts

Although the usual ratios have been calculated, they are based on published figures and must therefore be used with caution. True profits are not disclosed; the published profits are earnings after transfers to inner reserves. The existence of inner reserves must affect judgement on prudential ratios, for example, the capital/assets ratio, which was low throughout (or, alternatively, the Hongkong Bank operated with a high leverage). There were significant changes in both the information in and format of the published accounts; there were also changes in accounting practices. Additional information was required by the Hong Kong Companies Ordinance, the London Stock Exchange, and the British Companies Act. The changes were noted from time to time in the Bank's Annual Reports. Accounting changes were of sufficient impact as to affect the published rate of growth, particularly as between various key years;

---

[m] The annual rate of inflation in 1975 was 1.5%, in 1979 11.6%, and in 1980 16.1%. The average annual mean rate of inflation using the GDP deflator, 1962-69 was 2.4% (CV 7.7, Range −0.8-4.6); 1970-79 it was 8.5% (CV 40.5, Range 2.8-13.3); the latter period measured by changes in the consumer price index gives annual mean growth of 7.6% (CV 68.1, Range 1.5-18.3).

in a sense, the figures are not strictly comparable. The way in which these changes impacted on the accounts, however, was further affected by the practice of allocating the additional amounts consequent to accounting changes to inner reserves and, on occasion, returning the rough equivalent as a transfer to published reserves. The main changes in this category were in the handling of property and of investment in subsidiaries.

As for property accounts, a total $38 million was transferred to 'Premises' between 1962 and 1971 to write down the value of the Bank's property; but the practice then ceased, and, beginning in 1972, property was revalued at market, with a consequent impact of $200 million on the balance sheet, although not in published shareholders' funds – the whole amount being transferred to inner reserves. In 1971 the Bank's investments in major subsidiaries were revalued. Previously they had been shown at historical cost less amounts written off; they were now to be shown at ('or about') the Bank's proportionate share in their published net worth. The $180 million increase resulting from this exercise was, exceptionally, transferred directly to the Bank's published reserves. In 1976, by using the net asset value method of showing investment in subsidiaries, the resulting changes totalled $180 million, a sum transferred to inner reserves. Such revaluations then became matters for regular note in the accounts.

A survey of the tables

The main concern of this section is with the Bank as opposed to the Group, although the capital accounts should be considered on a Group basis. The figures being discussed are found in Tables 15.8 through 15.11A, pp. 732–37. The proportion of Bank assets to total Group assets is shown in Table 15.19; the proportion varied between 60% and 65% during the years 1962–1979.

Published shareholders' funds (Tables 15.8, 15.9, and 15.11)

The basic statement of the capital refers to that of the Corporation, that is, of the so-called Hongkong Bank Group. Accepting the existence of inner reserves, the accounts are straightforward. There is, however, a new development – the increase in reserves is less a consequence of transfers from Profit and Loss Account consequent to a vote of shareholders at the Annual Meetings, a point confirmed by the figures in Table 15.11. More important are the transfers from inner reserves; these are often made to reinstate published reserves, usually, but not always, after a capitalization issue.

The increase in paid-up capital occurs through the issue of 'bonus' shares, that is, by a capitalization issue, financed by transfers from published reserves, from inner reserves and/or from P&L Account (or some combination). The capitalization issue in 1965 was seen as part of the centenary celebrations, reflecting however both the pressures on the Bank's published capital position and on the traditional attitude of management. The continued growth of the Bank and inflationary pressures forced the Board to take a more serious view of the Bank's position. By 1973 there was consideration of long-term borrowing and of rights issues, but neither materialized in the period under consideration. The Bank relied on capitalizing reserves or, since the reserves were immediately replenished, on transferred inner reserves.

What, once again, were inner reserves? By definition they were unpublished shareholders' funds, of which only a portion were 'free', that is, in accounts for purposes undesignated. Inner reserves were the consequences of transfers for specific contingencies, of usual or extraordinary profits, and of some Board-approved portion of normal annual profits. All this is consistent with the Bank's traditional policies. Except where public confidence was visibly shaken and required specific reassurance, the Bank's contingency accounts had not been published; historically, publication had been an admission that, for the time being, shareholders and constituents had lost faith in management. Transfers to 'free' inner reserves can in part be explained in terms of the need to equalize dividends; for this purpose the published Reserve account and even a special 'equalization of dividends' account had proved unsuitable (see Volume I). A draw-down of reserves to pay dividends had proved unacceptable, the permissive provisions of the Bank's ordinance notwithstanding. Another important factor in the creation of inner reserves had been management's desire, especially under Sir Thomas Jackson, to build up the reserves and not be faced with the necessity of withstanding pressures for increased dividends with every favourable, but undoubtedly temporary, turn of the market.

From 1962 when the Board considered the annual accounts, it had to consider, first, total 'available' profits from the Hongkong Bank itself, that is, profits *after* transfer of funds to inner reserves for contingencies, unrealized exchange proceeds, and extraordinary profits. To available profits was added the dividends received by the parent corporation, the Hongkong Bank, from subsidiaries. On the basis of this latter total, the Board had to consider management's recommendations relative to (i) 'retention', that is, transfer to unallocated inner reserves and (ii) published profits. The Board would recommend for shareholder approval at the Annual Meeting allocations from published profits to published reserves, dividends, carry forward, and other purposes.

In view of the concern expressed by United States regulatory authorities, the Board had to comment on its uses of inner reserves. Only in 1973 and 1976 was there a decline in 'free' inner reserves. The Board's ability to even out changes in profitability came from variations in the annual allocation to inner reserves before declaring profits, that is, in variations in the difference between 'true' and 'published' profits of the Bank qua bank plus dividends from subsidiaries.

Part of the gross transfers to inner reserves were later revealed by the capitalization issues of 1965 and then annually from 1969, which were in large part financed by subsequent transfers from inner reserves. The Bank cannot, as a result of reassurances to regulatory authorities, use inner reserves as a means of paying dividends after transfer from inner reserves to current Profit and Loss Account. Nevertheless, with the exception of 1967, published profits have always shown an increase. But what of true profits? Although true profits have shown several exceptional variations, published profits can be and have been adjusted to a trend by varying the transfer *to* inner reserves; post-war the Board never withdrew *from* inner reserves to affect either published profits or, therefore, the level of the dividend.

At the 1973 Annual General Meeting Sayer acknowledged public interest in the matter of disclosure, informed the meeting that the matter had been considered by the Board, and concluded that disclosure did not appear appropriate. Later Sayer would stress that while disclosure might be useful to determine whether shareholders had been receiving appropriate returns, the system of inner reserves protected depositors who could be assured of additional protection beyond that declared in the balance sheet. This was comparable with the 'additional protection' depositors received in other jurisdictions from statutory bodies, the Federal Deposit Insurance Corporation, for example; such protection is not available in Hong Kong. Sayer would also refer to the volatility of the Bank's business and the impact this would have on both depositors and shareholders. He concluded with the view that as long as the Bank had major responsibilities to the banking system, as long as people in Hong Kong regarded it as a potential lender of last resort, whatever the actual position, then for so long the Bank needed reserves on which it could call without endangering the public's confidence in the Bank and therefore in Hong Kong's entire banking system in sensitive times. Central banks, Sayer noted, do not usually act as lenders of last resort in the sense of 'saving' financial institutions in difficulties; they have other institutions behind them. In 1973 the Hongkong Bank did not enjoy potential support from such sources; developments since 1982 suggest, however, that the Exchange Fund is playing not so much a new as an enhanced role in supporting the integrity of the banking system.

On other subjects: despite a reasonable rate of return on Hongkong Bank assets (Table 15.11), which fluctuated from a low of 0.66 in the Red Guard year of 1967 to an exceptional 1.08 in 1979, earnings had difficulty keeping pace with the Bank's capital requirements, the capital/assets ratio declined, and on at least two occasions the Bank's Chairman aired the possibility of the need for a rights issue – which was actually agreed to by shareholders in 1980. The high leverage which was consequent to this situation is evidence of the Group's expansionist policy, that is, of a high rate of growth of total assets, inflated though this figure is by the inclusion of the Bank's note issue of $6,184 million (or 7.7% of total Bank footings) at the end of 1979. The problems reflected by the ratios are not unusual in a period of inflation.

The capital position was nevertheless sound. With ratios between 4.5% and 5.9% for the Bank, the existence of inner reserves, and, most important, the absence of gearing in the capital structure of the corporation itself, even the low overall Group capital/assets ratios could be tolerated.

On the question of marketability, the problem had again risen by the early 1970s and the shares were again split on a ten for one basis, despite some debate in the Bank as to whether $2.50 was a convenient par value. As a consequence the number of shareholders did increase; there were 40,000 in March 1975 compared to less than 19,000 in 1970. By early 1978 about 70% of the capital of The Hongkong and Shanghai Banking Corporation was represented by shares whose holders had a Hong Kong registered address. This shift of ownership back to the East was one consequence of the closing of the London Register and its amalgamation with the Hong Kong Register in 1974.

Profits and dividends (Tables 15.8, 15.8A, 15.11, and 15.11A)
The published profits/capital ratio and the net return on assets were satisfactory but inconclusive as true profits were not published. The practice of issuing 'bonus' shares requires that any calculation relative to growth of dividends paid out should refer to the holding on a particular date. In Table 15.8, 1954 is used, prior to initiation of the new bonus issue policy. On that basis the dividend per share, $0.74, in 1979, becomes $1,914.80 on the one share held in 1954, on the obvious assumption that all bonus shares were retained (and that, contrary to the actual position, fractional holdings were permitted).

The practice of quoting dividends in terms of sterling ceased with the 1972 accounts. To assist in making the dollar figures in Table 15.8 comparable to previous dividend quotations, Table 15.8A has been added. Certainly from 1970 onwards the thinking was in terms of Hong Kong dollars, with odd sterling amounts quoted. Although this change was the consequence of the devaluation of sterling and the floating of the Hong Kong dollar, the previous system had been an anomaly, the origins of which were recalled in Chapter 13.

Allocations from P&L Account were made to dividends, property account, reserves, and charity (Tables 15.11 and 15.11A). On the question of charity, by 1975 Group contributions were totalling an average $3.6 million. In 1980 an

728 The Hongkong Bank Group, 1962–1980

Group earnings per share amounted to HK$1.46 in 1979 compared with HK$1.05 (as adjusted) in 1978 and have shown a compound annual growth rate of 23.76% during the twelve year period ending December 1979.

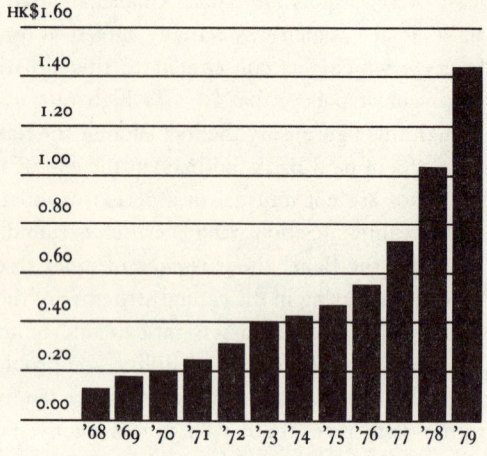

Figure 15.2 The Hongkong and Shanghai Banking Corporation
Earnings per share: Group
(Adjusted for bonus issues and share split)

Distribution for 1979 amounted to HK$0.74 per share on the capital as increased by the free scrip issue of one for two in April 1979 and shows a compound annual growth rate of 21.11% when compared with the HK$0.09 per share (as adjusted) paid in 1968.

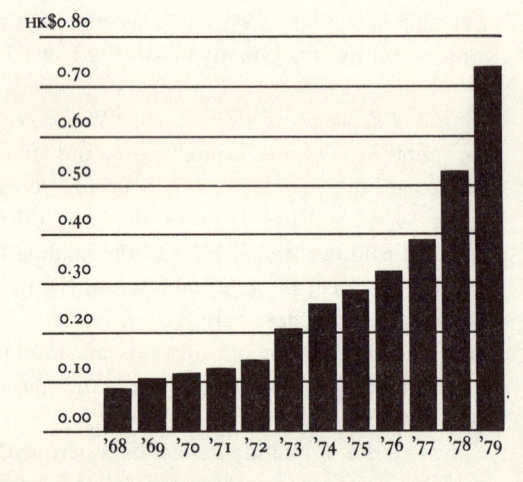

Figure 15.3 The Hongkong and Shanghai Banking Corporation
Dividend per share
(Adjusted for bonus issues and share split)

initial $50 million (and a further $50 million the following year) was set aside from current profits to fund the Hongkong Bank Foundation, which would focus primarily on Hong Kong but would also supervise the Group's charitable contributions elsewhere. Such a foundation was tax efficient and set a visible context for the Bank's charitable operations.

III. Policy, development, and performance

Net profit of the Group for 1979 at HK$1014 million represents an increase of 39.29% compared with the profit for 1978. Since 1968 the profit of the Group has increased at a compound annual rate of 23.90%.

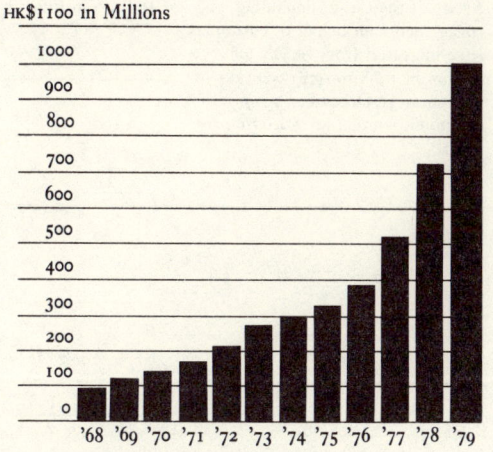

Figure 15.4 The Hongkong and Shanghai Banking Corporation Profit growth: Group

Since 1968 there has been an unbroken sequence of annual free scrip issues to shareholders and this, together with share exchanges, various transfers to published reserves and retained profits, has resulted in shareholders' funds increasing from HK$535 million in 1968 to a total of HK$3,709 million in 1979.

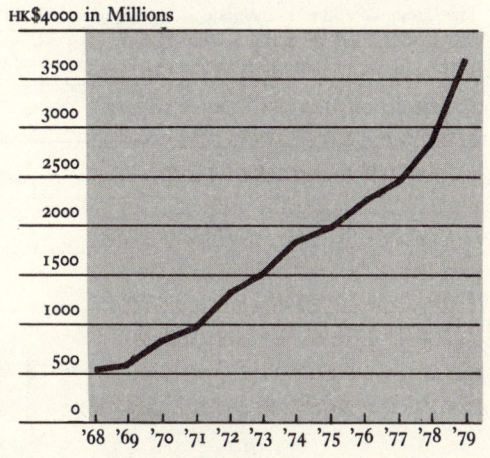

Figure 15.5 The Hongkong and Shanghai Banking Corporation Shareholders' funds: Group

Uses of funds (Table 15.10)

Table 15.10 shows selected balance items and ratios. The general picture is one of conservative management of funds, but there are specific lapses. Without at this time going through the chronology, the impact of the Red Guard period in 1967 and of the problems and depression of 1974/75 is apparent.

In the former case loans increased at the cost of liquidity; in the latter loans declined and liquidity rose to a high for the period of 64.4%, placing the Bank

Assets of the Group including engagements on behalf of customers have increased from HK$18.308 million in 1968 to HK$125.292 million at 31 December 1979, a compound annual growth rate of 19.11%.

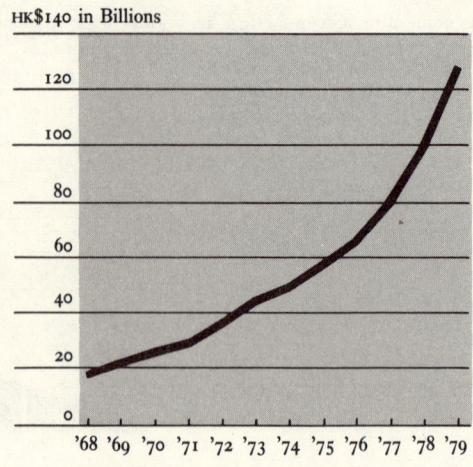

Figure 15.6 The Hongkong and Shanghai Banking Corporation
Total assets: Group

The Group continues to maintain a high degree of liquidity and at the end of December 1979 the advances to deposits ratio stood at 43.80%. Deposits from constituents have continued to grow steadily over the twelve year period resulting in a compound annual growth rate of 19.82%.

■ Total Assets
▨ Deposits
▨ Advances

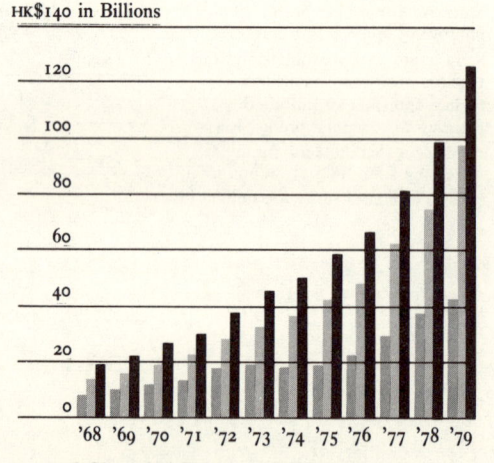

Figure 15.7 The Hongkong and Shanghai Banking Corporation
Advance/deposit growth: Group

fortuitously in a position to take advantage of the high interest rates which would prevail in the late 1970s. This had a positive impact on the Return on Assets (Table 15.11).

The growth in fixed assets cannot be seen consistently from the figures in Table 15.10 because of the varying methods of valuation, but the changes account for over 3.5% of the growth in the corporation's assets over the period. The increase in loans was greater than that of trade bills etc., but again the

III. Policy, development, and performance

comparison is marred by the change in definition of the latter category – in 1971 and after negotiable certificates of deposit are included – so that the item no longer reflects pure trade finance.

Rates of growth

The period 1968 through 1979 covers the recovery from the Red Guard troubles, the stock market boom of 1972/73, the depression of 1975, and the recovery and inflation up to the eve of HSBC's take-over of Marine Midland Banks. The figures for this significant period in the Bank's history confirm the growth which is evident from a glance at the tables (see also Figures III.1 and 2, pp. 563–64).

Issued capital, total profit as published, earnings per share, and dividends per share (adjusted for capitalization issues) all increased at the compound annual rate of approximately 23.5%. On the same basis total Group assets increased 19% – at approximately the same rate as shareholders' funds.

The chronology

Chief executive – J.A.H. Saunders
The Hongkong Bank's performance during the early years of this period was little affected by the closure of the branch in Rangoon, the withdrawal from Jakarta and the impact of *Konfrontasi*. Although the cost of providing banking services increased, the underlying economic strength of the region and the continued prosperity of Hong Kong offset the problems, and in March 1965 shareholders approved the first in a virtually annual series of bonus issues.

The 1965 Group accounts reflect the acquisition of Hang Seng Bank. The Hongkong Bank, confronted by a local banking crisis, was urged to act as a bank of last resort; this it resisted. Also in 1965 the Hongkong Bank signed its first significant computer contract with IBM for the installation of an on-line Electronic Data Processing system with the first focus on Savings Bank accounts and current accounts. This required an extension to be built on the west side of the Head Office building on Queen's Road. Without this the growth of branches and the consequent inflow of funds would have been impractical.

In 1965, the Hongkong Bank marked its centenary by increasing its authorized capital to $200 million in connection with a one for one capitalization issue, the $79 million required being financed from the Share Premium Account in the Reserve Fund, the latter to be reimbursed from inner reserves. The final dividend for 1964 was increased from 11s:0d plus a centenary cash bonus of 2s, with a note that no increase in the regular dividend for 1965 should

Table 15.8 *The Hongkong and Shanghai Banking Corporation Capital and dividends, 1962–1979**

(in millions of $)

		Capital resources					Shares			Book value		Dividend/share[e]	
Year	Assets	Paid up capital	Reserves[a]	P&L a/c balance[b]	Share-holders' funds[c]	Capitalization (bonus) issue x for y	Number (000)	Nominal value	Per share	Original (number)	holding[d]	as pub-lished	on original holding[d]
1946	2050.9	20.0	97.0	1.8	118.9	—	160.0	125.0	742.8	1.0	742.8	48.5	48.5
1961	7659.6	79.0	240.0	2.3	321.4	—	3161.8	25.0	101.6	12.5	1270.6	12.1	150.9
1962	9646.1	79.0	240.0	2.5	321.5	—	3161.8	25.0	101.7	12.5	1271.1	12.9	160.8
1963	10234.9	79.0	240.0	5.5	324.6	—	3161.8	25.0	102.6	12.5	1283.1	12.9	160.8
1964	10925.0	79.0	240.0	6.5	325.5	—	3161.8	25.0	103.0	12.5	1286.9	16.1	200.8
1965	12819.3	158.1	240.0	11.1	409.2	1 for 1	6323.7	25.0	64.7	25.0	1617.7	8.0	201.1
1966	14217.4	173.9	285.2	19.0	478.2	1 for 10	6956.1	25.0	68.7	27.5	1890.4	8.0	221.2
1967	15601.2	173.9	297.2	25.1	496.2	—	6956.1	25.0	71.3	27.5	1961.6	8.1	222.1
1968	18307.7	173.9	328.8	32.4	535.2	1 for 10	7651.7	25.0	76.9	27.5	2115.8	8.9	243.7
1969	21601.3	191.3	360.3	39.7	591.3	1 for 1	15303.3	25.0	77.3	30.25	2337.5	9.5	287.5
1970	26294.4	382.6	397.6	64.1	844.4	1 for 10	16833.7	25.0	55.2	60.5	3338.1	5.2	313.5
1971	29671.9	420.8	474.4	73.6	968.9	1 for 10	18517.0	25.0	57.6	66.55	3870.3	5.3[e]	350.1
1972	37040.1	462.9	749.5	99.5	1311.9	1 for 10	224272.5	2.5	70.9	73.2	5186.6	5.5	402.6
1973	44575.7	560.7	824.0	123.7	1508.4	1 for 5	277652.0	2.5	7.6	878.4	5908.4	0.63	553.4
1974	49487.1	694.1	1024.9	122.2	1841.3	1 for 5	347065.0	2.5	6.6	1054.2	6990.7	0.65	685.2
1975	57821.2	867.7	941.0	162.8	1971.4	1 for 4	381771.5	2.5	5.7	1317.7	7484.8	0.58	764.3
1976	66261.7	954.4	1189.5	128.9	2272.8	1 for 10	419948.6	2.5	6.0	1449.5	8629.2	0.60	869.7
1977	80479.4	1049.9	1298.6	137.9	2486.4	1 for 10	461943.5	2.5	5.9	1594.4	9439.9	0.65	1036.4
1978	98391.0	1154.9	1427.2	295.2	2877.3	1 for 10	692915.2	2.5	6.2	1753.8	10924.2	0.80	1403.1
1979	125292.5	1732.3	1635.9	341.2	3709.4	1 for 2			5.4	2630.8	18777.9	0.74	1946.8

* Consolidated Group Accounts.

[a] The figure for the Reserve Fund *includes* the amount transferred at the end of the period as approved by the shareholders at the subsequent meeting; figures for 1960 and 1961 include the Share Premium Account.

[b] The amount carried forward after all allocations, including the final dividend, have been made.

[c] Shareholders' funds (or 'primary capital') include capital paid up, published reserves (plus Share Premium Account from 1960 + balance on Profit and Loss Account after deduction for the final recommended dividend.

[d] Assume that the owner of one share in 1954 held onto bonus issues.

III. Policy, development, and performance

Table 15.8A *Hongkong Bank Sterling dividends, 1962–1971*[a]
(with dollar equivalents)

	£:s:d	@	=	$
1946	3:00	1/3		48.5
1961	0:15	1/3		12.1
1962	0:16	1/3		12.9
1963	0:16	1/3		12.9
1964	1:00	1/3		16.1
1965	0:10	1/3		8.0
1966	0:10	1/3		8.0
1967	0:10:8	1/3		8.0
1968	0:11:13	1/4½		8.9
1969	0:11:13	1/4½		9.5
1970	0:7:1	1/4½		5.2
1971	0:7:2⅜	1/4½		5.3

[a] Dividends declared in dollars after 1971 (see Table 15.8)

be anticipated in consequence of the increased number of shares (see Chapter 14).

The Bank's performance was weak in 1965. The dividend was nevertheless maintained, the 1966 decision was affected by the Board's desire to restore confidence in Hong Kong. A capitalization issue of $15.8 million was also authorized, of which $12.4 million came from the balance of the Share Premium Account. The Reserve Fund was replenished both by the traditional transfer from undistributed profits and by the now standard procedure of transfers from inner reserves. By the end of 1966 Hang Seng had more than recovered, and the increase in the Group's deposits was attributable mainly to developments in Hong Kong. The move of the Mercantile Bank's head office to Hong Kong was completed; integration of the BBME would be delayed until 1980. The contribution of the BBME to the Group was adversely affected by the Finance Act of 1965, and that bank paid no dividend to the HSBC until the law was changed effective for the year 1973.

At the annual meeting in 1968 the Chairman warned that, owing to changes in the exchange rates, 1967 figures were not directly comparable with those of 1966. Nevertheless the fall in Group Profit from $97.4 million to $88.7 was readily apparent. This was the only published profit decline since the Pacific War. Events in the Middle East (the Arab-Israeli War) and the spill over of China's Cultural Revolution, the Red Guard disturbances in Hong Kong, were

Table 15.9 *The Hongkong and Shanghai Banking Corporation Group consolidated and Hongkong Bank assets compared, 1962–1979*

(in millions of dollars or in percentages)

| | Group | | | Hongkong Bank | | | Assets (1946 = 100) | | | |
| | | | | | | | Group | | Bank | |
Year	Assets	Share-holders' funds	Capital/assets %	Assets	Bank assets/Group assets %	Capital/assets %	Index	increase %	Index	increase %
1946	2050.9	118.9	5.8	2050.9	100.0	5.8	100		100	
1961	7659.6	321.4	4.2	4774.0[a]	70.2	5.8	373		233	
1962	9646.1	321.5	3.3	5823.7[a]	60.4	5.5	470	26	284	22[b]
1963	10234.9	324.6	3.2	6343.1	62.0	5.1	499	6	309	9
1964	10925.0	325.5	3.0	6836.1	62.6	4.8	533	7	333	8
1965	12819.3	409.2	3.2	7950.1	62.0	5.1	620	17	388	16
1966	14217.4	478.2	3.4	8766.9	61.7	5.5	693	8	427	10
1967	15601.2	496.2	3.2	9529.2	61.1	5.2	761	10	465	9
1968	18307.7	535.2	2.9	11092.1	60.6	4.8	893	17	541	16
1969	21601.3	591.3	2.7	13229.7	61.2	4.5	1053	18	645	19
1970	26294.4	844.4	3.2	16223.7	61.7	5.2	1282	22	791	23
1971	29671.9	968.9	3.3	18999.7	64.0	5.1	1447	13	926	17
1972	37040.1	1311.9	3.5	23607.5	63.7	5.6	1806	25	1151	24
1973	44575.7	1508.4	3.4	28467.7	63.9	5.3	2173	20	1388	21
1974	49487.1	1841.3	3.7	31070.0	62.8	5.9	2413	11	1515	9
1975	57821.2	1971.4	3.4	35516.5	61.4	5.6	2819	17	1732	14
1976	66261.7	2272.8	3.4	39939.6	60.3	5.7	3231	15	1947	12
1977	80479.4	2486.4	3.1	48854.0	60.7	5.1	3924	21	2382	22
1978	98391.0	2877.3	2.9	62455.3	63.5	4.6	4797	22	3045	28
1979	125292.5	3709.4	3.0	80711.9	64.4	4.6	6109	27	3935	29

[a] 1961 figures exclude $600.7m Confirmed credits, guarantees and endorsements; the category is added to 1962 assets (1963 = $692.2m)

Table 15.10 *The Hongkong Bank*
Selected balance sheet items and ratios, 1962–1979

(in millions of dollars or percentages)

Year	(i) Assets	(ii) Index (1946 = 100)	(iii) Liquid assets[a]	(iv) Ratio (i)/(iii)	(v) Excess note issue	(vi) Total deposits	(vii) Liquidity ratio[b] %	(viii) Loans etc.	(ix) Loan/ deposit ratio %	(x) Invest- ments[f] (quoted)	(xi) Trade bills discounted, CDs	(xii) Fixed assets
1961	4774.0	233	1273	27	837.8	3363.1	37.9	1804	54	540	656	199
1962	5823.7	284	1424	24	925.8	3684.0	38.7	1942	53	573	761	201
1963	6343.1	309	1445	23	1013.8	4043.8	35.7	2153	53	624	845	232
1964	6836.1	333	1406	21	1153.8	4298.1	32.7	2544	59	580	836	314
1965	7950.1	388	2016	25	1425.8	4888.6	41.2	2682	55	574	899	318
1966	8766.9	427	2273	26	1481.8	5357.5	42.4	3058	57	553	886	358
1967	9520.2	465	2076	22	1825.8	5715.3	36.3	3447	60	520	845	358
1968	11092.1	541	2483	22	1659.1	6957.6	35.7	4333	62	539	1012	371
1969	13229.7	645	2738	21	1771.3	8445.3	32.4	5655	67	556	1167	380
1970	16223.7	791	4178	26	2039.3	10220.2	40.9	6340	62	535	1216	388
1971	18999.7	926	5672[c]	30	2303.3	11948.0	47.5	7191	60	547	1659[c]	643[a]
1972	23607.5	1151	5713	24	2667.3	15158.2	37.7	9587	65	730	2288	985[a]
1973	28407.7	1388	8565	30	2894.0	18734.6	45.7	10394	55	664	3148	918
1974	31070.0	1515	11532[e]	37	2979.0	19933.6	57.9	9120	46	642	2495	1291[d]
1975	35516.5	1732	14526	41	3286.0	22511.8	64.5	8747	39	734	3070	1434
1976	39939.6	1947	15524	39	3912.0	25514.4	60.8	10303	40	787	3893	1659[f]
1977	48854.0	2382	18197	37	4699.0	32514.2	56.0	13325	41	787	2644	1896
1978	62455.3	3045	22332	36	5794.0	42823.9	52.1	19353	45	801	3484	2278
1979	80711.9	3935	33893	42	6124.0	55800.0	60.7	22476	40	974	4633	2932

[a] The composition of this item changes: it begins with cash in hand and balances with other banks + money at call and short notice + British and other Government bills + trade bills discounted; it ends as cash and short-term funds + time deposits with banks payable within 12 months + trade bills discounted and bankers' certificates of deposit purchased. The major changes are noted by *c* and *e*, see below.
[b] The ratio is: liquid assets (iii) ÷ (vi), that is, current, deposit, and other accounts including inner reserves + authorized note issue.
[c] First year to include bankers' CDs as an item listed with trade bills.
[d] Revaluation of Bank premises.
[e] First listing, as a separate item, of time deposits with banks payable within 12 months.
[f] Revaluation of fixed assets on a new asset worth basis.

735

Table 15.11 *The Hongkong Bank**
Profits and dividends, 1962–1979

(in millions of dollars)

Year	Assets	Capital[a]	Capital/ assets[b] %	Profit	Profit/ Capital %	Return on assets	To dividends	To reserves[c]	Reserves[d]
1962	5823.7	321.5	5.5	45.8	14.2	0.79	40.7	0	240
1963	6343.1	324.6	5.1	47.7	14.7	0.75	40.7	0	240
1964	6836.1	325.5	4.8	55.8	17.1	0.82	50.8	0	240
1965	7950.1	409.2	5.1	60.5	14.8	0.76	50.9	0	240
1966	8766.9	421.3	4.8	67.2	16.0	0.77	56.0	0	240
1967	9529.2	423.1	4.4	63.0	14.9	0.66	56.2	0	240
1968	11092.1	434.3	3.9	74.9	17.2	0.68	61.7	10	250
1969	13229.7	457.7	3.5	90.7	19.8	0.69	72.7	10	260
1970	16223.7	680.9	4.2	114.2	16.8	0.70	79.4	10	270
1971	18999.7	925.3	4.9	133.8	14.5	0.70	88.6	10	460
1972	23607.5	1253.7	5.3	175.2	14.0	0.74	101.8	15	730
1973	28467.7	1440.8	5.1	240.5	16.7	0.84	140.9	20	797
1974	31070.0	1743.4	5.6	278.3	16.0	0.90	180.5	30	963
1975	35516.5	1854.4	5.2	312.3	16.8	0.88	201.3	40	820[e]
1976	39939.6	2161.7	5.4	356.4	16.5	0.89	229.0	50	1050
1977	48854.0	2317.2	4.7	428.4	18.5	0.88	273.0	60	1110
1978	62455.3	2645.3	4.2	592.4	22.4	0.95	369.6	100	1210
1979	80711.9	3402.2	4.2	869.5	25.6	1.08	512.8	150	1360

* Figures in this table refer to the Hongkong Bank itself; not to the Group.
[a] Shareholders' funds of the Hongkong Bank only.
[b] Compare this with the higher figures in Table 15.8; there the 'capital' is shareholders' funds of the Hongkong Bank Group consolidated accounts.
[c] Sums from current year's profits so transferred; other sums were transferred for special reasons from Profit and Loss Account at other times in the year.
[d] Includes 'Share Premium Account'; changes in reserves are due to factors other than those shown in this table.
[e] Due to draw down of Share Premium Account to finance bonus share issue.

responsible – this was also the year in which Lawrence Kadoorie resigned from the Board. During such crises the public prefer banknotes to bank deposits, even if the bank be a note-issuing bank. The 1967 expansion of the note issue resulted in a drawdown of interest-bearing funds in London and therefore of interest income at a time when the Bank (of England) rate was 7%. The losses resulting from devaluation of sterling were not included as the extent of the loss was still being negotiated with the Government; the anticipated amounts had, however, been covered by drawing down free inner reserves – although current

III. Policy, development, and performance

Table 15.11A *The Hongkong Bank Group Profits compared, 1962–1979*
(in millions of dollars)

Year	Bank profit	Group profit	To dividends
1962	45.8	50.7	40.7
1963	47.7	52.9	40.7
1964	55.8	59.4	50.8
1965	60.5	78.2	50.9
1966	67.2	97.4	56.0
1967	63.0	88.7	56.2
1968	74.9	105.0	61.7
1969	90.7	139.9	72.7
1970	114.2	160.0	79.4
1971	133.8	186.6	88.6
1972	175.2	238.4	101.8
1973	240.5	312.0	140.9
1974	278.3	333.7	180.5
1975	312.3	367.5	201.3
1976	356.4	440.0	229.0
1977	428.4	582.0	273.0
1978	592.4	808.6	369.6
1979	869.5	1014.0	512.8

profits ($63.0 million after transfers into inner reserves) were sufficient to cover both the dividend payout ($56.2 million) and the exchange loss.[n]

Although 1967 was a dramatic year, from the Hongkong Bank's viewpoint the events in Hong Kong itself were potentially of the greatest consequence. As it happened the Red Guard disturbances were temporary and supported by but a fraction of the population, virtually without long-run consequences. At the time, however, there were tense moments. Next door to the Hongkong Bank's Head Office the Bank of China had become something of a fortress, with barbed wire on the roof to prevent helicopter attack by Hong Kong forces, and with loud speakers blaring out key passages from the thoughts of China's Communist Party chairman. From the Supreme Court building on one side and from Beaconsfield House on the other, Government loudspeakers were set to drown out the revolutionary message. For those performing the more mundane tasks of banking, however, the noise did nothing for productivity. On reflection the

---

[n] The inner reserves cover would imply transferring funds from unallocated contingencies (free reserves) to a special account designed for the specific contingency of losses against devaluation. Such a transfer would not affect published accounts.

time was full of 'what if's' and 'if only's'; in 1966–1967, with many staff members in the volunteer forces, the problems seemed very real. As a further complication Hong Kong had early drawn its contracted water supply from China; negotiations for additional supplies could not even be started, and water was rationed by district.° Then in October 1967 the water supply from China was turned on again in accordance with the existing contract; Hong Kong and the Bank relaxed.

Equally dramatic from a financial point of view was the 1967 devaluation of sterling. For the first time a colonial territory on a *de facto* sterling exchange standard was given the opportunity to decide its own monetary future. The Government was given four hours to decide; it first opted for the full devaluation, there then followed three days of consultations, and the Hong Kong dollar was appreciated. This was a serious matter for the Bank, which, as a Sterling Area authorized bank, held the bulk of its reserves in sterling as required. Although the Government compensated on an *ex gratia* basis for the loss to the extent of $82.8 million, losses on account of Head Office and Hong Kong office were still $25.6 million, the Government seriously arguing that the Bank had after all enjoyed a high return on its sterling investments for many years. There were also losses to the account of other offices and the total was $38.4 million after $6.9 million in tax relief. The Board were informed that the Bank's ready sterling overbought position, £136 million, was now covered by the Exchange Fund. In the nineteenth century Hong Kong had argued that its monetary system had to take China's position into consideration. With 45% of the territory's food imports coming from the People's Republic, that policy remained valid. Nevertheless, as noted above, the Hong Kong Government's decision had a significant impact, and the Bank's published profits declined for the first time since the Pacific War.

Although Hong Kong had not completely recovered in 1968, confidence was partially restored; to prevent a total collapse of the market, the Bank continued to invest temporarily in property and bought on the stock exchange – subject to resale once the market rose. At the same time the recovery of Hong Kong's leading export market, the United States, had a significant impact. Profits increased once again. The year 1969 witnessed the opening of the Bank's new building in Mongkok; there was a further increase in profits due, the Chairman stated, to high liquidity and consequent ability to take advantage of high rates of interest. The tables do not reflect this directly, but the liquidity ratio is understated due to the existence of inner reserves within the total of deposit

---

° Important board meetings are said to have been postponed due to a conflict of interest – and cleanliness came before profits. An alternative explanation: profits could be obtained at any time, water could not.

liabilities. Hang Seng continued to grow; in 1969 their profits surpassed all previous figures.

The continued revival of Hong Kong in 1970 provided the occasion for a public statement on the Bank's equity involvement in shipping. The accounts for 1971 began the revaluation of subsidiaries discussed above. This change in accounting practice was related to the continuing problem of the capital/assets ratio which had reached, for the Group, a low of 2.7% in 1969. The Chairman referred to the possibility of a rights issue at the March 1972 meeting, but the need for this was avoided for another eight years. The Board meanwhile had specifically rejected the idea of long-term borrowing for capital purposes.

Sayer, who succeeded Saunders after the meeting, was under the impression that the Bank had never gone to shareholders for additional capital, although the records, now that they have been studied, reveal a public issue of shares in 1866 and four subsequent rights issues, the last being in 1922 (see Volumes I, II, and III). Nevertheless, there was concern that the call would not be well received by Chinese shareholders, that they might react with concern when an institution with apparently unlimited inner reserves should be forced to come 'begging'. The problem was, however, precisely to retain those inner reserves as such while presenting a balance sheet in which ratios could be explained and justified entirely by the figures actually revealed. The announcement the following year that, in line with other banking companies' practices, the Bank was revaluing its property at market, was not in this context surprising.

– *G.M. Sayer*

The year 1972 was important in a broader financial sense. Following the 1967 devaluation of sterling, various schemes had been developed for guaranteeing the value of Hong Kong's sterling reserves culminating in the Basel Agreement. Meanwhile the Hongkong Bank had been shifting a small proportion of its own reserves out of sterling – the percentage was now 89% (as opposed to the earlier 99%). Then in 1972 sterling was allowed to float and the Hong Kong dollar made no pretence of following; it was first linked to the U.S. dollar and then in 1974, with the end of the Bretton Woods post-war monetary settlement, the Hong Kong dollar itself was floated. This independence was at one level the sign of the break-up of the Sterling Area, on another a basis for the development of Hong Kong as a major financial centre. The Hongkong Bank set aside an exchange contingencies fund within its inner reserves. The Bank was once again an 'exchange bank'; it had to relearn the art of exchange operations. Men like Jackson, Henchmen, and Grayburn would have found it all strangely familiar.

The United Kingdom's guarantee of sterling applied to official accounts only. Accordingly the Bank's sterling was not protected as such. However, official accounts with the Bank were protected and provided the basis for the Hong Kong Government's guarantee to the banks. The Hongkong Bank, for example, bought otherwise unneeded non-interest bearing certificates of indebtedness from the Government, that is, it lent to the Exchange Fund, whose statutory right to borrow was increased for this purpose; payment was in sterling which the Government held in an account in the London Office; this transfer of sterling from Head Office's or Hong Kong office's London account to that of the Government converted the Bank's sterling into 'official' sterling, which was thus covered by the guarantees. The Government had been forced, however, to set limits even to this form of guarantee, the implication being that banks must invest their funds in currencies other than sterling. For the Hongkong Bank this too was an important but early step along the path to multinational status.

Unfortunately 1972 was the year of the stock market boom; it was also the year Wardley Limited was established. It is in one sense not fair to link the two developments, but the revival of confidence in Hong Kong had led to the need for expansion of existing industrial firms; to secure capital many had gone public legitimately and successfully. The majority of these new issues were undertaken by a department in the Bank's Hong Kong office. By 1972 the task had proved too great, too specialized to be properly handled within the commercial banking atmosphere of the Hongkong Bank itself, and Wardley Limited was founded as the Bank's merchant bank. At the same time, however, the market was being flooded with what Sandberg referred to as *lap sap* (rubbish) issues, and speculation was rife.[p]

Even though the Bank restricted itself to bona fide issues, the crowds of would-be investors and speculators filled the banking hall. The Dean of the Anglican Cathedral protested that normal business was impeded; the Bank asked if they could ease the crowding by using the cathedral's parish hall to make new issues; the Dean charitably agreed. The advertisements promoting the new issue of shares included, however, a picture of the cathedral itself. It was useless to protest that between the cathedral and the parish hall there was a key distinction – the latter was not sanctified; the poor and uneducated among the speculators were unresponsive to this manifestation of scholasticism and supposed, or chose to suppose, that the Church was behind the issue. Many would regret the Dean's decision.

The stock market boom with its many new issues caused liquidity crises for the smaller banks in Hong Kong, their customers withdrawing funds as deposits against share applications. In many cases these funds had been

[p] This was coincident with a very effective public campaign to clean up Hong Kong. The campaign was personified in the form of a litterbug monster, 'Lap Sap Chung'.

borrowed from the banks themselves ignoring the obvious impact of the inevitable clearing-house drain; to this extent the crises were self-made. Throughout the boom the Hongkong Bank had been powerless to act decisively as a central bank; it could push up inter-bank rates and restrict its own lending against shares, although at the cost of losing customers, but in the speculative atmosphere little more could be done. As the Hong Kong Stock Exchange operates on a cash basis, the Bank tried to keep pace with the workload as staff laboured into the night to remain current – and at the height of the speculation transactions fell only three days into arrears. This in itself set limits to the speculation and kept some order; nevertheless the authoritative market index, compiled by Hang Seng Bank, rose from 400 in early 1972 to reach 800 in the autumn; it topped 1770 in March 1973. Sayer was consulted by the Governor, the Exchange Banks raised interest rates, a Securities Advisory Council was formed, but eventually it was a minor incident, the discovery of a very few forged Hopewell Holdings share certificates, which pricked the market and caused the inevitable fall in 1973.

Sayer's concern for an efficient operation in London has been considered in Chapter 14. Early in his administration he was faced with a new example of 'Londonitis'. The original major shareholders of the Cross Harbour Tunnel Company had agreed with Government to offer 25% of the capital to the public. This was done, but two shareholders, Wheelock Marden and Hutchison, obtained sub-underwriters in London and shared the commissions. Unfortunately, the Bank, quite independently of this, raised interest rates and the issue failed. Brokers who had anticipated a small commission for no risk accused the Bank of deliberate obstruction. To avoid further recriminations the Bank offered to buy the shares from dissatisfied brokers; the brokers sold. One year later the market price of the shares had increased by a factor of three.

None of this adversely affected the general trend of the Hongkong Bank Group's increase in balance sheet figures, but the capital/assets ratio as a consequence remained low and the question of a rights issue was again raised in the 1974 meeting. Shares had been split on a ten for one basis and were consequently more easily marketed; furthermore, a trend to Hong Kong ownership was expected, a trend approved by Sayer and reinforced by the 1974 amalgamation of the share registers. The fact is that the Bank's shares then were particularly strong, being quoted on the market at rates which were at a premium even over true book value, and the share split had improved the position; it was a time, possibly, to acquire another bank. The capital ratio problem was viewed as sufficiently serious, however, for the Chairman to consider, but in the same breath to deny, the possibility of a slowdown in the Bank's growth.

The Hongkong Bank did in fact purchase an interest in Antony Gibbs

Holdings, but no major acquisition was made and there were other acquisitions, considered in the previous section. In June 1974 Sayer discussed with the Board his search for a company to buy into; in this context a decision, reflecting in a sense the inability of the Bank to find an investment more relevant to long-term development, was made to buy 6.9 million new Jardine stock in exchange for 8.5 million Hongkong Bank shares; the Bank consequently held 5% of Jardine's and an exception to the Bank's own shareholding restriction had to be made. The deal was announced as a long-term investment which would not involve any special relationship – membership on Jardine's board, for example; the deal was designed to give 'recognition to the strong business ties between the two organizations'.

Bank-commissioned studies were, however, soon to begin relative to the Bank's position in the United States – the Hongkong Bank of California was too small (and too unlucky) to be permitted to remain as it was or, alternatively, to be retained as the Bank's main financial venture in North America.

All this was consistent with Sayer's own concept of his role as chief executive. He had served as a deputy responsible for subsidiaries and this experience led him to stress proper delegation and information flows. To achieve this reorganization Sayer saw his first task as assembling his own team in Head Office. John Boyer had done well in Singapore; Sayer brought him up to Hong Kong to make possible Sandberg's move to the Deputy Chairman position, M.J. Pridham undertook the staffing tasks, I.H. Macdonald was brought into overseas operations, and P.E. Hammond into Group finances. The reorganization was not, however, complete. There were still executive directors without specific responsibilities on the Board.

Sayer took a moderate view on expansion. He was aware of the various restrictions in places of immediate interest, for example, Australia and Canada, but he was willing to consider proposals, especially in merchant banking. Development continued, but major changes waited.

The March 1975 Annual Meeting provided an opportunity to consider the Bank's progress in the decade since the centenary. Published shareholders' funds in the Group consolidated accounts had increased from $325 million to $1,841 million; Group profits from $59 million to $300 million; total Group assets from $10,925 million to $49,487 million. Sayer told the meeting, 'Our business has also moved away from the concept of regional retail banking to the much wider field of international financial services although the emphasis on meeting the requirements of our constituents in the Middle East, Far East and Pacific areas is still our primary objective.' This must not be interpreted as denying the importance of retail banking. In 1970 the Customer Services Department was instituted. From this there followed cash dispensers (first installed in 1971), the cheque card to enable withdrawal of funds from any branch, the 'autopay' system for payment of employees and the collection of accounts receivable, credit cards in the Master Charge and later the Visa systems, and Hong Kong dollar travellers cheques issued by the Bank's joint venture with Thomas Cook.

The world-wide depression of 1974/75 affected the Bank's operations, but financial support had to be given to Hong Kong industry both by Hang Seng and the Hongkong Bank. The latter also found it necessary to 'assist' the Hutchison Group by, as the Chairman put it, 'acquiring a large shareholding in the parent company thereby virtually guaranteeing all its obligations'.

In contrast there was a ceremonial opening of the Bank's New York office on the ground floor of the new World Trade Center's plaza. Sir Murray Maclehose, the Governor of Hong Kong, spoke on Hong Kong's problems before an American audience. The Bank's centenary was celebrated in the Philippines. Even in Indonesia, which the Bank had been virtually forced to abandon for a time, business was flourishing, and the Bank opened its new office building. And, although not as yet ready for a real decision, the Bank was feeling its way to a broader world base; it was in 1975 that a Representative Office was opened in Brazil following a favourable report on opportunities by the New York Manager, D.H. Leach.

The Hongkong Bank of California's performance, however, remained unsatisfactory. The Bank transferred US$5 million from Hong Kong to credit the capital account 'paid-in surplus'; with the permission of the State Banking Department this sum was then transferred on the end-1974 balance sheet to 'retained profits'. The purpose of this manoeuvre was to avoid showing loan losses and thus endangering confidence in the California subsidiary. Since, however, the published accounts state specifically that retained profits include US$5 million 'transferred from paid-in capital' and since balance sheet totals in 1974 were smaller than in 1973, it is difficult to suppose that the fact of loan losses would not have been apparent even to a casual reader. With such obvious difficulties exposed, it is difficult to understand the hesitations of senior Managers in disposing of the California subsidiary when this American strategy option was first presented by the Bank's consultants (see Chapter 16).

The Bank was from time to time caught in various difficulties in the several jurisdictions in which it operated; generally it was successful in avoiding contraventions of complex regulations. The following are two of possibly several more exceptions. In 1972 the Bank was involved in the planning for its new Kuala Lumpur office building, a development which required 'unusual concessions' by the Selangor State Government for which no local provision for the payment of a premium existed. The Bank decided instead to make a donation to UMNO Party funds; the transaction was mishandled and in 1976 the then Chief Minister of Selangor was successfully prosecuted; the Bank

Negara, the central bank, concluded that the Hongkong Bank had acted 'honestly but foolishly'.[q] Also in 1976 the Bank was found to have been in violation of U.K. Exchange Control since 1972, for which the Bank immediately offered voluntary compensation to the Government, ordered an investigation, and promised rigorous action. This was favourably received by the Treasury and the Bank of England and no prosecution took place, but the Bank was expected to make good lost foreign exchange to a potential total of US$6 million. The Bank accordingly set aside a sum in inner reserves; fortunately it was never required.

– *M.G.R. Sandberg*

The economic revival was slow, but the Hongkong Bank was in a good position to take advantage of rising interest rates. Its liquidity ratio, which had been increasing since 1972, was unusually high at 56% in 1977. The Bank could afford to contemplate the initial cost of acquiring Marine Midland Banks (MMBI) through the use of its own U.S. dollar liquid assets. Sandberg at the 1978 Annual Meeting was able to reassure shareholders that there was no need to consider a rights issue. MMBI began to affect the Group's balance sheets; the purchase in May 1978 of MMBI's US$100 million $7\frac{3}{4}$% subordinated note, which, being purchased by a wholly owned subsidiary, did not show on the accounts of the Bank itself, was included under 'advances to customers and other accounts' in the Consolidated Balance sheet.

As the Bank's profits increased (in 1978) by some 39% and the Hong Kong dollar continued strong, the Hong Kong Government lifted the moratorium on new foreign banks establishing in the territory. Even as Jackson had welcomed the entry of American banks into competition on the China coast at the turn of the century, so Sandberg spoke of 'healthy competition'. The Hongkong Bank's network of branches garnered the bulk of the territory's savings, and new banks expecting to buy these funds on the inter-bank market for relending would be disppointed. Citibank thought the consequent 'inversion of interest rates' unfair, and they protested to the press, a serious matter when the Bank was seeking regulatory approval for the purchase of MMBI, but Sandberg took the position that the Hongkong Bank wasn't put into the world to provide funds for Citibank – or any other rival.

There were, however, other ways to fund Hong Kong lending, and the foreign banks had come to the territory with a global strategy in mind, always aware of the changing economic and political policies of the People's Republic of China. Hong Kong was on its way to becoming the third largest financial centre in the world.

---

[q] A summary of these events may be read in Chee Peng Lim's account in King, ed. *Eastern Banking*, p. 372 (see Bibliography).

III. Policy, development, and performance

The last year of this pre-MMBI period, 1979, was another record year, with the Bank's profits increasing by 47%; Wardley's dividend was also a record at $47.5 million (1978 = $30 million). When announcing the capitalization of $1,039 million of reserves by a three for five 1980 bonus issue, Sandberg confirmed the Bank's policy of not buying in money. With a liquidity ratio of 60.7% for the Bank itself and the capital/assets ratio at least no worse at 3%, there seemed as yet *no need* for a change in capital policy. It was in this atmosphere of general well-being and success that in 1980 the Bank announced its plan to redevelop its Queen's Road site; the eventual consequences would be surprisingly controversial, both financially and architecturally.[r]

Exhaustive examination of the Hongkong Bank by various Federal and State regulatory agencies, including the Office of the Comptroller of the Currency and the Federal Reserve Board, found the corporation an acceptable partner for America's thirteenth largest bank, Marine Midland. The developments described in this and the previous two chapters were so ordered that this conclusion could be made against considerable doubt in certain banking and regulatory circles. Moreover the Hongkong Bank was particularly profitable, its shares at a premium, and the next corporate move seemed logical. There were however dangers. The Hong Kong Government had been reconsidering the basis of the Hong Kong dollar's international position, the end of the banking moratorium facilitated the fuelling of Hong Kong's latest boom, and the Hongkong Bank itself would be involved in the fallout. The consequent loss of financial confidence turned attention to the ever-nearing year of 1997 when Britain's hold on the New Territories would cease with the end of the 99-year lease negotiated in that year of concessions 1898 (see Volume II). In 1979 this problem had not as yet been resolved in such absolute or unfavourable terms.

This future history would not, therefore, affect the Bank's negotiations with MMBI, nor was 1979 a likely year to consider such dark matters. The Bank had taken twenty years to bring BBME's head office to Hong Kong; despite its aggressive behaviour in the late 1950s under an apparently reluctant Sir Michael Turner, despite the growth of the Group to nearly 400 companies, the fact is that no dramatic single acquisition had occurred since the acquisition of the British Bank of the Middle East and the Hang Seng Bank. The BBME acquisition transformed HSBC into an inter-regional bank, but for this to be meaningful in a management sense, integration of management had to be accomplished and this, as described in these chapters, took time. A reapprasial

---

[r] Nearby the Bank of China was also to redevelop according to plans designed by I.M. Pei, the American son of Pei Tsuyee, sometime chief executive officer of the Bank of China. This too will be a major architectural addition to central Hong Kong.

of the Bank's position in North America began under Sayer, then under Sandberg Marine Midland was identified, and by 1979 negotiations had all but been completed. This time, with success in 1980, The Hongkong and Shanghai Banking Corporation was dramatically transformed – after years as the greatest of the British overseas banks in the East, it had become at last a multinational bank and financial group.

Table 15.12 *The Hongkong and Shanghai Banking Corporation Companies owned 25% or more (31 December 1979)*

Name of company	Place incorporated	% held (i)	% held (ii)	Nature of business
Acceptor Enterprises	Hong Kong	45		Financial Services
Antony Gibbs Holdings	United Kingdom	40		Merchant Banking/Holding
Antony Gibbs Administration Services	United Kingdom		100	Group Management Service
Antony Gibbs Associates	United Kingdom		49	Investment Co. & Advisor on Investment
Antony Gibbs Financial Services	United Kingdom		100	Financial Planning
Antony Gibbs (Personal Financial Planning)	United Kingdom		100	Dormant
Lionel Sage (Life and Pension Consultants)	United Kingdom		100	Dormant
Lionel Sage (Pension Services)	United Kingdom		100	Dormant
Antony Gibbs Insurance Co.	United Kingdom		100	Insurance
Antony Gibbs (Insurance Holdings)	United Kingdom		100	Holding Co. for Insurance Group
Antony Gibbs Sage	United Kingdom		100	Insurance brokers
AG Underwriting Managers	United Kingdom		100	Dormant
Antony Gibbs Completion	United Kingdom		100	Provide completion guarantee
Antony Gibbs & Sons (Insurance)	United Kingdom		100	Holding Co.
Hogg Robinson and Antony Gibbs SA	Peru		35	Insurance broking
Antony Gibbs UK Insurance Brokers	United Kingdom		100	Dormant
Wardley Gibbs (Remaining 67% of equity held by Wayhong Holdings)	Hong Kong		33	Insurance Co.
Andrews Brighton Holt & Co.	United Kingdom		100	Dormant
Antony Gibbs Northern Insurance Brokers	United Kingdom		100	Dormant
Anton Underwriting Agencies	United Kingdom		99.8	Lloyds Syndicate Managers
Lionel Sage Underwriting Agencies	United Kingdom		98.5	do

Table 15.12 (cont.)

Name of company	Place incorporated	% held (i) (ii)	Nature of business
GH (Insurance Agencies) NV	Belgium	80	Insurance broking
Antony Gibbs Investment Management	United Kingdom	100	Investment Management
Antony Gibbs (Middle East)	United Kingdom	100	Agency & Merchanting
Duranton	United Kingdom	100	Agency & Merchanting
Antony Gibbs (O'seas Investments)	United Kingdom	100	Holding Co. for O'seas
Gibbs Bright Holdings Pty	Australia	100	Holding Co.
Gibbs Bright & Co. Pty	Australia	96.22	Holding and Insurance
East Coast Sawmills Pty	Australia	100	Sawmilling
Tamic International Pty	Australia	100	Dormant
Panelboard Pty	Australia	100	Manufacturer of wood based products
Panelboard Technical Services Pty	Australia	100	Group Service Co.
MT & MM Pty	Australia	100	Hardware retailers
Access Control Systems Pty	Australia	100	Security systems
Access Control Systems (Australia) Pty	Australia	60	Security systems
Gibbs Bright (New Guinea) Pty	New Guinea	100	Timber
Papua New Guinea Forest Exports Pty	New Guinea	100	Timber
Gibbs Bright (HK)	Hong Kong	100	Holding Co.
Silverbell	Hong Kong	100	Holders of patent rights
Gibbs Bright (New Zealand)	New Zealand	100	Timber
HT Russel & Sons Pty	Australia	100	Saw Millers, Timber Processors
Gibbs Bright Mercantile Insurance Co.	Australia	25	Insurance
Gibbs Bright Nominees Pty	Australia	100	Nominee Company
Great Northern Wool Dumping Pty	Australia	33.33	Dormant
Gibbs Y Cia S.A.C.	Chile	100	Manufacturer's rep.

Table 15.12 (cont.)

Name of company	Place incorporated	% held (i) (ii)	Nature of business
Sociedad Commercial y de Inversiones "Anton"	Chile	100	Investment Holding Co.
Gibbs, Williamson (Bolivia)	Bolivia	50	General Traders
Cayetana SA	Panama	49	Dealers in antiques and fine art
Antony Gibbs Pension Services	United Kingdom	100	Pensions
Antony Gibbs Securities	United Kingdom	100	Managers of special situations
Antony Gibbs Financial Services (C.I.)	Channel Islands	100	Financial planning
Diameco Investments	Jersey	100	Investment Co.
Angelot	Guernsey	100	Film Project Co.
Beauty Enterprises	Guernsey	100	Film Project Co.
Ariadne Films	Jersey	71.9	Film Projects Co.
Fiver	Guernsey	100	Film Project Co.
Hazel General Trading Co.	Guernsey	100	Film Project Co.
Watership Productions	Jersey	42.1	Film Projects Co.
Jonathan	Guernsey	100	Film Project Co.
La Perte Enterprises	Guernsey	100	Dormant
Merton Trading	Guernsey	100	Dormant
Ondine	Guernsey	100	Film Project Co.
Quadrant Trading Co.	Guernsey	100	Dormant
Spartan Enterprises	Guernsey	100	Film Project Co.
Bridgepalm	United Kingdom	100	Film Project Co.
Disappearance Project Co.	United Kingdom	77	Film Project Co.
Gelhood	United Kingdom	100	Commodity Funds
Harthover Projects Co.	United Kingdom	50.8	Film Project Co.
Ibsonville	United Kingdom	84.2	Commodity Funds
Pethurst International	United Kingdom	100	Film Project Co.
Pipkin Project Co.	United Kingdom	36.1	Film Project Co.
Rantcroft Securities	United Kingdom	100	Dormant
Spangshaw	United Kingdom	100	Dormant

Table 15.12 (cont.)

Name of company	Place incorporated	% held (i)	% held (ii)	Nature of business
Pipkin	United Kingdom		100	Film Project Co.
Harthover	United Kingdom		100	Film Project Co.
Antony Gibbs & Sons	United Kingdom		100	Management Co.
Antony Gibbs and Sons (Nominees)	United Kingdom		100	Nominees
Antony Gibbs Unit Trust Managers	United Kingdom		100	Unit Trust Management
Gibbs Y Cia S A	Peru		100	In liquidation
Antony Gibbs Ireland	Eire	100		Banking
Aspiration Land Investment	Hong Kong	50		Property Holding
Banking Computer Services Pte	Singapore	50		Computer Services
BC Facilities	United Kingdom	100		Dormant
Benteng Redevelopment Sdn Bhd	Malaysia	40		Property Holding
99 Bishopsgate	New Hebrides	100		Property Holding
Bowmaker (CA) (Pvt)	Rhodesia	33.3		Dormant
Lansdown Estate Private	Rhodesia		100	Farming
British and Chinese Corporation	United Kingdom	61		Dormant
The British Bank of the Middle East	United Kingdom	100		Banking
The British Bank of the Lebanon	Lebanon		95	Banking
Société Immobilière Atlas	Switzerland		100	Property Investment
Middle East Finance Co.	Dubai		90	Consumer Finance
BBME Nominees	United Kingdom		100	Dormant
The Bank of Iran and the Middle East (A further 17.5% held by HSBC)	Iran		17.5	Banking (Nationalized)
The Saudi British Bank	Saudi Arabia		40	Banking
Wardley Middle East (A further % held by HSBC)	Dubai		20	Merchant Banking
Hongkong & Shanghai Bank (Trustee)	United Kingdom		100	Trustee Services
Carlingford Holdings	New Hebrides	100		Holding Co.
Carlingford NH	New Hebrides		100	Investment Holding

III. *Policy, development, and performance* 751

Table 15.12 (*cont.*)

Name of company	Place incorporated	% held (i)	% held (ii)	Nature of business
Highclere Investments	New Hebrides		100	Dormant
Carlingford Investments	United Kingdom	100		Dormant
Collyer Quay Properties (Pte)	Singapore	100		Property Development
Concord International (Curaçao) NV	Netherlands Antilles	37.64		Holding Co.
EuroConcord Finance BV	Netherlands		100	Holding Co.
Concord Leasing Inc	USA		100	Dormant
Concord Leasing Services	United Kingdom		100	Services Co.
Concord Leasing (Antony Gibbs Holdings own further 20%)	United Kingdom		80	Leasing Co.
Concord Credit	United Kingdom		100	Leasing & Consumer Finance
Concorde Equipement SA	France		63	Leasing Co.
Concorde Finance SA	France		100	Consumer Finance
EuroConcord Leasing BV	Netherlands		100	Operating Co.
Concord Leasing GmbH	Germany		100	Leasing Co.
Concord Leasing GesmbH	Austria		100	Leasing Co.
US Concord Inc.	USA		100	Management Co.
Gatechurch Property Management	United Kingdom	100		Property Management
Gibbs Wardley Middle East	United Kingdom	40		Management Services
Hang Seng Bank	Hong Kong	61		Banking
Hang Seng Bank (Trustee)	Hong Kong		100	Trustee Services
Hang Seng Finance	Hong Kong		100	Deposit taking co. consumer credit
Hang Dah Chong Investments	Hong Kong		50	Property development
Hang Seng (Nominee)	Hong Kong		100	Nominee Service
Hang Tung Travel Service	Hong Kong		100	Travel Agents
Haseba Investment Company	Hong Kong		100	Investment Co.
Hong Kong Fintracon[a]	Hong Kong		20	Export Credit
Perpetual Publicity	Hong Kong		100	Advertising Agents
Sharps Pixley Wardley[a]	Hong Kong		15	Bullion Brokers
Yan Nin Development Co.	Hong Kong		100	Property Investment

[a] Companies listed as total group members' holdings exceed 25%

Table 15.12 (*cont.*)

Name of company	Place incorporated	% held (i)	(ii)	Nature of business
Hong Kong and Shanghai Thomas Cook	Hong Kong	50		Travellers' Cheque Issuing Co.
Hongkong & Shanghai Bank (Singapore) Trustee	Singapore	100		Trustee Services
Hong Kong and New Zealand Properties	New Hebrides	50		Property Owning
Honggroup Nominees	United Kingdom	100		Nominee Services
Hongkong & Shanghai Bank (Kuala Lumpur) Nominees	Malaysia	100		Nominee Services
Hongkong & Shanghai Bank (Malaysia) Trustee	Malaysia	100		Trustee Services
Hongkong & Shanghai Bank (Singapore) Nominee Pte	Singapore	100		Nominee Services
Hong Kong and Shanghai Banking Corporation (Nominees)	Hong Kong	100		Nominee Services
Hong Kong and Shanghai Banking Corporation (CI)	United Kingdom	100		Banking
Hong Kong and Shanghai Bank Trustee (Jersey)	Jersey		100	Trustee Services
Hong Kong and Shanghai Bank Nominees (Jersey)	Jersey		100	Nominee Services
Hong Kong and Shanghai Trustee (Guernsey)	Guernsey		100	Trustee Services
Hong Kong and Shanghai Trustee (Isle of Man)	Isle of Man		100	Trustee Services
Hong Kong Bank Serviços	Brazil	100		Representative Office
Hongkong Fintracon Ltd	Hong Kong	40		Export Credit
Isoba	Hong Kong	50		Property Holding
Kellett Investments	Hong Kong	100		Investment Holding
Kellett (New Hebrides)	New Hebrides	100		Investment Holding
Korean International Merchant Bank	South Korea	30		Merchant Banking
Mercantile Bank (Malaysia) Nominees	Malaysia	100		Nominee Services
Mercantile Bank (Singapore) Nominee Pte	Singapore	100		Nominee Services

Table 15.12 (cont.)

Name of company	Place incorporated	% held (i)	% held (ii)	Nature of business
Lion Corporate Services	Hong Kong	100		Secretarial Services
Mercantile Bank	United Kingdom	100		Banking
Mercantile Bank (Agency) Pte	India		100	Trustee Services
Mercantile Bank (Hong Kong Nominees)	Hong Kong		100	Nominee Services
Mercantile Bank (Nominees)	United Kingdom		100	Nominee Services
Crorebridge	New Hebrides		100	Finance Co.
Merino	Hong Kong	100		Banking
Mortgage And Finance	Brunei	100		Consumer Finance
Mortgage And Finance (Malaysia)	Malaysia	100		Consumer Finance
Oroton Investments	Hong Kong	100		Investment Holding
Guardforce	Hong Kong		51	Security Services
Pall Mall Nominees	United Kingdom	100		Nominee Services
Resources and Investment Finance	New Guinea	33.3		Merchant Banking
SDC International	Canada	68		Investment Holding
Wood Products International	Hong Kong		35.72	Timber
Aihco Hongkong	Hong Kong		100	Shipping and Timber
Kapunda Development Co. Pty	Australia		100	Pine plantation development
NV Wood Products International Europe	Belgium		100	Timber
Speedlink	Belgium	100		Telecommunications
South China Morning Post	Hong Kong	43.81		Publishing & Printing
Asher & Co. (HK)	Hong Kong		50	Stationery suppliers/security printers
Asia Magazines Distributors	Hong Kong		25	Magazine distributors
Asia Magazines	Hong Kong		34	Magazine publishers
Filmset	Hong Kong		100	Film typesetter/ book & magazine publisher
Lever Printing Factory	Hong Kong		100	Printing & Packaging

Table 15.12 (*cont.*)

Name of company	Place incorporated	% held (i)	% held (ii)	Nature of business
Panasia Book Distributors	Hong Kong		51	Wholesale Book dist
The Far Eastern Economic Review	Hong Kong		51	Magazine publishers
Yee Tin Tong Printing Press	Hong Kong		100	Printing
UDA Merchant Bankers	Malaysia	25		Merchant Banking
UDA Nominees	Malaysia		100	Nominee Services
Wayfoong Finance	Hong Kong	100		Real Estate Finance
Metway	Hong Kong		51	Consumer Finance
Wayfoong Credit	Hong Kong		100	Consumer Finance
Wayhong Holdings	New Hebrides	100		Insurance Holding
Citadel Insurance Co.	Hong Kong		40	Insurance Co.
Sirius Holdings NV (see Leith Investments)	Netherlands		50	Holding Co. for insurance interests
Sirius Insurance	Australia		100	Insurance Co.
Leith Investments	Hong Kong		40	Investment Co.
Sirius Holdings NV (see Citadel Insurance Co.)	Netherlands		50	Holding Co. for insurance interests
Middle East Insurance Holdings	Hong Kong		51	Holding Co.
Al Sagr Insurance Co. of Saudi Arabia	Saudi Arabia		40	Insurance Co.
Al Sagr Insurance Co. UAE	United Arab Emirates		40	Insurance Co.
Arthur Weller	Hong Kong		40	Insurance Broking
Arthur Weller Holdings NV	Netherlands		100	Holding Co.
Arthur Weller Australia Pty	Australia		100	Insurance Broking & Consulting
Insurex Pty	Australia		60	Computer Services
Gilman Weller Victoria Pty	Australia		31	Insurance Agency
Gilman Weller SA Pty	Australia		70	Insurance Agency
Arthur Weller NSW Pty	Australia		56	Insurance Agency
Wardley Gibbs (remaining 33% of equity held by Antony Gibbs & Sons (Insurance))	Hong Kong		67	Insurance Co.
Wayhong Insurance Agencies	Hong Kong		100	Insurance Brokers
Wayfoong Insurance Co.	Hong Kong		100	Insurance Co.
Wardley Insurance Co.	Hong Kong		70	Insurance Co.
Wardley Swire Assurance	Hong Kong		50	Insurance Co.

Table 15.12 (cont.)

Name of company	Place incorporated	% held (i)	(ii)	Nature of business
Sword Assurance	Hong Kong		100	Insurance Co.
East Point Reinsurance Management Company of Hong Kong	Hong Kong		30	Reinsurance Management
Wayhong Properties	New Hebrides	100		Property Holding
New Sydney Enterprise	Hong Kong		100	Property Holding
Liana Company	Hong Kong		100	Property Holding
Wayhong NH	New Hebrides	100		Investment Holding
Cannae	Hong Kong		50	Property Holding
PT Manning Development	Indonesia		75	Property Co.
Kellett Holdings NH	New Hebrides		100	Investment Co.
Wayhong Investment	Hong Kong		100	Holding Co.
Cathay Pacific Airways	Hong Kong		25	Airline
Associated Engineers	Hong Kong		30	Group Mechanical equipment
Cathay Holidays	Hong Kong		100	Tourist Promotion
Cathay Pacific Airways (London)	United Kingdom		100	European Centre of Sales & Promotion
Cathay Pacific (Netherlands) BV	Holland		100	Dormant
HK Aircraft Engineering Co.	Hong Kong		25	Aircraft maintenance
HAECO Investments	Hong Kong		100	Dormant
HK Airways	Hong Kong		100	Dormant
Securair	Hong Kong		50	Airport Security
Securair International	Hong Kong		100	Security
Swire Air Caterers	Hong Kong		75	Catering
Vogue Laundry Service	Hong Kong		27	Laundry
WHS Investments	Hong Kong		45	Investment
Regent Investment Holdings Inc.	Liberia		40	Holding Co.
Nikko Investment Co. Inc.	Liberia		100	Holding Co.
Floral Shipping Co. Inc.	Liberia		100	Holding Co.
Begonia Shipping Co.	Panama		100	Shipowning
Cactus Shipping Co.	Panama		50	Shipowning
Carica Shipping Inc.	Liberia		100	Shipowning
Carnation Shipping Co.	Panama		100	Shipowning
Heath Shipping Inc.	Liberia		100	Shipowning
Narcissus Shipping Co.	Panama		100	Shipowning
Primrose Shipping Co.	Panama		100	Shipowning
Regent Bellis Shipping Co.	Panama		100	Shipowning

Table 15.12 (*cont.*)

Name of company	Place incorporated	% held (i) (ii)	Nature of business
Regent Botan Shipping Co.	Panama	100	Shipowning
Regent Camellia Shipping Co.	Panama	100	Shipowning
Regent Cedar Shipping Inc.	Liberia	100	Shipowning
Regent Cosmos Shipping Inc.	Liberia	100	Shipowning
Regent Fleur Shipping Inc.	Liberia	100	Shipowning
Regent Violet Shipping Co.	Panama	100	Shipowning
Fortune Holdings	Liberia	100	Holding Co.
Liberian Lily Transports Inc.	Liberia	100	Shipowning
Regent Daffodil Shipping Inc.	Liberia	100	Holding/Ship Management
Regent Daisy Shipping Co.	Panama	50	Shipowning
Regent Tulip Shipping Co.	Panama	50	Shipowning
Regent Zinnia Shipping Inc.	Liberia	50	Shipowning
Resources Investment Inc.	Liberia	100	Holding Co.
Regent Petunia Shipping Inc.	Liberia	50	Holding/Ship Management
Regent Buttercup Shipping Inc.	Liberia	100	Shipowning
Regent Cherry Shipping Inc.	Liberia	100	Shipowning
Regent Orchid Shipping Inc.	Liberia	100	Shipowning
World Finance International	Bermuda	37.5	Shipowning/Holding Co.
Liberian Sparta Transports Inc.	Liberia	40	Holding Co.
Liberian Countess Transports Inc.	Liberia	100	Shipowning
Liberian Cougar Transports Inc.	Liberia	100	Holding Co.
Liberian Amethyst Transports Inc.	Liberia	100	Holding Co.
Liberian Athene Transports Inc.	Liberia	100	Shipowning
Liberian Raven Transports Inc.	Liberia	100	Shipowning

Table 15.12 (*cont.*)

Name of company	Place incorporated	% held (i) (ii)	Nature of business
Liberian Cypress Transports Inc.	Liberia	100	Shipowning
Liberian Tunny Transports Inc.	Liberia	100	Shipowning
Walnut Shipping Co.	Hong Kong	100	Shipowning
World Maritime	Bermuda	50	Shipowning/Holding Co.
Accord Tankers	Liberia	100	Shipowning
Allied Shipping Co.	Panama	100	Shipowning
Chancery Tankers	Liberia	100	Shipowning
Credo Shipping Co.	Panama	100	Shipowning
Francolyn Shipping	Hong Kong	100	Shipowning
Hendale Navigation Co.	United Kingdom	100	Shipowning
International Capital Corporation	Liberia	100	Finance
Juniper Shipping	Liberia	100	Shipowning
Lensbury Co.	Liberia	100	Shipowning
Liberian Atlas Transports Inc.	Liberia	100	Shipowning
Liberian Crest Transports Inc.	Liberia	100	Shipowning
Liberian Cross Transports Inc.	Liberia	100	Shipowning
Liberian Crown Transports Inc.	Liberia	100	Dormant
Liberian Emblem Transports Inc.	Liberia	100	Shipowning
Liberian Eternity Transports Inc.	Liberia	100	Shipowning
Liberian Express Transports Inc.	Liberia	100	Shipowning
Liberian Global Transports Inc.	Liberia	100	Shipowning
Liberian Hart Transports Inc.	Liberia	100	Shipowning
Liberian Onyx Transports Inc.	Liberia	100	Shipowning
Liberian Poniard Transports	Liberia	100	Shipowning
Liberian Poplar Transports Inc.	Liberia	100	Shipowning
Liberian Ruby Transports Inc.	Liberia	100	Dormant
Liberian Shield Transports Inc.	Liberia	100	Shipowning

Table 15.12 (cont.)

Name of company	Place incorporated	% held (i) (ii)	Nature of business
Liberian Skylark Transports Inc.	Liberia	100	Shipowning
Liberian Sickle Transports Inc.	Liberia	100	Shipowning
Liberian Silver Transports Inc.	Liberia	100	Shipowning
Liberian Sparta Transports Inc.	Liberia	60	Holding Co.
Liberian Countess Transports	Liberia	100	Shipowning
Liberian Stag Transports Inc.	Liberia	100	Shipowning
Liberian Stamina Transports Inc.	Liberia	100	Shipowning
Liberian Swift Transports Inc.	Liberia	100	Shipowning
Liberian Unity Transports Inc.	Liberia	100	Holding Co.
Bloomfield Co.	Liberia	30	Holding Co.
Marnav Property Holdings	Hong Kong	100	Property
Liberian Valient Transports Inc.	Liberia	100	Shipowning
Liberian Violet Transports Inc.	Liberia	100	Shipowning
Liberian Viscount Transports Inc.	Liberia	100	Shipowning
Liberian Whale Transports Inc.	Liberia	100	Shipowning
Liberian Zeus Transports	Liberia	100	Shipowning
Ludlow Navigation Co.	United Kingdom	100	Shipowning
Milestone Co.	Liberia	100	Shipowning
Poplar Navigation Inc.	Liberia	100	Finance
Proton Transports (Bermuda)	Bermuda	100	Holding
Skua Navigation	Hong Kong	100	Shipowning
The Windsor Shipping Co.	Hong Kong	100	Shipowning
Troya Corporation N.V.	Netherlands Antilles	100	Holding
Liberian Peony Transports Inc.	Liberia	100	Finance Co.
World Magnate Shipping	Hong Kong	100	Dormant
World Maritime (Bahamas)	Bahamas	100	Dormant
World Maritime Ltd, Hong Kong	Hong Kong	100	Dormant

Table 15.12 (*cont.*)

Name of company	Place incorporated	% held (i)	% held (ii)	Nature of business
World Planet Shipping	Hong Kong		100	Shipowning
World Shipping & Investment Co.	Hong Kong		34	Holding Co.
World Marine Transportation Inc.	Liberia		100	Holding Co.
Eastbourne Finance	Liberia		100	Finance
Grand Canyon Co.	Liberia		100	Holding Co.
Hakone Holdings	Panama		40	Holding Co.
Regent Shipping	Hong Kong		100	Ship Management
Liberian Clover Transports Inc.	Liberia		100	Shipowning
Liberian Courage Transports Inc.	Liberia		100	Shipowning
Liberian Expedience Transports Inc.	Liberia		100	Shipowning
Liberian Flame Transports Inc.	Liberia		100	Shipowning
Liberian Galaxie Transports Inc.	Liberia		100	Shipowning
Liberian Pristella Transports Inc.	Liberia		100	Shipowning
Liberian Tulip Transports Inc.	Liberia		100	Shipowning
Liberian Thrush Transports Inc.	Liberia		100	Shipowning
Liberian Ulysses Transports Inc.	Liberia		100	Shipowning
Liberian Wasp Transports Inc.	Liberia		100	Shipowning
Nightingale Shipping Co.	Panama		100	Shipowning
River Cape Shipping Co.	Panama		100	Shipowning
Tranquility Shipping Co.	Panama		100	Shipowning
Abberley Company	Liberia		45	Investment Co.
Wardley Investments Canada	Canada	100		Investment Holding
Gracechurch Holdings	Canada		100	Dormant
Wardley Canada	Canada		100	Industrial/Commercial finance
British Acceptance Corporation	Canada		100	Dormant
Wardley Realty	Canada		100	Real Estate/Mortgage Investments

Table 15.12 (cont.)

Name of company	Place incorporated	% held (i)	% held (ii)	Nature of business
Wardley	Hong Kong	100		Merchant Banking
Central Registration (HK)	Hong Kong		50	Share Registration
Fatima Estates	Hong Kong		100	Property
Ormskirk Co.	Hong Kong		50	Finance Co.
Sharps Pixley Wardley	Hong Kong		25	Bullion brokers
Stanbridge	New Hebrides		100	Finance Co.
Wardley Asia	Hong Kong		100	Finance Co./Management
Wardley Australia (Holdings)	Australia		100	Investment Holdings
Wardley Australia	Australia		100	Finance/Holding Co.
Finaway Pty	Australia		100	Dormant Property Construction Co.
Finaway Properties Pty	Australia		100	Property owner
Kingsgate Property Management	Australia		50	Hotel complex management
Orchard Shopping Village Pty	Australia		50	Shopping Centre Developers
Starbridge No. 1 Pty	Australia		37.5	Dormant
Wardley Australia Securities	Australia		100	Securities
Real Property Leases	Australia		33.3	Property leasing
Real Property Leases Pty	Australia		100	Property leasing
Wardley Leasing	Hong Kong		100	Leasing/Loans
Wardley Data Services	Hong Kong		100	Investment information
Wardley International	Bahamas		100	Dormant
Wardley Investments (NH)	New Hebrides		100	Dormant
Wardley Investment Services	Hong Kong		100	Investment Management
Pittencrieff Investments	Hong Kong		100	Investment Co.
Wardley Bond Management	Hong Kong		100	Unit Trust Management
Wardley International Management	Hong Kong		100	Unit Trust Management
Wardley Nikko Management	Hong Kong		50	Unit Trust Management
Wardley Securities	Hong Kong		100	Investment Banking
Wardley Services (New Hebrides)	New Hebrides		100	Nominee Service
Wardley (Malaysia)	Malaysia		100	Dormant
Wardley Nominees	Hong Kong		100	Nominee Service
Wardley (Singapore) Nominees	Singapore		100	Nominee Service
Wardley International Bank	Bahamas		100	Banking
Wardley International NV	Netherlands Antilles		100	Dormant

Table 15.12 (cont.)

Name of company	Place incorporated	% held (i)	% held (ii)	Nature of business
Wardley International BV	Netherlands		100	Dormant
Zulu Investments	Hong Kong		100	Lending
State Leasing (Hong Kong)	Hong Kong		50	Leasing
Wardley (Vila)	New Hebrides		100	Finance Co.
State Investment House Inc.	Philippines		25	Finance Co.
State Investment House (Hong Kong)	Hong Kong		100	Investment Co.
SIH (Vila)	New Hebrides		100	Finance Co.
Tenix	Hong Kong		100	Import/Export traders
State Leasing (Hong Kong)	Hong Kong		50	Leasing
Philippine Development and Industrial Corp.	Philippines		51	Limestone quarrying
Credit Finance and Industrial Corp.	Philippines		100	Finance Co.
State Land Investment Corp.	Philippines		25	Property Co.
WTL Limited	Hong Kong		100	Holding Co.
Investment and Securities (Thailand)	Thailand		39	Investment Co.
Wardley Thailand Limited	Thailand		100	Finance Co.
Investment and Securities (Thailand) (WTL Ltd owns a further 39%)	Thailand		1	Investment Co.
Wardley Investments (NZ)	New Zealand	100		Investment Holding
Wardley Middle East	Dubai	80		Merchant Banking
Wayfoong Mortgage And Finance (Singapore)	Singapore	100		Consumer Finance
Woodhall Co.	Hong Kong	50		Property Holding
Kellett N.V.	Netherlands Antilles	100		Investment & Management Co.B
HSBC Holdings BV	Netherlands		100	do

Boldface indicates a directly held subsidiary company of HSBC. In the column '% held', the percentage of a company (either subsidiary or associated) held directly by HSBC is listed under (i); the percentage of a company held indirectly is listed under (ii).

Source: U.S. Congress, 'Exhibit A', in *Foreign Acquisitions of U.S. Banks and Non-Banking Activities of Foreign Bank Holding Companies*, Hearings before a subcommittee of the Committee on Government Operations, House of Representatives, 96th Congress, second session, May 15 and June 25, 1980 (Washington, D.C. 1980), pp. 88–189.

16

THE ACQUISITION OF MARINE MIDLAND BANKS, INC., 1978–1980, I. STRATEGY AND INITIAL SUCCESS, THE SIGNING OF THE DEFINITIVE AGREEMENT*

> Marine Midland Banks, Inc. is a New York-based financial services institution with assets of more than [US] $24 billion. Its principal subsidiary, Marine Midland Bank, N.A., operates extensively throughout New York State and elsewhere in the U.S. and the world through a network of branches, other offices and correspondent banks. A special Marine Midland strength is its unique partnership with The Hongkong and Shanghai Banking Corporation, a leading global banking group and a 51% shareholder in Marine Midland.
>
> Marine Midland Banks, Inc., *Annual Report* (1984)

INTRODUCTION TO A PARTNERSHIP

THE SETTING

The transaction described

This is an account of the events whereby The Hongkong and Shanghai Banking Corporation on October 1, 1980, completed acquisition of 51.1% of the common stock of the Delaware-incorporated, New York-based, financial services institution and bank holding company, Marine Midland Banks, Inc. (MMBI), which owned 100% of the stock of America's then twelfth largest bank, Marine Midland Bank (MMB) of Buffalo, New York. The actual acquisition was by the Netherlands-incorporated HSBC Holdings, BV, a wholly owned subsidiary of Kellett, NV (Netherlands Antilles), which is in turn a wholly owned subsidiary of The Hongkong and Shanghai Banking Corporation (see Appendix to Chapter 15).

The consequences of this acquisition both to MMBI and to the Hongkong Bank are considered in Chapter 17. A glance at Table 16.1, however, will reveal that at the end of 1979, the year before the acquisition was completed, the total assets of MMBI were 62% of those of the HSBC, 96% of those of the Hongkong Bank itself. During 1980, the year the deal was effected the

---

* The abbreviations are restated in the Appendix to Chapter 17, p. 850. For general references, see the introduction to the end-notes, p. 936.

Table 16.1 *Hongkong Bank Group, Hongkong Bank, MMBI Comparative figures, 1978–1980*

end of:	Assets	Shareholders' equity
(in billions of Hong Kong dollars[a])		
1978		
Hongkong Bank Group	98.4	2.88
Hongkong Bank	62.5	2.65
Marine Midland Banks, Inc.	61.4	2.16
1979		
Hongkong Bank Group	125.9	3.71
Hongkong Bank	80.7	3.40
Marine Midland Banks, Inc.	77.7	2.38
1980		
Hongkong Bank Group	243.0	10.33
Hongkong Bank	104.3	9.18
Marine Midland Banks, Inc.	89.9	3.91
(in billions of U.S. dollars[a])		
1978		
Hongkong Bank Group	20.5	0.60
Hongkong Bank	13.0	0.55
Marine Midland Banks, Inc.	12.8	0.45
1979		
Hongkong Bank Group	25.3	0.75
Hongkong Bank	16.3	0.69
Marine Midland Banks, Inc.	15.7	0.48
1980		
Hongkong Bank Group	47.3	2.01
Hongkong Bank	20.3	1.79
Marine Midland Banks, Inc.	17.5	0.76

[a] Exchange rates for US$1.00: 1978, $4.80; 1979, $4.95; 1980, $5.135.

Hongkong Bank Group's total assets virtually doubled from $125.3 billion to $243 billion. For the first time since 1960 The Hongkong and Shanghai Banking Corporation had made a significant change of course; the regional 'China bank' was now a multinational corporation.

Described in the financial press as a 'finely sculptured deal', the transaction, after the June 1979 renegotiation, involved the Hongkong Bank's tendering for approximately 25% of the then existing common stock of MMBI at a price of US$25 a share and purchasing sufficient newly issued shares in two tranches at US$34 plus a factor which took performance improvement into account (US$1.42 as it happened) to give the Hongkong Bank 51.1% of the common stock of MMBI then outstanding. Pending approval of the transaction by the authorities, the Hongkong Bank (actually Kellett N.V.) on May 18, 1978, purchased a US$100 million $7\frac{3}{4}$% subordinated note, intended to rank as capital under certain specified conditions. As regulatory authority for the transaction was delayed, the Hongkong Bank exchanged this note on June 27, 1979, for a fifteen-year, 9% subordinated note of equivalent value, which consequently did rank as capital and which, after the final regulatory approval on January 28, 1980, was surrendered on March 4, 1980, in part payment of the first tranche.

When the deal was completed ahead of schedule on October 31, 1980, the HSBC had paid US$314 million, or 80% of book value, for control of MMBI's end-1980 assets of US$17,480 million, equivalent to US$1 per US$55.67 of assets. Foreign banks had been paying one and a half to two times book value to acquire an American bank.[1]

The transaction was unusual in that it set two share prices, that it held together during a prolonged period of negotiations with the regulatory authorities, that a subordinated note provided tangible evidence of HSBC's declared intention to inject funds into the capital-hungry MMBI, and that it was at the time the largest bank acquisition in United States history, thus arousing considerable political interest in a wide range of relevant banking regulatory and statutory issues. The history of the merger is covered in two chapters. Chapter 16 deals with the preliminary considerations, the contact with Marine Midland, and the signing of the Definitive Agreement. Chapter 17 deals with the process by which the agreement was finally implemented after regulatory approval – a timetable is appended.

The human element

Just as the mutual benefits to be derived from the transaction held it in place during a record period of negotiation, so the HSBC and MMBI officers and advisers formed a uniquely sympathetic team which proved capable of working together through difficult times and inconvenient hours. In the absence of this element the transaction might, for human reasons, have failed. The two factors combined to see the deal through.

From the first the consultants developed a sense that the Hongkong Bank had a vision and a purpose, which it was worth devoting considerable effort to assist them to realize. The two chief executive officers, Edward W. Duffy and Michael Sandberg, established a mutual respect which underlay the more general rapport of those HSBC and MMBI officers and advisers involved in the transaction. Advisers quickly sensed the feeling; it had been engendered at the first meetings in Honolulu and was referred to as 'the spirit of Hawaii'. The transaction was approached with the attitude that it could not fail, that any

I. Strategy and initial success 765

impediment was temporary, any misunderstanding correctable, any obstacle surmountable.

How this came about is part of the story of the Hongkong Bank's partnership with Marine Midland. It is also a justification for concluding that, in this case, 'partnership' was not simply a euphemism for 'holding company/subsidiary'; similarly, 'merger', a term widely used in describing the intended effect of the transaction, was not simply a euphemism for the legally accurate 'acquisition'.

The timetable

The first contact between the chief executive officers of the two banks in the context of the transaction was in January 1978; the timing was excellent. Three policy streams were in fact converging: (i) the HSBC had been developing its North American strategy at least since 1975 and had eventually identified Marine Midland, (ii) MMBI had been 'turned around' following disastrous decisions in the early 1970s, and since then its Board had become aware of (a) the need to increase capital and (b) the difficulty of doing so, and (iii) New York State had initiated a policy of economic development which welcomed foreign investment. Underlying all this was the passage, in 1978, of the International Banking Act (IBA), which by predicating 'national treatment' resolved many but, as will be described in the following section, not all of the legislative problems and public concerns relative to foreign banks and foreign bank acquisitions in the United States.

The actual negotiations between HSBC and MMBI were completed by May 1978 when the 'Definitive Agreement' was signed in Buffalo. The initial public reaction to the agreement was favourable and in the following months the transaction received regulatory approval from various agencies in the United States and elsewhere which were essential but relatively non-controversial (see Figure 16.1 and Appendix to Chapter 17, 'Timetable'). At the same time the MMBI prepared proxy statements and, prior to mailing to shareholders, sought the approval of the Securities and Exchange Commission (SEC). At this point there began a series of delays which, to any deal less favourable to all parties, would have been fatal.

After meeting SEC objections, MMBI secured shareholder approval for the Definitive Agreement on October 18, 1978. Application had already been made to the Federal Reserve Board and, since MMB was a State bank, to the New York State Banking Department. Concurrently arrangements were made for the sale of the Hongkong Bank of California in conformity with the terms of the Banking Holding Company Act of 1970 (12 USC §1842). Federal Reserve Board approval for the Definitive Agreement was obtained in March 1979, but a New York decision was postponed on the pretext of requiring further

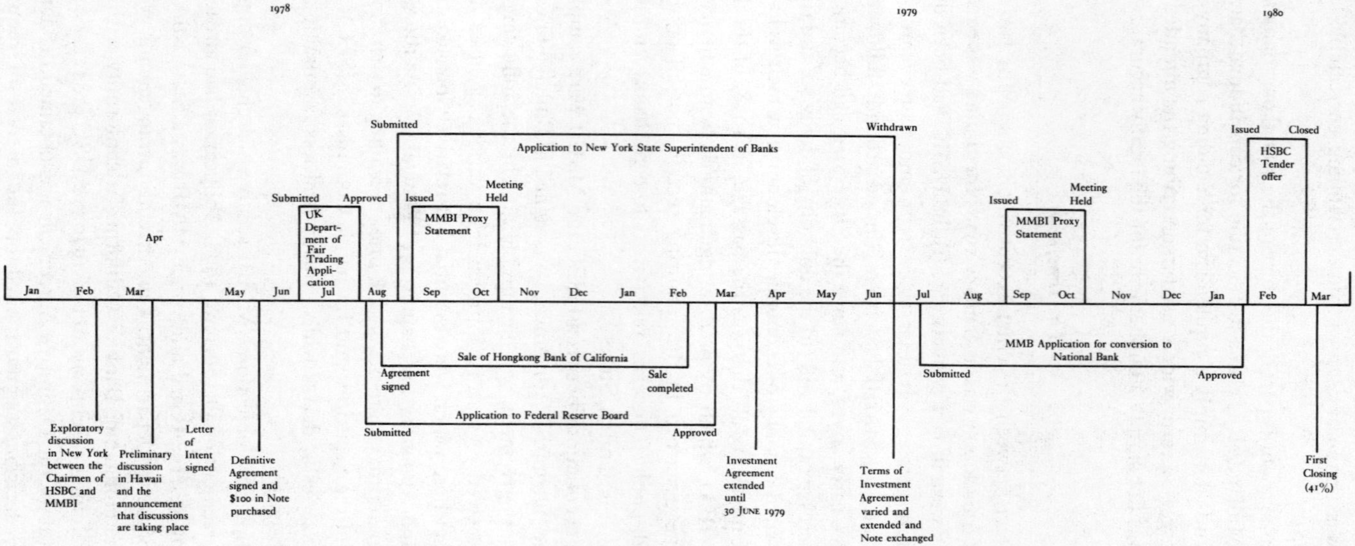

Figure 16.1 Marine Midland Banks, Inc.: progress of the transaction

information relative to HSBC's non-financial subsidiary and associated companies.

The two bank holding companies, HSBC and MMBI, agreed not to terminate the Investment Agreement prior to June 30, 1979. The feeling was growing, however, that New York State approval would not be forthcoming. Accordingly MMBI decided to apply to the Comptroller of the Currency and Administrator of the National Banking System in Washington, D.C., for permission to convert MMB into a national banking association; once this were granted, the Marine Midland Bank would apparently be beyond the jurisdiction of the New York State Banking Department, and, as Federal permission for the acquisition had been granted, the terms of the agreement could be put into immediate effect. In the meantime, however, MMBI's position had been improving, and, on June 27, the two parties amended the Definitive Agreement in favour of Marine Midland and extended the date of termination to June 30, 1980; the following day the application to the New York State Banking Department was withdrawn.

The amended agreement was approved by MMBI shareholders on October 17, 1979. The Comptroller of the Currency, aware of the political implications, made a careful study of MMB and in October sent a high-level team to study the Hongkong Bank in Hong Kong. Not until January 28, 1980, however, did the Comptroller finally approve MMB's application to convert. MMB converted to a national bank on February 1 and HSBC Holdings' tender for MMBI common stock was announced in the *Wall Street Journal* on February 4; the offer, which was successful, closed on March 3, and on the following day the 9% note was sold by Kellett to HSBC Holdings, the latter then paid this note and cash for newly issued MMBI shares, thus completing the first stage of the actual purchase. The second tranche was purchased on October 31, 1980, and the requirements of the Definitive Agreement were completed; the HSBC owned, through its wholly owned subsidiaries, a controlling 51.1% share in MMBI.

This schedule can be simplified. There were essentially four stages: (i) the negotiations between the two banks culminating in the May 1978 Agreement, (ii) the negotiations with regulatory agencies on the assumption that MMB would remain a State bank – these lasted to June 27, 1979, (iii) the negotiations relative to converting MMB from a State to a National bank to January 28, 1980, and (iv) the completion of the now approved transaction on October 1, 1980.

This period and these negotiations are crucial in the history of The Hongkong and Shanghai Banking Corporation. They will, therefore, be considered in some detail in the following sections.

THE REGULATORY AND BANKING ENVIRONMENT

The 1970s were important in the history of U.S. foreign banking. They were also, partly in consequence of this, a period of frequent legislative change accompanied by new regulatory interpretation. Furthermore, when unexpected developments occurred, even recent enactments proved unsatisfactory to at least part of the interested community. As one example, when the Hongkong Bank began its negotiations relative to the acquisition of Marine Midland Banks, Inc., in 1978, the initial atmosphere was friendly, but, as delays continued, there were increasing doubts in Congress and elsewhere not so much on the Bank's particular offer but on the unforeseen number of offers, banks, and funds involved. The number of foreign bank acquisitions had been increasing during the decade; in 1977 there were fourteen with total assets of US$920 million, but in 1978 there were seventeen and their assets totalled US$3,461 million; there would be fifteen acquisitions in 1979 involving total assets of US$12,638 million.

Although the following review benefits from hindsight, especially from Office of the Comptroller of the Currency (OCC) Staff analyses published in 1980, that is, after approval of the HSBC/MMBI transaction, the facts – and their misinterpretation – were both factors in the Hongkong Bank's American experience.[2]

'National treatment'

Foreign bank operations had been severely restricted by general State legislation, including outright prohibition. They were not, however, subject to the limitations of basic Federal restrictions, for example, those in the Douglas and MacFadden amendments to the Glass-Steagall Act of 1933. In consequence, foreign banks could, if permitted by State law, open branches or control banks in more than one State.

As long as foreign banks operated small branches designed to finance foreign trade, as indeed the Hongkong Bank of California was originally designed to undertake, there was little concern at the competitive advantage consequent to this unusual privilege. Domestic banks could, after all, found Edge Act Corporations, which would permit out-of-State offices for foreign trade finance. The increased presence of foreign banks and/or their U.S. incorporated subsidiaries forced the Congress to consider the problem.

The response was a series of enactments combined into the International Banking Act of 1978 (IBA), the provisions of which were designed to create 'national treatment', that is, equal treatment of domestic and foreign banks, in the United States. One consequence of this was that the Hongkong Bank in developing an American strategy had to be in place before passage of the act and, as will be seen below, HSBC opened or secured authority to open branches in key centres where this had been permitted before the provisions of the act came into force. The subsequent act 'grandfathered' these branches.

The act required a foreign bank to designate a 'home state'. In the home state the foreign bank can both operate branches and control a subsidiary. The Hongkong Bank can have a controlling interest in MMBI (in fact since December 1987 a 100% interest) and there are also branches of both the Hongkong Bank and Hang Seng Bank operating in New York as the 'home state'; also in New York the Hongkong Bank acquired (in 1985) the Golden Pacific Bank, then insolvent, and took over its offices as Hongkong Bank branches. However, outside the home state HSBC cannot operate a subsidiary, and it therefore had to divest itself of the HBC before acquiring MMBI; it can however – but subject to State laws – (i) continue to operate grandfathered branches and (ii) operate agencies, defined as offices permitted to take deposits which would be permitted by an Edge Act Corporation.[3]

At the same time the Federal Reserve Board, responding to the provisions of the IBA, authorized the establishment of nation-wide branching for both domestic and foreign-owned Edge Act Corporations. Bank-related financial operations of a bank holding company and loan-generating offices were also permitted nation-wide.

The possibilities of nation-wide operations were then significant and the atmosphere seemed favourable, despite the new but equalizing restrictions, to foreign banks and their subsidiaries.

'National treatment' should not, however, be confused with 'reciprocity'. The latter is a long-established U.S. policy goal, but it was not a mandatory factor in existing legislation nor was it in the implementation of the new legislation by the regulatory agencies. This would lead to misunderstandings.[4]

Acquisitions by foreign banks

The nature of the problem

The subject of acquisitions was not covered by the IBA but was dealt with in the Bank Holding Company Act of 1970 as supplemented by the Change of Control Act, 1978; this latter is not, however, relevant to the discussion.

To start a bank *de novo* in the United States, except in the case of a few small, limited-purpose branches, was prohibitively expensive; acquisition of an existing bank became increasingly common and, as noted above, was one factor which developed into a political impediment to the Hongkong Bank's acquisition of Marine Midland. To understand the developing concern of bankers and Congress some background is necessary.

Prior to 1970 there had been only five foreign acquisitions of U.S. banks, and these had been small with total assets of US$76.3 million. Acquisition was a phenomenon of the 1970s, but even then, it could be argued, as of March 31, 1980, only 109 U.S. banking organizations, less than 1% of the total, were foreign controlled (10% or more of equity) and these controlled assets of US$76.9 billion, some 4.5% of total banking assets. On the other hand, 26% of the 300 largest U.S. banks were foreign-owned, although even this may not appear dangerous to the control of the economy.

On 'danger', or less dramatically, 'importance', there are two further comments. The size of at least three transactions caused the overall problem to be exaggerated in the public mind, and then the question remained, Is this just the beginning?

Unfortunately, the first major bank acquisition was that of the Franklin National Bank, with assets of US$3.5 billion, by Michele Sindona in 1972. By 1974 the resulting management had forced the bank into an emergency situation from which only US$1.6 billion of assets remained; these were acquired on a rescue basis by the European-American Bank and Trust Company, an international consortium bank with members from Austria, Germany, Britain (Midland Bank), Belgium, and France; by end-1979 the bank's assets had grown to US$4.7 billion – the case was one of a bad and a good take-over. The bad take-over was, however, the one which seemed precedential and was to remain of continued interest.

The next major acquisition came in 1979. While the Hongkong Bank's transaction with MMBI was still in the delaying hands of the Superintendent of Banks for New York State, Muriel Siebert, the Standard Chartered Group acquired the Union Bank of California, the 25th largest (by size of deposits) in the United States.

The example of the Standard Chartered Group[a]

The Standard Chartered Group's chief executive officer responsible for the acquisition was (Sir) Peter A. Graham, (Sir) Michael Sandberg's friend from junior days in Tokyo and later manager of the Chartered Bank's Hong Kong operations. Although Chartered had moved into North America some ten years after the Hongkong Bank established HBC, its history followed the same pattern. The Chartered Bank of London (San Francisco), for example, bought Liberty National Bank (of San Francisco) in 1974 and the Commercial and Farmers Bank of Oxnard in 1977; it also had a limited but inadequate branch network. In 1976 Graham approached the Bank of California, which was at that time 14% owned by Baron Edmond de Rothschild (32% from

---

[a] The Standard Chartered Group was a 1969 merger of the Chartered Bank (of India, Australia and China) and the Standard Bank (of South Africa) – both banks had by the time of the merger dropped their geographic designations.

1979), but the offer met with board opposition and Graham withdrew. He returned a year later and began negotiations, eventually successful, with the Union Bank, into which would be merged the branches of the Chartered Bank of London. Graham was following a California strategy which would be specifically rejected by the Hongkong Bank.[5]

But the problem all this created was timing, the bunching in 1979.

There were in the same year as the Union Bank acquisition by Standard Chartered (1979), acquisitions involving in all assets of US$12.6 billion. Congress was uneasy. So, indeed, was Sandberg, who opened his daily newspaper concerned that he would read of yet another major take-over offer. Unless these developments could be shown to be exceptional, Congress would naturally be concerned. Equally to be expected was that the sensational aspects would be developed first, and, in this context, Franklin National was not forgotten.

Factors behind the acquisitions

There were two apparently obvious factors, low share prices and a 'cheap' U.S. dollar, which might explain developments. In the key years of 1974 and 1979 the earnings equity ratios of banks were particularly low; prices were at a significant discount over book value, and with 'troubled' banks the discount might run to 50% or more. The U.S. dollar was weak on the foreign exchange markets.

U.S. banks must be saved from being bought on the cheap by foreigners.

This led to a further concern. If U.S. banks were purchased cheaply, would not their deposit base be exploited in the interests of the foreign acquirer? Could the foreign bank or individual use those deposits to buy foreign exchange and invest American savings overseas at more profitable rates of interest? These fears aroused the interest of those concerned with local development, of community interest groups. The outflow of local savings to foreign lands (or even to the next State in the American Union) was a particularly worrying popular concern.

The more rational observer noted, however, that if foreigners wanted a U.S. investment, given the 'cheap' dollar, there were more effective ways of accomplishing this than by buying a bank, as they were doing, at a premium or, more likely, buying a troubled bank at something considerably in excess of its market valuation.

The strategic long-term factors seemed to be more interesting. Banking had become global; banks needed to diversify their assets, and they needed a dollar base. These themes were developed as the Hongkong Bank considered its American strategy. Furthermore the Hongkong Bank and the Standard Chartered had been oriented to business in the Third World; they were the inheritors through post-war rationalization, that is, through acquisition or merger, of British imperial banking. Even the Hongkong Bank with its strong Hong Kong base needed a U.S. dollar base of operations. As of March 31, 1980, the four largest foreign banks (or foreign bank subsidiaries) in the U.S. in terms of deposits, Marine Midland (HSBC), Union Bank (Standard Chartered), the European-American Bank, and the National Bank of North America (National Westminster) were either British or British-controlled or, in the case of the European-American Bank, had a substantial British interest (Midland, 20.125%).

Major foreign banks were also seeking to rationalize their world-wide operations; they were seeking a partner in a stable political base whose operations were complementary, whose own branch network would, perhaps, mesh with theirs. It was the positive developmental prospects which were underlying the acquisitions whatever tactical considerations may have resulted in the focus on 1978–1980. Indeed it was these factors that had sent American banks in search of partners overseas.

This much many observers accepted. But the developments nevertheless warranted investigation and the key question for the Hongkong Bank was whether such investigation would affect adversely the HSBC/MMBI merger transaction.

There was an additional rather esoteric factor.

The Bank Holding Company Act of 1956 defined 'bank holding company' as a company controlling two or more banks. Despite the fact that one purpose of the act was to prevent a holding company engaging in commercial activities, the definition used in fact permitted a primarily non-financial holding company to control *one* bank. The anomaly was corrected by amendment to the act in 1970, and the offending non-financial holding companies were given ten years to divest themselves of their subsidiary bank. One such bank, the First Western and Trust Company, was acquired in 1974 by Lloyds Group, but two were acquired in the crucial year of 1979: the National Bank of North America by National Westminster and La Salle National Bank by the Algemene Bank Nederland. Of these only the National Bank of North America was a large bank, 37th in terms of deposits, and the third largest foreign-owned bank in the United States (the fourth after the acquisition of MMBI by the HSBC); its assets of US$4.3 billion ranked it along with the Union Bank of California.[6]

Supervisory concerns
National banks are subject to various regulations controlling their operations, as, for example, that dividends must be paid out of net profits but provided there are adequate surplus funds; a National bank cannot lend to or make investments in any affiliated institution, including its parent bank holding company, in excess of 10% of the bank's capital stock and surplus. These

restrictions apply to the foreign bank holding company and include its overseas operations. The requirement that under certain conditions the branch of a foreign bank became insured by the FDIC led to further questions as to whether the entire bank was then subject to the additional restraints imposed by the FDIC; for practical purposes they were not subject to the FDIC. Nevertheless, the concern remained.

Such detailed regulatory authority raised two questions: (i) was the Hongkong Bank fully aware of what its involvement in the United States implied and (ii) was it possible for the regulatory agencies to supervise the Hongkong Bank's world-wide activities to the extent required? The first was probably the motive that lay behind the Comptroller of the Currency's demand that Sandberg have a final face-to-face meeting with him in Washington; the latter led to demands on several occasions that the Hongkong Bank agree to abide by certain rules or submit certain information.

In the nineteenth century the British Treasury had been similarly concerned. Its response was to require deposit of cash and securities under Government control and to encourage geographical limitation, but this latter was now precisely the point at issue. American banks were global, their overseas operations had to be monitored by U.S. agencies, was it not now possible to accept foreign banks on the national treatment basis?

The legislation clearly answered in the affirmative, but, as the number of acquisitions increased and as the size of the bank acquired became significant, there was pressure from Congress to ensure that the Office of the Comptroller of the Currency and the Federal Reserve Board appreciated the complexity of the task and secured the guaranteed cooperation of the foreign bank involved. All this would be further stressed in cases where, like the HSBC, the foreign bank holding company had considerable non-financial interests.

Non-financial activities and national treatment

The two trends in American financial legislation have been decentralization and separation of banking from commercial and industrial activities. One purpose of the Bank Holding Company Act was to prevent financial and non-financial business coming under a single management through the holding company device. National treatment suggests that foreign and domestic bank holding companies should be treated equally. However, the separation referred to is peculiar to a few countries, and such equal treatment would in consequence virtually prevent foreign banks in, say, Japan or continental Europe from opening a branch or acquiring a United States subsidiary.

As in the case of inter-state branching, foreign banks were at one time excluded from this legislation, although a foreign bank's U.S. subsidiary was subject to the restrictive U.S. approach. The IBA grandfathered existing operations, securities operations, for example, after consideration of possible foreign retaliation.

Would-be foreign acquirers have to apply for permission to acquire to, *inter alios*, the Federal Reserve Board, which is empowered by the IBA to modify the requirement of separation after taking the laws of the foreign bank's home country into consideration. The regulations are administered to ensure (i) that the foreign bank holding company is primarily engaged in banking and (ii) that their non-financial operations in the United States are minimized and conducted at 'arm's length'. The latter was particularly important in view of American business concern relative to possible unfair competition.

Specifically, a foreign bank holding company principally engaged in banking business outside the United States may own a foreign company principally engaged in business outside the United States, which company can in turn own a U.S. company that is engaged in the same general line of business or in a business related to that of the investor company. This explains the apparent concern, to be recounted below, of Muriel Siebert, the New York State Superintendent of Banks, and Congressman Benjamin S. Rosenthal when confronted with a long list of HSBC subsidiary and associated companies. The brewery, the film companies, the tankers – could these companies establish Hongkong Bank-financed subsidiaries in the United States? It was a question which could, if put with sufficient inaccuracy and lack of analysis, arouse considerable concern; it was a question which could be given considerable political content.

As the Hongkong Bank concluded its deliberations and approached the United States, there was therefore policy unease which could be and was triggered into a consideration of the legislation under which the Hongkong Bank first made its application. The Bank's case could be regarded critically by some because (i) of its size – it was the largest in the history of the United States, (ii) the Bank's non-disclosure policy, and (iii) its target, Marine Midland, was an up-State commercial bank with a broad retail deposit base.

The implications for the American banking system and for those responsible for its supervision have been stated in general terms above.

Concern for the adequacy of existing legislation caused attempts either to prevent consummation of the HSBC transaction with MMBI itself or to delay the transaction until it either fell victim to that delay or until the laws were changed adversely.

That, in any case, puts the potential development at its worst.

In fact, the HSBC/MMBI transaction was seen to be so mutually advantageous that most of those directly involved favoured grandfathering the agreement regardless of other developing considerations. The HSBC/MMBI merger was not necessarily seen as objectionable in itself; for most, this transaction was not the target. To this generalization there were exceptions. At times senior executives of the Hongkong Bank appeared to be unaware of the complexity of the problem and of the historical background to sufficiently understand apparently unintelligible reactions. Nevertheless, even had the Hongkong Bank been able to assess the situation accurately and been fully prepared, the impact of the few opposed would have remained a continuous concern. Delay itself was potentially sufficient to destroy the deal.

THREE STRATEGIES CONVERGE

Timing is an essential element in any business negotiation. Since ideal timing characterized the negotiations which led to the investment by the HSBC in MMBI, the first part of this account is on the three independently developed strategies which converged in January 1978 to make possible the developments which followed. Concurrently the Hongkong Bank was working out an American strategy, Marine Midland was preparing itself for the reality of a market in which an increased capitalization could only be achieved on reasonable terms by accepting a 'partnership', and Governor Hugh Carey's New York State Administration were already proving the success of a new economic policy stressing the encouragement of outside investment.

THE DEVELOPMENT OF THE HONGKONG BANK'S AMERICAN STRATEGY

A serious reconsideration of the Bank's role in the United States was forced by the continued poor performance of the Hongkong Bank of California (HBC). Behind this motivation lay the recognition of certain senior Hongkong Bank executives, for example, Michael Sandberg, the Deputy Chairman, and I.H. Macdonald, General Manager for Overseas Operations, that The Hongkong and Shanghai Banking Corporation (HSBC) had – despite its balance-sheet growth and its new geographical spread – stagnated conceptually. Although the Bank's shares were quoted on the market at above *true* book value, although the Bank was notoriously liquid, no advantage seemed to be taken of the situation. In 1975 the Chairman and chief executive, G.M. Sayer, authorized, albeit with some reservations, the President of the Hongkong Bank of California to retain consultants and determine an improved approach to the Bank's presence in California.

The consultants were encouraged to probe into further possibilities, including the acquisition of a bank on the Pacific coast outside California. At each meeting, it seemed, the Hongkong Bank was willing to commit itself further; this assumption proved premature.

The development of the Bank's American strategy can in fact be divided into two phases, the first was from 1975 to November 1976. But the expansionists had moved too quickly; there was a reaction, a return to rethink the future of the California bank and a hold on considerations farther afield. The period between November 1976 and October 1977, that is, for the balance of Sayer's chairmanship, was a hiatus. The second phase began then with the appointment of Sandberg as Chairman; it continued to a January 1978 telephone call from Sandberg to Duffy, chairman of Marine Midland Banks, asking simply if he would be available in New York for a discussion in the immediate future. The decision had been made; the negotiations were to start.

The first phase

Focus on California

Between 1973 and 1975 M.J. Calvert as President of the Hongkong Bank of California had the task of identifying and remedying problem loans. The HBC had been barely providing a satisfactory return on capital before consideration of losses; the situation throughout was precarious. In 1974, for example, when accumulated losses were written off, an additional US$5 million of capital had to be subscribed; Calvert then had the additional assignment of rethinking the HSBC's California role.

The Hongkong Bank had had an agency in San Francisco since 1875, it had found the restrictions imposed on an agency such that the Bank could no longer fulfil the post-war requirements of its Far Eastern constituents; the Hongkong Bank of California had been established in 1955 in consequence. Although initially founded to perform virtually as a branch of the parent company, even before it opened for business Turner had given it a broader brief – it was to act as a bank in its own right (see Chapter 12). As such it was at US$10 million undercapitalized for a general California operation, and, despite continued reference to international trade-related finance, HBC attempted general banking. HBC management had apparently been unable to restrain itself. HBC's Foreign staff senior management were unprepared for California domestic banking; Calvert's assignment was hardly premature.

The decision made, Calvert was transferred to head the Hongkong Bank's Malaysian operations. Before he left, he and R.W. Campbell, previously Manager for the Southern California branches, then the bank's President-designate, received instructions that Campbell would carry out the California review with the assistance of consultants. After consideration Booz, Allen and

Hamilton, Inc., were selected in October 1975, their team consisting of Warren Chinn, head of the firm's San Francisco office, and two banking consultants, John Poppen, at that time head of the Banking Practice section operating from Chicago, and Howard D. Adams.

At the first meeting Calvert and Campbell set the consultant's brief in terms of a review of California operations with a view to growth, a return of 15%, and a taxable income of about US$6 million following an investment in the range of US$25 to 30 million. As Campbell recognized, one obvious way to achieve expansion was to buy up small California banks in trouble, but this was impractical despite calls from the State Banking Superintendent's Office asking if HBC were interested. The Japanese were at that time paying up to 2.5 times book value for such banks, and then there would be the question of new management. This solution was too expensive for the HSBC. The advice of consultants was needed.

Warren Chinn put the possibilities this way. HBC was too small to be a successful retail bank and it had not carved out a position in the wholesale market; it was too small to be profitable in California. The Hongkong Bank had therefore four options, the first of which was, as noted above, ruled out immediately on grounds of cost: (i) set up retail branches across the State *de novo*, (ii) cut back to three offices, San Francisco, Los Angeles, and San Francisco Chinatown, concentrating on the finance of trade and agency business in the first two, taking advantage of specialized retail business in the last mentioned, (iii) buy a series of medium-sized banks and put together a profitable network, or (iv) acquire control, say 25 to 35%, of a substantial bank with branches in place. After discussion the options were narrowed to a pullback or acquisition.

Or put another way, by presenting unattractive or costly alternatives in California, the consultants were really suggesting that the Hongkong Bank might do better elsewhere. Macdonald accepted the suggestion on instructions from Head Office; the emphasis was to be on securing a control position in a larger bank, probably a Pacific Rim bank; the team consequently began looking outside California, submitting its report on this enlarged brief in August 1976.

The Bank's 'philosophy' considered
The proposal that the Hongkong Bank seek to acquire a controlling interest in a larger bank, while readily accepted in principle, had drawbacks and problems of its own. The proposal was acceptable because, as the consultants argued, the Foreign staff had never been accepted in California financial circles; they had remained for too short a period. In some cases this was because they had not performed well, in others because they had performed too well and were needed

elsewhere. Or, to put it bluntly, Foreign staff of the Hongkong Bank could not be expected to manage an American bank. Once this principle was accepted, the way was clear to consider buying control of a bank with the staff in place. As it became clear that California opportunities were limited, this in turn suggested that the consultants should think in terms of a positive U.S. policy without sentimental attachment to the heritage of HBC.

There was no specific turning point; the search for a satisfactory American presence just developed logically.

With the enlarged brief, there were more serious questions the consultants needed to ask the Hongkong Bank. If the Bank were to gain control of an American bank it could be achieved only with the permission of the regulatory authorities; the Bank would be questioned; what were its motives? Behind this was the constant popular concern that the foreign holding company would strip the assets of the acquired bank as in the case of the Franklin National Bank, or, less dramatically, transfer funds garnered in the areas served and use them in higher earning areas overseas. This concern would be discussed publicly later and the reality of the danger minimized by Governor Henry Wallich of the Federal Reserve Board, but the consultants were already asking.

In pre-war days the Hongkong Bank had been an Eastern bank. While China was on silver, the Bank's reserves were divided between silver and gold-denominated investments. After 1935 the Bank's reserves moved to London and its risks could be diversified worldwide through the London market. Post-war the Hongkong Bank began quietly building up reserves in the United States. In the 1950s the Bank already felt itself overexposed in Hong Kong, and within Hong Kong, overexposed in textiles. The acquisition of the Mercantile Bank did nothing to solve this problem; the acquisition of the British Bank of the Middle East, very little.

The Hongkong Bank's policy since the mid-1950s had been to spread its assets geographically. It was having difficulty achieving this (see discussion in Chapter 12). But certainly part of its American strategy was based on the intention of investing funds in America, up to 30% of the Bank's total assets, over the next ten to fifteen years, putting capital if not into the HBC then into some financial institution which would grow with the Bank. With trade expanding across the Pacific, the Bank would be on both sides of the deal. The long-run strategy made sense both in the historical tradition of the Bank and in context with trends in international trade and finance.

Having stated this intention, the Bank had to answer concerning its policy if the investment turned sour. What was its attitude relative to its responsibility for subsidiaries? This was a question Booz-Allen asked in 1976; it was one of the last guarantees required by the Comptroller of the Currency in December 1979. As the Bank had assured the U.S. Philippine authorities at the turn of the century, it stood behind its overseas branches; it now took the position that it stood behind its subsidiaries.

Meanwhile, through its own connections, through also the involvement of its New York office in the initial discussions relative to the IBA, the Bank was being introduced through Booz-Allen to a wider U.S. financial circle. The groundwork for a major acquisition was being laid, in part unconsciously, but in part in consequence of the realization that the Bank must grow now as it had in the late 1950s if it were to survive. There was no argument with Sayer's position that size for its own sake is not sound policy, a point particularly valid in view of the Hongkong Bank's own management concerns relative to its existing subsidiary and associated companies. But management was being reordered and a large U.S. acquisition with senior staff in place did not involve Foreign staff management; this was no longer the impediment. On the other hand size was a factor in the Bank's continued ability to serve its constituents. They too were growing, and their requirements in real and money terms were greater. Cathay Pacific's DC-3 was now more expensive; furthermore its DC-3 was now a 747; finance of Y.K. Pao's tankers made similar and increasing demands – and so through the whole range of the Bank's activities. If the market of the 1980s was to be served, the Hongkong Bank had to grow.

The consultants were meanwhile searching for an acquisition with management in place – but at a price.

An America-wide strategy

Despite the widened vision, the Bank asked the consultants to look first at the Pacific Rim. The ultimate consequences of this were that the Bank itself secured permission to open branches in Seattle and Portland in anticipation of the restrictive 'national treatment' provisions of the IBA. California with the then dominant Bank of America did not look promising. The Pacific Rim had its limitations. With the Hongkong Bank now talking of an investment of US$50 to 100 million, Booz-Allen had identified nineteen banks nation-wide in a list, which included Marine Midland Banks, submitted in September 1976. A preliminary screening by Booz-Allen had ruled out banks in 'unfriendly' states – as determined by six law firms retained by the consultants to avoid any possibility of leaks as to the client or the client's purpose; also ruled out were banks, otherwise suitable, whose principal shareholders would be unwilling to sell.

The final list was to be taken to Hong Kong for discussion between the consultants and Hongkong Bank's senior management on November 4–5, 1976. It was in Hong Kong that the fundamental disagreement would be identified.

Hong Kong, November 1976
In the Booz-Allen presentation to the Hongkong Bank's senior management the main recommendation was to authorize the consultants to narrow down the field and so lead eventually to the control of a significantly placed American bank. Secondly, the Bank was advised to proceed with opening branches in friendly states in anticipation of the passage of the IBA. As noted, this last led to opening in Portland and Seattle, later in Chicago; Texas would have caused political problems and a Representative Office only was opened in Houston; Miami was not recommended, possibly a mistake in view of its commanding position of Central and South American financial contacts.

This was all in line with previous instructions. Nevertheless, Booz-Allen presented the name of Marine Midland Banks (MMBI) as worthy of separate consideration. Its price was beyond the range mentioned by the Hongkong Bank, furthermore in 1976 its performance, as reflected by the Marine Midland Bank (MMB), newly established through the consolidation of ten regional banks, was particularly poor as bad loans from its several predecessor banks continued to be identified; net charge-offs peaked at US$93 million that year, they had totalled US$58.4 million the previous year. Booz-Allen realized, however, that, as MMB was in difficulty, any assistance offered would be sympathetically considered by the regulatory authorities and that the MMBI possibility should continue to be reviewed.

Later both Chinn and Adams would have the feeling that Sandberg was watching Marine Midland very closely from the beginning. This was the only bank which was both 'major' and 'practical'. More important, Sandberg was getting to know, and to appreciate, Ed Duffy, the MMBI chairman, at various international meetings.

Although the initial reception of the Booz-Allen report appeared favourable, within a week the Bank seemed to have reversed itself. Acceptance of the consultants' recommendations in reality meant selling off the Hongkong Bank of California and moving aggressively with an even greater investment into a country in which the Bank had admittedly done poorly. The belief that HBC could be turned around at a more reasonable price and that a large investment was too risky caused Sayer to water down the recommendation to the Board of Directors. All that was agreed was the opening of U.S. branches, a statement that management was considering an acquisition, and that the HBC was not to be sold for the present.

Despite this setback, Sayer did not withdraw the consultants, and there is reason to suppose that one of his main objections was timing. He would retire within the next nine months; he did not want to begin a major operation which he would not be able to complete.

The proposal to acquire a major U.S. bank was not simply a question of investment policy. Unlike the original brief which involved an investment of less than one-tenth the eventual cost of MMBI, this was a proposal to change the entire nature of The Hongkong and Shanghai Banking Corporation, and, quite naturally, there were many both within the Bank and within the community who questioned the wisdom of such a change. The Bank had, after all, been successful.

In consequence, however, of the Board's agreement to the modified recommendation, the consultants were retained, and they quietly worked on the problem of a major acquisition with an increased investment during what was recognized as a hiatus. During this period Booz-Allen became increasingly aware of the potential political difficulties the Bank might face, the point of contact was changed from San Francisco to the Hongkong Bank's New York Manager, D.H. Leach, and contacts were made in Washington.

The second phase

The Vancouver Meeting, October 1977
Booz-Allen had been convinced that the Hongkong Bank would come back to them in strength; accordingly they had continued to work on the Bank's American strategy in the hiatus. Then in late August 1977 they received encouragement from Chairman-designate Sandberg through Macdonald; they were also given new terms of reference. The investment was to be in excess of US$200 million, the target bank was to be a money centre bank, and the Hongkong Bank wanted to buy 51% of the voting capital.

The 51% requirement followed without question from the size of the investment the Bank was now willing to make. 'Control' of a kind is possible with 25% of the shares, but it is not full control; furthermore, under Hong Kong law only with over 50% of the equity can the balance sheets be consolidated. And yet there remained a major difficulty. With 51% the Hongkong Bank was in control and 'responsible'; the Bank's slow absorption of the Mercantile and its problems with HBC indicated a conflict between the need to acquire 51% and the ability to manage the acquisition. From this would be born the concept of 'partnership'; Hang Seng rather than Mercantile/BBME would be the model.

On reflection Sandberg had concluded that the tentative approach – small bank, small investment, minimum control – would be as unproductive in the long run as the HBC; furthermore such a policy would not change HSBC; it would not diversify its assets sufficiently nor would it compensate for the years of 'stagnation'. The Hongkong Bank had taken twenty years to settle the question of control of its wholly owned subsidiary, BBME; Sandberg was not the type of chief executive to tolerate drifting or part-measures. The Bank's

U.S. Strategy as part of a World Strategy had been given a new thrust and new terms of reference.

At a meeting of Bank officials – Leach, Campbell, and Macdonald – with the consultants in Vancouver, B.C., in October 1977 the signal was given to move ahead. The consultants presented a list of six banks: Bank of New York, Bankers Trust, Crocker National, Irving Trust, Marine Midland, and SeaFirst, but it was becoming clear that Sandberg was watching Marine Midland. Despite their list of banks, the consultants remained divided on a fundamental question: was 51% control by HSBC of any sizeable American bank a 'do-able' proposition? Howard Adams concluded that it was, although not necessarily with all the banks on the 'ideal' list. Indeed, this concern was increased by the opinions of the investment bankers, Salomon Brothers, who were now brought onto the team. The search must be for a willing seller; there was no reason, in their opinion, why an established, well-run American bank, Bank of New York, for example, would want to sell to a 'group of Britishers from Hong Kong'. There had to be a reason; then if the willing seller were not quite that willing, he might, under the right circumstances be encouraged by the regulators. Thus the focus had to be on Marine Midland.

At that time, however, MMB had in their portfolio US$400 million reduced rate or non-accrual loans; Booz-Allen remained concerned. They had been seeking a 'quality' bank.

October 1977–January 1978

During the lead-up to the Bank's final decision, the initiative moved from the consultants, Booz-Allen, to the investment bankers, Salomon Brothers, with their team led by James D. Wolfensohn, assisted principally by Craig Stearns. Sandberg and Wolfensohn, the latter from Australia, with City of London experience, an American wife, an interest in music, and the ideal personality for the task, established a rapport which saw the deal through.

The Bank had established counsel in Washington, Shaw, Pittman, Potts and Trowbridge (Steuart Pittman); the Bank's usual counsel in New York were otherwise involved, and Sandberg was advised to look elsewhere; accordingly Cleary, Gottlieb, Steen and Hamilton were brought in (James F. Munsell with Barry Fox).

Wolfensohn quickly contacted the priority banks, but there were no signs of interest. Now Howard Adams was faced with the immediate problem of Marine Midland and his concern that the Hongkong Bank, which had always sought partnership in a trouble-free bank, was being pressed into approaching a bank still in difficulty. He reexamined his figures and agreed on December 16, 1977, to recommend Marine Midland to his Hongkong Bank clients. He had made

I. Strategy and initial success

two findings: first, the Hongkong Bank was in a sufficiently sound position to bear the loss of US$200 million if a downturn in the United States economy were to undermine MMB's recovery, and, secondly, MMB was in much better shape than appeared from earlier analyses. Indeed it was a general failure to perceive the extent of MMB's turnaround which led to the undervaluation of its shares in the market and to some surprise when the terms of the Hongkong Bank's offer were made public.

The actual decision to approach Marine Midland was made in Hong Kong in December. The consultants were basically in agreement that this was in fact the only deal that could be done. Sandberg was attracted because it was the only major deal being proposed which would achieve the assets distribution that the Hongkong Bank really required. Anything short of Marine Midland was almost 'dabbling'. But it was a dramatic step and a difficult decision which would involve the reputation of the Bank, the time of its top executives, large expenditure of funds – and uncertain conclusions. However good MMB looked relative to what pessimists had expected, the bank still had problems.

All the team were present in Hong Kong except Wolfensohn, who would arrive later, presumably having told a client in London that Salomon's could no longer assist them in a major U.S. acquisition. Certainly the Hongkong Bank had become aware that there were others looking to the United States; later the New York State Banking Department let slip that Barclays Bank had been very interested in Marine Midland. In any case, there was need to move fast; the consultants felt the political atmosphere might tolerate one major bank acquisition, but possibly not two. This did not prove to be the case, but the situation was without precedent.

Sandberg authorized Wolfensohn to make a 'no-name' approach to Ed Duffy; the first step leading to the acquisition of Marine Midland Banks had been taken. But when Wolfensohn called, Duffy knew who was behind him; Marine Midland too had been thinking.

MARINE MIDLAND'S SEARCH FOR CAPITAL – AND A PARTNER

Background

1929–1975

The Marine Midland Corporation (MMC; later renamed Marine Midland Banks, Inc.) was formed as a bank holding company in September 1929 with sixteen bank affiliates, of which the Marine Midland Trust Company of the Mohawk Valley, in Utica, could trace a line back to 1812; MMC's primary purpose, as with many other bank groups and bank chains, was to overcome the limitations imposed on banking by State laws forbidding or restricting branch and/or interstate banking. The corporation's shares were underwritten and one million were sold at US$60 on the eve of the stock market crash; share prices had risen to US$80, they then fell to a little less than US$3, but the strong cash position of the corporation proved invaluable to its member banks during the coming depression.[7]

Unlike most bank holding companies, MMC was not conceived of primarily as an 'investment institution'. George F. Rand, Jr, the founder of MMC, had been president of the Marine Trust Company in Buffalo, New York, since 1925 and had been instrumental in the formation of smaller investment groupings which were to form the nucleus of MMC. He was an advocate of the advantages of sharing certain operational overheads and management supervision through a holding company; he saw MMC as forming a group which would be prepared, when State laws changed, to form an operating bank with State-wide branches.[8]

The original group of banks held by MMC did not include a New York City bank. This defect was remedied in 1930 by acquisition of the Fidelity Trust Company of New York which became, after the 1960s merger with Grace National Bank, the Marine Midland Grace Trust Company of New York – when Grace interests were subsequently bought out the 'Grace' name was omitted. By 1942, when Rand retired, MMC controlled 21 banks with 91 offices in 39 communities. These banks took advantage of increasingly liberal State laws relative to branching but were restricted as to acquisitions. Individual banks were seen as a strength to the Group and, with the succession of Charles Diefendorf, the up-State characteristic of the bank was confirmed, but with the difference that Diefendorf was able to acquire additional banks; there were mergers, and the beginnings of a major State-wide network was in evidence.

During the 1950s Marine Midland moved to rationalize through the merging of its local subsidiary banks into larger regional banks, the regions being defined for the purpose by new State legislation. When the New York Marine Midland Bank absorbed Grace National and became the largest in the system, there was potential competition between the New York money centre bank and the major up-State regional bank in Buffalo. Under the innovative management of men like Baldwin Maull, MMC, now known as Marine Midland Banks, Inc. (MMBI), was instrumental through Karl Hinke in the development, for example, of a national interbank credit card, Master Charge, in pioneering consumer finance, and in the finance of agribusiness; by the end of 1973 the system was serviced by two IBM 370/164 computers operating in the Marine Midland Center in Buffalo.

The dynamic growth of the Marine Midland system in the late 1960s and early 1970s was also a source of danger. First, the system was highly geared;

in 1969, for example, there was a US$50 million issue of $7\frac{5}{8}$% 25-year debentures. MMBI's total outstanding long-term debt (debentures) in 1978 was US$196.3 million. This type of borrowing had increased the banks' leverage, but at a cost. Secondly, the management question as between holding company supervision and local bank autonomy – paralleling the Hongkong Bank/Mercantile/BBME dilemma – was never fully resolved. Thirdly, the competition between the New York City bank and the up-State Buffalo bank had become increasingly difficult to rationalize. Fourthly, the system's move into overseas operations created control problems which were potentially dangerous.

Against all this was the possibility, realized by a law enacted in mid-1971, that the State would permit State-wide branch banking. There had already been consolidation in response to State authorization of regional banking, and Marine Midland Banks, Inc., confronted with the possibility of rival State-wide groups, which did not in fact materialize, resolved after considerable study to merge its eleven subsidiary banks into a single operating State (as opposed to 'National') bank with its head office in Buffalo at the earliest date possible – January 1, 1976.[b] By this merger certain problems were resolved, but the new Marine Midland Bank inherited the portfolios of the former subsidiary banks with their non-performing loans; it was this which had caused Booz-Allen and others to hesitate.

The years 1969–1975
The chief executive officer of MMC, J. Fred Schoellkopf, IV, died on December 7, 1969. His brief administration, of less than three years, had been a period of further expansion, with consolidated net income increasing by one-third. The record overseas was particularly dramatic. The Marine Midland Bank in New York City had representative offices in Frankfurt, Hong Kong, Mexico City, Madrid, Paris, and Tokyo; there was a full-service branch in London. The New York bank's wholly owned subsidiary, Marine Midland International Corporation, had interests in France, Spain, the Philippines, Malaysia, Costa Rica, Peru, and Canada. Then a new subsidiary, Marine Midland Overseas Corporation, was founded; it sold US$30 million debentures in Eurodollar financing and purchased equity in various European banks and other overseas financial operations.

Under Charles Winding, chief executive, 1970–1973, MMBI and its

[b] The United States has a dual banking system, administered by the particular State Government or the Federal Government respectively. Both State and National banks may belong to, and the vast majority do belong to, the Federal Deposit Insurance Corporation (FDIC); the National banks must and the larger State banks (including Marine Midland Bank) do belong to the Federal Reserve System. MMBI had eight State and three National bank subsidiaries; the Buffalo bank had been State chartered.

subsidiary banks apparently continued their success. In 1970 a wholly owned merchant bank, the International Marine Banking Company, was formed in London with a paid-up capital of US$27.7 million equivalent, but, surprisingly, with no Marine Midland representative on its board. By end-1973 it had offices in Beirut and Tokyo and had invested in a Canadian leasing subsidiary, an Irish bank, and a Venezuelan finance company. As a consequence of this overseas development, 20% of MMBI's earnings before securities transactions resulted from international operations in 27 offices in nineteen countries.

The system had grown; earnings, however, had not. While average deposits increased from US$5.7 billion in 1970 to US$9.7 billion in 1973 (70.2%), consolidated net income for common stock increased only from US$43.4 million to US$45.8 million (5.5%).

Edward W. Duffy became president of the holding company (MMBI) on January 1, 1973, chief executive on October 1, 1973, and chairman of the board on January 1, 1974. He had at one time been a banking examiner and had worked up through the Marine Midland system, serving successively as president or chairman of the Marine Midland banks of Northern New York, the Mohawk Valley, and Central. He had every reason to expect continued growth; there were already 100 domestic branches, basic organizational decisions had been made, and there was a balance, it appeared, between domestic and overseas operations.

At this point the international economy and the banking industry ran into difficulties and Marine Midland's own portfolio was exposed. There were the increase in oil prices and the depression of 1974/75, with the failure of the Franklin National Bank, the Herstadt Bank in Germany, and the secondary banking crisis in London giving the problems a specific impetus.

The main causes of MMBI's problems were their exposure to REIT (Real Estate Investment Trust) loans made by leasing and mortgage subsidiaries and to lending by the London merchant bank subsidiary. The restructuring of this latter operation by its New York parent involved heavy losses, but Marine Midland was determined to protect its international reputation – on this point MMBI and HSBC had identical policies. As a consequence net charge-offs (recognized losses) on a consolidated basis were US$25 million in 1974, US$58.4 million in 1975, and, as noted above, a peak US$93 million in 1976 – the process continued through 1980 by which year a total US$364.4 million had been written off, compared to a 1979 paid-up capital of US$62.6 million or total shareholders' equity of US$480.3 million.[9] In 1975, for example, non-income producing loans exceeded shareholders' equity. It could be argued that the survival of the bank depended on the orchestrated write-off of such loans in a way acceptable both to the regulators and to constituents.

As a consequence net income declined from US$40.2 million in 1974 to US$13.2 million in 1976 – it would be US$62.7 million in 1980; in 1976 the

I. Strategy and initial success

dividend was cut from US$1.80 to US$0.80 a share. The year 1976 appears to have been critical, but in part this reflects the fact that this was the year the banks were consolidated and certain problems were revealed in their entirety to the management of the newly constituted Marine Midland Bank – including two computer systems which did not interface. As MMBI non-executive director Charles G. Blaine commented,

[Duffy] had become chairman and chief executive officer of a very big bank in the United States that turned out to have a relatively substantial portion of poor assets, and he had to fight very hard just to keep the thing going – and he didn't have his own management team in place. He had to stem the tide of poor earnings; he had to put ten banks that had never operated as a single unit together; he had to get them operating in harness. I can't imagine a single set of problems more difficult for a bank chief executive officer to resolve than the combination that Duffy had: bad earnings, deteriorating loan portfolio, the merger of ten banks, putting together ten disparate management systems, putting his own management team in so that he could rely upon people, and a sharp recession both within the United States and world-wide...[10]

Financial analysts and journalists could not assess the 'Duffy factor'. Sandberg's underlying and continuing interest in Marine Midland was to a great extent based on his intuitive appreciation of just that 'unknown' in the Marine Midland equation – the competence of Edward Duffy.

In the meantime Duffy had put through measures which were to effect the eventual turnaround, including an economy program involving a 10% reduction of staff, the elimination of 'frills' – company airplanes, cars, country club memberships – and the virtual freezing of top executive salaries to the point that average remuneration fell considerably below the national average for the relevant category.

The search for capital

Duffy could save the bank; it was never '*in extremis*' as Franklin or the First Pennsylvania had been. Basically MMB was sound. Duffy could not, however, reconstitute it as a dynamic major banking force in the State without additional capital. The write-offs, as managed by Duffy, did not threaten the bank's solvency, but they did inhibit necessary growth. There were two ways of increasing capital: (i) obtain new capital from the equity market and (ii) obtain new capital from a partner at the possible cost of losing majority control of the bank to that partner. The former was preferable to the management and shareholders; the latter proved necessary.

The capital alternatives
There were two aspects to MMB's capital problem: (i) the low capital/assets ratio, say 3+%, which provoked the attention of regulators and (ii) the slowness of the process of increasing capital solely from earnings, given the need to pay out dividends at an acceptable rate. Aside from the prudential

aspects of the existing position, MMBI executives recognized that without an increase in capital a growth of assets in the existing highly levered situation was impractical; the bank was doomed to stagnate in an economy which was recovering from depression and needed bank intermediation. There was a role to play, but with the capital base then existing, MMB could not play it.

Paul Volcker, then the president of the Federal Reserve Bank of New York, on several occasions urged on the MMBI board of directors the need for a capital infusion. But neither he nor the board could suggest how such an infusion could be reasonably achieved.

Although the book value of shares was some US$33 in 1975, the market price of shares fell from a high of US20\frac{3}{8}$ to a low of US$10. This suggested that additional common stock could be sold at US$9+, a very unsatisfactory price for existing shareholders. Some watering of equity was seen to be unavoidable, but this was unacceptable – and Volcker appreciated the argument. Borrowing was not feasible, first because the bank was already highly geared and additional borrowed funds would not be acceptable; secondly, because, once again, the cost to existing shareholders would be too high. This left the possibility of preferred stock.

The objection to preferred stock was obvious. A heavy annual after-tax obligation would be fixed on Marine Midland during a period when the bank, already highly geared, should be, to the extent possible, using earnings after dividends to increase shareholders' equity. There was even question as to whether raising funds through a sale of preferred stock was feasible. An exhaustive study by Lehman Brothers Kuhn Loeb, conducted under the direction of Louis Glucksman in association with Blyth Eastman Dillon and Co., concluded that US$75 million could be raised by the issue of preferred stock through a public-oriented transaction. This did not make the proposal any the more attractive, but Marine Midland knew the possibility existed during the time they were negotiating with the Hongkong Bank for a US$200 million capital injection.

The partnership alternative

A corporation in difficulties is not always in a position to choose either a 'partner' or the terms of the 'partnership'. Marine Midland was a potential take-over target, although the unfriendly acquisition of any bank, but particularly of a major bank, would have been impossible from a political or regulatory point of view, and in fact had been ruled out by G. William Miller when chairman of the Board of Governors of the Federal Reserve Board in 1978.[c]

[c] Almost by definition an unfriendly take-over means one opposed by the board of directors. The non-executive directors are usually selected on the basis of their importance to the bank; this

I. Strategy and initial success

Nevertheless, MMBI did retain a law firm which specialized in take-over situations, Skadden, Arps, Slate, Meagher and Flom. At the same time both the board and the senior management began to face the 'take-over question' with the growing recognition that one of the non-negotiable terms might well be 51% of the equity.

In mid-November 1976 John R. Petty, a partner in Lehman Brothers and a friend of Glucksman, became president of Marine Midland Bank – his background an essential complement to Duffy's. His most recent experience had been in investment banking; he had also served successfully as Assistant Secretary to the Treasury for International Affairs in both the Johnson and Nixon administrations. In preliminary discussions with the board of directors Petty had argued that if the capital question could not be solved otherwise, the board must be willing to explore the question of a foreign equity investor with a major shareholding position.

In August [1976], when I was talking to the Directors and with Duffy, I received answers to my satisfaction that I would not come to the bank unless they were prepared to say then that, should our joint analysis (which I would lead the executive committee through) of the bank's future capital needs and competitive position reach the conclusion that more capital would be needed, that the conclusion also was that you could only find the amount of capital and the type of capital you needed off-shore, and if that further it came that you could only get it at an amount that involved control of the bank, that they would be prepared to consider it.

Behind this line of reasoning lay Petty's awareness of the box into which a combination of legislative provisions had put large problem banks. Banks were not, for the purposes of the present discussion (there were exceptions), permitted to operate full-service branches in more than one State; bank holding companies were not permitted to own banks in more than one State. This in itself was not necessarily the problem; there was at least one New York City bank which would have been willing to buy MMBI with its up-State network. But, if the bank were big enough to secure a controlling interest in MMBI, it was big enough to be in danger from anti-trust and/or other restrictive legislation.[12] The only solution, therefore, and one which was particularly annoying to major domestic U.S. banks, was for Marine Midland to seek a partner (or be sought by a partner) from overseas.

On the issue of control, the problem was more straightforward. What MMBI sought was a significant capital injection, which indicated an amount which

---

disaffection would make questionable the viability of an unfriendly take-over. In 1976 the Standard Chartered Bank had hoped to acquire the Bancal Tri-State Corporation, the holding company for the Bank of California, with its unusual tri-State banking charter; the Standard Chartered's deputy chief executive officer, Peter A. Graham, had assured the FRB, however, that he understood the acquisition must be on a friendly basis. Thus, as noted above, when he was turned down by the board of directors, he withdrew.[11]

would also be significant to the other bank. The smaller (in relative terms) the other bank, the more significant would the amount required appear and the more likely would be insistence on full control through a 51% equity investment. What remained at issue was the nature of the relationship following that 51% acquisition.

The coming of the Hongkong Bank
After several tentative approaches, two of which Marine Midland initiated, the MMBI Board agreed in 1977 not to pursue actively any form of public financing for the time being. Duffy and Petty appreciated, however, that, despite the progress made by MMB, the options available for the necessary increase in capital remained tenuous. In the meantime Petty continued to study quietly those banks he considered likely to be interested. The list included The Hongkong and Shanghai Banking Corporation. 'We didn't know much about the [HSBC],' Petty confessed, 'other than the fact that they had a Tiffany name and good people managing them. I put them on the list on the basis that if I were running that bank I sure as hell would get a major leg in a dollar-based area and the California branches are not going to be going anywhere.' In the fall of 1977 there was a more formal approach from an overseas bank, and then Wolfensohn called on a no-name basis. That did not mystify Marine Midland. As Petty recalls, 'Partly because of some analysis we had done, partly because of some intelligence we had, we knew exactly what he was talking about.'

NEW YORK STATE: THE ECONOMIC POLICY OF THE CAREY ADMINISTRATION

The recent economic history of the State of New York as characterized by Robert P. Morgado, executive secretary to the Governor, was one of depression, a failure to recover from the recession of the late 1960s, and a worsening of the position in the downturn of 1974. The task, as the newly elected Governor, Hugh Carey, saw it, was to encourage investment, open up foreign markets, cut back on Government red tape, reform the tax structure, create, in other words, the atmosphere and environment suitable for increased private investment.

Morgado later described the Administration's success as staged: (i) 1975/76, reordering the State's finances and public accounts and (ii) 1977/78, positive encouragement for the import (as opposed to the historic export) of capital. In this latter period, the focus was to be on three sectors: (i) the agricultural base, including the wine industry and dairy farming, (ii) tourism – with an annual promotional campaign of US$10 to US$15 million – and (iii) the service centres of the State's economy, financing, banking, and insurance.

New York State created a 'free zone' for insurance, supported the

International Banking Facilities Act, and took steps to virtually deregulate the banking industry relative, at least, to the removal of such anomalies as usury ceilings and excessive differentiation between commercial and savings banks.

Governor Carey would become directly involved in the Hongkong Bank acquisition of Marine Midland. As he saw it, Marine Midland, as the most important up-State bank, was an essential part of his recovery program. The injection into Marine Midland of US$200 million of capital, capable of being leveraged to support economic growth in important areas of the State and at the same time unavailable from any domestic source, was welcome. It confirmed the State's interest in the import of capital and the finance of new industry.

To achieve his goals Carey brought into the Government a team of capable officers, including Muriel Siebert as State Superintendent of Banks. She would implement the more liberal State banking system and encourage foreign banking in New York. But Muriel Siebert in her appointed role felt prudential and other responsibilities independent of her political power base; she also developed her own preferences for U.S. and State banking policies which were contrary to the provisions of the statutes she was obligated to enforce. She would have a powerful voice in the negotiations which were to follow HSBC's approach to Marine Midland.

A DEAL MADE: FROM THE FIRST CONTACT TO THE DEFINITIVE AGREEMENT

This period covers developments from Michael Sandberg's first telephone contact with Edward Duffy in January 1978 to the signing of the Definitive Agreement in May 1978. The period is characterized by the development of a sort of euphoria as the two parties, HSBC and MMBI, concluded an agreement which apparently met not only with the approval of the shareholders but also with that of the public. In a sense the relative ease with which the agreement was negotiated left the principals ill-prepared for the problems which the regulators and certain political figures, even when well-disposed to the agreement, would cause.

From a tentative beginning in New York City on Washington's Birthday weekend to a successful meeting in Hawaii on St Patrick's Day weekend, the tone and pace were set; the first public announcement drew few critical comments and these were, with the exceptions to be noted, routinely handled; the first examination by the Hongkong Bank of the Marine Midland in Buffalo and New York caused no additional problem, and only the question of the terms of the subordinated note created serious anxiety as the negotiators moved from a preliminary to the Definitive Agreement. The latter was signed on May 18, 1978.

FIRST CONTACTS

The immediate prelude

The schedule to February 1978

At the Vancouver meeting, October 5–6, 1977, the Hongkong Bank's expanded American strategy had been confirmed; Booz, Allen and Hamilton advised the assistance of Salomon Brothers, and the latter were first briefed on October 13 with an initial Hong Kong meeting on November 9 and a target for a first approach to a major U.S. bank set for February 1978.

John Petty passed through Hong Kong in November, but neither bank was ready for contact. Sandberg commented, 'I felt a bit of a hypocrite because I knew in my own mind what our target should be, but we hadn't made the decision, I hadn't seen the Board... and I had to talk to him as a normal senior executive from a correspondent bank.'

Petty was equally frustrated; HSBC was on his list and he assumed MMBI was on Sandberg's. He was curious. Nevertheless, he purposely ensured that in his meeting with Sandberg he was accompanied by junior staff; the discussion was about correspondent bank relationships.

At a second Hong Kong meeting on December 17, Booz-Allen reversed their position and endorsed an approach to Marine Midland. There were then three banks on the list. When the first two indicated no interest, Sandberg authorized the consultants to contact Marine Midland, but on a no-name basis because a wholly satisfactory analysis of that bank had not as yet been presented. Wolfensohn returned to New York and telephoned Duffy; this was followed on January 5, 1978, by a meeting between Wolfensohn and Chinn on behalf of the still unnamed principal and Duffy and John Petty, chairman and deputy chairman (and president of MMB) respectively, for MMBI. Warren Chinn of Booz-Allen recalls that he was asked if they represented a Japanese bank; once the reply to this was negative, Duffy and Petty were seen to realize who was being represented. At this point the MMBI executives were convinced that there was a sufficient basis for a meeting between the principals; Wolfensohn consequently returned to Hong Kong and so informed Sandberg.

In the meantime a final meeting had been held on January 24, at which the analysis of Marine Midland, still based on public information, was concluded; following this the Hongkong Bank's Board gave authorization to Sandberg to proceed.

The 'dream', partnership, and merger

The figures come first. They must then be placed aside.

The transaction has to be presented not in terms of cash flows and equity ratios but in terms of long-run purposes and policies, long-run potentials which

I. Strategy and initial success

can be game-played but cannot be proved. Or simply, as Wolfensohn saw it, 'We needed to sell a dream.'

Slow growth may not, it is true, be exciting but it is your own. The Hongkong Bank was actually asking the board of directors and the management of MMBI to agree to become a subsidiary of The Hongkong and Shanghai Banking Corporation. The constituent banks of Marine Midland had a long history; the towns of up-State New York had enjoyed considerable banking autonomy and State-wide banking had only been authorized from 1976. The Hongkong Bank was not negotiating in the atmosphere of an internationally oriented money centre but in Buffalo, New York. The bottom line wasn't everything.

Duffy was clear on one point from the beginning. Marine Midland was not interested in selling out. National Westminster would later complete the take-over of the National Bank of North America where, in essence, the latter sold out to the former. Duffy, however, wanted a partnership.

What did the Hongkong Bank want?

In Petty the Hongkong Bank found a man fully experienced in international finance; among the directors men like Felix Larkin of W.R. Grace and Co. and Robert W. Hubner of IBM had moved in an international business context; for the most part, however, the Hongkong Bank was dealing with men whose long-term focus was the tradition of Marine Midland; they were primarily concerned with their role as bankers and citizens of the State of New York. Certainly they recognized that the Hongkong Bank was offering a capital injection, but the Hongkong Bank was also asking for control. Were they justified in selling their heritage?

Faced with such a situation, what do you say?

One obvious response is that, after all, you don't really mean it. Certainly you need 51% for accounting purposes, for consolidation. What you have in mind, however, is a partnership. This is not an acquisition; this is a merger.

On the other hand, no matter what is said, no matter what is intended, you're not kidding anyone. Fifty-one percent is total control. On the whim of the Hongkong Bank the MMBI board of directors could be changed and/or the senior management replaced. Much of the concern for the transaction then and later was related to the likelihood of this happening. Those close to Marine Midland, advisers like Glucksman, recognized that, if Marine Midland management did not perform, the Hongkong Bank, no matter what assurances had been given, would have to move to protect its investment. Would they move short of this?

From the Hongkong Bank's viewpoint, the answer seemed self-apparent. They did mean what they said – a partnership approach, a merger of interests.

Sandberg particularly had moved towards Marine Midland because he appreciated its management. Certainly no one in the Hongkong Bank considered managing an American bank after their California experience – and the success of their Hang Seng 'partnership'. The Hongkong Bank intended to inject some US$200 milion of their shareholders' funds into Marine Midland for the purpose of spreading their assets; they chose Marine Midland because they had made an analysis paralleling that of MMBI's own management and advisers. What the Hongkong Bank wanted was a successful MMBI. But they wanted more; they wanted a global partnership. Sandberg and his associates actually saw the deal as a merger. Here was a concept not wholly sustainable at law which was nevertheless to be the basis of a multi-million dollar transaction.

In early 1986 John Petty was Chairman of the Board of MMBI, Duffy was Chairman of the Executive Committee; three MMBI directors were members of the Board of the Hongkong Bank and three members of the Hongkong Bank Board were directors of MMBI; MMBI's common stock was quoted at US$43.25 and total assets had touched US$24.5 billion (1979 = US$15.7 billion). The two holding companies and their subsidiaries were working in harness on a global basis. But when Wolfensohn and Chinn called on Duffy and Petty in January 1978, these facts were obviously not to hand.

[At the time]...the dream which we had was that the Marine Midland Bank, an American-based bank which had a primary emphasis in Latin America and North America...some activities in Europe, linked with a bank like the Hongkong Bank, which was dominant or at least an eminent and very powerful member of the community in the Far East, in the Pacific, in India and in the Middle East, with again a fairly modest penetration in Europe and not a great penetration in Latin America, could create a world-wide banking group where the component parts would be unlikely to be competitive with each other and which, if put together in an intelligent way, could lead to what we now (March 1980) have, which is a major world banking group, with separate but linked managements in each of these various areas, and give it the muscle to be able to compete in the top-fifty banking league in which it now is.

First calls and meetings

Identification by telephone
Shortly after the January 24th meeting in Hong Kong, Wolfensohn arrived back in Hong Kong, and he and Sandberg prepared to call Duffy. The resulting first expression of the 'dream' was not particularly dramatic.

After dinner at Sandberg's home on the Peak, Wolfensohn spoke to Duffy first, thereby linking the previous meeting with the personal call, then Sandberg spoke to the effect that 'we want to talk about interesting things which obviously one cannot, Ed, talk about on the telephone. Would you be free if I were in New York in a week's time?'

As Duffy recalls the historic moment, 'I had known Mike from one or two trips to Hong Kong and during IMF meetings, and he asked to come over to see me, which he did.'

Washington's Birthday weekend, February 17–21, 1978

Sandberg's first dinner meeting with Duffy and Petty didn't get very far. The 51% aspect overshadowed the 'partnership' concept of the deal. Marine Midland had been prepared in theory but the actual moment of confronting the reality was difficult. Duffy suggested that both parties think about it and get back to each other within two months. Sandberg was anxious not to get out of personal contact at this point and suggested, after taking Wolfensohn's advice, that the four meet again on the Tuesday before Sandberg returned to Hong Kong.

This was the crucial meeting. Sandberg stressed at the outset that this was a negotiation between two banks of virtually the same size, that there was no question of HSBC coming in and trying to run Marine Midland; this was to be a partnership right from the start. The point was made and taken. Sufficient common ground had been found and the four agreed that the preliminary discussions should be extended. They would meet again with their investment advisers in Hawaii.

The Hawaii meeting, March 17–19, 1978

The selection of Hawaii may be seen as a gesture of going 'half-way'; on the other hand HSBC/MMBI were not the first to select one of the Pacific islands for a winter business meeting despite the fine facilities back home. The fact that it was on the eve of the busy Easter season proved the 'clout' MMBI must have had with the hotel and travel industry.

The Hongkong Bank team consisted of the Chairman, Michael Sandberg, the Deputy Chairman, John Boyer, and the legal adviser, F.R. Frame, with legal and investment bank advisers. T. Welsh, then Manager Hong Kong, joined the team later. Marine Midland brought, in addition to their outside advisers, Ed Duffy, John Petty, and their general counsel, Frank J. Laski.

Initially the Hongkong Bank's advisers were concerned. Marine Midland were bringing along advisers from Skadden Arps, noted for their role in contested merger transactions, and Louis Glucksman, who had a reputation as one of the toughest negotiators on Wall Street. Had the spirit already engendered in the quiet private New York meetings been forgotten?

There were almost immediate reassurances. Glucksman's presence was due to his longtime association with John Petty and to Lehman Brothers' work on MMBI relative to the marketability of a preferred stock issue; Skadden Arps had been retained earlier, and their abilities were not confined to *contested* mergers. Glucksman particularly and possibly because of his reputation was a source of reassurance; he had already sensed the essential elements of the eventual deal.

'The spirit of Hawaii'
It could be argued that everything done at the Honolulu meeting had to be redone more carefully later; indeed, that was the admitted purpose of the meetings in New York and Buffalo which continued right to the signing of the Definitive Agreement in May. Nevertheless the deal was made in Honolulu: the key elements, (i) 51% and partnership, (ii) the subordinated note or, as some were to see it, the 'earnest money', and (iii) the basic structure of the transaction, were all agreed in principle before the move to more specific deliberations in New York.

The whole was, moreover, greater than the sum of the parts. Something happened in those hectic hours which produced an attitude to the potential transaction which saw both sides through difficult negotiations. Participants referred to it as 'the spirit of Hawaii'. In the negotiations which followed there was the underlying assumption that whatever the problem it could be solved, whatever temporary feelings were aroused in the course of discussions, the deal would nevertheless succeed.

Those like Peter Mullin of Skadden Arps, who went out with MMBI on what he thought was a 'long shot', felt the deal coming together, and there was consequently a growing excitement. The arrangements had been made at the last minute, Duffy and Laski had problems getting to Mass – the 17th was St Patrick's Day, the 19th was Palm Sunday.[d] Wolfensohn recalled that the Kahala Hilton was crowded and that there never seemed to be enough room. The last discussions in fact were held in the elevator lobby; the Easter vacationers had arrived and rooms had to be vacated, the hotel staff standing by to force-pack the luggage of anyone still trying to complete a memo. The request for a large table led to a query from the hotel's manager as to whether the boys were planning to gamble. From the pressure placed on management to find rooms, the suspicion appears to have developed that this might be a sort of international crap game.

It is in such chaos that rapport is often developed.

The course of the meeting
Despite the preliminaries in New York, at the beginning of the Hawaii meetings the parties appeared far apart. For Marine Midland to become a 51%

[d] In an interview with Shakespeare one would expect him to refer from time to time to St Crispin's and other holy days. There is something heartening in the fact that a major bank acquisition is remembered by its banker participants in relation to the Christian calendar.

I. Strategy and initial success

subsidiary of HSBC had an emotional content, not only for Duffy and the board but for the staff and, possibly, for the bank's constituents. Once more the partnership concept had to be stated and accepted. This done, the question of timing arose. Marine Midland proposed that HSBC buy in tranches over a period to extend to 1985; don't do it all at once, seemed to be the plea. Purchase over such an extended time would have made an agreement on price almost impossible and in any case Sandberg did not consider it sensible for HSBC to have a major project pending in this way. The tentative compromise, which in fact held despite regulatory delays, was for the final tranche to be paid and 51% ownership achieved in 1980.

Negotiations on price were muted for several reasons. First, any such formal discussion had first to be reported and made public; second, the Hongkong team had not visited Buffalo and had not examined Marine Midland's records. Discussion was in general terms, taking into account, for example, the difference between MMBI's book value and the price of its shares in the market. Several problems were noted: to buy 51% at book value was probably not justified and was excessively expensive; buying sufficient newly issued shares to achieve 51% at a price substantially below book value would be a watering of the present equity and be unacceptable to shareholders; buying presently issued shares at the market would be unsuccessful since shareholders would not sell in the more optimistic circumstances created by the offer itself.

All this pointed to a new issue at or near book value and an offer to shareholders substantially in excess of present market price. After frank discussions between Wolfensohn and Glucksman, the basis for the final price was established consistent with the points outlined, but the parties could not move further in Hawaii.

Although the proceedings between the February meetings and Hawaii were carefully protected, there had been an inexplicable movement of Marine Midland shares just prior to the Hawaii meeting.[e] Skadden Arps were concerned about a premature leakage, and plans were therefore made for an immediate release on return to the mainland. Gavin Anderson of Hill and Knowlton, public relations consultants, was notified to stand by in New York; a release would have to go out on Monday, March 20.

At the end of the two-day sessions the parties were in sufficient agreement on the outlines of the transaction to make a public statement that negotiations were in fact in progress. Marine Midland had accepted the concept of 51%, Hongkong Bank had accepted that the deal would not be finalized until 1980,

[e] Only the personal secretaries of the three MMBI principals knew of the meeting in Hawaii, and they were instructed to inform callers that Mr X was away for a long weekend. This was apparently not expected to suggest anything unusual.

partnership with an exchange of directors was understood, and there was recognition that the actual financial arrangements would be complex. Other more technical aspects of the understandings are listed in the Appendix timetable at the end of Chapter 17.

In sympathy with 'the spirit of Hawaii', the acquisition was not referred to by this term. The two bank holding companies were negotiating a merger with the intention of forming a partnership in a world-wide banking group. As this is what they accomplished, 'merger' and 'partnership' have become legitimate terms with which to describe the outcome.

EARLY REACTIONS

Back from Hawaii

John Petty flew to New York on Sunday and immediately that evening called on Paul Volcker, president of the Federal Reserve Bank of New York, at his home. Volcker was not disapproving. On Monday Petty called on the New York State Superintendent of Banks, Muriel Siebert, at the New York State Banking Department (NYBD). Petty considered her to be 'clearly pleased at the prospect and complimentary to Marine Midland'.

Sandberg had instructed his Deputy Chairman, John Boyer, and General Manager I.H. Macdonald to fly to New York from Hong Kong: Tom Welsh continued directly from Hawaii. Sunday afternoon and evening they met with Gavin Anderson to prepare a press release for distribution on Monday, March 20; the release would state that negotiations were underway and would identify and describe the Hongkong Bank. This latter presented a problem. The Bank was both a holding company and an operating bank, but Anderson was naturally trying to discover whether the Group (in 'Hongkong Bank Group') owned the Hongkong Bank or vice versa. The difficulty was that the 'Group' is not the title of a legal organization, merely of a concept. Later Hill and Knowlton would be commissioned to do a study of Hongkong's corporate identity problem.

Duffy returned directly to Buffalo to explain the position to his directors and staff and prepare material for the Hongkong Bank's team.[f]

With the release despatched, the New York Stock Exchange notified, and key regulators informed, the two teams could expect the first reactions – from the public and from the staffs.

---

[f] Certain of the support staff were rushing around securing sufficient tea to serve 'the Brits'. When they arrived Boyer, Macdonald, and Welsh asked for coffee. For the Mercantile's efforts re bourbon for Chase Manhattan and HSBC's purchase of California wine for MMBI executives, see Chapter 12.

I. Strategy and initial success

First reactions and public relations

Back in New York State

There was the predictable humour. At the New York airport a friend of MMB executive, Eugene T. Mann, arriving from Buffalo called out, 'I hear you've been Shanghaied!', to which Mann responded, 'You've got it wrong, these guys have been Buffaloed.' There were cartoons showing Marine Midland bankers using chopsticks in the corporation dining room and one drawing put a Chinese roof on the Buffalo Marine Midland Center. As Laski put it, the humour ran the whole range of 'Polish jokes'.

There was a little vagueness up-State about whether or not Hong Kong were in Japan, but that was to be expected. When Sandberg visited a Marine Midland branch in Binghamton, New York, he discovered that of the three ladies he was talking to not one had ever visited New York City. There was no reason why they should have, but it was interesting. And yet, despite this manifestation of pervading provincialism, the Oriental aspect of the proposed transaction seemed to cause little concern *per se*.

The Hongkong Bank's public relations efforts were focused on showing the Bank as a British bank with British management. This line became particularly relevent when it appeared that the Hongkong Bank's management, while British, were Hong Kong British, not stuffy 'City' British with whom up-State bankers would not, in their own opinion, have been able to establish a working relationship.[g] With Sandberg visiting Buffalo and Binghamton and other Hong Kong 'Brits' making their presence known in the State, the point was quickly made and fully accepted. Sandberg made two visits in the initial stages, and he came over well. Explanatory information was circulated, short video takes of Sandberg commenting on the meaning of the deal to up-State New York were transmitted to local stations, and that evening there might be: 'In Buffalo today the Chairman of the Hongkong and Shanghai Bank and the Chairman of Marine Midland signed an agreement in principle for the two banks to merge. We asked Michael Sandberg, the Chairman of the Hongkong Bank, what this would mean for New York State...' The Hongkong Bank and its Chairman received wide exposure.

---

[g] The difference had been noted many years before. A.M. Townsend (East in 1870), the Hongkong Bank's New York Manager, 1880–1901, reported in his autobiography that he got on well with Americans, one banker paying him the ultimate compliment, 'You don't speak with an English accent' – a point which would be very much in Macdonald's favour when testifying before a Congressional sub-committee, see below.

Townsend once gave a Western banker a letter of introduction to Sir Ewen Cameron, then the Hongkong Bank's London Manager. The American reported that 'he found Cameron all right, but could not get on with the other City men, who greeted him with an eye-glass and "Ha-Ha, what, ha, may be the nature of, ha-ha, your business, ha?" He said when a man comes into my office in Ohio, I simply say, "What the hell do you want?"'[13]

The main concern then and later was, quite rightly, not the nationality of the Hongkong Bank but the impact of the merger on the ability of Marine Midland to continue to serve its constituents. At its simplest, the fear was expressed by businessmen, who, as a class, are notoriously uninformed about how banks operate, that the deposits would 'go out to Hong Kong'. David Gruen of MMB asked one of his business friends, 'And if you then asked for a loan and were denied it because the funds were in Hong Kong...?'

'Oh, I'd take my business to another bank.'

'Precisely!' And Governor Henry Wallich of the Federal Reserve Board argued in the same terms before Congress.

Duffy put the concern in perspective:

The real question was about what responsibility a bank from Hong Kong would feel in supporting our traditional New York State operations, whether it was mortgage loans or personal loans. So it was there; there is no question about it. It wasn't something that you woke up in the morning and thought about, but you knew it was in the background.

And there was a certain fear for Buffalo itself. The city had lost considerable industry over the previous 50 years; its bank was the symbol of what was left, and citizens were anxious not to lose control of this last great asset; they opposed, although they did not put it this way, the 'Liverpoolization' of Buffalo.[h] In this the people of Buffalo had much in common with those of Edinburgh (see Chapter 18), if only Hongkong Bankers had had the prescience to take more careful note of it.

The public relations consultants focused therefore on the Bank's size and reputation and the responsibility of its management. That is why the subordinated note, to be discussed below, was an important part of the deal relative to its public acceptance. It provided Marine Midland with additional funds even before the merger had been effected; it was a significant indication of the Hongkong Bank's intentions.

The boards of directors

On the Marine Midland's board, Charles Blaine looked at the proposed merger from a historical position. The Hongkong Bank was doing on a global scale just what the 1929 founders had hoped for Marine Midland Corporation, when it

---

[h] The concern expressed in Edinburgh relative to the Royal Bank of Scotland Group was that, if acquired outside Scotland, the head office would be removed. This would not be the first and the fear was that a critical point would be reached at which the city would no longer be a prosperous, social, decision-making centre. The problems of Liverpool were ascribed in part to the moves to London of traditional Liverpool-based enterprises. There was no one left behind with the ability to lead in civic matters. Buffalo too had been a varied economic centre; many of its important industries had decreased in importance; Marine Midland remained the symbol of its status.

had, before passage of disabling legislation and the Depression, nation-wide ambitions. In a sense the merger was the fulfilment of that vision; one might have hoped the MMBI would have succeeded alone, but this had become impossible. The Hongkong Bank's intervention was therefore welcome. Those on the board with international businesses naturally welcomed the overseas facilities the merger would provide. Those looking to up-State constituents had to be and were reassured of the Hongkong Bank's intentions.

The Hongkong Bank's Board had been supportive throughout. There was no question of working without them; the directors of a bank holding company would be required to file considerable personal information with the Federal Reserve Board – and few Hong Kong businessmen were used to such exposure, even though confidential. But more than this, the Board were positively in favour of Sandberg's American strategy.

NEGOTIATIONS AND THE DEFINITIVE AGREEMENT

Although the regulatory authorities were kept advised from the beginning, the first task facing HSBC and MMBI was the formalization of the general principles agreed in Hawaii and the securing of shareholder approval. The Marine Midland Bank as a wholly owned subsidiary of Marine Midland Banks, Inc., presented no special problem in this last context; the focus was on MMBI. The Hongkong Bank team began its investigations in New York and Buffalo the week of March 20. Simultaneously the investment bankers led by Wolfensohn and Glucksman considered alternative formulations of the transactions and recommended the price. The preliminary agreement was signed on April 4. The annual meeting of MMBI shareholders was held on April 19, but, despite the intense interest created by the announcement of the preliminary agreement, the merger issue was naturally not on the agenda; Duffy was even on the verge of going too far to meet shareholders' questions; he had to be restrained by Frank Laski, MMBI's legal adviser.

The Definitive Agreement was signed on May 18.

The explanations and proxy materials were mailed to MMBI shareholders on September 6, the delay having been caused by problems with the Securities and Exchange Commission (SEC; see below). Shareholders voted 75% (95% of those represented and voting) in favour of the terms of the Definitive Agreement at a special meeting on October 18, 1978. The owners of Marine Midland had made their decision, but implementation of the Agreement was subject to the approval of the regulatory authorities. How this was obtained will be the subject of Chapter 17.

Early developments

Three Hongkong Bankers arrived in New York to negotiate a deal which would change the history of their China-coast, colonially chartered corporation. At their first meeting I.H. Macdonald was startled to find printed agendas with their names included and specific plans for the development of MMB on the basis of the projected US$200 million capital injection implied by the Hawaii discussions. There must, Macdonald said, have been a serious leak. MMB executives explained that they had been game planning the future and to feed in a specific assumption was, for the computer, a matter of seconds. As for the names – that presented little problem to New York's printing industry. Suddenly Macdonald felt like a country boy in the city, but typical of the China-coast tradition, the feeling did not last long, it merely focused attention once again on the significance of the steps being taken.

In fact, the Hongkong Bankers had had considerable experience, but not in the United States. Macdonald (East for the Mercantile Bank in 1948) had served in Chittagong and elsewhere in Pakistan and India, in Singapore, Malaya, Ceylon, and Mauritius. He had helped the Mercantile to move its head office from London to Hong Kong, served in its Hong Kong head office, as Manager for Indian operations of the Group in Bombay, and from 1973 as General Manager, Hong Kong, in charge of Overseas Operations. He would be the Group's Chief Executive Officer for the Americas; in 1980 he was the New York resident Executive Director of the Hongkong Bank Board and became a member of the MMBI Board and of its executive committee. John L. Boyer (East in 1949) had served in Rangoon, Osaka, and Calcutta before a career in Singapore, where he was Manager from 1971–1974; he became a General Manager in Hong Kong in 1974 and Deputy Chairman of HSBC in 1978. Tom Welsh had come East in 1953 and served in Ipoh, Kuala Belait, had been Manager in Seria, and moved on to Bangkok. He was Manager Tawau in 1968 and became Manager Jakarta in 1973, moving back to Hong Kong as Manager of the Main Office only in 1976. Welsh retired in 1985 as resident Executive Director in London.[1]

These three moved immediately to Buffalo where they found the executives of MMB '100% cooperative'. Although general familiarization was one objective, the main concern was with the state of MMB's portfolio. Had all the problems been identified? The accounting firms presented the actual figures, and the price to be offered by HSBC was advised by the investment bankers, by Wolfensohn after consultation with Glucksman. During these latter discussions, HSBC was quietly informed by Glucksman that there was an

---

[1] Welsh had been unaware that he would continue east from Hawaii to the cold of New York; he was given a special allowance to buy winter clothes.

'interloper', a bank which was very anxious to have an opportunity to bid for Marine Midland. This was an additional factor which caused the vital importance of the subordinated note.

The consequences

The Definitive Agreement – general terms

The transaction, as it was shaped into the preliminary agreement included the two-tier structure – HSBC would tender for 25% of the outstanding common stock, then trading between US$16¼ and US$14, at US$20; reserving the right to buy shares at market if the tender were not fully successful, the Bank would buy new shares in MMBI with an end-1977 book value of US$33+ for US$30.[14]

The eventual injection of capital promised to be in the US$200 million range, but that was a long way down the road, and the MMBI needed capital funds as soon as practical. This once again pointed to a subordinated note.

The Definitive Agreement has been described as containing something for everyone. The shareholder had an opportunity to sell all or part of his holdings at a then advantageous price. The Marine Midland would eventually have an injection of capital of US$200 million at US$30 per share; in contrast it could be argued that they might have been able to float a more limited preferred issue at US$15. It was true, as previously noted, that banks were being purchased at up to twice the book value, but the circumstances were different. First, the other banks were usually small banks in States in which banking, particularly branch banking, was expanding – in Florida, Texas, and California; secondly, despite the fact that MMB had been audited, its loan portfolio was in question, rightly or wrongly, as reflected in the market for the holding company's shares. Sandberg had never intended to buy at above book value and the Hongkong Bank opened at US$28 a share; the investment bankers reached the figure of US$30.

Marine Midland was to become a subsidiary. However, to sweeten this and to give the partnership concept reality, the MMBI board was empowered to nominate three of its members as members of the Hongkong Bank's Board of Directors. This arrangement was reciprocal, the Hongkong Bank would appoint three of its members – and no more – to the MMBI and MMB boards, but would not otherwise reorganize or change MMBI's board or management nor would it interfere in day-to-day management. Furthermore, the Hongkong Bank, which would acquire a total of 51.1% of the outstanding shares, was to be barred from acquiring any further common stock for a period of five years and then only if authorized by a majority of non-HSBC shareholders. This kept a large public interest in MMBI.

Whatever other consequences of such a situation, it meant that regulatory authorities would be particularly insistent that the Hongkong Bank played its promised role. These decisions could be, and were (by Muriel Siebert), later described as being merely 'pious statements', and it is true that, except for the agreement not to buy further common stock, they were not legally binding. Indeed, the proxy material informed shareholders that the HSBC did not, by the statements, limit its rights as a shareholder; since it would have 51.1% the statement noted that HSBC could vote its own board of directors and therefore its own management. These pious statements were, however, sincerely meant and were believed by experienced men, presumably because there was personal trust and confidence supplemented by an analysis which confirmed the deal made mutual sense of a kind which would be self-enforced by self-interest.

The role of the subordinated note
The subordinated note was a loan of US$100 million by the Hongkong Bank and its terms were the only serious misunderstanding of the negotiations. The underlying problem was that MMBI by signing an agreement with HSBC cut itself off from any other method of obtaining additional capital funds, at least until the agreement were either finalized after regulatory approval or called off. There was no thought that finalization would take more than six months or so – the eventual 1980 date would most certainly not have been considered feasible. If the agreement went through, all was well; if it did not, MMBI had been set back in its schedule for full recovery. Under the agreement HSBC would have the essential 51% of the equity in a deal which was attractive to MMBI, despite the control issue, because of the promised capital injection. MMBI simply needed some token of assurance.

From the Hongkong Bank's point of view, this was quite reasonable and indeed to HSBC's advantage since it meant that MMB's growth would not be delayed and the note would be used to pay for the first tranche of new shares when issued. The trouble was that for the $100 million to be treated as MMB capital by the regulators, the note had to be long-term, say fifteen years. But what if the deal collapsed through no fault of the HSBC? The note was to be at less than market rates and the Bank would, therefore, have funds tied up uneconomically in an institution in which it no longer had any vital interest.

The solution was for the note to be a minimum five-year loan; if the deal fell through because of the HSBC's refusal to cooperate with the regulatory investigations or otherwise 'pulled out', then the note would become a fifteen-year loan and rank as capital for regulatory purposes. If, therefore, the regulators – the SEC, the Federal Reserve Board (the Fed), the NYBD, or other agency – refused to sanction the merger, the note would remain a five-year note, but it would not be capital and could not therefore provide MMB with the capital it required. The dispute was over the exact circumstances under which the note would convert to a long-term (fifteen year) loan; foreseeing all possibilities and allowing for them were not easy tasks, and the position was not really clear at the time of the preliminary agreement.

Nevertheless, after the direct intervention of Duffy and Sandberg, the terms were eventually worked out for the Definitive Agreement as outlined above. The US$100 million would not be capital until triggered by the Hongkong Bank's pulling out unilaterally. The Hongkong Bank would not be stuck with a fifteen-year investment through either regulatory or legislative decisions. But what then had been accomplished for the deal and for MMB?

In the opinion of most participants, most especially of John Petty, the deal would not have been consummated without the US$100 million no matter on what specific terms. The Hongkong Bank's American strategy was based, Sandberg claimed, on the need to distribute the Group's assets; they *intended* to inject funds into MMB. Intent is easier to prove in the context of some significant move in the direction intended; as stated above, the note was a *bona fides* of the HSBC and was seen as such by all concerned – including the 'interloper'.

As it was not capital MMB could not leverage it into a multiple increase in assets. Nevertheless two benefits resulted: (i) US$100 million could be lent out within the five-year time frame in a way that permitted MMB to benefit from the margin between the lending rate and the $7\frac{3}{4}\%$ at which the note had been sold at par and (ii) the injection of funds *per se* and the implications of that injection made it possible for MMB's investment bankers, Lehman Brothers, to ensure the marketability of MMB's negotiable certificates of deposit to buyers with particularly high quality requirements and to prevent any further deterioration in MMB's credit ratings. Both the tangible and intangible consequences of this second benefit were significant.

Although this solution proved satisfactory when both parties assumed the deal would be consummated before the end of 1978 – the Definitive Agreement was originally valid through March 1979 – the terms of the note were a major feature in the renegotiations which extended the terms of the agreement once it had become clear that regulatory approval would not be immediately forthcoming.

Wolfensohn and Glucksman considered the agreement which they had put together was 'elegant'; the press called it 'finely sculptured'. Wolfensohn ascribed a great deal of the credit to Frame, the Hongkong Bank's legal adviser, to Macdonald (and behind him the Booz-Allen team) for his long-run approach to the American strategy, and to Sandberg as the Chief Executive responsible both for having the vision and perspective necessary to see through the run-up and for executing the subsequent policy, that is, for having the determination to put it through. Specific credit for particular ideas relative to the deal is, however, difficult to apportion since in discussion ideas come simultaneously and 'firsts' are not always recognized, even by those responsible.

There had been several disagreements, the most important had been the terms under which the note would be triggered. It was at such points that the spirit engendered in Hawaii and passed on, as it were, to all the negotiators carried them through. It was here also that the Americans stressed again that only *Hong Kong* Brits could have carried their American friends with them.

The agreement received the approval of both boards of directors. Sandberg was present for the May signing and spoke of the significance for New York State. Sandberg was interviewed by G. William Miller, then chairman of the Federal Reserve Board, later Secretary of the Treasury. Miller, who had lived in Shanghai and knew the reputation of the Hongkong Bank, was generally supportive, stating only that he would oppose any unfriendly or hostile takeover of small banks, thereby defusing that particular source of opposition. Sandberg was particularly grateful for the support of certain New York City bankers, among them David Rockefeller of Chase, Don Platten, and Gordon Wallace – there was support from Morgan Guaranty and Irving. John McGillicuddy of Manufacturers Hanover, like Walter Wriston of Citibank, was disturbed that anti-trust legislation barred him from doing what the Hongkong Bank was doing – and told Sandberg or Petty so.

There was, nevertheless, a general if temporary euphoria. The deal, well-informed advisers said, would go through quickly, and, for a time, this assessment appeared correct. But there would be surprising developments. These will be considered in the following chapter.

17

THE ACQUISITION OF MARINE MIDLAND BANKS, INC., 1978–1980, II. THE REGULATORS, CONGRESS, AND THE FINAL APPROVAL

CONGRESSMAN ROSENTHAL: You were pretty persevering in this deal.
I.H. MACDONALD, HSBC: We believe in it.
Congressional Hearings, May 15, 1980

Estimates varied: Sandberg was advised that the necessary regulatory approvals of the Definitive Agreement (see Chapter 16) would be obtained by the end of 1978; Frank Laski thought 90 days not impossible; James Munsell was more cautious – his estimate was nine to twelve months. The actual time from the signing of the Definitive Agreement to the final decision of the Comptroller of the Currency on January 28, 1980, was twenty months.

Possibly because the transaction seemed favourable to all parties, the principals and their advisers failed to be realistic about the prospects for speedy Federal and State approvals. Even when the regulators agreed with the underlying soundness of the agreement, they had their own departmental or long-term political concerns.[1] The SEC, for example, had long been arguing for full bank disclosure and this would impact on their handling of the HSBC information, regardless of the merits of the particular case.

Paradoxically, the turnaround of Marine Midland, which was becoming vaguely visible to the particularly astute, could be used as an excuse to reclassify the situation from urgent to routine. Departmental and political concerns could once again be brought into play.

Sandberg, Macdonald, and Petty made calls on Paul Volcker of the Federal Reserve Bank – he remained receptive but non-committal – and on Muriel Siebert, the New York State Superintendent of Banks. The impression Sandberg and Petty received was that she favoured the prospects. Thus the optimistic forecasts appeared reinforced and the two bank holding companies proceeded with their tasks.

* The abbreviations are restated in the Appendix to this chapter. For general references, see the introduction to the end-notes to Chapter 16, pp. 950–51.

THE FEDERAL AND STATE REGULATORS – THROUGH JUNE 1978

This section deals with the two parties' dealings with the regulators through June 27, 1979, when the HSBC withdrew its application seeking to vote its shares in Marine Midland from consideration by the New York State Banking Department. The main focus is on the SEC and the simultaneous submissions to the Federal Reserve and the State Banking Department. There were other submissions within this time period which can be noted briefly at this point.

THE ISSUES

There were four underlying and principal issues which should be read in the context of the earlier section (Chapter 16) on the regulatory and banking environment: (i) that a foreign bank should be able to do what a domestic bank was not permitted to do, despite the attempt to write 'national treatment' into the IBA, seemed unfair, (ii) that the Hongkong Bank was not really a bank at all but a conglomerate of various types of enterprise, (iii) that the Hongkong Bank did not reveal its true position and therefore could not be properly assessed, and (iv) the Definitive Agreement contained 'pious statements' which were unenforceable and that the Bank might act with impunity against the interests of depositors and/or borrowers.

There were several minor concerns, some legitimate, others wild. Of the latter the accusation, made by the U.S. Labor Party, that there was a conspiracy between the British Royal family, Zionists, Mao Tse-tung, and the Hongkong Bank to run an international dope ring suggested the presence of KGB funds to some observers, but the Party received considerable publicity and its charges had nevertheless to be heard by the agencies involved.[2] Arising from the concern as to the Hongkong Bank's intentions were more detailed objections relative to 'red-lining' and the two-tier price decision, indeed, of the terms of the deal itself, but these will be considered below.

Anti-trust concern had to be dealt with thoroughly, despite the minor importance – in the context of relevant legislation – of the Hongkong Bank's operation, but it did not create an impediment in the course of the transaction.[3]

Although the issues can be stated separately, they did not always affect the regulators in so clear-cut a fashion. In Siebert's concern there seemed to be an underlying response to the 'unfairness' aspect coupled with some mixture of the three further problems in varying proportions. Those opposing a measure do not always confine themselves to the issue with which they are really concerned; their purpose is to stop the transaction. This will become clear in

II. Final approval

the section on the regulators and the chronology. The issues can, however, be stated in their own right.

The negative impact of U.S. legislation on U.S. banking

The first principal issue was quite true and Sandberg appreciated why senior executives of, for example, Citibank, would be concerned, but that was not the fault of the Hongkong Bank; it was a consequence of U.S. legislation. The issue however took two courses. First, those concerned, bankers and regulators, lobbied Congress, and in the process such fundamental problems as the prohibition against interstate banking and the impact of foreign acquisitions on the domestic banking system came up for consideration. Fortunately for the parties, Congress did not insist on resolving the issues before settlement of the merger in question.

There would seem to be a spill-over from this bias against big banks into what came to be known as the up-State down-State policy, whereby the State Banking Department had prevented big New York City banks from acquiring up-State banks. That this should be applied to the Hongkong Bank depended on taking the Hongkong Bank's world-wide rather than its New York City operations into account and can only be made sensible if, in fact, the regulator had other factors in mind, particularly the complaints of New York City bankers that somehow the approval of Hongkong Bank would not be fair.[4]

The non-financial activities of the Hongkong Bank

That the non-financial activities of the Hongkong Bank should come under question was consequent to several factors, the first being the assumption by Congress that the matter was satisfactorily covered by the Bank Holding Company Act and the second being a question of whether the Hongkong Bank qualified even under the more generous provisions for a foreign bank holding company. This has been discussed in the preceding chapter, but the issue became confused with another and basically more important one, that is, the Bank's accounting and reporting methods. Thus one of Siebert's objections would be that the Bank had allegedly provided insufficient information to permit her to judge its application; specifically, they had failed to respond to questions concerning all associated companies in which, through a chain, they had a 25% interest. This issue was discussed in full before a sub-committee of the Congress in 1980 after the transaction had been fully approved.[5]

Underlying the financial/non-financial differentiation was, *inter alia*, the fear that the non-financial companies would achieve an unfair competitive advantage through loans from the associated bank at advantageous rates. As of December 31, 1979, HSBC estimated that its loans to companies in which it owned 25%

or more of the equity totalled US$350 million, or 4% of HSBC's total advances and other accounts as of that date. HSBC undertook to keep its business relations with MMBI and its non-financial operations at 'arm's length'.[6]

The Bank's accounts

The basic problem was that the Hongkong Bank's accounts, published or unpublished, are not drawn up according to GAAP, the American 'Generally Accepted Accounting Principles'. Peter E. Hammond, who handled the 'money-end' of the Bank and became involved with SEC negotiations, estimated that it would have taken some US$4 million to convert the Bank's accounts. At the beginning, there seemed to be no question that the American regulators expected such action to be taken, that they would be satisfied with the audited accounts plus explanations of accounting procedures. This was probably true; the question of forms and definitions was used to cover certain other disquiets.

The Hongkong Bank was also accused by the NYBD of being unwilling to provide the information required. This the Bank denied.[7] Siebert and others pointed to the lack of a Hong Kong central bank and, while on the one hand acknowledging the willingness of the Hong Kong Government to cooperate but on the other hand minimizing the existence of Hong Kong's regulatory banking ordinances and the role of the Commissioner of Banking, argued that the Hongkong Bank was therefore without regulatory supervision in its own jurisdiction. The long-discredited argument was brought out once more: did not the Hongkong Bank actually control the local authorities? There was, in other words, a general lack of understanding of the Hong Kong system, both by opponents and supporters of the transaction. The NYBD's objections were so obviously implausible that they seemed capable of explanation only in the context that Siebert was looking for excuses. Furthermore, the department's call for more and more information seemed to the Bank to be a delaying tactic; she did not like the merger and she knew that delay could kill a deal without any regulatory decision.

In this controversy over disclosure some time passed before the Hongkong Bank realized it would have to reveal its true profits and true position, that is, reveal inner reserves to the NYBD and to the Federal Reserve. But this was done before the end of 1978 and should not have been a factor in delaying any favourable decision.

The Bank's intentions

Bank take-overs and acquisitions had a bad name both in the City of London and in the United States. Banks had been acquired and their assets stripped. Calling the HSBC/MMBI transaction a 'merger' could be seen as a cynical

II. Final approval

disguise. The questions were, as the consultants had first asked them: What did the Hongkong Bank intend? and, Could the Bank prove it?

Just as Duffy could argue that he had confidence in Sandberg, so could Assemblyman Herman D. Farrell, Jr (74th district, Harlem) as chairman of the New York State Assembly Banks Committee, state that he was not so much concerned with what the Hongkong Bank intended to do as with what it could do. He stated his opposition to ordinary citizens carrying firearms not because he thought they would kill but because they might. There is no answer either to Duffy or to Farrell on these terms.

On the other hand, as there is no answer, the issue becomes one of political responsibility. Siebert eventually decided that she would not accept the Bank's explanations; Governor Carey had all the time been supportive. The Hongkong Bank's strategy was designed to inject funds into a North American institution.[8] The Federal Reserve Board's Henry Wallich argued that the Hongkong Bank would lose its investment in the United States if it were not supportive of Marine Midland's capital requirements and responsive to American attitudes towards the role of domestic banks. It thus made sense for the Hongkong Bank to act as promised. To judge the integrity of a bank, Wallich argued, you took the opinion of its peers; the reputation of the Hongkong Bank (coupled with a professional study of the Bank) was sufficient to let the transaction through.[9]

The finer points, for example, 'red-lining' (see below), become irrelevant if the Hongkong Bank were to leave the day-to-day operation of the MMB to MMB management. Red-lining was a particularly sensitive issue in New York where certain relatively depressed areas had possibly been neglected by banks – or, as the name implies, 'red-lined'. Enforcement of the legislation prohibiting such practices was through 'gatekeeping', that is, the Superintendent could only act effectively when and if the offending bank asked to undertake a certain course (open a branch, for example) which was discretionary with the State Banking Department. The MMB branches were, Siebert argued, in place. There would be no opportunity to correct any HSBC-inspired misdirection of investment.

The Bank, it was argued during Congressional questioning of Federal Reserve officers, might have good intentions, but was it not the central bank of Hong Kong and would it not therefore have political responsibilities which would override its intentions *vis-à-vis* Marine Midland and the needs of up-State New York? This was not one of Siebert's concerns and the Bank was at pains to deny its central bank role, claiming only that it acted as the Government's bankers, a point discussed in Chapter 8.

THE REGULATORS

The authorities involved[10]

The principals
The principal approvals necessary were (i) the SEC approval of the proxy material; (ii) the Federal Reserve approval for the acquisition of an American bank by an overseas bank holding company – an approval which would not be given until HSBC had divested itself of the Hongkong Bank of California; and, as Marine Midland Bank was a State-chartered bank, (iii) the approval of the Superintendent of Banks of New York State to actually vote the bank shares acquired. Without (i) nothing could happen; without (iii), any permission granted in (ii) would be, from the Hongkong Bank's point of view, useless. But – and the idea never occurred to anyone involved in 1978 – if (iii) approval were withheld, its relevance would cease if the Marine Midland Bank converted from a State to a National (banking) Association. In such a case, no third approval for the actual merger would be necessary, but the Comptroller of the Currency would have to approve MMB as a National (banking) Association, that is, as a Federally chartered bank.

This summary depends on there being no new legislated change in the rules of the game. Furthermore, it depends on there being no legislation pending which would provide the regulator an excuse to freeze any new permission to vote shares or change from a State to a National charter. At crucial moments the transaction seemed threatened with just such developments.

That the transaction survived the ordeal depended on its perceived soundness, the existence of a dual banking system in the United States making avoidance of one regulatory authority a possibility, the sympathetic approach of Hugh Carey, Governor of New York, to the deal, and the willingness of the Congress to exclude the HSBC/MMBI transaction from a moratorium enforced during consideration of, *inter alia*, necessary revisions to the International Banking Act. At another level it depended on the specific terms of the renegotiated agreement, effective July 1, 1979, and especially on the new terms for the subordinated note, on the tenacity of Sandberg and the encouragement he received from Wolfensohn, and on the growing appreciation of the legal problems by such experienced experts on the Hongkong Bank's team as Frank Frame, James Munsell, and Steuart Pittman. Marine Midland, with an equal commitment to the merger, fielded an equally competent team.

The 'other' authorities
With reference to the anti-trust implications of the merger, the Federal Trade Commission was involved, and Steuart Pittman drew up the necessary

arguments in full despite the minimal size of the Hongkong Bank in New York. The conclusion was that the impact of the merger on competition would exist; the degree was described as 'slight' but with offsetting advantages.[11] With reference to the sale of the Hongkong Bank of California, the Hongkong Bank were involved with the California State Banking Department (HBC was a State bank), the FDIC, and the Federal Reserve Bank of San Francisco. HBC was sold in early 1979 to the Central Bank of Oakland, which earlier had converted from a National to a State chartered bank.

The Hongkong Bank had also to deal with the Department of Justice and the Federal Trade Commission relative to the anti-trust implications of its non-financial activities; a presentation was made on October 10 and an exemption granted from further submissions on October 11. Events could, but rarely did, move rapidly.

There were overseas implications.

The issue in Australia was that Marine Midland had an interest in an Australia-based merchant bank. The Federal Reserve had instructed MMB to divest itself of this investment, but with the merger the instruction would no longer stand. In view of the fact that the Hongkong Bank had subsidiaries in Australia the merger was a matter to discuss with the Foreign Investment Revenue Board – on August 1, 1978, the board stated that there were no objections.

Approval of the transaction was granted by the Monopolies and Mergers Commission of the United Kingdom virtually as a matter of routine: both banks were active in London.

The transaction received a slight and temporary setback, which nevertheless received considerable notice in the press, when the Canadian Foreign Investment Review Board ruled adversely on the Hongkong Bank's acquiring control, through MMBI, of the latter's Canadian subsidiaries. Subsequent opinion among MMBI directors was simply that the application was uncoordinated and misadvised; the decision had no impact on the course of events relative to the merger and was later rejected.

The course of events, May 1978–June 1979

Following the May signing of the Definitive Agreement, MMBI and HSBC sought the approval of the three principal regulators simultaneously. MMBI was responsible for obtaining the approval of its own shareholders. To obtain this the MMBI board of directors needed to send out proxy materials which had been submitted to the SEC and to which the SEC had had no objections. The Hongkong Bank at the same time prepared submissions for the Federal Reserve Board and the New York State Banking Department.

The first problem came from the SEC, and the Hongkong Bank became involved.

SEC and full disclosure

The Hongkong Bank filed information about itself with the SEC on May 30, the preliminary proxy materials were sent by MMBI on July 7. SEC acceptance of the proxy materials was not obtained until late August. The problems were accounting principles and disclosure.

Michael Sandberg and other Hongkong Bank directors had long felt that, with the Bank's shares quoted in excess of true book value, every effort should be made to expand through acquisitions obtained through issue of additional Bank shares. Now, when the decision to expand in North America was made, the Bank, in conformity with the purpose of the acquisition, had to pay cash. This, the Bank expected, would render it unnecessary to make any presentation to the SEC involving disclosure of inner reserves. As the Definitive Agreement called for cash payments by the Hongkong Bank, there was no expectation that the SEC would require more than evidence of the Hongkong Bank's ability to pay the cash. This proved to be too narrow an interpretation of the SEC's responsibilities. The SEC took the quite reasonable position that 48.9% of the shares would remain in non-HSBC possession and that the decision of shareholders as to whether they should remain to be part of this minority in accordance with the Definitive Agreement would depend, in part, on their assessment of the management capability and resources of the HSBC. The past performance of the Hongkong Bank was therefore relevant, even though the Bank stated it did not intend to run MMB.

Specifically the SEC wanted the HSBC accounts restated in a form consistent with GAAP and they wanted to know the size of the Bank's inner reserves. The former demand was surprising since the SEC had accepted non-GAAP accounts from foreign financial firms before. The fact is that MMBI and HSBC had failed to take into consideration the size of the deal they had agreed to; the regulatory authorities would be particularly careful. On the question of inner reserves, the Bank at that point did not expect to have to reveal these figures to the regulatory authorities, but it was absolutely essential that they not be stated to the SEC which, unlike the Federal Reserve Board and the State Banking Department, were subject to all the disclosure provisions of the Freedom of Information Act.

The Hongkong Bank was facing Charles Ogilby, an SEC official who was well-known for his insistence that U.S. banks fully disclose their position. He had to be overruled. Peter Hammond was successful in convincing the staff that the Bank's position was better than that shown in the published figures and that

II. Final approval

inner reserves were not used to boost the annual profit statement or pay the annual dividend.

Although the Hongkong Bank had routinely been reporting to U.S. regulators in New York and California, the operation had been merely the U.S. end of a mainly foreign bank. This was the first Hongkong Bank encounter with regulators since it had declared its intention to own a major U.S. commercial bank. There was a legitimate difference, but for a time it seemed the deal would fail at the first hurdle. Barry Fox of Cleary, Gottlieb went to Hong Kong; for some six weeks he and Bank officers would try to put through acceptable statements, telex them to James Munsell in New York in the evening – Munsell would get a response back before the next working day in Hong Kong. Sandberg at the same time was responding to questions from Harold Williams of the SEC by telephone; Hammond was in New York.

The SEC were not prepared, however, to be responsible for derailing so large a deal at the first step. Accordingly the final solution, which was made exceptionally by the full Commission, was (i) the accounts should be presented as published with explanations relative to the differences between Hongkong Bank practices and GAAP and (ii) the inner reserves need not be disclosed. This last was undoubtedly consequent on acceptance by the SEC of a letter to the Bank from Hong Kong's Financial Secretary, Sir Philip Haddon-Cave, to the effect that it was Hong Kong Government policy that banks should have inner reserves and not be required to make full disclosure.

The shareholder reaction

This decision cleared the way for the proxy materials to be circulated. At the subsequent shareholders meeting some 95% of those voting were in favour of the transaction as detailed in the Definitive Agreement.

The MMBI board of directors refused, however, to advise shareholders on the sale of their shares. It is difficult to see how they could have acted otherwise, despite some pressure from the Hongkong Bank for them to take a position. The MMBI directors argued that shareholders held shares for diverse reasons which would in some cases argue for acceptance, in others not. Furthermore, if the directors argued too strongly that US$20 was a good price for shares which were once selling at around US$40 a share and were then selling between US17\frac{7}{8}$ and US14\frac{5}{8}$, what could be made of the argument that 48.9% were to remain in the possession of non-HSBC shareholders?

The directors' difficulty can be put this way. If the shareholders agreed that the HSBC partnership would be beneficial to MMBI, the latter's share price would rise back to US$40 (and it had actually gone to US$55 before the end of 1986); therefore it was wise for shareholders to hold on to their shares. But, if the shareholders acted in this way, then the Hongkong Bank's tender offer would fail and the transaction could become void; shares would then fall back to the former depressed levels. A *laissez-faire* approach was the only one feasible.

The higher-than-market tender offer, however, can also be seen as making the tender successful. There were major institutional investors who would take the opportunity to diversify by selling MMBI shares at a smaller loss – perhaps advantageously for tax reasons. There were also small-holders particularly in up-State New York. MMBI had acquired some 200 local banks by payment of MMBI shares; there were many shareholders who had in this way acquired less than a board lot, and even so small a holding had been split among heirs. These shareholders reacted individually, but the higher-than-market price was attractive.

The shareholders' decision in October 1978 was not an end to the matter. The Agreement was renegotiated in June 1979 and again presented to shareholders. The Hongkong Bank would meet with the SEC again.

The Federal Reserve Bank of New York and the Federal Reserve Board
The application under the Bank Holding Company Act for permission to buy a U.S. bank is a negotiated document. The Hongkong Bank first approached the Federal Reserve Bank of New York for post-agreement discussions on June 8, 1978, and, before the relevant application documents had been fully approved for submission to the Federal Reserve Board, the New York Fed sent a staff member, F. Piderit, to make a study of the Bank in Hong Kong. His one week visit and subsequent report would become matters of controversy later; had the Fed recognized that the very size of the transaction was likely to make it a political issue, no doubt their initial study would have been more comprehensive. As it was, it could be criticized for its necessarily general nature.[a]

The HSBC's draft submission was made to the New York Fed on July 13, and the final application on August 31; this was accepted and forwarded to the Federal Reserve Board of Governors in Washington on September 1. The Board now had, by law, 90 days to object to the HSBC purchase of MMBI. On March 16, 1979, some seven and a half months later, the Board finally approved the application of HSBC. Here the traditional interest of Hongkong Bankers in sports was useful: the 90 days worked like a fifteen minute football quarter; the

---

[a] During Congressional hearings in 1979 a discussion arose between the chairman, Benjamin S. Rosenthal, and the Federal Reserve representative, John Ryan, as to whether the late Mr Piderit had stayed at the Mandarin or the Peninsula. Both are excellent hotels, but Rosenthal had information that Piderit had chosen the Peninsula, thus requiring a ferry ride and a longer trip to the Bank, thus cutting the time available for serious investigation.[12] Hongkong Bank executives had not expected the discussion to turn on such fine points.

II. Final approval

clock was stopped under certain conditions, for time-outs, certain penalties. Similarly, if the FRB wanted further information, it submitted questions to the Bank and the clock was stopped until that information was provided.

The responsibility of the Federal Reserve Board was to determine whether the bank holding company had management competent to handle the resulting operations and was thus in a financial position to sustain its support of the banking subsidiary, in this case, Marine Midland. To determine this the Board had to obtain information as to the HSBC's true financial position. The Hongkong Bank was concerned with possible leaks with the dangers of random access to information through the Freedom of Information Act. Nevertheless the information had to be provided. The Hongkong Bank was subjected to a notional examination; examinations are confidential and cannot be revealed under the Freedom of Information Act; the Bank was therefore protected.

There were in fact three main factors in the delay. The first, as noted, was informational. The second had to do with intent of Congress relative to the IBA. The stated purpose of the IBA was equal or national treatment, therefore it could be argued that the Federal Reserve, as gatekeeper, should not permit the merger with MMBI unless the HSBC agreed to, *inter alia*, close its branches, except those in New York State, its home State under the terms of the act, and those in the one other State permitted under the act. The FRB could argue that the IBA facilitated foreign bank Edge Act corporations in lieu of commercial banking branches, but the Hongkong Bank argued that the requirement was excessive, without precedent, and unnecessary. In the end the FRB agreed; the proposals had never been put forward formally.

The third factor is neither clear cut nor particularly important. Where a State Supervisor or the OCC is required to rule on an acquisition, their ruling is usually submitted before the FRB, which has the authority to overrule, makes its own ruling.[13] The New York statute however was not concerned with the acquisition *per se* but with the subsequent voting of shares. Whatever the factors involved, however, they were not the ultimate cause of the State delays.

As the months passed both sides were arguing as to whether the 90 days had elapsed, that is, when had the clock started and when had there been time-outs? Legally, the HSBC could have taken a position that the 90 days were over and, as there had been no objection from the Fed, the merger could go forward. There were three problems to this course: (i) the Bank was not sure the courts would sustain the proposition relative to the lapse of the 90 days, (ii) a foreign bank seeking a bank merger was not in a position to challenge the 'system' in the U.S. – or in the United Kingdom as it would later develop, and (iii) more than this, the Definitive Agreement needed a positive statement of support from the Fed, it would not be safe (however legal) to 'sneak through'. In any case the NYBD had not as yet made its decision; the deal could not succeed by default.

The reasons for the 'delay' have been variously explained. The Hongkong Bank's operations with those of the Mercantile and BBME were complex, but the FRB analysts were competent to handle that. There was some thought that the Fed were waiting for the State, which had immediate responsibility for MMB, to make a decision first, and were pushed into a prior announcement by the clock. Or, more simply, the Fed could not delay once the Hongkong Bank of California had been fully and legally divested.

The matter was then still before the New York authorities.

The New York State Banking Department – (i) developing opposition

In the New York State Banking Act (Section 143-b) there is a provision requiring an institution that wants to control a New York State chartered bank to obtain the permission of the Superintendent to be able to vote the stock that it intends to acquire. The Superintendent may refuse such permission if she finds this 'reasonably necessary to protect the interests of the people of [New York State]'. More specifically, she is obligated to determine 'the character, responsibility and general fitness of the company' and 'whether the exercise of control may impair the safe and sound conduct' of the bank whose stock has been purchased.

The intent of the provision is commendable. But it almost seemed as if Siebert were confusing it with another enactment under which the Attorney-General could be requested to hold a public hearing on the suitability of a person or group attempting a take-over.[b] This latter law was directed at those attempting to gain control following which they were expected to strip a bank of its assets or otherwise misdirect its business; the Banking Act under which Siebert acted was regulatory in intent.

The provision calls for a decision by the Superintendent; Muriel Siebert was being asked to act as Superintendent of Banks in a statute-defined, quasi-judicial capacity and not as a political subordinate of the Governor. For this reason alone, Governor Hugh Carey, who had been persuaded to support the merger proposals in public, would have been politically unwise to remove the Superintendent, who served at his pleasure, merely on the grounds that he disagreed with a position which she had taken as part of her statutory and regulatory responsibility. That she was in fact taking a political policy position would be difficult to prove, nor could the Governor, without political cost, have removed her on the basis that she made no decision at all.

[b] This act is popularly referred to as the 'Chemical Bank law' because of the alleged attempt by S. Steinberg to take over that bank and the apparently adverse public and regulatory reaction to this possibility.

II. Final approval

The Hongkong Bank made preliminary application on July 13 and a final application on September 7 to be permitted to vote 51% of the shares of MMBI. By June 27, 1979, when the Hongkong Bank withdrew its application, no decision had been made. After the Bank had withdrawn its application, Siebert issued a 45-page statement as to why she was opposed to HSBC voting the shares. This had no legal significance, but there is sound reason for supposing that she would have issued the statement as a statutory decision had not the Bank acted first. For this reason, in what follows, the assumption is that the Superintendent was, possibly at an early date, certainly by the Spring of 1979, opposed to the implementation of the Definitive Agreement. The reason for this opposition is a matter of considerable disagreement and speculation, but the several factors involved can be discussed.

The difficulty of assessing the situation is due to the fact that Siebert in her public statements made comments which, if they in fact influenced her 'decision' (as defined above), could be considered *ultra vires*.

Clearly Siebert was concerned with the 'unfairness' of the situation; she did not like a foreign bank being able to come into the State and buy a bank which other New York banks would be quite willing and able to acquire were they not barred by the provisions of anti-trust legislation. She therefore took up this issue at the national level, testifying before Congress. With this position several Hongkong Bankers expressed their understanding, arguing only that (i) they did not make the laws and (ii) Siebert, although quite justified in calling Congressional attention to the problem, should not, as State Bank Superintendent, allow her disapproval of the then existing Federal laws to influence the execution of her duty as stated under State laws as they then stood.

These are non-controversial statements, but they would be impossible to formulate effectively in court.

Secondly, and probably less important, Siebert argued that the deal, with particular reference to the price of shares to shareholders, was unfair. Such matters of fairness are, however, resolved by the vote of the shareholders, which was in this case overwhelmingly supportive.

The general context of the Superintendent's decision was that the latest department examination of MMB indicated that it was no longer in danger and that the merger proposal could not be considered on an emergency basis. This put the informational aspect to the fore; the question was no longer simply survival but long-term development.

The reasons actually given in the official statement are: (i) the possible adverse policies which HSBC might impose on MMBI, (ii) the uncertain future of Hong Kong and therefore of the Hongkong Bank, (iii) the lack of supervisory authority in Hong Kong and the Hongkong Bank's potential as a bank of last resort in the territory, (iv) the failure of the Hongkong Bank to provide the information necessary for a decision, (v) the up-State/down-State argument (see above), and (vi) the inability of the New York State Banking Department to supervise the HSBC's role on a continuing basis. There is nothing new in these charges, except possibly the future of Hong Kong itself. Governor Wallich of the FRB thought the question irrelevant (see below); the wartime London precedent is all that the authorities could cite (see Chapter 1).

The Hongkong Bank for its part claimed that it had provided the New York Department the same material it had provided the Federal Reserve Board and that, at one point, Siebert's staff had informed the Bank that it had sufficient for a decision. But there was certainly a division of opinion among the staff of the Banking Department itself.

– (ii) explanations and reactions

The general expectation among MMBI executives and advisers was that, once the Federal Reserve Board had made its decision, the State would follow. Frank Laski cited precedents illustrating the cooperative approach of the State Banking Department, particularly in 1975 when MMBI was putting together its ten regional banks to form the single State-wide MMB. These examples were, however, during the incumbency of Siebert's predecessor, John G. Heimann, who had been appointed Comptroller of the Currency in Washington. But the Fed itself took longer than expected, the State kept asking for further information, and the meetings with the Superintendent became less and less satisfactory. By January Duffy, chairman of MMBI, recognized that there was a problem.

With the Definitive Agreement set to expire on March 30, 1979, the HSBC and MMBI agreed to extend its terms, without amendment, until June 30, by which time a decision from the State was expected. Indeed, during the next three months negotiations continued, with Siebert proposing various alternatives and safeguards, including an agreement relative to the composition of the MMBI board of directors. These recommendations are explained in her official statement.

Throughout this latter period, Carey and his administration were in support of the HSBC/MMBI merger; it was consistent with declared State policy. Carey and his Secretary, Robert P. Morgado, concurred in the view that Siebert was moving out of her role as a State regulator and taking a national political stand; Morgado saw the eventual report as an *ex post facto* justification of her basic anti-foreign position. James S. Dyson, as Commerce Commissioner, was another outspoken critic of Siebert; Attorney-General Abrahms was, on the contrary, the only senior State officer to give tentative support to her concerns.

Siebert's main problem that HSBC was a foreign bank would not necessarily

II. Final approval

be inconsistent with the Superintendent's positive role in attracting overseas financial institutions and forwarding the establishment of international banking facilities; these were 'foreign' functions. She was opposed to an alien bank assuming control of a major domestic deposit-taking bank on national policy considerations but, unless this concern could be brought within the context of existing State legislation, she ought, nevertheless, to permit the merger to go through.

At one point Siebert circularized central banks world-wide and asked if they would permit the take-over of one of their major clearing banks; the answers were negative. This was interesting but irrelevant; reciprocity was not the basis of existing banking law; it was only a U.S. policy goal.[14] Significantly, she did not contact Hong Kong.

Hermann Farrell, the chairman of the New York State Assembly's banking committee, had become concerned at the high percentage of New York banking assets which would be owned by 'alien' (defined as 'non-American', as opposed to 'foreign', 'non-New York State') banks. He did not object to a alien bank branching *de novo*, but, he was concerned with this particular merger. On the other hand, he did not make a political issue of it; his own constituents – 'they cared less, knew less' on this particular topic, but they could have been made to care had he chosen an irresponsible political course. Instead, his response was muted; he introduced a bill which would have provided a three-month moratorium to permit further study; his purpose was to give support to the Superintendent. In the event he was surprised to find considerable support and speedy passage in the Assembly; the bill however did not pass the State Senate and did not become law.

As for the principals, the HSBC and MMBI, their determination to proceed was made public in the decision to extend the agreement. Duffy was reluctant to take the only other step possible, changing MMB from a State bank to a National banking association. The reasons for this reluctance are understandable – it was difficult for him to accept that a deal approved overwhelmingly by the board of directors and the shareholders, agreed to by the Fed – a deal without significant political opposition up-State and publicly supported by the Governor and his administration – should be rebuffed by his own State's Bank Superintendent.

Nevertheless as time passed Duffy recognized that (i) the agreement would have to be further extended, but on renegotiated terms and (ii) the need to 'go the Federal road' was becoming increasingly obvious. There had been hints from Washington that such a course would be welcome; both Volcker and Heimann, by then chairman of the Federal Reserve Board and Comptroller of the Currency respectively, had been in New York during MMBI's difficulties. They would surely not oppose their resolution.

There was, however, a possible threat to the course of action which now seemed necessary. A law might be passed in New York State which in some way negated the effectiveness of a National charter. On March 6, 1979, in the State Senate, such a law was in fact introduced.

The 'Take-over' Bill and its veto

A comparison

In a very real sense during the mid-nineteenth century the British Empire had a dual banking system. Banks in colonial territories could be locally or imperially chartered. Imperial charters permitted the bank to operate in more than one colonial jurisdiction; colonial charters initially did not. Imperial charters, although they contained privileges not permitted in locally chartered banks (unless, like the Hongkong Bank, chartered according to the Colonial Banking Regulations), also contained saving clauses which negated the privileges if they proved contrary to local legislation. This eventually eliminated the special advantages of imperial charters.

In the dual system(s) – since each State differed – which evolved in the United States after the Civil War, there was no *a priori* advantage to either the National or State systems, the provisions of each changing from time to time in a process of what has been referred to by its critics as 'competition in laxity'. The National system was not, however, truly national in the sense of 'nationwide'. Federal legislation limited the inter-State capacity of National banking associations; furthermore, Federal banking legislation took cognizance of general State legislation, for example, on the right of any bank in the State to operate branches. On this latter *general* basis State legislation could prevent foreign-owned or controlled banks from operating in the State *as a class*, but the State could not supervise a particular Nationally chartered bank in a way which, since it required a separate decision of judgement, overrode a Federal decision. Such an ability would negate the point to National bank associations and undermine the National bank system supervised by the Comptroller of the Currency in Washington.

The 'Take-over' Bill: background and passage

Muriel Siebert and other State bank superintendents were therefore faced with apparent responsibility for the banks within their respective States but were in fact unable either to examine or influence the actions of specific National banks. Thus when National Westminster Bank made application to acquire the National Bank of North America, they applied to the FRB and the OCC; Siebert had no opportunity to comment.

For some weeks Muriel Siebert, as the Superintendent of Banks, would not be convinced that such indeed was the law; once convinced she was determined to remedy this apparent gap between her responsibilities as seen by an ill-informed public and her legal authority. Her problem was more complex and of longer standing then the question of the merger of MMBI and HSBC but its first impact would have been on that transaction.

Although this was the situation in all States of the Union, the position in New York had peculiar features. Briefly, the ability of the Superintendent to supervise bank holding companies was flawed by the definition of a bank holding company as one controlling two or more banks, but after 1975 the MMBI was a one-bank holding company. The relevant Federal legislation had since 1970 included the one-bank holding company.

Secondly, when this New York State omission became apparent in the Chemical Bank case, New York had chosen to enact additional legislation rather than redefine a bank holding company, but, and this is the relevant issue, the new legislation specifically exempted National banks from its provisions. The reasons for this exemption had not been matters of legislative debate, but it could be assumed that the draftsman, presumably counsel for Chemical Bank, took the pragmatic approach that the inclusion of National banks might infringe on the Federal jurisdiction and thus be unconstitutional.

In 1977 Siebert had first tried to remedy the defects of the State laws as she saw them. Her intention was to acquire the right to determine whether in the case of a 'merger' the controlling company had the right to vote its shares regardless of the status of the controlled bank.

In March 1978 similar legislation – in this case providing that the acquiring institution had to seek permission from the State Banking Board *prior to* the acquisition of *any* banking institution in the State – was again introduced and surprisingly passed both houses of the New York State legislature. If this bill (NY Senate A.2650) were signed by the Governor, there would be no purpose in MMB giving up its State charter for a National charter; the State Banking Superintendent could still rule on the acquisition of MMBI by HSBC apparently without regard to the State or National status of the subsidiary bank.

Siebert's support of this legislation was consistent with her overall policy goal – to be able to control all banks within the State. It was also consistent with her efforts at least as early as February 1979 to obtain the interest of the Congress in Washington to her perception of the dangers of foreign bank acquisitions. There were those in Washington who agreed, but the situation in the capital, as it affected the HSBC/MMBI merger, developed later in the year and will be considered separately below.

The Governor's veto

All MMBI and HSBC officers and advisers considered the Take-over Bill to be unconstitutional in that it intruded, without Federal permission, into Federal jurisdiction. The Take-over Bill did not seek to prevent all acquisitions, but pretended to permit an acquisition only after a favourable opinion had been obtained from the State Banking Board. If the bank were Nationally chartered, the issue would only arise after the OCC and the Fed had given a favourable decision. The proposed New York bill therefore would give its own Banking Board a veto on a specific Federal decision relative to a specific Nationally chartered bank. This challenged the very basis of the dual banking system.

The bill if signed into law could certainly have been challenged in the courts. All involved accepted, however, that in the HSBC/MMBI case such action was totally impractical. The Hongkong Bank as a foreign corporation could not be seen to be challenging the State; the court case would at the most optimistic estimate carry on beyond any date which could possibly be covered by an extension of the Definitive Agreement.

The only practical course was to urge the Governor to veto the bill. The transaction now rested on the willingness of the Governor to do so.

Duffy was in London with Sandberg at the International Monetary Conference at the end of May 1979. Both were somewhat on edge; the two parties were already renegotiating the Definitive Agreement, they had already planned to 'go the Federal road' if Siebert did not make a ruling quickly, and curious bankers did not improve the atmosphere by asking 'How's your deal going?' The fact is no one knew how it was going, but Duffy was clearly worried. He determined to telephone the Governor.

The Carey Administration itself was being challenged; a major New York bank was being hamstrung; the State's reputation for fast and sound decisions, a cornerstone of Carey's economic policy, was being undermined, and significant investment in up-State New York delayed. Nevertheless the issue had to be handled carefully, and in Albany the question of constitutionality seemed the easiest basis for a resolution. Accordingly, Morgado contacted John Heimann in Washington; Heimann saw immediately that the bill intruded into his jurisdiction. He too could wait for the bill to be passed and then, on behalf of the Federal Government, challenge its constitutionality, but quite reasonably he thought this process lengthy, uncertain, and costly. Thus, despite the fact that he might be said to be an interested party in the particular case – since it was obvious by then that, if the bill were vetoed, MMB would seek a National charter from Heimann's office – he called the attention of the Governor to his position.

This gave Carey the opportunity he required, but no immediate action was taken. The principals waited. If the Governor did not veto the bill within the time specified by the State constitution, the bill would become law without his signature.

With only six hours to spare Carey vetoed the Take-over Bill.

Governor Carey sent for Duffy and told him that the bill had been 'kiboshed', adding, there is nothing to stop MMB from becoming a National bank, is there? Duffy rang Sandberg, then on leave in London, and gave him the news. After this resolution to what can only be described as a 'cliff-hanger', Duffy sounded less despondent. As Sandberg recalls, 'I felt, Christ, here we go again, but you know, we've got to try.'

THE FEDERAL ROAD – THE AGREEMENT IMPLEMENTED

Since the original agreement between HSBC and MMBI, as extended, was due to expire on June 30, 1979, and, as the Superintendent of the New York State Banking Department had still not issued her official opinion, by May the two parties had come to a time of decision. Both parties sensed that if Siebert did issue an opinion on HSBC it would be unfavourable. This suggested that the only course was for the HSBC to withdraw its application from State consideration and for the MMB to apply for a National charter. Such a course of action would require a further extension of the Definitive Agreement, and Duffy recognized that, as his bank had improved considerably over the year, renegotiation would have to take place. In fact, renegotiation was underway throughout the crisis of the Take-over Bill.

The renegotiation was successful, the HSBC withdrew its application on June 27, MMB applied for a National charter from the Comptroller of the Currency the following day, and the FRB extended its approval of the merger for a further year.

Although the deal had been renegotiated, the new terms were more favourable to MMBI than the old, and there was some discussion as to whether it was necessary for MMBI to go back to its shareholders. To be safe, in view of the importance of the proposals, Duffy decided to call another special meeting and ask for another vote. This decision brought the Hongkong Bank once again before the SEC, this time with further problems. On October 17, 95% of the shareholders voting again approved the revised terms, and the parties made preparations for the tender offer.

Meanwhile political interest grew as Siebert went down to Washington, and it became apparent that the Bank Holding Company Act, the Change of Control Act, and the International Banking Act had not resolved all concerns when Congress were confronted with a major acquisition or, indeed, with a series of such acquisitions, some of which seemed to violate the principle of 'national treatment'. During the period after June 1979 the national political dimension cannot be ignored. The issue had moved out of New York State in more ways than one.

John Heimann was faced with an apparently simple question: should Marine Midland Bank be permitted a National charter? Usually this question is resolved on the basis of an examination, and the MMBI board expected that MMB would be found qualified. That was never the issue. Nevertheless Heimann did not actually approve the conversion for seven months, that is, until January 28, 1980. Heimann recognized that, whatever the situation had been when Piderit spent a week in Hong Kong for the FRB, the question of the merger had become political. Heimann concluded that the issue of the conversion could not be separated from that of the merger, and consequently he had to determine the facts relative to the Hongkong Bank. The latter accepted this; in October Heimann sent a team to Hong Kong to spend a month with the Bank; their conclusions were favourable. But still Heimann delayed; his purpose, declared afterwards, was to make a 'non-event' of his conversion approval. In this he was successful; the issue had been defused over time.

The conversion of MMB to Marine Midland Bank, N(ational) A(ssociation), removed it from the relevant jurisdiction of the New York Superintendent of Banks. The Fed's approval for the merger had been extended once again and remained in place. HSBC and MMBI therefore moved ahead to implement the revised agreement. Despite the delays the HSBC obtained 51.1% of the shares of MMBI by the end of 1980, the year agreed in the original Definitive Agreement.

PRELIMINARIES

Renegotiating the Definitive Agreement

Underlying the negotiations for a revised Definitive Agreement was the decision that the merger remained a sound proposition. There had, however, been developments since April 1978, and Duffy had to take them into account; furthermore, any extension of the agreement left both banks in a tentative position, but MMB was involved in the more serious risk. It was obvious that either Siebert would decide by June, in which case renegotiation was irrelevant, or she would not, in which case MMBI had to agree to seek a National charter for MMB. The risk, slight as some might assess it, was that the Office of the Comptroller of the Currency (OCC) might refuse the conversion or that legislation might be enacted at the Federal level to prevent consummation of the deal. At that point MMB, its capital unchanged, would be under New York jurisdiction and with a possibly very annoyed Superintendent.

MMBI could only agree to accept such a risk if there were a *quid pro quo*, and indeed there were objective reasons why more favourable terms should be granted by HSBC. The renegotiated agreement had therefore to take cognizance of Marine's improved earnings: the return on average shareholders' equity rose from 4.4% for 1978 to 8.1% for 1979. This was in part a consequence of MMBI's increased assets, and the capital/assets ratio was further eroded in consequence: with 1977 year-end assets of US$12.1 billion, the ratio of shareholders' equity to total assets (based on average daily balance) was 3.89; at the end of 1979 total assets had risen to US$15.7 billion, and the ratio had fallen to 3.14.

This focused attention on the fact that, under the existing agreement, the US$100 million note, although the acknowledged 'cement' of the deal, was a note of indeterminate length and as yet did not rank as capital; it had not therefore improved the capital position of Marine Midland Bank.

The question of price presented little difficulty; Sandberg accepted the necessity as obvious. The final decision was to raise the price offered to shareholders for existing common stock from US$20 to US$25, and the price of new shares from US$30 to US$34 – book value had increased from US$34.44 at the end of 1977 to US$35.91 at the end of 1978; it was US$36.87 as at June 30, 1979 – it would be US$38.29 at the end of 1979. Anticipating both this improvement and the possibility of delayed negotiations, MMBI insisted that the final price include an allowance for MMB's retained earnings in addition to the US$34. The injection of capital had thereby increased from US$200 million to US$226.8 million; it would eventually total just over US$234.3 million. This, too, HSBC accepted.

With book value at US$36.87, at the end of the transaction, that is, after the purchase of 6,666,667 shares by the HSBC at US$34, book value would be US$35.87. The one dollar difference was the amount of 'watering' of equity (2.7%). This the shareholders apparently considered a reasonable price to pay.

Just as the board of Marine Midland were now pursuing a risky course, so too HSBC was asked to take a risk. For a brief period the very expectation of US$200 million in additional capital was sufficient inducement for MMBI to delay any search for an alternative source of capital, but this situation could not continue. HSBC was asked, therefore, to convert the US$100 million subordinated note into an unconditional fifteen-year note at the increased but still concessionary rate of 9%. Under the original agreement there were circumstances under which the note would be limited to five years (see discussion above); under the renegotiated agreement, the note was fifteen years from the start – no matter what happened, no matter who was responsible should the deal in the end fail. Of the total, 10% was retained in the holding company and 90% put down into Marine Midland Bank as capital.

This justified the board of MMBI postponing once again any search for an alternative source of capital funds. HSBC on the other hand had advanced funds which were tied up for fifteen years at a rate substantially below the market. If the deal went through, the note, as before, would be used to buy part of the first tranche of new shares.

The decision to go National

There can be little question but that the motivation behind the application of MMB to become a National bank was the failure of the New York State Superintendent of Banks to make a timely decision. On the other hand, the decision to go National at some time was neither so obvious nor so unidimensional.

During June the pace of the negotiations with the State Banking Department intensified. Siebert attempted, as regulators often do, to write in certain conditions before her final decision on the right to vote the shares. The conditions, were, as a matter of record, totally unrealistic: the Bank would not be permitted to vote all its shares immediately, but only after a period and a review of its management by a 'Blue Ribbon Committee', a scheme which was so totally impractical that it did not warrant consideration. Furthermore, the Superintendent wished to dictate the composition by category of the MMBI directors, thereby infringing on the rights of shareholders. And all the time the delays continued; the accusations that information was being withheld, what certain directors referred to as unbusinesslike behaviour, all this led MMBI officers and directors to recall that, although they had long associations with the State, they had on previous occasions at least discussed the implications of converting to a National charter.

Quite reasonably John Heimann's unofficial estimate was that if the merger factor ranked ten, the other factors in the ultimate MMBI decision ranked at most two or three. Nevertheless, there were other factors.

There is a history in the United States of major banks moving from State to National jurisdiction and, on occasion when the regulatory environment suggests the advisability, from National to State. Chase Manhattan had moved from New York State jurisdiction some fifteen years previously; Marine Midland of Buffalo had been predominantly a State bank, but even it had some National bank history; of the banks merging in 1975 to form MMB, three had been National.

The fact is, moreover, that the largest American banks were National banks. It is true that there had been advantages to the New York State system, if only because the rules were embodied in statutes rather than regulations promulgated by an official and were consequently less likely to be challenged in court. Another then possible advantage was that, as long as MMB were a State bank,

II. Final approval

MMBI could spin off MMB's up-State branches and create a second bank, withdraw that from membership in the Federal Reserve, and thus save several millions of U.S. dollars annually as a consequence of not being subjected to the FRB's then stringent reserve requirements. A National bank, which must belong to the Federal Reserve System (FRS), would not have this option.

The advantages of the State system had, however, been decreasing over the previous few years due to the multiplicity of examinations – State, the FDIC, and the Fed – required by overlapping regulations differently stated. As a National bank MMB would be examined by the Office of the Comptroller of the Currency acting for the other agencies. The reserve requirements of the FRS were subsequently modified to meet the objections MMBI and other member banks were discussing.

There remained therefore 'sentiment', the feeling perhaps that one should not on the one hand argue that the merger would benefit the State and then remove the operating bank from the State's jurisdiction. Since State banks were charged for their examinations, the withdrawal of MMB would mean a considerable loss of revenue to the New York State Banking Department and a consequent loss of jobs. But these concerns could not survive the treatment received from the Superintendent nor the impact of her attitude on the future of a major New York institution, Marine Midland Bank. Furthermore, the Governor let it be known that he would not be offended.

Duffy himself had started his banking career as a National bank examiner. The Comptroller of the Currency, John Heimann, had previously been Superintendent of Banks in New York. MMB was not then going into the unknown. Heimann himself argued that the OCC was the best qualified banking regulator in the world; others argued that the U.S. banking legislation must soon be altered to permit at least intraregional banking and that one needed to be in the National system as soon as possible.

The arguments for going National were manifold, but, given the particular circumstances, what would be MMB's reception in Washington?

Jim Wolfensohn and John Heimann were close friends. As the possibility of going Federal developed, both men agreed never to meet or talk in private, and for over nine months they kept their agreement. They did, however, meet with their aides on official business. Wolfensohn put it this way: he felt that, if Heimann had pre-determined he would not approve conversion, he would have said so at an early official meeting.

Did Heimann encourage or invite the approach by MMBI officers? Officially, he did not. On the other hand the move was so obvious a probability that officers of both the MMBI and the HSBC were queried from time to time on the possibility. At the same time the delayed merger was very much a public matter and colleagues meeting representatives of either party inevitably asked some variation of 'How's Muriel treating you?' Heimann did the same; at cocktail parties he is reported to have made informal comments of the 'come down to Washington and discuss it' variety. Heimann did not want to undermine his former New York State Banking Department, but he, like many others, considered the merger sound.

In June Duffy, Petty, and Laski called formally at the Office of the Comptroller of the Currency and informed the Comptroller that they were considering conversion. He provided them official advice and a set of application forms.

The withdrawal of HSBC's application

The events

When Duffy and his colleagues returned from Washington, they reported to their board of directors and obtained permission to apply to the Comptroller of the Currency for a National charter for the Marine Midland Bank. Down in New York City at the same time Frank Frame of the Hongkong Bank and Frank Laski of the Marine Midland were having what proved to be a last attempt to secure from the Superintendent a response to HSBC's application to vote 51.1% of the shares of Marine Midland Banks, Inc., having once acquired them.

Following the board meeting, Duffy called Siebert and asked for a meeting. On June 27 he and Sandberg had their last formal meeting with Muriel Siebert. Duffy informed the Superintendent that they had waited a long time and still didn't know when a decision would be forthcoming from the department. They were, he continued, concerned that the decision might be qualified, if it were not negative, and that the directors had taken the position that Marine Midland could wait no longer; Marine Midland was, therefore, going to apply for a National charter.

There was a long silence at the end of which Sandberg said, 'And that means, Madam Superintendent, we must withdraw our application'. He handed her a letter to this effect.

Reactions

Whether the staff blanched or not is contested. The decision had an adverse impact on the department. But Siebert was not put down. She almost immediately informed the Governor that she was nevertheless going to issue the opinion she had been drafting, although now it would be merely an expression of her views without legal significance. The Governor argued that this would be pointless, that her failure to make a decision had damaged the State's reputation. However Siebert was not trying merely to block the HSBC/

II. Final approval

MMBI merger, she had definite broad policy objectives; checkmated in New York State she would go to Congress. The Hongkong Bank had not heard the last of Muriel Siebert.

In a letter dated June 23, 1981, she responded to my suggestion that she had, in fact, been relieved when the decision, as it were, went away.

> There is no basis whatsoever for such a view. As I indicated in the interview, I believe that states should have control over their banking structure. The fact that a bank can convert to a National charter in order to circumvent state control is part of having to live within the constraints of a dual banking system.
>
> Moreover, although I have frequently stated publicly that a national policy must be developed to deal with foreign acquisition of large American banks, I also believe that state authorities should retain the power to approve or disapprove proposed acquisitions of large banks in their particular state.

This is a legitimate position, right or wrong, for a State officer to take. Such ultimate policy objectives are not however a legitimate input into a statute-defined consideration of a specific application under section 143-b (3) of the State Banking Act.

FIRST STEPS AFTER THE JUNE 1979 DECISIONS

The purpose of the MMB conversion was, in very great part, to effect the conclusion of the Definitive Agreement as renegotiated. Therefore not only did MMB have to apply for a National charter from the OCC, but MMBI concluded that it would obtain shareholder approval for the renegotiated terms, submitting proxy material once again to the SEC; the MMBI had also to determine whether the Federal Reserve Board's approval remained valid or whether re-application were necessary. These problems were primarily the responsibility of MMBI, but the Hongkong Bank was nevertheless involved throughout.

The Federal Reserve Board

The possible need for reconsideration by the Federal Reserve Board (FRB) under the Bank Holding Company Act arose primarily as the result of hearings before Representative Rosenthal's (D. New York) sub-committee on legislative oversight (see below). There were two concerns: (i) had the FRB undertaken a sufficiently thorough investigation before the original approval and (ii) had they correctly interpreted the law relating to non-financial activities of bank holding companies (and, if so, should the legislation be reviewed?).

The quick answer is that the FRB did consider the original investigation adequate and did consider that it had interpreted the law correctly. In the absence of what FRB Chairman Paul Volcker determined to be new evidence, he refused to reopen the case for precedential reasons.

The real concern for HSBC was whether the FRB's original approval would remain valid, and the first information was that resubmission would be necessary. As the original investigation, although in fact adequate, could not in the new political atmosphere be redone at the same level, there would have to be a more thorough investigation. This would presumably have been in addition to the investigation planned by the OCC. The HSBC's main concern now was time. Fortunately, the Board's final opinion was that the original approval could be extended to cover the time necessary to conclude the deal despite the changes made in the agreement.

At this point the parties could turn to the next regulatory agency.

The SEC

The Hongkong Bank's Peter Hammond had appeared before the SEC in 1978 and, in accordance with the strict instructions of Michael Sandberg as chief executive, informed the staff that the Hongkong Bank would not reveal its inner reserves to anyone. Since then the Bank had explained its true position, with figures, to both the Federal Reserve Board and to the New York State Banking Department; it was about to make the same disclosure to the Office of the Comptroller of the Currency. During Congressional questioning of the Federal Reserve, the Board's staff informed the sub-committee that they had had access to the Bank's true figures.

Not only did the SEC now demand to see the same material but at the first in a new round of meetings virtually accused Hammond of bad faith. On reflection Hammond believes that he might have been well advised to explain the problem to the SEC as soon as the Bank had given additional information to the FRB, but the obvious difference between the two agencies had confused the issue. The SEC is disclosure-oriented, its purpose being to ensure that the shareholder is fully informed. The FRB is regulatory and through the bank examination process can keep information confidential.

The SEC would not, however, be denied the information. So Hammond appeared before them again, going through the Hongkong Bank's accounting procedures with figures; those present made notes as to how GAAP would handle various items and eventually came up with what they considered true profits. At the end of the day these notes were handed in and burned.

The SEC had originally assumed that HSBC's accounts must be hiding poor performance from shareholders. Their new concern was that the accounts misled shareholders in the other direction; the Bank was considerably stronger than the figures indicated. The problem then was whether, if MMBI shareholders were aware of the true position, they would sell their shares; they would perhaps wish to remain shareholders of a bank holding company

(MMBI) whose majority shareholder (HSBC) was so strong; the future would seem assured.

On the other hand, to repeat a previous argument, if 25% of the common stock then outstanding were not sold, the Hongkong Bank would not be able to consummate the transaction, and its strong position would be irrelevant.

In the end HSBC agreed to qualify its accounts by adding a statement to the effect that, *inter alia*,

> In assessing the financial information...it should be noted that: (a) as a result of the accounting practices followed by HSBC there are substantial inner reserves which are not included in shareholders' equity and (b) the unrealized foreign exchange gains and losses...(which are not reflected in HSBC's published profit) can be large.[15]

MMBI submitted on this basis. An SEC officer then contacted Sandberg to inform him that the information was unacceptable because it did not make full disclosure. Sandberg suggested that he contact his superiors. Somewhat later an apology came back; the accounts were indeed acceptable.

Before the Comptroller of the Currency

When the MMB applied to the OCC for conversion to a National banking association, John Heimann stressed that he didn't know what the outcome would be. He would make a full-fledged examination; the decision would be predicated upon whether the OCC would accept Marine Midland Bank as a National bank and not whether OCC would accept Marine Midland as a National bank *if the merger with HSBC went through*. But, as Heimann admitted from the first, he could not ignore the Hongkong Bank problem. In a sense the OCC undertook a full-scale familiarization of the Hongkong Bank and then, having satisfied themselves and stated their conclusions in public, returned to their statutory responsibility of making a decision on the basis of their examination of Marine Midland Bank as it then existed, that is, without the HSBC.

The examination of MMB itself calls for no particular comment. Heimann, as New York Bank Superintendent, had known of Marine Midland's problems in 1975 and 1976, but in his new position he had lost detailed contact. The OCC discovered points for debate with MMB management on several matters, all of which were resolved.

Almost as a separate exercise, the OCC began a process of familiarizing itself with HSBC. A three-man team, headed by Robert R. Bench, Assistant Chief National Bank Examiner and deputy director of the OCC's Multi-national Division, spent a full month in Hong Kong. The members of the team had some awareness of the Hongkong Bank and, through their examinations of

American banks, they were also familiar with Hong Kong and the Far East banking situation[c]. They reported and Heimann confirmed that HSBC were totally cooperative and provided all information required. This together with the favourable figures revealed provided convincing evidence that, contrary to the claims of the New York State Banking Department, the HSBC had furnished that department all the information which had been mutually agreed upon. There was no reason why HSBC should have been held back.

In the meantime and despite the fact that the merger had not as yet been approved, I.H. Macdonald moved into New York as the Hongkong Bank Group's permanent representative for the Americas. This move permitted structural and organizational changes in the Hongkong Bank Group's Head Office. From New York Macdonald stressed to his colleagues in Hong Kong that the OCC familiarization was the last chance; that there had to be total cooperation. Whether the reminder were necessary or not, the Bank reacted properly. Indeed, so did the OCC team. Only at the end were they prevailed on to accept a luncheon invitation, despite the fact that in Hong Kong hospitality of this kind is so much a matter of routine courtesy that it is excluded from the purview of the territory's ICAC (Independent Commission against Corruption).

The purpose of the OCC team was not confined to discovery of the figures, their quality and their meaning. They came to learn how the Hongkong Bank managed itself and how its management style would impact on Marine Midland should the merger be completed. In this their findings were particularly perceptive.

Briefly, the team noted that the Hongkong Bank was going through the same transformation from a transnational to a multinational bank that had been characteristic of leading American international banks some five to ten years previously. The Hongkong Bank had had a management style based on longstanding tradition appropriate to an operation within a well-defined region. When the Bank had acquired the Mercantile Bank and the BBME its region had been only slightly enlarged; it still operated with a tradition-conditioned staff in a semi-protected area.

The question the OCC team asked itself was whether, with the coming of competition within the traditional region, with the need for specialists, and with the move into global operations, the organizational structure, the personnel policies, and the technological overheads had changed and developed

---

[c] In ordinary conversation one would say that the OCC sent a team to 'examine' the Hongkong Bank. Unfortunately, the term 'examine' has a legal and even political overtone, and its use in the present context would be resented. An OCC examination is legally defined; the OCC has no jurisdiction in Hong Kong and cannot conduct an 'examination' here. The OCC in fact conducted in Hong Kong what in the United States would be an examination, but it has to be called for example, 'familiarization'. They have returned for this purpose on several occasions.

sufficiently. The OCC team therefore talked to the Hongkong Bank's M.J. Pridham (see Chapter 14), examined existing and planned organizational changes, and investigated the Group's computer and communications planning. All this proved satisfactory.

Even more encouraging to the U.S. regulators was the team's conclusion that the HSBC offer to MMBI was not undertaken in a planning vacuum. The proposal was part of a global strategy and the Bank's internal changes were focused on the needs prerequisite to becoming a multinational. The findings were reported to John Heimann in Washington.

As a third aspect of Heimann's handling of the Marine Midland conversion application, and one even further from the narrow requirements prescribed by statute, he had commissioned a series of studies on the impact of foreign acquisitions on the American banking scene. Several are cited in Chapters 16 and 17. He was aware of a banking bill before Congress, the Senate version of which called for a three-month moratorium on foreign bank acquisitions; he had determined that this should not affect his present investigations, but he was aware that Congress were directly interested. He could not plead the statutes, he and his office had to respond to both the statute and the current political reality.

The MMB and the HSBC could rely on a fair hearing. They were both aware, however, that there was concern in Washington relative to bank acquisitions and that the struggle to obtain regulatory approval for the merger had not as yet been achieved.

ON CAPITOL HILL

Foreign acquisitions as a political issue

Recent history
In one respect the timing of the proposed HSBC/MMBI merger was unfortunate. As noted in Chapter 16, the period 1978/79 was one which witnessed several foreign acquisition attempts, at least two of which were initiated after the Hongkong Bank's approach to MMBI and successfully completed before the HSBC/MMBI transaction. Had the HSBC/MMBI been the only such acquisition the issue would probably not have become of national political interest, although Muriel Siebert's concerns, being individual, would not have been affected.

The factors involved were the general change in the world banking environment, the specific need of non-financial holding companies to divest their one-bank holdings by 1980, and specific tactical advantages including what was described as the 'cheap dollar'.[16]

In February 1979 Muriel Siebert brought her concerns relative to foreign acquisitions and the position of would-be American purchasers before, among others, Senator William D. Proxmire (D. Wisconsin), chairman of the Senate Committee on Banking, Housing and Urban Affairs, and Henry S. Reuss (D. Wisconsin), chairman of the House Banking Committee. Reuss played no significant role in the developments, but Proxmire was sufficiently interested to initiate a study of the problem through the GAO (General Accounting Office).[d] By May or June 1979, at the time the HSBC was committing itself to a tie-up of US$100 million for fifteen years, Senator John Heinz (R. Pennsylvania) began to have general concerns and Representative B. Rosenthal (D. New York), after discussions with Siebert, became concerned with the HSBC/MMBI merger with special reference to the non-financial activities of the intended bank holding company, the HSBC.

There developed two main interests which concerned the Congress: (i) given that U.S. dollars were 'cheap', that there were several foreign acquisitions of U.S. banks pending regulatory approval – and that, for general reasons, there might well be more – did the situation warrant further study despite recent legislation, and, if so, should there be a moratorium until the study and consideration thereof had been completed – and, if so, should the case of the HSBC/MMBI be grandfathered? – and (ii) given existing legislation, had the Federal Reserve Board investigated sufficiently and decided properly in the HSBC case in view of its size and the HSBC's non-financial activities?

The larger issues are not of particular concern to the history of The Hongkong and Shanghai Banking Corporation. Neither Heinz nor Proxmire was concerned to stop the HSBC/MMBI deal *per se* and in the end, as Congress considered the Heinz rather than the Proxmire bill, Heinz did give specific assurance that any moratorium would grandfather the HSBC/MMBI merger. As it happened the moratorium was not voted until after Heimann had approved the MMB charter conversion, although he was naturally watching developments on Capitol Hill very closely. A third bill, one introduced in the House of Representatives by Rosenthal came closer to affecting the Hongkong Bank, but that was not passed even by the House, and Rosenthal's role was to be almost entirely related to the second of the two concerns listed above.

The attitude of the regulators

The Federal authorities, especially the FRB, on their part had some difficulty in understanding what the Congressional concern really was. There were

[d] Reuss's middle initial stood for 'Schoellkopf', the name of a family long associated with the Buffalo Marine Midland Bank; J.F. Schoellkopf had been chief executive of the Marine Midland Corporation from 1968 to 1969 (see above). On a less speculative point, two New York members of his committee, John LaFalce (D. 36th District) and Stanley N. Lundine (D. 39th District), were very supportive of the merger; this may be the more relevant fact.

sensational presentations of generally accepted information relative to foreign acquisitions. Federal Reserve Board Governor Henry Wallich, who testified relative to this subject, was the grandson of Hermann Wallich, sometime manager of the Shanghai branch of the Comptoir d'Escompte de Paris (see Volume I) in the 1860s, and had a scholarly as well as a family background to banking. He found it difficult to understand the vaguely articulated fears that foreign banks would somehow take the farmer's savings, the local businessman's deposits and put them somewhere 'overseas'. Wallich accepted the contention that banks were important beyond the actual numbers on the balance sheet, but neither he nor his associates could understand why these critics did not carry the analysis further, recognizing that those who purchased banks were not usually interested in stripping them and that there were regulatory agencies designed to prevent this from happening.

Testifying before the Senate Banking Committee on July 16, 1979, in connection with S.J.RES.92 (see below), Wallich went further. Although accepting that Marine Midland's share of the up-State market was significant, he considered that 'there are a large number of competitive alternatives available to business and consumers in these markets should Marine Midland for any reason falter in its service to these areas.' And he added,

> The acquisition of Marine Midland by a foreign bank is therefore not a cause for concern from the point of view of the provision of banking and financial services in these markets. Moreover, the Hongkong and Shanghai Bank is a commercial concern motivated by profits which as a consequence must recognize that failure to serve credit and financial needs in these markets will lead to a loss of its deposit and customer base.[17]

In reply to a question from Senator Heinz as to what would happen when the People's Republic of China takes over Hong Kong, he wrote,

> The Hongkong and Shanghai Banking group is a multinational corporation with assets and operations throughout the world. It is not therefore at all sure what the consequences would be for that organization as an independent commercial entity if the Peoples Republic of China were to take over Hong Kong. In any event, the political status of a country does not necessarily have an impact on the lending and deposit policies of banks headquartered in that country or on those of their foreign affiliates. Any U.S.-chartered bank, whether or not it is owned by a foreign bank, is subject to the laws of the United States. Federal bank supervisors have authority to prevent unsafe and unsound banking practices by U.S. banks.[18]

John Heimann had the difficult task of bridging the comprehension gap between genuinely concerned senators and professional regulators. In this the HSBC/MMBI merger agreement played a role, but it was not the focus of attack.

The course of events

The Proxmire and Heinz bills

Although Senators Proxmire and Heinz both introduced banking bills in the Senate in 1979, the focuses of their concerns were not identical. Proxmire, in the Populist tradition, was concerned with the impact of foreign acquisitions on the balance of compromises which had led to the present decentralization of the U.S. banking system. The situation was illogical; foreign banks could do what domestic banks could not do despite recent legislation. But the consequent political pressures were not necessarily directed at foreign bank holding companies; a whole range of domestic issues, including the virtual prohibition against interstate commercial banking (as defined), was under attack. Heinz, on the other hand, was probably not wedded to the system but was concerned with the actual issue of foreign ownership; he simply wanted a pause so that the issues, including foreign reciprocity, could be studied in context.

After preliminary studies a bill (S.J. RES. 92) was introduced into the Senate on June 26, 1979, and hearings were arranged by Proxmire for July 16 and 17. Although the Marine Midland acquisition was an important topic, the bulk of the discussion was on subjects as varied as interest rate differentials and the potential impact of new regulations relative to Edge Act corporations. Muriel Siebert inserted her report on the Hongkong Bank application into the record, but her concerns were effectively answered by Wallich, whose testimony has been cited above.

As nothing significant developed, Heinz subsequently offered an amendment which, *inter alia*, confirmed the request for a moratorium on foreign bank acquisitions. At the same time Rosenthal introduced a bill, HR 5937, which was specifically directed to the failure of the FRB to examine the Hongkong Bank's non-financial activities. This failed to attract the Senate since it could be argued that Rosenthal's facts were not established, and some consideration was given to the political position the Governor of New York had taken supportive of MMBI's actions. The conversion application, although it was an attempt to change regulators in order to achieve a specific goal, that is, to 'skirt Siebert', was not a State/Federal confrontation. There was nothing politically attractive about taking it up on this basis.

Of the three bills, although all required a moratorium, only Heinz's amendment seemed to permit the HSBC/MMBI to escape the general moratorium provisions. It was nevertheless ambiguous; its effect depended on the interpretation of whether the date were mid-1978 when the original application was filed or July 1979 after MMB had applied for a National charter. Steuart Pittman, who was watching developments for the Hongkong

Bank, called on Senator Heinz and determined that Heinz himself had no objections to the HSBC/MMBI merger being grandfathered, and a letter was sent to Pittman to this effect.

Nevertheless legislation was pending. The question was whether Heimann would be subjected to sufficient pressure to make it wise for him to postpone his approval of the charter conversion until the issues, broad and vague as they had become, had been resolved. His careful handling of the specific case, his success in obtaining full and favourable information in Hong Kong, and his obvious willingness not to press forward until lack of political interest had become widely apparent, while it caused concern in the Hongkong Bank, proved sound policy.

Legislative oversight – the Rosenthal hearings

Two sets of hearings before the House sub-committee on Commerce, Consumer and Monetary Affairs were held under the chairmanship of Benjamin S. Rosenthal: July 31 and August 1, 1979, and May 15 and June 25, 1980. The former focused on 'the operations of Federal Agencies in monitoring, reporting on, and analyzing foreign investments in U.S. banks', the latter was more a survey of what had happened – 'Foreign acquisitions of U.S. banks and the non-banking activities of foreign bank holding companies'.

The hearings were not oriented towards legislation but dealt with oversight; if the need for legislation were shown, the matter would be brought before the appropriate House committee. In consequence, the hearings tend to be wider ranging, but, despite charges that Rosenthal was publicity minded, the sub-committee did focus on problems needing explanation, especially in the consumer field. For these reasons the tone was particularly disturbing to Hongkong Bank officers and advisers, the former placing more weight on the hearings than perhaps they warranted.

During the first hearings, Muriel Siebert again had her report on the Hongkong Bank read into the proceedings, and the testimony of Heimann and Wallich once again offset her concerns. Heimann did, however, stress his intention of seeking full information from the Hongkong Bank before passing on the application of MMB for conversion.

Rosenthal enjoyed making debating points. In discussing the Hong Kong Government supervision of the Hongkong Bank, he manoeuvred Wallich into stating that the supervisors were appointed by the Crown, that they were in the traditions of the British Civil Service and therefore satisfactory.

ROSENTHAL: The British civil servant is traditionally beyond reproach having been appointed by the Crown; right?
WALLICH: At least one can find out something about him.

ROSENTHAL: That was not true when his picture was created 200 years ago; right? I am talking about Alexander Hamilton.
[Laughter]
When did this tradition change? [Laughter][19]

The issue here was the ability of regulators to prevent the type of predatory destruction wrought by Sindona on the Franklin National Bank.

ROSENTHAL: Mr Heimann will tell you what kind of review they made of the documents Mr Sindona produced before he ravaged and savaged the Franklin National Bank. They reviewed all those documents; right? He looked good up front, right?[20]

But, as Heimann pointed out, Sindona was an individual; the Hongkong Bank was an institution. The real protection was not, therefore, the research of the regulatory staffs but the reputation of the acquiring institution. Eventually Wallich made the point.

WALLICH: I think we can say we are dealing with a reputable bank. It has a high reputation among other banks. By what else other than its reputation among its peers can you judge it?[21]

The intention of Rosenthal's questions was to put the efficacy of the FRB's analysis so in question that the Fed could be induced to reopen the hearings or withdraw its approval. In this Rosenthal failed signally, but he was able, once again, to show that FRB interpretation of the 1970 Bank Holding Company Act favoured foreign bank holding companies by permitting them to engage in non-financial activities.

The most thorough investigation of the Hongkong Bank came after the conversion in May and June 1980. Here the purpose was not to stop a merger already in process of being implemented; nevertheless the attitude towards the Hongkong Bank appeared initially unfriendly. Once again one of the major witnesses was Muriel Siebert and again her complaint touched on 'disclosure', this time related to the Hongkong Bank's non-financial activities.

The Bank was by this time aware of its need to respond freely, and I.H. Macdonald, as the resident Executive Director of HSBC and director of MMBI, presented a wide range of material (see, for example, Table 15.12 in Chapter 15). His own analysis confirmed that HSBC was primarily a financial group with non-financial activities accounting for 1.35% of total assets and 10.18% of Group profit, despite the impressive list of associated companies presented by Siebert: 6 banks, 4 merchant banks, 16 film companies, 19 insurance companies, 76 ship companies, 1 major regional airline, and a major Hong Kong daily newspaper. As previously quoted, Macdonald concluded, 'We know of no method which would increase the non-financial assets above 5% or the non-financial net income above 15% of the comparable consolidated figures of HSBC.'[22] Siebert's presentation lacked the necessary analysis, but this would have undermined her position.

Laughter on Capitol Hill

At some point in the proceedings Rosenthal decided that Macdonald, with his twinkling eyes and heavy Scottish accent, was playing fair – an English accent would have taken the Congressmen back to 1775 again – and a certain amount of banter crept into the proceedings. Macdonald stressed that the Hongkong Bank had not just appeared; it had been in the United States since 1875, that is for over 100 years. The counter was that this might be true and the reputation of the Hongkong Bank might have been world-wide, but 'most of us had not even heard of you' nor had the Hongkong Bank ever been examined by U.S. regulatory authorities. Now the United States is so important to the Bank that an executive director had been assigned to reside in New York.

ROSENTHAL: Do you like New York?
MACDONALD: Very much, Sir. I have been rejuvenated since I came here. [Laughter]... I was a volunteer. I was involved at a very early stage in the development of the strategy that we followed in America, and I am very happy to be here.
ROSENTHAL: We are delighted to have you here....
MACDONALD: As of December 31, 1979, the total assets of HSBC were $19 billion, in round figures.
ROSENTHAL: ...You are bigger than the Hunts.[e]
MACDONALD: I do not own it all, Sir. [Laughter]...
This is very big bank, Sir, and I cannot pretend to know everything.
ROSENTHAL: The Hunts did not know how much they were worth either. [Laughter]...
Are you buying any real estate in New York?
MACDONALD: I have not bought any real estate, except the apartment I am now living in, Sir. It was rather expensive.
ROSENTHAL: But it is not expensive compared to Hong Kong.[23]

Reverting to whether the late Mr Piderit had stayed at the Mandarin or Peninsula, Rosenthal could not refrain from asking Macdonald if the Hongkong Bank owned the Peninsula. Macdonald knew the answer to that one: No.

In between these several exchanges, Macdonald gave additional information. The committee had begun to follow the details.

ROSENTHAL: You seem to have come out of it fairly well, though.
MACDONALD: Thank you.
ROSENTHAL: You have lost none of your charm; you are represented by distinguished counsel; you have bought an apartment in New York that has doubled in value since you bought it.
[Laughter]...

[e] The Hunt family (of Dallas, Texas) had been in the news because of their unsuccessful attempt to allegedly corner the silver market and their reputed wealth would have been well-known to those at the Hearings.

MACDONALD: May I proceed, Sir?
ROSENTHAL: Yes, I am dying to find out what the assets are of the nonbanking enterprises; this is like a suspense story – an Agatha Christie banking mystery. [Laughter].[24]

Back to the late Mr Piderit and the location of his hotel: Rosenthal compared the situation to someone coming to New York and staying at a Staten Island hotel; it would cut back on his work time. Macdonald quickly detected the flaw in this argument:

MACDONALD: In Hong Kong we all work very hard because the motto there is, 'If you don't work, you don't eat.' And everybody works six days a week there; the work ethic is very strong.

– which laid Macdonald [see colour plate 5] open to –

ROSENTHAL: And everyone is eating pretty well. [Laughter][25]

It would be unfair to suggest that this was the product of the session; it rather reflects an unbending, if you will, or an acceptance of HSBC's representative. The sub-committee continued to probe the extent of the corporation's non-financial activities, and the information submitted was of considerable worth.

This latter discussion has, however, been taken out of time sequence. The narrative should return to the point at which it can be determined that Congress is not about to strike out at the merger agreement, that the moratorium would not affect HSBC's application, and the OCC's team has returned with information from Hong Kong. The expectation in November was, therefore, for an early decision. There were nearly three more months to go.

THE CHARTER GRANTED

By the end of November the question of whether to permit the conversion of MMB was a matter entirely in the hands of the Comptroller of the Currency. In his determination to make it a 'non-event' Heimann had decided to hold public hearings, an unusual step in a case of this kind. He continued to liaise with key Congressional figures and he brought the HSBC Chairman, Michael Sandberg, over on a special trip to Washington for a briefing which has been variously described – 'charade' is a favourite term. Then there was the period during which his own department's budget was under review. During all these 'delays', as they were perceived by the parties involved, Heimann continued to reassure HSBC/MMBI and their advisers, but naturally uncertainties remained.

The saga ended on January 28. The conversion was approved.

II. Final approval

The Hearings

The Hongkong Bank's annual report for the key year of 1979 contained my well-illustrated account of the Bank's archives. Jim Wolfensohn's comment to me (why me?) was, 'I commend you on the literary skill, but in terms of economic reportage the [Annual Report is] not especially illuminating.' He went further. Despite the disclosures which the Hongkong Bank had made during the protracted negotiations, he noted, there was still room for those opposed to the merger to inject doubts, to keep asking, 'Yes, but what are they really doing?', to talk of breweries in Canada and carpet manufactories in Hong Kong – companies held, it is true, under special circumstances and usually through a chain of partly owned associates, but nevertheless visible on the list submitted to the regulatory authorities.

This lack of knowledge of the Hongkong Bank was not entirely due to the hesitation of the Bank. When the transaction was first announced, the Bank still had no press relations officer; it had no one specialized in providing information to the press, and the task was in any case a difficult one. There is a limit to the space even the most specialized journals can devote to explaining the history of an institution which requires four volumes merely to provide an outline. The Rosenthal hearings raised more questions than they answered; Heimann correctly assessed the situation; the public were still not satisfied that all questions had been answered. There was need, exceptionally, for public hearings.

The Hearings, which were scheduled and well advertised for Buffalo and New York City, brought out nothing new, but they added credibility to a credible system. And even the airing of well-known objections was an important element in the entire process.

The Community Reinvestment Act

One important purpose of the (Federal) Community Reinvestment Act of 1977 (CRA) is to prevent the 'red-lining' of certain districts within a bank's normal service area.[26] That is to say the CRA is designed to discourage discriminatory lending policies, including those which rule out lending for a project or to an individual mainly on the grounds that it or he is located in a district which is depressed or which for any other general reason seems to be undesirable. The act is part of a program to protect the inner city and other areas against discrimination. As such it is not a mandatory loan rationing enactment; it encourages the banks' boards to have a policy which will focus on ways to lend despite undesirable location.

At one level the concern expressed at the public hearings on this issue was an extension of the more general 'moving our savings overseas' theme, but it had two more reasonable aspects. First, the very move from a New York State to a National charter seemed to take the responsibility for implementation farther away from the State and its local interests. It was easier to lobby in New York with a locally responsive banking department than in Washington. Secondly, there was the feeling expressed by community affairs lobbyists that, even short of a dramatic stripping of assets by the foreign acquirer, foreign management must by its very nature show less interest in the concerns of a small up-State community or a depressed area in a larger New York town.

The CRA itself cannot contain a fully effective enforcement procedure. Only when the regulatory agencies act as gatekeepers can the policy of the bank be examined and the approval of whatever request has been made be granted subject to compliance with the act. Thus in the process of the conversion application examination Marine Midland was examined relative to CRA compliance with satisfactory results.

The only response that MMBI and HSBC could provide was to repeat (i) that the HSBC would leave the day-to-day running of the Marine Midland Bank, NA, in the hands of its own management and (ii) that the merger would not affect MMB's domestic lending policies. On this last, MMB was, after all, a money centre bank as well as an up-State bank; it had considerable overseas interests. The alternative use of funds overseas had not become possible only through the merger; MMB's position up-State was a consequence of its up-State lending policy and its compliance with the spirit of CRA. There was no reason to suppose that the Hongkong Bank, having made an investment of some US$300 million would disturb the basis of its subsidiary's success.

Book vs market value of shares

Although this had been a feature from the first public description of the deal, the question of the two prices was not fully understood and was protested at the public hearings by two shareholders from Indiana. Marine Midland Bank officers had already received informal queries from shareholders as to how they could qualify for the US$30 as opposed to the US$20 price, and Siebert took credit for having got an extra US$5.00 for the shareholder as a consequence of the tender price being raised during the renegotiation of June 1979.

Siebert's claim cannot be sustained. Duffy with the support of his board and based on MMBI's performance since the signing of the Definitive Agreement justified an improved price. The Superintendent of Banks was not involved.

Nevertheless the public had not fully accepted the proposition that, although the Hongkong Bank were willing to pay MMBI US$34+ for new shares, it was only willing to pay US$25 for the existing shares. The simple answer is that the two prices made it possible for the Bank to pay an agreed price for 51.1% of the common stock without significant watering of the stock held by the public.

By tendering at a lower price for 25% of the common stock, the Bank could afford to pay a price closer to book value for new stock. The shareholders who accepted the tender received more for their shares than the market valuation.

Immediately after the tender had been successful, the price of Marine Midland shares fell back again. The US$25 price then seemed like a bonus for those shrewd shareholders who had accepted the revised tender offer. The fact is that the turnaround of MMB, real as it undoubtedly was, had not been acknowledged; the impact of the Hongkong Bank's injection of capital funds had not been properly assessed. The continued questioning of the HSBC's intent, the continued criticisms of Muriel Siebert, and the Congressional hearings may have had their effect. The market had not been convinced, and those who sold out were deemed to have done well. With today's prices (November 1986) over US$44.00, these sceptics were proved mistaken. (And when the Bank offered to purchase the balance of the outstanding shares in 1987, the price rose to US$82.00.)

The only other witnesses at the Hearings were (i) representatives of the U.S. Labor Party, with their anti-Chinese, anti-Zionist tale of an international drug conspiracy financed by the Hongkong Bank and (ii) Muriel Siebert with her long-standing concerns. Heimann had managed another non-event. Surely now he was ready to approve the conversion.

The 'charade'

Sandberg had been pressing Heimann for action. At the October IMF meeting in Belgrade they had met quietly and Sandberg had asked, 'When?' Heimann explained that he had to take a step at a time and outlined a tentative schedule which he proved unable to keep.

Later in November 1979 Macdonald received a call from the OCC to the effect that the Comptroller of the Currency wanted to interview the Chairman of the Hongkong Bank personally. Both men were busy and the interview was set in the first week of December, apparently on the basis of mutual inconvenience. The expectation of the HSBC party was that this interview must be the prelude to an announcement on the conversion issue; perhaps the decision would be made at or immediately after the meeting, certainly by the end of the year.

Sandberg duly went. The interview lasted some two and a half hours. Heimann was delayed by telephone calls; he arrived late and had to leave early; Sandberg was taking the 1.00 p.m. Concorde and would reach Hong Kong after a 72-hour absence and in time to host his staff party. Heimann was supported by several top members of his staff; Sandberg had his team with him. As

Sandberg put it, 'I got there, and I still to this day haven't the faintest idea for why.'

The substance of the meeting appears to have been a sort of playlet in which Heimann at one time played Senator Proxmire and asked questions which his staff answered. Then Heimann warned Sandberg of what to expect from regulatory agencies and reminded him that in America the Congress could not be denied and that any confidentiality was subject to this proviso. The Congress would be reasonable; they accepted the principle of banking confidentiality; the OCC would resist disclosure; but after all this was said, the people's representatives were sovereign. 'It wound up', Sandberg recalls, 'with my signing the inevitable letter. Every time we did anything we always signed a letter of undertaking or something or other, that we would gather nuts in May or something like that, but nothing, nothing ever of any import.'

A few days later the OCC contacted Macdonald to advise him that, due to the complexity of the matter, a response to MMB's application could not be given before the end of the year. Word that the HSBC were increasingly concerned filtered through and Heimann telephoned Sandberg to reassure him that within three months – or possibly by the end of January, he would give a decision. Heimann at no time indicated what the decision would be. Sandberg's concern was two-fold: (i) every quarter the decision was delayed the cost of MMBI was increasing consistent with the terms of the renegotiated agreement and (ii) despite the fact that the threat of delay through moratorium appeared ended, some other legal impediment might be found to prevent consummation of the merger within a reasonable period.

John Heimann had had something more substantial in mind when he requested Sandberg to come over from Hong Kong for a meeting. They had never had a face-to-face meeting. They had met, it is true, from time to time informally at IMF or other meetings. But what if a Congressional committee asked Heimann, 'So much for the findings of your staff, so much for the statements of HSBC's lawyers and investment banking advisers, but what did their Chairman say? Have you had him in to discuss these points face-to-face?' Heimann wanted to be able to answer in the affirmative.

More than this: Heimann was concerned as to whether Sandberg had been properly and fully advised on the implications of coming to America. As the HSBC had been cooperative in the end, there was some indication that the Bank would have been cooperative from the beginning had they been properly instructed on the extent of disclosure necessary. Although Heimann may have been unaware of the facts, it is true that the Bank was not correctly appraised of the SEC's requirements; the Bank had not been informed it would be required to reveal the details of its inner reserve operations. In the end it did so, but had the lesson been taken? There was one last chance to determine

II. Final approval

whether there were any misunderstandings, any impediments. A personal confrontation with the Comptroller in Washington, D.C. was an essential last step.

Unfortunately, it was not the last step. The OCC's deliberations continued until the end of January.

From delay to approval

Sandberg was again in Washington on Robert Burns' birthday (January 25), 1980, and Macdonald was hoping the approval might come in time for a dual celebration. Heimann stressed that the timing was *his* timing not *their* timing and word did not come through to Macdonald until 4.00 p.m. on the 28th. The real factors involved in the delay are a matter of debate. One MMBI adviser was certain that at one point Heimann wavered, waiting for a clear signal from the Carter White House. The majority view however would appear to focus on Heimann's need to take political soundings, to wait until his department's budget allocation had been made, and not to endanger the overall banking policies, domestic and foreign, which the OCC were advocating along with the Federal Reserve Board.

Heimann's approval came while the whole issue of foreign banking and foreign acquisitions together with the implications relative to domestic banking legislation were under active consideration. In the first quarter of 1980 there were four foreign bank acquisitions involving U.S. domestic assets of US$16,483.9 million (of which Marine Midland Bank, N.A., constituted US$15,690 million); there were ten applications pending involving total assets of US$845.3 million.[27]

Heimann had promised Congress that foreign acquisitions would be a matter of study, and in 1980 the Office of the Comptroller published some fourteen research studies on various topics under the general heading, 'OCC Staff Papers pertaining to Foreign Acquisition and Control of U.S. Banks'; the most important of these from the point of view of this history are listed in the notes.[28] The issues had not been dreamed up by the New York State Superintendent of Banks; she had focused on unresolved policy issues in which the Hongkong Bank became entrapped. Through the OCC's conversion decision, the Bank had now broken loose and could at last implement the Definitive Agreement of May 1978 as renegotiated in June 1979.

By concentrated working the advisers had prepared the preliminary documents and then the tender offer by the Hongkong Bank's Netherlands-registered, 100%-owned subsidiary holding company, HSBC Holdings, had been sent out on February 1, with closing on March 3 (see Appendix Timetable). The price offered was US$25 for shares trading on January 31, 1980, between US21\frac{3}{8}$ and US20\frac{3}{4}$. The tender offer material was also sent to the

SEC, one of whose offices telephoned to ask why the HSBC's true financial position had not been included. There was a second telephone call to say never mind.

On March 4 the first closing occurred; the tender offer had been over-subscribed. HSBC Holdings had acquired 3,123,795 shares by tender for a consideration of US$78.1 million; it acquired a further 3,333,333 new shares at US$35.42 a share by the delivery of the subordinated note (with accrued interest) and an additional payment of approximately US$16.9 million. With the control of 41% of the stock thus secured, Michael Sandberg, J.L. Boyer, and I.H. Macdonald became, on March 5, directors of the MMBI and attended their first board meeting. E.W. Duffy, J.R. Petty, and R.W. Hubner became Hongkong Bank directors and attended the Bank's Board and annual meetings in Hong Kong. On October 1, 1980, the second closing occurred, involving the purchase of an additional 3,333,334 new shares for US$118.1 million, after which HSBC Holdings held 51.1% of the common stock of Marine Midland Banks, Inc., for a total consideration of approximately US$314 million. The source of funds for these transactions was intra-Group transfers, including a fifteen-year, 5% loan of US$80 million equivalent from Wayhong, NH, to HSBC Holdings, BV, and the purchase of US$120 million equivalent new shares in HSBC Holdings by Kellett, NV. All transactions were guaranteed by The Hongkong and Shanghai Banking Corporation.[29]

The Hongkong Bank's legal and investment banking fees in the United States relating to the transaction were reported to Congress as totalling US$4 million.[30]

The Hongkong Bank's acquisition of Marine Midland was the largest foreign bank acquisition in the history of the United States, but, as some political observers had feared, this record would not stand for long. In 1981 Midland Bank, the third largest London-based clearing bank, with total deposits of US$55 billion equivalent, in what some financial commentators have termed the worst banking decision in British history, acquired Crocker National Corporation, the holding company for Crocker National Bank, then the eleventh largest bank in the United States and whose end-1981 assets were US$23 billion compared to MMBI's US$18.7 billion. There were no controversial elements in the transaction, and the US$495 million of new capital for 57% of the stock was particularly welcome. Unlike the Hongkong Bank's experience, however, this partnership did not work out; Midland had to acquire 100% of the capital in 1985 and, having turned Crocker around with a new management team, sold out (non-performing loans excluded) to Wells Fargo Bank in 1986.

If the size of the HSBC/MMBI transaction did not long remain the largest in U.S. banking history, the extraordinary competence with which the

II. Final approval

Hongkong Bank and its advisers, under the direction of Michael Sandberg, considered their policy, evaluated potential targets, and selected their partner remained unchallenged.

By 1980, however, it was already clear that the acquisition of MMBI was not simply a surprising conclusion to the Hongkong Bank's search for an American strategy, a substitute, as it were, for the Hongkong Bank of California. The Hongkong Bank was now thinking globally; it had become a multinational corporation; there were boom times in Hong Kong; and for a period the HSBC was – among those whose shares were publicly traded – the largest in the world on the basis of market capitalization.[f] At the end of 1980 the Bank ranked 33rd on the basis of total assets. The process of acquiring MMBI had, however, been both expensive and exhausting. Management decided that time was required to take stock of the new situation, to develop the potential of the Group at a different level, and to consolidate.

Such a policy had been pursued before – from 1960 to 1977, from the acquisition of the BBME to the approach to MMBI. A seventeen-year period was a luxury no one was expecting, but even then events moved faster than anticipated, and the Hongkong Bank found itself once again, but under totally different circumstances, seeking to acquire a major overseas bank.

The impact of MMBI and the subsequent developments are the subject of a summary discussion in a final chapter.

---

[f] For December 31, 1980, HSBC's market capitalization was US$4.8 billion compared to BankAmerica Corp.'s US$4.4 billion and Standard Chartered's US$1.4 billion equivalent.

APPENDIX TO CHAPTER 17: THE TIMETABLE

THE HONGKONG AND SHANGHAI BANKING CORPORATION

Investment

in

MARINE MIDLAND BANKS, INC.

The companies and/or agencies actually responsible for taking a particular action are listed, using the abbreviations below, following the description of the action itself.

As used in this timetable:

BA&H	Booz, Allen & Hamilton Inc.
BED CO.	Blyth Eastman Dillon & Co., Incorporated.
Comptroller	The Comptroller of the Currency of the United States.
CSBD	The California State Banking Department.
CBO	Central Bank, N.A. of Oakland.
CGS&H	Messrs. Cleary, Gottlieb, Steen & Hamilton.
FDIC	The Federal Deposit Insurance Corporation.
FRB	The Board of Governors of the Federal Reserve System.
HBC	The Hongkong Bank of California.
HSBC	The Hongkong and Shanghai Banking Corporation.
LBKL	Lehman Brothers Kuhn Loeb Inc.
MM or MMB	Marine Midland Bank.
MMBI	Marine Midland Banks, Inc.
NYBD	The New York State Banking Department.
NY Fed	The Federal Reserve Bank of New York.
NYSE	The New York Stock Exchange.
OHR&S	Messrs. Orrick, Herrington, Rowley & Sutcliffe.
PLHB&H	Messrs. Phillips, Lytle, Hitchcock, Blaine & Huber.
SASM&F	Messrs. Skadden, Arps, Slate, Meagher & Flom.
SB	Salomon Brothers.
SEC	The Securities and Exchange Commission.
SPP&T	Messrs. Shaw, Pittman, Potts & Trowbridge.
Superintendent	The Superintendent of Banks of the State of New York.
Transaction	The proposed share purchase/tender offer by The Hongkong and Shanghai Banking Corporation.
WLR&K	Messrs. Wachtell, Lipton, Rosen & Katz.
W&VH	Messrs. Worst & von Haersolte.

II. Final approval

Date (1978)	Event
Fri., March 17– Sun., March 19	Initial meetings between representatives of HSBC and MMBI *re* Transaction. Discussions included: a. Objectives of Transaction including post-Transaction relationships. b. Development of mutually acceptable basic parameters for Transaction. c. Arrangements for representatives of HSBC to review and discuss with representatives of MMBI the condition, financial and other, of both MMBI and MM. d. Co-ordination and timing of necessary shareholder and regulatory approvals. e. Need for, and content of, a preliminary public announcement. f. Establishment of mechanisms to preserve confidentiality of details of discussions prior to approval of definitive proposal by respective Boards and to permit a rapid, coordinated response by HSBC and MMBI to an unexpected development which might warrant a premature public announcement as to the details of the proposed transaction. HSBC, MMBI, SB, LBKL, CGS&H, SASM&F.
Mon., March 20	Bank regulatory authorities advised in advance of contents of press release. MMBI. Press releases in New York, London and Hong Kong announcing exploratory talks taking place. HSBC, MMBI.
Week of March 20	Representatives of HSBC (both employees and professional advisers) with the assistance and cooperation of representatives of MMBI and MM, review condition, financial and other, of MMBI and MM, including review of investment and loan portfolio concentrations. HSBC, MMBI, MM. Determination by HSBC of appropriate structure for financing and holding securities of MMBI acquired in Transaction in light of applicable tax and other considerations and nature and method of disposition of HBC. HSBC, SB, CGS&H, SPP&T. SB and LBKL meet to explore alternative Transaction formulations. SB, LBKL.
Week of March 27	Continuation of review and investigation by representatives of HSBC. HSBC, MMBI. Representatives of HSBC and MMBI negotiate terms of a definitive proposal for Transaction. SB, LBKL.
By Fri., March 31	Draft Preliminary Agreement prepared. CGS&H, SASM&F. HSBC Board meets to authorize Transaction.
Sat., April 1– Mon., April 3	Meetings to discuss and revise successive drafts of Preliminary Agreement. HSBC, MMBI, SB, LBKL, BED CO., CGS&H, SASM&F.
Mon., April 3	Materials prepared for submission to Board of MMBI. MMBI, SASM&F.

	Presentation regarding HSBC made to meeting of MMBI Board, with Chairman of HSBC (and other executives of HSBC) attending and meeting Board members. HSBC, MMBI.
	Representatives of HSBC and MMBI meet informally with FRB, NY Fed, NYBD and other interested parties to advise on a confidential basis of terms of proposed Transaction as set out in Preliminary Agreement. HSBC, MMBI.
Tues., April 4	Board of MMBI meets to review and approve terms of proposed Transaction as set out in Preliminary Agreement. MMBI.
	Immediately after approval by MMBI Board MMBI and HSBC execute Preliminary Agreement.
	MMBI issues press release in New York announcing terms of Transaction (including proposed price) subject to, *inter alia*, shareholder and regulatory approval. HSBC arranges for similar press release in both London and Hong Kong at opening of business on April 5.
Wed., April 5	Joint press conference to announce Transaction. HSBC, MMBI.
Thurs., April 6	Meetings to discuss regulatory approvals and assignments. Preliminary meetings with the staff of the NY Fed and NYBD. MMBI, HSBC, PLHB&H, CGS&H, SPP&T.
Fri., April 7	Preliminary meeting with staff of Fed in Washington. SPP&T.
	Preparation of drafts of Investment Agreement and Note Purchase Agreement. CGS&H, SASM&F.
Tues., April 11	Exchange of drafts of Investment Agreement between counsel for HSBC and MMBI. CGS&H, SASM&F.
Wed., April 12	Meetings to discuss first draft of Investment Agreement. CGS&H, SASM&F.
Thurs., April 13	Prefiling conference with staff of NY Fed to discuss BHCA Application. MMBI, PLHB&H, CGS&H, SPP&T.
Fri., April 14	Draft of Note Purchase Agreement circulated. CGS&H. Annual General Meeting of HSBC. HSBC.
Sat., April 15	First draft of Investment Agreement circulated to all concerned. CGS&H.
Week of April 17	Meetings as necessary to discuss and revise Investment Agreement and Note Purchase Agreement. CGS&H, SASM&F.
	Commence preparation of FRB Application for Fed approval on FRB Y-1. SPP&T, PLHB&H.
	Commence preparation of Schedule 13D to be filed by HSBC with SEC within 10 days of execution of Investment Agreement. CGS&H.
Wed., April 19	Annual Meeting of MMBI. MMBI.
Sat., April 22	Revised draft of Investment Agreement and first draft of Note Purchase Agreement circulated to all concerned. CGS&H.
Weeks of April 24,	Meetings to discuss and revise successive drafts of the

II. Final approval

May 1 and May 8 and beginning of week of May 15	Investment Agreement and Note Purchase Agreement. SB, LBKL, CGS&H, SASM&F.
Thurs., May 4	Outline of information in HSBC FRB Application circulated. HSBC, SPP&T.
Tues., May 9	Approval of form of Investment Agreement and Note Purchase Agreement by Board of HSBC. HSBC.
Fri., May 12	Circulation of questionnaire to HSBC officers and directors. CGS&H, HSBC.
Wed., May 17	Approval of form of Investment Agreement and Note Purchase Agreement by Board of MMBI. MMBI.
Thurs., May 18	Execution of Investment Agreement and Note Purchase Agreement in Buffalo, New York. Closing of purchase of US$100 million note of MMBI in Buffalo, New York and New York City. HSBC, MMBI, SB, CGS&H, SASM&F, Kellett.
Mon., May 22	Commence preparation of preliminary proxy materials for Special Meeting of MMBI shareholders. MMBI, SASM&F, HSBC, CGS&H.
	Identification of and discussion with prospective purchasers and preliminary discussions with CSBD and the San Francisco Fed concerning disposition of HBC. HBC, HSBC, SB, OHR&S, BA&H.
Tues., May 30	Schedule 13D filed with SEC by HSBC. HSBC, CGS&H.
Fri., June 2	First draft of preliminary proxy materials circulated by MMBI. SASM&F.
	First draft of purchase agreement for HBC completed by OHR&S. HBC, SB, OHR&S, BA&H.
Wed., June 7	Circulation of first draft of HSBC FRB Application for comments. SPP&T.
Thurs., June 8	Meeting with NY Fed to discuss HSBC FRB Application. SPP&T, HSBC.
	Meeting with NYBD. SPP&T, HSBC.
Fri., June 9	Exchange of first drafts of preliminary proxy materials by MMBI and HSBC. SASM&F, MMBI, CGS&H, HSBC.
Week of June 12 through week of July 3	Circulation of drafts and proofs of preliminary proxy materials and meetings to discuss same. SASM&F, MMBI, CGS&H, HSBC.
Mon., June 12	Meeting with Peat, Marwick, Mitchell & Co. to discuss HSBC financial presentation in preliminary proxy materials. CGS&H.
Tues., June 13	Completion and mailing of bidding information package for HBC. HBC, SB, HSBC, OHR&S, BA&H.
Fri., June 16	Circulation of draft of preliminary proxy materials to Board of MMBI and certain other parties to Transaction. SASM&F, MMBI.
	Submission of draft HSBC Application to NY Fed. SPP&T.
Wed., June 21	Preliminary proxy materials distributed to Board of MMBI. MMBI, SASM&F.
Fri., June 23	Submission of HSBC Application to Australian Foreign

	Investment Review Board. HSBC.
	Submission of HSBC Application to Monopolies and Mergers Commission of the United Kingdom. HSBC.
Week of Mon., June 26	NY Fed visit to HSBC in Hong Kong. HSBC.
Mon., June 26	Confer with NY Fed *re* draft HSBC FRB Application. SPP&T, PLHB&H, CGS&H.
Months of July and August	Confer with NY Fed and Justice Department *re* draft HSBC FRB Application. SPP&T, PLHB&H.
Thurs., July 6	Purchase Agreement and information package for HBC mailed. HBC, SB, HSBC, OHR&S, BA&H.
Fri., July 7	Preliminary proxy materials filed with the SEC. MMBI, SASM&F.
Week of Mon., July 10	Submission of HSBC Application to Canadian Foreign Investment Review Board. HSBC.
Mon., July 10	Submission of draft HSBC FRB Application to NY Fed. SPP&T, HSBC.
Thurs., July 13	Submission of draft HSBC FRB Application to NYBD. SPPT&T, HSBC.
Mon., July 24	Bidding date for HBC. HBC, SB, HSBC, OHR&C, BA&H.
Tues., July 25	SEC comments by letter on preliminary proxy materials.
Fri., July 28	Meeting with SEC on comments on preliminary proxy materials. SASM&F, CGS&H, MMBI.
Week of Mon., July 31	Negotiation with CBO of price, unitary tax and other matters with respect to HBC. HBC, SB, HSBC, OHR&C, BA&H.
Mon., July 31	Meeting with SEC on comments on preliminary proxy materials. SASM&F, CGS&H, MMBI.
By Tues., August 1	Approval of Transaction by Australian Foreign Investment Review Board.
Fri., August 4	Meeting with SEC on comments on preliminary proxy materials. SASM&F, CGS&H, MMBI.
Week of August 7 through week of August 28	Telephone conferences and letters to SEC on comments on preliminary proxy materials. SASM&F, CGS&H, MMBI, HSBC.
Mon., August 7	HSBC enters into Agreement in Principle with CBO providing for sale of HBC to CBO. CBO, HSBC, OHR&S, SB, HBC, BA&H.
	Approval of Transaction granted by Monopolies and Mergers Commission of the United Kingdom.
Tues., August 15	Meeting with SEC on comments on preliminary proxy materials. SASM&F, CGS&H, MMBI, HSBC.
Wed., August 17	Submission of modified draft HSBC Application to NY Fed. SPP&T, HSBC.
Thurs., August 24	Publication of FRB Y-4 Notices of HSBC, Kellett and HSBC Holdings *re* nonbanking activities. SPP&T.
	HSBC enters into Purchase and Sale Agreement with CBO to dispose of HBC. HSBC, OHR&S, CBO, SB, HBC, BA&H.
Thurs., August 31	Submission of final FRB Application on Kellett and HSBC Holdings to NY Fed. HSBC, SPP&T.

II. Final approval

Months of September and October	Contact with FRB, Justice Department and NYBD as needed. SPP&T, PLHB&H.
Fri., September 1	FRB Applications of HSBC, Kellett and HSBC Holdings accepted by NY Fed and forwarded to FRB in D.C.
Tues., September 5	Opinion of SASM&F as to proxy materials delivered to HSBC. SASM&F. MMBI furnishes HSBC with (a) Proxy Statement Certificate, certifying no material change in MMBI, and (b) copies of definitive proxy materials. MMBI, SASM&F, CGS&H, HSBC.
Wed., September 6	Definitive proxy materials mailed to MMBI shareholders. MMBI, SASM&F.
Thurs., September 7	Submission of final HSBC application to NYBD. SPP&T, HSBC. MMBI issues press release on mailing of proxy statement. MMBI.
Thurs., September 28	Meeting on various U.S. regulatory approvals. SPP&T, HSBC, CGS&H.
Fri., September 29	Meeting with CSBD and FDIC in California regarding approvals of sale of HBC to CBO. SPP&T, HSBC, CGS&H.
Fri., September 29 to Mon., October 3	CBO converts from national bank to a California state bank.
Fri., October 6	CBO files application with FDIC to acquire shares of HBC. CBO files application with CSBD to acquire shares of HBC.
Tues., October 10	Submission of portions of FRB applications for Kellett, HSBC Holdings, HSBC to U.S. Department of Justice and U.S. Federal Trade Commission in compliance with requirements of the Hart-Scott-Rodino Antitrust Improvements Act of 1976 as to non-banking activities. SPP&T, HSBC.
Wed., October 11	HSBC receives notice from the Federal Trade Commission to the effect that the acquisition is exempt from any additional requirements of the Hart-Scott-Rodino Antitrust Improvements Act of 1976.
Wed., October 18	Special Meeting of MMBI shareholders approves proposed Transaction. MMBI, SASM&F.
Week of Mon., October 23	MMBI circulates for comments draft listing application required in connection with securities to be issued in Transaction. MMBI, SASM&F.
Wed., October 25	Amendment No. 1 to Schedule 13D filed with SEC by HSBC. CGS&H, HSBC, MMBI, SASM&F.
Tues., November 7	MMBI files draft listing application required in connection with securities to be issued in Transaction. MMBI, SASM&F.
Week of Mon., November 20	CGS&H circulates first draft of HSBC's assignment of its rights under the Investment Agreement to HSBC Holdings. CGS&H, HSBC, SASM&F, MMBI.

Fri., November 24	Canadian Foreign Investment Review Board decision on Transaction.
Wed., December 13	NYSE orally notifies MMBI of approval of listing of New Shares, subject to regulatory approvals. MMBI, SASM&F.
Fri., December 15	HSBC Holdings adopts resolutions accepting the assignment and authorizing the performance of the actions specified in the Investment Agreement. HSBC Holdings, CGS&H.
Wed., December 27	MMBI prepares and files with the Secretary of State of the State of Delaware any corporate charter amendment or certificate of designations and preferences required for creation of securities to be issued in capital investment. MMBI. CSBD approves sale of HBC to CBO.
(1979)	
Wed., January 24	FDIC approves CBO acquisition of HBC; closing to occur in Hong Kong on first Saturday following 15 days after approval and any stay period.
Wed., January 31	Delaware notice of intention to make tender offer sent to MMBI. HSBC Holdings, CGS&H.
Sat., February 24	HSBC sells HBC to CBO.
Fri., March 16	FRB approves applications of HSBC, Kellett and HSBC Holdings.
Week of Mon., March 26	CGS&H circulates draft of Dealer Manager Agreement. CGS&H, HSBC Holdings.
Fri., March 30	HSBC and MMBI exchange letters agreeing not to terminate Investment Agreement prior to June 30. HSBC, MMBI, CGS&H, SASM&F.
Mon., April 2	Delaware notice of intention to make a tender offer sent to MMBI. HSBC Holdings, CGS&H.
Tues., April 3	FRB General Counsel determines that HBC has been effectively divested.
Tues., April 10	HSBC files Amendment No. 2 to the Schedule 13D filed on May 30, 1978. HSBC, CGS&H.
Fri., April 13	Request for SEC no-action letter on simultaneous purchases of tendered shares and closing on first tranche of new securities to be issued in accordance with the Investment Agreement sent to the SEC. CGS&H, HSBC Holdings.
Week of Mon., April 16	CGS&H circulates revised Dealer Manager, Depositary, Forwarding Agent and Information Agent Agreements. CGS&H, HSBC Holdings. SB circulates tender offer side papers, including broker-dealer letter, client letter and newspaper advertisement. SB, WLR&K.
Fri., May 4	SEC issues no-action letter on simultaneous closing of purchases of tendered shares and first tranche of new securities to be issued in accordance with the Investment Agreement.

II. Final approval

Tues., May 15	Delaware notice of intention to make a tender offer sent to MMBI. CGS&H, HSBC Holdings.
Wed., June 27	Investment Agreement amended to extend date of termination option to June 30, 1980, to provide for conversion of MMB into national bank and to increase tender price and price of New Shares. MMBI, HSBC, CGS&H, SASM&F.
	Note Purchase Agreement amended to provide for exchange of the $7\frac{3}{4}$ percent note for a 15-year 9 percent note. MMBI, HSBC, CGS&H, SASM&F.
	Applications of HSBC, Kellett and HSBC Holdings to NYBD withdrawn. MMBI, HSBC.
Thurs., June 28	MMB files application with Comptroller for conversion into national bank. MMBI.
Fri., June 29	NY Fed confirms in writing its earlier oral extension of FRB approval of Transaction to Dec. 16, 1979. HSBC, SPP&T. NYSE reaffirms oral approval of listing of New Shares in light of revisions to Transaction, subject to Comptroller's approval. SASM&F, MMBI.
Mon., July 2	HSBC files Amendment No. 3 to the Schedule 13D filed on May 30, 1978. CGS&H, HSBC.
	Comptroller accepts MMB'S application for conversion into a national bank for filing. CGS&H, HSBC.
Week of Mon., July 2	Initial draft of proxy materials to be used for MMBI shareholder ratification of revised Transaction prepared and circulated. CGS&H, HSBC, MMBI, SASM&F.
Fri., July 6	Meeting to review initial draft and to discuss problem areas. CGS&H, SASM&F.
Week of Mon., July 9	Meeting with SEC to inform staff of planned filing. MMBI, SASM&F.
	First printed draft of proxy materials is circulated. CGS&H, HSBC, MMBI, SASM&F.
Week of Mon., July 16	Successive drafts of proxy materials are circulated and discussed. CGS&H, HSBC, MMBI, SASM&F.
Mon., July 25	Preliminary proxy materials filed with SEC. SASM&F, MMBI.
August through October	Comptroller's staff examined MMBI.
Fri., August 10	SEC staff gives preliminary comments on proxy materials to MMBI by telephone. SASM&F.
Wed., August 29	Definitive proxy materials prepared and cleared with SEC. CGS&H, HSBC, MMBI, SASM&F.
Fri., August 31	MMBI furnishes HSBC with (a) Proxy Statement Certificate, certifying no material change in MMBI, and (b) copies of definitive proxy materials, opinion of SASM&F as to proxy materials delivered to HSBC. MMBI, SASM&F, HSBC, CGS&H.
	Definitive proxy materials mailed to MMBI shareholders. MMBI, SASM&F.
Tues., October 4	Comptroller's staff arrived in Hong Kong for month-long examination of HSBC. HSBC.

Wed., October 17	MMBI shareholders' meeting held and revised Transaction ratified. MMBI, SASM&F.
Tues., October 23	Delivery notice of intention to make a tender offer sent. HSBC Holdings, CGS&H.
Fri., October 26	Amendment No. 4 to the Schedule 13D filed on May 30, 1978. CGS&H, HSBC.
Wed., December 12	Letter extending FRB approval of the Transaction to June 16, 1980 received. SPP&T.
(1980)	
Mon., January 28	Comptroller approved conversion of MMB into national bank.
	Press releases announcing Comptroller approval of conversion of MMB into national bank. HSBC, MMBI.
Week of Mon., January 28	Definitive tender offer documents completed. CGS&H, SASM&F, SB, WLR&K, HSBC Holdings, MMBI.
Wed., January 30	MMBI prepares and files with NYSE final listing application for New Shares. MMBI, SASM&F.
Thurs., January 31	NYSE approval of listing application for New Shares received. MMBI, SASM&F.
Fri., February 1	MMB converted to national bank. MMBI.
	MMBI delivers waiver of 3-day written notice requirement of Investment Agreement. MMBI, SASM&F.
	HSBC Holdings files Schedule 14D-1. CGS&H, HSBC Holdings.
	MMBI files Schedule 14D-9. MMBI, SASM&F.
	Documents delivered in accordance with Investment Agreement. MMBI, SASM&F, HSBC, HSBC Holdings, CGS&H.
	Tender offer commences; offer to purchase mailed to MMBI's shareholders. CGS&H, HSBC Holdings, SB, WLR&K.
	HSBC Holdings press release announcing commencement of Tender Offer. CGS&H, HSBC, HSBC Holdings.
Mon., February 4	Post-commencement newspaper advertisement of tender offer in Wall Street Journal. SB, CGS&H, HSBC, HSBC Holdings, WLR&K.
Thurs., February 14	Amendment No. 5 to Schedule 13D mailed by HSBC to SEC. HSBC, CGS&H.
Mon., February 25	HSBC Holdings delivers notification to MMBI of date of First Closing. CGS&H, HSBC Holdings.
Mon., March 3	Executed closing documents for First Closing examined and placed in escrow. CGS&H, HSBC, HSBC Holdings, MMBI, SASM&F.
	Tender offer expires. Depositary advises Holdings as to approximate number of shares tendered. HSBC Holdings, CGS&H.
Tues., March 4	HSBC Holdings press release announcing expiration of Tender Offer given to wire services. CGS&H, HSBC, HSBC Holdings.
	Shares issued by HSBC Holdings to Kellett and recorded on HSBC Holdings' share record book. W&VH.

II. Final approval

	9 percent Note sold by Kellett to HSBC Holdings. HSBC Holdings, CGS&H.
	First Closing occurs; closing documents for First Closing released from escrow; HSBC Holdings pays purchase price of New Shares by delivery to MMBI of 9 percent Note and cash and application of interest on 9 percent Note. CGS&H, HSBC, HSBC Holdings, SASM&F, MMBI, SB, WLR&K.
	Press release at 4:00 p.m. announcing completion of First Closing. CGS&H, HSBC Holdings.
Thurs., March 13	Guaranteed delivery period ends. CGS&H, HSBC, HSBC Holdings, SB.
Fri., March 14	Final proration determined, Press Release announcing final proration. CGS&H, HSBC Holdings.
	Form 3 of HSBC Holdings filed with SEC. CGS&H, HSBC Holdings.
Mon., March 17	Depositary mails cheques to tendering shareholders. CGS&H, HSBC Holdings.
After Mon., March 17	HSBC and HSBC Holdings make necessary filings with SEC, Dept of Commerce, and IRS. CGS&H, HSBC, HSBC Holdings.
	MMBI makes necessary filings with Dept of Commerce. MMBI, SASM&F.
	Resubmission of HSBC application to Canadian Foreign Investment Review Board. HSBC.
Wed., March 19	Form 8-K of MMBI filed with SEC. MMBI, SASM&F.
By Wed., December 31, 1980	Second Closing occurs. After Second Closing, HSBC Holdings holds approximately 51 percent of the shares of MMBI.

18

'HONGKONGBANK', THE HONGKONG BANK GROUP, 1980–1984*

> ...there shall from henceforth be no limit whatever to the duration of the period of [the Bank's] incorporation.
>
> Hongkong Bank Ordinance, No. 6 of 1929

In one sense 1979 might seem to have been a suitable year for the ending of this history. The implementation of the agreement with Marine Midland Banks, Inc. (MMBI), had an impact on The Hongkong and Shanghai Banking Corporation sufficient to create an apparent discontinuity and, therefore, it might seem reasonable to conclude that the Hongkong Bank, as previously known in its history, had virtually ceased to exist.

This, however, is unsatisfactory.

The acquisition of MMBI was not an opportunistic move with unforeseen consequences; it was part of a strategy developed by Michael Sandberg and his chief associates, many of whom had, as juniors, come East by P&O, lived in the Peak Mess or the Mercantile Bank's equivalent, and learned the traditions of the Bank from Managers some of whom had joined London Office immediately before the Great War. The lack of committees, the on-line hierarchy, indicates that they would have learned more of the Bank's regional role than of Sir Michael Turner's Board-approved policy of searching for extra-regional involvement. Nevertheless, their everyday experience would reveal deficiencies in the system, opportunities missed, lessons learned from other banks, from journals, from meetings. The Bank evolved not as a consequence of outside consultants, nor from lateral transfers at the middle levels, but from within the traditionally recruited Eastern staff of the Hongkong Bank itself.

Although startlingly different in so many ways, the post-1979 Bank is, nevertheless, a product of its history.

The importance of the Marine Midland acquisition is unchallenged, but it is an event representing the fulfilment of the Bank's policy trend since the mid-1950s, albeit the policy horizon was then still limited by self-imposed constraints and lack of perceived opportunity. The Bank had been preparing for MMBI in the context of a global strategy since at least 1976. This is not to suggest that the move was inevitable; a major, dramatic transaction required

---

* There are no end-notes for this chapter. Readers are referred to the bibliographical notes, p. 953.

the right chief executive, one who appreciated both the continuity he was developing and the dangers which he was incurring – and accepted the latter as necessary for the former. In this context the success of the MMBI acquisition did not complete the Bank's strategic requirements. Neither did the success cut the threads of the Bank's history.

As China's policies changed, the Hongkong Bank moved back carefully to Peking and to China's newly created Special Economic Zones; it was invited to supplement its Hong Kong based China-financing with on-the-scene offices. The new Head Office building was, among other things, a declaration of intent to remain in Hong Kong, where it continued to issue over 80% of the banknote currency and remained the principal bankers to the Government. Despite geographical diversification, the Bank's profits were more than 50% attributable to its Hong Kong activities.

In this chapter the first task is to state the consequences of Marine Midland and to note that the completion of the transaction was but one of several important developments in 1980.

The story of the Hongkong Bank Group, or, to use the new 'signature', HongkongBank, after 1980 will narrow down to a few topics which are consequent to events previously described. In this context, therefore, HSBC's attempt to acquire the Royal Bank of Scotland Group, a key part of its global strategy, will be noted. But, as with so many other developments, the full account must be reserved for a subsequent history.

The collapse of the Hong Kong share market in 1982 had its impact on the Bank; the temporary but severe lack of confidence in the dollar, at least partially in the context of uncertainty over the fate of Hong Kong in 1997, the subsequent Sino-British Joint Declaration, the renewed confidence in a dollar now pegged to the U.S. dollar, and the redevelopment of optimism relative to the economy of the territory are, however, events which will prove assessable only after several years. They are not yet subjects for a history.

THE YEAR IS 1980

A history of the Hongkong Bank in the year 1980 must refer first to the completion of the Marine Midland transaction, but in a new context; afterwards there will be consideration of other important acquisitions. The quantum jump shown in the tables as between 1979 and 1980 was due primarily to MMBI, but there were many important factors involved – and there were further developments unrelated to acquisitions. The Bank's Hong Kong branches were linked by an on-line computer system, making practical the introduction of an ETC (Electronic Teller Card) system; the system was introduced with an initial sixteen machines distributed over the urban area of

Hong Kong and was heralded by award-winning advertisements; the Hongkong Bank's VISA card was also launched – Master Charge had been available since 1975 – and both would give access to the ETC system. By 1985 these initial steps had been developed into a 'Super ETC' account system – 'all-electronic' personal banking in Hong Kong with 'revolving credit' facilities available 24-hours a day through 450 ETC machines (including Hang Seng's) throughout Hong Kong. Retail services at least had not been forgotten.

Looking to the future and with the passage of the Canadian Bank Act, the Hongkong Bank made immediate application to become a fully operational commercial bank and was in the first tranche of approved banks. By the end of 1986 the wholly owned subsidiary, Hongkong Bank of Canada, which had opened for business in October 1981, had become, with the acquisition of the Bank of British Columbia in 1986, that nation's third largest overseas bank (as measured by assets); the Hongkong Bank was also the largest in the United States and thus in North America. Back in 1980, the head office of the British Bank of the Middle East removed to Hong Kong, Antony Gibbs became a 100%-owned subsidiary, the Peking Representative Office was opened, the Bank's investment in Concord International, NV, a leasing and financial group, increased to 51%, Wardley International Bank, Nassau, opened for business in March – and there were new uniforms for the staff.

The immediate impact of Marine Midland

The celebration

The transaction whereby HSBC acquired 51.1% of MMBI was completed on October 1, 1980, in time to celebrate 100 years of the Hongkong Bank's presence in New York City. The original Bank-staffed agency had opened, at the request of its then merchant agents, Russell and Co., in 1880 in consequence of the growth of business. Despite the importance of the office in terms of the Bank's international trade financing, it remained a low-profile agency; like Paris and Hamburg, it was a service facility. The celebrations initiating the 'partnership' with Marine Midland were occasion for the Governor of Hong Kong and the Governor of New York State to speak of mutually beneficial economic consequences, and the Bank's award-winning 1980 Annual Report featured an essay by Anthony Sampson comparing Hong Kong and New York – the Pearl of the Orient with the Big Apple.[a]

---

[a] Both the 1980 and the 1982 annual reports were granted awards at the Mean Library of Ideas International Annual Report Show; the reports were designed by Henry Steiner and the 1980 report photographed by Ken Haas. The Staff of the Office of the Comptroller of the Currency were not so excited, but they were looking at it from a different perspective.

Congressman Benjamin S. Rosenthal was already asking the question. Accepting I.H. Macdonald's assessment of the growth of Hong Kong/U.S. trade, how would this benefit Buffalo? The Hongkong Bank's role through Marine Midland would be to establish manufacturing and trade contacts, to encourage investment flows. In the Fall of 1980 the Hongkong Bank, Macdonald reported to the Congressional sub-committee, would be sponsoring the first group of New York businessmen on a fact-finding trip to Hong Kong. Rosenthal could not refrain from asking whether they would be flying on Cathay Pacific.

But when the celebrations were concluded, there were hard questions to consider.

The capital/assets problem
The consolidation of accounts consequent to HSBC's ownership of over 50% of MMBI equity was a major factor in the increase of Hongkong Bank Group's assets from the $125.3 billion shown on the original end-1979 balance sheet to the $243.0 billion at the end of 1980. The 1979 figure, when revised to a basis comparable to that of 1980, was $109.5 billion, disclosing an even larger increase than the published figures would indicate. The fact is that a growth in assets of the magnitude involved with the MMBI merger would force the Hongkong Bank to reconsider the adequacy of its capital base.

The transaction had cost HSBC some US$314 million, say $1,500 million, which was paid in cash, the consequence of a series of intra-Group transactions which resulted in a payout which would be reflected in the consolidated accounts. The Group's ratio of shareholders' funds to total assets, including minority interests, calculated on an equity basis, was originally shown as 3.3% (4.2% for the Hongkong Bank itself), which is low and, although understated because of hidden reserves, was a matter of concern even before the payment for MMBI.

This was a manifestation of a long-term problem faced by a dynamically growing bank in an inflationary environment. In the case of the MMBI transaction, the Bank with its inner reserves was unable to offer scrip on the basis of a prospectus which would be satisfactory to the SEC; it had, therefore, to inject cash. From MMBI's point of view, that was the whole purpose of the operation. And yet at the end of 1980 the capital/assets ratio, as defined to include minority interests, had risen to 5.3%. How was this achieved?

The Bank's assets had included offsetting items (contra accounts) under the general heading 'Engagements on behalf of Customers', particularly confirmed credits, guarantees, and endorsements. By conforming more closely to standard practices, the Bank was able to eliminate all such items other than a small

($1 billion of $16.8 billion) item, 'Acceptances'. As shown in Table 15.3, this restatement reduced end-1979 assets from $125.3 billion to $109.5 billion, a move which would raise, retroactively, the capital/assets ratio to 3.8%.

Secondly, the Bank reexamined its accounting practices; it determined that it had been indulging in an expensive luxury by not valuing property at the market. Banks do not deal in real estate and, therefore, the Hongkong Bank had traditionally written down its property holdings, a practice which overstated the earnings/assets ratio. Now the practice, which had been standard, would from time to time be amended. Moreover, on accepting the principle that a more complex corporate organization could provide efficiencies, a bank could deal with property through specialized subsidiaries, and the Hongkong Bank accordingly established HS Property Management Company. The main result of this at the time was a 'one-off exercise' which determined that the Bank's property had been $5,187 million undervalued; this sum was accordingly credited to the Reserve Fund.

The 3 for 5 bonus share issue did not in itself increase published shareholders' funds, but the $1,039 million of the Reserve Fund capitalized was replaced from current income and from inner reserves (see Tables 15.2B and C). There was also additional paid-up capital of $13.9 million issued to former shareholders of Antony Gibbs.

The Reserve Fund increased from $1,640 million to $7,156 million in a single year, while the growth in assets was considerably less than anticipated because of the change in accounting procedures referred to above.

At the end of 1980 shareholders' funds, including minority shareholders of the Bank's major associated companies, were $12,984 million as opposed to end-1979 total of $4,178 million. The capital/assets ratio was accordingly 5.3% as compared to the 3.3% calculated on the historical basis.

The geographical impact

By the end of 1980 the Hongkong Bank Group's assets were some 38% in the East, 42% in the Americas, and 18% in Europe (see Figure 18.1). This distribution was achieved despite the growth of assets in the East and was partly due to the 100% acquisition of Antony Gibbs Holdings (see below). However, as stated, the percentages reflect two related but separate 'distribution' policies.

The first arose from the need to invest reserves outside the territory which was the source of the funds, especially Hong Kong. In several of the territories in which the Bank operated, its reserves were held by the country's central bank, which had its own foreign exchange policy. In Hong Kong there was no central bank, and, with the Hong Kong dollar floating, that is, no longer tied either to sterling or to the U.S. dollar, the Bank covered itself by holding reserve liquid assets in several currencies. This, however, was not the policy

Geographical Distribution of Group Assets
(Excluding contra accounts)

Group assets, less contra accounts, increased by more than 3% over 1983. They are shown here divided geographically among the Group's four principal regions of operation. The major increase in the Americas in 1980 resulted from acquisition of a majority shareholding in Marine Midland Banks, Inc.

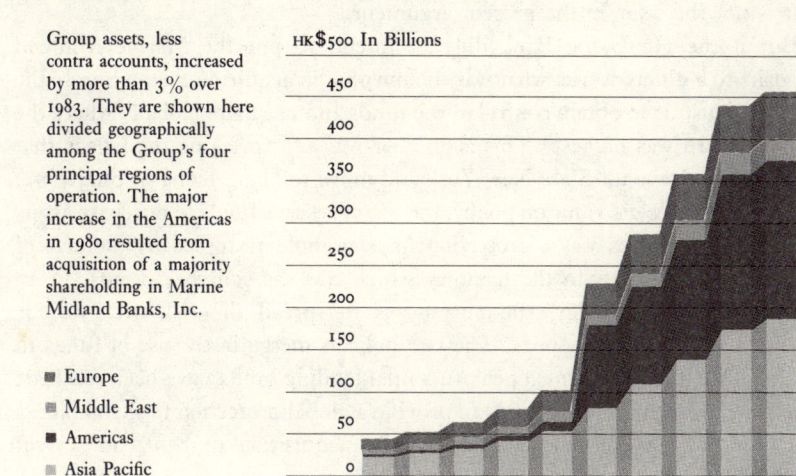

- Europe
- Middle East
- Americas
- Asia Pacific

Figure 18.1 Geographical distribution of assets, 1984 (Excluding contra accounts)

which motivated the Hongkong Bank to seek an American partner; it could always obtain U.S. dollar assets as a use of funds garnered in Hong Kong. This was but an extension of what the Federal Reserve Bank perceived as the Hongkong Bank's 'country bank' characteristics; the Bank stressed asset rather than liability management, it sought a sound deposit base or bases as a first objective; it then considered the appropriate uses of these funds.[b]

What Sandberg was achieving for the Hongkong Bank was a policy of distribution in addition to the reserve policy described. This involved securing new deposit bases from which new earning assets, loans and advances, could be acquired within that same area. This the Hongkong Bank had achieved minimally with the purchase of the Mercantile Bank; it had been somewhat more successful with the BBME, tapping the Middle East deposit base but with limited opportunity to acquire earning assets within the same region. The merger with Marine Midland on the other hand was ideally situated to

---

[b] In the United States deposits in a 'country' bank, for example, the Citizens Bank and Trust Company of Abilene, Kansas, in excess of the percentage which can be prudently loaned within the bank's service area are used to purchase Government paper of a kind unavailable in Hong Kong and/or passed on through correspondent banks, first to a correspondent bank in the Federal Reserve city of Kansas City and then possibly to Chicago or New York. The Hongkong Bank was doing the same with its Hong Kong deposits, albeit on an international basis.

accomplish Sandberg's policy with a single stroke – the Hongkong Bank acquired a new and major deposit base together with a region which would use the funds – and with a management and organizational structure in place, but that is not the issue in the present argument.

But if the Hongkong Bank did not intend to put the Marine Midland deposits to a different use, what was the purpose in acquiring them? Surely the purpose must be to obtain control of the funds and use them globally where the rate of return was highest? This is another way of expressing the fallacy that funds would leave up-State New York and move to Hong Kong or Singapore.

In the reserves distribution policy, the use of reserve funds to purchase assets in several currencies was a protection for shareholders forced by the lack of suitable reserve assets in the territory which was the source of funds. In an assets distribution policy, the purpose is to spread the risk over various activities in several economies. The two policies merge in the use of funds in excess of such requirements once prudential lending limits have been reached; it is the movement of these funds to provide a global protection to shareholders which is one key to purposes behind the acquisition of banks in several economies.

At the end of 1981 the Hongkong Bank's advances to customers was US$6.3 billion + Hang Seng's US$2.3 billion + Wardley's US$1 billion (= US$9.6 billion equivalent), MMB's US$11.0 billion. These loans were not all to Hong Kong or New York State borrowers respectively; their actual geographical distribution would require further analysis, but the figures make the point necessary to explain HSBC's purpose – they also reflect the different liquidity positions of the Hongkong Bank and Marine Midland.

There are, however, two supplementary ways of regarding the problem, that is by determining the source of (i) funds, that is, deposits and (ii) profits. A 1982 study by Vickers da Costa states that post-MMBI merger deposits were distributed 55% outside Hong Kong – although other research placed the percentage as high as 70%. Profits originating in Hong Kong accounted for some 65% of the total. This indicates the particular profitability of Hong Kong and the slightly unfavourable reaction of the market, as seen through a decline in price/earnings ratios, occasioned by HSBC's venture into what Hong Kong shareholders saw as lack of faith in the territory and/or a move into less progressive and less profitable economies.

In conclusion HSBC had achieved assets diversification as between East Asia (including Hong Kong) and the Americas (in 1980 almost entirely the United States); its position in Europe, despite the acquisition of Antony Gibbs, remained unsatisfactory. Fortunately, the Bank's global strategy had taken this into account. There remained in the United Kingdom a potential partner, an alliance which Sandberg saw as a sensible next step after a U.S. acquisition. Unfortunately, Standard Chartered's Peter Graham thought so, too.

Marine Midland itself had associated companies overseas; the Group's geographic coverage, especially in South America, was correspondingly enhanced. In Australia MMBI had an interest in Intermarine Australia Limited, which was merged with Wardley Limited's Australian subsidiary, Wardley Australia Limited. The latter was then owned 67% by Wardley Australia (Holdings), 20% by Marine Midland Bank, NA, and 13% by Tokai Bank of Nagoya, Japan (this last holding was subsequently sold to the Group). MMBI had in any case been under FRB pressure to divest, and the merger was not a 'take-over' precedent; as if to provide evidence of this, in 1981 MMB opened an office in Seoul. And in 1980 the Eurobond unit of Marine Midland Ltd, the London merchant banking subsidiary of MMBI, was transferred to Antony Gibbs.

Also in the United States, D.H. Leach, who had been Manager New York, was appointed in late 1979 on a post-retirement contract as Representative in the new Washington, D.C., office of the Bank's International Corporate Accounts Department. As such it was not involved in the Marine Midland negotiations, but was part of the Bank's attempt to coordinate its activities relative to its major international constituents.

The Hongkong Bank Group

The impact of the MMBI merger can be described in terms other than geographical.

In Table 18.1 the figures for the 'Hongkong Bank' are residual, that is, they are published assets/profits less the known assets/profits of other subsidiaries. Even with this imperfection, however, the 33% cutback in the Hongkong Bank's share and the 26% in Hang Seng's are dramatic; this is accounted for both by the acquisition of MMBI and the growth of Wardley. The sale of the Hongkong Bank of California is offset by the acquisition of 100% of Antony Gibbs.

Nevertheless, the impact on profits is quite different with the Hongkong Bank and Hang Seng together accounting for a higher percentage in 1980 than in 1975 – and the Hongkong Bank figure includes the loss from Antony Gibbs. The relatively poor performance of the Mercantile Bank in high tax areas is to be expected; the BBME had particularly difficult years politically, and the Saudi British Bank, although successful, would not be fully represented in the figures.

At first glance this would seem to suggest that the purchase of MMBI, although it had the right geographical impact, must have diluted profits per

Table 18.1 *The Hongkong and Shanghai Banking Corporation
Distribution of assets and profits, December 31, 1980*

	1975		1980	
Company	Assets[a]	Profits	Assets[a]	Profits
	percentages			
Hongkong Bank[b]	59.0		37.8	
		59.0		54.3
British Bank of the Middle East	21.9		8.7	
		14.6		7.9
Mercantile Bank	2.8		1.3	
		3.4		1.2
Hang Seng Bank	13.3		9.8	
		16.3		18.6
Marine Midland Banks, Inc.	—		36.6	
		—		9.0
Hongkong Bank of California	1.4		—	
		(3.1)		—
Wardley	1.6		4.4	
		7.6		11.3
Antony Gibbs	—		1.4	
		—		(34.0)
	$ bn	$ mn	$ bn	$ mn
Total assets	47.4		237.8	
Contra accounts	10.3		5.2	
Published Total	57.7		243.0	
Total net profits		333.2		1431.3
Minorities		34.3		328.4
Published net profits		367.5		1759.7

[a] Excluding contra accounts.
[b] A residual quantity.
Source: Report of Wood, Mackenzie and Co., 15 December 1981.

share. Thus is an unreasonable conclusion; in the context of percentages, the Hongkong Bank Group had reached relative saturation in its traditional region if prudential ratios were heeded. The allocation of the US$314 million from MMBI to, say, the Hongkong Bank for use in Hong Kong was not a feasible alternative.

Other developments in 1980

The People's Republic of China

By the mid-1970s there was evidence that China's foreign economic policy was undergoing significant change. The Hongkong Bank had retained its Shanghai branch throughout the Cultural Revolution and it had been operated with sufficient business to prevent loss; the remainder of the Hongkong Bank's China business had been conducted in Hong Kong. The first changes were the establishment in 1978 of a 'China Desk' in the Hong Kong office by O.J.L. Barnham (East in 1966), who subsequently became Manager Shanghai; he was succeeded by C.R. Page (East in 1975), a graduate in Chinese from Leeds University. An officially unrecognized representation in Guangzhou was established the following year.

In 1980 business had developed to a point where a Peking Representative Office, with M.P. Langley (East with the Mercantile Bank in 1948) as Representative, was authorized and established in October; in December Sandberg, as Chairman of the Bank, hosted a reception in Peking's Great Hall of the People. In Hong Kong the China Desk was further developed to bring together the various activities of the Group, including Wardley Limited, involved in China finance. The Bank's China Desk sent representatives, including the Japanese Regional officer resident in Hong Kong, to the China Trade Fair; they assisted constituents at the Fair, and from this developed the permanent representative alluded to above. Research staff were employed and the beginnings established of the China Office, which would be an integral part of the Group's China operations, both in Hong Kong and in China itself.

This expansion of activities affected the Shanghai branch, and there was a search for additional space with consequences beneficial to the Bank's history project. The Shanghai branch's files dating back to the early years of this century had been stored in a godown adjoining the rear of the Bank's office on Yuen Ming Yuen Street; as there was access on every floor, the Bank had requested permission to destroy this archival material to create more office space. When permission was granted, the Bank modified the request. Rather than burn the material could it be shipped to the new Group Archives in Hong Kong? This was approved by the responsible Shanghai officials; through the cooperation of the Chinese authorities, these records now constitute the largest part of the Hongkong Bank's historical records.

Antony Gibbs

Antony Gibbs was the first of all the members of the Hongkong Bank Group to be established. Some four years before the Bank of Utica (New York) was founded in 1812, the earliest of the banks which would eventually merge into Marine

Midland, Antony Gibbs was founded in London. Until 1972 the company was wholly owned by the Gibbs family, but there were difficulties and the company went public. The Bank began with a 20% equity stake in the holding company, Antony Gibbs Holdings in 1973. The following year, the Bank bought a further 20%, and in 1980, despite delays caused by senior executive involvement in the problems of the Marine Midland acquisition, there were negotiations, prompted by poor performance and encouraged by the Bank of England, which led to the acquisition of the remaining 60%.

During these years Antony Gibbs made no contribution to Group profits and in 1980 there was a $45 million loss; despite its long history, the company had lacked the ability to attract sufficient top staff. It had failed to develop; the Bank had no alternative but to take total control and change the management – David Macdonald, formally Deputy Chairman of Hill Samuel and Co., took over as chief executive of the subsidiary merchant bank, Antony Gibbs and Sons – but the right formula had not yet been found.

Antony Gibbs was valued at some £17.5 million (= $214.6 million); the 1980 purchase of 60% of the equity was effected, partly in cash, partly in shares (at a premium), to a total value of £10.6 million (= $130 million). This included the issue of six million new shares with a par value of $14 million (see Table 18.2C) with a total premium of $65.3 million. The attributable net asset value of this investment was $124.7 million at year-end exchange rates.

The purchase was part of the Bank's global strategy, this time through a United Kingdom based merchant bank. The plan was marred not only by the poor performance of Antony Gibbs but also by the fully expected decision of the Accepting Houses Committee not to permit Antony Gibbs, now overseas controlled, to remain a member. There were precedential reasons for this not related to the Hongkong Bank, but the decision focused attention once again on the Bank's need for an improved British presence.

British Bank of the Middle East

With P.E. Hutson as Chairman of the BBME in London and Kenneth Bradford the chief executive officer the way was open for a long delayed move of the head office of the bank to Hong Kong; this was effected on January 1, 1980. The integration of the two banks, the Mercantile and the BBME, with the Hongkong Bank had taken twenty years to accomplish.

Sandberg became Chairman of the BBME in Hong Kong and, among head office executives to be appointed directors, was J.A.P. Hill, who had originally been recruited by BBME and had served in the Middle East. Bradford returned to London as the Chairman's representative, the advisory committees were merged to form a single London Committee (see Table 14.4), while J.L.A. Francis relinquished his role as the BBME Secretary and became Manager (International Relations) in London.

There were three Group control policies: (i) for the Mercantile and BBME, total integration, (ii) for Hang Seng and MMBI, 'partnership', and (iii) for the specialist companies, their own management, with varying degrees of supervision and policy control. The argument that the BBME needed career specialists was no longer relevant in the planning of an international bank; local expertise had to be provided by increasingly senior local staff. The two 'integrated' banks nevertheless kept their individual corporate identity and accounts – for the time being.

In London arrangements were made for the Hongkong Bank to take over all the activities of the BBME's City office at 99 Bishopsgate. This meant that customers would receive back their Hongkong Bank cheque books. The first step to an effective solution had been taken.

The new Bank Act gave greater regulatory authority to the Bank of England and this affected the British Bank of the Middle East, which, despite its move to Hong Kong, remained London registered. To improve BBME's capital ratios, the Hongkong Bank agreed to buy the BBME's equity investment in the Saudi-British Bank. The Saudis, however, preferred their relationship with BBME, and the Hongkong Bank had consequently to inject a further £30 million of capital into its subsidiary; in addition the Bank granted unspecified date, subordinated loans ranking as capital and totalling US$90 million (from Nassau branch to a tax free BBME branch) for the same purpose.

Corporate identity

In 1899, a letter from the United Kingdom addressed simply 'T.J., China' was delivered without difficulty to Sir Thomas Jackson, the Chief Manager of the Hongkong and Shanghai Bank. This is hardly surprising, for is it not true that 'Far East' is defined as that area in which the term, 'the Bank', refers to The Hongkong and Shanghai Banking Corporation?

It was all quite straightforward! It is the East that needs identity, not the Bank! But that becomes irrelevant when the Bank opens in Chile or takes an equity share in the Equator Bank.[c] Nor does it solve the question of 'the Group'. In common with so many companies which moved from the area where they were well-known and from the single manufacture which they first produced, the Hongkong Bank needed, despite so many years of success, a corporate identity. The Bank had been in America for 100 years, but, as Congressman Rosenthal pointed out, they were still not known.

Marine Midland negotiations inspired Congressional discussions, and

[c] The Hongkong Bank had been involved with the Royal Bank of Canada in the Bahamas-incorporated Equator Bank, a merchant bank focused on West, Central, and East Africa. The Royal Bank withdrew as a consequence of changed policies. In 1981 HSBC, through Wardley, acquired 72% of the equity by a US$6.6 million purchase of new shares. Marine Midland Bank came in to the extent of 6%. The balance of the share capital continued to be held for a time by Hartford National Bank and Helmboldt, Montgomery and Co.

regulatory study papers had established an important point about the Hongkong Bank Group; it was a financial Group. The long list of companies, the strangeness of the titles, the excitement of 'discovery' had all come back to the point that, however calculated, their contribution was financially minimal. The Hongkong Bank Group might include shipping, newspapers, and airlines, but that is not what it was about and they could be explained.

The problem of 'corporate identity' nevertheless remained. What was the Hongkong Bank Group? Did the corporation have the right name? If at a Christmas party one of the games were 'identify the logos', would the Bank's be recognized?

V.A. Mason (East in 1919) had been troubled as early as World War II. Temporarily stranded in Australia he noted that Australian bankers gave their China business to HSBC but their India business to the Mercantile Bank of India or the Chartered Bank of India, Australia and China. Although he didn't put it this way, HSBC apparently had the wrong corporate image. Arthur Morse in London bluntly disagreed; the Hongkong Bank was sufficiently well known. And the discussion ended.

From time to time Hongkong Bankers venturing to the United States would be asked why they worked for a Communist bank, and the Hongkong and Shanghai Banking Corporation of California, Inc., seemed an unnecessarily contentious name for the 1950s.

For the most part chief executive officers did not carry the problem further than idiosyncratic but strongly held views on the capital 'T' for the initial definite article and the use of the ampersand. There were two main factors forcing a more professional approach. First was the growth of the Hongkong Bank Group, especially since this 'Hongkong Bank Group' was not the name of an incorporated holding company as analogy might lead one to suppose. There had already been efforts to use similar names for similar activities, for example, 'Wardley' for merchant banking; in 1980 the insurance companies included, where feasible, the identity name of 'Carlingford', which, as previously noted, was the name of the Manager's house in Bangkok. The BBME still had its palm trees, however, and the Hongkong Bank had its lions; there seemed to be no adequate unifying feature.

The second factor was the Marine Midland merger. As the Bank's U.S. public affairs consultants had warned, it was difficult to describe the Hongkong Bank, the Group, HSBC, concisely or cope with the several variant presentations of the basic name. For an initial review the Bank brought in both Hill and Knowlton's Corporate Identity Division and Hong Kong's Henry Steiner, who, as local consultant and designer of the Bank's annual reports, had already achieved some standardization.

Following the initial report, the bank commissioned Steiner to make specific recommendations; these would provide the basis of the new corporation image,

Figure 18.2 Hexagon and HongkongBank designs

including 'HongkongBank' and the hexagon logo. Traditionalists considered the Bank had been fortunate; it might like so many other diversified multinationals have become a set of initials. And it has been permitted to keep its lions – both sculptured and adopted.[d]

There were still other developments in 1980. The Hongkong Bank Foundation was established by Trust Deed with an initial contribution of $10 million – the

---

[d] The adopted lions are Krishna, the Gir lion, and his mate, Juna, sponsored by the Bentong Branch of the Hongkong Bank at the Zoo Negara, Federation of Malaysia. Every child visiting the zoo on Lion Day, 1983, was presented with a lion mask, a colouring contest entry form, a Hongkong Bank souvenir, and a special Lion Stick ice-cream coupon, redeemable, one assumes, on sight.

Board gave the Chairman authorization to transfer a further $40 million without consultation. The Foundation would reach $100 million the following year; it would be hindered by the fall in share prices, but by 1984 it would regain its intended capital worth.

At an entirely different level, a more tax effective property holding structure was designed with virtually separate companies for each property, held by property holding companies operating out of Nassau and held ultimately by the Hongkong and Shanghai Bank in Hong Kong. The estimated savings would be $14 million. At the same time certain properties were revalued to market less depreciation to improve the capital/assets ratio.

London operations and property management were restructured using HSBC Holdings UK, under HSBC Holdings, BV, in turn under Kellett, NV, The United Kingdom holdings company held HSBC Trustee Company, Gatechurch Property Management, Gatewood Investments, Ltd (for North Sea Oil operations), and Antony Gibbs Holdings, Ltd, which in turn held Antony Gibbs and Sons, Ltd. A corporate chain was also set up by Hongkong Shanghai (Shipping), Ltd in Nassau to operate through Wayfoong Shipping Services, Ltd. These operations can all be rationalized and grouped, as was done in Chapter 15 for earlier corporate development, but such a study is not yet part of 'history'.

Several relevant topics have been referred to in previous chapters. The Iloilo office, for example, was closed; Mandaluyong, Pasig, was opened. There were new developments. The Bank became involved in North Sea Oil operations through an equity participation in Cliff Oil (HK), Ltd. As for geographical expansion, the Bank opened in Fukuoka, expanded in Chile and Macau, decided to move quickly relative to an office in Milan, and set up yet another property chain from Wayhong (Bahamas), Ltd.

The history would seem in danger of becoming a (partial) chronicle without analysis. The solution is therefore to present main currents briefly, to describe the accounts, to follow threads, both corporate and personal, and to examine the final succession.

THE BANK'S ACCOUNTS, 1980–1984

This is not a financial analysis.

Background comments

Carefully calculated surveys of the Hongkong Bank have estimated that true profits, that is, profits before transfers to inner reserves, may have been 60% in excess of published profits. However the basis for this history has been the published accounts of the Bank, supplemented with indications as to the Bank's true financial position in periods when the difference had a significant meaning for the standing of the Bank, indeed, at times for the Bank's future. This procedure was possible because the Bank opened its Archives without reservation. If and when the Hongkong Bank moves to a policy of full disclosure, the new information will not be first published within the text of a commissioned history.

The structure of the Group, the Bank as holding company and operating bank, the intra-Group transfers, the layers of holding companies, the decisions made for tax purposes are all understandable at a descriptive level. An attempt to go behind the published figures, however, should only be attempted by those particularly qualified to do so.

In 1980 HSBC had completed a period of extraordinary growth. Net published profits doubled between 1960 and 1967, 1967 and 1971, 1971 and 1975, 1975 and 1978, and 1978 and 1980. This indicates quite clearly an accelerating rate of growth; true net earnings were considerably higher. This growth was internally financed; the corporation had no long-term debt and there had not been a rights issue since 1921. Despite warnings from Michael Sandberg that this rate of profit could not be maintained, some observers predicted that profits would double again at least by 1984. This was not achieved. The Bank's successes in 1980 and 1981 were to be followed by setbacks which, while leaving the Bank in an admittedly improved position, did not permit the global advance on all fronts which was part of Sandberg's long-term strategy.

In 1984 the Hongkong Bank was the fourteenth largest bank in the free world on the basis of its published shareholders' funds. This is a sounder measure than market capitalization of assets, even though, for a short period and on that basis the Bank had ranked first in the world.

Hong Kong had been enjoying one of its periodic land booms, and this had affected the price of all shares; although by 1980 the Hong Kong dollar was already declining from its 1977 peak value against the U.S. dollar, it was still approximately $5.14. In September 1982, the British Prime Minister, Margaret Thatcher, visited China and the '1997 issue' came into public focus, perhaps for the first time. The uncertainty caused a fall in the value of the dollar, although the exchange rate was eventually stabilized in 1984 and effectively linked to the U.S. dollar at approximately $7.80; stock market prices, which had fallen from the July 1981 Hang Seng Index high of 1810 to 901 (July 1964 = 100), began to recover, averaging 1,200 in the fourth quarter. The Bank's year-end accounts were published at the following exchange rates: 1981, $5.68; 1982, $6.50; 1983, $7.78; 1984, $7.82.

Although the Hong Kong economy remained supported by a growth in the China trade and domestic exports increased 26% and 32% in 1983 and 1984 respectively (14% and 17% in real terms), with the property market depressed

Table 18.2 *The Hongkong and Shanghai Banking Corporation Capital and dividends, 1980–1984*

(in billions of dollars except as stated otherwise)

Year	Assets	Capital resources					Shares				Book value $	Original holding			Dividend/Share	
		Paid up capital	Reserve Fund[c]	P & L A/c	Totals[a] (i)	(ii)	Capitalization issues[a] x for y	Number (million)	Nominal value $	Per share		(number)	$ (000)	as published $	pub-original holding $ (000)
1946	2.1	0.02	0.10	—	0.1		—	0.16	125.0	742.8		1.0	0.7	48.5	0.05
1961	7.7	0.08	0.24	—	0.3		—	3.16	25.0	101.6		12.5	1.3	12.1	0.15
1979	125.3	1.73	1.64	0.3	3.7	4.2	1 for 2	692.91	2.5	5.4		2,630.8	18.8	0.74	1.95
1980	243.0	2.8	7.2	0.4	10.3	13.0	3 for 5	1,114.2[e]	2.5	9.3		4,209.2	24.4	0.65	1.71
1981	304.2	3.9	9.5	0.6	14.1	17.3[b]	1 for 4	1,559.9[f]	2.5	9.0		5,261.5	29.6	0.64	3.37
1982	379.2	5.2	8.4	2.0	15.6	22.7	1 for 3	2,079.9[g]	2.5	7.5		7,015.4	32.9	0.55	3.86
1983	470.3	5.7	10.9	2.9	19.6	28.8	1 for 10	2,287.9	2.5	8.6		7,716.9	41.3	0.55	4.24
1984	481.6	7.2	11.4	2.3	20.9	31.5	1 for 4	2,859.9	2.5	7.3		9,646.1	44.0	0.46	4.44

(i) Published HSBC shareholder equity, comprised of paid-up capital + Reserve Fund + balance on P & L Account.
(ii) Total Group 'capital' resources:: (i) + minority interests in subsidiary companies + long-term borrowing.

[a] For reconciliation see Table 18.2A.
[b] Long-term borrowings do not appear until the 1982 Annual Report, and the 1981 figures were amended; this amendment is not given here, see Table 18.2A.
[c] Includes the Share Premium Account, see Table 18.2B.
[d] Read this column as follows, e.g. for [1980]: The paid-up capital was in part the consequence of a capitalization issue [3 for 5] during [1980], contributing to the number of shares as shown in the next column; for other factors involved, see special notes; see also Table 18.2C.
[e] Increase also due in part to issue of new shares to former shareholders of Antony Gibbs Holdings, Ltd.
[f] Increase also due in part to rights issue.
[g] Increase also due in part to balance of rights issue.

876

Table 18.2A *The Hongkong and Shanghai Banking Corporation Capital and dividends, 1980–1984*
Capital reconciliation

(in billions of dollars)

Year	(i)	+Minority interests	+Long-term borrowing MMBI	+Long-term borrowing Total	= (ii)
1979	3.7	0.468	—	0	4.2
1980	10.3	2.658	—	0	13.0
1981	14.1	3.209	1.754	1.808	19.1[a]
1982	15.6	3.962	3.051	3.186	22.4
1983	19.6	5.725	3.209	3.487	28.8
1984	20.9	6.223	4.170	4.438	31.5

(i) Published HSBC shareholder equity, comprised of paid-up capital + Reserve Fund + balance on P&L Account.

(ii) Total Group 'capital' resources: (i) + minority interests in subsidiary companies + long-term borrowing.

[a] Long-term borrowing for 1981 appears first in 1982 Annual report and is therefore not incorporated into other tables in this chapter on the general principle that readjustments are not made for retroactive revaluations.

the demand for loans increased slowly and interest rates remained low. The Hongkong Bank was revealed as exposed to serious losses on loans and advances, especially to the Carrian Group; the Bank's architecturally brilliant, but expensive new head office building was subject to much adverse but ill-informed comment. Once again the Bank found itself completing in depressed times a building which had been planned with community encouragement in boom times. The Bank's new Shanghai building had provoked similar comments in 1875.

Not surprisingly the price of the Bank's shares reached a high of over $18.00 (compared to published book value of $11.60) in 1980; prices declined very sharply in 1982 and were consistently below book value until the revival in 1986.

With this brief background some specific comments on Tables 18.2–5 should prove useful.

Accounting changes
The motivation for accounting changes would appear to have been (i) recognition of the desirability to conform to general bank accounting practices and (ii) the need to improve the capital ratios – the two were not unrelated. The

Table 18.2B *The Hongkong and Shanghai Banking Corporation*
Capital and dividends, 1980–1984
Reserve Fund and Share Premium Account reconciliation

(in billions of dollars)

Year-end			Of which: Share Premium
1979 Reserve Fund		1.636	0.000[a]
1980			
−Capitalization	(1.039)		
+from retained profits	0.209		
+from inner reserves	0.830		
+revaluation of property	5.187		
+increase in Share Premium Account	0.065		
+from current income	0.150		
+other adjustments	0.118	5.520	
1980 Reserve Fund		7.156	0.065
1981			
−Capitalization	(0.696)		
+from Share Premium Account	0.065		
+from inner reserves	0.400		
+from retained profits	0.231		
+net increase Share Premium Account	1.562		
+other adjustments	0.822	2.384	
1981 Reserve Fund		9.540	1.562
1982			
−adjust end-81 figures	(0.461)		
+exchange adjustment	0.078		
−Capitalization	(1.300)[b]		
+from inner reserves	0.068		
+from retained profits	0.440		
+other adjustments	0.012	1.162	
1982 Reserve Fund		8.378	0.262
1983			
+Exchange adjustments	0.158		
−Capitalization	(0.520)[c]		
+from inner reserves	2.420		
+from retained profits	0.504		
+other adjustments	0.007	2.569	
1983 Reserve Fund		10.944	0.00
1984			
−Exchange adjustments	(0.013)		
−Capitalization	(1.430)		
+from retained profits	1.947		
−other adjustments	(0.005)	0.499	
1984 Reserve Fund		11.443	0.00

[a] Share Premium Account = $359,000 only
[b] from Share Premium Account
[c] of which $262 million from Share Premium Account

Table 18.2C *The Hongkong and Shanghai Banking Corporation Capital and dividends, 1980–1984*
Paid-up capital and number of shares

Year-end		Shares issued (billion)		Paid-up capital (billions of $)	
1979 Shares/Paid-up capital			0.693		1.732
1980					
+bonus issue, 3 for 5	0.416		1.039		
+to Antony Gibbs shareholders	0.006	0.421	0.014	1.054	
1980 Shares/Paid-up capital			1.114		2.786
1981					
+bonus issue, 1 for 4	0.278		0.696		
+rights issue, 3 for 20	0.167	0.445	0.417	1.113	
1981 Shares/Paid-up capital			1.559		3.899
1982					
+bonus issue, 1 for 3	0.520		1.300		
+balance of rights issue	0.000[a]	0.521	0.001	1.301	
1982 Shares/Paid-up Capital			2.080		5.200
1983					
+bonus issue, 1 for 10	0.208	0.208	0.520	0.520	
1983 Shares/Paid-up capital			2.288		5.720
1984					
+bonus issue, 1 for 4	0.572	0.572	1.430	1.430	
1984 Shares/Paid-up capital			2.859		7.150

[a] $400,000

Hongkong Bank continued during the problems of 1983–1984 to make immediate provisions for bad or doubtful debts as it had in 1874–1875; the present provisions were probably more than offset by exchange profits in inner reserves during the years in question.

Coupled with the major changes relative to property account (see above) was the decision to depreciate premises at 2% and furniture on a straight line basis over its lifetime – previously, property had been written down as quickly as possible to zero and furniture had been written off immediately.

Table 18.3 *The Hongkong and Shanghai Banking Corporation Group consolidated and Hongkong Bank assets compared, 1980–1984*

(in billions of dollars)

	Group			Hongkong Bank				Assets (1946 = 100)			
								Group		Bank	
Year	Assets	Total Capital[b] Account	Capital/ assets %	Assets	Bank assets/ Group assets %	Share- holders' funds	Capital/ assets %	Index	incr. %	Index	incr. %
1946	2.1	0.1	5.8	2.1	100.0	0.1	5.8	100		100	
1961	7.7	0.3	4.2	5.4	70.2	0.3	5.6	373		262	
1979	125.3	4.2[c]	3.3	80.7	64.4	3.4	4.2	6112		3935	
1979	109.5[a]	4.2[c]	3.8	70.5[a]	64.4	3.4	5.7	5339		3357	
1980	243.0	13.0	5.3	104.3	42.9	9.2	8.8	11848	122	5090	52
1981	304.2	17.3	5.7	135.5	44.5	12.2	9.0	14833	25	6603	30
1982	379.2	22.8	6.0	163.5	43.1	12.9	7.9	18489	25	7980	21
1983	470.3	28.8	6.1	194.3	41.3	15.8	8.1	22931	24	9483	19
1984	481.6	31.5	6.5	206.4	42.9	16.8	8.1	23482	2	10073	6

[a] After adjustment to Engagements on Behalf of Customers Account; compatible with 1980–1985.
[b] As defined for column (ii) in Table 18.2.
[c] After adjustment explained in Tables 18.2 and 18.2A.

The Hongkong and Shanghai Banking Corporation

Consolidated Profit and Loss Account for the year ended 31 December 1984

1983 HK$m		Note		1984 HK$m
2,855	Net profit of The Hongkong and Shanghai Banking Corporation and its subsidiary companies	3		2,893
377	Share of net profits of associated companies			482
3,232				3,375
	Deduct:			
740	Profit attributable to minority interests in subsidiary companies			784
2,492	Profit attributable to the shareholders of The Hongkong and Shanghai Banking Corporation	4		2,591
	Deduct: Transfer to reserves			
250	The Bank		250	
254	Subsidiary and associated companies		267	
1,258	Dividends paid and proposed	5	1,316	1,833
730				758
2,028	Balance brought forward		2,922	
—	Deduct: Transfer to Reserve Fund		1,430	1,492
164	Exchange adjustments			20
2,922	Retained profits carried forward	6		2,270
HK$0.87	Earnings per share	7		HK$0.91

13 The Hongkong and Shanghai Banking Corporation, 1984, as seen through the published accounts
—from the 1984 *Annual Report*.
(i) Consolidated profit and loss account.

The Hongkong and Shanghai Banking Corporation

1983 HK$m		Note	1984 HK$m	1984 £m	1984 US$m
5,720	Share Capital	8	7,150	787	914
8,592	Reserve Fund	9	8,842	973	1,130
1,508	Retained profits	6	842	92	108
15,820			16,834	1,852	2,152
	Liabilities				
11,124	Hong Kong currency notes in circulation	11	11,754	1,293	1,503
155,588	Current, deposit and other accounts	12	166,410	18,311	21,278
8,618	Amounts due to subsidiary companies		6,646	731	850
846	Proposed dividend		887	98	113
231	Balance of drafts, remittances, etc. in transit between offices		110	12	14
2,058	Acceptances on behalf of customers		3,722	410	476
HK$194,285			HK$206,363	£22,707	US$26,386

F R Frame, *Secretary*
26 March 1985

Balance Sheet at 31 December 1984

1983 HK$m		Note	1984 HK$m	1984 £m	1984 US$m
	Assets				
47,962	Cash and short-term funds		49,839	5,484	6,373
21,266	Time deposits with banks payable within twelve months		19,328	2,127	2,471
9,115	Trade bills discounted and bankers' certificates of deposit purchased		9,418	1,036	1,204
11,064	Hong Kong Government certificates of indebtedness	11	11,694	1,287	1,495
2,172	Investments	14	2,987	329	382
70,752	Advances to customers and other accounts	13	77,307	8,506	9,885
22,730	Amounts due from subsidiary companies		23,159	2,548	2,961
185,061			193,732	21,317	24,771
5,856	Investments in subsidiary companies	16	6,658	733	851
223	Investments in associated companies	17	219	24	28
772	Bank premises and other properties	18	794	87	102
315	Furniture, plant and equipment	18	1,238	136	158
2,058	Liabilities of customers for acceptances		3,722	410	476
HK$194,285			HK$206,363	£22,707	US$26,386

Directors
M G R Sandberg
A J Archer
L S Dunn

(ii) The Hongkong Bank, balance sheet, December 31, 1984.

The Hongkong and Shanghai Banking Corporation

1983 HK$m		Note	1984 HK$m	1984 £m	1984 US$m
5,720	Share Capital	8	7,150	787	914
10,944	Reserve Fund	9	11,443	1,259	1,463
2,922	Retained profits	6	2,270	250	290
19,586			20,863	2,296	2,667
5,725	Minority interests in subsidiary companies		6,223	685	796
3,487	Long-term borrowings	10	4,438	488	568
28,798			31,524	3,469	4,031
	Other liabilities				
11,124	Hong Kong currency notes in circulation	11	11,754	1,293	1,503
411,280	Current, deposit and other accounts	12	422,403	46,479	54,009
846	Proposed dividend		887	98	113
336	Balance of drafts, remittances, etc. in transit between offices		137	15	18
17,931	Acceptances on behalf of customers		14,902	1,640	1,905
HK$470,315			HK$481,607	£52,994	US$61,579

F R Frame, *Secretary*
26 March 1985

Consolidated Balance Sheet at 31 December 1984

1983 HK$m		Note	1984 HK$m	1984 £m	1984 US$m
	Assets				
110,104	Cash and short-term funds	13	105,784	11,640	13,527
52,060	Time deposits with banks payable within twelve months		42,673	4,695	5,456
17,967	Trade bills discounted and bankers' certificates of deposit purchased		18,257	2,009	2,334
11,064	Hong Kong Government certificates of indebtedness	11	11,694	1,287	1,495
20,535	Investments	14	19,239	2,117	2,460
223,644	Advances to customers and other accounts	15	249,177	27,418	31,860
435,374			446,824	49,166	57,132
2,901	Investments in associated companies	17	3,101	341	397
13,192	Bank premises and other properties	18	14,784	1,627	1,890
917	Furniture, plant and equipment	18	1,996	220	255
17,931	Liabilities of customers for acceptances		14,902	1,640	1,905
HK$470,315			HK$481,607	£52,994	US$61,579

Directors
M G R Sandberg
A J Archer
L S Dunn

(iii) The Hongkong and Shanghai Banking Corporation, consolidated balance sheet, December 31, 1984.

14 The 1986 head office building under construction.
—from Ian Lambot and Gillian Chambers, *One Queen's Road Central.*

15 Chief executives:
Sir Michael Sandberg, CBE, 1977–1986.

Table 18.4A *The Hongkong Bank*
Selected balance sheet items and ratios, 1980–1984

(in billions of dollars or percentages)

Year	(i) Assets	(ii) Index (1946 = 100)	(iii) Liquid assets[a]	(iv) Ratio (i)/(iii)	(v) Excess note issue	(vi) Total deposits	(vii) Liquidity ratio[b] %	(viii) Loans etc.	(ix) Loan/deposit ratio %	(x) Investments (quoted)	(xi) Trade bills discounted, CDs
1961	4.8	233	1.3	27	0.8	3.4	38	1.8	54	.5	.7
1979	80.7	3935	33.9	42	6.1	55.8	61	22.5	40	0.97	4.6
1980	104.3	5090	45.2	43	7.3	72.8	62	32.1	44	1.07	5.2
1981	135.5	6603	59.4	44	8.6	103.5	57	41.4	40	1.15	6.3
1982	163.5	7980	72.3	44	9.9	131.3	55	54.3	41	1.41	6.7
1983	194.3	9483	78.3	40	11.1	155.6	50	70.8	46	1.86	9.1
1984	206.4	10073	78.6	38	11.7	166.4	47	77.3	46	2.66	9.4

[a] The composition of this item changes: it begins with cash in hand and balances with other banks + money at call and short notice + British and other govt bills + trade bills discounted; it ends as cash and short term funds + time deposits with banks payable within 12 months + trade bills discounted and bankers' certificates of deposit purchased.

[b] The ratio is: liquid assets (iii) ÷ [(vi), that is, current, deposit, and other accounts including inner reserves + authorized note issue].

Table 18.4B *The Hongkong and Shanghai Banking Corporation*
Selected Group consolidated balance sheet items and ratios, 1980–1984

(in billions of dollars or percentages)

Year	(i) Assets	(ii) Index (1946 = 100)	(iii) Liquid assets[b]	(iv) Ratio (i)/(iii)	(v) Excess note issue	(vi) Total deposits	(vii) Liquidity ratio[c] %	(viii) Loans etc.	(ix) Loan/deposit ratio %	(x) Investments (quoted)	(xi) Trade bills discounted, CDs
1961	4.8	233	1.3	27	0.8	3.4	37.5	1.8	54	0.5	0.7
1979	125.3 −15.8[a]	6110									
(adj)	109.5	5339	53.3	49	6.1	97.4	54.4	42.7	44	3.7	10.2
1980	243.0	11848	94.5	39	7.3	216.1	43.7	114.3	53	11.1	12.6
1981	304.2	14833	119.6	39	8.6	269.7	44.3	145.3	54	11.7	14.0
1982	379.2	18489	148.5	39	9.8	335.5	44.3	182.6	54	13.3	13.0
1983	470.3	22931	180.1	38	11.1	411.3	43.8	223.6	54	18.1	18.0
1984	481.6	23482	166.7	35	11.7	422.4	39.5	249.2	59	16.9	18.3

[a] Adjustment to eliminate certain Engagements on Behalf of Customers; compatible with 1980–1985 accounts.
[b] The composition of this item changes: it begins with cash in hand and balances with other banks + money at call and short notice + British and other govt bills + trade bills discounted; it ends as cash and short term funds + time deposits with banks payable within 12 months + trade bills discounted and bankers' certificates of deposit purchased.
[c] The ratio is: liquid assets (iii) ÷ [(vi), that is, current, deposit, and other accounts including reserves + authorized note issue].

Table 18.5 *The Hongkong and Shanghai Banking Corporation Profits, ratios, and dividends, 1980–1984*

(in billions of dollars)

Year	Assets	Total capital[b]	Capital/ assets %	Share- holders' equity[c]	Profit[a]	Profit Capital	Return on assets %	To dividends	Payout ratio %	To Reserve Fund from P&L A/c[e]	Reserve Fund[f]
1979	109.5[a]	4.2	3.8	3.7	1.014	27.4	0.93	0.513	50.6	0.177	1.636
1980	243.0	13.0	5.3	10.3	1.431	13.9	0.59	0.724	50.6	0.359	7.156
1981	304.2	17.3	5.7	14.1	2.003[g]	14.2	0.66	0.996	49.7	0.231	9.540
1982	379.2	22.4	5.9	15.6	2.357[h]	15.1	0.62	1.144	48.5	0.440	8.378
1983	470.3	28.8	6.1	19.6	2.492	12.7	0.53	1.258	50.5	0.504	10.944
1984	481.6	31.5	6.5	20.9	2.591	12.4	0.54	1.316	50.8	1.947	11.443

[a] Adjusted as noted in Table 18.3.
[b] HSBC shareholders' funds as defined for (ii) in Table 18.2.
[c] HSBC shareholders' funds as defined for (i) in Table 18.2.
[d] Attributable to shareholders of HSBC.
[e] Allocations to the Reserve Fund are not necessarily from current earnings as such; they are part of the 'capitalization process'; there were other allocations to the reserves of subsidiary companies.
[f] Includes the Share Premium Account. Changes in Reserve Fund attributable to other factors in addition to transfer from Profit and Loss Account.
[g] $2.116 billion by definition effective with 1982 accounts; see note 'h'.
[h] Equity accounting adopted: the total earnings of major associated companies are now included in the Group Consolidated Profit and Loss Account, previously only dividends received were included.

Provisions for doubtful debts were deducted from 'advances to customers and other accounts'; in 1980 general provisions were also deducted, a further negative impact on the total assets figure. Securities were no longer listed 'below market'; that cushion, so much used in the inter-war period, was a luxury the Bank's ratios could not afford. Equity accounting was applied to the profits of major associated companies effective with the 1982 accounts. This would eliminate one source of understatement of net earnings. The assets of subsidiary companies had been equity-accounted since 1975.

Although the six pages of notes attached to the accounts would appear extraordinary to Hongkong Bankers of the 1950s and before, they are minimal compared to the information provided by, for example, Marine Midland Banks, Inc. Nevertheless, they are useful. On the assumption that inner reserves transactions are handled consistently, a reasonable assumption in view of U.S. regulatory concern, the progress of HSBC can be determined from its published accounts.

Capital accounts

The Bank continued its policy of capitalization of reserves. As Table 18.2B shows, this capitalization was usually offset by transfers from retained earnings and from inner reserves. In 1980, 1981, and 1982 the scrip or bonus issue was partially financed from the Share Premium Account which had been funded from the premium at which new shares had been issued to former Antony Gibbs shareholders and from the premium of $9.50 per share on the 1981 rights issue.

There had from time to time been talk of a rights issue by both G.M. Sayer and Michael Sandberg. Clearly the reason for such an issue would be the need to improve the capital/assets ratio, and despite the improvements made by rearranging the accounts in 1980 the Board agreed that a rights issue was needed and should be made in 1981 on a three for twenty basis at a price of $12.00 (see Table 18.2C); it was underwritten by Wardley's and, as in 1921, was payable in two tranches.

A further increase in published shareholders' funds was achieved in 1983 by a transfer from inner reserves which was not immediately capitalized. The apparent decline in the Reserve Fund in 1981 was due to the draw down of the Share Premium Account as the source of funds for the bonus issue; the transfer from inner reserves in 1983 provided for a net growth of the Reserve Fund and a consequently improved capital/assets ratio.

The improved ratio in 1984 to a high of 6.5% was partly due to the decline in rate of increase of assets. The Bank was, moreover, aware that, with several bank failures in Hong Kong and a less optimistic atmosphere, there was discussion of new banking legislation which might specify prudential ratios.

The HSBC's total capital accounts already included long-term borrowing (see Table 18.2A), principally by MMBI, but also by the Hongkong Bank of Canada. In 1985 HSBC, the parent company, borrowed long-term for primary capital, with two flotations, in July and November, of undated Floating Rate Notes at $\frac{1}{4}$ of 1% over the three-month London Interbank Mean Rate totalling US$800 million (= $6.24 billion) thereby increasing total Group capital by 20% over its end-1984 level and changing the capital/assets ratio (other factors remaining unchanged) from the 6.5% in Table 18.5 to a strong 7.8%. (Further flotations to a total of $1.2 billion were made in 1986.) The Hongkong and Shanghai Banking Corporation had become 'geared' for the first time in its history.

Other accounts

Table 18.3 indicates clearly how the percentage of Bank to 'Group', that is, HSBC, assets declined from 64.4% to 42.9% as a result of the merger with MMBI. The index numbers also show how both the Group's and the Bank's rate of growth declined, especially in 1984. In 1980, as Table 18.4A indicates, the Hongkong Bank had a liquidity ratio of 62%, the Group's ratio was 43.7%, making it one of the most liquid international banks in the world.

Other ratios are marred by lack of disclosure, but they are those of an efficiently performing bank.

The figures presented suggest that The Hongkong and Shanghai Banking Corporation had met the cost of Marine Midland without difficulty, that its capital base had been restored from inner reserves, retained earnings, capital borrowing, and a rights issue, and that it was in a strong position in 1981 to continue the policies of financial and geographical diversification which were manifested in the MMBI partnership. This is the theme of the concluding sections.

FOLLOWING THE THREADS TO 1984 – (1) CORPORATE DEVELOPMENT

In the Fall of 1980 the Hongkong Bank had recruited Bernard Asher as General Manager, Planning. His long-range assignments were almost immediately set aside in view of the Bank's offer to the Royal Bank of Scotland Group; Asher was needed back in London to plan and coordinate the Bank's efforts. Dramatic as those events were and serious as was their failure, RBSG was but part of the HSBC's global strategy, and Asher's ability to contribute signalled a new level of understanding in Head Office.

Specialists had been brought in successfully for many years, but a corporate planner impinged directly on the traditional atmosphere at the top. Sandberg and his immediate contemporaries had not, it is true, been socialized by a long period in London Office, but they had experienced the Peak Mess and they shared the heritage. They were in a new age and had had over twenty years to adjust to a new world of banking. Nevertheless, a chief executive is entitled to his own team; he would not wish to work with a senior officer who was 'not one of us'.

The question, however, was the definition of 'us'. For the Hongkong Bank, to be one of 'us' had long meant time as a London junior and years of apprenticeship in the East. For a multinational financial group, 'us' had to be redefined to strip the concept of its particularistic implications. Experience within the corporation did not necessarily provide career executives with a diversity of expertise sufficient to meet all top management requirements, but the deficiencies could not be made up by the employment of an expert who was excluded from a full participatory role. The Bank's political advisers inter-war were respected by the Chief Managers, but they handed in their reports and returned to their specialist activities; they were not part of a banking management team.

The corporate planning officer had now to be part of a coordinated functioning team, in this case in Head Office itself. The ability of the chief executive to redefine 'us' was one of the management changes sought for – and found – by officers of the Office of the Comptroller of the Currency in their Hong Kong visit in October 1979.

Despite long-term plans a corporation can be faced with sudden opportunities and unexpected frustrations which make it difficult for an observer to detect the intended course. Thus the Bank's sudden decision to bid for the Royal Bank of Scotland Group in 1981 can appear opportunistic, whereas it was, and had to be, a basic part of the Bank's strategy pulled out of an ideal time sequence through no fault of the Bank.

Although the discussion which follows is but a brief survey, restricted in most cases to merely listing the major developments, there is a context. The Hongkong Bank Group was seeking (i) to complete its global policy relative to asset distribution and major deposit bases, (ii) to bring together a total range of financial services within a coordinated Group, and (iii) to take geographical factors into consideration, so that the Group would become truly 'global'. Marine Midland had confirmed the wisdom of planning – Sandberg had decided to approach MMBI and not Crocker National; with the employment of Asher and the establishment of an appropriate department, planning had been brought into the corporation; the success was integrated institutionally, and the events to be described should be read in this context.

Table 18.6 *The Hongkong and Shanghai Banking Corporation International network, 1984*

	Offices		Offices
Asia and Pacific		*Americas (cont.)*	
Australia	11	United States	317
Brunei Darussalam	10	Venezuela	1
China	5		
Hong Kong	411	*Europe*	
India	24	Belgium	1
Indonesia	5	Channel Islands	4
Japan	7	France	4
Republic of Korea	4	Gibraltar	1
Macau	7	Greece	1
Malaysia	44	Republic of Ireland	1
Mauritius	11	Italy	2
New Zealand	3	Netherlands	3
Pakistan	2	Spain	1
Papua New Guinea	2	Sweden	1
Philippines	4	Switzerland	2
Singapore	25	United Kingdom	34
Solomon Islands	1	West Germany	6
Sri Lanka	1		
Taiwan	1	*Middle East*	
Thailand	3	Bahrain	9
Vanautu	2	Cyprus	86
		Djibouti	1
Americas		Egypt	3
Argentina	2	Jordan	5
Bahamas	6	Lebanon	10
Brazil	2	Oman	6
Canada	1	Qatar	2
Chile	4	United Arab Emirates	18
Colombia	1	Yemen Arab Republic	1
Mexico	2	Saudi Arabia	24
Panama	2		

Geographical distribution

One way of stating the changes which had occurred in the Hongkong Bank Group between 1962 and 1984 is to note the practical difficulty of providing a comprehensive list of Group offices providing financial and banking services world-wide. For the 1960s and 1970s the list in this history excluded the British Bank of the Middle East and the offices of such subsidiaries as Wardley, but as the range of financial services widens and a more comprehensive picture of the Group as opposed to the Bank, narrowly defined, is required, the list must somehow be expanded and rationalized. At the end of 1984 there were 1,000 offices in 55 countries, as summarized in Table 18.6. As this history has been focused primarily on the Bank itself, the numbers may appear surprising; the figures are not directly comparable with those which could be derived from Table 13.3.

The growth of the Hongkong Bank Group is, however, obvious. In the summary which follows, only the major developments can be mentioned. Details have been left to another history.

General developments

The Hongkong Bank opened its own office in Switzerland, in Zurich, in 1980; the Group were now represented in the money centres of Frankfurt, Geneva, London, and Paris; the old Hamburg Branch remained and a second office was opened in Paris in 1985. The European network was broadened in 1982 with the Bank's new office in Milan, with a representative office in Stockholm in 1984, and a branch in Madrid in 1985. As a British overseas bank, the Hongkong Bank had pioneered in Europe in the nineteenth century, but its plans for expansion in the early 1920s were never carried through and its immediate post-war survey of Scandinavian opportunities proved premature. With the Bank's long history in the Philippines, its late arrival in Madrid may seem surprising, but in the past trade finance with the East as the hub had been the dominant consideration, and the Bank had played a role in Philippine-U.S. and Philippine-U.K. trade.

The Iloilo office was closed (see Chapter 14) and the licence transferred to the new industrial development in Pasig, Manila. There was expansion in the State of Brunei, and the establishment of a Representative Office in Taipei, Taiwan, which became a branch in 1984. The Bank's move into Korea had been tentative, with a Representative Office and participation in the Korea International Merchant Bank, but in 1982 permission was received to open a branch in Busan – again for trade finance – and the right to the Seoul office was not withdrawn. The Government needed a representative on hand, with the result that, exceptionally, the Hongkong Bank had two locations in the Republic of South Korea. The Seoul office subsequently became a fully operating branch.

The Bank's China Desk evolved into a major country or Area Office responsible for the operations of offices in Shenzhen (1982), Xiamen (1984), and Wuhan (1985); the Shenzhen office was up-graded to a full branch in 1984. There were then six offices in the People's Republic of China – there had been fourteen pre-war (see Table 9.1). The role of the Hong Kong Head Office, where the China Desk had become the separately incorporated 'Hongkong Bank China Services, Ltd', remained important, however, both for research back-up and for initial contacts. And there remained the Hong Kong based finance of trade and joint ventures.

Elsewhere in Asia, the Bank returned to Pakistan with a branch in Karachi in 1982, but expectations relative to branching in Sri Lanka did not develop (see Chapter 14). A representative office was opened in Fukuoka, Kyushu, recalling the years of the Bank's previous activity through its nearby Nagasaki branch, 1891–1929. Four new branches were established in Macau in 1983 and the Bank established a 'head office' in the territory for the development of full retail banking. Restrictions on new branches limited the Hongkong Bank's development in its other traditional areas of operation, for example, in Thailand. Nevertheless, in the Federation of Malaysia, the Hongkong Bank, under the management of M.J. Calvert, took maximum advantage of the opportunities available; it became the largest foreign bank in the nation.

The sale of Mercantile Bank Limited

In 1984 The Hongkong and Shanghai Banking Corporation sold the Mercantile Bank at a price in excess of its net asset value to Citibank, N.A. By this time it had become a virtual shell, with the exception of its office, sub-office, and licence in Bangkok, where it would continue to operate for an initial period under the Mercantile Bank name. The Mercantile's Hong Kong office became Hongkong Bank and customers were invited to remain; the Hongkong Bank also retained Mercantile Bank's historical archives. Even so, there remained loyalists who would have preferred some other wording than 'tidying up operation' for the virtual end of the Group's oldest exchange banking member.[e] The Indian and Japanese operations had been transferred to the Hongkong Bank at the end of 1982, Mauritius in 1983. The close-down in India was in three stages: (i) July to September 1982, establish the relationship between Mercantile Bank and HSBC, (ii) October to December, announce that the Hongkong Bank is coming to India, and (iii) January 1983 onwards the theme was 'HongkongBank has arrived!' In fact the Hongkong Bank had only just left; it had transferred its Indian branches to the Mercantile Bank in 1972 (see Chapter 13).

In Bangkok there had been a quick shuffle. The Hongkong Bank had moved to the Siam Center, leaving, as had the Mercantile Bank previously, its old site

---

[e] Mercantile Bank was chartered in 1857 as the Chartered Mercantile Bank of India, London and China and acquired by the HSBC in 1959. For a brief account, see my 'The Mercantile Bank's Royal Charter', in King, ed. *Asian Policy, History and Development* (Hong Kong, 1979), pp. 42–50, and the references to P.T. Lamb's history in the Bibliography.

by the river. The two sites would be developed into the de luxe Royal Orchid Hotel complex, in which the Hongkong Bank Group retained a 15% equity interest through Wayhong Properties, Ltd. The Bank cut back on its residential property, disposing of the Manager's home with its ties to the days of quiet living by the peaceful klongs, and then decided, in 1983 and in anticipation of the sale of the Mercantile, to switch the Hongkong Bank and the Mercantile Bank offices. To meet Thai banking regulations, this had to be, and was, accomplished overnight.

In 1984 the popularly revered Queen Rambhai-Barni, the consort of King Prachathipok, Rama VII, died; she had been a constituent of the Hongkong Bank for more than 50 years. S.W.P. Perry-Aldworth, Bangkok Accountant and Manager 1946–1953, recalled her visits to the Bangkok office and the reverence of the Thai staff as she inspected items held for her in the Bank. In her honour the Bank donated Baht 50,000 to the Vajira Hospital, one of her personal interests. The funds were to be used to furnish a private room; on the door would be a commemorative plate with the words, 'Donated by The Hongkong and Shanghai Banking Corporation in Memory of the beloved Queen Rambhai-Barni'.

In the days of ETCs and cost effectiveness, this was a reminder that the Hongkong Bank had been a pioneer in Siam and the bank of rulers and their ministers throughout the East.

The Americas and Australia
When I.H. Macdonald was established in New York as a resident executive director, his title covered 'the Americas', although HSBC's immediate preoccupation was with the United States and particularly with Marine Midland Banks. Thereafter there were three lines of development: (i) South America, especially Chile, (ii) Canada, and (iii) cooperative developments in the United States.

In 1980 A.M. Prado, who had joined the local Portuguese staff in Hong Kong, had become the Bank's first Macau Manager, and had moved on to become Representative in São Paulo, now became the first regional officer to join the International staff. In cooperation with the office in New York, with Macdonald and A.R. Petrie (East in 1951), who had been the first Manager in Kuching, Sarawak, Prado developed contacts in Chile. A branch was opened in Santiago in 1982 and a second in Valparaiso in 1983; in the latter city the Hongkong Bank had listed a merchant agent in 1865. There had been no further reference for 118 years.

The history of banking in both Australia and Canada had been influenced by the struggle to take away control of money and banking matters from the Imperial Treasury. The struggle had been won, not by Australia and Canada, since they did not exist as the relevant political entities, but by the individual colonies or provinces. The existing imperially chartered banks, for example, the Bank of British North America, were 'grandfathered'. With the establishment of united Commonwealth Governments, there developed a trend for nation-wide branching, which indeed had caught the imagination years earlier of George F. Rand of the Buffalo Marine Trust Company. But having seized control from the Treasury, the provincial Governments had not permitted entry to new overseas banks and the Commonwealth Governments had pursued the same policy.

The Hongkong Bank Group's development in Canada in the 1970s had been predicated on a change in legislation, which was eventually effected in 1980, and the Hongkong Bank of Canada was established in 1981 with head office in Vancouver and twelve branches elsewhere in Canada, its Group relations being coordinated at the top level through the Chairman, who was virtually *ex officio* the Bank's resident executive director in New York.

Change in Australia came one year later, but the HongkongBank of Australia, one of the first foreign banks to receive a licence under the new law, was not opened until 1986, when offices in Sydney, Melbourne, Brisbane, and Perth were established.

The Royal Bank of Scotland Group

Offers to purchase
There were four major United Kingdom clearing banks and there was a fifth, the Royal Bank of Scotland Group, including the venerable Royal Bank itself, founded by Royal charter in 1727, the largest of the three Scottish clearing banks, and Williams and Glyn's Bank, the fifth largest London clearing bank. If any bank intended to play a major role in Britain, the only practical way to achieve its purpose appeared to be the acquisition of the Royal Bank of Scotland Group. It was also apparently the case that the Bank of England would be unwilling to permit a foreign bank to acquire a British clearing bank; Muriel Siebert, the New York State Bank Superintendent, was allegedly told so in 1978. There were thus only three banks in the world that could have a practical interest: Lloyds Bank, which already had 16.4% of the ordinary capital of the Group, the Standard Chartered Bank, and The Hongkong and Shanghai Banking Corporation. If Lloyds be excluded because of monopoly considerations, that left only two.

These two inheritors of British overseas banking recognized that they needed to establish a U.S. dollar base and a European base. Both chose to move on the former first, and both were fatally delayed. For the Chartered Bank there was, however, a hiatus. Peter Graham was rebuffed by the Bank of California and, while he was planning his approach to the Union Bank of California, he met with Sir Michael Herries, sometime taipan of Jardine, Matheson and Co. and a former director of the Hongkong Bank, who had become the chairman of the Royal Bank of Scotland Group. Herries had in fact just taken over; he had his own internal priorities, but the suggestion of a combined British-based and overseas integrated operation under a single corporate cover seemed attractive – at a later date. Graham returned to his American strategy.

The Standard Chartered acquired the Union Bank in 1979, HSBC acquired Marine Midland in 1980. Graham and Sandberg then turned their minds to the execution of the final stage of their world strategies, but unfortunately only one (or, as it turned out, neither) could succeed.

In late 1980 there were rumours that Lloyds was seeking to acquire a larger interest in the Royal Bank of Scotland Group (RBSG). This forced the pace and Herries and Graham met again. Sandberg still felt the Bank's hands were tied; the final tranche of Marine Midland shares had not as yet been acquired; the deal had not been fully consummated and Sandberg was not yet prepared to initiate a major operation. He was actually in New York on March 19, 1981, when he was told of a rise in Royal Bank shares and the expectation of an announcement, relative to a take-over. While waiting for more authoritative information, Sandberg and Macdonald worked out a rough estimate of a reasonable price for a Group with 1980 assets of £6,147 million ($75,394 million), shareholders' funds of £495 million ($6,071 million), and after tax earnings per share of 30.7p ($3.77). Their rough conclusion: approximately 280 pence ($34.34) per share compared to the market price of RBSG of 88p ($10.79) prevailing before the pre-bid rise.

The Board of the RBSG announced that they and the Standard had reached an agreement their advisers felt 'fair and reasonable': for every five ordinary shares of RBSG, one share of Standard Chartered plus 50p cash. That worked out to 148p per share or just over half of Sandberg's desk top calculation. Sandberg's first reaction was to let it go; Standard Chartered had gone in first, obtained board approval, and cleared the transaction with the Bank of England.

Sandberg nevertheless concluded that the bid was inexplicably low, and he consequently resolved to make a counter offer. He felt he was not well received at the Bank of England; he felt he was not particularly welcome in Edinburgh. He recognized that, whatever else the Hongkong Bank's strategy might be, their offer had to be a 'blockbuster'; it had to be so high that it could not or at least would not be matched by the Standard Chartered. The Hongkong Bank's rights issue played no role in the timing or the decision; it was the price element which would not go away.

On April 9, 1981, the Hongkong Bank informed the RBSG board of its offer of eight shares of HSBC for five of RBSG, thus valuing the latter at 221p ($27.11) per share. This failed as a 'blockbuster'. At 214.6p ($26.32) the

Standard Chartered on April 23 came back with a revised offer which, critics claimed, topped, *under certain assumptions*, that of the Hongkong Bank. This revealed a weakness in the Hongkong Bank's position; the value of its offer depended on the market value of its shares; the price was declining, but in any case some questioned whether even in boom times the market could absorb the new shares should former RBSG shareholders decide to unload. This had been Michael Turner's concern during the first acquisitions in 1959.

Subsequent developments
The Hongkong Bank's offer was opposed by the Bank of England; they had agreed to the Chartered's first bid, and they were angered at being challenged, especially by a bank which offered twice the bid they had unwisely agreed to as being fair and reasonable. But the action of the Hongkong Bank in proceeding against the wishes of the central bank provided a weapon. The Hongkong Bank claimed that it would be a good citizen, that it would accept the central bank role of the Bank of England; but if this promise had any meaning, hostile observers were to argue, the Hongkong Bank should prove its intentions by withdrawing – it was a circular argument, a 'Catch-22' situation.

In the complex discussions which followed, much was made of the Hongkong Bank's overseas head office and the difficulty of ensuring an immediate response to the Governor's instructions. This first of all ignored more than a hundred years of Hongkong Bank cooperation with the Bank of England, and Sir Humphrey Atkins, Lord Privy Seal, stated clearly that anyone who claimed the Hongkong Bank were not British was incorrect. Secondly, the Bank of England's position contained some wishful thinking relative to the obedience of the major British clearing banks. In fact, Sandberg sought advice from the chairmen of two clearing banks; both advised him to move ahead.

On May 1, 1981, the Secretary for Trade and Industry referred the bids to the Monopolies and Mergers Commission. Here the Hongkong Bank and the equally frustrated Standard Chartered Bank fought shadow battles against unspecified charges based on unknown criteria, in contrast to the open approach to government typical of the United States. The Commission's report, published after the grant of a three-month extension to the normal six-month period allowed, issued a negative recommendation relative to both bids. The recommendation, which was not unanimous but which was subsequently supported by the Government, was based on two findings: the adverse effects (i) 'arising from the removal of ultimate control from Edinburgh...on career prospects, initiative and business enterprise in Scotland...damaging to the public interest of the United Kingdom as a whole' and (ii) of transferring, in the case of the Hongkong Bank's bid, 'ultimate control of a significant part of the clearing bank system outside the United Kingdom'. On this latter the Commission argued that there was a possible 'opening up of divergence of interest which would not otherwise arise' (pars. 12.16, 12.38–29). An almost petulant opposition by the Governor of the Bank of England and the unfathomable concerns of the Secretary of State for Scotland had been too much to overcome – at least, these, in the absence of any compelling argument in the Commission report, would seem to have been the deciding factors. In January 1982 the Hongkong Bank learned that it (and Standard Chartered) had failed. The European strategy lacked its major base. But more than this: 'Everyone', as Sandberg put it at the time, 'has lost.'

The Hongkong Bank's position
The events between March 1981 and January 1982 were dramatic, but, despite great efforts by Hongkong Bankers now considerably more experienced in acquisitions and the inevitable public scrutiny involved, the proposed transaction lacked those very qualities that had made the MMBI transaction successful. Briefly, the relevant HSBC/MMBI transaction features were (i) ideal timing, (ii) the development of a cooperative attitude, the 'spirit of Hawaii', (iii) the support of key political figures, and (iv) the dual banking system which permitted skirting an unfavourable regulator. Quite simply the Hongkong Bank had a proposal which met the MMBI's requirements: (i) capital injection and (ii) partnership.

In announcing the Standard Chartered's offer, the RBSG's board stated that 'they had felt that it would be in the best interests of shareholders, staff and customers if Royal Bank were to form an association with a financial institution which had a strong international presence to complement the Royal Bank's concentration in the U.K.'

The Hongkong Bank offered a concept which was termed 'Flagship Europe'. The Hongkong Bank offered a role in a partnership; the RBSG senior management professed to wanting neither the Flagship role nor the partnership, a position they defended only after redefining Europe to exclude the United Kingdom, thereby altering the sense of the Hongkong Bank's offer. The RBSG management did not wish to be the British/European base of a global banking group; they wanted to be an integral part of a British-based international bank. One could argue that the difference was one of emphasis, but this brings the problem to another level – under the circumstances there could be no quiet consideration of the relative merits. The RBSG board had taken a public position; it had been embarrassed by the higher bid; it was covered when the Standard Chartered matched it. The Hongkong Bank offer was dismissed as having no particular appeal sufficient to offset the Chartered Bank's financial and non-financial proposals.

But to go through the factors listed as positive in the MMBI merger: first, the *timing* was not ideal either for the Standard Chartered or for the Hongkong Bank; it was consequent to pressure from Lloyds Bank – the Hongkong Bank had targetted the Royal Bank of Scotland Group but it had been unable to go further; had the bid been higher, HSBC would not have intervened. Secondly, there had been, as already noted, no 'spirit of Hawaii'.

The Hongkong Bank had hoped that the Bank of England would remain neutral; it did not. The Hongkong Bank had hoped that its 'Scottish' background, both in origins and in staffing, coupled with its assurances of independent, partnership-style management from Edinburgh would engender Scottish support; it was clear that the Standard Chartered offer would tip the balance of power in favour of England. The Bank was partially successful; as between the Chartered and the Hongkong Bank, Scottish opinion favoured the Hongkong, but that in itself was insufficient. The Hongkong Bank could not, after all, really claim to be 'Scottish'.

What the vocal Scottish community apparently wanted was an independent Royal Bank of Scotland with its Scottish note-issuing rights intact. There were several levels to this feeling and some confusion as to whether the discussion was about the Royal Bank of Scotland (which in a sense had already lost its full independence) or the Royal Bank of Scotland Group, which included Williams and Glyn's and gave the whole a distinctly English flavour. If the Royal Bank were somehow to leave the Scottish clearing, the remaining two banks, both of which had English affiliations, might abandon their Scottish heritage; loss of a Scottish clearing would be another loss to the capital of Scotland, another downgrading of a proud and independent city.

In later interviews the concept 'Liverpoolization' was used. There were those in Edinburgh who professed concern at the drain of *community* leaders from the capital. Thus it was not enough to leave behind the man who made the business decisions; the 'manager' had to be able, for example, to initiate donations, to provide leadership and funds in major projects. When Q.W. Lee of the Hang Seng Bank testified before the Monopolies Commission the emphasis was on management independence; the Hang Seng's School of Commerce and its contribution to Hong Kong business research were a part of the evidence.

The actual gains to Scotland and to the shareholders and management of the RBSG were set forth in the Hongkong Bank's pamphlet, *Approach to an Alliance, Proposals for Partnership*, published in November 1981. But by this time too many had taken a dug-in position; the Hongkong Bank accordingly failed to gain the support of the Secretary of State for Scotland, George Younger, or the Bank of England. There was support in the Foreign Office and Treasury, but it was effective only in containing the criticism.

The Bank's offer was not permitted to go forward, but the real loss was to Edinburgh and to the Scottish economy. Had the Hongkong Bank succeeded, outside analysts have concluded that the Hongkong Bank Group's assets outside Hong Kong would have increased to some 70% of the total and that the Group's sources of profit would be divided 45% from Hong Kong and 55% from the remaining areas. The percentages, even if correct, are not the only consideration. Since the 1950s the Hongkong Bank's Board and chief executive officers have sought a sound diversification; with the MMBI merger a major portion of the strategy was achieved. The Bank, checked in Britain, as far as commercial banking was concerned, still had opportunities to develop financial product diversification. This, indeed, is the next thread to follow.

The development of the Hongkong Bank Group

A survey

Not all developments resulted in the formation of a new subsidiary nor were they consequent to acquisition. With the several banks which constitute the Group new methods, new products, and improved communications form a constant input into the Bank's in-house newspaper. There were also structural reorganizations.

J.R.M. Lewis, former Secretary of the Hongkong Bank, was, for example, appointed to head a new 'Private Banking' department, designed to provide personalized services to the Bank's wealthier constituents and with access to the Group's specialized subsidiaries, for example, a Wardley Investor Services Unit. The complexity of such an apparently straightforward development is illustrated in Figure 18.3.

The principal subsidiary and associated companies of the Hongkong Bank Group as they existed on December 31, 1984, are listed in Table 18.7. A total list would be subject to the same type of analysis as found in Chapter 15 for the period to 1979 or to a presentation similar to that attempted by I.H. Macdonald before a Congressional sub-committee in 1980.

The Hongkong Bank Group's holding company network had, however, become increasingly complex; for example, after the completion in October 1980, of the MMBI merger, that holding company was 51.1% owned through two 100%-owned subsidiaries, Kellett, NV, and HSBC Holdings, BV. This principle had subsequently been applied to a U.K. holding company, HSBC Holdings U.K., Ltd, which in turn had 100% ownership of seven 'group' holding companies, that is, companies which directly controlled a group of similar operating companies, for example, Antony Gibbs Holdings, Ltd, TKM International (Holdings) Ltd, which in turn held the operating companies. On

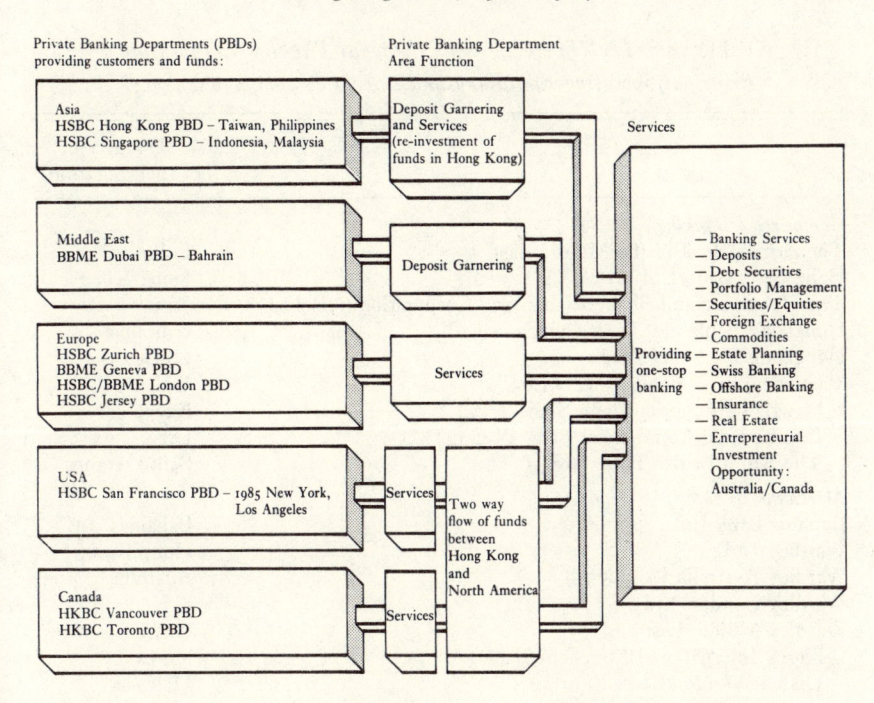

Hongkong Bank, 1980–1984

Private Banking Departments (PBDs) providing customers and funds:

- Asia
  HSBC Hong Kong PBD – Taiwan, Philippines
  HSBC Singapore PBD – Indonesia, Malaysia

- Middle East
  BBME Dubai PBD – Bahrain

- Europe
  HSBC Zurich PBD
  BBME Geneva PBD
  HSBC/BBME London PBD
  HSBC Jersey PBD

- USA
  HSBC San Francisco PBD – 1985 New York, Los Angeles

- Canada
  HKBC Vancouver PBD
  HKBC Toronto PBD

Private Banking Department Area Function

- Deposit Garnering and Services (re-investment of funds in Hong Kong)
- Deposit Garnering
- Services
- Services
- Services — Two way flow of funds between Hong Kong and North America
- Services

Services

Providing one-stop banking:
— Banking Services
— Deposits
— Debt Securities
— Portfolio Management
— Securities/Equities
— Foreign Exchange
— Commodities
— Estate Planning
— Swiss Banking
— Offshore Banking
— Insurance
— Real Estate
— Entrepreneurial Investment Opportunity: Australia/Canada

The relationship between client and group servicing units should be through each Private Banking Department.

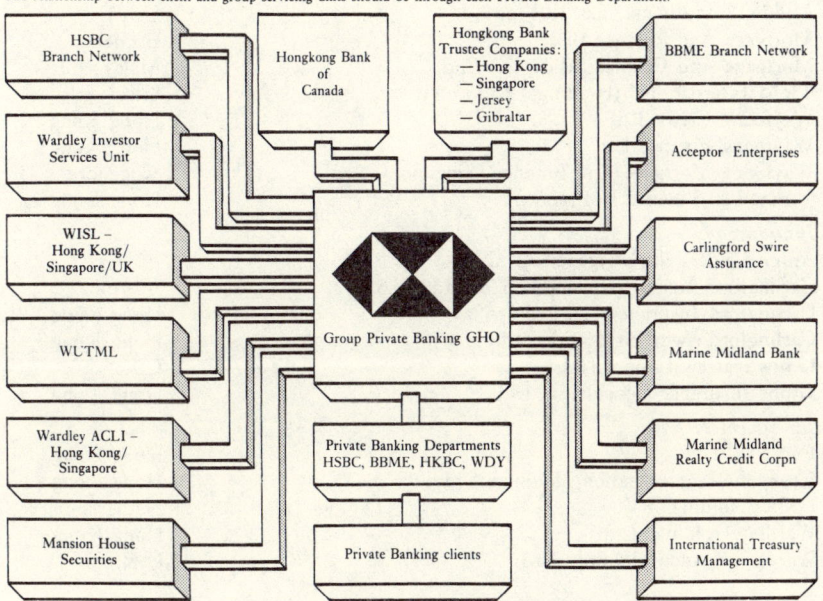

Units connected to **Group Private Banking GHO**:

- HSBC Branch Network
- Hongkong Bank of Canada
- Hongkong Bank Trustee Companies:
  — Hong Kong
  — Singapore
  — Jersey
  — Gibraltar
- BBME Branch Network
- Wardley Investor Services Unit
- Acceptor Enterprises
- WISL – Hong Kong/Singapore/UK
- Carlingford Swire Assurance
- WUTML
- Marine Midland Bank
- Wardley ACLI – Hong Kong/Singapore
- Private Banking Departments HSBC, BBME, HKBC, WDY
- Marine Midland Realty Credit Corpn
- Mansion House Securities
- Private Banking clients
- International Treasury Management

Figure 18.3 The Hongkong and Shanghai Banking Corporation Private banking chart

Table 18.7 *The Hongkong and Shanghai Banking Corporation Principal operating subsidiary and associated companies, 1984*[a]

	Country of Incorporation
Commercial Banking	
The British Bank of the Middle East	U.K.
Hang Seng Bank Ltd (61.48%)	Hong Kong
The Hongkong and Shanghai Banking Corporation (CI) Ltd	Jersey C.I.
Hongkong Bank and Trust Company Ltd	Gibraltar
Hongkong Bank of Canada	Canada
Marine Midland Banks, Inc. (51.05%)	U.S.A.
Hongkong Egyptian Bank SAE (40%)	Egypt
International Commercial Bank PLC (22%)	U.K.
The Saudi British Bank (40%)	Saudi Arabia
Merchant Banking	
Equator Bank Ltd	Bahamas
Wardley Ltd	Hong Kong
Wardley Australia Ltd (80%)[b]	Australia
Wardley London Ltd	U.K.
Wardley Middle East Ltd	U.A.E.
Korea International Merchant Bank (30%)	Korea
Utama Wardley Berhad (30%)	Malaysia
Finance	
Concord International (Curaçao) NV (70.2%)	N. Antilles
MetWay Ltd (51%)	Hong Kong
Middle East Finance Co. Ltd (90%)	U.A.E
Mortgage And Finance Bhd	Brunei
Mortgage And Finance (Malaysia) Bhd	Malaysia
TKM International (Holdings) Ltd	U.K.
Wayfoong Credit Ltd	Hong Kong
Wayfoong Finance Ltd	Hong Kong
Wayfoong Mortgage And Finance (Singapore) Ltd	Singapore
FortWay Finance Ltd (50%)	Hong Kong
Insurance	
Anton Underwriting Agencies Ltd (99.8%)[c]	
Carlingford Australia Insurance Co. Ltd (82.6%)	Australia
Carlingford Insurance Co. Ltd (70%)	Hong Kong
Carlingford Swire Assurance Ltd (74.5%)	Hong Kong
Gibbs Hartley Cooper Ltd	U.K.
Gibbs Insurance Consultants Ltd	Hong Kong
Investment Holding	
Fort Hall Ltd	Hong Kong
Grenville Transportation Holdings Ltd	Hong Kong
HSBC Holdings BV	Netherlands
Wardley Holdings Ltd	Hong Kong
Wardley London Holdings Ltd	U.K.

Table 18.7 (*cont.*)

	Country of Incorporation
Investment Services	
CM&M Group, Inc (through MMBI) (51%)	Delaware
Wardley International Management Ltd	Hong Kong
Wardley Investment Services Ltd	Bahamas
Wardley Marine International Investment Management Ltd[c] (75.5%)	U.K.
Wardley Unit Trust Managers Ltd	U.K.
James Capel & Co. (29.9%)[d]	U.K.
James Capel (Far East) Ltd (29.9%)[d]	Hong Kong
Wardley-ACLI Commodities Ltd (45%)[e]	Hong Kong
Wardley Nikko Management Ltd (50%)	Hong Kong
Financial Services	
International Treasury Management Ltd (75.5%)[f]	Hong Kong
Wardley Data Services Ltd	Hong Kong
Acceptor Enterprises Ltd (45%)	Hong Kong
Central Registration Hong Kong Ltd (50%)	Hong Kong
Dun and Bradstreet (HK) Ltd (50%)	Hong Kong
Hongkong and Shanghai Thomas Cook Ltd (50%)	Hong Kong
Trustee and Nominee Services	
Companies are located in the Channel Islands, Hong Kong, Gibraltar, India, Malaysia, Singapore, United Kingdom	
Transportation	
Cathay Pacific Airways Ltd (30%)	Hong Kong
World Finance International Ltd (37.5%)	Bermuda
World Maritime Ltd (50%)	Bermuda
World Shipping and Investment Co. Ltd (45%)	Cayman Islands
Printing and Publishing	
South China Morning Post Ltd (48.76%)[c]	Hong Kong

Notes:
Brunei   Negara Brunei Darussalam
C.I.   Channel Islands, United Kingdom
U.A.E.   United Arab Emirates

[a] Associated companies are indented. Group equity holdings are 100% except where indicated in parenthesis.
[b] Hongkong Finance Ltd (1986).
[c] sold.
[d] now a wholly owned subsidiary (1986).
[e] Wardley-Thomson Ltd (1986).
[f] Joint venture, HSBC/MMBI.

the other hand, there were some surprising direct involvements by the parent bank holding company, The Hongkong and Shanghai Banking Corporation. There, for example, is the 61%-owned British and Chinese Corporation, a dormant name from the dramatic past. HSBC's 40% investment in the Hongkong Egyptian Bank was also held direct – not through the BBME.

HSBC's major banking subsidiaries, the BBME, Hang Seng, and MMBI had their own networks of subsidiary and associated companies. The Bank's holding of 20% (in 1986, 21.3%) in the Cyprus Popular Bank, for example, came originally through BBME. The determining factors were tax and legal, geographical (national requirements), and practical. The tendency to split off specialized support activities as separate corporations increased – Cathay Pacific Airways, for example, had fourteen subsidiaries with such useful titles as Kai Tak Refuellers Co., Associated Engineers, Cathay Holidays, Vogue Laundry Service, and Swire Caterers.

HS Property Management was founded as a separate corporation in 1980, taking over the work of the in-house property department. In *Hongkong Bank News* (June 1984) there is a picture of Mrs L. Wong and Mrs V. Cierpicka of the Residences Department considering fabric and carpet samples. In the interwar period, the wife of a newly appointed Manager might be taken to visit the London Army and Navy Stores by a Manager's wife knowledgeable in the limitations imposed by 'someone' in Head Office – perhaps the Chief Manager himself. In the 1950s, Lady Turner, the wife of the Chief Manager, had toured with her husband inspecting properties and making recommendations which the local Manager might, or very possibly might not, implement.

As noted above, from the point of view of commercial banking, a breakthrough came with the founding of the Hongkong Bank of Canada in 1981 and of the HongkongBank of Australia in 1986. In merchant banking the rationalization of the Antony Gibbs heritage and the expanding role of Wardley Limited were important. For Group expansion across the range of financial services, the acquisition of TKM (Tozer, Kemsley and Millbourn) International (Holdings) was important in the acceptance business, and the Bank's 1974 maximum permitted equity investment (29.9%) in James Capel and Co., together with the Bank's previous joint venture Mansion House Securities, Ltd (HSBC 50%, Hang Seng 20%, and Evans Lowe 30%) brought HSBC into stockbroking. This was not, however, the final word from London; the Bank had been positioning itself for later changes in the regulations and the equity acquisition had been agreed after identification of James Capel as one of the top-quality houses in the City. The U.S. counterpart was MMBI's 1983 acquisition of CM&M (Carroll McEntry and McGinley) Inc., leading U.S. Government security dealers.

And there were other important developments.

Although the Group's banking activities came under increasing Government control in the Federation of Malaysia as part of the New Economic Policy, a proposal to require local incorporation and, therefore, a local majority of shareholders and directors, was not pushed by the central bank, the Bank Negara, although both the Hongkong Bank and Standard Chartered promised their cooperation. The Group's joint venture, the Saudi British Bank was permitted 'national treatment'; special restrictions on branching would be inapplicable.

Despite the proliferation of companies, the pattern remained reasonably clear. The public were assisted by the development of the 'HongkongBank' signature, as Sandberg called it, and by some standardization of names for functional groups, for example, Carlingford for insurance.

Other developments merit separate description.

Marine Midland and the United States

Although observers noted that Marine Midland upgraded its representative office to a full-service banking branch in Seoul in 1981 *after* the merger with HSBC, the actual trend was coordination of overseas operations with a stress on cooperative ventures. Thus MMB closed its Paris branch and its Edge Act office in Houston, Texas. This was the first stage in a major Group rationalization; Marine Midland would eventually close in Seoul and in other overseas centres, Latin America excepted. Instead MMBI would be the Group's 'flagship' in the United States, expanding domestically on the basis of its assured regional base.

The Hongkong Bank in 1982 had taken advantage of the IBA national treatment provisions to open an Edge Act bank in Houston – the Hongkong Bank International, with authorization to undertake international business. In 1984 the Hongkong Bank with the approval of the Banque de France established a second branch in Paris, taking over most of the staff – and certain corporate loans – of the MMB branch, which was then downgraded to a Representative Office.

There were two new joint ventures with Marine Midland: Wardley Marine International Investment Management and International Treasury Management Ltd. MMBI retained its interest in Wardley Australia. This latter joint subsidiary was agent for a syndicated loan for a US$100 million multicurrency financing of the Cooper Basin oil project; the Hongkong Bank and Marine Midland were lead managers. These positive developments, coupled with additional gearing in the form of US$125 million increase in primary capital through a Eurodollar note offering (underwritten by, *inter alios*, the 'Hongkong Bank Group') were to ensure Marine Midland's improved position.

Federal regulations require MMBI to report its dealings with its major shareholder. Throughout the period the Hongkong Bank had extended a line of credit to MMBI of US$30 million, at a commitment fee of 0.5%. In 1982, the Hongkong Bank Group had deposits of US$142 million with MMB and its subsidiaries (US$280.6 million end-1984); MMB's credit to the Group totalled US$642,000 in loans and nearly US$3 million of customers' acceptance liability (a total US$12.3 million end-1984). MMBI negotiated a US$50 million ten-year, subordinated note with HSBC (actually HSBC Holdings, BV) at a variable interest rate related closely to the London interbank rate.

The national-level banking debate of 1979–1980 did not result in the breakdown of inter-State banking prohibitions – with the single exception of acquisitions of large endangered banks. Nevertheless Marine Midland, as other major banks, was involved in 'positioning', either through what MMB referred to as its Enriched Correspondent Banks Relationships program (ENCOR) and/or equity investment, limited by the FRB however to 4.9% of the voting stock. In 1981 MMBI invested US$25 million in the Industrial Valley Bank and Trust Company of Philadelphia; in 1982 Marine Midland, with Hongkong Bank financing, invested US$70 million in newly issued non-voting preferred stock of the Centran Corporation, with warrants to purchase 2.3 million shares of common stock when current Federal legislation is amended to permit inter-State banking. Centran, with assets of US$3 billion, owns the Central National Bank of Cleveland and five smaller Ohio banks. Centran subsequently merged with Society Corporation of Cleveland, the combination becoming the second largest banking organization in Ohio. MMBI had also invested in Statewide Bancorp of New Jersey.

Under specific regulations a national banking association or bank holding company may have offices out-of-State. The Edge Act makes provisions for international business from such offices, and MMBI operated, for example, in Miami and, for a period, in Houston. A State might make an exception; in 1984 MMBI, under a new Delaware State law, established a commercial bank in Delaware, Marine Midland Bank (Delaware), NA. Also in 1984, reacting to new Federal Reserve regulations, MMBI applied for permission to open fourteen consumer finance offices across the United States.

The positioning exercises and office establishment brought immediate results, but there was a long-term plan; these actions were in preparation for future, full-scale, intra-regional or nationwide, inter-State banking, which, despite legislative inertia, would appear inevitable.

MMBI's development after its merger with the Hongkong Bank Group was encouraging. At the end of 1979, the year the Definitive Agreement was renegotiated, book value of MMBI's common shareholders' equity was US$38.29; at the end of 1984 it was US$52.88 and the annual dividend was increased to US$1.60 (1979 = US$0.80).

The improved capital position of MMBI had been achieved by the purchase of common stock by HSBC Holdings in 1980, by a further gearing through US$125 million of subordinated notes, and by retained earnings. During 1984 Federal regulators set minimum applicable guidelines for the primary capital ratio at 5.5%, for the total capital ratio 6%. MMBI's ratios were 6.91% and 8.48% respectively; in 1979 the primary capital ratio had been below 4%.

The Hongkong Bank/Marine Midland partnership had proved its success, and MMBI's performance was beyond the expectations of the most optimistic. There remained, then, in addition to the new capital resources (i) the Duffy/Petty factor and (ii) the international coordination of the two partners. Whatever else occurred between 1977 and 1986, Sandberg's contribution to the history of his Bank was made memorable by this one, well-considered, determined decision which constituted his American strategy.

As for the Hongkong Bank's own U.S. developments, in 1983 a new branch was opened in Flushing, New York, a community with a high percentage of Chinese Americans. Hang Seng also opened a full-service branch in New York's Chinatown – its first overseas. More important, however, for the Hongkong Bank's position in New York was the June 1985 closing of the offices of Golden Pacific National Bank, catering mainly to Chinese-American customers, and the FDIC's invitation to banks to bid for the US$120 million deposits. The Bank responded successfully within 48 hours and the branches opened within a week under the Hongkong Bank's name. But this, the new mini-bank in the Hongkong Bank Building, 5 East 59th Street, and indeed the building itself are beyond the limits of this history.

Developments in Britain
The Bank's British policy was not wholly concentrated upon acquisition of the RBSG. This section notes other dimensions.

Since 1973 HSBC's merchant banking presence had been represented by a minority holding in Antony Gibbs. This had proved unsuccessful, the Bank had taken a 100% interest in 1980, but in 1981 Sandberg had still to report unsatisfactory performance and the need to inject capital through a subordinated loan. By 1982 it had become clear that nothing further would be gained by linking the Hongkong Bank Group's British-based merchant banking activities to the traditional Antony Gibbs name. Accordingly, as part of a major restructuring and refinancing, and under the chairmanship of the Bank's retired Deputy Chairman, J.L. Boyer, the old name disappeared (with minor subsidiary company exceptions) and the merchant operations came under the general Wardley name – Wardley London Holdings Ltd.

At the commercial banking level these events coincided with a limited *de novo* expansion, with new branches in Leeds and Birmingham, virtually coincident with the return of retail banking from the BBME to the Hongkong Bank in the City. In 1984 there was a new emphasis. The Hongkong Bank would henceforth focus on corporate banking, current accounts would be accepted only on the basis of large minimum balances or a significant fee. The test would be strictly cost-effectiveness under a new 'corporate plan' and the focus was on the corporate customer who needed access to the Bank's worldwide facilities. Piecemeal *de novo* branching had proved too expensive, although only the Birmingham office was actually closed. The Hongkong Bank Group's representational functions had left the commercial bank offices and moved to the Office of the Executive Director for Europe.

The London solution, however, came only with the change of rules; the Bank sold Mansion House and in 1986 completed the purchase of 100% of James Capel. In 1983 the Antony Gibbs Holdings had become Wardley London Holdings; now, with James Capel as a subsidiary and with the promise offered through access to their highly qualified staff and virtually world-wide facilities, there was further rationalization with the Group's United Kingdom operations, including a successor merchant bank to Wardley, HongkongBank Limited.

The 1986 Head Office building

The redevelopment of 1, Queen's Road, Central, had been one of Sandberg's major initial goals, but the problems associated with the temporary relocation of Head Office and the Main Branch and with financial timing consistent with the Bank's other development commitments were in themselves considerable. The history of the Bank since 1946, however, provided sufficient justification for the redevelopment, and, despite the problems, the Board set November 1979 for architectural submissions. With the concurrence of Gordon Graham, the immediate past president of the Royal Institute of British Architects and the Bank's Architectural Adviser, only Foster Associates of the several firms submitting proposals were in fact invited to make a presentation; the firm was, in November 1979, duly commissioned. On that occasion, Sandberg told a press conference:

A complete redevelopment of the Queen's Road site is an expression born of the Bank's commitment to Hong Kong and of our confidence in Hong Kong's future as an international financial centre. We believe our new headquarters will not only meet the Group's needs for the foreseeable future but will also be an exciting building of which Hong Kong can be proud.

After consideration of various alternatives, including 'phased redevelopment', the decision was made to relocate temporarily in several buildings in central district – Head Office was in the new Admiralty development between Central and Wanchai, Main Branch moved into several floors of the China

Building to the west along Queen's Road at the corner of Pedder Street, although the annex to the old building was refitted as a retail office to enable business at the 1, Queen's Road, Central address to continue as long as possible.

With the innovative Norman Foster now commissioned, Hong Kong could expect a hi-tech building with 'new criteria which go beyond the traditional limits of architecture'. By dedicating the ground level to public use in the form of a 3,514 sq. metre plaza, the Bank was to secure Government permission for the plot ratio to be increased from 15 to 18:1; in consequence, the final design, a steel-framed building with suspended floors, would rise almost 178.8 metres above Des Voeux Road (on the north side) in 47 levels and reach 18.8 metres below through four basement levels. By the unique design there were economies of space – the new building would have some three times more usable floor space than its 1935 predecessor, that is, 70,398 of a total 99,171 sq. metres. Furthermore, experts concluded that the use of raised floors, thus permitting direct access to all services, and other innovations would reduce costs-in-use dramatically over the life of the building and further justify the Board's decision to move into what qualified critics saw as a building of the 21st century.

In 1986 the building, which, during construction, had involved some 4,000 workers, of whom 3,500 were on site, could be seen to have lived up to Foster's award-winning reputation and to Sandberg's, the Board's, and Hong Kong's highest expectations. Major architectural periodicals devoted whole issues to studies of the building and the editor of the *Architectural Review* confessed that he had never before felt so inadequate as when he had tried to translate his experience of the Bank into mere words and photographs. This was a work of art; it has been described as the first successful redesign of the huge impersonal office building on a human scale.

Although the year 1986 lies well this side of the limits of this Hongkong Bank history, no history covering even the outline of the period to 1984 would be complete without reference to the Bank's new building. Not, alas, for positive reasons – these remain visible as subjects of continued comment – but for negative reasons which threatened to sour Sandberg's administration and turn by rumour what some had heralded as an architectural wonder into nothing better than a costly display of traditional Hongkong Bank arrogance. One principal factor was the change in Hong Kong itself, its economic performance, its property and stock markets, and expectations relative to its long-term future. What the community had once urged on behalf of Hong Kong's prestige was now seen as the extravagance of a major private sector banking company. Giving a sort of focus to all this was the confused problem of cost – not actual cost but rumoured cost.

Nevertheless this is not the place to write the complex story of what, if anything, went wrong – not because the story can't be told but because it has been told. The usual polite excuse, 'this must be left for some future historian', has to be modified: Stephanie Williams' thorough study, *HongkongBank, the Building of Norman Foster's Masterpiece*, has already been published.[f]

The evidence suggests strongly that throughout 1980 the Bank's management became increasingly positive in their reactions relative to Foster's designs. They were aware of the high nominal cost, but this factor was neutralized by (i) costs-in-use analysis which suggested low costs by more reasonable criteria, (ii) the difficulty of comparing costs as between the usual commercial and a single-occupant, special-purpose designed high-rise, and (iii) the enthusiasm generated by Foster for his vision and his actual designs and the positive desire to see them executed in the interests of the Bank and its efficiency over the next half-century. R.V. Munden, who remained the executive director responsible, has stated that from the beginning management estimated expected total cost, including inflationary factors, to be some $5.7 billion. The Bank has announced that the *actual* costs were $5.129 billion (excluding certain listed items).

Unfortunately these are not the relevant figures. At a meeting in December 1980, the Board of Directors approved a figure for the 'shell' of $1,380 million. In mid-1982 it was this figure which the public set against leaked estimates of $5 billion – and higher, the figure of $8 billion was reached; furthermore, announcements were made that the Board of Directors were becoming directly involved and from this further rumours were generated touching on all involved from architect to major contractors to chief executive. Press comments began referring to 'the most expensive office building in the world', and the Bank would be on the defensive – at least until the building were completed and a full explanation provided.[g]

Williams' narrative would suggest that management had determined to approach the project, at least to some degree, as if it were a standard Bank building project. In this context management would place the cost before the Board for approval, but that cost would, as usual, be for the 'shell'; the fit-out

---

[f] What follows here is based on my reading in November 1987 of her final draft (as supplemented by correspondence with R.V. Munden), to which I have added my own interpretation. Those who have followed the complex story as related in her text will understand why I do not, in this general history, attempt to reargue the problems. I had earlier consulted Ian Lambot and Gillian Chambers' excellent but non-controversial study, *One Queen's Road Central, the Headquarters of HongkongBank since 1864* (Hong Kong, 1986), and several of the quotations, the architectural data, and Plate 14 are taken from this latter source.

[g] At the same time the Board had authorized redevelopment of the Chairman's house on the Peak. Unfortunately it had long been named 'Sky High', which provided punsters with an obvious target (no further pun intended) – and there were others.

to render the structure suitable for banking was a cost which fell within the range of business delegated by the Board to the Bank's chief executive. Then too the cost was stated in November 1980 prices and although inflationary and related estimates were provided the Board, these additions were not before the public.

By the nature of the relationship between Foster and the Bank, not all decisions relative to the building had been set at the time of the initial estimates; revisions were made even as yet newer technology became available. One of the revisions involved steel and eventually the potential delays and an unexpected cost overrun were of sufficient magnitude to require Board attention. Only then, in mid-1982, were the Board made aware of the *total* cost of the building, of the shell plus the 'banking' costs. The Board thereupon appointed its own sub-committee, reassessed the whole project, and at that stage agreed it should continue. Management had itself scaled down on certain proposals – there would, for example, be no swimming pool; the Board went further, but Foster's basic concepts and the design which had attracted all from the first were not affected.

What was needed to quiet public concern was a full, frank exposition of precisely what had happened. But the project was fast-moving; to pin-point the precise factors responsible for the concerns would have been contentious (or worse) even had it proved possible to do so. The Bank itself was changing dramatically during the period of construction, its own requirements were adjusting, and the only safe conclusion must be that the Bank was paying the cost of pioneering.

Perhaps the discussion can be summed up in terms of the Bank's semi-annual meeting in 1875. Then the Bank's American Chairman, W.H. Forbes, urged the disgruntled shareholders that the cost of the new Shanghai building would be proved less than paying rent and 'at the time the building was sanctioned, the Bank was in what he supposed even H. Kingsmill [the self-appointed devil's advocate] would have called a very flourishing condition.' To which the response was then (as now), 'Ah, but you've got into the hands of architects and builders.' (See Volume I, p. 206.)

In its own field of expertise, however, the Bank did well, buying foreign exchange forward; to this extent the fall of the dollar against the U.S. dollar did not materially affect costs, hence the ability to keep the final figure, despite major cost-overruns, within management's early estimates.

While Foster was accepting architectural awards, while his 'design and the achievement of John Lok/Wimpey [the contracting partners] and the many sub-contractors, are already stimulating the interest of architects the world over', while Sandberg could state, 'All of us can expect the distinctive outline of this building from now on to become the most visible symbol of its originality and advanced technology', there were many in Hong Kong, it seemed, who could only grumble.

William Purves, then Executive Deputy Chairman, put the matter in perspective.

This is our fourth building at One Queen's Road Central, and although it is of necessity on a vastly different scale from its predecessors, it has been designed from the onset to accomplish the same four basic functions...to serve the exacting demands of running a world-wide banking group in the era of instant communications, and doing so when necessary around the clock. [The building is also the] principal banking 'factory' containing all the plant and machinery required to conduct our business. Third, it is also our main branch, the focus for our large retail and commercial business here in Hong Kong. [The fourth function is to provide] the most advanced and secure vaults which the world is technically able to construct.

In other words, here was a dramatic, cost-efficient, international bank headquarters providing just those facilities that such a building ought to provide. The criticisms had been ill-conceived and short-sighted. A new building had to be; this one would prove its worth.

Perhaps the problem was with the lions. They had had to be relocated during the move; when they were returned and the building was officially opened with a gigantic celebration on April 17, 1986, the economy itself began to recover confidence. The markets began to improve. The value of Hong Kong's domestic exports continue to grow. New views were expressed and ultimately... But 'ultimately' is a reminder. This is a *history* of the Hongkong Bank; this chapter covers the years through 1984 only.

FOLLOWING THE THREADS TO 1984: (II) SHAREHOLDERS, DIRECTORS, AND THE ADVISORY COMMITTEE

Shareholders

During the years immediately before the Great War when jingoists were questioning whether the Hongkong Bank were not German rather than British, the Foreign Office stated its definition of a British bank as one with a majority of British shareholders. When, during the RBSG episode in 1981, the Bank of England put out suggestions that the Hongkong Bank was 'foreign', the Treasury pronounced that the Bank was a British overseas bank, which had long been, in fact, its official classification. But this too depended on the nationality of the Bank's 166,600 shareholders. The Bank is not subject to the relevant provisions of the Hong Kong Companies Act and has not released detailed information, however in testimony before the Monopolies and Mergers Committee (Report, p. 43), it was stated that on December 31, 1980, 73% of the shares were held by shareholders with registered addresses in Hong Kong, 20% United Kingdom, and 7% elsewhere.

The Hongkong Bank responded in its *Approach to an Alliance* pamphlet that its shareholders were 'predominantly' British subjects, but as critics of the Bank were quick to point out, most of these would be Chinese Hong Kong 'belongers'. The majority of the shares had returned to Hong Kong, despite the fact that they continue to be traded in both London and Hong Kong. The restriction on shareholding remains; without the permission of the Board no shareholder may be the beneficial owner of more than 1% of the total shares outstanding.

Until the 1960s the problem was to encourage a sufficient number of shareholders to attend the meeting to provide a quorum. More recently shareholders' meetings became a great Hong Kong gathering, moving first into a hotel ballroom then into the City Hall concert hall. For a time the meetings were followed by a buffet lunch, so that any calculation of annual dividends needs revision to the extent of say $75 (service and champagne included) per shareholder present. Hong Kong 'belongers' are experienced in buffet participation; Ed Duffy and John Petty had never seen anything quite like it and said so. In 1983 this bonus stopped; there was no place large enough to house the growing crowd. The equivalent sum was sent instead to charity; refreshments were confined to tea and biscuits with, as yet, no sign of escalation.

The Board of Directors and the London Committee

The Board of Directors

The Hongkong and Shanghai Banking Corporation's 1984 Board of Directors had changed remarkably not only since inter-war days but over the previous decade. First of all there were 21 members; Morse would have considered the number unworkable. He would also have questioned whether there were 21 people in Hong Kong qualified to be bank directors. But Hong Kong itself had grown and new sectors of the economy, the Mass Transit Railway, for example, might well be represented.

Only four of the companies represented on the Board in 1962 were represented in 1984/85 (see Table 15.3). Gilman and Co. were there and had been since 1864 – the only survivor of the Provisional Committee establishing the Bank, but the firm was now part of Inchcape, their very name would be threatened by any consideration of corporate rationalization. Inchcape, which was represented throughout, had taken over other firms with traditional Board membership: Gibb, Livingston and Co. (1869), Dodwell and Co. (1895), and Mackinnon, Mackenzie and Co. (1929). Directors from other companies represented in the Bank's history included the taipans of Butterfield and Swire/ John Swire and Sons HK (1914) and Jardine, Matheson and Co. (1877). In 1982 P.G. Williams, who had represented Dodwell's and then the Inchcape Group, died in London; he had served eighteen years as a director, the longest-serving since the war, and had been Deputy Chairman of the Bank, 1975–1980.

The fall-out of the old companies was offset by the drawing in of Chinese enterprises. This was noted in the press as representing a new departure; the Hongkong Bank was reaching out to the Chinese business community. This was an a-historical interpretation. The Bank had throughout its history been closely involved with Chinese enterprise. In earlier times this had been effected through the compradore. A legitimate comment might rather have been that the Bank switched from the traditional compradore system to the more usual board representation system less than a decade after the retirement of the last compradore; events in the 1970s and after confirmed a normal practice.

In 1982 Lydia S. Dunn was elected a director. She was the first woman to be so elected, but her role in Hong Kong business and on the Legislative Council suggests that this was not the reason for her election. The Canton Delta has had a relatively long history (in specific aspects) of what is now referred to as 'Women's Lib', and women in Hong Kong have been playing key managerial roles first within the traditional family business, that is, behind the curtain, and then in public companies. The Bank's acknowledgement of this would appear to have come relatively late; in fact, at the time only the Midland Bank among British banks had a woman director.

The Hongkong Bank's own executives had been represented since the early 1970s, (Sir) Q.W. Lee came on the Board from Hang Seng Bank in 1979 (retiring in 1985), and in accordance with the agreement one non-executive and two MMBI executive directors joined the parent Board in 1980. In 1984 there were two executive directors resident in New York and London respectively. Board membership now included executives of the Hongkong Bank and of its subsidiaries in addition to the non-executive directors, who, as in the past, are leading members of the Hong Kong community.

The London Advisory Committee

The composition of the London Advisory Committee (see Table 14.4) reflected several policy elements. First, the Bank's long association with the National Westminster had to be modified in view of the latter's development as a competitor in international banking; the Westminster, as the London and County Bank, had been represented on the Committee since the latter's founding in 1875, but when J.A.F. Binny retired in 1981 he was not replaced. Secondly, the Committee provided a forum for representatives of the several HSBC subsidiary companies in Hong Kong, especially with the dissolution of the BBME Advisory Committee and the coming of James Capel and Co. Thirdly, the advisory concept was broadened to take in former diplomats with experience in key areas, for example, Sir John Addis, son of Sir Charles Addis, for the Far East, and Sir Geoffrey Arthur (and more recently Sir James Craig) for the Middle East. The Chairman was the Executive Director, Europe, thus providing a direct link to the Board in Hong Kong. The developments were sound, but the Bank continued to consider it as purely advisory; little use if any was made of the Committee qua committee during the period of the RBSG offer, but the individual members were once again of considerable assistance.

FOLLOWING THE THREADS: (III) HONGKONG BANKERS

The succession

Sir Michael Sandberg
Before Michael Sandberg announced his intention to step down as HSBC's chief executive officer, he had been presented by the *International Herald Tribune* with the 'Innovative Banker Award' for the Pacific Area (1980) and designated 'Banker of the Year' by *Euromoney* on the vote of the chairmen of the 500 largest banks in the world (1982). These were fitting tributes from the profession for a banker who had transformed a traditional regional bank, still without losing that tradition, into a world-wide financial multinational corporation. During his administration the corporation's total assets had increased 38 times from $14,217 million (end-1976) to $545,610 million (= US$69,860 million), shareholders' funds 46 times from $478 million to $21,882 million. In June 1982 he had been awarded, as had several of his predecessors, the CBE, and in the 1986 Birthday Honours he became a Knight Bachelor. His many years of work for Hong Kong, especially his membership on the Executive Council in the difficult times during negotiations relative to the Sino-British Joint Declaration on the future of Hong Kong after 1997, had been recognized.[h]

In the mid-1970s financial journalists delighted in writing about this colonial anachronism, these amateur bankers. One can almost hear echoes of the Hongkong Bank's dignified London messenger replying to the question, 'Do you call this a bank?', with, 'No, Sir. This is an institution for learning young gentlemen to become bank clerks' (see Volume II). And while the journalists were interviewing Managers in air-conditioned offices tut-tutting that they *were* in air-conditioned offices and not out a-marketing, the Hongkong Bankers in

---

[h] In 1898 the Imperial Chinese Government leased territory to Britain, the New Territories, to be administered for 99 years as part of the Crown Colony of Hong Kong. Such had been the Colony's development that the life of the two sections, the ceded and the leased, had become irretrievably intertwined. The eventual solution was to permit 'two systems, one country', whereby the People's Republic of China would regain sovereignty of both sectors but would permit Hong Kong to retain its particular system, under Chinese rule, for a further 50 years. During the uncertainties of these negotiations, the economy and the dollar were endangered. The Bank's decision in November 1982 to finance *twenty-year* home mortgages was seen, in this context, as another manifestation of continued faith in the territory's economic future.

the field were pressing up the rivers of Sarawak, adopting orangutangs in Singapore, and generally doing what Hongkong Bankers have done to make the Bank the leading financial institution in the East. But, in addition, when the journalists had left, the generalist bankers led by Sandberg were listening to consultants and planning the acquisition of the thirteenth largest bank in the United States.

When Sandberg had become Chairman in 1977 he had set himself specified goals. Among these were the acquisition of an American bank and a European bank, the development of a new head office building, a strengthened capital base, the establishment of a charitable foundation, a revised personnel policy (including a more satisfactory retirement benefits scheme and earlier opportunities for executive staff), and published histories including that of the British Bank of the Middle East, catalogues of the Chinnery and numismatic collections, and a detailed study of the Hongkong Bank itself.[1] In all but one of these he succeeded; the European base had eluded him. With this record and after nearly ten years as Chairman, the time had come to announce the succession.

William Purves

Meanwhile William Purves (East in 1955) was moving up behind Sandberg. With Sandberg's recommendation he had been appointed Chief Accountant in 1970; in 1985 he was Deputy Chairman and in March 1986 Chief Executive Officer of The Hongkong and Shanghai Banking Corporation, designated to succeed Sandberg (East in 1949) as Chairman later in the year. When Purves became Chairman in December 1986, he was 54 years of age, thus ranking, with A.C. Hynes, second in age after A.C. Stephen (58); with 30 years in the East, Purves's length of service ranked after Stephen (35 years) and Barlow (33 years). One could argue that Stephen and Barlow were special cases; more accurately, all Chief Managers were special cases – the sample is not suitable for generalizations (see Appendix Table A). Sandberg, for example, was older than his three predecessors on retirement; the trend throughout the Bank was for a longer period in the East. What is important is that Purves's age, although reflecting his war service and later entry into the Bank's service, is also a statement that the general tradition of the 30 years in the East may need modification consistent with the policy of recall of top executives to Head Office positions after they had had senior managerial positions in the branches. In 1971 when Sandberg moved up to Manager Hong Kong and A.D.A.G. Mosley (East in 1950) had been transferred to meet a temporary emergency, Purves was

---

[1] The several history projects also yielded as by-products a collection of conference papers, *Eastern Banking* (London, 1983), and M. Harcourt Williams' *Catalogue of the Papers of Sir Charles Addis* (London, 1986).

Chief Accountant and then Manager Tokyo; he was temporarily a Manager in London Office and returned to take over Overseas (then 'International') Operations until his appointments as Director, Banking, then Deputy Chairman (1984) and heir presumptive. Sandberg's previous two deputies, J.L. Boyer (East in 1949) and P.E. Hammond (East in 1949), had been his contemporaries.

There are, however, two further observations of historical relevance. First, Purves had served, like Sayer, in six branches since coming East, but Sayer had not served long as a senior in Hong Kong. The broad branch experience which Purves enjoyed reflects back to the 1920s and earlier for a precedent; that he could serve in six branches and be in the running for chief executive was another consequence of career planning, shorter assignments, and a longer period in the East.

Secondly, there were unusual elements to Purves's path to the Chair. The strains of the years 1979 to 1981, during which time a top management team had focused on two major acquisition attempts – the first (MMBI) successful, the second (RBSG) a failure – were not without an impact on the Bank's performance. The dramatic collapse of the property boom and the Bank's over-involvement with unsuccessful enterprises, together with administrative criticism relative to the new Head Office building, caused more than local concern. Purves had been untouched by these events and was brought in as Director, Banking, to provide a visible statement of Sandberg's reaffirmation of traditional priorities. When Purves, by then Executive Deputy Chairman, was appointed chief executive, he did not immediately take over the chairmanship of the Bank. Since the 1969 revision of the Bank's regulations, which required that an executive of the Bank be the Chairman, Saunders and Sayer had retired directly from Hong Kong for personal reasons; this had not, however, set a precedent. The Board, moreover, were anxious about the impact of a change and had found Sandberg willing to remain for a time as Chairman, retaining the representational and community responsibilities, including membership on the Executive Council, while the new chief executive took over the management.

The Hongkong and Shanghai Banking Corporation was no longer the bank which Sandberg had taken over; with a staff of 46,000 in 1,200 offices and 55 countries, growth had led to greater complexity, manifest in part by the existence of some 520 subsidiary and associated companies. Although quite usual in other corporations, including Marine Midland, this sensible progression was nevertheless a first in Hongkong Bank history.

But there had been no real surprises.

Hongkong Bankers – other careers

On career specialization

In a lecture to Bank officers responsible for China research I commented on how Charles Addis in 1887, after his tour in Peking, had made his final decision on the question of 'banker' or 'China expert' (see Vol. I). One officer expressed surprise, 'I made that decision before joining the Bank.' He was reflecting changed procedures.

Like all juniors before him, when M.W. Bond (East in 1952) joined the Bank, he simply joined as a member of the Foreign (now 'International') staff as a junior in London. In the early 1960s the Hongkong Bank sought from among the Foreign staff members who would be willing to move into such specialized areas as computers, training, trustee work. Bond in fact founded and developed the Bank's training department, but in 1981 he was replaced by a specialist. In the great tradition, Bond then returned to banking, ending his career as the Bank's successful Representative in Seoul.

H.L. 'Peter' Pierce (East in 1948) had had a similar career switch. His army service had included language study at the School of Oriental and African Studies in London, and his decision to join the Bank reflected his Chinese language interest. Indeed, after a few months in Hong Kong he was assigned to Chungking and later to Shanghai; eventually he became Manager Iloilo and then in 1964–1965 Manager Colombo. Experience at the 'sharp end' of banking was not, however, appealing, and Pierce took the opportunity offered to return to Head Office as Assistant Controller, Methods Research. From this position he moved first to Manager, Methods Research, and then to Manager, Communications, where he was retained for a year on contract after his official retirement in 1978. At the end he was involved with the installation of the SWIFT system.

These switches in mid-career show commendable adaptability, but they are more easily undertaken during introductory years. Just as there had been no successor from within the Bank when E.G. Hillier died in Peking in 1924 or when Sir Charles Addis retired in 1922, so the Bank could not continue to rely on the existence of general bankers who would suddenly be available as communications or training experts. The Hongkong Bank had now to employ specialists, officers who would make their careers in the corporation without touching banking. As the young man remarked, 'I made my decision before joining the Bank.' And yet this development, although not without earlier precedent, stemmed primarily from the 1977 personnel policy decisions. The Bank had only been just in time to meet the challenge of the Marine Midland partnership.

The seniors – contrasting career patterns

In considering Purves's career the point was made that he was not alone in remaining East beyond the 30-year period. Among the 1985 General Managers were K.W. Barker (East in 1953), previously Manager Malaysia, R.V. Munden (East in 1951), sometime Manager Bombay, R.W. Campbell (East in 1954), previously President of the Hongkong Bank of California, D.G. Jaques (East in 1951), previously Manager Malaysia, all of whom returned to Head Office in a senior position – A.R. Petrie (East in 1951), previously Manager Singapore, became resident Executive Director Americas in succession to I.H. Macdonald. D.F.L. Turner (East in 1953) had been Manager India before being brought back to Head Office. R.C. Farrell (East in 1953) served in Kuala Belait, Tokyo, and Calcutta, but his career was then primarily in Hong Kong where he was active in the New Territories offices in the 1960s, serving as Manager in Yuen Long and Tsuen Wan; after a very brief tour as chief executive officer, Japan, he returned to Head Office and became a General Manager and then resident Executive Director in London.

Service could also be retained on a contract basis for a specific assignment, for example, B.J.N. Ogden as Controller, Group Archives, after retiring in 1979 as the Bank's Secretary. Similarly S.F. Fairchild, who had been raised in China and spoke Chinese, was sent to open the Bank's Taipei representative office; on retirement he was recalled on contract to convert the office to a branch. The Bank had to devise ways to retain valued officers beyond a retirement date better suited to the days before air conditioning, but this had to be done without disappointing the mid-career expectations of able younger executives. The broadening of Head Office and the expansion of that part of the Group managed by Hongkong Bankers permitted the policy to be effected.

The generation of Managers who joined the Bank in 1955 or earlier and who are now (1985) in Head Office had experience in the smaller branches – agencies or sub-agencies – in the Bank's traditional region. The Tawau office was described in Chapter 11. Those who learned banking from assorted Tawau planters, smugglers, merchants, and fishermen, include P.E. Hammond, Deputy Chairman of the Bank; T. Welsh, executive director, London; A.C.R. Chappell, General Manager, Finance; P.J. Wrangham (East in 1955), the last Chief Accountant and now General Manager, Hong Kong; and R.V. Munden, executive director. Tawau is but an example. J.M. Gray (East in 1956) served in Calcutta, Brunei Town, and Jesselton before becoming Manager Hamburg and returning to Hong Kong to become a General Manager and eventually an executive director.

If, however, the careers of younger General Managers are examined, only major branches are shown. R.E. Hale (East in 1961) served in Hamburg, Hong Kong, and Tokyo; P.W.S.C. Brockman (East in 1960) did serve in Ipoh and the Orchard Road branch, Singapore, but otherwise he too was in the major branches; Keith Whitson (East in 1965) served in Hamburg and Kuala Lumpur; J.R.H. Bond (East in 1964) in Bangkok, Singapore, and Jakarta; P.E. Selway-Swift (East in 1966) in Jakarta, Calcutta, and Singapore.

International staff officers in the first six years of service have still, in 1986, opportunities to serve in small offices in the Middle East, now that the BBME and Hongkong Bank staffs have been 'integrated', but these younger men will find their range increasingly narrowed. As noted previously, visas can be obtained for trainees, providing they do not replace a local officer, and this can be extremely valuable. The task of keeping the International staff 'general bankers' with grass roots experience in the smaller offices in the East has, however, become increasingly difficult.

Post-1977 personnel policies

The professionalization of the Hongkong Bank's personnel policies is not a subject which can be dealt with properly in this chapter. To the extent that the post-war history has been considered in terms of 'pressures' which required eventual relief, the changes after 1977 have, in a sense, been heralded, and it would prove frustrating to cut off without some reference to them. This is especially true in cases where personnel policy affected policies (or lack thereof) which have been frequently considered in the several chapters dealing with Hongkong Bankers. A major reform of considerable potential was the designation of 'Foreign' staff as 'International' staff, with two provisos: (i) the International staff would remain primarily British but that a higher proportion of non-British would be eligible for direct recruitment and (ii) Regional officers would be appointed to the International staff both on a temporary basis, that is, when asked to serve outside their own country or, in a limited number of cases, by actual transfer on a permanent basis. The direct recruitment of non-British to the International staff revives the long-standing policy of the 'London gate', but the concept of lateral transfer from Regional officer (or contract officer) status is new and provides, among other things, a potential solution to the problem of retaining highly qualified nationals in a country with limited Hongkong Bank Group opportunity.

The selection process was improved; thereafter the Bank pledged itself to consider such familiar problems in today's large corporation as 'man management', 'career planning', and 'appraisal'. But the changes begin in London, and, with this in mind – and to illustrate the limitations of the presentation – the first topic is New Beckenham and the playing fields which feature so prominently in the reminiscences of today's retired executives.

New Beckenham

When Stan Coles retired in 1981, D. Westerman, his son-in-law, was still working at the New Beckenham Sports Club and, indeed, he became Head Groundsman. Perhaps symbolic of the new age throughout the Bank, however, the overall supervision had devolved to a professional Secretary, G. Farncombe, based in the London Office. He worked both in Bishopsgate and in New Beckenham and inherited the Bank house on the grounds. From these twin vantage points, he could note the changes.

Pre-war the Sports Club had been primarily an extension of the socialization process of juniors in London Office; they played rugger together, many lived in digs nearby, and, having but minimal salaries, they found the Club, basic though it was, a place to spend the evenings, both for recreation and for studying for the Institute of Bankers examination.

The breakdown of this system had several origins: (i) the end of Saturday morning work and consequently the juniors were not pre-assembled for the afternoon train to New Beckenham, (ii) the old houses near the playing fields which had provided rooms for rent had been to a great extent replaced by flats, (iii) higher rents in inner London forced a wider dispersion of juniors while, in apparent contradiction, their higher initial salaries made it possible for juniors to join more conveniently located sports clubs, (iv) the shorter period in London for International staff after the 1977-inspired changes, (v) the alternative activities which had become socially acceptable. On joining the Bank, International (vice Foreign) staff juniors are briefed on the Club, but only three or four from any 'intake' can or will play during their approximately six months' London training period. The continued high use of the Club and playing fields is consequent to the broader use made of the facilities by Home staff, both male and female.

The new policies – 'man management'

The new policies would seem to be based in part on the proposition that today's eligible young people have higher expectations, that a bank cannot hire gentlemen clerks with the hope that an appropriate percentage will turn out, after fifteen years or more in routine assignments now handled by computers, to be capable exchange operators and Managers. (Symbolically the junior mess in Colombo office is now the computer room.) But, having recruited a 'higher' level of young person, the Bank must determine how to handle them, if only because they are expensive.

The first step also becomes more important. The Bank must ensure that it has appropriately qualified and motivated recruits. Today selection is made from a slightly older group with some post-'A'-level experience, including, almost without exception, a university degree. This selection is based on a formal interview process, including testing, lasting over at least two days, and the initial training is specifically organized as such; it is no longer an on-the-job learning process within London Office – nor is London Office now equipped to handle such supernumeraries.

All this means that the young International staff officer goes East with a different background, but he goes to be a different East – and a very different Bank.

'Man management' does not eliminate all elements of traditional China-coast discipline and paternalism. The young officer – for since 1987 both men and women have been recruited to the International staff – may still be transferred on short notice, but increasingly successful attempts are made to keep such postings within a career planning concept. The officer still may not marry during the first tour, but the first tour is a maximum two years. One is expected to undertake the assignment offered, but Managers are instructed to be more open in their discussion of Group policies, to encourage early initiative, to push down decision making to the lowest level at which a decision is capable of being made, to encourage participation by asking such questions as 'What are the policy alternatives?' and 'Which alternative would you recommend?' This last is no different from A.M. Mack's questioning of young Boyer and the injunction to be sure what he thought best was also best for The Hongkong and Shanghai Banking Corporation (see Vol. III, p. 344). But the wisdom of the approach is officially recognized and encouraged, the consequences handled under staff 'appraisal'. This encouragement has its offset. The Bank has to be more realistic about those who will not do well in banking and inform them at an appropriately early stage.

As in almost all major firms employing expatriates, the Bank provides housing and amenities, the latter often shared with the Regional officers. The former may include a period in the re-redesigned Cloudlands, the Peak Mess. Retention of the Mess is based partly on historical sentiment and partly on zoning regulations – the building must be used as a residence and is therefore also designed to accommodate resident courses for Regional officers brought to Hong Kong. The argument for the Mess as part of the socialization process is based on the long-standing assumption that a junior will thus meet a high proportion of fellow juniors; when they are all senior Managers in distant ports, they will retain a bond, they will remember each others' strong and weak points. The logic of this argument was often a matter of dispute, however. Some felt the Mess intellectually deadening, others questioned the facts – Grayburn, for example, had never been in Hong Kong as a junior. London had been more important. Today, the number of resident juniors as a percentage of all juniors is less than ever before, the senior Managers have more timely opportunities to meet their subordinate executives; in modern Hong Kong the

Mess could be thought of as isolating rather than socializing. There is, however, one assurance: with an international group of university graduates, the discussions are closer to those in an Oxford middle common room than to a nineteenth-century army mess; consideration of the finance of the annual ball, for example, can take some forty-five minutes without final resolution. The staggering number of basic principles involved surely warrants such full discussion; 'Fast decisions Worldwide' come later.

There are other matters, however, which do not change. The holiday bungalows are here, and the new launch suggests that Hongkong Bankers remain very much 'on an even keel'. The Bank has 100 private club debentures available in Hong Kong; these provide early membership for clubs with waiting lists. When the Banker is eligible in his own right, he returns the debenture for use by a more recent Hongkong Bank arrival. There have been, admittedly, subtle adjustments. As the old Mess boy, Ah Lam, put it to Norman Bennett as early as 1973, 'No longer the same, Master' or put another way, the marriage regulations may not have the same impact. And yet the new 'junior' has come, as of old, to begin a career, not a job. He would argue that the sociological changes have but a superficial impact, irrelevant to banking. For today's East, he would appear to be correct.

Career planning

Career planning is designed to solve two problems, assurance that qualified officers will be available to meet the Hongkong Bank Group's requirements on the one hand and a sufficiently clearly defined career path laid out to satisfy 'expectations' of the executive on the other. This section considers the latter problem.

At least since the early 1880s the Bank had made a clear distinction between a 'junior', 'banker's assistant', or 'bank clerk' and an appointed officer, that is, an Accountant, Sub-Manager, Assistant Manager, or Manager. This was never entirely a measure of responsibility; the Manager Shanghai might assign a 'junior' to head a department, for example, current accounts, with larger responsibilities and staff than in some of the smaller agencies. However, these departmental positions were at the discretion of the Manager; they did not come before the Board of Directors for approval. An appointment was a matter for the Board, it was a recognition of a permanent status change from clerk to banker, and it carried certain privileges, including, in the earliest days, the right to marry. However, the size of the Eastern staff grew faster than the number of available appointments; the number of years as a junior increased from five or six to more than fifteen by the mid-1890s. It was this delay, normal even in the 1950s, which made a career with the Hongkong Bank unacceptable to most university graduates.

By 1977 the technical advances and the changed use of local staff made it possible to cut back on the operational tasks which had to be undertaken by Foreign staff. The argument that, given a sufficiently long apprenticeship, the present International staff could operate the Bank alone in the face of a major labour dispute is not worth consideration. The desirability of operational experience for a general banker is therefore considered on its merits, the absolute specialization found in many major U.S. banks has been rejected as unsound, the preference for those with general experience confirmed, but the mix has been totally redesigned. Historical comparison is difficult because of the radical change in banking, the increased use of specialists, and the impact of Government regulations on work permits, but one could argue that the 'junior' years are to be confined to four to six years of 'general banking'. Even within that time, efforts are to be made to ensure diversity of experience both functional and geographical; experience should include some executive responsibility, including management of a small department or sub-branch.

The concept of 'appointment' has been discarded and Home leaves after the first six years have become annual. This latter is important because it makes for greater flexibility in assignment; appropriate promotion is no longer prevented because of long-leave expectations. These changes are particularly important in the middle phase (years seven to sixteen), during which the officer is supposed to receive continued broad experience but to be more often placed in positions which reflect his perceived special aptitudes. In the final phase, the officer is to be 'streamed' either into the area of functional expertise for which he shows particular aptitude or into general banking.

The appropriate overheads were set up to implement this and the related scheme for Regional officers.

Regional officers and local staff

Since the early 1960s there has been an increasing role for the Regional officer. Ideally, assignments are to be made without regard to international or regional status, with the exception that normally the latter will not be assigned outside his country, a qualification which consequently has certain indirect limitations in practice on the career of the Regional officer. The Regional officer has certain of the same perquisities of the International staff, although tax problems and comparability with other local employment terms may set a limit. Debentures are available for business clubs; the Bank pays 50% of the entrance fees, arguing, perhaps, that this after all is the officer's own country and he will remain there throughout his career and into retirement.

As noted above, to offset the career limitations he faces when he is the citizen of a country with only one or two Hongkong Bank offices, a policy has been devised to bring him for periods on secondment to Hong Kong. Alternatively, since 1980 Regional officers can become members of the International staff, and this may prove the ultimate solution. Nevertheless a high percentage have working spouses, and the frequent moves would not be universally welcome. But these are problems common to most multinational corporations. As noted, not until 1987 did the Hongkong Bank appoint a woman to the International staff, despite there having been senior Regional women officers.

For the local staffs life has become more organized, the counterpart of developments at New Beckenham. In Hong Kong, for example, there is a sports club with a membership of 6,000. The corporation's in-house news magazine, *HongkongBank News* (formerly *Group News*), has its counterparts in such regional publications as Malaysia's *Berita HongkongBank* which would include articles on, for example, Hong Kong artist Brian Tilbrook's murals for the new Kuala Lumpur office, the Batik motifs designed by M. Shahabudin for the Main Banking Hall, the coming of the new sculptured lions, stories of local staff honoured for long and/or meritorious service, staff parties, local branch news, and, in prominent place, sports events.

The focus now as always is on the Hongkong Bank team, and the team is understood now – as in fairness it was from the beginning – in the full corporate sense, the International staff, the Regional officers, and the local staff. The Board of Directors has over its history concerned itself with the eye operation of a Portuguese clerk, the widow of an Indian messenger, the emigration of a Russian guard. The difference is that the concern has become systematized; there are more activities in which the several communities can share; there are specialists on the staff whose task is to promote the sharing. Multinationalism begins in a single office.

HongkongBank, the Hongkong Bank group, is, then, continuing to develop geographically and to broaden its range of financial services. The Board of Directors is more broadly selected and the executive succession is in place. The various staffs are seen as part of the team coordinating both multicurrency credit facilities and intra-regional sports. The young man or woman can still be told in truth – as Sandy Moncur, the long-time and much respected London Accountant, told the young juniors in the 1920s and early 1930s, 'You are entering on a career not a job' (see Vol. III).

Although growth of the normally dynamic Hong Kong economy in 1985 was 1%, the Sino-British Joint Declaration on Hong Kong was in place and, with the revival of the economy in 1986, with the Bank's continued ability to raise capital (in 1987, for example, with a rights issue), the persistent needling relative to the cost of the new Head Office building ceased now that its merits can be demonstrated, the Bank would appear prepared to continue its dynamic contribution to local, intra-regional, and international finance.

With the 1987 cash investment of 14.9% of the capital of Midland Bank, even the Bank's problem of a European base would appear on the road to solution. Indeed by mid-1988 rationalization had reversed once again recent Bank European policies – HSBC was in the process of virtually ceasing retail operations in the United Kingdom and of withdrawing from the Continent – Frankfurt and Geneva excepted. Undoubtedly this history has suggested other potential points of strain. Although this study has made occasional reference to an event in 1985 or even 1988, as told here this history of the Bank properly ended with the inauguration of the successful partnership with Marine Midland. Incautiously perhaps for an economic historian, I have offered in Part III of Volume IV a survey of the events whereby the Bank prepared for change during the late 1970s and early 1980s. Under Michael Sandberg, who was himself building on the work of his immediate predecessors, Michael Turner, John Saunders, and G.M. Sayer, survival and dramatic growth were for the time ensured through transformation of The Hongkong and Shanghai Banking Corporation from an Eastern exchange bank, a regional China bank with a colonial and Treaty Port tradition, to a multinational financial group.

Success, however, is never assured. Despite the steady development of HongkongBank (Hongkong Bank group) since 1980, there have been setbacks, and the Hong Kong environment, while recovered from several economic and political shocks, has only just returned to its earlier buoyancy, while the aftermath of the property boom of the early 1980s has not yet been fully resolved. Meanwhile, with 1997 a matter of public discussion, questions must be asked about the Bank and the future; for these a history can provide relevant material for discussion, but it cannot be expected to offer an authoritative answer. The conclusions of this chapter and of this volume are, nevertheless, clearly optimistic; the Bank is *prepared* for the future. Furthermore, the law as embodied in Ordinance No. 6 of 1929 still stands:

the Bank shall continue to be and shall remain incorporated but there shall from henceforth be no limit whatever to the duration of the period of its incorporation.

APPENDIX TABLES

APPENDIX

BIBLIOGRAPHY

INDEX

APPENDIX TABLES

Table A. *The Hongkong and Shanghai Banking Corporation Chief Executives**

Dates	Name	Seniority in Bank	Chief Executive	Years East on Appointment	Branches served	Age on Appointment	Membership on Legco	Membership on Exco
na–1883	Victor Kresser	1865	1865–1870[a]	—	1	na	—	—
1837–1911	James Greig	1867	1870–1876	3[b]	1	33	1872[t]	—
1841–1915	Thomas Jackson	1866	1876–1886	10[b]	4	36	1884–86[c]	—
1842–1907	John Walter[d]	1868	1886–1887	18[b]	5	44	—	—
—	Thomas Jackson	—	1887–1889	—	—	—	—	—
na–1902	George Edward Noble	1866	1889–1890	23[b]	4	na	—	—
—	Thomas Jackson	—	1890–1891	—	—	—	—	—
1853–1930	Louis François David de Bovis	1872	1891–1893	19	6	38	—	—
—	Sir Thomas Jackson	—	1893–1902	—	—	—	—	—
na–1918	John Ross Middleton Smith	1882	1902–1910	20	5	na	—	—
1868–1931	Sir Newton John Stabb	1891	1910–1920	19	5	43	1919[t]	—
1862–1924	Alexander Gordon Stephen	1885	1920–1924	35	9	58	1921–23	1921–24
1870–1960	Arthur Harold Barlow	1891	1924–1927	33	7	52	—	—
1873–1940	Arthur Cecil Hynes	1897	1927–1930	29	6	54	1927–30	1928[t]
1881–1943	Sir Vandeleur Molyneux Grayburn	1904	1930–1941[e]	25	3	49	—	—
1892–1967	Sir Arthur Morse	1915	1941–1953[e]	26	4	49	—	1946–53
1905–1980	Sir Michael William Turner	1930	1953–1962	23	3	47	—	1954–62

1917–	Sir John Anthony Holt Saunders	1940[f]	1962–1972	16	3	45	1965–72[g]
1924–	Guy Mowbray Sayer	1947	1972–1977	24	6	48	1974–77
1927–	Sir Michael Graham	1949	1977–1986	28	3	50	1973–74 1978–86
1931–	Ruddock Sandberg	1955	1986–	30	6	54	1987–
	William Purves						

na = not available Legco = Legislative Council Exco = Executive Council

* The use of the term 'chief executives' enables the construction of a table stating who was actually in charge (except during brief periods of leave); the dates stated are not, therefore, precisely those given in an official list of 'chief managers'.

[a] There was no Chief Manager until 1868. Until then Kresser was de facto chief executive officer in consequence of his role as de facto executive secretary of the Court of Directors.

[b] Years in the Hongkong Bank in the East.

[c] Appointed after nomination as the elected representative of the Hong Kong General Chamber of Commerce.

[d] Walter was, as usual, first appointed as 'acting' Chief Manager, but he was not substantiated. Instead Jackson was recalled.

[e] 1941–43 Grayburn was interned but remained titular Chief Manager; Morse was Acting Chief Manager in London.

[f] East in 1946.

[g] Saunders was a temporary member for a short period in 1964.

[t] Temporary or substitute member.

Table B. *The Hongkong Bank Group*
Directors, Managers, and subsidiary companies, June 1986

HongkongBank

The Hongkong and Shanghai Banking Corporation
Incorporated in Hong Kong with limited liability

Head Office:
1 Queen's Road Central, Hong Kong

Board of Directors

Michael Graham Ruddock Sandberg, CBE, *Chairman*
William Purves, DSO, *Chief Executive and Deputy Chairman*
Li Ka-shing, *Deputy Chairman*
Denys Eamonn Connolly
Patrick Charles Samuel Deveson
Edward Walsh Duffy
Lydia Selina Dunn, CBE
Robert Conmac Farrell
Frank Riddell Frame
David Grand Jaques
Simon Lindley Keswick
James Wilson McKee, Jr.
Henry Michael Pearson Miles
Charles Wilfrid Newton
Alfred Ramsay Petrie, CBE
John Robert Petty
Helmut Sohmen
Jack Chi-Chien Tang, OBE

General Managers

Bernard Harry Asher
Kenneth William Barker
John Reginald Hartnell Bond
Peter William Sheppard Campbell Brockman
Robert Walker Campbell
John Malcolm Gray
Richard Edward Hale
John Estmond Strickland
Anthony Kenyon Daltry Townsend
David Franklyn Lewis Turner
Michael William Wells
Peter John Wrangham

Subsidiary Companies

African Queen Holdings Limited
Agile Nominees Limited
Allmann, Dorling & Co., Limited
American Interest Arbitrage Corporation
The Angel Trustee Company Limited
Angelot Limited
Antony Gibbs & Sons, Limited
Antony Gibbs Associates Limited
Antony Gibbs Completions Limited
Antony Gibbs Insurance Company Limited
Antony Gibbs Ireland Limited
Antony Gibbs (Middle East) Limited
Antony Gibbs (Overseas Investments) Limited
Antony Gibbs Pension Services Australia (Holdings) Pty Limited
Antony Gibbs Pension Services Australia Pty Limited
Antony Gibbs Pension Services Limited
Antony Gibbs (Personal Financial Planning) Limited
Antony Gibbs Securities Limited
Antony Gibbs, Simmers (Insurance Brokers) Limited
Antrobus Investments Limited
Ariadne Films Limited
Arrowhead Associates, Inc
Asian Pacific Investments Pty Limited
Aslore Pty Limited
Associated Bankers Insurance Company Limited
（銀聯保險公司）
Ausfic Investment Services Limited
Australian Pacific Management Services Pte Limited
B.A. Turner Limited
Basingstoke Holdings Limited
BBME Nominees Limited
Beauty Enterprises Limited
Benteng Redevelopment Sdn Bhd
99 Bishopsgate Limited
Bridgepalm Limited
The British and Chinese Corporation Limited
The British Bank of the Middle East
133759 Canada Limited
Capital Collections Limited
Carlingford Australia General Insurance Limited
Carlingford Australia Holdings Pty Limited
Carlingford Australia Insurance Company Limited
Carlingford BV
Carlingford Gibraltar Insurance Holdings Limited
Carlingford Insurance Agencies Limited
Carlingford Insurance Brokers Singapore Pte Limited
Carlingford Insurance Company Limited
Carlingford Insurance Representatives Limited
Carlingford International Limited
Carlingford Investments Limited
Carlingford Life and General Assurance Company Limited
Carlingford Limited
Carlingford NV
Carlingford PNG Limited (in liquidation)
Carlingford Services Limited
Carlingford Swire Assurance Limited
Carlingford Swire International Assurance Limited
Carroll McEntee & McGinley, Inc
Carsil Limited
Charles Investments Limited
Chelmer Shipping Company Limited
Chronogram Corporation
CM & M Asset Management Company, Inc
CM & M Futures, Inc
CM & M Futures (Singapore) Pte, Limited
CM & M Group, Inc
CM & M (U.K.) Limited
Collyer Quay Properties Limited
Colwyn Investments Limited
Concord Asset Management, Inc
Concord Credit Limited
Concord Export Finance Company Limited
Concord International (Curacao) NV
Concord Leasing (Asia) Pte Limited
Concord Leasing GmbH
Concord Leasing Inc
Concord Leasing Limited
Concord Leasing NV/SA
Concord Leasing Services Limited
Concorde Equipement SA
Concorde Finance et Cie SNC
Concorde Finance SARL
Concorde Location SA
Corylus Investments Limited
Cotswold Investments Limited
Cranleigh Investments Limited
Crorebridge Bank Limited
Crouch Shipping Company Limited
Dalbeattie Investment Limited
Deeside Investment Corporation
Diameco Investments Limited
Diana Investments Limited
Dominus Investments Limited
DPC Investments Limited
Dungeness Investment Limited

Table B (cont.)

Durness Investments Limited
Duveen & Walker Limited
Eastleigh Investments Limited
Educational Funding Services, Inc
Equator Advisory Services Limited
Equator Bank Limited
Equator Holdings Limited
Equator Investment Services Limited
Equator Leasing Incorporated
Equator Leasing One Incorporated
Equator Limited
Equator Overseas Services Limited
Equator Trade Services Limited
Equator U.S.A. Incorporated
ETC Machines Pte Limited
ETC Services Limited
ETSL Equator Trade Services Limited N.V.
EuroConcord Finance BV
EuroConcord Leasing BV
First Leasing Corporation
First Tower Shipping Corporation
Fitrust Corporation
Fiver Limited (in voluntary liquidation)
Foraker Investments Pty Limited
Fort Hall Limited
Gairloch Investments Limited
Galaxia Navigation Company Limited
Gatechurch Property Management Limited
Gatestock Limited
Gatewood Investments Limited
Gelhood Limited
GH (Insurance Agencies) NV
Gibbs & Company (Central Africa) (Private) Limited
Gibbs Hartley Cooper Administration Limited
Gibbs Hartley Cooper Bloodstock Limited
Gibbs Hartley Cooper Financial Risks Limited
Gibbs Hartley Cooper International Limited
Gibbs Hartley Cooper Limited
Gibbs Hartley Cooper Marine Limited
Gibbs Hartley Cooper North America Limited
Gibbs Hartley Cooper Re Limited
Gibbs Hartley Cooper Technical Services Limited
Gibbs Hartley Cooper UK Limited
Gibbs (Holding) Limited
Gibbs Insurance Consultants Limited
Gibbs Insurance Holdings Limited
Gibbs Liquidaciones de Seguros Limitada
Gibbs Y Cia S.A.C.
Gibbsure (Private) Limited
Gingerfield Limited
Gloxinia Investment Limited
Gracechurch Holdings Limited
The Grenelefe Corporation
Grenelefe Realty, Inc
Grenelefe Utility Corporation
Grenville Eastern Holdings Limited
Grenville Pacific Holdings Limited
Grenville Property Holdings Limited
Grenville Resources Holdings Limited
Grenville Transportation Holdings Limited
Guardforce International Limited
Guardforce Limited
(衛安有限公司)
Guttata Investment Limited
Hambauxon Company, Limited
(恒寶盛有限公司)
Hang Che Lee Company, Limited
(恒致利有限公司)
Hang Seng Bank (Bahamas) Limited
Hang Seng Bank, Limited
(恒生銀行有限公司)
Hang Seng Bank Trustee (Bahamas) Limited
Hang Seng Bank (Trustee) Limited
(恒生銀行信託有限公司)
Hang Seng Credit (Bahamas) Limited

Hang Seng Credit Limited
(恒生存款有限公司)
Hang Seng Finance (Bahamas) Limited
Hang Seng Finance Limited
(恒生財務有限公司)
Hang Seng (Nominee) Limited
(恒生(代理人)有限公司)
Hang Shun Lee Company, Limited
(恒順利有限公司)
Hang Tung Travel Service Limited
(恒通旅運有限公司)
Hang Yuan Management Limited
(恒潤管理有限公司)
Harbord Investment Limited
Harrogate Investment Limited
Harthover Project Public Limited Company
 (in members' voluntary liquidation)
Hartley Cooper & Co. Limited
Hartley Cooper & Warner Limited
Hartley Cooper Group (Staff Funds) Limited
Hartley Cooper Holdings Limited
Hartley Cooper Life & Pensions Brokers Limited
Hartley Cooper Overseas Holdings Limited
Hartley Cooper Trustees Limited
Hartley Cooper Underwriting Agency Limited
Haseba International Management Limited
(恒生國際管理有限公司)
Haseba Investment Company Limited
(恒生投資有限公司)
Haslemere Investment Corporation
Hazel General Trading Company Limited
HBL Holdings Limited
HBL Nominees Limited
Hexagon Productions Limited
Hexham Investment Limited
Heywood Shipping Limited
Highclere Investments Limited
 (in members' voluntary liquidation)
Himalaya Investments Limited
HK Management Limited
HKBG Holdings Limited
Honggroup Nominees Limited
Hongkong & Shanghai Bank (Kuala Lumpur)
 Nominees Sendirian Berhad
Hongkong & Shanghai Bank (Malaysia) Trustee Berhad
Hongkong & Shanghai Bank (Pension Trustee) Limited
Hongkong & Shanghai Bank (Singapore) Nominees
 Private Limited
Hongkong & Shanghai Banking Corporation
 (Nominees) Limited
Hongkong and Shanghai Bank Nominees (Jersey) Limited
Hongkong and Shanghai Bank Trustee (Jersey) Limited
The Hongkong and Shanghai Banking Corporation (CI)
 Limited
Hongkong and Shanghai Trustee (Guernsey) Limited
Hongkong and Shanghai Trustee (Isle of Man) Limited
Hongkong Australia Holdings Pty Limited
Hongkong Bancorp Inc
Hongkong Bank (Agency) Private Limited
Hongkong Bank and Trust Company Limited
Hongkong Bank and Trust Company (Nominees)
 Limited
Hongkong Bank Malaysia Berhad
Hongkong Bank (Malaysia) Nominees Sdn Bhd
Hongkong Bank of Canada
Hongkong Bank of Canada Leasing Limited
Hongkong Bank Servicos Limitada
Hongkong Bank Trustee Limited
Hongkong Bank Trustee (Singapore) Limited
Hongkong Finance Holdings Limited
Hongkong Finance Investments Limited
Hongkong Finance Limited
Hongkong International Trade Finance (Holdings)
 Limited

Table B (cont.)

Hongkong International Trade Finance (Japan) KK
Hongkong International Trade Finance Limited
Hongkong International Trade Finance (UK) Limited
Hongkong International Trade Finance (USA) Inc
Hongkong International Trade (Germany) Limited
Hongkong Resources Inc
Hongkong Shanghai (Properties) Limited
Hongkong Shanghai (Shipping) Limited
HongkongBank (Bahamas) Limited
HongkongBank China Services Limited
HongkongBank Financial Services (Gibraltar) Limited
HongkongBank International Trustee Limited
HongkongBank Limited
HongkongBank Nominees Limited
HongkongBank of Australia Limited
HongkongBank Pension Services Limited
HongkongBank Trustee Holdings Limited
Hop Wing Tai Property Limited
(合永泰地産有限公司)
H.S. Property Management Company Limited
HSBC Holdings BV
HSBC Holdings UK Limited
HSI Services Limited
(恒指服務有限公司)
Ibsonville Limited
Intermarine Australia Limited
Intermarine Limited
Intermarine Shipping Holdings (Jersey) Limited
Intermarket Securities Corporation
International Ship Finance (Liberia) Inc
International Ship Finance (Panama) Inc
International Treasury Management Inc
International Treasury Management Limited
Investors Arbitrage Corporation
Jackson Holdings BV
Jadmas Pty Limited
James Capel & Co
James Capel (Channel Islands) Eurobonds Limited
James Capel (Channel Islands) Limited
James Capel (Channel Islands) Nominees Limited
James Capel (Far East) Limited
James Capel Far East Nominees Limited
James Capel (Financial Futures) Limited
James Capel Financial Services Limited
James Capel Gilts Limited
James Capel International Asset Management Limited
James Capel International Limited
James Capel International S.A.
James Capel Investment Services (Jersey) Limited
James Capel (Nominees) Limited
James Capel Research Limited
James Capel (Second Nominees) Limited
James Capel Securities Inc
James Capel Unit Trust Management Limited
James Capel (USA) Limited
Jessie Investment Pte Limited
Jirbas Drilling Limited
Jonathan Limited (in voluntary liquidation)
Jungali Investment Limited
Kellett Investments Limited
Kellett NV
Kemsley & Co (New Zealand) Limited
Lady Margaret Maritime Corporation
Laurel Management Corporation
Laurhold Limited
Lee County Management Corporation
Liana Company Limited
Lion Corporate Services Limited
Lion International Management Limited
Llandudno Investments Limited
Lyndholme Limited
MAF Finance Limited
Makari Investment Limited
Marine CM & M Securities
Marine Midland Automotive Financial Corporation
Marine Midland Bank (Delaware), National Association
Marine Midland Bank, NA
Marine Midland Bank (Nominees) Limited

Marine Midland Banks, Inc
Marine Midland Business Credit Corporation
Marine Midland Business Loans, Inc
Marine Midland (C.I.) Limited
Marine Midland Capital Markets Limited
Marine Midland Consumer Credit Corporation
Marine Midland do Brasil, Limitada
Marine Midland (Export Finance) Limited
Marine Midland Finance NV
Marine Midland Holdings, Inc
Marine Midland International Bank
Marine Midland International Trust Company (Cayman) Limited
Marine Midland Leasing Corporation
Marine Midland (Leasing) Limited
Marine Midland Limited
Marine Midland Mortgage Corporation
Marine Midland Mortgage Servicing Corporation
Marine Midland National Corporation
Marine Midland National Finance Corporation
Marine Midland New Jersey Corporation
Marine Midland Overseas Corporation
Marine Midland Pennsylvania Corporation
Marine Midland Properties Corporation
Marine Midland Realty Credit Corporation
Marine Midland Securities, Inc
Marine Midland Southwest Corporation
Marine Midland Trade, Inc
Marine Options, Inc
Marine-Massachusetts Real Estate, Inc
Marinvest, Inc
Marmid Aircraft Leasing Corporation
Marmid Energy Corporation
Marmid Finance Limited
Marmid Life Insurance Company
Marmid United Corporation
Mayotte Limited (in members' voluntary liquidation)
Menorca Investments Limited
Meridian International Assurance (B) Sdn Berhad
Merino Limited
MetWay Limited
Miami Investment Limited
Michigan Investments Limited
Middle East Finance Company Limited
Middle East Insurance Holdings Limited
Milnethorpe Limited
Minnmar Corporation
Mortgage And Finance Berhad
Mortgage And Finance (Malaysia) Berhad
Mountain Trading Limited
New Sydney Enterprise Limited
New Town Management Corporation
Obelix Hong Kong Limited
Obelix Limited
Oleifera Investments Limited
Ondine Limited (in voluntary liquidation)
253014 Ontario Limited
Opalville Limited
Oristle Investment (No. 1) Limited
Oristle Investment (No. 2) Limited
Oristle Investment (No. 3) Limited
Oristle Investment (No. 4) Limited
Oristle Investment (No. 5) Limited
Oristle Investment (No. 6) Limited
Oristle Investment (No. 7) Limited
Oristle Investment (No. 8) Limited
Oristle Investment (No. 9) Limited
Oristle Investment (No. 10) Limited
Oristle Investment (No. 11) Limited
Oristle Investment (No. 12) Limited
Oristle Investment (No. 13) Limited
Oristle Investment (No. 14) Limited
Oristle Investment (No. 15) Limited
Oristle Investment (No. 16) Limited
Oristle Investment (No. 17) Limited
Oristle Investment (No. 18) Limited
Oristle Investment (No. 19) Limited
Oristle Investment (No. 20) Limited
Oroton Investments Limited
Oswesry Investments Limited

Table B (cont.)

Pakenham Investment Limited
Pall Mall Nominees Limited
Palmer Gould Evans Pty Limited
Pannoch Investments Limited
Pannoch Investments (Management) Limited
Papua New Guinea Forest Exports Pty Limited
250 Park Avenue Corporation
Perpetual Publicity Limited
(永年廣告有限公司)
Pethurst International Limited
Pethurst Limited
Pico Development Corporation
Pino Armadora S.A.
Pipkin Project Company Limited
Pittencrieff Investments Limited
PPF Limited
Public Financial Management, Inc
Pyracantha Investment Limited
Quadruped Limited (in voluntary liquidation)
1 Queen's Road Central Limited
Quelton Company NV
Rappresentanza Marine Midland Bank - New York S.R.L.
Reavcom Services, Inc
The Rhed Rhombohedron, Inc
Ronda Investment Limited
Silom Limited
Snowden Investments Limited
Sociedad Commercial Y de Inversiones "Anton" Limitada
Société Immobilière Atlas S.A.
Soham Investment Company Limited
(長康置業有限公司)
Solandra Investment Limited
Speedlink SA
Stanbridge International Bank Limited
State Equipment Finance Limited
(國家器材信貸有限公司)
State Leasing (Hong Kong) Limited
(國家租貸(香港)有限公司)
Strangford Investment Limited
Sword Assurance Limited
Sword International Limited
Taunton Investments Limited
Thames Company Limited
Tinker Properties Corporation
TKM (Australia) Limited
TKM (Far East) Limited
TKM (Germany) GmbH
TKM Limited
TKM Mid Americas Inc
TKM New Zealand Limited
TKM (Singapore) Pte Limited
TKM Trading (HK) Limited
TKM Trading GmbH
TKM (UK) Limited
TKM (USA) Financial Holdings, Inc
TKM (USA) Holdings Inc
Tobermory Investment Limited
ToMar Corporation
Townermar Corporation
US Concord Inc
Verbena Investment Limited
Victoria Branch Nominees Limited
Vinford Limited
Wardley Asia Limited
Wardley Australia (Holdings) Limited
Wardley Australia Leasing Limited
Wardley Australia Leasing (Victoria) Pty Limited
Wardley Australia Limited
Wardley Australia Management Limited
Wardley Australia Nominees Pty Limited
Wardley Australia Overseas Limited
Wardley Australia Property Management Limited
Wardley Australia Securities Limited
Wardley B.V.
Wardley Bond Management Limited
Wardley Cyprus Limited

Wardley Data Services Limited
Wardley Development Finance Limited
Wardley Export Finance Limited
Wardley Far East Capital Limited
Wardley Finance Limited
Wardley Fund Managers (Jersey) Limited
Wardley Funds Limited
Wardley Gibbs Limited
Wardley Gilt Fund Limited
Wardley Group Limited
Wardley Holdings Limited
Wardley International Bank Limited
Wardley International Bank (Vila) Limited
Wardley International BV
Wardley International Limited
Wardley International Management Limited
Wardley International NV
Wardley Investment Management Limited
Wardley Investment Services (Hong Kong) Limited
Wardley Investment Services (Japan) K.K.
Wardley Investment Services Limited
Wardley Investment Services (UK) Limited
Wardley Investments (NH) Limited
Wardley Investments (NZ) Limited
Wardley Leasing Limited
Wardley Limited
Wardley London Holdings Limited
Wardley London Limited
Wardley London Nominees Limited
Wardley London Property Services Limited
Wardley (Malaysia) Sendirian Berhad
Wardley Management Gibraltar Limited
Wardley Marine International Investment Management Limited
Wardley Middle East Holdings Limited
Wardley Middle East Limited
Wardley New Zealand Deposits Limited
Wardley New Zealand Limited
Wardley Nominees Limited
Wardley Nominees (Nassau) Limited
Wardley Property Management Limited
Wardley Retirement Services Limited
Wardley Securities Limited
Wardley Services (New Hebrides) Limited
Wardley Shipping Services Limited
Wardley (Singapore) Nominees Private Limited
Wardley Swire Holdings Limited
Wardley Swire International Limited
Wardley Thailand Limited
Wardley Trade Finance Limited
Wardley Unit Trust Managers Limited
Wardley-ACLI Commodities Australia Limited
Wardley-Thomson Futures H.K. Limited
Wardley-Thomson Futures (Singapore) Pte Limited
Wardley-Thomson Limited
Wardley-Thomson Nominees Limited
Wayfoong Credit Limited
Wayfoong Finance Limited
(滙豐財務有限公司)
Wayfoong Mortgage And Finance (Singapore) Limited
Wayfoong Plaza Limited
Wayfoong Property Agency Limited
(滙豐物業代理有限公司)
Wayfoong Shipping Services Limited
Wayhong (Bahamas) Limited
Wayhong Finance Limited
Waylee Holdings Limited
(in members' voluntary liquidation)
Waylee Investments Limited
Westminster Insurance Company Limited
Winnipeg Investments Limited
WISL International Limited
WISLI Nominees Limited
WISUK Nominees Limited
WTL Limited
Yan Nin Development Company Limited
(恩年發展有限公司)
Yick Lee Securities Limited

APPENDIX: THE HONGKONG AND SHANGHAI BANKING CORPORATION ORDINANCE
(as revised in 1983)

Chapter 70 of the Laws of Hong Kong

Originally 6 of 1929.
(Cap. 70, 1950.)

33 of 1939.
8 of 1946.
20 of 1948.
37 of 1950.
27 of 1953.
36 of 1957.
25 of 1961.
5 of 1965.
G.N. 761/65.
L.N. 60/69.
L.N. 127/73.
6 of 1978.
21 of 1978.

To amend the constitution of The Hongkong and Shanghai Banking Corporation.

(Replaced, 37 of 1950, Schedule)

[17 May 1929.]

Short title.

1. This Ordinance may be cited as The Hongkong and Shanghai Banking Corporation Ordinance.
(Replaced, 37 of 1950, Schedule)

Interpretation.

2. In this Ordinance, unless the context otherwise requires—

"auditor" means auditor of the bank;

(5 of 1866.)

"bank" means "The Hongkong and Shanghai Banking Corporation" created by virtue of the provisions of the Hongkong and Shanghai Bank Ordinance 1866, and continued by this Ordinance; *(Amended, 33 of 1939, Supp. Schedule, G.N. 840/40, and 37 of 1950, Schedule)*

"board" means board of directors and (if the context so requires) means the directors assembled at a meeting of the board;

"capital" means the share capital for the time being of the bank;

"chairman" means the chairman or his deputy presiding at any meeting of shareholders or of the board;

"chief accountant" means the person for the time being performing the duties of chief accountant of the bank at the head office;

"chief manager" means the person for the time being performing the duties of chief manager, and "acting chief manager" means the person for the time being performing the duties of acting chief manager of the bank; *(Amended, 8 of 1946, s. 2)*

"court" means the Supreme Court of the Colony and includes any judge or judges thereof, sitting either together or separately, in court on in chambers;

The Hongkong Bank Ordinance

"directors" means the directors for the time being of the bank or (if the context so requires) directors present and voting at a meeting of the board;

"dividend" includes any interim dividend, bonus or profits on any share;

"dollar" means dollar in Hong Kong currency;

"general meeting" means a general meeting of shareholders;

"head office" means the principal place of business in the Colony for the time being of the bank;

"incapacitated shareholder" means a shareholder being an infant, or an idiot or lunatic, or *non compos mentis*, or a bankrupt or one whose estate has, by the operation of law, become vested in any other person or persons in trust for or for the benefit of his creditors; *(Amended, 33 of 1939, Supp. Schedule, G.N. 840/40)*

"Ordinance" or "the Ordinance" means this Ordinance;

"ordinary resolution" means a resolution of a simple majority of shareholders at a general meeting;

"person" includes a firm, company or corporation;

"regulations" means the regulations of the bank for the time being in force;

"share" means share in the share capital of the bank;

"shareholder" or "holder of a share" or "holder of any share" means every person whose name is entered in any register of shareholders of the bank as a holder of any share or shares.

3. Notwithstanding the repeal of the Hongkong and Shanghai Bank Ordinance 1866, the bank shall continue to be incorporated by the name of "*The Hongkong and Shanghai Banking Corporation*", and by that name shall and may sue and be sued in all courts, and in that name shall continue to have perpetual succession, with a common seal which it may vary and change at its pleasure: — Incorporation. (5 of 1866.)

Provided that there shall be no limit whatever to the period of incorporation.
(Replaced, 33 of 1939, Supp. Schedule, G.N. 840/40, and 37 of 1950, Schedule)

4. (1) The regulations are hereby substituted for and shall replace the deed of settlement dated the 20th July 1867, and all the articles contained therein and any amendments thereof, and shall be for all purposes the regulations of the bank, and this Ordinance and the regulations shall be binding in all respects upon the bank and upon all persons whatsoever, whether shareholders or not, and shall regulate the rights and liabilities of all the above persons *inter se*, their heirs, executors, administrators, assigns or successors. *(Amended, 33 of 1939, Supp. Schedule, G.N. 840/40)* — Regulations of the bank; ordinance and regulations binding on all persons;

(2) At any time and from time to time it shall be lawful for the shareholders by special resolution to amend the provisions of the regulations or any of them: — power to amend regulations;

Provided that no such amendment shall be valid or have any force or effect until it has been approved by the Governor and published in the *Gazette*. Any such power to amend as aforesaid includes the power to amend, vary, rescind, revoke or suspend any regulation or any part thereof and the power to make any new regulation. *(Amended, 33 of 1939, Supp. Schedule, G.N. 840/40)*

proof of regulations.

(3) A copy of the regulations and of any such special resolution to amend, purporting to be certified by the Chief Secretary to be a correct copy, shall be received in all courts of justice, and for all purposes, as valid and sufficient evidence of the contents of the regulations and of the fact that such regulations have been duly approved and published in the *Gazette*.

Objects of the bank and conduct of its business;

5. (1) The objects of the bank shall be the carrying on the business of banking and as ancillary thereto the other businesses and objects set forth and contained in regulation 3 of the regulations, and the bank shall be at liberty to continue, commence, carry on and effect all or any of its objects at any of its establishments, that is to say, at its head office and also at its present branches, agencies and sub-agencies and also at any additional branches, agencies and sub-agencies whether in the Colony or elsewhere which may hereafter be established:

Provided that the business of the bank's branches, agencies and sub-agencies shall conform to the laws relating to banking whether passed before or after the date of this Ordinance in any of the territories in which the powers hereby conferred are exercised. *(Amended, 37 of 1950, Schedule, and 36 of 1957, s. 2)*

power to close establishments.

(2) The bank shall have power to close any of its establishments.

Power to sell and convert property taken as security.

6. It shall be lawful for the bank to sell, dispose of and convert into money any real or personal property of whatever description, mortgaged, charged, pledged or hypothecated to the bank or taken by it in satisfaction, liquidation or payment of any debt or liability.

Capital and increase thereof.

7. (1) The capital of the bank is $8,000 million divided into 3,200 million shares of $2.50 each. *(Amended, G.N. 761/65, L.N. 60/69, Gazette of 10.4.70, PN544, and L.N. 127/73, Resolutions 1 and 3, EGM 27/3/75, EGM 20/4/79, EGM 25/4/80, and EGM 9/4/81)*

(2) The capital of the bank may from time to time be increased by ordinary resolution. *(Replaced, 36 of 1957, s. 3)*

Alteration of capital.

8. The shareholders in general meeting shall, in addition to the power hereinbefore conferred of increasing the capital of the bank, have power by ordinary resolution—

(a) to consolidate and divide all or any of the capital of the bank into shares of larger nominal amount than its existing shares;

(b) to subdivide its shares or any of them into shares of smaller amount than is fixed by this Ordinance or by the regulations, so however that in the subdivision the proportion between the amount paid and the amount, if any, unpaid on each reduced share shall be the same as it was in the case of the share from which the reduced share is derived; *(Amended, 36 of 1957, s. 4(a))*

(c) to convert any paid-up shares into stock and reconvert that stock into paid-up shares of any amount; and *(Added, 36 of 1957, s. 4(c))*

(d) to cancel shares which at the date of the passing of the resolution in that behalf have not been taken or agreed to be taken by any person, and to diminish the amount of its capital by the amount of the shares so cancelled, and a cancellation of shares in pursuance of this section shall not be deemed to be a reduction of capital. *(Amended, 36 of 1957, s. 4(b))*

9. (1) The shareholders may be special resolution reorganize the capital, whether by the consolidation of shares of different classes or by the division of the shares into shares of different classes: *(Amended, 5 of 1965, s. 2)*

Reorganization of capital.

Provided that no preference or special privilege attached to or belonging to any class of shares shall be interfered with except by a resolution passed by a majority in number of shareholders of that class holding three-fourths of the share capital of that class and confirmed at a meeting of shareholders of that class in the same manner as a special resolution of the bank is required to be confirmed, and every resolution so passed shall bind all shareholders of the class.

(2) A copy of any such resolution shall be filed with the Chief Secretary within 7 days after the passing of the same or within such further time as the Governor may allow, and the resolution shall not take effect until such copy has been so filed.

10. (1) Subject to the provisions of subsection (2) and of the Bank Notes Issue Ordinance, the bank may in the Colony, but not elsewhere, issue, re-issue and circulate notes of the bank payable to bearer on demand. *(Amended, 21 of 1978, s. 3)*

Power to issue bearer notes.

(2) The bank shall not issue such notes of a denomination lower than five dollars in excess of such number as may, from time to time, be authorized by the Secretary of State.

(Replaced, 36 of 1957, s. 5)

11. (1) The total amount of the notes of the bank payable to bearer on demand actually in circulation shall subject to the provisions of subsection (3) not at any time exceed the equivalent of the sum of sixty million dollars. *(Amended, 37 of 1950, Schedule; 27 of 1953, s. 2 and 6 of 1978, s. 2)*

Amount of and security for note issue.

(2) The bank shall at all times keep deposited with the Crown Agents or with trustees appointed by the Secretary of

State or partly with the Crown Agents and partly with such trustees securities, approved by the Secretary of State, not less in value than the said sum of sixty million dollars. *(Replaced, 36 of 1957, s. 6(a). Amended, 6 of 1978, s. 2)*

(Cap. 66.)

(3) Notwithstanding the provisions of subsection (1), notes of the bank payable to bearer on demand may be issued and be in actual circulation to an amount in excess of the equivalent of the said sum of sixty million dollars, if there has been paid in accordance with section 4(1) of the Exchange Fund Ordinance to the Financial Secretary of the Hong Kong Government for the account of the Exchange Fund referred to in such Ordinance and against the issue to the bank of certificates of indebtedness as provided in such Ordinance an amount equal to the face value of such excess issue for the time being actually in circulation. *(Replaced, 37 of 1950, Schedule. Amended, 27 of 1953, s. 2; 36 of 1957, s. 6(b) and 6 of 1978, s. 2)*

(Cap. 66.)

(4) The securities deposited in accordance with subsection (2), and, as provided in section 4 of the Exchange Fund Ordinance, the whole of the amount paid in accordance with subsection (3) for the account of the Exchange Fund, shall be held as special funds exclusively available for the redemption of the said notes and in the event of the bank being wound up shall be applied accordingly so far as may be necessary, but without prejudice to the rights of the holders of such notes to rank with other creditors of the bank against the assets of the bank. *(Added, 36 of 1957, s. 6(c))*

Liability of shareholders.

12. In the event of the bank being wound up every shareholder shall be liable to contribute to the assets of the bank, in respect of any debts and liabilities of the bank, an amount not exceeding the amount, if any, unpaid on the shares held by him.

(Replaced, 36 of 1957, s. 7)

Form of contracts.

13. (1) Contracts on behalf of the bank may be made as follows— *(Amended, 33 of 1939, Supp. Schedule, G.N. 840/40)*

(a) any contract, which if made between private persons would be by law required to be in writing under seal, may be made on behalf of the bank in writing under seal and may in the same manner be varied or discharged;

(b) any contract, which if made between private persons would be by law required to be in writing signed by the parties to be charged therewith, may be made on behalf of the bank in writing, signed by any person acting under its authority, express or implied, and may in the same manner be varied or discharged;

(c) any contract, which if made between private persons would by law be valid although made by parol only and not reduced into writing, may be made by parol on behalf of the bank by any person acting under its authority, express or implied, and may in the same manner be varied or discharged.

(2) All contracts made according to this section shall be effectual in law and shall bind the bank and its successors and all other parties thereto, their heirs, executors, administrators or assigns or successors, as the case may be.

14. A bill of exchange or promissory note shall be deemed to have been made, accepted or indorsed on behalf of the bank if made, accepted or indorsed in the name of or by or on behalf or on account of the bank by any person acting under its authority. Bills of exchange and promissory notes.

15. The bank shall not discount, or in any manner advance money upon, bills of exchange, promissory notes or other negotiable paper in or upon which the name of any director or officer of the bank appears as drawer or acceptor, either on his individual or separate account, or jointly with any partner, or otherwise than as a director or officer of the bank to an amount exceeding one-tenth of the amount of the sum for the time being under discount or advanced by the bank, nor shall any director be allowed to obtain credit on his own personal guarantee. Limit of accommodation to directors and officers.

16. The total amount of the debts and liabilities of the bank of what nature or kind soever shall not at any time exceed the aggregate amount of the then existing *bona fide* assets and property of the bank. Limit of debts and liabilities.

(Amended, 36 of 1957, s. 8)

17. (1) Subject as hereinafter mentioned, the bank may be wound up by the Court, and all the provisions of the Companies Ordinance, with respect to the winding-up of companies registered thereunder shall apply to the bank as if expressly re-enacted in this Ordinance, save and except in such respects as the same may be altered or modified as hereafter mentioned or provided for. *(Amended, 33 of 1939, Supp. Schedule, G.N. 840/40, and 20 of 1948)* Winding-up and application. (Cap. 32.)

(2) The circumstances under which the bank may be wound up are as follows—

(a) in the event of the bank being dissolved or ceasing to carry on business or carrying on business only for the purpose of winding-up its affairs; or

(b) whenever the bank is unable to pay its debts; or

(c) whenever the court is of opinion that it is just and equitable that the bank should be wound up.

18. Nothing in this Ordinance shall affect or be deemed to affect the rights of Her Majesty the Queen, Her Heirs or Successors, or the rights of any body politic or corporate or of any other persons except such as are mentioned in this Ordinance and those claiming by, from or under them. Saving.

(Amended, 33 of 1939, Supp. Schedule, G.N. 840/40)

NOTES

Material from the Hongkong Bank Group Archives is not fully cited; the archives were in the process of being catalogued during the writing of this history.

Abbreviations used in the notes:

anon.	anonymous
BAAG	British Army Aid Group
B&CC	British and Chinese Corporation
BBME	British Bank of the Middle East
BT	Board of Trade
CCR	Chinese Central Railways
CO	Colonial Office
ECAFE	Economic Commission for Asia and the Far East
ed.	editor
esp.	especially
et seq.	and following
f.	folio
FO	Foreign Office
HK	Hong Kong
HSBC	Hongkong and Shanghai Banking Corporation
ibid	same
Kl	F.H. King Papers, Hongkong Bank Group Archives
LAC	London Advisory Committee
MMBI	Marine Midland Banks, Inc.
n.	note
OCC	Office of the Comptroller of the Currency
p.	page
pp.	pages
PP.MS.14	[Sir Charles S.] Addis Papers, the Library, School of Oriental and African Studies, University of London
S/O	semi-official
UN	United Nations

I HEAD OFFICE, LONDON: BANK OPERATIONS DURING THE PACIFIC WAR

1 A.C.C. Parkinson, Colonial Office, to Arthur Morse, Hongkong Bank, London, 16 December 1941, CO 129/590/4, 54065/41. The sequence of official correspondence, etc. is copied in several places including the minutes of the London Consultative

Notes to pp. 26–51

(Advisory) Committee, the F.H. King Letters, and various collections by J.R. Jones in the Group Archives.
2 *Ibid.*
3 Copies in *ibid.*
4 22 December 1941, CO 129/590/4, F13823/10.
5 Sir Vandeleur Grayburn to Arthur Morse, 19 December 1941, in London II, Box 26, item 321, Group Archives.
6 Message quoted in Edwin Ride, *BAAG, Hong Kong Resistance, 1942–1945* (Hong Kong, 1981), p. 200.
7 See minutes, London Advisory Committee (LAC), 23 December 1941, in Group Archives.
8 Villiers F. Caesar Hawkins of Stephenson Harwood & Tatham, to Morse, 10 April 1942, in F.H. King Letters, Kl.17.
9 Par. 2; a copy of the Order in Council will be found in the various J.R. Jones collections in Group Archives, see e.g. Appendix I to the chapter on 'War with Japan', in Jones, 'The Bank, 1876–1948'.
10 In Morse Papers, London Office II, Box 26, item 321, Group Archives.
11 Minutes, 26 March 1942, LAC, Group Archives.
12 Morse to Bruce, 31 December 1942, London Office II, Box 26, item 308.
13 Board of Directors, Minutes, 23 September 1943.
14 Addis diary, 5 January 1942, PP.MS.14/60, [Sir Charles S.] Addis Papers, Library, School of Oriental and African Studies.
15 See the Barlow file in the Morse Papers, London Office II, Box 26, item 304; on Morse's relations with Addis, see Volume III, Chapter 9.
16 A. Morse to W.C. Cassels, 14 September 1942, in F.H. King Letters, Kl.17, Group Archives.
17 *Ibid.*
18 Biographical information from J.R. Jones, ed. 'Personalities and Narratives', section on Arthur Morse.
19 Chief Manager's papers, Group Archives.
20 For Addis's relations with the University, see for example his diary, 10 January 1922, PP.MS.14/40; for the Treasurers, see University of Hong Kong, *Calendar, 1984–1985* (Hong Kong, 1984), p. 50.
21 T.J.J. Fenwick, oral history, pp. 31–32.
22 Addis diary, 8 June 1941, PP.MS.14/59.
23 *Ibid*, 28 November 1940, PP.MS.14/58.
24 *Ibid*, 3 October 1941, PP.MS.14/59.
25 H.E. Muriel, Autobiography, in Group Archives.
26 See Morse to Addis, 31 August 1943, London Office II, Box 26, item 297, Addis file, in Group Archives.
27 An article by Marius S. Jalet, the source of which is not given; it is found in Miscellaneous material sent to M. Collis, now in Group Archives.
28 Hongkong Bank Chairman's speech, Annual Meeting, 16 June 1943.
29 G.W. Stabb, oral history, p. 60.
30 'Scheme for dealing with salaries of interned British staff', referred to in Minutes of Board Meeting, 25 May 1944.
31 Addis to Morse, 20 June 1944, in Addis file cited; for the 1943 discussions, see Addis diary, 5 March 1943, PP.MS.14/61.
32 C.B. Terdre to J.R. Jones, 9 January 1963, in Jones, 'The Bank, 1876–1948', chapter on 'War with Japan', Appendix X.
33 Morse to H.M. Cook, 10 August 1945, in London II, Box 26, item 310.

34 Staff file, H.E. Muriel, Manager London Office, and A. Morse, 3 July 1946, in *ibid*, Box 28, item 489.
35 The principal source is the Hong Kong Reoccupation file in the Morse Papers, London II, Box 28, item 434. The main memo is dated 1 August 1945.
36 W. Webster, oral history, pp. 60–62, in Group Archives.
37 Board of Directors, Minutes, 3 June 1943.
38 *Ibid*, May 1945, and note dated 17 December 1945 in London II, Box 26, item 327.

2 THE BANK REESTABLISHED, 1945–1946

Oral history interviews referred to in this chapter were undertaken, unless otherwise specified, by Christopher Cook after an initial session with Cook and Frank H.H. King; the transcripts were edited by Catherine E. King.

1 M.G. Carruthers, oral history, p. 36.
2 Wendy, Lady Turner, oral history interview by Catherine E. King, p. 9.
3 O.P. Edwards, oral history, pp. 83–85.
4 Lady Turner, pp. 9–10.
5 F.J. Knightly, oral history interview by Cook and Frank H. H. King, p. 29 and M.F.L. Haymes, oral history, p. 42.
6 Lady Turner, pp. 23–24.
7 Maurice W. Turner, oral history, pp. 12–13.
8 Arthur Morse papers, London Office II files, Group Archives.
9 David J.S. King, 'On the Relations of the Hongkong Bank with Germany, 1864–1948', p. 101. A copy is in Group Archives.
10 J.R. Jones, 'Branches', Special Agencies, Hamburg section, copy in Group Archives.
11 The main sources for this section are an unidentified U.S. Army history, entitled 'Chapter XII, the Los Baños Raid', in the 'Miscellaneous materials sent to M. Collis' by J.R. Jones, and the diary of Max Haymes, a typed copy of which is in Group Archives.
12 Haymes, diary, typed copy, p. 239.
13 *Ibid*, pp. 253–54.
14 R. MacIntyre, 'Manila Office Foreign Staff', report in file 'Miscellaneous materials sent to M. Collis', in Group Archives.
15 A.I. Rabuco, oral history interview by Frank H.H. King, pp. 7–9.
16 J. F. Hulme file, Morse Papers, London Office II, Box 26, item 339.
17 See e.g. M.F. Key, *Hongkong before, during and after the War, an Account of the Stanley Civilian Internment Camp*, 2nd ed. (printed in Hong Kong by Ye Olde Printerie, 1946).
18 Natalie Davis, oral history interview, pp. 57–58.
19 T.J.J. Fenwick to Arthur Morse, 9 October 1945, General S/O File, London.
20 C. Key, War Office, to Morse, 11 October 1945, Hong Kong Reoccupation file, Morse Papers, London II, Box 28, item 434.
21 Morse to Key, 13 October 1945, in *ibid*.
22 Manager, China Light and Power Co., to Fenwick, 28 September 1945, in General S/O Correspondence, London.
23 Fenwick to Morse, a general report dated 16 September 1945, General S/O Correspondence, London.
24 Morse to Fenwick, 28 September 1945, in *ibid*.
25 Fenwick to I.H.C. Highet, 3 October 1945, in *ibid*.
26 F.H. King quoted in letter from Morse to H.E. Muriel, 19 October 1946, in F.H. King letters, Kl.18, Group Archives.

27 Articles in the *South China Morning Post* and *China Mail* (8 October 1946), copies in F.H. King letters cited.
28 F.R. Burch, oral history, p. 66.
29 *Ibid*.
30 Morse to S.A. Gray, 28 November 1945, Morse Papers, cited.
31 W.A. Stewart, oral history, p. 26.
32 Knightly, oral history, pp. 27–31.
33 A.C. Kennett to H.J. Prata, 22 November 1945, Morse Papers, Box 28, item 473.
34 E.C. Hutchison, oral history, pp. 51–55.
35 *Ibid*, p. 53.
36 P.A. Sellars, report dated 2–8 December 1945, in Rehabilitation File, Morse Papers, Box 28, item No. 473.
37 J.McG. Taylor, oral history, pp. 29–30.
38 G.S. Chambers, oral history interview by Frank H.H. King, pp. 26–28.
39 H.C.D. Davies, oral history, p. 37; see also references in Volume III.
40 G.W. Stabb, oral history, p. 67.
41 Bruce Tytler, *Here, There & (Nearly) Everywhere* (London, 1979), p. 253–54.
42 J.W.L. Howard, oral history, pp. 11–12.
43 R.G.L. Oliphant, oral history, pp. 27–28.
44 17 August 1945, in Morse papers, London II, Box 26, item 373.
45 J.R. Jones, ed. 'Branches', Indonesia section; see also his 'Personalities and Narratives', under Lydall, Edwards, and Mabey.
46 *Ibid*.
47 Statement issued by the British Chamber of Commerce, 18 March 1947, in *ibid*, pp. 74–75.
48 For specific complaints of discrimination against British banks, see, e.g. despatches from Batavia dated 23 July, 2, 6 August and 20 August 1946 in FO 371/53804, F10883/1/61; FO 371/53805, F11260/1/61; FO 371/53806, F11490/1/61; FO 371/53809, F12219/1/61.
49 From C.L. Edwards, Manager, Hongkong Bank, Batavia, 20 August 1946, in FO 371/53809, F12219/1/61.
50 Fenwick, oral history interview by Frank H.H. King, pp. 82–83, and Jones, 'Branches', Japan section, pp. 124–25.
51 V.A. Mason, oral history, edited by Mason and Gary Watson, p. 71.
52 *Ibid*, p. 81.
53 *Ibid*, p. 76.
54 *Ibid*, p. 77.
55 For messages re Mason's complaints etc., see, e.g. Duncan Wallace, Hongkong Bank junior Manager, London, to Foreign Office, 21 October 1947, FO 371/63827, F14209/14209/23; Gascoigne to MacDermot, 18 November and 15 December 1947, *ibid*, F16379/14209/23; also Duncan Wallace, to Foreign Office, dated 29 December 1947, *ibid*.
56 W.R. Hobbin, Mercantile Bank oral history, pp. 81–82.
57 V.A. Mason to A.M. Duncan Wallace, copy with latter's letter to F.S. Tomlinson, Foreign Office, dated 23 December 1947, in FO 371/63669, F16875.
58 Ena Coberly Gilbert, oral history, pp. 14–15.
59 Deutsche Bank to Hamburg Branch, Hongkong Bank, 5 September 1947, cited in David J.S. King, p. 101.
60 Quoted in Jones, 'Branches', Hamburg, p. 12.

3 POST-WAR POLICIES AND PROBLEMS: HEAD OFFICE, HONG KONG

1. 16 October 1945, Sir Arthur Morse Papers, London II, Box 25, item 357, Group Archives.
2. Morse to T.J.J. Fenwick, 17 November 1945, Box 28, item 473.
3. Shanghai file, Morse Papers, Box 28, item 477.
4. Morse to H. E. Muriel, Morse Papers, Box 28, item 489.
5. Muriel to Morse, May 1946, in *ibid*.
6. Morse to A.G. Kellogg, 18 February 1946, in Staff file, cited.
7. M.P. Langley, oral history interview by Frank H.H. King, p. 3.
8. Maurice W. Turner, oral history, p. 11; see also S.F.T.B. Lever, oral history, pp. 7–9.
9. G.A. Leiper, *A Yen for my Thoughts* (Hong Kong, 1982), pp. 37–38, 42, and 51.
10. The section on the duress notes is based on information in J.R. Jones's special file on the history of the note issue, a copy of which is in the file of Miscellaneous Material sent to M. Collis, and in CO 537/1369, Economic 1946, No. 15117/2; see also *ibid*, 19222/68/45 and 15104/4/47.
11. Muriel, autobiography, binder 5, Group Archives.
12. See, for example, Letter to the Editor, *Shanghai Herald* (21 November 1941), in FO 371/46149, F11579/13/10 of 12 December 1945.
13. See analysis in Frank H.H. King, *Money in British East Asia* (London, 1957).
14. Report of the Exchange Fund Advisory Committee on the Duress Note Issue, 19 November 1946, in file Economic 15117/2, Currency, Hong Kong, Notes Issued Under Duress, p. 30 (pencilled), CO 537/1369.
15. In addition to the references cited in note 10, there is a full statement of the course of events with the Morse quotations filed with the London Board Minute Book for the War Years, Group Archives.
16. *Ibid*.
17. *Ibid*.
18. Morse to Sydney Caine, 25 January 1946, CO 537/1369, file cited, p. 164.
19. Minutes of 5 February 1946 meeting, *ibid*, file cited, pp. 161–62.
20. Caine to Morse, 28 February 1946, in London Board Minute Book and in CO 537/1369, file cited, pp. 138–43. On the 'firm' style see Caine to D.M. MacDougall, 1 March 1946, *ibid*, F15117/2/46, p. 132.
21. Caine to Morse, cited in note 20.
22. W.R. Cockburn, Chief Manager, Chartered Bank of India, Australia and China, to Caine, 1 May 1946, and J.B. Crichton, Chief Manager, Mercantile Bank of India, to Caine, 1 May 1946, in *ibid*, pp. 73 and 78 respectively (pencilled numbers); on waiting to settle the problem, see Caine to Cockburn, Caine to Crichton, 31 May 1946, in *ibid*, pp. 58 and 59 respectively; see also Caine to MacDougall, cited in note 20, p. 133, final paragraph.
23. British Embassy to Foreign Office, 1 August 1942, and Foreign Office to Chungking, 12 August 1942, in FO 371/31717, F5453/5383/10, ff. 4–7; see also *ibid*, ff. 26–27, 30–35, 36–40, 50–55, 82–85; and in 1943, FO 371/35772, ff. 73–78, 85–86, 132–36.
24. Published in the *Hong Kong (British Military Administration) Gazette*, available also in CO 537/1369, reference cited, p. 41.
25. *Ibid*, II, 301 (6 April 1946), and draft announcement sent by Morse to Fenwick, copy in CO 537/1369, file cited, p. 134.
26. D.M. MacDougall to Caine, 15 April 1946, in CO 537/1369, reference cited, p. 82.

27 *Ibid.*
28 The Hongkong and Shanghai Banking Corporation, *Minutes of the 130th Meeting of Shareholders*, 1947, p. 7.
29 *Ibid*, 129th Meeting, 1946, p. 4.
30 For a sympathetic exposition of the problem, see G.B. Endacott, *Hong Kong Eclipse*, edited with additional material by Alan Birch (Hong Kong, 1978), esp. pp. 288–89.
31 Republic of the Philippines, Court of First Instance of Manila, Civil Case No. 71009, in CO 537/1374, attachment to Minute dated 25 January 1947, p. 14.
32 For discussion see Roy C. Ybañez, 'The Hongkong Bank in the Philippines', pp. 85–90, and J.R. Jones, 'Branches', section on the Philippines. The cases are: (i) *Hongkong Bank v Luis Parez Samanillo Inc. and the Registrar of Deeds of Manila*, and (ii) *Hongkong Bank v Estate of Ramon S. Araneta*; see also *Haw Pia v China Banking Corporation*, references in Jones, with copies in CO 537/1374.
33 Re National City Bank of New York: Note of a Meeting held on the 11th of July 1946, in CO 537/1374, 15488/17/46.
34 The Hongkong and Shanghai Banking Corporation, *Minutes of the 129th Meeting of Shareholders*, 1946, p. 5.
35 *Ibid*, 130th Meeting, p. 4.
36 *Ibid*, 131st Meeting, p. 6.
37 The file on debtor/creditor problems is in CO 537/1374.
38 Extract of a letter, Morse to Caine, 28 November 1946, CO 537/1374.
39 The Hongkong and Shanghai Banking Corporation, *Minutes of the 132nd Meeting of Shareholders*, 1949, p. 1.
40 *Ibid.*
41 *Ibid*, p. 12.
42 *Ibid*, 129th Meeting, 1946, p. 5.
43 Morse to A.H. Barlow, 8 September 1944, Box 26, item 304.
44 Morse to Muriel, 20 September 1944, Muriel file, Box 28, item 490.
45 *Supplement to the Hong Kong Government Gazette* 88, 9 (17 June 1946), the draft bill.
46 Muriel to Sir Edward Reid, 24 June 1946, London II, Box 28, item 434.

4 THE HONGKONG BANK AND THE REPUBLIC OF CHINA, 1945–1949

Oral history references cited in this chapter are to transcripts in the Hongkong Bank Group Archives. Unless otherwise noted, the interviews were conducted by Christopher Cook following preliminary discussion with the retiree by Cook and Frank H.H. King. The transcripts as quoted have been edited for purposes of style and brevity; meaning remains unchanged.

Hongkong Bank sources consulted included the minutes of the Board of Directors and the London Advisory Committee, the microfilm records of files entitled Shanghai, Nanking, and related topics in Head Office archives, and the Chairman's papers. With exceptions these references are not noted; they can be located by the date or writer, the files being chronological.

1 See, for example, the discussion on the responsibility for unissued notes, Chapter 5.
2 The continuity is based on Kia-ngau Chang, *The Inflationary Spiral, the Experience in China, 1939–1950* (New York, 1958); Shun-hsin Chou, *The Chinese Inflation, 1937–1949* (New York, 1963); and Frank H.H. King, 'Inflation and Hyperinflation in China, 1946–1948', M.A. Thesis, Stanford University, 1949.

3 The figures are taken from contemporary Shanghai publications as cited in King, pp. 157–65, see also the bibliography on p. 137; reference should also be made to tables in Chang and Chou, cited.
4 For a history of the Customs Gold Unit, see Frank H.H. King, 'Essays in China's Recent Monetary History, (i) The Customs Gold Unit', in King, *Asian Policy, History and Development – collected essays* (Hong Kong, 1979), pp. 83–88.
5 Chou, pp. 133 and 306–07n13.
6 See note 1 above.
7 F.C.B. Black, oral history interview, pp. 81–83.
8 *Ibid*, p. 83.
9 *Ibid*, p. 84.
10 *Ibid*, p. 83.
11 See discussion in Volume III.
12 J.F. Marshall, oral history interview, pp. 25–26.
13 *Ibid*, p. 25.
14 Nanking file in Head Office Archives.
15 Marshall, pp. 26–27.
16 *Ibid*, p. 27.
17 Black, p. 85.
18 R.P. Moodie, oral history interview (there was no preliminary interview), p. 39.
19 Black, pp. 85–86.
20 Moodie, p. 40.
21 *Ibid*, p. 40.
22 Black, pp. 86–87.
23 See discussion in Volume III, Chapter 7, and references in the [Sir Charles S.] Addis Papers, the Library, School of Oriental and African Studies: Diary entries for 22 and 28 December 1939, 3 and 5 January 1940; Montagu Norman to Lord Catto, 4 January 1940 (copy to Addis); Norman to Addis, 5 January 1940, in PP.MS.14/429.
24 Addis, diary, 2 February 1942, and Foreign Office minute of 16 May 1946, FO 371/53731, F5184/10.
25 Addis, diary, 27 May 1942.
26 *Ibid*, 29 May 1942.
27 G.V. Kitson (Foreign Office) to N.E. Young (Treasury), 23 April 1946, FO 371/53731, F5184/10. State Department correspondence with the American Group can be found in Thomas W. Lamont to Secretary of State, with memorandum, 893.516/11-1945, and other material on the file for 1945 and 1946; see also, correspondence between Lamont and the Hongkong Bank, J.P. Morgan and Co., and the Secretary of State, etc. in 893.516/9-1946, 893.516/6-1446, State Department, National Archives of the United States, Washington, D.C.
28 Minute relative to a letter from H.E. Muriel, Hongkong Bank, to Kitson, 16 April, 1946, in FO 371/53731, F5184/5184/10.
29 Foreign Office minute of 12 September 1946, quoting conversation with Miss Ashe of the Treasury, in *ibid*.
30 27 August 1946 in *ibid*.
31 This and other information on the company is found in BT31/31836/68872. For earlier references, see notes in Volume II.
32 Convenient summary histories written for specific CCR directors' meetings are found in Boxes C38 and 48, in Matheson and Co's holdings of CCR archives. For information in the public domain, see BT 31/36256/79679.

33 The main source of information on the B&CC is the file in Companies House; other information has been obtained from the files in Matheson and Co.
34 This and other information on capital changes is found in the B&CC's petition to the High Court of Justice, Chancery Division, Mr Justice Wynn-Parry, draft in B&CC Archives, Matheson and Co. See also the B&CC's letter to shareholders, dated 30 August 1951; for the main file, see Companies Office files, Companies House, London.
35 Letter to shareholders, cited.
36 London/HK Letter No. 786, 26 September 1951, in Box C45, Matheson and Co.
37 Note of a meeting with G.O.W. Stewart and his successor as the Hongkong Bank's London Manager, G.P. Stubbs, on Tuesday, 28 May 1968, in *ibid*, Matheson and Co.
38 Chou, pp. 80–81, esp. Tables 2.10 and 2.11.
39 Quoted in a memorandum from the Hongkong Bank in FO 371/63345, F12273. This file is an excellent source for consultation of copies of earlier loan agreements and related documents.
40 *Ibid*.
41 W.C. Cassels, Hongkong Bank, to British Embassy, Nanking, 13 June 1947, in FO 371/63345.
42 Draft of a response from Kitson to Muriel, November 1947, FO 371/63345, F12273/152/10.
43 *Ibid*.
44 Memorandum from the Hongkong Bank entitled 'Claim in the Matter of the Shanghai Municipal Council'; Foreign Office to Canton, 18 August 1949; and quotes from Chinese Ambassador cited in Foreign Office to S.A. Gray, Manager, London Office, Hongkong Bank, draft of 17 September 1949, FO 371/75809, F10485.
45 Foreign Office to Canton, reviewing the background, 17 August 1949, FO 371/75809, F10485/10139/10.
46 S.A. Gray, Hongkong Bank London Manager, to Foreign Office, 15 September 1949, in *ibid*.
47 *Ibid*.
48 Draft reply to Gray, 17 September 1949, in *ibid*.
49 N.C.C. Trench, 1 January 1951, FO 371/83275, FC10124/2.
50 *Ibid*.
51 Foreign Office to Gray, 27 December 1949, FO 371/75809, F18256/10139/10.
52 H.H. Thomas in Shanghai to N.E. Young, Treasury, 29 December 1947, p. 6, in FO 371/69564, Fxx502 [illegible].
53 Quoted in a letter Cassels to Inspector-General of the Chinese Customs Little, 19 January 1948, FO 371/69565, F3702.
54 *Ibid*, p. 8. For State Department references, with copies of certain letters from Cassels forwarded from Shanghai by J.T.S. Reed of National City Bank of New York, see 893.516/9-1746 CS/HH, State Department, National Archives.
55 Michael W. Turner to Colonial Secretary, 19 April 1960, in Colonial Secretary file, carton I, Chairman's files, Group Archives.
56 Turner to S.W.P. Perry-Aldworth, 9 September 1960, in Chairman's files.
57 Marshall, pp. 29–30.

5 THE HONGKONG BANK, POLICY AND PERFORMANCE, 1947–1961

The documentation for this chapter can be handled without end-notes as the sources and even the specific citations are obviously from the appropriate Hongkong Bank report.

The BBME history referred to is Geoffrey Jones, *Banking and Empire in Iran* and *Banking and Oil*, Volumes I and II of *The History of the British Bank of the Middle East* (Cambridge, 1986 and 1987).

6 THE CORPORATION, 1947–1962

1 Michael W. Turner to K. Brown (shareholder), 3 March 1960, in London file, Chairman's papers, Group Archives.
2 See Turner's replies to stockbrokers, e.g. 20 and 25 February 1960, in *ibid*.
3 Draft letter Colonial Office to Government of Hong Kong, 10 August 1948, CO 537/2812, file 15104/17/5/47.
4 *Ibid*.
5 Cable, Hong Kong to Colonial Office, 5 October 1950, CO 537/5451, and related communications.
6 See Frank H.H. King, *Money in British East Asia* (London, 1957), pp. 116–17.
7 J. Caldwell, oral history interview by Frank H.H. King, p. 18.
8 N.H.T. Bennett, oral history interview by Christopher Cook, p. 15.
9 *Ibid*, p. 16.
10 G. Follows, Financial Secretary, Hong Kong, to Sir Sydney Caine, Colonial Office, 12 February 1948, CO 537/2812, No. 4/2201/47.
11 Hong Kong to Colonial Office, 5 October 1959, CO 537/5451.
12 CO 537/2812, 4/2201/47.
13 *Ibid*.
14 CO 527/5451, minute dated 9 October 1950.
15 *Ibid*.
16 This matter is found in the Chairman's files: see, especially, (i) Arthur Clarke, Financial Secretary, to A.S. Adamson, 5 July 1951, Government file No. 2/2201/50, and related papers; (ii) Memorandum by J.R. Jones, 24 January 1961.
17 Submission by the Chief Manager, 7 March 1957, in Chairman's files; see also memo by J.R. Jones for the BBME dated 24 January 1961, in *ibid*.
18 Turner to Sir Arthur Morse, 15 November 1955, in Chairman's London file.
19 Turner to S.A. Gray, 30 December 1954, in *ibid*; see also Morse to Turner, 21 November 1955, in *ibid*.
20 Sir Edward Reid to Sir Michael Turner, 26 July 1961, in *ibid*.
21 See, for example, Turner to S.W.P. Perry-Aldworth, 1 April 1958, in *ibid*.
22 See Reid to Turner, 26 July 1961; Turner to Reid, 14 July 1961, in *ibid*.
23 Turner to Perry-Aldworth[?], 24 May 1961; Reid to Turner, 26 July 1961; G.O.W. Stewart to Turner, 3 August 1961, in *ibid*.
24 Morse to Turner, 7 April 1953, and Turner to Gray, 2 April 1953, in *ibid*.

7 HONGKONG BANKERS AND THE EMERGENCE OF HEAD OFFICE

1 G.W. Stabb, oral history interview, p. 15.
2 P.A. Sellars, oral history interview, pp. 62–63.
3 Sir Michael Turner, oral history interview, p. 32.
4 Miss Margaret Goldney, oral history interview by Frank H.H. King, pp. 11–12.

Notes to pp. 294-324

5 *Ibid*, p. 12.
6 *Ibid*, p. 8.
7 *Ibid*, p. 9.
8 *Ibid*, p. 8.
9 *Ibid*, pp. 9–10.
10 *Ibid*, pp. 12–13.
11 Turner, pp. 46–47.
12 Goldney, pp. 14–15.
13 Geoffrey Jones, *Banking and Empire in Iran*, Vol. I of *The History of the British Bank of the Middle East* (Cambridge, 1986), p. 108.
14 J. Caldwell, oral history interview, p. 2.
15 *Ibid*, pp. 23–24.
16 I.H. Bradford, oral history interview, p. 44.
17 A.M. Prado, oral history interview by Frank H.H. King, p. 3.
18 *Ibid*, p. 10.
19 *Ibid*.
20 *Ibid*, p. 11.
21 Sir Robert Ho Tung to Michael Turner, 7 August 1953, in Ho Tung file, Chairman's files, Group Archives.
22 Turner, p. 33.
23 *Snake Wine, a Singapore Episode* (reprinted, Kuala Lumpur, 1980), p. 21.
24 Morse to C.A.W. Ferrier, 9 July 1952, in Chairman's London file.
25 Gray to Morse, 17 March 1952, and Morse to Gray in Chairman's London file.
26 Turner to Gray, 10 February 1953, in Chairman's London file.
27 Turner to Gray, 1955, in Chairman's files.
28 Hongkong Bank, 'A brief summary of conditions of service on the Foreign Staff ruling at this date [22 January 1951]', 'Conditions of Service on the Foreign Staff ruling at 1st January 1954', and *ibid*, 1961, in Group Head Office, Personnel Department.

8 THE HONGKONG BANK IN HONG KONG, 1947–1962

Documentation for this chapter can be handled without end-notes as the sources and specific citations are obvious.

The information comes from the following Hongkong Bank sources: the annual reports, the minutes of the Board of Directors, the Chairman's correspondence files, J.R. Jones's collection 'Personalities', and oral histories. The last mentioned, undertaken by Christopher Cook in the usual way, include: N.H.T. Bennett, F.C.B. Black, I.H. Bradford, M. G. Carruthers, G. H. Cautherley, O.P. Edwards, D.G. Lachlan, R.P. Moodie, R.G.L. Oliphant, G.M. Sayer, Maurice W. Turner, and Sir Michael Turner.

General information on Hong Kong and on its money and banking system comes, as far as this chapter is concerned, from Y.C. Jao, *Banking and Currency in Hong Kong, a Study of Postwar Financial Development* (London, 1974); S.Y. Lee and Y.C. Jao, *Financial Structures and Monetary Policies in Southeast Asia* (1982); F.H.H. King, *Money in British East Asia* (London, 1957); and various Hong Kong Government annual reports, census and statistical publications, and its *Report of the Industrial Banking Committee* (1960), and U.N. surveys, especially those of ECAFE. Also of value was L.S. Pressnell, 'A Glimpse of Banking in Hong Kong', *Three Banks Review* (September 1961), pp. 22–23. For the open market, see King, 'The Hong Kong Open Market, 1954', in his edited *Asian Policy, History and Development* (Hong Kong, 1979), pp. 161–72. The reference to Citibank is Harold van B. Cleveland and Thomas F. Huertas, *Citibank, 1812–1970* (New York, 1985), esp. Chapters 3 and 4.

The comments on the new three-storey car park are taken from Executive Council minute 32 of 14 August 1956, and memos X.C.R. 272 of 30 July 1956, X.C.R. 291, and related documents in the Hong Kong PRO.

This chapter also refers to Y.C. Jao's study undertaken for the 1981 Hongkong Bank History Conference, 'Financing Hong Kong's Early Postwar Industrialization: the Role of The Hongkong and Shanghai Banking Corporation', in King, ed. *Eastern Banking* (London, 1983), pp. 545–74, and to the sources listed therein, particularly the following: M.G. Carruthers, 'Financing Industry', *Far Eastern Economic Review* (1966), pp. 367–70; R.A. Ma and E. Szczepanik, *The National Income of Hong Kong 1947–50* (Hong Kong, 1955); J.A.H. Saunders, 'The Hongkong and Shanghai Banking Corporation', *The Banker* (1970), pp. 755–59; E. Szczepanik, 'Financing the Postwar Economic Growth of Hong Kong', *Far Eastern Economic Review* (1956), pp. 781–83; and Szczepanik, *The Economic Growth of Hong Kong* (1958). Reference has also been made to Victor F.S. Sit's study for the Hongkong Bank History Conference, 'Branching of The Hongkong and Shanghai Banking Corporation in Hong Kong: a Spatial Analysis', in *Eastern Banking*, pp. 629–54.

Victor Sit refers to L. Kraar, 'Financial Fortress', *Fortune* (May 1976), and the reference cited in this chapter is on p. 187. Also of interest is P.A. Graham (of the Chartered Bank), 'Hong Kong's Banks and Financial Institutions', *The Banker* (July 1970), pp. 747–53.

Ian Macdonald's testimony, together with comments on other relevant issues, including the Hongkong Bank's role in the Colony, is available in House of Representatives (96th Congress, second session), Committee on Government Operations. *Hearings. Foreign Acquisitions of U.S. Banks and the non-banking activities of Foreign Bank Holding Companies* (15 May and 25 June 1980).

9 THE HONGKONG BANK IN CHINA, 1949–1962

1 J.F. Marshall, oral history interview, p. 30.
2 R.P. Moodie, oral history interview, p. 41.
3 *Ibid*, p. 42.
4 *Ibid*, p. 43.
5 O.P. Edwards, oral history interview, p. 95.
6 *Ibid*, pp. 94–95.
7 Arthur Morse to A.S. Adamson, 29 August 1951, and Morse to Cockburn, Chartered Bank, 4 January 1952, in Chartered Bank file, Chairman's papers, Group Archives.
8 H.L. Pierce, oral history interview by Frank H.H. King, p. 8.
9 *Ibid*, p. 12.
10 16 May 1951, China offices file, in Chairman's papers.
11 F.R. Burch, oral history interview, pp. 88–89.
12 *Ibid*, pp. 93–95.
13 Minutes of the London Advisory Committee, 16 April 1953, in Chairman's files.
14 *Ibid*, 4 June and 2 July 1953.
15 Burch, p. 88.
16 *Ibid*, pp. 91–92.
17 *Ibid*, p. 93.
18 W.T. Yoxall to Head Office, 11 October 1954, Group Head Office archives.
19 Burch, p. 93.

20 F.C.B. Black, oral history interview, p. 104.
21 Yoxall to Head Office, 30 August 1954, File 1860, microfilm, Head Office archives.
22 Michael Turner to Arthur Morse, 14 October 1954, in post-settlement file, Chairman's papers, Group Archives.
23 Turner to Yoxall, 15 July 1953, Shanghai file, Chairman's papers.
24 *Ibid.*
25 Turner to S.A. Gray, 26 April 1954, in China, Closure file.
26 Correspondence in the post-settlement file, Chairman's papers.
27 Report on the Trade Mission by F.C.B. Black to O. Skinner in Hong Kong, dated 27 November 1954, in *ibid* and in the Correspondent Banking Department files.
28 *Ibid.*
29 G.O.W. Stewart to S.W.P. Perry-Aldworth, 19 April 1960, in *ibid*.
30 Correspondence dated 10 May 1955 in *ibid*.
31 See discussions dated July 1951 in FO 371/92215, FC 10113/14.
32 The Chinese version is official. The English translation is PR 130.4/1 in Group Archives.
33 Anon., 'What the Lions Saw and Heard', a clipping without reference in the Head Office files sent from Shanghai.
34 Buchan to O. Skinner, Chief Inspector, Head Office, 1 November 1955, Head Office archives.
35 Correspondent Banking Department, Group Head Office files.
36 S.W.P. Perry-Aldworth, London Manager, to Michael W. Turner, Chief Manager, 5 June 1957, and Turner to Perry-Aldworth, 11 June 1957, in Head Office archives.
37 W.A. Stewart, oral history, pp. 67–68.
38 See discussion in Volume III; the quote is from an article on Mr Zee in *Hongkong Bank Group News* (November 1982), p. 17.
39 See note 33 in Chapter 4.
40 Yoxall to Head Office, 18 April 1955, in Head Office archives.
41 Michael Turner to Morse, 6 March 1956, Chairman's papers.
42 Stewart, pp. 72–73.
43 *Ibid*, p. 74.
44 *Ibid*, p. 73.
45 E.C. Hutchison, oral history interview, p. 78.
46 Stewart, p. 86.
47 *Ibid*, pp. 74–75.
48 *Ibid*, p. 75.
49 *Ibid*, p. 76.
50 *Ibid*, pp. 87–89.
51 Hutchison, p. 79.
52 *Ibid*, p. 82.
53 Stewart, pp. 86–87.

10 THE COMMERCIAL BANKING BRANCHES, 1947–1962

This chapter depends on branch correspondence, S/o's, the Chairman's correspondence, Annual Reports, and, especially, oral histories.

Reference was also made to the collections of J.R. Jones in Group Archives under the titles 'Personalities' and 'Branches'.

For the section on the Philippines overall, the continuity is based on Roy C. Ybañez,

'The Hongkong Bank in the Philippines', a research report commissioned for the Hongkong Bank History Project and supervised by the U.P. Business Research Foundation, Inc. Ybañez cites Frank Hodsoll, *Britain in the Philippines*, p. 21. There is also a quotation from the Central Bank of the Philippines, *Annual Report* (1949), p. 89.

General use was made in particular country studies of the following:

I. The Philippines
   A. The Hongkong and Shanghai Banking Corporation, Group Archives.
      (i) S/O Correspondence: Iloilo to Head Office, London and Manila for selected years in the inter-war period
      (ii) Iloilo agency and Manila files post-war.
      (iii) Oral history: HSBC staff – Robin W. Campbell, A.D.A.G. Mosley, Roberto E. Paredes, Alfonso I. Rabuco; Customers – Patrick Chiene, Patrick J. Ford, Carlos Jalandoni, and miscellaneous notes from the Jones collection.
   B. Personal correspondence and interviews: C.W.D. Hall, R.H. Lloyd, H.L. Pierce, G.W.E. True, W.E. Young
   C. United States of America. National Archives. Bureau of Insular Affairs, various files on banking.
   D. Published works
      Loney, Nicholas. *A Britisher in the Philippines or the Letters of Nicholas Loney*. Introduction by Margaret Hoskyn. Manila, 1964.
      Thursfield, R.P. *Topical Verses*. Privately published, 1914.
      Young, Walter H. *A Merry Banker in the Far East*. London, 1916.

II. Sri Lanka
   A. The Hongkong Bank Group Archives.
      1. J.R. Jones, 'Personalities': V.A. Mason, David McLean.
      2. Oral history transcripts: V.A. Mason, H.A. Greig, F.R. Burch, A.L. V.S. Giles, H.L. Pierce, B.J.N. Ogden, L.G. Atterbury.
      3. Group Head Office files, 1952–1982.
   B. Other sources consulted.
      1. H.L.D. Selvaratnam, 'Research Report on the Ceylon Branch' in Group Archives, commissioned as part of the Hongkong Bank History Project, Centre of Asian Studies. Mr Selvaratnam utilized materials found in Colombo and also drew on his experiences as Deputy Governor of the Central Bank of Ceylon.
      2. C. Loganathan, General Manager, Bank of Ceylon, 'Finance to the Ceylonese Exporter', in *Banking in Ceylon* (Institute of Chartered Accountants, Colombo, 1963).
      3. Government of Ceylon, Report of the Ceylon Banking Commission (1934 Sessional Paper XXII).
      4. ———, Da Silva Commission Report of 1966 [de Kretzer case].
      5. H.A. de S. Gunasekera, *From Dependent Currency to Central Banking in Ceylon* (1960).
      6. H.D. Andrée, *Progress of Banking in Ceylon* (Colombo, 1864).
      7. Central Bank of Sri Lanka, 'Examination Report of 1978'.
      8. ———, Copies of agreements on the procedure for the financing of imports with the Central Bank, May 1965 and December 1971.

Notes to pp. 463, 482, and 565   949

11   PIONEERING IN BORNEO – BRITISH NORTH BORNEO AND SARAWAK

This Chapter depends on branch correspondence, S/O's, the Chairman's correspondence, Annual Reports, and, especially, oral histories.

Reference was also made to the collections of J.R. Jones in Group Archives under the titles 'Personalities' and 'Branches'. Economic information was taken from the annual reports of the territories and from the UN, ECAFE surveys, especially for 1954; the relevant report was drafted by Frank H.H. King.

The following oral histories, now in Group Archives, were consulted: Max Haymes, F.J. Knightly, J.F. Marshall, G.P. Stubbs, and Maurice W. Turner.

12   THE HONGKONG BANK'S NEW SUBSIDIARIES, 1955–1961, AND THE
       ORIGINS OF THE HONGKONG BANK GROUP

The material has been obtained almost in its entirety from the microfilmed files of the Hongkong Bank now stored in Head Office, from the Board of Directors minute books, and from published annual reports and accounts. The files are listed under the banks and companies involved, chronologically; there are special files dealing with each acquisition. Dates and correspondence are cited in the text. The California State Banking Department files on the Hongkong Bank of California were consulted.

Quotations from members of the staff, unless the context otherwise indicates, are from their oral history interviews in Group Archives.

The draft of *Banking and Oil*, the second volume of Geoffrey Jones's *History of the British Bank of the Middle East* (Cambridge, 1987) was available for consultation – Chapter 3 is of particular importance and should be read in conjunction with the account presented here; data on Hongkong Bank retired staff on the Imperial Bank board was checked against Jones's first volume, *Banking and Empire in Iran*; certain 'Special Letters' files of the BBME were consulted in London. A typescript by Paul Lamb on the history of the Mercantile Bank is available in Group Archives and was published serially in *Group News*.

The reference to Jones's article on Continental banks is 'Lombard Street on the Riviera: British Clearing Banks and Europe, 1900–1960', in King, ed. *Eastern Banking* (London, 1983), pp. 753–77. The reference to the Lyons office is to Claude Fivel-Démoret, 'The Hongkong Bank in Lyon, 1881–1954: Busy but too Discreet?', in King, ed. *Eastern Banking*, pp. 467–517.

For the story of Chase Bank in this period, including a particularly naive version of its relations with the Mercantile Bank, see John Donald Wilson, *The Chase – The Chase Manhattan Bank, N.A., 1945–1985* (Boston, MA, 1986).

13, 14 AND 15   THE HONGKONG BANK GROUP, 1962–1980

The material for these chapters is taken almost entirely from the Annual Reports of the Hongkong Bank, from articles in *Group News*, staff lists, internal reports, and oral histories as cited. This has been interpreted through interviews of varying intensity with members of the Hongkong Bank staff at all levels.

References for material on Colombo, Iloilo, Sabah, and Sarawak are found in the notes to Chapters 10 and 11.

The tables are compiled from published balance sheets and lists of public companies found in the Annual Reports. The Appendix Table is taken from U.S. Congress, 'Exhibit A', in *Foreign Acquisitions of U.S. Banks and Non-Banking Activities of Foreign Bank Holding Companies*, Hearings before a subcommittee of the Committee on

Government Operations, House of Representatives, 96th Congress, second session, May 15 and June 25, 1980 (Washington, D.C., 1980), pp. 88–189.

The history of the Hang Seng Bank is based on (i) an interview with Q.W. Lee and (ii) Y.P. Ngan, 'Hang Seng Bank Limited: a Brief History', in King, ed. *Eastern Banking* (London, 1983), pp. 709–16.

These chapters do not attempt to provide a full background to Hong Kong banking, but to the extent that such information is provided, it is dependent on Y.C. Jao, *Banking and Currency in Hong Kong, a Study of Postwar Financial Development* (London, 1974). See also, H.J. Tomkins, *Report on the Hong Kong Banking System and Recommendations for the Replacement of the Banking Ordinance, 1948* (Hong Kong, April 1962). Jao's study of banking in Hong Kong is continued in his work with S.Y. Lee, *Financial Structures and Monetary Policies in Southeast Asia* (London, 1982). The rates of inflation quoted for Hong Kong are from his Table 2.14, p. 242, and his study is based on official Hong Kong Government statistics. CV = coefficient of variation.

For the structural changes in the corporation see, *inter alia*, the 1959 regulations, L.N. 61 of 1969, in Legal Supplement No. 2 to the *Hong Kong Government Gazette* (25 April 1969), pp. B184–88. Full use has been made of S.G. Redding's 'Organizational and Structural Change in The Hongkong and Shanghai Banking Corporation, 1950–1980', in King, ed. *Eastern Banking* (London, 1983), pp. 601–28. His references include, D.F. Channon, *British Banking Strategy and International Challenge* (London, 1977) and H. Mintzberg, *The Structuring of Organizations* (Englewood Cliffs, NJ, 1979), which have been consulted relative to the present study.

P.T. Lamb's history of the Mercantile Bank of India is in the Group Archives, but it has been published in *Group News*, (Spring 1973) pp. 12–15, (Autumn 1973) pp. 8–12, (Spring 1974) pp. 9–12.

The personnel report referred to is P.A. Management Consultants Limited, 'The Hongkong Bank Group, review of executive staff employment', supporting volume, 'Current Staffing Arrangements for Executive Staff, HSBC' (January, 1978). There is a similar volume for the BBME. The principal consultant was Roger Cadman, working in association with the Bank's General Manager, M.J. Pridham (East in 1950).

16 THE ACQUISITION OF MARINE MIDLAND BANKS, INC., 1978–1980, I. STRATEGY AND INITIAL SUCCESS, THE SIGNING OF THE DEFINITIVE AGREEMENT

The continuity in this chapter is based on a series of interviews by Christopher Cook and Frank H.H. King with key figures, officials, consultants, executives of the Hongkong Bank and Marine Midland Banks, and members of the Boards of Directors, most of whom were interviewed in 1980. The quotations, without other references, are from these interviews, copies of which are in Group Archives.

The background policy and statistical material is taken from a series of OCC Staff Papers. In certain cases there are specific references, but others, listed in the final notes, were also referred to.

1 M.G.R. Sandberg, Chairman, The Hongkong and Shanghai Banking Corporation, 'To all shareholders of HSBC', and Appendix I, in *Detailed information relating to the acquisition by HSBC Holdings B.V., a wholly owned subsidiary of The Hongkong and Shanghai Banking Corporation, of Shares of Common Stock of Marine Midland Banks, Inc.* (Hong Kong, 20 June 1980), pp. 1–5.

2 For the figures, see 'Foreign Acquisitions of U.S. Banking Organizations (1970–1980)', Table 4, in William A. Longbrake, Melanie R. Quinn, and Judith A. Walter,

Foreign Acquisitions of U.S. Banks: Facts and Patterns, OCC Staff Papers (Washington, D.C., 1980), p. 14.
3 For a general discussion of these developments, see John E. Shockey and William B. Glidden, *Foreign-controlled U.S. Banks: the Legal and Regulatory Environment*, OCC Staff Papers (1980), pp. 43n32 and 43–44n34. On the IBA, see Report No. 95-1073 to accompany H.R. 10899, 95th Congress, 2nd Session, 1978.
4 See Glidden, pp. 11–12 and 46; for general reference to U.S. policy on reciprocity, see Steven J. Weiss, *A Critical Evaluation of Reciprocity in Foreign Bank Acquisitions*, OCC Staff Papers (Washington, D.C., 1980), esp. pp. 23–28.
5 This information is taken from [Standard Chartered Bank], *Standard Chartered Bank: a Story Brought up to Date* (London, 1980), pp. 34–35 and 46–56; this book is the sequel, as far as the Chartered Bank's history is concerned, to Compton Mackenzie, *Realms of Silver* (London, 1954).
6 Judith A. Walter, *Foreign Acquisitions of U.S. Banks: Motives and Tactical Considerations*, OCC Staff Papers (Washington, D.C., 1980), pp. 36–37.
7 Baldwin Maull, 'Some Observations on Bank Holding Companies', *The Bankers Magazine* 155: 19–23 (Summer 1972), esp. p. 19.
8 For the historical background, this section depends on (i) an unpublished history of Marine Midland: Gerald C. Fischer, 'Wall to Wall Banks, the Marine Midland Story', taking the history to 1968, (ii) draft supplementary chapters by B. Maull, and (iii) Arthur B. Ziegler, 'Marine Midland Bank in an Analysis of Regulatory Environment and Corporate Structure', in King, ed. *Eastern Banking* (London, 1983), pp. 717–34. See also the Maull reference in note 7 above.
9 The figures are taken from the Annual Reports of MMBI.
10 Quotations from participants are taken from interviews conducted by Christopher Cook and Frank H.H. King, see general notes above.
11 Standard Chartered Bank, pp. 34–35.
12 For the full impact of statutory and regulatory impediments on acquisitions by domestic banks, see W. Paul Smith and Steven J. Weiss, *Potential Acquisition Partners for Large U.S. Banks: the Discriminatory Effects of Law and Policy*, OCC Staff Papers (Washington, D.C., 1980), esp. Table A-1, pp. 20–21.
13 A.M. Townsend, 'Early Days of the Hongkong and Shanghai Bank' (written in 1937, unpublished), p. 17, in Group Archives.
14 The details of the renegotiated agreement, together with a statement of the differences with the original agreement of May 1978, are found under cover of a letter from Frank J. Laski as Secretary, MMBI, to the Shareholders, dated August 31, 1979, and entitled *Notice of a Special Meeting of Shareholders to be held October 17, 1979* (Buffalo, New York). The material covered includes a summary of the Proxy Statement, the background, the actual Amended Agreement and Note Purchase Agreement, a description of common stock, and other information on the two banks.

17 THE ACQUISITION OF MARINE MIDLAND BANKS, INC., 1978–1980,
II. THE REGULATORS, CONGRESS, AND THE FINAL APPROVAL

1 See John E. Shockey and William B. Glidden, *Foreign-controlled U.S. Banks: the Legal and Regulatory Environment*, OCC Staff Papers (1980).
2 The U.S. Labor Party was responsible for a book entitled *Dope, Inc., Britain's opium war against the U.S.* authored 'by a U.S. Labor Party investigating team', i.e. Konstadinos Kalimtgis and others (New York, 1978). The book, which outlined an alleged conspiracy, included charges against the Hongkong Bank.

3 See Steven J. Weiss, *Competitive Standards applied to Foreign and Domestic Acquisitions of U.S. Banks*, OCC Staff Papers (1980). See especially Tables I and II, the latter dealing with the competitive impact of HBC's acquisition of Republic National Bank and Trust Company.
4 The up-State policy is described in Muriel Siebert, *Report of the Superintendent of Banks of New York State on the Proposed Acquisition by The Hongkong and Shanghai Banking Corporation of Marine Midland Banks, Inc.* (New York, 1979), especially the section on 'Historical Background of New York Policy', on pp. 6–15, and her conclusion that HSBC should be equated with a moderate-to-large New York City bank is found on p. 13.
5 U.S. Congress (96th, second session), House of Representatives, *Foreign Acquisitions of U.S. Banks and the non-Banking Activities of Foreign Bank Holding Companies*, Hearings, Commerce, Consumer and Monetary Affairs Subcommittee of the Committee on Government Operations (May 15 and June 25, 1980).
6 Information provided by the HSBC, found in *ibid*, p. 85.
7 See Siebert, p. 32, in which she acknowledges the willingness of the Hong Kong Financial Secretary to cooperate but minimizes the relevance and refers again to the Bank's failure to use GAAP.
8 The Hongkong Bank's motives were not inconsistent with the motives generalized in an OCC study by Judith A. Walter, *Foreign Acquisitions of U.S. Banks: Motives and Tactical Consideration*, OCC Staff Papers (1980).
9 U.S. Congress (96th, first session), House of Representatives, *The Operations of Federal Agencies in Monitoring, Reporting on, and Analyzing Foreign Investments in the United States. Part 4 – Foreign Investments in U.S. Banks*, Hearings, Commerce, Consumer and Monetary Affairs Subcommittee of the Committee on Government Operations (July 31 and August 1, 1979), p. 93.
10 See Shockey and Glidden (note 1 above) for a detailed listing.
11 See Weiss, *Competitive Standards*, Table I.
12 U.S. Congress, 1979 hearings (see note 9), p. 89.
13 See discussion in Shockey and Glidden, pp. 3–4 and related notes.
14 *Cf.* Weiss, *A Critical Evaluation of Reciprocity in Foreign Acquisitions*, OCC Staff Papers (Washington, D.C., 1980).
15 In MMBI, *Notice of a Special Meeting of Shareholders to be held October 17, 1979* (Buffalo, New York), section on The Hongkong and Shanghai Banking Corporation, p. 25.
16 William A. Longbrake, Melanie R. Quinn, and Judith A. Walter, *Foreign Acquisitions of U.S. Banks: Facts and Patterns*, OCC Staff Papers (Washington, D.C., 1980), Appendix V.
17 Wallich's written reply to a question by Senator Heinz in U.S. Congress (96th, first session), U.S. Senate, *Edge Corporation Branching; Foreign Bank Takeovers; and International Banking Facilities*, Hearings before the Committee on Banking, Housing, and Urban Affairs on Oversight on the International Banking Act...(July 16 and 20, 1979), p. 50.
18 *Ibid.*
19 U.S. Congress (96th, first session), House of Representatives, Commerce, Consumer and Monetary Affairs Subcommittee of the Committee on Government Operations, *The Operations of Federal Agencies...* p. 96.
20 *Ibid.*
21 *Ibid*, p. 97.
22 'Statement of I.H. Macdonald, Executive Director, The Hongkong and Shanghai Banking Corporation', in U.S. Congress (96th, second session), House of

Notes to pp. 842–860   953

Representatives, *Foreign Acquisition of U.S. Banks*... (May 15 and June 25, 1980), pp. 208–30, esp. pp. 225–27.
23 *Ibid*, extracts from pp. 70, 72, and 74.
24 *Ibid*, extracts from p. 76.
25 *Ibid*, extracts from p. 78.
26 Pub L No. 95–128, codified at 12 USS §2901 *et seq.*
27 Longbrake and others, *Foreign Acquisitions*, Table 4, p. 14.
28 In addition to the studies cited above, the following OCC Staff Papers are relevant and were consulted: Diane Page and Neal Soss, *Some Evidence on Transnational Banking Structure*, William A. Longbrake, *Prices Paid by Foreign Interests to Acquire U.S. Banks*, and Ellen S. Goldberg, *Analysis of Current Operations of Foreign-Owned U.S. Banks*, all published in 1980 by the OCC, Washington, D.C.
29 The information is found in the tender material issued by HSBC Holdings, BV, under the title, 'Offer to Purchase 3,121,000 Shares of Common Stock of Marine Midland Banks, Inc. for cash at $25.00 Net Per Share by HSBC Holdings, BV, a wholly owned subsidiary of The Hongkong and Shanghai Banking Corporation' (February 1, 1980). The material contains a summary of the history of the transaction and extracts from regulatory opinion.
30 U.S. Congress (96th, second session), House of Representatives, *Foreign Acquisitions of U.S. Banks*..., p. 50.

18   'HONGKONGBANK', THE HONGKONG BANK GROUP, 1980–1984

The general material in this chapter is taken from *HongkongBank News* and other Hongkong Bank sources, especially the Annual Reports. Lengthy interviews with Sir Michael Sandberg have provided the basis for the interpretation given to events the sources for which, by the nature of banking, cannot as yet be fully provided. The P.A. Consultants report and recommendations were important for the sections on the International and Regional officer staffs.

In addition use has been made of three financial reports:
(i) Wood, Mackenzie & Co., 'The Hongkong and Shanghai Banking Corporation ', dated 15 December 1981, (ii) Vickers da Costa, 'The Hongkong and Shanghai Banking Corporation, a study', January 1982, and (iii) Merrill Lynch International, 'The Hongkong and Shanghai Banking Corporation', May 1982.

The reference to Benjamin S. Rosenthal is found in: U.S. Congress (96th, second session), House of Representatives, *Foreign Acquisitions of U.S. Banks and the non-Banking Activities of Foreign Bank Holding Companies*, Hearings, Commerce, Consumer and Monetary Affairs Subcommittee of the Committee on Government Operations (May 15 and June 25, 1980), p. 79.

The brief description of the Hongkong Bank's role in the RBSG bids is based in part on in-depth interviews with participants, including Sir Michael Herries and Sir Peter Graham, to whom particular appreciation is due. For the reports of the Commission, see: Great Britain, Monopolies and Mergers Commission, *The Hongkong and Shanghai Banking Corporation, Standard Chartered Bank Limited, The Royal Bank of Scotland Group Limited, a report on the Proposed Mergers*, Cmnd 8472, January 1982.

Material on the new Head Office building is based on internal documents and Ian Lambot and Gillian Chambers, *One Queen's Road Central, The Headquarters of HongkongBank since 1864* (Hong Kong, 1986), a study commissioned by the Bank for the opening ceremonies in April 1986. I also read the final typescript of Stephanie Williams, *Hongkong Bank, the Building of Norman Foster's Masterpiece* (Boston and London, 1989), in which all aspects of the subject are considered in the context of full research access.

BIBLIOGRAPHY

The 'bibliography' is primarily a list of works consulted prefaced by an explanation of archival material and the oral history transcripts. The list covers only those materials relevant to Volume IV of the history of the Hongkong Bank. A separate bibliography has been provided for each volume.

ARCHIVAL COLLECTIONS

The most important source for Volume IV has been the several archives of the Hongkong Bank itself. 'Group Archives' are basically a historical collection, but in some cases brought up to date with the deposit of new material. Most conscientious in this regard was Sir Michael Sandberg himself, and the Chairman's papers and the Board's minute books were opened for the preparation of the history. There are, however, other collections, some of which are incomplete: these include the files of Hong Kong office and of Head Office – the chapters dealing with branches are, for example, dependent on the latter source.

The papers of the Bank's chief executives are preserved, and the Arthur Morse papers are essential for the study of the Bank during the 'Babylonian captivity'. Sandberg's interest in history had set an example which many retired staff members are following; private papers, photographs, and other memorabilia are reaching Group Archives. These include, for example, M.W. Bond's papers on the early problems of computerization and W.A. Stewart's files on Lunghwa Camp.

In the 1950s a circular newsletter for Managers was introduced. By the 1970s there were in-house publications, *Group Magazine*, *Group News*, and eventually branch or area news magazines which, while not usually reporting in depth, have provided useful guides to developments as the Hongkong Bank diversified. The Bank also publishes economic information and country studies.

Until approximately 1960 the centenary collections made by J.R. Jones remain of considerable usefulness, including the extracts from London Office undertaken by F.H. 'Towkay' King and of Shanghai branch by E.C. Hutchison. Group Archives has accessioned several reports undertaken specifically for this history, for example, those by D.J.S. King, Roy C. Ybañez, and H.L.D. Selvaratnam; on the conclusion of the project, papers and xeroxes accumulated from those sources which permit retention of research documents were also accessioned.

Volume IV continues the story of the British and Chinese Corporation; the records are kept by the Secretaries, Matheson and Co., by the Public Record Office, and by Companies House. For the end of the China Consortium, the Addis Papers in the School of Oriental and African Studies were once again consulted. By far the most important outside collection is that of the Hoover Institution, Stanford, especially the

A.N. Young Papers. Official files are often subject to the thirty-year rule, limiting the use of Treasury and Foreign Office Archives. The Information Bank of the New York Times Company was searched for references, and clipping files were also consulted in, for example, Kiel and Hamburg.

For the Hongkong Bank in the United States, the archives of the Federal Reserve, and the State Banking Departments of California and New York were consulted.

ORAL HISTORY

In addition to the Hongkong Bank Oral History Project, the story of the Marine Midland acquisition and the Royal Bank of Scotland attempt was detailed in several interviews as listed below. In general they are the work of Christopher Cook after a preliminary interview during which I usually initiated the questions, in some cases with B.J.N. Ogden present. The interviews were transcribed and then edited by Catherine E. King. The interviewee was asked to read and correct his typescript, which was then deposited in Group Archives.

Hongkong Bank oral history project

Foreign Staff (+ indicates that the officer's wife was interviewed by Catherine E. King): F.C.B. Black+, I.H. Bradford, F.R. Burch, M.G. Carruthers, G.S. Chambers, H.D.C. Davies, O.P. Edwards, T.J.J. Fenwick, A.D.M. Ford, A.L.V. St. Giles+, Margaret Goldney, H.A. Greig, M.F.L. Haymes+, J.W.L. Howard, E.C. Hutchison+, P.E. Hutson+, F.J. Knightly, D.G. Lachlan, S.F.T.B. Lever, V.A. Mason (edited with Gary Watson), R.P. Moodie, A.D.A.G. Mosley, B.J.N. Ogden, R.G.L. Oliphant, S.W.P. Perry-Aldworth, H.L. Pierce+, A.M. Prado, Sir Michael Sandberg+, G.M. Sayer+, P.A. Sellars, G.W. Stabb, G.O.W. Stewart, W.A. Stewart, G.P. Stubbs, J. McG Taylor, Maurice W. Turner+, Sir Michael Turner+, and W. Webster.
The author is grateful for additional comments by Sir John Saunders.
Widow: Mrs Natalie Davis; *daughter*: Tita [Stephen] de Gherardi.
Local Staff: Stan Coles, New Beckenham; M. Roche and L. Vincent, Lyons (by C. Fivel Démoret); Ena Coberly Gilbert, Hankow and Tokyo; Peter Lee Shun Wah, compradore, Hong Kong; Alfonso I. Rabuco, Iloilo.

Mercantile Bank oral history project

Foreign Staff, Mercantile Bank Ltd: D.K. Anderson+, L.C. Blanks+, P.T. Lamb, F.I.C. Herridge, C.C. Misselbrook, C.F. Pow, and Sunil Singh Roy.

Marine Midland oral history project

Hongkong Bank: Sir Michael Sandberg, J.L. Boyer, R.W. Campbell (also on Iloilo), F.R. Frame, P.E. Hammond, I.H. Macdonald, G.R. Ross (director).
Hongkong Bank consultants and advisers: Howard D. Adams, Gavin Anderson, Warren D. Chinn, Barry Fox, James F. Munsell, Steuart Pittman, W. Brown, Craig Stearns, James D. Wolfensohn, D.E. Connally.
Marine Midland: Edward W. Duffy, Charles G. Blaine (director), David Gruen, Karl Hinke, Robert W. Hubner (director); Felix Larkin (director), Frank J. Laski, Baldwin Maull, John R. Petty, Arthur B. Ziegler.
MMBI consultants and advisers: Louis Glucksman, John L. Kelsey, Robert C. Shehan, Peter Mullin, Michael Goldberg.
Federal: Robert R. Bench, F. Dahl, J. McAfee, R. Youngmeyer, Paul Freedenburg,

John G. Heimann, G. William Miller, John E. Ryan, Donald P. Tucker, Henry C. Wallich.
New York State: Hugh Carey, John S. Dyson, Herman D. Farrell, Jr., Robert P. Morgado, Muriel Siebert, Ernest Kohn, Geofredo Rodrigues.

Royal Bank of Scotland Group oral history project
Hongkong Bank: Sir Michael Sandberg, B.H. Asher, J.J.N. Dreaper, F.R. Frame, P.E. Hammond, W. Purves, P.E. Hutson, P.M. Anderson.
Hongkong Bank advisers: (merchant banking) Charles Hambro, John Clay, Christopher Sporborg, D.C. Macdonald, Richard Mead; (legal) David Shaw, Ian Threlfall, Richard Buxton; (academic) Andrew D. Bain, Tibor Barna; (public relations) Tim Traverse-Healy, George Hodge.
London Advisory Committee, Hongkong Bank: Sir Philip de Zulueta, Viscount W. Weir.
Royal Bank of Scotland Group: Sir Michael Herries, William Dacombe, Sidney Proctor.
Standard Chartered Group: Sir Peter A. Graham.
Other Scottish interviewees: Christopher Baur, Gavin Boyd, Ian Dalziel, Peter H.J. de Vink, Angus Grossart, James T. Laurenson, Iain More, Iain Noble, Thomas N. Risk.

LIST OF WORKS CONSULTED

*indicates a sometime member, however briefly, of the Hongkong Bank or Mercantile Bank staffs.

Anderson, Patrick. *Snake Wine, a Singapore Episode*. Reprinted, Kuala Lumpur, 1980.
Andrée, H.D. *Progress of Banking in Ceylon*. Colombo, 1864.
*Carruthers, M.G. 'Financing Industry'. *Far Eastern Economic Review* (1966), pp. 367–70.
Ceylon, Government of. Report of the Ceylon Banking Commission (1934 Sessional Paper XXII). *See also* Sri Lanka.
Chandler, Alfred D., Jr. *The Visible Hand: The Managerial Revolution in American Business*. Cambridge, MA, 1977.
Chang, Kia-ngau. *The Inflationary Spiral, the Experience in China, 1939–1950*. New York, 1958.
Channon, D.F. *British Banking Strategy and International Challenge*. London, 1977.
Chen, Chung-sieu. 'British Loans to China from 1860 to 1913, with special reference to the period 1894–1913'. Diss. University of London, 1940.
China Mail. Hong Kong.
Chou, Shun-hsin. *The Chinese Inflation, 1937–1949*. New York, 1963.
Cleveland, Harold van B. and Thomas F. Huertas. *Citibank, 1812–1970*. New York, 1985.
Cook, Christopher. 'The Hongkong and Shanghai Banking Corporation on Lombard Street'. In Frank H.H. King, ed. *Eastern Banking: Essays in the History of The Hongkong and Shanghai Banking Corporation*. London, 1983. Pp. 193–203.
Collis, Maurice. *Wayfoong, The Hongkong and Shanghai Banking Corporation*. London, 1965. Revised ed. with additional material by Frank H.H. King, published by the Hongkong Bank, 1979.
Couling, Samuel, ed. *The Encyclopaedia Sinica*. Shanghai, 1917. Reprinted, Hong Kong, 1983.

Cribb, Joe. *Money in the Bank. An Illustrated Introduction to the Money Collection of The Hongkong and Shanghai Banking Corporation.* London, 1987.
Cruikshank, Charles. *S.O.E. in the Far East.* Oxford, 1983.
Endacott, G.B. *Hong Kong Eclipse.* Edited with additional material by Alan Birch. Hong Kong, 1978.
Far Eastern Economic Review. Hong Kong.
Fischer, Gerald C. 'Wall to Wall Banks, the Marine Midland Story', unpublished history of Marine Midland. N.d.
Fivel-Démoret, Claude. 'The Hongkong Bank in Lyon, 1881–1954: Busy but too Discreet?'. In King, ed. *Eastern Banking.* London, 1983. Pp. 467–517.
Goldberg, Ellen S. *Analysis of Current Operations of Foreign-Owned U.S. Banks.* OCC Staff Papers. Washington, D.C., 1980.
Goodstadt, Leo. 'A Wary Reception for Hongkong Bank'. *Asian Banking*, pp. 29–39 (June 1981).
Graham, P.A. 'Hong Kong's Banks and Financial Institutions'. *The Banker*, pp. 747–53 (July 1970).
Gunasekera, H.A. de S. *From Dependent Currency to Central Banking in Ceylon.* Colombo, 1960.
Herrick, Tracy G. *Bank Analyst's Handbook.* New York, 1978.
Hongkong and Shanghai Banking Corporation. Hong Kong. *Annual Report.* 1940–1986.
Alliance for Progress. Hong Kong, 1981.
Berita Malaya.
Conditions of Service (various years)
Detailed information relating to the acquisition by HSBC Holdings B.V., a wholly owned subsidiary of The Hongkong and Shanghai Banking Corporation, of Shares of Common Stock of Marine Midland Banks, Inc. Hong Kong, 1980.
Group Magazine.
Group News then *HongkongBank News.*
Marine Midland Banks, Inc. Hong Kong, 1980.
Minutes of Shareholders' Meetings, 1946–49.
Wayfoong.
Hong Kong, Government of. *Hongkong Government Gazette.*
Annual reports.
Census and statistical publications.
Hong Kong (British Military Administration) Gazette.
Report of the Industrial Banking Committee. 1960.
Hsiao, Liang-lin. *China's Foreign Trade Statistics, 1864–1949.* Cambridge, MA, 1974.
*Jao, Y.C. *Banking and Currency in Hong Kong, a Study of Postwar Financial Development.* London, 1974.
'Financing Hong Kong's Early Postwar Industrialization: the Role of The Hongkong and Shanghai Banking Corporation'. In King, ed. *Eastern Banking.* London, 1983. Pp. 545–74.
Jones, Geoffrey. *Banking and Empire in Iran.* Vol. I of his *The History of the British Bank of the Middle East.* Cambridge, 1986.
Banking and Oil. Vol. II of his *The History of the British Bank of the Middle East.* Cambridge, 1987.
'Lombard Street on the Riviera: British Clearing Banks and Europe, 1900–1960'. In King, ed. *Eastern Banking*, London, 1983. Pp. 753–77.
*Jones, J.R. History Collections in the Hongkong Bank Group Archives: 'Personalities and Narratives'.

'The Bank, 1876–1948'.
'Branches'.
'Miscellaneous materials sent to M. Collis'.
Jones, Stephanie. *Two Centuries of Overseas Trading: the Origins and Growth of the Inchcape Group*. London, 1986.
[Kalimtgis, Konstadinos and others.] *Dope, Inc., Britain's opium war against the U.S.* 'By a U.S. Labor Party investigating team'. New York, 1978.
Keswick, Maggie, ed. *The Thistle and the Jade: a Celebration of 150 Years of Jardine, Matheson and Co.* London, 1982.
Key, M.F. *Hongkong before, during and after the War, an Account of the Stanley Civilian Internment Camp.* 2nd ed., Hong Kong, 1946.
King, Catherine E. 'The First Trip East – P&O via Suez'. In King, ed. *Eastern Banking*. London, 1983. Pp. 204–29.
King, David J.S. 'On the Relations of the Hongkong Bank with Germany, 1864–1948'. Research report in Hongkong Bank Group Archives, Hong Kong.
King, Frank H.H. 'Inflation and Hyperinflation in China, 1946–1948'. M.A. Thesis, Stanford University, 1949.
Money in British East Asia. London, 1957.
'Essays in China's Recent Monetary History, (i) The Customs Gold Unit'. In King, *Asian Policy, History and Development – collected essays*. Hong Kong, 1979.
'The Hong Kong Open Market, 1954'. In King, *Asian Policy, History and Development – collected essays*. Hong Kong, 1979.
Ed. *Eastern Banking, Essays in the History of The Hongkong and Shanghai Banking Corporation*. London, 1983.
Kraar, L. 'Hong Kong's Beleaguered Financial Fortress'. *Fortune*, pp. 187–91, 284 (May 1976).
'What the Hong Kong "Amateur" is Doing in New York'. *Fortune*, pp. 159–60 (August 1979).
*Lamb, P.T. 'The History of the Mercantile Bank Limited'. *Group News*, pp. 12–14 (Spring 1973), pp. 8–12 (Autumn 1973), pp. 9–12 (Spring 1974).
Lambot, Ian and Gillian Chambers. *One Queen's Road Central, the Headquarters of HongkongBank since 1864*. Hong Kong, 1986.
Lee, S. Y. and Y. C. Jao. *Financial Structures and Monetary Policies in Southeast Asia*. 1982.
Lee, T.A. 'The Financial Statements of The Hongkong and Shanghai Banking Corporation, 1865–1980'. In King, ed. *Eastern Banking*. London, 1983.
Leiper, G.A. *A Yen for my Thoughts*. Hong Kong, 1982.
Lim, Chee Peng, Phang Siew Nooi, and Margaret Boh. 'The History and Development of The Hongkong and Shanghai Banking Corporation in Peninsular Malaysia'. In King, ed. *Eastern Banking*. London, 1983. Pp. 350–91.
Loganathan, C. 'Finance to the Ceylonese Exporter'. In *Banking in Ceylon*. Colombo, 1963.
Loney, Nicholas. *A Britisher in the Philippines or the Letters of Nicholas Loney*. Introduction by Margaret Hoskyn. Manila, 1964.
Longbrake, William A. *Prices Paid by Foreign Interests to Acquire U.S. Banks*. OCC Staff Papers. Washington, D.C., 1980.
Longbrake, William A., Melanie R. Quinn, and Judith A. Walker. *Foreign Acquisition of U.S. Banks: Facts and Patterns*. OCC Staff Papers. Washington, D.C., 1980.
Ma, R.A. and E. Szczepanik. *The National Income of Hong Kong, 1947–50*. Hong Kong, 1955.
Mackenzie, Compton. *Realms of Silver*. London, 1954.

*Marshall, J.F. *Where the Wild Thyme Blows; some memoirs of service with the Hongkong Bank*. Grayshott, Surrey, England, 1986.
Maull, Baldwin. 'Some Observations on Bank Holding Companies'. *The Bankers Magazine* 155:19–23 (Summer 1972).
Merrill Lynch International. 'The Hongkong and Shanghai Banking Corporation'. May 1982.
Mintzberg, H. *The Structuring of Organizations*. Englewood Cliffs, NJ, 1979.
*Muriel, H.E. Autobiography. Typescript in Group Archives, Hong Kong.
New York Times Co. Data from 'The Information Bank' on the Hongkong Bank.
Ngan, Y.P. 'Hang Seng Bank Limited: a Brief History'. In King, ed., *Eastern Banking*. London, 1983. Pp. 709–16.
P.A. Management Consultants Limited. 'The Hongkong Bank Group, review of executive staff employment', supporting volume, 'Current Staffing Arrangements for Executive Staff, HSBC' (January, 1978). There is a similar volume for the BBME. The principal consultant was Roger Cadman, working in association with the Bank's General Manager, M.J. Pridham.
Page, Diane and Neal Soss. *Some Evidence on Transnational Banking Structure*. OCC Staff Papers. Washington, D.C., 1980.
Perry, F.E. *A Dictionary of Banking*. 2nd ed. London, 1983.
Powell, Ifor B. 'The British in the Philippines in the American Era, 1898–1946, (ii): the Banks'. *Bulletin of the American Historical Collection* 9,3:39–52 (July–September 1981), Manila.
Pressnell, L.S. 'A Glimpse of Banking in Hong Kong'. *Three Banks Review*. September 1961.
Redding, S.G. 'Organizational and Structural Change in The Hongkong and Shanghai Banking Corporation, 1950–1980'. In King, ed. *Eastern Banking*. London, 1983. Pp. 601–28.
Reed, Richard. *National Westminster Bank, a short history*. London, 1983.
Ride, Edwin. *BAAG, Hong Kong Resistance, 1942–1945*. Hong Kong, 1981.
Romualdez, Eduardo Z. 'Rehabilitation of the Philippine Banking Structure'. *Philippine Rehabilitation Journal* 1:22 (October 1949).
Rowley, Anthony. 'The Revolt of Hongkong's Foreign Banks'. *Institutional Investor*, pp. 135–36 (May 1979).
Ryder, F.R. and D.B. Jenkins, eds. *Thomson's Dictionary of Banking*. 12th ed. London, 1974.
*Saunders, J.A.H. 'The Hongkong and Shanghai Banking Corporation'. *The Banker*, pp. 755–59 (1970).
Shanghai Herald.
Shockey, John E. and William B. Glidden. *Foreign-controlled U.S. Banks: the Legal and Regulatory Environment*. OCC Staff Papers. Washington, D.C., 1980.
Siebert, Muriel. *Report of the Superintendent of Banks of New York State on the Proposed Acquisition by the Hongkong and Shanghai Banking Corporation of Marine Midland Banks, Inc*. New York, 1979.
Sit, Victor F.S. 'Branching of The Hongkong and Shanghai Banking Corporation in Hong Kong: a Spatial Analysis'. In King, ed. *Eastern Banking*. London, 1983. Pp. 629–54.
Sithi-Amnuai, Paul. *Finance and Banking in Thailand, a study of the commercial system, 1888–1963*. Bangkok, 1964.
Smith, Carl T. 'Compradores of the Hongkong Bank'. In King, ed. *Eastern Banking*. London, 1983. Pp. 93–111.

Smith, W. Paul and Steven J. Weiss. *Potential Acquisition Partners for Large U.S. Banks: the Discriminatory Effects of Law and Policy.* OCC Staff Papers. Washington, D.C., 1980.
South China Morning Post. Hong Kong.
Sri Lanka. Central Bank of Sri Lanka, 'Examination Report of 1978'.
 Copies of agreements on the procedure for the financing of imports with the Central Bank, May 1965 and December 1971.
 De Silva Commission, Report of 1966.
 See also Ceylon.
Standard Chartered Bank: a Story Brought up to Date. London, 1980.
Szczepanik, E. 'Financing the Postwar Economic Growth of Hong Kong'. *Far Eastern Economic Review*, 781–83 (1956).
 The Economic Growth of Hong Kong. 1958.
Thiravet Pramuanratkarn. 'The Hongkong Bank in Thailand: a Case of a Pioneering Bank'. In King, ed. *Eastern Banking.* London, 1983. Pp. 421–34.
Thomas, W.H. Evans. *Vanished China.* London, 1952.
*Thursfield, R.P. *Topical Verses.* Privately published, 1914.
Tillotson, G.H.R. *Fan Kwae Pictures, Paintings and Drawings by George Chinnery and other Artists in the Collection of The Hongkong and Shanghai Banking Corporation.* London, 1987.
Tomkins, H.J. *Report on the Hong Kong Banking System and Recommendations for the Replacement of the Banking Ordinance, 1948.* Hong Kong, 1962.
*Townsend, A.M. 'Early Days of the Hongkong and Shanghai Bank' (written in 1937, unpublished). A copy is in the Hongkong Bank Group Archives.
*Tytler, Bruce. *Here, There and (Nearly) Everywhere.* London, 1979.
United Kingdom, Monopolies and Mergers Commission. *The Hongkong and Shanghai Banking Corporation, Standard Chartered Bank Limited, The Royal Bank of Scotland Group Limited, a report on the Proposed Mergers*, Cmnd 8472. January 1982.
United States, Congress, House of Representatives. Report No. 95–1073 to accompany H.R. 10899, 95th Congress, 2nd Session, 1978.
(96th Congress, second session), Committee on Government Operations. *Hearings. Foreign Acquisitions of U.S. Banks and the non-Banking activities of Foreign Bank Holding Companies.* 15 May and 25 June, 1980.
 The Operations of Federal Agencies in Monitoring, Reporting on, and Analyzing Foreign Investments in the United States. Part 4 – Foreign Investments in U.S. Banks, Hearings, Commerce, Consumer and Monetary Affairs Subcommittee of the Committee on Government Operations. July 31 and August 1, 1979.
U.S. Labor Party, *see* Kalimtgis.
University of Hong Kong. *Calendar, 1984–1985.* Hong Kong, 1984.
Vickers da Costa. 'The Hongkong and Shanghai Banking Corporation, a study'. January 1982.
Walter, Judith A. *Foreign Acquisitions of U.S. Banks: Motives and Tactical Considerations.* OCC Staff Papers. Washington, D.C., 1980.
Weiss, Steven J. *Competitive Standards applied to Foreign and Domestic Acquisitions of U.S. Banks.* OCC Staff Papers. Washington, D.C., 1980.
 A Critical Evaluation of Reciprocity in Foreign Bank Acquisitions. OCC Staff Papers. Washington, D.C., 1980.
Williams, Stephanie. *Hongkong Bank: the Building of Norman Foster's Masterpiece.* Boston and London, 1989. (Seen in final draft form.)

Wilson, John Donald. *The Chase. The Chase Manhattan Bank, N.A., 1945–1985*. Boston, MA, 1986.

*Wodehouse, P.G. 'My Banking Career'. *The Hongkong Bank Group Magazine*, No. 6 (Summer 1975), pp. 13–16. Reprinted in King, *The History of The Hongkong and Shanghai Banking Corporation*. Cambridge, 1988. II, 180–81.

Wood, Mackenzie & Co. 'The Hongkong and Shanghai Banking Corporation'. December 15, 1981.

Ybañez, Roy C. 'The Hongkong Bank in the Philippines, 1899–1941'. In King, ed. *Eastern Banking*. London, 1983. Pp. 435–66.

'The Hongkong Bank in the Philippines'. A research report dated October 16, 1981. U.P. Business Research Foundation, Inc., Quezon City. TS in Group Archives.

Yip, Christopher L. 'Four Major Buildings in the Architectural History of The Hongkong and Shanghai Banking Corporation'. In King, ed. *Eastern Banking*. London, 1983. Pp. 112–38.

Young, Arthur N. *China's Wartime Finance and Inflation, 1937–1945*. Cambridge, MA, 1965.

Papers. Archives, Hoover Institution, Stanford, California.

Young, Walter H. *A Merry Banker in the Far East*. London, 1916.

Ziegler, Arthur B. 'Marine Midland Bank in an Analysis of Regulatory Environment and Corporate Structure'. In King, ed. *Eastern Banking*. London, 1983. Pp. 717–34.

INDEX

[Alphabetization is by *letter*. Names of Chinese cited in Chinese format (without comma) are accordingly alphabetized on the basis of their entire name. Names of British Bank of the Middle East (BBME), Hongkong Bank (HSBC), Mercantile Bank (MBLD), and Hongkong Bank of California (HBC) staff and their wives are marked with an asterisk. Names listed only in tables are not necessarily indexed. Hongkong Bank Group offices (including suburban offices) are listed under the principal city; Hong Kong offices are listed under 'Hong Kong'.]

abbreviations, xlvii–viii, 850, 936
Aberdeen, HSBC branch in, *see* Hong Kong
Abilene, Kansas, 865n
Accepting Houses Ctte, 716, 870
Adams, Howard D., 777, 780, 782–83
*Adamson, A.S., 61, 89–90, 94, 155, 279–80, 285, 294, 328, 351, 353, 358
*Addis, *Sir* Charles S., 202, 271, 300, 312, 376, 518, 531, 644, 686; and Morse, 31, 36–37, 39, 48; British and Chinese Corp., 31n, 166, 170; China Consortium, xxxv, 36–37, 165–66, 636–37; London Advisory Ctte, 581; London Manager, 14, 46, 579, 636, 637; on Grayburn, 48; on Indian experience, 71–72; on staff policy, 7, 497, 518, 592, 914; University of Hong Kong, 36n
Addis, *Sir* John, 644, 910
Adler, Solomon, 62
Africa, south of Sahara: HSBC and, 488, 500, 520–21, 527–28, 562, 695, 697, 871
Agricultural and Industrial Credit Corp., 653
*Aitkenhead, G.G., 467
Alexander, J.D., 272
Algemene Bank, 707, 772
*Allan, B.C., 468–69
Allied Banking Corp., purchase of Iloilo branch, 650–51
Al Sagr Insurance Co., 719
Amoy (Xiamen), 157, 381, 465, 888
Amsterdam, HSBC in, 609
Anderson, Gavin, 797
*Andrée, H.D., 460

Antony Gibbs (various): acquisition by HSBC, 560, 640, 647, 693, 741–42, 862, 864 (LAC's opinion) 642, (name) 695; in Hongkong Bank Group, 717–18, 866, 869–70, 874, 899, 900, (disappearance of) 903–04; in South America, 612; management, 312, 903; performance, 647, 868, 870, 903
Antony Gibbs Unit Trust Managers, 716
Approach to an Alliance, 895, 908–09
Arbuthnot, Latham and Co., 720
Architectural Review, 905
Army and Navy Stores, 900
Arthur, *Sir* Geoffrey, 911
Arthur Weller, 719
*Ash, S.H., 86
Ashburton, *Lord* (Alexander Baring), 31, 32
*Asher, Bernard, 885–86
Associated Engineers, 900
Association of Southeast Asian Nations (ASEAN), 647
Atkins, *Sir* Humphrey, 893
Atlas Consolidated Mining, 647
*Atterbury, L.G., 461, 542, 609, 653–54
Augustine Heard and Co., 684
Australia, 243, 431, 434; and HSBC, 49, 402–03, 469n, 488, 528, 604, 695, 697, 698, 719, 867, 891, 901; Foreign Investments Review Board, 813
Ava Bank, 205

Bacolod, HSBC and, 444, 445, 446, 448, 450
*Bacon, R.H.L., 711–12
Baguio, 81, 83

963

Bahrain, HSBC in, 609
*Baker, T.S., 35
Bancal Tri-State Corp., 789n
Banco di Roma, 700
Bandaranaike, Felix Dias, 655–56
Bandaranaike, Sirimaro, 653
Bandar Seri Begawan (Brunei Town), 464, 465
Bangkok: HSBC in, 84–85, 424, 473, 483, 889–90, (banknote issue) xli, (Suapah Rd) 311, 423, 550–51, 619; MBLD in, 550–51, 889–90, (Asoke Lane) 599, (Rajawongse Rd) 550–51, 599, 602. *See also* Carlingford
Bank Deutscher Länder, 106
Bankers Trust, 431, 782
banking
  competition, 187, 328, 424–25, 488, 517, 600, 628
  theory and practice: as art and science, 37; branch banking, 364, 424, 483; central banking functions, 203, 334–36, 342, 410–11, 573, 726; consequences of foreign ownership, 837, 843–44; industrial, 356–60, 618, 620–21, 625–28; liability management, 199, 865; post-war developments, 202, 203–04, 206–07, 328, 560, 561, 609, 864–66; role of exchange banks, 328, 349, 659, 666n. *See also* Hong Kong; Hongkong and Shanghai Banking Corporation (ii)
Bank Negara (Malaysia), 744, 901
banknotes
  Bank of England, for Hong Kong, 576, 702
  currency board system, 234–35
  'duress' issue and undestroyed: Pacific War issue, 9, 20, 51, 115–31, 134, 147, 215; potential future, responsibility for, 239–41, 575–76
  government vs private, 238–39, 242–43, 335, 573
  HSBC issue, history of, 573–78, (one-dollar issue) xl–xli, 242, 576
  HSBC issue, other references
    authorized/ excess issue, 120, 341n, 574, 576; circulation in South China, 153, 161, 236–38, 575, 576–77; cost of issue, 338n, 576–77, (labour involved) 233, 320; legal tender, 8, 118, 575; place of issue, 412; regulations, 241–43, 244, 246, 411, 565, 571, 931–32, (security for, reserves against) 576; size of issue, 119, 147, 236, 573, 577, 736, 861, 881–82
  Royal Bank of Scotland, 895

Bank of America/BankAmerica Corp., 1n, 442n, 499, 600, 647, 658, 849n
Bank of British Columbia, 862
Bank of British North America, 891
Bank of Calcutta, 482
Bank of California, 770–71, 789n, 892
Bank of Ceylon, 66–67, 342n, 455, 457–58, 461, 462, 658
Bank of Chettinad, 457
Bank of China
  National government, 59, 60, 95, 156, 161, 382
  People's Republic, 340, 373, 375, 382, 383, 390–94, 396–99, 404, 405–06, 410–11, 439, 612, 737, 745n
Bank of Communications, 156
Bank of England, 434, 615, 871
  Addis as director of, 31
  and BBME/MBLD acquisitions, 501, 508–09, 533, 634, 640
  and HSBC: general relations, 179, 240, 261, 267, 430, 634–35, 639, 674, 684; on war-time survival, 38, 41; responsive to, 341n, 343, 394, 519, 714
  and Royal Bank of Scotland, 891–96, 908
  banknotes of, for Hong Kong, 576, 702
  British overseas banking rationalization, 487, 498–99, 509, 519, 529, 532–33, 633, 640
  China Consortium, 165
  duress note issue, 124
Bank of Iran and the Middle East, 698, 710
Bank of Japan, 603
Bank of Kuwait and the Middle East, 706–07
Bank of Mauritius, 482
Bank of New South Wales, 49, 402
Bank of New York, 782
Bank of Seoul, 611–12
Bank of Thailand, 96, 430
Bank of Tokyo, 437
Bank of Utica, 869
Banque Belge, 393n
Banque de France, 901
Banque de l'Indo-Chine, 58, 167, 168n
Banque de Paris et des Pay-Bas, 168n, 526
Banque d'Outremer, 168
Banque Française du Commerce Extérieure, 441
Banque Worms, 720
Barclays Bank, 52, 528, 550
Baring, A. (*Lord* Ashburton), 31, 32
Baring Bros and Co., 31–33, 267, 340n
*Barker, K.W., 915
*Barlow, A.H., 31–33, 137, 268–71, 281, 438, 687–88
*Barnes, O.J., 35, 37, 71, 438, 519, 637

*Barnham, O.J.L., 869
Barrington, R.L., 587
Barton, H.D.M., 260–61, 272, 297, 674, 675
Basel Agreement, 139
Ba Swe, U, 205
Batavia, see Jakarta
BBME, see British Bank of the Middle East
Beaufort (Sabah), 311
*Beaumont, R., 602–03
Beijing, see Peking
Beirut, BBME in, 635, 684
Beith, B.D.F., 31–33
Belilios, H.R., 252
*Bell, W.H., 33
Bench, Robert R., 833–34
Benham, H.D., 248–49, 272
*Bennett, N.H.T., 230n, 236, 345, 424, 435, 587, 637, 641–42, 646, 669, 689, 690
Bermuda, 243, 500. See also under company titles
Bernard, Sir Dallas G.M., 31, 271–72, 530, 531–33, 542, 546–49, 644
Bessborough, Lord, 179
Bevan, Aneurin, 390
Bicester, Lord (R.H. Vivian-Smith), 499, 502
Binny, J.A.F., 271, 910
Birmingham, HSBC in, 903, 904
*Black, F.C.B.: China mission, 390, 392–93; Hankow, 94, 149, 157–59; Head Office, 280, 289, 290, 296, 311, 328, 359, 445; Shanghai, 163–64
*Blackhall, A.R.M., 109
Blackwood, J.A., 272
Blaine, Charles G., 787, 800–01
Blaker, Cedric, 248, 250, 272–73
*Blanks, L.C., 498
Blyth, Eastman, Dillon and Co., 788
Blyth, Greene, Jourdain and Co., 271
Bombay: BBME in, 516, 531, 602; HSBC in, 46–47, 204–05, (agent of BBME) 531, (profit) 45; MBLD in, 599
Bombay Burmah, 469
*Bond, J.R.H., 916
*Bond, M.W., 587, 914
Booz, Allen and Hamilton, 776–82, 785, 792, 805
Boustead and Co., 271
Bowmaker (C.A.), 204, 224, 251, 438, 497, 520, 527, 695, 697, 707, (branches) 520
Boxer Uprising and Indemnity, 172, 173, 174, 379
*Boyer, J.L., 286, 658, 742, 798, 802, 848, 903, 913, 918

*Bradford, I.H., 89, 303, 312, 328, 357, 361, 490, 631
*Bradford, Kenneth, 640, 870
*Bray, John, 714
Brazil: government bonds, 44, 518; HSBC and, 306, 528, 612, 743
Brisbane, HSBC and, 891
British Acceptance Co., 699, 700, 714
British Airways, 721
British and Chinese Corp. (B&CC): and Sir Charles Addis, 31n, 166, 438, 636; corporate history, 9, 14, 64–65, 167–68, 169–72, 224, 350n, 438, 695, 900; loan rescheduling and renegotiation, 14, 172–75, 178–79
British and Korean Corp., 9
British Army Aid Group (BAAG), 30, 114
British Bank of Iran and the Middle East, 482, 549
British Bank of the Middle East (BBME, formerly Imperial Bank of Persia)
acquisition of: attempt by Lombard, 531–32; by HSBC, 204, 211n, 216, 222, 225–27, 251, 267, 517, 523–24, 529, 535–39, (compulsory purchase of shares) 537–38, 539, (true profit stated) 536; negotiations with Grindlay's and HSBC, 523–24, 530, 533–34; negotiations with MBLD and HSBC, 510, 532–33
Board of Directors, 437, 523–24, 529–30; HSBC executive as chairman, 521, 526, 639; negotiations, 532–33, 537–38, 547–49; on London Advisory Ctte, 271–72, 543, 642; responsibilities, 545–47, 585
branches, 193, 414, 521, 526, 593, 597, 600, 602
capital, 485, 545, 547, 548–49, 552, (post-1960 equity asistance) 871
head office: location debate, 485, 640; move to Hong Kong, 870
history of, 3, 232n, 300–01, 530–31; charter, revised, 640; post-1960 history, 191–92, 635
post-1960 acquisition consequences: deposits with HSBC, 194, 226–27, 268, 543–45, 591, 603, 637, 638–39, 645–46; Group's U.K. retail business, 585, 638–39, 640, 871; HSBC staff in BBME, 543; management fee, 545; relations with HSBC, integration, 224, 247, 261, 289, 541–42, 543–49, 552–53, 641, 733, 865, 867–68, 870–71, 872, 910, (in amateur theatricals) 540
reserves, 222, 548–49, (inner) 537, 548

British Bank of the Middle East (*cont.*)
   sports: soccer, 669
   subsidiaries, 482, 549, 695–96, 699, 706–07, 713
British Bank of the Middle East (Morocco), 549
'British Borneo', 413, 415, 463–64, 487. *See also* British North Borneo; Brunei; Sarawak
British Council of Foreign Bondholders, 172, 173
British Export Trade Research Organization, 50
British North Borneo (Sabah)
   HSBC and, 99, 147, 190, 346, 413, 463–65, 474, 475–78, 600, (Dusuns) 474, (Leg Co/Ex Co) 473–74, 477
   North Borneo Development Board, 478
   railway, 478
British overseas banking, 508–09, 555; rationalization of post-war, 487, 498–99, 519, 529–30, 532–34, 633, 640
British Overseas Banks Assn, 438
British Wagon Co., 700
*Brockman, P.W.S.C., 915–16
*Brohier, E.O., 454
*Brown, J. McI., 433
*Bruce, R., 28
Brunei (Negara Brunei Darussalam), HSBC and, 147, 463, 464–65, 521
Brunei Town (Bandar Seri Begawan), HSBC in, 464, 465
*Buchan, D., 378, 390, 397, 400
Buffalo, 799–800, 863
Buffalo Marine Trust Co., 891
Bukit Terendak, 319
Bunbury, F.J., 533
*Burch, F.R., 89, 387–88, 458, 460, 462
Burma: HSBC and, 205, 516, 600, 712; Burma Agricultural and Products Board, 54–55. *See also* Rangoon
Busan (Pusan), HSBC in, 413, 612, 707n, 888
*Butter, J. McN., 100–01, 115, 301, 423
Butterfield and Swire, *see* Swire Group

Caine, *Sir* Sydney, 25, 116, 125–26, 133, 135, 234, 239, 341n, 580
Calcutta: HSBC in, 70, 71–72, 76, 235–36, 289, 303, 416, (profits) 45, 510; MBLD in, 599
Caldbeck, Macgregor and Co., 684, 685
*Caldwell, J., 108, 235–36, 285, 303
California: banking legislation and State Banking Department, 340n, 484, 488, 490, 496, 777, 813; HSBC policy in, 777–78; unitary tax, 491, 721; wine,

508n. *See also* Hongkong and Shanghai Banking Corp. of California; Los Angeles; San Francisco
California First Bank, 312
*Calver, G.A., 637, 640, 641, 646
*Calvert, M.J., 776–77, 889
Cambodia, HSBC in, 206, 600
*Cameron, A.G., 667–68
*Cameron, *Sir* Ewen, 14, 71, 202, 579, 636, 637, 686, 799n
Cameron Highlands, HSBC in, 319, 415–16, 424, 469n
*Campbell, Angela (*Mrs* R.W.), 648
Campbell, C.A., 31, 34, 50, 267, 271
*Campbell, R.W., 446, 648, 776–77, 782, 915
*Campbell, W.W., 102
Canada: evolution of the Hongkong Bank Group in, 490, 604, 697, 700, 716, 862, 890–91, (Bank Act) 862; Foreign Investment Review Board, 813. *See also* Hongkong Bank of Canada
Canton (Guangzhou), HSBC in, 93, 157, 381, 382, 423, 613
Canton Trust and Commercial Bank, 702
Carey, Hugh, 775, 790–91, 811, 812, 818, 820, 824–25, 830–31, 838
Carlingford (HSBC Bangkok residence), 230n, 669–70
Carlingford (HSBC insurance co.), 230n, 695, 718, 901
Carlingford investments, 698, 872
Carrian Group, 877
*Carrier, J., 78
Carroll McEntry & McGinley (CM&M), 900
*Carruthers, M.G., 282, 433, 437, 617, 630, 688, 703, 705
cart, Peking Manager's, 449
Carter, G.G.D., 273
*Cassels, W.C., 33, 34, 57, 58, 60, 61, 65, 150, 174, 178–79, 208
Cathay Pacific, 590, 693, 696, 697, 720–21, 863, 900, (subsidiaries) 900
Catto, *Lord* Catto of Cairncross, 642
*Cautherley, G.H., 328, 630
Cebu, 444
Central Bank of Ceylon, 457–58, 652, 662
Central Bank of China, 61, 156, 160, 162, 164, 177, 375
Central Bank of Oakland, 813
Central Bank of the Philippines, 442, 650
Central National Bank of Cleveland, 902
Central Registration (H.K.), 584
Central Reserve Bank (Nanking), 88, 153
Centran Corp., 902
Ceylon, *see* Sri Lanka
Ceylon State Mortgage Bank, 457

Index

Ceylon Trading Co., 459
*Chambers, G.S., 281, 424, 441n
*Chandler, F.W., 95
Chang Kia-ngau, 156
Channel Islands, HSBC and, 609, 610. *See also* Jersey; St Helier; St Peter's Port
*Chappell, A.C.R., 712, 915
Chartered Bank (of India, Australia and China), 27, 49, 50, 54, 62–63, 156, 228, 342n, 433, 482, 498, 501, 528, 529–30, 532, 562, 566, 770n, 872
 as business competition, 93, 100–01, 164, 235, 239, 338–39, 424, 431, 521;
 British North Borneo, 414, 464, 468, 469, 471–73, 474, 477–78; Colombo, 655–56; Hong Kong, 339–40, 615, 702–03; India, 71; Philippines, 442n, 447, 648; Sarawak, 465, 473, 521
 banknotes of, 115n, 236–38, 575, (duress note issue) 118, 124, 127
 China policy, 377, 389, 393, 395, 408
 See also Standard Chartered Group
Chartered Bank of London, 770
Chartered Mercantile Bank, 506n, 567, 575, 889n. *See also* Mercantile Bank
Charterhouse, Japhet and Thomasson, 699
Chase Manhattan (Asia), 712
Chase National (*then* Manhattan) Bank, 431, 499, 508–09, (and MBLD) 503, 507–11, (and Hang Seng) 703
Chefoo, 155
Chemical Bank, 1n, 818n, 823
Chen, K.P. (Kwang-pu), 58, 61
Chen, R.C., 156
*Cherepanoff, I. and N., 403
chettiars, 350
Cheung Kong (Holdings), 686, 711
Chicago, HSBC in, 611
Ch'i Chao-t'ing, 62, 375–76
Chile, HSBC and, 528, 612, 716, 874, 890
China
 banking regulations, 58–60, 150–51, 156, 160
 currency, 62, 71, 152–55, 164, 384–85, (conversion rates) 154, 386, 391
 economic conditions, 151–55, 158–59, 160–61, 162–64, 351, 861
 HSBC
  and Republic of: banknotes in, 395; war-time, 24, 55; post-war, 149–50, 182; role of, 158. *See also* Chungking
  People's Republic of, 251, 342, 375, 376–79, 381–83, 389–94, 396–97, 612–13: 'all-for-all' settlement, 9, 149, 187, 383, 389, 391–92, 393–95, 415, 612; post-1978, 861, 869,

888–89. *See also* Shanghai; Ta Hwa Agreement
  as a China bank, 149, 150, 182, 342, 383, 613, 763
  role, 149–51, 180–83
  See also Hongkong Bank China Services, Ltd
 loans and advances (pre-1941), 169, 170, 172–80, (impact on HSBC) 180–82; Boxer Indemnity 6% (1934), 179; Canton-Kowloon, 170, 178; Chuchow Repair Shop, 174; Nanking-Kiangsu, 174; Peking-Mukden, 170; Pukow-Sinyang, 169; Reorganization (1913), 173; Shanghai Municipal Council, 173, 175–77; Shanghai-Nanking, 170; Shanghai-Ningpo, 170, 178; Tientsin-Pukow, 169, 170, 178
 railways, 169, 170, 174, 178, 180
 trade, 164, 190, 342, 392–93, 396, 404
 See also Bank of China; Boxer Uprising; extraterritoriality; Sino-British Joint Declaration
China, Chinese Maritime Customs, 174, 179
China, Ministry of Finance, 58–60, 61, 178
China Association, 57, 391, 392–93, 438
China Consortium, xxxv, 11, 14, 31n, 37, 64–65, 165–67, 175
China Development Finance Corp., 170
China Light and Power Co., 55, 87, 252, 369, 722
China Resources Co., 396
Chinatowns, HSBC in, 495, 610, 611, 620, 903
Chinese Bondholders Committee, 178, 179
Chinese Central Railways, 9, 14, 167–69, 636
Chinese Currency Stabilization Board, 61, 62, 376, 394, 612
Chinese Currency Stabilization Fund, 62–64
Chinese Manufacturers Association, 625
Chinese University of Hong Kong, 615
Chinn, Warren, 777, 780, 792
Chinnery, George, xxxix, 912
Chou En-lai, 613
Chubb and Son's, 466
*Chung En Loi, 477
Chungking, HSBC in, 20, 59, 61–62, 157, 375–76, 381–82, (profit) 45, (representational role) 52, 60–61
*Cierpicka, V., 900
cigarettes, 467
Citibank/Citicorp [(First) National City Bank (of New York)], 1n, 84, 133, 156, 335, 442n, 444, 547, 604, 658, 702, 744, 806, 889, 943n54
Clague, J. Douglas, 114, 252–57, 273, 674–79, 683, 708, 711

Clark, A.G., 338
*Clark, N.E., 209, 289, 297, 584, 620
Cleary, Gottlieb, Steen and Hamilton, 782
*Cleland, D.F.C., 92, 380
*Clements, E.W.A., 375, 381
Cliff Oil (HK), 874
Cloudlands (Peak Mess), 143, 313, 664, 860, 918
*Clout, C.H., 690
Club de Recreio, 111
CM&M, 900
Cobbold, C.F., 509, 532, 533
*Coberley, Ena, 105
Cockburn, *Sir* William R.M., 27, 238, 377, 469
*Coles, Jim, 313
*Coles, Stan, 313, 669, 917
*Collete, H.A., 454, 457
Collar, Hugh, 273, 392
Collis, M., 265, 612, 616
Collyer Quay Properties, 722
Colombo
  HSBC in, 66–70, 301, 326, 350, 453–62, 652, 656, 917; ETC in, 660–62; labour problems, 47, 67–70, 453–57; profit, 68, 460, 654, 657; Ratmalana, 658
  MBLD in, 453, 456, 458–59, 461
  See also Sri Lanka
Colonial Development Corp., 467, 469
Columbine, Montague E., 54
Commercial and Farmers Bank of Oxnard, 770
Commercial Bank of Ceylon, 458, 652, 655–56
Commercial Bank of Greece, 532
Commerzbank, 700, 713
compradore (guarantee shroff)
  system, 7, 349, 484, 910
  change to local officers, 303, 310–11, 350, 465, 616
  decline and fall, 301, 309–11, 350, 352, 370, 436, 630
  post-war return of, 86, 88, 92–93, 94, 98
  role of, 88, 164, 205, 362, 374–75, 424, 453, 475, 476
  succession, 143, 465
Comptoir d'Escompte de Paris, 168n, 837
Compton, A.H., 30, 142
Concorde Equipement, 720
Concord(e) Finance, 720
Concord International, 720, 862
Continental Illinois Bank, 312
Cook, Christopher, 164
*Cook, H.M., 51
Cooke, S.J., 273, 674
*Cookes, C.I., 37, 490

copra, 467, 470, 472
*Cordiero, Henry E., 98
Council of Foreign Bondholders, 172, 173
*Courtney, H.A., 449
Cowperthwaite, *Sir* John, 341, 634, 704
Cox and Co., 531
Craig, *Sir* James, 911
Crédit Lyonnais, 168n, 700
Cribb, Joe, xl
Crocker National Bank, 600, 782, 848
Cross Harbour Tunnel Co., 693, 741
*Cruickshank, L.J.O., 282
*Cruse, P., 47
*Curran, M., 674
Customs Gold Unit (CGU), 152–53, 164
Cyprus. British overseas banking in, 482, 532
Cyprus Popular Bank, 900

Dairen, 155
*Dalgety, G.M., 37
D'Almeda, Leo, 521–22
*Danielson, J.G., 37, 80, 102, 105
Dao Heng Bank, 702
David Sassoon and Co., 248, 252, 684
*Davidson, G.L., 46
*Davies, E.J., 31, 35, 71, 641
*Davies, H.D.C., 96, 98
Davies, L.J., 30
*Davis, D.C., 286, 440
Deacon and Co., 684
*de Bovis, François, 71, 259, 281, 300
debtor/creditor relations, post-war, 20, 51, 116, 131–37, 147, 441–42
Delacour, J.H., 424
Delaware, banking legislation, 902
Denis frères, 95
Dent, Alfred, 463
Dent and Co., 257
*de Sousa, Vickers, 616
Deutsch-Asiatische Bank, 11, 14, 165
Deutsche Bank, 106
de Zulueta, *Sir* Phillip, 647, 715
*Dias, R., 454
Diefendorf, Charles, 784
Disappearance Project Co., 694
*Dods, W.K., 72
Dodwell and Co., 358, 459, 909–10
*Drake, R.N., 504
Drummond, J.D. (*Viscount* Strathallan), 170
Dublin, HSBC in, 610
Duffy, Edward W.: acquisition of MMBI, 783, 786–90, 792, 796–98, 811, 820, 824–25, 829–30, 844, 848, (relations with Sandberg) 764–65, 780, 787, 805; director, HSBC, 684, 909

Index

*Dunlop, T. McC., 81
Dunn, *Dame* Lydia S., 686, 910
*Dunnett, J.S., 37, 109, 282, 424, 600, 688, 700
duress notes, *see* banknotes
Dyson, James S., 820

Eastern Bank, 458, 482, 529, 652
East Point Reinsurance Co., 719
*Ebell, C.G.G., 69, 454, 457
Eccles, *Sir* David, 509
Economist Intelligence Unit, 621
Edinburgh: HSBC in, 609–10, 639; reaction to Royal Bank of Scotland bids, 892, 895. *See also* Scotland
*Edmondston, D.C., 34, 35, 36n, 71–72, 279, 687, (widow of) 143
*Edwards, C.L., 98, 100, 468
*Edwards, O.P., 59, 66, 76, 311, 350, 358, 361, 370, 374, 375–76, 379, 495, 631, 641, 722
*Edwards, R.P., 70, 431, 603
Elephant Lite Co., 460
Eley, *Sir* Geoffrey, 510, 532
Elizalde, Juan, 83
Elly Kadoorie and Sons, 252, 483, 684, 685
enamelware, 354–55
English, Scottish and Australian Bank, 528
Enriched Correspondent Banks Relationships (ENCOR), 902
Equator Bank, 562, 871
Euro-currency, 609, 672, 785, 901, (-bond) 867
European-American Bank, 770, 772
'even keel' policy, 2, 11, 633
Exchange Banks Association, 338
exchange rates: Chungking/London, 45; Hong Kong on London, 11, 570, 576; Netherlands East Indies, 101; U.S. dollar, 577, 875. *See also* Hong Kong, open market
Exporters Refinance Corp., 698, 699, 707
extraterritoriality, 20, 24, 51, 58, 90, 141, 150, 159, 565. *See also* United Kingdom, Treaty of 1943

*Fairchild, S.F., 915
Fan Kwae Pictures, xxxix, xl
Fanlingerers, 158n
Far East Bank, 702
Far Eastern Economic Review, Ltd, 351n, 483, 522, 697
*Farncombe, G., 917
Farrell, Herman D., Jr, 811, 821
*Farrell, R.C., 915

Federal Deposit Insurance Corp. (FDIC), 335, 491, 496, 726, 785, 813, 903
Federal Reserve Bank of New York, 635, 788, 798, 816–18
Federal Reserve Bank of San Francisco, 813
Federal Reserve Board and System (FRB): attitude and actions, 335, 726, 745, 785, 789n; HSBC and, 495, 867, 902; MMBI acquisition and, 773–74, 800, 801, 810, 812, 816–18, 825, 829, 831–32, 836–37, 840, 847, 865
Federation of Malaya (Malaysia), *see* Malaya (Malaysia), Federation of
feng-shui, 88, 362, 363, 483, 592, 629
Fengtien, *see* Mukden
*Fenwick, T.J.J., 36, 51, 57, 74, 86–87, 88n, 93, 96, 102, 108, 114, 125, 143, 280, 289, 290–91, 319, 377
*Ferrier, C.A.W., 85, 95
*Figg, M.J.S., 479–80
First National Bank of Chicago, 700
First National City Bank of New York, *see* Citibank
First State Bank of Encino, 611
First Western and Trust Co., 772
Fivel-Démoret, C., 525
Flanagan, B.T., 273
*Fonseka, C.S., 457
Foochow, HSBC in, 45, 57–58, 157
Forbes, W.H., 907
*Ford, A.D.M., 312, 389, 465
foreign banks and branches, national reactions to, 58–60, 205, 319, 336n, 340, 341–43, 430, 440, 442–43, 521, 523, 525, 534, 559, 560, 620, 647, 652, 654–57, 659, 695, 697, 709n, 889, 890–91, 900–01, (local incorporation requirement) 706, 719–20, (visa or work permit restrictions) 465, 664–65, 673, 916, 920
Foreign Exchange Stabilization Ctte (China), 156
Fortway, 720
Foster, Norman, 905–07
Foster Associates, 904
Fox, Barry, 782, 815
*Fox, S.J.H., 286, 378, 389, (President HBC) 490, 492, 494–96
*Foy, H.E., 473
*Frame, F.R., 584, 795, 805, 812, 830
France, HSBC in, 525–26. *See also* Lyons; Paris
*Francis, J.L.A., 639, 870
Frankfurt, HSBC in, 888, 922
Franklin National Bank, 770, 771, 778, 786, 787, 840

*French, J.J., 68, 96, 109, 280, 424
French Indo-China, *see* Cambodia; Haiphong; Phnom Penh; Saigon
*Frost, J.N., 70, 617
Fukuoka, HSBC in, 874, 889

*Gairdner, R.C., 291
*Garrett, G.W., 84, 651n, (widow of) 143
Gascoigne, *Sir* Alvary, 104
Gatechurch Property Management, 696, 874
Gatewood Investments, 874
Geddes, A., 531–32
Geneva: BBME in, 521, 526, 602, 609, 888, 922; HSBC and, 500, 521, 526
Germany: Anglo–German Debts Agreement, 108, HSBC and, 525–26. *See also* Frankfurt; Hamburg
Gerschenkron, Alexander, 620n
Gherardi, Tita (Stephen) de, xl
Gibb, Livingston and Co., 252, 358, 684, 685
Gibbs Bright Holdings, 716
Gibbs Nathaniel (Canada), 716
Gibbs y Cia SAC Representaciones, 716
Gibraltar, HSBC in, 413
*Giles, A.L.V.S., 62, 280, 457
Gillespie, R.D., 143
Gilman and Co., 248, 252, 674, 684, 685, 909
Glucksman, Louis, 788, 789, 793, 795–96, 801–02
gold, 153, 155, 442–43, 467, 608, 701, 704
Golden Pacific National Bank, 340n, 903
*Goldney, C.M., 285, 293–99, 583
Goldsack, G.M., 273
*Gonsalves, C.J., 300
Goode, *Sir* William, 478
Gooneshinha, A.E., 453
Goonetilleke, *Sir* Oliver, 205n
Gordon, R., 273, 385
Gracechurch Property Management, 722
Grace National Bank, 784
Graham, Gordon, 904
Graham, *Sir* Peter, 433, 770–71, 789n, 866, 891–92, 957
Grantham, *Sir* Alexander, 20, 240, 245, 259, 329, 341, 345, 508, 645
Gray, David, 313
*Gray, J.M., 313, 915
*Gray, S.A., 59, 61–62, 89, 93, 108, 155, 280, 285, 313, 392, 438
*Grayburn, *Sir* Vandeleur M.
as Chief Manager: before-1941, 2, 16, 45, 159, 214, 284, 483, 489, 531, (and staff) 286, 483, 580, (relations with government) 341; fall of Hong Kong, 25–27, 123; interned, 23, 26, 27
death of, 29–30, 48

early career, 279, 281, 918
opinion of Morse, 19, 20, 34–35
relations with London Office, 438, 633–34, 637, 641, ('Londonitis') 504n
*Gregoire, J.M., 461
*Greig, H.A., 69, 205n, 458
*Greig, J., 458n
Grieve, J., 446
Grindlays [National (Overseas) and,] Bank, 457–58, 522, 523, 527, 529, 699; negotiations with BBME and HSBC, 523–24, 530, 533–34
*Groves, A.C., 380
Guam, HBC/HSBC in, 611
Guangzhou, 423, 613. *See also* Canton
Guardforce, 696, 722
Guernsey, C.I., 413
gum copal, 470
gunny sacks, 71
Gurney, *Sir* Henry, 416

Haadyai, MBLD and, 551
Haas, Ken, 862n
Haddon-Cave, *Sir* Philip, 815
Ha'erbin, *see* Harbin
Hague Convention, 133
Haiphong, HSBC in, 95–96, 423
*Hale, R.E., 915
Hall, George, 126
*Hall, J., 518
Hall-Patch, E.L., 58–59
Halpern, E., 522
Hamburg, 106; British Military Authority in, 80, 102; HSBC in, 80, 102, 105–06, 305, 387, 439–40, 525
Hamm, J.H., 273
*Hammond, P.E., 286, 742, 814–15, 832, 913, 915
*Handcock, A.F., 81, 109, 444
Hang Seng Bank, 684
acquisition by HSBC, 340, 615, 693, 696, 698, 703–06
branches of, 368, 593, 598, 701
history, 311, 345, 701–06
in Hongkong Bank Group, 558, 625, 705, 733, 743, 862, 895, 900, 910
performance, 559, 739
subsidiaries of, 713, 717
Hankow, HSBC in, 93–94, 149, 157–59, 381–82, 433. *See also* Wuhan
Hannah, Malcolm, 477
Hanoi, 95
Harbin, 155; HSBC in, 402
*Harman, A.L., 469n, 476
Harper, Gilfillan and Co., 271
*Harries, H.E., 436n

Index

Harrisons and Crosfield, 413, 459, 464
Hartford National Bank, 871n
Hastings West Investment Co., 700
Hatton National Bank, 457, 652
Hawaii, plans for HBC in, 495
*Hawkins, V.A. Caesar, 277, 300, 530, 686
Hay, *Sir* John, 502
*Hayashi, S., 437
*Haymes, M.F.L., 77, 81–83, 286, 472–77, 478–79
HBC, *see* Hongkong and Shanghai Banking Corporation of California
Heard, A.F., 4
Heath and Co., 459
Heimann, John G. MMBI acquisition, 820, 821, 824, 826, 829–30, 833–35, 837, 839, 840, 842, 843, 845–47
Heinz, John, 836–37, 838–39
*Helbling, A.W., 469
Helmboldt Montgomery and Co., 871n
*Henchman, A.S., 37, 64, 89, 91, 109
Henry Steiner Associates, 208, 862n, 872–73
Herple, *Dr*, 92
*Herridge, F.I.C., 640, 646, 653
Herries, *Sir* Michael, 892, 953
Herstadt Bank, 786
*Heuck, E., 80
*Hibberd, E.E.F., 99
*Highet, I.H.C., 88n
Hill, E.R., 274
*Hill, J.A.P., 870
Hill and Knowlton, 797, 798, 872
*Hillier, E.G., 404, 914
Hill, Samuel and Co., 870
Hill-Wood, W.W.H., 31, 32
Hinke, Karl, 784
HK Aircraft Engineering, 696
Ho, H.T., 608
Ho, S.H., 701, 703, 705
*Hobbin, W.R., 104
Ho Chi Minh, 95
*Holden, M.McD., 469
Hong Kong
  banking, 508, 726, 744; branches, 206–07, 364–69; crises, 340, 702–03, 731, 740–41; HSBC in system, xxxvi, 8, 562, 567; moratorium and debts, 132–37, 145. *See also* debtor/creditor
  currency, 88, 123–24, 128, 131, 132, 201, 233–35, 236–43, 573–77, 702, 738, 739, 861, 931–32. *See also* banknotes
  disturbances, 576, 708, 711, 733, 737
  economic conditions, 53, 87–88, 96, 195, 324–26, 335–39, 344–45, 347–49, 557, 634, 731, 743, 875, 905–06, 908, 921, (financial centre) 712, 744
Hang Seng Bank, branches: Causeway Bay, Kowloon City, Mongkok, Shamshuipo, Tsimshatsui, Tsuen Wan, Yaumati, 701
  HSBC and, 55–57, 69, 84, 86–89, 202, 324, 778, (Statue Square) 88–89, 329–34
  as clearing house, 339, 577–78, 587
  as local bank, 190, 487, 518, 561–62, 581–82, 614–19, 620–32, (market share) 621–25
  branches, 362–72; Aberdeen, 363, 369, 629; Hung Hom, 363, 629; Kennedy Town, 369; Kwun Tong, 363, 616–18; North Point, 225, 328, 368, 369, 423, 616, 618–19; San Hui, 369; Shamshuipo, 363, 369, 629; Shaukiwan, 363, 629; San Po Kong, 363, 629; Sheung Shui, 369; Sai Ying Poon, 369; Taipo, 363, 629; Tsuen Wan, 363, 369, 629; Wanchai, 369; Yuen Long, 319, 369. *See also* Mongkok
  buildings, 302, 332; Head Office, 35, 143, 731, 738, 745, 861, 877, 904–08, 912, 921
  'central bank' functions, 8, 334–44, 577–78, 614–15, 702, 708, 711, 726, 738, 739, 740–41, (denial of central bank status), 335, 577, 811, (HSBC management of assisted banks) 615, 702, 708
  merchant banking, 712
  profits, 182, 326–27, 693, 861
  See also Hang Seng
industrialization, 202, 324, 326, 328, 344–45, 352–61, 430, 488, 618–19, 620–29, 630. *See also* Mongkok
Japan, early post-war contacts, 433–34
Mercantile Bank and, 598, 607
open market (for U.S. dollars), 202, 311, 345–46, 562, 701
post-1997, position of, 837, 861, 875, 904, 911, 921–22
post-war: planning for, 20, 55–57, 88; reopening of HSBC, 74; status, 34, 65
stock market: boom, 740–41, (Anglican cathedral and) 740; post-1980, 861, (stock exchange) 568
See also Hong Kong government
Hongkong and Shanghai Banking Corporation, The: (i) **historical summaries**
  from Vols. I–III, 1–16, 187–92, 214–15, 250–51, 275–77, 329–34, 349–51,

Hongkong and Shanghai Banking
    Corporation (i), (cont.)
    448–50, 463–64, 530–31, 557–64,
    565–67, 573–78, 578–80, 632–34,
    666n, 686–88
  history project, xxxvii–ix, 265–66, 401,
    612–13, 615–16, 635n, 668
Hongkong and Shanghai Banking
    Corporation, The: (ii) general
    accounting practices, xxxvi, 6, 27, 38,
    42–43, 44, 45, 53, 181, 208, 209–18,
    557, 569, 628n, 631, 723–24, 730–31,
    781, 809, 814–15, 833, 863–64, 877,
    879, 884; and GAAP, 810, 814, 832
  charges account, expense accounts, and
    control, 263, 449–50, 469, 489, 618–19
  disclosure, 569–70, 572–73, 723, 726,
    774, 810, 814–15, 819–20, 832–33, 840
  Hongkong Bank Group, impact of, 208,
    218–23, 224–27, 744
  inner reserves, 14, 34, 148, 195, 201,
    209, 211–15, 222, 244, 325, 560, 572,
    708–11, 725–27, 731, 737n, 739, 744,
    810, 884–85
  note issue, impact of, 201, 211
  Officers Good Service Fund, 110
  premises, 42, 200, 430, 593, 724, 738,
    864, 879
  profits and 'true' profits, 194–95, 200,
    209–12, 874
  reserve fund investments, valuation of,
    11, 884
  share premium account, 216, 221, 222,
    731, 733, 878, 884–85
advertising, 206, 446, 600, 617, 862
annual report, 208–09, 862, 862n
as British overseas bank, 341–42, 343, 525,
    555, 715, 888, 891–92, 893, 908
as 'central bank', denial of status, 334–35,
    341, 577, 811. See also Hong Kong
as China bank, 149, 150, 182, 342, 383,
    613, 763
as 'country bank', 864–65
as local bank, 3–4, 34, 72, 229, 249, 338,
    362–63, 371, 487, 555, 581–82, 904–05
branches and offices, 327, 364–72, 381–83,
    397, 594–97, 598–99, 601, 605–06,
    652, 731, 869, 874, 887–91
  branching in one city, 206, 289–90, 550,
    597–99, 600, 610, 611, 619–20, 648,
    874, 888, 901, 903. See also Hong
    Kong
  branch vs agency, 412–13, 431, (in U.S.)
    489–90, 611, 776
  capital assigned to, 90, 465, 593, 608,
    647, 659

control and lending 'limits', 289–90,
    415, 440, 441, 461, 470–71, 476, 483,
    582, 585–86, 612, 617, 618–19, 629;
    European 'head office', 527
  expansion, 147, 415–32, 562, 593–612,
    620
  management of, 316–18, 424–29, (Japan)
    432–34
  policy, 65–66, 193, 319, 326–28, 412–14,
    415–32, 462, 483, 560, 585–86;
    regarding BBME/MBLD, 515, 597,
    602–04
  regulations relative to, 442, 447–48,
    456–60, 461–62, 900
  representative offices, 593, 604, 608,
    610–11, 612–13, 698, 700, 707n, 743,
    780, 862, 866, 869, 888, 915
  sources and uses of branch funds,
    204–05, 362, 414, 424, 430–32, 440,
    441, 443, 444–448, 466, 479, 483, 578,
    598–99, 610, 617–19, 647, 652–53,
    658–59, 672, 699–700, 712, 744, 837
  types of, 412–13, 608–09, 616, 651,
    654–55
  See also Chinatowns; foreign banks and
    branches
buildings and land, 161, 249, 385, 436,
    466, 515, 669–70, 696, 698, 722, 743,
    874, 903, 913
  Hankow, 157–58
  Hong Kong: Head Office, 35, 143, 731,
    738, 745, 861, 877, 904–08, 912,
    921
  lions, 88, 401, 483, 611, 872–73, 908,
    921, (Krishna) 873n
  Shanghai, 384, 385, 395, 395–96, 877
  See also under various locations
business of: categories
  'financial group or industrial
    conglomerate?' 695, 697, 714, 721
  non-financial, 351n, 482, 520–22, 561,
    695–96, 697, 700, 707, 708, 714,
    720–22, 738–39, 741, 774, (U.S.
    regulatory concern) 773–74, 779,
    809–10, 813, 831, 835–36, 840–42,
    843. See also Wayhong
business of: listed
  adviser to governments, 341–43, 438,
    463; Hong Kong, 337, 338, 341, 741;
    Occupied Japan, 102–05, 432
  bankers to governments, 11, 66–67, 160,
    203–04, 239, 244, 336–40, 457, 458,
    459, 561, 614, 619, 624, 811, 890,
    (China) 11, 61–62, 156. See also Hong
    Kong government
  bullion dealing, 713

Chinese (and other local) customers, 88, 100, 349–50, 351–61, 364, 387, 468–69, 470–71, 474–75, 478, 616–18, 629–30, 649–51, (Dyaks) 479–80. *See also* Chinatowns
consumer finance, 328, 520–21, 719–20, 902
credit cards, 743, 862
equity investment, 6, 251, 349–51, 518, 520, 561, 647, 693, 696–97, 708, 711
exchange banking and remittances, 10, 35, 43–44, 62, 67, 71–72, 88, 94, 101, 158–59, 228, 233–36, 375–76, 387, 435, 442, 449, 628, 739
development of new categories, 525–28, 552
factoring, 719
government securities, colonial, 147
hire purchase, 616
industrial lending, 349–51, 358, 368, 371, 618–19, 621–29, 631–32, 743. *See also* Hong Kong
insurance, 206, 716–19
leasing, 719–20, 862
merchant banking, 5–6, 203, 647, 711–16, 740–41. *See also* under Wardley companies
motion pictures, 349
nominee, 609, 694
off-shore, 609, 647, 659
oil, North Sea, 874
private banking, 896–97
savings accounts, 445, 451, 466, 471, 479, 617–18, 649, 731. *See also* Hong Kong Savings Bank
trade finance, 55, 61, 66, 71, 73, 87, 88, 100, 104–05, 147, 149, 150, 164, 190, 325–28, 342, 345–46, 368, 391–94, 404, 430, 434–35, 442, 448, 459, 462, 464, 466–67, 470, 483, 489–90, 525–26, 609, 612, 652, 654, 659, 671–72, 862, 888
travellers cheques, 743
trustee, 413, 695
capital, 486, 560, 912
authorized, 221–22, 244, 513, 568, 615, 731
capitalization ('bonus') issues, 5, 195, 215, 244, 245, 560, 615, 724–25, 727, 732, 733, 876, 884
long-term borrowed, 5–6, 877, 885
paid-up, 10, 11–14, 191, 196, 215–16, 245–46, 500–01, 724–27, 864
rights issues, 5, 6, 11, 14, 727, 739, 741, 744, 884–85, 921
shareholders' funds, xxxv, 1, 11–14, 16, 38–41, 45, 188–89, 196–97, 513–14,

557, 563–64, 724–27, 729–30, 732, 734, 863–64, 875, 876–77, 880, 883
shares and shareholders, 108, 131, 223, 231, 500–01, 513–14, 569, 570, 725–27, 908–09; limitations on beneficial ownership, 232, 487, 508, 571–72, 741, 909; nominal value of, 222–23, 231–32, 512, 569, 727, 741; price, 38–39, 183, 223, 231, 537n, 877; reserved (or double) liability, 10, 245–46, 568, 576; share registers, 140–41, 569, 741, (Hong Kong) 43, 569, 727, (London) 40, 43, 221, 514, 535–36, 569, 727, (Shanghai) 140–41
corporate identity exercise, 798, 871–73, (earlier name problems) 228–30, 872
corporate organization and structure, xxxv, 4–6, 139–41, 191–92, 483, 578–80, 711–12, 745–46, 771, 834–35, 843, 849, (management) 247, 292, 817, 834
archives, 613
as holding company and operating bank, 4, 193, 195, 225, 230, 540, 564, 571, 591, 798, 874
China desk, 613, 869; area office, 888–89. *See also* Hongkong Bank China Services
Commercial Credit Dept, 360
Corporate Secretary and Office of, 568, 583–84
Customers Service Dept, 742
Industrial Banking Dept (variant names), 206, 310, 361, 629–32
Inspection and Inspectors Dept, 276, 280, 288, 289–90, 360–61
International Corporate Accounts, 867
mobile bank, 371
Personnel Dept, 276, 288, 290–92
Residences Dept, 900
subsidiaries, 247; basic policy towards, 482, 484–86, 517, 557, 561, 637, 645–46, 654–55, 694–95, 705, 792–94, 871, 895–96; control of, 497, 514, 581, 584–87, 707–08, 781–82; management fees, 491, 516
Training Dept, 672, 914
See also Hongkong Bank Group; Hong Kong Savings Bank
dividends, 27, 39, 108, 145–46, 193, 196–97, 199, 211, 214, 222, 231, 244, 328, 510, 511–13, 544, 569, 570, 591, 633, 721–22, 725–26, 727–28, 731–33, 736, 737, 876, 883, (free lunch bonus) 909
geographical distribution, 518–19, 524–28, 593–97, 605–06, 608–13, 864–66, 867, 868, 871, 874, 887–89, 896

Hongkong and Shanghai Banking
  Corporation (ii) (*cont.*)
  head office
    and London office, 14, 247–48, 268,
      518–19, 632–35, 642, 741–42
    development and structure of, 276,
      284–85, 286–99, 486, 578–79, 583–90,
      834
    emergency transfer of, 243, 638
    internal allocation of resources, 204–05,
      226, 381, 383, 387–88, 389, 430–31,
      435–36, 443, 447, 635, 653, 725
    in the East, 3, 14, 17, 20, 34, 74, 137,
      190, 249–50, 581, (historical problem)
      569–72
    London, wartime, 29, 33–34
  investment policy, 44–45, 70, 194, 199,
    201–02, 204, 213, 267, 268, 286–87,
    438–39
  liquidity, 198, 201, 211–12, 353, 364, 369,
    423, 431, 517, 560, 576, 624, 625, 729,
    730, 735, 738, 744, 745, 775, 866,
    881–82, 885, (defined) 193n
  marketing, 72–73, 160, 617, 618–19, 625,
    630, 632, 911–12
  performance, xxxv, 38–46, 145–48, 189,
    193–202, 207–12, 218–23, 326–28,
    361–62, 430, 510, 557, 663, 693,
    723–45, 866–68, 875–79, 911
  planning
    American strategy, xxxvii, 5, 552, 561,
      600, 617, 694, 746, 765, 775–83, 792,
      805–06, 807, 834–35, 841, 848–49,
      865, 903, 912. *See also* Marine
      Midland Banks, Inc.
    early exercises in, 486–89, 517–20,
      522–28, (wartime) 51–57
    global strategy, 860, 866–67, 875,
      885–87, 891–93, 896
  rank (relative to other banks), 1, 557, 849,
    862, 875, 889
  reserve funds and policies, 40, 44–45,
    194–96, 201, 211, 212–16, 244, 262,
    430, 634–35, 640, 724–27, 733, 736,
    738–39, 740, 864, 878–79, 883, 884–85
  sources and uses of funds, 6, 11, 43, 84,
    106, 147, 162, 163, 203–07, 356, 368,
    371, 423, 424–25, 430–32, 465, 610,
    624, 719–20, 774, 864–65
  tax as a policy factor, 249–50, 268, 287,
    295, 296, 312, 322–23, 383, 405, 430,
    432, 449, 460, 491, 527, 558, 569, 582,
    591, 603, 669n, 695, 707, 721, 874,
    920; in relations with BBME/MBLD,
    501, 502, 509, 515, 523, 524, 533,
    535–36, 539, 541–45, 548, 602, 603,
    638–39, 645, 700, 707, 871, 900; with
    HBC, 491
  technology, 295, 299, 497, 580, 581, 586,
    587–89, 731, 834–35, 861, 914, 920
    autopay, 617, 743
    electronic data processing (EDP), 586,
      587, 591, 731
    electronic teller card (ETC), 861–62, (in
      Colombo) 660–62
Hongkong and Shanghai Bank:
  (iii) staff
  graves of, 404, 436n, 651
  health, 28, 46, 47, 407, 416, 589n
  ladies, 292–93, 294–95, 306, 666, 918, 921,
    922; Expat Women's staff, 295
  leave, 320, 323, 666, 918
  level of living, 321–22, 449, 669–70, 671;
    mess life, 313, 664, 860, 918–19
  policies: basic, 6–8, 191, 275–76, 377–78
  policies: (i) Eastern (*then* Foreign, *then*
    International) staff, 6–7, 483–86, 558,
    663–64, 834–35, 860, 885–86
    control, 483–84, 495, (of BBME/
      Mercantile) 516, 540–41, 558, 603
    expert vs banker, staff 'up-grading', 7,
      202–03, 226, 284, 291, 312, 355, 497,
      518, 591–92, 667–68, 914, (university
      education), 518, 561, 592, 665–66,
      917–18; role of generalists, 578–79,
      587, 590, 664–65, 666
    integration with BBME/Mercantile,
      501–02, 516, 540–41, 542, 552, 558,
      602–03, 609, 613n, 639–40, 646,
      663–64, 667, 669
    marriage (and alternatives), 35, 94,
      113–14, 320, 322, 323, 670, 918–19;
      foreign wives, 113, 314; role of wives,
      48, 293. *See also* Turner, *Lady*
    promotion and careers, 27n, 31n, 37n,
      285–86, 287, 304, 316–19, 424–29,
      437, 465, 467, 469n, 492, 592–93, 613,
      613n, 802, 915–16; career planning,
      280, 288, 291, 319–20, 376–77, 425,
      451, 589–90, 916, 917–20; first
      assignments, 303, 304–05, 320, 666n,
      919; length of service/tours, 670
    recruitment, 2, 27n, 114–15, 291, 301,
      303, 311, 321–22, 646, 667–68, 916;
      Home to Foreign staff, 114; 'London
      gate', 276–77, 300, 302, 456, 540, (not
      through London) 114–15, 590, 916
  reporting, personnel, 292
  specialists, 7, 51, 114, 209, 276, 284,
    291, 520, 558, 579–80, 582, 587, 591,
    834, 885–86, 914, (China) 869,
    (contract executives) 664

training, 307–08, 320, 370, 437, 455, 456–57, 465, 477, 483–84, 496–97, 657, 668, 672–73, 918, (Dept) 672, 914, (exchange operations) 236, (in London) 8, 591
women as, 918, 921
policies: (ii) three-tiers, 6, 27n, 111, 300–05, (breakdown of) 1, 302–09, 558, 592, 616
Chinese (or other indigenous), 68–69, 111, 143, 301, 370, 374–75, 616, 630–32, 649, 650–51, 862, 920, 921, (French) 441. *See also* labour
Home staff, 640, 641, 669, (messengers) 47, 669, 917
local 'British', 300, 374, 375
Portuguese, burghers, White Russians, 7, 111, 162, 300–01, 302–03, 305–09, 310, 401–03, 461, 593, 616
policies: (iii) regional officers (title varies)
first steps, 275, 289, 302–05, 307–08, 369–70, 451–53, 455–57, 616–17, 629–30, 652, 653, 663
later developments, 304, 305, 308–09, 310–11, 468, 474, 590, 665–66, (business promotion officer) 630
senior positions, 305, 306, 311, 451, 456–57, 477, 630, 654, 673–74, 869, (communal membership) 666. *See also* Thambiah
transfer/secondment to international, 673, 890, 920–21
women as, 666
remuneration
bonuses, 209, 379, 671
cost of living allowance, 112, 209, 291, 321
salaries, 112–14, 161, 162–63, 320, 321, 322, 454, 465, 670–71
retirement, pensions, and/or death benefits, 28, 47, 48 108, 110–11, 112, 138, 147, 190, 218, 251, 291, 312, 321, 375, 400, 403, 411, 439–40, 441, 454, 653, 671, (Provident Fund) 109, 263, 321, 671, 912
size, 109, 110, 114, 190, 284–85, 287–88, 302, 314–15, 320, 663–66, 673; age distribution, 109–11, 315
sports, 114, 275, 313n, 322, 447, 592, 668–69, 917, 921, (soccer) 669
See also compradore; labour problems
Hongkong and Shanghai Bank: (iv) **Pacific War and immediate aftermath**
business, first post-war, 85–86, 86–87, 93, 94, 95, 105–06
clandestine operations, 24, 27
directors, fate of, 30

Head Office: to London, 19–21, 24–29, 31, 107; return to Hong Kong, 21, 53, 74, 137–45
internment: debts incurred during, 108–09; return from, 20, (arrangements in U.K.) 75–77, (Changi) 96, 433, (Columbia Country Club) 93, (Haiphong Rd) 90, (Los Baños) 81–83, (Lunghwa) 85, 89, 155, 954, (Santo Tomas) 81, 83, (Stanley) 85
manpower control, India, 108
Peak mess, 143. *See also* Cloudlands
remuneration, 46–49, 77, 81, 83, 92–94, 97–98, 109, 111, (widows and orphans) 143
repatriation, 24, 48, 75–78, 81, 85, 91, 93–94, 96, 99–100
staff: aging of, 109–11; local, 19, 68–70, 93, 94, 95, 98, 105, 111, (Staff Provident Fund, Hamburg) 80
staff: policy, 23, 51–52, 108–15; dependants, 19; Portuguese, 19, 86, 87, (remittances to) 19, 47–48; retirement and related benefits, 108
See also Japan, Pacific War; Macau
Hongkong and Shanghai Bank: (v) **Board of Directors**
chairmen, 19, 29, 248, 277, 674, 683, 684; Chief Manager as Chairman, 143–45, 248–50, 251, 258–64, 674–86; need for banker as, 248–50, 568, 674. *See also* under individual name
composition, 10, 14, 29, 141–43, 252–57, 262, 518, 531, 568, 583, 674–86, 711, 909–10, 926; Clague, 708; Lord Kadoorie, 684; MMBI directors on Board, 684, 685, 848
policies
branches, 159, 608, 650, 874
British Bank of the Middle East (BBME), 534–35, 536–37, 552
capital, 739
charity, 49–51, 143, 144, 148, 156, 251, 258, 264, 615–16, 649, 723, 890, 909. *See also* Hongkong Bank Foundation
China, 181, 266, 381–83, 388–89
disclosure, 725–26
diversification/expansion, 486–89, 500, 517–25, 527–28, 693, 860
Head Office move, 23, 25
history of Bank project, 265–66
Hongkong Bank Group, 265
insurance, 717–18
Marine Midland (MMBI) acquisition, 780, 801, 848

Hongkong and Shanghai Banking
Corporation (v), (*cont.*)
  Mercantile Bank, 499–500, 511, 534
  property, 251, 264, (1986 Head Office
    building), 904–06
  staff, 205, 264, 265, 275, 342–43, 343n,
    378–79, 403, 436–37, 456, 473n, 921
  subsidiaries, 485, 541–42, 551–53
  relationship with Chief Manager/chief
    executive, 248–50, 251, 257–64, 277,
    297, 332, 558, 568, 584, 674, 906
  reorganization and structural change, 5,
    250, 568, 683–84, 684–86; executive
    directors and, 674, 834
  role of, 14, 28, 30, 33, 131, 143, 208–09,
    247–52, 263–66, 277–78, 297, 332,
    485, 518, 571, 580, 587, 639, 674,
    704–05, 904–06
  wartime fate of, 30
Hongkong and Shanghai Bank: (vi) **Chief
  Manager/chief executive**
  as Chairman, 143–45, 248–50, 251, 257–64,
    674, 683
  as director, 29, 568, 674, 683
  definitions: Acting Chief Manager, 29,
    140; Deputy Chief Manager, 288n
  remuneration, 46, 217–18, 262–64, 321, 671
  role of, 28–29, 190, 247, 258–59, 263–64,
    335, 337–38, 341, 449, 518, 683, 689,
    (as exchange operator) 35, 143, 190,
    288–89, 293–97
  selection and succession, 27, 30, 34–35,
    258, 260–62, 277–84, 578, 686–90,
    912–13, 923, (Chief Accountant as
    prior post) 278, 279, 283, 287, 688–91,
    912, (refusal to be) 686
Hongkong and Shanghai Bank: (vii)
  advisory committees
  Ireland, Republic of, 610
  London
    advice from, 518, 641
    adviser to, 209
    'Board of Directors': wartime, 19,
      28–29, 31–33, 45–46, 109, 162, 251;
      duress note issue, 116, 124, 125–26,
      131; 'fall-back', 243, 642
    chairman, 636–37, 642, 646
    composition, 28, 31–33, 138, 142, 143,
      145, 267–72, 301, 438, 518–19, 531,
      543–44, 553, 633–34, 642–45, 685,
      910–11
    fee, 143, 217–18
    minutes of, 250–52
    organization of, 138, 145, 267, 519, 870
    role of, 27, 31, 71, 145, 179, 249,
      266–68, 438, 518–19, 581, 584,

635–36, 642–45, 911, (sub-committee
  during BBME/MBLD negotiations) 512,
  524, 535, 642
Macau, 608
Hongkong and Shanghai Banking
  Corporation of California, Inc. (HBC),
  xxxvi, 4, 191, 695, 742
  accounts, consolidation of, 219–20, 224
  board of directors, 491, 492, 496, 520
  branches, 193, 414, 431, 493, 494–95, 594,
    595, 596, 600, 610–11, (through
    acquisition) 600, 777
  capital, 204, 219, 227, 485, 493, 496, 521
  management, 247, 282, 495–96, 497, 520,
    600, 688, 776
  name, 229, 490
  performance, 493–97, 520, 721, 743, 868
  role of, 484, 489, 491, 492–93, 494–96, 520
  sale of, 611, 695n, 722, 780, 813, 818
  sources and uses of funds, 226, 490
  Turner, *Sir* Michael and, 488, 494–95
  See also Fox
Hongkong and Shanghai Bank (Nominees),
  500
Hongkong and Shanghai Bank (Trustee), 248,
  312
Hongkong and Shanghai Bank Trustees (Isle
  of Man), 413n
Hongkong and Shanghai Trustee (Guernsey),
  413
Hongkong and Whampoa Dock Co., 711
'HongkongBank', 692, 872–73, 901. *See also*
  Hongkong and Shanghai Banking
  Corporation
Hongkong Bank and Trust Co., 413n
Hongkong Bank China Services, Ltd, 889
Hongkong Bank Foundation, 264, 723,
  873–74, 912
Hongkong Bank Group, 485–86, 489, 745
  composition, 230, 233, 485–86, 693–97,
    706, 709–10, 747–61, 888, 926–29
  dormant companies, 695, 713 899–900.
    See also British and Chinese Corp.
  holding companies, 695, 707, 717–19,
    720–21, 864, 874, 896, 899
  non-financial, 696–97. *See also*
  under separate company names
  concept/definition, 230, 233, 485–86,
    590–91, 691–93, 771–72, 778, 798, 873
  development of, 517–22, 524, 552–53, 585,
    706–23, 864–66, 888
  intra-Group rationalization, 485–86,
    711–19, 922
  branches, 549–51, 593, 598, 599,
    602–04, 607–08, 637–39, 645, 654,
    655–56, 888–90, 901–04

financial, 226, 430, 486, 541–49, 602–03, 901–02
relationships within, 219, 225, 516–17, 540–43, 549–51, 584–85, 612, 645–46, 705, 711–19, 848, 871, 885, 900, 901–02
See also under separate company names
Hongkong Bank International, 901
HongkongBank News, 900, 921
HongkongBank of Australia, 698, 891, 900
Hongkong Bank of California, Inc., *see* Hongkong and Shanghai Banking Corp. of California
Hongkong Bank of Canada, 862, 885, 891, 900
Hongkong Bank Serviços, 612
Hongkong Bank, the Building of Norman Foster's Masterpiece, 906
Hongkong Egyptian Bank, 900
Hongkong Electric Co., 55, 252
Hong Kong Export Credit Insurance Corp., 632
Hongkong Finance, 469n, 698, 714
Hong Kong General Chamber of Commerce, 684
Hong Kong government,
 and HSBC
  banking regulator, xxxvi, 232, 245, 246, 336–40, 565, 567, 568–69, 570–71, 577–78, 702, 704, 810–11, 815, (Banking Advisory Ctte) 615, (Commissioner of Banking) 810
  guarantor of HSBC rescue operations, 88, 562, 615
  guarantor of sterling reserves, 739–40
  on note issue, 8, 336, 574–75. *See also* banknotes
 and Statue Square, 329–34, 615–16
 civil servants, 839–40
 debt moratorium, 53
 Dept of Agriculture and Fisheries, 360
 duress notes: proclamations and ordinances, 128–29. *See also* banknotes
 economic policy, 336, 337–38, 360, 614, (monetary policy/standard) 337–38, 577–78, 738, 739–40, 745, 861, 875, (Securities Advisory Council) 741
 exchange control, 87, 288, 345–46, 364, (Hongkong Banker as administrator of) 341, 345n
 Exchange Fund, 121, 123, 126, 337–38, 575–78, 740, (and banking system) 726, (certificates of indebtedness, transferability of) 236–38, (financing of Military Administration) 123

HSBC, principal bankers to, 239, 334, 337–39, 340–41, 349, 434, 561, 614, 861
Industrial Bank Committee, report of, 363
Japan, open trade account with, 105, 434–35
legislation, emergency, 23, 25, (Defence [Companies Temporary Transfer] regulations) 25
legislation, HSBC ordinances or amending, 560, 565
 No. 1 of 1865, 10
 No. 5 of 1866, 10, 565, 566
 No. 6 of 1929, 25, 121, 129, 568–72, 860, 922, (as revised) 930–35
 No. 8 of 1946, 53, 129, 139–41, 288n
 No. 13 of 1946, 129
 No. 37 of 1950, 228
 No. 27 of 1953, 129, 241–42
 No. 36 of 1957, 215–16, 242–43, 245–47, 576
legislation, other: banking, 810, (1949) 232, (1964) 232, 567, 615, (regulations) 565n, 570, 572, 702; companies ordinances, (1865) 565, 566, (others) 570, 723, 908; Debtor and Creditor (Occupation Period) Ordinance, No. 24 of 1948, 135–36; Note-issuing Banks Extension of Powers Ordinance, No. 21 of 1939, 129; Reconstruction of Records Ordinance, No. 1 of 1948, 141
loans, 147, 239
Hongkong Government Gazette, 567, 568, 571
Hong Kong LP Gas Co., 722
Hong Kong Productivity Centre, 632
Hong Kong Savings Bank, 341n, 362, 368, 371, 445, 731. *See also* savings accounts
Hongkong Shanghai (Shipping), 874
Hong Kong Trade Development Council, 632
Honiara, Guadalcanal, HSBC in, 609
*Hope, W.J., 51, 94–95, 285, 424, 441n
Hope and Co., 707
Hopewell Holdings, 741
Ho Tim, 705
Ho Tung, *Sir* Robert, 309
Houston: HSBC in, 597, 610, 780, 901; MMBI in, 901, 902
*Howard, C.H., son of, 143
*Howard, J.W.L., 99, 312, 435, 613, 688, 715
*Ho Wing (Ho Sai Wing), 86, 143, 309–10
HSBC, *see* Hongkong and Shanghai Banking Corporation
HSBC Holdings, BV, 762–63, 767, 848, 874, 896, 902

HSBC Holdings UK, Ltd, 874, 896
HSBC Trustee Co., 874
H.S. Property Management Co., 900
Hubner, R.W., 793, 848, (director HSBC) 684
Hui Sai Fun, 705
*Hulme, J.F., 84, 451
*Hunter, H.E.R., 463, 530
*Hutchison, E.C., 93–94, 157, 401, 405, 407–08, 410, (Shanghai letter file) 401, 612
Hutchison International (*then* Hutchison Whampoa), *see* John D. Hutchison
*Hutson, P.E., 610, 619, 689–90, 705, 870, (Chairman, BBME) 640
*Hutton, P.F., 690
*Huxter, J.R., 498
*Hyde, C.F., son of, 143
*Hynes, A.C., 279, 281, 912

IBA, *see* United States government
IBM, 587, 793
I.I. Tschurin and Co., 351, 696
illipe nuts, 479–80
Iloilo, HSBC in, 83–84, 207, 319, 424, 443–53, 456, 648–51, 874, (manager as British Vice-Consul) 449–50, (profits) 442, 445, 446, 649–50, ('safe' posting) 110
Imperial Bank of India, 459
Imperial Bank of Persia, 232n, 267, 300–01, 530–31, 566. *See also* British Bank of the Middle East
Imperial Chemical Industries (ICI), 143, 252
Inchcape Group, 684, 720, 909–10
India, 51, 59, 336n, 435, (army) 100
  and HSBC, 46–47, 70–73, 204, 326–27, 523, 531, 534–35, 607, 665, 673, 712, 889
  and Mercantile Bank (MBLD), 228–29, 498, 515, 518, 531, 534–35, 598–99, 602, 607, 889
  See also Bombay; Calcutta; exchange; Madras
Indian Bank, 457
Indian Overseas Bank, 457
Indonesia, 468, 469, 470; HSBC in, 206, 462, 599–600, 712, 743. *See also* Jakarta; Sourabaya
Industrial Valley Bank and Trust Co. of Philadelphia, 902
*Inoue, Mrs Utako, 105
Institute of Bankers, 7, 667
Intermarine Australia, 867
International Bank for Reconstruction and Development (IBRD; World Bank), 204, 312, 431, 623

International Commercial Bank, 697, 699–700, 707
International Labour Organization (ILO), 456
International Marine Banking Co., 786
International Monetary Fund (IMF), 234–35, 248, 341, 348, 443, 608
Investors' Chronicle, 538
Ionian Bank, 3, 482, 529
Ipoh, HSBC in, 99
Irano British Bank, 482
Irving Trust, 311, 700, 782, 806
Isle of Man, HSBC in, 413
Isphahani, 70
Issuing Houses Ctte, 716

*Jackson, D., 436n
*Jackson, *Sir* Thomas, 11, 231, 267, 276, 277, 286, 300, 325–26, 329, 337, 363, 403, 519, 530, 579, 636, 871, (statue) 89, 261n, 276, 332–33
*Jacques, D.G., 915
Jaffna: HSBC and, 658; MBLD in, 652
Jakarta (*formerly* Batavia), HSBC in, 85, 100–01, 326, 600, 731, (Kota office) 600, 620
James Capel and Co., 560, 900, 904, 910
Jao, Y.C., 344, 614, 620–28, 631, 702n
Japan:
  banking overseas, 435–36, 439
  China trade, 435
  Foreign Exchange Control Board (FECB), 433–34
  HSBC and, 51, 204, 369, 432–37, 488, 603–04, (public loans, repayment of) 433–34, (Sterling Area trade) 102–04, 434–35
  MBLD and, 104, 515, 889
  Pacific War: dealings with HSBC staff, 81–83, 85, 86, 89, 143, 332, 433
  payments in occupation currency, 43, 135–36, 441–42
  SCAP and, 102–05, 423, (British military currency) 104, (Foreign Banks Assn) 104
Japan Association, 438
Japhet and Thomasson, 699
*Jardine, R.A., 286, 312
Jardine, Fleming, 711
Jardine, Matheson and Co., 10, 261, 271, 335, 339, 358, 376, 482, 584, 684, 685, 711, 717, 719, (B&CC) 14, 168, 171–72, 174, 351n, (HSBC purchase of shares of) 742
Jaro, Panay, HSBC in, 651
Javasche Bank, de, 101
Jay (Hsieh Ch'i-chu), K.C., 394

Index

Jayawardene, Junius R., 656–57
J.D. Hutchison and Co., *see* John D.
Jersey, States of: HSBC and, 609, 610. *See also* Channel Islands; St Helier
Jesselton (*now* Kota Kinabalu, Sabah), HSBC in, 326, 464, 471, 472, 600
John D. Hutchison and Co. (*also* Hutchison International; Hutchison Whampoa), 252–57, 358, 674, 685, 686, 696, 708–11, 741
John Lok/Wimpey, 907
*Johnston, D.A., 37, 80, 109
Jones, Cyril E., 271, 645
Jones, Geoffrey, 497, 529, 635n
*Jones, J.R., 51, 114, 117, 125, 133, 177–78, 483, 580
Jones, Stephanie, 684n
joss, 1, 61, 88, 483, 592
J.P. Morgan and Co., xl, 167
jute, 70

Kadoorie, *Lord* Lawrence, 51, 252, 261, 274, 369, 521, 528, 534, 684, 736. *See also* Sir Elly Kadoorie and Sons
Kai Tak Refuellers, 900
Kandy: HSBC and, 658; MBLD in, 652
Karachi, HSBC in, 600
*Kaye, William, 276, 579n
*Keith, N.A., 448–49
Kellett Investments, 694, 707
Kellett, NV, 762–63, 848, 874, 896
*Kellogg, A.G., 27, 109, 114, 281, 300
*Kelly, A.B., 443, 450
*Kelly, Francis, 89
*Kennedy, A.M., 205n
Kennet of the Dene, *Lord* (E.H. Young), 531
*Kennett, A.C., 51, 93
Keswick, Henry, 711
Keswick, *Sir* John, 271, 274
Keswick, William, 530
Keswick, *Sir* William, 32, 33, 56, 170, 171, 271
King, Catherine E., xxxiii, 938
King, David J.S., 587n
*King, F.H., 88
Kingsmill, H., 263, 907
Kirkbride, *Sir* Alec, 272, 543
Kiuchi, Nobutani, 433–34
Kleinwort Benson, 713n
*Knightly, F.J., 77, 90–92, 282, 290, 463, 466–67, 468, 476, 488, 497, 520, 527, 583, 602, 646, 688, 700, 703–05, (HSBC director) 282, 674, 676–77, 678–79
Knowles, W.C.G., 274, 674, 675
Kobe, 69, 102; HSBC in, 437
*Koelle, F.T., 112, 300, 343n, 440, 587

Kondo, Michitaka, 433
Korea, HSBC in, 413, 611–12, 707n, 713, 888. *See also* Busan; Seoul
Korea Development Bank, 713
Korea Exchange Bank, 713
Korea International Merchant Bank, 413, 612, 707n, 713, 888
Kota Kinabalu, HSBC in, 600. *See also* Jesselton
Kraar, L., 368
*Kresser, V., 286, 300, 328
Kuala Belait, HSBC in, 416, 464, 465
Kuala Lumpur, 620; HSBC and, 97, 515, 620, 673, 743, 921, (Development Board) 620; MBLD in, 515, 550
Kuching, HSBC in, 464, 473
Kung, H.H. (Hsiang-hsi), 62
Kunming, 581; HSBC and, 59, 60
Kure, HSBC in, 102, 423
Kuwait, BBME and, 546–47, 707
Kwong On Bank, 702

Labor Party, U.S., 808, 845
labour problems, 47, 205, 266, 436, 666n; China, 182, 374–75, 376, 387–88, 406–07; Colombo, 47, 67–70, 453–57; Iloilo, 650–51; Japan, 433, 436–37, 603
*Lachlan, D.G., 497, 613, 618–19, 672
LaFalce, John, 836n
Lahad Datu, 476
Lam, B.Y., 701
*Lamb, P.T., 638, 889n
*Lambert, B.C., 667
Lambot, Ian, 906n
Landale, David, 142
Landeszentralbank, 106
*Langley, M.P., 115, 609, 869
Lapraik, Douglas, 252
Larkin, Felix, 793
La Salle National Bank, 772
Laski, Frank J., 795, 796, 799, 801, 807, 820, 830
Lau Chan Kwok, 705
*Laville, L.V.S., 587
*Law, C.J.D., 160, 356, 489
Lawman, T.H.R., 27
*Leach, D.H., 496, 743, 781, 867
*Learmond, D.P.G., 226, 497, 521
*Lee, J.S., 436n
*Lee, K.C., 59, 61, 375
Lee, *Sir* Quo Wei, 684, 701, 702–04, 705, 895, 910
Lee, T.N., 156
Leeds, HSBC in, 903
*Lee Shun Wah, Peter, 86, 310–11

Lehman Bros Kuhn Loeb, 788, 789, 795, 805
Leiper, G.A., 115n, 127
*Lendrum, M.B., 37
*Lever, S.F.T.B., 115, 283, 286
*Lewis, J.R.M., 896
*Liang, H.C., 94
Liang, Y.C., 608
Liberty National Bank, 770
Lidbury, Sir Charles, 27
Li Hung-Chang, 350
Li Ka Shing, 711
*Lim Bok Kee, 98
Lim Chee Peng, 744n
Lim Yew Hock, 343
Lion Corporate Services, 694, 696
Little, L.K., 179
Liu Chong Hing Bank, 614, 615
'Liverpoolization': Buffalo and, 800; defined, 800; Edinburgh and, 895
*Livesey, D.H. 450
Lloyd's, 716
Lloyds Bank, 115, 529, 531, 699, 707, 772, 891–92, 894
*Lo, Denis and Horace, 650
Lobo, P.H., 608
*Loch, John, 616–17, 630
Lombard Banking Group, 531–32
London, 799n
 Accepting Houses Ctte, 716, 870
 BBME in, 585, 638–39, 640, 903–04
 HSBC and, 715, 741, 871
  Chairman's representatives/executive director in, 639–40, 645
  London (main) Office, 540; building, 638–39, 641; juniors in, 8, 27n, 592, 635–37, 668–69, 917–18; profit, 45, 326, 327, 635, 736; role of, 215, 261, 268, 286–87, 291, 433, 438–39, 518–19, 569, 579, 592, 635–37, (retail business to/from BBME) 585, 638–39, 640, 871, 903–04
  other offices, 610, (Pall Mall office) 639
  training of regional officers, 307–08, 456–57, 477, 672–73
  See also Hongkong and Shanghai Bank, (vii) London Advisory Committee; International Commercial Bank
 importance of, 632–35
 Issuing Houses Ctte, 716
 MBLD in, 607
 secondary banking crisis, 786
 stock exchange, 221, 569, 634, 723
London and County Bank, 910. See also Westminster Bank
'Londonitis', 182, 633, (defined) 504n
London School of Economics, 85, 116n

Los Angeles, HBC and, 494, 497, 600; HSBC in, 494, 611
Los Angeles National Bank, 611
Lubman, Stanley, 386
Lucknow, 70
Lundine, Stanley N., 836n
*Lydall, W.H., 100, 440, 516, 525–26, 550–51, 585, 645
*Lyon-Mackenzie, G., 74, 86, 108, 109
Lyons, HSBC in, 78–80, 286, 416, 440–41, 525

*Mabey, H.A., 100–01, 236
MacArthur, Douglas, 102–03
Macau, 307; during Pacific War, 19, 24, 47–48; Hang Seng in, 704; HSBC and, 306, 522, 528, 608, 696, 874, 889
*McCallum, W.R., 8
McCloy, John L., 508
*McCormick, Hilary, 538
*McCutcheon, W.R., 497
Macdonald, David, 870
*Macdonald, I.H., 334, 337, 525, 697, 743, 892; acquisition of MMBI, 775, 777, 781, 782, 798, 799n, 807, 834, 840–42, 845–47, 848, 863; career, 802; Executive Director, Americas, 890; Royal Bank of Scotland Group, 892
Macdonogh, Sir George, 31, 32
MacDougall, D.M., 130
McGillicuddy, John, 806
MacGregor, D., 468
McGregor, J.F., 274
Macindoe, R.G., 32, 33, 267
*MacIntyre, R., 83
*Mack, A.M., 280, 289, 296, 615, 641, 645, 918
Mackinnon, Mackenzie and Co., 252, 909
*Mackintosh, Mary, 295
Maclaine, Watson and Co., 32, 33, 267
*McLean, David, xxxix–xl, 203, 231, 300–01, 463, 530, 578, 579n, 642, 686
Maclehose, Sir Murray, 743
McLennon, Derek, 712
*Macqueen, Angus, 637, 640
Madrid, HSBC in, 888
Mahaweli Development Scheme, 651
Makati, see Manila
Malacca, HSBC in, 99, 110
Malaya, Federation of, 133, 236, 340, 346, 415, 487, (Emergency) 97. See also Malaysia
Malayan Banking Agency, 53–54
Malayan currency area, 346, 464
Malayan People's Anti-Japanese Army, 97
Malayan Public Estates Owners Co., 55
Malayan Union, 97

Index

Malaysia, Federation of, 600, 603; HSBC in, 665–66, 673, 889, 900–01. *See also* Malaya
Malay States, 97, (Federated, govt of) 43n
Maldives, Republic of the, 662
*Manantan, Maria, 83
Manchester, HSBC in, 609
Mandaluyong, *see* Manila
Manila, HSBC in: main office, xl, 78, 79, 80–81, 83, 424, 441–42, 647–48, 649, (building) 52, 81, (to Makati) 620, 647, (profits) 441–42; Pasig office (Mandaluyong), 620, 648, 649–50, 874. *See also* Iloilo; Philippines
Mann, Eugene T., 799
Mansion House Securities, 900
Manufacturers Hanover Bank, 1n, 806
Marden, George, 206, 498–500, 502, 503, 517, 684–85
Marden, J.L., 685
Marine Midland Bank, NA (MMB), 801, 811, 813, 817, 866, 871n; branches, 867, 901; capital, 784–85, 804–05, (benefit from subordinated note) 805, 827; condition of, 782–83, 785, 819, 845; enriched correspondent banks relationship (ENCOR), 902; interstate consumer finance, 902; state vs federal charter, 767, 812, 821, 823, 824–26, 828–30, 833–35, 847. *See also* Marine Midland Banks, Inc.
Marine Midland Bank (Delaware), NA, 902
Marine Midland Banks, Inc. (MMBI)
 acquisition of, by HSBC
 and HSBC's American strategy, 780, 782–83, 811
 Board of Directors, 789, 793, 794, 800–01, 815–16, 820, 821, 827, 830, 844, (exchange of directors with HSBC) 692–93, 803, 848, 910
 capital problems, 787–88, 803, 827, 832–33
 concept, 'sell-out' or partnership, 765, 781, 789–90, 792–96, 803, 810–11, 903
 Definitive Agreement, 765–66, 801–06, 814; renegotiation of, 825, 847; subordinated note, importance of, 803, 804–05, 812, 827, 836
 negotiations: early, 791–95; expectations on timing, 807, 845; in Hawaii, 795–98. *See also* Definitive Agreement
 price, 763–64, 797, 808, 815, 844–45
 reactions to proposals, 798, 806, 820–21, 830–31, (Hong Kong 'Brits') 799; public relations, 799–800, 843
 shareholders, 801, 813, 815–16, 821, 825, 831

 summary, 762–67, 774–75, 847–48, (timetable) 765–67, 850–59
 See also Federal Reserve; Marine Midland Bank; United States
 described, 762
 history, 585, 783–87
 miscellaneous references, 340, 486–87, 520, 693, 744–46
 performance, 786–87, 794, 827, 844, 847–48, 868, 902–03
 post-1980, 591, 869–70; capital, 877, 885, 901–03; ENCOR, 902; offices, 901; relations, (with HSBC) 863, 901–03, (with regulators) 867
Marine Midland Corp., 783–85
Marine Midland Grace Trust Co., 784, 785
Marine Midland International Corp., 785
Marine Midland Ltd, 867
Marine Midland Overseas Corp., 785
Marine Midland Trust Co. of the Mohawk Valley, 783
Marine Trust Co. (Buffalo), 784
*Marshall, J.F., 160–62, 183, 373, 471–73, 616n
*Marshall, J.H.W., 452
*Martin, Connie, 400–401, 612–13
*Mason, V.A., 51, 68–69, 102–05, 108, 229, 432–33, 454, 457, 87
*Massey, B.P., 281, 312, 491, 492
*Massillamany, 453
Mass Transit Railway (H.K.), 334, 562, 712
Matheson and Co., 169, 171
*Mathews, C.P.B., 447
*Matthews, E.A., widow of, 143
Maull, Baldwin, 585, 784
Mauritius, 312; MBLD in, 271, 515, 599, 608, 889
MBLD, *see* Mercantile Bank Ltd
Mealing, *Sir* Kenneth, 271, 502, 503–04, 508, 513, 514, 551, 643, 645
Mees and Hope Group, 707
Melbourne, HSBC in, 891
Mendis, N.S.O., 459
Mercantile Bank (of India) Ltd (MBLD)
 acquisition attempt: by Chase, 507–10
 acquisition by HSBC, 204, 219, 221–22, 224–25, 251, 267, 497, 498–505, 507
 assets, 485
 banknote issue, 235, 576. *See also* banknotes
 Board of Directors, 437, 487; negotiations, (by Lord Bicester) 499, 502, (with BBME and HSBC) 509, 532–33; on London Advisory Ctte, 271, 543, (rationalization of committees) 645; role of, 485, 500–01, 503–04, 508, 511, 512–14, 550–51, 645; staff, concern for, 501–02

Mercantile Bank (of India) Ltd (MBLD) (cont.)
  branches, 193, 319, 395, 399n, 414, 550–51, 593, 594–97, 598–608, 620, 652–53; pre-acquisition, 342n, 431, 498, 504–05
  capital, 219, 221–22, 511, 513–14, 516, (restructuring of) 505–07, 509; reserves, 221, 244, 511, (inner) 503, 505, 511
  head office: location debate, 486, 502, 509, 514, 515, 638, 645; to Hong Kong, 604, 638, 645–46, 733
  name, change of, 228, 507
  post-acquisition: deposits with HSBC, 194, 225–27, 268, 516, 541–43; management fee, 545; relations with HSBC, 247, 289, 514–16, 540–43, 576, 584–85, 591, 604–08, 637–38, 653, 865, 868; role in Hongkong Bank Group, 191–92
  pre-1959, 3, 49, 115, 575
  registered office, 640
  sale of, by HSBC, 604, 889–90
  staff, 291, 308, 319, 514–16, 589
Mercantile Credits (Sydney), 698, 714
Metway, 720
Mexico, 442–43
Miami: HSBC and, 780; MMB in, 902
Mico Equities, 647, 717, 719
Middle East Insurance Holdings, 719
Middle East Finance Co., 720
Midland Bank, 633, 770, 772, 848, 910, 922
Milan, HSBC in, 874, 888
Miller, G. William, 788–89, 806
*Miller, K.A., 712
*Mills, M.E.H.G., widow of, 143
Ming Tak Bank, 702
Mintzberg, H., 583n
Miri, 465
Miskin, G., 30, 143
MMB, *see* Marine Midland Bank
MMBI, *see* Marine Midland Banks, Inc.
*Moncur, A., 921
*Moncur, D., 435n
Money in the Bank, xl
Mongkok, HSBC in: buildings, 362, 738; history of, 203, 328, 368, 369, 423, 617, 629, (specialized functions) 616; industrial finance, 310, 353–58, 360–61, 362–63, 624, 629–32; manager's post held by future chief executives, 688, 689; savings accounts, 363, 368
Monopolies and Mergers Commission, *see* United Kingdom
Monte Carlo, proposed HSBC office in, 441

Montreal Trust Co., 522
*Moodie, R.P.: career, 155, 279, 281, 282, 328, 686, (post-war return to Hong Kong) 86; in Hong Kong, 288, 289, 296, 350, 353–54, 579, (on China finance) 397–98; in Shanghai, 163–64, 373–75
*Moon, H.E., 72, 73
Morgado, Robert P., 790, 820, 824
Morgan, J.P., xl
Morgan, Grenfell and Co., 31–33, 166, 502n, 522
Morgan Guaranty, 431, 806
*Morrison, I.C., 436n
*Morrison, J.A.D., 37, 49, 86, 108, 114, 143, 292
Morrison, K.S., 30
*Morriss, E., 436n
*Morse, *Sir* Arthur
  as 'legend in his own time', 20, 284, 286, 293, 376, 637
  Board of Directors: composition, 260–61; role of, 33, 248–50, 252
  Bowmaker, 520, 527
  Chairman, HSBC, 33–34, 248, 257–58
  Chief Manager
    banknotes, Hong Kong, 156, 234–35, 237–38, 240 (duress notes), 116, 124, 125, 131
    branches, 466
    China, 39, 57, 60–61, 64–65, 99, 150–51, 156–57, (China Consortium) 166, (debts) 173–74, 176–77, 190
    conflicts with government, 8, 125, 134–35, 217, 329, 336n, 567, 634. *See also* duress notes; debtor/creditor
    debtor/creditor legislation, 117, 131–37, 441
    Far Eastern Relief Fund, 50–51
    Hong Kong office, 17, 53, 74, 138–39
    in Hong Kong, 139–48, 213, 251, 283, 293–94, 326, 342, 432, 443, 553, (banking policy) 199–201, (Iloilo) 443–44, 449
    in London, 16, 38, 39, 43, 45–46, (assuming charge) 23, 25, (China policy) 20, (India) 66, 106, (post-war) 75
    remuneration, 217–18
    return to the East, 87–88, 89, 100, 103
    staff policies, 7, 47–49, 94, 108, 109, 205, 218, 290–91, 293, 313n, (Eastern staff, China) 376–80, (repatriates) 75–77
    visit by first Japanese delegation, 433–34
    wartime planning, xxxv, 1, 415, 464

corporate name of Bank, 872
early career, 2, 34–37, 130–31
London (post-retirement), 261n, 294, 307
China policy, 438–39
London Advisory Ctte (LAC), 29, 32, 267, 268–71, 518, 519, 551, 637, 645
negotiations, 488, 500, (BBME) 524, 533, 547n, (MBLD) 509, 510, 551
on BBME board, 543
London Manager, 19, 449, 641, (selection as) 687
relations with: Barlow, 31, 137; Grantham, 341n; Grayburn, 29–30, 48; Reid, 37; Turner, 267–68, 277–79, 281, 294, 391, 438, 518, 637
University of Hong Kong: on breeding by lecturers, 114n; Treasurer, 36
*Morse, Margery, *Lady*, 36
Mortgage And Finance Co., 722
*Mosley, A.D.A.G., 452, 653, 689, 690, 912
'Mt Echo', Singapore, 669
*Moutrie, G.C., 106, 286, 312, 439
Muar, HSBC in, 99, 390, 424
Mukden, HSBC in, 157, 161–62
Mullin, Peter, 796
*Munden, R.V., 308–09, 906, 915
Munsell, James F., 782, 807, 812, 815
*Muriel, H.E., 21, 108, 116n, 125, 137–38, 166–67, 179, 271, 285, 438, 525, 634, (on Morse) 37
*Muriel, H.J.S., 653
*Murray, W.C., 57–58, 59, 61, 99, 109
*Musker, Harold, 526, 530, 547n, 602
Myanna Oil Corp., 712

*Nack, A., 80, 439–40, 587n
Nagasaki, HSBC in, 611, 889
Nagoya, MBLD/HSBC in, 603–04
Nanking, HSBC in, 156, 157, 159–61, 382, (profit) 160, 161
Nassau, HSBC in 862, 874
National and Grindlay's Bank, *see* Grindlay's Bank
National Bank of India, 313, 342n, 453, 529, 652
National Bank of North America, 772, 793, 822–23
National Bank of Scotland, 492
National City Bank, *see* Citibank
Nationale Handelsbank, 508
National, Overseas and Grindlay's Bank, *see* Grindlay's Bank
National Provincial Bank, 115. *See also* National Westminster
National Westminster Bank, 1n, 772, 793, 822–23. *See also* Westminster Bank

Nedbank, 720
Nederlandsch Indische Handelsbank, 442n
Nepal, 312
Netherlands, HSBC and, 52, 526, 609
Netherlands East Indies, 52, 100–01. *See also* Indonesia; Jakarta; Sourabaya
Newall, 'Red' (Citibank), 304
New Beckenham Sports Grounds, 114, 275, 302, 313, 321–22, 592, 668–69, 917
New York, City of
Golden Pacific National Bank and HSBC, 340n, 903
HSBC main office: 27n, 219, 430, 491, 496, 602–03, 743, 779, 862, 890, 903, (World Trade Center) 743; U.S. dollar funds, 430–31
HSBC other offices, 610, (Flushing) 903
New York State
Assembly, Banking Ctte, 811, 821
banking legislation and regulations, 784, 785, 790–91, 817, 818–19, 823, 831, ('take-over' bill vetoed) 822–25
economic conditions and plans, 790–91, 824
State Banking Department: MMBI acquisition, 770, 798, 807, 810–11, 812, 817, 818–21; 'up-State down-State' policy, 819–20
See also Siebert
New Zealand, HSBC and, 488, 700, 713
New Zealand Investment Co., 700
New Zealand Investment Mortgage and Deposit Co., 700
*Nicholson, J.C., 72
*Nicoll, F.E., 46–47
Nicoll, *Sir* John, 271
99 Bishopsgate, Ltd (Vila), 638, 694, 722
N.J. and S. Bardac, 168n
*Noble, G.E., 71
Norman, Montagu, 165–66
North Borneo Development Board, 478
Nu, *U*, 205

Ogden, *Sir* Alwyne, 93
*Ogden, B.J.N., 286, 583–84, 616–18, 915
Ogilby, Charles, 814
Ohio, MMBI in, 902
oil, 464–65, 874
*Oliphant, R.G.L.: early career, 100, 282; Manager Hong Kong and Deputy Chief Manager, 185, 283, 309, 324, 350–51, 368, 369, 527, 567, 615, 625, 688, 703–04, 722, (branching policy) 206–07, 289, 311, 370, 423; Manager Mongkok, 328, 353, 354–57, 360–61
Olver, J., 209

One Queen's Road Central, the Headquarters of HongkongBank since 1864, 906n
opium, xxxvi, 668n
Oriental Bank Corp., xxxix, 574
Orion, 700
Oroton Investments, 722
Osaka: HSBC in, 102, 423, 435; MBLD in, 603
*Ostrenko, A.T., 161, 402–03
Oversea-Chinese Banking Corp., 479

packing credits, 358–59, 626
*Page, C.R., 869
Pakistan, 236, 516; MBLD in, 600; HSBC in, 889
*Palisson, J., 441
P&O, 311, 313, 321, 592, 668
P&O Banking Corp., 482, 501
Panmure Gordon and Co., 716
Pao, *Sir* Y.K. (Yue-kong), 579, 686, 696–97, 721
Papua, New Guinea, 713
*Paredes, R.E., 451, 452–53, 649–50, (Mrs Paredes) 650
Paris: HSBC in, 80, 286, 423, 440–41, 888, 901, (Place Vendôme) 440; MMB in, 901
*Park, W., 37, 46, 109
*Parker, H.V., 81, 83, 281, 285, 433, 437, 440–41, 444, 531–32
Pasig, *see* Manila
*Paterson, B.O'D., 236, 672
Pearce, T.E., 30
Peat, Marwick and Mitchell, 536, 587
Pei, I.M., 745n
Pei Tsu-yi, 59, 60, 156, 745n
Peiping, *see* Peking
Peking, 410–11; HSBC in, 90–92, 380, 385, 423, 613, 862, 869
Pekin Syndicate, 64–65, 168
Penang, HSBC in, 97, 99
Peninsular and Oriental Steam Navigation Co., *see* P&O
People's Bank (Sri Lanka), 458, 658
Perera, N.M., 654–55
Perpetual Publicity Co., 694
*Perrin, A., 78, 80
*Perry-Aldworth, S.W.P., 180, 268, 281, 285, 424, 438–39, 440, 522, 528, 890; BBME/MBLD negotiations, 500–01, 502, 504–05, 508, 510–11, 512, 513, 524, 533, 536, 537–39, 540, 543, 547, 551; on boards of BBME/MBLD, 514, 543; on sub-ctte of London Advisory, 512, 524, 535
Perth, HSBC in, 891
Peru, 443
Petaling Jaya (Selangor), HSBC in, 319, 620

*Peter, *Sir* John C., 31
*Peterson, H.C., 496–97
*Petrie, A.R., 473, 890, 915
Petty, J.R.: acquisition of MMBI, 789–90, 792–94, 795, 798, 805, 807, 830, 848; director HSBC, 684, 909
Philadelphia National Bank, 720
Philippine Development Bank, 649
Philippine National Bank, 448
Philippines, 80–84, 312, 336n, 467, 469, 470
  banking legislation, 442, 523, 647, 649–51
  British ambassador, 449–50
  debtor/creditor legislation, 133, 441–42
  HSBC in, 54, 102, 430, 441–43, 444, 647, 649–51, 778, 888
  role of foreign banks, 441–42
  See also Iloilo; Manila
*Phillips, H.F., 161, 401
Phnom Penh, HSBC in, 423
Piderit, F., 816, 841–42
*Pierce, H.L., 319, 379–81, 448, 450, 456, 462, 914
Pitmann, Steuart, 782, 812, 838–39
Pitmann, Potts and Throwbridge, 782
Platten, D., 806
Poppen, John, 777
Portland (Oregon), HSBC in, 611, 780
Port Louis, 599
Port Vila (New Hebrides, *now* Vanuatu), HSBC in, 608–09
*Pow, C.F., 508, 645–46
*Prado, A.M., 306–09, 608, 890
*Prata, H.J., 93
Pratt, *Sir* John, 170
Pressnell, Leslie, xlii, 46n, 346
*Pridham, M.J., 742, 835
Private Development Corp. of the Philippines, 647
Proxmire, William D., 836, 838, 846
Pullen, W.G., 390
*Purves, William: early career, 322, 690; deputy chairman, 908; chief executive, 568n, 912–13
python, Bank's 469

Qantas, 431
Qingdao (Tsingtau), 383

*Rabino, Joseph, 300
*Rabuco, Alfonso I., 84, 448, 452, 649
*Raikes, J.H., 285
railways: China, 167–68, 169, 170, 174, 178, 180; Sabah, 478; Thailand, 431
Rambhai-Barmi, *Queen*, 890
Rand, George F., 784, 891

Rangoon, 70; HSBC in, 54, 96, 99, 205, 326, 559, 600, 603, 731, (in Simla) 28, 45
Ratmalana, *see* Colombo
RBSG, *see* Royal Bank of Scotland Group
Redding, S.G., 583, 586
'red-lining', 808, 811. *See also* Community Reinvestment Act
Reed, J.T.S., 943n54
Régie Générale de Chemins de fer et Travaux Publics, 168n
Reid, *Sir* Edward, 31–34, 124, 125, 131, 145, 249, 267, 439, 518–19, 634, 638; and BBME/MBLD, 499, 500, 502, 510, 511, 512, 524, 532, 534, 544, 551; on B&CC board, 170, 510–11; on sub-ctte of London Advisory, 512, 524, 535
REIT (real estate investment trust), 786
Republic National Bank (Beverly Hills), 340n, 600
Reserve Bank of India, 70, 599
Resources and Investment Finance, 713
Reuss, Henry Schoellkopf, 836
rice, 96, 112, 152, 153
*Rice, C.R., 68–69
Richardson, Gordon, 640, 893–94
Ride, *Sir* Lindsay T., 294
*Riollot, E., 80
Ritz Hotel, Paris, 440
Roberts, C.C., 30, 141–43, 274
Roberts, T.A., award, 69, 453
*Roche, M., 490
Rockefeller, David, 508, 806
Rogers, Cyril, 156
romanization, xxxix, 373n
Rosenthal, Benjamin S., 525, 774, 807, 816n, 831, 836, 838, 839–42, 863, 871
*Ross, D.M., 71, 98, 686
Ross, G.R., 684
Rothschild, *Baron* Edmond de, 770–71
Rotterdamsche Bank, 508
*Rowe, C.R., 450
Rowley Davies, 459
Roxas, Manuel A., 441
Royal Bank of Canada, 522, 871
Royal Bank of Scotland, 891, 895
Royal Bank of Scotland Group (RBSG)
  HSBC attempt to acquire, 861, 885, 886, 891–96; contrast with MMBI, 894–95; price, 892–93; status of MMBI acquisition, 892
  Standard Chartered attempt to acquire, 891–94
Royal Hong Kong Golf Club, 616
Royal Hong Kong Jockey Club, 616, 617
Royal Institute of British Architects, 904
Royal Orchid Hotel (Bangkok), 108, 670, 890

RoyWest Banking Corp., 697, 699, 707
rubber, 66, 342, 459, 464, 466–67, 474–76, 551, 624
Russell and Co., 252, 862
Russo-Asiatic Bank, 335
Ruttonjee, H., 325–26
Ryan, John, 816n
*Ryan, P.M., 656–57
*Rynd, P.G., 389

Sabah, *see* British North Borneo
Sacramento, HBC in, 495, 600
Saigon, HSBC in, 85, 94–95, 379, 424
St Andrew's Society, Shanghai, 408
St Helier (Jersey), HSBC in, 609
St Peter's Port (Guernsey), HSBC in, 413
Salisbury, Southern Rhodesia, 520
Salomon Bros., 782, 805, 829. *See also* Wolfensohn
Sampson, Anthony, 862
Samuel Montagu, 499
Sandakan, HSBC in, 464, 467–68, 475–76
*Sandberg, *Sir* Michael G.R., xxxvii–iii, 284, 667
  Chairman, 477, 568n, 584, 640, 660–61, 668, 744–46, 875, 884, 911–12, 913, 922
  building, 1986 head office, 904
  Marine Midland acquisition and planning, 775, 780, 781, 783, 792, 797, 799, 805–06, 807, 812, 814–15, 824–25, 830, 833, 842, 845–46, 848–49
  personnel policies, 589
  planning: American strategy, xxxvii, 486; United Kingdom, 866, 875, 912
  Royal Bank of Scotland, 633, 894
  selection as, 689, 690–91, (Sayer's reasons) 690
  early career, 286, 433, 630, 691, (personnel report) 292
  in Hong Kong to Deputy Chairman, 339, 613, 689, 690–91, 714–15, 740, (and Wardley) 711, (as Chief Accountant) 690–91
  Macau, chairman, local 'board', 608
  Singapore, 292
San Francisco, HSBC in, 45, 326–27, 424, 489–90, 600, 611, 698, 776. *See also* Hongkong and Shanghai Banking Corporation of California, Inc.
San Jose, CA, HBC in, 600
Santiago, HSBC in, 612, 890
São Paulo, HSBC and, 597, 608
Sarawak, 346, 463–65, 600; HSBC in, 478–81, 521, 911
Sassoon interests, 531
Saudi Arabia, 559

Saudi British Bank, 559, 695, 707, 867, 871,
    (national treatment) 901
*Saunders, Sir John A.H.
    Board of Directors, 4–5, 250, 261–62,
        674–77, 683
    chief manager/executive chairman, 6, 232,
        283–84, 341n, 486, 579, 621, 634–35,
        649, 674, 683, 731–39, 922
        branches/subsidiaries, 447, 585
        Hang Seng acquisition, 702, 704–05
        London, 641; London Advisory Ctte,
            642, 645
        policies, 562, 567, 597, 697–98, 700, 721,
            (MBLD in Hong Kong) 645–46
    early career, 98, 286, 468
    selection as Chief Manager, 259–62,
        282–84, 293, 686
savings accounts, 445, 451, 466, 471, 479,
    617–18, 649, 731. See also Hong Kong
    Savings Bank
*Sayer, G.M.
    American strategy, 775, 780
    chief executive, 232, 637, 646, 653, 658,
        671, 689, 694, 706, 714, 726, 739–44,
        746, 922; policies, 562, 572, 586, 653,
        (Board of Directors) 683, (Clague)
        708–11, (London) 633, 641
    early career, 114, 286, 352, 358, 359, 379,
        (general manager) 585, 689, (selection
        as chief executive) 688–90
Scandinavia, 398, 525
Schoellkopf, J. Fred, IV, 785, 836n
Scotland, and Royal Bank of, 895–96
*Scott, M.D., 285, 502, 525
Scroggie, J.G., 453
SDC International, 697
SeaFirst (First National Bank of Seattle), 782
Seattle, HSBC in, 611, 780
Securair, 696
*Self, D.N.H., 411, 612
*Sellars, P.A., 94, 113, 286, 290–91, 294, 296,
    403–04, 488, (Mme Sellars) 113
Selvaratnam, H.L.D., 458n
*Selway-Swift, P.E., 916
Selwyn-Clarke, P.S., 108–09
Senananyake, Dudley, 652
Seoul: HSBC in, 413, 597, 611–12, 707n, 888,
    914; MMB in, 867, 901
Seria, 465
Shahabudin, M., 921
Shanghai, 351, 352, 380, 385, 433, 837
    HSBC in, 84, 89–90, 155–57, 162–64, 191,
        251, 336, 349, 368, 382, 387, 396–402,
        404–11, 498, 612–13, 869, (banknotes)
        xli, 156–57, (capital assigned) 90,
        (cashier's orders) 164

discussions relative to branch, post-1949,
    390, 391, 393–94, 396
profits, 155, 181, 182, 326–27, 383, 387,
    399, 404, 612, 869
staff in, 89, 155–56, 300, 301, 373–75,
    376–81, 387–88, 391, 400–01,
    406–07. See also Hongkong and
    Shanghai Bank (iv), internment
Municipal Council, 9, 156, 175–77, 394
property, 384, 385, 399–400
social life, 379, 380–81, 385, 407–08
Shanghai Power Co., 386
*Shannon, O.J. (and family), 81, 83, 143
Shantou (Swatow), 76, 94, 156, 286, 378,
    492
Sharps Pixley, 713n
Sharps Pixley Wardley, 713
*Shen, H.J., 156, 630
Shenzhen, HSBC in, 888
Sheppard, R.J., 274
Shewan, Tomes and Co., 252
Shields, A.L., 30
*Shirreff, J.R.N., 602–03
Siam, see Thailand
Siebert, Muriel, 770, 774, 791, 798, 804, 807,
    808, 809–11, 818–19, 820–21, 822–23,
    830–31, 836, 838, 839–41, 845, 891
Siebs, H.A., 439
Siemssen and Co., 439
SIH (Vila), 713n
silver and silver standard, 11, 16, 72, 489,
    570, 574, 841n
silver yuan, 155
Simla, HSBC Rangoon office in, 28, 45
Sindona, Michele, 770, 840
Singapore, 56, 96, 97, 336n, 342–43, 346–47,
    433, 436, 470, 912, (People's Action
    Party) 343
    HSBC main office, 45, 84, 96–98, 229, 343,
        424, 436, 600, 603, 666, (Borneo
        branches) 415, (proposed wartime
        Head Office) 23, 25, 26
    HSBC other offices: Jurong, 620; Orchard
        Rd, 619; Tanglin, 423
    MBLD in, 516, 603
Sin Hwa Trust and Savings, 161
Sino-British Educational and Cultural
    Endowment Fund, 175
Sino-British Joint Declaration (on Hong
    Kong), 861, 911, 921
Sir Elly Kadoorie and Sons, 252, 483, 684,
    685
Sit, Victor F.S., 368, 369, 599
Skadden, Arps, Slate, Meagher and Flom,
    789, 795–96
*Skinner, O., 289, 290, 328, 489

*Slade, C., 114
Sloss, Duncan, 36, 130
*Smith, J.R.M., 259, 281, 686
*Snaith, A.L., 83, 312
Snake Wine, 311
*Soares, F.X., 48, 306, 307
Société Chérifienne de Gérance et de Banque, 549
Société de Bruxelles pour la Finance et l'Industrie, 168
Société Financière Privée, 716
Société Générale pour favoriser le développement du Commerce et de l'Industrie en France, 168n
Society Corp. (Cleveland), 902
Soong, T.V. (Sung Tsu-wen), 175
Sourabaya, HSBC in, 101, 115, 301, 423
*Sousa, V., 307-08
South China Morning Post, Ltd, 88, 351n, 483, 522, 697
*Spandau, F., 80
*'Specky' (Yang San Lin), 407
Speedlink, 588-89
Sri Lanka, 431, 574
  banking, 456-57, 652, 653-55, 657-58, (policy) 66-67, 652-53, 654-55, 656-57, 658-59
  development finance: Development Bank, 155, 312; Development Finance Corp., 204, 460
  FCBU, 659
  Free Trade Zone (FTZ), 657-59
  HSBC in, 305, 308, 336n, 342, 607, 652-62, 665. *See also* Colombo
  MBLD in, 607, 652-53, 656, 657
  politics, 69, 205n, 436, 454, 461, 652, 653-57, (Lanka Sama Samaja Party) 654, (Sri Lanka Freedom Party) 652, 656, (United National Party) 657
*Stabb, Effie (Townsend), *Lady*, 293
*Stabb, G.W., 98, 278, 416
*Stabb, *Sir* Newton, xxxv, 35, 259, 280n, 281, 282, 286, 438, 589, 636, 686
*Stacey, G.H., 155, 156, 285, 288, 374, 392, 433, 489, 498
Standard Bank (of South Africa), 528
Standard Chartered Group, 770-71, 772, 789n, 849n. *See also* Chartered Bank
State Bank of India, 659
State Investment House, 647, 713
State Mortgage Bank (Sri Lanka), 653
Statue Square, *see* Hong Kong
Stearns, Craig, 782
*Stedman, H.W., 651n
Steinberg, S., 818n
Steiner, Henry, 862n, 872-73

*Stephen, A.G., xl, 157, 280n, 281, 395, 592, 636, 912, (death) xl
*Stephen, *Mrs* A.G., xl
sterling, 577, 634, 736, (devaluations) 738, 739, 740
Sterling Area, 203, 341, 345-46, 430, 635, 738, 739, (Sterling Area Payments Agreements) 104
*Stewart, G.A., 306
*Stewart, *Sir* Gershom, 608
*Stewart, G.O.W., xxxviii, 70-71, 87, 208-09, 282-83, 686
  BBME and MBLD: negotiations, activities, role during, 485, 498, 500, 501, 502, 515, 534-35, 547, 553
  Deputy Chief Manager, 204, 209, 260, 288-89
  London Manager, 171, 259, 393n, 438, 526, 636, 641, 643-45, 699
*Stewart, J.B., 59, 84
*Stewart, W.A., 89, 90, 389-90, 400, 404-05, 954
*Stilliard, R., 312
Stockholm, HSBC in, 888
Stone, L.B., 274
Straits Settlements, 54. *See also* Malacca; Penang; Singapore
Straits Steamship Co., 468, 477-78
*Strauch, Wilhelm, 112
*Streatfield, E.P., 290-91
*Stuart, R.A., 26, 37, 49, 97-98, 108, 283, 285
*Stubbs, G.P., 283, 416, 469-71, 637, 642, (university graduate) 518
sugar, 444, 448
Sungei Patani, HSBC in, 99, 495
Sun Wah Hotel, 87
*Sutherland, Ian, 450
Sutherland, *Sir* Thomas, 10, 137, 284
Swatow, HSBC in, 76, 94, 156, 286, 378, 492
Swettenham, Frank, 341n
SWIFT, 914
Swire Caterers, 900
Swire Group (John Swire and Sons), 721, 909
Swiss National Bank, 609n
Switzerland, Hongkong Bank Group and, 488, 500, 522, 526, 602, 609n, 716. *See also* Geneva; Zurich
Sydney, HSBC and, 593, 698, 891
Sykes, *Sir* Frederick, 32, 33, 271

Tagg, G.T., 274
Ta Hwa (Enterprises) Agreement, 391, 392, 393-96
Taipei, HSBC in, 888, 915

988 Index

*Tait, J.F.G., 608
'take-over', 487, 502, 518, 788–89, 806, 810–11, (defined) 788n
*Taplin, R.W., 402
Tarakan, 468
Tawau, HSBC in, 464, 467–73, 476, 477, 915
*Taylor, J.D., 265
*Taylor, J.McG., 95, 285
tea, 66, 234, 459; vs coffee, 798n
Teluk Anson, HSBC in, 415, 424
Tenix, 713n
*Terdre, C.B., 49
textiles, 350, 431, 621, 622
Thailand, 431; HSBC in, 430, 516, 603; MBLD in, 516, 550–51, 603, (Haadyai) 551. *See also* Bangkok
Thalberg, H.A., 378
Thalgodapitiya Award, 455
*Thambiah, R., 301, 308, 457, 607, 654, 660–61, 658
Theo. H. Davies, 204, 495, 522
Thomas, W.H. Evans, 62–63
Thomas Cook, 457, 743
*Thompson, F.M., 495, 496–97
*Thomson, G.G., 466, 468
*Thomson, J.E.B., 424
*Thorn, L.H., 469
Tientsin (Tianjin), HSBC in, 35, 156, 157, 350, 381, 382, 388, 389
Tilbrook, B., 921
Tillotson, G.H.R., xxxix
timber, 469, 479–80
The Times, 555
Times of Ceylon, 460
TKM International (Holdings), 520, 899, 900
Tokai Bank, Nagoya, 867
Tokyo, HSBC in, 102–05, 204, 423, 433, 434, 435, 603, 669, 672, (profits) 432, (strikes) 433
Tomkins, H.J., 567, 615
*Tong, T.P., 86, 143, 309–10
*Townsend, A.M., xl, 27n, 799n
*Townsend, G.H., xl
Tozer, Kemsley and Millbourn (TKM), 520, 899, 900
Trench, *Sir* David, 645
*True, G.W.E., 96, 445, 448
Trust Corp. of the Bahamas, 204, 438, 522, 699
Tsingtau (Qingdao), 383
Tsuen Wan, 345, 355; HSBC in, 319
Turnbull, R.E., 54
*Turner, A.L., 436n
*Turner, D.F.L., 915
*Turner, Maurice W., 78, 115, 228, 236, 283, 286, 477–78, 674, 688, 705

*Turner, *Sir* Michael W.
  Chairman: BBME, 521, 526, 602; HSBC, 259
  chairmanship, views concerning, 248–50, 259
  Chief Manager
    banknotes, responsibility for, 241
    branches, 370, 414, 423, 432, 441, 443, 455, 469
    China, 180, 187, 190, 381–83, 390, 391, 392, 393, 398–99
    Ho Tung, *Sir* Robert, 309
    London, 439, 440
    management, 195, 289, 293, 295–99
    performance, 193
    policies, banking: general, 199, 201, 204–05, 353; new, 192, 206–07, 299, 326, (staff) 291, 342–43
    policy on acquisitions/expansion, 195, 485, 488, 497, 524–25, 553, 557, (insurance) 717; BBME, 529, 533–34, 537–39, 540, 543; HBC, 490, 492, 495–96; MBLD, 204, 498, 499, 503–04, 508–09, 515–16, (cash or scrip offer), 500, 502–03, 510, 511–14;
    subsidiaries, 521, 545–46, 550–51
    shares, nominal value, 231–32
    Statue Sq., 333
  early career, 328, 492, 531n, (university graduate) 518
  family life, 437. *See also* Turner, Wendy
  London, 267; London Advisory Committee, 519, 645
  return from internment, 76–78, 96
  succession to Chief Manager, 277, 278–81, 328, 686
*Turner, Wendy, *Lady*: post-war reunion, 76–78; role as wife of Chief Manager, 278–79, 900
Twining, *Sir* Edward Francis, *Lord*, 467
*Tytler, G.E. Bruce, 99, 108, 285

*Udal, E.R., 584, 608, 684, 714
Union Bank of California, 771, 772, 892
United Aid to China Fund, 50
United Kingdom, government of, 133, 634–35, 642
  Board of Trade, 509
  Colonial Office, 133–35, 232, 234–35, 240, 415, 464, 633
  Colonial Banking Regulations, 232, 566–67, 574–75
  Hong Kong's duress notes, 116, 123, 124–26
  HSBC: initial wartime policies, 19, 25–26; planning for post-war, 24, 49, 52–54, (Hong Kong Planning Unit) 54–57; regulations relevant to, 3–4, 10, 341–42

Directorate of office machinery, 57
exchange control, HSBC violation of, 744
Foreign Office, 104, 896
  China, 58, 71, 118, 166–67, 389, (debt repayment) 150–51, 173, 174–75, 176–77, 182, (embassy) 91, 116, 128, 158–59, 173–79, (Hankow, consul-general) 158, (Treaty of 1943) 20, 51, 150
  Hong Kong, 861
  Sino-British Joint Declaration, 861, 911, 921
  legislation: bank act, 871; companies acts, 207–08, 213, 216–18, 568–69, 723, (sec. 209) 513, 537–38, 545; finance act (1947), 111, 217, (1965) 733; reserved liability act (1879), 246, 506
military forces of, 92, 99
Monopolies and Mergers Commission: MMBI, 813; RBSG, 893–94, 895, 908
orders-in-Council, re HSBC: (1943) 19, 23, 24, 28–29, 58, 59, 63–64, 137, 140, 228, 243, 257, (1946) 53, 75, 138–39, (1954 draft) 243
Scottish Office, 894, 896
securities of, HSBC investment in, 44
Treasury, xl–xli, 63, 123, 229, 232, 235, 240, 245, 267, 337, 341–42, 343, 483, 638, 645, 744, 891, 896, (as HSBC regulator) 565–66, 574–75, 633, 908. *See also* Colonial Office
See also banknotes; Bank of England; British overseas banking; Sterling Area
United Nations: embargo, 341, 347–48
United Nations High Commissioner for Refugees, 402
United Nations Relief and Rehabilitation Agency (UNRRA), 152, 158
United States
  army, 82, 84, 91
  banking system, 767, 769, 785n, 809, 817, 822, 824, 828–29, 838, 902; anti-trust legislation, 789, 806, 812–13, 819; 'country bank' defined, 865n; foreign banks, acquisitions by, 769–73, 821, 823, 831, 835–37, 839–41, 848–49, (Standard Chartered) 770–71
  HSBC in, 519–20, 841
United States, Congress: MMBI acquisition Congressional concern/involvement, 768, 769, 773, 812, 819, 823, 835, 846
  House: Banking Ctte, 836; sub-ctte on Commerce, Consumer and Monetary Affairs, 839–42
  new legislation and moratorium, 836, 838–39, 846
  Senate, Ctte on Banking, 836–38, 863
United States, government of
  and HSBC (1941), 25, 28
  banking legislation, 809–10, 902, (national treatment) 768, 773, 817, 901
    Bank Holding Co. Act, 495, 610, 765, 769, 772, 773–74, 809, 825, 826–28, 831, 840
    Change of Control Act, 769, 825
    Edge Act, 769, 817, 838, 901
    Glass-Steagall Act (1933), 768
    International Banking Act, 610, 611, 697, 765, 768–69, 779–80, 812, 817, 825, 901
    International Banking Facilities Act, 791
  banking regulations, 81, 454, 769; relative to MMBI acquisition, 768, 772–74, 818, 832, 901, 902, (issues) 808–11, (summary) 812–13. *See also* California; New York State
  Community Reinvestment Act ('redlining'), 808, 811, 843–44
  Comptroller of the Currency (OCC), 765; MMBI acquisition, 767, 773, 778, 812, 826, 829–30, 833–35, (hearings) 843–45, (in Hong Kong) 833–34, 886
  Department of Justice, 813
  Federal Trade Commission, 812–13
  Freedom of Information Act, 572, 814, 817
  General Accounting Office (GAO), 836
  Securities and Exchange Commission (SEC), 572, 765; MMBI acquisition, 801, 812, 813–15, 825, 832–33, 846, 847–48
  State Department, 151; China policy, 58, 64, 152, 166–67, 347–48, 384, 392, 396n, 435, 704
  Treasury, 335, 384, 446
  See also Federal Deposit Insurance Corporation; Federal Reserve
University of Hong Kong, 114n, 134, 294, 620, 674, (relations with HSBC) 36, 615, (HKU Advisory Ctte) 36n
*Unthank, Audrey, 295
U.S. Labor Party, 808, 845

Valparaiso, HSBC in, 890
Vancouver, HSBC and, 490, 593, 700
*Van Geyzel, M., 454
Vanuatu, 608
*Veitch, A., 436n
Vickers, da Costa and Co., 712, 866
Vietnam, HSBC in, 206. *See also* Haiphong; Saigon
Vivian-Smith, R.H., *see* Bicester
Volcker, Paul, 788, 798, 807, 821, 831

Wall, B.J., 648
*Wallace, A.M. Duncan, 96, 104
Wallace, Gordon, 806
Wallich, Henry, 800, 811, 820, 837, 839–40
Wallich, Hermann, 837
*Walter, J., 686
*Wardle, C.R., 514, 516, 550–51
Wardley, 5, 203, 558–60, 562, 656, 691, 694, 696, 706, 708, 711–13, 740, 745, 867, 869, 871n, 884, 900
Wardley Australia, 695, 698, 713, 867, 901
Wardley Australia (Holdings), 695, 714
Wardley Canada, 706, 713–14
Wardley Corp., 698
Wardley Data Services, 708, 713
Wardley Gibbs, 718
Wardley House, 229, 230
Wardley Insurance, 719
Wardley International Bank, 713, 862
Wardley Investment Services, 694, 713, 896
Wardley Investments (NZ), 713
Wardley Investor Services Unit, 896
Wardley London Holdings, 903, 904
Wardley Marine International Investment Management, 901
Wardley Marine International Treasury Management, 901
Wardley Middle East, 714
Wardley Swire Assurance (*then* Carlingford Swire), 718
Wardley Vickers, 712
Wardley (Vila), 713
Warner, Barnes and Co., 441, 446, 448, 648
Washington, D.C., HSBC office in, 867
*Watson, J.S., 78, 80, 81
Wayfoong Credit, 719
Wayfoong Finance, 191, 203, 204, 225–26, 521, 552, 560–61, 627, 694, 719
Wayfoong Insurance, 718, 719
Wayfoong Mortgage And Finance, 720
Wayfoong Shipping Services, 874
Wayhong (Bahamas), 874
Wayhong Holdings, 718–19
Wayhong Investment, 695, 720–22
Wayhong, NH, 695, 697, 720, 848
*Webster, Patricia M., 360
*Webster, W., 49, 51, 53–54, 97, 441–42, 444, 450
Weiss, K., 483, 522
Wells Fargo Bank, 848
*Welsh, T., 640, 644, 795, 798, 802, 915
*Westerman, D., 917
Western Bank of Scotland, xxxix
Westminster Bank (National Westminster), 1n, 27, 32–33, 50, 244, 267, 700, 772, 793, 822–23, 910

*Wheatley, W.F., 47
Wheelock Marden, 741
Where the Wild Thyme Blows, 616n
whisk(e)y, 96, 508
Whitehead, T.H., 337
*Whitson, Keith, 916
WHS Investments, 696
*Wickremeneratne, L.Y., 609
*Wignaraja, *Dr* G., 454
*Williams, D.C., 380
Williams, Harold, 815
Williams, Margaret Harcourt, 912n
Williams, P.G., 909–10
Williams, Stephanie, 906
Williams and Glyn's Bank, 891, 895
Wilson, Dick, 522
Wilson, J.D., 509n
Winding, Charles, 785–86
Wing Lung Bank, 702
*Wodehouse, P.G., xxxv, 8, 308, 668, 672
Wolfensohn, James D., 782–83, 790, 792–93, 797, 801–02, 812
*Wong, Charlie, 469–70
*Wong, *Mrs* L., 900
*Wong Tau Sem, 475
wool, 434
World Bank, *see* International Bank for Reconstruction
World Maritime (Bermuda), 696
World Shipping and Investment Co., 696
World Wide (Shipping), 721
*Wrangham, P.J., 915
W.R. Grace and Co., 784, 793
Wright, C.A., 274
Wriston, Walter, 806
Wuhan, HSBC in, 888. *See also* Hankow
*Wu Mao-ting (Wu Jim Pah), 350
Wyllie, W., 708, 711
Wyte Gass, 610

Xavier, J., 307–08
Xiamen (Amoy), 157, 381, 465, 888

Yamanouchi, Saburo, 74, 90
*Yang San Lin, 407
Yangtze Valley Co., 168
*Yap, Daniel Siong Lin, 465
*Yasheroff, G., 403
Ybañez, Roy C., 947
Yokohama, HSBC in, 102–03, 249, 436, 669
Yokohama Specie Bank, 89, 99, 433
Young, Arthur N., 156
Young, E.H., *see* Kennet
Young, *Sir* Norman E., 240, 241, 329, 341n

*Young, W.E., 650
Younger, George, 893–94, 896
*Yoxall, W.T., 96, 155, 285, 312, 378, 380, 388, 389–90, 394, 395–96, 399, 460
Yuen Long, HSBC in, 319, 369

Yule, *Sir* David, 502n
Yule, Catto and Co., 502n

*Zee Tsung Yung, 400, 407
Zurich, HSBC in, 609, 888

HONGKONG BANK GROUP HISTORY SERIES

General Editor: FRANK H.H. KING

1 *Eastern Banking: Essays in the History of The Hongkong and Shanghai Banking Corporation* Edited by FRANK H.H. KING.
2 *Catalogue of the Papers of Sir Charles Addis* by MARGARET HARCOURT WILLIAMS, with an introduction by Roberta A. Dayer.
3 *The History of The British Bank of the Middle East* by GEOFFREY JONES.
   Volume I. *Banking and Empire in Iran.*
   Volume II. *Banking and Oil.*
4 *The History of The Hongkong and Shanghai Banking Corporation* by FRANK H.H. KING. 4 vols.

Related studies published for

THE HONGKONG AND SHANGHAI BANKING CORPORATION

Controller of Group Archives: A.I. DONALDSON

Money in the Bank. An Illustrated Introduction to the Money Collection of The Hongkong and Shanghai Banking Corporation by JOE CRIBB.
Fan Kwae Pictures. Paintings and Drawings by George Chinnery and Other Artists in the Collection of The Hongkong and Shanghai Banking Corporation by G.H.R. TILLOTSON.